Handbook for the
Strong Vocational Interest Blank

Edward K. Strong, Jr. 1884–1963

Handbook for the Strong Vocational Interest Blank

David P. Campbell

Stanford University Press, Stanford, California 1971

Stanford University Press
Stanford, California
© 1971 by the Board of Trustees of the
Leland Stanford Junior University
Printed in the United States of America
ISBN 0-8047-0735-9
LC 74-93495

To Phyllis and our interests,
Jim, Charlie, and Andy

Preface

This Handbook is a succession of dreary statistics about the most exciting topic in the world: a man's enthusiasm for his work. Under the guise of employment, men allow themselves to be manhandled physically (professional football players), to be subjected to public ridicule (politicians), to be displayed publicly (cocktail waitresses, Bunnies, and strippers) or to be deprived of all material possessions (priests and monks). The excitement of occupation has led men into more risks—undercover espionage, space travel, Antarctic exploration—than could money or fame; the fanatic commitment of some men to their jobs has probably caused more divorces than has marital infidelity; the possibility of better employment has created larger mass migrations than has religious fervor, and the absence of meaningful work has likely created more mental depression than any other single factor. For most people, where they work is where the action is.

Given the fascination of the subject, the following pages and pages of means, standard deviations, and correlations seem bland; yet I do not apologize for the endless numbers. Quite the contrary. Test results from over 100,000 diverse adults in over 400 occupations, some tested as many as four times over 40 years, are summarized here. And they were diverse adults, not captive subjects. In the main, the subjects were *not* college sophomores, not military recruits, not job applicants, not hospital patients, not clients, not inmates. The vast majority have been employed for at least three years, are successful in their jobs, and say they like their work; the samples included here constitute the most extensive collection of psychological tests from normal adults in the world.

Of course, this has not been one man's achievement. Professor Edward K. Strong, Jr., of Stanford University, who died in 1963, has been and will always be the dominant researcher in vocational interests. He established the area as a field of scholarship, and he is the genius on whose shoulders the rest of us stand. The last chapter of this book is an unabashed tribute to him. His wife, Margaret Strong, and I have communicated regularly in the past years, and understand each other better than most other dyadic combinations in this project.

I am grateful also to R. F. Berdie, K. E. Clark, J. G. Darley, Theda Hagenah, A. E. Smith, E. G. Williamson, and other administrators at the University of Minnesota, who have supported my work, especially by providing the necessary freedom. It is no accident, of course, that a majority of these administrators are among the world's leading experts in the field of vocational interests. The University's Computer Center, under the direction of Professor Marvin Stein, has assisted in maintaining a computer archives system over three generations of computers.

An important group whose contribution must be acknowledged en masse are those other investigators who have collected SVIBs from employed men or women and have loaned, or more often given, them to me for storage in our archives. Perhaps 20 percent of the data presented in the following pages was collected by others, and I'm grateful to those who shared their materials unselfishly. I have tried to indicate in the text, when appropriate, where the various samples came from. I am well aware of the possessive—almost paternal—feelings investigators have toward their data, and I wish to emphasize my gratitude to all who shared their material with me. (My requests for others' data were refused only three times: once by a police organization that was concerned with invasion of privacy, once by a research institute studying outstanding people—they were afraid such action would disturb their rapport with their subjects—and once because a deceased investigator's will tied up his materials through the lifetime of his subjects' children.)

In a project of this magnitude, the quality of the research staff takes on overwhelming importance. Because of my location within the Student Counseling Bureau at the University of Minnesota and consequent contact with those who have intimate contacts with large numbers of students, I have been able to skim off some of the best students at the University for research assistants. Following is a list of those most closely involved, roughly in chronological order: Charles Johansson, Suzanne DePree, Suzanne Eastes, Lenore Harmon, Walter Warfield, Bonnie Merton, Irena Elliott, Fred Borgen, Barbara Fraser, Judith Mack, Charlotte Kauppi, Jack Rossmann, Terry Cook, Sandy Cook, Abdalla Soliman, Joyce Dann, William Anderson, Iffat Shah, Dennis Gibson, Sandra Davis, Darwin Hendel, Deanna Berkenpas McQueen, Bruce Libby, Robert Peterson, Shirley Crawford, Nancy Lexvold Squire, Michael Vinitsky, Leota Krosch, Gloria Davis, Carol Chapman, Janice Otto, Jo-Ida Hansen. Their efforts were abetted for several years by Sandy Van Gelder, who also bore the major responsibility for the organization and preparation of this manuscript.

I am indebted above all to Charles Johansson, now Professor Johansson of Macalester College. He started working here eight years ago as a sophomore—a quiet, high-achieving math major. He finished a B.A. in three years, an M.A. in psychology in one more, and the Ph.D. in three more, in 1969. His talent for data processing was early apparent, and while still an undergraduate he assumed most of the day-to-day responsibility for the data handling and statistical analysis. He learned about the SVIB, computers, and psychology concurrently, and he learned more intimately than most the problems of maintaining consistency when everything else is constantly changing—the other staff, the techniques, the sources of funds, and the computers (from a Univac 1103 to a Control Data 1604 to a Control Data 6600). He was the only constant in this stream, and none of the others who worked with him will contradict me when I say flatly that without him it would never have been finished.

Some of the materials presented here appeared earlier in various journals of the American Psychological Association and the American Personnel and Guidance Association. I am grateful to those associations and the journal editors for permission to reprint them here. Chapter 11 originally appeared in *Advances in Psychological Assessment*, Vol. 1, edited by Paul McReynolds, published by Science and Behavior Books, Inc., Palo Alto, California, 1968.

The funds to support the research reported here have come from many sources. Various segments have been supported by Federal agencies—the U.S. Office of Education, the National Institute of Mental Health, the Office of Economic Opportunity, and the Department of Defense. Some portions have been financed by occupational organizations, such as the National Association of Funeral Directors, the Palmer School of Chiropractic Services, and the U.S. Army Topographic Command (the study of cartographers). Two of the commercial SVIB scoring services—National Computer Systems and TestScor—have contributed funds or services; NCS has been especially helpful, as they provided scoring for all of the re-standardization samples. The only guaranteed long-range source of research money has been the publisher, Stanford University Press; these funds, because of the lack of red tape and assurance of reasonable permanence, were worth at least twice those from other sources, which came and went with the political winds.

A word on statistics. Several thousand statistics are reported in this Handbook, mainly means, standard deviations, and correlations. I believe the information has been organized and presented in meaningful ways— showing trends, documenting differences, identifying themes—and I take considerable pride that this has been done without a single test of statistical significance. As I am bound to be faulted for this, I would like to explain my feelings.

I firmly believe that nothing in the history of scientific psychology has retarded progress as much as has the concept of statistical significance. This concept was originally developed to relieve the investigator of deciding what was important and—regrettably—a good many investigators have been willing to have that power taken out of their hands. Indeed, many feel a great deal of discomfort when deprived of the security of a significant, socially acceptable *t*-test.

I have two quarrels with this: first, any researcher who does not know his area well enough to know intuitively—with an intuition that replicates —when he has found a meaningful result can hardly be expected to advance the edge of truth very much. Second, factors whose influence can be detected only when compared with chance are so trivial that they might as well be ignored. Psychological findings established by "different from chance" methods are so chaotic that if laid end to end, they would make a pretty good table of random numbers.

So . . . no tests of significance in this Handbook. Rather the emphasis is on magnitude and replicability of differences, and consistency of trends.

This book is intended for all those who use the SVIB—counselors, researchers, teachers. Incorporated here are all of the ingredients of a test manual, technical information on scale development, some brief comments on use in various settings, and some case studies. This book is also intended as an archival record of changes in the SVIB since its introduction.

When working with a test such as the SVIB over a long time span, one learns to separate one's opposition into two categories: those who reject testing as a ridiculous enterprise, providing useless and perhaps dangerous information, and those who embrace psychological tests so warmly that they lose their common sense, and expect impossible answers. Hopefully the data presented here will help keep us on the middle ground. The SVIB will not destroy the world, nor will it singlehandedly bring occupational salvation.

DAVID P. CAMPBELL

Minneapolis, June 1970

Contents

1. A General Introduction to the SVIB 1
2. The Occupational Scales 25
3. The Men's Basic Interest Scales 87
4. The Women's Basic Interest Scales 158
5. The Nonoccupational Scales 194
6. The Administrative Indices 248
7. The Interests of Outstanding Men 260
8. Interpreting the Profile 273
9. Stability of Measured Interests within Occupations over Long Time Spans 315
10. Changing Interests over Time within Society in General 324
11. An Informal History of the SVIB 343

Appendices 367

   A. The 1966 Revision of the Men's SVIB and the 1969 Revision of the Women's SVIB   369

   B. The Occupational Criterion Groups   384

   C. The Men- and Women-in-General Samples   394

   D. The Various Forms of the SVIB Booklets   405

   E. The Forthcoming Revision of the Men's SVIB   441

   F. Item Composition of the Occupational Scales   473

References 497

Index 507

Tables

2. The Occupational Scales

2-1. Illustrative Items from the Army Officer Scale   26
2-2. Popular Items Among Both Army Officers and Men-in-General   27
2-3. Mean Scores for Various Groups on the Army Officer Scale   28
2-4. Intercorrelations Between the Men's Occupational Scales   36
2-5. Intercorrelations Between the Women's Occupational Scales   39
2-6. Tilton Percent Overlap Table   43
2-7. Concurrent Validity Characteristics of the Men's Occupational Scales   45
2-8. Concurrent Validity Characteristics of the Women's Occupational Scales   46
2-9. Mean Standard Scores for the Male Criterion Groups on the Occupational and Nonoccupational Scales   50
2-10. Mean Standard Scores for the Female Criterion Groups on the Occupational and Nonoccupational Scales   52
2-11. Predictive Validity of Men's Physician Scale   54
2-12. Mean Scores of Six Occupational Groups on Their "Own" Scale and on Their Five Other Highest-Score Scales, on High School Senior and Adult SVIB's   56
2-13. Interest Changes During College   58
2-14. Occupations 10 Years Later of Students with High Scores on Sales or Science Scales   59
2-15. Interest Ratings and Productiveness Among 181 Life Insurance Salesmen   66
2-16. Relation of "Own" Interest Scores to Satisfaction Ratings   67
2-17. Odd-Even and 30-Day Test-Retest Reliabilities for the Men's Occupational Scales   70
2-18. Median Test-Retest Correlations for the Men's Occupational Scales for Varying Ages and Test-Retest Intervals   82

3. The Men's Basic Interest Scales

3-1. Sample Item Intercorrelations   91
3-2. Men's Adventure Scale Item Intercorrelations   93
3-3. Men's Agriculture Scale Item Intercorrelations   93
3-4. Men's Art Scale Item Intercorrelations   93
3-5. Men's Business Management Scale Item Intercorrelations   94
3-6. Men's Law/Politics Scale Item Intercorrelations   94

3-7. Men's Mathematics Scale Item Intercorrelations 94

3-8. Men's Mechanical Scale Item Intercorrelations 95

3-9. Men's Medical Service Scale Item Intercorrelations 96

3-10. Men's Merchandising Scale Item Intercorrelations 96

3-11. Men's Military Activities Scale Item Intercorrelations 96

3-12. Men's Music Scale Item Intercorrelations 97

3-13. Men's Nature Scale Item Intercorrelations 97

3-14. Men's Office Practices Scale Item Intercorrelations 98

3-15. Men's Public Speaking Scale Item Intercorrelations 98

3-16. Men's Recreational Leadership Scale Item Intercorrelations 98

3-17. Men's Religious Activities Scale Item Intercorrelations 99

3-18. Men's Sales Scale Item Intercorrelations 99

3-19. Men's Science Scale Item Intercorrelations 100

3-20. Men's Social Service Scale Item Intercorrelations 100

3-21. Men's Teaching Scale Item Intercorrelations 101

3-22. Men's Technical Supervision Scale Item Intercorrelations 101

3-23. Men's Writing Scale Item Intercorrelations 101

3-24. Autonomy Cluster Item Intercorrelations 104

3-25. Compulsivity Cluster Item Intercorrelations 104

3-26. Reliabilities for Some Tentative Basic Interest Scales 106

3-27. Educational Level of Men's Basic Interest Scales Norm Sample 108

3-28. Job Satisfaction of Men's Basic Interest Scales Norm Sample 108

3-29. Teenage and Adult Mean Scores for the Basic Interest Scales Norm Group 109

3-30. Men's Basic Interest Scale Intercorrelations 110

3-31. Correlations Between the Men's Basic Interest and Occupational Scales 111

3-32. Basic Scale Means, Standard Deviations, and Test-Retest Correlations for Stanford Students Tested as Freshmen, Sophomores, Five Years After Graduation, and Fifteen Years After Graduation 117

3-33. Summary of the Test-Retest Statistics for the Men's Basic Interest Scales 125

3-34. Brief Descriptions of 180 Occupational Samples Whose Basic Scale Mean Scores Appear in Tables 3-35 to 3-56 132

3-35. Mean Scores on the Men's Adventure Scale 139

3-36. Mean Scores on the Men's Agriculture Scale 139

3-37. Mean Scores on the Men's Art Scale 140

3-38. Mean Scores on the Men's Business Management Scale 140

3-39. Mean Scores on the Men's Law/Politics Scale 141

3-40. Mean Scores on the Men's Mathematics Scale 141

3-41. Mean Scores on the Men's Mechanical Scale 142

3-42. Mean Scores on the Men's Medical Service Scale 142

3-43. Mean Scores on the Men's Merchandising Scale 143

3-44. Mean Scores on the Men's Military Activities Scale 143

3-45. Mean Scores on the Men's Music Scale 144

3-46. Mean Scores on the Men's Nature Scale 144

3-47. Mean Scores on the Men's Office Practices Scale 145

3-48. Mean Scores on the Men's Public Speaking Scale 145

3-49. Mean Scores on the Men's Recreational Leadership Scale 146
3-50. Mean Scores on the Men's Religious Activities Scale 146
3-51. Mean Scores on the Men's Sales Scale 147
3-52. Mean Scores on the Men's Science Scale 147
3-53. Mean Scores on the Men's Social Service Scale 148
3-54. Mean Scores on the Men's Teaching Scale 148
3-55. Mean Scores on the Men's Technical Supervision Scale 149
3-56. Mean Scores on the Men's Writing Scale 149
3-57. Mean Scores on the Basic Interest Scales for 853 Business School Professors in Six Different Fields 150
3-58. Basic Interest Scale Test and Retest Data for the Berdie-Schletzer Curricular Groups 152
3-59. Three Highest Test and Retest Means and Largest Gains for the Berdie-Schletzer Six Curricular Groups 153

4. The Women's Basic Interest Scales

4-1. Women's Art Scale Item Intercorrelations 159
4-2. Women's Biological Science Scale Item Intercorrelations 159
4-3. Women's Homemaking Scale Item Intercorrelations 159
4-4. Women's Law/Politics Scale Item Intercorrelations 160
4-5. Women's Mechanical Scale Item Intercorrelations 160
4-6. Women's Merchandising Scale Item Intercorrelations 161
4-7. Women's Medical Service Scale Item Intercorrelations 161
4-8. Women's Music Scale Item Intercorrelations 162
4-9. Women's Numbers Scale Item Intercorrelations 162
4-10. Women's Office Practices Scale Item Intercorrelations 162
4-11. Women's Outdoors Scale Item Intercorrelations 163
4-12. Women's Performing Arts Scale Item Intercorrelations 163
4-13. Women's Physical Science Scale Item Intercorrelations 164
4-14. Women's Public Speaking Scale Item Intercorrelations 164
4-15. Women's Religious Activities Scale Item Intercorrelations 165
4-16. Women's Social Service Scale Item Intercorrelations 165
4-17. Women's Sports Scale Item Intercorrelations 165
4-18. Women's Teaching Scale Item Intercorrelations 166
4-19. Women's Writing Scale Item Intercorrelations 166
4-20. Means and Standard Deviations on the Women's Basic Scales for the Women-in-General Norm Sample, and a Sample of High School Seniors 167
4-21. Intercorrelations for the Women's Basic Scales 168
4-22. Intercorrelations Between the Women's Occupational Scales and the Women's Basic Scales, Nonoccupational Scales, and Administrative Indices 169
4-23. Intercorrelations Between the Men's and Women's Basic Scales, Occupational and Nonoccupational Scales, and Administrative Indices 170
4-24. Test-Retest Statistics Over a Two-Week Interval for Set 1 and Set 2 of the Women's Basic Scales 171
4-25. Summary of the Test-Retest Statistics for the Women's Basic Interest Scales 175

4-26. Brief Descriptions of the 89 Occupational Samples Whose Basic
Scale Mean Scores Appear in Tables 4-27 to 4-45   177
4-27. Mean Scores on the Women's Art Scale   181
4-28. Mean Scores on the Women's Biological Science Scale   181
4-29. Mean Scores on the Women's Homemaking Scale   181
4-30. Mean Scores on the Women's Law/Politics Scale   182
4-31. Mean Scores on the Women's Medical Service Scale   182
4-32. Mean Scores on the Women's Mechanical Scale   183
4-33. Mean Scores on the Women's Merchandising Scale   183
4-34. Mean Scores on the Women's Music Scale   184
4-35. Mean Scores on the Women's Numbers Scale   184
4-36. Mean Scores on the Women's Office Practices Scale   185
4-37. Mean Scores on the Women's Outdoors Scale   185
4-38. Mean Scores on the Women's Performing Arts Scale   186
4-39. Mean Scores on the Women's Physical Science Scale   186
4-40. Mean Scores on the Women's Public Speaking Scale   187
4-41. Mean Scores on the Women's Religious Activities Scale   187
4-42. Mean Scores on the Women's Social Service Scale   188
4-43. Mean Scores on the Women's Sports Scale   188
4-44. Mean Scores on the Women's Teaching Scale   189
4-45. Mean Scores on the Women's Writing Scale   189
4-46. Mean Test and Retest Profiles on the Basic Scales for Nolting's
Female Curricular Samples   190
4-47. Highest Test and Retest Means and Largest Gains on the Basic
Interest Scales for Nolting's Female Curricular Samples   192

5. The Nonoccupational Scales

5-1. Intercorrelations Between Men's Academic Achievement (AACH)
Scale, High School Rank, Minnesota Scholastic Aptitude Test,
and Grade Point Average   196
5-2. Men's Academic Achievement (AACH) Scale and Undergraduate
Point Average: Means for Different Degree Levels in Minnesota
25-Year Follow-up Sample   197
5-3. Men's Academic Achievement (AACH) Scale, High School Rank,
and American Council of Education Examination: Means for
Different Degree Levels in Minnesota 10-Year Follow-up Sample   198
5-4. AACH Means and Standard Deviations for Samples at Various
Educational Levels   198
5-5. Items Weighted on the Men's Academic Achievement Scale   201
5-6. Mean Scores on the Men's Academic Achievement Scale for
178 Occupational Samples   202
5-7. Intercorrelations Between Women's Academic Achievement
(AACH) Scale, High School Rank, Minnesota Scholastic
Aptitude Test, and Grade Point Average   202
5-8. Items Weighted on the Women's Academic Achievement Scale   204
5-9. Women's Academic Achievement Scale (AACH) Means on Test
and Retest for Varying Educational Levels Among Nolting's
Sample of University of Minnesota Students   205

5-10. Women's Academic Achievement (AACH) Scale, Grade Point Average, Minnesota Scholastic Aptitude Test, and High School Rank: Means for Different Degree Levels in 25-Year Follow-up Sample   206

5-11. Mean Scores on the Women's Academic Achievement Scale for 78 Occupational Samples   206

5-12. Mean Scores on the Basic Interest Scale (Set 1) for Men Tested at Ages 17–49   210

5-13. Mean Scores on the Occupational Scales for Men Tested at Ages 17–49   212

5-14. Summary of SVIB Scale Gains and Losses with Age   213

5-15. Items Weighted on the Men's Age-Related Interests Scale   215

5-16. Test-Retest Statistics for 22 Samples on the Age-Related Scale   216

5-17. Mean Scores on the Age-Related Interests Scale   216

5-18. Correlations Between the Age-Related Interests Scale, Interest Maturity Scale, and Profile Stability, Using 191 Stanford University Seniors Tested in 1927 and Retested in 1949   220

5-19. Correlations Between the Age-Related Interests Scale, Interest Maturity Scale, and Profile Stability for 152 High School Seniors Tested in 1954 and Retested in 1964   221

5-20. Item Intercorrelations for the Men's Diversity of Interests Scale   222

5-21. Item Intercorrelations for the Women's Diversity of Interests Scale   222

5-22. Mean Scores on the Men's Diversity of Interests Scale   224

5-23. Mean Scores on the Diversity of Interests Scale for 87 Women's Occupational Samples   224

5-24. Validity Data on the Managerial Orientation Scale for the Validation and Cross-Validation Samples of Managers   227

5-25. Items Weighted on the Men's Managerial Orientation Scale   228

5-26. Mean Scores on the Men's Managerial Orientation Scale   229

5-27. Test-Retest Data for Ten Samples on the Managerial Orientation Scale   229

5-28. Mean Scores on the Managerial Orientation Scale for 22 Samples of Outstanding Men   231

5-29. Means and Standard Deviations on MFII, FMII Scales for MF Validation Samples   233

5-30. Items Weighted on the Masculinity–Femininity Scales (MFII and FMII)   234

5-31. Mean Scores on the FMII Scale for 75 Women's Occupational Samples   235

5-32. Mean Scores on the MFII Scale for 112 Men's Occupational Samples   235

5-33. Characteristics of Validation and Cross-Validation Samples for Men's Occupational Introversion–Extroversion (OIE) Scale   237

5-34. Validity Statistics for Men's Occupational Introversion–Extroversion (OIE) Scale   238

5-35. Mean Scores on the Men's Occupational Introversion–Extroversion Scale   238

5-36. Items Weighted on the Men's Occupational Introversion–Extroversion Scale   240

Tables

5-37. Characteristics of Validation and Cross-Validation Samples
for Women's Occupational Introversion–Extroversion Scale 241
5-38. Validity Statistics for Women's Occupational Introversion–
Extroversion (OIE) Scale 241
5-39. Mean Scores on the Occupational Introversion–Extroversion
Scale for 86 Women's Occupations 241
5-40. Items Weighted on the Women's Occupational Introversion–
Extroversion Scale 242
5-41. Items Weighted on the Men's Occupational Level Scale 244
5-42. Mean Scores on the Men's Occupational Level Scale 245
5-43. Items Weighted on the Men's Specialization Level Scale 246

6. The Administrative Indices

6-1. Examples of Item Weight on the Men's Form Check Index 250
6-2. Distributions of Raw Scores on the Form Check Indices for
Groups Answering Different Forms of the SVIB Booklet 251
6-3. Scoring Weights for the Men's Form Check Index 252
6-4. Scoring Weights for the Women's Form Check Index 252
6-5. Distributions of Raw Scores on the Unpopular Index for Two
Men's Test-Retest Groups 253
6-6. Scoring Weights for the Men's Unpopular Index 254
6-7. Scoring Weights for the Women's Unpopular Index 255
6-8. Distributions of Like, Indifferent, and Dislike Response Percentages
for 1,214 Men Tested at Age 16 and Retested at 52 255
6-9. Mean Percent "Like" Responses on First 100 Items for Men 256
6-10. Mean Percent "Dislike" Responses on First 100 Items for Men 256
6-11. Mean Percent "Like" Responses on First 128 Items for Women 257
6-12. Mean Percent "Dislike" Responses on First 128 Items for Women 257

7. The Interests of Outstanding Men

7-1. Mean Scores on the Science Basic Interest Scale for 19 Groups
of Outstanding Men 269

8. Interpreting the Profile

8-1. Examples of Items on the Mathematician Occupational Scale 284

10. Changing Interests Over Time

10-1. Item Weights for the Men's Cultural Change Scale 328
10-2. Correlations Between the Men's Cultural Change Scale and
the Men's Basic Interest Scale 331
10-3. Mean Scores on the Men's Cultural Change Scale Versus Year
Tested for 202 Male Occupational Samples 333
10-4. Items Weighted on the Women's Cultural Change Scale 336
10-5. Mean and Standard Deviations for the Old (1930's) and New
(1960's) Occupational Samples on the Women's Cultural
Change Scale 337

10-6. Mean Scores on the Women's Cultural Change Scale Versus Year
Tested for 95 Female Occupational Samples   338

10-7. Correlations Between the Women's Cultural Change Scale and
the Women's Basic Interest and Nonoccupational Scales   340

10-8. Mean Scores on the Occupational Introversion–Extroversion Scale
for Men in Various Marital Categories   342

11. An Informal History of the SVIB

11-1. Noteworthy Events in the History of the SVIB   348

11-2. Life Insurance Sales Production Versus Ratings on the SVIB
Life Insurance Salesman Scale   357

11-3. Distribution of Physician Interest Scores of Criterion Group and
of 137 Students Who Became Physicians   361

Appendix A

A-1. Test-Retest Reliabilities of 1938 Versus 1966 SVIB Scales   376

A-2. Percentage of Various Women's Occupational Samples Responding
"Like" to Religious People   379

A-3. Differences in Percent Responses for Two Groups Responding to
"Old" Revised Versus "New" Revised Women's Booklet   380

Appendix B

B-1. Description of Men's Criterion Groups   385

B-2. Description of Women's Criterion Groups   390

Appendix C

C-1. Item Response Percentages for the 1938 Men-in-General Sample
(Form M)   395

C-2. Item Response Percentages for the 1966 Men-in-General Sample
to the Common Items of Form M and Form T399   396

C-3. Item Response Percentages for the 1969 Men-in-General Sample
(Form T399)   400

C-4. Item Response Percentages for the 1946 Women-in-General Sample
(Form W)   402

C-5. Item Response Percentages for the 1969 Women-in-General Sample
(Form TW398)   403

Appendix D

D-1. Instructions for Converting Answers to Men's Booklet Form A to
Form M Order   434

D-2. Item Changes Between Men's Booklets Form M and Form T399   435

D-3. Form WA Items Omitted from Form W Booklet   437

D-4. Item Changes Between Women's Booklets Form W and
Form TW398   438

D-5. Item Numbers of the 249 Items Common to the Men's (Form T399
and T399R) and Women's (TW398 and TW398R) Booklets   440

Appendix E

E-1. Descriptions of the 1971 Men's Criterion Samples 445
E-2. Scale Characteristics of the 1971 Men's Scales 449
E-3. Mean Scores of the Criterion Samples on the 1971 Scales 450
E-4. Mean Scores of Miscellaneous Samples on the 1971 Scales 454
E-5. Scale Intercorrelations for the 1971 Scales 456
E-6. Correlations Between the 1971 Men's Occupational Scales and the Basic Interest Scales 459
E-7. Correlations Between the 1971 Men's Occupational Scales, and the Nonoccupational Scales, Like, Indifferent, Dislike Percentages, and the Holland Scales 460
E-8a. Means and Standard Deviations of the Scale Intercorrelation Sample—Occupational Scales 462
E-8b. Means and Standard Deviations of the Scale Intercorrelation Sample—All Other Scales 462
E-9. Item Composition of the Holland Scales 463
E-10. Mean Scores for 202 Samples on the Holland Realistic Scale 464
E-11. Mean Scores for 202 Samples on the Holland Intellectual Scale 465
E-12. Mean Scores for 202 Samples on the Holland Artistic Scale 466
E-13. Mean Scores for 202 Samples on the Holland Social Scale 467
E-14. Mean Scores for 202 Samples on the Holland Enterprising Scale 468
E-15. Mean Scores for 202 Samples on the Holland Conventional Scale 469
E-16. Scale Intercorrelations for the Holland Scales and Nonoccupational Scales 470
E-17. Intercorrelations Between the Male Basic Scales, and the Nonoccupational and Holland Scales 471

Appendix F

F-1. Items Weighted on the Men's Occupational Scales 474
F-2. Items Weighted on the Women's Occupational Scales 484

Figures

1. A General Introduction to the SVIB

1-1. Examples of items from the men's SVIB 3
1-2. Publisher's profile sheet for the men's SVIB 8
1-3. Publisher's profile sheet for the women's SVIB 9
1-4. Basic Interest scale means for 100 sales applicants and 100
employed salesmen 18
1-5. Basic Interest scale means for 91 medical school students,
tested as freshmen and retested as seniors 19

2. The Occupational Scales

2-1. Distribution of scores on Engineer scale for engineer criterion
group, men-in-general, and liberal arts college freshmen 44
2-2. Mean profiles for two groups of high school seniors, one with
high scores on the Life Insurance Salesman scale, the other
with high scores on the Physicist scale 72
2-3. Test-retest data over two weeks for 139 University of Minnesota
sophomores 72
2-4. Test-retest data over 30 days, for 102 U.S. Army Reserve Personnel 73
2-5. Test-retest data over three and a half years, for 189 Harvard
University freshmen 73
2-6. Test-retest data over three and a half years, for 91 University of
Minnesota Medical School freshmen 74
2-7. Test-retest data over three and a half years for 106 Medical
School "A" freshmen 74
2-8. Test-retest data over three and a half years for 82 Medical
School "B" freshmen 75
2-9. Test-retest data over eight to ten years, for 171 Minnesota
high school seniors 75
2-10. Test-retest data over ten years for 123 University of Minnesota
General College students 76
2-11. Test-retest data over ten years for 152 Missouri high school seniors 76
2-12. Test-retest data over 17 years for 92 psychologists 77
2-13. Test-retest data over 24 years for 47 YMCA secretaries 77
2-14. Test-retest data over 22 years for 220 Stanford University seniors 78
2-15. Test-retest data over 30 years for 48 Minnesota bankers 78
2-16. Test-retest data over 31 years for 229 Purdue engineering freshmen 79

2-17. Test-retest data over 36 years for 1,214 California teenagers   79

2-18. Profiles for E. G. Boring from 1927, 1948, and 1965   80

2-19. Test-retest data over two weeks for 112 University of Minnesota sophomore women   80

2-20. Test-retest data over four years for 38 Minnesota freshman women   84

2-21. Test-retest data over 15 years for 81 Connecticut College for Women freshmen   84

2-22. Test-retest data over 24 years for 134 psychologists   85

2-23. Test-retest data over 26 years for 91 University of Minnesota freshman women   85

3. The Men's Basic Interest Scales

3-1. Frequency distributions of item intercorrelations for both the men's and women's SVIB   90

3-2. Test-retest data over two weeks for 140 University of Minnesota College of Liberal Arts sophomores   113

3-3. Test-retest data over 30 days for 102 U.S. Army Reserve Personnel   114

3-4. Test-retest data over five months for 219 University of Minnesota general college freshmen   114

3-5. Test-retest data over 10 years for 123 University of Minnesota general college men   114

3-6. Test-retest data over three and a half years for 126 University of Missouri agricultural students   114

3-7. Test-retest data over three and a half years for 189 Harvard University freshmen   116

3-8. Test-retest data over three and a half years for 100 University of Minnesota College of Liberal Arts freshmen   116

3-9. Test-retest data over eight to ten years for 171 Minnesota high school seniors   116

3-10. Test-retest data over ten years for 152 Missouri high school seniors   116

3-11. Test-retest data over 22 years for 220 Stanford University seniors   118

3-12. Test-retest data over 22 years for 191 Stanford University graduate students   118

3-13. Test-retest data over 26 years for 93 University of Minnesota freshman men   118

3-14. Test-retest data over 31 years for 229 Purdue University engineering freshmen   118

3-15. Test-retest data over three and a half years for 2,800 Medical School freshmen from 26 medical schools   120

3-16. Test-retest data over three and a half years for 91 University of Minnesota Medical School students   120

3-17. Test-retest data over three and a half years for 106 Medical School "A" freshmen   120

3-18. Test-retest data over three and a half years for 82 Medical School "B" freshmen   120

3-19. Test-retest data over 11 years for 37 high school seniors who became Certified Public Accountants   122

3-20. Test-retest data over 17 years for 98 Iowa veterinarians   122

3-21. Test-retest data over 17 years for 92 psychologists   122
3-22. Test-retest data over 24 years for 47 YMCA secretaries   122
3-23. Test-retest data over 30 years for 48 Minnesota bankers   124
3-24. Test-retest data over 36 years for 1,214 California teenagers   124
3-25. Test-retest data over 36 years for 497 California teenagers (no college)   124
3-26. Test-retest data over 36 years for 214 California teenagers (B.A., B.S. degrees)   124
3-27. Test-retest data over 36 years for 72 California teenagers (M.A., M.S. degrees)   128
3-28. Test-retest data over 36 years for 17 California teenagers (LL.B. degrees)   128
3-29. Test-retest data over 36 years for 22 California teenagers (M.D. degrees)   128
3-30. Test-retest data over 36 years for 27 California teenagers (Ph.D., Ed.D. degrees)   128
3-31. Test and retest profiles for Salesman and Scientist samples over 36 years   154

4. The Women's Basic Interest Scales

4-1. Test-retest data over three and a half years for 56 University of Minnesota freshman women   172
4-2. Test-retest data over nine years for 327 University of Minnesota freshman women   172
4-3. Test-retest data over ten years for 56 University of Minnesota general college freshman women   172
4-4. Test-retest data over ten years for 81 Connecticut College freshman women   174
4-5. Test-retest data over 17 years for 142 women Ph.D. psychologists   174
4-6. Test-retest data over 25-year interval for 91 University of Minnesota freshman women   174

5. The Nonoccupational Scales

5-1. Relationship between age and scores on men's Academic Achievement scale   200
5-2. Academic Achievement (AACH) scale mean scores for outstanding people in ten occupations   207
5-3. Examples of items showing extreme correlations between age of respondents and percent responding "Like"   214
5-4. Mean scores on the Interest Maturity and Age-Related Interests scale for men tested at various ages   214
5-5. Age versus mean scores on the Age-Related Interests scale for test-retest samples, and a general curve   218

6. The Administrative Indices

6-1. Mean scores on men's profile for answer sheets marked all "Like," all "Indifferent," or all "Dislike"   258
6-2. Mean scores on women's profile for answer sheets marked all "Like," all "Indifferent," or all "Dislike"   258

7. The Interests of Outstanding Men

7-1. Mean SVIB profile for 12 prominent artists   262
7-2. Mean SVIB profile for 22 astronauts   262
7-3. Mean SVIB profile for Pulitzer Prize winning authors: 10 poets, 26 novelists and biographers   263
7-4. Mean SVIB profile for 16 corporation presidents   263
7-5. Mean SVIB profile for 91 Danforth Fellows   264
7-6. Mean SVIB profile for 132 federal judges   264
7-7. Mean SVIB profile for 13 top college football coaches   265
7-8. Mean SVIB profile for state governors: 8 Minnesota and 38 others   265
7-9. Mean SVIB profile for 43 McKnight Fellows (actors)   266
7-10. Mean SVIB profile for military officers: 91 generals and 21 admirals   266
7-11. Mean SVIB profile for outstanding musicians: 12 composers and 53 performers   267
7-12. Mean SVIB profile for Pulitzer Prize winning newsmen: 7 cartoonists and 47 writers and editors   267
7-13. Mean SVIB profile for psychologists: 50 APA presidents and 24 distinguished scientific contribution award winners   268
7-14. Mean SVIB profile for highly productive salesmen: 101 life insurance salesmen and 52 encyclopedia salesmen   268
7-15. Mean SVIB profile for scientists: 10 Noble Prize winners and 12 U.S. Medal of Science winners   269

8. Interpreting the Profile

8-1. Profile for Case Study #1   288
8-2. Profile for Case Study #2   288
8-3. Profile for Case Study #3   294
8-4. Profile for Case Study #4   294
8-5. Profile for Case Study #5   296
8-6. Profile for Case Study #6   296
8-7. Profile for Case Study #7   300
8-8. Profile for Case Study #8   300
8-9. Profile for Case Study #9   304
8-10. Profile for Case Study #10   304
8-11. Profile for Case Study #11   306
8-12. Profile for Case Study #12   306
8-13. Profile for Case Study #13   308
8-14. Profile for Case Study #14   308
8-15. Profile for Case Study #15   310
8-16. Profile for Case Study #16   310

9. Stability of Measured Interests Within Occupations

9-1. Mean profiles for 251 California lawyers tested in 1930 and 79 Minnesota lawyers tested in 1948   316
9-2. Mean profiles for 98 ministers tested in 1927 and ministers who were serving in the same churches in 1965   316
9-3. Mean profiles for 93 bankers tested in 1934 and bankers in the same jobs in the same banks in 1964   318

9-4. Mean profiles for 149 school superintendents tested in 1930 and the superintendents who were in the same school districts in 1965 ... 318

9-5. Mean profiles for 25 corporation presidents tested in 1935 and presidents of the same corporations tested in 1964 ... 320

9-6. Mean SVIB profiles for 25 early and 25 recent presidents of the American Psychological Association ... 320

10. Changing Interests Over Time

10-1. Response changes to item #27, "College professor" ... 326

10-2. Response changes to item #247, "Thrifty people" ... 326

10-3. Mean scores for old and new occupational samples on the Men's Cultural Change scale ... 329

10-4. Mean cultural change score versus year tested for 202 male occupational samples ... 332

10-5. Mean cultural change score versus year tested for 95 female occupational samples ... 339

11. An Informal History of the SVIB

11-1. Number of men's SVIB booklets printed annually: 1927–69 ... 346

11-2. Number of publications appearing annually on the SVIB: 1927–63 ... 347

Appendix A

A-1. Mean profiles of Policemen's scores on 1938 and 1966 scales ... 374

A-2. Mean profiles of Librarians' scores on 1938 and 1966 scales ... 374

A-3. Mean profiles of Psychologists' scores on 1938 and 1966 scales ... 375

A-4. Mean profiles of Lawyers' scores on 1938 and 1966 scales ... 375

Appendix D

D-1. The Cowdery Booklet (c. 1923) ... 408

D-2. The SVIB, Form A (1927) ... 410

D-3. The SVIB, Form M (1938) ... 414

D-4. The SVIB, Form T399 (1966) ... 418

D-5. The SVIB, Form WA (1933) ... 422

D-6. The SVIB, Form W (1946) ... 426

D-7. The SVIB, Form TW398 ... 430

Handbook for the
Strong Vocational Interest Blank

CHAPTER 1

A General Introduction to the SVIB

Men in different jobs have different interests. The Strong Vocational Interest Blank (SVIB) is a device to identify such differences among those occupations that college students usually enter. The SVIB accomplishes this by providing an index of the similarity between a person's interests and those of successful men (or women) in a wide range of occupations.

The specific techniques used in the SVIB are discussed below; briefly, what is done is to present the individual with a long list of activities and ask him to indicate which he likes and dislikes. His answers are analyzed in two main ways: first, by looking at his responses to clusters of related items, for example, mechanical activities; second, by comparing his responses to those of men (or women) already established in a wide range of activities. If his choices coincide with, say, engineers, then he receives a high score on the Engineer scale. If his answers are the opposite, that is, if he dislikes the activities that engineers like, he will receive a low score on the Engineer scale. The results of these analyses are printed out on a profile and, when used under the guidance of a well-trained counselor, can help the student better understand his unique pattern of interests.

If students and others making career decisions had the time to try out several occupations to determine if they enjoyed them, this inventory would not be needed. But, because that is impossible, some way of helping a student to understand how his preferences compare with those of people employed in various jobs can be useful. That is the primary function of the SVIB.

Many cautions should be noted, indeed emphasized. Psychological tests and inventories must be used wisely, and only by those who have some understanding of what these instruments can and cannot do. Because the problems that tests are used to solve—in general, making decisions about people—are common and, to those faced with them, frequently crucial, any technique that offers some systematic help is embraced warmly. A test that will "tell me what I should do" is eagerly sought by many students as a stable guide in a time of uncertainties; counselors who are advising students are also searching for objective methods to help lessen the student's feeling of uncharted floundering.

But no test or inventory can "tell me what I should do," and to imply that it can is inaccurate, unethical, and lessens the credibility in what it is the test can do. The SVIB cannot tell anyone where he can succeed; what it can do is act as a mirror to reflect back the individual's interests in a manner that allows him to compare his likes and dislikes with those of individuals in specified occupations. This is helpful information, but it must be integrated with the individual's other characteristics—his intelligence, special abilities, experience and other attitudes—before any definite decisions can be made.

This tendency for users to expect too much and exaggerate the results from the inventory is perhaps the biggest problem with using the SVIB; this point needs to be continually emphasized.

The Strong Blank is designed to help guide the student and the employee into areas where they are likely to find the greatest job satisfaction but not necessarily job success. Though there must be some substantial relationship between interest and quality of performance, it is, at present, not well understood. Perhaps interest has more to do with whether a task is attempted than with how well it is performed. Whether a student likes a course or not, he will earn about the same grade that he earns in other courses; his grades will depend on his abilities and general level of aspiration. But whether or not he elects to take a specific course, and succeeding courses in the series, depends on his interest in the subject matter. Thus, while measures of ability are needed to predict quality of performance, measures of interest are also needed to suggest areas that will be most stimulating.

Similarly, although a man's performance on the job depends on his abilities and motivation, whether or not he stays on the job will largely reflect whether he likes or dislikes it. For this reason, interest ratings are better indices of job persistence than of job success. In most selection techniques, too much attention is given to efficiency and too little to satisfaction and enjoyment—what does it avail us if our trainee becomes an immediate success, but then leaves the job?

All of our research confirms the summary statement published earlier by E. K. Strong, Jr.: "A person should consider seriously those occupations in which he receives high scores on the Strong Vocational Interest Blank before entering some unrelated occupation. On the other hand, he should scrutinize critically any occupation in which he receives a low score before accepting it as a final choice."

General Application

The primary use of the SVIB is for counseling high school and college students about their career choice, and the Strong Blank is oriented mainly toward that section of the occupational spectrum that college students usually enter—in general, business, social service occupations, the arts, and the professions. It is ordinarily not appropriate for use with unskilled, semi-skilled, and skilled trade occupations, because of both the item content and the research emphasis over the years. Practically all of the research has concentrated on men and women with some college experience; much less is known about the use of interest measures among blue-collar occupations.

In the 1969 revision of the women's booklet, many women's occupations at the nonprofessional level were tested and the results are presented in later chapters. While these data may help in working with women at this level, the emphasis on the profile is still on the professional and skilled occupations.

Test Materials

The basic SVIB documents are the *test booklets* containing the items, the *answer sheets* where individuals record their responses, and the *profile forms* that are used to report the results.

Test Booklets

There are 399 items in the men's SVIB booklet, 398 in the women's; to most of these, the individual is asked to respond "Like," "Indifferent," or "Dislike." The categories of response to the remaining items vary somewhat, but the three choice alternative is standard. An example of the items from the men's booklet is shown in Figure 1-1. The several forms of the booklet are discussed further below.

1 Actor	11 Auto Salesman
2 Advertising Man	12 Auto Racer
3 Architect	13 Auto Mechanic
4 Military Officer	14 Airplane Pilot
5 Artist	15 Bank Teller
6 Astronomer	16 Designer, Electronic Equipment
7 Athletic Director	17 Building Contractor
8 Auctioneer	18 Buyer of merchandise
9 Author of novel	19 Carpenter
10 Author of technical book	20 Cartoonist

FIG. 1-1. *Examples of items from the men's SVIB.*

Men's Booklet (Form T399). This is the 1966 revision of the men's booklet, designed for use with a separate answer sheet. Those who wish to reuse their test booklets—as most will—should use this form. This booklet can be used with any of the answer sheets provided by the various scoring services.

Users should be careful to distinguish between this booklet, Form T399, and the older 1938 booklet, Form M. The old booklet was yellow; the new one is blue. The old booklet had 400 items; one item has been dropped from the new one, leaving 399 items, to make it easier to discriminate between the old and new booklets and answer sheets.

Raw scores on the old and new forms are not equivalent, and old scoring weights applied to the revised booklet will provide meaningless figures. Although under certain conditions the old booklet can be scored with some of the new scales, to prevent confusion most users will want to switch to the new forms as soon as possible. As new scales become available, they will be designed for use with the new form, T399.

A copy of this booklet is in Appendix D.

Men's Booklet (Form T399R). This booklet contains precisely the same items as T399, but is designed so the respondent can mark his answers directly on the booklet. It is used in research projects to make the response task as simple as possible for the respondent. The front page of the booklet includes a short questionnaire, asking for such basic information as occupation, years of experience, and educational level. To score responses marked on this booklet, it is necessary to transfer them to answer sheets or IBM cards.

Men's Booklet (Form T399N). This booklet, available only from National Computer Systems, combines the booklet and answer sheet into a single form. The response positions are located on the test booklet itself, and, after the individual has filled in his answers, this booklet can be processed as an answer sheet. This makes the task easier for the respondent, though of course the booklet cannot be reused. Like the booklet above, this form has been designed for research projects and has a short questionnaire on the front page. With this booklet, the answers do not have to be transferred to other sheets; they can be scored directly. With two exceptions, Nos. 234 and 235, the T399N items are identical to T399 and T399R. See Appendix D for more information.

Women's Booklet (Form TW398). This is the 1969 revision of the women's booklet, analogous to the men's form T399, and is designed for use with a separate answer sheet. This is the form that should be adopted for most routine uses. Responses to this booklet cannot be scored on the old (1946) scoring scales.

A copy of this booklet is in Appendix D.

Women's Booklet (Form TW398R). This booklet is directly analogous to the men's booklet T399R, the form designed for research use, and the same comments apply. The front of the booklet has a short questionnaire, and the responses to the booklet must be transferred to an answer sheet or IBM cards for scoring.

Women's Booklet (Form TW398N). This booklet is directly analogous to the comparable men's booklet.

Older forms of the booklets. The earlier versions of the booklets cannot be used with the revised scoring scales, and they should be eliminated from most routine uses. Appendix D contains examples of all forms, and more complete information about the changes from form to form.

Some Background on the SVIB Booklets

The first men's form, published in 1927 by E. K. Strong, Jr. of Stanford University, had 420 items; the women's, published in 1933, had 410. In 1938, both booklets were revised and shortened to 400 items (to permit use of an IBM answer sheet—which could only accommodate 400). Strong selected the poorest 20 and 10 items, respectively, and discarded them; the remaining items were renumbered sequentially, so that most of the item numbers were changed by this revision.

The 1966 revision of the men's booklet and the 1969 revision of the women's booklet have continued this process of sifting out the poorer items; roughly 100 items from each booklet have been replaced, either because they were outdated, their validity was marginal, or, in a few cases, because they were in poor taste ("Deaf mutes"). In this revision cycle, all of the discarded items were replaced by new items, and the unchanged items retained their same numbers. The new items cover areas not well covered formerly, such as philosophic topics, art, and technological activities.

The item content of the SVIB has been oriented toward occupational topics, and the revisions have steadily increased that orientation. Personality-type items, such as "I get rattled easily," are less effective in separating occupational groups than items aimed directly at occupational activities, and most of them have been eliminated. Also, in the recent revisions, efforts were made to simplify the vocabulary and lower the required reading level. As the items stand now, they have survived several siftings, and should collectively serve as a useful tool in the measurement of interests.

More information on the historical development of the SVIB is included in Chapter 11.

The men's SVIB booklet is divided into several sections. The first contains 100 occupational titles, to which the respondent indicates either

"Like," "Indifferent," or "Dislike." Some examples are shown in Figure 1-1. This is the most powerful section of the test in terms of separating occupations from each other. The second section (36 items) contains school subjects, the third (49 items) various amusements and hobbies. The fourth section (48 items) includes general occupational activities, such as "Writing reports," "Teaching adults," and "Buying merchandise for a store." In the fifth section (47 items), the respondent indicates his liking, disliking, or indifference toward various kinds of people; some examples are "Energetic people," "Military men," "People who daydream a lot." The sixth section (40 items) has a forced-choice format; the person is presented with ten items and asked to select the three he most prefers and the three he least prefers. The seventh section (40 items) is a modified forced-choice format; the person is shown pairs of activities and asked to indicate which he prefers, or he may opt for saying he likes both equally well. The eighth and last section (39 items) contains statements about personal characteristics, such as "Win friends easily," "Am always on time with my work," and "Can prepare successful advertisements." To these the person is asked to check either "Yes" (it is true of me), "?" or "No."

The SVIB is the only major psychological inventory containing different types of item formats. Strong originally chose different forms because he wanted to compare several methods of asking questions to determine which was best. The research that has been done indicates that item content is far more important than item format, and apparently one style is not much better or worse than another. The variation in item style will be retained for the foreseeable future, both because a change would be extremely expensive and because a mixture of layouts does provide some variety for the individual who, after all, is being presented with a fairly long, possibly tedious task.

The above comments also apply to the women's booklet, though the precise layout from section to section differs somewhat. There are 249 items common to the men's (T399) and women's (TW398) forms.

Profile Forms

An individual's SVIB scores are normally reported on especially devised profile forms. The scoring services each produce their own profile forms, under license from the publisher. Examples are shown in Figures 1-2 (men's) and 1-3 (women's).

Across the top of the profiles are the Basic Scales; these scales contain items with high intercorrelations and the scale name summarizes the item content. The individual's scores are reported in standard score form in the column following the scale name; they are also plotted as hash marks on the right side of the form to give a visual impression of the patterns of the scores. This graphic presentation aids in interpretation by emphasizing the high and low scores.

On the men's profile, the solid vertical line at a standard score of 50 represents the mean score of a cross-section of 52-year-old men; the thin jagged line shows the mean score of these same men when they were about 16 years old. The differences between the two lines show changes that occurred with maturation.

On the women's profile, the line at 50 represents the mean of the Women-in-General sample; the jagged line indicates the mean score of a representative sample of high school senior girls. The two women's samples are not strictly comparable, as the Women-in-General sample probably contains more professional women than will come from the high school senior group. Thus, the differences between their means is due to both maturation and sampling differences.

More information on the Basic Scales is reported in Chapters 3 and 4.

Below the Basic Scales are two columns of Occupational Scales. These scales have been developed by identifying the characteristic interests of men, or women, in the specified occupations. On the profile, these scales have been arranged in groups according to their similarity, and special attention should be given to the patterns of scores in these groupings. The scales have been normed by using the criterion sample from the occupation, and their mean score has been set equal to 50 with a standard deviation of 10. Thus, engineers average 50 on the Engineer scale, artists 50 on the Artist scale, and so forth. The individual's standard score for each Occupational Scale is printed after the scale name, and is also plotted as a hash mark. These hash marks fall within letter-ratings, e.g., A, B+, B, B−, C+, C, which have been used to make interpretation easier. A ratings are considered "high," C ratings "low."

The shaded area on each Occupational Scale represents the middle third of the Men-in-General (MIG) group (actually, the MIG mean ±0.43 standard deviations), and provides information about how the average professional man or businessman scores on each scale. The women's profile has similar shaded areas, based on the middle third of the Women-in-General group.

At the bottom left hand side of the profile are several Non-Occupational Scales, identified only by initial. These scales, whose development and interpretation are discussed in Chapter 5, should be used only by those with sufficient training to avoid misinterpretation. These scores will add little to, indeed may detract from, the counseling process unless the counselor is very knowledgeable about their meaning.

Reprinted from the *1969 Supplement to the Manual for the Strong Vocational Interest Blanks*,
copyrighted by the Board of Trustees of the Leland Stanford Junior University and published by Stanford University Press

BASIC INTEREST SCALES

SCALE	PLOTTED SCORE
PUBLIC SPEAKING	30 40 50 60 70
LAW/POLITICS	
BUSINESS MANAGEMENT	
SALES	
MERCHANDISING	
OFFICE PRACTICES	
MILITARY ACTIVITIES	30 40 50 60 70
TECHNICAL SUPERVISION	
MATHEMATICS	
SCIENCE	
MECHANICAL	
NATURE	
AGRICULTURE	30 40 50 60 70
ADVENTURE	
RECREATIONAL LEADERSHIP	
MEDICAL SERVICE	
SOCIAL SERVICE	
RELIGIOUS ACTIVITIES	
TEACHING	30 40 50 60 70
MUSIC	
ART	
WRITING	

DOUBLE LINE = AVERAGE SCORE FOR 650 52-YEAR-OLD MEN.

OCCUPATIONAL SCALES

OCCUPATION	STD. SCORE	C	B—	B	B+	A		OCCUPATION	STD. SCORE	C	B—	B	B+	A
I DENTIST		20 30 40 50 60					VI	LIBRARIAN		20 30 40 50 60				
OSTEOPATH								ARTIST						
VETERINARIAN								MUSICIAN PERFORMER						
PHYSICIAN								MUSIC TEACHER						
PSYCHIATRIST							VII	C.P.A. OWNER						
PSYCHOLOGIST							VIII	SENIOR C.P.A.						
BIOLOGIST		20 30 40 50 60						ACCOUNTANT		20 30 40 50 60				
II ARCHITECT								OFFICEWORKER						
MATHEMATICIAN								PURCHASING AGENT						
PHYSICIST								BANKER						
CHEMIST								PHARMACIST						
ENGINEER								FUNERAL DIRECTOR						
III PRODUCTION		20 30 40 50 60					IX	SALES MANAGER		20 30 40 50 60				
ARMY OFFICER								REAL ESTATE SALESMAN						
AIR FORCE OFFICER								LIFE INS. SALESMAN						
IV CARPENTER							X	ADVERTISING MAN						
FOREST SERVICE MAN								LAWYER						
FARMER								AUTHOR-JOURNALIST						
MATH-SCIENCE TEACHER		20 30 40 50 60					XI	PRESIDENT-MFG.		20 30 40 50 60				
PRINTER								SUPP. OCCUPATIONAL SCALES						
POLICEMAN								CREDIT MANAGER						
V PERSONNEL DIRECTOR								CHAMBER OF COM. EXEC.						
PUBLIC ADMINISTRATOR								PHYSICAL THERAPIST						
REHABILITATION COUNS.								COMPUTER PROGRAMMER						
YMCA STAFF MEMBER		20 30 40 50 60						BUSINESS ED. TEACHER		20 30 40 50 60				
SOCIAL WORKER								COMMUNITY REC. ADMIN.						
SOCIAL SCIENCE TEACHER														
SCHOOL SUPERINTENDENT														
MINISTER														

NON-OCCUPATIONAL SCALES

AACH   AR   DIV   MFII   MO   OIE   OL   SL

ADMINISTRATIVE INDICES

TR   UNP   FC   LP   IP   DP

FIG. 1-2. *Publisher's profile sheet for the men's SVIB.*

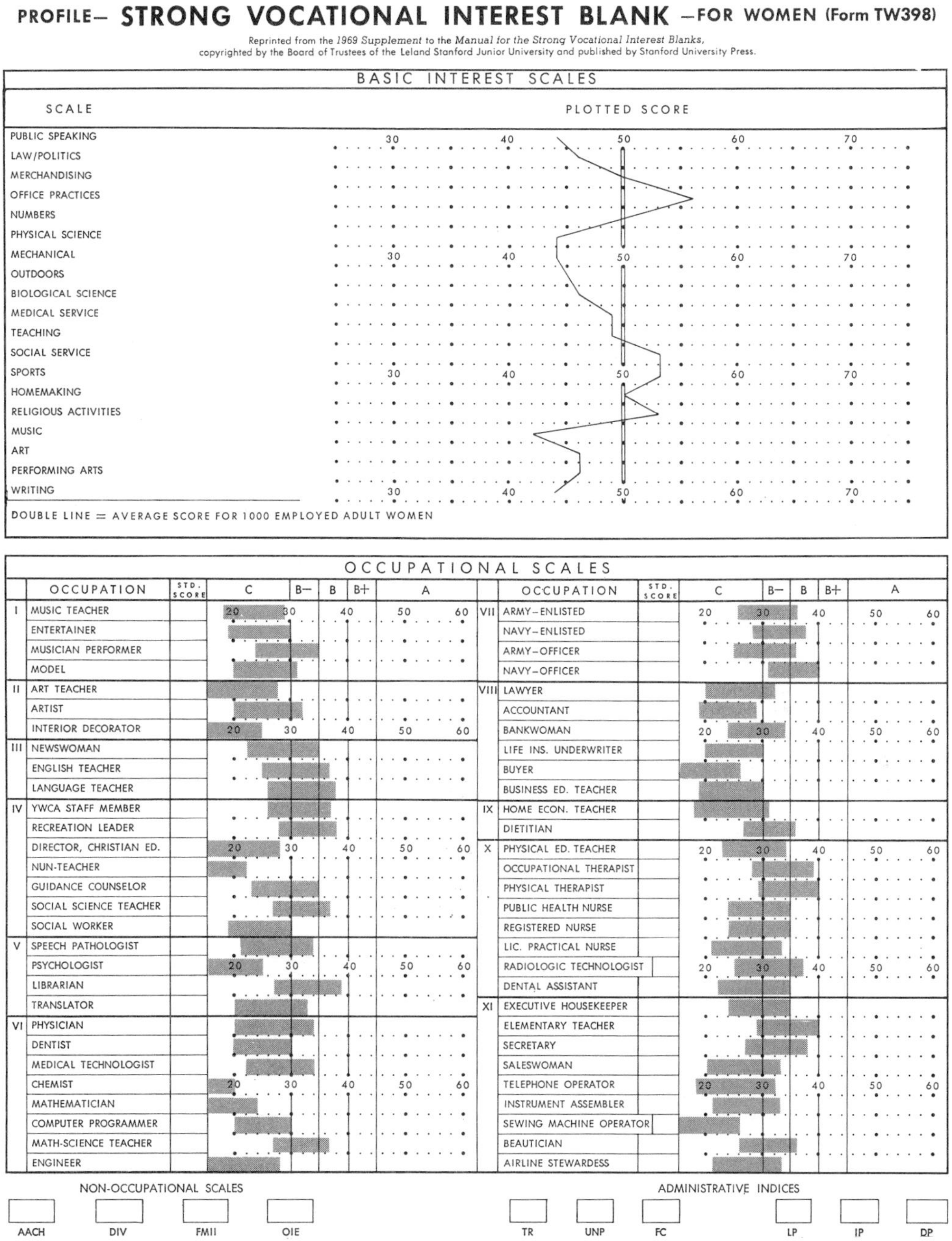

PROFILE— **STRONG VOCATIONAL INTEREST BLANK** —FOR WOMEN (Form TW398)

Reprinted from the *1969 Supplement* to the *Manual for the Strong Vocational Interest Blanks*,
copyrighted by the Board of Trustees of the Leland Stanford Junior University and published by Stanford University Press.

BASIC INTEREST SCALES

SCALE	PLOTTED SCORE
PUBLIC SPEAKING	
LAW/POLITICS	
MERCHANDISING	
OFFICE PRACTICES	
NUMBERS	
PHYSICAL SCIENCE	
MECHANICAL	
OUTDOORS	
BIOLOGICAL SCIENCE	
MEDICAL SERVICE	
TEACHING	
SOCIAL SERVICE	
SPORTS	
HOMEMAKING	
RELIGIOUS ACTIVITIES	
MUSIC	
ART	
PERFORMING ARTS	
WRITING	

DOUBLE LINE = AVERAGE SCORE FOR 1000 EMPLOYED ADULT WOMEN

OCCUPATIONAL SCALES

	OCCUPATION			OCCUPATION
I	MUSIC TEACHER		VII	ARMY—ENLISTED
	ENTERTAINER			NAVY—ENLISTED
	MUSICIAN PERFORMER			ARMY—OFFICER
	MODEL			NAVY—OFFICER
II	ART TEACHER		VIII	LAWYER
	ARTIST			ACCOUNTANT
	INTERIOR DECORATOR			BANKWOMAN
III	NEWSWOMAN			LIFE INS. UNDERWRITER
	ENGLISH TEACHER			BUYER
	LANGUAGE TEACHER			BUSINESS ED. TEACHER
IV	YWCA STAFF MEMBER		IX	HOME ECON. TEACHER
	RECREATION LEADER			DIETITIAN
	DIRECTOR, CHRISTIAN ED.		X	PHYSICAL ED. TEACHER
	NUN-TEACHER			OCCUPATIONAL THERAPIST
	GUIDANCE COUNSELOR			PHYSICAL THERAPIST
	SOCIAL SCIENCE TEACHER			PUBLIC HEALTH NURSE
	SOCIAL WORKER			REGISTERED NURSE
V	SPEECH PATHOLOGIST			LIC. PRACTICAL NURSE
	PSYCHOLOGIST			RADIOLOGIC TECHNOLOGIST
	LIBRARIAN			DENTAL ASSISTANT
	TRANSLATOR		XI	EXECUTIVE HOUSEKEEPER
VI	PHYSICIAN			ELEMENTARY TEACHER
	DENTIST			SECRETARY
	MEDICAL TECHNOLOGIST			SALESWOMAN
	CHEMIST			TELEPHONE OPERATOR
	MATHEMATICIAN			INSTRUMENT ASSEMBLER
	COMPUTER PROGRAMMER			SEWING MACHINE OPERATOR
	MATH-SCIENCE TEACHER			BEAUTICIAN
	ENGINEER			AIRLINE STEWARDESS

NON-OCCUPATIONAL SCALES

AACH   DIV   FMII   OIE

ADMINISTRATIVE INDICES

TR   UNP   FC   LP   IP   DP

FIG. 1-3. *Publisher's profile sheet for the women's SVIB.*

9

At the bottom right-hand side of the profile are the newly developed Administrative Indices. These are intended to detect errors in test administration and scoring, and are discussed further in Chapter 6.

The reverse side of the profile forms has an explanation of the various scales in nontechnical language, and can be used to help the student understand his results.

Answer Sheets

The answer sheets are produced by the various scoring agencies—under license from the publisher—for use with their own particular scoring machines and they are not interchangeable from service to service. Further information can be obtained from the scoring agencies.

Administering the Inventory

The SVIB can be administered individually, in groups, or by mail. The booklet and answer sheets contain adequate instructions, and most individuals can complete the inventory correctly with little supervision, especially those who have had prior experience with such answer sheets. Of course, the administrator should check to see that the instructions on the booklet and answer sheet have been followed. Most users will want to send the completed answer sheet to a test-scoring service and therefore must be careful to use the appropriate answer sheet. An important point in test administration is to maintain the answer sheets in good condition so that they can be properly scored. Dirty or crinkled answer sheets, messy erasures, or curled corners create problems at the scoring machine.

Instructions for completing the inventory are printed in the booklets, and additional instructions appear on the answer sheets. These should be followed very closely. The test administrator should also:

1. Reiterate that all the information requested on the answer sheet should be filled in.

2. See that the person understands how to use the name grid, when answer sheets with these grids are used.

3. Emphasize that all the marks should be heavy and dark.

4. Reiterate that one answer, and only one answer, should be marked for each question.

5. Check to see that the instructions for the forced-choice responses in Part VI are understood.

There is no time limit. Most people require from 25 to 45 minutes; virtually everyone finishes in an hour. A group of adult men took from 20 to 120 minutes to fill in the Blank, with the following spread:

Q3 .... 26 minutes
Median .... 30 minutes
Q1 .... 37 minutes

For 1,000 high school juniors, the ranges were:

Q3 .... 29 minutes
Median .... 36 minutes
Q1 .... 44 minutes

Eleven percent of the high school group required more than 50 minutes to fill in the Blank.

In administering the SVIB, users should be careful to distinguish between the older forms and the new revisions of the booklets. The differences between the forms have been discussed above.

When the individual has finished, the test administrator should scan the answer sheet to detect any gross errors; then the answer sheet can be mailed to the scoring service, who will score the answers and provide a profile of the results. Usually, answer sheets are scored and mailed back within a day or two of receipt. Some agencies offer optional services such as calculation of means and standard deviations for each scale for specified samples, and item frequency counts. For current price lists and descriptions of optional services, write the scoring services directly.

Appropriate Age Level for Use

The criterion groups used to standardize the SVIB averaged about 40 years of age. Because interests change very little after age 25, the SVIB is distinctly applicable for adults. Moreover, changes of interest with age are relatively mild between the ages of 20 and 25, so that here also the test is appropriate.

Evidence is mounting that occupational choice is determined to some extent in high school, and the inventory should be helpful in counseling students in this age range. But, because changes in interest scores are more likely between the ages of 16 and 20, the emphasis in interpreting scores for students in this age range should be on planning the general direction of a career, rather than on concentrating on one occupation, and the possibility of later change should be stressed.

Age 16 is the minimum age for normal use.

Required Qualifications for Those Using the SVIB

The minimum qualifications necessary for those using the SVIB are difficult to define because a paradox quickly appears, i.e., if a person is in a position where he *has* to make personnel decisions or give advice, the less training and experience he has, the more he should probably depend on "canned, empirical" techniques. However, this runs counter to the accepted thinking among psychologists which requires a person to have extensive training and supervised experience before using these methods. The answer, of course, is that untrained people should not be making these decisions but that is not always realistic.

Although most SVIB profiles can be adequately interpreted by an intelligent person with a little background information, the optimum use of the SVIB as part of a battery of psychometric devices will generally be achieved only by someone professionally trained in counseling or personnel work.

Anyone using the SVIB for counseling should have, as a minimum, some training in test construction and interpretation; some supervised counseling experience is also highly desirable. The optimum training would include an internship or experience in a practicum setting.

Those using the SVIB in personnel decisions should have some course work in test technology, and in personnel management techniques. A Master's degree in Psychology, Industrial Relations, or a similar field should be considered a minimum.

Use of the SVIB in Personnel Selection

The selection of employees should be based on relevant information; usually, the person's vocational interests are relevant to the employment decision, and an interest inventory is a more systematic means of assessing these than any other technique now available, including an interview. *When used by a professionally trained person*, a SVIB profile can provide useful information for evaluating an applicant, information which should be used analogously to any other empirical data about the person.

The use of rigid cutting scores is not recommended, except perhaps in the rare case where a company or organization has conducted an extensive study of the relationship between interest scores and performance in their institution. Where such studies have not been conducted, practitioners should be cautious in the use of interest inventories in selection.

The use of interest measures in employee *placement*, rather than *selection*, may be more fruitful, especially in large companies where a wide breadth of occupational possibilities is present. The use of interest inventories in counseling and reassignment of individual employees to activities they may find more satisfying has been described in various personnel textbooks, and this application of interest measures seems, at the moment, better justified by the research data.

Use of the SVIB by Untrained Persons to Study Their Own Interests

Can the man on the street gain any useful information about himself by looking at his SVIB profile without professional interpretation? *The Standards for Educational and Psychological Tests and Manuals*, published by the American Psychological Association (1966), states explicity that test manuals should not imply that any test can be interpreted by a person lacking proper training. While that position seems extreme, and is in fact violated by the vast majority of classroom tests, it is softened by including among those having the proper training, "Responsible, educated nonpsychologists such as school principals and business executives."

In the research on the SVIB, much experience has been accumulated in giving adults their profiles with only a general, written explanation of their scores. During 1965–67, some 20,000 adults filled in the SVIB for research purposes and they all received their profiles, by mail, as a courtesy in exchange for their help. While no systematic study has been done of the adequacy of the individual's self-interpretation, no catastrophes have come to light. And dozens of persons have commented favorably, by letter and in person, on being allowed to see their results. A frequent comment has been, "I've filled in dozens of questionnaires and tests but this is the first time I've ever received any feedback." There surely have been misunderstandings, especially the confusion between interests and abilities—"I'm glad to see I wouldn't make a very good funeral director"—but there have been some useful insights also, as the following from an academician who is in a position of some considerable influence, "It is startling to see my lack of common interests with psychologists."

In general, psychologists have been too secretive about their test scores; we had best be more concerned with how to communicate results, not how to protect them from scrutiny. Perhaps personality and ability measures are more sensitive, but giving persons normative information about their interests seems quite defensible.

In a sense, the veil of secrecy that psychologists have drawn over their test results resembles that drawn over salaries. Although the overt reason is to protect individuals from invidious comparisons, an equally potent covert motive is to protect the administrator from having to defend the inaccuracies, inconsistencies or inadequacies of his system. The recommendation made here is that anyone who fills in the SVIB should be allowed to see his results, with professional interpretation when possible, without it if there is no other way. If one impact of this policy is to generate pressure for more easily interpretable results, that will be all for the better.

Faking

Critics of the SVIB have leaned hard on the inventory for being "transparent" and "easily faked" (e.g., Rothney, 1967; Fricke, 1968). This section is a review of what is known about faking on the SVIB; it covers most of the published and some of the unpublished research on this topic, and the general conclusion is that the problem, while not completely absent, is not as severe as some would imply.

If one wishes to modify his SVIB answers, that is, to fake them, to affect his resulting scores, that is certainly possible. When investigators have asked students to sway their responses in specified directions, the scores always reflect this. Whether such faking actually happens in real life situations is more difficult to determine because closely parallel "honest" and "fake" test-taking situations are hard to produce. Some attempts have been made, and the relevant research is summarized below.

Gray's Literature Review

Clifton W. Gray, in a comprehensive literature review for his Ph.D. dissertation, has summarized the efforts of several decades:

Strong (1943) in 1927, Steinmetz (1932), Paterson (1946), Steward (1947), Benton and Kornhauser (1948), Kelso and Bordin (1948), Longstaff (1948), Wallace (1950), Garry (1953), and Gehman (1957) studied the fakability of the Strong.

Strong (1943, p. 684f) administered the inventory to a class of 34 engineering seniors and business graduates. He readministered it to the same group about one month later with instructions to fake high engineering scores. The mean gain was 18 standard score points.... Strong analyzed shifts on individual items and found that 59% of the items were answered the same while faking as they had been a month earlier. Of the remaining 41% which changed, 34% shifted by one category (e.g., Like to Indifferent, Indifferent to Dislike) and 7% shifted by two categories. Items showing the greatest changes were those "obviously related" (Strong, 1943, p. 686) to engineering.

Steinmetz (1932) used nearly the same procedure. His group of 46 junior college students took the Strong under standard directions and again three months later with instructions to fake good as Junior High School Principal. The mean score on 13 of 19 investigated occupational scales changed by an amount greater than one SD, 11 of these 13 pairs of means were from two to ten SDs apart.

Paterson (1946) reported a case study of a vocational misfit whose Kuder Preference Record scores but not his Strong scores confirmed his professed ambition and contradicted his background experiences in a way that suggested the Strong might be more subtle.

Steward (1947) administered the Strong to 31 university students for guidance purposes and again two days later with instructions to fake good as life insurance salesmen. The average gain was 131 raw score points on the life insurance key. [Note: this gain was on the old scoring scales where the item weights ranged from +4 to −4 DPC.]

Benton and Kornhauser (1948) gave the Strong to 34 undergradaute college students and again two days later with instructions to fake high physician interest. The mean physician score shifted from B minus to B plus, with the greatest shifts occurring, as with Steinmetz (1932) in the initially lowest scores.

Kelso and Bordin (1948) found 136 men in beginning psychology classes with "clear-cut" interest patterns. When instructed to simulate patterns different from theirs, they were able to "manipulate the patterns as readily as sophisticated subjects," although there was considerable variability in the stereotypes thus expressed (1948, p. 353).

Longstaff (1948) had 59 students in his evening extension class in applied psychology complete Strongs, first for getting information about themselves, then a second time for a study of its fakability. They were asked to depress certain interests and to fake good as carpenter, mathematician, engineer, physicist, chemist, artist, author-journalist, and musician. Of 35 male subjects, nearly half raised by two letter grades their score on chemist, artist, author-journalist, and musician, while a third were equally successful on engineer and physicist. Three-quarters of this group of men raised their score by one letter grade or more on all stipulated keys except carpenter.

Wallace (1950) administered the Strong to 238 male undergraduates in Medicine, engineering, and public accounting and at the same time obtained personal history data and a statement of vocational choice. He readministered the Strong with instructions to fake good in this chosen field. He defined "discrepants" and "nondiscrepants" according to whether the expressed and measured interest conflicted or coincided. He found that nondiscrepants faked significantly higher than discrepants, that they had more opportunity to gain information about the occupation of their choice than the discrepants, that they had less self-conflict about their choice, and that they "excelled" on 5 of 25 aspects of personal history.

Garry (1953) also following an "honest first–then fake" order, reported that 178 male college undergraduates in a general psychology course raised their mean score on the carpenter scale from minus 145 to plus 115 [raw scores based on ±4 weights]. Two groups of students, size 75 and 91, in an educational psychology course succeeded in faking good as president, lawyer, physician, and minister. The smallest mean gain was two-thirds SD for president in the smaller group. The median gain among the eight pairs of mean scores was about 1¾ SD (for physician) in both groups. The greatest gain was over 3 SDs for minister in the smaller group. Garry performed an item analysis of faked responses on the physician scale and noted that the differences from faking resulted from less than half of the keyed items. The items which students chose for faking were presumably more obviously related to the interests of the physician since they were items with the greatest weights. But significant differences between the most and the least successful fakers (high and low 27% according to faked physician score) occurred on as many unweighted as weighted items.

The most extreme distortion reported in this review was described by Gehman (1957). His 61 senior engineering students took the Strong in the "usual manner" (1957, p. 66). Three weeks later they simulated patterns of the social service group after hearing a description of the work such people do. Occupational Group II, physical science, dropped from a mean of 41.5 to 21, and its SD went from 10.7 to zero. The social service occupational group mean increased by 5 SDs, from 35 to 60. [Gray, 1959, pp. 10–14]

In two other unpublished studies, similar results have appeared. As part of an assessment project of 560 Veterans Administration Clinical Psychologist trainees conducted by Lowell Kelly of the University of Michigan, each trainee completed the SVIB three times, once in a regular way, once "faking masculine" and once "faking feminine." The intent was to measure their empathy for the MF dimension. The resulting statistics for their standard scores on the Masculinity-Femininity II scale were:

Test Instructions	Mean	SD
Fake masculine	74.2	7.7
Regular	49.0	10.7
Fake feminine	26.0	8.0

As the average man scores about 52, the average woman about 38 on this scale, these trainees successfully shifted their scores in the masculine or feminine direction as directed. Note, however, that they grossly exaggerated. If their task had been to "answer like the average man," it would have been a more difficult task.

In another unpublished study, Dunnette, Kirchner, and Jenson asked individuals who already scored high on the Accountant or Salesman scales to fake like successful accountants or salesmen respectively. They found that each group could raise their score on the appropriate scale even further but, more importantly, they found the shifts from the "regular" to "faking" answers were quite specific to the occupation, suggesting the absence of any global faking factor; thus, any general "Faking" scale would probably not work in all, or even most, settings.

Real-Life Faking

As Gray emphasized, all of these projects have depended on artificial situations where people were instructed to fake their answers—these results provide no information about what actually happens when people take tests. To fill this gap, for his Ph.D. research, Gray compared SVIBs completed by students seeing counselors versus SVIBs completed by those same students when applying for medical school some months later. He assumed, as does most everyone, that a student seeking counseling will complete the SVIB honestly, and that applicants to medical school will probably slant their answers in socially desirable ways. Thus, by comparing the two tests, one should be able to identify any faking that has occurred.

Gray located 278 males who had completed the SVIB either for high school counseling, during orientation week, or for counseling at the University of Minnesota, and who had also later completed the SVIB as part of the application procedure to the Medical School at Minnesota.

Gray concluded (Gray, 1959, p. 296):

> Forty-seven percent of the medical applicant group did not or could not raise their physician score between testing for counseling and testing for admission to medical school. Twenty-four percent raised their physician score enough to have a serious effect on its interpretation by an admissions officer; 29 percent raised their score by a less important amount. . . . Although the two Strongs of the medical applicants were separated by a mean time lapse of two and one-half years, the passing of time did not systematically affect the physician score; amount of change in physician score was not significantly related to amount of time lapse.

In another study of SVIB faking under real conditions, Kirchner compared the scores of 156 applicants for sales positions with those of 117 salesmen who had been on the job five years or more. The groups were split into industrial or retail sales positions for analysis. Kirchner concluded:

> Applicants . . . in both settings tended to score higher [than salesmen already employed] in Social Service and Business occupations and lower in Technical, Scientific, and, surprisingly, Sales. Apparently, applicants indicate a greater liking for things than do employed salesmen, which suggests the idea of completing the SVIB in the most socially acceptable fashion: i.e., liking much, disliking little (Kirchner, 1961, p. 276).

Other than the Navy studies discussed separately below, Gray's and Kirchner's studies are apparently the only published reports of possible faking on the SVIB administered under actual selection conditions; thus, their data are important. In preparing this Handbook, I tried to secure their data to present profiles of their samples to show the magnitude of the differences. In both cases, the original data were irretrievable; both authors were cooperative, however, and new samples were generated.

For the salesmen, another 100 applicants for sales positions at Minnesota Mining and Manufacturing (3M) were compared with 100 men tested after they were settled into their jobs. A comparison of their Basic Interest Scale profiles is shown in Figure 1-4. (See Chapter 3 for a discussion of the Basic Scales.)

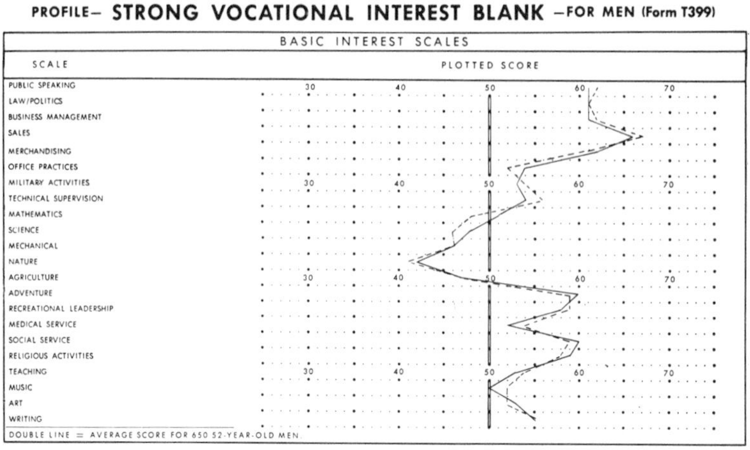

PROFILE— **STRONG VOCATIONAL INTEREST BLANK** —FOR MEN (Form T399)

FIG. 1-4. *Basic Interest scale means for 100 sales applicants (solid line) and 100 employed salesmen (broken line).*

As can be seen, there were a few differences, amounting to two or three points, but they were not dramatic. Contrary to Kirchner's earlier results, the applicants did score higher on the Sales scale, which may reflect their concern that they look like salesmen in answering the inventory. Still, one would hardly conclude that any massive faking has gone on; in the usual study described above, the magnitude of change under specific directions to fake has been more like a standard deviation or two, not just a few points.

Also, Kirchner's hunch that applicants marked more "Likes" than salesmen already employed was not borne out in these samples. The percent responses given by both groups to the first 100 items were:

	Like	Indifferent	Dislike	Total
Salesmen	39%	32%	29%	100%
Applicants	39%	30%	31%	100%

Gray's study of medical school applicants was not directly replicated, but some other relevant data on medical school students were available. In 1956, the freshman class at the University of Minnesota Medical School was tested with the SVIB, and they were retested upon graduation four years later as part of a larger study conducted by the Association of American Medical Colleges (Hutchins, 1964). Presumably as freshmen, they would be motivated to look good on the test; as seniors, they could afford to be more honest. A comparison of their freshmen and senior Basic Interest Scale profiles is in Figure 1-5.

Although the general shape of the profiles did not change much, several of the scales showed noteworthy differences. These students scored lower as seniors than they did as freshmen on the Social Service, Medical Service,

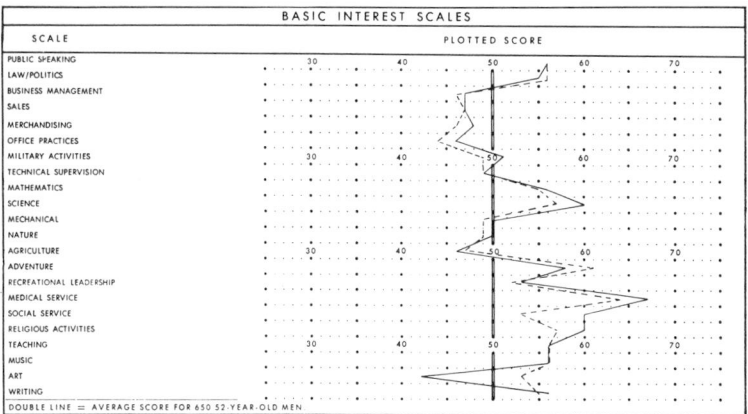

FIG. 1-5. *Basic Interest scale means for 91 medical school students, tested as freshmen (solid line) and retested as seniors (broken line).*

Science, and Religious Activities scales, all scales that would usually be considered "good" in relation to medical education. Either the medical school environment created these changes or, more likely, the freshmen were more inclined to give favorable answers than were the seniors, or both. In either event, with a few marked exceptions, the high scores stayed high, the low ones stayed low. The exceptions may reflect a relaxation by these students after the rigorous four-year program. The decrease in medical and social service interests, and the novel increase on the Adventure scale—novel because all other test-retest samples have shown a decrease on that scale (see p. 123)—all suggest a general loosening of the academic grip. These changes, incidentally, were not unique to the University of Minnesota; the same trends appeared in all of the 28 medical schools in the original study. See p. 119 for more information on this point.

Whatever the dynamics of the shifts, the relevant point here in this discussion of faking is that the profiles showed considerable consistency over the time period, even though the testing and retesting situations were different.

Investigations of Possible Faking
Among Navy ROTC Scholarship Applicants

Stephenson (1965) has reported some further information relevant to SVIB faking. In the Navy ROTC scholarship program, the interests of the applicant, as measured by the SVIB, are considered in the final decision, and the Navy wished to know if it was necessary for the inventory to be administered under tight control at a Navy testing station, or if the much simpler method of mailing it to the applicant could be used. In 1964, 213 applicants from several testing stations were given the SVIB to take home to complete; a matched sample completed the booklet at the testing station under standardized conditions. One might suspect that those answering at home, where they could discuss their answers with their parents, high school counselor, someone who had earlier won a scholarship, or perhaps even a Navy officer, might give somewhat different answers than those tested under strict conditions—yet Stephenson reported no differences in item responses between these two groups. He concluded: "The findings [show] that responses to the SVIB are not dependent upon place of test administration, at home or at the Recruiting Station, nor upon conditions of test administration, self or standard. . . . The findings suggest that research with [the SVIB] can employ the mail-out, mail-back procedure with little fear of biasing results" (Stephenson, 1965).

Abrahams, Neumann, and Githens (1968a, 1968b) have extended the research on the use of the SVIB for screening NROTC scholarship applicants. They first constructed a Navy Officer Retention scale by contrasting the SVIB responses of officers who remained in the Navy versus those who left after their obligated service, then collected more data from various groups to assess the degree of faking that may have occurred on this scale when the SVIB was filled out as part of the Navy ROTC application.

First, 122 men in a Navy Officer Candidate School were tested under the usual instructions, then they were retested and instructed to fake, i.e., "use all of the knowledge you have about the vocational interests of a career naval officer. Respond to the items as nearly like a CAREER naval officer as you can." (Underlining and capitals in original instructions.)

Under faking instructions, these students increased their scores on the Officer Retention scale by about two-thirds of a standard deviation, but the increase was by no means consistent—about 30 percent of the group actually lowered their scores. And while they shifted their responses to 120 item-responses by 20 percent or more, only one-fourth (30) of these were on the Officer Retention scale.

The investigators used the remaining 90 item-responses as a faking detection scale and applied it to other groups. Their results, among students tested first as applicants and retested routinely after arrival on campus, and among ROTC students tested routinely and then with instructions to fake, were consistent and, with their earlier research, led them to these conclusions:

1. When instructed to do so, some individuals can increase their scores [on the Officer Retention scale] by faking.

2. As indicated by scores on a specially constructed fake scale, there is a slight tendency for applicants to fake responses, although there is very little gain [1–2 points—DPC] on the Officer Retention scale.

3. From all available information, faking does not appear to be a serious problem and the continued use of the Officer Retention scale in officer selection is recommended (Abrahams, Neumann, and Githens, 1968*b*, p. 7).

In further research, these investigators, in cooperation with the Center for Interest Measurement Research, searched the records of routine testing programs to locate SVIB's for individuals who, at some time between 1965–1967, applied for an NROTC scholarship. Comparisons could then be made between SVIB's administered to the same people once under routine testing conditions and again under scholarship selection conditions. Of the 102 SVIB's that were located, approximately one-half were completed several months prior to NROTC selection and the other half several months after the NROTC administration. These data confirmed their earlier conclusions and definitely indicated that simulated faking information is no substitute for real-life faking information. Simulated faking is always much greater than actual faking.

Experimentally Induced Faking

Kroger has studied the influence of experimentally manipulating the test administration environment and he found sizable differences between two similar groups who were told they were being tested for ostensibly different purposes (Kroger, 1967). The first were Navy ROTC students from the University of California at Berkeley who were told they were being tested as part of a study to determine "what makes a good military officer," the second were similar students who were told they were participating in a study of "artistic creativity."

The testing of the first sample, a regular ROTC class, was done in an ROTC classroom by an officer in uniform; for this sample, the SVIB title was changed to "Military Interest Questionnaire."

To draw a second sample directly comparable to the first, Kroger contacted more students from the Navy unit, but their ROTC membership was never mentioned. These were approached directly as, they were told, part of "a representative sample of students," and asked to participate in a study of artistic creativity. As only 55 percent volunteered, there is some possibility that this second sample differed from the first sample where 90 percent volunteered. (This higher percentage probably came from the stronger social pressure in class to participate in what was construed as a "Navy study.")

The second sample was tested in a regular classroom by a psychologist who told them the purpose was to determine "what makes people artistically creative." To add credence to this, four paintings were hung in the front of the classroom and, before the testing started, each student was asked to name the painters and to rate his opinion of them. For this part of the study, the SVIB booklet was titled "Artistic Interest Questionnaire."

Kroger found that the two samples under these two different testing conditions, which he, curiously, described as "approximating those found in ordinary testing situations," gave different answers to the SVIB. On the two most appropriate scales, Artist and Army Officer, the samples had the following means:

| | | Mean Scores | |
| | | Artist | Army Officer |
Sample	N	Scale	Scale
"Military"	45	22	39
"Artistic"	55	30	33
Difference		−8	+6

The SDs for the groups were approximately 12 (Kroger, personal communication), so these mean differences were large enough to be of practical importance.

The results of this study are disturbing for they imply that the test-taking environment can subtly influence the scores by a factor of one-half to three-fourths of a standard deviation. Although it is the only study in the literature to suggest such a sizable effect, it is, in many respects, the best study of its kind so the results cannot be lightly dismissed.

What caused the two groups to give different answers? Was it the general demeanor, including the uniform, of the examiners? Was it the differential selection of the two samples? Was it the knowledge that they were participating in one case in a study of military effectiveness, in the other, artistic creativity? It apparently was not the difference in test titles for Kroger reported that in a subsidiary study where only the title of the inventory was changed, no biasing effect was detected.

Kroger's study is an imaginative one, and it has raised some concerns. A replication—with truly random samples—is needed. Even now, his data emphasize clearly that the SVIB should be administered in a neutral setting whenever possible.

Conclusions on Faking

Despite the gloss of objectivity in the above discussion, let us not delude ourselves into thinking that we understand much about the individual's test-taking strategy when he is filling in the SVIB for various purposes. To assume that a medical school senior, who may be suspicious that his internship will be affected by the test results, will be more honest than a freshman is a shaky assumption. To believe that a man settled in his job for five years is less threatened by a company psychologist than an applicant may be equally naive; neither the 3M salesman nor medical student studies are definitive—yet they are reassuring. Coupled with the results from the Navy ROTC studies, they strongly suggest that no massive distortion occurs. Against this positive conclusion, the findings from Kroger's "experimentally induced bias" stand out and call for caution.

With these conflicting results, no tidy, unassailable conclusions are possible. Still, one has to proceed on the available data. The following points seem reasonably well established:

1. People can and do raise their SVIB scores on specific scales when instructed to do so in experimental studies.

2. When instructed to fake, individuals generally increase their scores by roughly one to two standard deviations (10 to 20 standard score points).

3. When instructed to fake in a specified direction, say, "Like a man," individuals exaggerate their answers; in a sense, they answer much more "like a man" than does the average man.

4. In real-life situations, some people sometimes give different answers when they are applying for a job or advanced training than when they are seeking counseling, but the differences are mild, usually about one-third of a standard deviation (3 or 4 standard score points).

Finally, and briefly, although the possibility of faking is always present, the frequency and impact of this phenomenon is not such that we have to be especially paranoid about it.

The Detection of Faking

There are no routine techniques for the detection of faking on the SVIB because I have been uncomfortable about such procedures. When a person is asked, or required, to take an interest inventory, the examiner is entering into an implicit agreement with him to find out something about his interests. If the person—for any reason whatsoever—does not wish to provide straightforward information, that is his right. If he wishes to modify his answers in directions that he believes will make him appear more favorable, he would be foolish not to do so, and he should no more be penalized for that than for other attempts to make a good impression, such as showing up for an interview in a clean shirt and fresh haircut.

In no way should the SVIB become a contest between the test constructor and the person completing the inventory. Even if he sees it as a game of wits, as an opportunity to "pull the wool over the headshrinker's eyes," I do not particularly want to know that, but would rather accept his answers as honest and straightforward, knowing that I am going to be fooled occasionally. The techniques for using test results in personnel decisions are not so well established that we can claim infallibility, and, as decision errors will inevitably occur, the person should be allowed to protect himself against them in any way he sees fit, including having some choice in the data that he provides.

The practical disadvantages of this position are not as severe as one might initially think. As the data discussed in the previous section indicate—granted that they are not as extensive as one might wish—the impact of faking is probably neither massive nor frequent. And, even if it were, the outcomes might not be all bad. If, for example, one were hiring taxidermists, using a scale developed by testing established taxidermists, four situations could arise:

1. The applicant would have the interests of a typical taxidermist and score high on the scale.

2. The applicant would not have such interests, but would fake successfully and thus score high on the scale.

3. The applicant would not have such interests, and would fake unsuccessfully, thus scoring low on the scale. (Perhaps not too unlikely—after all, what are the interests of successful taxidermists?)

4. The applicant would not have taxidermists interests, would answer honestly, and would score low on the scale.

In the unlikely event that the score on the taxidermist interest scale was the sole employment criterion, the rejected applicants would include those who had neither the interests of taxidermists nor the insight to appear as if they did, the selected applicants would include those with taxidermy interests, and those capable of faking them.

This is not an entirely undesirable situation, certainly it is preferable to many of the alternatives. For these reasons, there are no "Lie" scales, no "Validity" scales, no "Good Impression" scales for the SVIB, and none are planned.

CHAPTER 2

The Occupational Scales

The SVIB has several types of scales: Occupational Scales, Nonoccupational Scales, Basic Interest Scales, and Administrative Indices. Historically, the Occupational Scales came first, and they still form the bulwark of the SVIB system.

Each Occupational Scale has been developed by contrasting the SVIB responses of men in a specified occupation (the criterion sample) with a group of Men-in-General, a sample of men from many diverse occupations. Each scale contains items that discriminate between the interests of these two groups; thus, an individual's score provides an index of the similarity between his interests and the characteristic interests of men in the designated occupation.

To develop each Occupational Scale, a sample of men (or women) from that occupation was selected and asked to fill in the SVIB. The samples were restricted to those who had at least three years experience, who said they enjoyed their work, and, where the necessary information was available, to those who met at least some minimum level of proficiency, such as licensing, certification, or some other index of proficiency. In general, the samples were selected to represent the "successful, satisfied man performing the occupation in the typical manner."

After the responses of each occupational sample had been collected, they were compared to the responses of the Men-in-General. Items showing large differences in response percentages (usually, 15–20 percent) between these two groups were included in the scoring scale for that occupation and the scale was normed by using the original occupational sample as the standardization sample. A raw-score-to-standard-score conversion was then applied to convert the raw scores into a standard score distribution where the occupational group had a mean score of 50 and standard deviation of 10. This same conversion is incorporated into the scoring procedure, so that any future scores can be compared to the criterion group distribution.

The heterogenenous item content of the Occupational Scales should be emphasized, especially in contrast to the Basic Interest Scales, discussed in the next chapters. The Occupational Scales are not internally consistent, nor are they intended to be; instead, they reflect *all* of the large differences in interests between the two samples and, thus, maximize group separation. The Basic Interest Scales use a different approach, that of emphasizing homogeneous item content, and the two types of scales are designed to complement each other.

An Example of the Derivation of an Occupational Scale: Army Officer

To illustrate the development of the Occupational Scales, some items selected for the Army Officer scale, an occupation familiar to almost everyone, are presented in Table 2-1. They are illustrative of the items showing substantial differences in response percentages between the Men-in-General and the Army Officer criterion sample, which included 463 Army Officers, all West Point graduates, with an average of 18 years experience in the mili-

TABLE 2-1. ILLUSTRATIVE ITEMS FROM THE ARMY OFFICER SCALE

Positive Weights

Architect	Military Officer
Civil Engineer	Military Drill
Building Contractor	Drilling in a military company
Watchmaker	
Inventor	Pursuing bandits in a sheriff's posse
	Secret Service Man
Governor of a State	Auto Racer
Judge	Foreign Correspondent
Criminal Lawyer	
	Make bets frequently
Manufacturer	Poker
Factory Manager	Golf
Shop Foreman	
Shop Work	Outside work vs Inside work
Carpenter	Continually changing activities
	Am able to meet emergencies quickly
Algebra	and effectively
Calculus	Usually get other people to do what
Physics	I want done
Mathematics	
Mechanical Drawing	

Negative Weights

Living in the city	Interviewing prospects in selling
Art galleries	When caught in a mistake I make
Sociology	excuses
Social Worker	Bird Watching
Social problem movies	Nature study
Giving "first aid"	Zoology
assistance	Physiology

tary. Most of them were field grade officers, that is, majors, lieutenant colonels, or colonels; all of them had been rated above average on the Army Officer Efficiency ratings.

In Table 2-1, the differentiating items have been grouped, by simple inspection, into clusters with similar content, and these demonstrate the relative complexity of the Occupational Scales, especially when compared to the Basic Scales. The clusters weighted positively include one dealing with mathematics, another with managerial type occupations—particularly those with a construction or engineering flavor—another includes adventuresome activities, another military pursuits, and so forth. The items weighted negatively do not cluster as readily and have not been put into any special groupings, but they also cover a wide range. Clearly, the scale is factorially complex.

The items listed in Table 2-1 are those that Army Officers respond to differently than do Men-in-General and are not necessarily the ones that are most popular among Army Officers, for those items might also be popular among other occupational groups. To demonstrate this, in Table 2-2 are listed some items that were answered "Like" by a majority of Army Officers, but which do not appear on the Army Officer scale because a majority of Men-in-General also answered "Like." The relevant percentages for both groups are included in Table 2-2. Again, this is to emphasize that

TABLE 2-2. POPULAR ITEMS AMONG BOTH ARMY OFFICERS
AND MEN-IN-GENERAL

| | Per Cent Responding "Like" | |
Item	Army Officer	Men-in-General
Advertising Man	53	40
Physician	58	49
Civics	55	56
Economics	56	56
Geography	84	75
History	76	72
Literature	57	59
Philosophy	54	58
Physical Education	61	55
Psychology	54	66
Spelling	52	51
Fishing	57	62
Hunting	52	51
Hiking	52	64
Bridge	57	48
Picnics	62	57
Symphony concerts	53	59
Sports page	63	56
Detective stories	57	52

The Occupational Scales

the items on the Occupational Scales are not always the most popular items among the men in that occupation, but rather the ones that distinguish them from Men-in-General.

After the items were identified for the Army Officer scale, the scale was normed by using the criterion sample raw score mean and standard deviation in the T-score conversion formula; thus, each score is converted into a distribution where the Army Officers have a mean of 50 and a standard deviation of 10.

The range of scores on the resulting scale is demonstrated in Table 2-3, which presents the mean scores of several occupational samples on the Army Officer scale. At the top, with a mean score of 50, is the criterion group of Army Officers. Next come several other military samples. The highest scoring civilians were the credit managers, and they scored only 32. Men-in-General scored 20, with most other occupations in this general range. At the bottom of the distribution, about four standard deviations away from the criterion group, were artists, authors, and ministers. When

TABLE 2-3. MEAN SCORES FOR VARIOUS GROUPS ON THE ARMY OFFICER SCALE

```
50  Army Officers
49
48
47
46  Air Force Officers
45  3 and 4 Star Generals and Admirals
44
43  Astronauts
42
41  Retired 3 and 4 Star Generals
40
39
38  West Point Cadets
37  Retired Army Colonels
36
35
34
33
32  Credit Managers
31
30  Engineers/Production Managers/Senior CPAs
29  Chamber of Commerce Executives
28  Forest Service Men/Public Administrators
27  Policemen
26  Physical Therapists/Corporation Presidents/Personnel Directors/Business Education Teachers
25  Chemists/YMCA Staff Members/Accountants
24  Purchasing Agents
23  Math-Science Teachers/CPA Owners/Office Workers/Sales Managers/Presidents, Manufacturing Concern
22  Physicists/Farmers/Rehabilitation Counselors
21  Biologists
20  Psychiatrists/Psychologists/Printers/Men-In-General
19  Osteopaths/Veterinarians/Physicians/Architects/Bankers/Pharmacists/Funeral Directors
18  Mathematicians/Social Workers/School Superintendents/Real Estate Salesmen
17  Music Teachers/Lawyers
16  Dentists/Social Science Teachers/Librarians/Musician Performers/Advertising Men
15  Life Insurance Salesmen
14
13
12  Ministers
11
10  Author-Journalists
9
8   Artists
```

their interests were analyzed in this manner, these three occupations proved to be very different from Army Officers.

Tables 2-1, 2-2, and 2-3 illustrate the main points in the development of the Army Officer scale; all of the other Occupational Scales have been developed in an analogous manner. More specific details on each step of the scale construction are given in the following sections.

Specific Techniques in the Construction of Occupational Scales

The specific details of the methods used in developing the original Strong Vocational Interest Blanks are reported in Professor Strong's book *Vocational Interests of Men and Women* (1943), and Appendix A of this Handbook elaborates on the specific changes in the recent revisions. Though the techniques have varied slightly in the various forms, the method remains essentially the same. The SVIB is administered to samples of men and women from various occupations—the criterion groups—and the responses of each of these groups are then compared to those of Men (or Women)-in-General (MIG). Items that the criterion groups answer differently from the MIG group are included in the Occupational Scales.

Occupational Criterion Samples

The composition of each criterion sample is important as this determines the characteristics of the eventual scale. The sampling method has varied from scale to scale but, in most cases, the following four standards have been used:

1. The person must be between 25 and 55 years old.

2. He must have been employed in the occupation for three years or more. This is taken as a minimum standard of both success and satisfaction.

3. He must indicate that he likes his work.

4. He must have met some minimum level of proficiency, when such indices are available; licensing, certification, advanced degrees, and supervisor's ratings are examples that have been used. The goal is to eliminate the incompetents, not to restrict the samples to only the outstanding members of the occupation.

In addition, many of the scales have been developed with the help of appropriate professional organizations; thus, the participants have had some identification with their profession. For example, most of the physicians used to develop the Physician scale were members of the American Medical Association.

The required size of the criterion sample is difficult to specify. In his earlier work in the 1920's and 1930's, Strong thought samples of about 200 were sufficient; later he became convinced that sample sizes of 400 were desirable, and his later samples were usually that large. Harmon, in more recent research (Harmon, 1968) has shown that large samples, while desirable, are not crucial if the item selection is done rigorously. Her work suggests that even samples of 50 can be used, given the appropriate conditions, though the resulting scales will be somewhat weaker than scales based on larger samples.

While no firm rules, buttressed by solid data, can be listed, the following guideline, based on a variety of statistics and experience, appears reasonable: samples of 400 are preferable, samples of 300 are sufficient, and samples of 200 are adequate. Scales based on smaller samples should be closely scrutinized, and the percentage difference cut off (discussed below) used in item selection should be raised.

In general, sample size is not as important as other characteristics such as job satisfaction and years of experience, and these factors should never be disregarded just to increase sample size.

Men-in-General

The use of a Men-in-General sample (MIG)—or, where appropriate, Women-in-General (WIG)—has always been central to the SVIB methodology. The SVIB was developed at a time—the 1920's—when tests, inventories, and questionnaires were still in their infancy but rapidly coming into vogue. In this period, Strong, building on the work of others, recognized that an individual's answers to an item on a questionnaire, taken on face value only, had little meaning until compared to some base rate, to "people-in-general," and he worked for years trying to understand just how a reference group should be constituted. His attempts are chronicled in his 1943 book, and only a few summary comments are presented here.

The main purpose of Men-in-General is to establish the general level of popularity of each item; this can then be compared with the rate of endorsement of the occupational sample to locate items that the members of the criterion sample answer differently from the reference sample. Thus, the crucial statistic used to decide whether an item is included in an occupational scale is the difference in response percentage between the criterion and reference samples, not the absolute level of response by the criterion sample. Items are weighted on the Occupational Scales only if the men in that occupation answered *differently* from the general reference group.

The biggest problem in this approach is how to determine the composition of the reference sample.

Strong's first MIG sample, gathered around 1925–27, simply included a few thousand men that he had had occasion to test in his exploratory work with the SVIB. Although this sample worked well as a reference group, particularly when viewed in historical perspective, its rather casual composition did not seem technically defensible. In an attempt to remedy this, Strong next collected a sample representative of all employed men, as defined by U.S. Census Bureau statistics. After a great deal of work, he found this group was unacceptable because it included too many unskilled and semi-skilled men; all business and professional men—be they accountants, lawyers, doctors, or teachers—seemed to have similar interests when compared against this MIG group. The sample used by Strong in his 1938 revision, and which was used until 1966, was a modification of this Census Bureau sample and included only men making a sufficient salary to justify placing them in the middle class or above category. Perhaps the best description would be "men in jobs that college students (not necessarily graduates) eventually enter."

In the 1966 revision of the men's SVIB, this MIG sample was initially used, mainly because we didn't wish to tamper with something that appeared to be working. But, as reported in some detail in Appendix A, a problem appeared—specifically, the sample had some "time bias." Some items were more, or less, popular among men tested in the 1930's than among men tested in the 1960's. (See also Chapter 10.) To overcome this flaw, the MIG sample was reconstituted to include men from a wide range of occupations, tested over the entire period 1927–65. Although this lessened the problem considerably, even this MIG sample is not entirely satisfactory. A new Men-in-General sample has been gathered, as described in Appendix C, and it will be used to construct scales for the new (T399) men's booklet.

Even after Strong's 40 years of work at Stanford, and the ten years of work at Minnesota, no routine formula can be specified for selecting a "Men-in-General" sample. However, the following points seem important:

1. The MIG sample should include the same general types of people as do the criterion groups.

2. The MIG sample should be highly diverse, so that most interest patterns will have some chance of being represented there.

3. Similarly, heterogeneity should be stressed to avoid any single dominant bias.

4. Finally, the group should be large enough to insure the stability of the item statistics.

Thus, a short description of a desirable MIG sample would be "a large, diverse, heterogeneous sample of the same sorts of people used to develop the Occupational Scales."

How to avoid a time bias in the reference sample is still a puzzle. One way would be to test the reference sample at the same time that all of the occupational samples are tested—which is what was done in the 1969 women's revision—but this will not solve all of the practical problems. We know from past experience that other scales will continue to be developed; to deny the development of these future scales would hamper research on new occupations; to include them on the profile will probably introduce some mild error created by the time bias. At the moment, an unresolved dilemma.

Because of these problems with the reference group, Kuder has suggested that the Men-in-General concept be done away with in favor of using only the criterion group's responses to establish the scale weights (Kuder, 1966). While that is certainly possible—Strong tried it in the early 1940's in his so-called "percentage weights" system (Strong, 1943, p. 619)— the problem of controlling for base rate popularity is still present, which is why Strong decided against this technique. With this method, as people across all occupations tend to like the same general activities, all of the popular items are weighted on all of the scales, thus creating a sizable "general popularity" factor. This factor is most visible when one scans an intercorrelation table of scales constructed in this manner because virtually all of the correlations will be positive, reflecting the general factor. Contrasting all of the occupational samples with a MIG sample removes this factor, and the scale intercorrelations range from high positive to high negative—see Table 2-4.

Whether one prefers the Strong-type scales, using criterion samples versus Men-in-General, or the Kuder-type using only the responses of the criterion samples, depends on whether he wishes to attend to the *unique* interests or the *most popular* interests of the criterion sample. At the moment, there are not enough published data, especially longitudinal data, on the latter type of scale to make a meaningful comparison; because the SVIB scales, based on the Men-in-General concept, have worked reasonably well, that technique will still be used to construct the SVIB Occupational Scales.

Two Men-in-General samples have been used in the data presented in this Handbook, both selected to represent a cross section of men mainly in the occupations that college students usually enter. Appendix C includes a detailed description of the MIG sample used here for item analysis; because this sample was constituted in 1965, it is labeled the 1965 MIG sample. Essentially, it represents the responses of men from the 54 occupations on the profile, with all occupations weighted equally.

The second MIG sample includes the 500 men selected by Strong in

1938 to represent a cross section of men in business and professional activities, and is labeled the 1938 MIG sample. In this sample, each occupation was represented approximately by its frequency in the general (middle class and higher) population. Because the 1965 MIG is too ponderous to score, the 1938 MIG sample was used to establish the validity statistics in Table 2-7. The use of this second sample does have the advantage of partially canceling out the effects of chance in item selection and provides a sort of "half-cross-validation."

The 1969 Women-in-General sample, used here for both item analysis and validity statistics, is described in detail in Appendix C; essentially it includes 20 women from each of 50 occupations, selected under the guidelines described above.

Appendix C contained a description of all of the reference samples discussed here and, for historical purposes, their SVIB item response percentages are also included. In addition, a third MIG sample, the 1969 MIG, is also described and their item response percentages are also listed; these figures will be used in the future to build new scales for the men's T399 booklet.

Establishing Scale Weights

Once item response percentages for the criterion sample and MIG are available, the next step is to construct the scale by identifying the items that discriminate between these groups. The precise method for selecting and weighting these discriminating items has varied throughout the history of the SVIB. (For background on these points, see Strong, 1943; Strong, Campbell, Berdie, and Clark, 1964; and Berdie and Campbell, 1968.) Gradually, the following system has evolved: those items showing "large" differences in percent response between the criterion and reference samples are identified and given unit weights in the appropriate direction. Though the precise rules have varied slightly from scale to scale, the following specific procedures are usually followed:

1. For each item, list the percentage of the criterion and reference samples selecting each of the three alternatives: Like, Indifferent, and Dislike. Then calculate the percentage difference for each response.

2. Identify those items showing 18 percent or larger differences on any of the three responses. If there are more than 100 such items, then discard the weaker items (first the 18 percent differences, then 19 percent, and so on) until 90–100 items remain. If there are fewer than 60 items, include the 17 percent differences, then the 16 percent and so on until roughly 60 items are available, though sometimes this won't be possible. It is impera-

tive—for reliability—to have a minimum of 40 items on each scale, and—for validity—to score only items with 14 percent or larger differences.

3. Assign the weights of +1 or −1, as appropriate, to the responses showing these large differences. Responses favoring the criterion group are weighted +1, and vice versa.

4. "Dimensionalize" these items. This is done by weighting the opposite end of the item in the reverse direction, that is, if the "Like" response to an item is weighted +1, the "Dislike" response should be assigned a weight of −1. This step—which is based on the assumption that each item is really a small dimension so that if one end is positive, the other should be negative—neither increases nor decreases the scale's validity, but it does improve the scale test-retest reliability by about 3–4 correlational points. For an example, see Johnson and Dunnette, 1968.

5. For those items already weighted, weigh the "Indifferent" response in the appropriate direction if the percent difference between the criterion group and Men-in-General exceeds 10 percent.

Some examples of assigning item weights are:

		L	I	D
Item A	Criterion sample percent response	60	30	10
	Men-in-General percent response	40	38	22
	Difference	+20	− 8	−12
	Assigned weight	+ 1	0	− 1
Item B	Criterion sample percent response	10	40	50
	Men-in-General percent response	3	28	69
	Difference	+ 7	+12	−19
	Assigned weight	+ 1	+ 1	− 1
Item C	Criterion sample percent response	30	40	30
	Men-in-General percent response	40	20	40
	Difference	−10	+20	−10
	Assigned weight	0	0	0

This last pattern of differences, showing the large difference on the Indifferent response, is rare and usually ignored because it does not conform to the assumption of item dimensionality.

Two Important Points: Empiricism and Relative Differences

Two points should be stressed about these scale building techniques. First, these procedures are strictly empirical; the items for each scale are selected not by subjective judgment but by actually testing the occupational groups to determine their responses.

Second, the items that are weighted on an occupational scale are not necessarily the ones that men in that occupation select most often—rather they are the items that men in that group answer *differently* from other men.

Norming, or the Establishing of Standard Scores

Once the items are selected and weighted, norms must be developed. For the SVIB Occupational Scales, the members of the criterion group are used to establish the norms. Their distribution of raw scores is converted to a distribution of standard scores with a mean of 50 and a standard deviation of 10 by applying the following conversion:

$$\text{standard score} = \frac{(X - M_c)}{SD_c} \; 10 + 50$$

where

$$X = \text{an individual's raw score}$$
$$M_c = \text{criterion group's raw score mean}$$
$$SD_c = \text{criterion group's raw score standard deviation}$$

The raw score means and standard deviations for this conversion are listed in Table 2-7 for the men's Occupational Scales, and in Table 2-8 for the women's Occupational Scales.

This conversion, which is a linear transformation and not a normalizing one, is then applied to all future results on this scale. The main purpose is to convert all scores to a common numerical scale. The resultant scores are frequently called T-scores, i.e., scores with a mean of 50 and standard deviation of 10. The main advantage of this system is that it is possible to determine quickly where any score falls within the criterion group distribution. For example, on each scale a standard score of 40 falls one standard deviation (10 points) below the mean of the criterion group.

A second advantage of standard scores is that they can be compared across scales. Thus a person's score on the Physician scale can be compared directly with his score on the Lawyer scale; what is actually being compared, of course, is his relative standing among physicians on their interest scale versus his standing among lawyers on their interest scale.

Because the mean standard score of each criterion group on their scale is 50, and the shaded area for each scale represents the middle third of the men-in-general group, the individual's score can be quickly compared to the average scores for both of these groups.

Occupational Scale Intercorrelations

The intercorrelations between the men's Occupational Scales are presented in Table 2-4, the women's in Table 2-5. These correlations, along with other data, were used to determine the order of the scales on the profile. See page 276 for a longer discussion of this point.

TABLE 2-4. INTERCORRELATIONS BETWEEN THE MEN'S OCCUPATIONAL SCALES
301 Stanford University Seniors, Class of 1927

Occupational and Nonoccupational Scales	Dentist	Osteopath	Veterinarian	Physician	Psychiatrist	Psychologist	Biologist	Architect	Mathematician	Physicist	Chemist	Engineer	Production Manager	Army Officer	Air Force Officer	Carpenter	Forest Service Man	Farmer	Math-Science Teacher	Printer	Policeman	Personnel Director	Public Administrator	Rehabilitation Counselor	YMCA Secretary	Community Recreation Admin.	Social Worker	Social Science Teacher	School Superintendent	Minister	Mean	S.D.
PHYSICAL THERAPIST	.15	.60	.33	.31	.29	-.21	.12	-.32	-.41	-.09	.08	-.11	.17	.24	.37	.20	.46	.04	.53	-.12	.49	-.14	.07	.15	.37	.34	.11	.03	-.10	.20	26.63	12.32
DENTIST		.73	.60	.82	.24	.09	.60	.71	.40	.64	.65	.61	-.01	-.23	-.12	.60	.33	.59	.19	.29	.09	-.78	-.77	-.74	-.64	-.71	-.71	-.61	-.63	-.30	31.59	11.68
OSTEOPATH			.63	.80	.42	-.01	.45	.29	.03	.34	.43	.29	.01	-.05	.08	.38	.44	.35	.31	-.00	.27	-.56	-.43	-.34	-.21	-.26	-.26	-.38	-.41	-.03	30.35	12.61
VETERINARIAN				.46	-.17	-.45	.07	.19	-.18	.10	.18	.27	.26	-.01	.02	.50	.51	.70	.07	.22	.41	-.44	-.45	-.50	-.18	-.22	-.53	-.27	-.47	-.48	23.00	9.98
PHYSICIAN					.56	.31	.73	.60	.39	.62	.65	.47	-.15	-.20	-.08	.33	.24	.33	.16	-.03	-.03	-.71	-.57	-.48	-.45	-.53	-.43	-.58	-.51	-.06	32.31	14.47
PSYCHIATRIST						.71	.64	.37	.35	.42	.43	.18	-.21	-.13	.04	-.17	-.09	-.30	.24	-.44	-.32	-.15	.00	.16	-.14	-.34	.17	-.30	-.01	.37	28.68	11.14
PSYCHOLOGIST							.62	.64	.76	.55	.44	.26	-.27	-.18	-.09	-.16	-.34	-.29	.09	-.22	-.61	-.13	-.03	.06	-.33	-.34	.11	-.32	.00	.26	29.62	10.85
BIOLOGIST								.64	.76	.86	.80	.63	-.10	-.17	-.01	.36	.17	.26	.40	-.05	-.20	-.57	-.41	-.37	-.59	-.63	-.39	-.60	-.36	.09	30.67	13.37
ARCHITECT									.71	.80	.72	.73	-.06	-.19	-.16	.49	.05	.47	-.05	.23	-.26	-.59	-.65	-.73	-.78	-.69	-.69	-.72	-.60	-.30	29.40	11.16
MATHEMATICIAN										.84	.63	.61	-.15	-.28	-.21	.25	.15	.19	.13	.04	-.43	-.41	-.37	-.37	-.73	-.74	-.40	-.52	-.20	.00	27.09	11.63
PHYSICIST											.90	.85	.14	-.03	.11	.55	.15	.42	.34	.15	-.19	-.57	-.49	-.58	-.79	-.80	-.63	-.80	-.54	-.23	24.57	13.75
CHEMIST												.86	.26	.17	.33	.57	.27	.43	.31	.17	-.05	-.58	-.46	-.62	-.73	-.73	-.67	-.85	-.67	-.34	32.20	15.81
ENGINEER													.45	.22	.32	.67	.34	.60		.21	-.02	-.45	-.43	-.69	-.80	-.78	-.81	-.88	-.65	-.53	29.94	12.89
PRODUCTION MANAGER														.65	.65	-.06	.39	.37	.28	.12	.39	-.06	.23	-.18	-.15	-.05	-.34	-.35	-.24	-.52	29.53	9.90
ARMY OFFICER															.87	-.19	.05	.05	.29	-.04	.36	.27	.36	.04	.10	.22	-.06	-.28	-.17	-.33	19.34	12.99
AIR FORCE OFFICER																-.16	.07	.07	.49	-.03	.36	.15	.25	.00	.06	.13	-.12	-.39	-.28	-.33	25.25	10.60
CARPENTER																	.55	.78	.42	.58	.40	.18	-.54	-.70	-.52	-.54	-.75	-.54	-.68	-.48	18.55	10.38
FOREST SERVICE MAN																		.57	.31	.20	.55		-.20	-.29	-.11			-.25	-.62	-.22	20.15	12.32
FARMER																			.17	.51	.29	.15	-.52	-.74	-.50	-.53	-.78	-.46	-.62	-.57	32.34	8.55
MATH-SCIENCE TEACHER																				.11	.20	-.27	-.06	-.10	-.13	-.12	-.21	-.25	-.21	.04	30.73	11.53
PRINTER																					.30	-.37	-.46	-.52	-.32	-.39	-.10	-.10	-.47	-.41	28.65	8.40
POLICEMAN																						.00	.04	-.08	.19	.18	-.14	.08	-.13	-.23	19.58	9.85
PERSONNEL DIRECTOR																							.80	.67	.51	.61	.62	.48	.64	.23	27.88	12.71
PUBLIC ADMINISTRATOR																								.72	.50	.66	.66	.45	.66	.33	31.49	10.96
REHABILITATION COUNSELOR																									.71	.74	.89	.66	.78	.62	25.70	10.25
YMCA SECRETARY																										.93	.74	.70	.51	.41	18.56	12.73
COMMUNITY RECREATION ADMIN.																											.75	.68	.60	.42	18.43	12.90
SOCIAL WORKER																												.72	.76	.69	25.12	12.34
SOCIAL SCIENCE TEACHER																													.71	.50	28.82	13.17
SCHOOL SUPERINTENDENT																														.66	24.90	13.11
MINISTER																															20.33	14.07

(table continued next page)

TABLE 2-4 (continued)

Occupational and Nonoccupational Scales	Mean	S.D.	Correlation with 1938 Scale	Academic Achievement	Occ. Introversion-Extroversion	Masculinity-Femininity	Occupational Level	Specialization Level	President, Mfg. Concern	Author-Journalist	Lawyer	Advertising Man	Life Insurance Salesman	Real Estate Salesman	Sales Manager	Mortician	Pharmacist	Banker	Purchasing Agent	Business Education Teacher	Chamber of Commerce Exec.	Credit Manager	Office Worker	Accountant	Senior CPA	CPA Owner	Music Teacher	Musician Performer	Artist	Librarian
Physical Therapist	26.63	12.32	.84	.11	-.30	.25	-.08	-.44	-.54	-.63	-.60	-.66	-.37	-.46	-.42	-.08	.29	-.40	-.32	.11	-.08	.09	-.04	-.24	-.21	-.59	-.04	.02	-.25	-.29
Dentist	31.59	11.68	.86	.27	.63	.24	-.44	-.34	-.16	.17	-.18	-.13	-.43	-.33	-.47	-.13	.35	-.26	-.13	-.75	-.79	-.72	-.40	-.44	-.25	-.31	-.38	.32	.68	-.10
Osteopath	30.35	12.61	.84	.27	.22	.23	-.35	-.34	-.34	-.17	-.33	-.38	-.40	-.41	-.49	-.07	.41	-.40	-.32	-.44	-.52	-.45	-.35	-.51	-.35	-.47	-.26	.22	.34	-.20
Veterinarian	23.00	9.98	.79	-.26	.28	.43	-.67	-.29	.02	-.15	-.22	-.38	-.04	.09	-.49	.38	.73	.11	.30	-.44	-.52	-.20	-.01	-.24	-.11	-.38	-.45	-.12	.18	-.20
Physician	32.31	14.47	.85	.45	.44	.14	-.24	-.20	-.30	.07	-.09	-.16	-.45	-.45	-.56	-.29	.20	-.56	-.43	-.79	-.68	-.76	-.63	-.68	-.46	-.33	-.23	.42	.69	.02
Psychiatrist	28.68	11.14	.80	.66	-.01	-.07	.44	.08	-.28	.25	-.06	-.23	-.44	-.45	-.51	-.56	-.18	-.57	-.67	-.37	-.27	-.41	-.59	-.59	-.39	.16	.11	.34	.31	.30
Psychologist	29.62	10.85	.82	.55	.27	-.12	.53	.17	-.11	.36	.11	.03	-.38	-.43	-.41	-.66	-.43	-.57	-.54	-.39	-.27	-.50	-.59	-.32	-.23	.16	.14	.36	.45	.52
Biologist	30.67	13.37	.89	.68	.53	.13	.14	-.13	-.37	.20	-.18	-.31	-.70	-.70	-.76	-.68	-.16	-.63	-.53	-.73	-.78	-.81	-.72	-.50	-.34	-.22	-.13	.37	.63	.22
Architect	29.40	11.16	.88	.27	.73	.10	-.15	-.03	.11	.51	.02	.16	-.39	-.26	-.32	-.33	-.08	-.26	-.11	-.84	-.70	-.80	-.53	-.32	-.17	-.16	-.26	.44	.86	.15
Mathematician	27.09	11.63	.91	.47	.65	.09	.18	.09	-.05	.13	.13	.30	-.38	-.31	-.47	-.25	-.31	-.26	-.22	-.64	-.74	-.74	-.56	-.22	-.13	.30	-.04	.30	.64	.37
Physicist	24.57	13.75	.96	.51	.74	.32	.04	-.12	-.10	.24	-.21	-.24	-.69	-.58	-.59	-.60	-.10	-.45	-.32	-.76	-.81	-.80	-.59	-.30	-.09	-.13	-.34	.26	.69	.08
Chemist	32.20	15.81	.94	.48	.65	.45	-.21	-.19	-.11	.03	-.37	-.29	-.77	-.64	-.58	-.64	.01	-.52	-.17	-.71	-.78	-.67	-.49	-.30	.03	-.21	-.52	-.07	.55	-.07
Engineer	29.94	12.89	.92	.29	.70	.57	-.12	-.09	.18	.03	-.29	-.29	-.63	-.42	-.35	-.42	.10	-.22	.14	-.64	-.73	-.56	-.33	-.00	.21	-.08	-.66	-.07	.48	-.26
Production Manager	29.53	9.90	.85	-.22	.10	.69	-.11	-.03	.32	-.51	-.40	-.45	-.28	-.08	.14	.06	.28	.18	.55	.11	-.07	.23	-.11	.44	.50	-.12	-.62	-.61	-.32	-.66
Army Officer	19.34	12.99	.83	-.13	-.15	.54	-.01	-.01	.12	-.51	-.40	-.51	-.27	-.15	.08	-.05	-.05	-.07	.23	.22	.23	.35	.20	.38	.53	-.10	-.47	-.19	-.41	-.48
Air Force Officer	25.25	10.60	—	-.02	-.11	.65	.17	-.09	.02	-.61	-.53	-.57	-.42	-.00	-.07	-.24	-.00	-.20	.15	.18	.08	.29	.14	.32	.50	-.17	-.49	-.46	-.39	-.52
Carpenter	18.55	10.38	.80	-.10	.61	.59	-.39	-.56	-.14	-.23	-.59	-.45	-.60	-.37	-.42	-.14	.26	-.03	.19	-.38	-.69	-.43	-.11	-.05	.08	-.47	-.49	.01	.31	-.36
Forest Service Man	20.15	12.32	.81	-.11	.16	.47	-.35	-.44	-.19	-.39	-.48	-.51	-.38	-.27	-.29	-.10	.22	-.07	.04	-.11	-.36	-.11	-.04	-.05	.04	-.52	-.47	-.19	-.04	-.47
Farmer	32.34	8.55	.73	-.19	.63	.53	-.37	-.36	-.10	-.09	-.32	-.27	-.30	-.30	-.17	.43	.43	-.37	-.21	-.40	-.40	-.38	-.06	-.04	.08	-.36	-.57	-.07	-.21	-.17
Math-Science Teacher	30.73	11.53	.86	.38	.12	.41	.17	-.43	-.48	-.64	-.75	-.82	-.72	-.72	-.61	-.46	.10	-.37	-.21	.03	-.40	-.09	-.05	.14	.14	-.26	-.22	-.07	-.17	-.02
Printer	28.65	8.40	.61	-.05	.51	.12	.03	-.57	-.06	.07	-.29	-.34	-.19	.01	-.09	.27	.18	.21	.26	-.08	.01	-.16	.14	.12	.18	.06	-.26	-.26	.18	-.02
Policeman	19.58	9.85	.74	-.34	-.10	.30	-.37	-.39	-.19	-.41	-.33	-.34	-.08	.01	-.02	.27	.29	.21	.26	.19	.01	.23	.38	.17	.14	-.39	-.26	-.28	-.29	-.47
Personnel Director	27.88	12.71	.74	-.23	-.64	-.16	.36	.43	.35	.15	.25	.15	.42	.36	.54	.19	-.26	.29	.21	.63	.76	.71	.38	.50	.27	.33	.25	-.37	-.62	-.02
Public Administrator	31.49	10.96	.71	-.06	-.65	-.16	.47	.35	.16	.10	.10	.24	.20	.36	.30	.09	-.28	.13	.04	.59	.65	.62	.24	.37	.18	.20	.20	-.44	-.67	-.03
Rehabilitation Counselor	25.70	10.25	.88	.03	-.73	-.40	.46	.34	-.08	-.13	.21	.06	.36	.16	.22	.37	-.26	.04	-.24	.65	.69	.57	.17	.14	-.09	.21	.53	-.16	-.55	.21
YMCA Secretary	18.56	12.73	.66	-.33	-.80	-.30	.08	.08	-.15	-.25	.08	.05	.50	.33	.33	.37	-.04	.05	-.08	.66	.78	.65	.30	.06	-.12	-.08	.48	-.07	-.56	-.04
Community Recreation Admin.	18.43	12.90	—	-.32	-.86	-.30	.17	.16	-.06	-.02	.05	.05	.47	.33	.37	.33	-.08	.07	-.04	.71	.72	.71	.08	.15	-.03	-.02	.42	-.17	-.65	-.10
Social Worker	25.12	12.34	.86	-.05	-.76	-.50	.46	.24	-.17	-.03	.28	.16	.40	.18	.20	.08	-.37	-.06	-.35	.57	.61	.48	.08	-.01	-.23	.10	.66	.05	-.46	.36
Social Science Teacher	28.82	13.17	.82	-.33	-.58	-.53	.07	.06	-.14	-.03	.27	.24	.56	.40	.30	.41	-.09	.38	-.02	.68	.61	.54	.40	.14	-.15	.09	.61	-.05	-.51	.24
School Superintendent	24.90	13.11	.79	.04	-.62	-.64	.38	.07	.01	.03	.40	.24	.44	.24	.26	.17	-.30	.22	-.30	.55	.43	.43	.17	-.26	-.13	.33	.60	-.14	-.47	.30
Minister	20.33	14.07	.89	.37	-.47	-.47	.43	.07	-.44	.04	.10	-.01	.05	-.24	-.27	-.20	-.42	-.30	-.67	.23	.23	.04	-.23	-.26	-.49	-.05	.76	.40	-.11	.62

(table continued next page)

TABLE 2-4 *(continued)*

Occupational and Nonoccupational Scales	Artist	Musician Performer	Music Teacher	CPA Owner	Senior CPA	Accountant	Office Worker	Credit Manager	Chamber of Commerce Exec.	Business Education Teacher	Purchasing Agent	Banker	Pharmacist	Mortician	Sales Manager	Real Estate Salesman	Life Insurance Salesman	Advertising Man	Lawyer	Author-Journalist	President, Mfg. Concern	Specialization Level	Occupational Level	Masculinity-Femininity	Occ. Introversion-Extroversion	Academic Achievement	Correlation with 1938 Scale	Mean	S.D.
LIBRARIAN	.30	.61	.61	.17	-.34	-.21	-.25	-.26	-.00	-.08	-.55	-.22	-.52	-.32	-.24	-.16	.01	.35	.29	.49	-.26	.39	.03	-.73	.04	.39	.80	30.41	10.19
ARTIST		.62	-.04	-.13	-.48	-.58	-.63	-.86	-.60	-.83	-.28	-.35	-.06	-.25	-.32	-.16	-.21	.32	.20	.71	-.00	-.21	-.05	-.11	.63	.23	.93	29.50	10.00
MUSICIAN PERFORMER			.48	-.24	-.61	-.58	-.47	-.51	-.25	-.43	-.55	-.07	-.23	-.21	-.36	-.24	-.10	.23	.46	.46	-.38	.03	-.18	-.50	.14	.27	.79	33.31	9.57
MUSIC TEACHER				.04	-.47	-.22	-.08	.09	.37	.28	-.44	.39	-.38	.10	-.00	.10	.35	.30	.29	.27	-.29	.29	.15	-.75	-.42	.07	.72	25.08	11.24
CPA OWNER					.46	.50	.29	.29	.34	.18	.24	.41	-.18	.11	.45	.40	.41	.44	.54	.27	.49	.23	.65	-.31	-.06	.16	.84	28.11	10.61
SENIOR CPA						.78	.57	.49	.19	.35	.53	.60	.01	.03	.32	.12	-.03	-.16	-.18	-.39	.34	.06	.09	.37	.06	-.10	.63	24.69	12.18
ACCOUNTANT							.73	.65	.39	.54	.59	.68	-.01	.19	.47	.28	.17	-.04	-.06	-.32	.43	.13	.21	.11	-.15	-.21	.78	23.03	12.19
OFFICE WORKER								.74	.48	.68	.64	.47	.30	.54	.56	.47	.39	.06	-.06	-.36	.29	-.16	.06	-.02	-.26	-.44	.83	27.50	11.27
CREDIT MANAGER									.80	.86	.41	.30	.10	.45	.62	.44	.70	.01	-.00	-.48	.27	-.14	.20	-.06	-.67	-.40	.83	23.42	12.54
CHAMBER OF COMMERCE EXEC.										.71	.19	.43	-.15	.44	.70	.59	.40	.37	-.35	-.06	.29	.20	.40	-.34	-.76	-.39	.90	28.48	11.36
BUSINESS EDUCATION TEACHER											.25	.72	.03	.35	.44	.33	.55	-.06	-.11	-.48	.08	.22	.08	-.16	-.58	-.35	.81	24.09	11.25
PURCHASING AGENT													.47	.58	.64	.66	.55	.17	.05	.01	.63	.20	.15	.33	-.00	-.56	.86	27.15	10.10
BANKER													.24	.66	.57	.20	.71	.32	.29	-.12	.44	-.37	.17	-.07	.11	-.49	.86	23.04	10.34
PHARMACIST														.55	.61	.73		-.13	-.23	-.28	.19	-.33	-.16	.28	.11	-.25	.71	23.45	8.56
MORTICIAN															.18			.38	.27	.02	.36	-.55	.16	-.17	-.25	-.60	.83	25.38	8.92
SALES MANAGER																.86	.81	.61	.49	.17	.71	-.13	.48	-.14	-.33	-.56	.88	26.35	11.14
REAL ESTATE SALESMAN																	.90	.71	.63	.35	.56	-.33	.41	-.25	-.23	-.60	.91	33.42	9.14
LIFE INSURANCE SALESMAN																		.73	.68	.35	.43	-.19	.47	-.48	-.42	-.46	.91	28.51	11.19
ADVERTISING MAN																			.79	.81	.47	-.08	.46	-.56	-.01	-.25	.89	31.57	10.84
LAWYER																				.73	.38	.00	.59	-.50	-.13	-.05	.92	36.97	9.95
AUTHOR-JOURNALIST																					.24	-.07	.34	-.50	.31	.04	.95	34.74	9.30
PRESIDENT, MFG. CONCERN																						-.05	.51	.09	.02	-.34	.79	25.61	9.73
SPECIALIZATION LEVEL																							.23	-.16	-.28	.39	.83	41.38	8.85
OCCUPATIONAL LEVEL																								-.29	-.23	.13	.79	58.46	6.79
MASCULINITY-FEMININITY																									.26	-.19	.95	45.20	9.18
OCCUP. INTROVERS'N-EXTROVERS'N																										.14	—	49.24	11.44
ACADEMIC ACHIEVEMENT																											—	50.28	10.06

Table 2-5. Intercorrelations Between the Women's Occupational Scales

	Entertainer	Musician Performer	Model	Art Teacher	Artist	Interior Decorator	Newswoman	English Teacher	Language Teacher	YWCA Staff Member	Dir., Christian Ed.	Nun-Teacher	Guidance Counselor	Soc. Sci. Teacher	Social Worker	Speech Pathologist	Psychologist	Librarian	Translator	Physician	Dentist	Med. Technologist	Chemist	Mathematician	Computer-Programmer	Math-Sci. Teacher	Engineer	Army-Enlisted	Navy-Enlisted
Music Teacher	29	58	03	42	-15	19	22	64	59	70	86	49	72	52	52	28	-01	21	-20	-27	-57	-51	-30	-38	-57	-44	-37	-39	-64
Entertainer		75	63	62	38	58	61	49	40	28	19	-19	15	-05	08	35	32	17	37	11	-24	-30	-15	-20	-24	-74	-32	-55	-53
Musician Performer			35	66	37	54	61	62	57	34	45	16	30	12	30	47	38	45	39	18	-26	-31	-00	-04	-33	-65	-25	-58	-64
Model				27	44	60	63	27	33	12	-09	-49	-07	-02	01	28	10	02	28	-13	-34	-50	-38	-25	-41	-71	-46	-40	-30
Art Teacher					40	62	53	48	35	34	34	11	23	-04	18	32	38	33	33	17	-12	-21	02	-06	-24	-57	-16	-59	-56
Artist						70	73	05	17	-27	-28	-09	-33	-28	-08	47	56	50	78	57	23	01	37	56	-07	-29	03	-35	-09
Interior Decorator							72	36	39	14	01	-23	02	-04	09	34	35	45	50	13	-15	-37	-06	03	-35	-61	-23	-53	-45
Newswoman								60	59	24	14	02	15	22	29	67	55	59	65	33	-15	-40	08	21	-37	-66	-22	-47	-43
English Teacher									86	60	68	28	67	65	52	42	18	47	13	-18	-56	-67	-31	-31	-58	-70	-47	-51	-73
Language Teacher										42	60	28	54	60	41	38	09	43	13	-24	-64	-72	-39	-28	-65	-66	-59	-55	-70
YWCA Staff Member											72	25	84	65	70	40	13	11	-15	-21	-42	-43	-24	-39	-40	-40	-18	-11	-45
Director, Christian Ed.												59	80	58	58	25	-04	12	-29	-27	-60	-49	-32	-40	-52	-39	-43	-41	-65
Nun-Teacher													42	29	29	18	04	18	-12	09	-16	-02	17	15	-10	14	02	-00	-11
Guidance Counselor														76	78	41	15	24	-15	-22	-45	-38	-21	-34	-37	-29	-23	-21	-59
Social Science Teacher															68	30	03	32	-13	-27	-42	-46	-26	-28	-42	-23	-23	-03	-39
Social Worker																57	35	40	11	05	-20	-20	01	-05	-26	-25	-07	-14	-45
Speech Pathologist																	80	62	65	55	10	-03	43	45	-05	-22	17	-18	-30
Psychologist																		67	84	79	46	**31**	70	67	31	-02	45	-16	-18
Librarian																			70	44	15	-04	44	51	-07	-16	-19	-21	-32
Translator																				71	42	22	60	68	22	-14	31	-20	-11
Physician																					74	65	89	84	51	27	63	06	19
Dentist																						84	82	71	71	61	83	45	55
Medical Technologist																							77	60	79	74	79	44	53
Chemist																								90	66	54	84	31	37
Mathematician																									55	48	70	25	40
Computer Programmer																										69	77	45	54
Math-Science Teacher																											71	66	68
Engineer																												62	60
Army-Enlisted																													84
Navy-Enlisted																													

(table continued next page)

TABLE 2-5 (*continued*)

	Diversity of Interests	Occupational Intro.-Extro.	Academic Achievement	Femininity-Masculinity	Airline Stewardess	Beautician	Telephone Operator	Sewing Machine Oper	Saleswoman	Secretary	Elementary Teacher	Instrument Assembler	Exec. Housekeeper	Dental Assistant	Radiol. Technologist	Lic. Practical Nurse	Registered Nurse	Pub. Health Nurse	Physical Therapist	Occ. Therapist	Phys. Ed. Teacher	Dietitian	Home Ec. Teacher	Bus. Ed. Teacher	Buyer	Life Ins. Underwriter	Lawyer	Navy Officer	Army Officer
Music Teacher	48	-58	10	46	34	-23	-06	-27	11	00	56	-54	26	-11	-47	12	43	54	-07	44	-20	19	47	05	01	31	-06	-45	05
Entertainer	06	-27	19	45	35	-26	-35	-55	-28	-24	-11	-56	-28	-42	-18	-30	23	15	-21	38	-42	02	07	-58	-32	-05	01	-15	-06
Musician Performer	16	-29	-01	62	11	-44	-42	-56	-56	-34	09	-67	-23	-45	-36	-20	24	24	-21	-13	-55	03	08	-55	-35	-04	08	-22	-05
Model	23	-13	-30	10	24	12	-37	-42	-28	03	-43	-32	-44	-45	-37	-61	-04	05	-56	-13	-36	-32	-07	-33	-00	25	13	16	-08
Art Teacher	20	29	39	59	15	-45	-45	-53	-35	-44	09	-64	-25	-54	-30	-26	-04	20	-10	70	-35	05	23	-62	-47	-21	-08	-27	-04
Artist	20	27	26	16	-56	-34	-52	-75	-40	-59	-11	-77	-37	-64	-59	-70	-42	-24	-48	-16	-52	-39	-54	-72	-34	-34	25	-13	-07
Interior Decorator	14	51	08	41	00	-21	-42	-55	-07	-09	-50	-67	-17	-40	-58	-20	36	43	-33	28	-51	-06	-03	-46	-06	14	25	15	-05
Newswoman	-14	29	39	25	-15	-45	-77	-75	-66	-44	-65	-76	-65	-84	-68	-71	-13	-34	-55	-59	-63	-34	-05	11	21	-35	48	40	27
English Teacher	26	21	21	54	-15	-77	-50	-50	-07	-09	44	-77	28	-68	-43	-20	36	43	33	28	-51	-04	-00	-19	-31	25	19	50	50
Language Teacher	22	-52	07	55	30	-41	-23	-50	-07	-01	28	-67	18	-40	-68	-28	27	40	-49	07	-55	-17	17	-14	-15	28	13	28	52
YWCA Staff Member	60	-32	11	15	16	-22	-24	-41	-10	-01	18	-84	-17	-18	-35	14	42	70	06	50	-01	19	50	-08	10	24	11	34	50
Director, Christian Ed.	49	-57	13	16	32	-22	-02	-50	15	-03	66	-54	40	38	-36	40	-34	45	47	17	08	50	38	06	06	24	-24	21	62
Nun-Teacher	22	-16	27	28	16	-24	-07	-05	05	-25	44	-25	-20	-11	-01	44	26	26	22	21	01	-09	18	01	02	-20	02	29	62
Guidance Counselor	22	-27	20	10	43	-32	-03	-24	-05	-05	40	-54	-09	-11	-34	14	56	70	08	36	-11	-25	38	18	09	48	60	46	50
Social Science Teacher	60	-74	04	31	29	-39	-03	-05	13	-05	27	-47	14	-42	-42	-01	37	56	-14	01	-15	19	-24	35	-01	-10	39	37	52
Social Worker	51	-60	31	16	17	-26	-02	-53	-12	-24	27	-58	58	-11	-11	-03	26	37	07	24	-19	15	-18	32	-18	-14	60	40	47
Speech Pathologist	-03	-38	53	00	-22	-76	-80	-85	-71	-86	-36	-75	-58	-70	-36	-48	-07	11	-13	06	-33	-07	-45	-51	-32	33	64	40	43
Psychologist	-08	-14	72	05	-32	-78	-78	-75	-82	-84	-45	-59	-39	-70	-14	-23	-22	15	02	17	-36	-34	-42	-66	-42	-07	57	35	40
Librarian	00	-11	58	30	-40	-44	-60	-53	-50	-50	-26	-62	-39	-61	-51	-43	-30	-18	-36	-05	-71	-07	-07	-38	-24	07	62	29	22
Translator	-32	12	57	11	-52	-22	-77	-63	-67	-67	-65	-48	-70	-72	-23	-62	-40	-35	-29	-06	-57	-21	-07	-69	-21	18	56	49	15
Physician	-24	12	71	-15	-56	-75	-86	-75	-72	-86	-36	-28	-58	-70	-36	-22	-07	11	06	07	-06	-07	-06	-68	-01	12	44	22	45
Dentist	-26	30	44	-37	-44	-43	-84	-75	-79	-59	-40	-54	-59	-23	-11	-22	-22	-34	40	-04	19	-34	-32	-08	13	30	29	45	27
Medical Technologist	-19	33	42	-35	-60	-16	13	13	-48	-40	-16	24	-37	-30	26	-17	-49	-43	66	07	19	09	-32	-16	-28	-12	33	42	33
Chemist	-39	17	71	-27	-81	-59	00	09	-74	-56	-56	-08	-57	-45	04	-11	-58	-50	33	02	-13	-19	-61	-19	31	-18	17	33	12
Mathematician	-09	33	57	-28	-60	-55	-01	-18	-27	-27	-04	-47	-08	-45	-42	-01	-34	-28	-41	43	-25	19	-27	-44	-12	35	18	33	24
Computer Programmer	07	33	37	-42	-81	-81	-07	09	-18	-18	-56	-09	05	-18	09	44	-50	-41	49	-26	53	19	-24	-09	-18	35	18	33	09
Math-Science Teacher	00	32	10	-55	-36	-18	24	44	10	-04	-04	58	-18	24	52	36	-39	-34	49	-26	53	19	-25	35	18	-14	42	17	00
Engineer	01	05	07	-47	-07	-05	-05	-05	-05	-04	-21	20	-09	41	52	20	-44	-47	27	-02	47	-40	-25	-41	00	50	42	54	28
Army-Enlisted	01	05	-07	-70	07	11	27	34	20	17	-40	52	24	39	41	20	-44	-38	27	-38	47	-40	-40	47	41	25	32	57	51
Navy-Enlisted	30	37	-16	-73	-30	26	15	39	07	07	-40	65	28	46	32	04	-52	-54	-46	-46	52	-05	-52	25	24	-02	12	28	55

(*table continued next page*)

40

TABLE 2-5 (continued)

This table is a correlation matrix (values are correlations ×100, decimal points omitted). Columns (left to right) and rows (top to bottom) represent the occupational and derived scales. Reading order follows the triangular (lower-left) structure.

	Army Officer	Navy Officer	Lawyer	Life Ins. Underwriter	Buyer	Bus. Ed. Teacher	Home Ec. Teacher	Dietitian	Phys. Ed. Teacher	Occ. Therapist	Physical Therapist	Pub. Health Nurse	Registered Nurse	Lic. Practical Nurse	Radiol. Technologist	Dental Assistant	Exec. Housekeeper	Instrument Assembler	Elementary Teacher	Secretary	Saleswoman	Sewing Machine Oper.	Telephone Operator	Beautician	Airline Stewardess	Femininity-Masculinity II	Academic Achievement	Occupational Intro.-Extro.
Diversity of Interests	32	-57	08	-29	22	09	41	09	45	33	30	43	36	03	19	44	-21	51	51	15	37	-07	28	-20	58			-58
Occupational Intro.-Extro.	-57	08	-29	-59	-12	-07	-22	-28	-00	-37	-08	-35	00	-03	23	-22	-47	-21	07	15	45	10	36	-52	-58	-02	-10	
Academic Achievement	29	09	35	-24	-54	-07	-30	-22	37	-09	-04	06	-31	-07	-74	-52	-48	-84	-28	23	18							
Femininity-Masculinity	-44	-59	-32	-34	-31	-29	46	13	-48	48	-14	34	39	03	-28	-15	04	-44	39	-01	05	-17	-02	-16	17			
Airline Stewardess	18	-41	-24	26	30	55	32	62	38	21	40	35	53	27	15	34	50	-03	40	47	56	03	25					
Beautician	-45	-22	-57	-01	45	80	37	31	31	-35	-02	02	22	14	59	40	70	16	80	61	73	65						
Telephone Operator	-24	-50	-54	-10	42	70	58	37	01	-17	12	-02	74	42	70	82	69	62	78	93	83							
Sewing Machine Oper.	-38	-30	-51	-22	43	63	35	33	-24	-14	-14	-05	59	36	78	63	84	40	66	75								
Saleswoman	-16	-51	-45	08	53	74	66	34	26	04	19	19	69	27	84	88	55	66	81									
Secretary	-21	-29	-38	15	59	76	48	-01	12	-25	03	13	28	02	65	62	55	35										
Elementary Teacher	-27	-84	-57	-00	38	75	19	51	54	73	10	67	10															
Instrument Assembler	-23	-02	-40	-24	39	51	08	49	-30	23	-20	43	56	71	43													
Exec. Housekeeper	-01	-47	-37	11	55	66	56	27	19	33	21	33	75	28	81													
Dental Assistant	-18	-37	-50	-08	47	44	36	51	-04	10	27	22	81	58														
Radiol. Technologist	00	-09	-31	-40	02	03	01	64	20	-05	03	60																
Lic. Practical Nurse	-16	-56	-48	-20	14	48	54	48	31	35	52																	
Registered Nurse	-21	-68	-45	-07	-19	23	58	45	83																			
Pub. Health Nurse	-21	-55	-34	11	-14	45	49	14	23																			
Physical Therapist	13	-25	-27	-32	-26	-11	-00	16	54	67																		
Occ. Therapist	-01	-59	-37	-32	-39	-34	50	43	10																			
Phys. Ed. Teacher	13	-06	-34	-05	10	12	11	19																				
Dietitian	08	-33	-15	-04	18	18	53																					
Home Ec. Teacher	-36	-80	-63	-08	18	34																						
Bus. Ed. Teacher	12	-10	10	38	64																							
Buyer	20	18	10	51																								
Life Ins. Underwriter	57	37	56																									
Lawyer	70	74																										
Navy Officer	55																											

41

The Occupational Scales

The correlations between the Occupational Scales and the Basic Interest Scales are given in the respective chapters on the Basic Scales.

Validity

Concurrent Validity: the separation of occupations

The criterion used to establish the concurrent validity of the SVIB scales has traditionally been "continued membership in an occupation," and the degree of validity is determined by how well a given occupational scale discriminates between men who are settled into that occupation and Men-in-General. A visual example of that discrimination for one scale, the Engineer scale, is shown in Figure 2-1. There are some problems with this criterion: Why, for example, should simple occupational membership be the criterion? Why not, instead, satisfaction in the occupation, or success there?

Part of the answer is that simple occupational membership has not, in fact, been used when it has been possible to avoid it. Inclusion in the criterion group has been limited in relevant ways—men have been asked if they like their jobs, and those who say "no" have been dropped. Where measures of success were available, they have been used. For example, as reported earlier, the Army Officer scale is based on West Point graduates only and, among them, only on officers who ranked above the median on the annual efficiency ratings.

Because satisfaction and success data are not always available, and because such data may not themselves be valid enough to use in defining group membership, a minimum of three years of experience has usually been required. This serves as a minimum of both satisfaction and success, as anyone who has persisted three years is at least minimally satisfied with his job, and at least successful enough to survive the first critical years. Further comments on the relationship between the SVIB scales and success and satisfaction can be found on p. 63.

Traditionally, the statistic used to indicate the degree of separation is the *percent overlap* suggested by Tilton (1937). This figure, with a range from zero to 100 percent, gives the percent of scores in one distribution that can be matched by scores in another distribution. When the distributions of the two groups are identical, the overlap is 100 percent. When the separation of the two groups is total, the overlap is zero percent.

Tilton has provided tables for calculating this statistic, using the means and standard deviations of the two groups in question. Using the formula

$$Q = \frac{M_1 - M_2}{\frac{SD_1 + SD_2}{2}}$$

TABLE 2-6. TILTON PERCENT OVERLAP TABLE

$$Q = \frac{M_1 - M_2}{\dfrac{SD_1 + SD_2}{2}}$$

Q	Per Cent Overlap	Q	Per Cent Overlap	Q	Per Cent Overlap	Q	Per Cent Overlap
0.00	100	0.63	75	1.35	50	2.30	25
0.02	99	0.66	74	1.38	49	2.35	24
0.05	98	0.69	73	1.41	48	2.40	23
0.08	97	0.72	72	1.44	47	2.45	22
0.10	96	0.74	71	1.48	46	2.51	21
0.12	95	0.77	70	1.51	45	2.56	20
0.15	94	0.80	69	1.54	44	2.62	19
0.18	93	0.82	68	1.58	43	2.68	18
0.20	92	0.85	67	1.61	42	2.74	17
0.23	91	0.88	66	1.65	41	2.81	16
0.25	90	0.91	65	1.68	40	2.88	15
0.28	89	0.94	64	1.72	39	2.95	14
0.30	88	0.96	63	1.76	38	3.03	13
0.33	87	0.99	62	1.79	37	3.11	12
0.35	86	1.02	61	1.83	36	3.20	11
0.38	85	1.05	60	1.87	35	3.29	10
0.40	84	1.08	59	1.91	34	3.39	9
0.43	83	1.11	58	1.95	33	3.50	8
0.46	82	1.14	57	1.99	32	3.62	7
0.48	81	1.17	56	2.03	31	3.76	6
0.51	80	1.20	55	2.07	30	3.92	5
0.53	79	1.23	54	2.12	29	4.11	4
0.56	78	1.26	53	2.16	28	4.34	3
0.58	77	1.29	52	2.21	27	4.65	2
0.61	76	1.32	51	2.25	26	5.15	1

* Source: J. W. Tilton, "The Measurement of Overlapping,"
J. educ. Psychol., 28, 656–60.

an index, Q, is calculated. Entering the overlap table (Table 2-6) with this index, the percent overlap of the two distributions can be calculated. From the formula we can see that the overlap is a function both of the size of the difference between the means (represented by the numerator) and of the variability of the two groups (represented by the denominator—note that the denominator represents the average of the two standard deviations).

Percent overlaps for each scale on the Men's SVIB are presented in Table 2-7. They range from 15 to 52, with a median of 31 percent overlap. On the women's scales, the percent overlaps, reported in Table 2-8, range from 14 to 52, with a median of 36. Such overlaps indicate that the separations between means is, on the average, about two standard deviations.

The next-to-last column in Tables 2-7 and 2-8 lists the number of SVIB items that make up each scale, and the last column shows the minimum

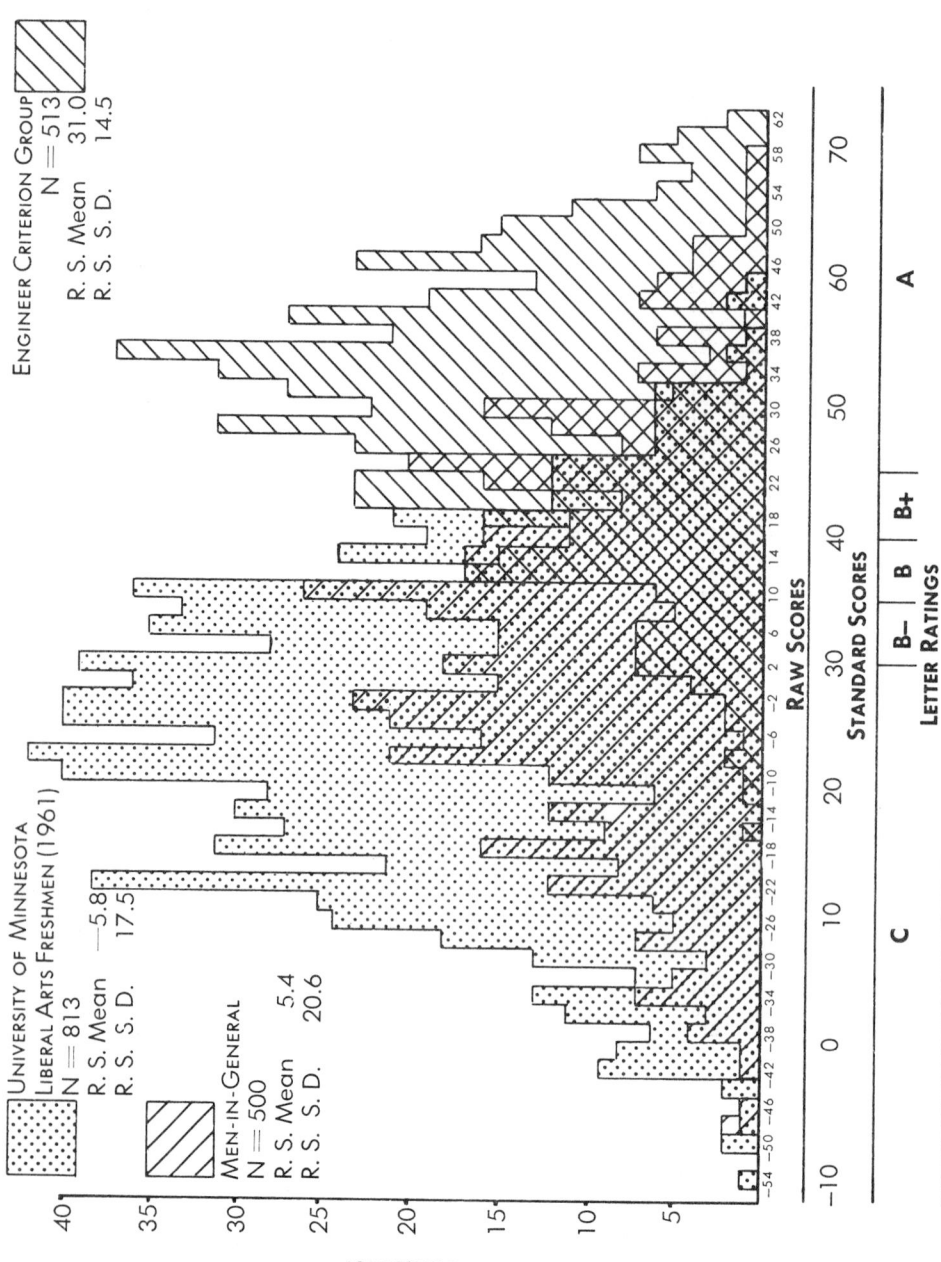

FIG. 2-1. *Distribution of scores on Engineer scale for engineer criterion group, men-in-general, and liberal arts college freshmen.*

TABLE 2-7. CONCURRENT VALIDITY CHARACTERISTICS OF THE
MEN'S OCCUPATIONAL SCALES
(Scores for criterion groups are raw scores; scores for
men-in-general group are standard scores)

Occupational and Nonoccupational Scales	Criterion Group			Men-in-General		Per Cent Overlap	Number of Items Scored	Min. Per Cent Difference Scored
	N	Mean	S.D.	Mean	S.D.			
DENTIST	235	24.8	13.6	31.5	11.3	38	72	15
OSTEOPATH	584	13.8	8.4	27.9	11.0	29	46	14
VETERINARIAN	310	28.0	13.9	26.9	11.0	29	74	17
PHYSICIAN	532	16.7	8.5	26.5	13.2	31	46	14
PSYCHIATRIST	401	23.5	9.8	21.0	12.5	20	52	17
PSYCHOLOGIST	1045	26.7	13.0	22.2	12.4	21	70	17
BIOLOGIST	342	30.4	12.7	23.6	13.4	26	64	17
ARCHITECT	238	40.1	18.7	29.7	12.2	36	96	17
MATHEMATICIAN	181	46.4	19.7	23.2	12.5	24	97	20
PHYSICIST	167	47.9	18.8	20.7	14.4	23	93	21
CHEMIST	292	26.2	11.1	26.6	15.4	36	59	16
ENGINEER	511	31.0	14.5	31.9	14.2	45	75	17
PRODUCTION MANAGER	212	13.3	9.6	35.9	11.2	51	44	14
ARMY OFFICER	463	29.2	10.9	20.4	12.7	19	65	17
AIR FORCE OFFICER	198	37.8	17.6	24.3	10.9	22	89	17
CARPENTER	179	36.2	15.4	24.5	13.3	27	90	17
FOREST SERVICE MAN	406	29.2	9.5	23.4	14.4	26	64	16
FARMER	240	23.8	15.2	36.1	10.7	50	65	15
MATH–SCIENCE TEACHER	288	16.9	10.1	27.6	12.0	31	53	15
PRINTER	269	18.3	11.7	31.6	10.1	36	60	15
POLICEMAN	251	26.8	12.0	23.8	10.6	20	71	17
PERSONNEL DIRECTOR	147	15.4	8.2	29.3	13.1	37	44	14
PUBLIC ADMINISTRATOR	534	13.7	8.2	33.6	12.0	45	35	14
REHABILITATION COUNSELOR	272	21.6	12.8	25.0	10.1	21	51	17
YMCA SECRETARY	184	32.6	14.9	16.6	13.1	15	91	17
SOCIAL WORKER	400	29.0	13.1	21.1	13.4	22	68	17
SOCIAL SCIENCE TEACHER	217	20.7	11.8	28.7	12.4	34	55	16
SCHOOL SUPERINTENDENT	189	24.0	10.7	25.1	12.9	28	62	15
MINISTER	249	35.3	12.2	16.3	15.5	19	74	17
LIBRARIAN	425	30.2	15.2	25.0	11.6	25	75	17
ARTIST	218	41.9	25.1	27.7	10.2	27	95	22
MUSICIAN PERFORMER	441	11.8	11.1	28.6	10.2	29	54	17
MUSIC TEACHER	490	20.2	10.9	22.6	11.6	20	57	17
CPA OWNER	353	18.1	9.4	29.6	11.3	34	51	15
SENIOR CPA	611	19.9	8.0	26.5	13.4	32	51	14
ACCOUNTANT	343	14.0	7.7	30.8	13.5	42	42	14
OFFICE WORKER	316	14.5	10.0	33.2	12.6	46	53	15
PURCHASING AGENT	217	15.8	12.5	36.0	11.6	52	59	15
BANKER	238	22.0	13.3	32.2	10.6	39	67	17
PHARMACIST	292	14.7	11.2	29.7	10.0	31	61	14
MORTICIAN	354	18.3	14.8	32.9	10.2	40	68	16
SALES MANAGER	228	18.2	12.1	32.5	12.4	43	56	16
REAL ESTATE SALESMAN	241	15.9	16.3	37.1	10.2	52	56	17
LIFE INSURANCE SALESMAN	310	22.0	15.7	31.6	12.1	41	68	17
ADVERTISING MAN	167	24.2	18.4	32.2	11.3	40	79	17
LAWYER	249	24.2	15.6	34.3	10.4	44	63	17
AUTHOR–JOURNALIST	242	36.2	30.0	31.8	9.9	36	98	21
PRESIDENT, MFG. CONCERN	165	15.6	9.4	34.5	12.1	48	47	15
CREDIT MANAGER	452	27.1	14.9	28.7	13.1	36	69	17
CHAMBER OF COMMERCE EXEC.	399	29.6	20.2	29.0	11.0	32	86	17
PHYSICAL THERAPIST	348	21.7	11.2	24.6	12.4	25	52	16
COMPUTER PROGRAMMER	503	24.0	8.1	24.2	13.0	32	66	15
BUSINESS EDUCATION TEACHER	322	18.7	13.4	27.6	11.7	30	57	17
COMMUNITY RECREATION ADMIN.	350	40.1	15.6	18.4	13.4	18	93	17
SPECIALIZATION LEVEL				36.9	10.6		33	10
OCCUPATIONAL LEVEL				59.6	8.6		70	15
MASCULINITY–FEMININITY				47.4	9.6		99	16
ACADEMIC ACHIEVEMENT				44.5	11.0		55	14
OCC. INTROVERSION–EXTROVERSION				48.8	11.8		81	20

45

	N*	Criterion Group Mean	SD	Women-in-General (N=1000) Mean	SD	Percent Overlap	Number of items scored	Minimum percent Difference scored
Accountant	335	21.6	12.4	23.8	12.2	24	67	15.6
Army Enlisted	218	8.7	15.0	31.0	11.2	37	70	16.6
Army Officer	307	22.3	14.4	30.6	12.3	39	73	14.6
Artist	296	58.4	24.2	25.9	13.8	31	96	24.6
Art Teacher	359	46.0	12.0	19.3	19.3	29	87	14.6
Bankwomen	271	17.5	15.7	29.3	11.6	34	72	16.6
Beautician	262	23.8	19.6	31.3	11.2	38	77	19.6
Business Education Teacher	300	36.3	19.2	24.4	12.4	26	88	16.6
Buyer**	198	25.5	12.4	21.6	9.9	16	83	14.6
Chemist	173	43.1	12.8	11.7	18.8	19	80	22.6
Computer Programmer**	262	19.8	11.1	25.2	11.6	25	90	12.0
Dental Assistant	417	24.6	15.2	28.7	14.6	39	75	14.6
Dentist**	188	25.5	13.6	25.0	11.6	25	76	15.6
Dietitian	327	13.1	8.4	31.5	11.6	40	37	13.6
Director,Christian Education	434	40.2	13.5	22.3	14.3	26	77	15.6
Elementary School Teacher	325	21.0	15.1	34.7	13.1	51	60	14.6
English Teacher	352	36.1	15.3	30.9	14.1	43	76	13.6
Engineer	322	25.7	12.9	22.4	13.9	25	69	15.6
Entertainer	104	33.2	15.2	24.5	13.7	29	77	18.6
Executive Housekeeper	280	27.6	16.2	29.6	13.2	38	82	15.6
Guidance Counselor	347	32.5	13.3	28.9	14.0	38	66	13.6
Home Economics Teacher	373	35.1	13.5	24.7	15.6	33	78	14.6
Instrument Assembler	89	26.0	17.6	27.2	14.0	34	86	18.6
Interior Decorator	172	48.4	14.2	17.9	16.7	23	89	19.6
Language Teacher	287	24.8	10.0	31.7	13.7	44	51	13.6
Lawyer	235	32.2	16.2	26.3	13.6	32	87	16.6
Librarian	410	24.4	10.9	33.0	14.7	49	55	13.6
Licensed Practical Nurse	222	33.3	18.3	26.9	13.8	33	86	17.6
Life Insurance Underwriter	187	26.2	14.0	24.6	11.4	24	77	15.6
Mathematician	119	41.9	13.8	16.2	17.2	22	77	28.6
Math-Science Teacher	308	24.6	19.9	32.1	12.1	44	82	15.6
Medical Technologist	345	24.9	15.5	27.7	14.3	36	73	15.6
Model**	70	33.1	15.2	25.8	12.7	29	84	17.6
Musician Performer	287	22.7	9.3	29.6	12.8	37	51	13.6
Music Teacher**	444	27.6	9.9	23.6	13.2	33	62	14.6
Navy Enlisted	213	17.0	18.0	33.0	10.9	42	77	16.6
Navy Officer	190	19.5	16.0	35.8	10.1	48	65	14.6
Newswoman	189	39.3	17.7	28.4	14.8	39	79	18.6
Nun-Teacher**	494	27.1	10.0	16.9	12.4	14	73	15.6
Occupational Therapist	594	27.8	14.4	33.7	12.9	48	66	14.6

TABLE 2-8 (*continued*)

	Criterion Group			Women-in-General (N=1000)		Percent Overlap	Number of items scored	Minimum percent Difference scored
	N*	Mean	SD	Mean	SD			
Physical Education Teacher (High School)	310	26.0	15.6	28.7	12.6	35	78	13.6
Physical Therapist	263	20.7	14.6	34.4	13.2	51	66	13.6
Physician	329	33.9	14.6	27.1	15.6	37	76	16.6
Psychologist	275	42.8	18.2	17.1	17.7	24	77	23.6
Public Health Nurse**	268	17.7	7.8	29.3	12.4	36	43	13.6
Radiologic Technologist	306	17.2	13.0	30.9	14.1	43	67	13.6
Recreation Leader	197	37.1	20.4	33.3	12.0	45	81	15.6
Registered Nurse	263	22.4	9.7	29.7	12.5	37	54	13.6
Saleswoman	241	31.7	17.3	26.1	15.2	35	79	18.6
Secretary	366	20.7	16.0	32.6	12.7	45	75	13.6
Sewing Machine Operator	294	29.4	14.8	18.7	16.0	23	80	25.6
Speech Pathologist	323	35.0	13.8	27.5	14.6	36	85	13.6
Social Science Teacher	182	22.5	12.2	32.1	11.6	41	56	13.6
Social Worker**	464	25.7	9.7	24.5	12.9	27	65	13.6
Stewardess	439	33.5	17.3	26.8	14.2	34	78	18.6
Telephone Operator	128	24.5	13.8	25.0	17.1	36	71	19.6
Translator	130	34.6	16.4	26.7	14.6	35	80	19.6
YWCA Staff Member	282	27.3	14.8	31.4	12.5	41	48	14.6

* This number deviates in some samples from N reported in Appendix B. The discrepancy is due to incompletely filled out forms--they were used in item analysis but not in the norming.

**These scales based on samples that filled in Form W or WA--see Appendix A.

percent difference in response rate between the MIG group and the criterion group accepted for that scale; the 15 percent difference for the Dentist scale, for example, means that item response differences greater than 15 percent were used to make up the Dentist scale.

No systematic attempt has been made to present cross-validation data for the SVIB scales, and some comment should be made about this omission. The purpose of cross-validation is to ensure that the methods used in scale development are not vulnerable to chance differences. The usual technique for doing this is to split the group under study into two portions, build the scale on one portion, and test its effectiveness (i.e., cross-validate) on the other. This technique has the disadvantage of denying the use of the latter data to the investigator in developing the scale—that is, he is forced to build his scale utilizing only a portion of the information that he actually has available.

Although such a situation is inevitable in the early stages of research, once the techniques for scale development have proved themselves, cross-validation is no longer necessary or even desirable; all available data should be used in scale development, which is generally what has been done here. The SVIB scales have stood up well in cross-validation studies, though there is usually a mild shrinkage when the relevant scale is applied to new samples. Some information on this point can be found in later sections, especially Appendix E. For example, the 1964 banker sample in Figure 2-15 is essentially a cross-validated sample collected 30 years after the validation sample. This sample averaged 46 on the Banker scale which, considering the time lag, compares favorably with the mean score of 50 of the validation sample. Also, the mean profiles in Chapter 7, which are from very successful men, provide further evidence of cross-validation endurance.

The above discussion has been concerned with how well the scales separate the occupational criterion groups from Men-in-General, but there is a second validity requirement, i.e., the scales must separate occupations from each other. The necessary data for those comparisons are in Table 2-9 for the men's scales and Table 2-10 for the women. They show that many occupations score high on another occupational scale, in a few cases as high as the criterion group itself. For example, the physicists scored higher (mean = 54) on the Chemist scale than the chemists did (mean = 50); clearly the Chemist scale cannot be used to distinguish between the interests of these two occupations. Paradoxically, the Physicist scale did separate them rather well. Physicists averaged 50 on their own scale, whereas chemists averaged only 38; on this scale the percent overlap between the two occupations was roughly 55 percent. Just why the two scales give different results, and why the relationship is not symmetrical, is not understood.

That the SVIB scales do not separate all possible pairs of occupations is probably not so much a reflection of poor validity as it is an indication of similarity in interests between some occupations. Thus, physicists, mathematicians, and engineers all score high on the Chemist scale—54, 46, and 44, respectively—but this is more likely an indication of common interests than of lack of validity.

Possibly, scales could be built that would separate occupational groups from Men-in-General, and also separate all occupations from each other. Although scales developed in such a manner would be valuable, they might have the disadvantage of concealing similarities between occupations. The SVIB is usually used to indicate a general area of interest to the client, rather than a specific occupation. One way to do this is to show him his scores on several related occupational scales—and to show him, in fact, that the occupations making up each family on the profile are indeed similar to each other in general interests.

The question of how to build scales that better discriminate between occupations, yet retain occupational similarities, is one deserving more research.

Predictive Validity: Occupational Membership

As the Strong Vocational Interest Blanks are widely used as aids in the guidance of young people, adequate validity in differentiating between adult occupations is not enough; the scores must also be stable over considerable periods of time, and there must be some agreement between them and subsequent vocation—that is, the test must have predictive validity.

Before grappling with the details of long-range predictive accuracy, a parenthetical comment might be inserted here. When reading the studies reported below, one longs for a straightforward statistic—some comment such as "The test was 60 percent accurate," or "Fifty-eight percent of the students were accurately predicted." But no simple summary statement emerges. Partially this is because people are pleasantly complex, and do not fit neatly into categories; thus, any classification system cannot be clean and sharp. Though better categorization systems might be possible, we haven't learned which variables are important.

Other specific problems which contribute to fuzzy validity statistics are discussed below in the various studies. Two of the more important ones are, first, men choose occupations for reasons other than interest; and second, men choose occupations that they eventually find do not interest them but where they feel locked in and cannot leave. When analyzing test results for such individuals, many quandaries appear. For good prediction purposes, should a dissatisfied individual have scored high or low on his particular occupational scale when tested earlier? If he scored high, the researcher can claim accurate prediction for the man is indeed currently in that occupation; if he scored low, again it could be considered an accurate prediction for he now says he is dissatisfied. Most researchers try to avoid setting up the analysis so that they win no matter what the outcome, but the point here is that it is difficult to know just how to do that.

No one closely associated with the SVIB wants to overstate the level of predictive accuracy, but it is difficult to work with this inventory over several years without becoming convinced that there is some substantial relationship between a person's scores and what he chooses to do with his life, especially for adults. Several studies are reviewed below to illustrate the empirical data supporting these beliefs.

Strong's study of Stanford students. Strong's classic follow-up of 663 Stanford University students showed fairly good predictive power for interest scores in 1927–30 in predicting occupations engaged in 18 years later

TABLE 2-9. MEAN STANDARD SCORES FOR THE MALE CRITERION GROUPS ON THE OCCUPATIONAL AND NONOCCUPATIONAL SCALES

Occupational and Nonoccupational Scales	Physical Therapist	Dentist	Osteopath	Veterinarian	Physician	Psychiatrist	Psychologist	Biologist	Architect	Mathematician	Physicist	Chemist	Engineer	Production Manager	Army Officer	Air Force Officer	Carpenter	Forest Service Man	Farmer	Math-Science Teacher	Printer	Policeman	Personnel Director	Public Administrator	Rehabilitation Counselor	YMCA Secretary
PHYSICAL THERAPIST	50	32	38	39	35	35	29	32	21	18	22	27	22	24	31	37	31	30	29	35	29	37	25	27	34	45
DENTIST	32	50	42	43	41	31	25	34	40	34	38	35	34	29	23	22	39	31	39	32	35	34	20	22	18	18
OSTEOPATH	41	47	50	48	44	37	28	34	31	25	29	31	26	24	23	25	31	28	33	31	29	32	20	24	25	26
VETERINARIAN	32	36	37	50	32	23	18	24	24	15	19	25	24	25	22	23	33	32	39	25	27	32	18	21	20	25
PHYSICIAN	39	44	45	42	50	43	34	43	36	33	38	36	29	22	25	25	26	26	32	30	26	27	18	23	23	23
PSYCHIATRIST	33	27	32	23	38	50	46	41	27	33	34	32	24	20	24	26	13	18	16	27	17	17	27	30	37	27
PSYCHOLOGIST	28	24	26	19	33	44	50	42	29	42	41	35	27	22	25	26	16	20	17	29	22	15	28	31	34	24
BIOLOGIST	32	33	32	28	39	40	41	50	34	45	48	40	33	22	26	28	24	28	28	32	24	23	22	27	25	21
ARCHITECT	22	35	29	27	32	28	30	34	50	39	42	36	40	30	26	24	36	30	33	25	31	25	25	25	17	15
MATHEMATICIAN	17	24	21	16	27	29	34	38	32	50	48	34	33	23	21	20	23	20	23	26	22	18	22	23	20	11
PHYSICIST	18	26	21	17	27	25	30	35	31	44	50	38	36	24	21	22	25	21	23	25	21	18	18	20	14	7
CHEMIST	26	35	30	25	35	34	35	43	38	46	54	50	44	33	32	33	28	28	30	33	28	26	24	26	17	12
ENGINEER	23	35	29	28	32	28	30	35	41	44	51	44	50	39	32	32	37	35	36	31	30	29	30	30	19	13
PRODUCTION MANAGER	29	34	32	34	29	26	27	27	32	30	36	39	45	50	41	40	44	40	38	34	36	39	40	37	29	28
ARMY OFFICER	26	16	19	19	19	20	20	21	19	18	22	25	30	30	50	46	26	28	22	23	20	27	28	28	29	27
AIR FORCE OFFICER	32	23	25	24	25	27	27	28	24	25	30	32	33	31	42	50	30	28	25	31	26	31	28	28	29	30
CARPENTER	22	29	23	28	21	14	13	20	31	24	29	26	31	28	23	25	50	32	34	26	34	34	17	17	12	14
FOREST SERVICE MAN	25	26	26	32	20	14	11	21	20	14	18	23	27	26	28	24	36	50	37	24	25	35	20	25	18	19
FARMER	31	39	36	45	33	25	24	32	36	32	36	36	38	35	31	30	44	42	50	34	37	38	27	29	22	26
MATH–SCIENCE TEACHER	36	33	31	30	30	29	30	34	25	38	39	37	32	29	31	36	36	31	32	50	34	33	25	27	29	28
PRINTER	28	34	28	32	26	20	21	25	29	27	28	30	29	31	26	27	45	33	37	31	50	40	24	24	23	24
POLICEMAN	26	27	27	27	20	15	9	14	18	12	15	20	24	27	25	24	36	32	28	24	30	50	23	21	19	23
PERSONNEL DIRECTOR	24	17	21	18	21	30	32	21	22	23	21	27	32	38	35	32	22	29	21	26	23	29	50	40	40	33
PUBLIC ADMINISTRATOR	34	26	31	28	29	39	42	35	29	29	30	33	35	41	45	44	28	40	30	34	30	35	47	50	48	41
REHABILITATION COUNSELOR	33	20	27	23	27	36	36	29	21	24	21	23	21	25	30	32	20	25	19	29	24	27	35	35	50	41
YMCA SECRETARY	33	13	20	22	17	21	20	16	8	5	3	9	7	14	23	28	14	19	14	21	17	22	22	22	32	50
SOCIAL WORKER	32	17	24	19	24	37	37	27	16	19	16	17	13	19	27	27	14	20	14	25	21	21	31	33	44	42
SOCIAL SCIENCE TEACHER	32	25	28	30	23	26	27	22	19	19	13	18	16	26	25	22	27	29	27	32	31	31	32	32	40	42
SCHOOL SUPERINTENDENT	22	20	21	19	22	29	30	23	17	28	21	19	21	26	24	20	15	22	20	26	18	20	35	34	38	31
MINISTER	22	16	18	12	20	26	27	24	16	24	18	12	10	10	11	10	10	12	12	19	15	13	22	21	29	28
LIBRARIAN	26	24	23	17	28	34	37	36	32	37	32	28	23	21	22	21	22	21	19	25	30	21	27	29	31	28
ARTIST	25	34	31	29	33	30	31	33	40	35	37	32	31	23	27	24	28	27	24	25	35	21	21	21	21	21
MUSICIAN PERFORMER	35	35	33	30	36	37	36	37	39	35	34	31	26	24	23	24	33	27	28	31	35	29	26	25	29	32
MUSIC TEACHER	28	22	24	21	25	29	30	27	25	26	21	16	14	17	20	21	19	17	18	25	24	20	25	24	33	37
CPA OWNER	19	25	23	22	25	25	28	25	32	34	28	28	31	29	26	26	20	22	23	26	23	22	30	29	29	22
SENIOR CPA	20	20	18	20	18	15	19	18	23	26	24	30	32	31	35	36	27	25	25	28	27	28	34	30	24	22
ACCOUNTANT	17	21	17	19	15	13	17	16	25	26	23	29	35	38	31	30	33	29	29	27	32	31	34	30	24	22
OFFICE WORKER	24	28	26	28	20	15	15	15	24	19	17	25	30	36	30	30	35	30	32	31	36	38	34	29	28	29
CREDIT MANAGER	31	20	24	28	22	25	24	19	19	15	13	22	23	32	35	37	25	27	25	28	27	29	36	33	39	40
CHAMBER OF COMMERCE EXEC.	31	22	27	27	25	30	31	24	24	19	16	22	23	29	35	36	22	27	24	26	28	28	36	34	39	43
BUSINESS EDUCATION TEACHER	30	20	24	27	21	24	25	20	17	20	16	20	20	29	31	33	28	27	26	30	29	28	35	34	38	31
PURCHASING AGENT	24	32	29	34	25	20	20	21	31	26	28	33	38	43	33	33	40	35	37	30	35	38	35	32	27	27
BANKER	20	28	26	32	22	18	16	16	26	23	20	22	28	33	25	22	35	31	34	25	32	33	29	28	26	23
PHARMACIST	32	35	36	42	32	25	20	23	22	19	21	28	25	30	23	23	32	27	33	30	30	33	24	24	27	27
MORTICIAN	29	34	35	40	29	24	20	20	28	18	18	23	26	33	27	25	34	30	33	26	31	33	29	29	30	34
SALES MANAGER	21	26	27	29	22	20	20	16	27	18	16	23	29	36	28	27	25	29	29	22	29	27	34	29	28	30
REAL ESTATE SALESMAN	29	33	33	37	30	27	27	24	33	27	24	28	32	36	32	31	35	36	37	28	34	36	35	34	35	36
LIFE INSURANCE SALESMAN	24	28	30	33	26	24	22	18	25	21	16	19	22	28	23	21	23	26	29	22	26	28	30	27	32	33
ADVERTISING MAN	23	30	29	28	29	29	29	27	36	28	25	27	28	30	26	22	24	27	27	21	32	26	31	29	29	29
LAWYER	27	34	34	32	35	36	35	33	36	28	25	27	29	31	30	26	24	30	31	27	29	31	34	35	33	29
AUTHOR–JOURNALIST	26	32	31	29	33	34	36	35	37	37	35	33	32	30	28	24	27	30	30	26	32	28	31	32	30	28
PRESIDENT, MFG. CONCERN	17	30	26	29	25	22	23	20	34	25	26	29	37	41	29	25	30	30	32	22	28	24	36	32	26	20
SPECIALIZATION LEVEL	41	33	35	28	39	52	55	51	42	48	48	44	41	39	44	46	32	36	31	42	36	33	45	46	48	42
OCCUPATIONAL LEVEL	54	57	58	57	60	62	62	60	62	61	61	60	63	62	62	60	48	56	55	55	50	51	64	63	63	59
MASCULINITY–FEMININITY	49	49	48	50	47	45	45	46	44	46	52	52	55	53	54	56	53	53	52	50	49	52	48	48	43	43
INTROVERSION–EXTROVERSION	43	53	50	50	51	45	48	52	55	58	60	56	54	49	46	43	54	50	54	49	52	47	42	44	39	35
ACADEMIC ACHIEVEMENT	51	48	49	44	55	59	59	62	50	61	60	56	50	44	49	49	38	43	41	51	41	42	48	50	52	44

TABLE 2-9 (*continued*)

Social Worker	Social Science Teacher	School Superintendent	Minister	Librarian	Artist	Musician Performer	Music Teacher	CPA Owner	Senior CPA	Accountant	Office Worker	Credit Manager	Chamber of Commerce Exec.	Business Education Teacher	Purchasing Agent	Banker	Pharmacist	Mortician	Sales Manager	Real Estate Salesman	Life Insurance Salesman	Advertising Man	Lawyer	Author-Journalist	President, Mfg. Concern	Occupational and Nonoccupational Scales
35	31	24	32	26	22	30	31	20	28	23	26	32	31	32	22	21	34	30	22	22	24	18	19	16	20	PHYSICAL THERAPIST
18	23	23	26	24	45	34	24	27	26	26	28	18	15	18	30	31	36	33	26	30	29	27	31	34	30	DENTIST
26	25	23	31	22	37	31	24	25	24	21	22	20	21	20	24	26	37	34	22	28	30	22	31	28	26	OSTEOPATH
18	23	17	19	13	26	23	19	21	24	21	24	22	21	21	27	30	36	36	26	31	30	21	23	20	26	VETERINARIAN
25	20	24	30	27	44	33	26	25	21	16	17	14	18	14	19	21	33	24	17	23	24	22	33	37	·23	PHYSICIAN
39	23	29	31	35	31	31	32	26	21	18	16	21	24	23	16	14	25	16	16	16	18	24	29	31	21	PSYCHIATRIST
37	24	30	32	39	34	31	32	30	24	22	17	20	25	26	17	16	21	15	16	15	15	27	29	37	22	PSYCHOLOGIST
27	20	27	29	34	38	30	28	25	23	20	16	15	16	18	16	17	24	15	13	13	13	19	25	33	20	BIOLOGIST
19	17	22	24	29	50	34	26	30	26	26	25	16	18	15	29	25	25	26	26	28	24	33	30	40	32	ARCHITECT
20	18	27	27	30	33	26	24	28	23	23	19	14	12	16	19	21	17	14	17	16	16	21	28	33	22	MATHEMATICIAN
12	9	19	19	22	32	23	16	23	21	20	16	9	6	10	18	16	17	12	14	12	10	17	21	27	21	PHYSICIST
15	14	22	18	26	38	30	19	29	29	27	23	17	11	14	28	19	26	17	21	18	13	22	25	29	29	CHEMIST
16	16	26	20	23	35	26	18	34	34	34	31	23	16	19	36	30	27	26	30	27	23	26	29	30	38	ENGINEER
26	28	32	26	23	22	26	25	37	39	42	40	38	31	32	44	39	34	37	42	36	32	30	30	22	44	PRODUCTION MANAGER
18	16	18	12	16	8	16	17	23	30	25	23	32	29	26	24	19	19	19	23	18	15	16	17	10	23	ARMY OFFICER
25	22	22	18	22	16	23	21	26	32	28	27	32	30	29	27	22	25	23	25	24	20	19	21	14	25	AIR FORCE OFFICER
10	17	12	14	16	28	25	17	18	23	24	25	16	9	18	27	25	24	25	19	23	16	16	14	17	23	CARPENTER
14	21	17	17	11	19	15	10	17	24	23	23	20	12	18	24	26	21	22	22	24	20	13	16	14	22	FOREST SERVICE MAN
21	30	26	27	24	37	30	24	31	33	33	33	27	23	27	36	38	36	37	32	37	33	27	30	30	36	FARMER
24	33	30	30	26	22	28	27	24	31	29	29	27	21	32	27	25	31	25	21	21	20	17	19	17	24	MATH-SCIENCE TEACHER
23	31	20	23	29	35	35	26	27	33	32	36	27	24	30	34	34	34	32	28	31	27	31	26	32	29	PRINTER
16	22	17	18	12	15	19	14	19	24	26	30	23	17	18	28	28	26	27	23	26	23	16	20	14	21	POLICEMAN
38	33	40	32	30	15	22	29	37	34	38	35	42	42	35	35	32	23	28	38	31	34	33	36	27	36	PERSONNEL DIRECTOR
47	41	44	41	39	22	28	38	39	38	40	36	45	46	42	36	37	31	33	37	31	33	35	37	31	38	PUBLIC ADMINISTRATOR
46	38	36	35	36	19	27	36	29	28	28	27	37	39	40	24	26	27	26	27	26	29	28	30	26	25	REHABILITATION COUNSELOR
35	31	22	28	22	10	21	30	14	18	16	18	30	38	32	15	15	20	23	20	21	25	20	16	13	13	YMCA SECRETARY
50	36	34	.39	38	19	29	37	23	22	21	20	32	39	35	16	20	21	22	22	21	25	27	28	28	18	SOCIAL WORKER
42	50	39	40	35	22	29	39	28	27	31	33	36	38	43	29	34	30	33	30	31	36	31	31	29	26	SOCIAL SCIENCE TEACHER
36	38	50	43	32	14	20	34	29	22	28	26	30	34	33	24	20	22	24	29	25	31	29	35	28	27	SCHOOL SUPERINTENDENT
34	28	33	50	33	23	26	36	16	11	13	14	17	24	22	9	14	13	15	15	13	21	21	23	27	13	MINISTER
38	30	31	38	50	40	38	41	29	26	25	24	24	29	29	20	23	24	21	21	21	22	33	31	43	22	LIBRARIAN
23	21	23	26	39	22	28	38	27	23	22	23	16	20	18	24	22	27	25	24	27	25	35	37	31	38	ARTIST
35	30	27	37	40	51	50	44	24	23	22	25	22	29	26	24	24	31	29	25	28	29	34	28	42	24	MUSICIAN PERFORMER
38	34	32	40	40	31	38	50	21	19	20	21	26	35	32	17	21	22	26	22	22	26	30	25	32	19	MUSIC TEACHER
25	26	32	24	28	24	23	25	50	40	41	35	34	30	31	32	36	27	28	33	30	32	32	38	31	35	CPA OWNER
17	21	20	11	21	9	18	16	41	50	43	39	41	27	33	33	33	25	27	30	26	23	21	24	12	28	SENIOR CPA
19	26	26	17	23	13	19	19	42	45	50	46	42	29	35	42	42	28	31	37	32	28	28	27	19	36	ACCOUNTANT
23	33	28	23	24	16	25	24	37	41	47	50	43	34	40	44	44	37	39	40	38	36	32	28	20	36	OFFICE WORKER
35	35	30	26	27	10	24	30	32	38	38	38	50	44	44	36	36	34	37	39	35	36	31	27	16	31	CREDIT MANAGER
40	35	34	34	33	22	29	36	32	32	32	33	42	50	39	31	30	30	34	37	35	38	37	33	30	31	CHAMBER OF COMMERCE EXEC.
34	39	31	29	29	13	25	33	29	32	35	36	42	38	50	32	35	32	34	33	34	34	27	23	17	29	BUSINESS EDUCATION TEACHER
22	29	28	20	21	23	25	22	35	38	43	43	39	32	34	50	44	39	42	45	42	38	34	31	24	43	PURCHASING AGENT
22	31	28	23	22	21	24	23	34	34	38	39	35	28	32	39	50	32	38	36	39	38	29	32	24	35	BANKER
22	28	22	21	18	23	25	22	26	25	33	35	34	25	34	50	41	35	34	35	35	34	27	24	21	29	PHARMACIST
28	33	28	28	24	26	29	31	29	30	33	36	35	36	33	39	40	41	50	40	41	43	34	31	27	36	MORTICIAN
26	28	28	23	20	24	23	24	33	30	36	38	37	39	32	40	38	36	40	50	44	45	44	33	30	42	SALES MANAGER
33	36	34	30	28	32	31	31	37	35	49	44	47	41	42	47	46	40	44	46	50	48	42	40	37	40	REAL ESTATE SALESMAN
30	33	32	31	24	28	28	30	31	26	30	34	33	37	31	33	37	33	39	42	44	50	38	37	34	35	LIFE INSURANCE SALESMAN
31	30	30	30	34	42	33	33	33	27	30	32	29	37	28	33	32	32	35	40	40	40	50	38	48	37	ADVERTISING MAN
35	34	39	36	34	38	33	33	41	36	37	40	37	35	37	30	37	30	32	36	37	40	39	50	47	36	LAWYER
32	30	32	33	37	45	36	34	34	29	29	29	26	32	26	30	30	30	30	32	33	33	41	39	50	33	AUTHOR-JOURNALIST
21	25	29	22	19	30	23	21	37	32	37	36	33	31	27	42	38	34	37	46	40	41	40	35	33	50	PRESIDENT, MFG. CONCERN
50	41	46	44	52	40	43	49	44	41	40	36	43	45	44	35	33	34	30	38	32	33	44	41	44	38	SPECIALIZATION LEVEL
60	57	66	60	58	57	55	60	66	59	62	60	63	65	59	62	61	59	59	67	63	65	65	65	63	66	OCCUPATIONAL LEVEL
41	43	43	39	36	39	40	36	46	50	48	47	48	43	45	51	47	46	45	48	47	43	41	44	37	49	MASCULINITY–FEMININITY
38	42	42	40	48	57	49	41	49	49	48	47	39	35	43	49	50	49	47	42	46	40	43	46	52	48	INTROVERSION–EXTROVERSION
51	45	53	52	58	48	49	53	52	49	46	42	46	46	45	40	41	47	39	41	37	42	44	49	49	44	ACADEMIC ACHIEVEMENT

TABLE 2-10. MEAN STANDARD SCORES FOR THE FEMALE CRITERION GROUPS ON THE OCCUPATIONAL AND NONOCCUPATIONAL SCALES

Columns are Criterion **Groups**; rows are **Scales**. Columns left blank (Art Teacher, Language Teacher, Recreation Leader, Nun-Teacher, Social Worker, Speech Pathologist, Dentist, Computer Programmer) have no group data; for the scale rows from Army-Enlisted through Airline Stewardess these columns are marked "Scores Not Available."

Scales \ Groups	Music Teacher	Entertainer	Musician Performer	Model (Cross-Validation)	Art Teacher	Artist	Interior Decorator	Newswoman	English Teacher	Language Teacher	YWCA Staff Member	Recreation Leader	Dir., Christian Ed.	Nun-Teacher	Guidance Counselor	Soc. Sci. Teacher	Social Worker	Speech Pathologist	Psychologist	Librarian	Translator	Physician	Dentist	Med. Technologist	Chemist	Mathematician	Computer Programmer	Math-Sci. Teacher
Music Teacher	24	18	32	25		26	23	33	33		33		41		35	32			25	28	22	20		13	19	20		21
Entertainer	50	44	30	35		34	35	28	26		24		21		28	22			31	23	33	25		19	20	20		12
Musician Performer	44	36	37	44		40	41	36	36		33		36		30	29			38	35	40	32		25	32	31		21
Model	43	44	27	33		35	38	27	25		26		21		21	23			27	24	30	22		18	17	19		13
Art Teacher																												
Artist	34	31	35	50		38	37	26	27		23		22		22	24			37	30	38	34		25	35	36		20
Interior Decorator	29	29	33	41		50	33	19	18		18		13		17	15			28	24	29	22		09	19	21		06
Newswoman	39	34	35	44		40	50	37	34		32		29		30	33			41	36	41	32		21	20	20		18
English Teacher	36	32	37	34		34	43	50	44		39		42		42	43			36	40	37	28		19	24	25		26
Language Teacher	38	31	38	36		36	43	50	50		38		43		43	42			36	41	37	28		18	26	30		28
YWCA Staff Member	32	33	34	26		32	35	37	34		50		45		43	37			39	33	30	29		23	27	24		25
Recreation Leader																												
Dir., Christian Ed.	18	17	27	16		17	19	33	31		37		50		37	32			22	26	16	17		13	15	14		21
Nun-Teacher	07	-01	18	13		06	08	21	22		19		32		25	22			16	20	12	18		20	21	19		24
Guidance Counselor	22	23	31	21		25	27	39	36		42		45		50	40			38	33	26	28		23	27	25		30
Soc. Sci. Teacher	28	26	31	26		29	38	44	43		40		41		44	50			37	39	33	30		24	29	29		32
Social Worker	17	16	24	23		23	28	30	28		38		35		40	33			40	30	28	32		24	30	27		22
Speech Pathologist	31	28	34	38		31	37	36	33		35		35		37	34			50	36	40	37		26	40	38		25
Psychologist	22	20	24	34		23	28	20	18		20		16		22	18			50	25	37	33		22	40	38		18
Librarian	32	26	40	47		42	46	43	41		36		40		40	41			50	50	48	40		31	26	46		32
Translator	34	32	31	45		35	41	30	30		25		29		24	27			47	35	50	38		28	42	42		24
Physician	26	26	29	41		29	32	23	24		25		22		25	23			46	32	42	50		42	52	48		33
Dentist	19	18	23	32		25	22	18	19		20		16		20	20			32	26	32	39		39	43	38		31
Med. Technologist	19	23	23	25		19	19	16	19		21		19		21	20			32	26	31	41		50	49	43		39
Chemist	04	03	13	23		08	12	07	10		09		08		12	09			35	19	29	33		30	50	44		26
Mathematician	13	08	18	32		15	20	14	18		12		14		15	16			37	24	33	33		26	46	50		28
Computer Programmer	23	29	24	21		21	23	19	22		21		17		20	20			30	24	29	29		37	39	39		36
Math-Sci. Teacher	20	22	26	23		22	21	27	30		29		30		32	32			31	30	28	26		43	44	45		50
Engineer	16	18	23	25		22	21	16	17		21		15		21	19			34	26	31	34		37	46	43		34
Army-Enlisted	25	22	23	22		22	24	26	26		32		29		32	30			27	29	27	29		34	30	30		35
Navy-Enlisted	29	29	26	27		26	26	25	26		30		27		27	28			27	29	28	33		39	34	34		35
Army Officer	30	27	30	27		32	38	33	30		40		31		37	35			40	34	35	34		30	35	31		28
Navy Officer	38	36	34	41		40	44	35	34		38		30		37	36			45	39	44	41		38	44	43		35
Lawyer	28	24	25	33		35	41	30	28		30		24		32	33			43	35	39	35		24	37	37		23
Accountant	17	21	25	23		19	24	27	30		31		16		29	33			19	38	29	29		31	19	24		41
Bankwoman	16	22	23	18		14	21	28	30		30		19		30	33			8	32	21	19		27	7	14		38
Life Ins. Underwriter	30	29	23	24		36	32	27	26		32		27		31	29			27	25	24	24		16	19	20		20
Buyer	19	18	16	18		29	20	18	18		20		17		23	20			16	20	17	20		22	18	18		20
Bus. Ed. Teacher	16	15	18	11		18	17	27	27		26		28		31	30			14	23	14	14		18	15	19		19
Home Ec. Teacher	18	25	30	12		27	15	27	27		26		29		28	27			12	20	11	15		20	12	10		28
Dietitian	25	32	27	22		31	27	27	28		50		29		33	30			34	30	31	39		40	40	32		37
Phys. Ed. Teacher (H.S.)	21	25	23	14		14	16	23	24		31		28		27	27			19	20	17	28		36	26	23		36
Occupational Therapist	32	37	44	34		34	30	33	32		37		37		35	31			37	32	33	38		38	35	29		32
Physical Therapist	25	30	29	22		22	22	27	28		34		32		33	30			32	29	29	42		49	42	36		43
Public Health Nurse	23	25	26	20		18	22	31	30		33		38		36	32			28	27	22	32		32	24	20		28
Registered Nurse	26	29	26	17		20	23	31	30		34		36		33	32			25	25	24	34		36	24	18		29
Licensed Practical Nurse	18	18	19	14		16	13	21	23		24		29		26	23			16	22	18	27		26	25	22		32
Radiologic Technologist	26	30	21	19		19	20	20	22		23		21		24	22			24	23	27	37		49	35	29		36
Dental Assistant	22	24	19	-12		19	14	22	23		23		28		26	24			13	21	18	24		36	21	18		34
Executive Housekeeper	21	22	24	15		27	19	26	26		29		33		33	28			18	26	19	24		31	22	19		33
Instrument Assembler	23	23	18	16		19	16	18	20		19		19		19	21			12	19	17	22		33	22	22		32
Elementary Teacher	27	26	34	22		25	24	38	38		35		46		39	39			24	33	24	27		33	26	26		39
Secretary	33	34	26	20		31	30	33	33		32		33		32	33			16	28	22	19		25	13	16		30
Saleswoman	20	22	19	09		21	15	24	24		22		26		26	25			08	21	13	15		24	11	11		29
Sewing Machine Operator	11	11	10	07		10	05	11	13		09		15		12	13			00	12	06	10		21	10	12		24
Telephone Operator	19	20	15	06		14	12	20	21		19		24		22	20			05	17	12	15		26	11	11		29
Beautician	33	34	27	24		30	25	26	27		28		28		26	27			16	24	20	22		28	18	21		30
Airline Stewardess	35	40	26	12		28	27	28	25		30		25		28	27			20	20	20	17		21	12	10		20
Academic Achievement	44	41	50	52		46	50	50	51		48		48		49	49			59	53	57	56		52	62	60		51
Diversity of Interests	49	51	52	41		48	50	54	51		54		53		54	53			50	51	48	49		50	47	45		52
Femininity-Masculinity II	49	47	54	56		54	50	53	54		46		51		48	48			49	53	53	47		42	46	45		42
Occupational Intro.-Extro.	47	45	48	54		46	44	45	48		40		43		41	43			43	48	49	51		56	52	56		56

TABLE 2-10 (*continued*)

Army-Enlisted	Navy-Enlisted	Army Officer	Navy Officer	Lawyer	Accountant	Bankwoman	Life Ins. Underwriters	Buyer	Business Ed. Teacher	Home Economics Teacher	Dietitian	Physical Ed. Teacher	Occupational Therapist	Physical Therapist	Public Health Nurse	Registered Nurse	Lic. Practical Nurse	Radiologic Technologist	Dental Assistant	Executive Housekeeper	Instrument Assembler	Elementary Teacher	Secretary	Saleswoman	Sewing Machine Oper.	Telephone Operator	Beautician	Airline Stewardess	Groups / Scales
18	13	23	19	24	22	24	28	29	28	23	22	26	20			22	22	14	21	25	16	33	23	24	18	20	18	22	Music Teacher
18	19	24	25	25	17	16	27	12	19	19	20	24	21			23	17	22	20	16	17	18	22	19	12	18	25	36	Entertainer
23	21	30	29	32	26	24	33	21	25	27	21	32	26			28	25	23	24	25	20	29	26	26	19	22	22	29	Musician Performer
21	22	24	27	28	21	22	33	16	20	21	20	23	20			24	17	23	23	18	23	19	27	23	20	21	30	36	Model
																													Art Teacher
19	22	25	29	30	23	18	27	14	20	23	20	27	22			22	18	22	16	18	18	21	18	15	17	14	20	19	Artist
09	07	20	22	27	19	14	28	07	18	19	04	21	10			10	03	07	05	13	08	11	13	12	04	04	13	17	Interior Decorator
24	21	34	34	39	24	21	35	17	22	26	21	28	22			26	16	21	16	18	16	23	23	18	12	14	19	29	Newswoman
26	20	34	30	38	27	28	34	33	31	28	26	30	25			30	23	21	24	25	18	34	30	27	18	22	21	33	English Teacher
24	20	33	30	39	30	30	36	37	32	28	28	30	25			30	21	20	23	25	20	36	33	28	20	25	24	33	Language Teacher
33	26	40	35	37	31	30	39	32	32	31	33	36	30			32	26	25	27	31	22	30	29	27	18	24	24	38	YWCA Staff Member
																													Recreation Leader
19	13	22	17	20	16	19	24	26	28	20	25	27	23			27	25	15	22	25	12	33	21	22	16	19	17	24	Dir., Christian Ed.
19	17	17	14	14	16	16	11	22	17	16	22	20	21			20	26	18	18	22	15	28	13	17	20	17	10	09	Nun-Teacher
28	19	35	29	35	29	30	34	36	34	31	31	32	29			32	28	23	27	32	18	34	27	26	16	22	18	31	Guidance Counselor
32	26	38	35	43	33	33	36	39	33	32	32	30	21			33	27	26	27	30	23	35	32	29	23	26	22	32	Soc. Sci. Teacher
25	18	33	28	36	25	25	31	24	22	29	21	30	20			28	27	22	21	27	16	25	20	20	11	16	11	20	Social Worker
24	19	34	32	39	28	21	34	20	22	28	24	31	26			28	20	22	20	20	13	25	18	14	05	11	12	23	Speech Pathologist
13	10	23	23	28	19	8	16	05	10	19	11	22	16			33	27	15	06	12	04	07	03	10	06-02	06-02	02	12	Psychologist
30	25	40	38	46	38	32	36	32	28	36	19	33	27			27	26	23	22	29	20	32	28	25	19	20	14	21	Librarian
22	22	30	32	37	29	21	26	16	17	26	17	27	23			22	17	22	16	18	16	18	19	12	11	13	12	21	Translator
27	28	30	33	34	29	19	25	13	20	32	28	32	34			30	29	32	23	22	17	21	15	12	13	14	13	18	Physician
28	29	26	27	27	28	24	23	20	22	30	26	27	30			24	31	31	28	26	26	21	19	20	25	22	19	15	Dentist
32	35	27	29	24	31	27	19	22	26	34	32	32	39			32	39	41	34	31	33	25	23	25	30	30	24	23	Med. Technologist
14	14	17	18	18	19	7	06	04	05	18	11	16	17			10	13	14	06	09	04	07-01-04-00	00-08-04						Chemist
16	18	18	20	24	24	14	12	11	07	19	14	15	16			11	12	14	07	10	09	12	06	00	07	06	00-02		Mathematician
27	30	26	29	24	33	25	18	24	24	27	28	26	29			25	20	30	23	21	29	20	25	19	22	26	23	26	Computer Programmer
37	38	31	32	30	41	38	28	41	35	37	38	31	37			33	38	38	37	36	38	35	32	33	39	37	31	25	Math-Sci. Teacher
30	29	30	29	29	36	26	22	21	17	27	22	24	25			19	22	26	20	23	22	16	17	14	18	18	12	16	Engineer
50	46	40	37	33	39	40	35	*(Scores Not Available)*	40	25	31	35	27	30	*(Scores Not Available)*	27	35	35	34	38	40	29	34	36	39	38	32	30	Army-Enlisted
46	50	37	38	31	37	37	32		36	28	32	39	30	34		32	37	40	37	36	43	30	35	35	42	40	39	32	Navy-Enlisted
44	37	50	45	43	38	34	39		32	24	33	31	30	28		28	23	28	25	31	25	24	29	24	16	22	18	33	Army Officer
43	41	47	50	46	43	37	41		33	28	38	35	33	33		32	28	31	32	32	27	33	27	25	27	28	34		Navy Officer
29	23	37	36	50	38	32	40		25	16	29	18	22	20		21	16	20	17	21	16	18	22	17	12	14	12	22	Lawyer
39	37	38	43	38	50	41	33		35	20	35	25	25	31		19	26	28	30	35	30	32	37	28	22	27	30	24	Accountant
40	37	34	37	32	45	50	33		39	25	35	37	25	31		22	31	39	37	41	35	38	45	37	29	37	35	27	Bankwoman
27	20	30	29	38	33	33	50		27	21	26	20	20	19		21	18	17	22	25	18	21	24	27	18	19	22	28	Life Ins. Underwriter
28	24	24	24	26	31	35	32		28	22	25	16	18	19		18	25	23	27	31	28	20	28	34	29	26	25	21	Buyer
29	26	25	22	25	35	39	28		50	30	25	26	19	20		21	25	21	29	31	32	30	35	35	34	35	29	23	Business Ed. Teacher
16	16	17	16	14	20	25	19		34	50	32	27	31	27		28	28	22	30	33	29	34	30	33	32	34	32		Home Ec. Teacher
30	29	31	31	31	35	35	33		33	43	50	31	34	37		36	40	44	50	43	41	33	35	30	33	39	32		Dietitian
34	37	27	27	20	25	27	23		31	33	28	50	32	38		37	36	38	37	31	34	31	29	33	34	36	34		Phys. Ed. Teacher (H.S.)
30	29	33	30	26	25	25	25		26	41	34	36	50	42		40	38	36	33	34	30	38	31	30	28	31	30	38	Occupational Therapist
38	40	32	32	26	31	31	26		32	37	48	46	41	50		45	47	47	44	39	37	37	32	36	37	39	34	37	Physical Therapist
27	26	25	23	25	19	25	26		29	35	33	36	38	40		43	41	36	36	35	28	36	30	31	30	31	30	33	Public Health Nurse
26	26	25	25	23	22	25	24		25	37	33	39	44			50	44	39	39	33	27	34	30	11	28	31	30	36	Registered Nurse
31	31	22	20	19	26	31	24		31	31	32	30	28	36		33	50	37	42	40	35	34	29	40	42	41	33	26	Lic. Practical Nurse
38	42	28	30	22	28	29	22		26	30	34	39	34	43		40	47	50	45	37	40	29	31	36	40	40	37	35	Radiologic Technologist
34	36	23	23	19	24	29	26		37	33	31	33	27	35		50	41	41	33	38	41	43	37	35					Dental Assistant
36	32	29	25	25	35	41	32		40	38	37	29	30	32		31	43	34	41	50	40	35	37	45	44	44	36	31	Executive Housekeeper
35	39	23	24	19	30	33	30		35	30	28	31	25	30		27	36	36	37	36	50	30	35	40	45	42	27		Instrument Assembler
34	32	29	25	27	32	38	30		45	44	36	37	37	38		37	46	43	41	50	40	46	46	46	40	35			Elementary Teacher
36	36	31	31	29	37	45	35		49	35	30	31	29	29		32	33	33	41	39	45	36	50	44	46	46	45	41	Secretary
31	29	22	20	20	28	37	28		40	33	29	24	23	27		26	39	30	40	40	40	34	36	50	46	44	38	31	Saleswoman
24	26	12	12	10	22	29	15		30	24	20	19	14	19		18	32	25	30	31	37	25	27	36	50	39	35	16	Sewing Machine Oper.
31	32	19	17	15	27	37	22		40	36	22	22	28			27	41	33	41	39	43	33	38	45	50	50	41	30	Telephone Operator
33	36	26	28	24	30	35	32		35	35	30	35	28	30		32	35	35	38	36	43	33	38	41	46	43	50	30	Beautician
27	26	28	26	23	24	27	30		28	30	25	29	28	27		30	23	28	30	27	28	26	33	33	23	30	34	50	Airline Stewardess
45	42	51	48	52	48	42	44		43	43	48	43	49	48		47	44	44	40	42	37	45	40	38	35	38	32	40	Academic Achievement
49	47	50	48	52	53	52	52		55	53	51	51	53	52		52	52	50	51	52	49	53	52	53	48	53	50	56	Diversity of Interests
38	38	44	42	46	42	44	43		43	47	45	38	50	45		45	45	40	42	44	37	50	46	45	41	42	42	44	Femininity-Masculinity II
48	54	42	46	42	49	49	40		50	50	49	51	48	53		50	54	54	52	48	57	52	51	51	62	55	57	42	Occupational Intro.-Extro.

TABLE 2-11. PREDICTIVE VALIDITY OF MEN'S PHYSICIAN SCALE
(1938 scale)

Letter Ratings and Scores	Percentage Earning Letter Rating Shown, for Each Group		
	Criterion Group	137 Students Who Became Physicians	Graduate Business Students
A	71	64	1
B+	13	13	2
B	8	10	4
B−	5	8	10
C	3	5	83
Mean Score ...	50	47.8	
S.D.	10	10.3	

(Strong, 1955). For example, 137 of these students became physicians. The distribution of their scores on the Physician scale (using the 1938 scoring key) is given in Table 2-11 with comparable data for the physician criterion group and for a group of graduate business students; the physicians-to-be scored nearly as high as the criterion group.

How many of the students had high scores on the Physician scale and did not become physicians? Among the total sample, 132 had "A" ratings (see p. 274 for a description of these letter grades) and 67 had "B+" ratings on the Physician scale; 53 percent of the former group became physicians, but the remaining 47 percent did not scatter into every imaginable pursuit. Five percent became dentists or biologists, occupations that correlate over .80 with physicians in interests. Eight percent became architects, psychologists, and chemists (correlation .70 to .75), and 14 percent became engineers, writers, and geologists (correlation .52 to .62). Altogether, 80 percent of those with "A" ratings either became physicians or entered occupations whose interests correlate .50 or higher with those of physicians.

Of the 67 students with "B+" ratings on the Physician scale, 21 percent became physicians; 3 percent, biologists, 10 percent, architects, psychologists, or chemists; and 28 percent, engineers, writers, or geologists—a total of 62 percent. Thus, a college student's score on the Physician scale was a fairly impressive predictor of the likelihood of his being in the medical profession, or a related field, 18 years later.

Strong's book on this study, published in 1955, reports in detail his findings on the long-term predictive accuracy of his inventory. In his report, he grappled with the issues of base rate prediction, specificity of the criterion, and so forth. This work led him to conclude that the odds were 3-to-1 that a man would enter an occupation where he had an "A" rating, and 5-to-1 against his entering an occupation where he had a "C" rating. These summary statements are subject to misinterpretation, and the interested scholar should check Strong's original report to understand precisely how these ratios were determined.

Data on SVIB scores versus eventual job satisfaction among these Stanford students are given in a later section, and in Table 2-16. They show that men scoring low on their occupational scale were much more likely to express job discontent than those scoring high.

Berdie-Schletzer studies of Minnesota students. In two other prediction studies, Berdie (1960, 1965) has reported, for students graduating from medical school, law school, dental school, journalism school, engineering school, architectural school, and as accounting majors from a business school, the SVIB scores for inventories completed by these students while they were high school seniors. His results show that these seven groups differed considerably in their measured interests while they were in high school but not always in the expected direction. Although each group scored high on the relevant scale, they also scored high on other scales. Thus, 49 percent of the future medical school graduates scored within the "A" range on the Physician scale, but 59 percent scored within that range on the Osteopath scale. And although 50 percent of the future law school graduates scored within the "A" range on the Lawyer scale, 75 percent of the same group scored in that range on the Real Estate Salesman scale.

Schletzer (1963) retested some of the students from the Berdie groups after they had settled into their occupations, an average of eight to ten years after the original high school testing. Though the samples were small and conclusions must be guarded, the data are reported in some detail because they are so crucial for the use of the SVIB with high school populations.

Table 2-12 reports the mean for each group on its "own" scale, both for the test SVIB (taken during the fall of the high school senior year) and the retest SVIB (taken after two or three years of occupational experience). The five other highest scale means are also reported for each group at each testing.

The results indicate poor to moderately good predictive power over this 8-to-10-year period for the high school senior SVIBs. The best prediction was for the M.D. group, which averaged 43 on the Physician scale. This was within the B+ range, and higher than their average score on any other scale. (This apparent inconsistency with Berdie's report stems from the different ways in which the data were reported. Berdie was working with

Test (High School Senior) Occupational Scale	Mean Score	Retest (Adult) Occupational Scale	Mean Score
Accountants (N = 24)			
ACCOUNTANT	36	ACCOUNTANT	38
OFFICE MAN	44	SENIOR CPA	47
REAL ESTATE SALESMAN	41	CPA	42
SENIOR CPA	40	OFFICE MAN	39
PURCHASING AGENT	39	PUBLIC ADMINISTRATOR	38
PRINTER	37	REAL ESTATE SALESMAN	37
Dentists (N = 30)			
DENTIST	39	DENTIST	42
FARMER	42	PHYSICIAN	47
MATH–SCIENCE TEACHER	40	OSTEOPATH	45
PHARMACIST	40	FARMER	37
PRINTER	38	CHEMIST	37
VETERINARIAN	38	BIOLOGIST	36
Doctors (N = 27)			
PHYSICIAN	43	PHYSICIAN	54
OSTEOPATH	39	BIOLOGIST	44
MATH–SCIENCE TEACHER	38	PSYCHIATRIST	43
PHARMACIST	37	OSTEOPATH	42
DENTIST	37	CHEMIST	40
FARMER	36	PSYCHOLOGIST	39
Journalists (and Advertising) (N = 21)			
AUTHOR–JOURNALIST	32	AUTHOR–JOURNALIST	36
REAL ESTATE SALESMAN	39	ADVERTISING MAN	43
PRINTER	38	SOCIAL WORKER	42
ADVERTISING MAN	37	REHABIL. COUNSELOR	40
SALES MANAGER	36	REAL ESTATE SALESMAN	39
MUSICIAN	36	MUSIC TEACHER	39
Lawyers (N = 32)			
LAWYER	36	LAWYER	43
REAL ESTATE SALESMAN	43	PUBLIC ADMINISTRATOR	42
SALES MANAGER	42	PERSONNEL DIRECTOR	39
OFFICE MAN	39	REAL ESTATE SALESMAN	39
LIFE INS. SALESMAN	39	REHABIL. COUNSELOR	39
SOCIAL SCIENCE TEACHER	38	SOCIAL WORKER	39
Mechanical Engineers (N = 38)			
ENGINEER	39	ENGINEER	38
MATH–SCIENCE TEACHER	44	AIR FORCE OFFICER	47
AIR FORCE OFFICER	43	ARMY OFFICER	42
FARMER	43	PRODUCTION MANAGER	40
PRINTER	40	CHEMIST	40
CHEMIST	40	MATH–SCIENCE TEACHER	37

the 1938 scores; the data presented here are based on the 1966 scoring system.) The poorest prediction was in the group of journalism graduates; those students averaged only 32 on the Author-Journalist scale when they were high school seniors. However, many of them were actually in advertising positions when followed up as adults, and the group mean on the Advertising Man scale was 37. This may be a more meaningful estimate of the SVIB's predictive power for this group.

Overall, the results from high school testing have indicated that the SVIB can be used with students at this level to indicate general direction of career but not specific occupation. For example, the accountant group, when high school seniors, scored high on the Office Worker, Senior CPA, Purchasing Agent, and Real Estate Salesman scales, as well as on the Accountant scale. This pattern would suggest business activities to most counselors, but not necessarily the accounting field.

The data collected by Schletzer from these men after they had settled into their occupations indicate that the SVIB successfully differentiated between adult occupational groups. Two of the six groups—doctors and lawyers—had a higher average score on their own scale than on any other scale. In the other four groups, each group's average score on its own scale was usually among the top two or three scores, and the other high scores were on closely related scales; e.g., the accountants scored slightly higher on the CPA and Senior CPA scales than they did on the Accountant scale.

Though they concern reliability more than validity, Schletzer's data can be examined for changes in the interest patterns of these young men from their high school senior days to a period some years after college graduation. Table 2-13 presents the five scales showing the greatest increase and the five showing the greatest decrease.

The nature of the five highest scales on test versus the five highest on retest indicates that these students had shifted from reporting mainly technical and nonprofessional interests to reporting a similarity of interests with professional men.

The scales showing the greatest increase were those commonly termed "social service"; those showing the greatest decrease were those characteristic of skilled tradesmen or small businessmen. These findings agree closely with those reported by Strong (1943).

More information on these changes can be found in the chapter covering the Basic Interest Scales.

Campbell's study of Minnesota high school students. Further information concerning the predictive validity of the SVIB for high school youths is available from a longitudinal study dealing with students with two

TABLE 2-13. INTEREST CHANGES DURING COLLEGE (N = 172)

Scale	Test Mean	Scale	Retest Mean	Change
		Scales with Highest Scores		
PRINTER	36	PUBLIC ADMIN.	35	
REAL EST. SALES	36	AIR FORCE OFFICER	35	
FARMER	36	PHYSICIAN	34	
PURCHASING AGENT	35	LAWYER	33	
PHARMACIST	35	REAL EST. SALES	33	
		Scales Showing Greatest Increase		
PSYCHIATRIST	18		30	+12
PSYCHOLOGIST	21		31	+10
SOCIAL WORKER	20		29	+ 9
PERSONNEL DIR.	21		29	+ 8
PUBLIC ADMIN.	28		35	+ 7
		Scales Showing Greatest Decrease		
PRINTER	36		26	−10
PHARMACIST	35		26	− 9
FARMER	36		28	− 8
POLICEMAN	25		18	− 7
CARPENTER	25		18	− 7

clearly defined interest patterns; those with high scores in the Sales area (Group IX), and those with high scores in the Physical Science area (Group II).

Briefly, what was done was to identify approximately 100 students in high school graduation classes of 1953 and 1954 who had shown dominant patterns in the Sales areas while they were students, and to follow up these students ten years later to determine what occupations they were in. The same procedure was followed with students who had had high scores in the Physical Science area.

Files of the Minnesota State-Wide Testing Program were sifted to locate profiles for the first group by selecting all profiles with scores above 45 on the Life Insurance Salesman scale; to assemble the second group, all of the profiles with scores above 40 on the Physicist scale were selected. The resulting two group profiles are shown in Figure 2-2 (see p. 72). Obviously, they represent two very different patterns of interests.

Table 2-14 lists the occupations of each of these groups ten years later. As can be seen, the men who had had high sales interests usually took actual sales positions or went into other occupations requiring considerable verbal contact with others. Those with scientific interests, on the other hand, went

TABLE 2-14. OCCUPATIONS 10 YEARS LATER OF STUDENTS WITH HIGH SCORES ON
SALES OR SCIENCE SCALES

High Sales° Scores (N = 72)		High Science† Scores (N = 90)	
Occupations	Per Cent	Occupations	Per Cent
Life Insurance Sales	10	Engineering	37
Other Sales	32	Math–Chemists–Physicists	8
Business–Persuasion (Public Relations, etc.)	12	Other Scientists	12
Social Service–Persuasion (Minister, Lawyer, etc.)	22	Technical and Skilled Trades	14
		Technical Teachers	3
		Farmers	3
Unrelated	24	Unrelated	22

° SALES MANAGER, REAL ESTATE SALESMAN, LIFE INSURANCE SALESMAN
† PHYSICIST, CHEMIST, ENGINEER

primarily into scientific—or in general, "thing, not people oriented"—occupations.

For these two groups, the predictability of the SVIB seems extremely good. One caution should be raised, however: those groups both include interest patterns that are relatively rare among high school populations; several thousand profiles were sifted to find those that would fit the criteria. As the results from the Berdie-Schletzer group show, this kind of accuracy cannot be expected for most students, probably because their interest patterns are not sufficiently crystallized that early in life. When definite patterns are present, they are quite predictive; when they are not, the counselor should be cautious.

Harmon's study of Minnesota women. Harmon has completed an analogous study, using women entering the University of Minnesota. She abstracted her study as follows:

The use of "usual occupation" instead of "current occupation" as a criterion was used to study the predictive validity of the Women's SVIB. One hundred and sixty-nine women who had scored an A or B+ on the Social Worker scale and a contrasting group of 125 who had scored A or B+ on the Laboratory Technician scale in 1953–55 were located in 1966–67 and asked about their vocational history and current vocational commitment. Thirty-nine percent of the former group and 36% of the latter group reported "usual occupation" appropriate to their SVIB scores; however, 44% and 40% respectively reported no "usual occupation." Among those reporting some career commitment, the predictive validity of the women's SVIB was essentially equal to the validity of the men's forms, but the SVIB was of no help in identifying which women would report commitment (Harmon, 1968).

McArthur's study of Harvard Men. In 1939, 63 sophomores at Harvard completed the SVIB as participants in the Study of Adult Development; 14 years later McArthur compared their adult occupations with their earlier test scores (McArthur, 1954; McArthur and Stevens, 1955). Perhaps the most important finding was that the SVIB's predictive accuracy for Harvard students from private high schools was not as good as for those from public high schools. McArthur's explanation was that students from public schools were more apt to enter Ambitious Careers ("hope and confidence that higher occupational goals can be obtained") while students from private schools were more apt to follow Responsive Careers ("Job progression which parents or relatives expect worker to follow"—such as physician, lawyer, or trustee). The SVIB was a better predictor in the former group while expressed intent was better in the latter group, probably because the private school boys—in the higher socio-economic levels—were basing their career choices on family traditions, not their own inclinations. As McArthur and Stevens said, "We now have some evidence that people to whom the Strong does not apply are, indeed, responding to pressures other than their own interests" (McArthur and Stevens, 1955, p. 188).

To determine the overall level of predictive accuracy, McArthur classified each profile as a "Good Hit," "Poor Hit," or "Clean Miss." Using only the 43 cases where he had a "direct" scale, that is, a scale for the occupation the man entered, he found 51 percent Good Hits, 16 percent Poor Hits, and 33 percent Clean Misses. When he removed the private school boys from his calculations, the percent of Clean Misses dropped to 25 percent, leaving a prediction ratio of 3 to 1, essentially the same level Strong found in his study of Stanford students.

McArthur also presented mean scores for men on their "own occupation" scale versus men not in that occupation. All of his occupational samples scored higher on their own scale than did other men with the differences ranging from one-half to one and one-half standard deviations, with a median of about one. Though his samples were quite small, the data are important because such validity figures are difficult to accumulate.

McArthur also reported on job satisfaction versus SVIB score; again, as in Strong's study, those men scoring low on the relevant SVIB scale were much more likely to express discontent than were those who scored high. Some of these discontented ones were the upper-class students who always "knew"—from family pressure, not their own interests—what they would do. McArthur and Stevens put it thus: "one striking illustration of this trend to accurately predict [by expressed, not inventoried interests] career 'interests' that offer little personal gratification is the fact that eight out of the eleven men in our group who attended the best New England private schools, and who were undeniably members of the upper class and undoubtedly knew the behavior of doctors, lawyers, and trustees from firsthand experience, predicted their careers with perfect accuracy—but five of these eight now wish to change occupations" (McArthur and Stevens, 1955, p. 189).

From his research, McArthur drew the following conclusions:

1. The SVIB has at least the validity claimed for it as a measure of interests. [He was referring here to Strong's conclusions from his studies of Stanford students—DPC.]

2. Its most rigorous validation criterion will be the prediction of actual behavior, but even that criterion is met at least one time in two.

3. We may regard as critical for understanding of the test . . . future calculations as to how much other factors, such as economic conditions, family pressures, etc. affect a man's occupational career (McArthur, 1954, p. 352).

Trimble's study of Missouri high school seniors. In another follow-up study of high school seniors, Trimble (1965) studied SVIB scores versus occupations 10 years later of boys in the upper half of their class in several St. Louis suburban high schools; Trimble selected them as typical of the population that the SVIB is usually used with. Of the group he started with ($N = 218$), he was able to locate and collect the necessary data from 180, a commendable 82 percent. Of these 180, 110 had some graduate work, 148 had four year degrees, and all but six had attended college.

Trimble used McArthur's approach, described above, of assigning each person to one of three categories: Good Hit, Poor Hit, or Clean Miss. His findings, using only "direct" scales, i.e., scales with exactly the same name as the occupation the person entered, were:

	Percent
Good Hit	49
Poor Hit	17
Clean Miss	34
Total	100 ($N = 120$)

Trimble summarized: "When one predicts the future occupation to be *one* of the direct occupational scales on which the individual scores an A or B+ [standard score of 40 or above], he will be correct about two times out of three." This is slightly lower than Strong's and McArthur's findings of "three out of four," perhaps because Trimble was dealing with slightly younger students.

Trimble also reported his findings in terms of "Own Group" mean score versus "Other Group" mean score; for example, the scores on the Physician scale for those who become physicians versus those who didn't. On the average, the "Own Group" scored about one standard deviation higher than the "Other Group" on the appropriate scale; couched in percentage overlap between the two distributions, that would be roughly equal to 60 percent overlap.

Finally, he compared the hit rate between two subgroups: those apparently happy in their occupation and those expressing some discontent. Once again, his figures showed that those men in occupations not meshing with their SVIB profile were more apt to express occupational discontent than were the remainder of the group, though—as in the other studies—the number expressing any discontent was a minority, 50 out of 177.

One other aspect of Trimble's work is worth citing. He identified, and reported the frequency of, several possible contaminating factors that would effect the predictive accuracy of interest inventories. Though none of these factors appeared often enough to permit analyses, they certainly had some impact on his results, and future researchers should be cognizant of them.

1. Subject expressed dissatisfaction with occupation 29%
2. Probable criterion contamination [subject reported that the earlier SVIB results played a major part in his occupational choice] 10
3. Subject continued in parent's, or similar, occupation 30
4. Subject strongly influenced by "significant other" in occupational choice...... 31
5. Subject recalled treating interest inventory very casually when completing it in high school 18
6. Subject still aspired to different occupation when retested 36

All of these factors, excepting the second one, could cause a decrease in *apparent* predictive accuracy. As we learn more about which of these are important, and then control them in future studies, a more accurate estimate will emerge of the long-range accuracy of interest inventories.

Brandt's study of University of Iowa students: normals versus deviants.
Brandt (1967; Brandt and Hood, 1968) has reported a SVIB predictive validity study with an imaginative twist; he looked at the predictability of "normal" versus "deviant" students. Using MMPI profiles from students who had come to the University of Iowa Counseling Service, he identified a sample who had at least three scores, including either the Schizophrenia or Psychasthenia scales, over 70; he used these as his "deviant" sample, and most experts would agree that they were exhibiting a great deal of emotional distress. A contrasting sample of "normals"—students with all MMPI scores under 70—were used for comparison. Each sample contained roughly 150 students.

Most of these students had been tested between 1956 and 1964; working in 1966, Brandt located and secured current occupational information from 92 percent, an excellent return. To evaluate the predictive validity of the SVIB, he also used McArthur's system of classifying each case as a Good Hit, Poor Hit, or Clean Miss, and reported the following results:

	Normals	Deviants	Total
Good Hit	56%	37%	48%
Poor Hit	17	24	20
Clean Miss	27	39	32
Total	100	100	100

The differences between the normals and deviants were large and both statistically and practically significant; the psychic distress somehow interfered with the students' quests for jobs that fit their interests.

As Brandt pointed out, the effect may be a complicated one involving an interplay between "maladjustment"—MMPI defined—and specific types of vocational interests. Those students with wild MMPI profiles tend to be more oriented toward the arts than other students, and this is reflected in their vocational interests and, thus, their SVIB patterns. Because occupations in the arts are fewer in number, these students may not have had as many opportunities to find positions consonant with their measured interests. This is speculation—no direct data are available—but it fits in well with other research and Brandt was probably correct in suggesting that this was at least part of the explanation for his findings.

The overall level of predictive validity in Brandt's samples was below that found in the other studies. Partially, of course, this was due to the inclusion of the deviant students, but even among the normals the hit rate was below the usual 3-to-1 ratio. One explanation for this might be that all of his normals were drawn from students seeking educational or vocational counseling, and this would have eliminated those students who were very clear as to their final goals.

Brandt also collected some information on occupational satisfaction and reported, as did Strong, McArthur, and Trimble, that those cases classified as Good Hits reported that they enjoyed their work more than did those classified as Clean Misses.

Other Criteria: Ability, Success, Satisfaction

These validity results indicate that the SVIB can effectively separate occupational groups, and that it has moderate validity in predicting the general occupational area that men will be in some years later, but these studies have all used "membership in an occupation" as the criterion for validity. Users of the SVIB will also be interested in the relationship between SVIB scores and other criteria, such as ability, success and satisfaction. Though not nearly as much work has been done here as with occupational membership, some information is available.

Measured interests and tested abilities. Aptitude-test scores and interest-inventory scores have seldom yielded correlations much above .30, and the figures are usually lower. There are some hints, however, that a good study incorporating a wide range of ability tests and interest scales, and using a highly heterogeneous population, might reveal some common variance between interests and abilities. For example, with a group of Stanford students, correlations between the Thorndike Intelligence Test and some of the SVIB scales were moderate in size, but interesting in direction: .38 with the Psychologist scale, .35 with Mathematician and Chemist, .34 with Physicist, −.33 with Banker, −.26 with Life Insurance Salesmen, and −.25 with Office Worker (Strong, 1959). There seems to be an intellectual versus business dimension here that is reflected in both the interest and the ability scores.

Measured interests and success or achievement. Most of the work done thus far with the SVIB has been concerned with occupational persistence, rather than occupational success, and the SVIB scales have been better predictors of whether a man will remain on the job than whether he will be above average in his performance. These results might be partially explained by the nature of our samples: most men who remain in an occupation can be presumed to have at least an average amount of interest in it, but by definition half of them are below average on any relative measure of success. Although all members of an occupation may earn scores well above men-in-general on an interest measure, only half of them will achieve above-average success in their occupation.

Nevertheless, some recent reports indicate that there may be a substantial relationship between measured interests and success if we will but look for it in the proper manner. For example, a series of studies by Whitehorn and Betz (1960) and Betz (1962, 1963) seem to have demonstrated that the therapist's success in dealing with hospitalized schizophrenics is related to his scores on the Lawyer (high scores associated with success) and Math-Science Teacher (low scores associated with success) scales. In a related paper, McNair, Callahan, and Lorr (1962) have indicated that the therapist with the reverse pattern of scores (high Math-Science Teacher and low Lawyer) is more successful with neurotic out-patients. Thus, differential success in one occupation is related to scores on scales for other occupations. (A SVIB scale for describing the differences in interests between Whitehorn's and Betz's successful and unsuccessful therapists has been reported by Campbell, Stephens, Uhlenhuth, and Johansson, 1968.)

A similar finding occurred in a study of the interests of past presidents of the American Psychological Association. These 50 men, all of whom are outstanding successes in their field, scored precisely the same on the Psychologist scale as did psychologists-at-large. Yet there were meaningful differences between the two groups in their scores on other SVIB scales. The APA presidents scored one-half standard deviation higher on the physical science scales, whereas the psychologists-at-large scored about that much higher on the social-service scales (Campbell, 1965b).

Positive, but modest, relationships between measured interests and success can be found, if one searches for them directly. Stone (1960) reported the development of an SVIB scale that differentiated between superior and inferior students in an advanced shorthand course. Within his validating sample, his scale showed a 45 percent overlap. Though the overlap increased to 62 percent in the cross-validation sample, this still constituted a separation of a full standard deviation.

Two of the SVIB Nonoccupational scales were developed by comparing the interests of more successful versus less successful individuals. The Academic Achievement scale contrasts the interests of those who did well in school versus those who did poorly; the Managerial Orientation scale was developed by comparing the interests of highly rated industrial managers versus poorly rated ones. Both scales have moderate validity, and the rank-ordering of the means of other occupations is quite meaningful. Detailed information on these scales is given in Chapter 5.

Other studies of the relationship between SVIB scales and success include the impressive study by Kelly and Fiske (1951) of success among clinical psychology students. Using a variety of criteria to evaluate success, they reported the SVIB second only to the Miller Analogies Test in predicting quality of performance, though neither was very accurate.

One of the earliest studies of SVIB scores and success, completed in the early 1930's, concerned life insurance salesmen. The figures, reported in Table 2-15, indicate a substantial relationship between interest scores and sales production (Strong, 1943).

Bills (1952) has reported that 40 percent of a group of men rating high in life insurance sales interests became successful salesmen, whereas only 9 percent of those scoring low stayed on the job and became productive.

Ferguson (1958, p. 190) more recently has reported that, among life insurance salesmen, performance acts as some sort of moderator variable between scores on the Life Insurance Salesman scale and termination of employment. Specifically, "For all agents we find no difference between the termination rates of those with the interests of successful salesmen and

TABLE 2-15. INTEREST RATINGS AND PRODUCTIVENESS AMONG
181 LIFE INSURANCE SALESMEN

Average Annual Production	N	Per Cent of Salesmen with Each Letter Rating				
		C	B—	B	B+	A
$ 0 to 49,000...........	19	31	20	17	21	2
50,000 to 99,000	37	44	20	33	26	13
100,000 to 149,000	29	12	20	17	8	18
150,000 to 199,000	40	6	20	28	16	26
200,000 up	56	0	20	5	29	41
Total	..	100	100	100	100	100
N	181	16	5	17	38	105

those without. But for agents whose performance is average or above average, we find that those with the interests of successful salesmen terminated less frequently than those without. In other words, when the ability (performance) differential drops out, the interest differential takes over."

Priebe (1968) compared 50 "high income" farmers with 50 "low income" farmers and found no differences between their SVIB profiles. His total sample, which included only men who had been farming at least three years and who reported that they liked their work, scored 54 on the Farmer scale, higher than the original criterion group. While the scale, developed in the 1930's still represents the interests of satisfied farmers in the 1960's, once again an SVIB Occupational Scale proves not to be related to success within an occupation as we usually measure it.

Benjamin (1967), working with data provided by William LeBold at Purdue University, has studied the relationship between measured interests of college freshmen and several occupational variables collected 31 years later, an extraordinary time span. He concluded,.

Interests were related meaningfully to important occupational criteria, including job function, level of supervisory responsibility, salary and creative potential. . . . These relationships . . . were more readily demonstrative in a concurrent setting than in a predictive setting. However, in almost all cases there were relationships which had existed in the predictive setting but were now more fully developed . . . individuals, as a result of personal characteristics developed quite early in life, do seek out and select an occupation which allows for the expression of these characteristics. But they also as a result of [occupational experiences] . . . tend to become more like others in the same occupation (Benjamin, 1967, p. 109).

The relationships mentioned by Benjamin were not high enough over the 31-year period to suggest that the SVIB can, in any practical way, be used to make detailed predictions for college freshmen over 30 years. His data did show generally reasonable trends, which appeared stronger when the men were retested as adults. The mean profiles for his sample are given in Figure 2-16 for the Occupational Scales, and in Figure 3-13 for the Basic Interest Scales.

More relevant information on success and the SVIB scales is reported in Chapter 7, which includes the mean profiles for several groups of outstanding men.

Measured interests and job satisfaction. Most men are apparently satisfied with their work. Hoppock, Robinson, and Zlatchin (1948) reported the median figure from 133 studies of "percent of satisfied employees" as 79 percent satisfied, and Robinson (1953) reported the median of 201 analogous percentages as 85 percent. With so little variance in job satisfaction, the relationship with measured interests cannot be very high, and most studies have reported only modest correlations—.20 to .30—between the relevant SVIB scale and some index of job satisfaction. Some examples are Hutchinson's (1952) study of women elementary school teachers, where the correlation was .26; Schwebel's (1951) study of pharmacists, correlation .30; and Kate's (1950) study of clerical workers correlation .21. Schletzer's long-range study of University of Minnesota students found essentially no correlation (Schletzer, 1966).

In his 18-year follow-up of former Stanford graduates, Strong (1955) presented relevant data on this issue for a sample of men scattered over a wide range of college level occupations. Again, his correlations were in the .20 to .30 range. But a higher relationship may have been concealed by the usually high level of satisfaction. Table 2-16 reports the percentage of men in Strong's study reporting job dissatisfaction with their work, for various levels of SVIB scores on their "own" (job-relevant) scores. These data show that although a sizable majority of people reported satisfaction at all levels, the percentage of dissatisfied among those scoring very low

TABLE 2-16. RELATION OF "OWN" INTEREST SCORES TO SATISFACTION RATINGS
(N = 655; expressed in percentages)

Interest Scores (1938 Scales)	Satisfaction Ratings (on a 5-Point Scale)			
	Test Group		Retest Group	
	4 and 5	Below 4	4 and 5	Below 4
55 to 70	89	11	93	7
45 to 54	89	11	88	12
40 to 44	85	15	79	21
35 to 39	81	19	77	23
30 to 34	68	32	69	31
−10 to 29	75	25	68	32

in the original tests results (SVIB completed as Stanford students) was twice that of those scoring high and four times as high in the retest (adult) results. Clearly the dissatisfied man was more likely to be a low scorer than a high scorer on the relevant scale.

The same trend appeared in McArthur's follow-up of Harvard men and Trimble's study of Missouri high school students, both reported in more detail above. Although both of them found only a few men dissatisfied with their work, those who were had usually scored lower on the relevant scale when tested some years earlier as students. Brandt's work with "normals" and "deviants," also reported earlier, gave further evidence that those men in occupations consonant with their SVIB profile were more likely to report that they enjoyed their work.

Perry-Cannon study of computer programmers. In a series of studies on computer programmers, Perry and Cannon (1967) have neatly summarized the general themes of research on occupational groups with the SVIB. Their findings were:

1. A scoring scale based on the responses of experienced programmers who say they like their work discriminated well between programmers and men-in-general. The percent overlap between the criterion group and Men-in-General was 26 percent, and this increased to only 27 percent on cross-validation.

2. There was almost no relationship ($r = .11$) between success, as measured by adjusted salary, and scores on this programmer scale.

3. Although the general level of job satisfaction was quite high, there was a substantial tendency for those who scored low on the programming scale to express more job dissatisfaction. Four times as many low scorers as high scorers expressed dissatisfaction (14 to 3 percent respectively), although 86 percent of the low scorers did report that they liked their work.

These findings, based on large, carefully selected samples and well-done analyses, are so typical of the other research findings scattered throughout the professional literature that the Perry-Cannon research can be viewed as the "model SVIB replication study."

Reliability

Stability of Responses to Individual SVIB Items

An individual's answers to the individual SVIB items fluctuate somewhat from day to day. For example, over a 30 day period, people will typically change about 25 percent of their answers. Virtually all of these changes will be a one category shift, that is, from "Like" to "Indifferent" or "Indifferent" to "Dislike" or vice versa; a maximum of one or two percent of the responses will be changes from "Like" to "Dislike" or the reverse. Scale scores are much more stable as the stability in interest measures comes from drawing items together into reasonably long scales where the changes in answers tend to cancel each other out. The following discussion deals mainly with scale reliability, which is the important issue as these are the data that are actually used in counseling.

Odd-Even Reliabilites

The Occupational Scales for the SVIB are based on specific differences between the criterion groups and Men-in-General. These differences are not necessarily correlated, and there is no reason to expect these scales to be internally consistent, other than the expectation that generally clusters of similar items will tend to discriminate occupational groups from Men-in-General. For example, items about scientific activities will always be found on the Occupational Scales for scientists—but so will items concerning preferences for art, music, and working alone. The point is that there is nothing built into the scale construction technique that will directly affect the scale's internal consistency. Thus, for these empirical scales, the best index of scale reliability is some measure of stability over time, such as a test-retest correlation, not some index of homogeneity.

However, for the sake of completeness, odd-even reliabilities are reported in Table 2-17 for the men's Occupational Scales. They are based on the answer sheets from the 30-day test-retest sample ($N = 102$), discussed below. These correlations were calculated by scoring each individual's answer sheet using only the responses to the odd-numbered items and correlating these scores for each scale—across the entire sample—with the analogous score from the even-numbered items. The correlations were then "corrected" by using the Spearman-Brown formula, which adjusts for the fact that the correlations were based on only half of the test.

The 30-day test-retest sample was used here so that the odd-even reliabilities could be compared with short-term test-retest reliabilities. Two sets of odd-even correlations were calculated, one using the *test* administration responses, the second using the *retest* responses. Both sets of data are in Table 2-17, and demonstrate that these figures are consistent from one administration to the other.

As expected, the odd-even reliabilities were lower than the test-retest reliabilities, with median correlations of about .70 (or .80 when corrected) and .90 respectively.

TABLE 2-17. ODD-EVEN AND 30-DAY TEST-RETEST RELIABILITIES FOR THE
MEN'S OCCUPATIONAL SCALES

	Test-Retest Correlation[a]	TEST ADMINISTRATION		RETEST ADMINISTRATION	
		Odd-Even Correlation	with Spearman-Brown correction	Odd-Even Correlation	with Spearman-Brown correction
I DENTIST	.90	.69	.82	.67	.80
OSTEOPATH	.79	.39	.56	.39	.56
VETERINARIAN	.89	.62	.76	.64	.78
PHYSICIAN	.86	.56	.72	.56	.72
PSYCHIATRIST	.90	.63	.77	.62	.76
PSYCHOLOGIST	.90	.76	.87	.63	.77
BIOLOGIST	.91	.78	.88	.72	.84
II ARCHITECT	.91	.77	.87	.81	.89
MATHEMATICIAN	.91	.82	.90	.75	.86
PHYSICIST	.93	.78	.88	.74	.85
CHEMIST	.94	.78	.88	.80	.89
ENGINEER	.92	.79	.88	.76	.87
III PRODUCTION	.86	.50	.67	.53	.69
ARMY OFFICER	.89	.64	.78	.73	.84
AIR FORCE OFFICER	.90	.72	.84	.80	.89
IV CARPENTER	.93	.80	.89	.76	.86
FOREST SERVICE MAN	.90	.61	.76	.65	.79
FARMER	.89	.67	.80	.70	.82
MATH-SCIENCE TEACHER	.82	.48	.65	.32	.48
PRINTER	.86	.58	.73	.61	.76
POLICEMAN	.86	.42	.59	.46	.63
V PERSONNEL DIRECTOR	.86	.65	.79	.57	.73
PUBLIC ADMINISTRATOR	.90	.60	.75	.65	.79
REHABILITATION COUNS.	.90	.71	.83	.69	.82
YMCA STAFF MEMBER	.88	.78	.88	.76	.86
SOCIAL WORKER	.92	.80	.89	.74	.85
SOCIAL SCIENCE TEACHER	.91	.71	.83	.75	.86
SCHOOL SUPERINTENDENT	.87	.67	.80	.66	.79
MINISTER	.89	.69	.81	.70	.82
VI LIBRARIAN	.95	.69	.81	.71	.83
ARTIST	.91	.82	.90	.89	.94
MUSICIAN PERFORMER	.90	.69	.81	.76	.86
MUSIC TEACHER	.89	.66	.79	.69	.82
VII C.P.A. OWNER	.84	.48	.65	.60	.75
VIII SENIOR C.P.A.	.79	.56	.71	.49	.65
ACCOUNTANT	.85	.42	.59	.46	.63
OFFICEWORKER	.89	.49	.65	.48	.65
PURCHASING AGENT	.90	.69	.82	.60	.75
BANKER	.89	.60	.75	.70	.82
PHARMACIST	.85	.37	.54	.36	.53
FUNERAL DIRECTOR	.91	.74	.85	.72	.84
IX SALES MANAGER	.92	.75	.85	.73	.84
REAL ESTATE SALESMAN	.90	.79	.89	.79	.89
LIFE INS. SALESMAN	.93	.80	.89	.80	.89
X ADVERTISING MAN	.91	.80	.89	.83	.90
LAWYER	.90	.76	.86	.73	.84
AUTHOR-JOURNALIST	.90	.84	.91	.85	.92
XI PRESIDENT-MFG.	.84	.55	.71	.46	.63
SUPP. OCCUPATIONAL SCALES					
CREDIT MANAGER	.91	.77	.87	.75	.86
CHAMBER OF COM. EXEC.	.93	.85	.92	.83	.91
PHYSICAL THERAPIST	.86	.57	.73	.59	.74
COMPUTER PROGRAMMER	.86	.57	.73	.65	.79
BUSINESS ED. TEACHER	.90	.72	.84	.73	.84
COMMUNITY REC. ADMIN.	.92	.73	.85	.84	.91

a = Test-retest means and standard deviations can be found in Figure 2-4

Test-Retest Reliability Data for the Men's Occupational Scales

The SVIB is used mainly for counseling students about their future careers, and for the selection and placement of employees. The nature of these uses demands that SVIB scores show some stability over broad time spans. The student should not base his career plans on data that fluctuate from day to day, nor should employees be assigned to positions on the basis of unstable measurements. Some psychological instruments are designed primarily to reflect day-to-day fluctuations of mood; interest inventories are not. Rather, they seek to measure preferences that are stable enough to warrant consideration in laying long-range plans. Test-retest data, pertinent to this point, are reported in Figures 2-1 through 2-23 for several groups over several time intervals. Means, standard deviations, and test-retest correlations are reported for most groups, not only for the development of reliability data but also because the figures provide considerable normative data. Securing and organizing these test-retest profiles was a substantial task, and there are a few gaps in the data. Some of the groups were scored before some of the recently developed scales were available; for a few of the samples, only means and standard deviations, not correlations, are available.

The members of the two week test-retest groups (Figure 2-3) were students drawn from introductory psychology classes at the University of Minnesota—volunteers for this project. They were predominately sophomores from the University's College of Liberal Arts.

The 102 men composing the 30-day test-retest group (Figure 2-4) were members of a U.S. Army Reserve unit from Fort Snelling, Minnesota. They were mostly college graduates, and their median age was about 25. They were spread throughout a wide range of civilian occupations, with mild concentrations in the advertising and newspaper fields.

The three and one-half year test-retest group (Figure 2-5) included Harvard University students who were tested late in their freshman year and retested as seniors. They form part of a longitudinal study conducted by Dr. Stanley King and Dr. Bruce Finnie of Harvard University.

Test-retest reliability data have been calculated for several samples of medical school students tested in the fall of their freshmen year (1956) and retested in the spring of their senior year (1960) in medical school. They were participants in a longitudinal study initiated by Dr. Helen Gee, then Director of Research for the Association of American Medical Colleges and reported on by Dr. Edward Hutchins, a more recent incumbent of that position (Hutchins, 1964). Data for three medical schools are reported in Figures 2-6, 2-7, and 2-8; the first is for the University of Minnesota Medical School, the other two are from two other schools, chosen for geographic and "prestige" diversity. Although the three sets of data are fairly similar, there are some differences that might be related to school characteristics. For example, on the Academic Achievement scale (AACH), which reflects interest in doing well in academic endeavors, the "good" school freshmen class had a mean of 64, the Minnesota freshmen averaged 60, the "poor"

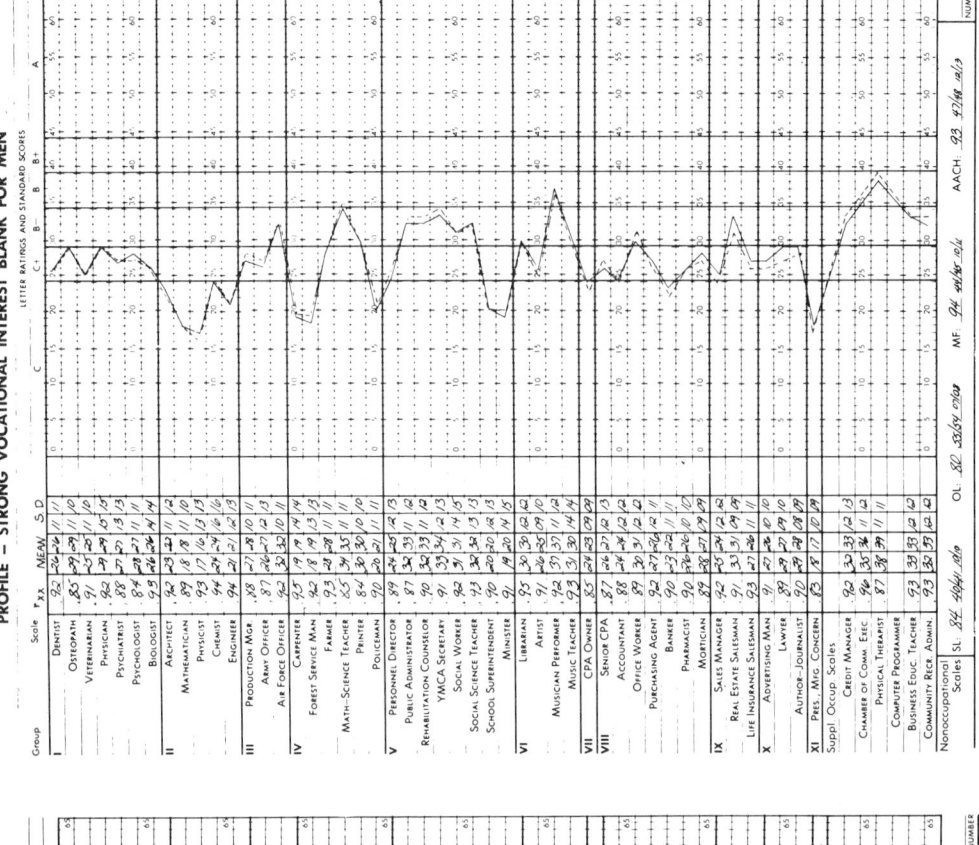

PROFILE – STRONG VOCATIONAL INTEREST BLANK FOR MEN

FIG. 2-2. Mean profiles for two groups of high school seniors, one with high scores on the Life Insurance Salesman scale (solid line), the other with high

PROFILE – STRONG VOCATIONAL INTEREST BLANK FOR MEN

FIG. 2-3. Test-retest data over two weeks for 139 University of Minnesota sophomores.

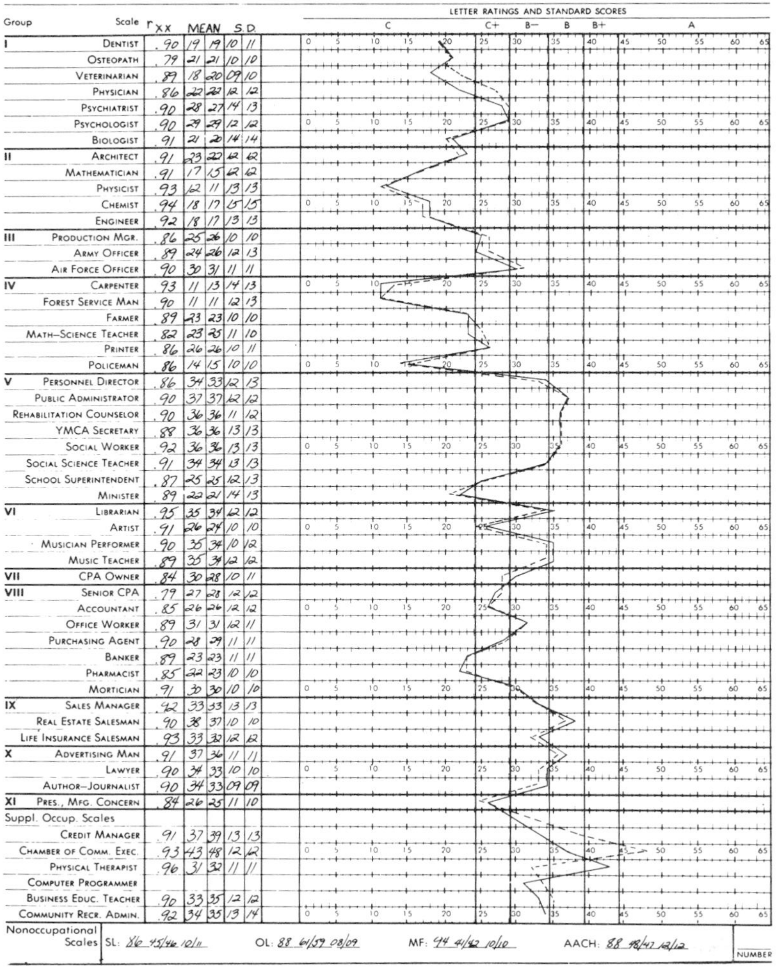

FIG. 2-4. Test-retest data over 30 days, for 102 U.S. Army Reserve Personnel.

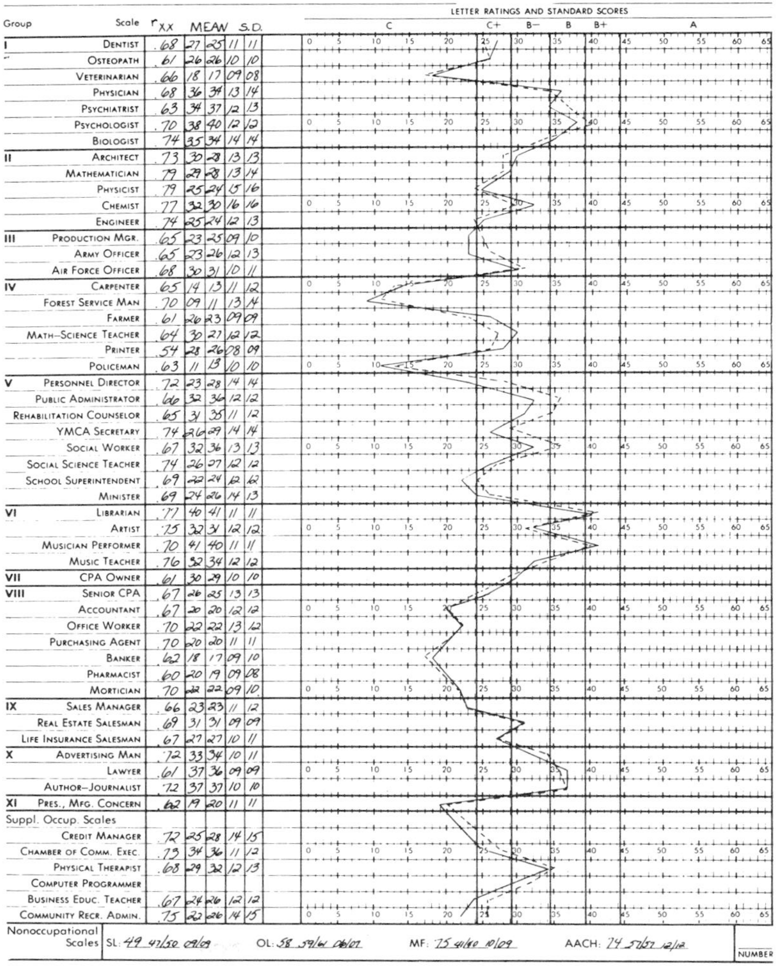

FIG. 2-5. Test-retest data over three and a half years, for 189 Harvard University freshmen.

73

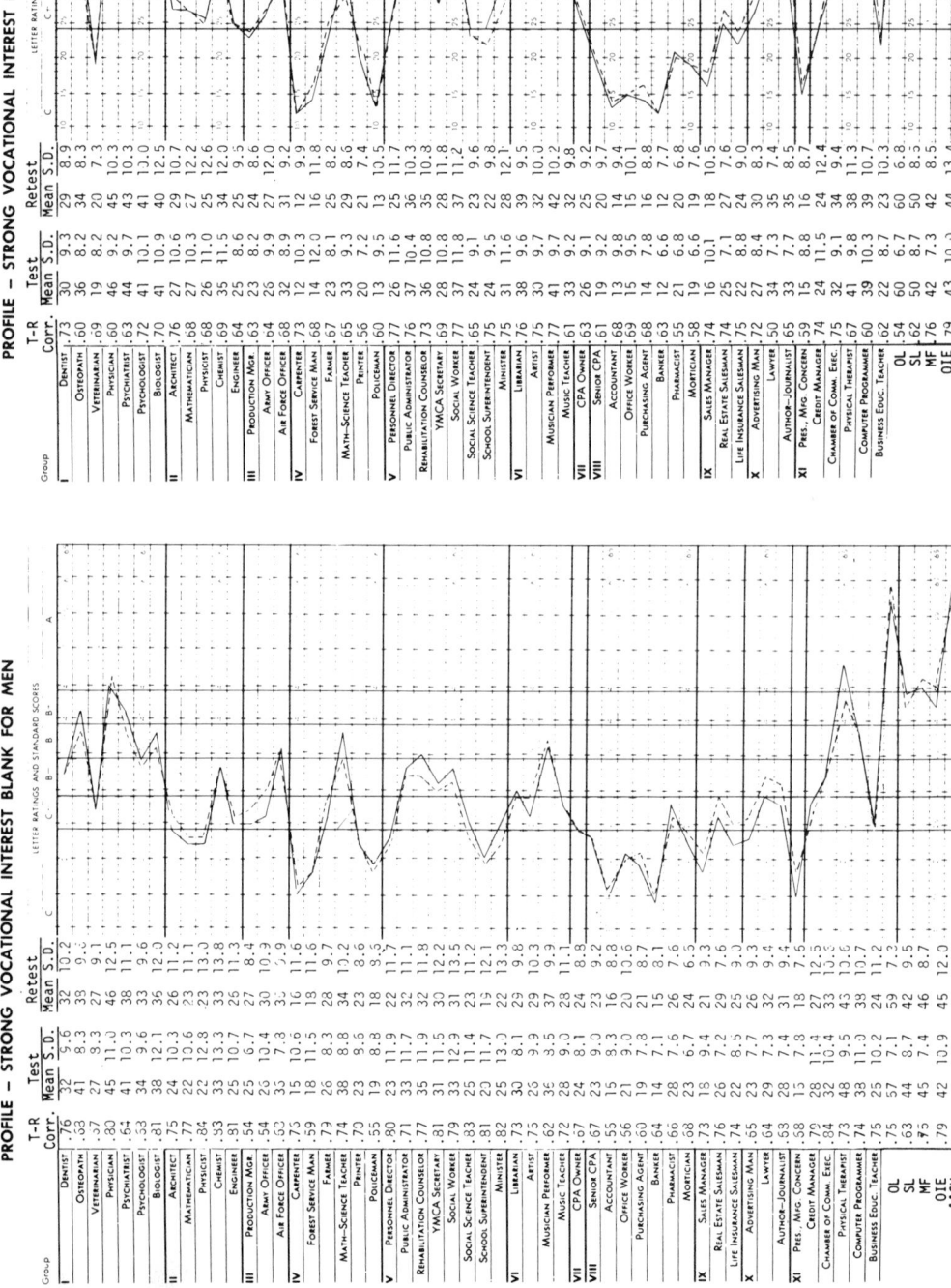

PROFILE – STRONG VOCATIONAL INTEREST BLANK FOR MEN

PROFILE – STRONG VOCATIONAL INTEREST BLANK FOR MEN

FIG. 2-6. Test-retest data over three and a half years, for 91 University of Minnesota Medical School freshmen.

FIG. 2-7. Test-retest data over three and a half years for 106 Medical School "A" freshmen.

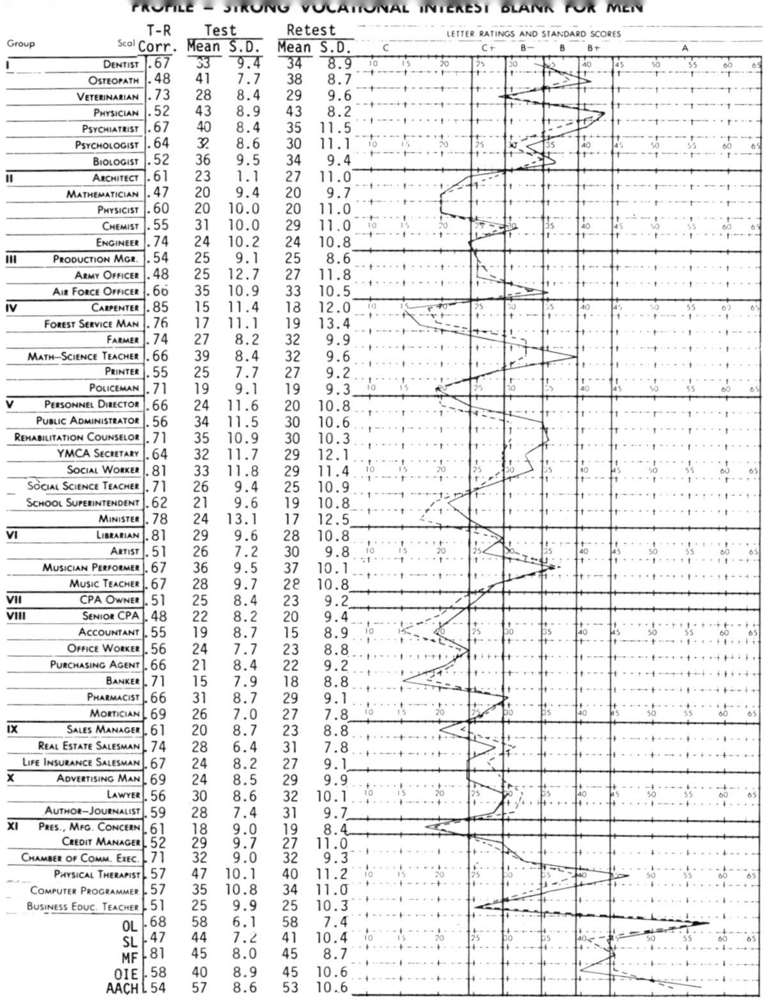

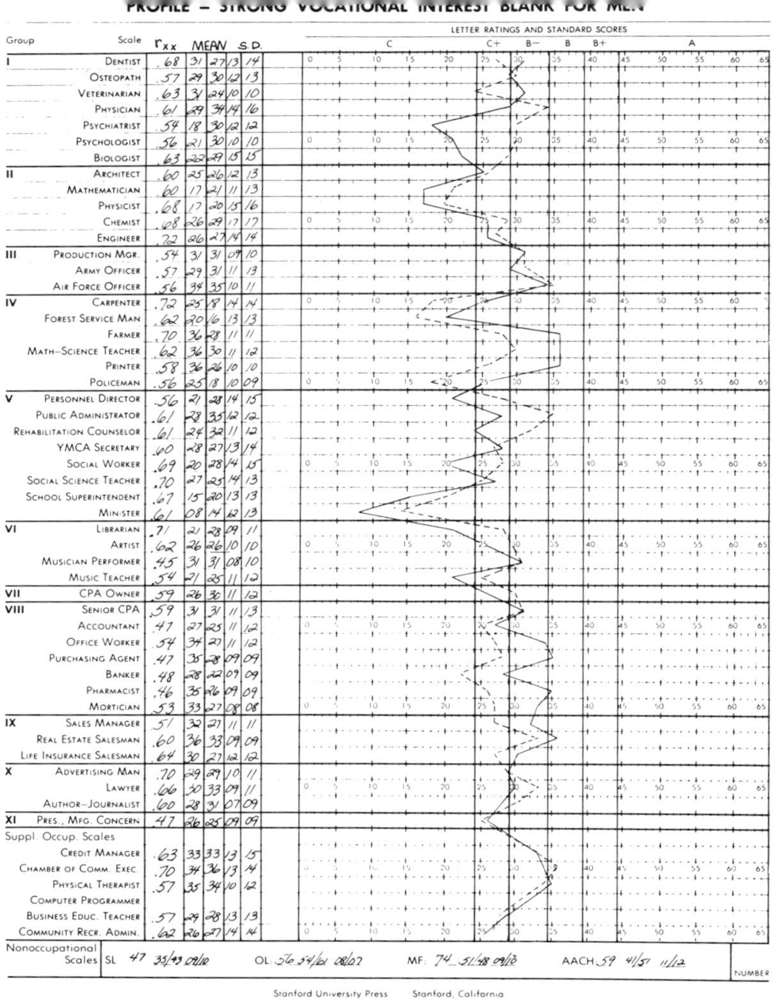

FIG. 2-9. *Test-retest data over eight to ten years, for 171 Minnesota high school seniors.*

FIG. 2-8. *Test-retest data over three and a half years for 82 Medical School "B" freshmen.*

75

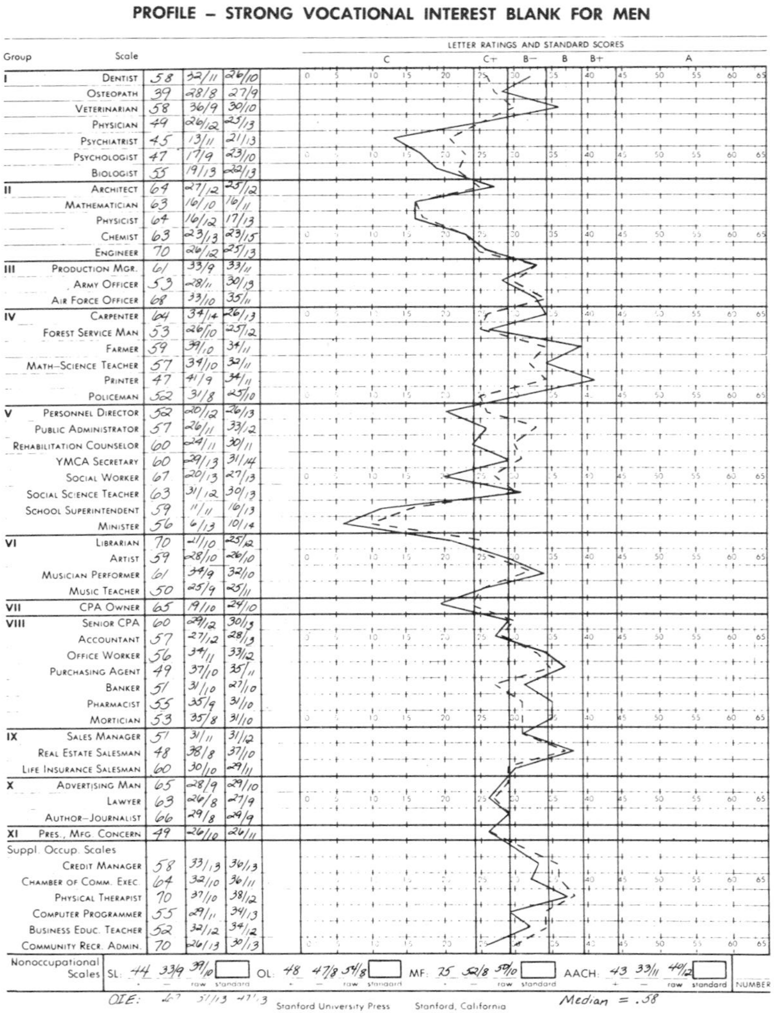

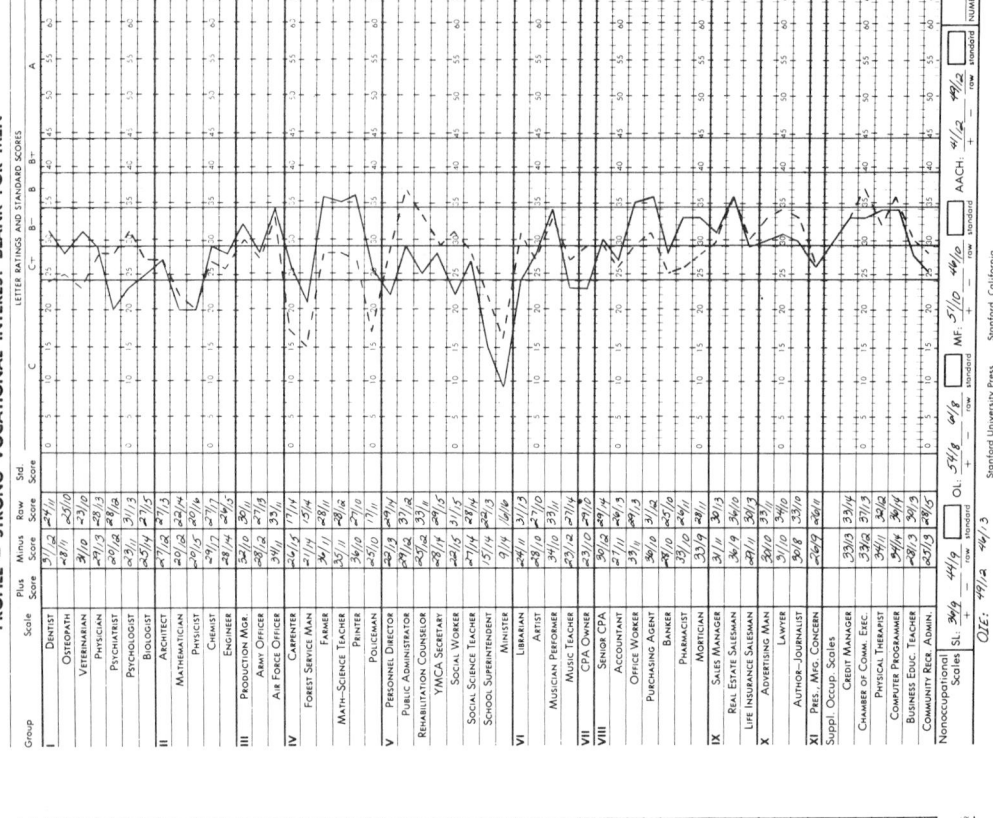

FIG. 2-10. Test-retest data over ten years for 123 University of Minnesota General College students.

FIG. 2-11. Test-retest data over ten years for 152 Missouri high school se-niors.

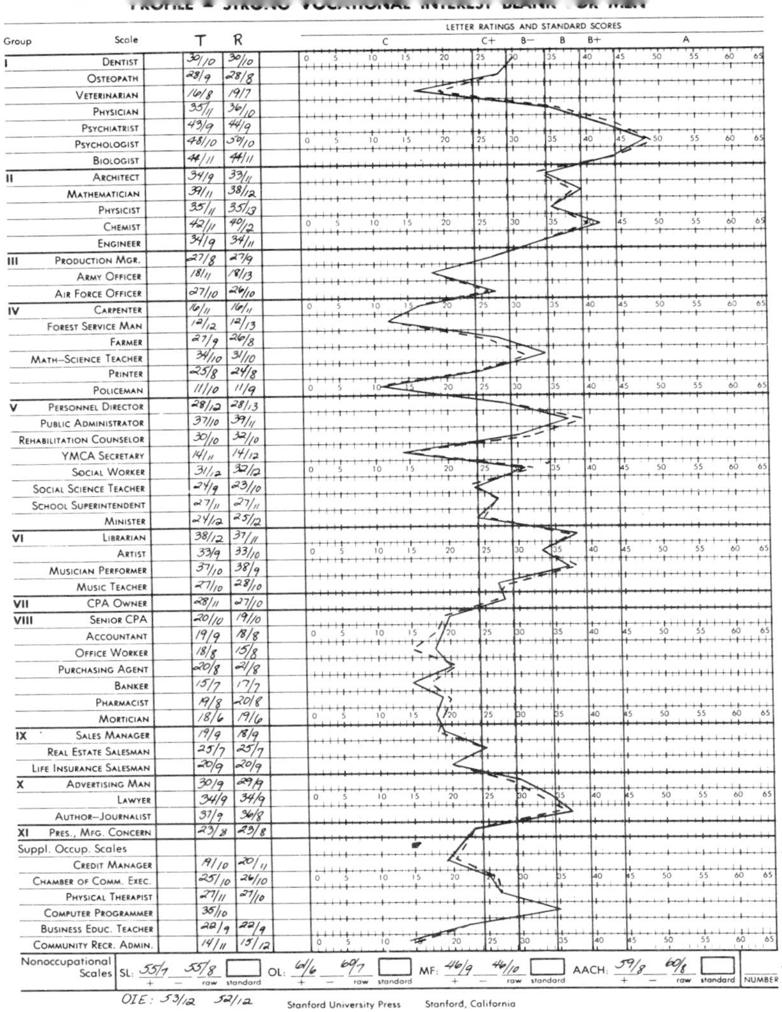

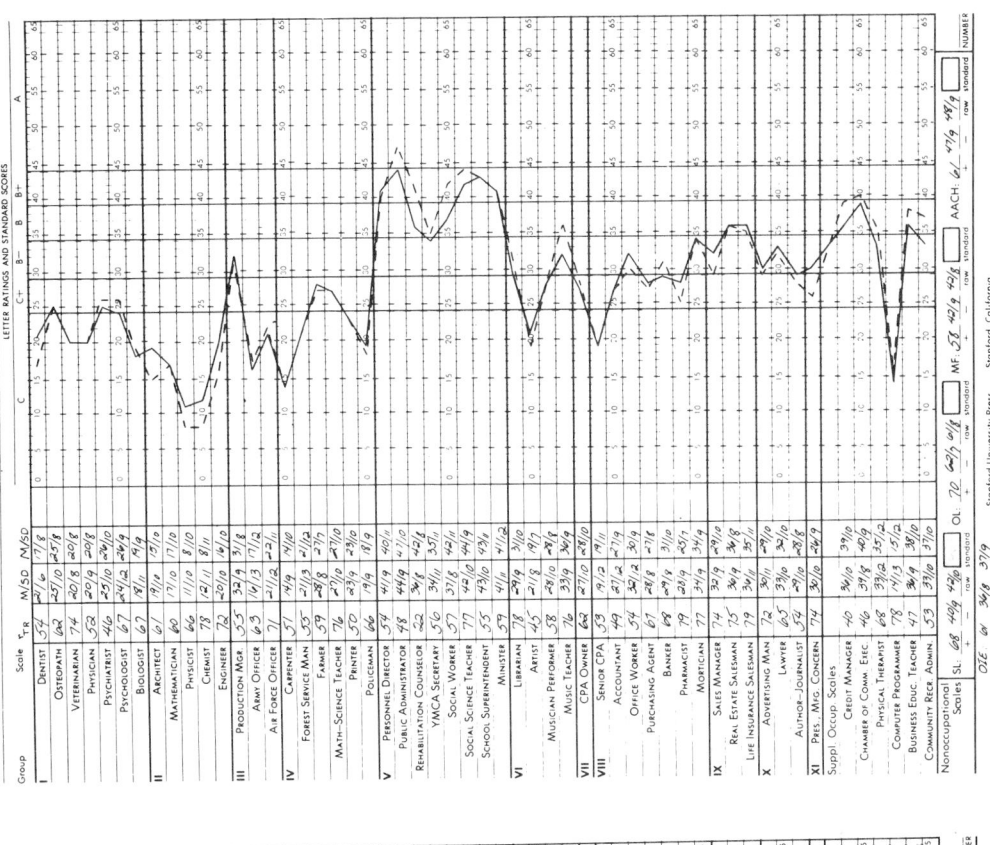

FIG. 2-12. Test-retest data over 17 years for 92 psychologists.

FIG. 2-13. Test-retest data over 24 years for 47 YMCA secretaries.

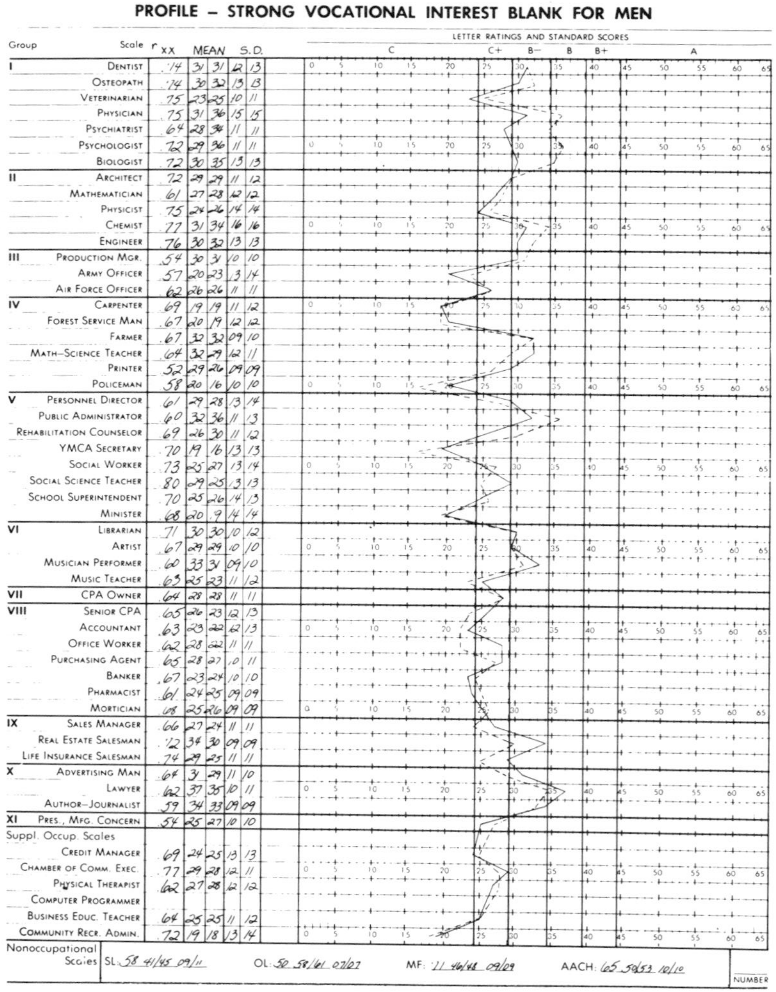

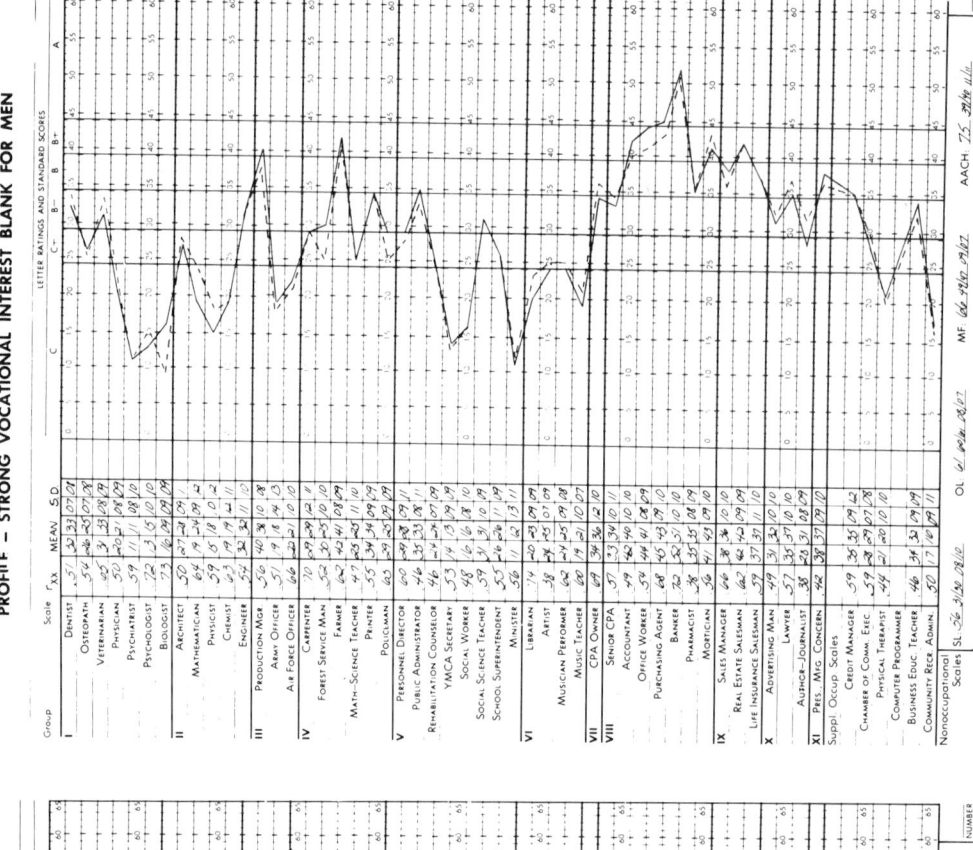

PROFILE – STRONG VOCATIONAL INTEREST BLANK FOR MEN

FIG. 2-15. *Test-retest data over 30 years for 48 Minnesota bankers.*

PROFILE – STRONG VOCATIONAL INTEREST BLANK FOR MEN

FIG. 2-14. *Test-retest data over 22 years for 220 Stanford University seniors.*

Group	Scale	Test M	Test SD	Retest M	Retest SD	r
I	Dentist	36	10	27	10	44
	Osteopath	27	8	25	9	32
	Veterinarian	30	8	26	9	53
	Physician	27	11	26	10	43
	Psychiatrist	15	10	23	12	43
	Psychologist	20	8	26	10	46
	Biologist	27	11	26	12	44
II	Architect	35	11	29	11	43
	Mathematician	27	10	23	12	48
	Physicist	30	12	25	13	46
	Chemist	40	12	34	14	41
	Engineer	42	10	36	12	41
III	Production Mgr.	42	8	43	10	36
	Army Officer	31	10	37	11	30
	Air Force Officer	37	8	38	9	32
IV	Carpenter	37	11	26	12	62
	Forest Service Man	25	11	21	11	56
	Farmer	42	9	34	10	51
	Math–Science Teacher	38	8	31	9	28
	Printer	42	9	28	10	37
	Policeman	30	9	17	9	39
V	Personnel Director	22	11	32	12	39
	Public Administrator	26	11	38	11	43
	Rehabilitation Counselor	18	9	26	10	36
	YMCA Secretary	17	11	20	12	47
	Social Worker	11	10	21	12	41
	Social Science Teacher	20	10	22	10	42
	School Superintendent	10	10	20	12	47
	Minister	2	11	11	13	53
VI	Librarian	18	8	22	10	54
	Artist	31	9	24	9	43
	Musician Performer	31	7	27	9	36
	Music Teacher	16	8	21	10	38
VII	CPA Owner	22	9	26	10	37
VIII	Senior CPA	34	9	35	10	26
	Accountant	33	10	31	10	35
	Office Worker	33	10	29	10	41
	Purchasing Agent	42	9	38	10	51
	Banker	30	8	28	9	47
	Pharmacist	31	7	27	9	37
	Mortician	31	7	30	9	42
IX	Sales Manager	29	9	30	11	41
	Real Estate Salesman	34	7	33	8	42
	Life Insurance Salesman	24	8	26	10	43
X	Advertising Man	27	8	27	8	38
	Lawyer	29	8	28	8	44
	Author–Journalist	30	7	27	7	38
XI	Pres., Mfg. Concern	29	9	32	11	40
Suppl. Occup. Scales						
	Credit Manager	26	11	35	12	46
	Chamber of Comm. Exec.	25	9	33	11	49
	Physical Therapist	29	10	30	11	43
	Computer Programmer	34	10	40	11	33
	Business Educ. Teacher	23	11	30	11	49
	Community Recr. Admin.	15	12	25	13	37

Nonoccupational Scales: SL: 33/9 43/10 r = .36; OL: 51/7 62/7 r = .41; MF: 57/6 55/8 r = .53; AACH: 40/10 47/10 r = .50

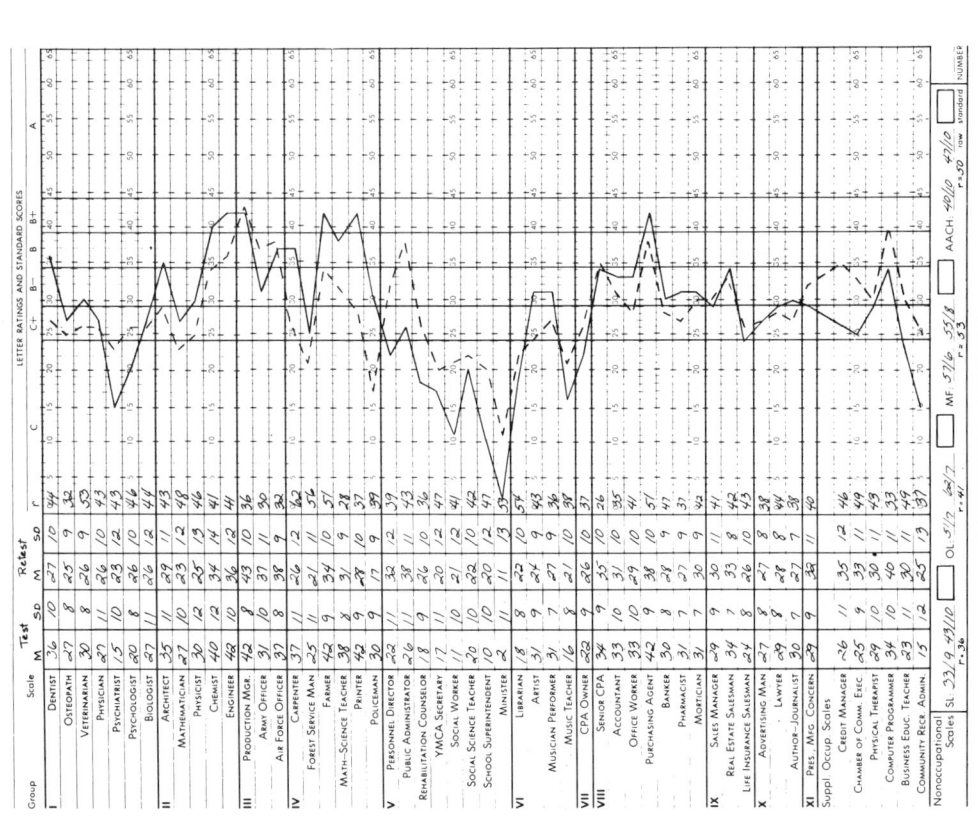

FIG. 2-16. *Test-retest data over 31 years for 229 Purdue engineering freshmen.*

Group	Scale	'30	'66	r
I	Dentist	39/10	31/12	.45
	Osteopath	29/9	29/10	.31
	Veterinarian	35/8	30/11	.48
	Physician	29/11	28/13	.39
	Psychiatrist	11/11	21/14	.46
	Psychologist	16/8	24/12	.44
	Biologist	24/11	25/14	.51
II	Architect	34/11	29/12	.44
	Mathematician	24/11	21/12	.41
	Physicist	24/12	21/15	.49
	Chemist	31/12	29/16	.52
	Engineer	34/12	31/14	.54
III	Production Mgr.	37/8	36/11	.42
	Army Officer	20/12	27/13	.38
	Air Force Officer	27/10	30/11	.42
IV	Carpenter	37/12	30/16	.63
	Forest Service Man	29/11	26/13	.46
	Farmer	45/9	37/12	.54
	Math–Science Teacher	33/10	30/11	.33
	Printer	45/9	36/12	.48
	Policeman	35/9	23/11	.42
V	Personnel Director	18/11	24/14	.41
	Public Administrator	22/11	32/13	.37
	Rehabilitation Counselor	17/9	25/12	.44
	YMCA Secretary	20/12	21/14	.48
	Social Worker	13/11	22/14	.49
	Social Science Teacher	27/11	27/13	.52
	School Superintendent	10/11	18/13	.51
	Minister	6/6	12/15	.50
VI	Librarian	21/8	26/11	.57
	Artist	34/10	28/10	.39
	Musician Performer	36/8	33/11	.41
	Music Teacher	20/9	23/12	.46
VII	CPA Owner	20/9	23/10	.43
VIII	Senior CPA	26/10	27/12	.35
	Accountant	29/10	27/12	.33
	Office Worker	34/10	30/11	.41
	Purchasing Agent	40/9	36/11	.43
	Banker	34/9	30/11	.48
	Pharmacist	33/7	30/10	.42
	Mortician	35/8	30/11	.48
IX	Sales Manager	31/8	28/12	.41
	Real Estate Salesman	39/8	35/10	.42
	Life Insurance Salesman	31/9	27/12	.48
X	Advertising Man	32/10	29/10	.37
	Lawyer	33/9	29/9	.41
	Author–Journalist	34/9	29/9	.34
XI	Pres., Mfg. Concern	28/8	28/11	.24
Suppl. Occup. Scales				
	Credit Manager	12	14	.44
	Chamber of Comm. Exec.	9	12	.54
	Physical Therapist	11	11	.33
	Computer Programmer	10	13	.46
	Business Educ. Teacher	11	12	.38
	Community Recr. Admin.	12	14	.48

Nonoccupational Scales: SL: 30/9 38/11 .35; OL: 48/8 55/10 .43; MF: 52/7 51/9 .58; AACH: 34/11 42/13 .51

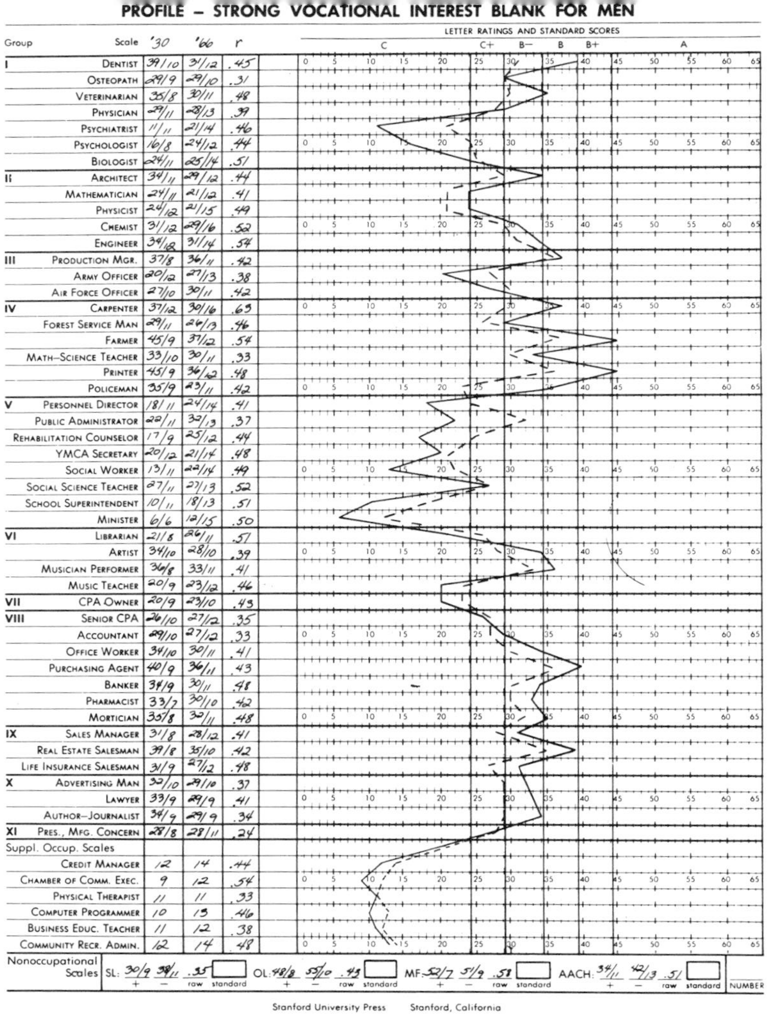

FIG. 2-17. *Test-retest data over 36 years for 1,214 California teenagers.*

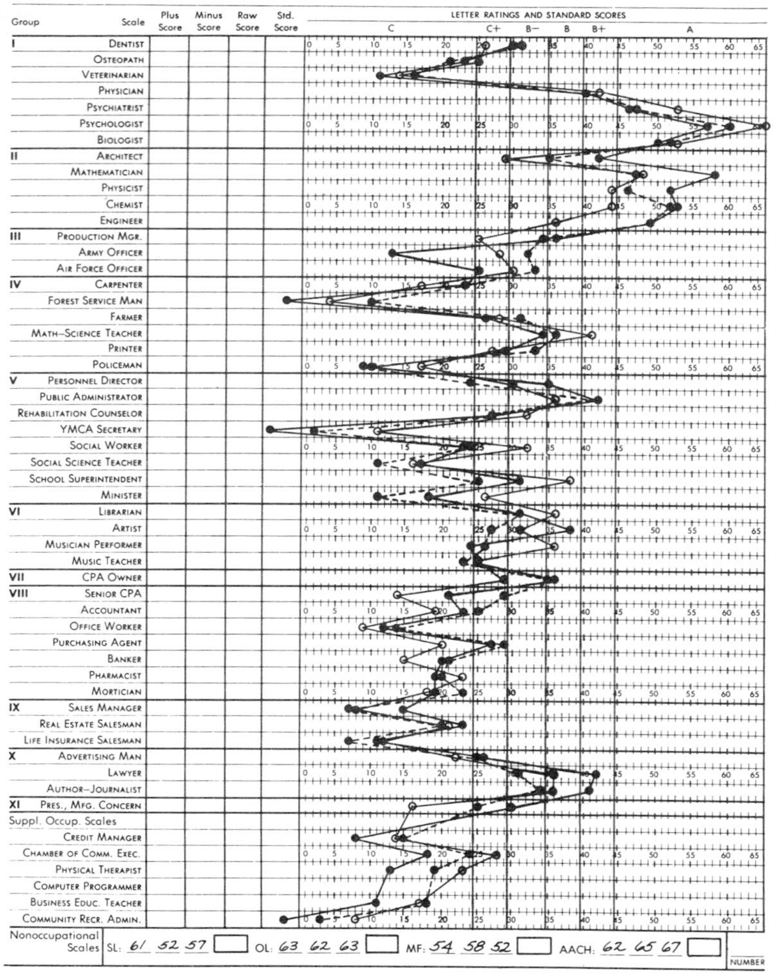

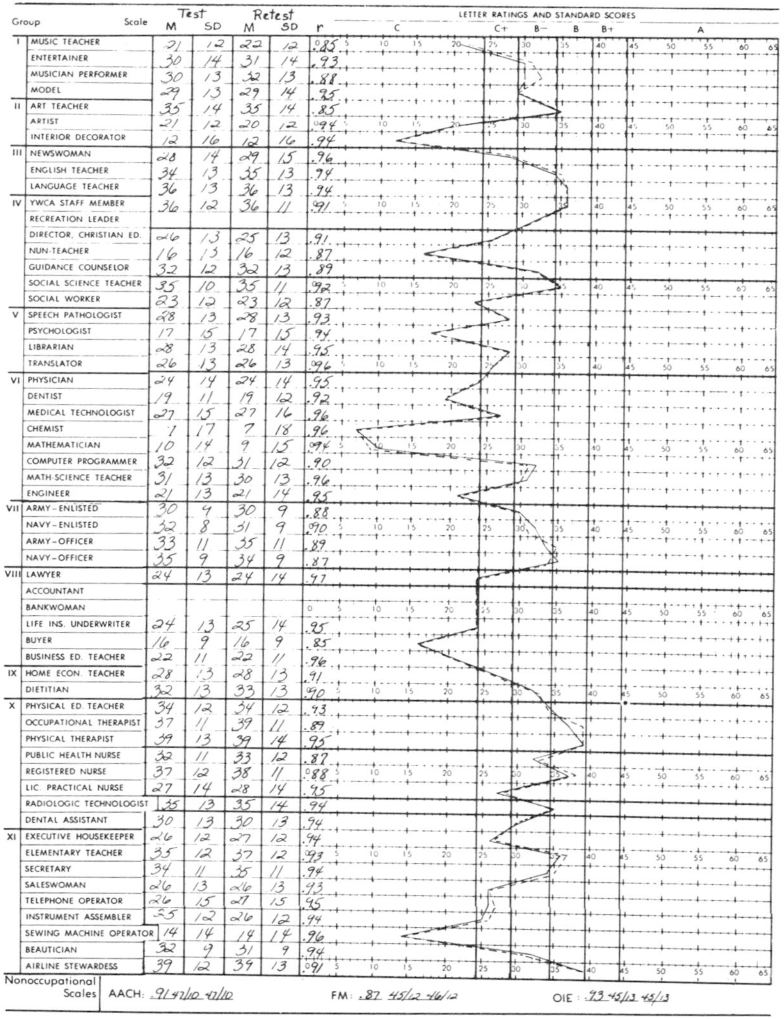

FIG. 2-19. Test-retest data over two weeks for 112 University of Minnesota sophomore women.

FIG. 2-18. Profiles for E. G. Boring from 1927, 1948, and 1965. Solid line connects 1927 scores; dashed line, 1948 scores; circled line, 1965 scores.

school class averaged 57. Interestingly, all three classes showed a decrease on this scale over the four-year medical school period. A longer discussion of the interest changes in medical school is on p. 119.

The participants in the 8-10-year test-retest group (Figure 2-9) were graduates of the University of Minnesota in several professional areas. The group, tested originally by Berdie and retested by Schletzer, is described at some length in the section on predictive validity (p. 55).

Results are available from two samples tested and retested over ten years. The data from the first of these, presented in Figure 2-10, were gathered from students who entered the University of Minnesota's General College, a division of the University that serves essentially a junior college function. They were originally tested as freshmen in 1956 and retested in 1966 by the General College Student Personnel Office, under the direction of G. Gordon Kingsley.

The second 10-year test-retest sample (Figure 2-11) was collected by Trimble (1965). These were Missouri high school seniors in the upper half of their class; almost all of them went on to college. Trimble's work was discussed earlier in the section on validity, p. 61.

Figure 2-12 contains profile scores for 92 psychologists first tested by E. K. Strong, Jr. in either 1927 or 1935 when he was collecting the original psychologist criterion group; these men were retested about 17 years later by Kriedt (1949) in 1948 when he restandardized the Psychologist scale. Test-retest correlations have not been calculated for this sample.

In 1951, Verburg (1952) retested, after their retirement, some of the YMCA Secretaries originally tested by Strong between 1927 and 1930. Their profiles over the 22-year period are in Figure 2-13. As can be seen, their scores on the YMCA Secretary scale were not very high. This scale was revised in 1966, and now is based on a sample of YMCA staff members tested in 1961. This failure of the early group to score high on the more recent scale is one of the few instances where a SVIB scale has failed to hold up over time.

The participants in the 22-year test-retest group (Figure 2-14) were graduates of Stanford University in 1927, retested by Strong in 1949 (Strong, 1955).

The men in the 30-year test-retest group (Figure 2-15) were all bankers; they were about 40 years old when initially tested in 1934, and about 70 when retested in 1964 (Campbell, 1966).

These test-retest statistics for adults over long time spans show reasonably good stability; the median correlation over 22 years was .67 for the Stanford seniors, and .56 over 30 years for the Minnesota bankers, even though this latter group was fairly homogeneous. The information presented in the next two figures, Figure 2-16 and 2-17, came from teenagers tested and retested over 30 years later, and these reliability figures are lower.

The data in Figure 2-16 are based on 229 engineering freshmen, about 18 years old, at Purdue University, tested in 1935 and retested in 1966 (Benjamin, 1967); their median test-retest correlation was .42.

Figure 2-17 contains the test-retest data for 1214 California teenagers, first tested at age 16 in 1930 by E. K. Strong, Jr. in his early research, and retested in 1966-68 by our staff at the University of Minnesota. Their median correlation was .44, also low, and shows that the SVIB scores are not very stable over a 35 year period for 16 year old boys—but that is a very rigorous test of stability.

Test-retest statistics on the Basic Interest Scales are given in Chapter 3 for all of the above groups and several others. The nature of changes that occur over time is also presented with those data.

Johansson and Campbell (1969) have used some of these test-retest samples to calculate the median test-retest correlations for different ages and different test-retest intervals; Table 2-18 summarizes their findings.

TABLE 2-18. MEDIAN TEST-RETEST CORRELATIONS FOR THE MEN'S OCCUPATIONAL SCALES FOR VARYING AGES AND TEST-RETEST INTERVALS

Age at first testing	Test-Retest Interval					
	Two Weeks	1 Year	2–5 Years	6–10 Years	11–20 Years	20+ Years
17–18	—	.80	.70	.65	.64	—
19–21	.91	.80	.73	.67	.67	.64
22–25	—	—	.78	.69	.75	.72
26+	—	—	.77	.81	.80	—

The median correlations ranged from about .90 over short spans down to .64 over longer intervals. The important influences of both age initially tested and length of interval is apparent in Table 2-18.

Stability of Scores over Time for a Single Individual

One figure is presented here to demonstrate the stability of scores for a single individual. The profiles in Figure 2-18, initially published in a study of the vocational interests of former presidents of the American Psychological Association (Campbell, 1965), are based on SVIBs completed by Professor E. G. Boring of Harvard University. The similarity of these profiles demonstrates the stability of the SVIB scores for a single individual over 38 years. This example is not atypical; many others could be substituted.

(When he was asked for permission to publish his SVIB results, Boring replied, "No, I have no objection to your putting my record on the Strong Vocational Interest Test into the public domain. Even if people don't already know that I am a good engineer and a good chemist, they must have realized that I am a poor life-insurance salesman, and there are certainly some that have long thought of me as a second-rate psychologist. So go to it.")

Test-Retest Data for the Women's Occupational Scales

Figures 2-19 through 2-22 present test-retest data for the women's Occupational Scales for five samples tested over two weeks, 3½, 15, 17, and 26 years respectively. Most of these samples are smaller than the men's samples, and the figures may not be as reliable. They are presented, however, because this type of information is quite important, and these data are the best that are available. Except where indicated, these statistics are, of necessity, based on the 1946 women's scales, as the old booklets cannot be scored on the new scales.

The first sample (Figure 2-19) included 112 University of Minnesota students, mostly sophomore volunteers from the introductory psychology course. The 1969 scales were used here as these students had completed the new booklet.

The second sample (Figure 2-20) consists of 38 women who were initially tested before entrance to the University of Minnesota and retested just before graduation 3½ years later. They were all students at the College of Liberal Arts. Other data on this sample suggest there is an intellectual bias in this sample, no doubt due to the self-selection in volunteering to fill out the inventory before graduation.

The third sample (Figure 2-21) included 81 women, formerly students at Connecticut College for Women. They were initially tested as 19 year old sophomores in 1939, and retested 15 years later by Dr. Ross Thomas (1955).

The fourth sample (Figure 2-22) included 134 women psychologists who were first tested in 1941 by E. K. Strong to establish his original psychologist key on the women's form, and retested 17 years later (Campbell and Soliman, 1968). Because these psychologists were retested with the new form of the women's Strong, the scores reported here are from a set of interim scales that are compatible with both the old and new women's booklets. As they are shorter than the final scales for the 1969 booklet, these reliability figures are probably conservative estimates. See Appendix A for a longer discussion of these interim scales.

The fifth sample (Figure 2-23) contained 91 women who were first

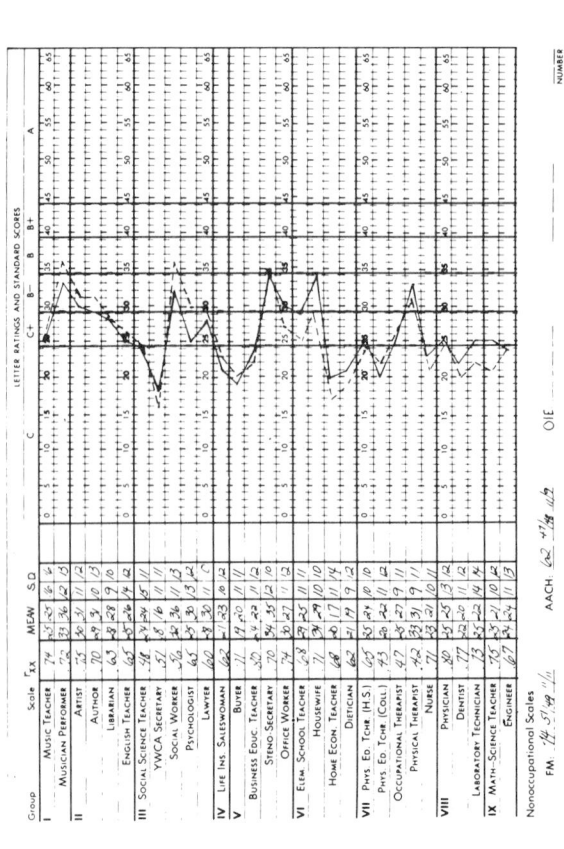

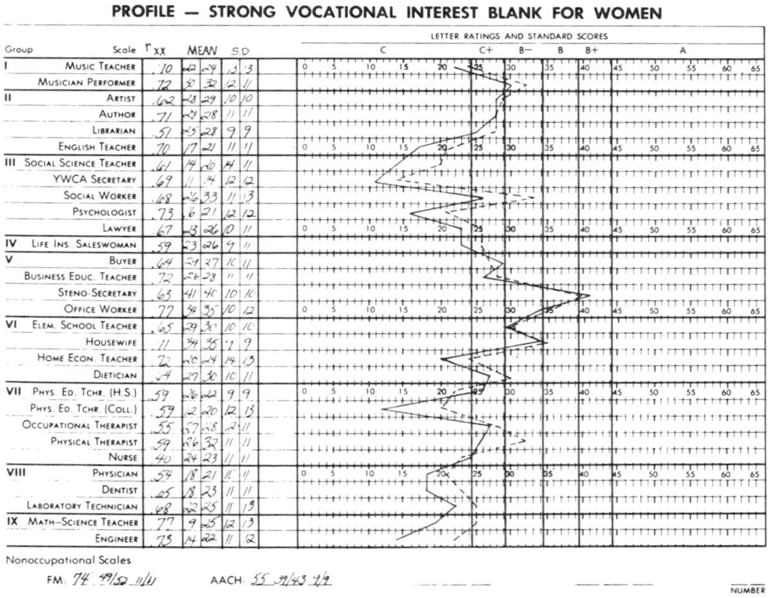

FIG. 2-21. *Test-retest data over 15 years for 81 Connecticut College for Women freshmen.*

FIG. 2-20. *Test-retest data over four years for 38 Minnesota freshman women.*

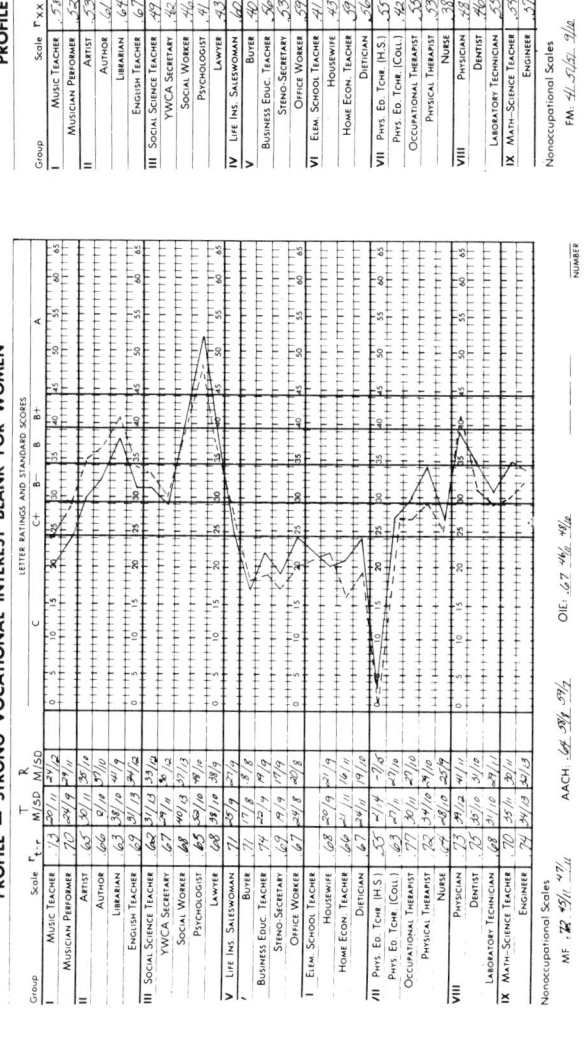

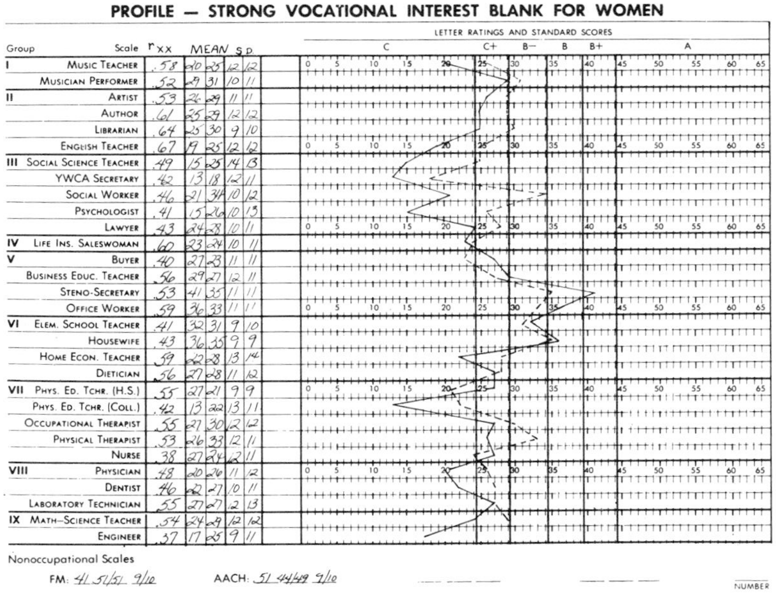

FIG. 2-23. *Test-retest data over 26 years for 91 University of Minnesota freshman women.*

FIG. 2-22. *Test-retest data over 24 years for 134 psychologists.*

tested in the years 1933–36, usually as incoming students to the University of Minnesota College of Liberal Arts. They were retested roughly 26 years later, in 1962, as part of a study on the effectiveness of counseling (Campbell, 1965). About 99 percent of those in the initial study were located, and about 90 percent completed the inventory in 1962.

While these test-retest data for both men's and women's samples permit some estimate of the degree of stability found statistically, the changes in content are hard to describe when working with the Occupational Scales. Test-retest data for most of these same samples on the Basic Interest Scales, scales that are homogeneous in content, are presented in Chapter 4, and in that chapter is a longer discussion of the nature of the changes.

General Conclusions on Stability

The major conclusion from these test-retest data is that the stability of an individual's scores on the SVIB varies with his age when first tested and the length of the interval between testing. After age 25, people's interests appear to change very little; between 20 and 25 some mild changes may appear, but the usual finding is one of considerable stability; between the ages of 15 and 20 there will be some people whose results show considerable change. Psychologists working with people in this age range should beware of the possibility of marked change, and the client certainly should be advised of it.

Professor Strong has said informally that the change between age 15 and 25 could be divided in thirds—the first third occurring between age 15 and 16, the second between 16 and 18, the last between 18 and 25. That summary is only a guideline, but it fits well with the data that have been accumulating.

More information on change with age can be found in the chapters on the Basic Interest Scales, and in the discussion of the Age-Related Interest Scale.

CHAPTER 3

The Men's Basic Interest Scales

The regular SVIB scales in use before 1969 were developed by comparing the responses of men in specific occupations with those of a Men-in-General group. The major advantage of these empirical scales is that they include all of the discriminating items for each occupation in one scale; this makes interpretation for that one occupation fairly easy. With these scores, a counselor can say something like, "You have interests similar to lawyers." However, the heterogeneous nature of empirical scales makes further psychological interpretation difficult. If the individual asks the obvious, "What does it mean to have interests similar to lawyers?", the counselor must fall back on what he has learned about lawyers from other sources. Although the occupational groupings and the individual's other high scores on the SVIB profile provide some general flavor, interpretation is still shallow except when done by well-trained, sophisticated counselors who have had considerable experience in working with the SVIB, and who have studied the research literature.

A second major disadvantage is that there is no limit to the potential number of these empirical scales; in theory one could be developed for each occupation . . . but there are over 16,000 occupations listed in the *Dictionary of Occupational Titles*. In current practice, to compensate for this relatively narrow coverage of the occupational world, the counselor usually extrapolates from the available SVIB scales to other occupations not listed on the profile. For example, if a student inquires about geology, scores on the Engineer and Chemist scales are probably relevant. Some such extrapolation will be inevitable, no matter what the final method used, but it should be as easy and direct as possible.

A third disadvantage is that these empirical, Occupational Scales are difficult to work with in research studies. If an investigator wishes to study men who have survived in a specific occupational setting versus those who have not, he finds it cumbersome to compare these two groups on all of the empirical scales. While he can, and frequently does, calculate the mean differences on each of the scales, the resulting statistics are neither parsimonious nor easily interpretable.

The empirical success of the SVIB has created most of these problems. Because the scales are useful and do provide an easily interpretable score *for a specific occupation,* there has been considerable pressure to build more of them, further increasing the complexity of the profile. From all indications, this will continue as more occupations feel the need for self-study. This is good, for this detailed psychometric information on a wide variety of jobs is quite useful, but this prospect makes it even more imperative to develop a simpler way to summarize the results.

Construction of the Basic Interest Scales

What both the counselor and researcher need is another system of scoring to supplement the Occupational Scales, a system containing relatively few scales, but scales which could be used to generalize beyond a single occupation. Clark, in his research with the Minnesota Vocational Interest Inventory, has shown that one way to do this is to work with measures that reflect interests in one type of activity or in closely related activities, i.e., homogeneous content scales (Clark, 1961).

Similar scales have been constructed for the SVIB by identifying clusters of items with high intercorrelations, for both the Men's and Women's booklet. The items in these clusters have been assigned scoring weights, and termed "Basic Interest Scales." Further details of scale construction are reported below.

Set 1 and Set 2 Scales

There are actually four sets of scales, two for the Men's booklet, two for the Women's. The first set, Set 1, for each sex is based on the item pool common to all published forms of the booklet. The Men's Set 1 scales can be used with any of the following booklets:

Form A and B (published in 1927 and revised slightly in 1930)
Form M (published in 1938)
Form T399 and T399R (published in 1966)

The men's Set 2 scales include the new items added in the 1966 revision (T399 and T399R) and can only be used with those booklets.

Analogously, for the Women's booklet, the Set 1 scales can be used with:

Form WA or WB (published in 1933)
Form W (published in 1946)
Form TW398 and TW398R (published in 1969)

The Women's Set 2 scales take advantage of the revised item pool of the 1969 revision and can only be used with the revised (1969) booklets.

The Set 1 scales, both men's and women's, have been developed for research purposes. Anyone who wishes to score individuals tested in earlier years—for example, participants in longitudinal studies—must have scales compatible with earlier forms of the booklet.

The Set 2 is simply the first set expanded to include the items added to the SVIB in the 1966 (Men's) and 1969 (Women's) revisions. In the revisions, a definite attempt was made to improve the coverage in areas relatively neglected in the original item pools such as art, religion, and music. As a result, scales for those areas are longer and more adequate in Set 2, and current users of the SVIB should use these scales.

Because much of the normative data presented below are from groups tested before the booklets were revised in 1966 and 1969, only the Set 1 scales are used unless specifically noted otherwise. The correlations between the like-named Men's Set 1 and Set 2 scales are listed in Table 3-29; the median correlation was .98, so the two sets are essentially interchangeable. However, the Set 2 scales are slightly more reliable over time (see Table 4-24) so are preferred.

Eliminated Items

Two restrictions were applied to the individual items before scale construction began. First, to eliminate the highly popular and unpopular ones, no item was used if any of the responses, LIKE, INDIFFERENT, or DISLIKE, had less than 15 percent response among a sample of men-in-general. Second, none of the items numbered 281–320 in the Men's booklet, 256–295 in the Women's, were included. Those are the items grouped in tens where the respondent is to select the three he likes best, the three he likes least, and mark the remaining four indifferent. Those items have somewhat different psychometric characteristics than the remaining SVIB items, they are more troublesome for the respondents, and, in anticipation of future revisions, they have not been used in these scales.

Item Intercorrelations

The next step in scale construction was to generate an item intercorrelation matrix. Using the responses from a sample of 500 men-in-general (or women, as appropriate), a Pearson product-moment correlation was calculated between each pair of items by assigning the values +1, 0, and −1 respectively to the LIKE, INDIFFERENT, and DISLIKE responses, then treating

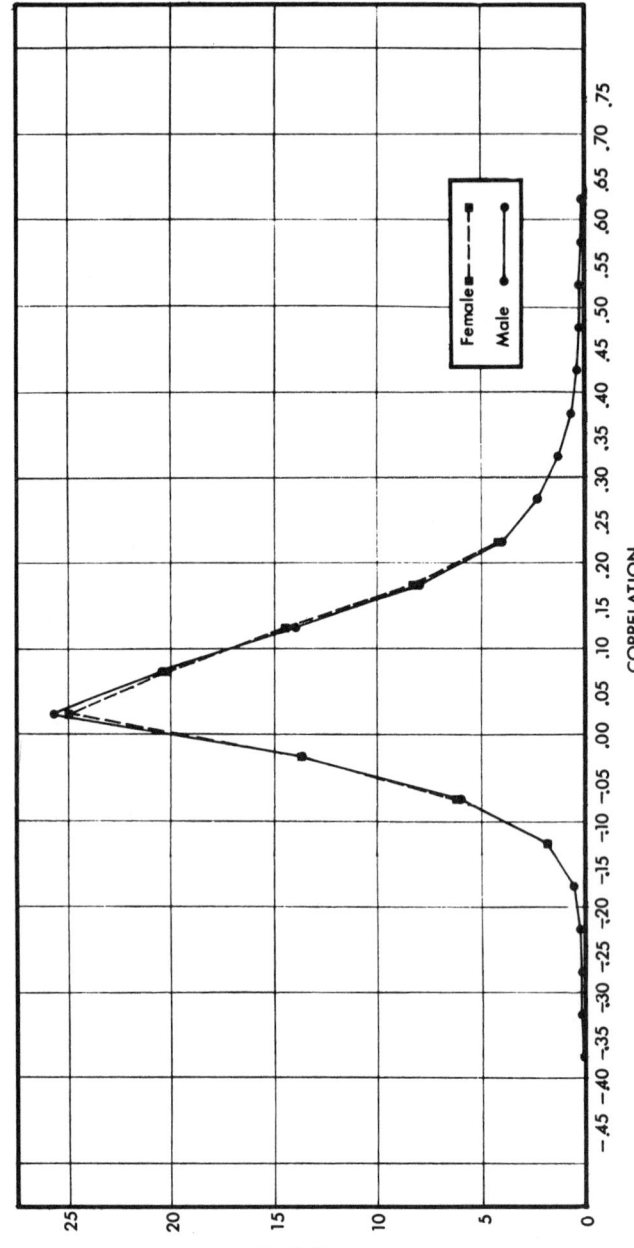

FIG. 3-1. *Frequency distributions of item intercorrelations for both the men's and women's SVIB.*

TABLE 3-1. SAMPLE ITEM INTERCORRELATIONS[a]

High Positive Correlation

Item 101 (Algebra) vs. 102 (Arithmetic)

		Algebra			
		L	I	D	Total
	L	51	12	06	69
Arithmetic	I	03	11	06	19
	D	01	01	10	12
Total		55	24	22	100

r = .63

Low Positive Correlation

Item 115 (Geometry) vs. 144 (Chess)

		Geometry			
		L	I	D	Total
	L	16	04	03	23
Chess	I	24	12	06	42
	D	15	11	09	35
Total		55	27	18	100

r = .21

High Negative Correlation

Item 1 (Actor) vs. 349 (Listening to a story vs. Telling a story)

		Actor			
		L	I	D	Total
	L	09	19	24	52
Listening	I	06	10	16	33
	D	08	04	04	15
Total		23	33	45	100

r = −.19

[a] Each cell entry is the proportion of 500 Men-in-General selecting that combination of responses.

one item as the X axis, the other as the Y axis. Examples of three such correlations are shown in Table 3-1, including a high positive, a low positive, and a high negative correlation. As there were almost no large negative correlations, except between forced-choice items where they were artifically created, −.19 qualified here as "high."

The next step was to decide exactly how to build the scales. The intent was to cluster items with "high" intercorrelations, but how high is "high," e.g., should only items with intercorrelations of .20, or .30, or maybe even .60 or .80 be used? To gain some knowledge here, a frequency distribution, using all of the correlations in the item intercorrelation matrix, was constructed for both the Men's and Women's forms; they are reproduced in Figure 3-1. As can be seen, the two distributions, both based on about 45,000 item intercorrelations, were remarkably similar.

Several conclusions can be drawn from these distributions:

1. The item intercorrelations were generally low, mostly around zero, practically all between ±.20.

2. The distributions were slightly positively skewed. This mild effect could be caused by any of several factors such as a slight response set, or overrepresentation of some content areas.

3. There were not many high correlations. In the initial matrix for the Men's booklet, even the highest were only .79 between the items "Mathematics" and "Arithmetic," and .78 between "Surgeon" and "Physician"; among the remaining correlations, only five percent were above .25, and only one percent above .35. This strongly suggests that the items are relatively specific, that the respondents pay a great deal of attention to the unique aspects of each item.

4. There were no large negative correlations. This indicates that, at the item level, there is little tendency for people who like one item to all dislike another. (This is peculiar for large negative correlations certainly appear at the scale level, ranging up to −.88 between the Social Science Teacher and Engineer scales.) In constructing the Basic Scales, only a few items with negative correlations were included, even though a lower absolute value of correlation was accepted.

After the matrices had been calculated, various searching techniques were used, with the aid of the computer when possible, to locate smaller matrices containing perhaps 5–25 items, all having high intercorrelations. Using Figure 3-1 as a guide, "high" was defined as above .30 though it was sometimes necessary to drop lower. The absolute minimum was set at .20 but even that was violated occasionally, especially when the correlations were negative.

Item Composition of the Men's Basic Interest Scales

Twenty-two Basic Scales were finally constructed for the Men's booklet; item intercorrelation matrices for each of them are listed in Tables 3-2 to 3-23. A similar set of scales was developed for the Women's SVIB; they are discussed in the next chapter.

In these matrices, two correlations are presented for each pair of items. Those above the diagonal were generated from Strong's 500 Men-in-General, tested during the 1930's, and were the correlations used to cluster the items into scales. The correlations below the diagonal are based on another sample of 500 Men-in-General who filled in the 1966 booklet. (Many of them were actually tested in 1964 and 1965, using a pre-publication version of this booklet.) The intercorrelations remained high in the second group,

TABLE 3-2. MEN'S ADVENTURE SCALE ITEM INTERCORRELATIONS[a]

Item Number	Item	211	14	231	12	334	86	277	337	321
211	Pursuing bandits in a sheriff's posse		24	26	37	23	44			
14	Airplane pilot	25		27	37	16	22			
231	Climbing along edge of precipice	23	12		25	19	10			
12	Auto Racer	28	40	11		22	32			
334	Taking a chance	13	05	16	17		11			
86	Secret Service Man	42	29	15	30	14				
277	Men who live dangerously	21	22	20	25	16	27			
337	Thrilling, dangerous activities	36	18	26	28	62	25	31		
321	Airline pilot	18	51	13	23	12	18	22	30	

(Set 1 brackets items 211 through 86; Set 2 brackets items 211 through 321)

a = decimal points have been omitted

TABLE 3-3. MEN'S AGRICULTURE SCALE ITEM INTERCORRELATIONS

Item Number	Item	37	102	342	345	76	191	230
37	Farmer		65	24	22	64	28	-34
102	Agriculture	58		27	28	44	32	-18
342	Outside work	21	27		40	30	26	-25
345	Physical activity	20	19	40		18	25	-10
76	Rancher	67	54	26	18		29	-30
191	Handling horses	28	28	20	16	35		-16
230[a]	Living in a city	-24	-17	-24	-18	-21	-06	

(Set 1 and Set 2 bracket items 37 through 230)

a= item weighted negatively

TABLE 3-4. MEN'S ART SCALE ITEM INTERCORRELATIONS

Item Number	Item	5	20	43	104	163	194	233	84	141	39	183	253	263	352
5	Artist		49	45	53	37	35	30	56						
20	Cartoonist	54		37	35	28	21	22	40						
43	Interior Decorator	38	26		38	26	42	35	46						
104	Art	65	46	38		50	38	30	38						
163	Art galleries	49	36	34	50		32	36	37						
194	Decorating a room with flowers	33	21	42	35	36		39	33						
233	Looking at a collection of antique furniture	30	15	26	33	42	39		33						
84	Sculptor	67	48	37	57	51	30	31							
141	Sketching pictures of wild animals	45	35	27	46	41	35	29	42						
39	Art Museum Director	48	38	39	48	50	26	31	59	38					
183	Magazines about art and music	44	29	29	49	60	34	35	48	37	46				
253	Artistic men	50	31	39	49	40	33	30	45	34	39	40			
263	Prominent artists	44	31	20	39	47	27	36	44	33	44	50	56		
352	Music and art events vs Athletic events	35	21	19	33	42	15	18	38	26	41	50	22	34	

(Set 1 brackets items 5 through 84; Set 2 brackets items 5 through 352)

TABLE 3-5. MEN'S BUSINESS MANAGEMENT SCALE ITEM INTERCORRELATIONS

Item Number	Item	33	35	58	65	81	206	226	347	196	42	85	96	177	278
33	Employment Manager		44	27	44	36	30	29	-15	44	33	34			
35	Factory Manager	47		49	41	34	32	32	-10	29	28	28			
58	Manufacturer	28	54		35	38	25	38	-11	27	18	22			
65	Office Manager	57	48	34		50	33	36	-24	28	40	43			
81	Sales Manager	47	42	37	42		36	42	-24	26	34	44			
206	Meeting and directing people	33	27	18	28	36		36	-17	39	31	26			
226	Developing business systems	30	34	34	39	41	29		-22	33	19	26			
347a	Technical vs Supervisory responsibility	-30	-22	-17	-28	-37	-28	-26		-17	-18	-09			
196	Interviewing men for a job	50	31	21	40	39	45	33	-27		22	22			
42	Hotel Manager	44	33	22	38	38	31	20	-30	30		35			
85	Manager, Chamber of Commerce	48	34	25	45	42	32	31	-22	30	38				
96	Travel Bureau Manager	41	27	25	35	32	27	19	-17	25	43	39			
177	Business methods magazines	34	37	37	33	45	24	48	-28	34	21	31	21		
278	Prominent businessmen	28	31	33	30	35	29	30	-24	29	23	26	22	37	

a= Item weighted negatively

TABLE 3-6. MEN'S LAW/POLITICS SCALE ITEM INTERCORRELATIONS

Item Number	Item	41	47	48	51	52	72	160	359
41	Governor of a state		51	42	31	35	51		
47	Judge	55		41	38	48	34		
48	Labor Arbitrator	39	48		33	22	39		
51	Criminal lawyer	45	50	35		42	36		
52	Corporation lawyer	34	46	30	52		22		
72	Politician	62	48	44	43	34			
160	Electioneering for office	50	33	35	34	28	65		
359a	Dog trainer vs Juvenile parole officer	-25	-23	-26	-23	-12	-24	-18	

TABLE 3-7. MEN'S MATHEMATICS SCALE ITEM INTERCORRELATIONS

Item Number	Item	101	103	107	115	120	128
101	Algebra		63	61	67	75	36
103	Arithmetic	65		48	51	79	32
107	Calculus	62	47		56	59	44
115	Geometry	67	50	62		65	50
120	Mathematics	76	77	63	66		42
128	Physics	50	38	55	53	48	

TABLE 3-8. MEN'S MECHANICAL SCALE ITEM INTERCORRELATIONS

Item Number	Item	19	56	94	186	189	190	122	132	148	187	121	185	188	368	13	32	45	55	61	30	88	24	180	98	128	16	22	216
19	Carpenter		51	47	40	65	40	39	55	26	35	46	36	36	33	49	28	26	37	32	38	42	32	24	37	30			
56	Machinist	47		66	47	44	62	41	55	34	55	40	48	48	39	63	45	37	57	45	36	51	36	29	45	29			
94	Toolmaker	49	73		46	46	46	40	52	37	42	36	35	35	36	54	39	35	40	51	40	57	33	18	55	32			
186	Repairing a clock	35	45	49		48	48	39	42	44	58	36	60	60	43	40	35	33	30	32	33	30	29	28	39	28			
189	Cabinetmaking	57	43	49	48		46	47	57	33	41	51	40	47	41	36	29	35	30	31	40	39	34	31	39	34			
190	Operating machinery	42	57	55	51	52		39	49	43	60	42	45	56	43	47	38	32	37	37	26	32	28	38	27	34			
122	Mechanical Drawing	32	41	42	38	44	40		62	41	35	61	38	39	39	28	31	27	25	30	55	31	39	32	22	35			
132	Shop Work	50	55	58	45	58	61	57		34	44	64	42	44	44	42	37	33	30	36	45	43	31	35	28	38			
148	Solving mechanical puzzles	23	33	35	40	31	37	33	30		39	32	38	37	36	27	36	39	23	30	33	30	26	34	29	30			
187	Adjusting a carburetor	33	52	55	66	45	62	33	52	39		37	63	69	40	54	34	30	35	37	29	27	30	36	29	24			
121	Industrial Arts	40	38	41	30	44	40	59	59	25	31		37	39	42	35	24	29	22	24	40	30	25	33	20	27			
185	Making a radio of Hi Fi set	29	38	39	55	45	43	35	44	39	52	32		64	43	41	42	36	30	29	30	24	32	33	34	24			
188	Repairing electrical wiring	32	45	47	62	53	60	39	50	37	67	30	53		41	38	39	29	31	27	31	29	25	34	28	24			
368	Have mechanical ingenuity	27	39	40	43	41	46	37	44	36	45	34	44	46		26	28	41	25	22	28	26	20	32	22	34			
13	Auto Mechanic	47	59	55	46	36	53	29	47	32	62	32	36	43	35		36	28	45	39	27	46	24	26	42	27			
32	Electrical Engineer	29	49	49	41	38	40	36	36	38	44	28	47	48	33	40		41	40	41	34	42	56	27	27	37			
45	Inventor	24	30	32	30	33	34	19	26	31	30	21	36	32	41	24	40		30	34	29	33	25	32	28	32			
55	Locomotive Engineer	37	53	46	28	23	38	25	34	18	34	28	20	23	13	42	29	17		37	18	39	23	24	35	25			
61	Mining Superintendent	17	28	30	19	17	30	22	25	22	27	24	20	24	18	29	30	25	28		36	50	40	17	34	28			
30	Draftsman	80	42	45	34	32	33	62	41	27	33	41	28	28	27	33	40	17	31	22		38	37	24	34	27			
88	Shop Foreman	33	52	54	29	29	42	33	42	25	40	34	22	31	23	41	34	15	41	44	33		29	21	41	37			
24	Civil Engineer	30	41	43	24	31	38	36	34	31	32	31	31	30	30	34	57	34	29	36	39	30		14	24	31			
180	Popular mechanics magazines	32	45	45	45	39	50	43	51	38	49	42	42	46	42	38	34	29	31	25	33	36	28		15	21			
98	Watchmaker	34	46	54	49	31	30	25	30	25	36	26	30	30	23	42	33	23	38	24	31	31	24	27		24			
128	Physics	17	24	27	28	20	22	22	19	36	26	17	31	28	28	20	37	33	14	23	18	14	38	24	19				
16	Designer, Electronic equipment	26	38	40	33	32	31	29	27	39	34	26	48	36	34	37	65	45	22	30	34	26	50	30	33	41			
22	Electronics Technician	29	45	46	36	32	37	32	34	36	43	27	49	40	29	40	68	37	29	28	40	31	54	35	36	35	68		
216	Looking at things in a hardware store	33	34	36	30	37	39	25	39	23	32	29	28	36	26	26	24	19	25	21	19	24	25	43	18	18	20	23	

TABLE 3-9. MEN'S MEDICAL SERVICE SCALE ITEM INTERCORRELATIONS

Item Number	Item	29	67	69	93	130	136	192
29	Dentist		40	40	45	21	23	25
67	Pharmacist	42		31	30	23	30	21
69	Physician	38	32		78	31	23	36
93	Surgeon	42	32	76		27	24	38
130	Physiology	22	26	39	33		34	28
136	Zoology	17	24	28	29	48		15
192	Giving first aid assistance	49	46	47	46	41	38	

(Set 1 and Set 2)

TABLE 3-10. MEN'S MERCHANDISING SCALE ITEM INTERCORRELATIONS

Item Number	Item	80	99	81	219	18	42	85	220	65	92	68	346	96	177
80	Retailer		59	48	51	52	36	40	48	44	30				
99	Wholesaler	55		58	44	48	33	45	39	47	41				
81	Sales Manager	52	48		47	48	34	44	44	50	38				
219	Buying merchandise for a store	53	49	50		54	32	31	61	32	26				
18	Buyer of merchandise	54	52	51	58		36	33	44	44	32				
42	Hotel Manager	36	30	38	38	36		35	32	44	32				
85	Manager, Chamber of Commerce	34	36	42	36	36	38		30	47	41				
220	Displaying merchandise in a store	41	39	34	59	42	31	33		32	26				
65	Office Manager	37	39	42	36	41	38	45	27		35				
92	Stockbroker	29	34	37	30	31	26	30	20	26					
68	Public Relations Man	35	35	53	38	41	42	51	36	42	31				
346	Work in an import-export business vs Work in research lab	28	30	36	31	35	33	24	28	20	21	37			
96	Travel Bureau Manager	34	31	32	32	33	42	39	27	35	28	41	27		
177	Business methods magazines	32	36	45	34	37	21	31	27	33	38	34	19	21	

(Set 2, Set 1)

TABLE 3-11. MEN'S MILITARY ACTIVITIES SCALE ITEM INTERCORRELATIONS

Item Number	Item	4	123	151	210	237
4	Military Officer		49	42	59	
123	Military Drill	52		66	68	
151	Drilling in a military company	53	81		61	
210	Drilling soldiers	59	68	74		
237	Military Men	52	44	43	47	

(Set 2, Set 1)

96

TABLE 3-12. MEN'S MUSIC SCALE ITEM INTERCORRELATIONS

Item Number	Item	62	63	66	167	183	352	152	157	149	261
62	Musician		50	57	40						
63	Music Teacher	56		52	27						
66	Orchestra Conductor	58	51		34						
167	Symphony Concerts	39	34	47							
183	Magazines about art and music	43	41	46	54						
352	Music and art events vs Athletic events	34	27	35	48	50					
152	Playing the piano	49	37	42	30	30	22				
157	Jazz concerts	26	20	28	25	30	08	29			
149	Religious Music	28	30	26	34	32	21	21	13		
261	Musical geniuses	43	34	44	39	46	33	35	23	25	

Set 1 / Set 2 bracket annotations appear to the left of the table.

TABLE 3-13. MEN'S NATURE SCALE ITEM INTERCORRELATIONS

Item Number	Item	37	50	102	106	125	136	147	193	230	326	194	76	214
37	Farmer		40	65	33	35	26	34	40	-34	-14	19	64	
50	Landscape Gardener	37		40	35	43	32	43	51	-17	-22	43	33	
102	Agriculture	58	42		42	44	34	39	42	-18	-08	29	44	
106	Botany	21	28	32		51	50	44	39	-09	-10	22	22	
125	Nature Study	25	33	35	47		47	64	45	-08	-16	32	25	
136	Zoology	13	22	20	57	45		41	30	01	-05	21	24	
147	Bird watching	24	31	23	36	48	34		48	-17	-20	30	28	
193	Raising flowers and vegetables	33	44	40	28	30	16	24		-17	-32	51	24	
230a	Living in the city	-24	-08	-17	00	-03	01	-06	-03		25	-01	-30	
326a	Selling things house to house vs Gardening	-24	-34	-22	-19	-22	-12	-21	-26	13		-15	-11	
194	Decorating a room with flowers	15	41	23	25	27	22	29	37	02	-13		13	
76	Rancher	67	34	54	19	23	13	16	30	-21	-22	13		
214	Being a forest ranger	34	30	37	22	37	21	26	26	-19	-24	17	37	

Set 1 / Set 2 bracket annotations appear to the left of the table.

a= Item weighted negatively

Table 3-14. Men's Office Practices Scale Item Intercorrelations

Item Number	Item	15	21	25	65	74	80	99	105	135	36	321
15	Bank Teller		69	32	31	39	34	30	40	32		
21	Cashier in bank	81		25	35	36	37	37	43	27		
25	City or State Employee	25	26		19	27	26	18	31	30		
65	Office Manager	39	40	22		48	44	47	40	21		
74	Private Secretary	35	33	22	31		38	34	35	32		
80	Retailer	32	30	13	37	19		59	32	25		
99	Wholesaler	30	29	09	39	19	55		33	23		
105	Bookkeeping	40	37	17	34	22	28	29		39		
135	Typewriting	20	17	13	20	17	14	15	28			
36	Income Tax Accountant	43	40	17	34	24	23	55	19			
321a	Airline pilot vs Airline ticket agent	-18	-20	-15	-13	-08	-13	-04	-15	-07	-14	

a= Item weighted negatively

Table 3-15. Men's Public Speaking Scale Item Intercorrelations

Item Number	Item	131	199	72	26	41	160	75	68
131	Public Speaking		66	34	29	34			
199	Making a speech	67		39	31	29			
72	Politician	42	43		22	51			
26	Minister, Priest or Rabbi	25	29	21		23			
41	Governor of a state	40	47	62	27				
160	Electioneering for office	38	43	65	18	50			
75	Radio Announcer	34	32	32	24	30	29		
68	Public Relations Man	38	28	39	21	34	35	39	

Table 3-16. Men's Recreational Leadership Scale Item Intercorrelations

Item Number	Item	7	70	79	127	143	171	12	350	280	60	352
7	Athletic Director		55	44	44	32	41	26	25	34		
70	Playground Director	55		40	27	13	27	22	20	20		
79	Sports page reporter	51	43		26	31	49	26	24	23		
127	Physical Education	62	42	40		26	27	16	26	31		
143	Boxing	32	24	25	32		33	20	20	19		
171	Sports pages in newspapers	39	29	48	38	20		20	14	31		
12	Auto racer	13	09	14	10	24	04		20	10		
350	Playing baseball vs Watching baseball	29	20	17	31	19	08	12		22		
280	Athletic men*	44	27	38	48	26	39	08	20			
60	Professional baseball player	59	38	57	47	27	43	18	33	39		
352a	Music and art events vs Athletic events	-41	-16	-30	-31	-18	-49	-10	-07	-33	-37	

*=Inadvertently left out of Set 1 scales

a= Item weighted negatively

TABLE 3-17. MEN'S RELIGIOUS ACTIVITIES SCALE ITEM INTERCORRELATIONS

Item Number	Item	26	100	250	124	149	161	169	181
26	Minister, Priest, or Rabbi		52	46					
100	Worker in YMCA	30		36					
250	Religious people	35	30						
124	Bible History	46	27	45					
149	Religious Music	39	30	42	46				
161	Going to church	47	30	57	46	43			
169	Church young people's group	35	45	52	46	46	59		
181	Reading the Bible	39	26	51	61	52	56	51	

Set 1: 26, 100, 250
Set 2: 124, 149, 161, 169, 181

TABLE 3-18. MEN'S SALES SCALE ITEM INTERCORRELATIONS

Item Number	Item	11	54	77	80	81	90	95	197	326	335	68
11	Auto Salesman		43	49 '	33	32	42	49	35			
54	Life Insurance Salesman	43		49	33	36	41	42	41			
77	Real Estate Salesman	54	52		39	41	50	44	44			
80	Retailer	34	35	41		48	39	38	30			
81	Sales Manager	43	41	48	52		47	48	54			
90	Specialty Salesman	43	50	51	45	57		54	43			
95	Traveling Salesman	43	44	45	38	52	56		51			
197	Interviewing prospects in selling	44	45	47	36	66	59	52				
326	Selling things house to house vs Gardening	30	33	29	18	33	38	34	42			
335a	Definite salary vs Commission on what is done	-16	-15	-20	-07	-32	-28	-26	-35	-32		
68	Public Relations Man	31	35	40	35	53	41	38	49	21	-17	

Set 1: 11, 54, 77, 80, 81, 90, 95, 197
Set 2: 326, 335a, 68

a = Item weighted negatively

TABLE 3-19. MEN'S SCIENCE SCALE ITEM INTERCORRELATIONS

Item Number	Item	83	212	23	49	108	6	10	128	107	136	114	16	22	34	346	264
83	Scientific Research Worker		67	54	50	41	43	47	37	35	35	35					
212	Doing research work	67		42	39	36	29	41	41	34	32	27					
23	Chemist	57	44		52	63	35	39	33	36	38	30					
49	Laboratory Technician	54	40	54		39	37	44	31	36	31	26					
108	Chemistry	38	30	57	37		25	25	50	38	36	30					
6	Astronomer	40	36	41	31	26		37	29	30	31	34					
10	Author of technical book	46	46	38	27	26	30		29	32	23	20					
128	Physics	41	36	45	32	50	34	33		44	30	32					
107	Calculus	33	29	34	22	40	30	30	55		19	19					
136	Zoology	33	28	31	25	28	32	30	27	21		41					
114	Geology	28	26	28	24	27	34	26	30	20	43						
16	Designer, electronics equipment	50	41	55	46	37	38	39	41	31	20	22					
22	Electronics Technician	49	37	58	54	32	33	32	35	25	19	21	68				
34	Geologist	44	37	44	39	32	47	32	34	24	40	61	36	37			
346a	Work in import-export business vs work in a research laboratory	-50	-47	-35	-33	-27	-26	-31	-28	-23	-20	-12	-30	-31	-21		
264	Outstanding scientists	31	27	30	25	26	24	32	28	17	28	24	23	19	18	-20	

a = Item weighted negatively

TABLE 3-20. MEN'S SOCIAL SERVICE SCALE ITEM INTERCORRELATIONS

Item Number	Item	89	100	133	184	228	229	359
89	Social Worker		59	49	40	26	32	
100	Worker in YMCA	46		34	28	30	35	
133	Sociology	47	23		41	22	33	
184	Social Problem Movies	49	24	47		14	20	
228	Contributing to charities	22	20	21	24		51	
229	Raising money for a charity	34	28	22	27	50		
359a	Dog trainer vs Juvenile Parole Officer	-29	-13	-26	-29	-15	-14	

a = Item weighted negatively

TABLE 3-21. MEN'S TEACHING SCALE ITEM INTERCORRELATIONS

Item Number	Item	82	27	63	203	202	53	59	387
82	School Teacher		68	48	38	36	40		
27	College Professor	63		37	44	29	38		
63	Music Teacher	34	26		18	21	39		
203	Teaching adults	48	44	23		45	18		
202	Teaching children	38	22	24	53		25		
53	Librarian	40	34	35	18	17			
59	High School Principal	57	46	29	32	28	31		
387	Have patience when teaching others	23	22	13	34	26	06		18

Set 1 brackets items 82 through 53. Set 2 brackets items 82 through 387.

TABLE 3-22. MEN'S TECHNICAL SUPERVISION SCALE ITEM INTERCORRELATIONS

Item Number	Item	35	58	61	88	347
35	Factory Manager			49	43	46	-10
58	Manufacturer	54		37	33	-11
61	Mining Superintendent	40	38		50	10
88	Shop Foreman	45	35	44		09
347a	Technical vs Supervisory responsibility	-22	-17	01	-02	

Set 1 and Set 2 bracket items 35 through 347a.

a = Item weighted negatively

TABLE 3-23. MEN'S WRITING SCALE ITEM INTERCORRELATIONS

Item Number	Item	9	57	71	31	53	78	119	40	112	172	165	170
9	Author of Novel		67	47	51	31	36	33	38	34	31		
57	Magazine Writer	65		51	63	43	48	35	38	43	32		
71	Poet	52	50		41	41	33	31	30	32	51		
31	Editor	52	57	43		37	50	39	47	43	29		
53	Librarian	28	36	37	34		31	30	26	26	32		
78	Reporter, General	42	54	39	53	28		25	51	26	24		
119	Literature	51	42	48	43	30	40		26	54	40		
40	Foreign Correspondent	47	51	38	51	25	54	36		29	18		
112	English Composition	48	47	40	44	35	40	57	32		30		
172	Poetry	44	40	67	37	35	32	52	28	41			
165	Writing a one-act play	58	64	55	50	37	46	43	45	46	44		
170	Biographies	38	37	33	32	33	32	42	26	34	44	40	

Set 1 brackets items 9 through 172. Set 2 brackets items 9 through 170.

indicating that these clusters are stable over time and from one group to another.

The latter group also provided item intercorrelations for the new SVIB items added in the 1966 revision; several of those items were added to the scales after reviewing these figures. The expansion of the scales with these new items constitutes "Set 2" of the Basic Scales.

Item Weights

Once the items had been selected for each scale, scoring weights were established by assigning the weight of +1 to the "Like" response, and −1 to the "Dislike" response. In the few cases where the item intercorrelations were negative, these weights were reversed, i.e., −1 for "Like" and +1 for "Dislike."

Some Considerations in Scale Construction

To recapture exactly the methods used in searching out these submatrices is difficult; a combination of computer searching, hunches, and intuition was employed to decide which items should be grouped together. As general guidelines, two standards were closely followed: first, each decision was based on statistical evidence so that no two items were clustered together unless it was empirically defensible; second, the other major concern was with eventual interpretation. Thus, considerable attention was paid to item content. Occasionally, an item with relatively high correlations with a cluster of items was not included with them because the item simply seemed out of character. One such example was the item "Sculptor" and the "Science" cluster. Although that item correlated fairly high with science items such as "Scientific Research Worker" ($r = .38$), "Chemist" ($r = .30$), and "Astronomer" ($r = .37$), it was not included with them because it just didn't seem to belong.

Scanning the item intercorrelation clusters indicates that some item content areas are better represented in the SVIB item pool than others. In the mechanical area, for example, many items were available while in the Religious Activities area, only three items were available for the Set 1 scales. Normally three items would not be enough to constitute a scale but because more items in this area were available for Set 2, such a scale was constructed.

When working with item intercorrelations, a cluster of interrelated items will emerge if enough items are available concerning any one type of activity. But if an activity is not represented in the SVIB item pool, then no scale to measure interests in that area can be constructed. Although the SVIB item pool does have considerable diversity, especially in occupational activities, certain omissions can be quickly identified by scanning the analogous intercorrelation matrix for the women's SVIB. For example, one scale available for the women's form but not the men's has been labeled "Homemaking" and contains the following items:

Caterer	Cooking
Cook	Sewing
Housekeeper	Preparing dinner for guests
Home Economics Teacher	Trying new cooking recipes
Doing your own laundry work	Home Economics

Whether or not such a scale would be useful on the men's profile can only be an academic question here; because these items have never been included in the men's booklet, this scale is not available for use in comparing male occupational groups.

In constructing these scales, some difficult decisions arose over the issue of scale interrelationships. Statistically, there would be some advantage in having completely independent scales, especially ones with no overlapping items. However, such scales might not be the most accurate reflection of the structure of interests; some interest dimensions are related, and some SVIB items tap more than one dimension.

One such quandary appeared in the three scales: Sales, Merchandising, and Office Practices. The correlations between these scales are high: .78, .63, and .79, respectively, and there is probably only one underlying dimension—Business. Yet, there were three fairly distinct clusters of items and, as they merit differing interpretations, they were retained as separate scales. Whenever such an arbitrary decision had to be made, the overwhelming consideration was to improve the final interpretability of the scales, not to satisfy intermediate psychometric requirements. The eventual impact of these decisions can be seen below in Table 3-30 where the scale intercorrelations are reported.

"Personality" Scales

The scales which appeared first in the scale construction stage were those that researchers in interest measurement have learned to expect: Sales, Science, Mechanical, Social Service, and so forth. But we were also interested in constructing scales that would represent more traditional personality dimensions, such as Aggressiveness or Compulsivity.

Several attempts to build such scales from the SVIB item pool were singularly fruitless. Neither our computer algorithms nor our intuition located clusters of items that held together statistically. To illustrate the difficulties, intercorrelations for items selected to represent the dimensions of "Autonomy" and "Compulsivity" are shown in Tables 3-24 and 3-25. The

TABLE 3-24. AUTONOMY CLUSTER ITEM INTERCORRELATIONS

Item Number	Item	299	335	336	351	338	367	392
299	Freedom in...doing work		-16	13	-06	-06		
a335	(neg) Commission on what is done vs salary	-14		-25	-04	24		
336	Work for yourself	18	-29		-01	-31		
a351	(neg) Amusement alone...	-12	-00	07		07		
a338	(neg) Work for self in small business	-10	25	-48	05			
367	Prefer working alone	06	01	-00	-22	-01		
392	Dislike taking orders	08	-06	17	-09	-14	09	

a = Items with negative weights

TABLE 3-25. COMPULSIVITY CLUSTER ITEM INTERCORRELATIONS

Item Number	Item	105	223	227	334	341	344	380	362	366	373	385	389
105	Bookkeeping		20	26	-01	-09	-02	17					
223	Methodical work	21		14	-10	-21	-02	30					
227	Saving money	22	14		-24	-03	-08	15					
a334	(neg) Playing safe	-10	-14	-10		03	14	-06					
a341	(neg) Work with many details	-09	-27	-03	06		-08	-19					
a344	(neg) Similarity in work	-10	-10	-08	19	00		10					
380	Plan work in detail	12	28	18	-06	-18	-01						
362	Make decisions immediately	03	-11	-07	20	09	07	-10					
366	Keep detailed records of expenses	19	21	21	-15	-11	-13	29	-11				
373	Am always on time with my work	06	14	11	-11	-01	-09	25	07	13			
385	Am slow going and sure	-01	10	08	-21	01	-08	12	-29	06	-02		
389	Pay attention to details (very little)	-14	-26	-12	14	29	04	-37	17	-32	-13	-10	

a = Item weighted negatively

level of homogeneity of these "clusters" fell far short of the minimal standards of statistical coherence which were followed in forming the occupationally oriented Basic Scales, and these personality clusters were dropped. These failures could be attributed to either a lower cohesiveness of personality clusters, or to the inadequacies of the SVIB item pool in the personality domain.

Finally, to gain some experience with such a personality scale, the Adventure scale was forced into existence. Items with a derring-do flavor were separated out, their intercorrelations were scanned, and those with at least mild positive correlations, generally larger than .10, were clustered together. (See Table 3-2 for the complete matrix of correlations.) As will be seen later, the resulting scale worked reasonably well—a group of astronauts scored highest, 2.50 standard deviations above the lowest scoring occupations of school superintendents and mathematicians—but, still, the scale seems to have less occupational relevance than the other, more homogeneous scales. For example, on the other scales, scores increase with age, especially with occupational experience, but scores on the Adventure scale *decrease* with age.

In general, our attempts to build homogeneous personality scales were unsuccessful. Paradoxically, at least some empirically derived personality scales can be generated from the SVIB item pool as reported in Chapter 5 where the Masculinity-Femininity and Occupational Introversion-Extroversion scales are discussed.

An Initial Check on Scale Reliability

Relatively few items are available in the SVIB for any single content area; thus, most of these scales are short and one of the first concerns was with scale stability. Building short scales, no matter how pure, could conceivably result in scales with unacceptable reliabilities. To check this, several tentative scales of varying lengths were constructed and their long-term reliabilities were compared. Six content areas were selected and two test-retest samples were used. The first samples included 102 members of an Army Reserve unit tested twice over a 30-day interval; the second included 191 Stanford University seniors tested first in 1927 and retested in 1949. Test-retest correlations for both of these samples for several tentative scales of differing lengths are reported in Table 3-26. Within each content area, the scales were formed from the "best" items available; thus, the eight item Science scale has those items with the highest intercorrelations, the sixteen item scale contains the initial eight plus the next eight, and so forth.

Several conclusions can be drawn from these reliability calculations:

1. On the Science scales, the relationship between scale length and reliability was approximately the same, whether split-half or test-retest reliability coefficients were used. As the major concern with the SVIB is long-term stability, test-retest reliability is more important, and that statistic was used for the other comparisons.

TABLE 3-26. RELIABILITIES FOR SOME TENTATIVE BASIC INTEREST SCALES

Content Area	Number of items	Corrected Split-half Reliability	Test-Retest Reliability 30-day	22-year
Science	8	.82	.86	.66
	16	.89	.91	.72
	24	.90	.88	.66
	32	.92	.91	.73
Mechanical	14		.93	.73
	21		.94	.70
	25		.94	.70
Sales	8		.89	.47
	16		.91	.50
Writing	4		.85	.60
	7		.83	.59
	9		.84	.61
	20		.88	.67
Public Speaking	7		.87	.67
Mathematics	5		.88	.75
Median Test-retest correlation for 53 Occupational SVIB scales			.91	.67

2. In general, the expected relationship appeared between scale length and reliability—the longer scales were more reliable—but the relationship was by no means perfect. The shortest Mechanical scale (14 items, r = .73) was more reliable over 22 years than the longest (25 items, r = .70). The most reliable scale over the 22-year period was the five item Mathematics scale (r = .75).

3. There was considerable difference between the content areas in the reliability of scales of equal length. Thus, the eight item Sales scale, seven item Writing scale, seven item Public Speaking scale, and five item Mathematics scale had 22-year test-retest reliabilities ranging over a considerable span: .47, .59, .67 and .75 respectively. This range could be caused either by differing degrees of homogeneity within the scales, the nature of the interest clusters involved, the composition of the test-retest samples, or all three factors.

4. These reliabilities were roughly equivalent to those of the regular SVIB Occupational Scales. The loss due to scale shortness was apparently offset by the gain attributable to scale homogeneity. (The Occupational

Scales have roughly 60–75 items; see Table 3-33 for further reliability comparisons.)

The general conclusion is that short scales, if their content is homogeneous, can be as reliable as long scales. Thus, in constructing the Basic Interest Scales, the conflicting goals of purity of content, measured by item intercorrelations, and longest possible scale length were stressed.

Norms for the Men's Basic Interest Scales

Raw scores on the Basic Interest Scales are meaningless for most purposes because item popularity varies from scale to scale. For example, the "average" man answers "Like" to four more items on the Mechanical Scale than he answers "Dislike" to, but on the Sales Scale he reverses and answers "Dislike" to two more items than "Like." Simply adding up the number of "Likes" and subtracting the "Dislikes" on each scale would be misleading without comparing the results to the base rate popularity.

Converting the raw scores to standard scores by scoring some norm group is one way of reflecting the base rates as this permits ready comparison between the individual's scores and those of a reference group. When this conversion is used, the composition of the norm group is important for it greatly influences the interpretation of the scores.

The Norm Group

The particular sample used to norm the Men's Basic Scales was selected for two reasons: first, the 647 men in the sample represent a diverse cross-section of the occupational world; and second, two completed SVIBs were available for each man, one from age 16 and another from age 52. These men were first tested by Strong in 1930 when they were 16 years old, in his study of the relationship between age and interests (Strong, 1931), and they were retested in 1966–67 to study the relationship between teenage interests and adult occupations. When retested, their mean age was 51.8, with a standard deviation of 1.50. To describe them as "16-year-olds" when first tested and "52-year-olds" when retested provides brief and essentially correct labels. They make an especially good norm group as norms can be established, using the same people, for both teenagers and adults. This advantage of being able to directly compare 16-year-olds with 52-year-olds, using the same samples, is offset slightly by the disadvantage that the 16-year-olds were drawn from the 1930 population, not the current generation, but this is a small price to pay for being able to use the identical group as both teenagers and adults.

When Strong originally gathered this sample in 1930, he included a wide

TABLE 3-27. EDUCATIONAL LEVEL OF MEN'S BASIC INTEREST SCALES NORM SAMPLE

Level	N	Percent
Less than H.S. graduate	94	14
H.S. graduate	139	22
Some college	170	26
B.A., B.S.	149	23
M.A., M.S.	50	8
M.D., D.D.S., L.L.B.	26	4
Ph.D., Ed.D.	19	3
Total	647	100

TABLE 3-28. JOB SATISFACTION OF MEN'S BASIC INTEREST SCALES NORM SAMPLE

Please check one of the following which best describes how you feel about your job:

Percent
Checking

18   It is exactly what I have wanted to do.

28   It is approximately what I have wanted to do.

40   It is something I entered, due to circumstances more or less beyond my control, but I am now satisfied in it.

2   It is a career which is tolerable but not really what I would like to do.

1   It is an unsatisfactory and unrewarding career.

0.3   It is a career that I strongly dislike and I wish I could leave for some other.

range of students from many schools and locations, both urban and rural. They were not a strictly random sample—"haphazard" would be more accurate. There were 1,943 in his original sample. When the norming of the Basic Interest Scales was done in 1967, 647 of them had been located and retested. Eventually, 1,214 were located and retested, and results for this total sample are presented in Figure 3-24. As can be seen, there were virtually no differences between the mean scores of the first 647 used here, and the total sample.

Further demographic data for the norm sample are presented in Table 3-27—educational level—and Table 3-28—job satisfaction. This sample had, on the average, 18 years of experience in their current jobs, which means that they did not enter their "career" positions until age 34.

Raw-Score-to-Standard-Score Conversions

The mean scores for the norm group on both sets of scales are listed in Table 3-29. For the adults, only the raw score statistics are listed; these are the figures that are used to convert an individual's raw scores into standard scores by using the formula on p. 35. This conversion is exactly identical to that performed on the Occupational Scales.

The adult group was used here because both Set 1 and Set 2 scores were available for them; because the teenagers were tested in 1930 with the old booklet, only Set 1 scores are available for them, and their means are reported in standard score points. With the exceptions of Adventure, Recreational Leadership, and Military Activities scales, their means on all of the scales were slightly below the adult mean of 50.

Correlations between the Set 1 and Set 2 scales with the same name are reported in Table 3-29 also, and they indicate the two sets are essentially identical with the mild exceptions of Religious Activities and Music; even their correlations (.89 and .91) are high enough so that the scales can be used interchangeably.

TABLE 3-29. TEENAGE AND ADULT MEAN SCORES FOR THE BASIC INTEREST SCALES NORM GROUP

| | Adult Scores (Age 52)* | | | | Teenage Scores (Age 16)** | | |
| | Set 1 | | Set 2 | | Set 1 | | Correlations Between the Set 1 and Set 2 Scales |
	Mean	SD	Mean	SD	Mean	SD	
Public Speaking	-0.93	2.67	-1.41	3.94	46.6	9.2	.94
Law/Politics	-0.82	3.39	-1.41	4.08	45.4	9.6	.97
Business Management	0.43	5.03	1.03	6.01	43.9	9.5	.98
Sales	-2.58	4.15	-3.73	5.11	46.1	8.7	.96
Merchandising	-0.87	4.89	-0.58	6.54	44.1	9.6	.98
Office Practices	-1.63	3.63	-2.72	4.27	47.8	11.3	.98
Military Activities	-1.12	2.62	-1.02	3.04	50.9	9.4	.98
Technical Responsibility	0.28	2.28	0.28	2.28	44.5	11.3	1.00
Mathematics	2.39	3.35	2.39	3.35	45.4	10.2	1.00
Science	1.90	5.23	2.78	7.31	45.6	10.6	.98
Mechanical	4.54	10.97	5.40	12.07	47.5	9.1	1.00
Nature	2.67	5.06	3.08	5.44	43.3	10.3	.99
Agriculture	1.12	3.23	1.12	3.23	49.0	9.2	1.00
Adventure	-0.80	2.48	-0.23	3.53	57.2	11.1	.96
Recreational Leadership	0.80	3.66	1.92	4.86	52.9	9.7	.98
Medical Service	-0.02	3.28	-0.02	3.28	45.5	10.4	1.00
Social Service	-0.87	2.71	-0.90	3.05	47.3	8.7	.98
Religious Activities	-0.76	1.41	-1.18	3.79	46.9	9.2	.89
Teaching	-0.29	2.91	-0.17	3.65	40.8	9.0	.96
Music	-0.28	2.37	-0.63	4.68	46.6	10.1	.91
Art	-0.54	4.16	-1.28	6.63	46.0	9.3	.95
Writing	-0.66	5.09	-0.72	6.02	45.7	9.2	.98

*Raw scores (the adult norm group has a standard score mean of 50, SD of 10 on all scales)
**Standard Scores

Scale Intercorrelations

The intercorrelations between the Men's Basic Interest Scales are presented in Table 3-30. Those above the diagonal are based on the Set 1 scales, using the scores of a sample of 1927 Stanford University graduates; those below the diagonal are based on the Set 2 scales, using the scores of the adult norm sample. Using these intercorrelations as a guide, the scales have been ordered on the profile so that the adjoining ones tend to be related.

The correlations between the Men's Basic Interest Scales and the Occupational Scales are in Table 3-31 for a sample of individuals who completed both the Men's and Women's booklets.

Correlations between the Men's and Women's Basic Interest Scales, Non-occupational Scales and Administrative Indices are given in Table 4-23, in the following chapter, based on the same sample.

TABLE 3-30. MEN'S BASIC INTEREST SCALE INTERCORRELATIONS

	1	2	3	4	5	6	7	8	9	10	11	12	13	14	15	16	17	18	19	20	21	22
1 Public Speaking		.72	.46	.25	.36	.10	.12	.04	-.16	-.22	-.18	.05	.09	.04	.28	.23	.35	.45	.37	.32	.21	.46
2 Law/Politics	.78		.62	.33	.53	.24	.12	.15	-.05	-.13	-.13	.01	.08	.19	.31	.25	.22	.20	.22	.15	.11	.37
3 Business Management	.58	.54		.67	.86	.63	.31	.41	-.06	-.17	.04	.00	.17	.24	.31	.17	.26	.22	.13	-.02	-.04	.09
4 Sales	.51	.42	.69		.78	.63	.36	.29	-.10	-.15	.08	.11	.27	.22	.35	.13	.32	.32	.12	-.04	-.08	.01
5 Merchandising	.57	.49	.86	.80		.79	.27	.41	-.09	-.13	.11	.13	.21	.20	.31	.24	.28	.27	.14	.04	.03	.14
6 Office Practices	.30	.29	.56	.48	.66		.24	.38	.06	-.01	.24	.16	.16	.22	.18	.16	.29	.31	.20	.06	-.07	.06
7 Military Activities	.25	.21	.26	.17	.22	.19		.37	-.01	.14	.19	.21	.28	.36	.29	.21	.19	.20	.20	.10	-.02	-.02
8 Technical Responsibility	.03	.10	.32	.16	.25	.23	.11		.24	.43	.65	.29	.31	.22	.08	.22	.06	.11	-.02	-.02	-.02	-.15
9 Mathematics	-.05	.06	.10	-.02	-.02	.08	.08	.26		.56	.43	-.05	-.13	.00	-.08	-.02	-.20	-.11	-.03	-.11	-.16	-.27
10 Science	-.09	-.03	-.09	-.21	-.17	-.04	.04	.42	.53		.58	.39	.20	.07	-.08	.29	.01	-.03	.06	.02	.12	-.12
11 Mechanical	-.19	-.16	-.01	-.06	-.03	.09	.12	.60	.37	.64		.33	.31	.17	-.06	.14	.02	.03	.02	-.01	.13	-.20
12 Nature	-.04	-.12	-.13	-.15	-.06	-.02	.06	.18	.03	.40	.34		.76	.13	.19	.41	.26	.21	.20	.16	.34	.14
13 Agriculture	-.09	-.14	-.10	-.02	-.03	-.10	.09	.18	.01	.14	.27	.73		.29	.44	.28	.28	.20	.07	-.03	.14	-.01
14 Adventure	.21	.22	.11	.14	.09	-.19	.21	.25	.09	.20	.23	.08	.20		.45	.23	.08	.04	-.08	.02	.14	.04
15 Recreational Leadership	.23	.20	.23	.25	.28	.19	.24	.14	.04	-.05	.11	.07	.20	.34		.27	.36	.32	.15	.01	.10	.16
16 Medical Service	.19	.19	.13	.10	.13	.10	.12	.22	.19	.49	.31	.43	.22	.19	.15		.30	.21	.25	.19	.25	.13
17 Social Service	.49	.50	.35	.35	.39	.34	.16	.05	.02	.03	-.04	.12	.03	.03	.23	.25		.63	.45	.23	.24	.37
18 Religious Activities	.37	.19	.23	.22	.28	.31	.18	.15	.07	.13	.15	.27	.17	.00	.23	.17	.52		.43	.25	.08	.27
19 Teaching	.51	.45	.28	.16	.25	.25	.14	.08	.08	.28	.06	.26	.04	.08	.13	.36	.52	.39		.62	.34	.51
20 Music	.31	.21	.12	.08	.15	.15	.05	.05	.03	.30	.11	.27	.03	.05	-.05	.34	.41	.42	.53		.50	.59
21 Art	.24	.18	.01	.04	.07	.00	.02	.07	-.04	.33	.16	.41	.08	.13	-.08	.39	.36	.24	.44	.68		.57
22 Writing	.54	.47	.26	.14	.26	.18	.10	.05	.02	.24	-.05	.21	-.03	.17	.07	.28	.45	.26	.63	.55	.59	

Set 1 correlations above diagonal calculated on sample of Stanford University Seniors, 1927 (N=301)
Set 2 correlations below diagonal calculated on cross-section sample of 52-year old men (N=647)

	Public Speaking	Law/Politics	Business Management	Sales	Merchandising	Office Practices	Military Activities	Technical Supervision	Mathematics	Science	Mechanical	Nature	Agriculture	Adventure	Recreational Leadership	Medical Service	Social Service	Religious Activities	Teaching	Music	Art	Writing
Physical Therapist	31	31	21	23	21	16	38	39	18	42	57	56	58	46	65	66	47	47	37	24	26	23
Dentist	-58	-56	-68	-53	-55	-29	-04	-32	06	26	06	29	14	05	-16	20	-40	-17	-27	-03	11	-08
Osteopath	-12	-13	-39	-27	-30	-17	08	-08	14	42	23	52	33	21	09	61	03	21	11	20	24	12
Veterinarian	-21	-13	-06	09	02	03	15	04	-13	-05	14	21	48	27	21	20	-33	-12	-45	-45	-34	-50
Physician	-28	-26	-75	-63	-68	-59	-16	-30	17	46	-01	32	08	10	-10	40	-14	-03	08	18	22	21
Psychiatrist	11	09	-31	-36	-31	-38	-20	-18	12	39	-11	16	-21	-07	-16	31	31	11	41	50	49	51
Psychologist	-10	-11	-49	-59	-54	-52	-44	-28	17	32	-14	-04	-33	-21	-37	-02	-06	-21	19	27	23	37
Biologist	-32	-36	-74	-74	-73	-56	-20	-24	28	57	12	33	06	-00	-20	21	-19	-03	15	23	24	23
Architect	-64	-68	-78	-75	-71	-55	-35	-41	00	13	-11	03	-13	-20	-42	-25	-51	-36	-29	04	18	01
Mathematician	-50	-53	-74	-77	-78	-48	-37	-41	29	26	-18	-09	-30	-35	-51	-21	-38	-17	-06	12	04	04
Physicist	-55	-55	-70	-73	-74	-46	-24	-21	36	48	13	05	-10	-12	-37	-05	-47	-20	-16	05	-02	-09
Chemist	-50	-42	-58	-60	-61	-39	-13	-01	46	66	32	13	03	09	-13	12	-50	-21	-18	02	-02	-07
Engineer	-55	-42	-33	-40	-43	-18	-04	10	43	49	41	-04	-01	01	-19	-10	-56	-29	-39	-23	-29	-40
Computer Programmer	-06	11	03	-14	-16	-10	09	39	63	71	60	09	07	38	18	19	-32	-11	-09	-01	-14	-10
Production Manager	09	11	55	46	41	43	36	57	27	18	58	-03	21	20	20	-06	-22	01	-21	-24	-37	-50
Army Officer	30	38	43	33	31	27	52	65	47	43	75	19	43	59	48	20	-12	12	-06	-12	-28	-17
Air Force Officer	29	41	43	36	28	25	45	69	50	57	79	14	31	55	45	26	-08	11	-01	-11	-24	-17
Carpenter	-44	-44	-13	-08	-12	16	14	18	03	09	50	14	32	11	04	-21	-43	-15	-34	-25	-17	-35
Forest Service Man	-08	-02	12	12	11	25	33	30	11	19	53	53	70	42	39	18	-07	15	-16	-24	-19	-25
Farmer	-40	-37	-17	-10	-12	06	10	10	-00	04	31	21	43	17	04	-13	-51	-17	-49	-44	-37	-51
Math-Science Teacher	-13	-04	05	06	-01	29	21	44	53	69	68	27	29	25	28	38	-03	20	10	-01	-07	-17
Printer	-31	-27	-07	-01	03	23	04	00	-28	-26	13	-01	13	08	03	-29	-35	-26	-44	-34	-12	-17
Policeman	14	22	35	40	36	45	60	37	-05	02	47	21	44	45	47	20	02	17	-12	-13	-09	-14
Personnel Director	55	54	75	55	60	27	21	39	03	-11	10	-14	-05	02	22	-06	33	17	19	06	-07	04
Public Administrator	65	60	68	50	51	29	29	47	17	13	28	06	09	16	26	12	38	29	33	15	-00	13
Rehabilitation Counselor	59	55	47	34	39	14	02	15	-07	-10	-12	05	-07	-07	13	15	70	35	58	31	28	44
YMCA Secretary	59	55	54	52	52	23	22	25	-21	-20	00	09	24	28	51	22	62	33	36	13	15	21
Comm Rec Administrator	69	57	62	60	59	29	29	30	-15	-16	11	20	30	26	51	20	58	37	38	13	14	23
Social Worker	62	52	27	21	25	-01	-02	-01	-25	-19	-22	10	-07	-04	10	14	67	33	55	41	43	57
Social Science Teacher	41	35	46	45	53	43	07	-05	-49	-58	-35	-06	-03	-17	17	-05	59	28	36	10	16	23
School Superintendent	52	33	39	27	35	22	-03	-00	-03	-18	-24	01	-15	-29	-11	03	55	38	56	39	25	36
Minister	33	10	-09	-09	-02	-05	-16	-18	-06	-06	-19	33	02	-19	-08	18	63	49	68	69	66	70
Librarian	-12	-24	-47	-47	-34	-26	-48	-53	-20	-17	-52	01	-36	-42	-49	-12	19	02	31	54	61	59
Artist	-55	-62	-82	-75	-72	-64	-44	-58	-19	-05	-33	03	-14	-21	-39	-23	-30	-33	-21	06	24	13
Musician Performer																						
Music Teacher																			56	58	61	57
CPA Owner																			-01	04	-18	00
Senior CPA																			-32	-27	-49	-38
Accountant																			-25	-15	-27	-30
Office Worker																			-31	-25	-24	-35
Credit Manager																			08	-05	-13	-08
Chamber of Comm E																			18	10	05	21
Business Ed Teach																			19	-01	-04	-08
Purchasing Agent																			-47	-47	-53	-70
Banker																			-35	-32	-35	-44
Pharmacist																			-29	-31	-26	-45
Mortician																			-19	-17	-09	-24
Sales Manager																			-36	-32	-31	-30
Real Estate Sale																			-35	-39	-35	-33
Life Insurance S																			-09	-11	-11	-04
Advertising Man																			-21	-03	10	17
Lawyer																			-01	05	-05	20
Author-Journalis																			-16	05	16	25
President-Mfg Co																			-42	-36	-37	-42

Test-Retest Reliability

Through the years, many samples have been tested and retested over various time intervals with the SVIB; results for some were presented in the preceding chapter on the Occupational Scales. Further information is presented below, using their scores from the Basic Interest Scales. The information is useful for two purposes; one, to study the reliability of the Basic Scales, and two, to study the changes that have taken place among various samples. For this latter purpose, the Basic Interest Scales are particularly useful for they permit the specific identification of the content of the shifts in interests, as opposed to requiring that this content be inferred from looking at the changes occuring on the Occupational Scales.

The profiles from each sample are not discussed in detail; only the unique features of each sample are covered. A summary below discusses general trends over all samples and points out some of the more noteworthy findings, but the reader is urged to look over each profile for the test-retest samples. Test-retest data are difficult to collect, and expensive, but they are very valuable—indeed, indispensable—for the understanding of change over time.

When a sample has been tested and retested, there are many ways that the results can be summarized. Three methods have been used here and they represent three levels of increasing analytic complexity and—not incidentally—cost. The first is the simple presentation of test and retest means; these can be calculated simply by multiplying the group percentage response to each item by the item weight, and summing over all items.

The second method is to calculate test and retest means and standard deviations; this permits an evaluation of mean changes in terms of sample standard deviation units, but this technique does not require that each individual's test results be matched with his retest results.

The third method is to calculate test-retest correlations along with the means and standard deviations; this statistic gives some indication of the stability of each individual's score in the two distributions. Of the three techniques, this is the most informative, also the most expensive. Each of the three approaches are used in the following tables and figures; which one was used depended on the resources that were available when the calculations were done.

All of the data in the following reliability tables are based on the Set 1 Basic Scales as most of these groups completed the Form M (1938) booklet; as the Set 2 scales are usually longer, their reliabilities should be slightly higher. (In the next chapter, in Table 4-24, is a direct comparison of the test-retest reliabilities of the two sets of women's Basic Interest Scales.)

Test-Retest Data From College Students: 2 Weeks to 31 Years

Only a brief description of most of the test-retest groups is included here; more information can be found in Chapter 2, where the test-retest results on the Occupational Scales were presented for most of the groups. More information, including the mean age for each sample, is given in Table 3-33.

The two-week test-retest sample (Figure 3-2) contained mostly sophomores at the University of Minnesota, all volunteers from the University's introductory psychology course.

The 30-day sample (Figure 3-3) included officers and men from an Army Reserve Unit at Fort Snelling, Minnesota. Almost all of them had college degrees. Their occupations were widely scattered, with a mild concentration in the advertising and mass media fields.

The students in King's five-month sample (Figure 3-4) were tested during the fall of their freshman year in the University of Minnesota's General College, which essentially serves a junior college function, and retested the following spring (King, 1957).

The General College 10-year sample (Figure 3-5) were tested as freshmen in 1956 and retested 10 years later in 1966.

Figure 3-6 has test-retest profiles for 126 students majoring in agriculture at the University of Missouri. These data were collected by Betty Heifner.

The Harvard students (Figure 3-7), tested in the spring of their freshman year and retested in the fall of their senior year, were participants in an extensive longitudinal study being conducted by Stanley King and Bruce Finnie of Harvard University.

The University of Minnesota College of Liberal Arts sample (Figure 3-8)

PROFILE– STRONG VOCATIONAL INTEREST BLANK –FOR MEN (Form T399)

BASIC INTEREST SCALES

SCALE	r_{t-r}	T M/SD	R M/SD
PUBLIC SPEAKING	.89	55/10	55/10
LAW/POLITICS	.88	55/9	56/10
BUSINESS MANAGEMENT	.90	51/11	52/11
SALES	.89	50/10	51/10
MERCHANDISING	.89	52/10	53/10
OFFICE PRACTICES	.83	50/10	52/10
MILITARY ACTIVITIES	.91	49/10	49/10
TECHNICAL SUPERVISION	.74	49/10	50/10
MATHEMATICS	.94	50/10	51/11
SCIENCE	.94	51/10	52/10
MECHANICAL	.94	47/10	48/11
NATURE	.90	45/9	47/9
AGRICULTURE	.88	46/10	47/10
ADVENTURE	.80	58/8	59/9
RECREATIONAL LEADERSHIP	.90	51/10	53/10
MEDICAL SERVICE	.89	55/10	57/10
SOCIAL SERVICE	.83	57/10	58/11
RELIGIOUS ACTIVITIES	.83	56/11	57/11
TEACHING	.88	55/9	56/9
MUSIC	.89	53/10	54/10
ART	.93	52/10	53/10
WRITING	.92	53/9	55/10

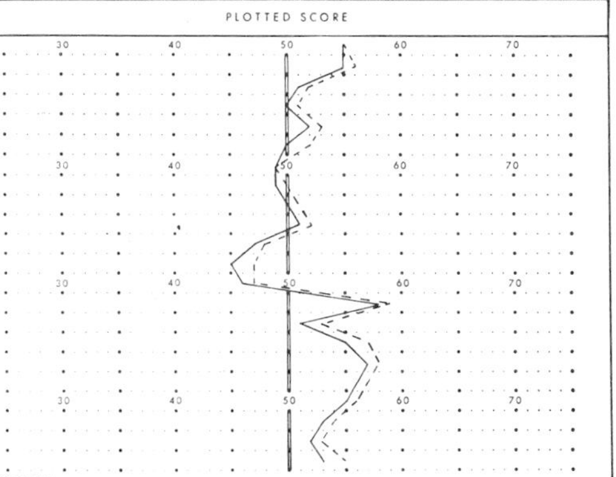

DOUBLE LINE = AVERAGE SCORE FOR 650 52-YEAR-OLD MEN

FIG. 3-2. *Test-retest data over two weeks for 140 University of Minnesota College of Liberal Arts sophomores.*

PROFILE— **STRONG VOCATIONAL INTEREST BLANK** —FOR MEN (Form T399)

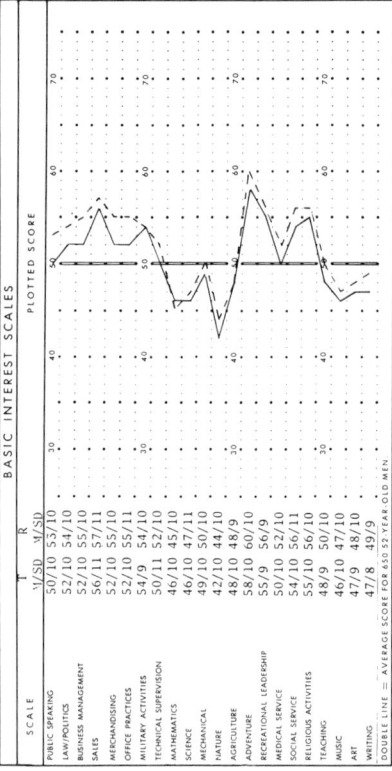

SCALE	T M/SD	R M/SD
PUBLIC SPEAKING	50/10	53/10
LAW/POLITICS	52/10	54/10
BUSINESS MANAGEMENT	52/10	55/10
SALES	56/11	57/11
MERCHANDISING	52/10	55/10
OFFICE PRACTICES	52/10	55/11
MILITARY ACTIVITIES	54/9	54/10
TECHNICAL SUPERVISION	50/11	52/10
MATHEMATICS	46/10	45/10
SCIENCE	46/10	47/11
MECHANICAL	49/10	50/10
NATURE	42/10	44/10
AGRICULTURE	48/10	48/9
ADVENTURE	58/10	60/10
RECREATIONAL LEADERSHIP	55/9	56/9
MEDICAL SERVICE	50/10	52/10
SOCIAL SERVICE	54/10	56/11
RELIGIOUS ACTIVITIES	55/10	56/10
TEACHING	48/9	50/10
MUSIC	46/10	47/10
ART	47/9	48/10
WRITING	47/8	49/9

DOUBLE LINE = AVERAGE SCORE FOR 650 52 YEAR OLD MEN

FIG. 3-4. *Test-retest data over five months for 219 University of Minnesota general college freshmen.*

PROFILE— **STRONG VOCATIONAL INTEREST BLANK** —FOR MEN (Form T399)

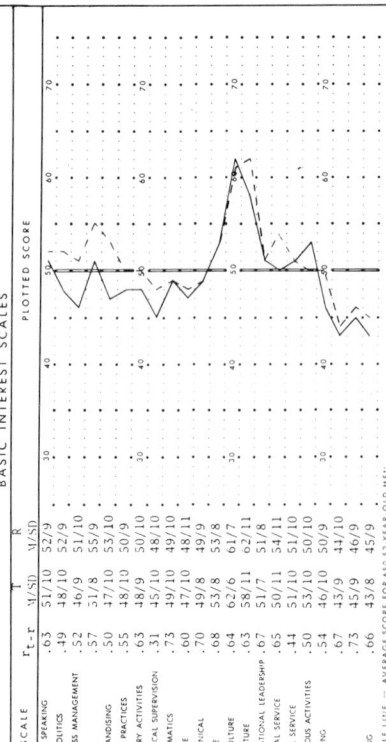

SCALE	rt-r	T M/SD	R M/SD
PUBLIC SPEAKING	.63	51/10	52/9
LAW/POLITICS	.49	48/10	52/9
BUSINESS MANAGEMENT	.52	46/9	51/10
SALES	.57	51/8	55/9
MERCHANDISING	.50	47/10	53/10
OFFICE PRACTICES	.55	48/10	50/9
MILITARY ACTIVITIES	.63	48/9	50/10
TECHNICAL SUPERVISION	.31	45/10	48/10
MATHEMATICS	.73	49/10	49/10
SCIENCE	.60	47/10	48/11
MECHANICAL	.70	49/8	49/9
NATURE	.68	53/8	53/8
AGRICULTURE	.64	62/6	61/7
ADVENTURE	.63	58/11	62/11
RECREATIONAL LEADERSHIP	.67	51/7	51/8
MEDICAL SERVICE	.65	50/11	54/11
SOCIAL SERVICE	.44	51/10	51/10
RELIGIOUS ACTIVITIES	.53	53/10	50/10
TEACHING	.54	46/10	50/9
MUSIC	.67	43/9	44/10
ART	.73	45/9	46/9
WRITING	.66	43/8	45/9

DOUBLE LINE = AVERAGE SCORE FOR 650 52 YEAR OLD MEN

FIG. 3-6. *Test-retest data over three and a half years, for 126 University of Missouri agricultural students.*

PROFILE— **STRONG VOCATIONAL INTEREST BLANK** —FOR MEN (Form T399)

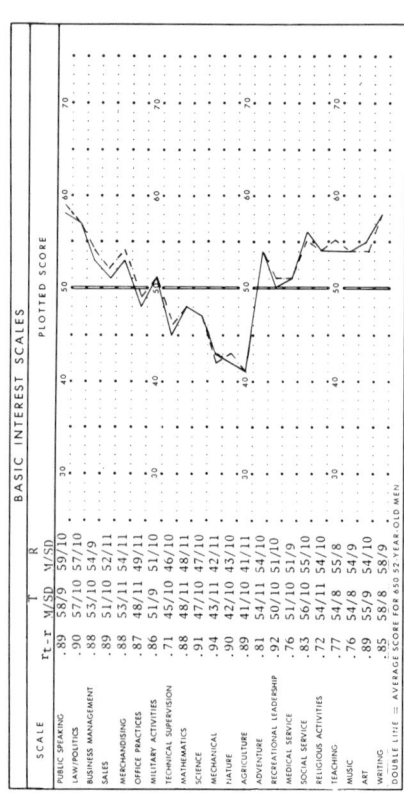

SCALE	rt-r	T M/SD	R M/SD
PUBLIC SPEAKING	.89	58/9	59/10
LAW/POLITICS	.90	57/10	57/10
BUSINESS MANAGEMENT	.88	53/10	54/9
SALES	.89	51/10	52/11
MERCHANDISING	.88	53/11	54/11
OFFICE PRACTICES	.87	48/11	49/11
MILITARY ACTIVITIES	.86	51/9	51/10
TECHNICAL SUPERVISION	.71	45/10	46/10
MATHEMATICS	.88	48/11	48/11
SCIENCE	.91	47/10	47/11
MECHANICAL	.94	43/11	42/11
NATURE	.90	42/10	43/10
AGRICULTURE	.89	41/10	41/11
ADVENTURE	.81	54/11	54/10
RECREATIONAL LEADERSHIP	.92	50/10	51/10
MEDICAL SERVICE	.83	56/10	55/10
SOCIAL SERVICE	.76	51/10	51/9
RELIGIOUS ACTIVITIES	.72	54/11	54/10
TEACHING	.77	54/8	55/8
MUSIC	.76	54/8	54/9
ART	.89	55/9	54/10
WRITING	.85	58/8	58/9

DOUBLE LINE = AVERAGE SCORE FOR 650 52 YEAR OLD MEN

FIG. 3-3. *Test-retest data over 30 days for 102 U.S. Army Reserve Personnel.*

PROFILE— **STRONG VOCATIONAL INTEREST BLANK** —FOR MEN (Form T399)

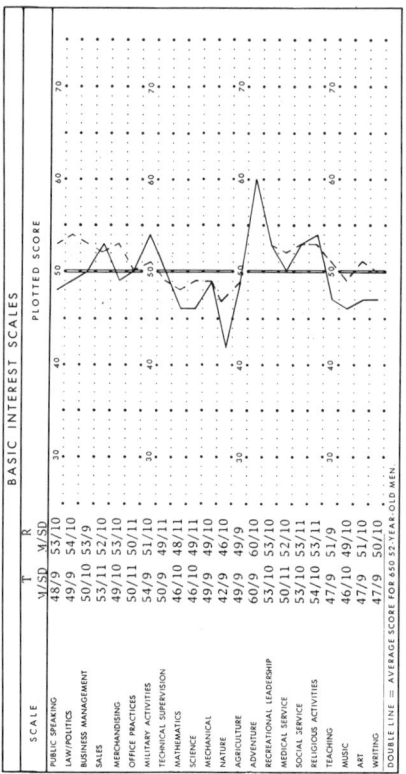

SCALE	T M/SD	R M/SD
PUBLIC SPEAKING	48/9	53/10
LAW/POLITICS	49/9	54/10
BUSINESS MANAGEMENT	50/10	53/9
SALES	53/11	52/10
MERCHANDISING	49/10	53/10
OFFICE PRACTICES	50/11	50/11
MILITARY ACTIVITIES	54/9	51/10
TECHNICAL SUPERVISION	50/9	49/11
MATHEMATICS	46/10	48/11
SCIENCE	46/10	49/11
MECHANICAL	49/9	49/11
NATURE	42/9	46/10
AGRICULTURE	49/9	49/9
ADVENTURE	60/9	60/10
RECREATIONAL LEADERSHIP	53/10	53/10
MEDICAL SERVICE	50/11	52/10
SOCIAL SERVICE	53/10	53/11
RELIGIOUS ACTIVITIES	54/10	53/10
TEACHING	47/9	51/9
MUSIC	46/10	49/10
ART	47/9	51/10
WRITING	47/9	50/10

DOUBLE LINE = AVERAGE SCORE FOR 650 52 YEAR OLD MEN

FIG. 3-5. *Test-retest data over 10 years for 123 University of Minnesota general college men.*

was tested on entrance to college and retested during the spring of their senior year. The retesting was strictly voluntary, and some clear effects of self-selection are apparent in Figure 3-8, which also includes the mean profile for the entire freshman class. Those who volunteered as seniors were, as freshmen, already more interested in academic activities than were their peers, and they continued to change in that direction. For example, on the Teaching scale, the entire freshman class scored 49, this subset scored 52, and increased that to 57 on retest. Another instance of the same trend but in reversed direction was the Office Practices scale where the entire class scored 49, the subset 48, and on retest 46. Thus, in comparing the sample of seniors with the entire freshman class, evidence can be found both for change and for biased selection and—an important point—the two sources of difference were closely related. The changes tended to occur in those areas where the groups differed most initially.

Reliability results for a sample of University of Minnesota freshmen tested and retested over 8–10 years are presented in Figure 3-9. Further information on this sample can be found in Table 3-58 in the validity section.

The Missouri high school seniors 10-year test-retest sample (Figure 3-10) were students in the upper half of their class; most went on to college. They were studied by Trimble (1965), and the results of his research have been presented earlier, on p. 61.

Stanford students tested four times over 19 years. Test-retest reliabilities for the Basic Scales are available over several time spans on a sample of men who were studied several times by E. K. Strong, Jr. He tested them originally as freshmen at Stanford in 1930, retested them the following year as sophomores, once more in 1939 five years after they had graduated and finally, in 1949, 15 years after they had graduated from Stanford (Strong, 1955). Table 3-32 has the mean profiles for the group at each testing and the test-retest correlations over the various intervals. The number tested varied from one time to another, and is reported at the bottom of the table for each comparison. From these data, one can draw the following conclusions:

1. On most of the scales, the mean scores of this diverse group of students resembled the norm group's mean of 50. As freshmen, their most significant deviations were their low scores on the Nature and Teaching scales, 43 and 45 respectively, and their high score of 56 on the Adventure scale.

2. Nineteen years later, when retested, their interests had shifted mainly in these same three areas and, on the Nature and Adventure scales, they closely resembled the norm group. On the Teaching scale, however, the shift had carried them beyond the norm group to a score of 53.

PROFILE— **STRONG VOCATIONAL INTEREST BLANK** —FOR MEN (Form T399)

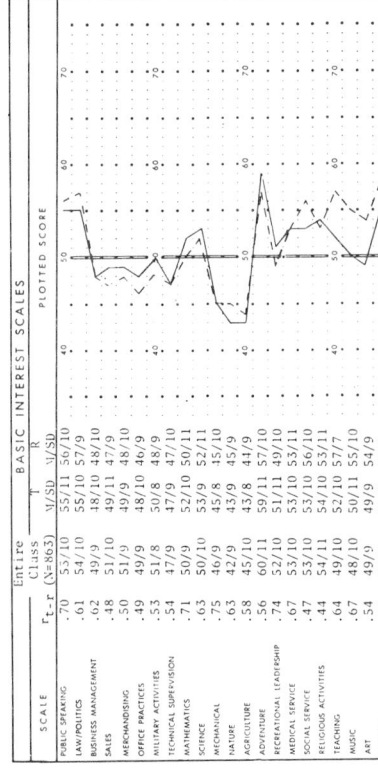

SCALE	r_{t-r}	T M/SD	R M/SD
PUBLIC SPEAKING	.71	57/11	58/10
LAW/POLITICS	.50	58/10	61/9
BUSINESS MANAGEMENT	.72	46/11	47/12
SALES	.57	45/9	45/9
MERCHANDISING	.66	45/10	45/11
OFFICE PRACTICES	.58	43/11	43/10
MILITARY ACTIVITIES	.52	45/8	46/8
TECHNICAL SUPERVISION	.52	43/11	45/12
MATHEMATICS	.71	53/10	52/10
SCIENCE	.70	53/10	52/11
MECHANICAL	.67	42/10	45/11
NATURE	.68	42/10	44/10
AGRICULTURE	.71	42/10	44/10
ADVENTURE	.64	56/12	57/12
RECREATIONAL LEADERSHIP	.81	47/11	49/11
MEDICAL SERVICE	.67	52/10	52/11
SOCIAL SERVICE	.54	51/10	53/11
RELIGIOUS ACTIVITIES	.51	51/11	50/11
TEACHING	.63	54/10	57/10
MUSIC	.60	58/10	58/9
ART	.56	53/9	56/9
WRITING	.65	60/8	62/8

DOUBLE LINE = AVERAGE SCORE FOR 650 52-YEAR-OLD MEN

FIG. 3-7. *Test-retest data over three and a half years for 189 Harvard University freshmen.*

PROFILE— **STRONG VOCATIONAL INTEREST BLANK** —FOR MEN (Form T399)

SCALE	r_{t-r}	Entire Class (N=863)	T M/SD	R M/SD
PUBLIC SPEAKING	.70	53/10	55/11	56/10
LAW/POLITICS	.61	54/10	55/10	57/9
BUSINESS MANAGEMENT	.62	49/9	48/10	48/10
SALES	.48	51/10	51/10	47/9
MERCHANDISING	.50	51/9	49/9	48/10
OFFICE PRACTICES	.49	49/9	48/10	46/9
MILITARY ACTIVITIES	.53	51/8	50/8	48/9
TECHNICAL SUPERVISION	.54	47/9	47/9	47/10
MATHEMATICS	.71	50/9	52/10	50/11
SCIENCE	.63	50/10	53/9	52/11
MECHANICAL	.75	45/8	45/8	45/10
NATURE	.63	42/9	43/9	45/9
AGRICULTURE	.58	45/10	43/8	41/9
ADVENTURE	.56	60/11	59/11	57/10
RECREATIONAL LEADERSHIP	.74	52/10	52/10	49/10
MEDICAL SERVICE	.67	53/10	53/10	53/11
SOCIAL SERVICE	.47	53/10	53/10	56/10
RELIGIOUS ACTIVITIES	.44	54/11	54/10	53/11
TEACHING	.64	49/10	52/10	52/11
MUSIC	.67	48/10	50/11	55/10
ART	.54	49/9	49/9	54/9
WRITING	.64	52/9	55/9	58/8

DOUBLE LINE = AVERAGE SCORE FOR 650 52-YEAR-OLD MEN

FIG. 3-8. *Test-retest data over three and a half years for 100 University of Minnesota College of Liberal Arts freshmen.*

PROFILE— **STRONG VOCATIONAL INTEREST BLANK** —FOR MEN (Form T399)

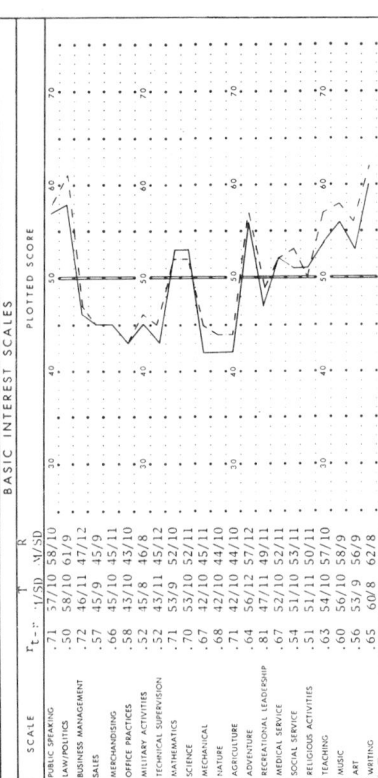

SCALE	r_{t-r}	T M/SD	R M/SD
PUBLIC SPEAKING	.67	53/11	57/11
LAW/POLITICS	.70	53/11	57/11
BUSINESS MANAGEMENT	.46	49/10	50/10
SALES	.38	53/10	48/10
MERCHANDISING	.52	50/10	50/10
OFFICE PRACTICES	.56	51/10	46/10
MILITARY ACTIVITIES	.43	53/9	50/9
TECHNICAL SUPERVISION	.37	48/10	47/11
SCIENCE	.60	52/10	53/9
MECHANICAL	.72	48/10	48/11
NATURE	.64	42/10	45/11
AGRICULTURE	.53	43/10	44/10
ADVENTURE	.47	58/11	57/11
RECREATIONAL LEADERSHIP	.65	52/10	50/10
MEDICAL SERVICE	.56	52/10	55/10
SOCIAL SERVICE	.44	52/10	52/10
RELIGIOUS ACTIVITIES	.38	52/10	53/11
TEACHING	.36	45/9	53/9
MUSIC	.55	46/10	51/9
ART	.57	45/8	50/10
WRITING	.63	49/9	53/10

DOUBLE LINE = AVERAGE SCORE FOR 650 52-YEAR-OLD MEN

FIG. 3-9. *Test-retest data over eight to ten years for 171 Minnesota high school seniors.*

PROFILE— **STRONG VOCATIONAL INTEREST BLANK** —FOR MEN (Form T399)

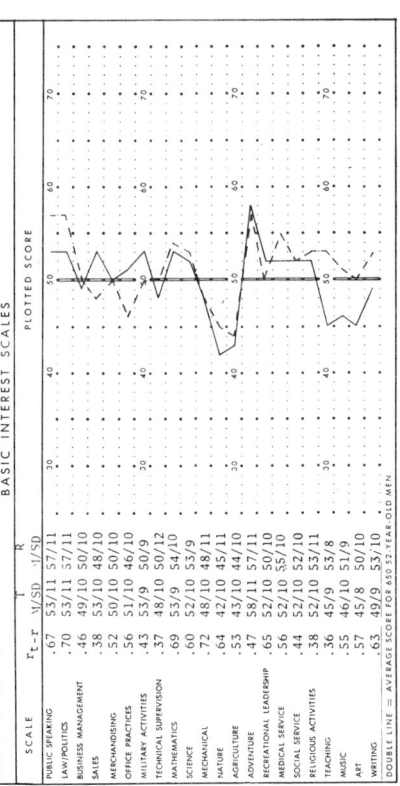

SCALE	r_{t-r}	T M/SD	R M/SD
PUBLIC SPEAKING	.59	54/11	56/11
LAW/POLITICS	.38	52/11	57/10
BUSINESS MANAGEMENT	.45	49/10	52/11
SALES	.54	52/11	49/10
MERCHANDISING	.45	50/10	51/11
OFFICE PRACTICES	.49	49/10	46/10
MILITARY ACTIVITIES	.41	52/9	49/10
TECHNICAL SUPERVISION	.40	48/10	47/11
MATHEMATICS	.66	50/11	50/11
SCIENCE	.53	52/11	51/10
MECHANICAL	.66	47/11	45/11
NATURE	.64	43/10	43/11
AGRICULTURE	.65	47/12	44/11
ADVENTURE	.46	57/11	55/12
RECREATIONAL LEADERSHIP	.75	51/11	49/11
MEDICAL SERVICE	.47	51/11	51/11
SOCIAL SERVICE	.38	51/11	51/11
RELIGIOUS ACTIVITIES	.46	54/11	50/11
TEACHING	.32	45/9	53/9
MUSIC	.58	45/10	51/11
ART	.53	47/9	51/9
WRITING	.67	49/10	53/10

DOUBLE LINE = AVERAGE SCORE FOR 650 52-YEAR-OLD MEN

FIG. 3-10. *Test-retest data over ten years for 152 Missouri high school seniors.*

TABLE 3-32. BASIC SCALE MEANS, STANDARD DEVIATIONS, AND TEST-RETEST CORRELATIONS FOR STANFORD STUDENTS TESTED AS FRESHMEN, SOPHOMORES, FIVE YEARS AFTER GRADUATION, AND FIFTEEN YEARS AFTER GRADUATION

	1930 Mean	1930 SD	'30-'31 r_{tr}	1931 Mean	1931 SD	'30-'39 r_{tr}	'31-'39 r_{tr}	1939 Mean	1939 SD	'30-'49 r_{tr}	'31-'49 r_{tr}	'39-'49 r_{tr}	1949 Mean	1949 SD
Public Speaking	52.2	9.8	.79	52.8	9.8	.51	.57	52.3	9.5	.54	.59	.66	52.1	9.7
Law/Politics	52.2	9.7	.79	53.8	10.1	.54	.56	53.6	9.1	.51	.56	.66	53.6	9.8
Business Management	49.2	10.3	.76	51.1	10.5	.54	.51	52.4	10.5	.48	.55	.78	51.9	10.2
Sales	47.9	8.7	.70	48.9	9.3	.48	.49	47.8	9.3	.46	.50	.81	48.5	9.6
Merchandising	50.3	10.2	.72	51.5	10.7	.52	.57	51.7	10.8	.51	.56	.81	51.3	10.6
Office Practices	51.2	10.7	.69	52.3	11.2	.48	.57	51.3	10.2	.46	.54	.72	49.7	10.5
Military Activities	51.9	9.9	.78	50.4	9.8	.63	.67	49.5	10.0	.56	.62	.74	49.0	9.6
Technical Supervision	47.8	11.8	.68	49.1	10.6	.51	.51	51.4	11.1	.51	.50	.69	51.4	11.8
Mathematics	51.1	9.9	.84	51.2	9.9	.75	.71	52.7	9.2	.73	.70	.87	52.1	9.5
Science	49.2	10.4	.82	49.1	10.0	.64	.72	52.4	10.0	.65	.72	.76	51.6	9.4
Mechanical	47.1	10.5	.85	46.7	10.3	.72	.77	48.6	11.2	.72	.70	.85	49.1	11.4
Nature	43.3	10.4	.81	43.4	10.6	.62	.68	47.2	10.2	.52	.53	.72	50.1	10.3
Agriculture	47.0	9.8	.77	46.9	9.8	.61	.67	47.5	9.8	.60	.60	.76	49.1	10.5
Adventure	56.1	11.2	.75	57.3	11.4	.54	.55	52.0	11.1	.59	.55	.68	50.1	10.8
Recreational Leadership	51.3	8.8	.77	51.9	9.1	.57	.68	49.9	9.5	.63	.67	.79	49.1	10.2
Medical Service	48.7	10.4	.80	48.3	9.9	.66	.66	49.8	11.1	.56	.61	.76	50.6	10.0
Social Service	49.2	9.7	.70	48.6	9.7	.34	.44	48.2	9.7	.38	.49	.77	49.0	9.9
Religious Activities	45.5	9.3	.68	44.3	9.5	.36	.37	44.7	9.7	.31	.31	.56	46.1	10.2
Teaching	44.8	9.6	.69	46.6	9.9	.45	.48	50.7	8.9	.40	.53	.62	52.7	9.2
Music	48.5	8.9	.75	49.0	9.2	.58	.51	51.3	8.1	.53	.51	.63	51.8	9.0
Art	47.9	9.3	.80	48.7	9.9	.59	.60	51.5	9.8	.56	.61	.79	51.2	10.1
Writing	51.4	9.8	.79	53.5	10.0	.67	.73	53.9	10.2	.64	.72	.81	54.9	9.6
N's for test-retest correlations			253			175	159			202	178	137		
Median test-retest correlations			.77			.56	.57			.54	.56	.76		

117

PROFILE— **STRONG VOCATIONAL INTEREST BLANK** —FOR MEN (Form T399)

BASIC INTEREST SCALES

SCALE	rt-r	T M/SD	R M/SD
PUBLIC SPEAKING	.59	53/10	52/10
LAW/POLITICS	.56	54/10	54/10
BUSINESS MANAGEMENT	.55	51/11	52/10
SALES	.50	49/9	49/10
MERCHANDISING	.56	52/11	51/11
OFFICE PRACTICES	.54	53/11	50/11
MILITARY ACTIVITIES	.62	50/10	49/10
TECHNICAL SUPERVISION	.50	49/11	51/12
MATHEMATICS	.70	51/10	51/10
SCIENCE	.72	49/10	51/10
MECHANICAL	.70	47/10	49/12
NATURE	.53	43/10	50/11
AGRICULTURE	.60	47/10	49/11
ADVENTURE	.55	57/12	50/11
RECREATIONAL LEADERSHIP	.67	52/10	49/10
MEDICAL SERVICE	.61	48/10	50/10
SOCIAL SERVICE	.49	49/10	46/10
RELIGIOUS ACTIVITIES	.31	44/9	46/10
TEACHING	.53	47/10	53/9
MUSIC	.51	49/9	51/9
ART	.61	48/10	51/10
WRITING	.72	53/11	55/10

DOUBLE LINE = AVERAGE SCORE FOR 650 52-YEAR OLD MEN

FIG. 3-11. *Test-retest data over 22 years for 220 Stanford University seniors.*

PROFILE— **STRONG VOCATIONAL INTEREST BLANK** —FOR MEN (Form T399)

BASIC INTEREST SCALES

SCALE	Rt-r	T M/SD	R M/SD
PUBLIC SPEAKING	.68	53/10	53/10
LAW/POLITICS	.71	53/11	52/10
BUSINESS MANAGEMENT	.52	48/10	48/10
SALES	.44	46/8	46/9
MERCHANDISING	.50	47/9	47/10
OFFICE PRACTICES	.56	48/10	47/11
MILITARY ACTIVITIES	.63	50/10	49/10
TECHNICAL SUPERVISION	.40	47/11	49/11
MATHEMATICS	.75	50/10	53/9
SCIENCE	.76	53/10	55/9
MECHANICAL	.70	45/11	48/11
NATURE	.63	48/11	51/10
AGRICULTURE	.60	47/10	48/10
ADVENTURE	.54	52/12	46/10
RECREATIONAL LEADERSHIP	.68	50/10	46/10
MEDICAL SERVICE	.73	53/11	54/11
SOCIAL SERVICE	.48	50/10	50/11
RELIGIOUS ACTIVITIES	.47	47/12	48/12
TEACHING	.47	52/10	53/9
MUSIC	.66	53/8	50/9
ART	.56	51/9	50/9
WRITING	.67	54/9	54/9

DOUBLE LINE = AVERAGE SCORE FOR 650 52-YEAR OLD MEN

FIG. 3-12. *Test-retest data over 22 years for 191 Stanford University graduate students.*

PROFILE— **STRONG VOCATIONAL INTEREST BLANK** —FOR MEN (Form T399)

BASIC INTEREST SCALES

SCALE	rt-r	T M/SD	R M/SD
PUBLIC SPEAKING	.46	54/9	57/10
LAW/POLITICS	.25	52/10	56/9
BUSINESS MANAGEMENT	.49	50/10	53/10
SALES	.37	50/10	51/10
MERCHANDISING	.49	51/11	53/10
OFFICE PRACTICES	.48	52/11	51/11
MILITARY ACTIVITIES	.35	52/10	53/10
TECHNICAL SUPERVISION	.31	44/10	47/10
MATHEMATICS	.63	45/10	48/11
SCIENCE	.49	49/10	50/10
MECHANICAL	.61	44/9	45/10
NATURE	.37	44/9	47/9
AGRICULTURE	.40	43/8	44/9
ADVENTURE	.44	51/11	51/11
RECREATIONAL LEADERSHIP	.50	52/9	50/10
MEDICAL SERVICE	.36	52/11	53/10
SOCIAL SERVICE	.35	54/9	56/10
RELIGIOUS ACTIVITIES	.46	52/11	53/13
TEACHING	.35	47/10	54/8
MUSIC	.66	53/10	53/11
ART	.45	49/10	52/11
WRITING	.57	55/9	57/10

DOUBLE LINE = AVERAGE SCORE FOR 650 52-YEAR OLD MEN

FIG. 3-13. *Test-retest data over 26 years for 93 University of Minnesota freshman men.*

PROFILE— **STRONG VOCATIONAL INTEREST BLANK** —FOR MEN (Form T399)

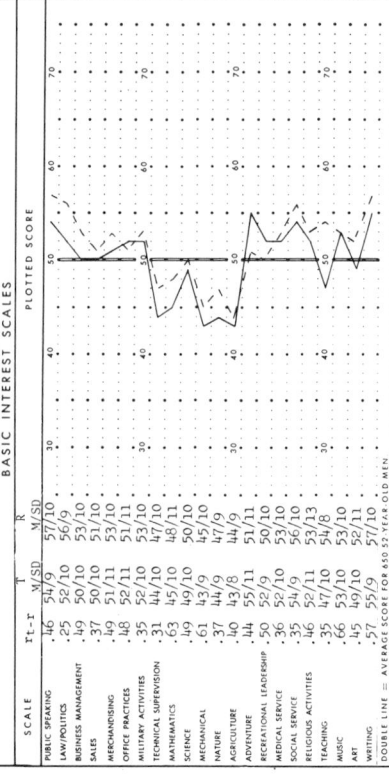

BASIC INTEREST SCALES

SCALE	T M/SD	R M/SD
PUBLIC SPEAKING	49/10	51/9
LAW/POLITICS	47/9	49/10
BUSINESS MANAGEMENT	49/10	51/10
SALES	48/9	51/10
MERCHANDISING	47/10	49/9
OFFICE PRACTICES	49/10	48/9
MILITARY ACTIVITIES	55/10	53/10
TECHNICAL SUPERVISION	54/10	55/10
MATHEMATICS	57/5	57/6
SCIENCE	52/9	53/8
MECHANICAL	55/8	54/8
NATURE	41/11	46/11
AGRICULTURE	45/10	47/10
ADVENTURE	56/12	52/10
RECREATIONAL LEADERSHIP	49/10	48/9
MEDICAL SERVICE	46/9	48/10
SOCIAL SERVICE	47/9	49/9
RELIGIOUS ACTIVITIES	49/10	50/10
TEACHING	45/10	49/10
MUSIC	47/9	49/9
ART	45/9	47/10
WRITING	47/9	48/9

DOUBLE LINE = AVERAGE SCORE FOR 650 52 YEAR OLD MEN

FIG. 3-14. *Test-retest data over 31 years for 229 Purdue University engineering freshmen.*

3. If we assume that a three-point change is the smallest difference worth attending to, the following shifts occurred over time within this sample.

Gains		Losses	
Teaching	8 points	Adventure	6 points
Nature	7 points	Military Activities	3 points
Music	4 points		
Writing	4 points		
Art	3 points		
Business Management	3 points		
Technical Supervision	3 points		

These changes are very similar to those found among the other college educated test-retest samples; perhaps "middle-aging intellectual responsibility" is a descriptive summary of those trends.

4. Their scores on the remaining scales over this 19-year period changed very little; interests in areas such as Public Speaking, Mathematics, Science, and Religious Activities were, as measured by these scales, surprisingly constant.

5. Among the test-retest correlations reported at the bottom of Table 3-32, the most intriguing finding was that the stability over the ten-year adult span, 1939–1949 ($r = .76$), was equal to the one-year freshman-sophomore period ($r = .77$)—further support for the familiar finding that interests are remarkably stable after age 25.

Data from two other samples of Stanford students tested and retested are reported in Figures 3-11 and 3-12. The first were tested during their senior year (1927) and retested 22 years later in 1949. The second sample were tested as graduate students in 1927 and also retested in 1949 (see Strong, 1955).

In 1936, many of the students entering the University of Minnesota were subjects in a study of the effectiveness of counseling (Williamson and Bordin, 1937). Several of them completed the SVIB as part of that counseling. In 1962, these men were located again to assess the long-term impact of their earlier counseling and retested with the SVIB. Their results are presented in Figure 3-13.

Freshman students entering the engineering program at Purdue were tested in 1935 and retested in 1966, 31 years later (Benjamin, 1967). Data from that sample are in Figure 3-14.

Medical School Students Tested as Freshmen, Retested as Seniors

The Medical School four-year test-retest means (Figure 3-15) are based on the 2,800 students from 26 medical schools in the Association of Ameri-

Fig. 3-15 (top left)

PROFILE— STRONG VOCATIONAL INTEREST BLANK —FOR MEN (Form T399)

BASIC INTEREST SCALES

SCALE	Test Mean	Retest Mean
PUBLIC SPEAKING	57	57
LAW/POLITICS	56	58
BUSINESS MANAGEMENT	47	46
SALES	47	47
MERCHANDISING	47	46
OFFICE PRACTICES	44	43
MILITARY ACTIVITIES	50	49
TECHNICAL SUPERVISION	48	48
MATHEMATICS	54	53
SCIENCE	58	55
MECHANICAL	48	48
NATURE	49	49
AGRICULTURE	48	48
ADVENTURE	57	59
RECREATIONAL LEADERSHIP	52	51
MEDICAL SERVICE	65	62
SOCIAL SERVICE	58	52
RELIGIOUS ACTIVITIES	57	56
TEACHING	55	56
MUSIC	56	56
ART	54	54
WRITING	56	56

DOUBLE LINE = AVERAGE SCORE FOR 650 52-YEAR-OLD MEN.

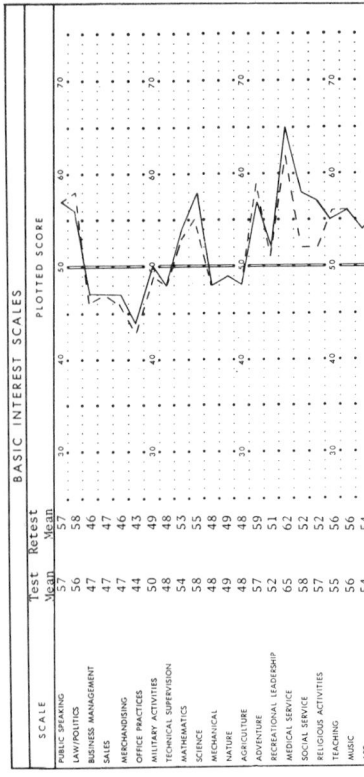

FIG. 3-15. Test-retest data over three and a half years for 2,800 Medical School freshmen from 26 medical schools.

Fig. 3-16 (top right)

PROFILE— STRONG VOCATIONAL INTEREST BLANK —FOR MEN (Form T399)

BASIC INTEREST SCALES

SCALE	$r_{t\text{-}r}$	T M/SD	R M/SD
PUBLIC SPEAKING	.81	56/11	56/11
LAW/POLITICS	.62	55/9	56/8
BUSINESS MANAGEMENT	.67	47/9	46/10
SALES	.70	47/9	47/9
MERCHANDISING	.65	48/10	46/10
OFFICE PRACTICES	.60	46/8	44/9
MILITARY ACTIVITIES	.63	51/9	49/8
TECHNICAL SUPERVISION	.45	49/9	49/11
MATHEMATICS	.79	56/6	55/7
SCIENCE	.63	60/6	57/8
MECHANICAL	.67	50/8	49/10
NATURE	.60	50/7	49/8
AGRICULTURE	.61	46/9	47/9
ADVENTURE	.65	58/10	61/11
RECREATIONAL LEADERSHIP	.75	53/9	52/9
MEDICAL SERVICE	.59	67/4	64/6
SOCIAL SERVICE	.68	60/10	53/11
RELIGIOUS ACTIVITIES	.68	60/12	57/12
TEACHING	.63	56/8	56/8
MUSIC	.72	56/9	56/9
ART	.81	53/9	53/9
WRITING	.69	56/8	55/8

DOUBLE LINE = AVERAGE SCORE FOR 650 52-YEAR-OLD MEN.

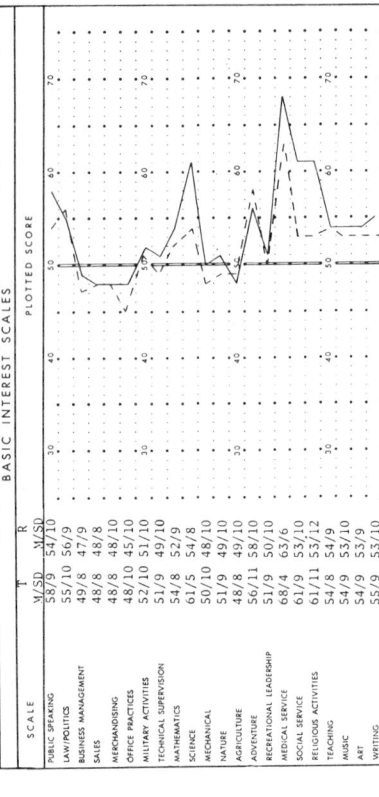

FIG. 3-16. Test-retest data over three and a half years for 91 University of Minnesota Medical School students.

Fig. 3-17 (bottom left)

PROFILE— STRONG VOCATIONAL INTEREST BLANK —FOR MEN (Form T399)

BASIC INTEREST SCALES

SCALE	T M/SD	R M/SD
PUBLIC SPEAKING	57/9	58/10
LAW/POLITICS	58/9	61/9
BUSINESS MANAGEMENT	45/9	46/9
SALES	45/7	45/9
MERCHANDISING	44/8	45/10
OFFICE PRACTICES	41/8	40/8
MILITARY ACTIVITIES	48/8	47/9
TECHNICAL SUPERVISION	47/10	48/10
MATHEMATICS	57/5	56/7
SCIENCE	59/6	56/8
MECHANICAL	50/8	48/9
NATURE	50/9	51/10
AGRICULTURE	49/9	50/10
ADVENTURE	55/11	58/11
RECREATIONAL LEADERSHIP	51/10	51/11
MEDICAL SERVICE	64/5	60/7
SOCIAL SERVICE	58/10	53/10
RELIGIOUS ACTIVITIES	54/13	50/12
TEACHING	59/8	58/9
MUSIC	60/6	60/7
ART	57/8	58/8
WRITING	61/7	61/7

DOUBLE LINE = AVERAGE SCORE FOR 650 52-YEAR-OLD MEN.

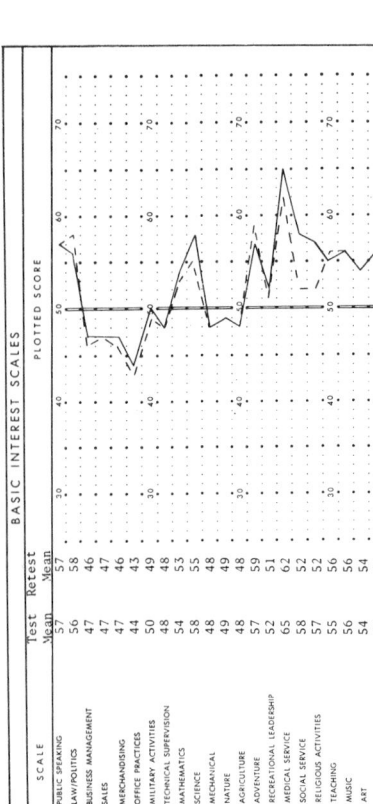

FIG. 3-17. Test-retest data over three and a half years for 106 Medical School "A" freshmen.

Fig. 3-18 (bottom right)

PROFILE— STRONG VOCATIONAL INTEREST BLANK —FOR MEN (Form T399)

BASIC INTEREST SCALES

SCALE	T M/SD	R M/SD
PUBLIC SPEAKING	58/9	54/10
LAW/POLITICS	55/10	56/9
BUSINESS MANAGEMENT	49/8	47/9
SALES	48/8	48/8
MERCHANDISING	48/8	48/10
OFFICE PRACTICES	48/10	45/10
MILITARY ACTIVITIES	52/10	51/10
TECHNICAL SUPERVISION	51/9	49/10
MATHEMATICS	54/8	52/9
SCIENCE	61/5	54/8
MECHANICAL	50/10	48/10
NATURE	51/9	49/10
AGRICULTURE	48/8	49/10
ADVENTURE	56/11	58/10
RECREATIONAL LEADERSHIP	51/9	50/10
MEDICAL SERVICE	68/4	63/6
SOCIAL SERVICE	61/9	53/10
RELIGIOUS ACTIVITIES	61/11	53/12
TEACHING	54/8	54/9
MUSIC	54/9	53/10
ART	54/9	53/9
WRITING	55/9	53/10

DOUBLE LINE = AVERAGE SCORE FOR 650 52-YEAR-OLD MEN.

FIG. 3-18. Test-retest data over three and a half years for 82 Medical School "B" freshmen.

can Medical Colleges' longitudinal study (Hutchins, 1964). The noteworthy changes were the substantial decreases in mean scores on the following scales:

Social Service .... 6 points
Religious Activities .... 5 points
Medical Service .... 3 points
Science .... 3 points

These decreases were on scales that had quite high averages initially, and might be explained by simple regression toward the mean. But that phenomenon is not common among the Basic Scale scores, as the remainder of the test-retest profiles show; rather, these changes are specific to medical school students.

Mean profiles for the freshman class from three individual medical schools are presented in Figures 3-16, 3-17, and 3-18 to demonstrate that these changes are consistent over all, or most, medical schools. The first school is the Universty of Minnesota; the other two were selected for geographical diversity and also because of their difference in "perceived excellence of medical education." Because the changes in mean scores were somewhat unexpected, these three replications have been presented here to demonstrate that it was a general trend. Whether one looks at Minnesota, or the "better" school, or the "poorer" school, the same shifts appeared. Over the four years of medical school, the main changes were decreases in Social Service, Medical Service, Science, and Religious Activities scales and a mild increase on the Adventure scale.

The two-point gain on the Adventure scale, though a small change, is significant here because virtually every other sample tested and retested over the span of a few years or more has shown a decrease on that scale. This pattern of changes once again suggests strongly that the medical school students are relaxing after their arduous four years; more has been said on this point on pp. 19 and 71.

Occupational Samples Tested and Retested: 11 to 30 Years

Figure 3-19 contains the mean test-retest profiles over 11 years for a small group of Certified Public Accountants, studied by Rhode (1966). The test statistics are based on SVIBs completed by these men when they were high school seniors or college freshmen; the retest statistics are based on SVIBs completed by them after they had entered their profession, on the average, 11 years after they had entered college. All of them were from Minnesota, and were practicing in the state when retested.

PROFILE— STRONG VOCATIONAL INTEREST BLANK —FOR MEN (Form T399)

BASIC INTEREST SCALES

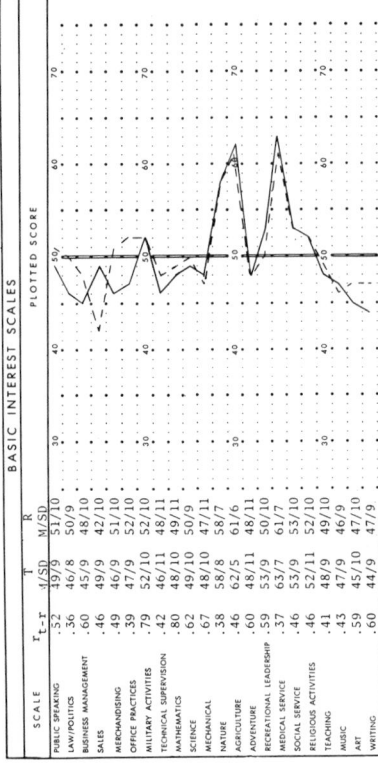

SCALE	r_t-r	T M/SD	R M/SD
PUBLIC SPEAKING	.50	51/9	57/9
LAW/POLITICS	.36	54/10	60/7
BUSINESS MANAGEMENT	.06	54/9	56/6
SALES	.17	59/9	51/10
MERCHANDISING	.12	57/9	56/8
OFFICE PRACTICES	.38	57/10	53/8
MILITARY ACTIVITIES	.41	52/10	48/8
TECHNICAL SUPERVISION	.09	47/8	46/11
MATHEMATICS	.25	54/7	55/6
SCIENCE	.49	47/11	49/9
MECHANICAL	.55	45/9	45/10
NATURE	.75	37/10	42/10
AGRICULTURE	.65	56/12	41/12
ADVENTURE	.35	51/11	50/10
RECREATIONAL LEADERSHIP	.68	47/10	51/11
MEDICAL SERVICE	.60	50/11	52/10
SOCIAL SERVICE	.57	52/11	53/10
RELIGIOUS ACTIVITIES	.45	51/8	51/8
TEACHING	.50	45/9	51/10
MUSIC	.62	46/10	51/10
ART	.29	42/8	46/10
WRITING	.49	46/8	49/9

DOUBLE LINE = AVERAGE SCORE FOR 650 52-YEAR-OLD MEN

FIG. 3-19. Test-retest data over 11 years for 37 high school seniors who became Certified Public Accountants.

PROFILE— STRONG VOCATIONAL INTEREST BLANK —FOR MEN (Form T399)

BASIC INTEREST SCALES

SCALE	r_t-r	T M/SD	R M/SD
PUBLIC SPEAKING	.52	49/9	51/10
LAW/POLITICS	.36	46/8	50/9
BUSINESS MANAGEMENT	.60	45/9	48/10
SALES	.46	49/9	42/10
MERCHANDISING	.49	46/9	51/10
OFFICE PRACTICES	.39	47/9	52/10
MILITARY ACTIVITIES	.79	52/10	52/10
TECHNICAL SUPERVISION	.42	46/11	48/11
MATHEMATICS	.80	48/10	49/11
SCIENCE	.62	49/10	50/9
MECHANICAL	.67	48/10	47/11
NATURE	.38	58/8	58/7
AGRICULTURE	.60	62/5	61/6
ADVENTURE	.37	63/7	61/7
RECREATIONAL LEADERSHIP	.59	53/9	50/10
MEDICAL SERVICE	.46	53/9	53/10
SOCIAL SERVICE	.46	52/11	52/10
RELIGIOUS ACTIVITIES	.46	48/9	49/10
TEACHING	.41	47/9	46/9
MUSIC	.43	45/10	47/10
ART	.59	45/10	47/10
WRITING	.60	44/9	47/9

DOUBLE LINE = AVERAGE SCORE FOR 650 52-YEAR-OLD MEN

FIG. 3-20. Test-retest data over 17 years for 98 Iowa veterinarians.

PROFILE— STRONG VOCATIONAL INTEREST BLANK —FOR MEN (Form T399)

BASIC INTEREST SCALES

SCALE	r_t-r	T M/SD	R M/SD
PUBLIC SPEAKING	.70	52/3	52/10
LAW/POLITICS	.62	51/10	50/10
BUSINESS MANAGEMENT	.67	44/10	45/10
SALES	.58	43/8	44/8
MERCHANDISING	.61	44/9	44/9
OFFICE PRACTICES	.62	46/9	44/9
MILITARY ACTIVITIES	.76	48/9	49/9
TECHNICAL SUPERVISION	.44	47/11	47/10
MATHEMATICS	.79	53/9	54/9
SCIENCE	.59	59/6	59/6
MECHANICAL	.82	48/10	48/10
NATURE	.63	49/10	50/9
AGRICULTURE	.64	43/10	44/9
ADVENTURE	.67	48/11	45/10
RECREATIONAL LEADERSHIP	.73	44/9	41/10
MEDICAL SERVICE	.68	55/7	55/6
SOCIAL SERVICE	.57	49/9	51/9
RELIGIOUS ACTIVITIES	.54	43/9	46/10
TEACHING	.63	57/7	56/7
MUSIC	.68	54/9	53/9
ART	.69	55/8	53/9
WRITING	.64	58/7	57/7

DOUBLE LINE = AVERAGE SCORE FOR 650 52-YEAR-OLD MEN

FIG. 3-21. Test-retest data over 17 years for 92 psychologists.

PROFILE— STRONG VOCATIONAL INTEREST BLANK —FOR MEN (Form T399)

BASIC INTEREST SCALES

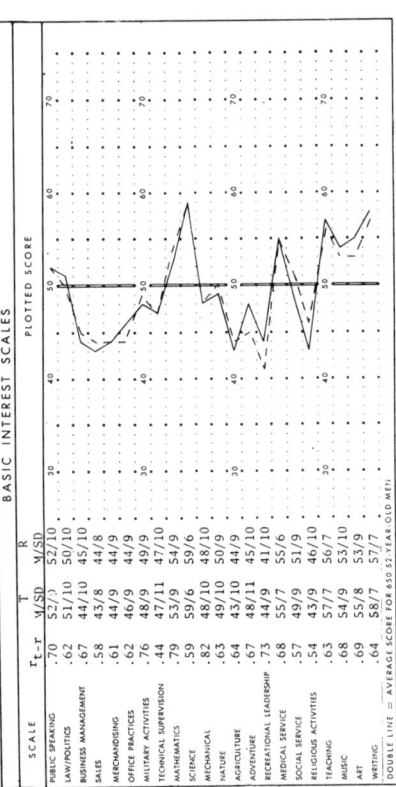

SCALE	r_t-r	T M/SD	R M/SD
PUBLIC SPEAKING	.40	60/8	62/6
LAW/POLITICS	.67	53/8	56/9
BUSINESS MANAGEMENT	.32	58/7	58/9
SALES	.63	55/10	56/9
MERCHANDISING	.40	55/8	55/8
OFFICE PRACTICES	.50	54/10	56/10
MILITARY ACTIVITIES	.66	51/10	50/9
TECHNICAL SUPERVISION	.61	47/12	49/12
MATHEMATICS	.82	49/10	49/10
SCIENCE	.78	49/9	47/9
MECHANICAL	.79	47/11	47/10
NATURE	.75	51/10	52/8
AGRICULTURE	.73	48/10	49/9
ADVENTURE	.53	46/10	45/10
RECREATIONAL LEADERSHIP	.72	52/9	51/8
MEDICAL SERVICE	.65	54/9	52/8
SOCIAL SERVICE	.14	70/5	72/4
RELIGIOUS ACTIVITIES	.32	71/7	72/6
TEACHING	.62	56/9	58/8
MUSIC	.68	54/8	54/9
ART	.12	55/8	52/8
WRITING	.72	57/8	58/8

DOUBLE LINE = AVERAGE SCORE FOR 650 52-YEAR-OLD MEN

FIG. 3-22. Test-retest data over 24 years for 47 YMCA secretaries.

Test-retest data are available for four samples containing men initially tested as adults as part of their occupation's criterion group, and retested some time later for other purposes. Those samples are:

1. 92 veterinarians, retested over a 17-year interval 1949–66 (Figure 3-20). (Hannum, 1950; Hannum and Alsip, 1966.)

2. 92 psychologists, retested over a 17-year average interval, 1927, 1935–48 (Figure 3-21).

3. 47 YMCA secretaries, retested over a 22-year interval 1927, 1931–51 (Figure 3-22). (Verburg, 1952.)

4. 48 bankers, retested over a 30-year interval, 1934–64 (Figure 3-23). (Campbell, 1966.)

More information on these samples can be found in Chapter 2.

The Basic Interest Scale profiles for these four occupational samples demonstrate the degree of stability over long time spans among adults. The means were stable; the highs stayed high, the lows remained low and, except in the Veterinarian sample, there were hardly any changes exceeding two standard score points.

Teenagers, Categorized by Eventual Educational Achievement, Retested 36 Years Later

Figures 3-24 through 3-30 contain test-retest profiles for samples of males first tested in 1930–31 when they were 16 years old, and retested 36 years later during 1966–68 when they were about 52 years old. The total sample was collected by E. K. Strong, Jr. for various of his research projects, especially his study of the relationship between age and measured interests (Strong, 1931). Of the 1,943 boys tested in 1930, 1,214 (63 percent) were retested in 1966–67. Twenty-five percent could not be located currently, four percent refused to cooperate in this study, and eight percent were deceased.

Conclusions from the Basic Interest Scale Test-Retest Data

Although each of the test-retest profiles in Figures 3-2 through 3-30 is worthy of scanning by anyone interested in the stability of interests, general trends are difficult to see by looking at each sample separately. To help in intrepretation, Table 3-33 has been prepared. Here are listed several basic facts for each sample, including the average age when first tested, the test-retest interval, the median reliability coefficient, when available, for both the Basic Interest Scales and the Occupational Scales, and the sizable mean changes between test and retest.

BASIC INTEREST SCALES

PLOTTED SCORE

SCALE	r_t-r	T M/SD	R M/SD
PUBLIC SPEAKING	.30	49/8	50/9
LAW/POLITICS	.59	51/7	50/10
BUSINESS MANAGEMENT	.35	52/7	49/9
SALES	.62	53/9	52/10
MERCHANDISING	.24	51/8	49/9
OFFICE PRACTICES	.42	60/8	59/9
MILITARY ACTIVITIES	.59	51/10	48/9
TECHNICAL SUPERVISION	.26	45/10	42/10
MATHEMATICS	.58	50/9	50/10
SCIENCE	.67	44/8	42/10
MECHANICAL	.72	45/11	43/11
NATURE	.61	52/8	50/11
AGRICULTURE	.39	49/8	49/9
ADVENTURE	.42	44/9	39/7
RECREATIONAL LEADERSHIP	.55	46/8	45/10
MEDICAL SERVICE	.38	46/9	45/10
SOCIAL SERVICE	.51	51/8	53/9
RELIGIOUS ACTIVITIES	.51	50/10	52/11
TEACHING	.41	42/8	43/9
MUSIC	.66	49/11	47/10
ART	.56	47/9	45/10
WRITING	.60	46/8	46/8

DOUBLE LINE = AVERAGE SCORE FOR 650 52-YEAR-OLD MEN

FIG. 3-23. *Test-retest data over 30 years for 48 Minnesota bankers.*

BASIC INTEREST SCALES

PLOTTED SCORE

SCALE	r_t-r	T M/SD	R M/SD
PUBLIC SPEAKING	.45	47/9	50/10
LAW/POLITICS	.39	46/9	50/10
BUSINESS MANAGEMENT	.32	44/10	50/10
SALES	.29	46/9	50/10
MERCHANDISING	.32	44/10	50/10
OFFICE PRACTICES	.34	48/12	50/10
MILITARY ACTIVITIES	.33	51/10	50/10
TECHNICAL SUPERVISION	.20	45/12	50/10
MATHEMATICS	.48	45/10	50/10
SCIENCE	.43	45/10	50/10
MECHANICAL	.47	48/9	50/10
NATURE	.42	44/10	50/10
AGRICULTURE	.40	50/10	50/10
ADVENTURE	.34	57/11	50/10
RECREATIONAL LEADERSHIP	.50	53/10	50/10
MEDICAL SERVICE	.35	45/10	50/10
SOCIAL SERVICE	.26	48/9	50/10
RELIGIOUS ACTIVITIES	.31	47/10	50/10
TEACHING	.28	40/9	50/10
MUSIC	.43	46/10	50/10
ART	.38	46/9	50/10
WRITING	.46	45/9	50/10

DOUBLE LINE = AVERAGE SCORE FOR 650 52-YEAR-OLD MEN

FIG. 3-24. *Test-retest data over 36 years for 1,214 California teenagers.*

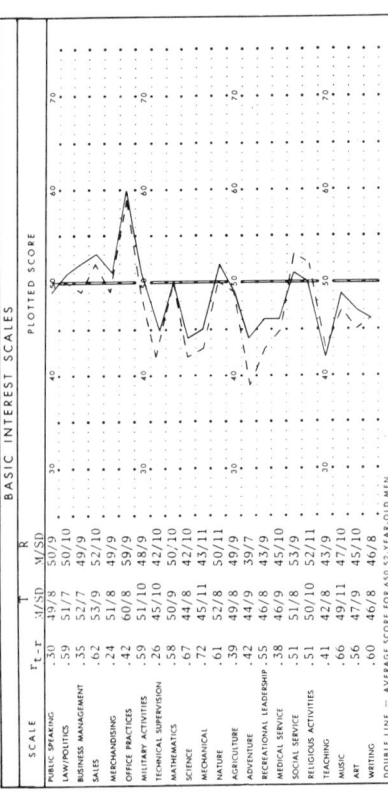

FIG. 3-25. *Test-retest data over 36 years for 497 California teenagers (no college).*

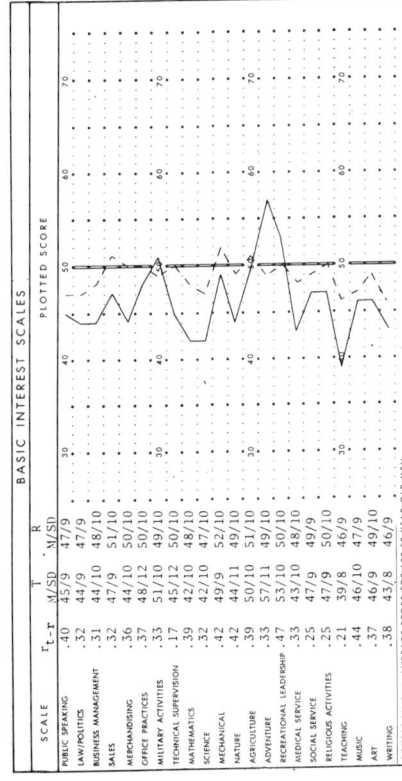

FIG. 3-26. *Test-retest data over 36 years for 214 California teenagers (B.A., B.S. degrees).*

TABLE 3-33. SUMMARY OF THE TEST-RETEST STATISTICS FOR THE MEN'S BASIC INTEREST SCALES

le	N	Test Age	T-R Interval	Median Test-Retest Correlations Basic Scales	Occ Scales	Mean Changes of 3 points or more Increase	Decrease
Minnesota sophomores	140	19	2 weeks	.89	.91	none	none
Reserve Personnel	102	26	30 days	.88	.91	none	none
Minnesota General lege students ssentially junior ollege students)	219	18	5 months	n/a	n/a	Public Speaking 3 Business Management 3 Merchandising 3 Office Practices 3	none
Minnesota General lege students	123	18	10 years	n/a	n/a	Law/Politics 5 Public Speaking 4 Merchandising 4 Nature 4 Teaching 4 Art 4 Business Management 3 Science 3 Music 3 Writing 3	Military Activities 3
Missouri Agricultural dents	126	18	3 1/2 years	n/a	n/a	Law/Politics 4 Business Management 5 Sales 4 Merchandising 4 Adventure 4 Medical Service 4	Religious Activities 3
ard Freshmen	189	18	3 1/2 years	.65	.68	Law/Politics 3 Teaching 3 Art 3	none
Minnesota Liberal s Freshmen	100	18	3 1/2 years	.62	n/a	Teaching 5 Music 5 Art 5 Social Service 3 Writing 3	none
Minnesota Freshmen beral Arts, Engineering, d Business)	171	18	8-10 years	.56	n/a	Teaching 8 Music 5 Art 5 Public Speaking 4 Law/Politics 4 Writing 4 Nature 3 Medical Service 3	Sales 5 Office Practices 5 Military Activities **3**
ouri H.S. Seniors	152	17	10 years	.51	n/a	Teaching 8 Music 6 Law/Politics 5 Art 4 Writing 4 Business Management 3	Religious Activities 4 Sales 3 Office Practices 3 Military Activities 3
Minnesota Liberal s Freshmen	93	18	26 years	.46	n/a	Teaching 7 Law/Politics 4 Public Speaking 3 Business Management 3 Technical Superv'n 3 Mathematics 3 Nature 3 Art 3	Adventure 4
ue Engineering Freshmen	229	18	31 years	n/a	n/a	Nature 5 Teaching 4 Sales 3	Adventure 4

(table continued next page)

TABLE 3-33 (*continued*)

Sample	N	Test Age	T-R Interval	Median Test-Retest Correlations Basic Scales	Occ Scales	Mean Changes of 3 points or more Increase	Decrease
Stanford University Freshmen retested as sophomores (1931)	253	18	1 year	.77	n/a	Writing 3	none
retested 5 years after graduation (1939)	175	18	9 years	.56	n/a	Teaching 6 Nature 4 Art 4 Business Management 3 Technical Superv'n 3 Science 3 Music 3 Writing 3	Adventure 4
retested 15 years after graduation (1949)	202	18	19 years	.54	n/a	Teaching 8 Nature 7 Music 4 Writing 4 Business Management 3 Technical Superv'n 3 Science 3 Art 3	Adventure 6
5 years (1939) vs 15 years (1949) after graduation	137	27	10 years	.76	n/a	none	none
Stanford Seniors (1927-1949)	220	22	22 years	.56	n/a	Nature 7 Teaching 6 Art 3	Adventure Office Practices Recreational Ldrship
Stanford Graduate students	191	c.25	22 years	.62	n/a	Mathematics 3 Mechanical 3 Nature 3	Adventure Recreational Ldrship Music
U of Minnesota Medical School freshmen	91	21	3 1/2 years	.66	.73	Adventure 3	Social Service Science Medical Service Religious Activities
Medical School "A" freshmen	106	21	3 1/2 years	n/a	.68	Law/Politics 3 Adventure 3	Social Service Medical Service Religious Activities Science
Medical School "B" freshmen	82	21	3 1/2 years	n/a	.65	(Adventure 2)	Social Service Religious Activities Science Medical Service Public Speaking Office Practices
Medical School freshmen from 26 schools (1956-1960)	2800	21	3 1/2 years	n/a	n/a	(Adventure 2)	Social Service Religious Activities Science Medical Service
Minnesota CPA's*	37	18	11 years	.41	n/a	Public Speaking 6 Law/Politics 6 Teaching 6 Nature 5 Music 5	Sales 6
Iowa Veterinarians	98	32	17 years	.48	n/a	Merchandising 5 Office Practices 5 Law/Politics 4 Business Management 3 Writing 3	Sales 5 Recreational Ldrship

TABLE 3-33 (*continued*)

le	N	Test Age	T-R Interval	Mean Test-Retest Correlations Basic Scales	Occ Scales	Mean Changes of 3 points or more Increase		Decrease	
hologists	90		17 years	.64	n/a	Religious Activ.	3	Adventure	3
								Recreational Ldrship	3
Secretaries	47	40	22 years	.66	.61	none		none	
esota Bankers	48		30 years	.53	.56	none		Adventure	4
								Business Management	3
								Military Activities	3
								Technical Supervision	3
								Recreational Ldrship	3
fornia Teenagers-Total*	1214	16	36 years	.38	n/a	Teaching	10	Adventure	7
						Business Management	6		
						Merchandising	6		
						Nature	6		
						Technical Superv'n	5		
						Mathematics	5		
						Science	5		
						Medical Service	5		
						Writing	5		
ollege*	497	16	36 years	.34	.38	Teaching	7	Adventure	8
						Merchandising	6		
						Mathematics	6		
						Science	5		
						Nature	5		
						Medical Service	5		
						Technical Superv'n	5		
, B.S. degree*	214	16	36 years	.36	.44	Teaching	10	Adventure	6
						Business Management	7		
						Nature	7		
						Law/Politics	6		
						Merchandising	6		
						Music	6		
						Art	6		
						Writing	6		
						Public Speaking	5		
						Technical Superv'n	5		
, M.S. degree*	72	16	36 years	.38	.48	Teaching	12	none	
						Writing	8		
						Business Management	8		
						Technical Superv'n	7		
						Law/Politics	6		
						Medical Service	6		
						Social Service	6		
						Public Speaking	5		
						Nature	5		
						Art	5		
degree*	17	16	36 years	.42	.43	Teaching	16	none	
						Nature	8		
						Music	8		
						Writing	8		
						Art	7		
						Medical Service	6		
						Religious Activ.	5		
degree*	22	16	36 years	.30	.43	Teaching	8	Adventure	7
						Nature	7	Military Activities	5
						Technical Superv'n	5		
						Medical Service	5		
., Ed.D degree*	27	16	36 years	.50	.58	Teaching	14	Adventure	9
						Music	8		

*For these samples, only changes of 5 points or more are listed

PROFILE— **STRONG VOCATIONAL INTEREST BLANK** —FOR MEN (Form T399)

BASIC INTEREST SCALES

SCALE	r_{t-r}	T M/SD	R M/SD
PUBLIC SPEAKING	.45	48/9	53/10
LAW/POLITICS	.50	47/10	53/10
BUSINESS MANAGEMENT	.32	43/9	51/11
SALES	.26	46/8	48/11
MERCHANDISING	.33	45/10	49/11
OFFICE PRACTICES	.33	46/11	50/11
MILITARY ACTIVITIES	.34	50/10	48/10
TECHNICAL SUPERVISION	.20	42/11	47/9
MATHEMATICS	.60	49/11	49/11
SCIENCE	.17	42/11	49/11
MECHANICAL	.47	44/9	47/10
NATURE	.42	45/11	53/10
AGRICULTURE	.37	48/10	47/11
ADVENTURE	.27	54/11	50/10
RECREATIONAL LEADERSHIP	.10	51/10	49/10
MEDICAL SERVICE	.34	46/10	51/10
SOCIAL SERVICE	.27	47/8	53/11
RELIGIOUS ACTIVITIES	.42	47/10	51/11
TEACHING	.43	45/10	57/10
MUSIC	.61	50/11	54/10
ART	.35	49/10	51/10
WRITING	.57	48/10	56/11

DOUBLE LINE = AVERAGE SCORE FOR 650 52-YEAR-OLD MEN

FIG. 3-27. *Test-retest data over 36 years for 72 California teenagers (M.A., M.S. degrees).*

PROFILE— **STRONG VOCATIONAL INTEREST BLANK** —FOR MEN (Form T399)

BASIC INTEREST SCALES

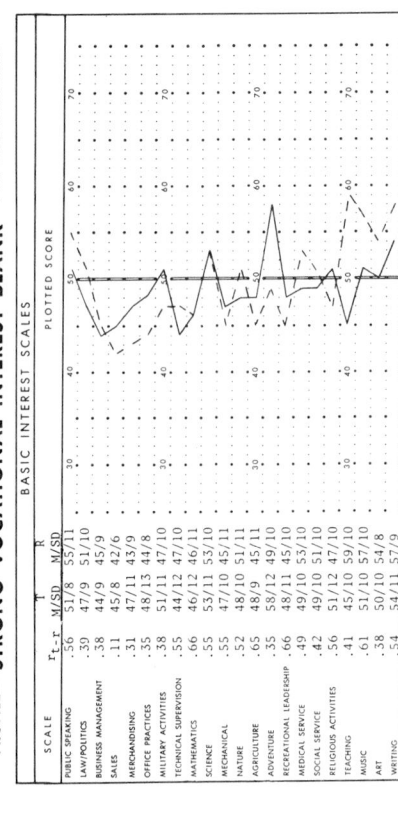

SCALE	r_{t-r}	T M/SD	R M/SD
PUBLIC SPEAKING	.60	56/9	57/9
LAW/POLITICS	.58	57/9	59/9
BUSINESS MANAGEMENT	.31	46/10	47/8
SALES	-.41	47/8	44/6
MERCHANDISING	-.24	46/11	46/8
OFFICE PRACTICES	.44	47/11	47/10
MILITARY ACTIVITIES	.28	48/6	47/8
TECHNICAL SUPERVISION	.21	44/9	47/9
MATHEMATICS	.43	48/8	51/10
SCIENCE	.21	48/9	52/6
MECHANICAL	.51	43/6	46/9
NATURE	.55	41/11	49/10
AGRICULTURE	.42	46/10	46/9
ADVENTURE	.65	53/10	51/11
RECREATIONAL LEADERSHIP	.52	51/9	50/7
MEDICAL SERVICE	-.26	48/10	54/10
SOCIAL SERVICE	-.42	50/9	52/10
RELIGIOUS ACTIVITIES	.49	44/7	49/10
TEACHING	.20	39/7	55/7
MUSIC	.42	42/6	50/7
ART	.43	45/8	52/10
WRITING	.26	51/9	59/11

DOUBLE LINE = AVERAGE SCORE FOR 650 52-YEAR-OLD MEN

FIG. 3-28. *Test-retest data over 36 years for 17 California teenagers (LL.B. degrees).*

PROFILE— **STRONG VOCATIONAL INTEREST BLANK** —FOR MEN (Form T399)

BASIC INTEREST SCALES

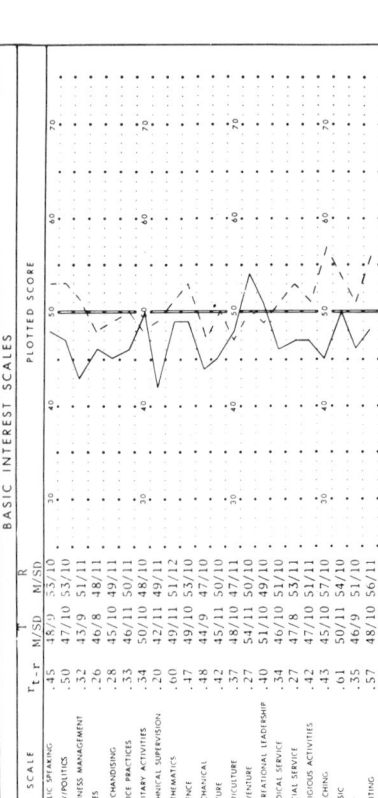

SCALE	r_{t-r}	T M/SD	R M/SD
PUBLIC SPEAKING	.30	48/10	47/10
LAW/POLITICS	.29	46/9	49/9
BUSINESS MANAGEMENT	.56	44/9	42/9
SALES	.28	45/8	46/8
MERCHANDISING	.55	43/9	44/10
OFFICE PRACTICES	.50	47/12	46/9
MILITARY ACTIVITIES	.57	55/10	50/12
TECHNICAL SUPERVISION	.00	42/10	47/9
MATHEMATICS	.29	53/8	55/7
SCIENCE	.27	54/11	58/9
MECHANICAL	.57	48/10	50/10
NATURE	.68	47/10	54/6
AGRICULTURE	.47	47/10	50/9
ADVENTURE	.52	53/8	47/10
RECREATIONAL LEADERSHIP	.75	52/10	51/8
MEDICAL SERVICE	.26	59/13	64/7
SOCIAL SERVICE	.31	50/10	53/10
RELIGIOUS ACTIVITIES	.33	48/10	51/10
TEACHING	.11	47/9	55/11
MUSIC	.14	52/11	54/10
ART	.29	49/10	53/9
WRITING	.01	46/7	49/9

DOUBLE LINE = AVERAGE SCORE FOR 650 52-YEAR-OLD MEN

FIG. 3-29. *Test-retest data over 36 years for 22 California teenagers (M.D. degrees).*

PROFILE— **STRONG VOCATIONAL INTEREST BLANK** —FOR MEN (Form T399)

BASIC INTEREST SCALES

SCALE	r_{t-r}	T M/SD	R M/SD
PUBLIC SPEAKING	.56	51/8	55/11
LAW/POLITICS	.39	47/9	51/10
BUSINESS MANAGEMENT	.38	44/9	45/9
SALES	.11	45/8	42/6
MERCHANDISING	.31	47/11	43/9
OFFICE PRACTICES	.35	48/13	44/8
MILITARY ACTIVITIES	.38	51/11	47/10
TECHNICAL SUPERVISION	.55	44/12	47/10
MATHEMATICS	.66	46/12	46/11
SCIENCE	.55	53/11	53/10
MECHANICAL	.55	47/10	45/11
NATURE	.52	48/10	45/11
AGRICULTURE	.65	48/9	45/11
ADVENTURE	.35	58/12	49/10
RECREATIONAL LEADERSHIP	.66	48/11	45/10
MEDICAL SERVICE	.49	49/10	53/10
SOCIAL SERVICE	.42	49/10	51/10
RELIGIOUS ACTIVITIES	.56	51/12	47/10
TEACHING	.41	45/10	59/10
MUSIC	.61	51/10	57/10
ART	.38	50/10	54/8
WRITING	.54	54/11	57/9

DOUBLE LINE = AVERAGE SCORE FOR 650 52-YEAR-OLD MEN

FIG. 3-30. *Test-retest data over 36 years for 27 California teenagers (Ph.D., Ed.D. degrees).*

From Table 3-33 and the test-retest profiles, the following conclusions can be drawn:

1. The stability of the Basic Interest Scale scores varies with age first tested and length of test-retest interval. Of these two factors, the former is the more crucial.

2. The magnitude of the correlations ranged from a low of approximately 40 for teenagers retested over a 36-year period to a high of about .90 for groups retested over a few weeks. For adults, the correlations rarely dropped below .50 no matter what the time span; for test-retest intervals of 20–30 years, the correlations were usually in the .55 to .65 range.

3. These test-retest correlations for the Basic Scales were slightly but consistently lower than those for the Occupational Scales, undoubtedly because the latter contained many more items, but this difference between types of scales was much less than the differences between samples of differing ages or test-retest intervals.

4. The means for all samples on most scales changed little; the majority were within three points on test and retest. There was, however, a consistent tendency for the means to increase slightly with age.

5. The most consistent and largest decrease was on the Adventure scale; mean scores on this scale dropped for every sample, excepting the medical school students. Other scales which showed fairly consistent but smaller losses were the Recreational Leadership and Military Activities and, to a lesser extent, the Sales scale.

6. Easily the largest gainer was the Teaching scale, and the gains were most prominent among those groups with the most education. The student groups gained at least one-half standard deviation on this scale and, in the most extreme case, the California teenagers who went on to earn law degrees increased their scores by 16 points, over one and one-half standard deviations. Again, the medical school students were prominent exceptions to this trend; their Teaching mean score was almost constant.

7. The other scale showing a general increase was the Nature scale, though the shifts were generally smaller than on the Teaching scale. Why this scale should show consistent gains is not obvious—perhaps it is a reaction against our increasing urbanization.

8. Other consistent increases among the student samples were on the Music, Art, and Writing scales. These "cultural" shifts should be satisfying to university faculties as they typify the liberal arts orientation of the curricula. Reasonably enough, the Purdue engineering students showed less gain than did the students from the liberal arts colleges.

9. There were other specific changes in many of the samples, but they

were specific to the group studied. The reader must scan the data to identify them for himself; most of the changes seem intuitively reasonable.

10. Attention should be drawn to the lack of increasing mean scores on the Social Service scales. Other research (e.g., Strong, 1943, 1955) has shown that scores on the Group V Occupational Scales, the Social Service grouping, tend to increase with age. The findings with the Basic Scales suggest this is because those scales include many of the items on the Teaching, Art, Music, Writing, and Nature scales, items that do increase in popularity with age and education. Responses to the specific social service items do not appear to change much.

11. The last points to be emphasized here are the general stability of the mean profiles, even when the test-retest correlations were low, and the general reasonableness of the high and low scores among the various samples. Except for the teenagers retested 36 years later, mean changes of three points (approximately one-third SD) appeared on less than one-third of the scales, but the means did vary substantially more than that between samples. On the Social Service scale, for example, the average score ranged from 47 for the Purdue engineering freshmen to 72 for the YMCA Secretaries, a spread of two and one-half standard deviations. The general finding here, even among young people and over long intervals, is that vocational interests, as reflected by responses to the SVIB, are stable, and related to career choice.

Some elaboration may be needed on this point. This general finding of stability does not mean that interests do not change; simple introspection suggests strongly that they do. What the SVIB results demonstrate is that the changes tend to be in related areas. To illustrate: while one might find the interests of an aging professor shifting from research and teaching to writing and administration, these are not large shifts relative to the entire domain of interests—they are all academic in nature. If we found the professor's interests changing to resemble those of life insurance salesmen, Army Officers, or building contractors, then those would be large shifts. But, the well-publicized exceptions notwithstanding, such changes are rare. Stability, almost to the point of rigidity, is the dominant feature.

Validity of the Basic Interest Scales

There is no single way to establish the validity of any test or inventory as no one index can adequately represent the relationship between test behavior and real world behavior. Even in those situations where the test is designed for a specific purpose, for example, in the Medical School Aptitude Test, it is not clear which aspect of medical school performance should be used as the criterion. For measures of interests, the situation is even more confusing as there are no criteria that have even the relative clarity of medical school accomplishments. How can the validity of, say, a measure of interests in Religious Activities be studied?

The establishment of validity for measures that are not oriented to specific criteria depends on the collection and organization of a vast amount of data covering several aspects of the inventory. All psychological tests and inventories have some potential validity—for persons do not give random answers—but until the relationships between the test behavior and an individual's actions are thoroughly studied, using many diverse approaches, the meaning of the scores remains obscure.

In this vein, a substantial amount of information, showing that scores on the Basic Interest Scales are related to the occupation that the individual chooses is presented here. The preceding section on reliability contained results for several occupations; many more are presented in this section. The concept of occupational membership is used here because it has proved valuable in earlier work with the SVIB; it is objective; hardly anyone finds fault with it; and it is closely related to the intended purpose of the SVIB, i.e., as an aid in vocational counseling.

Content Validity

Content validity refers to the actual content of the scales. For these Basic Scales, a certain amount of content validity is assured as each item has survived both a statistical and an intuitive screening to determine that, within each scale, the items are related. For example, one has some confidence that when a person answers "Like" or "Dislike" to the items Algebra, Arithmetic, Calculus, Geometry, Mathematics, and Physics, he is revealing something about his interests in mathematics.

However, although content validity is quite helpful in scale interpretation, by itself it reveals nothing about the relationship between an individual's interests and his actual behavior. For such information, concurrent and predictive validity statistics are needed.

Concurrent Validity: Mean Scores for 180 Occupational Samples

Concurrent validity refers to the power of the test to distinguish between specified groups at the current moment. For example, can these scales discriminate between the interests of men who *are* currently salesmen or scientists? This is in contrast to predictive validity where the issue is whether the scales can identify differences between boys who *will become* scientists or salesmen.

Sample	N	Year Tested	Investigator	Brief Description
Accountants	345	1932	E.K. Strong, Jr.	Junior accountants
Actors-1937	30	1937	E.K. Strong, Jr.	From the Pasadena Playhouse
Actors-1966	32	1966	CIMR[1]	McKnight Fellows from the Tyrone Guthrie Theatre in Minneapolis
Advertising Men-1931	169	1931	E.K. Strong, Jr.	Agency managers and account executives
Advertising Men-1968	228	1968	CIMR	Account executives listed in the Standard Directory of Advertising Agencies (June,1968)
Agricultural Extension Agents	65	1968	J.W. Longest	University of Maryland Extension personnel
Air Force Officers	200	1960	Col. Frank Winter	Air Force Officers in advanced training at Wright Patterson Air Force Base
Animal Husbandry Professors	82	1967	CIMR	University faculty members
Anthropologists	473	1967	J.E. Rossmann,O.J.Lips, & Shirley Beran	University faculty members, all Ph.D.s
Architects-1933	240	1933	E.K. Strong, Jr.	Architects, mostly from California
Architects-1968	208	1968	CIMR	Architects listed in the 1968 directory of the American Institute of Architects (AIA)
Army Officers-1950	463	1950	Army Personnel Research Office	Above average officers, mostly field grade, all West Point graduates
Army Officers-1969	712	1969	CIMR	Graduates from West Point, classes of 1950-1962
Army Sergeants	119	1969	CIMR	E-7's or higher, drawn from Washington, D.C. D.O.D. telephone directory,(1968-69)
Artists-1933	231	1933	E.K. Strong, Jr.	123 painters, 79 commercial artists, 20 sculptors and 9 cartoonists
Artists-1968	178	1968	CIMR	Artists listed in Who's Who in American Art (1966 edition)
Astronauts	16	1966	CIMR	Astronauts, mostly military officers
Astronomers	47	1967	CIMR	Drawn from Faculties in Physics and Astronomy in the United States
Authors	248	1931	E.K. Strong, Jr.	Roughly, 60 percent journalists, 40 percent authors
Bankers-1934	247	1934	E.K. Strong, Jr.	Bankers from the upper midwest, mostly from Minnesota
Bankers-1964	102	1964	CIMR	Bankers from upper midwest, mostly from Minnesota, drawn from same banks as preceding sample.
Bankers-1969	171	1969	CIMR	Presidents & vice-presidents of banks listed in Martindale, Hubbell Law Directory
Biologists	342	1959	C.A. Lindsay	All listed in American Men of Science
Business School Professors	868	1968	J.G. Rhode	Faculty from schools offering the Ph.D. in business
Business Education Teachers	323	1956	R.V. Bacon	Public school business teachers of 7 western sta
Buyers-1946	158	1946	E.K. Strong, Jr.	Buyers from Bullock's and the Emporium,both department stores in California
Buyers-1969	176	1969	CIMR	National sample of dept. store buyers drawn from Sheldon's Retail Directory (1969)

(table continued next page)

TABLE 3-34 (*continued*)

ample	N	Year Tested	Investigator	Brief Description
penters-1936	181	1936	E.K. Strong, Jr.	Union members; 55 percent from California, 24 percent from Minnesota, 21 percent miscellaneous
penters-1969	97	1969	CIMR	Drawn from city directories of 12 cities
tographers	466	1969	A.L. Benton	Civilian employees of the U.S. Army Topographic Command
s-1944	612	1944	E.K. Strong, Jr.	Senior Certified Public Accountants
-1965	304	1965	J.G. Rhode	Minnesota Certified Public Accountants
mber of Commerce Execs	400	1960	E.K. Strong, Jr.	Chamber of Commerce & Trade Assoc. executives
mists-1931	297	1931	E.K. Strong, Jr.	Industrial chemists
mists-1969	250	1969	CIMR	Listed in American Men of Science-Physical and Biological Sciences, 11th edition
ropractors	378	1969	CIMR	National sample of practicing chiropractors
onels	62	1967	CIMR	Retired Army colonels
lege Professors	421	1969	CIMR	All college or university professors, from a wide range of disciplines
munity Recreation Directors	350	1964	K.B. Roys	National sample of community recreation directors
puter Programmers	542	1964	D.K. Perry & W.M. Cannon	Nonsupervisory, experienced programmers, both scientific and business
poration Presidents-1935	169	1935	E.K. Strong, Jr.	From mostly small or medium-sized companies
poration Presidents-1965	25	1965	CIMR	Drawn from same companies as preceding sample
nty Welfare Workers	55	1946	Strate	Members of the County Welfare Merit System of Minnesota
nty Sheriffs	111	1967	R.E. Packard	County sheriffs from Utah
dit Managers	452	1958	E.K. Strong, Jr.	National sample
forth Fellows	93	1966	J.E. Rossmann & Joseph Bentley	Danforth Foundation Fellows-aspiring college professors
tal Educators	210	1969	CIMR	All on dental school faculties
tists-1932	239	1932	E.K. Strong, Jr.	Representative sample of California dentists
tists-1969	232	1969	CIMR	164 general practitioners, 68 practitioner/educators
artment Store Managers	257	1969	M.D. Dunnette	From Penney's department stores
nomists	99	1967	J.E. Rossmann & O.J. Lips	University faculty members
ctricians	120	1969	CIMR	Drawn from city directories
nentary Teachers	115	1965	C.A. Winkle	Minnesota elementary teachers
nentary Teachers	54	1965	Beulah Hegdahl	North Dakota elementary teachers
lish Teachers	223	1968	CIMR	Minnesota high school teachers
ineers-1928	513	1928	E.K. Strong, Jr.	Diverse sample of engineers
ineers-1968	1028	1968	J.C. Johnson	National sample of engineers
mers-1936	241	1936	E.K. Strong, Jr.	Farmers, mostly from Pacific Northwest
mers-1967	77	1967	K.R. Krause	South Dakota farmers
mers-1968	235	1968	D.W. Priebe	Minnesota farmers
tball Coaches	13	1966	CIMR	Taken from list of top 25 college football coaches based on their lifetime won-loss record

(table continued next page)

133

TABLE 3-34 (*continued*)

Sample	N	Year Tested	Investigator	Brief Description
Forest Service Men	406	1936	E.K. Strong, Jr.	Mostly U.S. Forest Service personnel
Food Scientists	130	1968	C.O. Willis	Mostly Ph.D.s, all in food production or processing research
Foresters	260	1968	CIMR	Listed in the directory of the Society of American Foresters
Funeral Directors-1945	360	1945	E.K. Strong, Jr.	National sample
Funeral Directors-1969	320	1969	CIMR	Members of the National Funeral Directors Association
Generals and Admirals	51	1965	CIMR	Three and four star Army generals and Navy admirals
Governors	28	1965	CIMR	Former state governors
Guidance Counselors-1950	275	c.1950	Brown	
Guidance Counselors-1968	44	1968	Janet Francis & Gloria Blanton	APGA members, all from North Carolina
High School Counselors	203	1967	H.B. Engen	Iowa high school counselors
Highway Patrolmen	288	1968	CIMR	Minnesota highway patrolmen
Interior Decorators	192	1967	CIMR	Members, American Institute of Interior Design
Interpreters	50	1966	CIMR	Language interpreters for the U.S. State Dept.
Investment Fund Managers	237	1969	CIMR	"Money Managers", those responsible for investing large sums of money
Journalists	27	1969	CIMR	British newspaper reporters
Judges	132	1967	CIMR	Federal district judges
Lawyers-1927	251	1927	E.K. Strong, Jr.	California lawyers
Lawyers-1949	79	1949	R.F. Berdie & Theda Hagenah	Minnesota lawyers
Lawyers-1969	177	1969	CIMR	Listed in the Martindale-Hubbell Law Directory (1968) Vol. I-IV
Legislators	86	1967	Richard Willow	Senators and representatives from the Minnesota State Legislature
Librarians	425	1959	J.S. Winters	Sampled from professional librarian organizations
Machinists	118	1948	E.K. Strong, Jr.	Journeyman machinists
Mathematicians-1929	181	1929	E.K. Strong, Jr.	Mostly college professors
Mathematicians-1969	223	1969	CIMR	Listed in American Men of Science-Physical and Biological Sciences, 11th edition
Math-Science Teachers-1936	289	1936	E.K. Strong, Jr.	High school math-science teachers
Math-Science Teachers-1968	463	1968	W.J. Lonner & S.E. Williamson	Drawn from NSF science institute courses
Medical Technologists	252	1968	CIMR	Members of American Society of Medical Technologists
Ministers-1927	250	1927	E.K. Strong, Jr.	Mostly west coast protestants
Ministers-1965	97	1965	CIMR	Drawn from same churches as preceding sample
Ministers-1969	498	1969	Dayton Hultgren	National sample of protestant ministers
Minneapolis Symphony	53	1966	CIMR	Members of Minneapolis Symphony Orchestra
Musicians-1952	450	1952	E.K. Strong, Jr.	Mainly performing musicians

TABLE 3-34 (*continued*)

ample	N	Year Tested	Investigator	Brief Description
sicians-1969	225	1969	CIMR	Minneapolis and St. Paul union members, and members of the Minneapolis Symphony
sic Teachers	493	1952	E.K. Strong, Jr.	Drawn from subscribers of the Music Journal
sic Teachers	150	1946	Kleist	
SA Scientists	93	1966	J.C. Johnson & M.D. Dunnette	Scientists and engineers employed by the National Aeronautics and Space Administration
AL Members	42	1966	CIMR	Members of the National Institute of Arts & Letters
vy Officers	645	1965	R.R. Stephenson & N.M. Abrahams	Career naval officers
wsmen	283	1967	CIMR	Newspaper reporters and television news broadcasters
fice Workers	326	1928	E.K. Strong, Jr.	
tometrists	405	1963	N.E. Acree	Members of the American Optometric Association
teopaths	585	1939	E.K. Strong, Jr.	
rsonnel Directors-1927	147	1927	E.K. Strong, Jr.	
rsonnel Directors-1969	231	1969	CIMR	Listed in the College Placement Annual,1969 edition- Personnel directors, personnel managers of companies with over 500 employees
troleum Engineers	385	1965	J.B. Alford	Texas petroleum engineers
armacists-1947	309	1947	M. Schwebel	New York pharmacists
armacists-1968	205	1968	CIMR	Members of the Minnesota Pharmaceutical Association
otographers	258	1967	CIMR	Mostly news photographers and photojournalists
ysical Therapists-1957	350	1957	E.K. Strong, Jr.	Members, American Physical Therapy Association
ysical Therapists-1966	72	1966	R.T. Flint	Minnesota physical therapists
ysicians-1927	175	1927	E.K. Strong, Jr.	Mainly west coast physicians
ysicians-1949	534	1949	E.K. Strong, Jr. & A.C. Tucker	Random sample of the American Medical Association
ysicians-1969	239	1969	CIMR	Random sample of the American Medical Association
ysicians; Sub-samples:				
Internists	209	1949	E.K. Strong, Jr. & A.C. Tucker	Representative sample of those boarded in designated specialty
Neurological Surgeons	48	1949	E.K. Strong, Jr. & A.C. Tucker	" "
Orthopedic Surgeons	71	1949	E.K. Strong, Jr. & A.C. Tucker	" "
Pathologists	155	1949	E.K. Strong, Jr. & A.C. Tucker	" "
Pediatricians	96	1949	E.K. Strong, Jr. & A.C. Tucker	" "
Physiatrists	460	1966	G.T. Athelstan	" "
Psychiatrists-1949	404	1949	E.K. Strong, Jr. & A.C. Tucker	" "
Psychiatrists-1967	89	1967	CIMR	Minnesota Psychiatrists, Psychotherapists and Clinical Psychologists

(*table continued next page*)

135

TABLE 3-34 (*continued*)

Sample	N	Year Tested	Investigator	Brief Description
Radiologists	111	1949	E.K. Strong, Jr. & A.C. Tucker	Representative sample of those boarded in designated specialty
Surgeons	188	1949	E.K. Strong, Jr. & A.C. Tucker	" "
Urologists	84	1949	E.K. Strong, Jr. & A.C. Tucker	" "
Physicists-1927	172	1927	E.K. Strong, Jr.	Mostly college professors
Physicists-1968	230	1968	CIMR	Drawn from Faculties in Physics and Astronomy in the U.S.
Pilots	510	1941	E.K. Strong, Jr.	Strong's original Aviator group
Policemen-1933	254	1933	E.K. Strong, Jr.	Police officers from several cities
Policemen-1968	44	1968	L.J. Klappauf	Racine, Wisconsin policemen
Policemen-1969	196	1969	CIMR	Minneapolis policemen
Political Scientists	177	1967	J.E. Rossmann & O.J. Lips	University faculty members
Priests	287	1966	Rev. Roy Lepak	Minnesota priests
Printers	270	1936	E.K. Strong, Jr.	
Production Managers	216	1935	E.K. Strong, Jr.	
Psychologists-1931	174	1931	E.K. Strong, Jr.	
Psychologists-1947	149	1947	E.K. Kelly	Veterans Administration clinical psychologists
Psychologists-1949	1045	1949	P.H. Kriedt	Ninety percent of American Psychological Association membership
Psychologists (Exp)	256	1949	P.H. Kriedt	Experimental psychologists, subset of the total group
Psychologists-1967	252	1967	CIMR	Random sample from the American Psychological Association Directory (1966 edition)
Public Administrators-1941	550	1941	E.K. Strong, Jr.	Public administrators from a variety of public agencies
Public Administrators-1969	189	1969	CIMR	Chapter officers of the American Society for Public Administrators
Pulitzer Prize winners	84	1965	CIMR	Pulitzer Prize winners, mostly journalists and novelists
Purchasing Agents-1931	219	1931	E.K. Strong, Jr.	
Purchasing Agents-1969	164	1969	CIMR	Members of Twin City Association of Purchasing Agents
Rehabilitation Counselors	272	1949	N.E. Acree	Vocational Rehabilitation counselors from the Veteran's Administration
Salesmen, Automobile	135	1929	E.K. Strong, Jr.	
Salesmen, Computer	190	1964	C.I. Stein	Control Data Corporation computer salesmen
Salesmen, Encyclopedia	49	1966	CIMR	Outstanding World Book Encyclopedia salesmen
Salesmen, Life Insurance-1931	310	1931	E.K. Strong, Jr.	
Salesmen, Life Insurance-1966	76	1966	CIMR	Life Insurance Salesmen who sold at least $2,000,000. annually

TABLE 3-34 (*continued*)

Sample	N	Year Tested	Investigator	Brief Description
Salesmen, Life Insurance-1969	250	1969	CIMR	Selected from the directory of the Minnesota State Association of Life Underwriters-- included members of the Million Dollar Club in Minnesota
Salesmen, 3M Co.	100	c.1960	W.K. Kirchner	Salesmen of the Minnesota Mining and Manufac- turing Company
Salesmen, 3M Co., applicants	100	c.1960	W.K. Kirchner	Men applying for sales positions at 3M Company
Salesmen, PG&E	179	1939	E.K. Strong, Jr.	Appliance salesmen, Pacific Gas & Electric Company, California
Salesmen, Real Estate-1932	243	1932	E.K. Strong, Jr.	California realtors
Salesmen, Real Estate-1969	175	1969	CIMR	Selected sample from the State of Minnesota roster of Licensed Real Estate Brokers and Salesmen
Salesmen, Steel	61	1966	R.F. Berdie	Structural steel salesmen
Sales Managers-1932	228	1932	E.K. Strong, Jr.	
Sales Managers-1968	199	1968	CIMR	Members, Twin City Sales and Marketing Executives Club
School Superintendents-1930	190	1930	E.K. Strong, Jr.	From cities of 10,000 or larger
School Superintendents-1965	153	1965	E.K. Strong, Jr.	Drawn from same school districts as preceding sample
School Superintendents-1969	207	1969	CIMR	Random sample of the directory of the American Association of School Administrators
Skilled Tradesmen	339	1969	CIMR	Combined samples of carpenters, electricians, and tool & die makers
Social Science Teachers - 1936	217	1936	E.K. Strong, Jr.	High school social science teachers
Social Science Teachers - 1969	239	1969	CIMR	Random sample from the directory provided by the Minnesota Department of Education
Social Workers-1953	400	1953	R.L. McCornack	National sample, most with M.A. degrees
Social Workers-1967	54	1967	CIMR	Drawn from 1966 Directory of Professional Social Workers
Sociologists	198	1965	J.E. Rossmann & O.J. Lips	University faculty members
Student Personnel Workers	192	1961	A.B. Clark III	Members, American College Personnel Association
Teaching Brothers	451	1967	Rev. O'Toole	Catholic priests, all teachers
Tool & Die Makers	122	1969	CIMR	Drawn from city directories
Unitarian Ministers-1929	69	1929	E.K. Strong, Jr.	
Unitarian Ministers-1950	113	1950	E.K. Strong, Jr.	
Veterinarians-1949	310	1949	T.E. Hannum	Iowa veterinarians
Veterinarians-1966	510	1966	T.E. Hannum & J.E. Alsip	Iowa veterinarians
Vocational Agriculture Teachers	395	1969	C.D. Norenberg	Vocational agricultural teachers from Minnesota, Iowa, and South Dakota
YMCA-Physical Directors	216	1927	E.K. Strong, Jr.	YMCA physical directors
YMCA-Secretaries	113	1927	E.K. Strong, Jr.	YMCA secretaries
YMCA Staff	184	1961	H.G. Seashore	YMCA Staff Members (comparable to combination of original physical directors and secretaries)
TOTAL	43,033			

[1]CIMR = Center for Interest Measurement Research, University of Minnesota

137

The relevant data for concurrent validity are presented in Tables 3-35 through 3-56. For each of the Basic Scales, the means of 180 occupational samples are rank-ordered, thus permitting at a glance an evaluation of the power of the scale to separate occupations.

These occupational samples represent the majority of adult men who have been tested for research purposes with the SVIB since it was first published in 1927; further information on each is listed in Table 3-34, and in Appendix B. For the most part, most of these occupational samples include men with at least three years of experience who say they like their work.

One large block of these samples came from Professor Strong's files, including those groups used to build the initial SVIB Occupational Scales, another block came from the work of the Center for Interest Measurement Research at Minnesota, and the remainder came from various other investigators working with the SVIB. Practically everyone in the latter group who was asked for his data was cooperative—if the information had not been lost or discarded—and this cooperation is gratefully acknowledged here.

The mean scores in Tables 3-35 through 3-56 are reassuring. Occupations that should score high did so; military officers scored highest on the Military Activities scale, ministers scored highest on the Religious Activities scale, scientists scored highest on the Science scale and so on—there were virtually no surprises. Clearly, scores on these scales are related, in a highly significant fashion, to the occupations of adult men. Anyone who would understand these scales thoroughly must spend some time studying these tables of means, both to learn more about the relative levels of scores on each scale, and to learn more about each occupation.

High and low scores on the Basic Interest Scales. The rank-ordered means in Tables 3-35 to 3-56 provide a firmer foundation for ascertaining the importance of scores at various levels. Scanning these tables suggests that scores above 58 or 59 are high enough to be important from an occupational standpoint; scores below 42 or 43 indicate important areas of rejection, at least among adults. Thus, scores above 58 should be considered HIGH, those below 42 LOW. Some sharpening of this interpretation will obviously be necessary, especially with teenagers and especially with the Adventure scale where high scores will likely decrease over time, but these figures can be used as initial landmarks.

Though these data are positive and meaningful, one disappointing aspect was the magnitude of differences between extreme groups. On most of the scales, the range from the highest mean to the lowest was about 20 standard

TABLE 3-35. MEAN SCORES ON THE MEN'S ADVENTURE SCALE

Mean Standard Score

66 Astronauts
65
64 County Sheriffs
63
62
61 Policemen(1969)/Highway Patrolmen/Policemen(1968)
60 Salesmen,3M applicants/Dept Store Mgrs
59 Salesmen,3M/Policemen(1933)/Salesmen,Computer/Army Officers(1969)
58 Air Force Officers/Navy Officers/Sales Mgrs(1968)
57 Investment Mgrs/Salesmen,Steel/Pilots
56 Actors(1966)/YMCA Staff/Petroleum Engineers/Math-Sci Teachers(1968)/NASA Scientists/Journalists(British)/Advertising Men(1968)/Electricians/Engineers(1968)/Physical Therapists(1966)
55 Photographers/Elem Teachers(Minn)/Comm Rec Direcs/Computer Programmers/Food Scientists/Purchasing Agents(1969)/Foresters/Tool & Die Makers
54 Personnel Direcs(1969)/Physicians(1969)/Soc Sci Teachers(1969)/Army Sergeants/Football Coaches/Skilled Tradesmen/Buyers(1969)/CPA(1965)/Army Officers(1950)/Legislators/Newsmen/Salesmen,Life(1966)/Social Workers(1967)
53 Cham Comm Execs/Salesmen,Auto/Forest Service Men/Physical Therapists(1957)/Machinists/English Teachers/Funeral Direcs(1969)/Salesmen,Life(1969)/Public Admins(1969)/Salesmen,Real Estate(1969)/Cartographers/Chiropractors/Ministers(1969)
52 Vets(1966)/YMCA PD/Optometrists/Ministers(1965)/Orthopedic Surgeons/Lawyers(1969)/Interpreters/Architects(1968)/Psychiatrists(1967)/Teaching Brothers/Carpenters(1969)/Elem Teachers(NDak)
51 Chemists(1969)/Dentists(1969)/Dental Educators/Medical Techs/Musicians(1969)/Salesmen,Encyclopedia/Generals & Admirals/Danforth Fellows/CPA(1944)/Corp Pres(1965)/Neurological Surgeons/Farmers(1968)/Psychologists(1967)/Guidance Counselors(1950)
50 Bus School Profs/School Supers(1969)/Priests(1966)/Sociologists/Credit Mgrs/Salesmen,PG&E/Printers/Carpenters(1936)/School Supers(1965)/Physicists(1968)/Astronomers/College Profs/Voc Ag Teachers
49 Radiologists/Urologists/Farmers(1936)/Surgeons/Mpls Symphony/Osteopaths/Math-Sci Teachers(1936)/Student Personnel Workers/Buyers(1946)/Pharmacists(1968)/Actors(1937)/Bankers(1969)/Artists(1968)/County Welfare Workers/Unitarian Ministers(1929)
48 Mathematicians(1969)/Psychologists(1947)/Salesmen,Real Estate(1932)/Public Admins(1941)/Pediatricians/Chemists(1931)/Biologists/Bankers(1964)/Physiatrists/Bus Ed Teachers/Farmers(1967)/Musicians(1952)/Anthropologists
47 Accountants/Social Workers(1953)/Psychologists(1931)/Office Workers/Unitarian Ministers(1950)/Economists/Production Mgrs/Ag Extension Agents/Psychologists(Exp)/Personnel Direcs(1927)/Funeral Direcs(1945)/Physicians(1949)/Psychiatrists(1949)/Animal Husbandry Profs/Artists(1933)/Vets(1949)/Colonels
46 Guidance Counselors(1968)/Pharmacists(1947)/Soc Sci Teachers(1936)/Physicians(1927)/Engineers(1928)/Purchasing Agents(1931)/Political Scientists/Sales Mgrs(1932)/Librarians/Dentists(1932)/Lawyers(1949)/Lawyers(1927)/Pathologists/Authors/Interior Decorators/Governors/Advertising Men(1931)/Music Teachers(1946)
45 Rehab Counselors/Architects(1933)/YMCA Secs/Salesmen,Life(1931)/High School Counselors/Pulitzer Prize/Ministers(1927)/Psychologists(1949)/Music Teachers(1952)/Internists
44 Judges
43 Bankers(1934)/Corp Pres(1935)/Physicists(1927)
42
41 School Supers(1930)
40 Mathematicians(1929)/NIAL Members

TABLE 3-36. MEAN SCORES ON THE MEN'S AGRICULTURE SCALE

Mean Standard Score

63 Farmers(1967)/Farmers(1968)
62 Voc Ag Teachers
61 Farmers(1936)/Vets(1949)
60 Vets(1966)
59 Foresters/Forest Service Men/Animal Husbandry Profs/Ag Extension Agents
58
57
56 Highway Patrolmen
55 County Sheriffs
54 Pilots
53 Policemen(1969)/Carpenters(1969)/Army Officers(1950)/Generals & Admirals
52 Electricians/Food Scientists/Football Coaches/Skilled Tradesmen/Orthopedic Surgeons/Math-Sci Teachers(1968)/Policemen(1968)
51 Tool & Die Makers/Army Officers(1969)/Chiropractors/Elem Teachers(NDak)/Salesmen,Encyclopedia/Policemen(1933)/Comm Rec Direcs/Physical Therapists(1957)/Astronauts/Governors
50 Physical Therapists(1966)/Physicians(1969)/Salesmen,Real Estate(1969)/Colonels/YMCA PD/Salesmen,PG&E/Biologists/Urologists/Legislators/Osteopaths
49 School Supers(1969)/Purchasing Agents(1969)/Cartographers/Public Admins(1941)/Radiologists/Carpenters(1936)/Surgeons/Salesmen,Life(1966)/Petroleum Engineers/Neurological Surgeons/NASA Scientists/Actors(1937)
48 Dentists(1969)/English Teachers/Engineers(1968)/Funeral Direcs(1969)/Medical Techs/Salesmen,Life(1969)/Soc Sci Teachers(1969)/Sales Mgrs(1968)/Army Sergeants/Salesmen,Real Estate(1932)/YMCA Secs/Salesmen,Steel/Salesmen,Life(1931)/YMCA Staff/Dentists(1932)/Bankers(1934)/Ministers(1927)/Journalists(British)/Salesmen,Computer/Funeral Direcs(1945)/Air Force Officers/Navy Officers/Physiatrists/Machinists/Guidance Counselors(1950)
47 Bankers(1969)/Dental Educators/Dept Store Mgrs/Salesmen,3M applicants/Salesmen,3M/Soc Sci Teachers(1936)/Pediatricians/Physicians(1927)/Credit Mgrs/Photographers/Elem Teachers(Minn)/Sales Mgrs(1932)/CPA(1944)/Bankers(1964)/Corp Pres(1965)/Physicians(1949)/Artists(1933)/Pharmacists(1968)
46 Guidance Counselors(1968)/Personnel Direcs(1969)/College Profs/Chemists(1931)/Engineers(1928)/School Supers(1930)/Unitarian Ministers(1950)/Production Mgrs/Personnel Direcs(1927)/Salesmen,Auto/Corp Pres(1935)/Bus Ed Teachers/Pathologists/Math-Sci Teachers(1936)/Lawyers(1969)/Chemists(1969)/County Welfare Workers/Music Teachers(1946)
45 Rehab Counselors/Priests(1966)/Cham Comm Execs/Architects(1933)/Social Workers(1953)/Office Workers/Printers/High School Counselors/Actors(1966)/Optometrists/Computer Programmers/Lawyers(1949)/School Supers(1965)/Psychiatrists(1949)/Social Workers(1967)/Music Teachers(1952)/Musicians(1952)/Internists/Anthropologists/Buyers(1946)/Interpreters/Artists(1968)/Unitarian Ministers(1929)/Advertising Men(1968)/Architects(1968)/Investment Mgrs/Teaching Brothers/Public Admins(1969)/Ministers(1969)/Buyers(1969)
44 Pharmacists(1947)/Accountants/Psychologists(Exp)/Purchasing Agents(1931)/Lawyers(1927)/Newsmen/Ministers(1965)/Advertising Men(1931)/Physicists(1927)/Psychologists(1949)/Authors/Musicians(1969)
43 Bus School Profs/Psychologists(1931)/Mpls Symphony/Danforth Fellows/Interior Decorators/NIAL Members/Student Personnel Workers/Physicists(1968)/Astronomers
42 Mathematicians(1969)/Psychiatrists(1967)/Psychologists(1947)/Sociologists/CPA(1965)/Librarians/Pulitzer Prize/Judges/Mathematicians(1929)/Psychologists(1967)
41 Economists
40 Political Scientists

139

TABLE 3-37. MEAN SCORES ON THE MEN'S ART SCALE

Mean Standard Score

65	Architects(1968)/Interior Decorators/Artists(1968)
64	Architects(1933)/Actors(1966)
63	Artists(1933)
62	Actors(1937)
61	
60	Photographers
59	Musicians(1969)/Mpls Symphony/NIAL Members
58	Advertising Men(1968)/Pulitzer Prize
57	Unitarian Ministers(1950)/Librarians/Danforth Fellows/Musicians(1952)/Journalists(British)
56	Advertising Men(1931)/Physiatrists/Music Teachers(1952)/Anthropologists/Neurological Surgeons/Psychologists(1967)/Physicists (1968)/Dental Educators/English Teachers/Psychiatrists(1967)/College Profs
55	Psychologists(1947)/Psychologists(1931)/Elem Teachers(Minn)/Ministers(1927)/Ministers(1965)/Orthopedic Surgeons/Authors/ Astronomers/Physicians(1969)/
54	Dentists(1969)/Teaching Brothers/Ministers(1969)/Elem Teachers(NDak)/Priests(1966)/Sociologists/Social Workers(1953)/ Pediatricians/Biologists/Economists/Psychologists(Exp)/Dentists(1932)/Newsmen/Psychiatrists(1949)/Unitarian Ministers (1929)/Music Teachers(1946)
53	Investment Mgrs/Mathematicians(1969)/Public Admins(1969)/Chiropractors/Salesmen,3M/YMCA Secs/Urologists/Personnel Direcs (1927)/Political Scientists/Judges/Physical Therapists(1957)/Psychologists(1949)/Social Workers(1967)/Pathologists/ Machinists/NASA Scientists/Chemists(1969)/Interpreters
52	Bus School Profs/Guidance Counselors(1968)/Medical Techs/Cartographers/Salesmen,3M applicants/YMCA PD/Radiologists/ Physicians(1927)/Salesmen,PG&E/Carpenters(1936)/Surgeons/Salesmen,Encyclopedia/Comm Rec Direcs/YMCA Staff/Computer Programmers/Generals & Admirals/Physicists(1927)/Physicians(1949)/Internists/Student Personnel Workers/Policemen(1968)
51	Food Scientists/Personnel Direcs(1969)/Physical Therapists(1966)/Buyers(1969)/Rehab Counselors/Cham Comm Execs/Public Admins(1941)/Office Workers/Engineers(1928)/Printers/Corp Pres(1935)/Optometrists/Bus Ed Teachers/Osteopaths/Astronauts/ Mathematicians(1929)/Buyers(1946)/Ag Extension Agents/Lawyers(1969)/County Welfare Workers
50	Dept Store Mgrs/Engineers(1968)/School Supers(1969)/Football Coaches/Foresters(1969)/Tool & Die Makers/Accountants/Soc Sci Teachers(1936)/Chemists(1931)/Credit Mgrs/Salesmen,Life(1931)/School Supers(1930)/High School Counselors/Funeral Direcs (1945)/Policemen(1933)/Army Officers(1950)/Legislators/School Supers(1965)/Salesmen,Life(1966)/Math-Sci Teachers(1936)/ Math-Sci Teachers(1968)
49	Salesmen,Real Estate(1932)/Salesmen,Steel/Air Force Officers/Production Mgrs/Salesmen,Auto/Forest Service Men/Pilots/ Sales Mgrs(1932)/Salesmen,Computer/CPA(1944)/Navy Officers/Lawyers(1927)/Governors/Pharmacists(1968)/Funeral Direcs(1969)/ Policemen(1969)/Soc Sci Teachers(1969)/Carpenters(1969)/Sales Mgrs(1968)/Purchasing Agents(1969)/Skilled Tradesmen/Colonel
48	County Sheriffs/Electricians/Army Sergeants/Army Officers(1969)/Physical Therapists(1947)/Farmers(1936)/Purchasing Agents(1931)/ Lawyers(1949)/Animal Husbandry Profs/Petroleum Engineers/Guidance Counselors(1950)
47	Bankers(1969)/Salesmen,Life(1969)/Salesmen,Real Estate(1969)/Vets(1966)/CPA(1965)/Bankers(1934)/Bankers(1964)/Corp Pres (1965)/Highway Patrolmen
46	Vets(1949)/Voc Ag Teachers
45	Farmers(1967)
44	
43	Farmers(1968)

TABLE 3-38. MEAN SCORES ON THE MEN'S BUSINESS MANAGEMENT SCALE

Mean Standard Score

63	Dept Store Mgrs
62	Salesmen,3M applicants
61	Personnel Direcs(1969)/Sales Mgrs(1968)/Salesmen,3M/Credit Mgrs
60	Cham Comm Execs/Salesmen,Encyclopedia/Bus Ed Teachers
59	YMCA Secs/Personnel Direcs(1927)/Salesmen,Computer/County Welfare Workers/Buyers(1969)
58	Salesmen,Steel/Comm Rec Direcs
57	Rehab Counselors/Accountants/Office Workers/Salesmen,PG&E/Sales Mgrs(1932)/YMCA Staff/School Supers(1965)/Buyers(1946)/ Policemen(1968)/Dentists(1969)/Salesmen,Life(1969)/School Supers(1969)/Purchasing Agents(1969)
56	High School Counselors/Purchasing Agents(1931)/Legislators/Funeral Direcs(1969)/Public Admins(1969)/Salesmen,Real Estate (1969)/Army Officers(1969)
55	Public Admins(1941)/Corp Pres(1935)/Funeral Direcs(1945)/CPA(1965)/Production Mgrs/Army Officers(1950)/CPA(1944)/Ag Extension Agents/Bankers(1969)/Football Coaches
54	Guidance Counselors(1968)/Army Sergeants/Soc Sci Teachers(1936)/Social Workers(1953)/Salesmen,Life(1931)/Air Force Officers Salesmen,Auto/Navy Officers/Bankers(1964)/Governors/Guidance Counselors(1950)
53	Salesmen,Real Estate(1932)/School Supers(1930)/Bankers(1934)/Generals & Admirals/Corp Pres(1965)/Salesmen,Life(1966)/ Pharmacists(1968)/Advertising Men(1968)/Soc Sci Teachers(1969)
52	YMCA PD/Petroleum Engineers/Student Personnel Workers/Machinists/County Sheriffs/Food Scientists/Colonels/Voc Ag Teachers
51	Bus School Profs/Investment Mgrs/Policemen(1969)/Cartographers/Chiropractors/Ministers(1969)/Elem Teachers(Minn)/Pharmacists (1947)/Elem Teachers(NDak)/Forest Service Men/Social Workers(1967)/Music Teachers(1952)/Lawyers(1969)
50	Policemen(1933)/Optometrists/Lawyers(1949)/Ministers(1965)/Math-Sci Teachers(1936)/Advertising Men(1931)/Highway Patrolmen Interpreters/Engineers(1968)
49	Foresters/Psychologists(1947)/Priests(1966)/Librarians/Computer Programmers/Ministers(1927)/Physical Therapists(1957)
48	English Teachers/Medical Techs/Physical Therapists(1966)/Tool & Die Makers/Vets(1966)/Engineers(1928)/Printers/Unitarian Ministers(1950)/Carpenters(1936)/Farmers(1936)/Pilots/Interior Decorators/Music Teachers(1946)
47	Economists/Physiatrists/Psychologists(1949)/Orthopedic Surgeons/Vets(1949)/Journalists(British)
46	Electricians/Teaching Brothers/Musicians(1969)Skilled Tradesmen/Pediatricians/Chemists(1931)/Urologists/Lawyers(1927)/ Newsmen/Psychiatrists(1949)/Farmer(1967)/Osteopaths/Astronauts/Farmers(1968)/Math-Sci Teachers(1968)/Psychologists(1967)
45	Sociologists/Radiologists/Judges/Animal Husbandry Profs/Musicians(1952)/NASA Scientists/Architects(1968)/Dental Educators/ Physicians(1969)/Psychiatrists(1967)/Carpenters(1969)
44	Psychologists(1931)/Surgeons/Political Scientists/Dentists(1932)/Neurological Surgeons/Chemists(1969)
43	College Profs/Architects(1933)/Psychologists(Exp)/Physicians(1949)/Internists/Unitarian Ministers(1929)
42	Biologists/Danforth Fellows
41	Physicians(1927)/Photographers/Mpls Symphony/Pathologists
40	Actors(1966)/Physicists(1927)/Mathematicians(1929)/Authors
39	Mathematicians(1969)/Anthropologists/Physicists(1968)/Actors(1937)
38	Pulitzer Prize/Astronomers
37	Artists(1968)
36	Artists(1933)/NIAL Members

140

TABLE 3-39. MEAN SCORES ON THE MEN'S LAW/POLITICS SCALE

Mean Standard Score

63	Football Coaches
62	Judges/Legislators
61	Soc Sci Teachers(1969)/Public Admins(1969)/Salesmen,3M applicants/Salesmen,3M/Political Scientists/Salesmen,Computer/ Governors/Lawyers(1969)/Policemen(1968)
60	Cham Comm Execs/Dept: Store Mgrs/Personnel Direcs(1969)
59	Lawyers(1949)/Sales Mgrs(1968)
58	County Sheriffs/Guidance Counselors(1968)/Policemen(1969)/School Supers(1969)/Army Officers(1969)/Ministers(1969)/Social Workers(1953)/Credit Mgrs/CPA(1965)/Economists/Navy Officers/Lawyers(1927)/Newsmen/Salesmen,Life(1966)/Student Personnel Workers/Guidance Counselors(1950)
57	Bus School Profs/Investment Mgrs/Salesmen,Life(1969)/Rehab Counselors/Unitarian Ministers(1950)/Air Force Officers/ Salesmen,Encyclopedia/Comm Rec Direcs/Army Officers(1950)/School Supers(1965)/Social Workers(1967)/Highway Patrol/Interpreter
56	Priests(1966)/Sociologists/Salesmen,Steel/High School Counselors/Personnel Direcs(1927)/YMCA Staff/Generals & Admirals/ Bus Ed Teachers/Danforth Fellows/Psychologists(1967)/Journalists(British)/Advertising Men(1968)/Psychiatrists(1967)
55	English Teachers/Salesmen,Real Estate(1969)/Chiropractors/Buyers(1969)/Public Admins(1941)/Soc Sci Teachers(1936)/School Supers(1930)/Elem Teachers(Minn)/Ministers(1965)/Astronauts/Ag Extension Agents/County Welfare Workers
54	Psychologists(1947)/Policemen(1933)/Optometrists/Computer Programmers/Corp Pres(1965)/Petroleum Engineers/Funeral Direcs (1969)/Physical Therapists(1966)/Purchasing Agents(1969)/Army Sergeants
53	YMCA Secs/Salesmen,PG&E/Actors(1966)/CPA(1944)/Physiatrists/Physical Therapists(1957)/Psychiatrists(1949)/Psychologists(1949) NASA Scientists/Pharmacists(1968)/Bankers(1969)/Food Scientists/Teaching Brothers/College Profs
52	Accountants/Pediatricians/Office Workers/Salesmen,Life(1931)/Salesmen,Auto/Librarians/Bankers(1934)/Ministers(1927)/ Orthopedic Surgeons/Anthropologists/Neurological Surgeons/Buyers(1946)/Math-Sci Teachers(1968)/Engineers(1968)/Physicians (1969)/Cartographers/Colonels/Vocational Ag Teachers/Elem Teachers(NDak)
51	Vets(1966)/Salesmen,Real Estate(1932)/Psychologists(1931)/Radiologists/Urologists/Psychologists(Exp)/Pulitzer Prize/Banker (1964)/Astronomers/Chemists(1969)/Actors(1937)/Unitarian Ministers(1929)/Dentists(1969)/Medical Techs/Foresters
50	Architects(1968)/Dental Educators/Mathematicians(1969)/Printers/Production Mgrs/Purchasing Agents(1931)/Pilots/Sales Mgrs (1932)/Machinists/Physicists(1968)
49	Pharmacists(1947)/YMCA PD/Corp Pres(1935)/Biologists/Photographers/Surgeons/Forest Service Men/Animal Husbandry Profs/ Music Teachers(1952)/Physiatrists/Math-Sci Teachers(1936)/Electricians/Musicians(1969)/Tool & Die Makers
48	Carpenters(1969)/Skilled Tradesmen/Funeral Direcs(1945)/Mpls Symphony/Advertising Men(1931)/Physicians(1949)/Musicians(1952)/ Authors/Music Teachers(1946)
47	Engineers(1928)/Farmers(1936)/Dentists(1932)/Pathologists/Vets(1949)/Farmers(1968)
46	Physicians(1927)/Chemists(1931)/Carpenters(1936)/Mathematicians(1929)/Interior Decorators/NIAL Members/Artists(1968)
45	Architects(1933)/Farmers(1967)
44	Physicists(1927)
43	
42	Artists(1933)

TABLE 3-40. MEAN SCORES ON THE MEN'S MATHEMATICS SCALE

Mean Standard Score

61	Astronauts
60	Physicists(1927)/Mathematicians(1929)/Physicists(1968)
59	Mathematicians(1969)/Astronomers/NASA Scientists
58	Engineers(1968)/Air Force Officers/Computer Programmers/Salesmen,Computer/Petroleum Engineers/Chemists(1969)
57	Engineers(1928)/Army Officers(1950)
56	Chemists(1931)/Colonels/Army Officers(1969)/CPA(1965)/Economists/Generals & Admirals/Corp Pres(1965)/Math-Sci Teachers (1968)
55	Psychologists(Exp)/Optometrists/CPA(1944)/Navy Officers/Animal Husbandry Profs/Machinists
54	Electricians/Food Scientists/Medical Techs/Physicians(1969)/Cartographers/Tool & Die/Psychologists(1931)/Danforth Fellows/Physiatrists/Math-Sci Teachers(1936)
53	Architects(1968)/Bus School Profs/Foresters/Skilled Tradesmen/College Profs/Accountants/Pediatricians/School Supers(1930)/ Biologists/Urologists/Production Mgrs/Elem Teachers(Minn)/Pilots/School Supers(1965)/Psychologists(1949)/Pathologists/ Orthopedic Surgeons/Neurological Surgeons
52	Psychiatrists(1967)/Purchasing Agents(1969)/Architects(1933)/Radiologists/Credit Mgrs/Salesmen,Steel/Corp Pres(1935)/ Forest Service Men/Bankers(1964)/Psychiatrists(1949)/Policemen(1968)/Pharmacists(1968)
51	Bankers(1969)/Dental Educators/School Supers(1969)/Carpenters(1969)/Football Coaches/Voc Ag Teachers/Salesmen,3M/Public Admins(1941)/Office Workers/Personnel Directors(1927)/Surgeons/Sales Mgrs(1932)/Lawyers(1949)/Physicians(1949)/Internists/ Psychologists(1967)/Highway Patrolmen
50	Psychologists(1947)/Vets(1966)/Pharmacists(1947)/Sociologists/Salesmen,PG&E/High School Counselors/Carpenters(1936)/ Farmers(1936)/Purchasing Agents(1931)/Judges/Legislators/Physical Therapists(1957)/Bus Ed Teachers/Student Personnel Workers/Investment Mgrs/Teaching Brothers
49	Rehab Counselors/Physicians(1927)/Salesmen,Auto/Banker(1934)/Lawyers(1927)/NIAL Members/Governors/Guidance Counselors (1950)/County Welfare Workers/Dentists(1969)/Guidance Counselors(1968)/Physical Therapists(1966)/Policemen(1969)/Public Admins(1969)/Salesmen,Real Estate(1969)/Army Sergeants/Elem Teachers(NDak)
48	Dept Store Mgrs/Personnel Direcs(1969)/Salesmen,Life(1969)/Sales Mgrs(1968)/Musicians(1969)/Chiropractors/Buyers(1969)/ Salesmen,3M applicants/YMCA PD/Policemen(1933)/Political Scientists/Mpls Symphony/Comm Rec Direcs/Dentists(1932)/ Ministers(1927)/Osteopaths/Anthropologists/Vets(1949)/Buyers(1946)/Ag Extension Agents/Unitarian Ministers(1929)/Music Teachers(1946)
47	Ministers(1969)/Cham Comm Execs/YMCA Secs/Salesmen,Life(1931)/Printers/Unitarian Ministers(1950)/Funeral Direcs(1945)/ Salesmen,Encyclopedia/Lawyers(1969)/Interpreters
46	County Sheriffs/Priests(1966)/Salesmen,Real Estate(1932)/Photographers/Actors(1966)/Librarians/YMCA Staff/Ministers(1965)/ Salesmen,Life(1966)/Farmers(1968)/Music Teachers(1952)/Musicians(1952)
45	Funeral Direcs(1969)/Soc Sci Teachers(1936)/Social Workers(1953)/Social Workers(1967)/Farmers(1967)/Advertising Men(1931)
44	Soc Sci Teachers(1969)
43	Advertising Men(1968)/English Teachers/Newsmen/Artists(1968)
42	Pulitzer Prize/Artists(1933)/Interior Decorators
41	
40	Authors/Journalists(British)
39	
38	
37	Actors(1937)

141

TABLE 3-41. MEAN SCORES ON THE MEN'S MECHANICAL SCALE

Mean Standard Score

61 Machinists
60
59 Tool & Die Makers
58 Electricians/Skilled Tradesmen
57
56 Carpenters(1969)/Air Force Officers/Carpenters(1936)/Orthopedic Surgeons
55 Engineers(1968)/Policemen(1968)
54 Voc Ag Teachers/Radiologists/Pilots/Army Officers(1950)/Farmers(1967)/Neurological Surgeons/Highway Patrolmen
53 Policemen(1969)/Cartographers/Engineers(1928)/Urologists/Physicists(1927)/Petroleum Engineers/NASA Scientists
52 Physical Therapists(1966)/Foresters/Psychologists(Exp)/Computer Programmers/Physical Therapists(1957)/Astronauts/
    Math-Sci Teachers(1936)/Farmers(1968)/Chemists(1969)
51 County Sheriffs/Food Scientists/Medical Techs/Purchasing Agents(1969)/Chemists(1931)/Printers/Production Mgrs/Surgeons/
    Forest Service Men/Policemen(1933)/Navy Officers/Physiatrists/Math-Sci Teachers(1968)/Physicists(1968)
50 Dental Educators/Colonels/Army Officers(1969)/Elem Teachers(NDak)/Pediatricians/Salesmen,PG&E/Farmers(1936)/Optometrists/
    Salesmen,Computer/Generals & Admirals/Pathologists/Astronomers
49 Architects(1968)/Dentists(1969)/Physicians(1969)/Chiropractors/Biologists/Dentists(1932)/CPA(1944)/Psychiatrists(1949)/
    Osteopaths/Ag Extension Agents/County Welfare Workers
48 Army Sergeants/Architects(1933)/YMCA PD/Psychologists(1931)/Credit Mgrs/Personnel Direcs(1927)/Elem Teachers(Minn)/
    Physicians(1949)/Psychologists(1949)/Pharmacists(1968)/Music Teachers(1946)
47 Mathematicians(1969)/School Supers(1969)/Musicians(1969)/Vets(1966)/Public Admins(1941)/Accountants/Salesmen,Auto/
    Purchasing Agents(1931)/Comm Rec Direcs/Ministers(1927)/Bankers(1964)/Corp Pres(1965)/Animal Husbandry Profs/Bus Ed
    Teachers/Internists/Mathematicians(1929)/Vets(1949)
46 Dept Store Mgrs/Ministers(1969)/Salesmen,3M applicants/Salesmen,3M/YMCA Secs/Physicians(1927)/Salesmen,Steel/Office
    Workers/Unitarian Ministers(1950)/High School Counselors/Corp Pres(1935)/Mpls Symphony/YMCA Staff/Musicians(1952)/
    Guidance Counselors(1950)
45 Funeral Direcs(1969)/Psychiatrists(1967)/Salesmen,Real Estate(1969)/College Profs/Psychologists(1947)/Rehab Counselors/
    Pharmacists(1947)/Social Workers(1953)/CPA(1965)/Photographers/Social Workers(1967)
44 Bankers(1969)/English Teachers/Personnel Direcs(1969)/Soc Sci Teachers(1969)/Teaching Brothers/Public Admins(1969)/
    Priests(1966)/Cham Comm Execs/Soc Sci Teachers(1936)/School Supers(1930)/Funeral Direcs(1945)/Sales Mgrs(1932)/
    Legislators/Bankers(1934)/Ministers(1965)/School Supers(1965)/Music Teachers(1952)/Artists(1933)/Buyers(1946)/
    Psychologists(1967)
43 Bus School Profs/Guidance Counselors(1968)/Sales Mgrs(1968)/Buyers(1969)/Salesmen,Real Estate(1932)/Sociologists/
    Economists/Librarians/Anthropologists/Student Personnel Workers/Artists(1968)/Unitarian Ministers(1929)
42 Advertising Men(1968)/Investment Mgrs/Salesmen,Life(1969)/Danforth Fellows/Lawyers(1969)/Interpreters
41 Salesmen,Encyclopedia/Actors(1966)/Lawyers(1949)/Advertising Men(1931)/Governors/Journalists(British)
40 Football Coaches/Salesmen,Life(1931)/Lawyers(1927)/Interior Decorators/Actors(1937)
39 Judges/Newsmen
38 Political Scientists/Pulitzer Prize/Salesmen,Life(1966)/Authors/NIAL Members

TABLE 3-42. MEAN SCORES ON THE MEN'S MEDICAL SERVICE SCALE

Mean Standard Score

64 Dentists(1969)/Physical Therapists(1966)/Dentists(1932)/Physical Therapists(1957)/Pharmacists(1968)
63 Dental Educators/Medical Techs/Vets(1966)/Urologists/Physiatrists/Osteopaths/Vets(1949)
62 Physicians(1969)/Pharmacists(1947)/Radiologists/Pediatricians/Surgeons/Physicians(1949)/Neurological Surgeons
61 Physicians(1927)
60 Optometrists/Psychiatrists(1949)/Pathologists/Internists/Orthopedic Surgeons
59 YMCA PD/Animal Husbandry Profs
58 Biologists/Funeral Direcs(1969)/Chiropractors
57 Food Scientists/Psychologists(1947)/Math-Sci Teachers(1936)/Policemen(1968)
56 Psychologists(Exp)/Comm Rec Direcs/YMCA Staff/Guidance Counselors(1968)/Psychiatrists(1967)/Ministers(1969)
55 County Sheriffs/Dept Store Mgrs/Policemen(1969)/Psychologists(1931)/Psychologists(1949)/Math-Sci Teachers(1968)/
    Highway Patrolmen
54 Football Coaches/Voc Ag Teachers/Elem Teachers/Salesmen,3M applicants/Rehab Counselors/Priests(1966)/Social Workers
    (1953)/Chemists(1931)/Elem Teachers(NDak)/Policemen(1933)/Ministers(1927)/Social Workers(1967)/Astronauts/Chemists(1969)
53 YMCA Secs/Unitarian Ministers(1950)/High School Counselors/Funeral Direcs(1945)/Salesmen,Computer/School Supers(1965)/
    Student Personnel Workers/Psychologists(1967)/Guidance Counselors(1950)/Ag Extension Agents/Journalists(British)/
    County Welfare Workers/School Supers(1969)/Teaching Brothers/Foresters
52 Engineers(1968)/Soc Sci Teachers(1969)/Purchasing Agents(1969)/Cartographers/Army Officers(1969)/College Profs/Salesmen,
    3M/Soc Sci Teachers(1936)/Credit Mgrs/Air Force Officers/Mpls Symphony/Army Officers(1950)/Computer Programmers/
    Legislators/Danforth Fellows/Ministers(1965)/Salesmen,Life(1966)/Petroleum Engineers/NASA Scientists/Unitarian
    Ministers(1929)
51 Cham Comm Execs/Public Admins(1941)/Salesmen,PG&E/Forest Service Men/Pilots/Navy Officers/Musicians(1952)/Governors/
    Astronomers/English Teachers/Personnel Direcs(1969)/Musicians(1969)/Tool & Die Makers
50 Sociologists/Salesmen,Steel/Office Workers/School Supers(1930)/Personnel Direcs(1927)/Farmers(1936)/Salesmen,Auto/
    Librarians/CPA(1944)/Music Teachers(1952)/Bus Ed Teachers/Anthropologists/Machinists/Lawyers(1969)/Advertising Men
    (1968)/Public Admins(1969)/Sales Mgrs(1968)
49 Music Teachers(1946)/Salesmen,Life(1931)/Printers/CPA(1965)/Production Mgrs/Photographers/Actors(1966)/Generals &
    Admirals/Physicists(1968)/Buyers(1946)/Actors(1937)/Interpreters/Artists(1968)/Bankers(1969)/Electricians/Salesmen,
    Life(1969)/Salesmen,Real Estate(1969)/Army Sergeants/Skilled Tradesmen/Colonels/Buyers(1969)
48 Accountants/Economists/Carpenters(1936)/Salesmen,Encyclopedia/Sales Mgrs(1932)/Pulitzer Prize/Judges/Lawyers(1949)/
    Newsmen/Bankers(1964)/Physicians(1927)/NIAL Members/Architects(1968)/Bus School Profs/Mathematicians(1969)
47 Investment Mgrs/Carpenters(1969)/Salesmen,Real Estate(1932)/Engineers(1928)/Corp Pres(1935)/Purchasing Agents(1931)/
    Bankers(1934)/Lawyers(1927)/Corp Pres(1965)/Artists(1933)
46 Architects(1933)/Political Scientists/Advertising Men(1931)/Mathematicians(1929)/Authors/Interior Decorators
45 Farmers(1967)
44 Farmers(1968)

142

TABLE 3-43. MEAN SCORES ON THE MEN'S MERCHANDISING SCALE

Mean Standard Score

```
65  Dept Store Mgrs
64
63  Buyers(1969)
62  Salesmen,3M
61  Sales Mgrs(1968)/Salesmen,3M applicants/Bus Ed Teachers/Buyers(1946)
60
59  Credit Mgrs
58  Funeral Direcs(1969)/Salesmen,Life(1969)/Purchasing Agents(1969)/Cham Comm Execs/Salesmen,PG&E/Salesmen,Encyclopedia/
    Pharmacists(1968)
57  Salesmen,Real Estate(1969)/Salesmen,Steel/Office Workers/Salesmen,Computer/County Welfare Workers
56  Personnel Direcs(1969)/Pharmacists(1947)/YMCA Secs/Funeral Direcs(1945)/Salesmen,Auto/Purchasing Agents(1931)/Policemen(1968
55  Comm Rec Direcs
54  Advertising Men(1968)/Bankers(1969)/School Supers(1969)/Soc Sci Teachers(1969)/Football Coaches/Rehab Counselors/
    Accountants/Soc Sci Teachers(1936)/High School Counselors/CPA(1965)/Sales Mgrs(1932)/YMCA Staff/Interior Decorators/
    Guidance Counselors(1950)
53  Guidance Counselors(1968)/Public Admins(1969)/Salesmen,Real Estate(1932)/Air Force Officers/Legislators/School Supers(1965)/
    Ag Extension Agents/Army Sergeants
52  County Sheriffs/Policemen(1969)/Army Officers(1969)/Voc Ag Teachers/Elem Teachers(NDak)/Salesmen,Life(1931)/Personnel
    Direcs(1927)/Elem Teachers(Minn)/Army Officers(1950)/CPA(1944)/Navy Officers/Bankers(1964)/Salesmen,Life(1966)
51  Food Scientists/Chiropractors/Ministers(1969)/YMCA PD/Corp Pres(1935)/Optometrists/Bankers(1934)/Petroleum Engineers/
    Math-Sci Teachers(1936)/Highway Patrolmen
50  English Teachers/Investment Mgrs/Cartographers/Vets(1966)/Public Admins(1941)/Social Workers(1953)/Advertising Men(1931)/
    Lawyers(1969)
49  Production Mgrs/Librarians/Computer Programmers/Generals & Admirals/Physical Therapists(1957)/Music Teachers(1952)/
    Machinists/Bus School Profs/Physical Therapists(1966)/Colonels
48  Engineers(1968)/Foresters/Musicians(1969)/Tool & Die Makers/Priests(1966)/School Supers(1930)/Printers/Urologists/
    Policemen(1933)/Lawyers(1949)/Ministers(1965)/Corp Pres(1965)/Physiatrists/Student Personnel Workers/Governors/Music
    Teachers(1946)
47  Dentists(1969)/Electricians/Medical Techs/Teaching Brothers/Carpenters(1969)/Skilled Tradesmen/Radiologists/Carpenters(1936)
    Farmers(1936)/Pilots/Ministers(1927)/Animal Husbandry Profs/Social Workers(1967)/Farmers(1967)/Osteopaths/Orthopedic
    Surgeons/Astronauts/Vets(1949)/Farmers(1968)/Interpreters
46  Architects(1968)/Psychologists(1947)/Pediatricians/Unitarian Ministers(1950)/Forest Service Men/Musicians(1952)/Math-Sci
    Teachers(1968)/NASA Scientists/Journalists(British)
45  Physicians(1969)/Sociologists/Chemists(1931)/Economists/Dentists(1932)/Psychiatrists(1949)/Psychologists(1949)/Neurological
    Surgeons/Psychologists(1967)
44  Dental Educators/Psychiatrists(1967)/Judges/Psychologists(1931)/Engineers(1928)/Surgeons/Mpls Symphony/Lawyers(1927)/
    Newsmen/Physician(1949)/Internists
43  Architects(1933)/Biologists
42  College Profs/Physicians(1927)/Psychologists(Exp)/Actors(1966)/Political Scientists/Chemists(1969)/Unitarian Ministers(1929)
41  Photographers/Pathologists/Mathematicians(1929)
40  Danforth Fellows/Physicists(1927)
39  Mathematicians(1969)/Authors/Anthropologists/Actors(1937)/Artists(1968)
38  Pulitzer Prize/Artists(1933)/Physicists(1968)/Astronomers
36  NIAL Member
```

TABLE 3-44. MEAN SCORES ON THE MEN'S MILITARY ACTIVITIES SCALE

Mean Standard Score

```
66  Colonels
65
64  Army Officers(1950)/Generals & Admirals/Policemen(1968)
63
62  Army Officers(1969)
61  Policemen(1933)/County Sheriffs
60  Air Force Officers
59  Army Sergeants/Highway Patrolmen
58  YMCA PD/Pilots/Policemen(1969)
57
56  Navy Officers/Astronauts/Governors
55  Football Coaches/Comm Rec Direcs
54  School Supers(1969)/Salesmen,3M applicants/Rehab Counselors/Public Admins(1941)/Credit Mgrs/Office Workers/Salesmen,PG&E/
    YMCA Staff/Legislators/Salesmen,Computer/Physical Therapists(1957)/County Welfare Workers
53  Salesmen,3M/Vets(1966)/Cham Comm Execs/Engineers(1928)/Personnel Direcs(1927)/Salesmen,Auto/Optometrists/CPA(1944)/Farmers
    (1967)/Osteopaths/Vets(1949)/Machinists/Dept Store Mgrs/Funeral Direcs(1969)/Medical Techs/Personnel Direcs(1969)/Physical
    Therapists(1966)/Soc Sci Teachers(1969)/Purchasing Agents(1969)/Chiropractors/Elem Teachers(NDak)
52  Accountants,Soc Sci Teachers(1936)/Salesmen,Steel/Production Mgrs/Farmers(1936)/Purchasing Agents(1931)/Funeral Direcs(1945)
    Lawyers(1927)/School Supers(1965)/Bankers(1964)/Bus Ed Teachers/Petroleum Engineers/Math-Sci Teachers(1936)/Pharmacists
    (1968)/Dental Educators/Engineers(1968)/Food Scientists/Sales Mgrs(1968)/Cartographers/Voc Ag Teachers
51  Salesmen,Real Estate(1932)/Pharmacists(1947)/Salesmen,Life(1931)/High School Counselors/Carpenters(1936)/Salesmen,
    Encyclopedia/Elem Teachers(Minn)/Forest Service Men/Sales Mgrs(1932)/Dentists(1932)/Animal Husbandry Profs/Orthopedic
    Surgeons/Advertising Men(1931)/Buyers(1946)/Guidance Counselors(1950)/Lawyers(1969)/Bankers(1969)/Dentists(1969)/
    Electricians/Physicians(1969)/Salesmen,Life(1969)/Public Admins(1969)/Salesmen,Real Estate(1969)/Foresters/Skilled
    Tradesmen/Tool & Die Makers
50  Architects(1933)/YMCA Secs/Physicians(1927)/School Supers(1930)/Printers/CPA(1965)/Urologists/Bankers(1934)/Lawyers(1949)/
    Physicians(1949)/Physiatrists/Salesmen,Life(1966)/Music Teachers(1952)/Student Personnel Workers/Farmers(1968)/Math-Sci
    Teachers(1968)/Journalists(British)/Music Teachers(1946)/English Teachers/Teaching Brothers/Carpenters(1969)/Physicians(1969)
49  Advertising Men(1968)/Judges/Priests(1966)/Social Workers(1953)/Chemists(1931)/Surgeons/Computer Programmers/Corp Pres
    (1935)/Newsmen/Psychiatrists(1949)/Social Workers(1967)/Neurological Surgeons/Interpreters
48  Architects(1968)/Ministers(1969)/Psychologists(1931)/Radiologists/Biologists/Psychologists(Exp)/Ministers(1927)/
    Authors/Ag Ext Agents/NASA Scientists/Pathologists
47  Bus School Profs/Guidance Counselors(1968)/Investment Mgrs/Psychologists(1947)/Librarians/Ministers(1965)/Physicists(1927)/
    Psychologists(1949)/Musicians(1952)/Internists/Interior Decorators/Actors(1937)/Unitarian Ministers(1929)
46  Pediatricians/Unitarian Ministers(1950)/Economists/Photographers/Political Scientists/Pulitzer Prize/Artists(1933)/
    Mathematicians(1929)/Psychiatrists(1967)/College Profs
45  Musicians(1969)/Sociologists/Corp Pres(1965)/Anthropologists/Psychologists(1967)/Astronomers/Chemists(1969)
44  Mpls Symphony/Danforth Fellows/NIAL Members
43  Mathematicians(1969)/Physicists(1968)
42  Actors(1966)/Artists(1968)
```

TABLE 3-45. MEAN SCORES ON THE MEN'S MUSIC SCALE

67	Music Teachers(1952)/Music Teachers(1946)
66	
65	Musicians(1969)
64	Actors(1966)/Musicians(1952)
63	Mpls Symphony
62	
61	Danforth Fellows
60	NIAL Members/Actors(1937)/Artists(1968)/Ministers(1969)
59	Astronomers
58	Librarians/Ministers(1965)
57	Unitarian Ministers(1950)/Ministers(1927)/Physiatrists/Psychologists(1967)/Physicists(1968)/Architects(1968)/Psychiatrists (1967)
56	English Teachers/Mathematicians(1969)/College Profs/Psychologists(1947)/Pediatricians/Economists/Photographers/Political Scientists/Pulitzer Prize/Journalist(British)/Interpreters/Unitarian Ministers(1929)
55	Advertising Men(1968)/Physicians(1969)/Teaching Brothers/Priests(1966)/Sociologists/Social Workers(1953)/Elem Teachers (Minn)/Newsmen/Psychiatrists(1949)/Interior Decorators/Anthropologists/Chemists(1969)
54	Dental Educators/Guidance Counselors(1968)/Public Admins(1969)/YMCA Secs/Psychologists(1931)/Biologists/Social Workers (1967)/Artists(1933)/Pathologists/Internists
53	Radiologists/Psychologists(Exp)/Computer Programmers/Physical Therapists(1957)/Psychologists(1949)/Orthopedic Surgeons/ Neurological Surgeons/Student Personnel Workers/County Welfare Workers/Bus School Profs/Medical Techs/Physical Therapists ((1966)/Chiropractors/Elem Teachers(NDak)
52	Dentists(1969)/Investment Mgrs/Personnel Direcs(1969)/Salesmen,3M applicants/Cham Comm Execs/Architects(1933)/Soc Sci Teachers(1936)/YMCA PD/Credit Mgrs/Printers/Urologists/Surgeons/Optometrists/Comm Rec Direcs/Salesmen,Computer/ School Supers(1965)/Physicians(1949)/Bus Ed Teachers/Mathematicians(1929)/Math-Sci Teachers(1936)/Advertising Men(1931)/ Ag Extension Agents
51	Engineers(1968)/Cartographers/Football Coaches/Public Admins(1941)/Accountants/Chemists(1931)/Office Workers/High School Counselors/Personnel Direcs(1927)/Salesmen,Encyclopedia/YMCA Staff/Legislators/CPA(1944)/Physicists(1927)/Salesmen,Life (1966)/Osteopaths/NASA Scientists/Pharmacists(1968)/Lawyers(1969)
50	Dept Store Mgrs/Food Scientists/Funeral Direcs(1969)/Salesmen,Life(1969)/School Supers(1969)/Purchasing Agents(1969)/ Buyers(1969)/Rehab Counselors/Salesmen,3M/Pharmacists(1947)/Salesmen,Steel/Salesmen,PG&E/School Supers(1930)/CPA(1965)/ Carpenters(1936)/Salesmen,Auto/Army Officers(1950)/Generals & Admirals/Judges/Navy Officers/Corp Pres(1965)/Animal Husbandry Profs/Astronauts/Authors/Machinists/Buyers(1946)/Math-Sci Teachers(1968)
49	Physicians(1927)/Salesmen,Life(1931)/Engineers(1928)/Production Mgrs/Policemen(1933)/Pilots/Dentists(1932)/Funeral Direcs (1945)/Air Force Officers/Bankers(1964)/Policemen(1968)/Policemen(1969)/Soc Sci Teachers(1969)/Sales Mgrs(1968)/Colonels
48	Bankers(1969)/Foresters/Army Officers(1969)/Vets(1966)/Farmers(1936)/Purchasing Agents(1931)/Forest Service Men/Sales Mgrs(1932)/Bankers(1934)/Lawyers(1949)/Corp Pres(1935)/Lawyers(1927)/Petroleum Engineers/Vets(1949)/Guidance Counselors (1950)
47	Salesmen,Real Estate(1969)/Army Sergeants/Skilled Tradesmen/Tool & Die Makers/Salesmen,Real Estate(1932)/Governors/ Highway Patrolmen
46	County Sheriffs/Electricians/Carpenters(1969)
45	Voc Ag Teachers
44	Farmers(1967)
43	Farmers(1968)

TABLE 3-46. MEAN SCORES ON THE MEN'S NATURE SCALE

60	Voc Ag Teachers
59	Foresters/Farmers(1936)/Animal Husbandry Profs/Ag Extension Agents
58	Forest Service Men
57	Vets(1949)
56	Vets(1966)/Biologists
55	Orthopedic Surgeons
54	Radiologists/Urologists/Physiatrists
53	Food Scientists/Physicians(1969)/Elem Teachers(NDak)/Pediatricians/Surgeons/Ministers(1927)/Physical Therapists(1957)/ Farmers(1967)/Osteopaths/Pathologists/Neurological Surgeons/Farmers(1968)
52	Dental Educators/Medical Techs/Public Admins(1941)/YMCA Secs/Dentists(1932)/Physicians(1949)/Psychiatrists(1949)/ Artists(1933)/Internists/NIAL Members/Highway Patrolmen/Math-Sci Teachers(1968)/Actors(1937)
51	YMCA PD/Physicians(1927)/Comm Rec Direcs/Generals & Admirals/Math-Sci Teachers(1936)/Artists(1968)/Chemists(1969)/ Unitarian Ministers(1929)/Dentists(1969)/Physical Therapists(1966)/Chiropractors
50	English Teachers/Electricians/Policemen(1969)/School Supers(1969)/Purchasing Agents(1969)/Cartographers/Skilled Tradesmen, Tool & Die Makers/College Profs/Rehab Counselors/Architects(1933)/Chemists(1931)/School Supers(1930)/Unitarian Ministers (1950)/High School Counselors/Mpls Symphony/School Supers(1965)/Anthropologists/Governors/Guidance Counselors(1950)/ NASA Scientists/Pharmacists(1968)/Journalists(British)/County Welfare Workers/Policemen(1968)
49	Architects(1968)/Guidance Counselors(1968)/Psychiatrists(1967)/Soc Sci Teachers(1969)/Carpenters(1969)/Ministers(1969)/ Psychologists(1947)/Soc Sci Teachers(1936)/Social Workers(1953)/Psychologists(1931)/Credit Mgrs/Psychologists(Exp)/ Personnel Direcs(1927)/Carpenters(1936)/Elem Teachers(Minn)/Policemen(1933)/Librarians/Pulitzer Prize/Army Officers(1950)/ Bankers(1934)/Legislators/CPA(1944)/Psychologists(1949)/Music Teachers(1952)/Interior Decorators/Machinists
48	County Sheriffs/Engineers(1968)/Colonels/Pharmacists(1947)/Sociologists/Accountants/Engineers(1928)/Actors(1966)/Pilots/ Optometrists/Lawyers(1949)/Corp Pres(1935)/Corp Pres(1945)/Ministers(1965)/Physicists(1968)/Bus Ed Teachers/ Musicians((1952)/Astronauts/Mathematicians(1929)/Authors/Student Personnel Workers/Music Teachers(1946)/Physicists(1968)/ Astronomers
47	Funeral Direcs(1969)/Public Admins(1969)/Salesmen,Real Estate(1969)/Football Coaches/Musicians(1969)/Army Officers(1969)/ Priests(1966)/Office Workers/Salesmen,Life(1931)/Salesmen,PG&E/Printers/Production Mgrs/Photographers/Sales,Encyclopedia/ Judges/YMCA Staff/Computer Programmers/Corp Pres(1965)/Bankers(1964)/Social Workers(1967)/Petroleum Engineers/ Psychologists(1967)/Lawyers(1969)
46	Salesmen,Real Estate(1932)/Economists/Sales Mgrs(1932)/Danforth Fellows/Navy Officers/Buyers(1946)/Advertising Men(1968)/ Bankers(1969)/Mathematicians(1969)/Personnel Direcs(1969)/Teaching Brothers/Army Sergeants
45	Cham Comm Execs/Salesmen,Steel/CPA(1965)/Purchasing Agents(1931)/Political Scientists/Air Force Officers/Lawyers(1927)/ Newsmen/Advertising Men(1931)/Interpreters/Bus School Profs/Dept Store Mgrs/Investment Mgrs
44	Salesmen,Life(1966)/Salesmen,Life(1969)/Sales Mgrs(1968)/Buyers(1969)
43	Salesmen,Auto/Salesmen,Computer
42	Salesmen,3M
41	Salesmen,3M applicants

144

TABLE 3-47. MEAN SCORES ON THE MEN'S OFFICE PRACTICES SCALE

Mean Standard Score

Score	
75	Bus Ed Teachers
74	
73	
72	
71	Bankers(1934)/Bankers(1964)
70	County Welfare Workers
69	Office Workers
68	Accountants/Soc Sci Teachers(1936)/Credit Mgrs/Policemen(1968)
67	
66	Guidance Counselors(1950)/Bankers(1969)/Dept Store Mgrs/Elem Teachers(NDak)
65	Rehab Counselors/High School Counselors/Comm Rec Direcs/Math-Sci Teachers(1936)/Guidance Counselors(1968)/Army Sergeants/Voc Ag Teachers
64	Salesmen,3M/YMCA Secs/Salesmen,PG&E/CPA(1965)/CPA(1944)/School Supers(1965)/Ag Extension Agents/Pharmacists(1968)/Funeral Direcs(1969)/School Supers(1969)/Soc Sci Teachers(1969)/Buyers(1969)
63	Colonels/Public Admins(1941)/Purchasing Agents(1931)/Policemen(1933)/Legislators/Funeral Direcs(1945)/Buyers(1946)
62	Public Admins(1969)/Purchasing Agents(1969)/Salesmen,Real Estate(1969)/Ministers(1969)/Salesmen,3M applicants/Pharmacists(1947)/Farmers(1967)/Governors/Highway Patrolman
61	County Sheriffs/English Teachers/Cartographers/Vets(1966)/Cham Comm Execs/YMCA PD/School Supers(1930)/Printers/Carpenters(1936)/Elem Teachers(Minn)/Salesmen,Auto/Librarians/Army Officers(1950)/YMCA Staff/Ministers(1927)/Air Force Officers/Farmers(1968)
60	Policemen(1969)/Salesmen,Life(1969)/Army Officers(1969)/Salesmen,Real Estate(1932)/Social Workers(1953)/Salesmen,Steel/Personnel Direcs(1969)/Farmers(1936)/Forest Service Men/Optometrists/Navy Officers/Ministers(1965)/Music Teachers(1952)
59	Medical Techs/Personnel Direcs(1969)/Physical Therapists(1966)/Teaching Brothers/Football Coaches/Chiropractors/Priests(1966)/Salesmen,Encyclopedia/Sales Mgrs(1932)/Computer Programmers/Lawyers(1949)/Generals & Admirals/Physical Therapists(1957)/Petroleum Engineers/Vets(1949)/Music Teachers(1946)
58	Salesmen,Life(1931)/Production Mgrs/Salesmen,Computer/Corp Pres(1935)/Physiatrists/Animal Husbandry Profs/Osteopaths/Interior Decorators/Student Personnel Workers/Machinists/Math-Sci Teachers(1968)/Lawyers(1969)/Bus School Profs/Carpenters(1969)/Sales Mgrs(1968)/Foresters/Skilled Tradesmen/Tool & Die Makers
57	Electricians/Musicians(1969)/Urologists/Social Workers(1967)
56	Dentists(1969)/Engineers(1968)/Food Scientists/Psychologists(1947)/Sociologists/Radiologists/Pediatricians/Unitarian Ministers(1950)/Pilots/Dentists(1932)/Mathematicians(1929)/Journalists(British)
55	Dental Educators/Judges/Psychologists(1931)/Chemists(1931)/Lawyers(1927)/Corp Pres(1965)/Psychologists(1949)/Musicians(1952)/Orthopedic Surgeons/Unitarian Ministers(1929)
54	Biologists/Economists/Political Scientists/Mpls Symphony/Physicians(1949)/Psychiatrists(1949)/Advertising Men(1931)/Psychologists(1967)/NASA Scientists/Interpreters/Advertising Men(1968)/Investment Mgrs/Physicians(1969)/College Profs
53	Architects(1968)/Mathematicians(1969)/Psychiatrists(1967)/Engineers(1928)/Psychologists(Exp)/Newsmen/Physicists(1927)/Salesmen,Life(1966)/Internists/Astronauts/Neurological Surgeons/Chemists(1969)
52	Physicians(1927)/Surgeons/Pathologists
51	Architects(1933)/Actors(1966)/Pulitzer Prize/Astronomers/Physicists(1968)
50	Danforth Fellows/Authors/Anthropologists/Actors(1937)
49	Photographers/NIAL Members
48	Artists(1968)
47	Artists(1933)

TABLE 3-48. MEAN SCORES ON THE MEN'S PUBLIC SPEAKING SCALE

Mean Standard Score

Score	
67	Legislators
66	Governors
65	Unitarian Ministers(1950)/Ministers(1965)
64	Ministers(1969)
63	Football Coaches/Priests(1966)/Cham Comm Execs/Salesmen,Computer/Political Scientists/Salesmen,Encyclopedia
62	Salesmen,3M applicants/Ministers(1927)/School Supers(1965)/Salesmen,Life(1966)/Unitarian Ministers(1929)/Public Admins(1969)/Sales Mgrs(1968)
61	Salesmen,3M/Comm Rec Direcs/Danforth Fellows/Social Workers(1967)/Ag Extension Agents/Soc Sci Teachers(1969)/YMCA Secs/Social Workers(1953)/YMCA Staff/Judges/Newsmen/Student Personnel Workers/Lawyers(1969)/Advertising Men(1968)/Personnel Direcs(1927)/Salesmen,Life(1969)/School Supers(1969)
60	Sociologists/Economists/Elem Teachers(Minn)/Lawyers(1949)/Dept Store Mgrs/English Teachers/Funeral Direcs(1969)/Guidance Counselors(1950)
59	Soc Sci Teachers(1936)/Salesmen,Steel/High School Counselors/Generals & Admirals/Navy Officers/Astronauts/Guidance Counselors(1950)/Interpreters/Policemen(1968)
58	Rehab Counselors/Credit Mgrs/School Supers(1930)/Air Force Officers/Actors(1966)/Lawyers(1927)/Salesmen,Real Estate(1969)/Army Officers(1969)/Chiropractors/Vocational Ag Teachers/Buyers(1969)/Elem Teachers(NDak)
57	Public Admins(1941)/CPA(1965)/Optometrists/Corp Pres(1965)/Music Teachers(1952)/Bus Ed Teachers/Bus School Profs/County Sheriffs/Investment Mgrs/Policemen(1969)
56	Salesmen,Life(1931)/Librarians/Pulitzer Prize/Army Officers(1950)/Physiatrists/Animal Husbandry Profs/Psychologists(1967)/Journalists(British)/Psychiatrists(1967)/Teaching Brothers/Army Sergeants
55	Psychologists(1947)/YMCA PD/Salesmen,PG&E/Personnel Direcs(1927)/Computer Programmers/Physical Therapists(1957)/Psychologists(1949)/Bankers(1969)/Physical Therapists(1966)/Purchasing Agents(1969)/Petroleum Engineers/Neurological Surgeons/Highway Patrolmen/Actors(1937)/County Welfare Workers
54	Vets(1966)/Pediatricians/Sales Mgrs(1932)/Psychiatrists(1949)/Orthopedic Surgeons/Anthropologists/Math-Sci Teachers(1968)/Music Teachers(1946)/Physicians(1969)/Cartographers/Foresters/College Profs
53	Psychologists(1931)/Funeral Direcs(1945)/Biologists/Urologists/Salesmen,Auto/Internists/Math-Sci Teachers(1936)/Architects(1968)/Dentists(1969)/Dental Educators/Engineers(1968)/Medical Techs/Musicians(1969)/NIAL Members/Buyers(1946)
52	Salesmen,Real Estate(1932)/Accountants/Radiologists/Photographers/Psychologists(Exp)/Surgeons/Policemen(1933)/CPA(1944)/Bankers(1964)/Osteopaths/Authors/Interior Decorators/Advertising Men(1931)/NASA Scientists/Chemists(1969)
51	Office Workers/Printers/Production Mgrs/Purchasing Agents(1931)/Mpls Symphony/Bankers(1934)/Physicians(1949)/Musicians(1952)/Pathologists/Machinists/Colonels
50	Electricians/Pharmacists(1947)/Farmers(1936)/Pilots/Vets(1949)/Astronomers
49	Physicians(1927)/Corp Pres(1935)/Forest Service Men/Dentists(1932)/Mathematicians(1929)/Physicists(1968)/Mathematicians(1969)/Carpenters(1969)/Skilled Tradesmen/Tool & Die Makers
48	Chemists(1931)/Engineers(1928)/Physicists(1927)/Farmers(1968)/Artists(1968)
47	Architects(1933)/Carpenters(1936)
46	Farmers(1967)
45	Artists(1933)

145

TABLE 3-49. MEAN SCORES ON THE MEN'S RECREATIONAL LEADERSHIP SCALE

Mean Standard Score

```
61  YMCA PD
60
59  Football Coaches/Salesmen,3M applicants/Comm Rec Direcs
58  County Sheriffs/Salesmen,3M/YMCA Staff/Physical Therapists(1957)
57  Dept Store Mgrs/Policemen(1968)
56  Physical Therapists(1966)/Policemen(1969)/Soc Sci Teachers(1969)/Highway Patrolmen
55  Policemen(1933)
54  Sales Mgrs(1968)/Salesmen,Steel/Elem Teachers(Minn)/Salesmen,Auto/Salesmen,Computer
53  School Supers(1969)/Purchasing Agents(1969)/Army Officers(1969)/Soc Sci Teachers(1936)/Salesmen,Life(1966)/Social
    Workers(1967)/Machinists/Math-Sci Teachers(1968)/Guidance Counselors(1950)
52  Electricians/Personnel Direcs(1969)/Salesmen,Life(1969)/Tool & Die Makers/Credit Mgrs/CPA(1965)/Pilots/Army Officers
    (1950)/Legislators/Air Force Officers/Math-Sci Teachers(1936)/Ag Extension Agents
51  English Teachers/Army Sergeants/Cartographers/Foresters/Skilled Tradesmen/Chiropractors/Voc Ag Teachers/YMCA Secs/
    Salesmen,PG&E/Forest Service Men/School Supers(1965)/Osteopaths/Petroleum Engineers/Orthopedic Surgeons/Astronauts/
    Vets(1949)/Buyers(1946)/Pharmacists(1968)
50  Vets(1966)/Cham Comm Execs/Printers/High School Counselors/Urologists/Computer Programmers/Generals & Admirals/CPA(1944)/
    Newsmen/Bus Ed Teachers/NASA Scientists/County Welfare Workers/Advertising Men(1968)/Bankers(1969)/Dentists(1969)/
    Food Scientists/Funeral Direcs(1969)/Physicians(1969)/Carpenters(1969)/Salesmen,Real Estate(1969)/Buyers(1969)
49  Rehab Counselors/Social Workers(1953)/Office Workers/Salesmen,Life(1931)/Personnel Direcs(1927)/Salesmen,Encyclopedia/
    Optometrists/Dentists(1932)/Navy Officers/Ministers(1965)/Bankers(1964)/Physiatrists/Neurological Surgeons/Farmers(1968)/
    Journalists(British)/Lawyers(1969)/Engineers(1968)/Guidance Counselors(1968)/Teaching Brothers/Public Admins(1969)/
    Ministers(1969)/Elem Teachers(NDak)
48  Priests(1966)/Salesmen,Real Estate(1932)/Pharmacists(1947)/Public Admins(1941)/Accountants/Radiologists/Pediatricians/
    Production Mgrs/Carpenters(1936)/Farmers(1936)/Surgeons/Purchasing Agents(1931)/Sales Mgrs(1932)/Animal Husbandry Profs/
    Farmers(1967)/Student Personnel Workers/Governors/Medical Techs/Investment Mgrs
47  Dental Educators/Colonels/School Supers(1930)/Unitarian Ministers(1950)/Lawyers(1949)/Ministers(1927)/Funeral Direcs
    (1945)/Lawyers(1927)/Corp Pres(1965)/Physicians(1949)/Psychiatrists(1949)/Musicians(1952)
46  Architects(1968)/Psychologists(1947)/Physicians(1927)/Chemists(1931)/Bankers(1934)/Advertising Men(1931)/Music Teachers
    (1946)
45  Sociologists/Engineers(1928)/Danforth Fellows/Corp Pres(1935)/Music Teachers(1952)/Internists/Psychologists(1967)/
    Interpreters/Bus Ed Teachers/Psychiatrists(1967)
44  Musicians(1969)/College Profs/Psychologists(1931)/Photographers/Mpls Symphony/Judges/Pathologists/Actors(1937)/Chemists
    (1969)/Unitarian Ministers(1929)
43  Architects(1933)/Biologists/Economists/Actors(1966)/Pulitzer Prize/Psychologists(1949)/Artists(1933)/Authors
42  Psychologists(Exp)/Political Scientists/Librarians
41  Mathematicians(1969)/Anthropologists/Physicists(1968)/Artists(1968)
40  Physicists(1927)/Astronomers
39  Mathematicians(1929)/Interior Decorators
38  NIAL Members
```

TABLE 3-50. MEAN SCORES ON THE MEN'S RELIGIOUS ACTIVITIES SCALE

Mean Standard Score

```
71  YMCA Secs/Ministers(1927)
70  Ministers(1965)
69  YMCA Staff
68
67  Priests(1966)/Ministers(1969)
66  YMCA PD
65
64  Unitarian Ministers(1950)
63
62  Unitarian Ministers(1929)/Guidance Counselors(1968)/Elem Teachers(NDak)
61  Comm Rec Direcs/Legislators/Ag Extension Agents
60  Teaching Brothers/Rehab Counselors/Physical Therapists(1957)
59  Football Coaches/Salesmen,3M/Cham Comm Execs/Social Workers(1953)/High School Counselors/School Supers(1965)/Student
    Personnel Workers/Guidance Counselors(1950)
58  Salesmen,3M applicants/Credit Mgrs/Salesmen,Encyclopedia/Elem Teachers(Minn)/Danforth Fellows/Salesmen,Life(1966)/Social
    Workers(1967)/Music Teachers(1952)/Farmers(1968)/County Welfare Workers/Policemen(1968)/English Teachers/Funeral Direcs
    (1969)/School Supers(1969)
57  Medical Techs/Physical Therapists(1966)/Salesmen,Life(1969)/Soc Sci Teachers(1969)/Voc Ag Teachers/Soc Sci Teachers(1936)
56  Salesmen,Steel/Optometrists/Salesmen,Life(1969)/Physiatrists/Bus Ed Teachers/Highway Patrolmen
55  Dept Store Mgrs/Personnel Direcs(1969)/Purchasing Agents(1969)/Salesmen,Real Estate(1969)/Chiropractors/Sociologists/
    School Supers(1930)/CPA(1965)/Funeral Direcs(1945)/Farmers(1967)/Math-Sci Teachers(1968)/Pharmacists(1968)
54  Electricians/Policemen(1969)/Sales Mgrs(1968)/Vets(1966)/Librarians/Salesmen,Computer/Math-Sci Teachers(1936)/Governors/
    Machinists
53  County Sheriffs/Food Scientists/Carpenters(1969)/Public Admins(1969)/Cartographers/Foresters/Skilled Tradesmen/Tool & Die
    Makers/Colonels/Army Officers(1969)/Computer Programmers/Judges/Lawyers(1949)/Air Force Officers/Animal Husbandry Profs/
    Petroleum Engineers/Music Teachers(1946)
52  Dentists(1969)/Physicians(1969)/Army Sergeants/Musicians(1969)/Buyers(1969)/Salesmen,Life(1931)/Policemen(1933)/Mpls
    Symphony/Navy Officers/Astronauts/Vets(1949)/Lawyers(1969)
51  Bankers(1969)/Dental Educators/Engineers(1968)/Psychiatrists(1967)/Public Admins(1941)/Radiologists/Office Workers/Personnel
    Direcs(1927)/Salesmen,Auto/Bankers(1934)/Political Scientists/Newsmen/Generals & Admirals/Orthopedic Surgeons/Neurological
    Surgeons/NASA Scientists/Chemists(1969)
50  Advertising Men(1968)/Architects(1968)/Bus School Profs/College Profs/Pharmacists(1947)/Accountants/Pediatricians/Biologists/
    Urologists/Economists/Pulitzer Prize/Army Officers(1950)/CPA(1944)/Corp Pres(1965)/Musicians(1952)/Osteopaths/Astronomers
49  Mathematicians(1969)/Psychologists(1947)/Salesmen,PG&E/Printers/Production Mgrs/Farmers(1936)/Actors(1966)/Sales Mgrs(1932)/
    Physicians(1969)/Interior Decorators/Buyers(1946)/Psychologists(1967)/Journalists(British)/Interpreters
48  Carpenter(1936)/Purchasing Agents(1931)/Corp Pres(1935)/Psychologists(1949)/Mathematicians(1929)/NIAL Members/Physicists(1968)
47  Investment Mgrs/Salesmen,Real Estate(1932)/Engineers(1928)/Photographers/Surgeons/Forest Service Men/Dentists(1932)/Lawyers
    (1927)/Physicists(1927)/Psychiatrists(1949)/Actors(1937)/Artists(1968)
46  Pilots/Pathologists/Internists
45  Architects(1933)/Physicians(1927)/Chemists(1931)/Authors/Anthropologists/Advertising Men(1931)
44  Psychologists(1931)/Psychologists(Exp)
43  Artists(1933)
```

146

TABLE 3-51. MEAN SCORES ON THE MEN'S SALES SCALE

Mean Standard Score

Score	
68	Salesmen,Life(1969)
67	Salesmen,3M applicants
66	Salesmen,3M/Sales Mgrs(1968)
65	
64	Salesmen,Real Estate(1969)/Salesmen,PG&E/Salesmen,Encyclopedia
63	Salesmen,Auto/Salesmen,Computer
62	Dept Store Mgrs/
61	Salesmen,Steel/Salesmen,Life(1931)/Salesmen,Life(1966)/Buyers(1946)
60	Buyers(1969)
59	Salesmen,Real Estate(1932)/Sales Mgrs(1932)/Bus Ed Teachers
58	
57	Policemen(1968)/Funeral Direcs(1969)
56	YMCA Secs/Credit Mgrs/Legislators/Pharmacists(1968)
55	Advertising Men(1968)/Purchasing Agents(1969)/Voc Ag Teachers/Pharmacists(1947)/Cham Comm Execs/Funeral Direcs(1945)
54	Office Workers/High School Counselors/Ag Extension Agents/County Welfare Workers/Soc Sci Teachers(1969)
53	Food Scientists/Personnel Direcs(1969)/Policemen(1969)/Chiropractors/Rehab Counselors/Soc Sci Teachers(1936)/YMCA Staff/School Supers(1965)/Machinists
52	Bankers(1969)/County Sheriffs/Guidance Counselors(1968)/Physical Therapists(1966)/School Supers(1969)/Ministers(1969)/Elem Teachers(NDak)/YMCA PD/Corp Pres(1935)/Air Force Officers/Purchasing Agents(1931)/Comm Rec Direcs/Bankers(1934)/Advertising Men(1931)/Bankers(1964)/Farmers(1967)/Farmers(1968)/Guidance Counselors(1950)/Highway Patrolmen
51	Army Sergeants/Vets(1966)/Corp Pres(1965)/Petroleum Engineers/Vets(1949)/Lawyers(1969)
50	English Teachers/Carpenters(1969)/Cartographers/Football Coaches/Skilled Tradesmen/Tool & Die/Army Officers(1969)/Social Workers(1953)/CPA(1965)/Production Mgrs/Personnel Direcs(1927)/Carpenters(1936)/Optometrists/Physical Therapists(1957)/Accountants/Music Teachers(1952)/Interior Decorators/Math-Sci Teachers(1936)/Governors/Music Teachers(1946)
49	School Supers(1930)/Farmers(1936)/Elem Teachers(Minn)/Policemen(1933)/Ministers(1927)/Navy Officers/Ministers(1965)/Electricians/Engineers(1968)/Investment Mgrs/Public Admins(1969)/Musicians(1969)
48	Priests(1966)/Printers/Army Officers(1950)/CPA(1944)/Physiatrists/Social Workers(1967)/Osteopaths/Journalists(British)/Bus School Profs/Dentists(1969)/Medical Techs/Teaching Brothers/Foresters
47	Public Admins(1941)/Radiologists/Unitarian Ministers(1950)/Urologists/Forest Service Men/Pilots/Computer Programmers/Lawyers(1949)/Animal Husbandry Profs/Musicians(1952)/Orthopedic Surgeons/Math-Sci Teachers(1968)/Physicians(1969)/Colonels
46	Architects(1968)/Psychiatrists(1967)/Psychologists(1947)/Dentists(1932)/Generals & Admirals/Astronauts/Neurological Surgeons/Student Personnel Workers/Interpreters
45	Dental Educators/Pediatricians/Chemists(1931)/Engineers(1928)/Surgeons/Librarians/Physicians(1949)/Psychiatrists(1949)/Psychologists(1949)/Psychologists(1967)/NASA Scientists
44	Sociologists/Mpls Symphony/Judges/Newsmen/Lawyers(1927)/Internists/Chemists(1969)/Unitarian Ministers(1929)
43	College Profs/Architects(1933)/Psychologists(1931)/Physicians(1927)/Biologists/Economists/Photographers
42	Psychologists(Exp)/Actors(1966)/Political Scientists/Danforth Fellows/Pathologists/Mathematicians(1929)/Actors(1937)/Artists(1968)
41	Mathematicians(1969)/Pulitzer Prize/Physicists(1927)/Artists(1933)/Authors
40	Anthropologists/Physicists(1968)/Astronomers
39	NIAL Members

TABLE 3-52. MEAN SCORES ON THE MEN'S SCIENCE SCALE

Mean Standard Score

Score	
62	Physicists(1927)
61	Chemists(1931)/Physicists(1968)/Chemists(1969)/Astronomers
60	Medical Techs/Biologists/Psychologists(Exp)/Pathologists
59	Psychologists(1931)/Animal Husbandry Profs/Neurological Surgeons/NASA Scientists
58	Mathematicians(1969)/Pediatricians/Urologists/Internists/Mathematicians(1929)/Math-Sci Teachers(1936)
57	Dental Educators/Engineers(1968)/Food Scientists/Physicians(1969)/Radiologists/Engineers(1928)/Air Force Officers/Physiatrists/Psychiatrists(1949)/Psychologists(1949)/Orthopedic Surgeons/Astronauts/Math-Sci Teachers(1968)
56	Cartographers/Psychologists(1947)/Surgeons/Anthropologists
55	Physical Therapists(1966)/Psychiatrists(1967)/College Profs/Physicians(1927)/Economists/Optometrists/Computer Programmers/Danforth Fellows/Physicians(1949)/Physical Therapists(1957)/Petroleum Engineers/Machinists
54	Electricians/Tool & Die Makers/Army Officers(1950)/Pharmacists(1968)
53	Dentists(1969)/Foresters/Pilots/Dentists(1932)/Generals & Admirals/Osteopaths/Psychologists(1967)/Policemen(1968)
52	Skilled Tradesmen/Colonels/Army Officers(1969)/Vets(1966)/Pharmacists(1947)/Public Admins(1941)/Architects(1933)/Sociologists/School Supers(1930)/Mpls Symphony/Salesmen,Computer/CPA(1944)/Navy Officers
51	Bus School Profs/Chiropractors/Voc Ag Teachers/Elem Teachers(NDak)/Rehab Counselors/YMCA PD/Unitarian Ministers(1950)/Production Mgrs/Personnel Direcs(1927)/Elem Teachers(Minn)/Librarians/Ministers(1927)/NIAL Members/Student Personnel Workers/Unitarian Ministers(1929)
50	Accountants/High School Counselors/Corp Pres(1935)/Farmers(1936)/Forest Service Men/Political Scientists/Policemen(1933)/School Supers/Architects(1968)/Policemen(1969)/Musicians(1969)/Corp Pres(1965)/Musicians(1952)/Artists(1933)/Vets(1949)/Interpreters/County Welfare Workers
49	County Sheriffs/School Supers(1969)/Teaching Brothers/Purchasing Agents(1969)/Ministers(1969)/YMCA Secs/Social Workers(1953)/Credit Mgrs/Salesmen,PG&E/Printers/Photographers/Judges/Lawyers(1949)/Highway Patrolmen/Ag Extension Agents/Artists(1968)/Music Teachers(1946)
48	Public Admins(1969)/Army Sergeants/Salesmen,3M/Priests(1966)/Salesmen,Steel/Office Workers/CPA(1965)/Purchasing Agents(1931)/Pulitzer Prize/Comm Rec Direcs/Lawyers(1927)/Music Teachers(1952)/Bus Ed Teachers/Actors(1937)/Journalists(British)
47	Guidance Counselors(1968)/Investment Mgrs/Football Coaches/Soc Sci Teachers(1936)/Carpenters(1936)/Actors(1966)/Sales Mgrs(1932)/YMCA Staff/Legislators/Ministers(1965)/Social Workers(1969)/Governors
46	Dept Store Mgrs/English Teachers/Carpenters(1969)/Salesmen,3M applicants/Cham Comm Execs/Advertising Men(1931)/Bankers(1964)/Authors/Guidance Counselors(1950)/Lawyers(1969)
45	Bankers(1969)/Funeral Direcs(1969)/Personnel Direcs(1969)/Soc Sci Teachers(1969)/Salesmen,Encyclopedia/Salesmen,Auto/Newsmen
44	Advertising Men(1968)/Salesmen,Real Estate(1969)/Salesmen,Life(1931)/Funeral Direcs(1945)/Bankers(1934)
43	Sales Mgrs(1968)/Buyers(1969)/Salesmen,Real Estate(1932)/Buyers(1946)/Farmers(1968)
42	Salesmen,Life(1966)/Farmers(1967)/Interior Decorators
41	Salesmen,Life(1969)

TABLE 3-53. MEAN SCORES ON THE MEN'S SOCIAL SERVICE SCALE

Mean Standard Score

69	YMCA Secs
68	
67	Social Workers(1953)/YMCA Staff/Ministers(1965)
66	Ministers(1969)/Social Workers(1967)
65	YMCA PD/Ministers(1927)/County Welfare Workers/Guidance Counselors(1968)
64	Guidance Counselors(1950)
63	Soc Sci Teachers(1969)/Rehab Counselors/Priests(1966)/Unitarian Ministers(1950)/High School Counselors
62	Soc Sci Teachers(1936)/Teaching Brothers/Elem Teachers(NDak)
61	Psychologists(1947)/Comm Rec Direcs/Student Personnel Workers/Policemen(1968)
60	Salesmen,3M/Legislators/Physical Therapists(1957)/Ag Extension Agents
59	English Teachers/School Supers(1969)/Salesmen,3M applicants/Sociologists/Elem Teachers(Minn)/Danforth Fellows/ School Supers(1965)/Music Teachers(1952)
58	Psychiatrists(1967)/Salesmen,Encyclopedia/Bus Ed Teachers/Journalists(British)
57	School Supers(1930)/Psychologists(1967)/County Sheriffs/Dept Store Mgrs/Physical Therapists(1966)
56	Funeral Direcs(1969)/Personnel Direcs(1969)/Salesmen,Life(1969)/Public Admins(1969)/Voc Ag Teachers/Cham Comm Execs/ Credit Mgrs/Librarians/Physiatrists/Salesmen,Life(1966)/Math-Sci Teachers(1936)/Governors/Interpreters/Music Teachers (1946)
55	Chiropractors/Buyers(1969)/Pediatricians/Salesmen,Life(1931)/Policemen(1933)/Political Scientists/Mpls Symphony/ Funeral Direcs(1945)/Psychiatrists(1949)/Machinists/Unitarian Ministers(1929)
54	Bus School Profs/Policemen(1969)/Sales Mgrs(1968)/Football Coaches/Pharmacists(1947)/Public Admins(1941)/Salesmen,Steel/ Personnel Direcs(1927)/Optometrists/Lawyers(1949)/Psychologists(1949)/Musicians(1952)/Vets(1949)/Pharmacists(1968)/ Lawyers(1969)/Math-Sci Teachers(1968)/Highway Patrolmen
53	Advertising Men(1968)/Medical Techs/Physicians(1969)/Purchasing Agents(1969)/Salesmen,Real Estate(1969)/Army Sergeants/ Musicians(1969)/Vets(1966)/Salesmen,PG&E/CPA(1965)/Economists/Actors(1966)/Newsmen/Bankers(1964)/Farmers(1967)/ Osteopaths/Buyers(1946)
52	Judges/Office Workers/Printers/Carpenters(1936)/Salesmen,Auto/Bankers(1934)/Salesmen,Computer/CPA(1944)/Internists/ Actors(1937)/Dentists(1969)/Dental Educators/Cartographers/College Profs
51	Electricians/Investment Mgrs/Skilled Tradesmen/Tool & Die Makers/Colonels/Accountants/Radiologists/Urologists/ Photographers/Forest Service Men/Computer Programmers/Corp Pres(1935)/Air Force Officers/Physicians(1949)/Orthopedic Surgeons/Interior Decorators/NIAL Members/Farmers(1968)/Chemists(1969)
50	Bankers(1969)/Food Scientists/Foresters/Army Officers(1969)/Salesmen,Real Estate(1932)/Production Mgrs/Psychologists (Exp)/Farmers(1936)/Sales Mgrs(1932)/Pulitzer Prize/Lawyers(1927)/Corp Pres(1965)/Anthropologists/Neurological Surgeons/Astronomers/Physicists(1968)
49	Architects(1968)/Engineers(1968)/Mathematicians(1969)/Carpenters(1969)/Psychologists(1931)/Physicians(1927)/Biologists/ Surgeons/Purchasing Agents(1931)/Dentists(1932)/Navy Officers/Animal Husbandry Profs/Petroleum Engineers/Pathologists/ Advertising Men(1931)/Artists(1968)
48	Army Officers(1950)/Mathematicians(1929)/NASA Scientists
47	Architects(1933)/Chemists(1931)/Engineers(1928)/Pilots/Generals & Admirals/Physicists(1927)/Astronauts/Authors
46	Artists(1933)

TABLE 3-54. MEAN SCORES ON THE MEN'S TEACHING SCALE

Mean Standard Score

66	Music Teachers(1952)
65	
64	Music Teachers(1946)
63	Elem Teachers(Minn)/School Supers(1969)
62	English Teachers/Guidance Counselors(1968)/Ministers(1969)/Librarians/Danforth Fellows/Ministers(1965)/School Supers(1965)/ Ag Extension Agents
61	Soc Sci Teachers(1969)/Teaching Brothers/Elem Teachers(NDak)/School Supers(1930)/Unitarian Ministers(1950)/High School Counselors/Ministers(1927)/Bus Ed Teachers/Student Personnel Workers
60	Rehab Counselors/Soc Sci Teachers(1936)/Social Workers(1967)/Math-Sci Teachers(1968)
59	Dental Educators/Football Coaches/Voc Ag Teachers/Priests(1966)/Sociologists/Mpls Symphony/Comm Rec Direcs/YMCA Staff/ Physiatrists/Psychologists(1967)/Guidance Counselors(1950)/Unitarian Ministers(1929)
58	Physical Therapists(1966)/Psychiatrists(1967)/College Profs/Social Workers(1953)/Biologists/Actors(1966)/Political Scientists/Mathematicians(1929)/Math-Sci Teachers(1936)/Neurological Surgeons/Astronomers
57	Bus School Profs/Mathematicians(1969)/Psychologists(1947)/Psychologists(1931)/Pediatricians/Legislators/Physical Therapist (1957)/Psychologists(1949)/Physicists(1968)/Policemen(1968)
56	Personnel Direcs(1969)/Physicians(1969)/Public Admins(1969)/Army Officers(1969)/YMCA Secs/Economists/Psychiatrists(1949)/ Animal Husbandry Profs/Musicians(1952)/Pathologists/Internists/Anthropologists/Chemists(1969)
55	Dept Store Mgrs/Medical Techs/Musicians(1969)/YMCA PD/Psychologists(Exp)/Judges/Salesmen,Encyclopedia/Optometrists/ Pulitzer Prize/Generals & Admirals/Navy Officers/Physicists(1927)/Orthopedic Surgeons/NIAL Members/Interpreters
54	Salesmen,3M applicants/Cham Comm Execs/Credit Mgrs/Air Force Officers/Surgeons/Computer Programmers/Lawyers(1949)/Dentists (1969)/Colonels/Salesmen,Computer/Newsmen/Journalists(British)/Lawyers(1969)
53	Advertising Men(1968)/Chiropractors/Salesmen,3M/Radiologists/Photographers/Army Officers(1950)/Salesmen,Life(1966)/ Astronauts/Artists(1968)
52	Engineers(1968)/Food Scientists/Cartographers/Buyers(1969)/Vets(1966)/CPA(1965)/Urologists/Personnel Direcs(1927)/Corp Pres(1965)/Physicians(1949)/Governors/NASA Scientists/Pharmacists(1968)/County Welfare Workers
51	Architects(1968)/Policemen(1969)/Salesmen,Life(1969)/Sales Mgrs(1968)/Purchasing Agents(1969)/Army Sergeants/Foresters/ Public Admins(1941)/Chemists(1931)/Petroleum Engineers/Interior Decorators/Machinists
50	Investment Mgrs/Physicians(1927)/Salesmen,Steel/CPA(1944)/Highway Patrolmen/Actors(1937)
49	Bankers(1969)/County Sheriffs/Accountants/Lawyers(1927)/Bankers(1964)/Osteopaths
48	Funeral Direcs(1969)/Tool & Die Makers/Salesmen,PG&E/Printers/Policemen(1933)/Dentists(1932)/Vets(1949)
47	Electricians/Salesmen,Real Estate(1969)/Skilled Tradesmen/Pharmacists(1947)/Architects(1933)/Officer Workers/Salesmen,Life (1931)/Production Mgrs/Advertising Men(1931)/Authors(1931)/Buyers(1946)
46	Carpenters(1969)/Engineers(1928)/Corp Pres(1935)/Carpenters(1936)/Farmers(1936)/Salesmen,Auto/Forest Service Men/Pilots/ Artists(1933)
45	Sales Mgrs(1932)
44	Funeral Direcs(1945)/Bankers(1934)/Farmers(1967)/Farmers(1968)
43	Salesmen,Real Estate(1932)/Purchasing Agents(1931)

TABLE 3-55. MEAN SCORES ON THE MEN'S TECHNICAL SUPERVISION SCALE

Mean Standard Score

```
0  Production Mgrs
9
8  Army Officers(1950)
7  Dept Store Mgrs
6  Machinists/Corp Pres(1935)/Salesmen,3M applicants
5  Personnel Direcs(1969)/Purchasing Agents(1969)/Army Officers(1969)/Personnel Direcs(1927)/Purchasing Agents(1931)/Credit
   Mgrs/Air Force Officers/Corp Pres(1965)/Salesmen,Steel/Salesmen,Computer
4  Sales Mgrs(1968)/Navy Officers/Salesmen,PG&E/Bus Ed Teachers/Salesmen,3M/Petroleum Engineers
3  Policemen(1968)/School Supers(1969)/Tool & Die Makers/County Welfare Workers/Generals & Admirals/Cham Comm Execs/Sales
   Mgrs(1932)/Accountants/Carpenters(1936)/County Sheriffs
2  Policemen(1969)/Buyers(1969)/Colonels/Buyers(1946)/CPA(1944)/Engineers(1928)/Office Workers/Public Admins(1941)/Football
   Coaches/School Supers(1965)/Comm Rec Direcs
1  Foresters/Bankers(1969)/Public Admins(1969)/Skilled Tradesmen/Voc Ag Teachers/Army Sergeants/YMCA Secs/Printers/Forest
   Service Men/Pilots/Soc Sci Teachers(1969)/Engineers(1968)/Governors
0  Soc Sci Teachers(1969)/Bankers(1934)/Farmers(1968)/Food Scientists/Salesmen,Life(1969)/Salesmen,Real Estate(1969)/
   Electricians/Farmers(1967)
9  Lawyers(1969)/Funeral Direcs(1969)/Carpenters(1969)/Pharmacists(1968)/Bankers(1964)/Guidance Counselors(1950)/School
   Supers(1930)/Chemists(1931)/Funeral Direcs(1945)/Math-Sci Teachers(1936)/Policemen(1933)/Salesmen,Auto/Highway Patrolmen
8  Guidance Counselors(1968)/Cartographers/Elem Teachers(NDak)/Orthopedic Surgeons/Ag Extension Agents/High School Counselors
   YMCA PD/Salesmen,Real Estate(1932)/Farmers(1936)/Rehab Counselors/Bus School Profs/English Teachers
7  Ministers(1969)/Chiropractors/Optometrists/Psychologists(1931)/YMCA Staff/Social Workers(1953)/Physical Therapists(1957)/
   CPA(1965)/Salesmen,Life(1931)/Lawyers(1949)/Elem Teachers(Minn)/Computer Programmers/Salesmen,Life(1966)/Astronauts
6  Advertising Men(1968)/Music Teachers(1946)/Urologists/Radiologists/Advertising Men(1931)/Ministers(1927)/Pharmacists(1947)
   Physical Therapists(1966)/NASA Scientists/Judges/Vets(1966)/Public Admins(1969)
6  Investment Mgrs/Interpreters/Osteopaths/Student Personnel Workers/Pediatricians/Neurological Surgeons/Vets(1949)/Ministers
   (1965)/Priests(1966)/Economists/Math-Sci Teachers(1968)/Physiatrists/Social Workers(1967)
4  Physicians(1969)/Dentists(1969)/Musicians(1969)/Lawyers(1927)/Music Teachers(1952)/Dentists(1932)/Psychiatrists(1949)/
   Unitarian Ministers(1950)/Journalists(British)
3  Chemists(1969)/Animal Husbandry Profs/Surgeons/Psychologists(1949)/Librarians/Medical Techs/Teaching Brothers/Newsmen
2  Architects(1968)/Unitarian Ministers(1929)/Physicians(1949)/Psychologists(Exp)/Musicians(1952)/Physicists(1927)/
   Psychiatrists(1967)/Interior Decorators
1  Physicists(1968)/College Profs/Dental Educators/Physicians(1927)/Internists/Psychologists(1947)/Mathematicians(1929)/
   Architects(1933)/Psychologists(1967)/Political Scientists
0  Pathologists/Biologists/Sociologists/Mpls Symphony
9  Photographers/Astronomers
8  Mathematicians(1969)/Authors
7  Anthropologists/Artists(1968)/Pulitzer Prize/Danforth Fellows
6  Artists(1933)/Actors(1937)
5  Actors(1966)/NIAL Members
```

TABLE 3-56. MEAN SCORES ON THE MEN'S WRITING SCALE

Mean Standard Score

```
4  Unitarian Ministers(1950)/Librarians/Pulitzer Prize/Newsmen/Journalists(British)
3  English Teachers/Actors(1966)/Authors/Unitarian Ministers(1929)
2  Political Scientists/Danforth Fellows/NIAL Members/Actors(1937)
1  Ministers(1965)
0  Advertising Men(1968)/Psychiatrists(1967)/Psychologists(1947)/Judges/Photographers/Ministers(1927)/Sociologists/
   Psychologists(1967)/Interpreters/Artists(1968)
9  Ministers(1969)/Anthropologists/Neurological Surgeons/Social Workers(1953)
8  Guidance Counselors(1968)/College Profs/Economists/Elem Teachers(Minn)/Legislators/Social Workers(1967)/Music Teachers
   (1952)/Student Personnel Workers/Advertising Men(1931)/Cham Comm Execs/Psychologists(1931)/Lawyers(1969)
7  Bus School Profs/Public Admins(1969)/Rehab Counselors/Priests(1966)/Mpls Symphony/Lawyers(1949)/School Supers(1965)/
   Physiatrists/Psychiatrists(1949)/Psychologists(1949)/Governors/YMCA Secs/Pediatricians
6  Teaching Brothers/Football Coaches/School Supers(1930)/Psychologists(Exp)/Salesmen,Encyclopedia/Lawyers(1927)/Musicians
   (1952)/Physicists(1968)
5  Architects(1968)/Investment Mgrs/Personnel Direcs(1969)/Physicians(1969)/Salesmen,3M applicants/Salesmen,3M/Printers/
   High School Counselors/Biologists/Personnel Direcs(1927)/Comm Rec Direcs/Army Officers(1950)/Generals & Admirals/Artists
   (1933)/Internists/Interior Decorators/Public Admins(1941)/Soc Sci Teachers(1936)/Astronomers
4  Dental Educators/Mathematicians(1969)/School Supers(1969)/Soc Sci Teachers(1969)/Musicians(1969)/Elem Teachers(NDak)/
   Credit Mgrs/YMCA Staff/Salesmen,Life(1966)/Bus Ed Teachers/Orthopedic Surgeons/Radiologists/County Welfare Workers/
   Music Teachers(1946)
3  Colonels/Urologists/Surgeons/Computer Programmers/Salesmen,Computer/Navy Officers/Physical Therapists(1957)/Pathologists/
   YMCA PD/Machinists/Chemists(1969)/Ag Extension Agents
2  Army Officers(1969)/Chiropractors/Buyers(1969)/Salesmen,Steel/Office Workers/Salesmen,Life(1931)/Salesmen,PG&E/Air Force
   Officers/Optometrists/CPA(1944)/Physicians(1949)/Astronauts/Mathematicians(1929)/Architects(1933)/Policemen(1968)
1  Bankers(1969)/Dentists(1969)/Medical Techs/Policemen(1969)/Sales Mgrs(1968)/Army Sergeants/Cartographers/Corp Pres(1935)/
   CPA(1965)/Sales Mgrs(1932)/Animal Husbandry Profs/Accountants/Chemists(1931)/Buyers(1946)/Guidance Counselors(1950)
0  Dept Store Mgrs/Engineers(1968)/Food Scientists/Physical Therapists(1966)/Salesmen,Life(1969)/Purchasing Agents(1969)/
   Foresters/Forest Service Men/Policemen(1933)/Pilots/Corp Pres(1965)/Osteopaths/Petroleum Engineers/Math-Sci Teachers(1936)/
   Salesmen,REal Estate(1932)/Physicians(1927)/Math-Sci Teachers(1968)/NASA Scientists/Pharmacists(1968)
9  Engineers(1928)/Production Mgrs/Salesmen,Auto/Dentists(1932)/Bankers(1934)/Physicists(1927)/Pharmacists(1947)/Highway
   Patrolmen
8  Funeral Direcs(1969)/Salesmen,Real Estate(1969)/Vets(1966)/Funeral Direcs(1945)/Farmers(1936)/Purchasing Agents(1931)/
   Bankers(1964)
7  County Sheriffs/Voc Ag Teachers/Carpenters(1936)
6  Tool & Die Makers/Vets(1949)
5  Electricians/Skilled Tradesmen
4
3  Carpenters(1969)/Farmers(1967)
2  Farmers(1968)
```

149

score points, or two standard deviations. While that is a substantial separation (if reported in percentiles, that would be the difference between the 15th and 85th percentiles), still it is less than the three or four standard deviations found between extreme scores on the Occupational Scales. To achieve purity of content and easier interpretation, empirical validity has suffered.

Scores for seven subgroups of business school professors. Further information on the use of the Basic Scales for concurrent comparisons of occupations has been provided by Rhode (1969). He collected hundreds of SVIBs from men in one occupation—business school professor—and divided them into categories according to their specialty. The mean profile for each specialty subgroup is shown in Table 3-57. Three conclusions are obvious; first, the highest and lowest mean scores of the groups are, again, intuitively reasonable. For the total sample, the highest means were those for the Teaching, Writing, Law/Politics and Public Speaking scales, and the lowest were for the Mechanical and Agriculture scales. Second, where the groups differed from each other, the differences were meaningfully related to their activities; thus, the accounting subgroup scored higher on the Office Practices scale than did the others, the management subgroup scored highest on the Business Management scale, the statistics subgroup scored highest on the Mathematics scale, the marketing subgroup was highest on the Merchandising scale, and the Industrial Relations subgroup was highest on both the Law/Politics and Social Service scales. Third, the differences

TABLE 3-57. MEAN SCORES ON THE BASIC INTEREST SCALES FOR 853 BUSINESS SCHOOL PROFESSORS IN SIX DIFFERENT FIELDS

SCALE	Accounting	Finance	Management	Statistics	Marketing	Industrial Relations	Misc[a]	Total Group
N=	165	100	156	79	183	39	131	853
Public Speaking	55	55	56	53	58	59	55	56
Law/Politics	56	57	57	55	57	62	57	57
Business Management	52	49	55	47	53	51	51	52
Sales	47	46	47	44	53	46	46	48
Merchandising	51	47	49	45	54	48	48	50
Office Practices	53	47	46	44	48	46	46	48
Military Activities	47	46	49	45	48	47	46	47
Technical Supervision	47	46	50	48	45	48	49	47
Mathematics	56	54	53	59	51	47	52	53
Science	51	50	51	55	49	51	51	51
Mechanical	44	41	44	45	40	42	44	43
Nature	46	44	45	46	44	50	46	45
Agriculture	43	41	43	44	43	45	44	43
Adventure	48	50	50	51	50	52	50	50
Recreational Leadership	46	45	45	44	45	48	44	45
Medical Service	48	47	48	49	47	49	48	48
Social Service	54	55	55	52	54	57	53	54
Religious Activities	53	48	50	49	49	53	49	50
Teaching	57	56	57	57	56	58	57	57
Music	53	52	54	55	52	55	53	53
Art	51	51	52	53	52	54	52	52
Writing	56	55	57	56	58	59	56	57

[a] Includes faculty from many other diverse areas such as Industrial Psychology, Transportation, and Computer Specialists.

between the subgroups, though reasonable, were much smaller in magnitude than are differences between unrelated occupations; the largest difference on any scale was only 12 points (the statisticians' 59 on the Mathematics scale versus the Industrial Relations' 47), and most of the means were within 2 or 3 points of each other.

Predictive Validity

Berdie-Schletzer curricular samples over 8–10 years. The predictive validity of these scales can be demonstrated by reanalyzing some SVIBs collected by Berdie and Schletzer (Berdie, 1960; Schletzer, 1963). Berdie identified students who graduated from the University of Minnesota in curricula that are closely tied to eventual occupations, specifically: Accounting, Dentistry, Journalism (which has a looser tie than the others), Law, Mechanical Engineering, and Medicine. Each of these students had completed the SVIB as high school seniors, and Berdie's report indicated that there were substantial relationships between their high school SVIB profiles and the curricula they selected. Schletzer, for her Ph.D. dissertation, located and retested these same students approximately four years after they graduated from the University of Minnesota, roughly eight to ten years after the initial testing.

The relevant data are presented in the next two tables. In Table 3-58 are listed, for the total group, test-retest correlations, test and retest means and standard deviations. For each of the occupational subgroups, the test and retest means are presented, and the mean changes larger than four points are identified. Four points, which is four-tenths of a SD, is probably the smallest practical difference worth attending to among these small samples.

As an aid to interpretation of the data in Table 3-58, Table 3-59 was prepared. In this table are listed for each subgroup (1) their three highest scores as high school seniors, (2) their three highest scores on retest, when they were roughly 3–4 years beyond their final degree, and (3) the three largest gains for each sample, which frequently were not among the highest scores on either testing.

Although, again, there is no one index to determine the predictive efficiency of these scales, the results are reassuringly meaningful. The scales that each group scored highest on, both at test and retest, were, with a few exceptions, those most related to their work. The exceptions were almost all due to the "Adventure" scale; this was among the three highest scores for five of the samples at test, and remained among the highest for three at the retest. This personality scale just doesn't operate as do the vocational interest scales. Other than this scale, the other high scores were appropriate. The

TABLE 3-58. BASIC INTEREST SCALE TEST AND RETEST DATA FOR THE BERDIE-SCHLETZER CURRICULAR GROUPS

	TOTAL SAMPLE						Accountants (N=24)			Dentists (N=30)			Journalists (N=21)			Lawyers (N=32)			Mechanical Engineers (N=38)			Physicians (N=26)		
	r_{t-r}	M	SD	M	SD	Ch	Test M	Retest M	C	Test M	Retest M	C	Test M	Retest M	C	Test M	Retest M	C	Test M	Retest M	C	Test M	Retest M	C
1. Public Speaking	.67	53	10.8	57	11.0	+4	52	55		46	47		55	61	+6	63	65		50	54	+4	54	59	+5
2. Law/Politics	.70	53	10.6	57	10.6	+4	55	60	+5	47	50		54	59	+5	61	66		50	55	+5	52	55	
3. Business Management	.46	49	10.3	50	10.5		54	56		46	43		51	53		56	54		46	51	+5	45	43	
4. Sales	.38	53	10.1	48	9.5	-5	58	50	-8	50	44	-6	58	54	-4	58	49	-9	50	49		48	42	-6
5. Merchandising	.52	50	9.9	50	10.4		56	56		47	45		52	54		56	52		47	50		46	43	
6. Office Practices	.56	51	10.2	46	9.9	-5	61	55	-6	50	43	-7	49	47		55	48	-4	47	45		46	42	-4
7. Military Activities	.43	53	9.0	50	9.4		53	48	-5	52	52		53	51		55	52		53	51		50	46	-4
8. Technical Supervis'n	.37	48	9.6	50	11.7		46	50	+4	48	47		46	42	-4	47	45	-5	53	61	+8	46	48	
9. Mathematics	.69	53	8.6	54	9.6		54	57		53	53		44	41		49	50		59	60		57	59	
10. Science	.60	52	9.5	53	9.3		48	50		54	55		46	45		46	47		58	58		60	60	
11. Mechanical	.72	48	9.9	48	10.9		45	46		49	49		45	41	-4	42	42		57	58		45	47	
12. Nature	.64	42	9.8	45	10.6		38	39		44	49	+5	41	40		39	41		44	47		46	50	+4
13. Agriculture	.53	43	10.0	44	10.1		40	40		43	46		42	40		40	41		47	47		45	44	
14. Adventure	.47	58	10.5	57	11.0		56	53		59	56		57	59		59	56		62	61		55	53	
15. Recreational Leadership	.65	52	9.8	50	9.8		55	52		53	53		51	49		53	49	-4	51	53		46	47	
16. Medical Service	.56	52	9.8	55	10.5		48	50		57	63	+6	48	49		50	50		49	52		62	64	
17. Social Service	.44	52	9.6	52	9.7		55	54		50	50		53	56		53	53		48	49		55	51	-4
18. Religious Activities	.38	52	10.4	53	11.3		52	53		50	52		54	55		54	52		50	53		54	56	
19. Teaching	.36	45	9.3	53	8.3	+8	46	54	+8	42	52	+10	47	55	+8	46	53	+7	42	51	+9	46	55	+9
20. Music	.55	45	10.3	51	9.4	+6	48	51		44	48	+4	48	52	+4	50	53		41	49	+8	48	56	+8
21. Art	.57	45	8.5	50	9.8	+5	43	46		45	51	+6	48	55	+7	45	49	+4	44	49	+5	45	51	+6
22. Writing	.63	49	9.2	53	10.1	+4	50	51		43	45		58	64	+6	56	60	+4	44	49	+5	48	54	+6
Median	.56																							

TABLE 3-59. THREE HIGHEST TEST AND RETEST MEANS AND LARGEST GAINS
FOR THE BERDIE-SCHLETZER SIX CURRICULAR GROUPS

	Accountants		Dentists		Journalists	
Test Means	Office Practices	61	Adventure	59	Writing	58
	Sales	58	Medical Service	57	Sales	58
	Merchandising	56	Science	54	Adventure	57
	Adventure	56				
Retest Means	Law/Politics	60	Medical Service	65	Writing	64
	Mathematics	57	Adventure	56	Public Speaking	61
	Business Management	56	Science	55	Law/Politics	59
	Merchandising	56			Adventure	59
Gains	Teaching	46-54	Teaching	42-52	Teaching	47-55
	Law/Politics	55-60	Medical Service	57-63	Art	48-55
	Technical Supervision	46-50	Art	45-51	Writing	58-64
					Public Speaking	55-61

	Lawyers		Mechanical Engineers		Physicians	
Test Means	Public Speaking	63	Adventure	62	Medical Service	62
	Law/Politics	61	Mathematics	59	Science	60
	Adventure	59	Science	58	Mathematics	57
Retest Means	Law/Politics	66	Technical Supervision	61	Medical Service	64
	Public Speaking	65	Adventure	61	Science	60
	Writing	60	Mathematics	60	Public Speaking	59
					Mathematics	59
Gains	Teaching	45-53	Teaching	42-51	Teaching	46-55
	Law/Politics	61-66	Technical Supervision	53-61	Music	48-56
	Art	45-49	Music	41-49	Art	45-51
	Writing	56-60			Writing	48-54

accountants scored highest on the business-oriented scales: Office Practices, Sales, and Merchandising; the dentists and physicians scored highest on the Medical Service and Science scales, and so forth.

The patterns of high scores on both the test and retest administrations again make it very clear that the scales have a substantial relationship to the individual's occupational choice.

Salesmen and scientists over 36 years. Further predictive validity information has been developed by studying two subsets of individuals from the Basic Scales norm group. As these men have been tested twice, once in 1930 as 16-year-olds and again in 1966 as 52-year-olds, their test results can be related to their adult occupations.

When retested as adults, these men were asked to fill in a short checklist describing their jobs. This checklist contained "semantic differential" type items, that is, pairs of statements reflecting opposite extremes, and each man was asked to indicate where his job fell on a line between these pairs. Two of the items were "sales vs. non-sales" and "science vs. non-science." From the total sample, two subgroups of individuals were identified, using their answers to these two items. The first included 101 men who marked

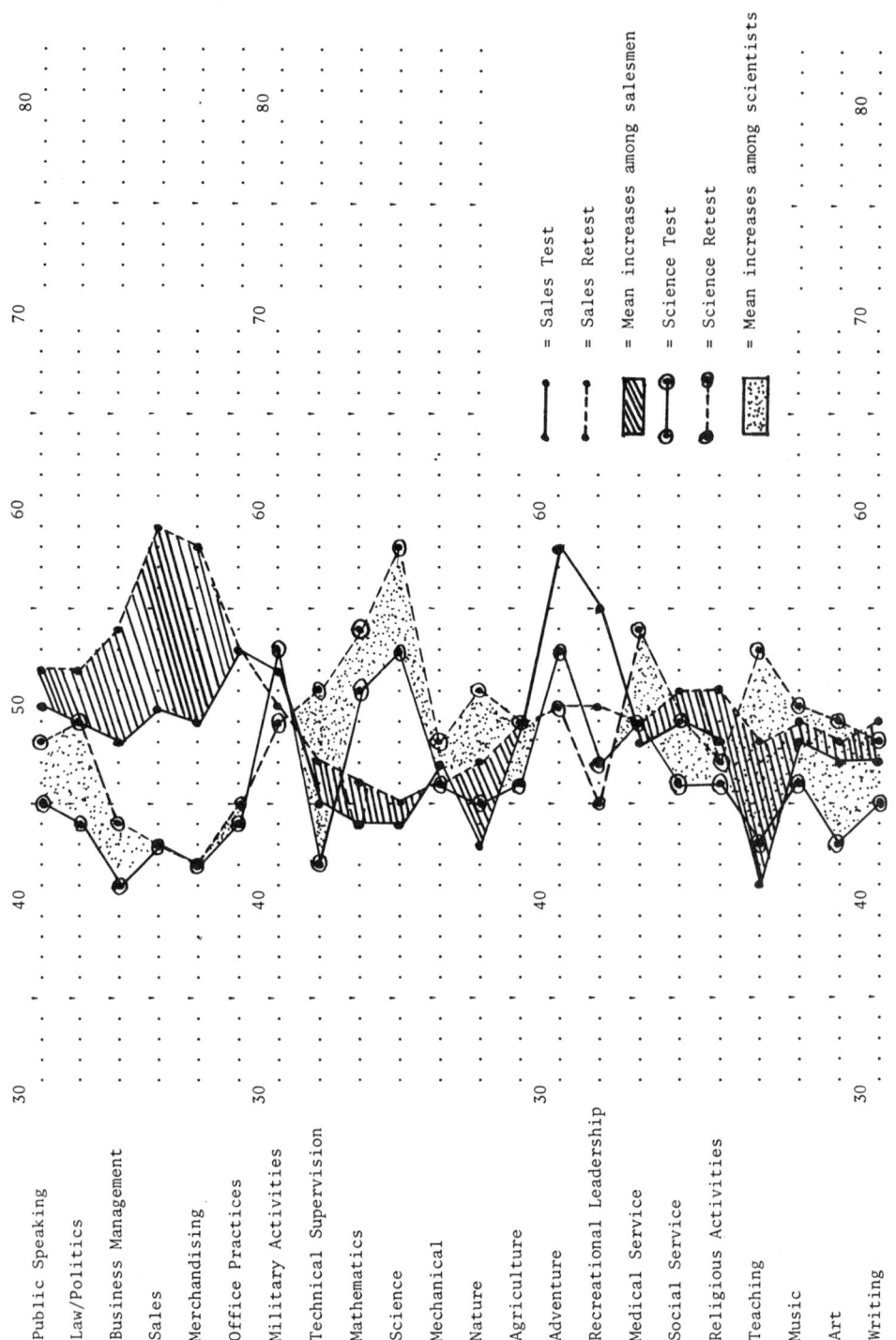

FIG. 3-31. *Test and retest profiles for Salesman and Scientist samples over 36 years.*

154

the opposing extremes, "sales, non-science" as descriptive of their jobs; the other sample included 42 men who marked the other extremes, "science, non-sales." The following diagram shows graphically how these groups were selected and reports the number in each group:

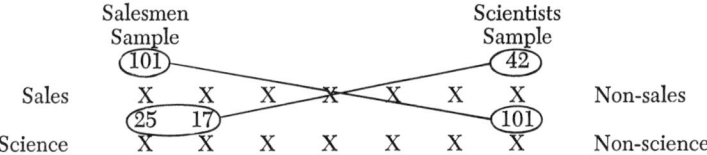

The test (age 16) and retest (age 52) SVIB Basic Scale profiles for these two groups are presented in Figure 3-31.

As the mean profiles indicate, the Sales and Science scales separated these groups fairly well at age 16 and by age 52 the difference had increased. At age 16, the differences were roughly one standard deviation, increasing to about 1.5 or 2 standard deviations between the adults. The larger differences between the adult samples were created because the salesmen increased more on the sales-oriented scales, the scientists on the science-oriented scales, not because either of them had decreasing scores. Whether these increases came before or after the occupational experience can't be determined from these data; the latter seems more plausible.

These mean differences on the Basic Scales, though large and statistically far beyond the chance level, were not as large as the differences between these two samples on the regular SVIB occupational scales. For example, on the Chemist and Sales Manager scales, the samples had the following test and retest means:

Chemist Scale Means

	Test	Retest
Scientists	39	43
Salesmen	26	17
Difference	13	26

Sales Manager Scale Means

	Test	Retest
Salesmen	35	41
Scientists	27	20
Difference	8	21

These larger differences, exceeding 2 standard deviations among the adult samples, can probably be traced to the relative heterogeneity of the occupational scales compared to the Basic Scales. Each of these two occupational scales, Chemist and Sales Manager, contains both science and sales components. In the Chemist scale, these components are weighted positively and negatively respectively; in the Sales Manager scale, the reverse is true. Thus the occupational scales take advantage of both components for maximum separation, while the Basic Scales sacrifice some of this differentiability for easier interpretability. Note again that there were differential increases (and, contrary to the findings on the Basic Scales, actual decreases on the nonappropriate scale) on these scales for these two differing samples.

This chapter has been almost solely concerned with the construction and evaluation of scales to measure specific areas of vocational interests. An important next step is to learn something about the application of these scales.

Uses of the Basic Interest Scales

Use in Understanding How Interests Are Organized

One result of this work was to reveal more about the organization of interests. The clusters of items were not forced; for the most part, they fell out of the intercorrelation matrix relatively cleanly and their make-up reflects something of the basic dimensions underlying the items. In this sense, some clusters that did not appear are noteworthy. The failure of personality clusters to appear has already been noted. Another interesting omission was anything resembling a "prestige" cluster—it might have contained items such as "Corporation President," "Governor," and, perhaps, "College Professor." This might indicate that status per se is not an important determinant of item choice; yet the item popularities, as measured by percent responding "Like," strongly suggest that status does play some role—another paradox.

The clusters that were formed merit extensive study as they have some psychological integrity, so to speak. One observation can already be made, i.e., item clustering tends to follow vertical, not horizontal, divisions in the occupational world. Thus, the Science scale includes high and low laboratory positions, the Office Practices scale includes high and low office positions. This strongly suggests that the unifying feature is the activity involved, not the more tangential aspects of the work.

Use in Applied Settings

Because the Basic Interest Scales are new, no one has had much experience with them in applied settings and any comments about interpretation must be tentative.

Still, after recognizing this caution, we should be able to make considerable use of the Basic Scales in understanding an individual's SVIB results.

Each of these scales has items concentrated in one area; if a person has a high score, above 57 or 58, this means he has consistently indicated more interests in this area than does the average person; in fact, he has marked as many "Likes" (and as few "Dislikes") as do people who have selected an occupation in that area. The task of the counselor is to help this person understand this about himself, and to plan accordingly.

The overall pattern of the Basic Scale scores are important. If an individual has high scores in two or more areas, he should seek information about career possibilities which might mesh well with all of his high scores. An example of this was found in an adult who had three high scores: Religious Activities, Law/Politics, and Writing. He currently is in Public Relations work for a large religious institution.

The task of the counselor in working with these scores is to help the individual find outlets—usually, an occupation—for his unique patterns of scores. This means the counselor must be well informed about the interest patterns of many occupations—specifically, the data presented in Tables 3-35 through 3-56 and, for the women, Tables 4-27 through 4-45.

The Basic Scales should be used in conjunction with the regular Occupational Scales. An individual's high and low scores on the Occupational Scales can be better understood by inspecting his scores on the Basic Scales. The combination of these two types of scales, the one oriented directly to the occupations, the other dealing with homogeneous content, should make it possible to better understand each individual's preferences.

Though the Basic Scales should be useful in evaluating an individual's responses to the SVIB, they are intended to supplement, not supplant, the regular Occupational Scales. The Occupational Scales still permit greater diversity and complexity in profile patterns than do the Basic Scales as the unique items remaining in the SVIB, not included in any of the Basic Scales, are important. To restrict our measurements to these 22 factors in the belief that the valid variance in the interest domain has been covered, or even the valid variance in the SVIB item pool, would be a mistake.

CHAPTER 4

The Women's Basic Interest Scales

Basic Interest Scales have been developed for the Women's booklet, directly analogous to the men's scales. General comments on these scales and details of scale construction have already been covered in Chapter 3; in this chapter are the relevant statistics for the Women's Basic Scales.

Item Composition of the Women's Basic Interest Scale

The items in each scale and their intercorrelations are presented in Tables 4–1 through 4–19. The items were taken from the Form W booklet (Set 1) and the revised booklet, TW398 (Set 2). The correlations above the diagonals are based on the responses of Strong's 1946 sample of 500 Women-in-General; those below the diagonal are based on the Women-in-General sample used to develop the 1969 Occupational Scales. Item response percentages for both groups are in the appendix. As with the men's scales, these items are scored by assigning +1 weights to the "Like" responses, −1 weights to the "Dislike" responses.

Norms for the Women's Basic Interest Scales

To norm the women's scales, the sample of 1,000 Women-in-General described in Appendix C was used; their raw score means and SDs on both the Set 1 and Set 2 scales are reported in Table 4-20. These are the figures to be used for the raw-score-to-standard-score conversions.

For comparative purposes, the standard score mean and standard deviations on the Set 1 scales for a general sample of high school senior girls, about age 17, is also given in Table 4-20. These girls were a cross section of the Minnesota high school population, tested in 1965 by Joselyn for his Ph.D. dissertation (Joselyn, 1968).

Table 4-20 also contains the correlations between the same named Set 1 and Set 2 scales. Those correlations, like the men's, are quite high, and the scales can be considered interchangeable, though the Set 2 scales are slightly longer and are preferred.

TABLE 4-1. Women's Art Scale Item Intercorrelations

Item Number	Item	6	19	28	49	50	103	112	131	162
6	Artist		47	36	52	31	56	46		
19	Cartoonist	46		32	53	27	41	27		
28	Costume Designer	49	39		46	58	35	30		
49	Illustrator	57	51	47		41	49	40		
50	Interior Decorator	43	31	53	45		31	30		
103	Sculptor	60	44	41	55	33		38		
112	Art Teacher	53	47	33	49	32	54			
131	Sketching pictures of wild animals	41	43	22	44	23	40	49		
162	Magazines about art and music	46	18	26	34	26	41	39	29	

TABLE 4-2. Women's Biological Science Scale Item Intercorrelations

Item Number	Item	13	16	77	78	111	391	203
13	Bacteriologist		75	55	47	45	39	
16	Biologist	69		45	50	41	40	
77	Pharmacist	49	40		45	41	29	
78	Physician	43	41	48		77	38	
111	Surgeon	45	39	43	70		32	
391	Physiology	35	39	37	31	26		
203	Watching an open-heart operation	41	39	36	47	53	30	

TABLE 4.3 Women's Homemaking Scale Item Intercorrelations

Item Number	Item	21	27	48	115	178	185	186	189	205	371	206
21	Caterer		52	31	42	22	40	21	34	39	39	
27	Cook	44		52	45	23	59	25	44	47	41	
48	Housekeeper	26	35		42	32	43	23	36	36	41	
115	Home Economics Teacher	24	29	27		26	37	28	36	34	53	
178	Doing your own laundry work	18	23	32	20		25	39	26	27	25	
185	Cooking	27	59	29	26	29		31	55	71	49	
186	Sewing	13	22	22	25	18	26		25	30	30	
189	Preparing dinner for guests	21	41	23	19	12	57	14		53	42	
205	Trying new cooking recipes	22	50	21	27	22	69	24	49		42	
371	Home Economics	20	31	25	35	33	31	41	16	32		
206	Organizing cupboards and closets	13	22	27	19	30	19	20	12	24	26	

TABLE 4-4. WOMEN'S LAW/POLITICS SCALE ITEM INTERCORRELATIONS

Item Number	Item	45	53	56	57	81	172	193	370	392	160
45	Governor of a State		52	51	37	42	42	25	28	34	
53	Judge	50		57	51	36	34	27	31	33	
56	Corporation Lawyer	44	42		53	41	34	27	31	33	
57	Criminal Lawyer	40	46	59		37	28	13	13	23	
81	Politician	60	41	36	42		33	32	28	39	
172	Being head of a civic improvement program	34	31	35	27	37		28	27	30	
193	Discussions of politics	36	31	30	30	45	31		37	55	
370	Civics (government)	22	21	22	15	24	27	43		56	
392	Political Science	32	29	30	30	41	26	60	56		
160	Electioneering for office	48	36	28	37	62	39	42	28	33	

Set 2 brackets items 45–392; Set 1 brackets items 53–392; item 160 is separate.

TABLE 4-5. WOMEN'S MECHANICAL SCALE ITEM INTERCORRELATIONS

Item Number	Item	32	52	64	101	102	140	176	177	340	384	38	135	151	163	353	385
32	Draftsman		36	52	45	30	30	42	39	28	54						
52	Inventor	26		42	45	40	29	25	32	31	41						
64	Mechanical Engineer	40	35		42	38	31	49	43	33	53						
101	Scientific Illustrator	34	40	45		58	29	30	32	29	41						
102	Scientific Research Worker	18	40	45	58		26	29	31	28	32						
140	Solving mechanical puzzles	24	30	43	32	31		34	35	27	38						
176	Operating machinery	21	28	44	24	33	38		65	48	52						
177	Repairing electrical wiring	29	29	46	37	34	45	55		52	51						
340	Have mechanical ingenuity	21	26	35	26	24	37	33	41		46						
384	Mechanical Drawing	55	32	45	34	23	34	40	39	38							
38	Electronics Technician	35	31	60	38	35	30	37	38	18	31						
135	Looking at things in a hardware store	25	16	20	22	12	24	36	37	22	30	14					
151	Popular mechanics magazines	31	29	42	33	31	46	48	50	40	40	36	41				
163	Making a radio or hi-fi set	29	36	42	33	37	40	40	46	28	32	37	24	41			
353	Enjoy tinkering with small hand tools	31	22	35	30	26	35	45	50	50	42	29	39	47	32		
385	Woodworking	40	30	36	29	22	29	43	46	42	57	25	36	45	37	53	

Set 2 brackets items 32–385; Set 1 brackets items 32–384.

TABLE 4-6. WOMEN'S MERCHANDISING SCALE ITEM INTERCORRELATIONS

Item Number	Item	4	18	37	46	47	59	61	94	98	107	120	207	122
4	Advertiser		35	23	23	33	24	26	25	32	26	19	30	
18	Buyer of merchandise	32		40	35	45	20	60	24	49	47	37	43	
37	Employment Manager	32	29		25	42	19	31	17	33	29	32	25	
46	Hostess	20	31	21		48	12	34	24	31	30	38	29	
47	Hotel Manager	30	37	44	45		19	36	22	43	29	38	33	
59	Life Insurance Saleswoman	24	17	19	14	17		11	48	24	32	16	14	
61	Manager, Women's Style Shop	22	51	20	41	29	18		23	45	46	43	51	
94	Real Estate Saleswoman	32	32	26	21	29	44	24		32	34	43	51	
98	Retailer	32	53	32	29	34	29	41	36		53	31	43	
107	Specialty Saleswoman	29	37	29	35	32	37	44	33	51		37	41	
120	Tea Room Proprietress	09	24	21	42	40	25	35	22	33	38		30	
207	Displaying merchandise in a store	25	40	17	26	24	17	46	21	47	39	23		
122	Travel Bureau Manager	29	35	34	29	45	18	33	26	33	31	26	27	

Set 2 { Set 1 }

TABLE 4-7. WOMEN'S MEDICAL SERVICE SCALE ITEM INTERCORRELATIONS

Item Number	Item	13	16	31	54	72	77	78	111	174	235	391	2	85	90	127	197	203
13	Bacteriologist		75	30	60	27	55	47	45	26	17	39						
16	Biologist	69		28	53	24	45	50	41	27	17	40						
31	Dietitian	26	21		32	26	37	33	24	15	15	20						
54	Laboratory Technician	54	44	34		35	57	39	41	19	12	25						
72	Nurse	30	26	32	40		27	34	32	38	32	23						
77	Pharmacist	49	40	37	56	32		45	41	14	08	29						
78	Physician	43	41	25	37	41	48		77	35	20	38						
111	Surgeon	45	39	16	32	30	43	70		35	15	32						
174	Giving "first aid" assistance	18	19	21	29	41	21	30	25		35	24						
235	Physically sick people	12	19	19	17	28	21	22	22	24		16						
391	Physiology	35	39	20	27	24	37	31	26	29	23							
2	Dental Assistant	20	15	31	44	36	30	16	13	15	10	19						
85	Nurse's Aid	14	12	31	33	62	77	18	10	32	28	19	34					
90	Veterinarian for small animals	26	25	17	17	25	23	30	29	24	12	17	16	20				
127	X-Ray Technician	46	38	35	64	43	52	37	34	25	22	26	53	36	21			
197	Taping a bruised ankle	29	30	29	32	45	26	38	37	49	36	30	15	31	24	30		
203	Watching an open-heart operation	41	39	14	35	41	36	47	53	29	25	30	26	26	26	36	39	

Set 1 / Set 2

TABLE 4-8. WOMEN'S MUSIC SCALE ITEM INTERCORRELATIONS

Item Number	Item	69	70	119	141	152	236
69	Music Composer		69	51	47	26	
70	Musician	71		44	60	39	
119	Music Teacher	58	60		43	20	
141	Playing the piano	39	53	40		32	
152	Symphony concerts	36	39	32	27		
236	Musical geniuses	44	44	41	31	43	

(Items 69–152 = Set 1; Set 2 indicated in margin.)

TABLE 4-9. WOMEN'S NUMBERS SCALE ITEM INTERCORRELATIONS

Item Number	Item	3	108	297	362	363	368	398	215
3	Income Tax Accountant		51	34	28	35	48	49	
108	Statistician	52		46	30	29	47	67	
297	Statistician vs Social Worker	24	33		20	21	43	51	
362	Algebra	23	24	21		59	55	32	
363	Arithmetic	27	29	11	63		52	37	
368	Calculus	32	40	24	50	45		55	
398	Statistics	39	57	30	26	34	41		
215	Making statistical charts	35	55	39	25	29	35	52	

(Items 3–398 = Set 1; Set 2 indicated in margin.)

TABLE 4-10. WOMEN'S OFFICE PRACTICES SCALE ITEM INTERCORRELATIONS

Item Number	Item	14	17	20	74	75	83	108	109	123	366	395	44	66	89	95	121	192
14	Bank Teller		60	64	48	36	28	39	36	37	51	39						
17	Bookkeeper	44		63	54	36	33	42	44	42	69	41						
20	Cashier in bank	81	50		50	38	30	38	38	38	49	36						
74	Office Clerk	56	51	56		52	44	35	57	53	48	44						
75	Office Manager	41	51	46	59		45	29	41	32	37	37						
83	Private Secretary	35	34	35	47	46		23	58	44	31	38						
108	Statistician	36	45	41	42	37	28		29	27	42	30						
109	Stenographer	38	43	43	58	44	57	46		69	39	57						
123	Typist	42	45	46	59	44	49	39	70		42	47						
366	Bookkeeping	35	68	40	46	42	30	42	41	44		50						
395	Shorthand	23	29	22	36	22	32	27	41	43	39							
44	Hospital Records Clerk	49	41	52	55	35	33	32	44	46	32	26						
66	Courtroom Stenographer	36	29	35	38	32	46	36	47	46	29	34	40					
89	Railroad Reservations Clerk	40	26	42	50	29	28	30	41	37	27	27	47	38				
95	Receptionist	42	28	41	41	41	38	23	36	40	25	19	40	30	31			
121	Supervisor in telephone office	45	35	47	46	44	32	32	42	45	30	24	45	33	44	38		
192	Operating office machines	40	45	44	58	48	40	40	51	52	46	37	41	36	34	31	48	
204	Checking typewritten material for errors	25	27	27	37	29	23	31	29	34	28	26	32	21	25	22	29	36

(Items 14–395 = Set 1; Set 2 indicated in margin.)

TABLE 4-11. Women's Outdoors Scale Item Intercorrelations

Item Number	Item	40	55	132	139	175	386	143	151	328
40	Farmer		38	24	26	39	25			
55	Landscape Gardner	29		22	33	48	32			
132	Camping out	28	16		26	30	28			
139	Bird watching	26	38	18		38	60			
175	Raising flowers and vegetables	26	51	25	44		37			
386	Nature Study	21	40	26	50	40				
143	Hiking	29	15	52	24	22	22			
151	Popular mechanics magazines	26	27	21	34	30	31	14		
328	Be married to a rancher vs be married to a corporation executive	41	14	28	23	20	26	23	16	

TABLE 4-12. Women's Performing Arts Scale Item Intercorrelations

Item Number	Item	1	33	69	70	76	86	93	100	103	114	372	236	243
1	Actress		45	13	13	30	44	47	30	23	36	34		
33	Dramatist	61		36	34	38	41	36	51	43	32	58		
69	Music Composer	30	38		69	50	24	30	37	43	27	22		
70	Musician	30	33	71		46	25	30	24	36	29	22		
76	Opera Singer	42	48	54	49		33	54	30	37	35	26		
86	Professional Dancer	55	45	40	39	44		35	29	36	57	28		
93	Radio-TV Singer	49	44	44	37	57	58		36	29	35	30		
100	Scenario Writer	33	42	46	31	41	32	33		38	26	40		
103	Sculptor	34	40	47	34	37	38	30	40		27	29		
114	Dancing Teacher	38	35	40	37	33	65	46	28	32		24		
372	Dramatics	51	54	32	33	40	46	42	28	34	36			
236	Musical geniuses	29	35	44	44	35	25	27	27	27	25	23		
243	Ballet dancers	34	33	30	30	35	46	29	28	34	36	44	35	

163

TABLE 4-13. Women's Physical Science Scale Item Intercorrelations

Item Number	Item	11	22	52	64	102	199	368	369	377	390	38	159	166	240	320
11	Author of technical book		32	27	37	44	39	42	27	30	32					
22	Chemist	40		34	34	53	33	36	62	31	45					
52	Inventor	32	32		42	40	29	30	24	32	31					
64	Mechanical Engineer	38	44	35		38	23	48	28	33	37					
102	Scientific Research Worker	37	59	40	45		61	31	37	39	35					
199	Doing research work	31	47	43	37	60		28	28	32	27					
368	Calculus	26	40	24	39	37	34		40	29	48					
369	Chemistry	32	61	19	33	44	40	43		32	51					
377	Geology	23	35	37	28	35	32	17	23		42					
390	Physics	23	46	23	43	41	42	57	53	30						
38	Electronics Technician	29	37	31	60	35	30	38	29	20	39					
159	Performing scientific experiments	31	57	44	39	63	55	40	46	39	47	31				
166	Science fiction magazines	32	33	27	32	34	31	22	28	28	29	32	39			
240	Outstanding scientists	23	37	36	22	40	36	20	28	36	25	23	40	36		
320	Be married to a research scientist vs Be married to a sales executive	20	38	26	24	42	38	27	29	25	27	20	41	38	21	

(Items 11–390 bracketed as Set 1; all items bracketed as Set 2.)

TABLE 4-14. Women's Public Speaking Scale Item Intercorrelations

Item Number	Item	24	33	81	91	92	172	173	181	182	184	195	394	160
24	College Professor		22	17	28	21	23	08	18	16	29	17	23	
33	Dramatist	35		17	37	42	14	16	17	18	25	08	32	
81	Politician	28	31		30	26	33	34	19	26	30	16	32	
91	Radio Announcer	19	28	22		57	32	18	25	25	43	21	46	
92	Radio Program Director	23	27	31	61		31	21	26	24	30	23	35	
172	Being head of a civic improvement program	26	24	37	28	36		39	34	41	41	36	38	
173	Expressing judgments publicly, regardless of what others say	24	17	33	20	17	37		27	28	33	23	36	
181	Interviewing men for a job	27	23	30	18	27	38	27		64	30	34	30	
182	Interviewing clients	24	18	24	20	28	32	24	66		35	40	30	
184	Making a speech	25	26	32	24	22	37	30	22	26		35	67	
195	Meeting and directing people	21	20	26	19	24	39	27	38	39	37		29	
394	Public Speaking	24	29	27	28	24	37	23	23	24	63	34		
160	Electioneering for office	24	27	62	26	25	39	33	31	28	36	24	28	

(Items 24–394 bracketed as Set 1; all items bracketed as Set 2.)

TABLE 4-15. WOMEN'S RELIGIOUS ACTIVITIES SCALE ITEM INTERCORRELATIONS

Item Number	Item	67	128	183	227	365		65	149	153	169
67	Missionary		36	40	43	39					
128	YWCA Staff Member	29		31	29	28					
183	Going to church	37	20		61	46					
227	Religious people	40	24	57		43					
365	Bible History	38	11	42	45						
65	Church Worker	56	35	56	51	45					
149	Religious music	35	21	42	46	49		49			
153	Reading the Bible	42	23	54	52	64		52	60		
169	Church young people's group	49	29	49	48	41		63	42	51	

TABLE 4-16. WOMEN'S SOCIAL SERVICE SCALE ITEM INTERCORRELATIONS

Item Number	Item	67	79	84	106	124	128		39	73
67	Missionary		25	27	32	21	36			
79	Playground Director	28		34	35	25	27			
84	Probation Officer	27	34		46	36	24			
106	Social Worker	36	38	36		38	42			
124	Vocational Counselor	24	36	38	36		37			
128	YWCA Staff Member	29	29	27	25	25				
39	Manager of children's nursery at resort hotel	32	52	19	34	23	27			
73	Policewoman	33	31	53	31	22	21		21	

TABLE 4-17. WOMEN'S SPORTS SCALE ITEM INTERCORRELATIONS

Item Number	Item	8	79	132	133	134	200	253	296	389		63	143	246
8	Athletic Director		49	23	19	20	22	37	56	52				
79	Playground Director	48		23	04	12	23	23	34	27				
132	Camping out	30	31		19	20	09	18	15	25				
133	Golf	23	16	28		19	03	14	06	16				
134	Horseback riding	21	12	38	29		12	22	10	21				
200	Acting as cheer-leader	33	29	16	20	23		21	20	22				
253	Women athletes	39	23	24	22	17	13		34	36				
296	Physical education director vs Magazine writer	47	30	25	15	12	13	39		53				
389	Physical Education	58	36	32	22	21	32	48	55					
63	Professional Golfer	35	21	21	57	21	30	29	17	28				
143	Hiking	26	30	52	20	31	17	21	12	22		14		
246	Athletic men	30	24	18	22	16	29	39	21	34		28	17	

TABLE 4-18. WOMEN'S TEACHING SCALE ITEM INTERCORRELATIONS

Item Number	Item	79	104	112	113	115	116	117	118	119	190	373	164
79	Playground Director		30	15	20	29	36	27	40	29	32	28	
104	School Principal	37		29	34	35	40	53	28	31	33	43	
112	Art Teacher	23	28		28	25	32	24	26	42	29	23	
113	Commercial Teacher	28	35	39		40	40	39	33	30	27	37	
115	Home Economics Teacher	27	33	34	44		26	35	32	30	29	33	
116	Grade School Teacher	38	42	31	40	36		47	57	38	41	45	
117	High School Teacher	27	49	32	36	34	52		30	36	47	49	
118	Kindergarten Teacher	44	26	30	33	27	65	33		35	44	37	
119	Music Teacher	24	34	43	34	36	37	39	39		29	30	
190	Teaching children	36	30	21	24	25	49	32	52	25		42	
373	Education (teacher training)	27	36	22	30	22	59	40	43	24	45		
164	Leading a Girl Scout troop	51	26	17	24	28	41	25	43	29	38	30	

Set 2, Set 1 (bracketed groupings as indicated in margin)

TABLE 4-19. WOMEN'S WRITING SCALE ITEM INTERCORRELATIONS

Item Number	Item	9	10	33	35	42	49	60	80	96	97	100	380	71	165
9	Author of children's books		49	24	34	25	38	44	38	25	23	29	32		
10	Author of novel	59		45	49	34	37	62	48	40	24	46	40		
33	Dramatist	25	39		46	39	42	46	50	35	26	51	37		
35	Editor	32	46	39		46	35	56	45	47	30	47	52		
42	Foreign Correspondent	29	35	37	38		39	44	33	48	29	38	38		
49	Illustrator	36	37	40	37	35		39	42	23	20	38	28		
60	Magazine Writer	46	65	42	48	34	43		53	50	35	55	53		
80	Poet	41	50	48	42	34	46	50		37	27	52	38		
96	General Reporter	22	35	25	46	40	25	42	31		55	44	52		
97	Women's Page Reporter	23	28	27	41	28	21	41	26	58		35	40		
100	Scenario Writer	32	45	42	41	28	42	46	51	33	34		44		
380	Journalism	31	44	27	43	30	19	45	32	38	30	32			
71	News Photographer	18	29	19	33	39	28	30	27	46	34	32	23		
165	Writing a one-act play	39	52	51	45	32	40	53	56	36	28	52	40	27	

Set 2, Set 1 (bracketed groupings as indicated in margin)

TABLE 4-20. MEANS AND STANDARD DEVIATIONS ON THE WOMEN'S BASIC SCALES
FOR THE WOMEN-IN-GENERAL NORM SAMPLE, AND A SAMPLE OF
HIGH SCHOOL SENIORS

	Women-in-General Sample* (N=1000)				Joselyn High School Seniors** (N-923)		Correlations between the Set 1 and Set 2
	Set 1		Set 2		Set 1		
	Mean	SD	Mean	SD	Mean	SD	Scales
Public Speaking	.65	5.47	.09	5.81	44.3	9.5	.99
Law/Politics	- .76	4.48	-1.32	4.88	45.6	10.1	.99
Merchandising	-1.37	5.83	-1.14	6.31	50.4	8.6	.99
Office Practices	-3.27	6.15	-5.43	9.37	56.2	10.0	.98
Numbers	-1.29	3.86	-1.66	4.32	49.6	8.3	.99
Physical Science	- .49	5.04	- .55	6.95	43.5	9.4	.98
Mechanical	-1.81	4.97	-2.81	7.59	44.5	8.2	.97
Outdoors	1.42	3.02	1.80	4.05	45.3	9.6	.95
Biological Science	.39	3.99	.11	4.08	46.5	10.4	.97
Medical Service	- .01	5.29	-1.14	7.84	49.4	10.4	.96
Teaching	- .07	5.56	- .11	5.98	49.2	9.0	.99
Social Service	- .29	3.18	- .80	4.07	52.6	9.1	.97
Sports	.80	4.33	1.88	5.30	53.4	8.0	.97
Homemaking	1.99	4.76	2.31	5.08	50.5	8.5	.99
Religious Activities	.87	2.60	1.77	4.74	53.3	8.5	.96
Music	1.54	2.74	1.96	3.09	42.1	11.6	.99
Art	2.00	3.96	2.48	4.81	46.5	9.9	.99
Performing Arts	.67	6.07	1.42	6.67	45.6	9.0	.99
Writing	2.07	6.44	2.40	7.44	44.1	9.5	.99

* Raw Scores   ** Standard Scores

Scale Intercorrelations

The intercorrelations for the Women's Basic Scales are given in Table 4-21, along with the means and standard deviations for the group used to calculate these figures. On the basis of these correlations, the scales have been ordered on the profile so that the adjoining ones tend to be positively correlated.

The correlations between the Women's Basic Scales and Occupational Scales are in Table 4-22. These figures are helpful in understanding the makeup of the Occupational Scales as they show the degree of relationship between these scales and each of the more homogeneous Basic Scales.

The correlations between the Men's Basic Scales and Women's Basic Scales are reported in Table 4-23. That table also contains all of the intercorrelations between the Men's and Women's Nonoccupational Scales and

TABLE 4-21. INTERCORRELATIONS FOR THE WOMEN'S BASIC SCALES

Scale	Mean	SD	Dislike Percent	Indifferent Percent	Like Percent	Total Responses	Unpopular Items	Form Check	OIE	FM II	Diversity of Interests	AACH	Writing	Performing Arts	Art	Music	Religious Activities	Homemaking	Sports	Social Service	Teaching	Medical Science	Biological Science	Outdoors	Mechanical	Physical Science	Numbers	Office Practices	Merchandising	Law/Politics
Public Speaking	56	9	-42	01	48	-02	-06	-12	-85	-08	50	25	51	40	25	21	25	03	23	39	41	20	22	15	15	12	07	11	29	75
Law/Politics	57	10	-38	10	34	-02	-07	-16	-70	-24	50	21	31	19	04	07	17	-07	21	30	22	20	25	08	13	15	14	17	23	
Merchandising	47	9	-53	12	50	09	-09	-14	-39	07	53	-32	11	21	24	04	18	44	22	39	22	26	-01	-02	02	-14	-02	54		
Office Practices	43	8	-55	27	36	-06	00	-36	-08	-02	41	-24	-01	-01	01	-05	34	34	19	29	11	24	-03	05	19	02	32			
Numbers	54	10	-28	21	10	05	-01	-58	01	-21	18	41	06	00	-06	07	-03	-02	13	-06	-02	18	22	13	41	58				
Physical Science	58	10	-30	12	22	-01	02	-70	-04	-18	11	64	11	14	12	19	-02	-06	20	-05	00	28	56	34	71					
Mechanical	55	12	-31	13	22	05	12	-31	-05	-26	16	35	06	07	15	09	02	-04	31	-04	05	32	30	50						
Outdoors	48	10	-35	09	31	-07	-09	-29	-15	-24	28	37	31	33	38	28	32	30	47	33	05	38	31							
Biological Science	54	9	-37	06	36	-12	01	-41	-17	-02	15	37	24	27	21	20	06	01	19	20	18	82								
Medical Service	52	9	-61	18	51	-06	-10	-04	-20	05	34	12	20	33	29	24	30	28	38	44	37									
Teaching	52	11	-52	07	54	-08	-29	-18	-48	32	53	-01	43	42	50	40	38	49	44	72										
Social Service	52	10	-61	14	57	-05	-05	-05	-46	25	54	-08	41	39	45	25	52	47	50											
Sports	52	9	-38	08	36	-06	-06	-04	-33	-14	39	07	20	23	20	15	42	18												
Homemaking	45	11	-45	06	47	01	-11	-07	-17	46	36	47	26	38	46	29	34													
Religious Activities	45	11	-29	18	44	-09	-19	-22	-26	30	39	28	17	73	53	27														
Music	52	10	-48	-09	64	-02	-22	-15	-25	49	33	40	47	75																
Art	50	10	-44	-06	62	05	-28	-24	-30	64	38	38	71																		
Performing Arts	52	10	-48	-08	60	06	-22	-23	-40	51	40		74																	
Writing	53	8	-55	08	18	-02	-15	25	-10	42	42																			
Academic Achievement	53	10	-12	06	59		-34	07	-58	23	18																			
Diversity of Interests	53	10	44	-20	36		-07		-02	23																				
Femininity-Masculinity II	40	13	42	05	-49																									
Occ. Extra-Introversion	44	12	29	24	-01																									
Form Check	2	5	04	-30	-02																									
Unpopular Items	1	1	-50	-01																										
Total Responses	398	1	-62	-37																										
Like Percentage	36	14																												
Indifferent Percentage	30	16																												
Dislike Percentage	34	17																												

TABLE 4-22. INTERCORRELATIONS BETWEEN THE WOMEN'S OCCUPATIONAL SCALES AND THE WOMEN'S BASIC SCALES, NONOCCUPATIONAL SCALES, AND ADMINISTRATIVE INDICES

	PUBLIC SPEAKING	LAW POLITICS	MERCHANDISING	OFFICE PRACTICES	NUMBERS	PHYSICAL SCIENCE	MECHANICAL	OUTDOORS	BIOLOGICAL SCIENCE	MEDICAL SERVICE	TECHNICAL	SOCIAL SERVICE	SPORTS	HOMEMAKING	RELIGIOUS ACTIVITIES	MUSIC	ART	PERFORMING ARTS	WRITING	AACH	DIV	FM II	OIE	FORM CHECK	UNPOPULAR RESPONSES	TOTAL RESPONSES	LIKE PERCENTAGE	INDIFFERENT PERCENTAGE	DISLIKE PERCENTAGE
Music Teacher	50	21	23	23	23	25	-18	14	-09	04	69	48	-01	39	47	54	37	46	40	10	48	46	-58	21	-27	-12	47	-22	-20
Entertainer	21	-03	-01	-37	-28	-03	-16	06	17	09	16	11	-08	14	-16	48	57	74	55	19	06	45	-27	12	-03	01	40	-36	00
Music Performer	26	-04	-13	-34	-22	-02	-14	17	06	06	28	14	-14	18	18	66	55	71	56	40	62	29	-13	16	-20	-04	33	-25	-05
Fashion Model	04	-04	02	-49	-51	-44	-14	-35	-16	-30	-15	-14	-31	-15	-43	13	13	19	10	-30	10	16	-29	37	10	12	-06	-33	35
Art Teacher	13	-04	-04	-42	-25	-10	-43	-20	08	-01	-35	-14	03	32	05	49	69	56	57	24	66	10	-25	33	-27	-04	37	-36	02
Artist	-26	-31	-66	-80	-05	-03	-13	-06	-07	-41	-41	-55	-46	-43	-50	02	-04	-05	-05	26	-51	27	17	27	-21	05	-38	-43	73
Interior Decorator	21	-11	-13	-71	-28	-20	-33	-09	-17	-40	-07	-30	-29	-04	-29	17	34	28	28	08	-14	16	-23	29	-01	00	-03	-45	46
Newswoman	48	29	09	-20	-27	-32	-44	-01	-04	-36	42	35	-03	-27	-29	39	45	28	43	26	39	54	-52	36	-23	06	41	-23	44
English Teacher	27	12	02	02	18	-49	-65	-21	11	-26	29	32	-03	23	21	32	26	53	40	21	22	55	-32	51	-18	01	17	-21	07
Language Teacher	78	57	43	20	-11	-37	-05	14	11	16	58	60	33	17	32	29	34	42	48	07	55	15	-84	11	-18	00	57	-15	-34
YWCA Staff Member	27	09	20	06	01	07	-26	17	11	17	58	64	27	21	44	44	35	41	48	11	60	49	-57	26	-18	00	48	-13	-29
Director, Christian Ed	15	20	-23	02	07	19	-17	20	-01	05	39	55	28	44	55	30	01	03	11	13	51	16	-16	06	-08	-13	55	-13	-01
Nun-Teacher	15	09	34	17	-11	-06	-18	-17	-05	16	35	23	00	00	30	34	01	37	11	27	22	60	-74	19	-26	-04	15	-04	-35
Guidance Counselors	67	55	25	17	-05	02	-18	20	-01	05	32	43	23	28	44	30	29	37	43	20	16	28	-58	22	-29	-07	30	-07	-20
Soc Sci Teacher	57	68	25	17	-03	19	-34	-17	-05	-05	35	56	28	10	27	34	17	41	11	04	51	16	-16	19	-21	07	55	-13	-35
Social Worker	54	55	08	00	-13	02	-15	24	29	-07	32	43	23	-40	27	30	17	37	31	31	39	39	60	15	-29	08	28	-04	-20
Speech Pathologist	47	18	-44	-52	31	52	18	05	35	-02	11	-18	-07	-22	-18	04	07	20	30	53	-03	16	-38	16	-07	13	00	-07	15
Psychologist	23	18	-44	-52	31	52	18	20	13	29	-02	-31	-07	-33	-36	02	15	-15	20	72	00	05	-11	-06	13	00	-07	-16	12
Librarian	19	16	-35	-31	15	15	-10	-07	30	-01	-14	-31	-20	-22	-12	12	10	14	31	58	30	11	12	-15	11	11	07	-15	20
Translator	-01	03	-37	-11	10	30	-05	-05	19	01	-33	-46	-52	-44	-54	15	05	10	19	57	-32	-15	12	05	07	07	-20	-20	36
Physician	-16	-03	03	-53	31	67	36	23	51	20	-23	-13	-07	-51	-25	-13	-06	-05	05	71	-15	-24	13	-20	06	02	-16	-08	21
Dentist	-16	-32	-63	-53	45	31	63	19	44	26	-37	-35	-14	-44	-34	-15	-19	07	-19	44	-24	-37	30	-47	16	06	-15	10	03
Medical Tech	-22	-05	-23	-09	53	82	66	25	53	45	-25	-38	-08	-40	-34	-05	-18	-22	-05	42	-26	-35	33	-54	16	01	-05	14	-09
Chemist	01	-02	-53	-27	76	76	57	24	45	15	-42	-55	-06	-43	-16	01	-16	-22	-30	71	-19	-12	17	-36	12	03	-15	03	10
Mathematician	-16	-08	-72	-41	57	74	34	09	19	-15	-23	-55	-24	-58	-27	-08	-33	-22	-21	57	-27	-39	33	-18	12	07	-46	-05	36
Computer Programmer	-20	-02	-19	08	37	61	61	05	23	23	-23	-23	11	-25	-19	-08	-11	-29	-15	37	-09	-42	33	-12	10	10	-10	-28	-05
Math Sci Teacher	-01	-01	-11	34	53	74	50	20	13	15	-21	-23	12	-23	01	-08	-18	-58	-53	10	-09	-55	32	-08	03	03	-24	28	-18
Engineer	-11	20	-20	06	10	77	75	20	30	18	-24	-32	10	-39	-03	-33	-51	-18	-10	50	01	-47	05	-45	18	01	-05	11	-11
Army Enlisted	13	27	14	44	30	27	45	-07	01	07	-32	-13	17	-45	02	-33	-49	-40	-35	-07	05	-70	05	-45	27	01	-11	24	-13
Navy Enlisted	-23	-08	-14	17	21	31	45	-04	-20	08	-50	-35	13	-51	-15	-33	-55	-55	-10	-16	-30	-73	07	-39	34	07	-40	22	07
Army Officer	66	70	18	10	28	29	37	01	00	08	00	06	22	-37	-01	01	-05	07	24	29	32	-44	57	-32	16	03	24	03	-23
Navy Officer	03	18	-34	-30	13	50	77	01	-20	-36	-65	-61	-25	-78	-47	-31	-53	-41	-31	09	-35	-59	08	-04	30	06	-13	03	49
Lawyers	42	53	-24	-22	19	16	03	-24	-19	-25	-48	-45	-12	-60	-20	-06	-28	-37	-29	35	-01	-58	07	-29	23	05	-21	12	22
Accountant	08	23	-01	29	60	36	39	-07	01	-18	-14	-13	-12	-23	-27	-25	-48	-35	-29	10	20	07	07	-03	11	05	08	12	07
Bankwoman	08	20	48	79	36	36	-06	-19	-23	-06	-36	-32	00	-37	-20	-27	-37	-34	-04	-39	20	03	-03	-21	23	16	06	12	-23
Life Underwriter	56	56	28	03	-14	-29	-23	-38	-17	-22	-48	-45	00	-24	04	-12	-29	-13	-04	-24	22	-34	-59	19	06	-03	06	-17	11
Buyer	03	07	49	41	05	-20	-01	-37	-30	-15	-22	-16	-01	-02	-11	-24	-35	-34	-33	-54	09	-31	-12	-08	14	-05	01	10	09
Bus Ed Teacher	07	17	54	75	-12	-30	-06	-25	-11	-11	07	-21	12	18	-23	-37	-37	-29	-33	-53	26	-07	-07	-07	-03	-05	06	18	-21
Home Econ Teacher	06	-04	63	42	-12	-30	-09	17	-06	24	56	52	22	85	36	22	45	29	18	-30	41	46	-22	03	-20	-08	55	-04	-43
Dietitian	17	19	43	32	36	47	28	27	18	55	31	24	24	60	36	26	23	11	11	-22	39	13	-28	-35	-10	-10	55	-03	-44
Phys Ed Teacher	-02	08	21	26	10	23	33	22	28	46	21	30	62	-01	18	-26	-23	-29	-33	-22	09	39	00	-32	13	-01	06	25	-29
Occupational Therapist	31	14	20	01	00	66	40	45	43	56	71	59	40	51	33	17	03	03	58	37	45	-48	-37	-47	-28	-08	67	-01	-56
Physical Therapist	07	16	16	26	38	52	52	23	64	79	34	41	61	18	13	09	09	09	03	45	33	-14	-08	-08	-09	-07	35	25	-56
Public Health Nurse	19	13	19	16	-44	-23	-36	23	41	62	60	66	27	43	33	00	13	09	21	30	34	34	-35	26	-23	-12	53	-11	-21
Registered Nurse	18	15	35	14	-23	-07	-23	23	41	62	58	43	38	56	50	33	44	42	21	01	39	34	-30	26	-25	-08	53	-04	-48
Lic Prac Nurse	-20	04	36	62	18	-07	50	26	56	67	32	43	40	49	59	13	05	06	13	-04	43	36	-03	14	-06	-14	37	07	-54
Radiological Tech	-03	12	12	32	26	60	50	-04	23	44	-05	40	40	05	32	06	00	-06	-08	06	03	39	23	-37	-06	-14	19	23	-38
Dental Assistant	-15	-08	32	77	16	60	17	13	08	32	21	37	25	05	32	-15	-17	-15	-15	-40	-28	-15	11	-54	-04	-07	18	26	-40
Exec Housekeeper	14	11	53	78	18	47	28	17	04	06	28	31	31	57	10	14	08	03	-03	-31	-15	15	23	-32	-05	-15	47	31	-45
Instrument Assembler	-48	-30	11	51	19	54	33	26	-15	37	-30	-15	07	03	-05	-40	-38	-47	-55	-47	44	-44	22	-28	22	-15	-24	05	-08
Elementary Teacher	15	06	17	54	18	30	-01	-01	15	64	70	64	25	71	68	-05	36	30	-47	-07	-21	39	51	-21	-12	-01	49	-05	-60
Secretary	-15	-09	41	66	03	-44	-25	-28	44	-14	-02	-10	07	32	13	-40	-10	-15	-18	-74	15	-07	-21	05	-26	-03	07	20	-16
Saleswoman	00	10	09	00	03	-22	-03	-06	-13	23	17	33	37	53	29	04	04	-02	-16	-49	37	-07	05	-16	03	-09	35	-10	-41
Sewing Machine Operator	-43	-35	26	63	-12	09	04	01	-27	03	-15	-07	-07	28	21	-28	-28	-44	-52	-48	-07	30	45	-19	-01	-12	-10	19	-09
Telephone Operator	-15	-06	16	09	09	-11	04	04	-17	03	11	31	23	50	31	-11	-02	-07	-16	-48	-02	34	10	-17	-24	-08	25	28	-47
Beautician	-43	-38	33	35	-52	-25	-25	-28	-14	00	-18	00	00	22	-03	-30	-28	-34	-50	-84	-20	58	36	09	03	-11	-20	06	12
Airline Stewardess	41	32	77	41	-10	-13	-03	06	12	34	43	57	37	45	17	17	45	46	39	-28	17	17	-52	-08	-06	00	71	-10	-51

TABLE 4-23. INTERCORRELATIONS BETWEEN THE MEN'S AND WOMEN'S BASIC SCALES, OCCUPATIONAL AND NONOCCUPATIONAL SCALES, AND ADMINISTRATIVE INDICES

Men's Scales \ Women's Scales	Public Speaking	Law/Politics	Merchandising	Office Practices	Numbers	Physical Science	Mechanical	Outdoors	Biological Science	Medical Service	Teaching	Social Service	Sports	Homemaking	Religious Activities	Music	Art	Performing Arts	Writing	AACH	Diversity of Interests	FM II	OIE	Form Check	Unpopular Items	Total Responses	Like Percent	Indifferent Percent	Dislike Percent
Public Speaking	81	68	27	17	02	04	08	10	11	14	23	30	23	05	37	13	08	27	32	11	46	-12	-72	-11	05	-03	38	-01	-31
Law/Politics	70	84	23	17	00	09	12	00	17	16	15	30	24	-07	20	-03	-01	13	25	04	44	-33	-65	-17	03	-02	31	05	-31
Business Management	49	45	72	51	03	-09	11	-09	11	11	20	24	23	22	17	-06	-06	00	-02	-28	46	-24	-52	-18	03	-05	35	06	-35
Sales	37	36	62	39	-07	-13	08	-11	-10	09	14	17	28	12	16	-12	-13	-05	-09	-31	38	-32	-40	-17	14	04	21	09	-26
Merchandising	38	34	83	48	-09	-20	01	-07	-09	14	22	26	22	32	17	-05	01	07	04	-36	49	-09	-47	-21	-03	-03	39	09	-39
Office Practices	07	18	59	81	12	-13	-10	-03	-09	18	13	26	19	32	17	09	04	-02	-07	-33	21	00	-11	-03	06	-08	34	14	-42
Military Activities	22	17	29	34	05	08	24	18	11	23	13	17	38	17	25	-03	04	-01	13	-09	21	-13	-20	-19	14	-03	31	04	-30
Technical Supervision	29	24	30	26	18	37	53	24	23	23	07	07	36	03	21	26	-08	14	01	11	26	-33	-24	-46	-05	-02	17	20	-33
Mathematics	-03	11	-12	13	71	66	36	22	28	25	-07	-13	16	05	09	20	10	08	08	52	19	-11	04	-35	01	-07	09	10	-17
Science	04	08	-18	-01	49	88	63	37	52	48	05	-06	16	05	13	20	11	14	01	59	06	-07	02	-54	-14	-15	21	10	-26
Mechanical	17	13	-18	08	31	22	89	52	34	44	10	02	36	08	07	12	42	08	08	24	27	-19	-10	-66	10	-15	26	09	-36
Nature	10	08	02	18	00	29	58	85	34	44	33	38	39	41	36	27	16	14	32	31	24	-02	-09	-29	-01	-03	35	13	-29
Agriculture	09	06	08	04	-01	14	32	65	19	31	24	15	67	18	07	04	11	21	07	59	24	-19	-20	-35	16	-14	28	00	-29
Adventure	25	25	09	00	09	39	37	30	30	24	10	34	37	-09	28	11	14	21	21	16	26	-21	-21	-20	02	-01	20	13	-29
Recreational Leadership	30	28	17	14	10	10	30	28	24	24	26	34	32	23	33	03	16	36	23	-06	25	-32	-33	-35	02	-07	49	00	-41
Medical Service	21	24	13	10	07	37	21	30	73	81	32	32	30	23	07	22	14	31	21	-22	24	09	-21	-22	-07	-10	43	11	-30
Social Service	39	34	24	24	13	-06	-10	15	09	27	56	66	33	30	45	24	28	27	30	26	47	25	-53	-29	-35	-06	43	-07	-36
Religious Activities	26	18	10	13	-02	07	06	34	12	29	36	46	30	29	91	31	29	26	17	04	35	20	-26	09	-17	-18	29	13	-33
Teaching	43	23	07	-01	00	10	01	20	16	24	71	43	40	30	36	45	30	36	38	34	41	35	-43	05	-32	-02	37	01	-26
Music	20	07	06	24	-01	12	02	24	14	20	35	23	23	30	31	83	57	65	47	27	36	61	-26	00	-34	-11	44	-14	-27
Art	14	-02	05	-06	-20	04	01	33	14	20	37	31	02	42	15	53	80	65	56	39	36	73	-26	06	-29	-07	47	-14	-21
Writing	38	22	-03	-03	-02	04	-06	27	12	07	31	29	11	20	18	47	56	60	82	39	39	47	-43	-06	-28	-01	42	-15	-27
Academic Achievement	08	05	-34	-22	38	34	07	27	45	33	20	07	-02	08	14	45	56	33	34	73	11	38	-07	-06	-26	-03	23	-07	-12
Age-Related Interests	15	10	-13	-09	11	30	25	47	26	27	36	07	06	21	23	30	26	16	21	46	14	35	-19	-09	-29	-11	27	-07	-16
Cultural Change	67	65	15	-03	07	19	02	-01	26	24	23	30	23	-31	13	12	01	23	28	25	36	-21	-64	-09	02	04	27	-05	-25
Diversity of Interests	41	42	39	30	14	13	28	35	38	52	53	44	45	-10	35	36	40	23	39	23	66	17	-47	-26	-13	-09	57	06	-54
Fem.-Masc. II	06	23	-03	08	19	17	19	-24	00	05	-25	-21	13	-39	-15	-51	-63	-49	-43	-24	-19	-88	01	-22	29	-02	-33	22	07
Managerial Orientation	46	33	-07	-12	18	17	15	-06	00	05	18	-21	13	-12	-14	04	-04	05	08	-06	14	-33	-50	-22	04	10	16	-09	-05
OCC Extra-Introversion	-75	-62	-37	-08	07	-02	-02	-12	-11	-21	-49	-44	21	-15	-35	-27	-25	-36	-38	-06	-59	-02	89	05	17	08	-44	03	34
Occupational Level	32	31	-03	-20	12	10	-11	-14	11	-02	06	-07	-04	-11	-02	16	-07	03	08	57	13	01	-43	15	-02	03	21	-09	22
Specialization Level	37	27	-15	-17	28	39	26	06	15	14	14	29	-19	16	35	32	-01	30	40	05	21	17	-34	21	-23	08	21	-09	-09
Form Check	28	34	13	10	-06	-03	-03	-01	17	-02	25	29	16	-29	11	11	-01	08	11	05	21	11	-35	21	-28	-03	-17	03	-17
Unpopular Items	-14	-27	13	10	-07	39	26	06	17	14	-20	02	-23	17	-29	-12	-01	01	01	29	-26	00	29	05	37	01	-07	-23	27
Total Responses	05	04	-20	-16	-07	-03	-18	-05	02	-19	-02	-03	16	-18	-16	-04	03	00	06	23	-07	-06	09	09	01	16	-04	02	01
Like Percentage	51	40	39	32	20	25	32	35	13	35	36	41	41	33	30	36	42	45	45	-08	55	19	-53	-27	10	-08	81	-36	-35
Indifferent Percentage	01	09	07	20	20	19	26	09	26	26	07	11	11	03	10	-11	03	-06	-08	09	-28	-28	06	06	-23	10	-07	83	-52
Dislike Percentage	-43	-42	-39	-46	-24	-38	-52	-38	-32	-54	-37	-40	-44	-24	-37	-19	-25	-32	-29	-21	-54	12	38	54	15	10	-38	-52	80

170

Administrative Indices. Most of the same named scales from the men's and women's scales are highly correlated, though in a few cases the correlations are not quite high enough for the scales to be considered equivalent forms. Usually, however, they are quite similar.

Test-Retest Reliability

Test-retest statistics for the Women's Basic Scales are presented in Figures 4-1 through 4-6 and Table 4-24 and 4-25.

As with the men's scales, these data are very valuable for studying the scales' stability, and for studying the characteristics of various groups. Again, although some summary comments are below, the reader should scan the profiles himself.

The two-week test-retest sample (Table 4-24) included women students in the introductory psychology course at the University of Minnesota, volunteers for this project. They completed the new revised booklet TW398, so reliability statistics were calculated for both the Set 1 and Set 2 scales, for

TABLE 4-24. TEST-RETEST STATISTICS OVER A TWO-WEEK INTERVAL FOR SET 1 AND SET 2 OF THE WOMEN'S BASIC SCALES

Scale	Number of Items Set 1	Set 2	Two Week Test Retest Correlations Set 1	Set 2	Test Mean/SD Set 1	Set 2	Retest Mean/SD Set 1	Set 2
Public Speaking	12	13	.86	.88	53/10	53/10	53/9	54/10
Law/Politics	9	10	.91	.92	54/11	55/11	56/11	56/11
Merchandising	12	13	.88	.87	53/9	53/9	52/9	53/9
Office Practices	11	18	.90	.92	50/9	50/9	50/9	51/9
Numbers	7	8	.92	.91	51/10	50/10	50/10	50/11
Physical Science	10	15	.94	.94	51/11	51/10	50/11	51/11
Mechanical	10	16	.92	.94	49/9	48/10	50/10	49/10
Outdoors	6	9	.88	.89	48/10	48/9	49/10	49/10
Biological Science	6	7	.89	.89	53/10	54/10	53/10	54/10
Medical Service	11	17	.90	.91	54/10	55/10	54/10	55/10
Teaching	11	12	.84	.85	53/9	54/9	55/9	55/9
Social Service	6	8	.83	.83	53/9	54/9	54/8	55/8
Sports	9	12	.92	.93	54/9	54/9	54/9	55/9
Homemaking	10	11	.87	.88	51/9	51/9	53/8	53/8
Religious Activities	5	9	.90	.92	49/10	48/10	49/10	49/11
Music	5	6	.86	.87	51/10	51/10	53/10	53/10
Art	7	9	.86	.86	52/10	52/10	54/9	54/9
Performing Arts	11	13	.92	.92	53/10	53/10	54/10	54/10
Writing	12	14	.86	.88	53/8	53/8	54/8	54/8

SCALE	$T\text{-}R_r$	Test M/SD	Retest M/SD	PLOTTED SCORE
				BASIC INTEREST SCALES
PUBLIC SPEAKING	.60	52/10	55/8	
LAW/POLITICS	.58	54/11	57/10	
MERCHANDISING	.50	49/7	52/8	
OFFICE PRACTICES	.50	49/7	47/8	
NUMBERS	.63	50/10	48/9	
PHYSICAL SCIENCE	.73	51/9	49/10	
MECHANICAL	.69	47/9	48/11	
OUTDOORS	.62	45/9	48/11	
BIOLOGICAL SCIENCE	.50	51/10	51/11	
MEDICAL SERVICE	.58	51/10	50/11	
TEACHING	.55	48/10	50/10	
SOCIAL SERVICE	.65	51/9	51/10	
SPORTS	.68	51/9	51/9	
HOMEMAKING	.64	45/9	46/10	
RELIGIOUS ACTIVITIES	.56	49/10	45/10	
MUSIC	.54	48/10	54/8	
ART	.53	48/9	54/8	
PERFORMING ARTS	.43	48/8	54/8	
WRITING	.60	51/9	54/8	

DOUBLE LINE = AVERAGE SCORE FOR 1000 EMPLOYED ADULT WOMEN

FIG. 4-1. *Test-retest data over three and a half years for 56 University of Minnesota freshman women.*

SCALE	$T\text{-}R_r$	Test M/SD	Retest M/SD	PLOTTED SCORE
				BASIC INTEREST SCALES
PUBLIC SPEAKING	.54	47/9	50/9	
LAW/POLITICS	.53	47/9	49/10	
MERCHANDISING	.44	50/8	53/9	
OFFICE PRACTICES	.57	50/8	48/9	
NUMBERS	.66	51/8	49/9	
PHYSICAL SCIENCE	.57	49/10	50/10	
MECHANICAL	.52	47/9	51/10	
OUTDOORS	.48	48/10	52/9	
BIOLOGICAL SCIENCE	.46	50/10	52/10	
MEDICAL SERVICE	.49	51/10	51/9	
TEACHING	.36	51/9	56/8	
SOCIAL SERVICE	.37	52/9	53/9	
SPORTS	.58	53/8	52/9	
HOMEMAKING	.54	50/9	54/9	
RELIGIOUS ACTIVITIES	.48	53/8	49/10	
MUSIC	.54	48/11	52/10	
ART	.45	49/10	56/7	
PERFORMING ARTS	.51	48/9	51/9	
WRITING	.58	48/9	51/9	

DOUBLE LINE = AVERAGE SCORE FOR 1000 EMPLOYED ADULT WOMEN

FIG. 4-2. *Test-retest data over nine years for 327 University of Minnesota freshman women.*

SCALE	$T\text{-}R_r$	Test M/SD	Retest M/SD	PLOTTED SCORE
				BASIC INTEREST SCALES
PUBLIC SPEAKING	.73	45/8	45/11	
LAW/POLITICS	.54	44/9	47/10	
MERCHANDISING	.62	53/7	55/8	
OFFICE PRACTICES	.36	54/7	53/9	
NUMBERS	.54	47/7	47/10	
PHYSICAL SCIENCE	.65	42/9	45/10	
MECHANICAL	.71	43/8	46/10	
OUTDOORS	.49	43/8	46/10	
BIOLOGICAL SCIENCE	.56	46/10	50/11	
MEDICAL SERVICE	.55	50/10	53/10	
TEACHING	.61	51/9	52/10	
SOCIAL SERVICE	.54	55/8	54/10	
SPORTS	.63	56/8	53/9	
HOMEMAKING	.35	49/8	50/10	
RELIGIOUS ACTIVITIES	.25	53/7	50/9	
MUSIC	.74	43/11	47/12	
ART	.61	46/10	50/10	
PERFORMING ARTS	.67	46/9	48/10	
WRITING	.59	44/9	46/10	

DOUBLE LINE = AVERAGE SCORE FOR 1000 EMPLOYED ADULT WOMEN

FIG. 4-3. *Test-retest data over ten years for 56 University of Minnesota general college freshman women.*

172

comparative purposes. The two sets of scales gave virtually identical results—the median correlations in each instance was .89—though the Set 2 reliabilities were one or two correlational points higher on 12 of the 19 scales, with five ties. Although the two sets appear virtually interchangeable, the Set 2 scales should be used whenever possible to take advantage of their slightly greater length.

By necessity, all of the following samples have been scored on the Set 1 scales as they had been tested with the old (Form W) booklet.

The 3½-year sample (Figure 4-1) included women who entered the University of Minnesota College of Liberal Arts in the fall of 1961, and who volunteered to complete the SVIB during the spring of their senior year. The sample is directly analogous to the sample of men in Figure 5-7.

Test-retest statistics are reported in Figure 4-2, for 327 University of Minnesota freshman women retested over a ten-year interval by Nolting (1967). In the predictive validity section below, this sample is discussed in greater detail.

Freshman women from the University of Minnesota's General College were retested ten years later in a project conducted by that college's Student Personnel Committee, under the direction of G. Gordon Kingsley (Figure 4-3).

Women from the freshman class of Connecticut College for Women were retested 10 years later by Ross Thomas (1955) (Figure 4-4).

E. K. Strong tested 380 women psychologists in 1942 to establish the first Psychologist scale for the women's SVIB. In 1966, 142 of these (81 percent of the 178 that were still listed in the APA directory) completed the inventory a second time; their test-retest data are in Figure 4-5. One unique feature of this sample was that they showed a decrease on 16 of the 19 scales, and an increase on only one scale—a two point gain on Religious Activities. See Campbell and Soliman (1968) for more information on this sample.

Ninety-one freshman women tested on entrance to the University of Minnesota's College of Liberal Arts in the years 1933–36 were retested 26 years later in 1962 as part of a larger study of the effectiveness of counseling (Campbell, 1965). The reliability data from this sample are in Figure 4-6.

Table 4-25 summaries the reliability data from these test-retest samples. The correlations were roughly equal to those found among the male samples; again, age when tested and length of test-retest interval were the most important factors.

The mean changes of three points or more are listed in Table 4-25 for

PROFILE— **STRONG VOCATIONAL INTEREST BLANK** —FOR WOMEN (Form TW398)

BASIC INTEREST SCALES

SCALE	T-R$_r$	Test M/SD	Retest M/SD
PUBLIC SPEAKING	.62	49/9	50/10
LAW/POLITICS	.49	49/10	52/10
MERCHANDISING	.34	55/9	55/9
OFFICE PRACTICES	.58	49/8	50/8
NUMBERS	.77	48/11	49/11
PHYSICAL SCIENCE	.56	45/8	47/10
MECHANICAL	.62	47/10	49/10
OUTDOORS	.57	48/11	50/10
BIOLOGICAL SCIENCE	.57	46/10	49/9
MEDICAL SERVICE	.52	47/11	48/8
TEACHING	.55	46/10	47/10
SOCIAL SERVICE	.50	50/10	49/9
SPORTS	.65	53/9	49/9
HOMEMAKING	.52	45/11	50/9
RELIGIOUS ACTIVITIE	.48	48/8	49/8
MUSIC	.40	51/10	50/9
ART	.53	49/11	51/9
PERFORMING ARTS	.64	51/10	51/9
WRITING	.60	51/10	52/9

DOUBLE LINE = AVERAGE SCORE FOR 1000 EMPLOYED ADULT WOMEN

FIG. 4-4. *Test-retest data over ten years for 81 Connecticut College freshman women.*

PROFILE— **STRONG VOCATIONAL INTEREST BLANK** —FOR WOMEN (Form TW398)

BASIC INTEREST SCALES

SCALE	T-R$_r$	Test M/SD	Retest M/SD
PUBLIC SPEAKING	.59	54/8	53/8
LAW/POLITICS	.55	52/9	50/9
MERCHANDISING	.61	47/9	43/8
OFFICE PRACTICES	.65	49/8	46/8
NUMBERS	.71	57/10	55/10
PHYSICAL SCIENCE	.64	60/7	58/8
MECHANICAL	.72	56/10	51/9
OUTDOORS	.68	52/10	51/10
BIOLOGICAL SCIENCI	.58	58/6	55/7
MEDICAL SERVICE	.61	55/7	50/7
TEACHING	.53	50/8	49/9
SOCIAL SERVICE	.53	51/8	48/8
SPORTS	.75	46/7	43/8
HOMEMAKING	.60	45/10	44/10
RELIGIOUS ACTIVITI	.65	41/10	43/10
MUSIC	.71	51/10	51/10
ART	.69	50/10	49/10
PERFORMING ARTS	.72	50/8	49/9
WRITING	.69	51/9	51/9

DOUBLE LINE = AVERAGE SCORE FOR 1000 EMPLOYED ADULT WOMEN

FIG. 4-5. *Test-retest data over 17 years for 142 women Ph.D. psychologists.*

PROFILE— **STRONG VOCATIONAL INTEREST BLANK** —FOR WOMEN (Form TW398)

BASIC INTEREST SCALES — PLOTTED SCORE 4-6

SCALE	T-R$_r$	Test M/SD	Retest M/SD
PUBLIC SPEAKING	.38	50/9	50/10
LAW/POLITICS	.38	49/10	51/10
MERCHANDISING	.30	52/8	53/9
OFFICE PRACTICES	.52	52/10	51/9
NUMBERS	.52	49/8	50/10
PHYSICAL SCIENCE	.54	49/9	51/9
MECHANICAL	.49	48/8	51/8
OUTDOORS	.52	50/9	50/10
BIOLOGICAL SCIENC	.55	50/10	53/10
MEDICAL SERVICE	.58	52/10	53/10
TEACHING	.55	46/10	50/9
SOCIAL SERVICE	.27	49/9	50/10
SPORTS	.43	51/8	47/8
HOMEMAKING	.49	45/9	49/9
RELIGIOUS ACTIVITI	.32	49/8	49/10
MUSIC	.55	51/10	52/9
ART	.38	48/9	51/10
PERFORMING ARTS	.55	53/8	51/10
WRITING	.47	53/8	53/9

DOUBLE LINE = AVERAGE SCORE FOR 1000 EMPLOYED ADULT WOMEN

FIG. 4-6. *Test-retest data over 25-year interval for 91 University of Minnesota freshman women.*

TABLE 4-25. SUMMARY OF THE TEST-RETEST STATISTICS FOR THE WOMEN'S BASIC INTEREST SCALES

Sample	N	Test Age	Test-Retest Interval	Median T-R coefficient	Mean Changes of 3 points or more Increase		Decrease	
Univ. of Minnesota sophomores	112	19	2 weeks	89	none		none	
Univ. of Minnesota CLA freshmen	56	17	3½ years	58	Music	6	Religious Activities	4
					Art	6		
					Performing Arts	6		
					Public Speaking	3		
					Law/Politics	3		
					Merchandising	3		
					Outdoors	3		
					Writing	3		
Univ. of Minnesota freshmen	327	17	10 years	.52	Art	7	Religious Activities	4
					Teaching	5		
					Mechanical	4		
					Outdoors	4		
					Homemaking	4		
					Music	4		
					Public Speaking	3		
					Merchandising	3		
					Performing Arts	3		
					Writing	3		
Univ. of Minnesota General College freshmen	56	17	10 years	.59	Biol. Science	4	Sports	3
					Music	4	Religious Activities	3
					Art	4		
					Law/Politics	3		
					Physical Science	3		
					Mechanical	3		
					Outdoors	3		
					Medical Service	3		
Connecticut College freshmen	81	17	10 years	.56	Homemaking	5	Sports	4
					Law/Politics	3		
					Biol. Science	3		
Psychologists	142	40	24 years	.65	none		Mechanical	5
							Med. Service	5
							Merchandising	4
							Off. Practice	3
							Biol. Science	3
							Social Service	3
							Sports	3
Univ. of Minnesota CLA freshmen	91	17	26 years	.49	Teaching	4	Sports	4
					Homemaking	4		
					Mechanical	3		
					Biol. Science	3		
					Art	3		

all of these test-retest samples to aid in identifying general trends. Only two scales showed consistent gain or loss over all of the samples; the Art scale generally showed a gain, the Sports scale a loss. Other gainers were the Music, Performing Arts, Teaching and Outdoors scales; the only other loser was the Religious Activities scale. These changes again are generally consistent with those found in the men's samples.

Of course, one of the most obvious conclusions is that all of the samples, excepting only the psychologists, showed increases on a number of scales. The psychologists were also the only group to be tested initially as adults. As the scores on the Basic Scales can be increased only by responding "Like" to more items, these data suggest that the vocational interests of teenage girls may be somewhat constricted but that they expand, probably with education. The data from the highly educated women psychologists suggest that at some point this trend may be reversed.

Validity
Concurrent Validity: Mean Scores for 89 Occupational Samples

Mean scores on the Women's Basic Interest Scales are presented in Tables 4-27 through 4-45 for samples of women in a wide range of occupations. Some basic information on each of these samples is listed in Table 4-26. Again, as with the men, the rank-ordering of the occupations is quite reasonable. Scores of 57 or 58 are "high" in the sense that they are usually associated with a relevant occupation; scores of 42 or 43 are low. As with the Men's Basic Scales, all available occupational samples have been included here. Some of the samples are small, many were collected several years ago, some of them are ill-defined; yet, collectively, these tables provide a wealth of information about women's occupations. Counselors, personnel workers, and others who would wish to learn more about the interest patterns of employed women should scan all of these tables.

Because they were used as the norm sample, the 1969 Women-in-General have an average of 50 on each scale.

Predictive Validity

The best predictive validity information on the women's Basic Interest Scales comes from Nolting's follow-up study of various curricular groups at the University of Minnesota (Nolting, 1967). He went through the graduation lists of the years 1958 to 1965, and identified women who had graduated in the following areas: Art, Elementary Education, Home Economics, Occupational Therapy, Library Science, Medicine (M.D.'s) and Social Work. He selected these particular ones because students who major in these are likely to be eventually employed in these same fields, in contrast to those majoring in areas such as History or Spanish. Then Nolting went back through the University's orientation test files, and some high school files, to locate SVIBs completed by these women years earlier. With these tests in hand, he approached the women once again and retested them. He was able to collect a sample of 327, with an average interval between test and retest of 9 years.

TABLE 4-26. Brief Descriptions of the 89 Occupational Samples Whose
Basic Scale Mean Scores Appear in Tables 4-27 to 4-45
(More information on the recent samples, marked with asterisks,
can be found in Appendix B)

Sample	N	Year Tested	Investigator	Brief Description
Academically gifted women-- grads	591	1950-58	Patricia Faunce	Freshmen entering U of M College of Liberal Arts with ACE test score above 80 percentile and HS rank percentile above 90. Eventually earned at least a BA degree.
Academically gifted women-- nongrads	448	1950-58	Patricia Faunce	Same as above. Did not graduate.
Accountants	335	1968	CIMR	American Society of Women Accountants*
Army Enlisted	218	1967	CIMR	Senior enlisted WAC's (E-7, 8, 9)*
Army Officers	307	1967	CIMR	WAC Captains, Majors, and Lt. Col*
Artists	402	1934,41	E. K. Strong, Jr.	Portrait, landscape, and still-life painters, sculptors, and commercial artists.
Artists	297	1967	CIMR	Non-commercial artists, listed in Who's Who in American Art*
Art Teachers	359	1967	CIMR	From Iowa, Massachusetts, Texas, and California*
Authors	402	1934,41	E. K. Strong, Jr.	Journalists and authors of short stories, articles, fiction, children's books, plays, and poems.
Bankwomen	271	1968	CIMR	Listed in the 1968 Yearbook of the National Association of Bank-Women*
Beauticians	262	1967	CIMR	Licensed beauticians in Minnesota*
Business Education Teachers	250	c1941	H. F. Koepke, Jr.	From public secondary schools in seven midwestern states. About equal numbers of teachers of accounting, general business, typewriting, shorthand, selling, office practices, and business English.
Business Education Teachers	300	1967	CIMR	Mostly from Minnesota, Iowa, and Colorado*
Buyers	204	1942	E. K. Strong, Jr.	Heads of merchandise departments, nearly all in department stores.
Chemists	173	1966	CIMR	From American Chemical Society Directory, all with Ph.D.'s.
County Welfare Workers	54	1946	Marvin Stein	Members of County Welfare Merit System, Minnesota
Dental Assistants	418	1966	CIMR	Members of the American Dental Assistant Association*
Dentists	195	1934,42	E. K. Strong, Jr.	Most of the women dentists in the country at the time.
Dietitians	416	1941	E. K. Strong, Jr.	Representative sample from across the United States. Majority working in hospitals.
Dietitians	327	1967	CIMR	Members of the American Dietetic Association*
Directors, Christian Education	434	1967	CIMR	From Presbyterian, Methodist, Lutheran and Baptist churches across the U.S.*
Elementary School Teachers	325	1966	CIMR	In urban, suburban, and rural schools in Minnesota*
English Teachers	293	1934	E. K. Strong, Jr.	Teachers rated average and superior, from Pacific Coast and New York.

(table continued next page)

177

TABLE 4-26 (*continued*)

Sample	N	Year Tested	Investigator	Brief Description
English Teachers	352	1967	CIMR	Mostly from Minnesota, Iowa and Colorado*
Engineers	325	1959	E. K. Strong, Jr.	Mostly in the Society of Women Engineers.
Entertainers	104	1966-67	CIMR	Entertainers listed in Variety magazine*
Executive Housekeepers	281	1967	CIMR	Members of the National Executive Housekee Association*
Guidance Counselors	347	1967	Janet Francis & Gloria Blanton	Members of the National Association of School Counselors*
Home Economics Teachers	420	1941	E. K. Strong, Jr.	Names supplied by State Departments of Education and State Home Economics Bureau
Home Economics Teachers	373	1967	CIMR	Mostly from Minnesota, Iowa, and Colorado
Housewives	402	1934	E. K. Strong, Jr.	Most were members of PTA's in California; some from L. M. Terman's study of married and divorced women; rest from miscellaneou sources.
Interior Decorators	172	1966	CIMR	Members of the American Association of Interior Decorators*
Instrument Assemblers	89	1966	CIMR	Assembly line workers in electronics firm*
Laboratory Technicians	356	1941	E. K. Strong, Jr.	Selected from lists furnished by the American Medical Technologists Association American Society of Clinical Pathologists, and hospitals across the country.
Language Teachers	287	1967	CIMR	Minnesota, Iowa, Colorado, Wisconsin teach
Lawyers	373	1934,41	E. K. Strong, Jr.	About half collected from Middle Atlantic, Great Lakes, and Pacific Coast states. Remainder collected with help of Mrs. Dorothea Dyer and Miss Helen Cirese, vice-president of National Association of Women Lawyers.
Lawyers	235	1967	CIMR	Selected from Martindale-Hubbell Law Directory, 1966*
Librarians	425	1934	E. K. Strong, Jr.	129 public librarians, 66 college librarians, 48 public school librarians, 56 reference librarians, 25 children's librarians, 32 cataloguers, 44 members of library school faculties, and 25 miscellaneous. Names drawn from list supplied by American Library Association.
Librarians	410	1967	CIMR	Selected from Who's Who in Library Science
Licensed Practical Nurses	222	1967	CIMR	Members of the American Federation of Licensed Practical Nurses*
Life Insurance Saleswomen	205	1937,41	E. K. Strong, Jr.	All with excellent sales records. Collecte with the help of Dr. M. A. Seder, Miss Beatrice Jones, Equitable Life Assurance Society, and Dr. A. K. Kurtz, Life Insurance Sales Research Bureau.
Life Insurance Underwriters	188	1967	CIMR	Members of tne Women Leaders Round Table; sold at least $250,000 in one year*
Mathematicians	119	1966	· CIMR	Members of the American Mathematical Society, all with Ph.D's*

TABLE 4-26 (*continued*)

Sample	N	Year Tested	Investigator	Brief Description
Math-Science Teachers	467	1934,41	E. K. Strong, Jr.	Teachers rated average or superior, from Pacific Coast and New York City.
Math-Science Teachers	308	1967	CIMR	Mostly from Minnesota, Iowa and Colorado*
Medical Technologists	345	1967	CIMR	Members of the American Society of Medical Technologists*
Models	72	1965	CIMR	From several modeling agencies in the U.S.
Music Performers	290	1952	E. K. Strong, Jr.	Developed with the assistance of Music Journal.
Music Teachers	450	1952	E. K. Strong, Jr.	Developed with the assistance of Music Journal.
Navy Enlisted	213	1967	CIMR	WAVES in their second or further enlistment*
Navy Officers	191	1967	CIMR	WAVE line officers*
Nun-Teachers	494	1961	Sister Olheiser	Roman Catholic sister-teachers from 41 states.
Newswomen	189	1966	CIMR	Editor and Publisher's Year Book*
Nurses	396	1934	E. K. Strong, Jr.	75 percent from New York State, mainly from New York City. Collected with help of Mrs. Eleanor Perry Wood, Educational Records Bureau, New York City. Most employed in hospitals, others as visiting nurses or school nurses, or in miscellaneous categories.
Occupational Therapists	162	1942	E. K. Strong, Jr.	Graduates of five schools of occupational therapy. Obtained through assistance of Sarah M. Ahearne, Field Secretary, National Tuberculosis Association.
Occupational Therapists	607	1966	R. T. Flint & L. D. Miller	National sample and Minnesota state sample*
Office Workers	427	1947	E. K. Strong, Jr.	278 general office workers, 89 bookkeepers, 13 secretaries, 16 department managers, 15 office managers, 9 secretary-treasurers, and 5 general managers. Work in all cases primarily with figures, not linguistic.
Photographers	30	1966	CIMR	Members of the American Society of Magazine Photographers*
Physical Education Teachers	101	1939	Patricia Collins	Four years' training in physical education and five years' training experience; all high school teachers.
Physical Education Teachers	100	1954	Rosena M. Wilson	All college teachers
Physical Education Teachers	310	1967	CIMR	Mostly Minnesota, Iowa and Colorado high schools*
Physical Education Teachers	226	1968	Roy E. Warman	All college and university teachers
Physical Therapists	450	1957	Sarah S. Rogers	Developed with the assistance of the American Physical Therapy Association, New York.
Physical Therapists	267	1966	R. T. Flint	From Minnesota*
Physicians	142	over several years	Betty H. Mawardi	All holding M.D. degrees from Western Reserve University School of Medicine, Cleveland, Ohio.
Physicians	414	1934,41	E. K. Strong, Jr.	Representative sample from across the U.S.

(table continued next page)

TABLE 4-26 (*continued*)

Sample	N	Year Tested	Investigator	Brief Description
Physicians	329	1967	CIMR	Drawn from the American Medical Association Directory, 1965*
Psychologists	380	1942	E. K. Strong, Jr.	Members of the American Psychological Association.
Psychologists	275	1966	CIMR	Members of the American Psychological Association, all with Ph.D.'s*
Public Health Nurses	268	1966	Constance Carmody	All working in public health agencies*
Radiologic Technologists	307	1967	CIMR	Members of the American Society of Radiologic Technologists*
Registered Nurses	263	1967	CIMR	Nurses with baccalaureate degrees licensed in Minnesota*
Saleswomen	243	1966	CIMR	Drawn from the sales staff of Dayton's, Inc. of Minneapolis, a large department store*
Secretaries	452	1934,47	E. K. Strong, Jr.	181 stenographers, 123 stenographer-secretaries, 127 secretaries, and 19 executive secretaries. Work in all cases primarily linguistic; none were included who spent any appreciable time with figures.
Secretaries	366	1967	CIMR	Members of the National Secretaries Association or from several midwestern corporations*
Sewing Machine Operators	295	1967	CIMR	Munsingwear employees from five states*
Social Science Teachers	395	1934,41	E.K. Strong, Jr.	Teachers rated average and superior, from Pacific Coast and New York.
Social Science Teachers	183	1967	CIMR	Mostly from Minnesota, Iowa and Colorado*
Social Workers	464	1953	R. L. McCornack	Members of the American Association of Social Workers*
Speech Pathologists	353	1965	Hildred Schuell	Members of the American Speech and Hearing Association*
Stewardesses	443	1966	CIMR	Northwest Orient Airlines stewardesses*
Telephone Operators	129	1966	CIMR	Northwestern Bell Telephone Company operators from Minnesota and Colorado*
Translators	130	1966-67	CIMR	American Translators Association members and interpreters*
Visiting Nurses	322	1959	Eileen Koehler	Visiting Nurses Association, Buffalo, New York.
Wives-Animal Husbandry Profs	106	1967	CIMR	Wives of Ph.D. Animal Husbandry Professors*
Wives-Physicists	80	1967	CIMR	Wives of Ph.D. Physicists*
Wives-Social Workers	82	1967	CIMR	Wives of Ph.D. Social Workers*
YWCA Secretaries	202	1934	E. K. Strong, Jr.	Developed with the assistance of the National Board of YWCA, from 43 states.
YWCA Staff Members	282	1967	CIMR	Minimum of BA degree, national sample*

TABLE 4-27. MEAN SCORES ON THE WOMEN'S ART SCALE

Art Teachers

Interior Decorators/Occupational Therapists (1966)/Artists (1934)
Artists (1967)/Stewardesses
Occupational Therapists (1942)/Entertainers
Models/Wives-Physicists
Home Economics Teachers (1967)/Newswomen/Musicians/Psychologists (1966)/Wives-Social Workers/English Teachers (1967)
Photographers
Wives-Animal Husbandry Professors/Translators/Elementary Teachers/College PE Teachers (1954)/Army Officers
Speech Pathologists
Social Workers/Authors/Psychologists (1942)/YWCA Staff (1967)/Librarians (1967)/Nurses (1934)/Engineers
Home Economics Teachers (1941)/Secretaries (1934)/Directors, Christian Education/Language Teachers/Music Teachers
English Teachers (1934)/Visiting Nurses/Physicians (Western Reserve)/Physical Therapists (1966)/Secretaries (1967)
Registered Nurses/Physical Therapists (1957)/Nongrads/Public Health Nurses/Physicians (1967)/Guidance Counselors
Grads/Beauticians/Librarians (1934)/Dentists/County Welfare Workers/YWCA Staff (1934)/College PE Teachers (1968)
Social Science Teachers (1934)/Nun-Teachers/Navy Officers/HS PE Teachers (1939)/Social Science Teachers (1967)
Exec Housekeepers/Radiologic Technologists/Buyers/Medical Technologists/Dietitians (1967)/Office Workers
Lab Technicians
HS PE Teachers (1967)/Lawyers (1967)/Dental Assistants/Life Underwriters/Physicians (1934)/Lawyers (1934)
Chemists/Housewives/Saleswomen/Telephone Operators
Dietitians (1941)/Math-Science Teachers (1934)/Instrument Assemblers/Army Enlisted/Business Education Teachers (1941)
Licensed Practical Nurses/Life Insurance Sales (1937)/Mathematicians/Bankwomen/Accountants
Math-Science Teachers (1967)/Business Education Teachers (1967)/Navy Enlisted
Sewing Machine Operators

TABLE 4-28. MEAN SCORES ON THE WOMEN'S BIOLOGICAL SCIENCE SCALE

Laboratory Technicians
Medical Technologists/Physicians (1934)
Physicians (1967)/Dentists
Physicians (Western Reserve)/HS PE Teachers (1939)/Physical Therapists (1957)/Chemists
Physical Therapists (1966)/Licensed Practical Nurses
Psychologists (1942)/Radiologic Technologists/College PE Teachers (1954)
Registered Nurses/Nurses (1934)/Visiting Nurses/Dietitians (1941)/College PE Teachers (1968)
Public Health Nurses/Dental Assistants/Occupational Therapists (1966)/HS PE Teachers (1967)
Occupational Therapists (1942)/Dietitians (1967)/Psychologists (1966)/Translators/Math-Science Teachers (1967)
Math-Science Teachers (1934)
Speech Pathologists/Home Economics Teachers (1941)
Engineers/Stewardesses
Grads/County Welfare Workers/Army Enlisted/Wives-Physicists/Nongrads
Social Workers/Mathematicians/Nun-Teachers/Exec Housekeepers/Home Economics Teachers (1967)/Navy Enlisted
Wives-Social Workers
Army Officers/Navy Officers/Lawyers (1934)/Guidance Counselors/YWCA Staff (1934)/Wives-Animal Husbandry Professors
Social Science Teachers (1934)
Entertainers/Librarians (1967)/Elementary Teachers/Secretaries (1934)/Housewives/Telephone Operators/YWCA Staff (1967)
English Teachers (1934)/Librarians (1934)/Art Teachers
Saleswomen/Office Workers/Artists (1934)/Photographers/English Teachers (1967)/Language Teachers/Social Science
Teachers (1967)/Lawyers (1967)/Musicians/Business Education Teachers (1941)
Life Insurance Sales (1937)/Models/Authors/Artists (1967)/Directors, Christian Education/Instrument Assemblers
Life Underwriters/Secretaries (1967)/Buyers/Accountants/Bankwomen
Newswomen/Beauticians/Sewing Machine Operators/Business Education Teachers (1967)/Music Teachers
Interior Decorators

TABLE 4-29. MEAN SCORES ON THE WOMEN'S HOMEMAKING SCALE

Home Economics Teachers (1967)
Home Economics Teachers (1941)

Dietitians (1941)
Dietitians (1967)
Executive Housekeepers/Telephone Operators/Sewing Machine Operators/Licensed Practical Nurses
Saleswomen/Housewives
Elementary Teachers/Wives-Animal Husbandry Professors/Beauticians
Registered Nurses/Dental Assistants/Instrument Assemblers/Wives-Social Workers/Stewardesses/Occupational Therapists (1966)
Visiting Nurses/Secretaries (1967)/Physical Therapists (1966)/Public Health Nurses/County Welfare Workers
Directors, Christian Education
Business Education Teachers (1967)/Occupational Therapists (1942)/Language Teachers/Social Science Teachers (1934)
Business Education Teachers (1941)/Social Workers/Math-Science Teachers (1967)
Physical Therapists (1957)/Musicians/English Teachers (1967)/YWCA Staff (1934)/Music Teachers/Art Teachers
Office Workers/Interior Decorators
YWCA Staff (1967)/Medical Technologists/Social Science Teachers (1934)/Lab Technicians/Wives-Physicists
HS PE Teachers (1967)/Math-Science Teachers (1934)/Radiologic Technologists/Guidance Counselors/Bankwomen
Nun-Teachers/Secretaries (1934)/English Teachers (1934)/Dentists/Nurses (1934)/Librarians (1967)/Newswomen
Physicians (Western Reserve)/College PE Teachers (1954)/Buyers
Physicians (1967)/Entertainers/Engineers/Nongrads/Navy Enlisted/HS PE Teachers (1939)/Life Underwriters
Life Insurance Sales (1937)/Accountants
Models/Speech Pathologists/Chemists/Navy Officers/Grads/Librarians (1934)/Translators
Psychologists (1942)/Army Officers/Psychologists (1966)/Lawyers (1967)/Lawyers (1934)/Physicians (1934)/College PE
Teachers (1968)
Army Enlisted/Mathematicians/Photographers/Authors/Artists (1934)/Artists (1967)

TABLE 4-30. MEAN SCORES ON THE WOMEN'S LAW/POLITICS SCALE

```
63 Lawyers (1934)
62 Lawyers (1967)
61
60
59
58 Social Science Teachers (1967)
57
56 Army Officers/Newswomen
55 Social Science Teachers (1934)/Life Underwriters/Psychologists (1966)
54 Navy Officers/YWCA Staff (1967)
53 Speech Pathologists/Stewardesses/Guidance Counselors/Life Insurance Sales (1937)/Social Workers/Grads/Engineers
   Accountants
52 Nongrads/Army Enlisted/Librarians (1967)/Translators/County Welfare Workers/YWCA Staff (1934)/Bankwomen
51 Models/Psychologists (1942)/Wives-Physicists/Physicians (Western Reserve)/Chemists/Visiting Nurses/English Teachers (1967)
   Language Teachers/Wives-Social Workers/Photographers/Physicians (1967)
50 Business Education Teachers (1941)/Registered Nurses/English Teachers (1934)/Physicians (1934)/Dietitians (1967)
   Interior Decorators/Business Education Teachers (1967)/College PE Teachers (1968)
49 Secretaries (1934)/Mathematicians/Physical Therapists (1957)/Public Health Nurses/Directors, Christian Education
   Physical Therapists (1966)/Entertainers/Nurses (1934)/Occupational Therapists (1966)/Secretaries (1967)
   Wives-Animal Husbandry Professors/Navy Enlisted/Nun-Teachers
48 College PE Teachers (1954)/HS PE Teachers (1939)/Math-Science Teachers (1934)/Office Workers/Buyers
   Medical Technologists/Housewives/Musicians/Librarians (1934)/Radiologic Technologists/Dentists/Music Teachers/Authors
   HS PE Teachers (1967)/Elementary Teachers/Dietitians (1941)/Art Teachers
47 Exec Housekeepers/Math-Science Teachers (1967)/Licensed Practical Nurses/Home Economics Teachers (1941)/Saleswomen
   Dental Assistants/Home Economics Teachers (1967)
46 Occupational Therapists (1942)/Telephone Operators/Lab Technicians
45 Instrument Assemblers
44 Artists (1967)/Artists (1934)/Sewing Machine Operators
43 Beauticians
```

TABLE 4-31. MEAN SCORES ON THE WOMEN'S MEDICAL SERVICE SCALE

```
62 Licensed Practical Nurses/Laboratory Technicians
61 Medical Technologists
60 Physicians (1934)/Dentists/HS PE Teachers (1939)
59 Dental Assistants/Physical Therapists (1957)/Nurses (1934)/Physical Therapists (1966)/Radiologic Technologists
58 Registered Nurses
57 Physicians (1967)/Visiting Nurses/Dietitians (1941)/Public Health Nurses/Physicians (Western Reserve)
56 Occupational Therapists (1942)
55 Chemists/Home Economics Teachers (1941)/Dietitians (1967)/Occupational Therapists (1966)/College PE Teachers (1954)
54 Psychologists (1966)/HS PE Teachers (1967)/Math-Science Teachers (1934)/College PE Teachers (1968)
53 Executive Housekeepers/Nun-Teachers/Math-Science Teachers (1967)/County Welfare Workers/Stewardesses
52 Grads/Engineers/Speech Pathologists/Nongrads/Home Economics Teachers (1967)
51 Army Enlisted/Wives-Social Workers/Telephone Operators/Translators/Saleswomen/Navy Enlisted/Wives-Animal Husbandry
   Professors/Housewives/Social Workers
50 Wives-Physicists/YWCA Staff (1934)/Psychologists (1966)/Elementary Teachers
49 Secretaries (1934)/Office Workers/Sewing Machine Operators/Guidance Counselors/Lawyers (1934)/Instrument Assemblers
   Army Officers/Social Science Teachers (1934)
48 Musicians/Directors, Christian Education/YWCA Staff (1967)/Business Education Teachers (1941)/Buyers/Navy Officers
   Mathematicians/Life Insurance Sales (1937)
47 Entertainers/English Teachers (1934)/Secretaries (1967)/Beauticians/Librarians (1967)/Life Underwriters
   Librarians (1934)/Social Science Teachers (1967)/Language Teachers (1967)
46 Models/English Teachers (1967)/Art Teachers (1967)/Music Teachers/Lawyers (1967)/Artists (1934)/Bankwomen
45 Business Education Teachers (1967)/Authors/Photographers/Accountants
44 Newswomen
43 Interior Decorators/Artists (1967)
```

TABLE 4-32. MEAN SCORES ON THE WOMEN'S MECHANICAL SCALE

Engineers

Chemists

Medical Technologists/Dentists/Lab Technicians/Physical Therapists (1957)/Occupational Therapists (1942)/Math-Science
Teachers (1934)/Occupational Therapists (1966)/Mathematicians
College PE Teachers (1954)/College PE Teachers (1968)
Psychologists (1942)/Math-Science Teachers (1967)/Physicians (1934)
Radiologic Technologists/Physicians (Western Reserve)/Physicians (1967)/Art Teachers/Instrument Assemblers
Physical Therapists (1966)/Army Enlisted
Army Officers/Navy Enlisted/Psychologists (1966)/Dietitians (1941)/Artists (1934)/Home Economics Teachers (1941)
Visiting Nurses/Nurses (1934)/Translators/Exec Housekeepers/HS PE Teachers (1939)/Navy Officers/Licensed
Practical Nurses
Dietitians (1967)/Photographers/Nun-Teachers/Office Workers/HS PE Teachers (1967)/Accountants
YWCA Staff (1934)/Interior Decorators/Home Economics Teachers (1967)/Business Education Teachers (1941)/Wives-Physicists
Telephone Operators/Artists (1967)
Nongrads/Lawyers (1934)/Sewing Machine Operators/Dental Assistants/YWCA Staff (1967)/Wives-Animal Husbandry Professors
Librarians (1967)/Social Workers/Speech Pathologists/Housewives/Grads/Librarians (1934)
Secretaries (1934)/Social Science Teachers (1934)/County Welfare Workers/Stewardesses/Guidance Counselors
Registered Nurses/English Teachers (1934)/Public Health Nurses/Elementary Teachers/Buyers/Business Education
Teachers (1967)/Musicians/Bankwomen
Saleswomen/Lawyers (1967)/Music Teachers/Life Insurance Sales (1937)/Wives-Social Workers/Newswomen/Secretaries (1967)
Entertainers/Authors/Directors, Christian Education/Models/Beauticians
English Teachers (1967)/Language Teachers/Social Science Teachers (1967)/Life Underwriters

TABLE 4-33. MEAN SCORES ON THE WOMEN'S MERCHANDISING SCALE

1 Saleswomen
0
9 Buyers
8 Stewardesses
7 Life Underwriters/Home Economics Teachers (1967)
6 Life Insurance Sales (1937)/Home Economics Teachers (1941)/Business Education Teachers (1941)/Business Education
Teachers (1967)
5 Exec Housekeepers/Dietitians (1941)
4 Secretaries (1967)/Office Workers/Interior Decorators/County Welfare Workers/Bankwomen
3 Dietitians (1967)/Beauticians/YWCA Staff (1967)/Secretaries (1934)/Instrument Assemblers/Guidance Counselors
HS PE Teachers (1939)/Telephone Operators/Army Enlisted/Housewives
2 Dental Assistants/Wives-Animal Husbandry Professors/Elementary Teachers/English Teachers (1967)/Social Science
Teachers (1967)
1 Visiting Nurses/Army Officers/Occupational Therapists (1942)/YWCA Staff (1934)/Models/Art Teachers (1967)
Wives-Social Workers/Music Teachers/Sewing Machine Operators/Occupational Therapists (1966)/Directors,
Christian Education/Social Science Teachers (1934)/Nongrads/Accountants
0 Social Workers/Licensed Practical Nurses/Language Teachers/Grads
9 Physical Therapists (1966)/Navy Officers/Entertainers/English Teachers (1934)/Public Health Nurses/Math-Science
Teachers (1934)/Nurses (1934)/Registered Nurses/Math-Science Teachers (1967)/Muscians/HS PE Teachers (1967)
8 Lawyers (1934)/Physical Therapists (1957)/Navy Enlisted/Lawyers (1967)/Engineers/Radiologic Technologists
Speech Pathologists/Librarians (1967)/College PE Teachers (1968)
7 Psychologists (1942)/College PE Teachers (1954)/Laboratory Technicians/Dentists/Wives-Physicists/Newswomen
Nun-Teachers
6 Medical Technologists/Librarians (1934)
5
4 Psychologists (1966)/Translators/Physicians (1967)
3 Physicians (1934)/Physicians (Western Reserve)
2 Artists (1934)/Authors
1 Chemists
0 Artists (1967)/Photographers/Mathematicians

TABLE 4-34. MEAN SCORES ON THE WOMEN'S MUSIC SCALE

```
62 Music Teachers
61
60 Musicians
59
58
57 Entertainers
56
55 Directors, Christian Education
54 Language Teachers/Psychologists (1966)/Wives-Physicists/HS PE Teachers (1939)
53 Nun-Teachers/Wives-Social Workers/College PE Teachers (1954)/English Teachers (1934)/Elementary Teachers/Nurses (1934)
   Occupational Therapists (1966)/YWCA Staff (1934)/Occupational Therapists (1942)
52 YWCA Staff (1967)/Translators/Art Teachers/English Teachers (1967)/Visiting Nurses/Secretaries (1934)/Housewives
   Physical Therapists (1966)/Physicians (Western Reserve)/Librarians (1967)/Public Health Nurses/Speech Pathologists
   Stewardesses/Chemists/Registered Nurses/Social Workers
51 Wives-Animal Husbandry Professors/Psychologists (1942)/Physical Therapists (1957)/Interior Decorators/Artists (1934)
   Army Officers/Lab Technicians/Office Workers/Models/Artists (1967)/Librarians (1934)/Physicians (1967)
   County Welfare Workers
50 Newswomen/Social Science Teachers (1967)/Authors/Grads/Social Science Teachers (1934)/Mathematicians/Engineers
   Photographers/Guidance Counselors/Nongrads/Math-Science Teachers (1934)/Medical Technologists/Buyers/Secretaries (1967)
   Licensed Practical Nurses/Physicians (1934)
49 Exec Housekeepers/Lawyers (1934)/Business Education Teachers (1941)/Life Insurance Sales (1937)/Dietitians (1967)
   Dietitians (1941)/Saleswomen/Navy Officers/Life Underwriters/Home Economics Teachers (1967)/Lawyers (1967)
   Dentists/College PE Teachers (1968)
48 Home Economics Teachers (1941)/Dental Assistants/HS PE Teachers (1967)/Telephone Operators/Business Education
   Teachers (1967)/ Radiologic Technologists/Accountants
47 Army Enlisted/Math-Science Teachers (1967)/Navy Enlisted/Bankwomen
46 Instrument Assemblers
45 Beauticians/Sewing Machine Operators
```

TABLE 4-35. MEAN SCORES ON THE WOMEN'S NUMBERS SCALE

```
63 Math-Science Teachers (1967)/Accountants
62 Math-Science Teachers (1934)/Mathematicians/Engineers
61
60 Chemists
59 Office Workers
58 Business Education Teachers (1941)
57 Bankwomen
56 Psychologists (1942)/Business Education Teachers (1967)
55 Medical Technologists/Psychologists (1966)
54 Dietitians (1941)
53 Physicians (Western Reserve)/Dietitians (1967)/Lab Technicians/College PE Teachers (1954)/Army Enlisted
   Lawyers (1934)/Physicians (1967)/Nun-Teachers/Exec Housekeepers/College PE Teachers (1968)
52 Nongrads/Instrument Assemblers/Physicians (1934)/Lawyers (1967)/Guidance Counselors/Buyers/Grads/Telephone Operators
   Dentists/Navy Enlisted/Sewing Machine Operators/Saleswomen
51 YWCA Staff (1934)/Physical Therapists (1966)/Home Economics Teachers (1941)/Life Insurance Sales (1937)/Army Officers
   Licensed Practical Nurses/Nurses (1934)/Housewives/Visiting Nurses/Radiologic Technologists/Physical Therapists (1957)
50 Elementary Teachers/Wives-Animal Husbandry Professors/HS PE Teachers (1939)/Navy Officers/Life Underwriters
   Social Science Teachers (1934)/Secretaries (1967)/Dental Assistants/HS PE Teachers (1967)/Translators
   County Welfare Workers/Librarians (1967)/Librarians (1934)
49 Secretaries (1934)/Wives-Physicists/Home Economics Teachers (1967)/Occupational Therapists (1942)/English Teachers (1934)
48 Social Workers/Registered Nurses/Social Science Teachers (1967)/Speech Pathologists/YWCA Staff (1967)
   Language Teachers/Beauticians/Music Teachers/Directors, Christian Education
47 Occupational Therapists (1966)/Stewardesses/Interior Decorators/Musicians/Public Health Nurses/Wives-Social Workers
46 Art Teachers/English Teachers (1967)/Photographers
45 Artists (1934)/Entertainers/Artists (1967)
44 Newswomen/Models/Authors
```

TABLE 4-36. MEAN SCORES ON THE WOMEN'S OFFICE PRACTICES SCALE

Business Education Teachers (1967)

Business Education Teachers (1941)

Office Workers/Bankwomen
Sewing Machine Operators/Secretaries (1967)/Telephone Operators

Secretaries (1934)/Saleswomen
Dental Assistants/Accountants
Housewives/Math-Science Teachers (1967)/Math-Science Teachers (1934)/Exec Housekeepers
Army Enlisted/Instrument Assemblers
Licensed Practical Nurses/Wives-Animal Husbandry Professors/Navy Enlisted/Nun-Teachers/Elementary Teachers
Buyers/YWCA Staff (1934)/Dietitians (1941)/Lawyers (1934)/HS PE Teachers (1939)/Guidance Counselors
Directors, Christian Education
Beauticians/Home Economics Teachers (1967)/Nongrads/Nurses (1934)/Home Economics Teachers (1941)/County Welfare Workers
Stewardesses/Life Insurance Sales (1937)/Social Science Teachers (1934)/Army Officers/Dietitians (1967)
Social Science Teachers (1967)/Lab Technicians/Radiologic Technologists/Wives-Social Workers/Life Underwriters
Engineers/Language Teachers/Grads/Lawyers (1967)/English Teachers (1967)/Occupational Therapists (1942)/HS PE Teachers (1967)
Dentists/Visiting Nurses/Music Teachers/English Teachers (1934)/Physical Therapists (1966)/YWCA Staff (1967)
Medical Technologists/Psychologists (1942)/Physical Therapists (1957)/College PE Teachers (1954)/Librarians (1967)
Librarians (1934)/Wives-Physicists/Musicians/Navy Officers/Social Workers
Occupational Therapists (1966)/Registered Nurses/Public Health Nurses/College PE Teachers (1968)
Physicians (1934)/Mathematicians/Entertainers/Chemists/Translators
Physicians (Western Reserve)/Physicians (1967)/Art Teachers/Psychologists/Speech Pathologists
Models/Interior Decorators
Newswomen/Authors
Artists (1934)
Photographers/Artists (1967)

TABLE 4-37. MEAN SCORES ON THE WOMEN'S OUTDOORS SCALE

56 Occupational Therapists (1942)/YWCA Staff (1934)
55 Physicians (Western Reserve)/Artists (1934)/Physicians (1934)/Nurses (1934)/Dentists/Physical Therapists (1957)
   Housewives/College PE Teachers (1954)/College PE Teachers (1968)
54 Licensed Practical Nurses/Home Economics Teachers (1941)/HS PE Teachers (1939)/Math-Science Teachers (1934)
   Lab Technicians/Librarians (1934)/County Welfare Workers/Social Science Teachers (1934)/English Teachers (1934)
53 Dietitians (1941)/Occupational Therapists (1942)/Elementary Teachers/Wives-Animal Husbandry Professors/Physical
   Therapists (1966)/Art Teachers/Psychologists (1942)/Physicians (1967)/Visiting Nurses/Chemists
52 Home Economics Teachers (1967)/Authors/Social Workers/Public Health Nurses/Medical Technologists/Sewing Machine
   Operators/Lawyers (1934)
51 Photographers/Artists (1967)/Exec Housekeepers/HS PE Teachers (1967)/Registered Nurses/Telephone Operators
   Wives-Physicists/Life Insurance Sales (1937)/Buyers/Engineers
50 Office Workers/Secretaries (1934)/YWCA Staff (1967)/Directors, Christian Education/Nun-Teachers/Wives-Social Workers
   Navy Enlisted/Librarians (1967)/Business Education Teachers (1941)/Dietitians (1967)/Army Officers/Music Teachers
   Math-Science Teachers (1967)/Radiologic Technologists/Interior Decorators/Saleswomen
49 Musicians/Army Enlisted/Psychologists (1966)/Translators/Newswomen/Mathematicians/Social Science Teachers (1967)
48 English Teachers (1967)/Dental Assistants/Instrument Assemblers/Stewardesses/Beauticians/Guidance Counselors
   Navy Officers/Language Teachers/Secretaries (1967)
47 Business Education Teachers (1967)/Speech Pathologists/Lawyers (1967)/Bankwomen/Accountants
46 Life Underwriters/Entertainers
45 Models/Nongrads
44 Grads

TABLE 4-38. MEAN SCORES ON THE WOMEN'S PERFORMING ARTS SCALE

```
60 Entertainers
59
58
57 Musicians
56 Models
55 Stewardesses/Music Teachers/HS PE Teachers (1939)
54 English Teachers (1967)/Newswomen/Art Teachers/Psychologists (1966)/Interior Decorators
53 Translators/Authors/English Teachers (1934)/Language Teachers/Artists (1967)/Secretaries (1934)/Wives-Physicists
52 YWCA Staff (1967)/Speech Pathologists/Nongrads/Photographers/Artists (1934)/Wives-Social Workers
   Occupational Therapists (1966)
51 Directors, Christian Education/Grads/Librarians (1967)/Army Officers/College PE Teachers (1954)/Nurses (1934)
   Lawyers (1967)/Guidance Counselors
50 Social Workers/Lawyers (1934)/Psychologists (1942)/Life Underwriters/Visiting Nurses/Nun-Teachers/Physicians (1967)
   Occupational Therapists (1942)
49 Elementary Teachers/Physical Therapists (1957)/Secretaries (1967)/Registered Nurses/Saleswomen/Life Insurance Sales (1937
   Wives-Animal Husbandry Professors/Social Science Teachers (1967)/Housewives/Physical Therapists (1966)
   Office Workers/Physicians (Western Reserve)/Buyers/Social Science Teachers (1934)/Navy Officers/College PE Teachers (1968
48 YWCA Staff (1934)/Librarians (1934)/Public Health Nurses/Engineers/Business Education Teachers (1941)/County
   Welfare Workers/HS PE Teachers (1967)/Lab Technicians/Chemists/Dentists/Dental Assistants/Physicians (1934)
   Radiologic Technologists/Telephone Operators/Beauticians
47 Dietitians (1967)/Exec Housekeepers/Mathematicians/Home Economics Teachers (1967)/Licensed Practical Nurses
   Dietitians (1941)/Math-Science Teachers (1934)/Home Economics Teachers (1941)/Medical Technologists/Accountants
46 Army Enlisted/Business Education Teachers (1967)/Bankwomen
45 Instrument Assemblers/Navy Enlisted/Math-Science Teachers (1967)
44
43 Sewing Machine Operators
```

TABLE 4-39. MEAN SCORES ON THE WOMEN'S PHYSICAL SCIENCE SCALE

```
66 Chemists
65
64 Engineers
63
62 Mathematicians
61 Medical Technologists
60 Laboratory Technicians
59 Math-Science Teachers (1934)/Psychologists (1942)/Physicians (Western Reserve)
58 Physicians (1934)/Physicians (1967)/Psychologists (1966)
57 Math-Science Teachers (1967)/Dentists
56 Translators
55 Physical Therapists (1957)/Radiologic Technologists/College PE Teachers (1954)
54 Dietitians (1941)/Physical Therapists (1966)/Dietitians (1967)/College PE Teachers (1963)
53 Nurses (1934)/Licensed Practical Nurses/Visiting Nurses/Home Economics Teachers (1941)/Lawyers (1934)
52 Occupational Therapists (1942)/Occupational Therapists (1966)/Army Officers/Wives-Physicists/Speech Pathologists
   Grads/Army Enlisted
51 Social Science Teachers (1934)/Lawyers (1967)/Navy Enlisted/Navy Officers/HS PE Teachers (1939)/Nongrads
   Artists (1934)/Nun-Teachers/Librarians (1967)/Librarians (1934)/Exec Housekeepers/Registered Nurses (1967)
   Photographers/English Teachers (1934)/Accountants
50 YWCA Staff (1934)/Wives-Animal Husbandry Professors/Art Teachers/Social Workers/Public Health Nurses/Dental Assistants
   Office Workers/Guidance Counselors
49 Home Economics Teachers (1967)/HS PE Teachers (1967)/County Welfare Workers/Instrument Assemblers
   Business Education Teachers (1941)/Artists (1967)
48 Secretaries (1934)/Stewardesses/Authors/Life Insurance Sales (1937)/Housewives/Telephone Operators/Newswomen
   Elementary Teachers/Social Science Teachers (1967)
47 Language Teachers/Buyers/YWCA Staff (1967)/Saleswomen/Musicians/Wives-Social Workers/Entertainers/Music Teachers
   Interior Decorators
46 Business Education Teachers (1967)/Directors, Christian Education/English Teachers (1967)/Sewing Machine Operators
   Life Underwriters/Bankwomen
45 Secretaries (1967)/Models
44
43 Beauticians
```

TABLE 4-40. MEAN SCORES ON THE WOMEN'S PUBLIC SPEAKING SCALE

YWCA Staff (1967)
Speech Pathologists/Lawyers (1934)/Lawyers (1967)
Guidance Counselors/Life Underwriters/Psychologists (1966)/Army Officers
Directors, Christian Education
County Welfare Workers/English Teachers (1967)/Stewardesses/Life Insurance Sales (1937)/Music Teachers
Newswomen/Social Workers/Social Science Teachers (1967)/Psychologists (1942)
YWCA Staff (1934)/Models/Translators
Musicians/Navy Officers/Interior Decorators/Language Teachers/Librarians (1967)/Entertainers/Grads/Army Enlisted
Art Teachers/Engineers
Nongrads/Social Science Teachers (1934)/College PE Teachers (1968)/Accountants
College PE Teachers (1954)/Occupational Therapists (1966)/Dietitians (1967)/HS PE Teachers (1939)/Exec Housekeepers
Photographers/Authors/Wives-Social Workers/Business Education Teachers (1967)/Visiting Nurses/Bankwomen
English Teachers (1934)/Chemists/Physicians (1967)/Dietitians (1941)/Wives-Physicists/Registered Nurses
Buyers/Physical Therapists (1957)/Home Economics Teachers (1967)
Home Economics Teachers (1941)/Public Health Nurses/Physicians (Western Reserve)/HS PE Teachers (1967)/Nun-Teachers
Physicians (1934)/Elementary Teachers/Saleswomen/Secretaries (1934)/Wives-Animal Husbandry Professors
Secretaries (1967)
Mathematicians/Physical Therapists (1966)/Dental Assistants/Housewives/Librarians (1934)/Occupational Therapists(1942)
Navy Enlisted/Artists (1967)/Office Workers/Math-Science Teachers (1967)/Licensed Practical Nurses/Dentists
Nurses (1934)/Telephone Operators/Radiologic Technologists/Math-Science Teachers (1934)
Medical Technologists
Artists (1934)/Instrument Assemblers/Beauticians
Lab Technicians
Sewing Machine Operators

TABLE 4-41. MEAN SCORES ON THE WOMEN'S RELIGIOUS ACTIVITIES SCALE

Directors, Christian Education

YWCA Staff (1934)

Nun-Teachers/Licensed Practical Nurses
Sewing Machine Operators
Saleswomen/Exec Housekeepers/Guidance Counselors/YWCA Staff (1967)
Elementary Teachers/Telephone Operators/Home Economics Teachers (1967)
Dental Assistants/Registered Nurses/Music Teachers/HS PE Teachers (1967)/Visiting Nurses/Wives-Animal Husbandry
Professors/Beauticians/County Welfare Workers
Radiologic Technologists/English Teachers (1967)/Language Teachers/Business Education Teachers (1967)/Secretaries (1967)
Social Science Teachers (1967)/Math-Science Teachers (1967)/Public Health Nurses/Physical Therapists (1966)
Housewives/Army Enlisted/Bankwomen
Nongrads/Medical Technologists/Physical Therapists (1957)/Grads/Instrument Assemblers/Dietitians (1967)/Navy Enlisted
Business Education Teachers (1941)/Life Underwriters/Musicians/Wives-Social Workers/Social Workers/Social Science
Teachers (1934)/Stewardesses
Occupational Therapists (1966)/Home Economics Teachers (1941)/Librarians (1967)/Army Officers/Art Teachers
Accountants/College PE Teachers (1968)
Office Workers/Math-Science Teachers (1934)/Buyers/Dietitians (1941)/Occupational Therapists (1942)/Engineers
Nurses (1934)
Physicians (1967)/Speech Pathologists/College PE Teachers (1954)/Secretaries (1934)/Life Insurance Sales (1937)
HS PE Teachers (1939)/English Teachers (1934)/Lawyers (1967)
Chemists/Navy Officers/Entertainers/Newswomen/Physicians (Western Reserve)/Interior Decorators
Models/Mathematicians/Lawyers (1934)/Wives-Physicists
Dentists/Lab Technicians/Artists (1934)/Authors/Librarians (1934)
Physicians (1934)/Artists (1967)
Translators/Psychologists (1942)
Psychologists (1966)

Photographers

TABLE 4-42. MEAN SCORES ON THE WOMEN'S SOCIAL SERVICE SCALE

```
60 YWCA Staff (1967)/YWCA Staff (1934)/Directors, Christian Education
59
58 County Welfare Workers
57
56 Guidance Counselors/HS PE Teachers (1967)/Social Workers
55 Registered Nurses/Nun-Teachers
54 Public Health Nurses/Army Enlisted/Licensed Practical Nurses/Stewardesses/Visiting Nurses/Wives-Social Workers
53 Home Economics Teachers (1967)/Elementary Teachers/Occupational Therapists (1966)/Physical Therapists (1957)
   Physical Therapists (1966)
52 HS PE Teachers.(1939)/Social Science Teachers (1967)/Nongrads/Exec Housekeepers/Telephone Operators/Grads
   Saleswomen/Secretaries (1967)/Business Education Teachers (1967)/Dental Assistants/English Teachers (1967)
   Housewives/Psychologists (1942)
51 Radiologic Technologists/Army Officers/Beauticians/Instrument Assemblers/Wives-Animal Husbandry Professors
   Navy Enlisted/College PE Teachers (1954)/College PE Teachers (1968)
50 Occupational Therapists (1942)/Social Science Teachers (1934)/Language Teachers/Nurses (1934)/Home Economics
   Teachers (1941)/Sewing Machine Operators/Math-Science Teachers (1967)
49 Music Teachers/Business Education Teachers (1941)/Dietitians (1967)/Lawyers (1934)/Medical Technologists/Bankwomen
48 Speech Pathologists/Physicians (Western Reserve)/Secretaries (1934)/Math-Science Teachers (1934)/Office Workers
   Dietitians (1941)/Life Insurance Sales (1937)/Engineers/English Teachers (1934)/Musicians
47 Psychologists (1966)/Life Underwriters/Art Teachers/Physicians (1967)/Librarians (1967)/Navy Officers/Dentists
46 Lawyers (1967)/Physicians (1934)/Lab Technicians/Buyers/Wives-Physicists/Entertainers
45 Newswomen/Models/Accountants
44 Librarians (1934)/Chemists/Translators
43 Authors
42 Mathematicians/Interior Decorators
41 Photographers/Artists (1934)
40 Artists (1967)
```

TABLE 4-43. MEAN SCORES ON THE WOMEN'S SPORTS SCALE

```
63 HS PE Teachers (1939)/HS PE Teachers (1967)
62
61
60 College PE Teachers (1968)
59 College PE Teachers (1954)
58
57 Physical Therapists (1957)/Stewardesses
56 Physical Therapists (1966)
55
54 YWCA Staff (1967)/Navy Enlisted
53 Telephone Operators/Beauticians/Radiologic Technologists/Nurses (1934)/Army Enlisted/Registered Nurses/Housewives
52 Elementary Teachers/Licensed Practical Nurses/Nongrads/Dental Assistants/Occupational Therapists (1966)
   Wives-Social Workers/Grads
51 Occupational Therapists (1942)/Public Health Nurses/YWCA Staff (1934)/Visiting Nurses/Nun-Teachers/Sewing Machine
   Operators/Home Economics Teachers (1941)/Directors, Christian Education/Medical Technologists/Home Economics
   Teachers (1967)
50 Secretaries (1967)/Saleswomen/Instrument Assemblers/Dietitians (1941)/Army Officers/Lab Technicians
   Exec Housekeepers/Physicians (1934)/Secretaries (1934)/Dentists/Math-Science Teachers (1934)/Math-Science Teachers (1967)
49 Buyers/Office Workers/Guidance Counselors/Wives-Animal Husbandry Professors/Navy Officers/Engineers
   Business Education Teachers (1967)/County Welfare Workers/Physicians (Western Reserve)/Business Education
   Teachers (1941)/Bankwomen
48 Social Science Teachers (1934)/Dietitians (1967)/Social Science Teachers (1967)/Life Insurance Sales (1937)
   Lawyers (1934)/English Teachers (1934)/Entertainers/Physicians (1967)/Life Underwriters/Social Workers
47 Music Teachers/Art Teachers/English Teachers (1967)/Librarians (1934)/Musicians/Accountants
46 Psychologists (1942)/Language Teachers/Models
45 Speech Pathologists/Artists (1934)/Librarians (1967)/Chemists/Lawyers (1967)/Mathematicians
44 Newswomen/Psychologists (1967)/Wives-Physicists/Interior Decorators/Photographers
43 Authors/Translators
42
41 Artists (1967)
```

TABLE 4-44. MEAN SCORES ON THE WOMEN'S TEACHING SCALE

Elementary Teachers/Directors, Christian Education
Home Economics Teachers (1967)
Music Teachers
Art Teachers/Nun-Teachers/HS PE Teachers (1939)/Home Economics Teachers (1941)/Business Education Teachers (1967)
HS PE Teachers (1967)/Occupational Therapists (1966)
Stewardesses/Guidance Counselors/Wives-Social Workers/College PE Teachers (1968)
YWCA Staff (1967)/English Teachers (1967)/Social Science Teachers (1934)/Social Science Teachers (1967)
Language Teachers/College PE Teachers (1954)/Housewives/Public Health Nurses/Business Education Teachers (1941)
Wives-Animal Husbandry Professors
Math-Science Teachers (1934)/Visiting Nurses/Math-Science Teachers (1967)/English Teachers (1934)/Registered Nurses
Speech Pathologists/YWCA Staff (1934)/Secretaries (1967)
Saleswomen/Physical Therapists (1966)/Telephone Operators/Musicians/Licensed Practical Nurses/Exec Housekeepers
Physical Therapists (1957)/Social Workers/Wives-Physicists/Dental Assistants/Occupational Therapists (1942)
Psychologists (1942)/Grads/Instrument Assemblers
Nurses (1934)/Sewing Machine Operators/Dietitians (1967)/Nongrads/Entertainers/County Welfare Workers/Beauticians
Office Workers/Librarians (1967)/Psychologists (1966)/Army Officers/Army Enlisted/Physicians (Western Reserve)
Bankwomen
Secretaries (1934)/Engineers/Radiologic Technologists
Life Insurance Sales (1937)/Lawyers (1934)/Buyers/Navy Enlisted/Dietitians (1941)/Life Underwriters/Interior Decorators
Medical Technologists/Models/Physicians (1967)/Accountants
Translators/Dentists/Physicians (1934)/Newswomen/Lawyers (1967)
Chemists/Navy Officers/Mathematicians/Artists (1967)
Lab Technicians/Photographers/Artists (1934)/Authors
Librarians (1934)

TABLE 4-45. MEAN SCORES ON THE WOMEN'S WRITING SCALE

Newswomen

Authors/English Teachers (1967)
Photographers
Translators/English Teachers (1934)
Psychologists (1966)
Models/Librarians (1967)/Entertainers/YWCA Staff (1967)/Army Officers
Stewardesses/Speech Pathologists/Language Teachers/Lawyers (1967)/Grads/Wives-Physicists/Social Science Teachers (1967)
Psychologists (1942)/Guidance Counselors
Interior Decorators/Secretaries (1934)/Lawyers (1934)/Directors, Christian Education/Art Teachers/Social Workers
Nongrads/Wives-Social Workers/Musicians/Librarians (1934)/Artists (1934)
Life Insurance Sales (1937)/County Welfare Workers/Social Science Teachers (1934)/Artists (1967)/Occupational
Therapists (1966)/Life Underwriters
Physicians (Western Reserve)/Elementary Teachers/Nun-Teachers/Music Teachers/Visiting Nurses/Navy Officers
YWCA Staff (1934)/Nurses (1934)/Secretaries (1967)/Army Enlisted
Physicians (1967)/Wives-Animal Husbandry Professors/Engineers/Buyers/Registered Nurses/Occupational Therapists (1942)
Public Health Nurses/Physical Therapists (1957)/Housewives/College PE Teachers (1954)/College PE Teachers (1968)
HS PE Teachers (1939)/Business Education Teachers (1941)/Office Workers/Dietitians (1967)/Home Economics
Teachers (1967)/Chemists/Saleswomen/Physical Therapists (1966)/Business Education Teachers (1967)
Physicians (1934)/Dentists/Radiologic Technologists/Lab Technicians/Telephone Operators/Dietitians (1941)
Exec Housekeepers/Accountants/Bankwomen
Home Economics Teachers/Dental Assistants/Medical Technologists/Licensed Practical Nurses/Math-Science Teachers (1934)
Mathematicians/Navy Enlisted/HS PE Teachers (1967)
Math-Science Teachers (1967)
Instrument Assemblers
Beauticians
Sewing Machine Operators

TABLE 4-46. MEAN TEST AND RETEST PROFILES ON THE BASIC SCALES FOR NOLTING'S FEMALE CURRICULAR SAMPLES

	Total Sample						Art Majors (N=29)			Elem. Ed. Majors (N=38)			Home Econ. Majors (N=133)			Occ. Therapy Majors (N=60)			Library Science Majors (N=26)			Physicians (N=15)			Social Work Majors (N=21)		
	r	M	SD	M	SD	Ch	Test M	Retest M	Ch	Test M	Retest M	Ch	Test M	Retest M	Ch	Test M	Retest M	Ch	Test M	Retest M	Ch	Test M	Retest M	Ch	Test M	Retest M	Ch
Public Speaking	.54	47	9.2	50	9.2		46	48		50	50		47	51	+4	43	46		49	52		48	50		51	58	+7
Law/Politics	.53	47	9.1	49	9.7		47	48		49	51		46	48		45	46		50	52		53	52		53	57	+4
Merchandising	.44	50	7.8	53	8.8	-4	50	51		53	55		51	56	+5	47	49		49	50		45	44		49	53	+4
Office Practices	.57	50	8.2	48	9.0		46	42	-4	49	48		52	50		48	45		48	49		47	46		48	47	
Numbers	.66	51	8.2	49	9.2		46	45		48	49		53	50		48	46		50	48		55	53		51	48	
Phys. Science	.57	49	9.7	50	9.8		47	49		46	48		48	51		55	57		49	49		62	61		48	50	
Mechanical	.52	47	9.0	51	9.5	+4	48	54	+6	43	47	+4	47	51	+4	49	54	+5	46	47		55	53		46	46	
Outdoors	.48	48	10.3	52	9.2	+4	49	54	+5	44	51	+7	48	53	+5	49	53	+4	47	52	+5	48	48		45	51	+6
Biol. Science	.46	50	9.7	52	9.6		48	50		44	47		49	50		51	50		50	51		63	61		48	47	
Med. Service	.49	51	9.6	51	9.3		46	47		48	47		51	52		57	56		49	46		61	58		49	50	
Teaching	.36	51	8.6	56	8.2	+5	48	51		54	60	+6	52	58	+6	51	54		48	51		46	50	+4	51	57	+6
Social Service	.37	52	9.0	53	8.8		50	45	-5	52	53		52	54		54	52		48	50		52	50		54	59	+5
Sports	.58	53	8.5	52	9.1		49	47		54	53		54	54		55	53		48	45		50	49		54	53	
Homemaking	.54	50	8.9	54	8.9	+4	47	49		47	52	+5	55	59	+4	49	52		46	49		42	49	+7	46	52	+6
Relig. Activities	.48	53	8.1	49	9.6	-4	52	43	-9	53	51		54	52		53	47	-6	52	50		48	43	-5	55	51	-4
Music	.54	48	10.7	52	9.6	+4	49	55	+6	52	55		44	50	+6	49	53	+4	51	54		49	54	+5	47	54	+7
Art	.45	49	9.6	56	7.0	+7	59	60		50	56	+6	47	55	+8	53	57	+4	49	54		46	52	+6	43	56	-13
Performing Arts	.51	48	8.6	51	9.2		52	55		50	52		46	49		47	51	+4	52	54		45	50	+5	47	54	+7
Writing	.58	48	9.3	51	8.9		54	56		51	53		47	48		47	49		54	57		45	50		49	57	+9

When retested, these women were in their late 20's, the prime child bearing and rearing ages, and many of them were not working. Nolting reported the employed percentage in each group at retest as:

Medicine	100%	Art	65%
Library Science	80	Home Economics	53
Social Work	75	Elementary Education	44
Occupational Therapy	73		

The test and retest means on the Basic Scales for each of the curricular groups are listed in Table 4-46; mean changes larger than four points are noted especially. Table 4-47 summarizes the highest test and retest means, and the largest gains for each subsample.

Although there is, again, no one index of validity to inspect, the results look very reasonable. The art majors, for example, scored highest on the Art scale, with a mean of 59 when originally tested, and a mean of 60 when retested. This was their highest mean and the highest mean on the Art scale for any of the samples. The mean scores of the physicians, though this sample contained only 15 women, was equally reasonable. When tested as 17-18-year-olds, they had their highest means on the Biological Science (63), Physical Science (62), and Medical Service (61) scales, far higher than the other samples. Like the male medical students discussed earlier, these women showed some regression on these scales. Interestingly, the largest increase among these women physicians was the seven point gain on the Homemaking scale.

The largest gain over all of these samples was on the Outdoors scale, which parallels the increase found on the Nature scale among the male samples. And, again like the men, the other noteworthy general increases were on the Teaching, Music, and Art scales.

In general, these results demonstrate a moderately good level of predictive validity, and better concurrent validity. Although the criterion—that of educational curriculum—is not completely satisfactory, as some individuals will leave for other areas of employment, the proper groups consistently scored highest on the proper scales.

A Concluding Comment

The general comments made earlier on the interpretation and use of the Men's Basic Interest Scales are appropriate for the Women's Basic Scales also, and do not need to be repeated in this chapter. In general, the psychometric characteristics of the women's scales are quite similar to the men's, and these scales can be used in the same ways.

There is nothing in these data to suggest that the relationship between

TABLE 4-47. HIGHEST TEST AND RETEST MEANS AND LARGEST GAINS ON THE
BASIC INTEREST SCALES FOR NOLTING'S FEMALE CURRICULAR SAMPLES

Category	Highest Test Means		Highest Retest Means		Largest Gains	
Art Majors	Art	59	Art	60	Mechanical	48-54
	Writing	54	Writing	56	Music	49-55
	Performing Arts	52	Performing Arts	55	Outdoors	49-54
	Religious Activities	52	Music	55		
Elementary	Teaching	54	Teaching	60	Outdoors	44-51
Education Majors	Sports	54	Art	56	Teaching	54-60
	Merchandising	53	Merchandising	55	Art	50-56
	Religious Activities	53	Music	55		
Home Economics Majors	Homemaking	55	Homemaking	59	Art	47-55
	Sports	54	Teaching	58	Teaching	52-58
	Religious Activities	54	Merchandising	56	Music	44-50
Occupational	Medical Service	57	Physical Science	57	Mechanical	49-54
Therapy Majors	Sports	54	Art	57	Outdoors	49-53
	Social Service	54	Medical Service	56	Music	49-53
					Art	53-57
					Performing Arts	47-51
Library Science Majors	Writing	54	Writing	57	Outdoors	47-52
	Performing Arts	52	Music	54		
	Religious Activities	52	Performing Arts	54		
Physicians	Biological Science	63	Physical Science	61	Homemaking	42-49
	Physical Science	62	Biological Science	61	Art	46-52
	Medical Service	61	Medical Service	58	Music	49-54
					Performing Arts	45-50
					Writing	45-50
Social Work Majors	Religious Activities	55	Social Service	59	Art	43-56
	Social Service	54	Public Speaking	58	Writing	49-57
	Sports	54	Law/Politics	57	Public Speaking	51-58
			Teaching	57	Music	47-54
			Writing	57	Performing Arts	47-54

192

women's interests and occupational characteristics is any different from that found among men. Yet, occupational planning for young women will necessarily be different from that done by young men because of their different roles. How to integrate these matters of interests into the realities of a young wife and mother's life is not well understood but, as the strategies of planning must be supplemented somehow, these scales should provide some systematic data to help direct the feminine decisions.

CHAPTER 5

The Nonoccupational Scales

The Nonoccupational scales* are the prime examples of the sheer empiricism that has dominated the development of the SVIB. These scales are simply collections of items that discriminate between two selected groups; for example, the Masculinity-Femininity scale contains items that men and women answer differently. Each of these scales was developed with a specific purpose in mind, and data relevant to these purposes are reported here. On the basis of this information, most of which has only recently been available, some of these scales seem to be serving their function well, others not so well. One, the Interest Maturity scale, designed by Strong in the 1930's to predict which individuals would show changing interests with maturation, hasn't worked at all and was dropped from the profile in 1966.

The Nonoccupational scales vary considerably in age. The oldest, the Masculinity-Femininity scale, first appeared on the profile in about 1936, but the version that is discussed in this Manual was developed in 1967. The Occupational Level scale appeared in the 1930's—its development was described in Strong's 1943 book—and exists today essentially unchanged. The other older scale, the Specialization Level scale, also has not been changed since it was created in 1952.

These older scales create a problem for the test author and publisher. Probably they should be retired. The newer Academic Achievement scale is a better predictor of academic persistence than the Specialization Level scale, and the new Managerial Orientation scale will serve many of the functions of the Occupational Level scale.

Yet we know from past experience that removing any scale from the profile creates problems. Practitioners have learned from experience how to interpret the scores, and researchers have found novel uses for many of the scales. For example, in an imaginative series of studies, Kunce (1966a,

* Some of the scores in this *Handbook* are based on slightly revised scales.

b, 1967) demonstrated that an Accident Proneness Index, generated by subtracting the SVIB Banker scale score from the SVIB Aviator scale score, was moderately and consistently related to accident frequency. Unfortunately, in the 1966 revision of the men's form, the Aviator scale was dropped in favor of the newer Air Force Officer scale, and thus Kunce's index was destroyed. To minimize these problems, the two older Nonoccupational scales are being left on the profile, at least for this revision cycle.

The Nonoccupational scales are not simple to use in counseling and *their use should be restricted to professionally trained people who are aware of the pitfalls.* To minimize their visibility on the profile, the scores are reported under the scale abbreviations only; presumably this will limit their use to those with at least enough familiarity with the SVIB to know the scale names.

Each of the Nonoccupational scales is discussed further below.

Academic Achievement Scale (AACH—Men and Women)

The Academic Achievement (AACH) scale is an attempt to identify patterns of interests associated with good scholarship. The scale includes items that differentiate between good and poor students and is moderately effective, as will be shown, in predicting grades and eventual educational level.

Scale Development—Men's Form

The AACH validation group consisted of 462 freshman men who completed the SVIB during orientation activities in the College of Science, Literature, and the Arts of the University of Minnesota in the fall of 1961; a cross-validation sample of 250 was held out from the same class.

A second cross-validation group included adults tested in 1962 as participants in a 25-year follow-up study of University of Minnesota students (Campbell, 1965*a*). Because they took the SVIB 25 years after college, they represent a peculiar kind of validity generalization—a retrodictive rather than predictive approach.

Within the validation group, an index based on an equally weighted combination of high school rank (HSR) and first-year college grade-point average (GPA) was calculated for each student. The group was then rank-ordered on this index, and the SVIB item response frequencies for the top 40 percent and the bottom 40 percent were compared. Items showing 14 percent or greater differences were included in the scale. If the difference favored the high-achieving group, the response was weighted +1. Differences favoring the low achievers were weighted −1.

No attempt was made to control for level of ability in the selection of high and low achievers. Others have tried this approach in attempts to predict achievement variance independent of mental ability, but the results have not been impressive. (See Young and Estabrooks, 1936; Mosier, 1937; Williamson, 1937; Martin, 1964.) In the current research an attempt was made simply to locate an "academic-achievement" dimension within the pool of SVIB items.

Scores on this scale have been converted to standard scores using a group of 1927 Stanford University graduates as the norm group.

Validity: Prediction of College Grades

The freshman sample and the 25-year follow-up sample were scored on the AACH scale, and correlations were computed with HSR, GPA, and the Minnesota Scholastic Aptitude Test (MSAT). These data are presented in Table 5-1. They show that, within the validation sample, the AACH scale was the best single predictor of GPA (.52). However, there was considerable shrinkage in both cross-validation samples (.36 and .35), and HSR became the best predictor (.55 and .46).

Multiple correlations were computed, using GPA as the dependent variable, and the AACH scale, HSR, and MSAT as independent variables. These figures are also reported in Table 5-1.

Inspection of the cross-validation samples shows that when the achievement score was added to either HSR or MSAT, it increased the correlation with GPA by about .06. However, the gain in adding the AACH scale to

TABLE 5-1. INTERCORRELATIONS BETWEEN MEN'S ACADEMIC ACHIEVEMENT (AACH) SCALE, HIGH SCHOOL RANK, MINNESOTA SCHOLASTIC APTITUDE TEST, AND GRADE POINT AVERAGE

	MSAT	HSR	GPA	Mean	S.D.	Multiple Correlations with Grade Point Average	
			1961 Validation Freshmen (N = 462)				
AACH	.38	.48	.52	41.5	14.0	AACH, MSAT	.55
MSAT		.24	.37	43.4	11.8	HSR, MSAT	.55
HSR			.48	71.6	19.4	AACH, HSR	.59
GPA				1.9	.8	AACH, HSR, MSAT	.61
			1961 Cross-Validation Freshmen (N = 250)				
AACH	.23	.32	.36	44.5	12.2	AACH, MSAT	.49
MSAT		.27	.41	43.8	11.3	HSR, MSAT	.62
HSR			.55	70.6	20.9	AACH, HSR	.59
GPA				1.9	.9	AACH, HSR, MSAT	.63
			25-Year Follow-up Cross-Validation Sample (N = 283)				
AACH	.30	.24	.35	48.3	11.9	AACH, MSAT	.50
MSAT		.29	.44	57.7	11.3	HSR, MSAT	.56
HSR			.46	69.9	23.2	AACH, HSR	.52
GPA				2.1	.8	AACH, HSR, MSAT	.59

196

the combined prediction of both MSAT and HSR was negligible. Whatever variance is tapped by the AACH scales is measured almost equally well with the MSAT and HSR.

Still, the scale is moderately valid when used alone or with one of the other measures and, because it is a different way of measuring "grade-getting behavior," further information is reported below to help counselors make use of this measure.

Validity: Prediction of Eventual Educational Level

Further evidence of the validity of the AACH scale was gathered by comparing the mean scores of subsamples from the 25-year follow-up sample who had earned different college degrees. The resulting data, presented in Table 5-2, show a progression from low scores for men who earned no degrees to high scores for men who earned the Ph.D. The average undergraduate grade point for each of the groups is also listed, and the grades, of course, show the same progression.

The magnitude of these differences on the AACH scale was large enough to be practically worthwhile. There was almost a full standard deviation between the Ph.D.'s and the B.A.'s—with the M.A.'s falling halfway between—and about a half standard deviation between the B.A.'s and those who dropped out before earning a degree.

Note that these Minnesota graduates of about 1940 averaged approximately the same as the Stanford graduates of 1927. To make a direct comparison we would have to know how many advanced-degree earners were included in the Stanford group, and that information is not available.

A second follow-up group that was available consisted of students who graduated from Minnesota high schools in 1953 or 1954. This group, which was followed up primarily to determine the relationship between their SVIB profiles and their eventual occupations (see p. 57), was divided into groups according to degree earned, and these groups were compared on their scores on the AACH scale. These figures are reported in Table 5-3, as well as information on other measures related to scholastic achievement.

TABLE 5-2. MEN'S ACADEMIC ACHIEVEMENT (AACH) SCALE AND UNDERGRADUATE POINT AVERAGE: MEANS FOR DIFFERENT DEGREE LEVELS IN MINNESOTA 25-YEAR FOLLOW-UP SAMPLE

Degree Level	N	AACH Mean	Undergraduate GPA (A = 4.0)
Ph.D.	16	58	2.9
M.A.	27	52	2.5
B.A.	101	47	2.4
None	85	42	1.7

TABLE 5-3. MEN'S ACADEMIC ACHIEVEMENT (AACH) SCALE, HIGH SCHOOL RANK,
AND AMERICAN COUNCIL OF EDUCATION EXAMINATION: MEANS FOR
DIFFERENT DEGREE LEVELS IN MINNESOTA 10-YEAR FOLLOW-UP SAMPLE

Degree Level	N	AACH Mean	HSR Mean (Percentile)	ACE Mean (Percentile)
Ph.D.	7	62	96	92
M.A.	18	45	82	74
B.A.	69	39	72	65
None	75	29	48	48

Again, the figures show a substantial relationship between scores on the AACH scale and eventual level of education, but the absolute level of the scores is lower than in the previous sample; for example, the B.A.'s in the 25-year sample scored 47, those in the 10-year sample scored 39. This is probably due to the difference in age levels at the time of testing, because— as we shall see—scores on the AACH scale increase with age, at least during college attendance.

Scores related to attained educational level are available for one more sample, a group of men first tested as teenagers, then retested 36 years later as adults. They were initially tested in 1930 by E. K. Strong, in his studies on the relationship between age and interests (Strong, 1931). In 1966–67, many of those men, now age 52, were retested with the SVIB and they were also asked to furnish information on their educational and occupational history. Roughly 1,200 of the original 1,943 were located and retested. Further information on this project can be found on p. 107. These men were separated into several categories according to their educational level, and the mean score on the AACH scale was calculated for each level. Those data are presented in Table 5-4. The data for those with "some college" are not included here as they were difficult to categorize accurately.

The progression of means among the groups when originally tested was quite orderly, moving from 29 for those who would never attend college

TABLE 5-4. AACH MEANS AND STANDARD DEVIATIONS FOR SAMPLES AT
VARIOUS EDUCATIONAL LEVELS
(Tested at age 16 and retested at age 52)

	N	Test Mean	SD	Retest Mean	SD	Growth
No College	497	29	10	36	11	+7
B.A., B.S.	214	38	11	47	11	+9
M.A., M.S.	72	41	11	53	13	+12
M.D.	22	48	12	58	13	+10
Ph.D., Ed.D.	27	44	13	58	8	+14

to 44 among those who would eventually earn the doctorate, and 48 among those graduating from medical school.

When retested as adults, the groups showed an even greater separation; there were 22 points, or roughly two standard deviations, between the extreme groups. However, even the samples with no higher education increased seven points on the AACH scale, suggesting once again that the scores are somewhat related to age.

Reliability

Test-retest reliability of the AACH scale over several time intervals is presented in Figures 2-1 through 2-23 in Chapter 2, which contain the test-retest data for several samples; these results indicate that the AACH scale is reliable over short time spans for most individuals, and over longer time periods for adults. However, in some groups tested and retested over their college days, there was a definite increase in the mean score. See, for example, the 8–10-year University of Minnesota test-retest sample (Figure 2-9, p. 75) where the mean increased from 41 to 51. Clearly, scores on this scale increase during the college years for some students, although no such changes were found in the Harvard sample (Figure 2-5), which had a very high mean as freshmen. This comparison between Harvard and Minnesota students suggests that Harvard attracts students who are quite academically oriented as freshmen and who show little change in this characteristic; Minnesota, on the other hand, as a large, public, Midwestern University, attracts freshmen who initially are only mildly interested in things academic but who show sizable shifts in these characteristics during their college days.

To fully explore the relationship between age and AACH scores, scores on this scale should be available for a sample tested every year for several years. For reasons that are patently obvious, such a sample is difficult to come by. However, an attempt has been made to put together test-retest samples in such a way as to generate an age curve; a complete description of this approach is included below under the discussion of age-related interests (see p. 208).

Essentially, what was done was to combine samples tested and retested at various ages into one sample, categorized by age. The results of sampling in this manner cannot be fully understood; there are almost certainly sampling biases that are obscured; and comparability of all samples at all ages is not guaranteed. Still, it is the best sample in existence for studying the change of interests with age.

Mean scores on the AACH scale were calculated for each age group to

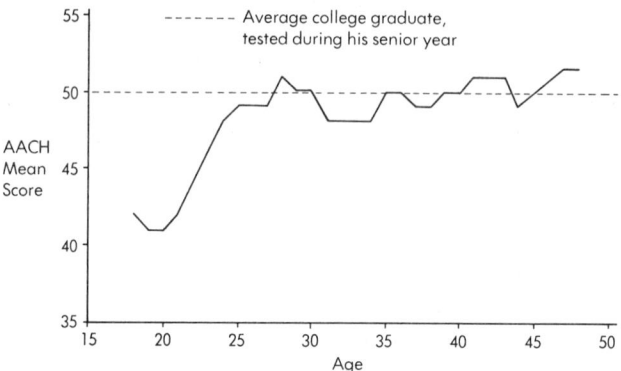

FIG. 5-1. *Relationship between age and scores on men's Academic Achievement scale.*

produce the curve for the AACH scale presented in Figure 5-1. The curve has been smoothed by using three-year floating averages. (The dotted line at 50 represents the average college graduate, tested during his senior year.)

Growth took place predominantly during the college years, especially in the immediate postgraduation years when many of these people were in professional and graduate schools. The scores leveled off at about age 28, and remained essentially constant from then on. These data, and the data reported earlier, suggest strongly that increased education is associated with high scores on this scale but, of course, which is cause and which is effect is not clear. Whether students who are developing these interests tend to seek more education, or whether increased education changes one's interests, cannot be determined from these data.

Construct Validity

The preceding data indicate the AACH scale is reliable over short time periods, fairly stable over longer time spans, and moderately valid in predicting grades and eventual educational level but, as yet, nothing has been said about the nature of the scale itself. If the AACH scale is to be useful in applied situations such as counseling and advising settings, the practitioner needs to know more about what the scale actually measures. Shrewd clinical utilizations of psychological tests depend more on the establishment and understanding of the underlying constructs than on supporting empirical data.

The items on the men's AACH scale are listed in Table 5-5. Those weighted positively include clusters of scientific and intellectual endeavors, general aesthetic interests, and some concern with personal efficiency. The negative weights emphasize business activities, particularly sales, and skilled trades.

An extra caution may be appropriate here. The weighted items on the AACH scale, and all of the other Nonoccupational scales, are listed in this chapter to help SVIB users understand what interests are tapped by each scale. Although scanning the items is useful in understanding the scales, this frequently leads to overinterpretation. Armchair explanations of why two groups differ on an item are easy to generate— but many of them fold under closer scrutiny. So while the reader should look over the item content carefully, he must avoid making wild jumps beyond this information. Studying both the item content and the rank-ordering of the occupational sample means on each scale is probably the best way to gain further insight into each scale, for this allows one to see both the item content and the empirical results for each scale.

TABLE 5-5. ITEMS WEIGHTED ON THE MEN'S ACADEMIC ACHIEVEMENT SCALE

Items Weighted Positively		Items Weighted Negatively	
Item Number	Item	Item Number	Item
9	Author of novel	2	Advertising Man
10	Author of technical book	11	Auto Salesman
23	Chemist	13	Auto Mechanic
27	College Professor	17	Building Contractor
53	Librarian	18	Buyer of merchandise
66	Orchestra Conductor	35	Factory Manager
67	Pharmacist	56	Machinist
69	Physician	81	Sales Manager
71	Poet	90	Specialty Salesman
82	School Teacher	139	Hunting
83	Scientific Research Worker	143	Boxing
101	Algebra	180	Popular mechanics magazines
103	Arithmetic	187	Adjusting a carburetor
107	Calculus	190	Operating machinery
108	Chemistry	282	Operate the new machine
112	English Composition	317	Chairman, Entertainment Committee
115	Geometry	345	Physical activity vs Mental activity
118	Modern Languages		
120	Mathematics		
128	Physics		
130	Physiology		
136	Zoology		
142	Hiking		
167	Symphony concerts		
172	Poetry		
192	Giving "first-aid" assistance		
199	Making a speech		
203	Teaching adults		
212	Doing research work		
240	Optimists		
243	People who assume leadership		
289	Teach others the use of the machine		
295	Opportunity to make use of all one's knowledge and experience		
347	Technical responsibility vs Supervisory responsibility		
353	Reading a book vs Watching TV or going to a movie		
378	Can write a concise, well-organized report		
380	Plan my work in detail		

65	Astronomers/Danforth Fellows
64	
63	Physicists(1968)
62	NIAL Members
61	Biologists/Chemists(1969)/Mathematicians(1969)
60	Pathologists/Mathematicians(1929)
59	Psychiatrists(1967)/Anthropologists/College Profs/Political Scientists/Economists/Psychologists(1947)/Internists/Neurological Surgeons
58	Physicians(1969)/Psychologists(1967)/Physiatrists/Pediatricians/Psychologists(1949)/Psychologists(Exp)/Physicists(1927)/Psychiatrists(1949)/Sociologists
57	Dental Educators/Librarians/Unitarian Ministers(1950)
56	Animal Husbandry Profs/Unitarian Ministers(1929)
55	Medical Techs/Judges/Astronauts/Student Personnel Workers/Surgeons/Chemists(1931)/Pulitzer Prize
54	Business School Profs/Actors(1966)/Mpls Symphony/Urologists/Physicians(1949)
53	NASA Scientists/School Supers(1930)/Ministers(1927)/Ministers(1965)/School Supers(1965)/Computer Programmers
52	Teaching Brothers/Math-Sci Teachers(1968)/Artists(1968)/Physicians(1927)/Interpreters/Radiologists/Music Teachers(1952)/Elem Teachers(Minn)
51	Food Scientists/Guidance Counselors(1968)/Investment Mgrs/Dentists(1969)/Ministers(1969)/Priests/Optometrists/Orthopedic Surgeons/Rehab Counselors
50	Actors(1937)/Social Workers(1953)/Math-Sci Teachers(1936)/Lawyers(1949)/Architects(1968)/English Teachers/Colonels/Public Admins(1969)/Newsmen/Social Workers(1967)/Generals & Admirals
49	Physical Therapists(1966)/Engineers(1968)/Photographers/Guidance Counselors(1950)/Physical Therapists(1957)/Engineers(1928)/Lawyers(1927)/Navy Officers/CPA(1965)/Architects(1933)
48	Lawyers(1969)/School Supers(1969)/Army Officers(1969)/Musicians(1952)/CPA(1944)/Army Officers(1950)/Authors/Public Admins(1941)/Salesmen,Computer/Football Coaches/Air Force Officers/Music Teachers(1946)
47	Musicians(1969)/Pharmacists(1968)/Osteopaths/Personnel Direcs(1927)/Corp Pres(1965)/Petroleum Engineers
46	Cartographers/Chiropractors/Legislators/Governors/Elem Teachers(NDak)/Dentists(1932)/YMCA PD/YMCA Secs/Artists(1933)/Pharmacists(1947)
45	Advertising Men(1968)/Personnel Direcs(1969)/Foresters/Vets(1966)/Cham Comm Execs/Accountants/Comm Rec Direcs/Credit Mgrs
44	Interior Decorators/Ag Extension Agents/High School Counselors/Business Ed Teachers/Soc Sci Teachers(1936)
43	Salesmen,Life(1966)/YMCA Staff/Production Mgrs/Advertising Men(1931)/County Welfare Workers
42	Bankers(1969)/Policemen(1968)/Soc Sci Teachers(1969)/Salesmen,Encyclopedia/Corp Pres(1935)/Office Workers/Vets(1949)
41	Army Sergeants/Bankers(1964)/Salesmen,Life(1931)/Forest Service Men/Pilots/Salesmen,3M
40	Voc Ag Teachers/Machinists/Sales Mgrs(1932)/Policemen(1933)/Printers/Salesmen,3M applicants
39	Funeral Direcs(1969)/Policemen(1969)/Purchasing Agents(1969)/Buyers(1969)/Salesmen,Steel/Bankers(1934)/Farmers(1936)/Purchasing Agents(1931)
38	Salesmen,PG&E/Dept Store Mgrs/Sales Mgrs(1968)/Tool & Die Makers
37	Salesmen,Life(1969)/Electricians/Highway Patrolmen/Buyers(1946)/Funeral Direcs(1945)/Salesmen,Real Estate(1932)
36	Skilled Tradesmen/Carpenters(1936)
35	County Sheriffs/Salesmen,Real Estate(1969)
34	Salesmen,Auto
33	
32	Carpenters(1969)
31	
30	
29	
28	
27	
26	Farmers(1968)/Farmers(1967)

TABLE 5-7. INTERCORRELATIONS BETWEEN WOMEN'S ACADEMIC ACHIEVEMENT
(AACH) SCALE, HIGH SCHOOL RANK, MINNESOTA SCHOLASTIC APTITUDE TEST,
AND GRADE POINT AVERAGE

	MSAT	HSR	GPA	Mean	S.D.	Multiple Correlations with Grade Point Average	
1961 Validation Freshmen (N = 658)							
AACH	.41	.44	.42	40.9	11.5	HSR, MSAT	.63
MSAT		.38	.47	44.7	11.9	AACH, MSAT	.53
HSR			.56	78.1	17.2	AACH, HSR	.60
GPA (1st year)				2.1	0.8	AACH, HSR, MSAT	.64
1961 Cross-Validation Freshmen (N = 400)							
AACH	.39	.38	.29	40.8	11.5	HSR, MSAT	.61
MSAT		.34	.51	45.9	11.9	AACH, MSAT	.52
HSR			.50	80.0	15.6	AACH, HSR	.51
GPA (1st year)				2.1	0.8	AACH, HSR, MSAT	.61
25-Year Follow-up Cross-Validation Sample (N = 292)							
AACH	.40	.28	.42	48.6	9.9	HSR, MSAT	.69
MSAT		.43	.57	55.9	11.8	AACH, MSAT	.61
HSR			.59	79.4	19.3	AACH, HSR	.65
GPA (1st year)				2.2	0.7	AACH, HSR, MSAT	.71

In seeking an understanding of the underlying dimensions of the AACH scale, it is useful to rank-order occupations by their scores on this scale and then look at the extremes. For this purpose, mean scores on the AACH scale for 178 occupational samples are reported in Table 5-6. Again, the rank-ordering of the occupations reflects the intellectual vs. business nature of the AACH scale; all of the scientific and intellectual occupations scored at one end of the scale, and the businessmen and skilled trades groups were at the other end. The occupations were spread out over almost four standard deviations, or about the same range we might expect to find in the mean IQ's of these occupational groups. Interestingly, the rank-ordering was about what we would expect to find if the occupations were ranked according to mean IQ—even though the data in Table 5-1 indicate that the AACH scale is only mildly related to ability (r = .30 with MSAT).

The correlation between the mean AACH score and the mean educational level of these occupations was .81, illustrating once again the degree of relationship between these interests and eventual educational level. (Note that this is a correlation between group means and must be interpreted cautiously.)

Women's AACH Scale

An Academic Achievement scale for the women's form was developed analogously to the men's form. This scale is the same one as was formerly used on the women's Form W booklet and uses only items common to the two forms. Validity statistics for the women's AACH scale are presented in Table 5-7 and the figures look very much like the men's statistics. Again the scale was moderately valid when used alone or with one of the other measures, but it did not add appreciably to a multiple correlation using HSR and MSAT.

Again, to help in interpretation, the items weighted on the Women's Academic Achievement scale are listed in Table 5-8. Two samples are available to check the long-term validity of the women's AACH scale. The first included the women from Nolting's research, already described on p. 176. All of them were college graduates so there is some restriction in range; even so, Nolting reported the data shown in Table 5-9 which shows considerable separation between groups earning different levels of degrees. The physicians scored quite high as teenagers, two standard deviations above those who eventually earned BA or BS degrees, but did not show any increase. Those earning Bachelor's or Master's degrees did show gains of six or seven points, though the rank-ordering remained the same.

The second sample included the women from the 25-year follow-up

TABLE 5-8. ITEMS WEIGHTED ON THE WOMEN'S ACADEMIC ACHIEVEMENT SCALE

Items Weighted Positively		Items Weighted Negatively	
Item Number	Item	Item Number	Item
11	Author of technical book	15	Beauty Specialist
13	Bacteriologist	18	Buyer of merchandise
22	Chemist	46	Hostess
24	College Professor	123	Typist
51	Interpreter	156	Women's pages
52	Inventor	171	Being the first to wear the very latest fashions
68	Art Museum Director		
69	Music Composer	202	Entertaining others
70	Musician	241	Fashionably dressed people
76	Opera Singer	292	Chairman, Entertainment Committee
80	Poet	296	Physical education director vs Magazine writer
92	Radio Program Director		
100	Scenario Writer	319	Physical activity vs Mental activity
102	Scientific Research Worker	336	Win friends easily
117	High School Teacher	361	Make bets Often...Sometimes...Rarely
139	Bird watching	387	Penmanship
141	Playing the piano	389	Physical Education
193	Discussions of politics		
270	Opportunity to make use of all one's knowledge and experience		
274	Freedom in working out one's own methods of doing the work		
330	Going to a play vs Going to a dance		
349	Can write a concise, well-organized report		
362	Algebra		
363	Arithmetic		
367	Botany		
368	Calculus		
369	Chemistry		
378	Geometry		
381	Ancient Languages		
382	Modern Languages		
386	Nature Study		
392	Political Science		

study of counseling (Campbell, 1965a); again, as with the parallel sample of men, this is a retrodictive situation because these individuals took the SVIB at about age 45, roughly 20 years after most of them had completed their education.

The appropriate figures are presented in Table 5-10. Once again the progression of means over the degree levels was quite regular, and there were almost two standard deviations between those earning no degrees and those earning the Ph.D. degree.

All of the women's occupational groups have been scored on the AACH scale, and the means are reported in Table 5-11. Again, to understand the essence of the scale, it is helpful to look at the groups scoring highest and lowest. The occupations scoring high were essentially the same ones that scored high on the men's scale, i.e., the scientific and intellectual ones. However, whereas the business, sales, and skilled trades occupations scored low on the men's scale, among the women the unskilled scored lowest. That would undoubtedly be true among the male samples, if test results were available for some unskilled occupations.

TABLE 5-9. Women's Academic Achievement Scale (AACH) Means on Test and Retest for Varying Educational Levels Among Nolting's Sample of University of Minnesota Students

Degree Earned	N	AACH Test Mean (age 17)	AACH Retest Mean (age 26)
M.D.	15	59	59
M.A., M.S.W.	45	47	53
B.A., B.S.	256	40	47

Use of the Academic Achievement Scales

The AACH scale is an example of one way to develop new tools to use with students, but a great deal of thought must be given to how these tools are to be used; there is some danger that the routine application of scales with only moderate validity may be deterimental to the overall goal of educational institutions. There may be a tendency for high scores on the AACH scale to be treated as "good," and low scores to be considered "bad," especially by those most immersed in academic enterprises. Such intellectual snobbery should be avoided. Although this scale is related to academic achievement, there are other worthwhile patterns of achievement in our society, and they are likely related to other interest patterns.

To emphasize this point, scores on the AACH scale have been gathered from several groups of men, all of them outstanding successes. These men were tested for the University of Minnesota's "Interest Archives," a program to preserve the interest profiles of the outstanding people of our time. The scores for each group are reported in Figure 5-2; each X represents a single individual, and the heavy vertical bar in each case represents the group mean. (Mean scores from other outstanding groups are reported in Chapter 7.)

Starting from the top of the table, the first group consists of high-producing life insurance salesmen. Each of them placed over $2 million of insurance in the preceding year.

The second group is made up of Army and Navy officers with the rank of Lieutenant General, or Vice-Admiral, or higher. These are all outstanding officers.

The third group consists of some of the country's most outstanding college football coaches. These men were all among the top 25 currently active football coaches in terms of lifetime won-lost records as of fall, 1965.

The fourth group consists of 17 corporation presidents, all of them from companies listed in the top 100 largest American companies in the 1964 *Fortune* magazine survey.

TABLE 5-10. WOMEN'S ACADEMIC ACHIEVEMENT (AACH) SCALE, GRADE POINT
AVERAGE, MINNESOTA SCHOLASTIC APTITUDE TEST, AND HIGH SCHOOL RANK:
MEANS FOR DIFFERENT DEGREE LEVELS IN 25-YEAR FOLLOW-UP SAMPLE

Degree Level	N	Mean	S.D.	N	Mean	S.D.
		Final GPA			MSAT	
No degree	158	1.7	0.6	131	50.1	12.1
B.A.	177	2.5	0.6	155	59.0	10.3
M.A.	22	2.7	0.5	20	61.0	9.6
Ph.D.	5	3.5	0.4	4	73.3	3.8
		HSR			AACH	
No degree	157	70.2	21.1	123	45.0	9.5
B.A.	177	85.5	14.4	152	50.2	8.9
M.A.	22	85.6	18.0	21	56.0	8.2
Ph.D.	5	98.2	1.2	4	64.0	3.4

TABLE 5-11. MEAN SCORES ON THE WOMEN'S ACADEMIC ACHIEVEMENT SCALE FOR
78 OCCUPATIONAL SAMPLES

```
62 Chemists 66 a
61
60 Mathematicians 66/Psychologists 66
59
58
57 Translators/Psychologists 42
56 Physicians 67/Physicians 34
55 Math-Science Teachers 34/Engineers
54 English Teachers 34
53 Librarians 67
52 Artists 67/Lawyers 67/Medical Technologists 67/Photographers 66/Authors 34/Librarians 34/Social Science Teachers 34
   YWCA Secretaries 34/Lawyers 34/Speech Pathologists
51 Language Teachers 67/Math-Science Teachers 67/Army Officers/Artists 34/PE Teacher (College) 54/Dentists 34
   Laboratory Technicians 41
50 Art Teachers 67/English Teachers 67/Newswomen 66/Social Workers 53
49 Guidance Counselors 67/Occupational Therapists 66/Social Science Teachers 67/Music Teachers 52/Physical Therapists 57
48 Accountants 67/Dietitians 67/Directors, Christian Education 67/Physical Therapists 66/Navy Officers/YWCA Staff 67
   Music Performers 52/Nurses 34
47 Nurses 67/Life Insurance Saleswomen 37/Dietitians 41/Occupational Therapists 42
46 Interior Decorators 66/Home Economics Teachers 41
45 Elementary Teachers 66/Army-Enlisted/Business Education Teachers 41/PE Teacher (high school) 39
44 Entertainers/Licensed Practical Nurses 67/Life Insurance Underwriters 67/Radiologic Technologists/Housewives
43 Business Education Teachers 67/Executive Housekeepers 67/Home Economics Teachers67/ PE Teachers (high school)67
   Navy-Enlisted/Stenographer-Secretary 34
42 Bankwomen 68/Office Workers 47
41 Models/Buyers 42
40 Stewardesses 66/Dental Assistants 66/Secretaries 67
39
38 Saleswomen/Telephone Operators
37 Instrument Assemblers
36
35 Sewing Machine Operators
34
33
32 Beauticians
```

        a = 66 refers to year tested

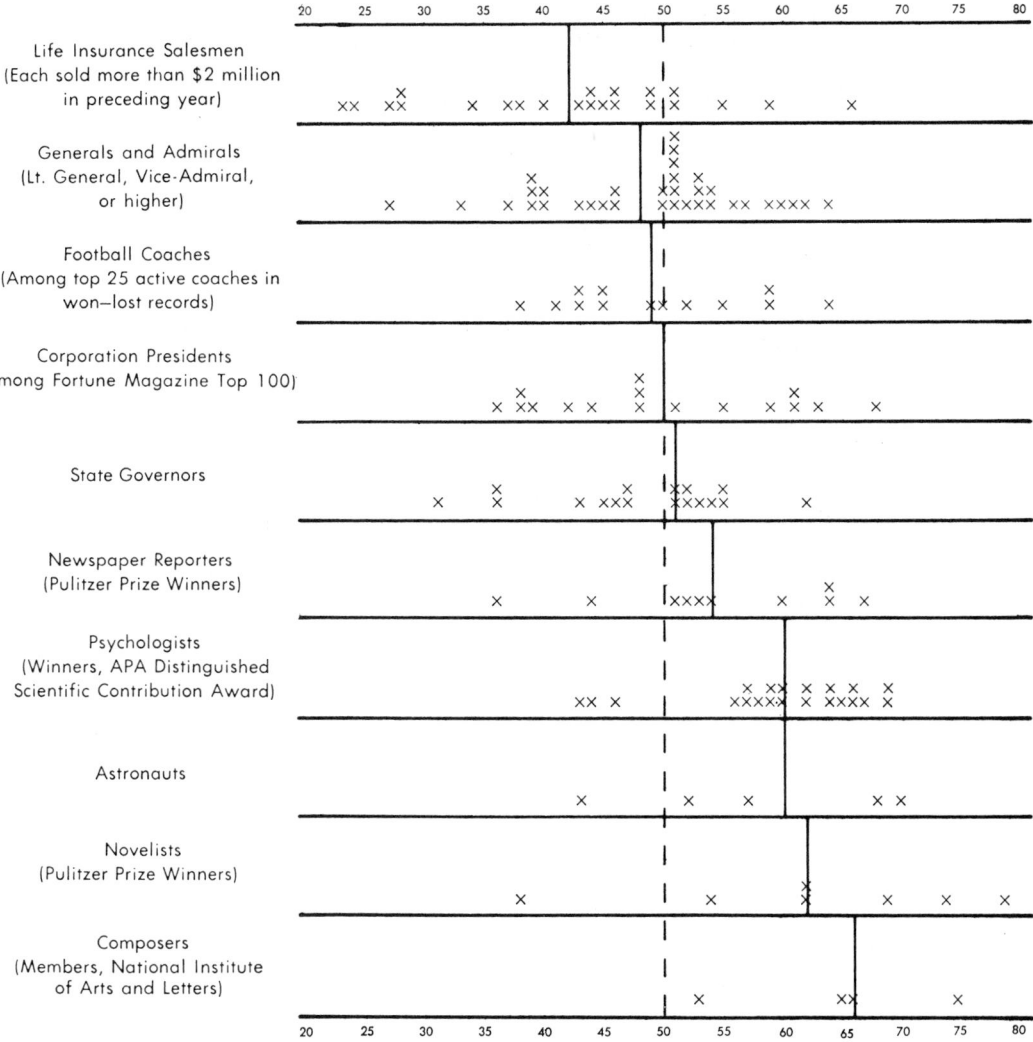

FIG. 5-2. *Academic Achievement (AACH) scale mean scores for outstanding people in ten occupations. (N in each case is the number of X's shown; solid vertical bar in each group is group average.)*

The fifth group consists of former state governors. Seven of them were from Minnesota, the rest from states scattered all over the nation.

Those in the sixth group are all Pulitzer Prize winning reporters.

The seventh group is made up of many of this country's most prominent psychologists, those who have been awarded the American Psychological Association's Distinguished Scientific Award.

The eighth group consists of five astronauts, mostly from among those now in training for future flights.

The ninth group represents Pulitzer Prize winning novelists.

Finally, the four members of the last group are among this country's best-known composers, all members of the National Institute of Arts and Letters.

The means in Figure 5-2 tend to follow about the same pattern as the occupational means in Table 5-6, indicating that scores on this scale have more to do with the type of occupation selected than with success in those occupations. Furthermore, the range of scores within each group should be noted, especially at the low end. Some men with interests antagonistic to academic affairs have made it in a big way, though usually in other areas.

The main point here is that any interest, or personality, scale related to academic achievement must be used wisely, especially in student selection, as it represents only one kind of achievement.

But if an interest inventory scale related to grades is not to be routinely used for selection, what then is its function? First, to serve as a research tool to better understand the educational process. Second, as an aid to counselors who need the best possible data about their clients. Counselors have little enough information about why some students succeed and others don't; anything that can be put into their hands to help them give more individualized attention to that student sitting across the desk from them will be welcome. The AACH scale may prove beneficial in that setting.

Age-Related Interests Scale (AR-Men)

This scale includes those items whose popularity varies with the age of the person completing the inventory. Thus, teenagers score low, old men score higher. Roughly, scores range as follows:

Age	Mean Score
17	30
25	40
50	50

Emphatically, these are only approximations; many qualifications have to be made.

In its development, the AR scale parallels an earlier scale for the SVIB, the Interest Maturity scale. In Strong's early work with men of various ages, he identified items that had differing rates of endorsement between 15-year-old boys and 55-year-old men. Later, he found that there was not much difference between his 25-year-olds and 55-year-olds, so the final scale was based on the 15–25-year comparison. Strong's major rationale was to provide an index that would be related to whether or not an individual's profile would change. Presumably, a person who had the interests of adults would be less likely to change than someone whose interests resembled those of teenage boys.

Several projects, such as those of Hoyt (1957) and Stordahl (1954) showed conclusively that the Interest Maturity scale was not related to profile stability, and in the 1966 revision the Interest Maturity scale was dropped.

However, even if this prediction task is not possible, it is important to learn as much as possible about the changes of interests with age for the SVIB is used to help individuals make relatively long-term plans and, thus, the counselor should be well informed about the longitudinal development of interest patterns.

To assess the change of vocational interests with age, one should have a carefully selected sample tested initially at about age 15 and then retested each year or two well into adulthood. Again, no such sample is available; instead, we must make do with a series of samples, tested and retested at various ages. However, with these data, one can approximate the effect of testing the same group each year.

Age Samples

To generate a curve of age-related interests, several test-retest samples, all containing men who attended college for at least a few years and most graduating, were drawn together. The bulk of these included those Stanford students tested and retested by E. K. Strong for a variety of projects; another subset included those University of Minnesota students studied by Berdie (1960) and retested 8 to 10 years later by Schletzer (1963). All had been tested at least twice, some as many as four times, over intervals ranging from 5 to 22 years. Their individual booklets were sorted into categories by age, that is, all of the booklets collected from 17-year-olds were put into one pile, the 18-year-olds in the next, 19-year-olds in the next and so on. Thus, an individual tested at 19 and retested at 26 would be included in the samples for those ages, another tested at 19 and retested at 27 would be in the first sample with the former person, but would be in a different

TABLE 5-12. MEAN SCORES ON THE BASIC INTEREST SCALE (SET 1) FOR MEN TESTED AT AGES 17–49

	17	18	19	20	21	22	23	24	25	26	27	28	29	30	31	32	33-34	35-36	37	38	39-40	41-42	43	44	45	46	47-48	49	TRENDS
Age = / N =	204	229	186	113	121	116	89	76	112	159	210	174	98	87	88	75	64	53	83	86	42	39	61	87	66	51	63	63	
Public Speaking	54	52	53	53	53	52	51	53	52	53	53	53	52	55	50	52	52	52	53	53	51	52	53	54	51	52	51	52	–
Law/Politics	53	53	53	54	53	54	52	52	52	54	54	54	52	56	52	53	52	52	54	54	52	55	54	53	51	52	50	50	
Business Management	50	49	51	52	52	52	52	49	49	51	51	49	47	50	49	51	47	47	48	49	53	50	52	52	51	48	48	47	
Sales	51	48	49	49	50	50	47	46	47	48	47	46	45	47	47	50	47	47	48	49	49	48	50	49	49	46	47	46	I I
Merchandising	51	50	51	51	51	51	49	47	49	50	50	49	47	49	49	51	49	48	51	52	51	49	52	51	47	47	47	45	I I
Office Practices	51	51	51	52	50	50	50	50	48	51	50	49	48	51	51	50	48	50	49	50	50	50	52	51	48	48	48	47	
Military Activities	52	51	51	49	52	51	50	50	47	53	50	49	50	51	52	50	51	50	52	52	50	50	52	54	48	48	50	47	
Technical Supervision	48	48	48	49	48	51	47	48	47	53	50	52	48	51	54	51	49	49	54	51	51	53	53	54	49	51	52	47	
Mathematics	53	51	49	49	50	49	49	48	50	53	52	52	51	51	52	51	53	49	54	51	51	53	54	54	49	51	52	52	
Science	51	49	49	48	49	49	50	51	51	48	53	52	54	51	54	49	47	50	50	51	53	55	54	54	52	54	55	54	
Mechanical	46	47	46	46	45	46	44	44	45	48	46	47	45	48	50	49	47	47	51	48	49	47	49	51	49	49	48	49	++
Nature	41	43	43	45	43	45	45	47	45	46	46	47	48	46	49	48	47	49	50	50	50	47	51	50	51	50	51	52	
Agriculture	43	47	47	48	46	48	47	46	45	46	46	46	46	46	49	48	47	47	49	50	49	50	49	48	48	48	46	44	+++
Adventure	57	57	58	57	55	55	54	51	52	54	53	53	51	53	52	52	50	50	49	51	51	51	49	47	48	49	46	45	I I
Recreational Leadership	50	51	52	53	51	51	49	50	49	51	50	50	49	51	49	49	49	50	49	49	51	45	50	51	48	46	48	54	I I
Medical Service	50	49	50	49	48	50	50	52	52	51	52	52	54	53	54	52	50	52	51	50	54	51	51	51	51	53	55	54	++
Social Service	51	48	49	49	46	47	47	47	49	48	49	48	49	51	47	48	47	49	50	48	53	49	50	47	48	49	41	41	
Religious Activities	50	46	44	45	44	45	44	47	46	46	46	46	47	54	44	45	44	46	50	46	53	45	48	48	46	50	47	49	+++
Teaching	45	45	46	46	47	47	50	52	51	51	52	52	52	54	52	52	52	54	55	52	52	54	53	52	52	53	53	52	
Music	48	48	44	49	50	52	52	52	51	51	51	51	52	54	52	50	51	53	54	50	52	54	50	50	49	50	52	50	+
Art	46	48	49	49	51	51	52	52	51	50	51	51	52	51	50	51	51	52	52	50	52	51	50	50	50	51	51	50	+
Writing	51	52	53	53	53	53	54	55	54	54	54	53	55	56	52	54	54	56	56	54	54	51	56	53	53	54	53	54	+

sample in the latter instance. The net effect of this, hopefully, is to generate samples that are directly comparable from one age to another.

The final samples contained a total of roughly 1,000 men, tested a total of 2,895 times. The numbers at each age are given in Table 5-12, where the mean scores on the Basic Scales are reported for each age sample.

Though these samples are the best available for studying interest changes over time, they are not altogether perfect; some bias may have crept into some of the age samples. For example, the 17-year-olds and, to a lesser extent, the 18-year-olds, seem "older" than the other samples—at least there are bulges in the age curves in those years (see Table 5-12, 5-13). Even with such limitations in mind, the samples are still exceedingly valuable for studying age trends.

Mean Scores for the Age Samples on the SVIB Scales

These age samples were first scored on the existing SVIB scales to see what trends would emerge. The mean for each sample is listed in Table 5-12 for the Basic Interest Scales and in Table 5-13 for the Occupational and Nonoccupational scales. At the right hand edge of each table is a column summarizing the trends. Three pluses (or minuses) show a major increase (or decrease); two indicate a mild increase, one a minor increase. These signs were assigned by simple inspection—in general, major trends were defined as those showing a change of approximately a full standard deviation, mild trends were those between one-half and a full SD, and minor trends those under one-half SD. For easier interpretation, these trends are summarized in Table 5-14.

The major increases were in the intellectual, academic areas; the decreases centered around the adventuresome activities, and business endeavors. These changes are quite similar to those already reported in the discussion of test-retest reliability of the Basic Scales.

While these trends are noteworthy, even the largest differences between any of the age samples are substantially less than the differences found between occupational samples. As a source of variance, age is not nearly so important as occupation.

Construction of an Age-Related Interest Scale

The purpose of constructing an age-related interest scale was to pull together all of these trends into one index. This index might then be used to assess the "psychological age" of an individual's interests. To construct such a measure, a correlation coefficient was calculated for each item response between age and the percent of each age sample selecting that

211

TABLE 5-13. MEAN SCORES ON THE OCCUPATIONAL SCALES FOR MEN TESTED AT AGES 17–49

Occupational Scale	17	18	19	20	21	22	23	24	25	26	27	28	29	30	31	32	33/34	35/36	37	38	39/40	41/42	43	44	45	46	47/48	49+	Trend
Physical Therapist	30	26	26	26	24	26	25	25	27	28	28	28	29	30	28	27	26	28	27	27	30	25	28	27	27	27	29	27	
Dentist	30	30	29	29	29	29	31	32	32	28	28	29	32	28	32	28	28	30	26	26	27	26	27	28	29	30	34	31	
Osteopath	27	26	26	25	24	27	27	28	29	27	28	29	31	29	31	28	27	29	27	26	28	26	26	28	29	30	34	31	
Veterinarian	28	26	25	24	24	25	23	23	23	23	23	23	22	26	24	22	23	21	24	23	19	23	25	28	24	26	24		
Physician	27	25	25	23	23	25	29	30	31	27	29	31	34	30	31	27	27	31	28	25	28	29	27	28	30	33	36	34	++
Psychiatrist	18	18	20	19	19	20	24	28	27	26	27	29	31	29	28	27	28	30	28	26	29	33	29	27	28	29	33	33	+++
Psychologist	22	21	22	22	23	22	26	29	30	29	29	31	32	30	29	29	31	31	33	29	31	36	31	31	29	33	33	34	+++
Biologist	22	21	20	20	20	22	27	28	29	27	27	30	32	28	30	26	29	30	29	25	27	32	28	28	29	33	33	35	+++
Architect	26	29	27	27	29	28	30	30	30	28	28	29	30	26	30	28	30	30	28	28	28	27	27	29	28	31	29	30	
Mathematician	20	22	20	21	21	21	24	27	26	24	24	25	27	23	26	22	25	26	25	21	22	29	24	24	23	28	26	30	++
Physicist	19	21	18	19	20	20	23	24	24	23	22	23	25	21	26	21	23	23	23	20	21	26	22	23	21	26	25	26	++
Chemist	30	30	28	28	30	29	32	32	33	33	32	33	34	30	36	32	32	32	32	29	30	34	33	33	30	34	33	33	+
Engineer	28	29	28	29	30	30	30	31	30	31	30	30	30	28	35	31	32	28	30	30	30	31	31	33	31	33	31	32	+
Production Manager	32	33	33	34	34	35	31	31	29	34	33	32	35	35	35	33	29	33	34	34	31	34	37	33	32	32	31		
Army Officer	26	26	25	25	24	24	21	18	21	28	26	26	23	26	27	26	23	22	30	30	25	25	30	32	23	24	22	22	-
Air Force Officer	32	30	29	28	29	29	26	25	27	32	30	29	27	30	30	29	27	26	31	30	29	29	31	32	26	27	26	25	-
Carpenter	23	24	22	22	22	23	20	19	20	22	20	19	19	18	24	21	20	20	21	20	20	16	20	23	21	22	20	21	
Forest Service	18	21	21	22	20	23	20	19	19	22	20	19	19	20	24	21	21	20	20	21	23	16	20	21	23	20	20	20	
Farmer	35	35	34	34	34	35	33	32	32	32	31	31	31	29	34	32	31	31	30	31	31	27	31	33	34	33	32	32	
Math-Science Teacher	34	33	30	30	29	30	30	29	30	31	30	30	30	30	33	29	28	27	28	28	30	29	26	30	29	30			
Printer	35	36	35	35	34	33	32	30	30	30	29	28	29	30	30	28	29	28	27	28	27	28	29	28	27	26	27		-
Policeman	23	25	24	23	22	24	21	20	19	20	19	19	19	21	22	20	20	19	16	17	19	15	17	18	18	18	17		-
Personnel Director	23	26	28	29	29	30	28	28	26	30	30	29	26	31	29	31	29	32	32	32	31	32	31	29	29	26	26		
Public Administrator	28	28	30	30	29	31	30	31	31	35	34	34	32	37	33	35	36	34	37	36	38	39	38	38	37	36	34	35	++
Rehabilitation Counselor	24	22	23	24	23	24	24	25	25	27	28	28	27	30	25	28	28	30	30	32	32	29	18	22	20	17	18	18	+
YMCA Secretary	24	22	23	22	21	21	20	18	19	21	20	21	19	22	16	20	19	19	20	22	22	16	20	18	19	15	16	15	--
Community Recreation Director	23	21	21	21	21	20	19	18	18	21	21	21	19	23	17	21	20	20	21	20	20	20	17	18	18				-
Social Worker	21	20	22	22	21	22	23	25	24	24	25	25	25	29	22	26	26	28	27	27	29	27	24	26	26	25	26		+
Social Science Teacher	28	28	30	30	29	29	28	29	27	27	27	27	27	29	25	28	28	29	27	28	28	26	26	24	28	25	26	26	-
School Superintendent	17	20	20	21	20	20	21	24	21	21	22	23	22	26	21	23	23	25	23	23	24	27	25	23	24	24	28		++
Minister	10	11	12	12	11	13	16	19	16	13	15	15	18	19	12	15	15	20	17	14	17	19	15	13	15	18	19	21	++
Librarian	24	25	26	26	26	29	31	30	28	29	29	32	30	27	27	28	30	27	28	32	27	26	27	30	28	30			+
Artist	27	28	27	27	28	28	29	30	30	27	27	28	29	26	28	27	28	29	27	26	27	27	25	26	28	29	29	29	
Music Performer	32	33	32	32	32	32	34	34	33	29	30	31	33	30	29	29	31	34	30	29	30	29	27	30	31	32	32		
Music Teacher	22	21	22	22	21	22	24	24	24	21	22	24	25	24	19	21	23	23	23	23	22	20	23	24	22	25			
C.P.A. Owner	28	26	26	27	28	26	29	29	28	29	29	30	28	28	28	30	25	29	28	26	32	29	27	26	27	27	25		
Senior C.P.A.	32	31	30	31	33	30	29	26	27	33	30	29	27	28	29	30	28	24	31	31	27	30	30	31	24	26	22	22	--
Accountant	29	30	30	32	31	30	26	25	25	30	29	27	24	29	27	29	29	27	27	29	30	23	24	21	20				---
Office Worker	35	35	35	37	35	35	32	30	29	31	30	29	26	29	30	28	25	28	29	29	27	29	28	26	24	24	21		---
Credit Manager	31	29	30	30	30	30	24	26	25	30	29	27	25	30	28	26	31	33	30	32	32	29	26	25	23				--
Chamber of Commerce Executive	33	31	33	33	32	30	28	29	31	32	31	29	33	27	32	30	30	32	34	31	32	32	30	29	27	26			-
Business Education Teacher	28	27	28	29	28	28	26	24	25	28	28	26	24	28	25	29	26	27	29	31	29	28	30	28	27	24	25	24	-
Purchasing Agent	35	35	35	35	35	31	29	32	31	29	30	30	30	33	32	28	31	33	30	28	28	29	26	27	25	26			--
Banker	28	28	28	30	28	28	25	25	24	25	24	24	23	24	25	25	25	24	24	27	25	24	26	26	27	26	25	24	--
Pharmacist	31	27	27	27	26	27	25	25	25	26	24	24	24	27	26	24	23	24	25	27	23	26	26	28	24	28	24		--
Mortician	31	30	30	30	30	30	28	27	25	26	24	24	26	26	26	28	27	26	26	29	29	25	27	28	29	28	26	25	--
Sales Manager	32	32	34	33	35	33	30	28	27	28	28	28	25	27	27	31	29	25	26	30	29	26	29	29	29	24	25	22	-
Real Estate Salesman	36	37	38	38	38	38	36	35	34	33	33	33	32	33	32	34	31	31	35	33	32	33	32	34	31	30	29		--
Life Insurance Salesman	30	30	32	32	32	32	31	29	28	26	27	27	24	28	27	25	24	27	26	25	26	29	24	26	23				--
Advertising Man	31	32	33	32	34	33	34	33	32	29	30	31	31	30	28	31	31	31	28	31	29	30	29	29	31	29	29	28	-
Lawyer	33	33	34	34	34	34	36	37	35	32	33	35	35	35	32	32	34	34	31	32	32	35	32	31	34	33	34	33	
Author-Journalist	30	32	33	32	33	33	35	36	34	31	32	33	34	31	31	32	33	34	31	32	30	33	31	30	32	32	32	32	
President, Manufacturing Co.	27	28	29	29	32	30	28	28	26	28	28	27	25	25	28	31	29	24	28	30	29	27	29	31	30	27	27	25	

Non-Occupational

	17	18	19	20	21	22	23	24	25	26	27	28	29	30	31	32	33/34	35/36	37	38	39/40	41/42	43	44	45	46	47/48	49+	Trend
Specialization Level	37	37	38	38	39	38	39	41	41	43	43	43	43	42	43	43	44	45	44	43	47	46	44	42	44	43	45		++
Occupational Level	55	55	55	56	57	57	58	58	58	59	60	59	59	58	59	60	58	60	61	60	63	62	60	60	60	60	59		++
Masculinity-Femininity	49	49	48	48	48	48	46	45	46	49	48	47	45	48	50	49	48	46	48	49	48	46	48	51	48	49	47	48	
Occupational Introversion-Extroversion	49	50	48	49	49	48	50	50	51	49	49	49	50	46	51	49	49	50	48	47	47	49	47	49	49	51	50	50	
Academic Achievement	43	41	41	41	42	43	47	49	49	48	49	50	52	49	49	47	49	49	51	46	49	54	51	49	48	52	53	52	+++

TABLE 5-14. SUMMARY OF SVIB SCALE GAINS AND LOSSES WITH AGE

		Increases	
	Basic Scales	Occupational Scales	Non-Occupational Scales
Major increase	Teaching Nature	Psychiatrist Psychologist Biologist	Academic Achievement
Mild increase	Science Medical Service	Physician Mathematician Physicist Public Administrator School Superintendent Minister	Specialization Level Occupational Level
Minor increase	Music Art Writing	Chemist Engineer Rehabilitation Counselor Social Worker Librarian	

		Decreases	
Major decrease	Adventure	Office Worker	
Mild decrease	Recreational Leadership	YMCA Staff Member Senior CPA Accountant Credit Manager Chamber of Commerce Exec. Purchasing Agent Pharmacist Mortician Sales Manager Real Estate Salesman Life Insurance Salesman	
Minor decrease	Law/Politics Merchandising Office Practices Sales	Army Officer Air Force Officer Printer Policeman Social Science Teacher Banker Advertising Man Business Education Teacher Community Recreation Director	

response. Item responses showing correlations of .65 and above were selected for inclusion in the scale. If the correlation was positive, the item response was weighted positively; if the correlation was negative, the weight was negative. Examples of two extreme item correlations, and the data they are based on, are given in Figure 5-3. For the first item, "Raising flowers and vegetables," the correlation between age of the sample and percent responding "Like" was .88. Thus, this response was given a weight of +1 on the Age-Related Interest scale. For the second item, "Climbing along edge of precipice," the analogous correlation was −.91, and this response was weighted −1.

The items were then dimensionalized (see p. 34) by weighting the op-

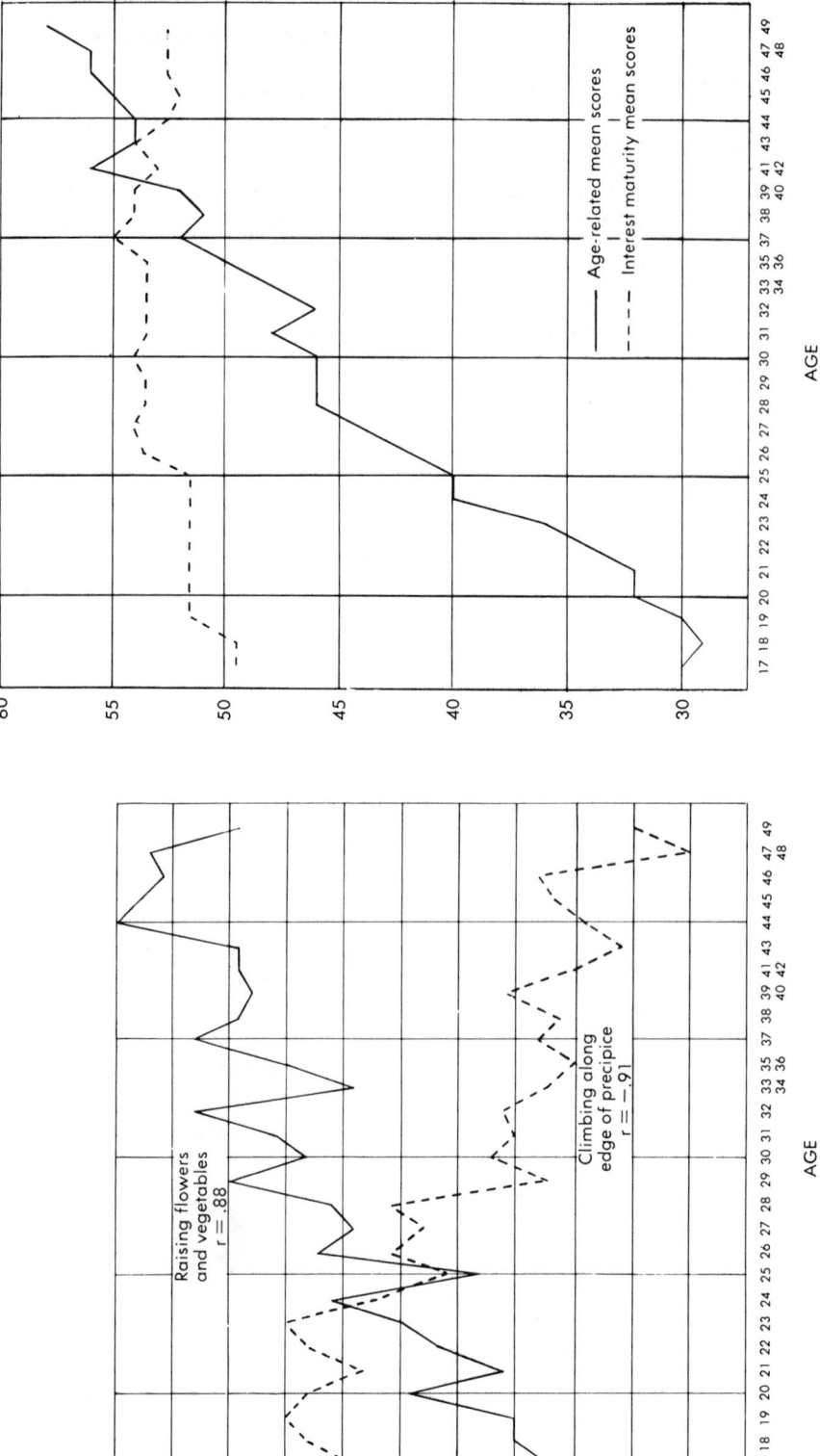

FIG. 5-4. *Mean scores on the Interest Maturity and Age-Related Interests scale for men tested at various ages.*

FIG. 5-3. *Examples of items showing extreme correlations between age of respondents and percent responding "Like."*

posite end of each item in the opposite direction. Eighty-one items were included in the scale; to help in scale interpretation, they are listed in Table 5-15.

The scale was normed by using the same group of men used to norm the Basic Scales (see p. 107), essentially a cross-section of 52-year-old men; thus, a standard score of 50 corresponds roughly to age 50.

TABLE 5-15. ITEMS WEIGHTED ON THE MEN'S AGE-RELATED INTERESTS SCALE

Items Weighted Positively		Items Weighted Negatively	
Item Number	Item	Item Number	Item
6	Astronomer	1	Actor
10	Author of technical book	2	Advertising Man
19	Carpenter	12	Auto Racer
27	College Professor	14	Airplane Pilot
37	Farmer	15	Bank Teller
50	Landscape Gardener	21	Cashier in bank
69	Physician	72	Politician
73	Printer	110	Dramatics
76	Rancher	127	Physical Education
82	School Teacher	139	Hunting
94	Toolmaker	159	Formal dress affairs
102	Agriculture	185	Making a radio or hi-fi set
106	Botany	187	Adjusting a carburetor
113	Geography	195	Arguments
114	Geology	200	Organizing a play
122	Mechanical Drawing	211	Pursuing bandits in a sheriff's posse
125	Nature Study	230	Living in the city
134	Spelling	231	Climbing along the edge of a precipice
173	Detective stories	246	Emotional people
182	Educational movies or TV	280	Athletic men
189	Cabinetmaking	288	Prepare the advertising for the machine
193	Raising flowers and vegetables	293	Opportunity for promotion
198	Interviewing clients	296	Opportunity to ask questions and to
202	Teaching children		consult about difficulties
203	Teaching adults	297	Opportunity to understand just how
207	Taking responsibility		one's superior expects work to be done
228	Contributing to charities	317	Chairman, Entertainment Committee
233	Looking at a collection of antique	318	Chairman, Membership Committee
	furniture	326	Selling things house to house vs
272	Carelessly dressed people		Gardening
295	Opportunity to make use of all one's	334	Taking a chance vs Playing safe
	knowledge and experience	342	Outside work vs Inside work
299	Freedom in working out one's own	343	Work in which you move from place to
	method of doing the work		place vs Work where you stay in one place
300	Co-workers--congenial,competent,	345	Physical activity vs Mental activity
	and adequate in number	350	Playing baseball vs Watching baseball
314	Member of a Society or Club	391	Lend money to acquaintances..only
316	Chairman, Educational Committee		certain people...hardly anyone
319	Chairman, Program Committee	393	When caught in a mistake, I make
330	Talk others into doing something		excuses usually...seldom...practically
	vs Order others to do something		never
353	Reading a book vs Watching TV	399	Make bets often...sometimes...rarely
	or going to a movie		
364	Usually get other people to do what		
	I want done		
376	Able to meet emergencies quickly		
	and effectively		
378	Can write a concise, well-organized		
	report		
379	Have good judgment in appraising		
	values		
380	Plan my work in detail		
381	Follow up subordinates effectively		
382	Put drive into the organization		
383	Stimulate the ambition of my associates		
398	My advice is asked for By many...By few...		
	By almost nobody		

Sample	Investigator (ref)	N	Test-Retest Interval	Test Age	Retest Age	Age-Related Scale Test Mean	Test SD	Retest Mean	Retest SD
U.of Minnesota sophomores	D.P. Campbell	140	2 weeks	19	19	39	9.6	39	10.3
U.S. Army Reserve	D.P. Campbell	120	30 days	26	26	41	10.3	42	10.8
Minnesota High School Juniors	E.G. Joselyn(1968)	923	5 months	16	17	30	n/a	29	n/a
U.of Missouri Agriculture students	B. Heifner; W. Anderson	126	3.5 years	18	21	37	9.5	41	9.2*
Harvard Freshmen	S.H. King	189	3.5 years	18	21	40	10.2	44	9.9
U. of M. GC Freshmen	L.A. King(1957)	219	9 months	18	19	24	9.7	35	10.1
U.of M. CLA Grads	D.P. Campbell	100	4 years	18	21	35	9.8	42	8.4
U.of M. Med School Freshmen	H.H. Gee; E.B. Hutchins (1964)	91	4 years	21	25	47	10.2	45	9.4
Medical School "A" Freshmen	"	111-106	4 years	21	25	50	9.7	49	9.3
Medical School "B" Freshmen	"	98-82	4 years	21	25	48	9.1	45	10.0
U.of M.Graduates	R.F. Berdie(1960); V.M. Schletzer (1963)	171	8-10 years	18	27	32	9.3	45	8.8
U.of M. GC Followup	G.G. Kingsley	123	10 years	18	28	33	10.2	44	9.7
Missouri H.S. Seniors	J.T. Trimble(1965)	152	10 years	18	28	32	8.7	40	9.7
Iowa Veterinarians	T.E. Hannum(1950); J.E. Alsip (1966)	98	17 years	32	48	51	9.0	52	8.5
Psychologists	P.H. Kriedt (1949)	91	17 years	39	56	53	9.6	58	8.6
YMCA Secretaries	W.A. Verbrug (1952)	47	22 years	40	63	52	10.5	58	8.6
Minnesota Bankers	D.P. Campbell(1966)	48	30 years	40	70	46	7.6	50	8.6
Purdue Engineering Grads	W.K. LeBold; Darrell Benjamin (1967)	229	31 years	18	49	37	13.7	47	13.6
Stanford Freshmen									
1930	E.K. Strong, Jr.	253		18		31	10.4		
1931	"	253	1 year	19		31	10.6		
1939	"	175	9 years	27		45	10.3		
1949	"	202	19 years	37		52	9.4		
Stanford Seniors(1927-1949)*	"	220	22 years	21	43	33	9.6	54	9.2
Stanford Grad. Students(1927-1949)*	"	191	22 years	c.25		41	9.7	58	9.2
California Teenagers	D.P. Campbell	1214	36 years	16	52	29	9.1	49	10.1
No College	"	497	36 years	16	52	28	8.9	46	9.8
B.A. Degree	"	214	36 years	16	52	29	9.0	52	10.0
M.A. Degree	"	72	36 years	16	52	32	10.0	55	8.2
Ph.D. Degree	"	27	36 years	16	52	32	10.0	65	8.2

*Sample added after calculations for Figure 5-5 were completed

TABLE 5-17. MEAN SCORES ON THE AGE-RELATED INTERESTS SCALE

60 Neurological Surgeons/Pathologists
59 Biologists
58 Internists/Pediatricians/Psychiatrists(1949)
57 Animal Husbandry Profs/Physiatrists/Surgeons/Rehab Counselors/School Supers(1965)
56 Chemists(1969)/School Supers(1969)/Dental Educators/Judges/NIAL Members/Psychologists(1947)/Orthopedic Surgeons/Urologists/Psychologists(1949)/Social Workers(1953)/Public Admins(1941)
55 Guidance Counselors(1968)/Physicians(1969)/Psychiatrists(1967)/Foresters/Colonels/Voc Ag Teachers/Ag Extension Agents/Generals & Admirals/Student Personnel Workers/Radiologists/Psychologists(Exp)/Guidance Counselors(1950)/Librarians/School Supers(1930)/Corp Pres(1965)/Unitarian Ministers(1950)
54 Public Admins(1969)/Anthropologists/College Profs/Physicists(1968)/Music Teachers(1952)/Physicians(1949)/Mathematicians(1969)/Physicists(1927)/Ministers(1927)
53 Pulitzer Prize/Credit Mgrs/Architects(1933)/Lawyers(1949)/County Welfare Workers/Architects(1968)/Food Scientists/Mathematicians(1969)/Medical Techs/Astronomers/Interior Decorators/Governors/Artists(1968)
52 Dentists(1969)/Psychologists(1967)/Political Scientists/Economists/High School Counselors/Business Ed Teachers/Engineers(1928)/Chemists(1931)/Army Officers(1950)/Personnel Direcs(1927)/Ministers(1965)/Sociologists
51 Elem Teachers(NDak)/Optometrists/Physicians(1927)/Physical Therapists(1957)/Corp Pres(1935)/Production Mgrs/Vets(1949)/YMCA Secs/Forest Service Men/Football Coaches/Music Teachers(1946)/Business School Profs/Investment Mgrs/Personnel Direcs(1969)/Cartographers/Ministers(1969)/Social Workers(1967)/Mpls Symphony
50 Machinists/Buyers(1946)/Osteopaths/Bankers(1969)/Lawyers(1969)/Purchasing Agents(1969)/Army Officers(1969)/Chiropractors/Engineers(1968)/Vets(1966)
49 Physical Therapists(1966)/Policemen(1968)/Priests/NASA Scientists/Salesmen,Encyclopedia/Bankers(1964)/Cham Comm Execs/CPA(1944)/Dentists(1932)/Advertising Men(1931)/Accountants/Bankers(1934)/Pharmacists(1947)/Computer Programmers/Comm Rec Dir/Elem Teachers(Minn)/Air Force Officers
48 Sales Mgrs(1932)/Soc Sci Teachers(1936)/Authors/Farmers(1936)/Purchasing Agents(1931)/Navy Officers/Petroleum Engineers/CPA(1965)/Advertising Men(1968)/English Teachers/Tool & Die Makers/Math-Sci Teachers(1968)/Danforth Fellows/Astronauts/Pharmacists(1968)
47 Policemen(1969)/Soc Sci Teachers(1969)/Teaching Brothers/Skilled Tradesmen/Musicians(1969)/Legislators/Newsmen/Photograph/Actors(1933)/Interpreters/Musicians(1952)/YMCA Staff/Lawyers(1927)/Funeral Direcs(1945)/Math-Sci Teachers(1936)/YMCA PD/Artists(1933)/Carpenters(1936)/Unitarian Ministers(1929)
46 Carpenters(1969)/Funeral Direcs(1969)/Dept Store Mgrs/Army Sergeants/Buyers(1969)/Highway Patrolmen/Salesmen,PG&E/Salesmen,Computer
45 County Sheriffs/Sales Mgrs(1968)/Salesmen,Real Estate(1969)/Electricians/Salesmen,Life(1966)/Office Workers
44 Salesmen,Life(1969)/Policemen(1933)/Salesmen,Life(1931)/Printers/Pilots
43 Salesmen,Steel/Farmers(1967)/Salesmen,Real Estate(1932)
42 Farmers(1968)/Actors(1966)
41 Salesmen,3M applicants
40 Salesmen,3M/Salesmen,Auto

Validity

The validation data for the AR scale are shown in Figure 5-4, where the mean score for each age sample is plotted. For comparative purposes, the Interest Maturity mean score is also shown. The AR means increased with age, as they should, indicating that the scale development achieved its initial purpose; scores on the AR scale are clearly related to age tested. In contrast, the Interest Maturity scale means changed only slightly over this age span.

To further study the relationship between age and scores on the Age-Related scale, several other samples that have been tested and retested over various periods were scored; the statistics for each sample are in Table 5-16, and the AR means for these groups are plotted against age tested in Figure 5-5.

The data in Table 5-16 and Figure 5-5 provide some very informative cross-validation data on the AR scale. Scores on this scale clearly increase with age, in a negatively accelerating curve. The total increase was greatest among those with the most education; even though they started at a higher level, they gained more.

The only exceptions to the increase in score with age were the three medical school samples, and the reversal was clear, consistent, and puzzling. Perhaps this is another manifestation of the readiness of these students to relax after the weary grind of medical school. Such an interpretation is compatible with the changes already reported on the Basic Interest scales for these medical school students (p. 119).

The other samples clearly show an increase with age on the AR scale, and the increase is related to educational level. This tendency is best demonstrated by the California teenager samples (described more fully on p. 107). Whatever interest changes appear with age on this scale are magnified by education.

Some of this may be a product of the method of scale construction. All of the students in the AR scale criterion samples were college students; most of them graduated. This scale, therefore, includes not only items that change in popularity with age, but also with education.

This relationship with higher education also appeared in the correlations between the AR scale and the other SVIB scales, reported in Chapter 3. The highest positive correlations with the AR scale were as follows:

Biologist	.57	Mathematician	.38
Academic Achievement	.55	Psychologist	.37
Psychiatrist	.48	Physicist	.36
Minister	.45		

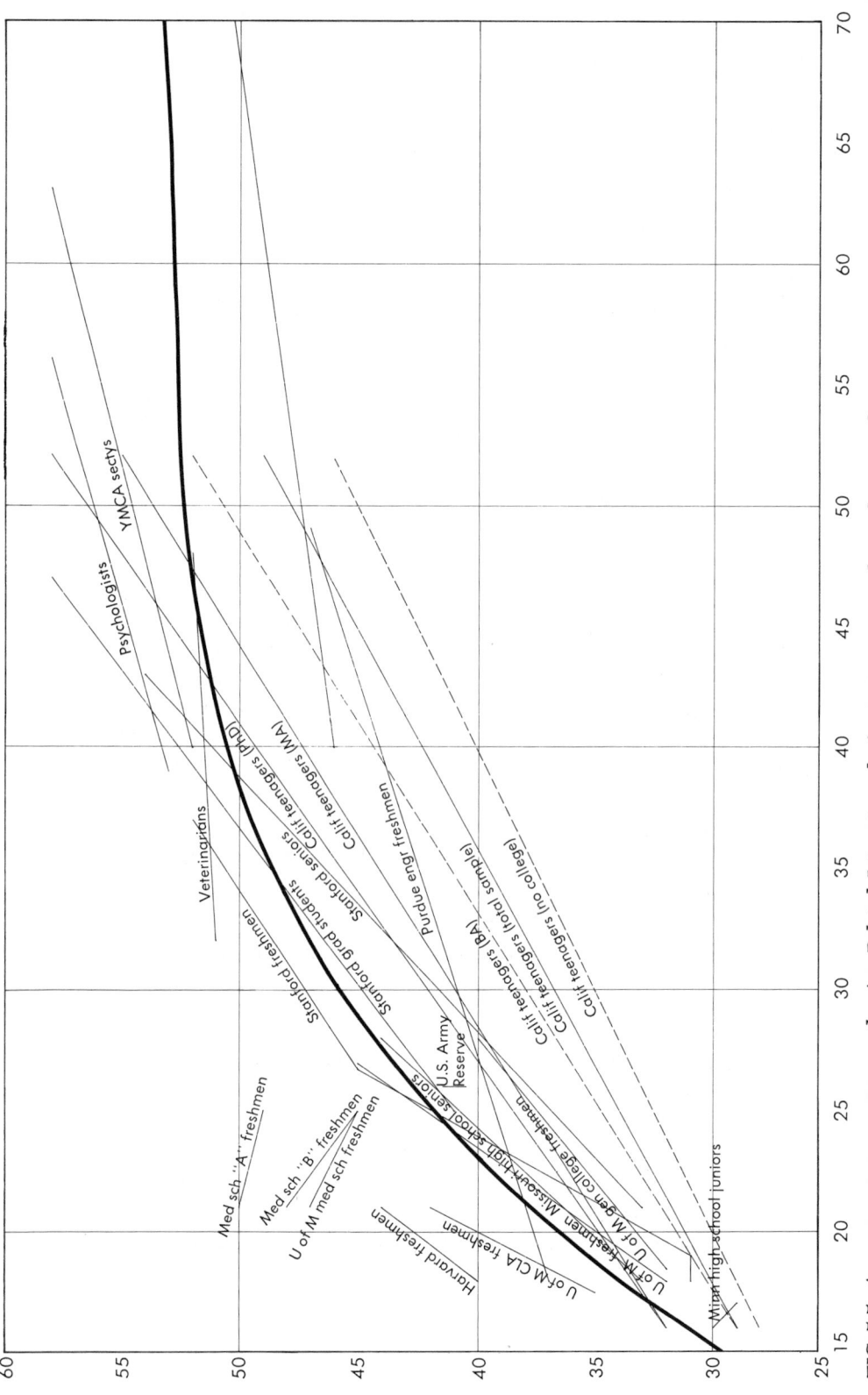

FIG. 5.5. Age norms mean norms on the Age-Related Interests scale for test-retest sample and ...

The largest negative correlations with the AR scale were as follows:

Sales Manager .... −.56   Purchasing Agent .... −.44
Real Estate Salesman .... −.56   Funeral Director .... −.43
Life Insurance Salesman .... −.48   Chamber of Commerce Executive −.41

Obviously, the highest correlations were with the scales based on the most educated occupations and, curiously, the familiar sales-science split appeared once again.

Mean Scores on the AR Scale for the SVIB Occupational Samples

The same tendency for high scores to go with higher education can be seen in Table 5-17 which includes the AR means for the occupational samples that have been tested with the SVIB. The range of scores for these adult groups was considerable, from 40 to 60, over two standard deviations. The occupations scoring high have the highest educational levels, and, curiously, are those most involved in medical science.

A Mathematical Curve for the Maximum Rate of Change of Interest with Age

The data presented in Table 4-13 and plotted in Figure 5-5 were used to generate a curve to express the relationship between the AR scale and age tested. Actually, several curves were constructed to find the one with the most reasonable fit with the data. The best analytical solution, using the sum of squares as a criterion, was not necessarily the best overall solution, for the calculations could not adjust for the fact that the oldest sample had a relatively low educational level—thus the best-fitting curve tailed off at the higher end.

The curve finally selected—and plotted in Figure 5-5—can be represented by the formula

$$Y = a_1X^3 + a_2X^2 + a_3X + b ,$$

where Y is the Age-Related Interest scale score and X is the age.

$$a_1 = -1.42 \qquad a_3 = -.045$$
$$a_2 = 2.69 \qquad b = .0003$$

This curve probably should be described as the relationship between age and *maximum* change of interests, for it is based on that subset of SVIB items showing greatest change.

This curve is something of an experiment. The specification of a mathematical relationship between age and interest change is a novelty, and caution should be exercised until the novelty is well studied.

The shape of this curve shows that the potential for maximum change is rapid over the teenage and young adult years, and considerably slower after age 40. The rate of change tapers off considerably in the age 30, 40, and 50 range but does not completely disappear.

These findings have some implications for norms for interest inventories, as different segments of the age curve might well have different norms. Before adopting that system, however, there is more to learn. For example, if different norms were available for different ages, should an individual's responses be compared with the norms for his age group, or for the group matching his score on the AR scale?

Prediction of Profile Change Using the AR Scale

The most obvious possibility for the practical application of the AR scale is for the prediction of profile change. If those teenagers who score high on this scale have stable interests and those who score low have changing interests, then counselors should know this and act accordingly. To study this possibility, a sample of Stanford University seniors, originally tested in 1927 and retested in 1949, were used to test the power of the AR scale to predict which individuals would show changed profiles. This group was chosen because the long test-retest interval—22 years—should permit some profile changes to appear.

Table 5-18 has the correlations between the AR scale, the IM scale for comparative purposes, the profile test-retest correlations (calculated by considering the individual's test scores as the X variable, his retest scores as the Y), and a normalized transformation of the profile correlation.

As can be seen, neither the AR nor IM scale was correlated with profile stability; the correlations were very low—for the IM scale, they were actually negative. While the mean score on the AR scale increased drastically from 42 to 59 (the IM scale did not increase at all), very little of this increase was directly related to the extent of profile change.

(The calculation of change by using correlations between profiles is not

TABLE 5-18. CORRELATIONS BETWEEN THE AGE-RELATED INTERESTS SCALE, INTEREST MATURITY SCALE, AND PROFILE STABILITY, USING 191 STANFORD UNIVERSITY SENIORS TESTED IN 1927 AND RETESTED IN 1949

Variable	Mean	SD	AR (t)	IM (t)	AR (r)	IM (r)	r	z_r
Age Related Interests (test)	42	10.0		.22	.50	.10	.10	.17
Interest Maturity (test)	52	6.2			.17	.57	-.15	-.19
Age Related Interests (retest)	59	10.0				.30	.02	.03
Interest Maturity (retest)	52	6.3					-.20	-.23
Profile Correlation (r)	.77	.13						.95
Fisher's z_r	1.09	.33						

TABLE 5-19. CORRELATIONS BETWEEN THE AGE-RELATED INTERESTS SCALE, INTEREST MATURITY SCALE, AND PROFILE STABILITY FOR 152 HIGH SCHOOL SENIORS TESTED IN 1954 AND RETESTED IN 1964

Variable	Mean	SD	AR (t)	IM (t)	AR (r)	IM (r)	r	$\bar{z}_r$
Age Related Interests (test)	33	10.2		.40	.47	.15	.09	.10
Interest Maturity (test)	49	6.9			.09	.40	.15	.14
Age Related Interests (retest)	44	10.1				.28	-.10	-.07
Interest Maturity (retest)	52	6.4					-.07	-.07
Profile Correlation (r)	.65	.23						.96
Fisher's $\bar{z}_r$	.88	.42						

completely satisfactory. Because one of the basic assumptions of the correlation coefficient is violated, that of independence of observations, the size of the coefficient is inflated. For example, the median correlations between randomly paired profiles is about .55 [Joselyn 1968]. However, several methods have been used to assess profile similarity. All seem to be highly related, so the test-retest profile correlations were used as a handy method.)

These same calculations were made on a second sample, this time a sample tested at an earlier age, i.e., the Missouri high school seniors studied by Trimble (see p. 61). They were first tested as high school seniors, and retested 10 years later. The data showing the relationships between the AR and IM scales and profile correlations for this sample are in Table 5-19; they show essentially the same low relationships as were found in the sample of Stanford seniors.

So, a paradox.

Here is a scale that is definitely related to age, but not to change over time. No use, other than research, is recommended for this scale. Because a great deal of development work has been done, and the validity data clearly show the scale is related to age, the AR scale is being included on the profile so that more can be learned.

In general, it should not be used in counseling settings.

Diversity of Interests Scale (DIV—Men and Women)

This scale was developed along with the Basic Interest Scales, but in an essentially reverse manner. The Basic Scales contain items with high intercorrelations; the Diversity of Interests Scale has items with low or zero intercorrelations, that is, none of the items correlate, either positively or negatively, with any of the other items in the scale.

The rationale behind this was to find some way to study breadth of in-

TABLE 5-20. ITEM INTERCORRELATIONS FOR THE MEN'S DIVERSITY OF INTERESTS SCALE

Item Number	Item	3	21	42	62	69	101	106	123	134	139	143	145	184	191	195	202	205	215	217	224	225	230	2
3	Architect		08	-02	06	-02	11	16	02	00	03	-03	-01	03	-04	03	06	07	11	07	11	04	-03	
21	Cashier	00		25	04	02	14	04	10	19	08	02	06	13	03	-05	14	12	09	11	14	-05	09	
42	Hotel Manager	-05	26		08	12	-11	00	11	12	03	)8	03	11	05	06	05	09	09	17	-03	12	15	
62	Musician	05	09	06		13	-04	09	05	09	-04	06	-03	15	00	02	19	07	05	-02	05	-02	05	
69	Physician	17	05	14	10		02	12	03	04	01	13	01	06	16	03	13	03	03	-02	01	03	02	
101	Algebra	09	07	-01	-05	07		07	00	07	-05	01	14	01	-08	-01	08	-01	03	00	09	04	-02	
106	Botany	12	02	-06	16	25	04		06	03	09	-01	-11	15	08	08	18	-03	05	-02	08	-01	-09	
123	Military Drill	00	13	14	00	04	00	02		-03	08	09	-01	01	13	00	04	02	09	-06	12	04	-02	
134	Spelling	03	11	06	12	06	03	14	02		05	-02	07	-01	-01	10	03	20	03	04	-03	06		-
139	Hunting	10	07	00	-14	11	05	06	16	-06		16	15	-02	17	-06	-01	-01	-09	12	-03	05	03	
143	Boxing	05	06	09	-03	05	03	02	23	06	23		22	04	12	08	-03	02	00	15	-04	-02	-01	
145	Poker	03	12	13	00	06	09	-04	01	01	16	09		-11	00	06	-06	07	-02	06	-08	03	13	-
184	Social problem movies	08	09	13	20	09	-02	09	-04	12	-08	06	-01		01	06	23	06	04	05	06	-01	10	
191	Handling horses	15	08	06	04	18	07	14	11	04	26	23	07	05		01	07	01	02	19	-03	08	-16	
195	Arguments	04	05	08	05	06	02	-03	02	-02	03	06	13	23	06		00	07	11	05	-14	10	06	
202	Teaching children	04	07	07	16	10	00	12	06	10	02	11	-01	22	15	14		12	14	-02	02	-02	06	
205	Being called by a nickname	00	06	07	04	05	02	00	10	-02	05	05	06	03	10	06	17		06	07	01	01	03	
215	Writing reports	04	14	08	11	00	05	06	00	15	-10	-02	-05	10	00	12	15	08		02	10	03	09	-
217	Bargaining ('swapping')	00	00	13	-01	00	09	00	12	05	12	20	19	04	16	13	06	07	-02		-09	16	00	
224	Regular hours for work	01	18	-04	04	-07	-01	05	07	06	01	09	-04	04	04	-11	01	05	10	-05		-15	-03	
225	Continually changing activities	08	01	11	01	05	12	03	03	-01	03	-02	08	10	12	17	06	,02	12	12	-16		-01	
230	Living in the city	02	09	22	09	08	08	00	00	05	-11	01	18	20	-06	11	06	02	08	05	-03	04		
231	Climbing along edge of precipice	12	03	02	06	08	08	10	06	-01	11	12	07	07	17	18	06	08	08	09	-10	16	04	
233	Looking at a collection of antique furniture	15	02	08	13	13	-03	23	04	08	03	12	01	20	12	01	12	00	05	13	02	02	05	

Note: Correlations above diagonal based on Strong's Men-in-General sample tested in 1930's. Correlations below diagonal based on Men-in-General sample tested in 1964-65.

TABLE 5-21. ITEM INTERCORRELATIONS FOR THE WOMEN'S DIVERSITY OF INTERESTS SCALE

Item Number	Item	4	12	17	58	84	136	142	144	155	171	178	180	188	190	201	210	225	235	364	372	378	397
4	Advertiser		14	05	08	11	12	07	14	16	18	14	19	13	06	07	14	00	-04	08	14	02	04
12	Airplane Pilot	24		01	-04	00	04	11	06	08	11	-01	03	07	05	10	17	07	03	09	14	07	04
17	Bookkeeper	02	-04		21	03	04	09	17	03	-07	13	-10	-07	09	10	01	01	08	-09	-09	16	08
58	Librarian	-01	-10	16		04	-04	-06	07	04	-14	11	02	-02	13	08	-11	-01	02	02	12	-03	02
84	Probation Officer	17	28	09	07		04	10	14	05	01	06	08	18	19	14	09	05	10	-03	19	02	-03
136	Bridge	14	12	08	05	12		06	14	14	02	04	07	00	-02	01	05	-03	-05	-09	09	08	-03
142	Amusement Parks	10	16	14	02	22	07		16	-03	16	12	01	06	07	07	14	18	09	-04	10	02	02
144	Conventions	19	03	19	11	09	15	23		16	09	15	02	21	03	12	03	04	13	-01	04	10	00
155	Financial pages in newspapers	19	17	06	10	05	21	03	16		-03	-01	,08	13	-01	09	03	05	11	01	00	09	05
171	Being the first to wear the very latest fashions	22	06	01	-05	07	18	23	11	08		-01	14	05	-01	00	19	16	-05	09	07	-07	-01
178	Doing your own laundry work	-13	-06	26	12	-01	-04	05	09	03	-03		-04	10	16	03	-01	03	13	04	00	02	05
180	Arguments	13	11	-02	-02	16	10	15	07	03	17	06		19	-02	04	22	15	-05	03	14	03	-09
188	Starting a conversation with a stranger	14	01	-02	01	09	19	09	08	13	20	02	13		10	10	14	21	06	12	13	-02	00
190	Teaching children	00	11	05	11	17	05	19	05	-04	-02	10	-01	17		05	01	10	15	16	13	-03	08
201	Writing reports	13	05	04	23	14	04	09	15	19	-04	04	12	09	06		06	12	07	07	07	12	12
210	Continually changing activities	22	25	-04	-02	17	13	24	09	05	17	-16	21	10	00			16	-08	07	16	06	-02
225	Emotional people	12	08	02	02	18	17	11	00	00	21	-08	26	16	06	13	18		11	15	19	03	01
235	Physically sick people	-11	-06	15	17	06	08	-04	03	07	-12	21	-09	02	14	03	-03	17		04	-01	06	08
364	Art	16	05	-21	05	-05	09	-07	-06	05	-02	-16	02	05	04	09	08	06	-03		16	08	-04
372	Dramatics	10	09	-19	-04	07	16	11	08	05	15	-05	14	19	05	15	13	15	01	02		00	10
378	Geometry	-05	07	19	04	02	14	04	04	07	-03	00	08	08	05	03	05	03	02	04	-11		-02
397	Spelling	00	-11	22	18	05	03	15	10	05	04	21	-10	11	05	09	-05	04	18	-03	09	-06	

Note: Correlations above diagonal from Strong's Women-in-General sample tested in 1930's. Correlations below diagonal based on Women-in-General sample tested in 1966-67.

222

terests. This concept, a familiar one in everyday conversation—"He certainly has wide interests"—has received little attention from researchers in interest measurement, mainly because of the technical problems involved. The main hurdle is that of ipsitivity or, more generally, the use of items and scales that are inevitably related to some extent. Simply counting up the numbers of "Likes" that an individual reports or the number of scales that he scores high on, as an indication of the breadth of his interests, can be misleading because of the relationship between the items or scales. Take, as an extreme example, the following five items: Be a chemist; Be an engineer; Be a physicist; Be a metallurgist; Be a car salesman.

Someone who answers "Like" to four of the five does not necessarily have broader interests than someone who picks only one—the former person might simply have scientific interests, the latter, sales interests.

To build an index of breadth of interests, one needs items that are truly unrelated so that responding to one item has no relationship to responding to another. Additionally, the items should be diverse enough to guarantee some reasonable coverage of the entire universe of activities. Those two goals guided the development of the Diversity of Interests scales.

Scale Construction

The two Diversity of Interests scales, one for the Men's booklet and one for the Women's, were constructed by using the same item intercorrelation matrices used to build the Basic Scales. These matrices were scanned to find items with low intercorrelations; those items selected are listed, with their intercorrelations, in Tables 5-20 (Men's) and 5-21 (Women's). The correlations above the diagonal are from Strong's original sample of men-in-general (or women) and were the figures used in scale development; those below the diagonal are from a second sample, and provide a replication.

The intent here was to include items with zero, or at least very low, intercorrelations. The guideline used was .00 ± .20, and practically all of the correlations actually fell between +.15 and −.05. As can be seen in Tables 5-20 and 5-21, there was some regression upward in the second samples but nothing serious—these are essentially unrelated items.

Norming

These scales, both the men's and women's, have been normed by using the same samples used to norm the Basic Scales.

There is only one form for each scale, that is, there is nothing parallel to the Set 1 and Set 2 Basic Scales. The men's scale can be used with any

TABLE 5-22. MEAN SCORES ON THE MEN'S DIVERSITY OF INTERESTS SCALE

```
61  Policemen(1968)
60  Salesmen,3M applicants
59  Comm Rec Direcs/Salesmen,3M
58  Dept Store Mgrs/Ministers(1969)/Physical Therapists(1966)/YMCA PD/Elem Teachers(Minn)/Air Force Officers
57  Policemen(1969)/Elem Teachers(NDak)/Physical Therapists(1957)/YMCA Staff/Math-Sci Teachers(1936)/Army Officers(1950)/C
    Mgrs/County Welfare Workers
56  Soc Sci Teachers(1969)/English Teachers/Legislators/Orthopedic Surgeons/Guidance Counselors(1950)/Business Ed Teachers
    Policemen(1933)/Soc Sci Teachers(1936)/Forest Service Men/Rehab Counselors/Salesmen,Computer/School Supers(1965)
55  Guidance Counselors(1968)/Medical Techs/Physicians(1969)/Psychiatrists(1967)/School Supers(1969)/County Sheriffs/Purch
    Agents(1969)/Voc Ag Teachers/Social Workers(1967)/Highway Patrolmen/Math-Sci Teachers(1968)/Physiatrists/High School
    Counselors/Pharmacists(1968)/Machinists/Urologists/Social Workers(1953)/Cham Comm Execs/CPA(1944)/Office Workers/YMCA
    Public Admins(1941)/Petroleum Engineers/Football Coaches
54  Student Personnel Workers/Psychologists(1947)/Salesmen,PG&E/Pediatricians/Neurological Surgeons/Radiologists/Osteopath
    School Supers(1930)/Accountants/Personnel Direcs(1927)/Psychiatrists(1949)/Navy Officers/Ministers(1965)/CPA(1965)/Uni
    Ministers(1950)/Food Scientists/Personnel Direcs(1969)/Public Admins(1969)/Cartographers/Foresters/Army Officers(1969)
    Ag Extension Agents/Vets(1966)/Generals & Admirals
53  Funeral Direcs(1969)/Teaching Brothers/Sales Mgrs(1968)/Army Sergeants/Skilled Tradesmen/Tool & Die Makers/Chiropracto
    Electricians/Priests/Danforth Fellows/Actors(1966)/Governors/Salesmen,Steel/Buyers(1946)/Optometrists/Surgeons/Music
    Teachers(1952)/Librarians/Vets(1949)/Ministers(1927)/Pilots/Computer Programmers/Salesmen,Auto/Music Teachers(1946)
52  Carpenters(1969)/Dental Educators/Musicians(1969)/Colonels/Buyers(1969)/Animal Husbandry Profs/Engineers(1968)/Astrona
    Bankers(1964)/Internists/Pathologists/Biologists/Physicians(1949)/Dentists(1932)/Production Mgrs/Chemists(1931)/Carper
    (1936)/Printers/Sociologists/Lawyers(1949)/Unitarian Ministers(1929)
51  Advertising Men(1968)/Architects(1968)/Bankers(1969)/Lawyers(1969)/Salesmen,Life(1969)/Dentists(1969)/Salesmen,Real Es
    (1969)/Newsmen/Psychologists(1967)/NASA Scientists/Judges/Salesmen,Encyclopedia/Mpls Symphony/Actors(1937)/Interprete
    Psychologists(1949)/Psychologists(Exp)/Musicians(1952)/Sales Mgrs(1932)/Funeral Direcs(1945)/Bankers(1934)/Salesmen,Li
    (1931)/Purchasing Agents(1931)
50  Business School Profs/Chemists(1969)/Investment Mgrs/College Profs/Economists/Physicians(1927)/Engineers(1928)/Lawyers
    Corp Pres(1935)/Salesmen,Real Estate(1932)/Farmers(1936)/Architects(1933)
49  Interior Decorators/Salesmen,Life(1966)/Advertising Men(1931)/Pharmacists(1947)
48  Anthropologists/Photographers/Physicists(1968)/Corp Pres(1965)
47  Astronomers/Political Scientists/NIAL Members/Farmers(1967)/Pulitzer Prize
46  Mathematicians(1969)/Farmers(1968)/Artists(1968)/Mathematicians(1929)/Physicists(1927)
45  Artists(1933)
44  Authors
```

TABLE 5-23. MEAN SCORES ON THE DIVERSITY OF INTERESTS SCALE FOR
87 WOMEN'S OCCUPATIONAL SAMPLES

```
56  Stewardesses
55  Business Education Teachers '67
54  Guidance Counselors/ YWCA Staff '67 / English Teacher '67
53  Social Science Teachers '67/ Occupational Therapists '66/ Directors, Christian Education/ Engineers/ Visiting Nurses
    Salesladies/ Elementary Teacher '66/ Home Econ Teachers '67/ Telephone Operators
52  H. S. PE Teachers '39/ BA Nurses/ Nongrads/ Business Ed Teachers '41/ Secretaries '67/ Physical Therapists '66
    Life Insurance Sales '67/ Art Teachers/ LP Nurse/ Physical Therapists '57/ Grads/ Exec Housekeepers/ Math-Science Teache
    Lawyers '67/ Housewives
51  Dental Assistants/ Language Teachers/ Nun-Teachers/ Wives-Social Workers/ Office Workers/ Lawyers '34/
    County Welfare Workers/ Librarians '67/ Dietitians '67/ HS PE Teachers '67/ Occupational Therapists '42/ Music Teachers
    Models/ Wives--Animal Husbandry Profs
50  Social Workers/ Home Econ Teachers '41/ Life Ins Sales '37/ YWCA Secretary/ PH Nurse/ WAC Officers/ Psychologists '66/
    Speech Pathologists/ Secretaries '34/ Social Science Teachers '34/Nurse '34/ Radiologic Technologists/ Newswomen
    Buyers/ Medical Technologists/ Beauticians
49  Dietitians '41/ Music Performers/ WOMEN-IN-GENERAL/ Math-Science Teachers'34/ Physicians '67/ WAC Enlisted
    Instrument Assemblers/ Psychologists '42/ Entertainers
48  College PE Teachers/ Interior Decorators/ Sewing Machine Operators/ Translators/ Wives--Physicists/ WAVE Officers
47  English Teachers '34/ Chemists/ WAVE Enlisted/ Photographers
46  Lab Technicians/ Physicians (Western Reserve)/ Dentists
45  Mathematicians/ Librarians/ Physicians '34
44
43  Authors
42  Artists '34
41  Artists '67
```

form of the men's booklet, the women's with any form of the women's booklet.

Validity

There are no standard validity statistics for the Diversity of Interests scales because there is no apparent way to identify a criterion group of people with broad interests. The difficulty stems, in part, from the murkiness of the concept "breadth of interests." For example, one might use judge's ratings as validating criteria, but some initial attempts have convinced me that the average person, and the average psychologist, has little specific knowledge about the range of interests among his acquaintances. If one sees a friend coming out of the library with books on sailing, raising tropical flowers, playing the stock market, programming computers, and digging among Greek ruins, he might conclude that his friend has broad interests when, in fact, the friend is showing a preference for one narrow, specific activity—reading.

Although no traditional validity indices are available, considerable normative data have been generated by scoring all of the occupational samples on these scales: the mean scores for the men's samples are in Table 5-22, for the women in Table 5-23. The scales do not spread the occupations apart very far, only about 15 points, or 1½ standard deviations; thus, these scales have less relevance for occupational membership than do scores on the more traditional SVIB scales. Whether these scores have any stronger relationship with other variables that are important for assessment has yet to be determined.

One trend is apparent in the rank-ordering of the mean scores in Tables 5-22 and 5-23. Curiously, among both the male and female samples, those occupations usually termed "creative"—artists, authors, photographers, research scientists—scored at the low end of the scale, indicating they have restricted interests, at least as defined by this scale. That is a peculiar finding, especially as it runs counter to one's intuitive feeling about creativity. Perhaps a certain narrowness in the activities that one finds interesting is necessary for creative output.

Interpretation

If the concept of breadth of interests is a valid one, and if the Diversity of Interests scale measures it, then the two scales—one for men, one for women—should be highly related, but the correlation between the two scales among a miscellaneous group that had answered both the men's and women's form was .66, only moderately high, and suggests that caution should be used in generalizing from these scales.

At the moment, no interpretation of this scale can be offered, only an operational definition. A high score, perhaps 57–58 or above, indicates that the individual has answered "Like" to a relatively larger number of *unrelated* activities than the average person; low scores of roughly 42–43 or below indicate the converse.

The scale is presented here as a novel collection of items—all unrelated—but definitely as an experimental measure which is not yet understood. Placing the score on the profile will make it available for many research projects and, hopefully, more information will be garnered on this measure.

Managerial Orientation Scale (MO-Men)

This scale was developed by Nash (1966), working as a doctoral candidate under the direction of Marvin Dunnette at the University of Minnesota. In an earlier literature review (Nash, 1965) he concluded that preference measures have consistently related to various criteria of managerial effectiveness, and he was encouraged by this to develop a SVIB scale related to these criteria.

Scale Construction

Nash's project was completed before the 1966 revision of the SVIB, and only 41 of his original 57 items survived the revision. Johnson and Dunnette (1968) have redone the Nash analysis, using only the items included in the 1966 revision, as follows:

Briefly, the development of the scale was based on data from and about the 468 managers (employed in about 13 different Twin Cities firms) who took part in the study reported earlier by Mahoney, Jerdee, and Nash (1960). A variety of organization levels and types of managerial jobs were represented in this sample, including about 25 percent from the top managerial level of their organizations, 30 percent from the middle, and 45 percent at the lowest level. About 32 percent were engaged in production supervision, 53 percent in office supervision, and 15 percent in the supervision of technical personnel.

The criterion of managerial effectiveness was obtained by pooling alternation rankings made by the subjects' superiors. One to six rankings were available for each subject. The inter-rater reliabilities ranged from .08 to .95, with a median of .65.

The entire sample was split into two sub-samples of about equal size, matched on criterion scores, company, type of work, and organization level. The upper and lower thirds [on the supervisor's ratings] of the first group were used for item analysis of the SVIB responses. The second group was used for cross-validation of keys developed on the first.

TABLE 5-24. VALIDITY DATA ON THE MANAGERIAL ORIENTATION SCALE FOR THE
VALIDATION AND CROSS-VALIDATION SAMPLES OF MANAGERS

| | Validation (Item Analysis) Samples | | |
	Highly Effective (N=61)	Middle (N=68)	Low Effective (N=74)
Mean	50	38.1	28.7
SD	10	12.0	10.9
	Percent Overlap 34 percent (High-Low)		
	Cross-Validation Samples		
	(N=79)	(N=74)	(N=74)
Mean	45	40.5	36.8
SD	11.2	10.6	12.4
	Percent Overlap 73 percent (High-Low)		

Validity

The MO scale was constructed by using the items showing item response percent differences of 15 percent or more between the high and low effectiveness groups in the validation sample. The resulting scale was applied to both the validation and cross-validation samples, and the results are shown in Table 5-24. The scale was normed by using the "High Effectiveness" sub-sample; other scores should be compared against their standard score mean of 50 and SD of 10. The scale worked well in the initial sample, showing a percent overlap of 34 percent, but there was considerable shrinkage in the cross-validation sample, where the percent overlap increased to 73. The correlation between the scale and the managerial effectiveness ratings was .33 in the cross-validation sample, just high enough to be enticing.

Although this index of validity is modest in size, the scale clearly has a "managerial flavor" to it, as demonstrated by both the item content, listed in Table 5-25 and by the mean MO scores for several occupations listed in Table 5-26.

Clearly, as Johnson and Dunnette said, "Those scoring higher on the scale are in occupations which presumably place a premium on aspirational, risk-taking, action-oriented, and dominating behaviors. Those scoring low tend to belong to the more analytical, aesthetic and subprofessional occupations which place a premium on behaviors actually antagonistic to the leading and forceful patterns characteristic of managerial activities and functions."

TABLE 5-25. ITEMS WEIGHTED ON THE MEN'S MANAGERIAL ORIENTATION SCALE

Items Weighted Positively		Items Weighted Negatively	
Item Number	Item	Item Number	Item
4	Military Officer	25	City or State employee
5	Artist	53	Librarian
14	Airplane Pilot	55	Locomotive engineer
18	Buyer of merchandise	66	Orchestra Conductor
65	Office Manager	98	Watchmaker
101	Algebra	109	Civics (government)
107	Calculus	117	Ancient Languages
129	Psychology	134	Spelling
140	Tennis	135	Typewriting
146	Bridge	224	Regular hours for work
159	Formal dress affairs	235	Conservative people
172	Poetry	246	Emotional people
191	Handling horses	292	Steadiness and permanence of work
195	Arguments	294	Courteous treatment from superiors
198	Interviewing clients	329	Do a job yourself vs Tell somebody
199	Making a speech		to do the job
210	Drilling soldiers	341	Work with few details vs Work with
243	People who assume leadership		many details
285	Supervise the manufacture of a machine	342	Outside work vs Inside work
299	Freedom in working out one's own methods of doing the work	347	Technical responsibility vs Supervisory responsibility
333	Activity that produces tangible returns vs Activity which is enjoyed for its own sake		
338	Work in a large corporation with little chance of becoming president until age 55 vs Work for self in small business		
361	Usually start activities of my group		
368	Have mechanical ingenuity		
369	Have more than my share of novel ideas		
376	Able to meet emergencies quickly and effectively		
382	Put drive into the organization		
398	My advice is asked for by many... by few...by almost nobody		

Reliability

To learn something of the stability of the preferences on the MO scale, Johnson and Dunnette computed the test and retest means and correlations for several samples tested just prior to, during, or shortly after graduation from college. Those data are in Table 5-27. The test and retest means are quite similar in each sample, even over periods up to 20 years, and the test-retest correlations are fairly substantial. Johnson and Dunnette concluded, "The managerial effectiveness pattern of preferences . . . apparently appears rather early (before, during, or shortly after college) and persists over time. . . . This particular pattern is not subject to changes over time in the societal or cultural milieu, and apparently reflects highly stable differences in individuals' likes and dislikes rather than any systematic response tendencies subject to economic, occupational, or cultural conditions prevalent at the time of taking the SVIB."

Finally, here is their summary conclusion on the Managerial Orientation scale:

TABLE 5-26. MEAN SCORES ON THE MEN'S MANAGERIAL ORIENTATION SCALE

Salesmen,Computer

Sales Mgrs(1968)
Dept Store Mgrs/Salesmen,3M/Salesmen,3M applicants
Generals & Admirals
Football Coaches/Air Force Officers/Investment Mgrs/Personnel Direcs(1969)/Army Officers(1969)
Salesmen,Encyclopedia/Astronauts/Cham Comm Execs/Army Officers(1950)/Corp Pres(1965)
Buyers(1969)/Governors/Salesmen,Life(1966)
Advertising Men(1968)/Bankers(1969)/Food Scientists/Salesmen,Life(1969)/School Supers(1969)/Engineers(1968)/Salesmen,Steel/
Sales Mgrs(1932)/School Supers(1965)/CPA(1965)/Credit Mgrs
Lawyers(1969)/Public Admins(1969)/Purchasing Agents(1969)/Corp Pres(1935)/Production Mgrs/Personnel Direcs(1927)/Navy
Officers/Petroleum Engineers
Salesmen,Real Estate(1969)/Legislators/Buyers(1946)/YMCA Staff/Advertising Men(1931)/Purchasing Agents(1931)/Public Admins
(1941)/Comm Rec Direcs
Architects(1968)/Business School Profs/Interior Decorators/Social Workers((1967)/NASA Scientists/High School Counselors/
Student Personnel Workers/Optometrists/Engineers(1928)/Rehab Counselors/Computer Programmers
Chemists(1969)/Funeral Direcs(1969)/Psychiatrists(1967)/Policemen(1968)/Foresters/Colonels/Psychologists(1967)/Economists/
Guidance Counselors(1950)/School Supers(1930)/Accountants
Physicians(1969)/Dental Educators/Army Sergeants/Psychologists(1947)/Bankers(1964)/Surgeons/Psychologists(1949)/Business
Ed Teachers/Lawyers(1927)/Funeral Direcs(1945)/YMCA PD/YMCA Secs/Elem Teachers(Minn)/Lawyers(1949)
Dentists(1969)/Cartographers/Voc Ag Teachers/Chiropractors/Ag Extension Agents/Judges/Pharmacists(1968)/Psychologists(Exp)/
Social Workers(1953)/CPA(1944)/Office Workers/Salesmen,Life(1931)/Salesmen,Real Estate(1932)/Psychiatrists(1949)/Ministers
(1965)/Unitarian Ministers(1950)
Vets(1966)/Physiatrists/Physicists(1968)/Guidance Counselors(1968)/Medical Techs/County Sheriffs/College Profs/Animal
Husbandry Profs/Math-Sci Teachers(1968)/Danforth Fellows/Salesmen,PG&E/Orthopedic Surgeons/Neurological Surgeons/Chemists
(1931)/Bankers(1934)/Architects(1933)/County Welfare Workers
Mathematicians(1969)/Physical Therapists(1966)/Policemen(1969)/Soc Sci Teachers(1969)/Ministers(1969)/Newsmen/Actors(1966)/
Photographers/Interpreters/Internists/Pathologists/Music Teachers(1952)/Biologists/Physical Therapists(1957)/Physicists
(1927)/Forest Service Men/Pilots/Salesmen,Auto
Teaching Brothers/Astronomers/Priests/Political Scientists/Highway Patrolmen/Physicians(1927)/Urologists/Physicians(1949)/
Osteopaths/Math-Sci Teachers(1936)/Sociologists
English Teachers/Tool & Die Makers/Machinists/Actors(1937)/Pediatricians/Dentists(1932)/Vets(1949)/Ministers(1927)/Soc Sci
Teachers(1936)/Pharmacists(1947)
Carpenters(1969)/Musicians(1969)/Anthropolgists/Electricians/Skilled Tradesmen/Elem Teachers(NDak)/Radiologists/Mathematician
(1929)/Authors/Unitarian Ministers(1929)
Librarians/Farmers(1936)/Music Teachers(1946)
NIAL Members/Artists(1968)/Artists(1933)
Musicians(1952)/Pulitzer Prize
Mpls Symphony/Policemen(1933)/Printers
Carpenters(1936)/Farmers(1968)

Farmers(1967)

TABLE 5-27. TEST-RETEST DATA FOR TEN SAMPLES ON THE MANAGERIAL
ORIENTATION SCALE

Test-Retest Interval	Number Tested	Test Mean	Retest Mean	Test-Retest Correlations
2 weeks	140	39	38	.84
30 days	102	44	44	.85
1 year	253	36	37	.66
8 years	160	36	38	.44
9 years	175	36	39	.48
10 years	137	38	39	.70
17 years	165	37	37	.52
18 years	178	37	38	.47
19 years	202	36	39	.52
22 years	191	36	37	.53

The Nonoccupational Scales

These data provide further support for arguing that potentially effective managers may be identified by a specific pattern of likes and dislikes. . . . We should caution, however, that the relationship is by no means a large one, accounting probably for no more than ten percent of the overall variance in the job effectiveness of managers. Still, the preferences are clearly volitional in tone, suggesting outcome preferences involving independence of thought, risk-taking, a rejection of regimentation [?? DPC] and a striving for positions of dominance in inter-personal contacts (Johnson and Dunnette, 1968).

Mean Scores for 22 Outstanding Groups

Like the AACH scale, the MO scale reflects interests related to competence in a specific area, i.e., management; it is not a general correlate success in all endeavors. To demonstrate this, mean scores for several outstanding groups are presented in Table 5-28; the number in each group is the first number in parentheses after the group name, the second number is the group SD on the MO scale.

While the groups might differ on some absolute level of success—whatever that means—and though they differ greatly in age, there is no question that most of the men in all of these samples would be considered outstanding by any reasonable criterion. More information on each group is given below, and their other SVIB scores are reported in Chapter 7.

Artists: All members of the National Institute of Arts and Letters (NIAL).
Cartoonists: Political cartoonists; all have been awarded the Pulitzer Prize.
Minneapolis Symphony: Members of an excellent symphony orchestra.
Poets: Either members of NIAL, or have been awarded the Pulitzer Prize.
Authors: Pulitzer Prize winners, either as novelists or biographers.
Journalists: Pulitzer Prize winners, either as reporters or editors.
Composers: NIAL members, or Pulitzer Prize winners.
McKnight Fellows: Young actors awarded a fellowship to study at the Tyrone Guthrie Theater in Minneapolis.
Danforth Fellows: College students who have been awarded a graduate fellowship to prepare for college teaching.
Federal Judges: District judges.
DSC Psychologists: Winners of the American Psychological Association's top scientific award, the Distinguished Scientific Contribution Award.
Medal of Science Winners: Winners of the country's top scientific honor.
Nobel Prize Winners: Self-explanatory.
APA Presidents: Past Presidents of the American Psychological Association.
Minnesota Governors: Eight of the last ten Minnesota governors.
Non-Minnesota Governors: Governors from other states, none currently in office.
Encyclopedia Salesmen: World Book salesmen with outstanding production records.
Life Insurance Salesmen: Salesmen from two companies, all sold minimum of $2,000,000 annually, 1965–66.
Generals: Active and retired, all with at least three stars, many with four.

TABLE 5-28. MEAN SCORES ON THE MANAGERIAL ORIENTATION SCALE FOR
22 SAMPLES OF OUTSTANDING MEN
(First number in parentheses is group N; second is group SD)

```
52 Corporation Presidents (16/9.9)

51

50 (Validation Sample of Highly Effective Managers)

49

48

47 College Football Coaches (13/6.3)

46 Generals (91/8.6); Admirals (21/7.5); Astronauts (22/7.0)

45 Encyclopedia Salesmen (52/8.2); Life Insurance Salesmen (101/9.2)
   (Cross-Validation Sample of Highly Effective Managers)
44

43 Non-Minnesota Governors (38/9.3)

42

41 Minnesota Governors (8/10.1)

40 Nobel Prize Winners (12/9.6); APA Presidents (50/9.3)

39 Medal of Science Winners (12/10.4)

38 Danforth Fellows (91/9.2); Federal Judges (132/8.4); DSC Psychologists (24/7.0)

37 (Cross-Validation Sample of Low Effective Managers)

36 McKnight Fellows (43/10.2)

35 Composers (12/11)

34

33

32

31 Journalists (47/10.6)

30

29 Authors (26/8.7); (Validation Sample of Low Effective Managers)

28 Minnesota Symphony (53/9.8); Poets (10/6.2)

27 Artists (12/5.8); Cartoonists (7/10.2)
```

Admirals: Same as generals.
Astronauts: Self-explanatory.
College Football Coaches: Thirteen of the U.S.'s top 25 coaches at major universities, as measured by lifetime won-lost records.
Corporation Presidents: From the U.S.'s largest 100 corporations, as determined by *Fortune* magazine's 1964 listing.

The MO means in Table 5-28 suggests strongly that this scale reflects interests in managerial activities in the traditional sense, and appears to do it rather well, but it is not a measure of success in all settings. Though the samples in Table 5-28 are small, the rank-ordering is very meaningful, and clearly oriented toward the management of large groups.

The occupations at the bottom of the table are about as far from the business world as one can get, and they are also—with the possible exception of the symphony members—lone-wolf jobs; certainly they demand little in the way of managerial talents. As one moves up the scale, there is a distinct and increasing emphasis on occupations where one must manage others, culminating in military, athletic, and business leadership positions. The top group, the corporation presidents, averaged even higher (mean of 52) than did the validation group of good managers (mean of 50).

These data are quite supportive of Nash's, and Johnson and Dunnette's conclusions, especially the latters' summary comments: "Those scoring highest on the scale are in occupations which presumably place a premium on aspirational, action-oriented, and dominating behaviors" (Johnson and Dunnette, 1968, p. 8).

While more experience must be gained before we know precisely how to use the MO scale, the care that went into its construction and its favorable validity statistics have earned it a place on the regular SVIB profile.

Masculinity-Femininity Scale (MFII-Men, FMII-Women)

The Masculinity-Femininity scale was the first of the Nonoccupational scales; Strong (1943, p. 216) wrote extensively on its development. In 1967, the MF scale was revised by Charles Johansson at the University of Minnesota so that it could be used with all forms of both Men's and Women's booklets. When used with the Women's booklet, the scoring weights are reversed, and the scale is named Femininity-Masculinity. To avoid confusion with earlier scales, the scales have been labeled Masculinity-Femininity II and Femininity-Masculinity II; this terminology should be used in any research reports on these scales.

Masculinity-Femininity scales are built by comparing the test responses of men and women, and the exact samples of men and women used are important as they determine the nature of the scale. One of the problems in selecting samples is to make certain that they are similar in all respects except sex. A cross-section of women versus a cross-section of men is probably not an acceptable sampling because the samples would not be equivalent in all respects—for example, more of the men would undoubtedly be employed and thus the scale would be based to some extent on the differences between employed and non-employed people.

Scale Construction

To generate equivalent samples, Johansson used samples from 18 occupations, listed in Table 5-29, where both males and females had been tested.

TABLE 5-29. MEANS AND STANDARD DEVIATIONS ON MFII, FMII SCALES FOR
MF VALIDATION SAMPLES

		Male Samples (MFII Scores)					Female Samples (FMII Scores)			
		Raw Score		Standard Score			Raw Score		Standard Score	
Occupation	N	Mean	SD	Mean	SD	N	Mean	SD	Mean	SD
Artist	218	-5.6	6.8	39.6	8.8	388	14.8	6.0	57.3	8.5
Author-Journalist	242	-2.7	7.5	43.3	9.8	387	14.2	6.7	56.4	9.4
Business Educ. Teacher	322	6.0	8.4	54.6	10.9	249	6.7	7.5	46.0	10.6
Dentist	235	5.2	7.0	53.6	9.1	188	5.8	7.5	44.7	10.6
Engineer	511	5.3	7.5	53.7	9.7	322	3.9	7.9	42.0	11.1
Lawyer	249	3.9	7.8	51.8	10.1	370	7.5	7.1	47.1	9.9
Librarian	425	-5.8	7.7	39.3	9.9	420	14.6	6.2	57.0	8.7
Life Insurance Sales	310	5.3	7.4	53.6	9.6	201	8.4	7.2	48.3	10.1
Math-Science Teacher	288	7.2	7.2	56.1	9.4	466	8.0	7.4	47.8	10.4
Musician Performer	441	-1.3	8.2	45.1	10.6	287	13.1	6.7	55.0	9.4
Music Teacher	490	-2.2	8.3	44.0	10.7	444	12.4	6.4	54.0	9.1
Office Worker	316	5.0	7.6	53.2	9.8	425	7.1	7.6	46.5	10.7
Physical Therapist	348	7.1	8.1	56.1	10.4	399	5.0	7.9	46.0	10.6
Physician	532	4.3	8.1	53.4	10.5	413	7.6	8.0	47.3	11.2
Psychologist	1045	3.5	8.2	51.4	10.6	378	8.8	7.6	48.8	10.7
Social Science Teacher	217	5.7	7.9	54.1	10.2	392	11.6	6.7	52.8	9.5
Social Worker	400	2.7	8.1	50.3	10.5	464	10.1	7.0	50.7	9.8
YMCA-YWCA Staff Member	113	0.6	7.1	47.6	9.2	197	13.1	6.4	54.9	9.1
TOTAL		2.46	7.71	50.0	10.0		9.59	7.10	50.0	10.0

For each of the SVIB items common to all forms of the Men's and Women's booklets, a "male percent response" was generated by equally weighting the responses of the 18 male samples. In a similar manner, a "female percent response" was generated. Then those two percentages were compared, item by item, and items with a 15 percent difference were selected for the final scale. (See p. 33 for a discussion of item weighting.) The selected items are listed in Table 5-30, along with their numbers on the respective booklets.

Norming

To norm the scales, the men from these 18 occupations were used for the MFII scale, the women for the FMII scale. Table 5-29 also includes the data for all of the samples used in developing the scale. The percent overlap between the men and women in these 18 occupations was 42 percent.

TABLE 5-30. ITEMS WEIGHTED ON THE MASCULINITY-FEMININITY SCALES
(MFII AND FMII)

Item Number in Men's Booklet	Item Number in Women's Booklet	Items Weighted in Masculine Direction
7	8	Athletic Director
29	30	Dentist
41	45	Governor of a State
51	57	Criminal Lawyer
137	133	Golf
190	176	Operating machinery
188	177	Repairing electrical wiring
196	181	Interviewing men
213	200	Acting as cheer-leader
388	355	Discuss my ideals with others
399	361	Make bets often...sometimes...rarely
128	390	Physics

		Items Weighted in Feminine Direction
5	6	Artist
43	50	Interior Decorator
44	51	Interpreter
50	55	Landscape Gardener
53	58	Librarian
62	70	Musician
71	80	Poet
74	83	Private Secretary
84	103	Sculptor
163	148	Art Galleries
167	152	Symphony concerts
172	157	Poetry
194	179	Decorating a room with flowers
224	209	Regular hours for work
228	212	Contributing to charities
255	232	Foreigners
104	364	Art
117	381	Ancient Languages
118	382	Modern Languages
119	383	Literature

This method of constructing an MF scale has both advantages and disadvantages. Using men and women from the same occupation has the advantage of matching the groups, at least roughly, on many relevant characteristics such as educational level and general type of occupational activity. Using only items common to all SVIB booklets permits ready comparison of scores from sample to sample, no matter which form of the booklet was used to test them.

But there are also two main disadvantages. First, using only occupational samples where both men and women are available restricts one to those occupations where both men and women can be found (and, in fact, have been tested with the SVIB)—this eliminates the most masculine and feminine occupations as, for example, no female farmers or forest rangers have been tested, nor male secretaries nor home economics teachers. The second major disadvantage is that restricting the scale to items common to all booklets makes it impossible to use the most masculine and feminine items because they only appear in the appropriate booklet, e.g., the items "Loco-

MII mean ore	(MFII*)	
58	26	Artists (1934)
57	27	Librarians (1934)/Authors/English Teachers (1934)
56	28	Artists (1967)
55	29	Musician Performers/YWCA Staff (1934)
54	30	Interior Decorators/Art Teachers/Language Teachers/Music Teachers
53	31	English Teachers (1967)/Librarians (1967)/Social Science Teachers
52	32	
51	33	Directors, Christian Education/Social Workers/Occupational Therapists (1942)/Nurses (1934)
50	34	Elementary Teachers/Occupational Therapists (1966)/Photographers/Newswomen/Secretaries (1934)
49	35	Psychologists (1966)/Entertainers/Psychologists (1942)/Housewives/Home Economics Teachers (1941) WOMEN-IN-GENERAL (1946)
48	36	Social Science Teachers (1934)/Guidance Counselors/Buyers/Life Insurance Sales (1937)/Math-Science Teachers (1934)
47	37	Home Economics Teachers (1967)/Physicians (1934)/Physicians (1967)/Office Workers/College PE Teachers (1954) Lawyers (1934)
46	38	Chemists/YWCA Staff (1967)/Secretaries (1967)/WOMEN-IN-GENERAL (1967)/Business Education Teachers (1941) Lab Technicians
45	39	Licensed Practical Nurses/Saleswomen/Mathematicians/Physical Therapists (1966)/Registered Nurses/Lawyers (1967) Dietitians (1967)/Dietitians (1941)/Dentists
44	40	Stewardesses/Army Officers/Executive Housekeepers/Physical Therapists (1957)
43	41	Life Underwriters/Math-Science Teachers (1967)/Business Education Teachers (1967)/HS PE Teachers (1939)
42	42	Dental Assistants/Beauticians/Engineers/Telephone Operators/Navy Officers/Medical Technologists
41	43	Sewing Machine Operators
40	44	Radiologic Technologists
39	45	
38	46	Army Enlisted/Navy Enlisted/HS PE Teachers (1967)
37	47	Instrument Assemblers

* For comparative purposes, the MFII equivalent of each FMII score is listed here. The conversion is not exactly perfect, because of rounding error, but it is within one standard score point.

TABLE 5-32. MEAN SCORES ON THE MFII SCALE FOR 112 MEN'S
OCCUPATIONAL SAMPLES

63	Salesmen,Computer
62	County Sheriffs
61	Petroleum Engineers/Air Force Officers/Sales Mgrs(1968)/Voc Ag Teachers/Highway Patrolmen
60	Pilots/Dept Store Mgrs/Farmers(1968)
59	Policemen(1969)/Salesmen,Life(1969)/Purchasing Agents(1969)/Salesmen,Real Estate(1969)/Army Officers(1969)/Electricians/ Salesmen,Steel/Farmers(1967)/Vets(1949)/CPA(1965)/Salesmen,3M/Salesmen,3M applicants
58	Funeral Direcs(1969)/Policemen(1968)/Skilled Tradesmen/Tool & Die Makers/Carpenters(1969)/Engineers(1968)/Vets(1966)/ High School Counselors/Machinists/Optometrists/Army Officers(1950)/Navy Officers/Comm Rec Direcs/Credit Mgrs
57	Pharmacists(1968)/Bankers(1969)/School Supers(1969)/Soc Sci Teachers(1969)/Army Sergeants/Foresters(1967)/Animal Husbandry Profs/Math-Sci Teachers(1968)/Astronauts/Salesmen,PG&E/Bankers(1964)/Cham Comm Execs/YMCA Staff/Forest Service Men/ Purchasing Agents(1931)/Football Coaches/Salesmen,Auto
56	Food Scientists/Legislators/Ag Extension Agents/Guidance Counselors(1950)/Physical Therapists(1957)/Production Mgrs/Sales Mgrs(1932)/Math-Sci Teachers(1936)/Policemen(1933)/Pharmacists(1947)/Corp Pres(1965)
55	Personnel Direcs(1969)/Physical Therapists(1966)/Cartographers/Chiropractors/Buyers(1969)/NASA Scientists/Governors/ Salesmen,Life(1966)/Buyers(1946)/Orthopedic Surgeons/Business Ed Teachers/CPA(1944)/Osteopaths/Funeral Direcs(1945)/ Salesmen,Real Estate(1932)/Farmers(1936)/Computer Programmers/County Welfare Workers
54	Medical Techs/Dentists(1969)/Generals & Admirals/Engineers(1928)/Corp Pres(1935)/Chemists(1931)/Soc Sci Teachers(1936)/ Accountants/Bankers(1934)/Salesmen,Life(1931)/Personnel Direcs(1927)/Rehab Counselors/Public Admins(1941)/School Supers (1965)
53	Urologists/Radiologists/Surgeons/Dentists(1932)/Office Workers/YMCA PD/Carpenters(1936)/Lawyers(1949)/Business School Profs/ Investment Mgrs/Lawyers(1969)/Public Admins(1969)/Colonels
52	Chemists(1969)/Guidance Counselors(1968)/Dental Educators/Social Workers(1967)/Salesmen,Encyclopedia/Elem Teachers(NDak)/ Student Personnel Workers/Psychologists(Exp)/Physicians(1949)/Lawyers(1927)/Printers
51	Internists/Pediatricians/Psychologists(1949)/Psychiatrists(1949)/Elem Teachers(Minn)
50	Advertising Men(1968)/Physicians(1969)/Physicians(1927)/Pathologists/Social Workers(1953)/School Supers(1930)
49	Biologists/Physicists(1927)/Music Teachers(1946)/Psychologists(1967)/Newsmen/Economists
48	Mathematicians(1969)/Psychiatrists(1967)/Judges/Physiatrists/Psychologists(1947)/Advertising Men(1931)/YMCA Secs
47	Teaching Brothers/College Profs/Political Scientists/Physicists(1968)/Neurological Surgeons/Sociologists
46	Musicians(1969)/Ministers(1969)/Astronomers
45	Architects(1968)/English Teachers/Priests/Musicians(1952)/Mathematicians(1929)
44	Photographers/Interpreters/Music Teachers(1952)/Ministers(1965)/Architects(1933)
43	Anthropologists/Authors/Unitarian Ministers(1950)
42	Danforth Fellows/Ministers(1927)/Unitarian Ministers(1929)
41	
40	Actors(1937)
39	Mpls Symphony/Librarians/Artists(1933)
38	Pulitzer Prize/Artists(1968)
37	Interior Decorators
36	Actors(1966)
35	
34	
33	
32	
31	NIAL Members

235

motive Engineer" and "Professional Baseball Player" are only in the Men's booklet; "Dietitian" and "Fashion Model" are only in the Women's booklet. Hopefully, these disadvantages are offset by the advantages described earlier.

Meaning of the MFII and FMII Scales

The mean FMII scores for several women's occupational groups are listed, in rank order form, in Table 5-31, and this listing emphasizes that the FMII scale is oriented toward *intellectual femininity* with the stress on art, music, and verbal activities—not on homemaking, children, or domestic concerns.

The Women-in-General sample scored 46; somewhere in the usual interpretation, the counselor should insert something like "The average FMII score of a cross-section of women drawn from many occupations is about 46."

In the left-hand side of Table 5-31 are listed the MFII equivalent of each FMII score; this shows where each of these samples would score if the items were weighted in the masculine direction. Thus, for example, the most "feminine" of the women's occupations—artists and authors—had a mean score of 28 on the MFII scale.

Scores on the MFII scale for 112 male occupational samples are listed in Table 5-32. High scores belong to those male occupations oriented to the outdoors, adventuresome activities, and to business. These scores are probably determined as much by a man's dislikes as likes, and, on this scale, those dislikes would include art, music, literature—i.e., feminine and cultural activities.

A Masculinity-Femininity score can be troublesome to use, as men are prone to interpret the score as relevant to their virility—or lack of it. Counselors should be certain to dispel any such ideas. Educated men in particular score toward the feminine end, which usually means they like books and art, to go to concerts, to work inside and keep their hands clean, to be kind to others, activities that are typically "feminine" in society as a whole.

Because of these problems, this scale should be used only by well-trained professionals who can integrate this score with the other information they have on their clients.

Occupational Introversion-Extroversion Scale
(OIE—Men and Women)

Personality theorists have long known of the importance of the introversion-extroversion dimension in understanding human behavior, as it is a dichotomy that continually reasserts itself in research findings. Because of the importance of this dimension, an effort was made to develop a SVIB scale that would help us to understand the relationship between introversion-extroversion and occupational membership.

Scale Construction and Validity—Men's Form

Using the Social Introversion-Extroversion scale from the Minnesota Multiphasic Personality Inventory, college students with high scores (plus one standard deviation, i.e., 60 and above) and low scores (minus one standard deviation i.e., 40 and below) were separated out, and their SVIB response percentages were compared. Among the male sample, 81 items showing at least 20 percent differences were identified, and these became the OIE scale for the men's booklet. Raw scores are converted to standard scores so that "introverts" average about 60, "extroverts" about 40, using the average of their raw score statistics.

Characteristics of the male validation sample and a holdout cross-validation group are reported in Table 5-33 and the validity statistics are shown in Table 5-34. The scale did a respectable job of separating the two extremes, and the difference held up well on cross-validation, though there was some shrinkage.

TABLE 5-33. CHARACTERISTICS OF VALIDATION AND CROSS-VALIDATION SAMPLES FOR MEN'S OCCUPATIONAL INTROVERSION–EXTROVERSION (OIE) SCALE

	Validation (N = 486)		Cross-Validation (N = 200)	
	Mean	S.D.	Mean	S.D.
GPA, MSAT, HSR				
First-Year Grade Point Average (A = 4.0)	1.9	0.8	2.0	0.9
Minnesota Scholastic Aptitude Test	43.3	11.3	44.2	12.2
High School Rank	71.5	19.3	72.0	20.0
Minnesota Multiphasic Personality Inventory				
Hypochondriasis	51.4	7.8	50.8	7.7
Depression	51.7	10.6	51.8	10.1
Hysteria	56.5	7.2	56.6	7.6
Psychopathic Deviate	57.5	9.8	58.1	9.5
Masculinity–Femininity	57.9	10.4	58.2	10.1
Paranoia	54.0	7.8	54.1	7.8
Psychasthenia	56.5	10.4	56.4	9.4
Schizophrenia	58.1	11.0	57.2	10.4
Hypomania	57.8	10.6	58.0	11.6
Social Introversion	48.2	9.5	47.9	9.2

TABLE 5-34. VALIDITY STATISTICS FOR MEN'S OCCUPATIONAL INTROVERSION–
EXTROVERSION (OIE) SCALE
(MMPI is the Minnesota Multiphasic Personality Inventory)

Sample	N	OIE Scale		Per Cent Overlap	Correlation with MMPI Social Introversion
		Mean	S.D.		
Validation					
Introverts	79	62.4	10.2	22	.59
Extroverts	100	37.6	9.9		
Middle	307	47.9	11.4		
Total	486	48.1	13.2		
Cross-Validation					
Introverts	30	60.8	12.8	32	.51
Extroverts	42	38.8	9.3		
Middle	128	49.8	11.4		
Total	200	48.3	12.4		

TABLE 5-35. MEAN SCORES ON THE MEN'S OCCUPATIONAL INTROVERSION–
EXTROVERSION SCALE

59 Physicists(1927)
58
57 Farmers(1968)/Farmers(1967)/Mathematicians(1929)/Artists(1933)
56
55 Mathematicians(1969)/Carpenters(1969)/Astronomers
54 Electricians/Skilled Tradesmen/Chemists(1931)/Architects(1933)
53 Anthropologists/Tool & Die Makers/NASA Scientists/NIAL Members/Physicists(1968)/Artists(1968)/Physicians(1927)/Engineers
    (1928)/Carpenters(1936)/Farmers(1936)
52 Pathologists/Psychologists(Exp)/Dentists(1932)/Authors/Pilots
51 Mpls Symphony/Biologists/Printers
50 Chemists(1969)/Radiologists/Physicians(1949)/Pulitzer Prize
49 Animal Husbandry Profs/Math-Sci Teachers(1968)/Engineers(1968)/Internists/Urologists/Surgeons/Osteopaths/Vets(1949)/Fores
    Service Men
48 Architects(1968)/Dentists(1969)/Musicians(1969)/Colonels/College Profs/Astronauts/Photographers/Pediatricians/Musicians
    (1952)/Math-Sci Teachers(1936)/Bankers(1934)/Purchasing Agents(1931)/Pharmacists(1947)/Computer Programmers
47 Medical Techs/Dental Educators/Foresters/Cartographers/Economists/Vets(1966)/Machinists/Actors(1937)/Bankers(1964)/
    Orthopedic Surgeons/Neurological Surgeons/Psychologists(1949)/CPA(1944)/Librarians/Corp Pres(1935)/Production Mgrs/
    Petroleum Engineers
46 Physicians(1969)/Interior Decorators/Political Scientists/Actors(1966)/Pharmacists(1968)/Office Workers/Funeral Direcs(19
    Accountants/Salesmen,Real Estate(1932)/Music Teachers(1946)
45 Optometrists/Lawyers(1927)/Policemen(1933)/Army Officers(1950)/Navy Officers/Teaching Brothers/Army Sergeants/Highway
    Patrolmen
44 Business School Profs/Food Scientists/Investment Mgrs/Physical Therapists(1966)/Purchasing Agents(1969)/Voc Ag Teachers/
    Psychologists(1967)/Elem Teachers(NDak)/Advertising Men(1931)/Psychiatrists(1949)/Corp Pres(1965)/Sociologists/Unitarian
    Ministers(1929)/Danforth Fellows/Physiatrists
43 Bankers(1969)/Policemen(1969)/Army Officers(1969)/Generals & Admirals/Interpreters/Physical Therapists(1957)/Public Admir
    (1941)/CPA(1965)
42 County Sheriffs/Salesmen,Real Estate(1969)/Chiropractors/Newsmen/Sales Mgrs(1932)/Air Force Officers/Salesmen,Auto/Lawyer
    (1949)
41 Funeral Direcs(1969)/Psychiatrists(1967)/Buyers(1969)/Priests/English Teachers/Ag Extension Agents/Buyers(1946)/Psycholog
    (1947)/Salesmen,PG&E/Music Teachers(1952)/Business Ed Teachers/School Supers(1930)/Personnel Direcs(1927)/County Welfare
    Workers
40 High School Counselors/Ministers(1927)/Soc Sci Teachers(1936)/Salesmen,Life(1931)/Elem Teachers(Minn)
39 Lawyers(1969)/Soc Sci Teachers(1969)/Judges/Salesmen,Steel/Student Personnel Workers/YMCA PD
38 Advertising Men(1968)/Policemen(1968)/School Supers(1969)/Public Admins(1969)/Guidance Counselors(1950)/Rehab Counselors/
    Credit Mgrs
37 Guidance Counselors(1968)/Personnel Direcs(1969)/Salesmen,Life(1969)/Dept Store Mgrs/Ministers(1969)/Social Workers(1953)
    Ministers(1965)/Unitarian Ministers(1950)
36 Social Workers(1967)/YMCA Secs/School Supers(1965)/Football Coaches
35 Governors/Salesmen,Life(1966)/Cham Comm Execs/YMCA Staff
34 Legislators/Comm Rec Direcs
33 Sales Mgrs(1968)/Salesmen,Computer
32 Salesmen,Encyclopedia
31 Salesmen,3M
30 Salesmen,3M applicants

To help establish the construct validity of the scale, all of the SVIB male criterion groups were scored on the scale; the results of this scoring are reported in Table 5-35. These scores indicate a "thing versus people" dichotomy, with the emphasis on helping people. High scores were found among the scientific and skilled trades occupations; low scores were found among the social-service occupations and among business occupations requiring a great deal of face-to-face contact with others.

The items weighted on the men's OIE scale are listed in Table 5-36, separated into those weighted positively, or toward introversion, and those weighted negatively, or toward extroversion. The OIE item weights were determined before the technique of "dimensionalizing" item weights had been established (see p. 33); thus, some of the item weights do not fit the usual patterns.

The item content of the OIE scale again supports the "things versus people" dichotomy.

Scale Construction and Validity—Women's Form

An OIE scale for the women's booklet was constructed analogously to the men's scale. From a sample of freshman women who entered the University of Minnesota in 1961, 100 who scored at least one standard deviation above the men (T score $\geq$ 60) on the MMPI Social Introversion-Extroversion scale were compared with 96 who scored one SD below (T score $\leq$ 40). Some demographic and psychometric characteristics of these students are reported in Table 5-37.

Fifty-seven SVIB items showing at least 20 percent difference in response rate between those two groups were gathered into the women's OIE scale.

Again, norming was done by using the average raw score mean and standard deviations for these two groups in the conversion formula, thus locating the standard score mean of 50 halfway between them. The validity and conversion statistics are reported in Table 5-38. The correlation between the MMPI SIE scale and the SVIB OIE scale among a sample of university women was .58, not high enough to assume the scales are measuring essentially the same attitudes.

Mean OIE scores for the women's occupations are listed in Table 5-39. The occupations scoring high and those scoring low, roughly one and one-half to two standard deviations apart, clearly represent two different occupational approaches. The high scoring samples work with things or numbers—with the exception of the beauticians. Curiously, these women, who work closely with people, scored toward the extreme introverted end. Perhaps they see themselves as working with "things."

Items Weighted Positively (in introversion direction)		Items Weighted Negatively (in extroversion direction)	
Item Number	Item	Item Number	Item
6	Astronomer	1	Actor
185	Making a radio or hi-fi set	2	Advertising Man
241	Pessimists	7	Athletic Director
282	Operate (manipulate) the new machine	11	Auto Salesman
284	Determine the cost of operation of the machine	41	Governor of a State
		47	Judge
313	Treasurer of a Society or Club	51	Criminal Lawyer
314	Member of a Society or Club	52	Corporation Lawyer
331	Deal with things vs Deal with people	71	Poet
335	Definite salary vs Commission on what is done	72	Politician
		79	Sports page reporter
348	Present a report in writing vs Present a report verbally	89	Social Worker
		90	Specialty Salesman
349	Listening to a story vs Telling a story	95	Traveling Salesman
		110	Dramatics
355	A few close friends vs Many acquaintances	111	Economics
		112	English Composition
393	When caught in a mistake, I make excuses usually...seldom... practically never	119	Literature
		126	Philosophy
		127	Physical Education
		131	Public Speaking
		133	Sociology
		137	Golf
		143	Boxing
		153	Amusement parks
		159	Formal dress affairs
		172	Poetry
		192	Giving "first-aid" assistance
		195	Arguments
		196	Interviewing men for a job
		197	Interviewing prospects in selling
		198	Interviewing clients
		199	Making a speech
		200	Organizing a play
		201	Starting a conversation with a stranger
		202	Teaching children
		203	Teaching adults
		206	Meeting and directing people
		207	Taking responsibility
		209	Adjusting difficulties of others
		213	Acting as cheer-leader
		215	Writing reports
		221	Expressing opinions openly, regardless of what others say
		229	Raising money for a charity
		236	Energetic people
		240	Optimists
		243	People who assume leadership
		246	Emotional people
		258	Very old people
		287	Sell the machine
		288	Prepare the advertising for the machine
		290	Interest the public in the machine through public addresses
		311	President of a Society or Club
		317	Chairman, Entertainment Committee
		319	Chairman, Program Committee
		330	Talk others into doing something vs Order others to do something
		351	Amusement where there is a crowd vs Amusement alone or with one or two others
		361	Usually start activities of my group
		363	Win friends easily
		365	Usually liven up the group on a dull day
		375	Can correct others without giving offense
		376	Able to meet emergencies quickly and effectively
		378	Can write a concise, well-organized report
		382	Put drive into the organization
		383	Stimulate the ambition of my associates
		386	Can smooth out tangles and disagreements between people
		388	Discuss my ideals with others
		398	My advice is asked for by many... by few...by almost nobody

	Validation (N=537)		Cross-Validation (N=300)	
	Mean	S.D.	Mean	S.D.
GPA, MSAT, HSR				
First-Year Grade Point				
Average (A=4.0)	2.1	0.8	2.2	0.8
Minnesota Scholastic				
Aptitude Test	44.9	12.0	45.6	11.7
High School Rank	79.5	16.4	78.6	16.9
Minnesota Multiphasic				
Personality Inventory				
Hypochondriasis	48.6	6.2	48.3	6.9
Depression	48.2	8.0	49.2	8.4
Hysteria	54.3	7.3	54.0	8.0
Psychopathic Deviate	57.0	8.9	57.0	9.5
Masculinity-Femininity	48.1	8.7	48.3	9.0
Paranoia	54.8	8.3	55.4	8.7
Psychasthenia	53.4	7.8	54.3	8.2
Schizophrenia	55.0	7.7	55.5	8.3
Hypomania	57.4	9.8	58.0	10.4
Social Introversion	48.8	9.4	50.1	8.3

TABLE 5-38. VALIDITY STATISTICS FOR WOMEN'S OCCUPATIONAL INTROVERSION–EXTROVERSION (OIE) SCALE
(MMPI is the Minnesota Multiphasic Personality Inventory)

		OIE Scale			Correlation with MMPI
Sample	N	Mean	S.D.	Percent Overlap	Social Introversion Scale
Validation					
Introverts	100	61.0	10.2	25	.58
Extroverts	97	38.1	9.7		
Middle	340	48.9	10.1		
Total	537	48.2	9.7		
Cross-Validation					
Introverts	47	58.7	12.7		
Extroverts	34	38.5	8.8	35	.58
Middle	219	49.0	11.0		
Total	300	48.9	12.2		

TABLE 5-39. MEAN SCORES ON THE OCCUPATIONAL INTROVERSION–EXTROVERSION SCALE FOR 86 WOMEN'S OCCUPATIONS

Sewing Machine Operators

Laboratory Technicians

Beauticians/Instrument Assemblers
Artists (1934,1941)/Mathematicians/Math-Science Teachers(1967)/Medical Technologists/Dentists
Math-Science Teachers(1934,1941)/Telephone Operators
Artists(1967)/Licensed Practical Nurses/Radiologic Technologists/Navy-Enlisted
Physical Therapists(1966)/Public Health Nurses/Nurses(1934)/Office Workers/Physicians/Physicians(1934,1941)/Wives-
Animal Husbandry Professors
Housewives/Librarians(1934)/Secretaries(1934,1947)/Wives-Physicists/Chemists/Dental Assistants/Elementary Teachers
Home Economics Teachers(1941)/Nun-Teachers/Occupational Therapists(1942)/H.S. Physical Education Teachers(1967)/
Physicians(1967)/Saleswomen/Secretaries(1967)
Authors/Business Education Teachers(1941)/Dieticians(1941)/Physical Therapists(1957)/Wives-Social Workers/Business
Education Teachers(1967)/Home Economics Teachers(1967)/Registered Nurses/Photographers
English Teachers(1934)/Engineers/Dieticians(1967)/Executive Housekeepers/Translators/Bankwomen/Accountants
Buyers/Music Performers/Visiting Nurses/Art Teachers/Language Teachers/Librarians(1967)/Occupational Therapists(1966)/
Army-Enlisted
H.S. Physical Education Teachers(1939)/Social Science Teachers(1934,1941)/Entertainers/College Physical Ed Teachers(1968)
College Physical Education Teachers(1954)/Interior Decorators/Navy-Officers
Models/Psychologists(1942)/Social Workers/English Teachers(1967)
Newswomen/Music Teachers
Directors, Christian Education/Psychologists(1966)/Social Science Teachers(1967)/Life Insurance Saleswomen(1937,1941)/
Y.W.C.A. Secretaries
Lawyers(1934,1941)/Speech Pathologists/Stewardesses/Lawyers(1967)/Army-Officers
Guidance Counselors
Life Insurance Underwriters(1967)/Y.W.C.A. Staff Members

TABLE 5-40. ITEMS WEIGHTED ON THE WOMEN'S OCCUPATIONAL INTROVERSION–
EXTROVERSION SCALE

Items Weighted Positively (in introversion direction)		Items Weighted Negatively (in extroversion direction)	
Item Number	Item	Item Number	Item
15	Beauty Specialist	18	Buyer of merchandise
72	Nurse	33	Dramatist
259	Determine the cost of building and furnishing the house	35	Editor
		45	Governor of a State
288	Treasurer of a Society	81	Politician
289	Member of a Society	91	Radio Announcer
306	Deal with things vs Deal with people	108	Statistician
322	Present a report in writing vs Present a report verbally	144	Conventions
		145	Formal dress affairs
323	Listening to a story vs Telling a story	155	Financial pages in newspapers
		157	Poetry
330	Going to a play vs Going to a dance	172	Being head of a civic improvement program
		173	Expressing judgments publicly, regardless of what others say
333	A few close friends vs Many acquaintances	181	Interviewing men for a job
		182	Interviewing clients
356	Worry about mistakes a good deal...Very little...Never	184	Making a speech
		187	Organizing a play
		188	Starting a conversation with a stranger
		189	Preparing dinner for guests
		191	Teaching adults
		193	Discussions of politics
		194	Reading editorial columns
		195	Meeting and directing people
		196	Taking responsibility
		198	Adjusting difficulties of others
		200	Acting as cheerleader
		201	Writing reports
		202	Entertaining others
		286	President of a Society
		310	Taking a chance vs Playing safe
		325	Amusement where there is a crowd vs Amusement alone or with one or two others
		331	Thrilling, dangerous activities vs Quieter, safer activities
		334	Usually start activities of my group
		336	Win friends easily
		337	Usually get other people to do what I want done
		339	Usually liven up the group on a dull day
		346	Can correct others without giving offense
		352	Stimulate the ambition of my associates
		354	Can smooth out tangles and disagreements between people
		370	Civics (government)
		372	Dramatics
		375	English Composition
		380	Journalism
		392	Political Science
		394	Public Speaking
		396	Sociology

The lowest scoring occupations are definitely people-oriented, and in a variety of settings—social service, sales, managerial, and legalistic. "Extroverted interests," as reflected by the OIE scale, are found in a wide range of jobs where there are opportunities for a great deal of face-to-face contact with others.

The items weighted on the women's OIE scale are listed in Table 5-40; again inspection of the item content can help understand the meaning of high and low scores.

Scale Name

The name *"Occupational* Introversion-Extroversion" has been chosen for these measures, even though the standardization work was based on the MMPI *Social* Introversion-Extroversion scale, because the emphasis here is on the individual's occupational orientation, and the scale is to be used to help the individual make job-oriented decisions.

Occupational Level Scale (OL—Men)

The Occupational Level (OL) scale was developed by identifying items that differentiated unskilled workers from Strong's 1938 Men-in-General group. A low score indicates interests similar to those of manual laborers; a high score means that the person has responded to the items the way most business and professional men do.

Various proposals have been advanced on the psychological meaning of this scale, including measures of "drive" and "level of aspiration." In an exhaustive survey of the literature, Carkhuff and Drasgow (1963) concluded that the OL scale could most accurately and simply be considered a measure of the "socioeconomic level" of the individual's interests.

Because the OL scale is not an easy scale to interpret, only those who have had considerable experience with the scale should use it. The scale remains on the profile now only because many practitioners have indicated that they find it useful.

Mean scores for all of the men's occupational samples on the OL scale are reported in Table 5-42.

The items on the OL scale are listed in Table 5-41 as an aid in understanding the scale. The scoring weights here are based on those used when the scale was first developed. Those weights, which ranged from plus four to minus four, have been converted to plus or minus one weights as discussed by Strong, Campbell, Berdie, and Clark (1964), essentially by replacing weights of three or four by the weight of one, with the appropriate algebraic sign, and assigning zero weights to the remainder. The revision of these weights, and scoring of all of the occupational samples, was done before the technique of "dimensionalizing" item weights had been developed (see p. 33) and it has not been possible to redo all of this work, using that item weighting technique.

Specialization Level Scale (SL—Men)

The Specialization Level (SL) scale was developed by comparing the SVIB responses of a group of medical specialists with those of a group of

TABLE 5-41. ITEMS WEIGHTED ON THE MEN'S OCCUPATIONAL LEVEL SCALE

Items Weighted Positively		Items Weighted Negatively	
Item Number	Item	Item Number	Item
52	Corporation Lawyer	13	Auto Mechanic
81	Sales Manager	25	City or State Employee
101	Algebra	29	Dentist
107	Calculus	43	Interior Decorator
108	Chemistry	55	Locomotive Engineer
111	Economics	56	Machinist
114	Geology	86	Secret Service Man
120	Mathematics	88	Shop Foreman
126	Philosophy	94	Toolmaker
128	Physics	97	Funeral Director
129	Psychology	100	Worker in YMCA
136	Zoology	139	Hunting
137	Golf	143	Boxing
146	Bridge	153	Amusement Parks
198	Interviewing clients	187	Adjusting a carburetor
206	Meeting and directing people	188	Repairing electrical wiring
207	Taking responsibility	190	Operating machinery
240	Optimists	231	Climbing along the edge of a precipice
287	Sell the machine	241	Pessimists
295	Opportunity to make use of all one's knowledge and experience	274	Socialists
		282	Operate (manipulate) the new machine
299	Freedom in working out one's own methods of doing the work	292	Steadiness and permanence of work
		293	Opportunity for promotion
311	President of a Society or Club	297	Opportunity to understand just how one's superior expects work to be done
328	Develop plans vs Execute plans		
330	Talk others into doing something vs Order others to do something	329	Do a job yourself vs Tell somebody to do the job
333	Activity which produces tangible returns vs Activity which is enjoyed for its own sake	332	Plan for immediate future vs Plan for five years ahead
		335	Definite salary vs Commission on what is done
344	Great variety of work vs Similarity in work	345	Physical activity vs Mental activity
353	Reading a book vs Watching TV or going to a movie	347	Technical responsibility vs Supervisory responsibility
361	Usually start activities of my group	368	Have mechanical ingenuity (inventiveness)
364	Usually get other people to do what I want done	391	Lend money to acquaintances...only certain people...hardly anyone
376	Able to meet emergencies quickly and effectively		
378	Can write a concise, well-organized report		
379	Have good judgment in appraising values		
381	Follow up subordinates effectively		
386	Can smooth out tangles and disagreements between people		
398	My advice is asked for by many... by few...by almost nobody		

doctors-in-general (see Holmen, in Strong and Tucker, 1952). The rationale was that this approach would eliminate the items dealing with medical interests, which both groups would presumably select, and differences in response rate between the two groups would appear on those items relating to the desire to specialize. When the resultant scale was used to score the specialist and the doctors-in-general samples, it distinguished between them moderately well—the overlap was 62 percent. Although this degree of separation was substantially less than that of the average occupational scale, it was high enough to indicate that these groups had somewhat different interests. Further research by Holmen (1954) demonstrated that the

TABLE 5-42. MEAN SCORES ON THE MEN'S OCCUPATIONAL LEVEL SCALE

7	Investment Mgrs
5	
5	
4	
3	
2	
1	Corp Pres(1965)
0	Salesmen,Life(1966)
9	Salesmen,Encyclopedia/Sales Mgrs(1968)/Governors
8	Corp Pres(1935)/Sales Mgrs(1932)/Salesmen,Computer
7	School Supers(1930)
6	Lawyers(1927)/Advertising Men(1931)/Salesmen,Life(1931)/School Supers(1965)/Lawyers(1949)/Bankers(1969)/Lawyers(1969)/Personnel Direcs(1969)/Salesmen,Life(1969)
5	Cham Comm Execs/Personnel Direcs(1927)/CPA(1965)/Football Coaches/Judges/Generals & Admirals
4	Advertising Men(1968)/Dept Store Mgrs
3	Buyers(1946)/Engineers(1928)/Production Mgrs/Salesmen,Real Estate(1932)/Public Admins(1941)/Credit Mgrs/Salesmen,3M applicants/Business School Profs/Psychiatrists(1967)/Public Admins(1969)/Economists/Salesmen,Steel
2	Internists/Accountants/Authors/Rehab Counselors/Purchasing Agents(1931)/Food Scientists/School Supers(1969)/Buyers(1969)/Interior Decorators/Legislators
1	Student Personnel Workers/Mathematicians(1929)/YMCA Secs/Bankers(1934)/Army Officers(1950)/Psychiatrists(1949)/Architects (1933)/Salesmen,3M/Physicians(1969)/Colonels/Army Officers(1969)/Psychologists(1967)
0	Architects(1968)/Chemists(1969)/Guidance Counselors(1968)/Engineers(1968)/Salesmen,Real Estate(1969)/Newsmen/Political Scientists/Danforth Fellows/NIAL Members/Psychologists(1947)/Physicians(1927)/Neurological Surgeons/Pathologists/Psychologists(1949)
9	Bankers(1964)/Pediatricians/Surgeons/Guidance Counselors(1950)/Office Workers/Chemists(1931)/Physicists(1927)/Navy Officers/Petroleum Engineers/Unitarian Ministers(1950)/Mathematicians(1969)/College Profs/Physiatrists/Physicists(1968)/High School Counselors
8	Optometrists/Actors(1937)/Social Workers(1953)/Biologists/CPA(1944)/Physicians(1949)/Funeral Direcs(1945)/Ministers(1927)/Pharmacists(1947)/Air Force Officers/County Welfare Workers/Purchasing Agents(1969)/Social Workers(1967)/Astronauts/Photographers
7	Funeral Direcs(1969)/Dental Educators/Dentists(1969)/Foresters/Anthropologists/Animal Husbandry Profs/Urologists/Radiologists/Music Teachers(1952)/YMCA Staff/Ministers(1965)/Sociologists/Computer Programmers/Pulitzer Prize/Comm Rec Direcs/Unitarian Ministers(1929)
6	Salesmen,PG&E/Interpreters/Orthopedic Surgeons/Psychologists(Exp)/Business Ed Teachers/Osteopaths/Elem Teachers(Minn)/Salesmen,Auto/Teaching Brothers/Chiropractors/Priests/NASA Scientists/Vets(1966)/Actors(1966)/Pharmacists(1968)
5	Ministers(1969)/Astronomers/Artists(1968)/Librarians/Soc Sci Teachers(1936)/YMCA PD
4	Dentists(1932)/Vets(1949)/Forest Service Men/Medical Techs
3	Artists(1933)/Soc Sci Teachers(1969)/Musicians(1969)/Cartographers/Army Sergeants/English Teachers/ Ag Extension Agents/Math-Sci Teachers(1968)
2	Musicians(1952)/Math-Sci Teachers(1936)/Farmers(1936)/Music Teachers(1946)/Physical Therapists(1966)/Mpls Symphony
1	Policemen(1968)/Voc Ag Teachers
0	Physical Therapists(1957)/Pilots
39	Elem Teachers(NDak)/County Sheriffs
38	Policemen(1969)
37	
36	Policemen(1933)/Highway Patrolmen
35	Machinists/Printers/Electricians/Tool & Die Makers/Skilled Tradesmen
34	Carpenters(1969)
33	Carpenters(1936)
32	
31	
30	Farmers(1968)
29	
28	Farmers(1967)

scale also separated Ph.D. chemists from B.A. chemists. Tentatively, the scale may be interpreted as measuring a desire or willingness to narrow one's interests to become a specialist in an occupational field through advanced study.

The medical-specialist criterion groups were used to develop the norms; thus, medical specialists have a standard score mean of 50 and a standard deviation of 10 on the SL scale.

Table 2-9 reports the average score on this scale for each of the occupational criterion groups. Low scores were earned by:

Veterinarians 28
Farmers 31
Carpenters 32
Morticians 32
Real Estate Salesmen............. 28

With the exception of the veterinarians, all of these groups had educational levels only slightly above the high school graduation level.

High average scores on the Specialization Level scale were earned by:

Psychologists 55
Psychiatrists 52
Librarians 52
Biologists 51
Social Workers 51

TABLE 5-43. ITEMS WEIGHTED ON THE MEN'S SPECIALIZATION LEVEL SCALE

Items Weighted Positively		Items Weighted Negatively	
Item Number	Item	Item Number	Item
3	Architect	93	Surgeon
9	Author of novel	192	Giving "first-aid" assistance
10	Author of technical book	250	Religious people
27	College Professor	280	Athletic men
31	Editor	292	Steadiness and permanence of work
66	Orchestra Conductor	317	Chairman, Entertainment Committee
83	Scientific Research Worker	342	Outside work vs Inside work
84	Sculptor		
199	Making a speech		
203	Teaching adults		
206	Meeting and directing people		
209	Adjusting difficulties of others		
212	Doing research work		
215	Writing reports		
241	Pessimists		
251	Irreligious people		
274	Socialists		
296	Opportunity to ask questions and to consult about difficulties		
316	Chairman, Educational Committee		
328	Develop plans vs Execute plans		
338	Work in a large corporation with little chance of becoming president until age 55 vs Work for self in small business		
378	Can write a concise, well-organized report		
382	Put drive into the organization		
383	Stimulate the ambition of my associates		

With few exceptions, the men in each of these groups held at least one advanced degree and many held the Ph.D.

Scores on this scale have some relevance for the student contemplating graduate school, inasmuch as a low score (say, below 35) would not augur well for satisfaction with graduate school experiences.

Items weighted on the SL scale are listed in Table 5-43; they have not been dimensionalized—see explanatory comment above in the OL section.

For further information on the SL scale, see Stewart (1964).

CHAPTER 6

The Administrative Indices

The Need for Error Detection

In the administration, scoring, and utilization of tests, procedural errors can occur and constant attention is necessary to insure accuracy. To this end, several new SVIB scales have been developed to help identify problems. These scales, called Administrative Indices, capitalize on the computer's capacity to process the individual's responses in an almost limitless manner, and their main use will be to identify procedural errors in test administration and scoring. As the widespread use of tests continues, and as more and more agencies install scoring devices, more extensive routine checks are essential. Although all of the scoring agencies use internal quality control checks, the intent here is to provide some routine information, which will be visible on the profile, to reassure the user that correct procedures have been followed.

Mistakes can happen in an infinite number of ways; some possible ones are:

1. The examiner might give the wrong form of the SVIB to the person being tested, especially during the transition period between the old and revised booklets.

2. The examinee might not understand directions, or might inadvertently overlook portions of the inventory. While the test administrator should, and does, catch most of these mistakes, a few may slip by.

3. The examinee might deliberately attempt to create inaccuracy, either by faking his answers in some specific way—and there is no defense against this—or by trying to slip a little bit of chaos into the system. The latter, which usually occurs in research situations, includes the person who simply goes through the inventory answering randomly or in some set pattern such as LID, LID, LID, etc.; another instance would be the pair of identical twins who deliberately gave exactly the same answers. The frequency of these "deliberate chaos" situations is hard to determine, but they turn up in research projects at the rate of 1 in every 5,000 or 10,000 persons tested, and no doubt a few others are undetected.

4. The scoring service might incorrectly score the answer sheet. While a variety of errors can occur in scoring, the most common ones arise at the point where the examinee's answers are transferred from the answer sheet to the scoring machine's internal storage, that is, at the "Read" stage. If the answer sheet has been mishandled, crinkled, soiled, if it has been printed poorly, if the person has not marked his responses carefully, if there are messy erasures—all of these can create problems. Although the scoring services have procedures to detect and remedy such problems, further checks are still useful.

None of the problems described above occur very often and, when they do, they are usually detected. Still, the more checks that are available on the total system performance, the better, and the Administrative Indices have been incorporated into the scoring scheme to insure that each answer sheet receives at least a few basic checks.

Total Responses Index (TR)

This index gives the total number of responses made to the inventory; for the men's form it should be 399, for the women's, 398. If the examinee omits items or makes multiple responses, that will be reflected here (unless, of course, these two errors cancel each other out). Although significant scoring inaccuracy does not occur until 30, 40, or even more items are omitted, it is prudent to explore what has happened whenever this number falls outside of the 390–410 range. (Note: some scoring services record here the number of *legitimate* responses. Multiple responses, i.e., two responses to an item, are illegitimate and consequently are not counted, so the total number of responses can never be more than the total number of items.)

When Forms T399N or TW398N are used, the Total Responses will only be 383 or 382, respectively, because of the layout of the forced choice sections of those booklets.

Form Check Index (FC)

As both the men's and women's SVIB have recently been revised, there is some danger that the old and new versions will become confused, even though there are several safeguards to prevent that. As a further check, this index indicates, with high probability, which form of the booklet the individual responded to. For the men's form, the score pertains to the Form M (1938) versus Form T399 (1966) comparison; for the women's form, Form W (1946) versus Form TW 398 (1969).

This index is based on the items that were changed in the recent revisions. Some of the old and new items had considerably different levels of endorse-

TABLE 6-1. EXAMPLES OF ITEM WEIGHTS ON THE MEN'S FORM CHECK INDEX

ITEM NUMBER	Men-in-General Percent Response			Scoring Weight on Form Check Scale		
	L	I	D	L	I	D
64 old item: "Office Clerk"	7	28	65			
new item: "Psychologist"	50	32	18			
Difference	+43	+04	-47	+1	0	-1
161 old item: "Fortune Tellers"	6	30	64			
new item: "Going to church"	46	34	20			
Difference	+40	+04	-44	+1	0	-1

ment, especially as one reason for replacing the older ones was extreme popularity or unpopularity and those responses showing differences were used in this index. Specifically, when the difference was 40 percent or greater, the response was weighted +1 or −1 as appropriate.

To illustrate the item selection, two examples from the men's booklet are presented in Table 6-1.

The item content of the Form Check Index is completely meaningless; the items were selected solely because they had extremely different popularity rates from those preceding them in the earlier version of the booklet.

Form Check scores are presented in Table 6-2 for a sample of 510 boys who completed the old (Form M) booklet in 1963 as high school seniors and an interim form of the revised (Form T399) booklet in 1964 as entering freshmen at the University of Minnesota; similar data are included in Table 6-2 for a sample of high school senior girls who filled in the old booklet (Form W) and then completed the new one (Form TW398) roughly 8 years later. (The latter group were the subjects in Nolting's research, discussed on p. 176.)

As can be seen in Table 6-2, Form Check raw scores of −8 or below are inevitably associated with the older booklet; scores of −4 or higher, with the revised forms. Scores between these two points are indeterminate.

Before the Form Check score is printed on the profile, a constant of 9 points is added to each score. The effect of this is to convert all scores higher than −9, which are those associated with the revised booklet, T399 or TW398, to positive scores. Lower scores are printed out as negative numbers, and indicate potential problems. As the revised booklets should be used for most routine applications, the Form Check scores should usually be positive. A negative Form Check score indicates that the person probably used the older booklet and, unless there is some particular reason for this, this indicates an error in test administration.

In a few cases, perhaps 1 in 500 or 1,000, an individual will receive a

TABLE 6-2. DISTRIBUTIONS OF RAW SCORES ON THE FORM CHECK INDICES FOR
GROUPS ANSWERING DIFFERENT FORMS OF THE SVIB BOOKLET

	Scores on Men's Form Check Index					Scores on Women's Form Check Index			
Raw Score	Test (Form M) Frequency		Retest (Form T399) Frequency		Raw Scores	Test (Form W) Frequency		Retest (Form TW398) Frequency	
	N	%	N	%		N	%	N	%
*-15	148	29			*-15	149	46	1	--
-14	63	12			-14	32	10		
-13	56	11			-13	26	8		
-12	61	12			-12	40	12		
-11	49	10	1	--	-11	18	6		
-10	54	11	--	--	-10	23	7		
- 9	29	6	1	--	- 9	7	2		
- 8	22	4	1	--	- 8	12	4	1	--
- 7	12	2	2	--	- 7	6	2		
- 6	6	1	8	2	- 6	3	1	2	1
- 5	5	1	14	3	- 5	2	1	2	1
- 4	2	--	22	4	- 4	1	1	4	1
- 3	2	--	34	7	- 3	1	--	5	2
- 2	1	--	47	9	- 2	1	--	5	2
- 1			57	11	- 1			13	4
0			60	12	0			13	4
1			73	14	1			20	6
2			53	10	2			25	8
3			49	10	3			23	7
4			37	7	4			23	7
5			24	5	5			25	8
6			16	3	6			33	10
7			6	1	7			29	9
8			4	1	8			24	7
9			1	--	9			18	6
10					10			19	6
11					11			15	5
12					12			10	3
13					13			11	3
14					14			2	1
15					15			1	--
N	510		510		N	324		324	
Mean	-12.6*		0.5		Mean	-13.8*		5.2	
SD	3.2		3.1		SD	4.1		4.5	

NOTE: Before the FC Index score is profiled, a constant--9 points-- is added;
thus, scores below the dotted line in this table become positive and can
be ignored. Scores above the dotted line remain negative and should be
treated as flags for possible problems. See text for more information.

* Due to a procedural error, all scores ≤ -15 were treated as -15; thus these means
are slightly in error.

negative Form Check score, even though he used the correct booklet. In
checking out such cases, the individual's responses to the items on the Form
Check Index can be studied. For this purpose, those items are listed in
Table 6-3 for the men's, Table 6-4 for the women's. Usually the individual
has marked a very large number of dislikes, and that will trigger off this
index.

Unpopular Index (UNP)

The Unpopular Index contains only those item responses selected by
seven percent or less of the Men-in-General sample or five percent or less of

TABLE 6-3. SCORING WEIGHTS FOR THE MEN'S FORM CHECK INDEX

Old Item (Form M)	Item Number	Weights			New Item (Form T399)
Office Clerk	64	1	0	-1	Psychologist
Driving an automobile	141	-1	0	0	Sketching pictures of wild animals
Collecting postage stamps	150	1	0	0	Camping out
"Rough house" initiations	157	0	0	-1	Jazz concerts
Fortune tellers	161	1	0	-1	Going to church
Museums	164	-1	0	0	Leading a Boy Scout troop
Musical comedy	166	-1	0	0	Science fiction magazines
Snakes	170	1	0	-1	Biographies
Travel movies	183	-1	0	0	Magazines about art and music
Meeting new situations	208	-1	0	0	Making statistical charts
Looking at a collection of rare laces	232	1	0	-1	Discussing the purpose of life
People who borrow things	238	0	0	-1	Aggressive people
Nervous people	257	1	0	0	Babies
Side-show freaks	260	1	0	-1	Outspoken people with new ideas
People who talk very loudly	268	0	0	-1	Republicans
Bolshevists	275	0	0	-1	Nonconformists
Men who use perfume	278	1	0	-1	Prominent businessmen
House to house canvassing vs Retail selling	325	0	0	-1	Taking dancing lessons vs Taking singing lessons
Repair auto vs Drive auto	327	0	0	-1	Repaint autos vs Grease autos
Work which interests you with modest income vs Work which does not interest you with large income	337	-1	0	0	Thrilling, dangerous activities vs Quieter safer activities
Nights spent at home vs Nights away from home	352	0	0	1	Music and art events vs Athletic events
Fat men vs Thin men	357	1	-1	0	Vocational counselor vs Public health officer
Jealous people vs Conceited people	359	0	-1	0	Dog trainer vs Juvenile parole officer
Can carry out plans assigned by other people	370	-1	0	0	Can prepare successful advertisements
Win confidence and loyalty	385	-1	0	1	Am slow-going and sure rather than quick-moving
Usually ignore the feelings of others...Consider them sometimes...Carefully consider them	390	1	0	-1	Worry about mistakes...a good deal...very little. never
Borrow frequently (for personal use)...Borrow occasionally..Practically never borrow	396	1	0	0	In my family, I am the Oldest (or only) child... Youngest...Neither oldest nor youngest

TABLE 6-4. SCORING WEIGHTS FOR THE WOMEN'S FORM CHECK INDEX

Old Item (Form W)	Item Number	Weights			New Item (Form TW398)
Traveling Saleswoman	122	1	0	-1	Travel Bureau Manager
Wife	127	-1	0	1	X-Ray Technician
Dancing	129	-1	0	1	Chess
Musical Comedy	151	-1	0	1	Popular mechanics magazines
Plays	153	-1	0	1	Reading the Bible
"Good Housekeeping" magazine	163	-1	0	1	Making a radio or hi-fi set
"National Geographic Magazine"	166	-1	0	1	Science fiction magazines
"New Republic"	167	-1	0	1	Business methods magazines
"Reader's Digest"	168	-1	0	1	Nightclubs
"True Story" magazine	169	1	0	-1	Church young people's groups
Discussions of economic affairs	192	-1	0	1	Operating office machines
Meeting new situations	197	-1	0	1	Taping a bruised ankle
People who have done you favors	230	-1	1	1	Famous chefs
"Mannish" women	243	1	0	-1	Ballet dancers
Men who are indifferent to you	246	1	-1	1	Athletic men
Nervous people	247	1	0	-1	Babies
Work which interests you with modest income vs Work which does not interest you with large income	312	-1	0	0	Experiment with new beauty preparations vs Experiment with new office equipment
People who are always prompt and expect others to be on time also vs People who are seldom on time and who do not mind if others are late	327	-1	0	1	Spend a great deal of time on make-up before going out vs Go out without make-up
Can carry out plans assigned by other people	341	-1	0	1	Prefer working alone to working on committees
Can discriminate between more or less important matters	342	-1	0	1	Do my best work early in the morning
Am inclined to keep silent (reticent) in confidential and semi-confidential affairs	343	-1	0	1	Can prepare successful advertisements
Get "rattled" easily	348	1	0	-1	My grades in high school were a fairly accurate reflection of my abilities
Win confidence and loyalty	353	-1	0	1	Enjoy tinkering with small hand tools
Borrow frequently (for personal use)...Borrow occasionally...Practically never borrow	359	1	0	-1	In my family, I am the Oldest (or only child... Youngest...Neither youngest nor oldest

the Women-in-General sample; thus, this is an index on which virtually everyone should score very low.

The scoring weights for the Unpopular Indices are all minus 1's. After each person's raw score is calculated, but before it is printed on the profile, a constant—8 points—is added to each score. Because most people choose less than 8 of these responses, most scores will be positive. Frequency distributions for two test-retest samples are listed in Table 6-5, and they demonstrate that almost everyone chooses less than eight of these responses. Anyone who chooses more than eight of these negatively weighted responses will still have, after the constant of 8 is added, a negative score.

A negative Uupopular Index score on the profile indicates something is probably wrong; either the person didn't understand the directions, or was marking randomly, or was using the wrong booklet—any of a number of explanations might be true—and a thorough check should be made. While

TABLE 6-5. DISTRIBUTIONS OF RAW SCORES ON THE UNPOPULAR INDEX FOR TWO MEN'S TEST-RETEST GROUPS

RAW SCORE	Basic Scale Norm Group				High School Seniors--College Freshmen			
	Test (Age 16--Form M)		Retest (Age 52--Form T399)		Test (H. S.--Form M)		Retest (College--Form T399)	
	N	%	N	%	N	%	N	%
0	161	25	326	50	170	33	189	37
-1	157	24	181	28	125	25	161	31
-2	126	19	81	12	91	18	82	16
-3	71	11	36	6	53	10	35	7
-4	56	9	23	4	34	7	22	4
-5	30	5	1	--	20	4	13	3
-6	17	3	1	--	7	1	3	1
-7	9	1	1	--	7	1	3	1
-8	8	1			2	--	1	--
-9	7	1			1	--		
-10	5	1						
-11	2	--						
-13								
-14	1	--						
N	650		650		510		510	
M	-2.1		-0.9		-1.6		-1.2	
SD	2.2		1.1		1.7		1.4	

NOTE: Before profiling, a constant--8 points--is added to each score; thus, scores above the dotted line become positive and can be ignored.

TABLE 6-6. SCORING WEIGHTS FOR THE MEN'S UNPOPULAR INDEX

Item Number	Item	Weights		
97	Funeral Director	-1	0	0
113	Geography	0	0	-1
116	History	0	0	-1
129	Psychology	0	0	-1
182	Educational movies or TV	0	0	-1
207	Taking responsibility	0	0	-1
234	Progressive people	0	0	-1
236	Energetic people	0	0	-1
240	Optimists	0	0	-1
241	Pessimists	-1	0	0
242	People who are natural leaders	0	0	-1
245	People who have made fortunes in business	0	0	-1
271	Fashionably dressed people	0	0	-1
276	Independents in politics	0	0	-1
280	Athletic men	0	0	-1
375	Can correct others without giving offense	0	0	-1
376	Am able to meet emergencies quickly and effectively	0	0	-1
398	My advice is asked for...by many...by few...by almost nobody	0	0	-1

an occasional individual might generate a negative score simply because he has an uncommonly large number of unpopular preferences, the usual explanation will be some flaw in the system.

For help in checking out problem cases, the items on the Unpopular Indices are listed in Tables 6-6 and 6-7.

Like, Indifferent, and Dislike Indices (LP, IP, DP)

Among the Administrative Indices are three that report the percentages of Like, Indifferent, and Dislike responses for the individual; these are based on only his (or her) responses to the job titles in the Occupations section of the booklet: on the men's form, the first 100 items—on the women's, the first 128 items.

Again, the purpose is to provide a rough screen to detect if anything has gone wrong. Inevitably, there will be those psychologists who attribute psychological importance to the percentage of Likes versus Dislikes, or something such, but currently almost nothing is known about this. While the future may prove these indices to have some deeper meaning, especially as they will now be readily available for research, for now they are to be used only to identify situations of doubtful accuracy. If, for example, an individual answers 100 percent of the items "Like," some checking should be done.

These three indices are based on the first 100 items (or 128 for the women) on the booklet, no matter which form is used. If any comparisons are made between groups, the groups must have answered the same form of the booklet for the comparison to be meaningful.

TABLE 6-7. SCORING WEIGHTS FOR THE WOMEN'S UNPOPULAR INDEX

Item Number	Item	Weights		
59	Life Insurance Saleswoman	-1	0	0
125	Waitress	-1	0	0
148	Art galleries	0	0	-1
152	Symphony concerts	0	0	-1
154	Movies	0	0	-1
179	Decorating a room with flowers	0	0	-1
194	Reading editorial columns	0	0	-1
200	Acting as cheer-leader	-1	0	0
212	Contributing to charities	0	0	-1
223	People who are natural leaders	0	0	-1
232	Foreigners	0	0	-1
241	Fashionably dressed people	0	0	-1
255	People who have made fortunes in business	0	0	-1
300	House-to-house canvassing vs Retail selling	-1	0	0
316	Working for men vs Working for women	0	0	-1
347	Able to meet emergencies quickly and effectively	0	0	-1
350	Have good judgment in appraising values	0	0	-1
356	Worry about mistakes...a good deal..very little...never	0	0	-1
361	Make bets...often...sometimes...rarely	-1	0	0
383	Literature	0	0	-1
393	Psychology	0	0	-1

Table 6-8 contains distributions of the Like, Indifferent, and Dislike percentages for 1,214 men tested at age 16 and retested at age 52. These figures demonstrate that there are a few people who choose one response almost exclusively, but they are rare. Most individuals come closer to a 33–33–33 split. Table 6-8 does show a definite tendency for the teenagers to mark "Dislike" more often than the adults (50 vs. 35 percent).

Men (and women) in different occupations do show differing rates of Like, Indifferent, and Dislike responding. Tables 6-9 and 6-10 have the men's occupations rank-ordered according to their Like and Dislike per-

TABLE 6-8. DISTRIBUTIONS OF LIKE, INDIFFERENT, AND DISLIKE RESPONSE PERCENTAGES FOR 1,214 MEN TESTED AT AGE 16 AND RETESTED AT 52

Percentage Interval	Like				Indifferent				Dislike			
	Test		Retest		Test		Retest		Test		Retest	
	N	%	N	%	N	%	N	%	N	%	N	%
90-99	1	0.1	1	0.1	7	0.6	3	0.2	39	3.2	10	0.8
80-89	1	0.1	2	0.2	14	1.2	15	1.2	117	9.6	26	2.1
70-79	2	0.2	6	0.5	35	2.9	42	3.5	121	10.0	34	2.8
60-69	7	0.6	10	0.8	49	4.0	94	7.7	188	15.5	86	7.1
50-59	11	0.9	40	3.3	99	8.2	167	13.8	174	14.3	127	10.5
40-49	43	3.5	111	9.1	142	11.7	272	22.4	150	12.4	185	15.2
30-39	134	11.0	257	21.2	233	19.2	262	21.6	164	13.5	224	18.5
20-29	310	25.5	345	28.4	241	19.9	202	16.6	109	9.0	238	19.6
10-19	428	35.3	341	28.1	217	17.9	104	8.6	84	6.9	169	13.9
0-9	277	22.8	101	8.3	177	14.6	53	4.4	68	5.6	115	9.5
TOTALS	1214	100.0	1214	100.0	1214	100.0	1214	100.0	1214	100.0	1214	100.0
Mean Percent	18.9		25.7		30.4		39.1		50.0		35.2	
S.D.		11.9		13.3		19.5		17.5		23.9		20.0	

TABLE 6-9. MEAN PERCENT "LIKE" RESPONSES ON FIRST 100 ITEMS FOR MEN

```
41  Policemen(1968)/Dept Store Mgrs
40
39  Salesmen,3M/Salesmen,3M applicants
38  Salesmen,Computer
37
36  Personnel Direcs(1969)
35  Comm Rec Direcs/Elem Teachers(Minn)/Business Ed Teachers/Rehab Counselors/Guidance Counselors(1968)/High School Counselo
34  Machinists/YMCA Staff/Air Force Officers/Food Scientists/Physical Therapists(1966)/Policemen(1969)/Soc Sci Teachers(1969
    County Sheriffs/Public Admins(1969)/Salesmen,Steel/Ministers(1969)/Ag Extension Agents
33  Elem Teachers(NDak)/Army Officers(1950)/Credit Mgrs/School Supers(1969)/Purchasing Agents(1969)/Army Officers(1969)/
    Legislators/English Teachers/Engineers(1968)/Salesmen,Encyclopedia/Physiatrists
32  Navy Officers/Computer Programmers/Football Coaches/Neurological Surgeons/Cham Comm Execs/Physical Therapists(1957)/
    Advertising Men(1968)/Teaching Brothers/Sales Mgrs(1968)/Psychologists(1967)/Social Workers(1967)/Highway Patrolmen/
    Actors(1966)/Pharmacists(1968)
31  Ministers(1965)/Orthopedic Surgeons/Unitarian Ministers(1950)/County Welfare Workers/Medical Techs/Physicians(1969)/
    Psychiatrists(1967)/Salesmen,Life(1969)/Cartographers/Tool & Die Makers/Voc Ag Teachers/NASA Scientists/Math-Sci Teacher
    (1968)/Salesmen,Life(1966)
30  Petroleum Engineers/School Supers(1965)/Student Personnel Workers/Optometrists/Psychologists(1947)/Salesmen,PG&E/Urologi
    Radiologists/Social Workers(1953)/Guidance Counselors(1950)/Funeral Direcs(1969)/Dental Educators/Dentists(1969)/
    Chiropractors/Buyers(1969)/Priests/Generals & Admirals
29  Chemists(1969)/Lawyers(1969)/Salesmen,Real Estate(1969)/Army Sergeants/Foresters/College Profs/Musicians(1969)/Judges/
    Danforth Fellows
28  CPA(1965)/Sociologists/Pediatricians/Psychologists(1949)/Psychologists(Exp)/CPA(1944)/Librarians/Math-Sci Teachers(1936)
    Pilots/Psychiatrists(1949)/Public Admins(1941)/Business School Profs/Investment Mgrs/Skilled Tradesmen/Colonels/Newsmen/
    Political Scientists/Economists/Astronauts
27  Bankers(1964)/Surgeons/Music Teachers(1952)/Office Workers/Policemen(1933)/Soc Sci Teachers(1936)/Personnel Direcs(1927)
    Bankers(1969)/Electricians/Animal Husbandry Profs/Vets(1966)/Governors/Mpls Symphony
26  Buyers(1946)/Interpreters/Biologists/Osteopaths/YMCA PD/YMCA Secs/Accountants/Printers/Architects(1968)/Astronomers/
    Photographers/Physicists(1968)
25  Corp Pres(1965)/Internists/Pathologists/Chemists(1931)/Funeral Direcs(1945)/Ministers(1927)/Pharmacists(1947)/Music
    Teachers(1946)/Mathematicians(1969)/Anthropologists/Interior Decorators
24  Farmers(1967)/Musicians(1952)/Production Mgrs/Carpenters(1936)/Salesmen,Auto/Lawyers(1949)/Carpenters(1969)
23  Physicians(1949)/Sales Mgrs(1932)/Purchasing Agents(1931)/Unitarian Ministers(1929)/Artists(1968)
22  Pulitzer Prize/Actors(1937)/Engineers(1928)/Dentists(1932)/Corp Pres(1935)/School Supers(1930)/Advertising Men(1931)/Vet
    (1949)/Salesmen,Real Estate(1932)/Salesmen,Life(1931)/Farmers(1968)/NIAL Members/Forest Service Men
21  Physicists(1927)/Bankers(1934)/Farmers(1936)
20  Mathematicians(1929)/Architects(1933)
19  Physicians(1927)/Lawyers(1927)
18  Artists(1933)/Authors
```

```
55  Authors
54  Artists(1933)
53  NIAL Members
52
51
50
49  Physicians(1927)/Lawyers(1927)/Physicists(1927)
48  Actors(1937)/Advertising Men(1931)/Mathematicians(1929)
47  Artists(1968)/Corp Pres(1935)/Salesmen,Real Estate(1932)/Architects(1933)
46  Pulitzer Prize/Engineers(1928)/Sales Mgrs(1932)/Salesmen,Life(1931)
45  Anthropologists/Interior Decorators/Photographers/Farmers(1967)
44  Purchasing Agents(1931)
43  Pathologists/Dentists(1932)/Chemists(1931)/Mathematicians(1969)
42  Farmers(1968)/Actors(1966)/Internists/Physicians(1949)/Vets(1949)/Funeral Direcs(1945)/Pharmacists(1947)/Lawyers(1949)
41  Investment Mgrs/Political Scientists/Danforth Fellows/Physicists(1968)/Buyers(1946)/Surgeons/Production Mgrs/Bankers
    (1934)/Farmers(1936)
40  College Profs/Newsmen/Psychologists(1947)/Psychologists(1949)/Psychologists(Exp)/Musicians(1952)/Biologists/Carpenters
    (1936)/Forest Service Men/Salesmen,Auto/Unitarian Ministers(1929)
39  Corp Pres(1965)/Osteopaths/Pilots/Astronomers/Economists/Salesmen,Life(1966)/Mpls Symphony
38  Student Personnel Workers/Interpreters/School Supers(1930)/Accountants/Psychiatrists(1949)/Bankers(1969)/Carpenters(1969
    Psychologists(1967)/NASA Scientists/Judges/Governors
37  Architects(1968)/Business School Profs/Psychiatrists(1967)/Personnel Direcs(1927)
36  Chemists(1969)/Lawyers(1969)/Salesmen,Life(1969)/Teaching Brothers/Dentists(1969)/Musicians(1969)/Advertising Men(1968)/
    Music Teachers(1952)/CPA(1944)/Office Workers/Printers/Rehab Counselors/Public Admins(1941)
35  Salesmen,PG&E/Bankers(1964)/Radiologists/Policemen(1933)/Food Scientists/Salesmen,Real Estate(1969)/Colonels/Animal
    Husbandry Profs/Engineers(1968)/Astronauts
34  Personnel Direcs(1969)/Physicians(1969)/Dental Educators/Foresters/Skilled Tradesmen/Buyers(1969)/Electricians/Vets(1966
    Salesmen,Encyclopedia/Sociologists/Urologists/Librarians/YMCA PD/Unitarian Ministers(1950)/Music Teachers(1946)
33  High School Counselors/Pediatricians/Neurological Surgeons/Social Workers(1953)/Cham Comm Execs/Guidance Counselors(1950
32  Generals & Admirals/Salesmen,Steel/Funeral Direcs(1969)/Guidance Counselors(1968)/County Sheriffs/Sales Mgrs(1968)/Army
    Sergeants/Army Officers(1969)/Priests/Social Workers(1967)/Petroleum Engineers/CPA(1965)/Optometrists/YMCA Staff/Soc Sci
    Teachers(1936)
31  Dept Store Mgrs/Public Admins(1969)/Tool & Die Makers/Math-Sci Teachers(1968)/Computer Programmers/Football Coaches/
    Machinists/Army Officers(1950)/Salesmen,3M applicants
30  Navy Officers/Math-Sci Teachers(1936)/Ministers(1927)/Medical Techs/School Supers(1969)/Chiropractors
29  Purchasing Agents(1969)/English Teachers/Elem Teachers(NDak)/Orthopedic Surgeons/Physical Therapists(1957)/YMCA Secs/
    Credit Mgrs/Air Force Officers/Salesmen,3M/County Welfare Workers
28  Soc Sci Teachers(1969)/Cartographers/Voc Ag Teachers/Ag Extension Agents/Physiatrists/Pharmacists(1968)/School Supers
    (1965)/Elem Teachers(Minn)
27  Ministers(1969)/Highway Patrolmen/Salesmen,Computer/Ministers(1965)/Business Ed Teachers
26  Physical Therapists(1966)/Policemen(1969)/Legislators
25
24
23  Comm Rec Direcs
22  Policemen(1968)
```

TABLE 6-11. MEAN PERCENT "LIKE" RESPONSES ON FIRST 128 ITEMS FOR WOMEN

42 Stewardesses
41
40
39
38
37
36 Guidance Counselors
35 YWCA Staff/Home Economics Teachers (1967)
34 Occupational Therapists/Business Education Teachers (1967)/Saleswomen/Director, Christian Education
   Dental Assistants
33 Wives-Social Workers/Secretaries (1967)/Telephone Operators/Elementary Teachers/Army Enlisted
   Business Education Teachers (1941)/Exec Housekeepers/Army Officers/County Welfare Workers
32 Wives-Animal Husbandry Professors/Psychologists (1966)/Psychologists (1942)/Visiting Nurses/Public
   Health Nurses/Licensed Practical Nurses/Registered Nurses/Radiologic Technologists/Physical Therapists(1966)
   Dietitians (1967)/Nun-Teachers/Social Science Teachers/Entertainers
31 Home Economics Teachers (1941)/Art Teachers/Language Teachers/HS PE Teachers (1939)/Nongrads/HS PE Teachers (1967)
   Dietitians (1941)/Secretaries (1934)/Social Workers
30 Engineers/Physical Therapists (1957)/Speech Pathologists/Occupational Therapists (1942)/YWCA Staff (1934)/Grads
   Office Workers (1947)/Newswomen/Librarians (1967)/Math-Science Teachers (1967)/Social Science Teachers (1934)
   Instrument Assemblers/Medical Technologists
29 Nurses (1934)/Physician (Western Reserve)/Music Teachers/Musician Performers/English Teachers (1934)
   Lawyers (1934)/Wives-Physicists/Sewing Machine Operators/Life Underwriters/Translators/Beauticians/Models
   College PE Teachers (1954)/Math-Science Teachers (1934)
28 Housewives/Lab Technicians/Navy Enlisted/Lawyers (1967)/Physicians (1967)/Buyers/Navy Officers
27 Dentists/Life Ins Sales (1937)/Interior Decorators
26 Chemists
25 Physicians (1934)/Authors (1934)
24
23 Photographers/Librarians (1934)/Artists (1934)
22 Artists (1967)
21 Mathematicians

TABLE 6-12. MEAN PERCENT "DISLIKE" RESPONSES ON FIRST 128 ITEMS FOR WOMEN

57 Artists (1967)
56
55
54
53 Photographers
52 Artists (1934)
51 Authors
50
49 Mathematicians
48
47
46 Librarians
45 Newswomen/Interior Decorators
44 Chemists/Physicians (Western Reserve)/Physicians (1934)/Models
43 Physicians (1967)/Navy Officers/Psychologists (1966)/Life Underwriters/Translators/
42 Lawyers (1967)
41 Public Health Nurses/Sewing Machine Operators/Speech Pathologists/Librarians (1967)/Beauticians/Wives-Physicists
40 Entertainers/Life Insurance Sales (1937)/Dentists/Navy Enlisted
39 Nun-Teachers/Buyers/Lab Technicians/English Teachers (1934)/Music Teachers/Musician Performers
38 College PE Teachers (1954)/Psychologists (1942)/Language Teachers/Lawyers (1934)/Medical Technologists
   Art Teachers/Dietitians (1967)/Math-Science Teachers (1967)
37 Social Workers/Instrument Assemblers/HS PE Teachers (1939)/Radiologic Technologists/Social Science Teachers
   Dietitians (1941)/Math-Science Teachers (1934)/Grads/County Welfare Workers/Social Science Teachers (1967)
   Nurses (1934)
36 English Teachers (1967)/Office Workers (1947)/Wives-Animal Husbandry Professors/Guidance Counselors
   Secretaries (1934)/Engineers/Physical Therapists/Registered Nurses/Nongrads/Occupational Therapists (1966)
   Army Enlisted
35 Army Officers/Wives-Social Workers/Directors, Christian Education/Exec Housekeepers/Secretaries (1967)
   Visiting Nurses
34 YWCA Staff/Home Economics Teachers (1967)/Elementary Teachers/Physical Therapists (1966)/YWCA Staff (1934)
33 Housewives/Business Education Teachers (1941)/Licensed Practical Nurses/Occupational Therapists (1966)
   Dental Assistants/Business Education Teachers (1967)
32 Telephone Operators
31 Saleswomen
30 HS PE Teachers (1939)
29 Stewardesses

PROFILE— STRONG VOCATIONAL INTEREST BLANK —FOR MEN (Form T399)

BASIC INTEREST SCALES

SCALE	All L	I	D
PUBLIC SPEAKING	74	54	33
LAW/POLITICS	68	53	39
BUSINESS MANAGEMENT	68	48	28
SALES	75	57	40
MERCHANDISING	72	51	29
OFFICE PRACTICES	77	56	35
MILITARY ACTIVITIES	70	53	37
TECHNICAL SUPERVISION	62	49	36
MATHEMATICS	61	43	25
SCIENCE	65	46	27
MECHANICAL	69	46	22
NATURE	61	44	28
AGRICULTURE	62	47	31
ADVENTURE	76	51	25
RECREATIONAL LEADERSHIP	65	46	28
MEDICAL SERVICE	71	50	29
SOCIAL SERVICE	69	53	37
RELIGIOUS ACTIVITIES	74	53	32
TEACHING	72	50	29
MUSIC	73	51	30
ART	73	52	31
WRITING	71	51	31

DOUBLE LINE = AVERAGE SCORE FOR 650 52-YEAR-OLD MEN

OCCUPATIONAL SCALES

	OCCUPATION	L	I	D
I	DENTIST	17	27	46
	OSTEOPATH	41	15	27
	VETERINARIAN	20	29	40
	PHYSICIAN	26	19	35
	PSYCHIATRIST	42	6	10
	PSYCHOLOGIST	28	19	30
	BIOLOGIST	20	13	32
II	ARCHITECT	6	22	51
	MATHEMATICIAN	4	15	48
	PHYSICIST	9	6	40
	CHEMIST	22	12	31
	ENGINEER	18	18	39
III	PRODUCTION	40	23	32
	ARMY OFFICER	55	13	-11
	AIR FORCE OFFICER	61	18	-5
IV	CARPENTER	14	32	40
	FOREST SERVICE MAN	29	20	10
	FARMER	18	41	51
	MATH-SCIENCE TEACHER	48	39	19
	PRINTER	24	49	45
	POLICEMAN	42	16	13
V	PERSONNEL DIRECTOR	58	14	4
	PUBLIC ADMINISTRATOR	66	19	0
	REHABILITATION COUNS.	62	13	4
	YMCA STAFF MEMBER	57	18	-1
	SOCIAL WORKER	55	22	0
	SOCIAL SCIENCE TEACHER	43	37	21
	SCHOOL SUPERINTENDENT	41	8	15
	MINISTER	39	10	3
VI	LIBRARIAN	28	32	32
	ARTIST	10	22	57
	MUSICIAN PERFORMER	30	35	48
	MUSIC TEACHER	36	26	27
VII	C.P.A. OWNER	30	14	32
VIII	SENIOR C.P.A.	29	29	21
	ACCOUNTANT	45	24	19
	OFFICEWORKER	49	32	22
	PURCHASING AGENT	24	33	57
	BANKER	25	28	42
	PHARMACIST	31	23	43
	FUNERAL DIRECTOR	27	26	48
IX	SALES MANAGER	30	25	40
	REAL ESTATE SALESMAN	28	32	53
	LIFE INS. SALESMAN	27	23	45
X	ADVERTISING MAN	14	25	60
	LAWYER	20	20	49
	AUTHOR-JOURNALIST	17	24	59
XI	PRESIDENT-MFG.	19	17	47
	SUPP. OCCUPATIONAL SCALES			
	CREDIT MANAGER	60	33	2
	CHAMBER OF COM. EXEC.	54	28	16
	PHYSICAL THERAPIST	65	28	-3
	COMPUTER PROGRAMMER	56	13	4
	BUSINESS ED. TEACHER	62	32	10
	COMMUNITY REC. ADMIN.	53	21	-4

NON-OCCUPATIONAL SCALES

	AACH	AR	DIV	MFII	MO	OIE	OL	SL
L	60	49	91	36	48	23	60	54
I	33	29	48	62	24	49	33	41
D	21	30	5	57	23	87	61	18

ADMINISTRATIVE INDICES

	TR	UNP	FC	LP	IP	DP
L	399	6	12	100	0	0
I	399	8	7	0	100	0
D	399	-8	-2	0	0	100

FIG. 6-1. *Mean scores on men's profile for answer sheets marked all "Like," all "Indifferent," or all "Dislike."*

PROFILE— STRONG VOCATIONAL INTEREST BLANK —FOR WOMEN (Form TW398)

BASIC INTEREST SCALES

SCALE	L	I	D
PUBLIC SPEAKING	72	50	27
LAW/POLITICS	73	53	32
MERCHANDISING	72	52	31
OFFICE PRACTICES	75	56	37
NUMBERS	72	54	35
PHYSICAL SCIENCE	72	51	29
MECHANICAL	75	54	33
OUTDOORS	68	46	23
BIOLOGICAL SCIENCE	67	50	33
MEDICAL SERVICE	73	51	30
TEACHING	70	50	30
SOCIAL SERVICE	72	52	32
SPORTS	69	46	24
HOMEMAKING	67	45	24
RELIGIOUS ACTIVITIES	65	46	27
MUSIC	63	44	24
ART	64	45	26
PERFORMING ARTS	67	48	28
WRITING	66	47	28

DOUBLE LINE = AVERAGE SCORE FOR 1000 EMPLOYED ADULT WOMEN

OCCUPATIONAL SCALES

	OCCUPATION	L	I	D
I	MUSIC TEACHER	42	2	2
	ENTERTAINER	34	14	23
	MUSICIAN PERFORMER	35	16	17
	MODEL	11	20	45
II	ART TEACHER	31	0	-8
	ARTIST	0	11	52
	INTERIOR DECORATOR	5	6	27
III	NEWSWOMAN	17	11	39
	ENGLISH TEACHER	41	12	12
	LANGUAGE TEACHER	26	15	24
IV	YWCA STAFF MEMBER	50	21	13
	RECREATION LEADER	67	22	-3
	DIRECTOR, CHRISTIAN ED.	40	2	0
	NUN-TEACHER	30	3	14
	GUIDANCE COUNSELOR	57	7	-5
	SOCIAL SCIENCE TEACHER	48	18	15
	SOCIAL WORKER	59	13	8
V	SPEECH PATHOLOGIST	21	19	29
	PSYCHOLOGIST	23	0	12
	LIBRARIAN	27	21	29
	TRANSLATOR	20	21	38
VI	PHYSICIAN	24	19	30
	DENTIST	30	25	33
	MEDICAL TECHNOLOGIST	45	31	23
	CHEMIST	22	7	11
	MATHEMATICIAN	1	19	38
	COMPUTER PROGRAMMER	35	37	27
	MATH-SCIENCE TEACHER	39	38	37
	ENGINEER	43	33	17
VII	ARMY-ENLISTED	46	47	43
	NAVY-ENLISTED	29	50	52
	ARMY-OFFICER	52	36	17
	NAVY-OFFICER	26	38	50
VIII	LAWYER	25	24	35
	ACCOUNTANT	31	30	34
	BANKWOMAN	41	34	36
	LIFE INS. UNDERWRITER	28	21	35
	BUYER	29	13	30
	BUSINESS ED. TEACHER	39	27	23
IX	HOME ECON. TEACHER	52	11	-4
	DIETITIAN	64	23	5
X	PHYSICAL ED. TEACHER	38	31	28
	OCCUPATIONAL THERAPIST	64	25	-3
	PHYSICAL THERAPIST	60	35	11
	PUBLIC HEALTH NURSE	41	13	13
	REGISTERED NURSE	53	23	1
	LIC. PRACTICAL NURSE	54	33	10
	RADIOLOGIC TECHNOLOGIST	57	38	22
	DENTAL ASSISTANT	53	36	15
XI	EXECUTIVE HOUSEKEEPER	58	24	8
	ELEMENTARY TEACHER	28	47	42
	SECRETARY	60	33	12
	SALESWOMAN	43	38	31
	TELEPHONE OPERATOR	52	32	11
	INSTRUMENT ASSEMBLER	25	26	36
	SEWING MACHINE OPERATOR	47	38	17
	BEAUTICIAN	24	36	22
	AIRLINE STEWARDESS	65	13	-5

NON-OCCUPATIONAL SCALES

	AACH	DIV	FMII	OIE
L	57	87	48	29
I	46	47	20	53
D	27	7	25	83

ADMINISTRATIVE INDICES

	TR	UNP	FC	LP	IP	DP
L	398	3	-1	100	0	0
I	398	8	9	0	100	0
D	398	8	19	0	0	100

FIG. 6-2. *Mean scores on women's profile for answer sheets marked all "Like," all "Indifferent," or all "Dislike."*

centage responses (the Indifferent percentages have not been presented here as they are simply 100 minus the Like and Dislike percentages); Tables 6-11 and 6-12 contain the same information for the women's occupations.

There was a considerable range in these percentages; compare, for example, the Stewardesses 42 percent Likes with the Mathematicians 21 percent. How much of this difference is due to some response set—a general tendency to say "Like"—and how much is due to item content is impossible to tell.

Profiles for Answer Sheets Marked All Like, All Indifferent, or All Dislike

Figures 6-1 and 6-2 show the scale scores on the men's and women's profiles that result when answer sheets are marked with all L's, all I's, or all D's.

For the Basic Scales, with a few exceptions, the "L" score represents the maximum, the "D" score the minimum possible scores. The exceptions are those few scales that have a few negative weights on the "L" response and positive weights on the "D" response.

A Final Note

The Administrative Indices cannot identify every problem that may arise, but they will provide a constant systematic check that will detect some cases of faulty performance. Some experience with them will be necessary before exact procedures can be specified, and this experience will probably suggest new methods of error detection. This is one area where test constructors have not kept pace with their machinery. Many more checking operations could be routinely performed by machine, and the net effect should be a more accurate, dependable system.

CHAPTER 7

The Interests of Outstanding Men

The Interest Archives

The University of Minnesota has established a program, entitled "The Interest Archives," to collect and preserve for posterity some information on the vocational interests of the outstanding people of our time.

The impetus for this project came from Professor Strong's files. Shortly before his death in 1963, his records—22 filing cabinets full—were shipped to Minnesota. When these were being inventoried, several documents emerged that had historic as well as scientific value, for example, the SVIB booklets completed by H. L. Mencken and Edna St. Vincent Millay. Those and similar ones were separated for special attention, and "The Interest Archives" were born. Many other prominent individuals have since been asked to participate by filling in the SVIB, and hundreds have. The mean SVIB profiles for some of these groups are presented below.

The issue of the individual's privacy is an important one here. Psychological tests have been severely criticized in recent years, and some of these criticisms are valid. One concern has been that test results might be used to the individual's disadvantage in ways that he had never anticipated. Although situations where an individual's SVIB profile could be used to his detriment are not likely, several safeguards are used here to avoid any possibility whatsoever of this. The individual has complete veto power over the publication of his own results; the files are maintained only by occupational category such as "scientist" or "corporation president"; there has been no attempt to make them into a data bank with all sorts of access (for example, to sort out all of the men with, say, a low MF score is impossible); the names have been removed from the working files, and the inventories are listed by code number only.

A central protection is that the individual's dignity is the paramount concern. No research purpose is important enough to single out anyone in an embarrassing manner. Most psychologists feel much more strongly about this than does the man-in-the-street; the American Psychological Association's Code of Ethics reflects this, and that policy is stringently followed with these data.

Finally, the potential for embarrassment is not very great. Men and women are open about their interests and the "measurement of interests" is a less threatening activity to the layman than the "measurement of IQ or personality." Most men, if they have the time, are willing to fill in the SVIB and few of them are secretive about their profile.

An example of this was the publication of the individual profiles for 50 past presidents of the American Psychological Association in the *American Psychologist* (Campbell, 1965*b*). All of those still living were asked for their permission to do this and none refused. Most of them were quite interested in the report and very willing to have their profiles published. This has been, as far as I can determine, the only time that any psychological test results have ever been published, specifically identifying the man's name, and there has been no negative reaction. Again, I believe this is because vocational interests are less threatening and more understandable than other constructs used in psychological assessment.

In the following figures, mean SVIB profiles are presented for 22 samples of outstanding men, including the APA presidents. The main reason for including these data here is that they are, of course, inherently interesting. To note, for example, that the astronauts scored highest on the Adventure scale is fascinating; to note that the prominent authors, who vicariously relate the escapes of others, scored lowest is wryly amusing; and to note that the McKnight Fellows (actors at the Tyrone Guthrie Theater) scored next to highest is perplexing—astronauts and actors?—an unlikely combination.

Each of the following samples has its unique characteristics and the reader should look over each profile, paying especial attention to the high and low scores for each group. A brief description of each sample follows, and, clearly, all of the men in each of these samples have achieved notable success in their chosen fields.

Brief Descriptions of the Samples and Their SVIB Profiles

Artists (N = 12). All hold membership in the National Institute of Arts and Letters, which is perhaps the most prestigious artistic organization in the United States.

Astronauts (N = 22). Mostly military officers with strong technical backgrounds. All have survived a rigorous selection procedure.

Authors. Poets (N = 10), Novelists and Biographers (N = 26). All have

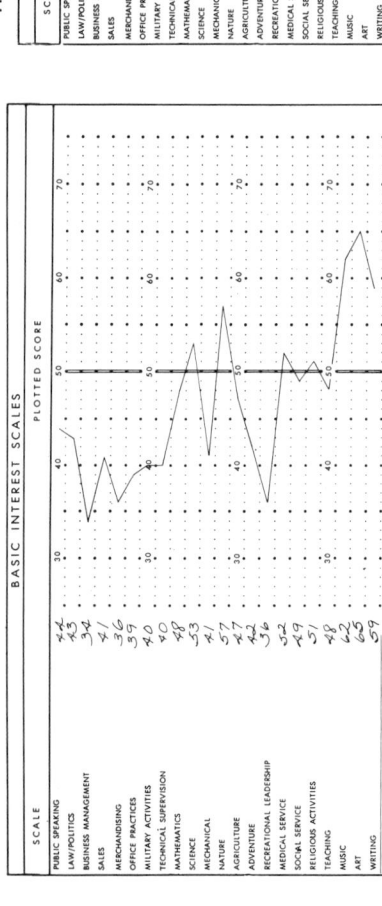

FIG. 7-1. *Mean SVIB profile for 12 prominent artists.*

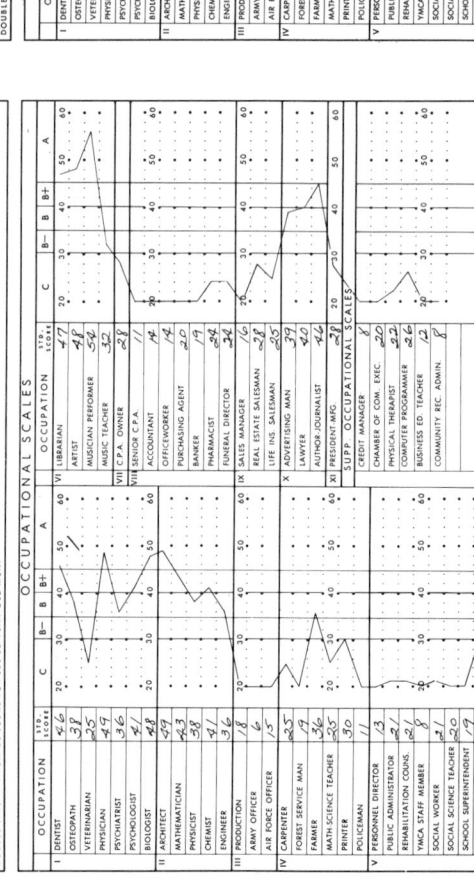

FIG. 7-2. *Mean SVIB profile for 22 astronauts.*

262

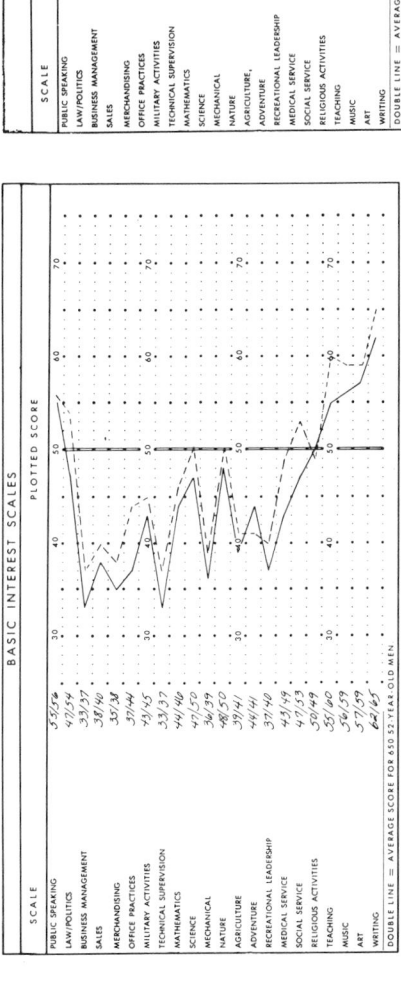

FIG. 7-3. Mean SVIB profile for Pulitzer Prize winning authors: 10 poets (solid line); 26 novelists and biographers (broken line).

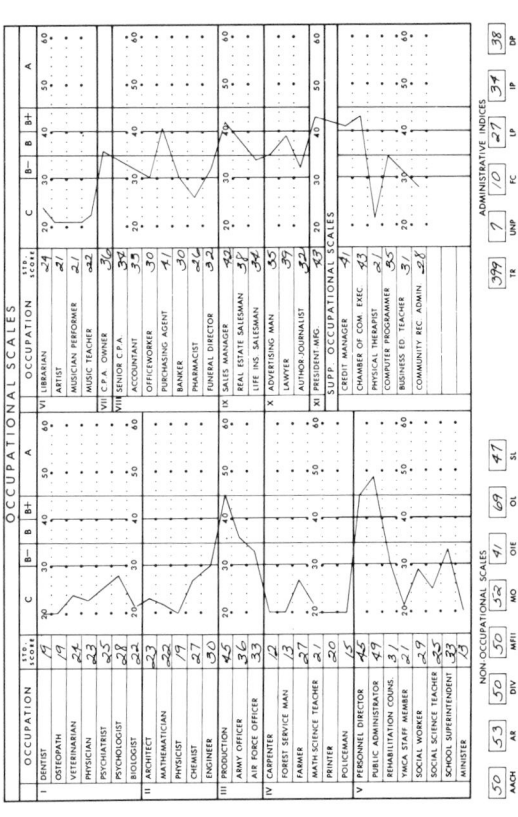

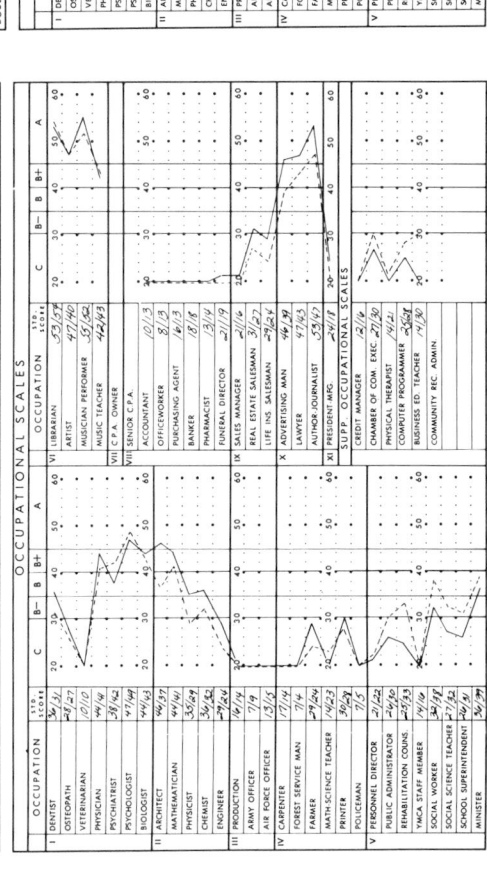

FIG. 7-4. Mean SVIB profile for 16 corporation presidents.

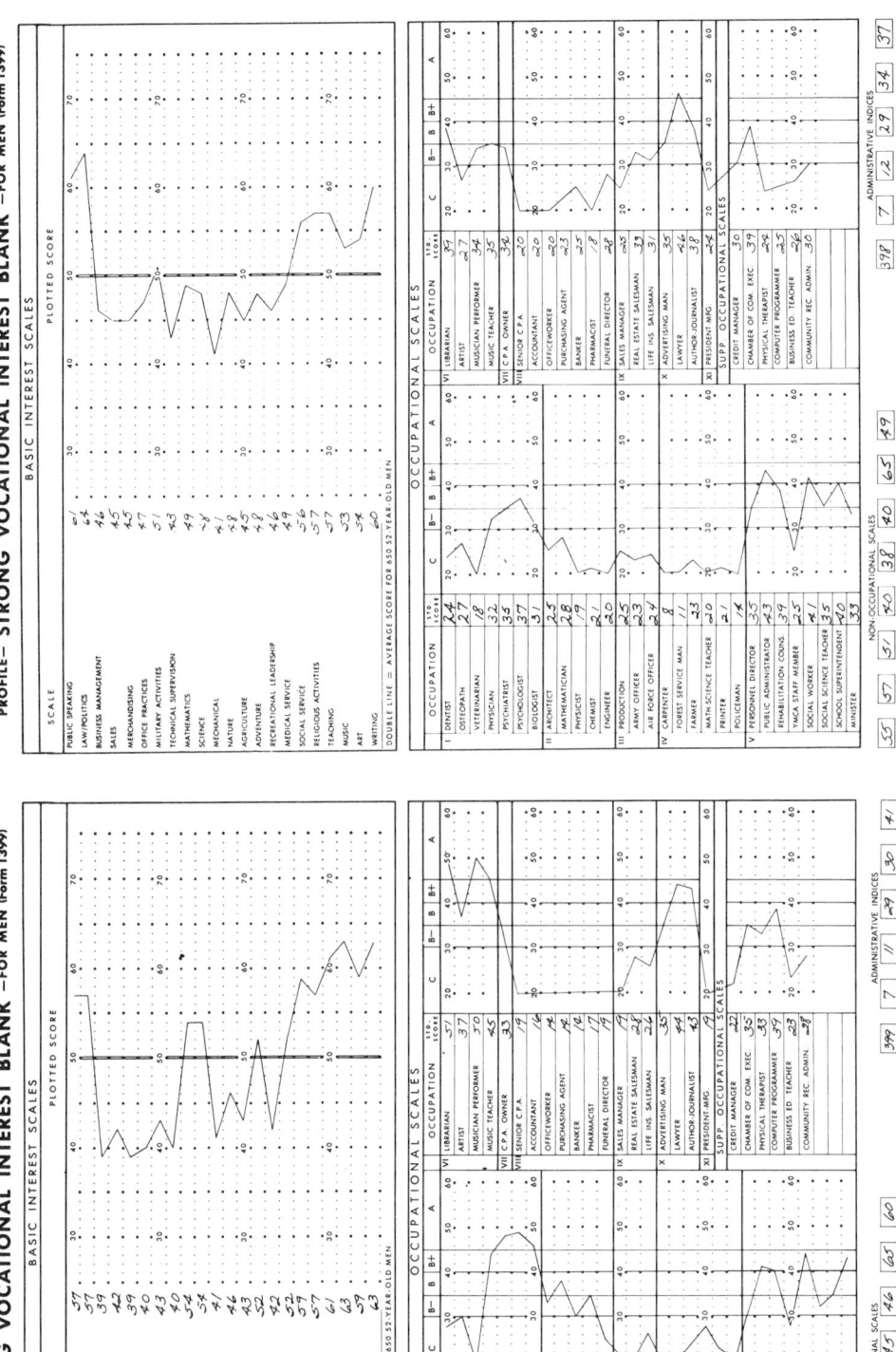

FIG. 7-5. Mean SVIB profile for 91 Danforth Fellows.

FIG. 7-6. Mean SVIB profile for 132 federal judges.

PROFILE— **STRONG VOCATIONAL INTEREST BLANK** —FOR MEN (Form T399)

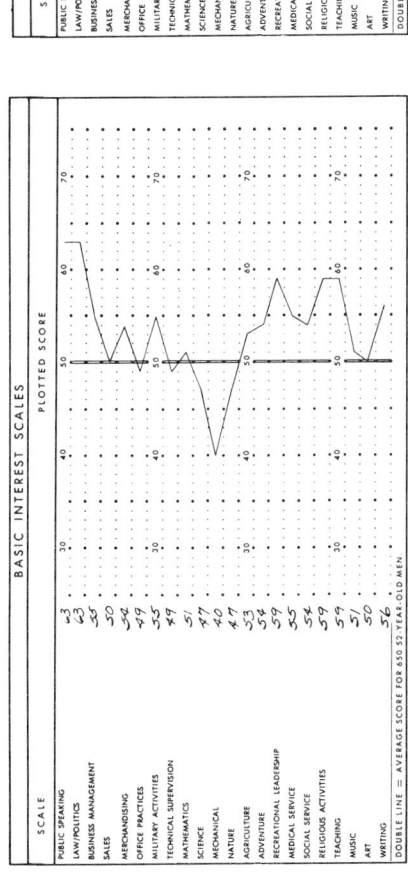

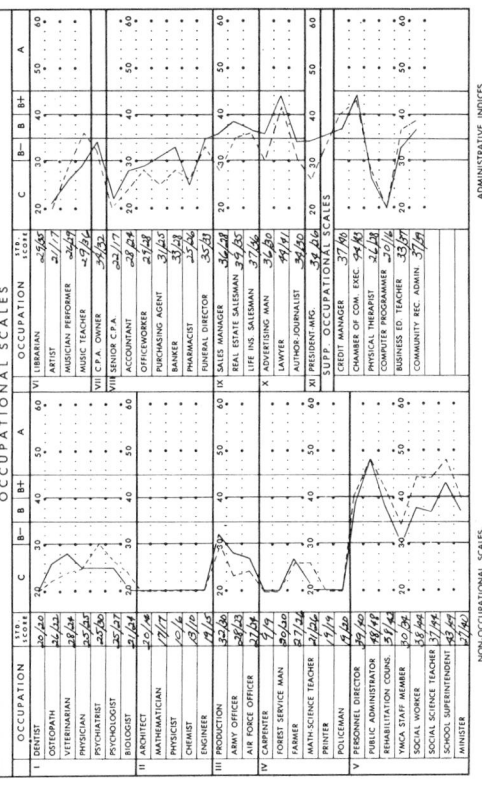

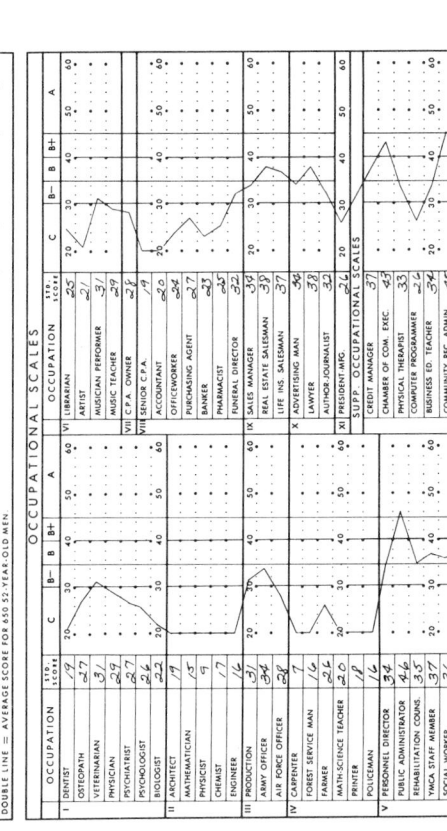

FIG. 7-7. *Mean SVIB profile for 13 top college football coaches.*

FIG. 7-8. *Mean SVIB profile for state governors: 8 Minnesota (broken line) and 38 others (solid line).*

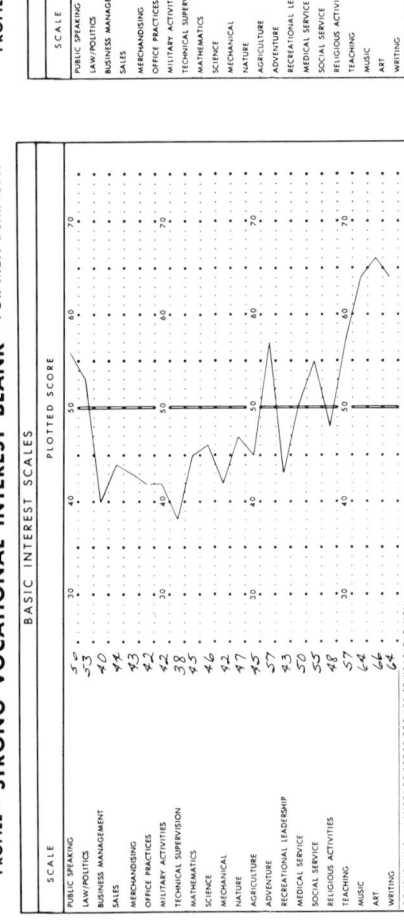

PROFILE— STRONG VOCATIONAL INTEREST BLANK —FOR MEN (Form T399)

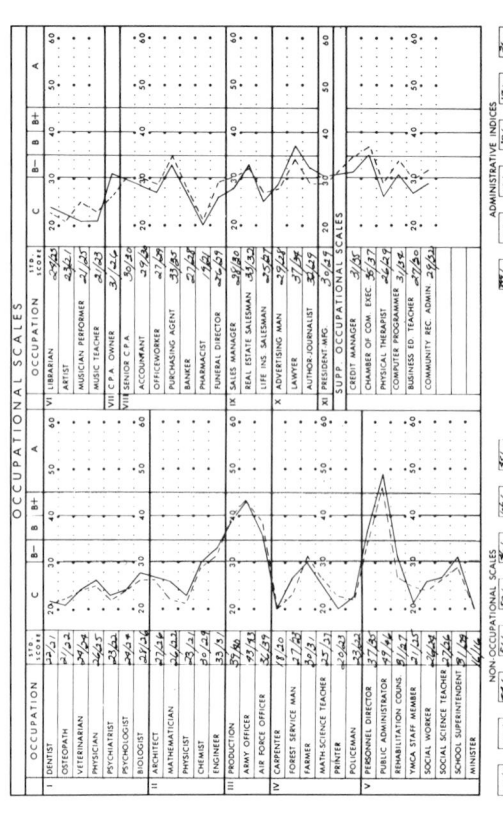

PROFILE— STRONG VOCATIONAL INTEREST BLANK —FOR MEN (Form T399)

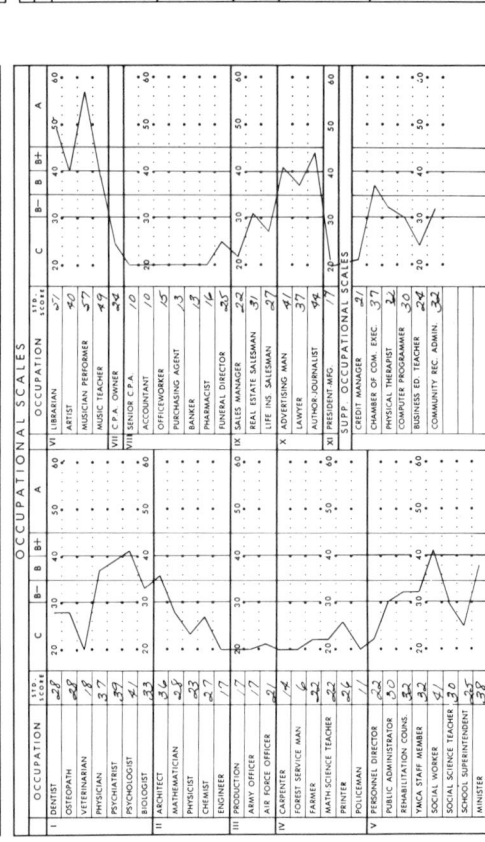

FIG. 7-9. Mean SVIB profile for 43 McKnight Fellows (actors).

FIG. 7-10. Mean SVIB profile for military officers: 91 generals (solid line) and 91 colonels (broken line).

266

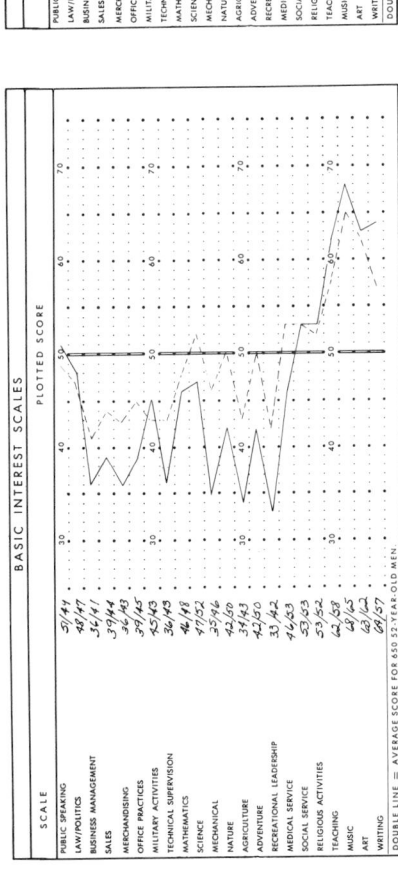
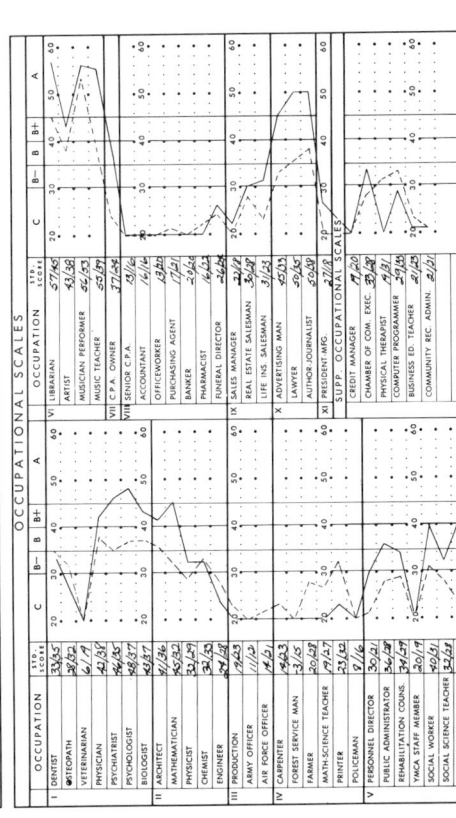

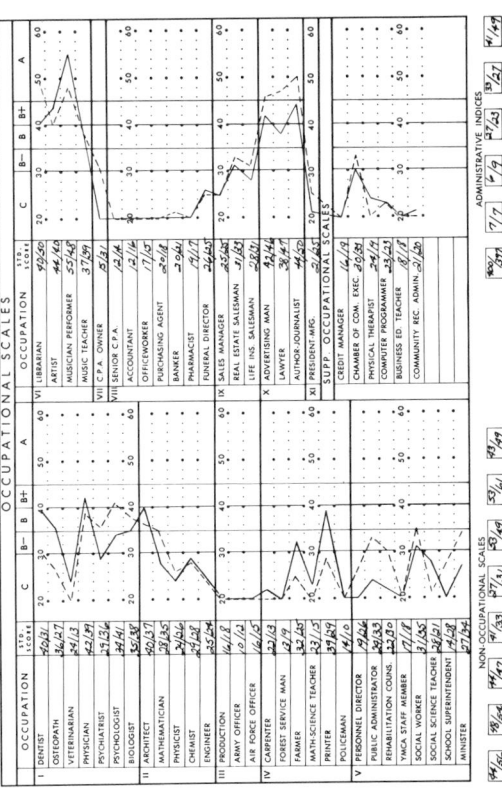

FIG. 7-11. *Mean SVIB profile for outstanding musicians: 12 composers (solid line) and 53 performers (broken line).*

FIG. 7-12. *Mean SVIB profile for Pulitzer Prize winning newsmen: 7 cartoonists (solid line) and 47 writers and editors (broken line).*

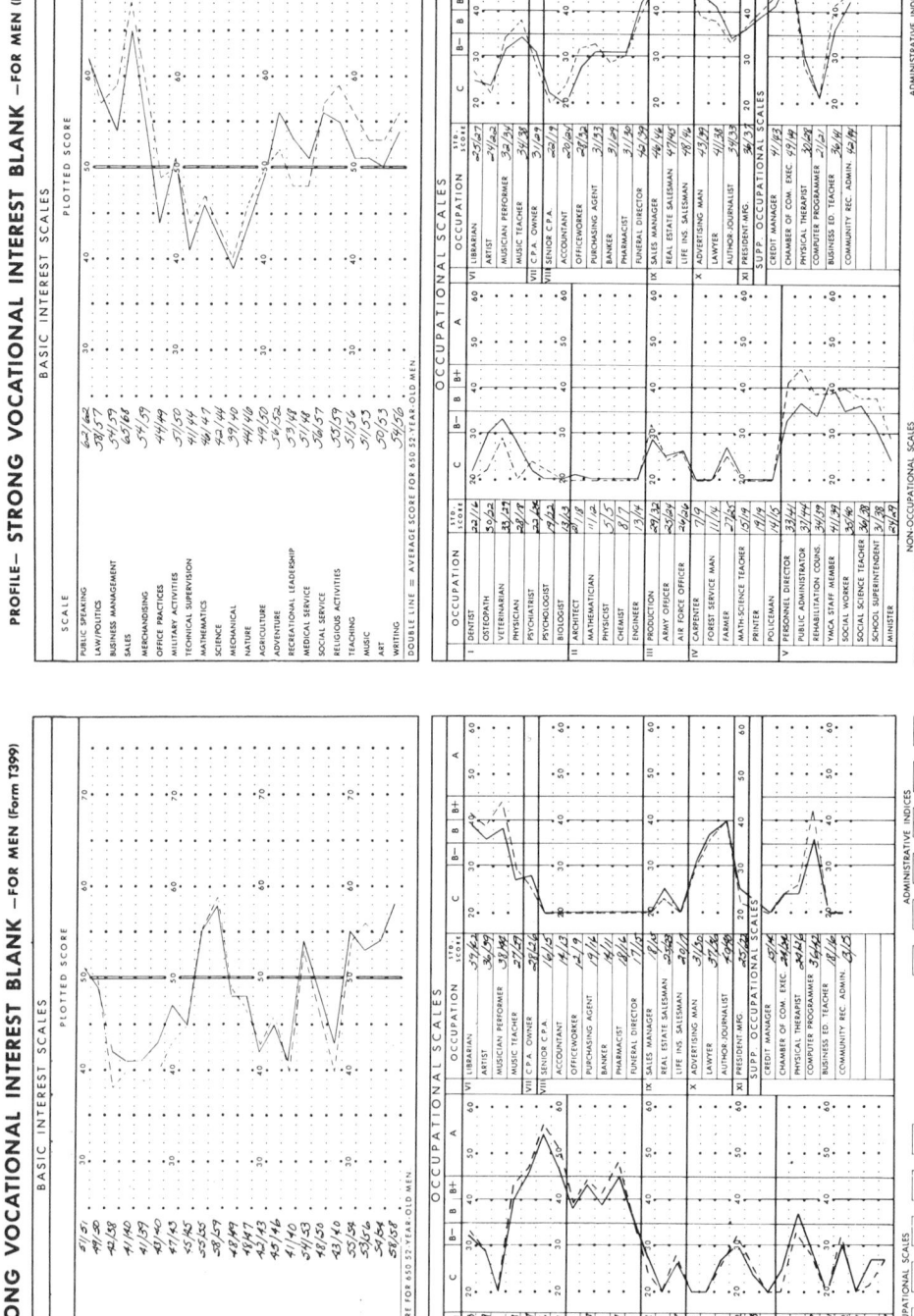

FIG. 7.13. Mean SVIB profile for psychologists: 50 APA presidents (solid line) and 24 distinguished scientific contribution award winners (broken line).

FIG. 7-14. Mean SVIB profile for highly productive salesmen: 101 life insurance salesmen (solid line) and 52 encyclopedia salesmen (broken line).

TABLE 7-1. MEAN SCORES ON THE SCIENCE BASIC INTEREST SCALE FOR 19 GROUPS OF OUTSTANDING MEN

64 U. S. Medal of Science Winners (N=12)

63

62

61

60

59 APA Distinguished Scientific Contribution Award Winners (N=24)

58 Nobel Prize Winners (N=10); Astronauts (N=22); APA Presidents (N=50)

57

56

55

54 Danforth Fellows (N=91)

53

52 Generals and Admirals (N=112); Symphony Members (N=53)

51

50 Novelists (N=26); Corporation Presidents (N=16)

49

48 Federal Judges (N=132); Governors (N=46)

47 Poets (N=10); Football Coaches (N=13); Composers (N=12); Journalists (N=54)

46 McKnight Fellows--actors (N=43)

45

44 Encyclopedia Salesmen (N=52)

43

42 Life Insurance Salesmen (N=101)

PROFILE— **STRONG VOCATIONAL INTEREST BLANK** –FOR MEN (form T399)

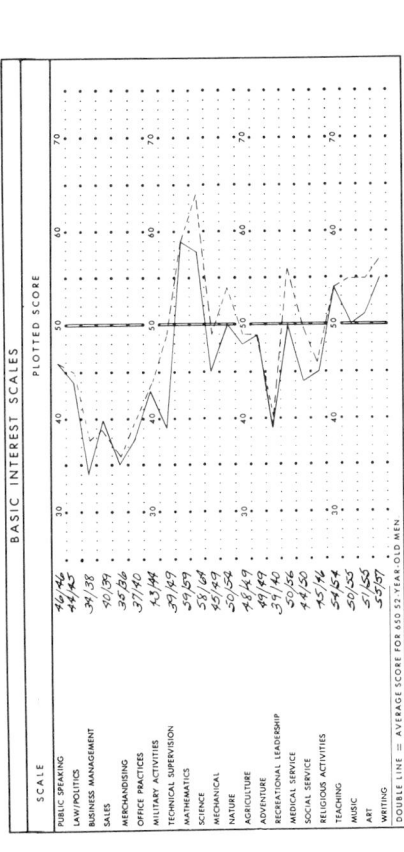

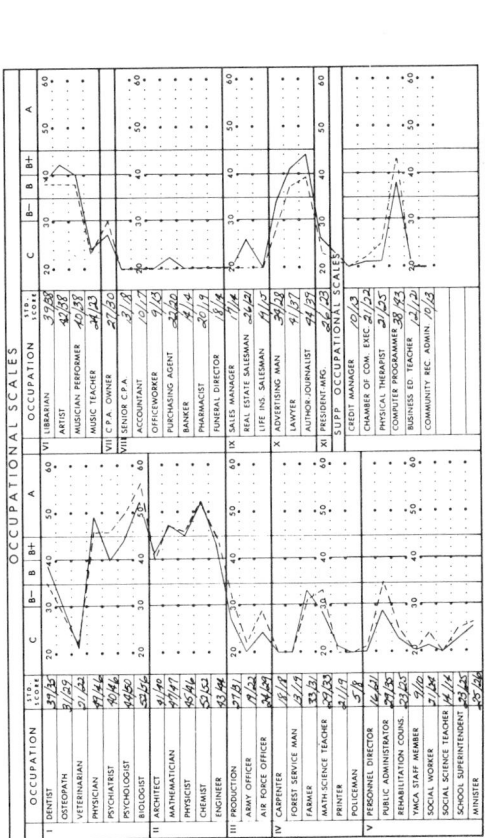

FIG. 7-15. *Mean SVIB profile for scientists: 10 Nobel Prize winners (solid line) and 12 U.S. Medal of Science winners (broken line).*

269

been awarded the Pulitzer Prize or hold membership in the National Institute of Arts and Letters.

Corporation Presidents (N = 16). Chief Executive Officers from companies listed as among the 100 largest U.S. corporations by *Fortune* magazine in 1964.

Danforth Fellows (N = 91). All have been awarded excellent fellowships given to outstanding graduate students—in any field—who plan to enter college teaching. Data were collected by Bentley and Rossmann (1969).

Federal Judges (N = 132). Mostly Federal District judges, with a few from the U.S. Supreme Court and Court of Appeals.

Football Coaches (N = 13). When tested in 1965, these men were among the top 25 active college coaches in lifetime won-loss records at major colleges and universities.

Governors. Minnesota (N = 8) and Others (N = 38). All former state governors, tested after leaving office. Includes 8 of the last 9 Minnesota governors.

McKnight Fellows. Actors (N = 43). Men mostly in their mid-20's, and early 30's, who have been awarded highly favored graduate scholarships to study at the Tyrone Guthrie Theater and University of Minnesota in Minneapolis.

Military Officers. Generals (N = 91) and Admirals (N = 21). Includes men with 3 stars or more (Lt. General or General, Vice-Admiral or Admiral). When tested in 1966–67, a substantial number of the Generals were retired; all Admirals were on active duty.

Musicians. Composers (N = 12) and Performers (N = 53). The composers have been awarded the Pulitzer Prize for music, or hold membership in the National Institute of Arts and Letters. The performers were all members of the Minneapolis Symphony Orchestra (now called the Minnesota Symphony Orchestra).

Newsmen. Cartoonists (N = 7), Writers and Editors (N = 47). All have been awarded the Pulitzer Prize.

Psychologists. American Psychological Association Presidents (N = 50) and winners of the APA Distinguished Scientific Contribution award (N = 24). Includes APA presidents extending back to 1910. There is some overlap between the two groups. Taken together, they include a large fraction of the prominent psychologists in America.

Salesmen. Life Insurance (N = 101) and Encyclopedia (N = 52). The life insurance salesmen all have produced more than $2,000,000 annual sales; the encyclopedia salesmen were honored by their firm as the outstanding performers of the year (1965).

Scientists. Nobel Prize Winners (N = 10) and U.S. Medal of Science Winners (N = 12). Mostly physicists or chemists earning Nobel Prizes or the U.S. Medal of Science. All very prominent.

Some Comments

The scores presented in Figures 7-1 to 7-15 demonstrate several points:

First, the patterns of scores on the Basic Interest Scales are eminently reasonable. The artists scored highest on the Art scale, the scientists scored highest on the Science scale, the salesmen scored highest on the Sales scale, the judges scored highest on the Law/Politics scale, the Generals and Admirals scored highest on the Military Activities scale. The lowest scores for each group, while not so intuitively obvious, also seem reasonable; thus, the composers were lowest on Recreational Leadership; the newsmen lowest on the Mechanical scales, and prominent psychologists were lowest on the Business Management scale.

Second, the scores on the Occupational Scales were also reasonable and, where appropriate, the specific occupation's scale usually held up well in these samples, and provided evidence of cross-validation robustness. The psychologists, for example, scored 55 on the Psychologist scale, one-half SD above the criterion sample (they scored lowest, about 5, on the Policeman scale, or 4½ SD below the criterion sample of policemen). Other instances are apparent on the profiles.

Third, no readily apparent pattern of "successful" interests appeared, that is, there is no "success in all fields" theme. Instead, these outstanding men have mean profiles more like their mediocre colleagues than they do like outstanding people in other fields. Once again, vocational interests, as we now measure them, are more indicative of occupational direction than of occupational success. To some extent, this may be a "restriction in range" phenomenon. A good example of this was presented earlier in the section on the Managerial Orientation scale; the data for that scale showed that good managers scored highest, then poor managers, and below them, men in "anti-managerial" settings, such as artists and musicians. Men who have managed to survive in a managerial setting have achieved at least some success and have somewhat similar interests to those managers who stand out from the pack; the men who are the most different—who score lowest— are those who decline to enter the race initially. That same phenomenon probably is operating with the other SVIB scales, for if one isolates groups demonstrating high achievement in a wide range of activities, then sizable differences in their interest patterns appear as demonstrated in the mean profiles for the outstanding men.

This is an important point, and a further illustration may be helpful in emphasizing it. Scores on a measure of scientific interests have never been shown to be related to scientific achievement, yet look at the distribution of mean scores on the Science Basic Interest Scale presented in Table 7-1 (p. 269). At the very top are the Medal of Science winners, next come the psychologists who have been awarded the APA's Distinguished Scientific Contribution award, the Nobel Prize winners, and the astronauts. At the bottom of the Science scale distribution are, as always, the salesmen. Clearly the mean scores on the Science interest scale are related to achievement in the field of science. Yet the same rank-ordering of occupations appears when one looks at the distributions of scores of more-or-less average men in each occupation, as is done in Table 3-52 (p. 147). Within occupations, interest inventory scales are not, and perhaps can never be, very effective in separating the spectacular successes from the merely adequate. Still, the latter does represent, after all, success of some note; those not in the occupation are not blessed with even the distinction of being "merely adequate."

CHAPTER 8

Interpreting the Profile

The main purpose of this Handbook is to outline the development of the SVIB and to present the basic psychometric data that the user needs. This is not the place for an extensive discussion of how the SVIB is to be used in practice; textbooks on counseling and personnel administration can more adequately serve that function.

However, some discussion may be useful, especially on those topics peculiar to the SVIB. This chapter covers topics such as the meaning of the Letter Ratings, the interpretation of High and Low Scores, the derivation and implications of the occupational groupings on the profile, frequent problems in interpretation and also presents some case studies for illustrative purposes.

Introducing the Client to the SVIB

M. David Galinsky and Irene Fast (1969) have written on the use of the SVIB with identity problems; much of what they say is relevant to most counseling uses of the inventory. Specifically, they have said, regarding the briefing of the client before the testing:

> The aim [in the discussion prior to the client's taking the test] is to make clear to him the structure of the test, the form in which the results will be presented to him, and the mode of reaching an interpretation. Any opportunities to deal with concerns about the possible results, unrealistic hopes or fears about the test, and possible relationships between the results and the client's background and interests should be utilized then.
> A useful way to clarify the structure of the test and the mode of presentation of the results is to show him a sample profile and discuss its characteristics with him. An attempt may be made to clarify that each score represents a comparison between the way he responded to the test and the way people in the particular occupational group (e.g. engineers) did . . . it is emphasized that each score is no more than a comparison between the client's responses and those of the professional group; the interpretive problem in counseling, then, is to account for the scale scores in terms of the client's own present and past experiences. It is

often useful to illustrate some of the kinds of misinterpretation that can occur and to suggest that as much time will be taken over the interpretation of the results as is necessary to deal with *all* the material relevant to the client's problem of decision.

There are several possible benefits from this way of using the test. First, the belief that the test results can offer a magical solution to the client's problems is mitigated by a clarification of its actual use. Second, the opposite and generally accompanying wish that the test will offer nothing, and, therefore, can be taken without fear of arousing anxieties is also found to be untenable. Third, the client is not forced into a passive role by the mystery of the test and the superior knowledge of the counselor. On the contrary, his realistic wishes to solve his problem are encouraged by showing him how he himself can explore the meanings of the results with his own goals in mind.

A frequent reaction to removal of the possibility of magical results from the test, and awareness of the possibility of gaining real information from it, is that fears of finding out "the truth" are mobilized. This reaction often takes the form of complaints that interest tests can be faked, that tests taken in the past have been of no use, or that friends have had uniformly poor experiences with tests. Predictably, the reaction is strongest in those clients whose yearning for test results has been most fervent.

Underlying the defensive assertion that test results could lead to nothing is very often the fear that they might indeed reveal something about which the client already has some apprehension. Among the most common fears are that the test results will present final proof that the client is not fit for any valued profession, that some dreadful perversion lurks inside him, or that he will have to accept an identification he has always fought. An example is the case of an engineering freshman who, six months earlier, had transferred out of engineering and was now considering moving back into it. His great reluctance to deal with the meaning of his high score on the engineer scale of the SVIB finally resulted in his admitting that his father, an engineer, had had a nervous breakdown. For him to be like engineers confirmed his fears for his sanity. . . .

Several factors facilitate the exploration and technical handling of these fears during, rather than prior to, the discussion of the test structure and use. First, because the fears are aroused by the imminence of finding out the results, their clarity and intensity is likely to make it easier to recognize them. Second, because the client understands the reality of the test situation, it is easier for him to recognize his complaints about the test as displacements and to attempt to discover and understand the underlying fears. Finally, because dealing with these anxieties becomes an integral part of his own attempt to solve his problem, rather than an externally imposed hurdle to overcome before he can get the test results he wants, his motivations to deal with his fears are likely to be more appropriate and his efforts in dealing with them are likely to be more successful.

Letter Ratings

The SVIB standard scores are sometimes difficult to explain to a person inexperienced in psychological and statistical techniques. As a solution to this problem, for many years Strong recommended a system of letter grades: A, B+, B, B−, and C. The letter ratings and corresponding standard scores are as follows:

A	45 and above	B−	30–34
B+	40–44	C	below 29
B	35–39		

Using this system, about two-thirds of the men in a criterion group are rated A by their own scale and another one-sixth are rated B+. Less than 2 percent of them score in the C range on their own scale.

Figure 2-1 (p. 44) shows the relationship between raw scores, standard scores, and letter ratings on the Engineer scale for the engineer criterion group, the Men-in-General group, and a group of liberal arts freshmen from the University of Minnesota.

Considerable research has shown that a person with an A rating on a given scale has interests similar to those of people successfully engaged in that occupation and would likely enjoy that work; a C rating means that he does not have such interests; and a B+, B, or B− rating means that although he probably has those occupational interests we cannot be as sure of it as we can with the A ratings.

Particular emphasis should be given to the C ratings, as these clearly identify occupational areas where the individual has few interests. A person with a C rating on a given occupational scale is rarely engaged in that occupation or, if so engaged, is often an indifferent success who will soon drop out or who is doing the work in some more or less unusual manner. The unusual situation is illustrated by a physician with a rating of C on the Physician scale who is a successful superintendent of a large hospital.

Occupational Groups

Most writers concerned with the interpretation of the SVIB (Darley, 1941; Darley and Hagenah, 1955; Layton, 1958; Stephenson, 1961) place more emphasis on the pattern of scores within the occupational groupings than on any single score. For one reason, scales cannot be developed for all possible occupations, and experienced counselors can often interpret the SVIB profile in reference to other occupations that a student is considering. For example, a student considering geology might well be expected to have some high scores in Group II; a would-be landscape architect might show higher scores on certain Group IV scales than on the Architect scale.

Another advantage of using occupational groups is that they help the student think of families of occupations rather than fixating on a single occupation.

The groups on the men's profile have been labeled as follows:

I.	Biological Science	VII.	CPA Owner
II.	Physical Science	VIII.	Business and Accounting
III.	Technical Supervision	IX.	Sales
IV.	Technical and Skilled Trades	X.	Verbal–Linguistic
V.	Social Service	XI.	President, Manufacturing Concern
VI.	Aesthetic–Cultural		

On the women's profile, the following labels have been assigned:

I.	Music/Performing	VII.	Military/Managerial
II.	Art	VIII.	Business
III.	Verbal–Linguistic	IX.	Home Economics
IV.	Social Service	X.	Health-Related Services
V.	Verbal–Scientific	XI.	Nonprofessional
VI.	Scientific		

The original groupings were established by Strong, using both the results of several factor analyses and a visual inspection of the scale intercorrelations. In establishing the current profile, the following four types of data, listed here in decreasing order of importance, were considered:

1. **Mean scores of the occupations on the scales.** If two criterion groups scored high, roughly above 40, on each other's scales, the two occupations were usually grouped together.

2. **Intercorrelations between the scales.** If two scales correlated highly, roughly above .65, the two occupations were usually grouped together.

3. **Similarity of educational requirements for the occupation.** Other things being equal, occupations with similar educational requirements were grouped together. For example, on the men's profile, groups with biological-science backgrounds were left together, though there were suggestions in the data that other groupings could be used—e.g., the veterinarians were a more rugged, masculine, outdoors-oriented occupation than the other biological scientists, and might well have been grouped with the Technical and Skilled Trades occupations in Group IV.

4. **History.** Other things being equal, the groups were left as they have always been. For example, the data suggest that funeral directors might be grouped either with the general business occupations (Group VIII) or with the sales occupations (Group IX). Since they have traditionally been located in Group VIII on earlier profiles, they were left there.

In the interpretation of the profile, groups containing a majority of A and B+ ratings are labeled "primaries"; those containing a majority of B and B+ ratings are "secondaries." Groups with a majority of scores below the shaded areas are called "rejects."

Although the occupational groupings are a convenient shorthand to use in discussing profiles, especially in counseling settings where they make a great deal of sense to students, the above comments on the problems of grouping should make it clear that the categories deserve only a mild degree of reification. As the Basic Scales become more widely used and understood, they will take over many of the functions of the occupational groups.

Low Scores

In both guidance and selection settings, occupations that are not in harmony with the person's interests should usually be eliminated from consideration. If a college student with a B− rating on the Physician scale says he wants to be a physician, he should be told that very few physicians score that low. If he persists, the counselor can add that perhaps he is similar to these few exceptional physicians and may find a home in a more-or-less unusual area of medicine, but that he must remember that there are few people with interests like his who are practicing physicians. If his score is even lower, perhaps in the C range, the counselor can state more positively that the student does not score like physicians, that he had better consider something else.

Less than 2 percent of an occupational group score below 25 on their own scale; scores this low indicate very few common interests with men in that occupation. Usually the student or client will agree that he has little interest in the areas where he has low ratings, and he may want to move quickly to a discussion of his high scores. But low scores are useful in interpreting high scores. A man who has low scores on the Engineer and Chemist scales and on the Group IV (Technical and Skilled Trades) scales is not likely to enjoy production management even though he has a high rating on that scale. If the high rating on the Production Manager scale is combined with fairly high scores on personnel, sales management, and office work, his scores indicate business administration interests, but not particularly production management. Another example is that of a man with an A rating on the CPA Owner scale and low ratings on the Accountant, Office Worker, and Senior CPA scales. Such a man might like to manage a CPA office, but he probably would not enjoy the preliminary work necessary to reach such a position.

Darley and Hagenah (1955) made a special study of what they call reject patterns, i.e., profiles where most of the scores in a particular group are low. They interpret such patterns as active rejection of the occupational activities of that group rather than mere indifference or lack of interest. Identification of such rejections is essential in understanding the individual's occupational interests, since our dislikes probably mold our lives as much or more than our likes.

High Scores

About two-thirds of the men in a given occupation score above 45 on their own scale. If a man scores that high, he surely has many interests in common with these men. Usually, individuals have several high scores, and interpretation of these scores varies depending on whether they are (1) concentrated in one area, (2) concentrated in two or more areas, (3) scattered over many areas, or (4) below the A or even B+ ratings.

High Scores Concentrated in One Area

Some profiles have all of the high scores in one group. Here the interpretation is apparent—the person should strongly consider the occupations with the highest scores, or others closely related. If, for example, a student receives an A rating on the Engineer scale, B+ ratings on Physicist and Chemist, a B rating on Mathematician, and has no other A or B+ ratings, he should be encouraged to enter some phase of engineering, assuming he has the necessary abilities. If he says he strongly prefers chemistry or physics, these occupations would be quite appropriate. Interest measures are not precise indicators; they indicate only general direction, and any occupation closely related to a scale with an A rating would be suitable. The chances are good that the student in this example could well be satisfied, as far as his interests are concerned, in any physical-science occupation.

High Scores Concentrated in Two or More Areas

Where high scores are concentrated in two or more areas, a person could select one of the options and ignore the alternatives. But a better solution would be to find an area which could provide expression for all of his varied interests. An example is that of a student who had A ratings in Author–Journalist and Advertising Man, B+ in Forest Service Man, and B in most of the other occupations in Group IV (Technical and Skilled Trades). Several years later he reported that he was engaged in publicity work for the National Park Service and thoroughly enjoyed his work. He was employed in work typical of his primary interests but related also to his secondary interests. This particular combination of interests was unusual, since the median correlation between the Author–Journalist scale and the Group IV occupations is −.29. Though this man's interests were centered in two diverse areas, he found opportunity to enjoy both.

In another example, Layton (1958) discusses a salesman who had high scores on the three sales occupations and also several high scores on the Group V (Social Service) scales. His job required him to high-pressure retailers into buying more of his product than they could hope to sell. After a while, he could no longer face his customers and began to lose repeat sales. Such persons are often happier in sales jobs where the emphasis is on providing personal service to the customer, or in fund-raising and public contact work for nonprofit organizations.

One further example is that of a student with a B+ rating on the Artist scale, an A rating on Architect, and several B+ and B ratings in the business activities. He spent a year in a school of architecture but disliked the mathematics and strength-of-materials courses. He switched to business school but this did not interest him very much either. After a long conference in which he named numerous business activities involving art, he finally brightened and said, "I guess I would really like some phase of interior decoration, package design, or something else along that line." In this example, the highest scores served as a focus for the discussion of all possible activities, particularly those having some relationship to his secondary interests.

Many students have demonstrated this capacity to ferret out activities that appeal to them, once they are helped to concentrate on a relatively small area and are given some time to do this.

Widespread Interests

Occasionally a profile has a large number of A or B+ ratings scattered throughout several groups.

In most cases of widespread interests, the highest scores are relatively low. Many businessmen demonstrate this type of profile. Among Stanford students who eventually entered business, the highest average scores were Office Worker 42, Real Estate Salesman 40, Accountant and Purchasing Agent 39, Sales Manager 38, Personnel Director and Production Manager 36. Although many of these students had one or more A ratings, the group's mean profile had only two B+ ratings. In contrast, students who later became engineers, lawyers, physicians, and dentists had, on the average, an A rating, i.e., scores over 45, in their own profession (Strong, 1955).

Usually, persons with widespread but relatively low interest scores are content to work in any one of such areas. Business students shift from one major to another, and later on shift from one business function to another. Advancement in pay or position seems to be more important than interest in the activities. This is in striking contrast to the professional man, whose high scores are typically restricted to a small area; such men seek a specific type of activity. Many of these, who have deserted their primary interest for appreciable increases in pay or position, have later expressed dissatisfaction, and some have returned to their original work.

No High Scores

The really tough counseling assignment occurs when a person has no A ratings, few if any B+ ratings, and does not have interests characteristic of business. In most cases the person simply does not possess the interests of any of the occupations for which there are scoring keys. Possibly he has interests akin to those of some unusual occupation for which we cannot score today, e.g., mariner. Some of these men, however, impress counselors as being definitely devoid of interests associated with occupational pursuits. Often such persons verbalize complete confusion and uncertainty as to what they like and dislike.

No High or Low Scores

Where there are no high or low scores, the SVIB cannot suggest occupational choices. Such a person must be counseled with reference to other test data and his personal history. Some research has suggested that the lack of any pattern on the Strong Blank is related to maladjustment; a person may be too fearful and unsure of himself to commit himself thoroughly to any vocation, or may be characteristically indecisive and ambivalent about most choices confronting him. With young people, the lack of high scores may be associated with immaturity (Layton, 1958).

Two studies using college students with low profiles—that is, few or no A or B+ scores—have recently been completed. The first was by Athelstan (1966); he identified 151 male freshmen, entering the University of Minnesota in 1961, with low profiles. He also selected 199 other freshmen to serve as controls, then located and retested both groups in 1965. He secured data from 76 percent of the total group. His findings were as follows:

1. The low profile subjects did not differ from the controls in age, scholastic aptitude, high school rank, dropout rate, or personality as measured by the MMPI.

2. The low profiles did not appear to be due to random responding or other unusual test-taking behavior.

3. The test means of the low profile groups differed significantly from

those of the control group, but not as markedly as would be expected in view of the great difference in the appearance of their profiles.

4. On retest, the two sets of means converged, though the low profile group did show a tendency toward higher scores in the business areas.

5. The interest profiles of the low profile sample were nearly as reliable on retest as those of the control sample. Many scores rose considerably in the low profile sample, but the relative levels within individual profiles remained fairly stable.

6. The item responses, on initial test, differed for the two groups, mainly because the low profile group gave more "Dislike" responses. On retest, the low profile group showed more changes, and the differences between the groups became less pronounced.

7. Only 15 percent of the low profile subjects had low profiles on retest. Those who did exhibited more uncertainty in their vocational planning than did the remainder of the group, but no other differences in various vocational or educational experiences could be located.

Athelstan summarized his study: "The findings suggest that low profiles may be used in vocational counseling much as any others would be. The chief indication that this may be warranted is the tendency of the profiles to rise over-all on retest, while their shape remains relatively stable" (Athelstan, 1966, p. 89).

Scheller (1967) has completed a similar study of low profiles; he was specifically concerned with the predictive validity of these profiles. His sample was drawn from low-profile students entering the College of Liberal Arts (N = 117) and the Institute of Technology (College of Engineering) (N = 156) in the fall of 1956. Among both groups he found that 22 percent did not have any primary interest patterns, as defined by Darley and Hagenah (1955) on their profiles. These students were matched with controls from the same classes and, in 1966, he attempted to locate these people and observe their occupational progress. He located approximately 90 percent of both groups and was able to retest about 65 percent.

He found, like Athelstan, that there was no difference in the academic aptitude nor persistence between those with "flat" profiles and a group of control subjects. His conclusions were:

1. The predictive validity of an SVIB secondary interest pattern when this is the highest pattern on the profile, is as high as that of a primary pattern when the profile has one or more primary interest patterns.

2. The concurrent validity, on retest, of either patterns or scale scores is as high for individuals who 10 years earlier had low profiles as it is for control subjects with "normal" profiles.

"For these samples, the secondary pattern, when it is the strongest pattern on the profile, has the predictive accuracy of a primary pattern.... These findings should serve to increase the counseling utility of SVIB profiles that do not exhibit any primary interest patterns" (Scheller, 1967, pp. 81–82).

The results of these two studies suggest strongly that, among college students, the general elevation of the profile is not as important as the shape. The highest scores, even when they are numerically low, should be used as the best indications of the student's direction of interests.

Common Interpretive Problems
Mistaking Interests for Abilities

The major problem in interpretation, overshadowing all others by a substantial margin, is untangling the difference between interests and abilities. Practically everyone views the SVIB scores as "telling me what I would be good at." Telling them once that these are measures of preferences, not abilities, is not sufficient. It must be pounded in, drummed in, emphasized in as many ways as one can imagine. Specific examples are necessary: A high score on the Science Basic Interest Scale does not mean the individual has an illustrious scientific career ahead; a high score on the Physicist Occupational Scale does not mean the individual is in any sense superior to the other members of his department; a high score on the Academic Achievement Scale is no guarantee of intellectual brilliance. Still, the temptation to interpret each of these scores as suggested is very strong, even among the best-informed psychologists.

Recently I tested, as part of a symposium, most of the members of a university psychology department. Their profiles were handed back to them at an evening cocktail party; for about five minutes it was quiet as they peered over their results, then they began comparing profiles and chortling, "Lookee here, my Psychologist score is 3 points higher than yours," and "How did you ever get a Ph.D. with an Academic Achievement score of 45?" and "It looks like we can trust our wives with Joe here—with an MF score of 35, he's no threat." All this was said in jest but, nevertheless, those with high Psychologist scores and especially high Academic Achievement scores were clearly more pleased and more comfortable with their results than the others. That this occurred among men who are much better informed than the average test-taker dramatizes the need for continual emphasis on what these scores are reflecting.

Again and again and again—these scores are measures of interests, more specifically of consistency of interests. On the Basic Scales, the scores reflect the consistency of the individual's responses to the items in the designated content area; on the Occupational Scales, the scores reflect the consistency between the individual's responses and the modal responses of the men or women in the designated occupation.

The relationship between SVIB scores and performance is not clear, so any interpretation must be tentative but what seems to be true is that interests determine which arena a man will choose to perform in, not his level of performance. Thus, both outstanding and mediocre scientists have about the same interests, as do outstanding and mediocre managers, or engineers or whatever. Interests are better indicators of occupational persistence than of occupational excellence.

Inconsistencies Between the Basic Interest and Occupational Scales

One interpretative problem arises when the Basic Scales and Occupational Scales appear to contradict each other. Instances of this occur when a profile has a high score on a Basic Scale but low scores on the Occupational Scales that are directly related to the Basic Interest area. For example, a student might have a high score on the Mathematics Basic Interest Scale but a low score on the Mathematician and Physicist Occupational Scales, or a profile might have a high score on the Social Service Basic Scale, but only moderate or low scores in Group V—the administrative and social service occupations.

Such situations provide excellent examples of the effects of the different strategies of scale building used for the Basic Interest and Occupational Scales and properly interpreted, they can give the student (the counselor too) considerable insight into what the scores mean for each type of scale.

The Basic Interest Scales reflect the individual's answers to the items directly concerned with the designated activity; his score on the Mathematics Basic Scale, for example, is based on his answers to only these items:

Algebra	Geometry
Arithmetic	Mathematics
Calculus	Physics

The "Like" responses are all weighted positively; the "Dislikes" negatively; thus, the only way an individual can score high is to say he likes mathematics courses—the only way he can score low is to report dislikes.

In contrast, the Occupational Scales have many more items and are much more heterogeneous in content. The Mathematician Occupational Scale for example, has 86 items, covering a very wide range of subjects and activities. Each item was included because it was an item that mathematicians responded differently to than did Men-In-General.

The heterogeneity of item content of the Occupational Scales is illustrated in Table 8-1 where many of the items on the Mathematician Occu-

TABLE 8-1. EXAMPLES OF ITEMS ON THE MATHEMATICIAN OCCUPATIONAL SCALE

Items Weighted Positively

Astronomer	Algebra	Go to symphony concerts
Author of Technical Book	Calculus	Teach adults
Designer, electronic equipment	Geometry	Do research work
Scientific Research Worker	Mathematics	
Statistician	Physics	

Items Weighted Negatively

Auctioneer	Auto Salesman	Fishing
Advertising Man	Life Insurance Salesman	Hunting
Public Relations Man	Real Estate Salesman	Boxing
Employment Manager	Specialty Salesman	Drilling in a military company
Radio Announcer	Traveling Salesman	Handling Horses
Sports Reporter		Going to church
Buyer	Chamber of Commerce Exec.	Leading a Boy Scout Troop
Office Manager	Military Officer	Going to night clubs
Wholesaler	Athletic Director	Planning a large party
Retailer	Playground Director	Giving "first aid" assistance
	Secret Service Man	
	Shop Foreman	
	Draftsman	

pational Scale are listed. Again, these items were selected because of the large difference in response frequencies between mathematicians and Men-in-General, and that was the only criterion. There was no attempt to screen them for any special type of content.

In Table 8-1 the items have been separated into positively and negatively weighted clusters, and then into subsets of items of similar content. The number and diversity of these clusters emphasize the many different ways that mathematicians differ from other men in their interests. The mathematicians are particularly interesting here as they have more items weighted negatively than most occupations. This means that one way of scoring high on the Mathematician Scale is to answer "Dislike" to all of these items. Thus, one way to "look like a mathematician" would be to share their aversions—a different way of expressing communality of interests than usually considered. Again, this is a further illustration of the differences between the Basic and Occupational Scales.

An analogous presentation could be made for several other pairs of scales where apparent inconsistencies occur—Art and Artist; Social Service and Social Worker; Military Activities and Army Officer. The explanation is always the same; the Basic Interest Scales are relatively homogeneous, and the high scores can only be earned by indicating preferences for those specific activities. In contrast, the Occupational Scales are heterogeneous, and the high scores can be earned in many different ways, including having the same pattern of dislikes as the men in the specified occupation.

When there is a conflict between the two types of scales, the Basic Scale score will virtually always be high, the related occupational scale low. Seldom, if ever, will the inverse occur; that is, one will hardly ever see a high score on the Artist, Mathematician or Minister Scales unless the Art, Mathematics or Religious Activities scores, respectively, are also high.

Such conflicts on the profile provide an opportunity to discuss the all-encompassing nature of occupations, for they emphasize vividly that interest in one specific activity is usually not sufficient for one to enjoy that area as an occupation. An intense interest in mathematics is only one element in the interests of professional mathematicians. Artists are unique in other ways than their interest in artistic activities; men in social service settings stand apart from other men on factors other than the "pure service" concerns.

There will be cases where the inconsistencies might be a valuable asset. Interests in sales and interests in science are negatively correlated; that is true among the Basic Scales, where the correlation is $-.15$, and especially true among the Occupational Scales—the correlation, for example between Sales Manager and Physicist is $-.59$. Again, this emphasizes the relative breadth of the Occupational Scales—sales managers and physicists differ dramatically in areas other than their interests in sales and science. Any individual showing the unlikely combination of interests in both sales and science would have many options open to him in the area of technical sales.

An Overemphasis on "Belonging"

The major purpose of interest inventories in counseling is to suggest occupational areas where the individual will enjoy the work, and the entire thrust of this Handbook has been to document that this approach is possible and important—yet it can be overdone. Most men are not in occupations where they score highest; at best, probably no more than one-third are. (The exact percentage is difficult to determine and is not especially meaningful as it depends on the number of scales on the profile and the degree of relationship between scales. If a profile has only a few scales, the chances are greater that the individual has his highest score on his occupational scale; as the number of scales increases, the probability obviously drops. Further, if the individual is in an occupation where there are many closely related ones on the SVIB profile—such as Sales Manager, which has the related scales of Realtor and Life Insurance Salesman—then the chances are good that his highest score will be in one of the closely related occupations.) To suggest that the only good outcome is for the person to be in the occupation where he scores highest is too restrictive, and ignores two important facts of the occupational world; first, the considerable diversity within any occupation and second, the freedom most professional men, and many others, have to mold their jobs to suit themselves.

When there is a major discrepancy between an individual's profile and his occupation (or intended occupation), his attention should be drawn to it, and he had best realize that the activities he enjoys are not those enjoyed by the majority of men in the occupation he is contemplating. Not infrequently, the person will have already recognized the difference and have it justified to himself; e.g., a medical school applicant, low on the Physician scale, high on the Farmer scale, said "Yes, I know I'm different— I don't want to be one of those high-powered research types—I want to go back and practice in Black Duck, Minnesota."

The emphasis on deviancy from the norm, whether for the student contemplating a career where he scores low, or for the employee already established, should be that his pattern of interests will indeed be related to the type of occupational environment that he will find compatible on a day-to-day basis, and he should then decide if he can achieve that environment within the setting he is contemplating. If he is "deviant," the solution may be to plan for it, perhaps even exploit it, rather than to change for the sake of compatibility.

All of this is not to suggest that congruence between the interest pattern and an occupation is unimportant—it certainly is—but other factors are important too, and may be overriding.

Case Studies

However adequate one's training or experience, his special skill with any particular test depends on his knowledge of and experience with that specific instrument. The following sample cases are presented to provide some initial experience for those who are not well acquainted with the Strong Blank.

The first six cases are taken from some of the longitudinal files on the SVIB. These men were first tested with the SVIB in 1930, when they were 15 or 16 years old, by E. K. Strong. Most of them were high school juniors and they were part of the sample studied by Strong for his 1931 book, *Change of Interests With Age*. Strong retested them a year later (1931), and again five years later (1936). Because most of those selected for this third study were college students, most of these case studies concern men with college degrees. As such, they likely have had more freedom to follow their interests than the average person, and for many of them there is a strong relationship between what they intended to do as young men and what they are doing today, 30 years later.

In his methodical way, Strong carefully filed and preserved the data from all of these men, and in 1966, when they were retested for further followup, it was possible to merge all of their files. Sixty-six men were located who had been tested four times (1930, 1931, 1936, 1966), and the following six cases are drawn from that group.

As these men were studied primarily to establish the stability of interests, little other biographic information has been collected thus far. The case studies are based on only one-page questionnaires filled out at each testing along with the SVIB. Some narrative imagination has been used to extrapolate between testings, and some fiction has been stirred in to protect their anonymity.

Although these men were tested with the SVIB as students, they probably never received any feedback on their results—certainly if they did, the information would have been very skimpy, as the scoring systems of those days were quite meager. Their career decisions were made, for the most part, without any knowledge of their test results.

The reports here are brief, calling attention to the more important aspects of each case. A closer inspection of each set of four profiles is educational, and the reader is urged to study them. One obvious conclusion of close study is that the relationship between the teenager's measured interests and his eventual occupation is not necessarily as direct as has been implied in earlier chapters. Another is that shifts can occur in individual cases that are larger than one might expect after reading the general findings on stability. Even when the group statistics look very meaningful, studying the diversity of individual cases can be quite sobering, and this step should be an integral part of any instructional program on the SVIB.

Another implication from these studies is that the SVIB works best when needed least. If a student has a dominant interest, say in science, then he knows it, and it is no surprise to find it on the profile. (This does not necessarily mean the inventory is of no use in such cases; to spend 45 minutes filling in the answer sheet and $1 to score it is not an unreasonable cost to be told you're on the right track.)

Finally, the case studies clearly show that the concurrent validity of the SVIB is better than the long-range predictive validity. There is a 36-year gap between first and last testings of these men, and there are many changes on the profiles. And, in general, the changes are in the direction of conformity to the pattern of their occupations.

Case 1 (Figure 8-1)

Steve grew up on a ranch, and has been involved in agriculture all of his life. His career has differed from the usual rancher's son in at least two

PROFILE— STRONG VOCATIONAL INTEREST BLANK —FOR MEN (Form T399)

BASIC INTEREST SCALES

SCALE	1930	1931	1936	1966
PUBLIC SPEAKING	46	57	61	65
LAW/POLITICS	35	49	61	52
BUSINESS MANAGEMENT	35	51	61	51
SALES	37	54	59	54
MERCHANDISING	35	58	54	48
OFFICE PRACTICES	43	68	71	43
MILITARY ACTIVITIES	54	54	58	70
TECHNICAL SUPERVISION	47	62	62	57
MATHEMATICS	58	61	61	61
SCIENCE	54	52	54	62
MECHANICAL	51	63	61	59
NATURE	47	57	63	61
AGRICULTURE	65	65	68	56
ADVENTURE	61	65	65	73
RECREATIONAL LEADERSHIP	59	61	64	56
MEDICAL SERVICE	59	65	65	65
SOCIAL SERVICE	50	46	50	53
RELIGIOUS ACTIVITIES	41	48	55	63
TEACHING	41	41	61	41
MUSIC	51	47	55	55
ART	34	46	49	51
WRITING	36	45	51	53

DOUBLE LINE = AVERAGE SCORE FOR 650 52-YEAR-OLD MEN

Non-Occupational Scales

	1930	1931	1936	1966
AACH	46	26	44	55
DIV	61	64	66	61
MFII	68	73	66	65
MO	25	33	46	58
OIE	59	47	41	35
OL	58	42	52	66
SL	26	31	36	43
AR	28	25	44	63

Administrative Indices

	1930	1931	1936	1966
TR	400	400	400	399
UNP	6	6	8	7
FC	-3	-3	-3	6
LP	14	38	40	38
IP	26	42	47	34
DP	60	20	13	28

OCCUPATIONAL SCALES

Group	OCCUPATION	1930	1931	1936	1966
I	DENTIST	48	38	27	27
	OSTEOPATH	32	40	28	25
	VETERINARIAN	38	48	38	28
	PHYSICIAN	46	26	18	30
	PSYCHIATRIST	23	9	12	37
	PSYCHOLOGIST	20	13	11	28
	BIOLOGIST	40	21	12	32
II	ARCHITECT	40	22	12	24
	MATHEMATICIAN	28	13	3	17
	PHYSICIST	39	19	9	24
	CHEMIST	46	26	20	43
	ENGINEER	46	31	32	39
III	PRODUCTION	40	38	51	56
	ARMY OFFICER	31	49	55	53
	AIR FORCE OFFICER	38	45	43	47
IV	CARPENTER	42	41	30	16
	FOREST SERVICE MAN	36	51	55	31
	FARMER	61	50	39	31
	MATH-SCIENCE TEACHER	45	58	42	34
	PRINTER	36	37	25	16
	POLICEMAN	33	35	33	24
V	PERSONNEL DIRECTOR	12	24	38	47
	PUBLIC ADMINISTRATOR	16	27	50	54
	REHABILITATION COUNS.	9	10	32	28
	YMCA STAFF MEMBER	15	21	35	25
	SOCIAL WORKER	4	13	26	28
	SOCIAL SCIENCE TEACHER	11	31	35	12
	SCHOOL SUPERINTENDENT	0	12	23	29
	MINISTER	-1	-4	9	10
VI	LIBRARIAN	12	10	14	9
	ARTIST	37	21	11	16
	MUSICIAN PERFORMER	34	28	16	19
	MUSIC TEACHER	9	13	10	13
VII	C.P.A. OWNER	25	26	29	33
VIII	SENIOR C.P.A.	30	28	34	39
	ACCOUNTANT	29	34	40	46
	OFFICEWORKER	27	37	37	31
	PURCHASING AGENT	36	41	33	37
	BANKER	27	29	26	22
	PHARMACIST	35	32	24	24
	FUNERAL DIRECTOR	28	30	32	22
IX	SALES MANAGER	23	32	24	26
	REAL ESTATE SALESMAN	35	35	29	27
	LIFE INS. SALESMAN	19	23	19	16
X	ADVERTISING MAN	22	14	14	24
	LAWYER	37	22	19	24
	AUTHOR-JOURNALIST	34	16	13	25
XI	PRESIDENT-MFG.	29	26	18	33

SUPP. OCCUPATIONAL SCALES: CREDIT MANAGER; CHAMBER OF COM. EXEC.; PHYSICAL THERAPIST; COMPUTER PROGRAMMER; BUSINESS ED. TEACHER; COMMUNITY REC. ADMIN.

NON-OCCUPATIONAL SCALES: AACH AR DIV MFII MO OIE OL SL

ADMINISTRATIVE INDICES: TR UNP FC LP IP DP

FIG. 8-1. *Profile for Case Study #1.*

PROFILE— STRONG VOCATIONAL INTEREST BLANK —FOR MEN (Form T399)

BASIC INTEREST SCALES

SCALE	1930	1931	1936	1966
PUBLIC SPEAKING	39	50	57	61
LAW/POLITICS	41	58	58	61
BUSINESS MANAGEMENT	35	51	65	55
SALES	37	54	56	61
MERCHANDISING	37	54	68	60
OFFICE PRACTICES	41	54	57	46
MILITARY ACTIVITIES	62	50	58	70
TECHNICAL SUPERVISION	28	57	62	67
MATHEMATICS	58	58	61	58
SCIENCE	48	54	62	64
MECHANICAL	47	60	53	57
NATURE	49	55	45	57
AGRICULTURE	56	53	47	50
ADVENTURE	57	65	65	61
RECREATIONAL LEADERSHIP	59	61	56	53
MEDICAL SERVICE	38	59	56	68
SOCIAL SERVICE	35	46	57	38
RELIGIOUS ACTIVITIES	41	48	41	48
TEACHING	30	37	41	58
MUSIC	34	34	43	55
ART	39	54	44	59
WRITING	40	41	49	53

DOUBLE LINE = AVERAGE SCORE FOR 650 52-YEAR-OLD MEN.

Non-Occupational Scales

	1930	1931	1936	1966
AACH	32	33	38	52
DIV	55	61	59	53
MFII	69	69	75	61
MO	30	33	54	48
OIE	64	51	31	40
OL	49	46	63	60
SL	23	33	36	44
AR	15	22	26	58

Administrative Indices

	1930	1931	1936	1966
TR	40	40	40	39
UNP	3	1	0	0
FC	-7	-5	-4	2
LP	13	33	32	54
IP	24	37	32	35
DP	63	30	36	11

OCCUPATIONAL SCALES

Group	OCCUPATION	1930	1931	1936	1966
I	DENTIST	43	32	20	39
	OSTEOPATH	24	32	22	47
	VETERINARIAN	26	35	12	47
	PHYSICIAN	32	22	12	43
	PSYCHIATRIST	3	4	15	31
	PSYCHOLOGIST	7	9	6	25
	BIOLOGIST	26	17	11	29
II	ARCHITECT	41	25	14	24
	MATHEMATICIAN	31	14	8	9
	PHYSICIST	34	18	12	17
	CHEMIST	41	34	30	36
	ENGINEER	46	36	36	30
III	PRODUCTION	42	48	48	41
	ARMY OFFICER	29	44	43	52
	AIR FORCE OFFICER	38	44	44	50
IV	CARPENTER	40	38	22	25
	FOREST SERVICE MAN	38	48	33	26
	FARMER	49	48	38	31
	MATH-SCIENCE TEACHER	42	45	40	38
	PRINTER	50	43	31	25
	POLICEMAN	43	39	34	20
V	PERSONNEL DIRECTOR	18	20	43	25
	PUBLIC ADMINISTRATOR	16	36	49	38
	REHABILITATION COUNS.	13	18	26	28
	YMCA STAFF MEMBER	11	23	33	31
	SOCIAL WORKER	-3	10	15	24
	SOCIAL SCIENCE TEACHER	18	32	30	24
	SCHOOL SUPERINTENDENT	-1	8	20	12
	MINISTER	-10	-8	-2	2
VI	LIBRARIAN	11	7	7	16
	ARTIST	35	22	13	21
	MUSICIAN PERFORMER	31	21	12	30
	MUSIC TEACHER	10	6	8	17
VII	C.P.A. OWNER	21	29	36	37
VIII	SENIOR C.P.A.				
	ACCOUNTANT	38	47	51	21
	OFFICEWORKER	40	51	57	23
	PURCHASING AGENT	54	51	53	31
	BANKER	40	37	28	13
	PHARMACIST	35	28	36	37
	FUNERAL DIRECTOR	38	32	39	34
IX	SALES MANAGER	30	31	48	24
	REAL ESTATE SALESMAN	45	40	41	23
	LIFE INS. SALESMAN	28	28	32	16
X	ADVERTISING MAN	34	16	21	22
	LAWYER	36	25	31	17
	AUTHOR-JOURNALIST	39	21	19	20
XI	PRESIDENT-MFG.	25	17	38	23

SUPP. OCCUPATIONAL SCALES: CREDIT MANAGER; CHAMBER OF COM. EXEC.; PHYSICAL THERAPIST; COMPUTER PROGRAMMER; BUSINESS ED. TEACHER; COMMUNITY REC. ADMIN.

NON-OCCUPATIONAL SCALES: AACH AR DIV MFII MO OIE OL SL

ADMINISTRATIVE INDICES: TR UNP FC LP IP DP

FIG. 8-2. *Profile for Case Study #2.*

aspects: first, his mother had a college degree and worked in advertising; second, Steve went into the academic side of agriculture, earning a B.S. degree and then working at a state university as an agricultural extension agent. At the same time, he owns and manages his own beef cattle ranch.

He was first tested with the Strong Blank in 1930, at age 16, when he was a junior in high school. On the cover sheet, he reported that he intended to go through college, that the school subjects he liked best were drawing and math, and that he intended to become an architect.

He reported his father's education as "high school graduate" and occupation as "rancher"; his mother's education as "college graduate" and occupation as "advertising."

His SVIB profile shows strong interest in mathematics and science, interests that held up in all four testings from 1930 to 1966. The first profile also shows a high score on the Law/Politics scale; that score stayed high on the second and third testings, when he was a high school senior and college senior respectively, but dropped on the adult testing. The Music scale was also high on the first testing, but on no other.

On the first testing, at age 16, his interests, as reflected by the Occupational Scales, were most similar to engineers, architects, and chemists—a very science-oriented grouping—and also to purchasing agents, farmers, and artists. His stated interests in drawing and art showed up in the Artist and Architect scales, though not, surprisingly, on the Art Basic scale. His scores on the Group V occupations—the social service and administrative occupations—were low, and his Occupational Introversion-Extroversion score was high, all indicating a rejection of activities dealing with people. This factor is also reflected in the moderately high score on the science occupational scales, and on the farmer and artist scale; all of these occupations reject the "people-oriented" items. In contradiction, the Law/Politics score was high. This score seems in opposition to the rest of the profile, and it may be meaningful that interests in that area have disappeared in the adult testing, even though there has been a sizable overall shift toward more extroverted preferences.

When he was tested a year later at age 17, as a high school senior, he was consistent in his report of biographical data; he still said that drawing and math were his favorite subjects, but mentioned that he intended to learn more about "art, advertising, and salesmanship." He had changed his occupational goal to advertising, and said his long-range plan was to be a manager of a store or head of an advertising agency. He attributed this interest in merchandising to the influence of an uncle.

His profile at that time shows considerable shifts from the earlier one. The Mathematics and Science scales were still high, as was Law/Politics, but a host of other scales were also high for the first time, most notably those clustered at the top of the profile: Public Speaking, Business Management, Sales, Merchandising, Office Practices and Technical Supervision. The Music scale dropped 10 points, and the Occupational Introversion-Extroversion scale dropped 15 points. That much change is probably atypical, even for a 16- to 17-year-old youth.

There is no hint in the file, other than the comment about the uncle, as to why this change occurred.

The next time that Steve appears in this file is 1936, five depression years later. From various sources, his life can be pieced together, though there is no overall narrative in his own words. He spent three years at the state university. Then he transferred to another branch that had a stronger agricultural program. (Later, as an adult, he recollected that he had decided on a career in agriculture during his sophomore year.) During those years, he worked on a ranch in California and on a cattle ranch in Arizona. One summer he worked at a resort and when retested, as a college senior, was working as a technician in the Genetics Department.

When retested as a senior, he indicated that he had been interested in both architecture and advertising earlier (accurate recall) but had rejected those in favor of animal husbandry; he listed his long-range goal as "managing or owning a cattle ranch." The next gap in the file is long—thirty years—from 1936 to 1966. In 1966, he reported his occupation as "Farm advisor, University Extension Service" and added "I also own and operate a beef cattle ranch." He has held this position since 1939, and he reported that he decided on this work during his second year of college, about 1932.

Several questions were asked in different ways about his job satisfaction, and he consistently reported that he thoroughly enjoyed his work. For example, when asked to select the one statement from a list of rank-ordered statements, he picked the most extreme one, "My job is exactly what I have wanted to do."

His adult profile, excepting one score, was congruent with his current occupation; his Agriculture, Nature, Science and Mathematics Basic scales scores were all high, as was Public Speaking and Adventure, and all of these are relevant interests for an academically oriented rancher. The exception was the low score on the Teaching scale; anyone engaged in university extension work might be expected to enjoy those activities more, and almost everyone with a Bachelor's degree scores relatively high on that scale.

He showed a strong conservative pattern with his high score on the Military Activities and Religious Activities; these scores, along with the high scores mentioned above in the practical, realistic areas, suggest strongly that he is a traditionalist in the world of ideas, very likely a Republican. Yet he defies easy classification because of his wide range of interests—his Diversity of Interests score has been above 60 on all four testings, placing him in the upper 15 percent of the population in terms of the breadth of activities that he reports preferences for.

It is instructive to look at his four profiles for trends and inconsistencies. His practical orientation—reflected in the Military, Mechanical, and Agricultural scales—has been constant over all testings though the absolute level was lower when he was 16. (At age 16, his Like Percentage was low (LP = 14) so that he could not score high on very many scales; in fact, considering how low that percentage was, he had a surprising number of high scores.) His Medical Service scale score was high on all four testings, and that is hard to integrate into his occupational pattern; it may—this is pure speculation—it may represent an area of fantasy, one that is likely to remain unfulfilled for there is no support for the biological sciences among his Occupational Scales.

He may think that he enjoys medical services activities, but he certainly doesn't have interests resembling those of a dentist, physician, or even a biologist.

The one major and dramatic shift on the profile is highlighted by the progression of scores on the Occupational Introversion-Extroversion scale; he became remarkably extroverted in his preferences. At age 16, he scored 59, which is far toward the introverted end of the scale; as a college freshman only a year later, he had moved to 47, slightly on the extrovertish side of the midpoint; when a college senior, he progressed to 41; and as an adult he scored 35, the score of an extremely outgoing man. This trend was directly supported by his scores on the Public Speaking scale of 46, 57, 61, 65, and by lesser and occasionally inconsistent shifts on such basic scales as Sales and Teaching.

His interests in writing have also shown a steady progression upward of almost 20 points.

All of these trends are mirrored more or less directly in the Occupational scales. His earliest profile showed high scores on the scientific and practical scales—Engineer, Chemist, Farmer, Dentist. On the three subsequent testings, his interests in people began appearing, so that the adult profile is dominated by the realistic, practical, yet people-oriented scales such as Production Manager, Army Officer, and Public Administrator. Such a shift, along with the Occupational Introversion-Extroversion scores, reflects a growing self-confidence in dealing with others.

His scores on the Age-Related scales progressed nicely from the mid-20's at age 16 and 17, to 44 at age 22, to 63 at age 53; however, there is a unique aspect in the "aging" of his interests, for his score on the Adventure scale has increased at every testing, a novel pattern. Almost all men show a decided decrease in these adventuresome, derring-do activities.

Case 2 (Figure 8-2)

Walter appears to have had the best of a good many worlds; fate has given him many opportunities and he has used them wisely.

Today he is a dentist, probably because of opportunities created by World War II.

He grew up in a highly educated family; his father was a civil engineer, his mother a college graduate. As a high school student, he reported being most interested in math, chemistry, and English. When he was a high school sophomore (1928) he worked for a summer in Yosemite Forest cutting brush, for which he earned $100 per month—a handsome amount. He went back every summer for the next seven years, working his way up through Head Chainman ($100 per month), Cat Skinner ($195 per month), Straw boss ($150 per month—the depression hit), and ranger ($140 per month). During his four college years, 1932–36, those jobs were undoubtedly choice plums and Walter's performance there was undoubtedly high, or he would not have continued on and up.

In 1936, he earned a B.A. in economics, reporting that his favorite subjects were economics, geology, and engineering, and from 1936 to 1941 he sold petroleum products.

Then the war came; at age 28—a brand new father—he went off to the Navy as an officer. His background of managing men in the forest, his technical leanings, and his college education were the type of highly useful skills that the U.S. could tap among its civilians thrown abruptly into service, and the empirical prediction of his performance as a Navy officer would be high—unfortunately, no specific data are available on that point—but when V-J Day came five years later, he was the commanding officer of a Navy ATA.

Wars are terrible, but a small side benefit is that men like Walter are permitted a reassessment of their goals. He reassessed, decided he wanted to be a professional man, and in 1946—at age 33—he entered dental school on the G.I. Bill. Four years later he emerged with a D.D.S. degree and a second child. Today he says about his job: "It is exactly what I have wanted to do."

His four SVIB profiles (Figure 8-2) from the various testings are compatible with his career, but not especially predictive. His earliest profile, at age 16, actually had the highest Dentist score (43) of all four testings—the other high scores were on the practical, masculine-oriented scales: engineer, farmer, purchasing agent. His Masculinity-Femininity score has always been high, and that is probably the best single reflection of his dominant interests. All of his profiles emphasize this aspect, with scales such as Army Officer, Production Manager and Veterinarian being high on various testings. He has always had low scores on the social service and artistic occupational scales.

He comes across as a realistic, competitive, capable, and confident person; probably he runs a taut—and successful—ship at both home and the office. He has had an exciting, stimulating life from the National Forests through the wartime Pacific to a tough professional school into a useful and rewarding career. He has won, and is probably bemused that the youth of today can't understand the benefits of his kind of striving.

Case 3 (Figure 8-3)

Greg was another who knew what he wanted, did it, and is now happy in it. As a high school junior, he wrote that his eventual goal was writing for a newspaper. He said the same thing a year later, and repeated it five years later, as a college senior majoring in political science. He went to work as a reporter and, except for a stint in World War II, has been so employed ever since. Even in the army he had a journalist assignment.

When tested at age 52, he was still a reporter, concentrating on labor-management news, and had a strong interest in manpower policy, labor statistics, and the like.

On the job satisfaction form, he checked the next-to-the-top category, "My job is approximately what I have wanted to do."

All four of his SVIB profiles (Figure 8-4) are congruent with his occupation; he has always expressed preferences for writing and speaking, and his highest Occupational Scale scores have been in the verbal areas—Advertising, Management, Sales, and—as an adult—in the administrative areas. His strongest aversions have been, and still are, mathematics and mechanical activities, a very common pattern among journalists and other verbally-oriented occupations.

Note that his LP, IP, and DP percentages changed drastically from age 21 to 52:

	1930	1931	1936	1966
LP	15	19	23	59
IP	47	41	21	3
DP	37	40	56	38

Through the years, the breadth of activities that he finds enjoyable have expanded markedly.

PROFILE— STRONG VOCATIONAL INTEREST BLANK —FOR MEN (Form T399)

BASIC INTEREST SCALES

SCALE	1930	1931	1936	1966
PUBLIC SPEAKING	68	61	65	72
LAW/POLITICS	55	55	61	64
BUSINESS MANAGEMENT	43	53	65	47
SALES	54	54	49	56
MERCHANDISING	50	52	60	60
OFFICE PRACTICES	46	52	52	52
MILITARY ACTIVITIES	70	70	70	70
TECHNICAL SUPERVISION	38	38	38	62
MATHEMATICS	28	28	25	25
SCIENCE	58	50	46	56
MECHANICAL	33	29	32	38
NATURE	47	45	39	53
AGRICULTURE	37	37	31	43
ADVENTURE	53	57	57	61
RECREATIONAL LEADERSHIP	45	53	56	45
MEDICAL SERVICE	44	44	44	41
SOCIAL SERVICE	42	46	53	46
RELIGIOUS ACTIVITIES	48	48	48	48
TEACHING	54	54	58	65
MUSIC	50	51	47	60
ART	44	34	34	51
WRITING	63	63	61	55

PLOTTED SCORE 30 40 50

DOUBLE LINE = AVERAGE SCORE FOR 650 52-YEAR-OLD MEN

Non-Occupational Scales

	1930	1931	1936	1966
AACH	49	36	39	44
DIV	50	41	61	59
MFII	58	65	66	52
MO	35	33	54	32
OIE	48	39	40	44
OL	50	51	74	65
SL	44	41	56	49
AR	30	19	33	42

Administrative Indices

	1930	1931	1936	1966
TR	40	40	40	39
UNP	1	0	3	3
FC	-6	-3	-7	5
LP	15	19	23	59
IP	47	41	21	3
DP	37	40	56	38

OCCUPATIONAL SCALES (STD. SCORE: C 20, B−, B, B+, A 60)

	OCCUPATION	1930	1931	1936	1966
I	DENTIST	33	18	11	15
	OSTEOPATH	19	16	13	30
	VETERINARIAN	21	20	12	24
	PHYSICIAN	30	26	4	33
	PSYCHIATRIST	11	17	30	48
	PSYCHOLOGIST	16	15	37	47
	BIOLOGIST	24	11	17	33
II	ARCHITECT	26	13	13	18
	MATHEMATICIAN	20	10	-3	19
	PHYSICIST	8	-3	5	13
	CHEMIST	21	4	11	21
	ENGINEER	16	7	31	11
III	PRODUCTION	14	16	21	15
	ARMY OFFICER	5	17	29	27
	AIR FORCE OFFICER	21	21	1	34
IV	CARPENTER	16	7	12	-1
	FOREST SERVICE MAN	15	17	15	9
	FARMER	37	26	13	20
	MATH-SCIENCE TEACHER	30	25	25	13
	PRINTER	39	33	18	25
	POLICEMAN	20	24	52	18
V	PERSONNEL DIRECTOR	10	30	58	25
	PUBLIC ADMINISTRATOR	26	43	50	54
	REHABILITATION COUNS.	25	41	44	53
	YMCA STAFF MEMBER	37	40	45	46
	SOCIAL WORKER	28	42	56	46
	SOCIAL SCIENCE TEACHER	38	47	37	43
	SCHOOL SUPERINTENDENT	23	29	26	23
	MINISTER	20	27		27
VI	LIBRARIAN	39	33	29	35
	ARTIST	26	26	24	29
	MUSICIAN PERFORMER	37	35	13	40
	MUSIC TEACHER	25	31	31	34
VII	C.P.A. OWNER	16	25	26	32
VIII	SENIOR C.P.A.				
	ACCOUNTANT	20	12	28	6
	OFFICEWORKER	26	26	33	15
	PURCHASING AGENT	33	30	39	17
	BANKER	27	24	23	9
	PHARMACIST	30	29	32	27
	FUNERAL DIRECTOR	27	25	34	30
IX	SALES MANAGER	35	44	53	36
	REAL ESTATE SALESMAN	38	45	45	38
	LIFE INS. SALESMAN	41	48	43	34
X	ADVERTISING MAN	45	48	56	42
	LAWYER	40	45	42	42
	AUTHOR-JOURNALIST	38	40	44	45
XI	PRESIDENT-MFG.	21	22	41	26

SUPP. OCCUPATIONAL SCALES (20 30 40 50 60)

- CREDIT MANAGER
- CHAMBER OF COM. EXEC.
- PHYSICAL THERAPIST
- COMPUTER PROGRAMMER
- BUSINESS ED. TEACHER
- COMMUNITY REC. ADMIN.

NON-OCCUPATIONAL SCALES: AACH, AR, DIV, MFII, MO, OIE, OL, SL

ADMINISTRATIVE INDICES: TR, UNP, FC, LP, IP, DP

FIG. 8-3. *Profile for Case Study #3.*

PROFILE— STRONG VOCATIONAL INTEREST BLANK —FOR MEN (Form T399)

BASIC INTEREST SCALES

SCALE	1930	1931	1936	1966
PUBLIC SPEAKING	61	68	65	68
LAW/POLITICS	67	67	58	61
BUSINESS MANAGEMENT	59	55	67	65
SALES	54	59	61	66
MERCHANDISING	50	54	66	68
OFFICE PRACTICES	52	57	54	57
MILITARY ACTIVITIES	47	58	50	70
TECHNICAL SUPERVISION	38	52	47	42
MATHEMATICS	43	43	49	49
SCIENCE	37	46	43	39
MECHANICAL	42	50	46	35
NATURE	41	43	41	43
AGRICULTURE	43	43	43	40
ADVENTURE	41	53	49	45
RECREATIONAL LEADERSHIP	64	67	64	64
MEDICAL SERVICE	47	50	50	47
SOCIAL SERVICE	50	57	53	50
RELIGIOUS ACTIVITIES	55	48	55	63
TEACHING	44	54	48	61
MUSIC	47	51	47	47
ART	39	44	44	39
WRITING	47	35	59	67

PLOTTED SCORE 30 40 50

DOUBLE LINE = AVERAGE SCORE FOR 650 52-YEAR-OLD MEN

Non-Occupational Scales

	1930	1931	1936	1966
AACH	29	30	29	38
DIV	52	68	53	52
MFII	70	62	71	60
MO	40	20	38	37
OIE	31	33	30	30
OL	52	46	55	61
SL	34	47	41	52
AR	20	36	25	37

Administrative Indices

	1930	1931	1936	1966
TR	40	40	40	39
UNP	0	1	0	0
FC	-4	-1	-6	3
LP	21	23	20	31
IP	24	72	68	51
DP	54	5	12	18

OCCUPATIONAL SCALES (STD. SCORE: C 20, B−, B, B+, A 60)

	OCCUPATION	1930	1931	1936	1966
I	DENTIST	15	14	7	2
	OSTEOPATH	10	12	6	2
	VETERINARIAN	18	26	25	19
	PHYSICIAN	8	12	-5	-6
	PSYCHIATRIST	4	15	9	1
	PSYCHOLOGIST	8	18	10	11
	BIOLOGIST	2	6	-2	-5
II	ARCHITECT	11	5	6	6
	MATHEMATICIAN	4	-1	-3	4
	PHYSICIST	-1	-6	-3	-4
	CHEMIST	3	1	-5	-6
	ENGINEER	2	-1	4	-2
III	PRODUCTION	32	29	32	26
	ARMY OFFICER	15	31	29	32
	AIR FORCE OFFICER	18	27	29	28
IV	CARPENTER	19	21	17	9
	FOREST SERVICE MAN	18	16	23	-4
	FARMER	32	32	27	19
	MATH-SCIENCE TEACHER	14	34	27	30
	PRINTER	43	39	41	28
	POLICEMAN	36	37	27	22
V	PERSONNEL DIRECTOR	45	34	46	43
	PUBLIC ADMINISTRATOR	37	37	42	47
	REHABILITATION COUNS.	31	35	39	43
	YMCA STAFF MEMBER	52	48	40	42
	SOCIAL WORKER	41	45	45	47
	SOCIAL SCIENCE TEACHER	43	48	49	54
	SCHOOL SUPERINTENDENT	27	29	28	41
	MINISTER	17	19	9	19
VI	LIBRARIAN	22	26	18	24
	ARTIST	21	14	10	7
	MUSICIAN PERFORMER	39	38	25	24
	MUSIC TEACHER	32	33	27	38
VII	C.P.A. OWNER	29	35	37	44
VIII	SENIOR C.P.A.				
	ACCOUNTANT	30	21	38	33
	OFFICEWORKER	38	36	50	46
	PURCHASING AGENT	41	27	45	39
	BANKER	31	27	33	34
	PHARMACIST	27	23	30	31
	FUNERAL DIRECTOR	41	28	36	38
IX	SALES MANAGER	45	27	47	48
	REAL ESTATE SALESMAN	49	34	46	43
	LIFE INS. SALESMAN	49	34	39	40
X	ADVERTISING MAN	40	24	32	40
	LAWYER	38	27	26	38
	AUTHOR-JOURNALIST	32	22	22	28
XI	PRESIDENT-MFG.	27	13	21	28

SUPP. OCCUPATIONAL SCALES (20 30 40 50 60)

- CREDIT MANAGER
- CHAMBER OF COM. EXEC.
- PHYSICAL THERAPIST
- COMPUTER PROGRAMMER
- BUSINESS ED. TEACHER
- COMMUNITY REC. ADMIN.

NON-OCCUPATIONAL SCALES: AACH, AR, DIV, MFII, MO, OIE, OL, SL

ADMINISTRATIVE INDICES: TR, UNP, FC, LP, IP, DP

FIG. 8-4. *Profile for Case Study #4.*

This man's career seems very predictable from his own expressed plans—there was no apparent need for any testing, interest inventories or counseling for him. Considering this, his comments in a letter returned with his completed SVIB are relevant and fascinating: "My own recent studies [as a labor reporter] in this 5 county metropolitan area have led me to these conclusions: (1) The U.S. has one of the most haphazard systems of matching men and jobs in the civilized world. (2) The economic waste, and personal unhappiness and frustration from our present methods are staggering . . ."

Needless to say, he has been an avid participant in this research project.

Case 4 (Figure 8-4)

Today, Wilbur is the merchandise manager for a large department store, responsible for all purchasing.

On the three early testings, he listed the following on the SVIB cover sheet as his career goals: age 16, Lawyer; age 17, Criminal Lawyer; age 22, Merchandise or personnel manager in large department store.

This is another case where the stated goal was an accurate predictor, though at age 22 (1936) Wilbur had already been employed for four years in the department store where he is today. His progression upward was from clerk (1932–38) to buyer (1938–59) to merchandise manager (1959–present).

He reports today that he thoroughly enjoys his work, and checked the comment: "It is a career I entered due to circumstances more or less beyond my control, but now I am satisfied in it."

Wilbur's is a case of a boy moving early into an occupational area that was compatible with his measured interests, and there he stayed. The only only other possibility he considered—law—was probably not accessible to him, both because of economics—his father was a carpenter with a fourth-grade education, his mother had eight years of schooling—and because of his own lack of an academic orientation. Though he always has scored high on the SVIB Law/Politics scale, his score on the Lawyer Occupational Scale was never high, and his score on the Academic Achievement scale was always low, strongly suggesting that he would never have been comfortable in a law school environment.

At all four testings, his SVIB profile has been compatible with the work he is in. The Business Management Scale has always been high, as have the Sales and Merchandising Scales. Among the occupation scales, the sales, business, and administrative scales show the high scores. The Mathematics, Science, and Nature scales have been low—this is characteristic of sales-

PROFILE– STRONG VOCATIONAL INTEREST BLANK –FOR MEN (Form T399)

BASIC INTEREST SCALES

SCALE	1930	1931	1936	1966
PUBLIC SPEAKING	39	50	39	42
LAW/POLITICS	38	44	44	41
BUSINESS MANAGEMENT	39	39	37	35
SALES	39	39	37	37
MERCHANDISING	33	31	31	31
OFFICE PRACTICES	32	32	32	32
MILITARY ACTIVITIES	39	50	39	39
TECHNICAL SUPERVISION	33	47	52	38
MATHEMATICS	61	58	61	61
SCIENCE	67	65	64	60
MECHANICAL	44	49	54	50
NATURE	41	49	43	47
AGRICULTURE	43	50	53	50
ADVENTURE	49	49	41	41
RECREATIONAL LEADERSHIP	42	40	48	37
MEDICAL SERVICE	65	65	65	59
SOCIAL SERVICE	46	42	42	57
RELIGIOUS ACTIVITIES	41	41	41	41
TEACHING	51	51	51	54
MUSIC	47	43	43	47
ART	44	44	37	42
WRITING	41	45	41	40

DOUBLE LINE = AVERAGE SCORE FOR 650 52-YEAR-OLD MEN.

Non-Occupational Scales

	1930	1931	1936	1966
AACH	64	58	63	70
DIV	48	52	44	43
MFII	58	66	62	51
MO	46	47	42	51
OIE	55	49	55	55
OL	61	60	60	71
SL	39	47	39	39
AR	47	49	49	66

Administrative Indices

	1930	1931	1936	1966
TR	399	400	400	399
UNP	0	0	0	0
FC	-5	-3	0	5
LP	11	13	15	10
IP	15	20	21	21
DP	74	67	64	69

OCCUPATIONAL SCALES

Group	OCCUPATION	1930 (STD. SCORE)	1931	1936	1966
I	DENTIST	42	42	41	38
	OSTEOPATH	44	42	41	41
	VETERINARIAN	19	23	31	23
	PHYSICIAN	50	50	54	55
	PSYCHIATRIST	38	43	43	46
	PSYCHOLOGIST	36	36	45	47
	BIOLOGIST	48	51	49	53
II	ARCHITECT	38	34	34	38
	MATHEMATICIAN	39	35	41	47
	PHYSICIST	46	42	50	48
	CHEMIST	53	52	53	50
	ENGINEER	47	47	48	49
III	PRODUCTION	38	36	36	37
	ARMY OFFICER	10	19	15	6
	AIR FORCE OFFICER	27	38	33	23
IV	CARPENTER	19	19	22	14
	FOREST SERVICE MAN	27	38	24	23
	FARMER	34	33	34	35
	MATH-SCIENCE TEACHER	32	34	38	23
	PRINTER	22	16	22	5
	POLICEMAN	21	23	16	8
V	PERSONNEL DIRECTOR	15	18	27	29
	PUBLIC ADMINISTRATOR	17	28	30	37
	REHABILITATION COUNS.	25	27	27	27
	YMCA STAFF MEMBER	21	23	17	13
	SOCIAL WORKER	15	23	19	23
	SOCIAL SCIENCE TEACHER	9	5	11	16
	SCHOOL SUPERINTENDENT	20	20	22	34
	MINISTER	20	18	13	28
VI	LIBRARIAN	28	22	20	31
	ARTIST	39	39	41	40
	MUSICIAN PERFORMER	34	30	35	29
	MUSIC TEACHER	19	16	14	22
VII	C.P.A. OWNER	7	12	12	17
VIII	SENIOR C.P.A.				
	ACCOUNTANT	12	10	16	3
	OFFICEWORKER	11	10	12	0
	PURCHASING AGENT	20	17	33	23
	BANKER	14	7	12	12
	PHARMACIST	29	26	31	26
	FUNERAL DIRECTOR	19	16	14	19
IX	SALES MANAGER	23	23	18	14
	REAL ESTATE SALESMAN	27	32	28	27
	LIFE INS. SALESMAN	22	20	19	22
X	ADVERTISING MAN	30	30	21	28
	LAWYER	39	39	36	43
	AUTHOR-JOURNALIST	39	38	35	41
XI	PRESIDENT-MFG.	21	24	16	26
SUPP. OCCUPATIONAL SCALES	CREDIT MANAGER				
	CHAMBER OF COM. EXEC.				
	PHYSICAL THERAPIST				
	COMPUTER PROGRAMMER				
	BUSINESS ED. TEACHER				
	COMMUNITY REC. ADMIN.				

NON-OCCUPATIONAL SCALES: AACH AR DIV MFII MO OIE OL SL

ADMINISTRATIVE INDICES: TR UNP FC LP IP DP

FIG. 8-5. *Profile for Case Study #5.*

PROFILE– STRONG VOCATIONAL INTEREST BLANK –FOR MEN (Form T399)

BASIC INTEREST SCALES

SCALE	1930	1931	1936	1966
PUBLIC SPEAKING	53	65	50	50
LAW/POLITICS	58	67	58	55
BUSINESS MANAGEMENT	35	43	53	51
SALES	37	39	54	56
MERCHANDISING	33	40	52	52
OFFICE PRACTICES	32	38	54	54
MILITARY ACTIVITIES	39	50	50	39
TECHNICAL SUPERVISION	28	28	47	47
MATHEMATICS	40	49	43	55
SCIENCE	33	39	48	52
MECHANICAL	31	33	43	50
NATURE	31	39	47	53
AGRICULTURE	31	37	50	50
ADVENTURE	45	41	57	41
RECREATIONAL LEADERSHIP	40	40	59	48
MEDICAL SERVICE	35	38	53	56
SOCIAL SERVICE	50	50	57	64
RELIGIOUS ACTIVITIES	41	41	55	48
TEACHING	34	51	61	61
MUSIC	47	43	68	60
ART	34	37	56	61
WRITING	40	49	61	69

DOUBLE LINE = AVERAGE SCORE FOR 650 52-YEAR-OLD MEN.

Non-Occupational Scales

	1930	1931	1936	1966
AACH	34	42	41	54
DIV	43	41	53	59
MFII	62	62	46	42
MO	34	37	18	28
OIE	44	40	33	32
OL	58	63	46	52
SL	33	46	39	51
AR	22	31	37	46

Administrative Indices

	1930	1931	1936	1966
TR	40	40	40	39
UNP	0	0	0	0
FC	-9	-8	-9	5
LP	4	6	16	23
IP	10	19	76	68
DP	85	75	8	9

OCCUPATIONAL SCALES

Group	OCCUPATION	1930 (STD. SCORE)	1931	1936	1966
I	DENTIST	37	27	32	21
	OSTEOPATH	16	22	30	40
	VETERINARIAN	9	8	18	15
	PHYSICIAN	28	20	20	27
	PSYCHIATRIST	15	17	21	42
	PSYCHOLOGIST	16	19	9	30
	BIOLOGIST	17	24	11	24
II	ARCHITECT	36	25	16	17
	MATHEMATICIAN	31	32	10	18
	PHYSICIST	20	17	-3	6
	CHEMIST	14	16	6	9
	ENGINEER	20	27	7	10
III	PRODUCTION	34	31	18	9
	ARMY OFFICER	4	13	12	7
	AIR FORCE OFFICER	10	18	13	19
IV	CARPENTER	21	18	16	10
	FOREST SERVICE MAN	5	15	23	21
	FARMER	38	33	27	19
	MATH-SCIENCE TEACHER	18	23	32	31
	PRINTER	30	22	31	23
	POLICEMAN	27	26	29	12
V	PERSONNEL DIRECTOR	25	35	30	35
	PUBLIC ADMINISTRATOR	24	38	31	39
	REHABILITATION COUNS.	19	25	29	46
	YMCA STAFF MEMBER	27	25	38	34
	SOCIAL WORKER	20	26	39	55
	SOCIAL SCIENCE TEACHER	34	42	56	46
	SCHOOL SUPERINTENDENT	28	41	38	36
	MINISTER	19	24	38	50
VI	LIBRARIAN	28	24	41	47
	ARTIST	37	25	21	18
	MUSICIAN PERFORMER	44	29	46	46
	MUSIC TEACHER	34	32	46	37
VII	C.P.A. OWNER	25	30	24	14
VIII	SENIOR C.P.A.				
	ACCOUNTANT	25	29	20	12
	OFFICEWORKER	34	28	30	17
	PURCHASING AGENT	40	33	25	16
	BANKER	39	38	31	22
	PHARMACIST	27	22	29	14
	FUNERAL DIRECTOR	40	32	28	22
IX	SALES MANAGER	42	33	23	16
	REAL ESTATE SALESMAN	50	47	32	25
	LIFE INS. SALESMAN	49	45	32	23
X	ADVERTISING MAN	48	42	28	22
	LAWYER	55	56	36	35
	AUTHOR-JOURNALIST	46	38	25	24
XI	PRESIDENT-MFG.	41	34	15	14
SUPP. OCCUPATIONAL SCALES	CREDIT MANAGER				
	CHAMBER OF COM. EXEC.				
	PHYSICAL THERAPIST				
	COMPUTER PROGRAMMER				
	BUSINESS ED. TEACHER				
	COMMUNITY REC. ADMIN.				

NON-OCCUPATIONAL SCALES: AACH AR DIV MFII MO OIE OL SL

ADMINISTRATIVE INDICES: TR UNP FC LP IP DP

FIG. 8-6. *Profile for Case Study #6.*

men's profiles. Many salesmen have high scores on the Adventure Scale, but Wilbur doesn't. Perhaps this is related to his choosing a retailing environment rather than a person-to-person sales job.

His Managerial Orientation score is only moderate; probably he does not aspire to the activities related to running a large chain of stores. His Occupational Introversion-Extroversion score has always been a hail-fellow-well-met. In the booklet, he reported liking golf, bridge, amusement parks, stag parties, conventions, nightclubs, large parties, and telling jokes. He dislikes art galleries, symphony concerts, carelessly dressed people, methodical work, and nonconformists. He clearly is a lively fellow in the typical business mold, and merchandising is a good area for him.

Case 5 (Figure 8-5)

Lewis's case is simple and straightforward. When he was 15, he wrote, "I want to be a professor of biochemistry or an M.D." When he was 16, "I want to be an M.D. doing research on disease." When he was 21, "I intend to be a physician on the staff of a large hospital, on the faculty of a good medical school, and practicing on the side." At 51, he reports his job as "Physician—Vice President for research . . . do medical research and related administration." He checked the following on the job satisfaction questionnaire: "This is approximately what I have wanted to do."

Lewis grew up in an educated family—both his parents were college graduates—and his academic interests were prominent early in life. At age 15, his SVIB Academic Achievement score was 64, higher than the average for adult Ph.D.'s. After graduating from high school, he went east to one of the better universities, majored in Biological Science, and went on to one of the leading medical schools.

His SVIB profiles consistently showed dominant interests in math and science, especially the biological sciences. Those Basic Scales were always high, and the Occupational Scales for Physician, Chemist, and Biologist were the highest ones. There were few other competing interests; his Diversity of Interests score was never high, and went lower on the last two testings. He never checked "Like" to more than 15 occupations. This concentration of interest and early commitment to science is a common feature in the careers of scientists.

For Lewis, there was never any question, either in his mind or from the SVIB profile, that he would end up in scientific research in the biological sciences. This doesn't mean an absence of agonizing career decisions; he undoubtedly pondered long over various alternatives. And he apparently was faced with at least one decision that the SVIB can't help with—a choice of geography. He today lives in the Midwest, one of the few from Strong's early sample to migrate away from California. Perhaps his intensive interests in medical research led him to ignore geographic considerations and to follow his career wherever the proper facilities beckoned.

Case 6 (Figure 8-6)

When Allen was 15, he wrote on the front of his SVIB booklet, "I plan to be a lawyer." When he was 16, he wrote, "I plan to practice law." When he was 21, a college senior, he wrote, "I plan to be an actor," and continued, "My folks think I should be a lawyer, but I know my own abilities and interests better than they do." At age 52, he reported the following information: occupation—Lawyer; years of experience—8; at what age did you decide on this work?—36. On the job satisfaction questionnaire, he checked, "This is a tolerable career but not really what I would like to do."

His career has not been smooth-flowing, and there are some gaps in the files. As a college senior in 1936, he was certain that he wished to be an actor, and was intent on following that path. The only information on the next 11 years is that eight of them were spent in a TB sanitarium. From 1947 to 1957, he listed his occupation only as "administrative assistant." During this period, he earned a law degree in night school; and finally, in 1958 at age 44, he became a lawyer. He never married.

His profiles reflect his stated interests; the first one, from 1930, had the highest occupational score on the Lawyer scale, and the Musician Performer score was also high. On the Basic Scales, Law/Politics and Public Speaking were the high scores. (He couldn't have very many high scores; his "Like Percentage" was only 4, and he marked "Dislike" to 85 percent of the occupations listed in the booklet.)

His second profile, 1931, was even more markedly like a lawyer. His Lawyer score was 56, well up in the range, and his score on the Law/Politics scale was a very high 67. He still marked "Like" to only 6 percent of the occupations.

There was a large shift in his measured interests between 1931 and 1936, his college years. The Lawyer scale fell off 20 points, and the Law/Politics scale fell 10 points, though it remained high. He reported much more interest in teaching, music, art, and writing; among the occupational scales, his highest score was on the Social Science Teacher scale, the next highest were Music Teacher and Musician Performer. Surprisingly, his score on the Adventure scale went up 16 points; among most men, that score slowly declines with age.

His adult profile resembled the college senior profile fairly closely; the

Teaching, Music, Art, and Writing scales were still high, and the Social Service scale was also high. On the Occupational Scales, the high scores were still in the Group V (Social Service and Administration)—such as the Social Worker and Social Science Teacher scales—and in Group VI (Cultural/Aesthetic)—Musician Performer and Librarian. The Adventure scale dropped back to its original level.

The Lawyer Occupational scale was again low.

His profile as a college senior and as an adult today is much more representative of a friendly, outgoing (Occupational Introversion-Extroversion score of 32), socially conscious teacher or counselor than it is of a corporation lawyer. He is likely concerned with atypical legal activities, such as providing services for the poor, or perhaps doing some legal work for various charities or artistic institutions. Or he might simply be carrying out his legal practice 40 hours per week, and spending his interests on these other activities as hobbies. Whatever, it is a safe prediction that he is not driven to succeed in the classic legal mold.

That he is an outgoing, verbal fellow can be documented by his reply when we asked him for information in the followup study. Through an error in our office, we sent him the second letter before the first. In the second letter, we said that we had not heard from him and wondered if we had the right person; if not, we would like to begin looking elsewhere. He wrote back: "As gently as you have reminded me that I have probably been derelict in my ordinary duties of response, may I persuade you to believe that the fault was not mine."

He went on to say, merrily, that he had been initially contacted by phone, and explained that he would be delighted to provide any information asked for, and concluded: "Obviously, you must have concluded by this time that I am both Allen——— and the fellow you are looking for. Any attempt by you to begin 'tracking (my) namesake elsewhere' would be looked upon as an unjustified assailment of my disgusting ego."

From the counseling standpoint, a good interpretation of the SVIB profile at age 15 might not have helped him; any advice based on that profile would have pointed directly at law. Presumably, even if he had gone straight through law school after the B.A., he would today still be a lawyer and reporting, "It is a tolerable career, but not really what I want to do."

Case 7 (Figure 8-7)

The profile in Figure 8-7 has been included to illustrate a specific point, i.e., the robustness of the individual's scores under different mental sets. This man, an Army sergeant, was sent a routine request, asking him to fill

PROFILE– STRONG VOCATIONAL INTEREST BLANK –FOR MEN (Form T399)

BASIC INTEREST SCALES

SCALE	RES	SGT
PUBLIC SPEAKING	56	61
LAW/POLITICS	61	53
BUSINESS MANAGEMENT	65	67
SALES	73	65
MERCHANDISING	59	59
OFFICE PRACTICES	45	45
MILITARY ACTIVITIES	37	37
TECHNICAL SUPERVISION	44	49
MATHEMATICS	37	37
SCIENCE	43	50
MECHANICAL	36	39
NATURE	42	42
AGRICULTURE	53	56
ADVENTURE	53	59
RECREATIONAL LEADERSHIP	30	34
MEDICAL SERVICE	38	35
SOCIAL SERVICE	30	37
RELIGIOUS ACTIVITIES	32	35
TEACHING	45	34
MUSIC	34	34
ART	47	53
WRITING	58	53

DOUBLE LINE = AVERAGE SCORE FOR 650 52-YEAR-OLD MEN

Non-Occupational Scales

	RES	SGT
AACH	35	34
DIV	35	32
MFII	55	57
MO	47	47
OIE	42	48
OL	71	72
SL	28	33
AR	43	46

Administrative Indices

	RES	SGT
TR	383	382
UNP	6	5
FC	8	7
LP	25	23
IP	23	22
DP	52	55

OCCUPATIONAL SCALES

Group	OCCUPATION	RES (STD. SCORE)	SGT
I	DENTIST	23	25
	OSTEOPATH	23	19
	VETERINARIAN	24	29
	PHYSICIAN	23	22
	PSYCHIATRIST	12	11
	PSYCHOLOGIST	26	26
	BIOLOGIST	17	28
II	ARCHITECT	29	37
	MATHEMATICIAN	18	19
	PHYSICIST	13	19
	CHEMIST	10	21
	ENGINEER	27	34
III	PRODUCTION	18	34
	ARMY OFFICER	16	17
	AIR FORCE OFFICER	19	25
IV	CARPENTER	14	21
	FOREST SERVICE MAN	20	22
	FARMER	32	37
	MATH-SCIENCE TEACHER	7	5
	PRINTER	25	27
	POLICEMAN	7	7
V	PERSONNEL DIRECTOR	36	37
	PUBLIC ADMINISTRATOR	37	38
	REHABILITATION COUNS.	39	30
	YMCA STAFF MEMBER	26	19
	SOCIAL WORKER	29	20
	SOCIAL SCIENCE TEACHER	29	22
	SCHOOL SUPERINTENDENT	26	17
	MINISTER	20	13
VI	LIBRARIAN	29	28
	ARTIST	31	32
	MUSICIAN PERFORMER	30	25
	MUSIC TEACHER	28	21
VII	C.P.A. OWNER	32	41
VIII	SENIOR C.P.A.	13	20
	ACCOUNTANT	15	28
	OFFICEWORKER	22	27
	PURCHASING AGENT	34	40
	BANKER	28	33
	PHARMACIST	31	34
	FUNERAL DIRECTOR	34	36
IX	SALES MANAGER	49	47
	REAL ESTATE SALESMAN	53	52
	LIFE INS. SALESMAN	50	46
X	ADVERTISING MAN	49	51
	LAWYER	39	39
	AUTHOR-JOURNALIST	42	42
XI	PRESIDENT-MFG.	45	50
SUPP. OCCUPATIONAL SCALES	CREDIT MANAGER	30	26
	CHAMBER OF COM. EXEC.	48	45
	PHYSICAL THERAPIST	10	10
	COMPUTER PROGRAMMER	21	24
	BUSINESS ED. TEACHER	42	37
	COMMUNITY REC. ADMIN.	36	27

NON-OCCUPATIONAL SCALES: AACH AR DIV MFII MO OIE OL SL
ADMINISTRATIVE INDICES: TR UNP FC LP IP DP

FIG. 8-7. *Profile for Case Study #7.*

PROFILE– STRONG VOCATIONAL INTEREST BLANK –FOR MEN (Form T399)

BASIC INTEREST SCALES

SCALE	1968
PUBLIC SPEAKING	46
LAW/POLITICS	39
BUSINESS MANAGEMENT	35
SALES	42
MERCHANDISING	37
OFFICE PRACTICES	40
MILITARY ACTIVITIES	50
TECHNICAL SUPERVISION	27
MATHEMATICS	61
SCIENCE	63
MECHANICAL	50
NATURE	54
AGRICULTURE	56
ADVENTURE	53
RECREATIONAL LEADERSHIP	40
MEDICAL SERVICE	56
SOCIAL SERVICE	56
RELIGIOUS ACTIVITIES	45
TEACHING	50
MUSIC	64
ART	67
WRITING	58

DOUBLE LINE = AVERAGE SCORE FOR 650 52-YEAR-OLD MEN

Non-Occupational Scales

	1968
AACH	66
DIV	55
MFII	46
MO	25
OIE	53
OL	54
SL	43
AR	46

Administrative Indices

	1968
TR	396
UNP	8
FC	4
LP	22
IP	30
DP	48

OCCUPATIONAL SCALES

Group	OCCUPATION	1968 (STD. SCORE)
I	DENTIST	52
	OSTEOPATH	45
	VETERINARIAN	39
	PHYSICIAN	53
	PSYCHIATRIST	28
	PSYCHOLOGIST	29
	BIOLOGIST	55
II	ARCHITECT	40
	MATHEMATICIAN	34
	PHYSICIST	38
	CHEMIST	48
	ENGINEER	42
III	PRODUCTION	19
	ARMY OFFICER	10
	AIR FORCE OFFICER	27
IV	CARPENTER	30
	FOREST SERVICE MAN	26
	FARMER	42
	MATH-SCIENCE TEACHER	32
	PRINTER	39
	POLICEMAN	24
V	PERSONNEL DIRECTOR	15
	PUBLIC ADMINISTRATOR	14
	REHABILITATION COUNS.	14
	YMCA STAFF MEMBER	15
	SOCIAL WORKER	11
	SOCIAL SCIENCE TEACHER	6
	SCHOOL SUPERINTENDENT	5
	MINISTER	22
VI	LIBRARIAN	33
	ARTIST	44
	MUSICIAN PERFORMER	44
	MUSIC TEACHER	22
VII	C.P.A. OWNER	29
VIII	SENIOR C.P.A.	26
	ACCOUNTANT	14
	OFFICEWORKER	16
	PURCHASING AGENT	14
	BANKER	15
	PHARMACIST	26
	FUNERAL DIRECTOR	21
IX	SALES MANAGER	13
	REAL ESTATE SALESMAN	22
	LIFE INS. SALESMAN	20
X	ADVERTISING MAN	35
	LAWYER	33
	AUTHOR-JOURNALIST	40
XI	PRESIDENT-MFG.	21
SUPP. OCCUPATIONAL SCALES	CREDIT MANAGER	12
	CHAMBER OF COM. EXEC.	21
	PHYSICAL THERAPIST	37
	COMPUTER PROGRAMMER	33
	BUSINESS ED. TEACHER	15
	COMMUNITY REC. ADMIN.	9

NON-OCCUPATIONAL SCALES: AACH AR DIV MFII MO OIE OL SL
ADMINISTRATIVE INDICES: TR UNP FC LP IP DP

FIG. 8-8. *Profile for Case Study #8.*

in the inventory for the study of Army sergeants. He complied, listing his occupation as "sergeant" but indicating that he didn't enjoy his work. He also mentioned being a part-time realtor for several years. When he returned the forms, he sent a short note, asking for another copy. In a few days, he returned the second form, this time indicating his occupation as "realtor" and that he enjoyed this work.

What he had clearly done was to answer the inventory the first time thinking, "I am a sergeant, I am a sergeant, I am a sergeant..." and answered the second time thinking, "I am a realtor, I am a realtor, I am a realtor...," and now he was curious about the differences that would appear in his test scores. As the profile in Figure 8-7 shows, the two approaches differed hardly at all, with the exception of two or three scales. The Sales Basic Interest scale score went up, but it was already very high, and was a dominant score on both profiles. The Teaching Basic Interest scale score also went up several points; just why is not clear. The Military Activities scored stayed low both times; actually, his score (37) is the lowest possible score on that scale.

Interestingly, his percentage of "Likes," "Indifferents," and "Dislikes" stayed almost constant; 25–23–52 versus 23–22–55.

The point here is that, contrary to most people's intuition about their test behavior, there is considerable consistency even under different strategies.

Case 8 (Figure 8-8)

The SVIB should typically not be used by students under 15 or 16, and probably not even with immature youths at those ages. Yet these ages are only guidelines; if a student can handle the vocabulary, and if he is cognizant of the world of work, then some information can be gained from looking at his SVIB scores. To pressure young boys and girls into premature career choices, or even to suggest indirectly that they must have a choice is not wise, I think; they need time to stare at clouds, and throw stones in lakes, and pretend that their last name is Bernhardt, or Namath, or Armstrong. Still, some fascinating information can be gained by looking at SVIB profiles from young students.

Figure 8-8 has the profile for a 10-year-old boy, a fifth-grader. He is a "typical" little boy, with scuffed sneakers, a long history of cuts and abrasions, and an almost perfect record of losing his father's tools. He is also bright, with excellent reading skills; most of his standardized test scores are at the 9th and 10th grade levels. He had no trouble reading the Strong, though his attention span was not sufficient to complete it in one sitting; he worked over the booklet in spare moments over several days.

His results document what his parents attest to—that he is fascinated by science. His highest scores on the Basic Interest Scales fell into two areas; math-science and the arts; music, art, and writing. This pattern is typical of academically oriented scientists, and the strong rejection of the scales at the top of the profile, especially the business activities, also supports that pattern of interests.

The same pattern appeared, as it should, among the Occupational Scales; the high scores were in Group I and II, the sciences, with some moderately high ones in Groups VI and X, the art-oriented occupations. The lowest ones were in Groups VIII and III, the business and technical-supervisory occupations; the Group V scores—public administration and social service occupations—were also low.

All of this was summed up in the Academic Achievement scale score—66, quite high for a college student, let alone a ten-year-old—and this score, particularly in concert with the rest of the profile, strongly suggests that the boy is destined for some type of academic-intellectual-scientific career.

There was no particular purpose in giving him the inventory, simply curiosity on his part and his parents'. What was accomplished was that the three of them had, so they reported, a fascinating two-hour conversation about the role of work in an individual's life, and about the possible different styles of life. His father commented later, "We talked about things that I never knew he was interested in, and he had insights that I never imagined him capable of." Clearly, the most important end served was family communication.

This knowledge of the boy's interests, by itself, does not provide any direct answers to the parents' questions of how he should be treated with respect to career development. Two extreme viewpoints could be adopted: one, by recognizing that the boy is a bookish, scholarly dreamer who should be allowed to pursue his interests unimpeded; the other by concluding, "Well, his preferences will insure his education in those areas; what we should do is lean on him to insure some breadth and diversity in his life by acquainting him with shop work, athletic activities, and some business philosophy."

In this particular family, the mother opts for the former, the father for the latter—the future should be interesting.

Case Studies—Women

Because the optimum use of the SVIB with women requires intimate recognition of the special problems they have in making career choices, I have asked one of my feminine colleagues, Dr. Lenore Harmon of the Department of Student Counseling at the University of Wisconsin, Milwaukee, to prepare some case notes on the profiles of some of her women clients. Her insights are especially useful, for she is well grounded in interest measurement, is an excellent counselor and has firsthand knowledge of the quandaries of the career woman who is also a wife and mother. These notes were originally used in a Workshop on Interest Inventories, sponsored by Iowa State University, conducted by Donald Zytowski.

The next cases, 9 through 15, are drawn from her current counseling activities; they are all recent cases, tested with the 1969 revision, and no long-term followup information is yet available.

Case 9 (Figure 8-9)

The major theme in this profile is business interests, though the Numbers score is lower than that of many women in business. This woman, according to the profile, seems willing to take on managerial responsibilities and to seek out new situations. Some type of sales or merchandising occupation might suit her; a specific possibility might be interior decorating. The other high Occupational Scale scores are not supported by the Basic Scales.

This girl was a senior in Business Administration; she took the SVIB to confirm her vocational choice. When she entered the university, she chose between interior decoration and business, electing the latter because she was unsure of her talent in design. In business, she has specialized in management courses and has avoided accounting and quantitative analysis as much as possible. She hopes to be employed at the middle management level and is willing to go anywhere in the world. She expects to marry but is in no hurry. She defines an "opportunity" as a chance to get ahead in business; her mother defines an "opportunity" as one of her brother's boy friends.

Case 10 (Figure 8-10)

This is the profile of another girl with strong interests in mathematics and science who has, in fact, earned a B.S. degree in economics. When tested, she was finishing up a Master's degree in economics where she was a Teaching Assistant; she, too, took the SVIB to confirm her occupational plans. She has considered going on for the Ph.D., but realizes that it is the freedom of the college professor which attracts her, not the nature of the work, and is quite sure she would hate writing a thesis or anything else, and she is now looking for a job as a business analyst or researcher.

She entered graduate school mainly because she found, as a girl with a bachelor's degree in economics, she was offered only programming and low-level research jobs. With a graduate degree, she hopes that more stimulating opportunities will be available.

PROFILE— STRONG VOCATIONAL INTEREST BLANK —FOR WOMEN (Form TW398)

BASIC INTEREST SCALES

SCALE	PLOTTED SCORE
PUBLIC SPEAKING	60
LAW/POLITICS	73
MERCHANDISING	52
OFFICE PRACTICES	56
NUMBERS	72
PHYSICAL SCIENCE	71
MECHANICAL	66
OUTDOORS	43
BIOLOGICAL SCIENCE	40
MEDICAL SERVICE	43
TEACHING	40
SOCIAL SERVICE	42
SPORTS	50
HOMEMAKING	43
RELIGIOUS ACTIVITIES	40
MUSIC	44
ART	55
PERFORMING ARTS	60
WRITING	43

Non-Occupational Scales

AACH	57
DIV	62
FMII	52
OIE	37

Administrative Indices

TR	398
UNP	7
FC	4
LP	39
IP	20
DP	41

DOUBLE LINE = AVERAGE SCORE FOR 1000 EMPLOYED ADULT WOMEN

OCCUPATIONAL SCALES

	OCCUPATION	STD SCORE
I	MUSIC TEACHER	13
	ENTERTAINER	25
	MUSICIAN PERFORMER	24
	MODEL	22
II	ART TEACHER	13
	ARTIST	30
III	INTERIOR DECORATOR	26
	NEWSWOMAN	23
	ENGLISH TEACHER	19
	LANGUAGE TEACHER	24
IV	YWCA STAFF MEMBER	40
	RECREATION LEADER	35
	DIETITIAN	11
V	DIRECTOR CHRISTIAN ED	11
	NUN-TEACHER	40
	GUIDANCE COUNSELOR	46
	SOCIAL SCIENCE TEACHER	38
	SOCIAL WORKER	43
VI	SPEECH PATHOLOGIST	40
	PSYCHOLOGIST	40
	LIBRARIAN	20
	TRANSLATOR	28

	OCCUPATION	STD SCORE
VII	ARMY-ENLISTED	47
	NAVY-ENLISTED	39
	ARMY-OFFICER	53
	NAVY-OFFICER	58
VIII	LAWYER	56
	ACCOUNTANT	58
	BANKWOMAN	39
	LIFE INS UNDERWRITER	36
	BUYER	33
	BUSINESS ED TEACHER	26
IX	HOME ECON TEACHER	16
	DIETITIAN	45
	PHYSICAL ED TEACHER	24
	PHYSICAL THERAPIST	25
	OCCUPATIONAL THERAPIST	40
	PUBLIC HEALTH NURSE	9
	REGISTERED NURSE	12
	LIC PRACTICAL NURSE	19
	RADIOLOGIC TECHNOLOGIST	25
	DENTAL ASSISTANT	20
XI	EXECUTIVE HOUSEKEEPER	29
	ELEMENTARY TEACHER	17
	SECRETARY	25
	SALESWOMAN	15
	TELEPHONE OPERATOR	13
	INSTRUMENT ASSEMBLER	21
	SEWING MACHINE OPERATOR	1
	BEAUTICIAN	46
	AIRLINE STEWARDESS	28

FIG. 8-10. *Profile for Case Study #10.*

PROFILE— STRONG VOCATIONAL INTEREST BLANK —FOR WOMEN (Form TW398)

BASIC INTEREST SCALES

SCALE	PLOTTED SCORE
PUBLIC SPEAKING	52
LAW/POLITICS	65
MERCHANDISING	64
OFFICE PRACTICES	47
NUMBERS	38
PHYSICAL SCIENCE	45
MECHANICAL	47
OUTDOORS	46
BIOLOGICAL SCIENCE	40
MEDICAL SERVICE	36
TEACHING	35
SOCIAL SERVICE	37
SPORTS	28
HOMEMAKING	40
RELIGIOUS ACTIVITIES	48
MUSIC	31
ART	57
PERFORMING ARTS	40
WRITING	48

Non-Occupational Scales

AACH	39
DIV	47
FMII	49
OIE	42

Administrative Indices

TR	396
UNP	7
FC	5
LP	24
IP	30
DP	46

DOUBLE LINE = AVERAGE SCORE FOR 1000 EMPLOYED ADULT WOMEN

OCCUPATIONAL SCALES

	OCCUPATION	STD SCORE
I	MUSIC TEACHER	16
	ENTERTAINER	25
	MUSICIAN PERFORMER	23
	MODEL	44
II	ART TEACHER	25
	ARTIST	33
III	INTERIOR DECORATOR	48
	NEWSWOMAN	43
	ENGLISH TEACHER	36
	LANGUAGE TEACHER	32
IV	YWCA STAFF MEMBER	37
	RECREATION LEADER	32
	DIETITIAN	9
V	DIRECTOR CHRISTIAN ED	-8
	NUN-TEACHER	26
	GUIDANCE COUNSELOR	45
	SOCIAL SCIENCE TEACHER	23
	SOCIAL WORKER	27
VI	SPEECH PATHOLOGIST	17
	PSYCHOLOGIST	41
	LIBRARIAN	35
	TRANSLATOR	

	OCCUPATION	STD SCORE
VII	ARMY-ENLISTED	39
	NAVY-ENLISTED	32
	ARMY-OFFICER	47
	NAVY-OFFICER	50
VIII	LAWYER	47
	ACCOUNTANT	39
	BANKWOMAN	39
	LIFE INS UNDERWRITER	49
	BUYER	46
	BUSINESS ED TEACHER	22
IX	HOME ECON TEACHER	24
	DIETITIAN	33
X	PHYSICAL ED TEACHER	12
	OCCUPATIONAL THERAPIST	23
	PHYSICAL THERAPIST	12
	PUBLIC HEALTH NURSE	12
	REGISTERED NURSE	10
	LIC PRACTICAL NURSE	16
	RADIOLOGIC TECHNOLOGIST	18
	DENTAL ASSISTANT	30
XI	EXECUTIVE HOUSEKEEPER	19
	ELEMENTARY TEACHER	43
	SECRETARY	25
	SALESWOMAN	17
	TELEPHONE OPERATOR	21
	INSTRUMENT ASSEMBLER	13
	SEWING MACHINE OPERATOR	34
	BEAUTICIAN	
	AIRLINE STEWARDESS	38

VI PHYSICIAN 10
DENTIST 11
MEDICAL TECHNOLOGIST 16
CHEMIST -3
MATHEMATICIAN 9
COMPUTER PROGRAMMER 23
MATH SCIENCE TEACHER 21
ENGINEER 19

FIG. 8-9. *Profile for Case Study #9.*

Incidentally, she confirmed her high Mechanical score when she reported that she has just bought her first car and is learning to change the oil and make minor repairs.

Case 11 (Figure 8-11)

This profile belongs to a woman of wide interests who might consider physical sciences and art as potential vocational choices. Actually, social service occupations, occupations which place her "on stage," secretarial, and sales occupations would all be appropriate choices, from an interest standpoint, if she has the necessary talents.

This young woman illustrates another type of conflict that women face in making vocational decisions. She is an extremely attractive 21-year-old with a degree in communication. Her professors call her talented and see her as a good candidate to become a "television personality." She has had extensive experience in radio and a little experience in modeling and television commercials. She is interested specifically in mass media merchandising of fashion, but she is also interested in marriage.

She belongs (nominally now) to a small and strict religious subgroup from which she learned that women should be quiet and submissive wives, marrying early and inside the group. Though she is creative and bright, she tends to present herself as young and flighty. She is offered secretarial and clerical jobs in advertising and television; those she says, quite accurately, "I can do blindfolded." To pursue the responsible jobs she wants, she must throw off the ultrafeminine role which she now plays to avoid being classed as too independent for marriage.

The SVIB suggests the conflict between her homemaking interests and the masculinity of her vocational interests but it does not resolve her conflicts. To become a career woman, especially a sophisticated, beautiful celebrity, would flout her religious upbringing and scare men away. To play the lost little girl may get her a husband, but not the career she wants (and not the type of husband she wants, either). In counseling, she is beginning to recognize this conflict and resolve it. Most recently she has changed jobs in an attempt to get a fresh start in presenting herself as more competent and self-confident.

Case 12 (Figure 8-12)

This profile is a clear-cut example of interests in mathematics and science; on that, the Basic and the Occupational Scales agree quite well.

Unfortunately, this is another illustration of a conflict situation—this time between interests and circumstances. The profile belongs to a 40-year-old woman, a recent divorcee, with a young child. She sought coun-

PROFILE— STRONG VOCATIONAL INTEREST BLANK —FOR WOMEN (Form TW398)

Fig. 8-12 (Case Study #12)

BASIC INTEREST SCALES

SCALE	PLOTTED SCORE
PUBLIC SPEAKING	55
LAW/POLITICS	57
MERCHANDISING	49
OFFICE PRACTICES	58
NUMBERS	65
PHYSICAL SCIENCE	69
MECHANICAL	66
OUTDOORS	58
BIOLOGICAL SCIENCE	55
MEDICAL SERVICE	58
TEACHING	59
SOCIAL SERVICE	52
SPORTS	63
HOMEMAKING	51
RELIGIOUS ACTIVITIES	50
MUSIC	50
ART	53
PERFORMING ARTS	55
WRITING	48

DOUBLE LINE = AVERAGE SCORE FOR 1000 EMPLOYED ADULT WOMEN

Non-Occupational Scales: AACH 61, DIV 64, FMII 22, OIE 55

Administrative Indices: TR 398, UNP 7, FC 16, LP 29, IP 63, DP 9

OCCUPATIONAL SCALES

	OCCUPATION	STD SCORE		OCCUPATION	STD SCORE
I	MUSIC TEACHER	10	VII	ARMY-ENLISTED	36
	ENTERTAINER	14		NAVY-ENLISTED	42
	MUSICIAN PERFORMER	23		ARMY-OFFICER	23
	MODEL	12		NAVY-OFFICER	32
II	ART TEACHER	20	VIII	LAWYER	20
	ARTIST	35		ACCOUNTANT	35
	INTERIOR DECORATOR	33		BANKWOMAN	33
III	NEWSWOMAN	13		LIFE INS. UNDERWRITER	13
	ENGLISH TEACHER	-3		BUYER	-3
	LANGUAGE TEACHER	29		BUSINESS ED. TEACHER	29
IV	YWCA STAFF MEMBER	30	IX	HOME ECON. TEACHER	29
	RECREATION LEADER	30		DIETITIAN	30
	DIRECTOR CHRISTIAN ED.	17	X	PHYSICAL ED. TEACHER	53
	NON-TEACHER	9		OCCUPATIONAL THERAPIST	43
	GUIDANCE COUNSELOR	24		PHYSICAL THERAPIST	56
	SOCIAL SCIENCE TEACHER	28		PUBLIC HEALTH NURSE	25
	SOCIAL WORKER	17		REGISTERED NURSE	38
V	SPEECH PATHOLOGIST	22		LIC. PRACTICAL NURSE	35
	PSYCHOLOGIST	21		RADIOLOGIC TECHNOLOGIST	48
	LIBRARIAN	20		DENTAL ASSISTANT	38
	TRANSLATOR	25	XI	EXECUTIVE HOUSEKEEPER	22
VI	PHYSICIAN	36		ELEMENTARY TEACHER	37
	DENTIST	29		SECRETARY	27
	MEDICAL TECHNOLOGIST	49		SALESWOMAN	27
	MATHEMATICIAN	26		TELEPHONE OPERATOR	36
	COMPUTER PROGRAMMER	56		INSTRUMENT ASSEMBLER	35
	MATH SCIENCE TEACHER	51		SEWING MACHINE OPERAT.	24
	ENGINEER	50		BEAUTICIAN	
				AIRLINE STEWARDESS	27

FIG. 8-12. Profile for Case Study #12.

PROFILE— STRONG VOCATIONAL INTEREST BLANK —FOR WOMEN (Form TW398)

Fig. 8-11 (Case Study #11)

BASIC INTEREST SCALES

SCALE	PLOTTED SCORE
PUBLIC SPEAKING	70
LAW/POLITICS	63
MERCHANDISING	64
OFFICE PRACTICES	60
NUMBERS	40
PHYSICAL SCIENCE	38
MECHANICAL	38
OUTDOORS	33
BIOLOGICAL SCIENCE	57
MEDICAL SERVICE	57
TEACHING	54
SOCIAL SERVICE	64
SPORTS	50
HOMEMAKING	61
RELIGIOUS ACTIVITIES	55
MUSIC	63
ART	39
PERFORMING ARTS	58
WRITING	52

DOUBLE LINE = AVERAGE SCORE FOR 1000 EMPLOYED ADULT WOMEN

Non-Occupational Scales: AACH 36, DIV 65, FMII 35, OIE 30

Administrative Indices: TR 398, UNP 6, FC 6, LP 57, IP 16, DP 27

OCCUPATIONAL SCALES

	OCCUPATION	STD SCORE		OCCUPATION	STD SCORE
I	MUSIC TEACHER	34	VII	ARMY-ENLISTED	43
	ENTERTAINER	41		NAVY-ENLISTED	33
	MUSICIAN PERFORMER	41		ARMY-OFFICER	46
	MODEL	41		NAVY-OFFICER	36
II	ART TEACHER	-13	VIII	LAWYER	28
	ARTIST	8		ACCOUNTANT	23
	INTERIOR DECORATOR	5		BANKWOMAN	42
III	NEWSWOMAN	24		LIFE INS. UNDERWRITER	48
	ENGLISH TEACHER	41		BUYER	36
	LANGUAGE TEACHER	45		BUSINESS ED. TEACHER	36
IV	YWCA STAFF MEMBER	56	IX	HOME ECON. TEACHER	33
	RECREATION LEADER	50		DIETITIAN	47
	DIRECTOR CHRISTIAN ED.	36	X	PHYSICAL ED. TEACHER	36
	NON-TEACHER	9		OCCUPATIONAL THERAPIST	22
	GUIDANCE COUNSELOR	48		PHYSICAL THERAPIST	32
	SOCIAL SCIENCE TEACHER	49		PUBLIC HEALTH NURSE	38
	SOCIAL WORKER	35		REGISTERED NURSE	43
V	SPEECH PATHOLOGIST	27		LIC. PRACTICAL NURSE	30
	PSYCHOLOGIST	1		RADIOLOGIC TECHNOLOGIST	32
	LIBRARIAN	22		DENTAL ASSISTANT	44
	TRANSLATOR	25	XI	EXECUTIVE HOUSEKEEPER	37
VI	PHYSICIAN	6		ELEMENTARY TEACHER	37
	DENTIST	5		SECRETARY	56
	MEDICAL TECHNOLOGIST	-11		SALESWOMAN	40
	CHEMIST	-6		TELEPHONE OPERATOR	42
	MATHEMATICIAN	17		INSTRUMENT ASSEMBLER	31
	COMPUTER PROGRAMMER	17		SEWING MACHINE OPERATOR	13
	MATH-SCIENCE TEACHER	23		BEAUTICIAN	39
	ENGINEER	11		AIRLINE STEWARDESS	60

FIG. 8-11. Profile for Case Study #11.

seling because a pre-1969 SVIB, taken in a psychology course at a community college, disturbed her. It suggested occupational and physical therapy, engineering, and math-science. She had been taking courses toward an accounting degree at the community college. The counselor suggested she take the new (1969) SVIB for women, suspecting that she would get high scores on some of the professional-level business scales like Accounting and Bankwoman.

The new SVIB only brought the conflict into sharper focus. None of her highest scores were related to the business area except the Basic Scale for Numbers. The new profile confirmed her earlier scores on medical service occupations, engineering, teaching, mathematics, and science. In the ensuing discussion with the counselor, she pointed out that she had begun in aeronautical engineering 25 years before at a large university and would do so again if she were in the same circumstances. However, today she is a woman alone with a preschool child. She couldn't get any engineering or specialized science courses at her local community college; and even if she could, to go back and take them now would not be practical. Accounting, at least, allows her to work with numbers, and she intends to finish that degree. After graduation she hopes to find a job that will not involve any great responsibility which would conflict with her family responsibilities.

Case 13 (Figure 8-13)

This profile also has a clear-cut pattern, with math and science interests predominating. Once again, there is a conflict, but fortunately, as contrasted to the preceding case, the profile offers some alternative suggestions.

This junior, a tall, attractive and poised young lady, came to the counseling office because after completing some 35 credits of chemistry and zoology, she had finally conceded that she would be a misfit in the laboratory. She didn't like lab work and she didn't do it well. As she did perform well in the theoretical phases of chemistry and zoology, her grades did not reveal her difficulty, but she herself was well aware of her practical limitations.

Testing revealed interests and intellectual abilities consistent with her choice of medical technology, but she scored in the bottom decile for women on a manual dexterity test. She remarked wryly that her efforts at typing and playing the piano were about as successful as her chemistry experiments. After some discussion she decided to register for an introductory psychology course, an accounting course, and a statistics course in a search for a more compatible area. Her strictly scientific background has left her

PROFILE— **STRONG VOCATIONAL INTEREST BLANK** —FOR WOMEN (Form TW398)

FIG. 8-13. Profile for Case Study #13.

BASIC INTEREST SCALES

SCALE	Plotted Score
Public Speaking	52
Law/Politics	55
Merchandising	58
Office Practices	43
Numbers	72
Physical Science	64
Mechanical	44
Outdoors	48
Biological Science	62
Medical Service	62
Teaching	47
Social Service	50
Sports	52
Homemaking	40
Religious Activities	53
Music	57
Art	55
Performing Arts	49
Writing	55

Non-Occupational Scales: AACH 58, DIV 60, FMII 38, OIE 53

Administrative Indices: TR 396, UNP 8, FC 16, LP 37, IP 27, DP 35

DOUBLE LINE = AVERAGE SCORE FOR 1000 EMPLOYED ADULT WOMEN

OCCUPATIONAL SCALES (STD SCORE)

	OCCUPATION	STD SCORE
I	MUSIC TEACHER	12
	ENTERTAINER	19
	MUSICIAN PERFORMER	20
	MODEL	27
II	ART TEACHER	32
	ARTIST	32
	INTERIOR DECORATOR	28
III	NEWSWOMAN	35
	ENGLISH TEACHER	25
	LANGUAGE TEACHER	22
IV	YWCA STAFF MEMBER	41
	RECREATION LEADER	34
	DIRECTOR CHRISTIAN ED	25
	NUN/TEACHER	46
	GUIDANCE COUNSELOR	46
	SOCIAL SCIENCE TEACHER	37
	SOCIAL WORKER	43
V	SPEECH PATHOLOGIST	51
	PSYCHOLOGIST	59
	LIBRARIAN	42
	TRANSLATOR	45
VI	PHYSICIAN	49
	DENTIST	28
	MEDICAL TECHNOLOGIST	44
	CHEMIST	41
	MATHEMATICIAN	37
	COMPUTER PROGRAMMER	49
	MATH SCIENCE TEACHER	41
	ENGINEER	44
VII	ARMY ENLISTED	37
	NAVY ENLISTED	25
	ARMY OFFICER	47
	NAVY OFFICER	50
VIII	LAWYER	49
	ACCOUNTANT	43
	BANKWOMAN	32
	LIFE INS UNDERWRITER	31
	BUYER	28
	BUSINESS ED TEACHER	19
IX	HOME ECON TEACHER	18
	DIETITIAN	44
X	PHYSICAL ED TEACHER	32
	OCCUPATIONAL THERAPIST	34
	PHYSICAL THERAPIST	45
	PUBLIC HEALTH NURSE	34
	REGISTERED NURSE	25
	LIC PRACTICAL NURSE	21
	RADIOLOGIC TECHNOLOGIST	30
	DENTAL ASSISTANT	15
XI	EXECUTIVE HOUSEKEEPER	26
	ELEMENTARY TEACHER	26
	SECRETARY	19
	SALESWOMAN	14
	TELEPHONE OPERATOR	6
	INSTRUMENT ASSEMBLER	18
	SEWING MACHINE OPERATOR	2
	BEAUTICIAN	19
	AIRLINE STEWARDESS	34

PROFILE— **STRONG VOCATIONAL INTEREST BLANK** —FOR WOMEN (Form TW398)

FIG. 8-14. Profile for Case Study #14.

BASIC INTEREST SCALES

SCALE	Plotted Score
Public Speaking	50
Law/Politics	47
Merchandising	53
Office Practices	73
Numbers	54
Physical Science	46
Mechanical	41
Outdoors	46
Biological Science	42
Medical Service	51
Teaching	67
Social Service	59
Sports	58
Homemaking	65
Religious Activities	57
Music	40
Art	59
Performing Arts	49
Writing	48

Non-Occupational Scales: AACH 27, DIV 56, FMII 51, OIE 53

Administrative Indices: TR 393, UNP 6, FC 11, LP 45, IP 35, DP 20

DOUBLE LINE = AVERAGE SCORE FOR 1000 EMPLOYED ADULT WOMEN

OCCUPATIONAL SCALES (STD SCORE)

	OCCUPATION	STD SCORE
I	MUSIC TEACHER	14
	ENTERTAINER	17
	MUSICIAN PERFORMER	2
	MODEL	22
II	ART TEACHER	-5
	ARTIST	5
	INTERIOR DECORATOR	22
III	NEWSWOMAN	-1
	ENGLISH TEACHER	8
	LANGUAGE TEACHER	26
IV	YWCA STAFF MEMBER	21
	RECREATION LEADER	33
	DIRECTOR CHRISTIAN ED	27
	NUN/TEACHER	41
	GUIDANCE COUNSELOR	25
	SOCIAL SCIENCE TEACHER	13
	SOCIAL WORKER	32
V	SPEECH PATHOLOGIST	33
	PSYCHOLOGIST	8
	LIBRARIAN	1
	TRANSLATOR	-14
VI	PHYSICIAN	11
	DENTIST	-1
	MEDICAL TECHNOLOGIST	14
	CHEMIST	-17
	MATHEMATICIAN	-4
	COMPUTER PROGRAMMER	19
	MATH SCIENCE TEACHER	35
	ENGINEER	7
VII	ARMY ENLISTED	36
	NAVY ENLISTED	34
	ARMY OFFICER	15
	NAVY OFFICER	16
VIII	LAWYER	5
	ACCOUNTANT	22
	BANKWOMAN	45
	LIFE INS UNDERWRITER	17
	BUYER	21
	BUSINESS ED TEACHER	47
IX	HOME ECON TEACHER	54
	DIETITIAN	36
X	PHYSICAL ED TEACHER	35
	OCCUPATIONAL THERAPIST	34
	PHYSICAL THERAPIST	36
	PUBLIC HEALTH NURSE	38
	REGISTERED NURSE	36
	LIC PRACTICAL NURSE	41
	RADIOLOGIC TECHNOLOGIST	37
	DENTAL ASSISTANT	48
XI	EXECUTIVE HOUSEKEEPER	52
	ELEMENTARY TEACHER	58
	SECRETARY	59
	SALESWOMAN	55
	TELEPHONE OPERATOR	64
	INSTRUMENT ASSEMBLER	45
	SEWING MACHINE OPERATOR	53
	BEAUTICIAN	48
	AIRLINE STEWARDESS	42

with no basis for a more definite decision, so she will defer choosing a final direction as long as possible.

Her high grades, high Academic Achievement score, and general career aspirations strongly suggest that she will eventually consider graduate school; this pattern coupled with the low scores on the Homemaking and Office Practices scales—the two Basic Scales most saturated with the "traditional feminine role"—further suggest that she will seek a professional career. If so, her intelligence and general competence will serve her well, though she will almost certainly marry—a prediction based on her physical and social attractiveness—and thus will have to deal with the classic career-home conflict.

Case 14 (Figure 8-14)

This profile belongs to a woman who has interests in teaching, secretarial work, and homemaking; elementary education might be a possibility for her, but her low Academic Achievement score suggests that she may find the training as a teacher too long and unrewarding.

In this case, the SVIB profile reflects the conflict quite accurately. These scores belong to a young freshman of limited academic ability who entered college primarily because her parents wanted her to. She entered the school of education, and after only six weeks of the first semester, she came to the Department of Student Counseling because she was not enjoying school, and not doing well either. During counseling, she considered business subjects, home economics, training as an executive housekeeper, and secretarial work. She rejected teaching and home economics because they required four years of college, and executive housekeeping because of the supervisory functions involved. Finally, to her parents' consternation, she dropped out of college. She intends to seek employment in an office setting and explore the possibilities for further secretarial training. She will probably eventually find her greatest satisfaction in a "typical" feminine role.

Case 15 (Figure 8-15)

This profile is one with few high scores—none on the Basic Scales and only three "B+'s" on the Occupational Scale for Model, Secretary, and Airline Stewardess. It suggests either a conflicted or very restricted occupational outlook. Both explanations are partially true, but for a special reason. This is the profile of a freshman who, until recently, thought that she would teach the language of the European country in which she was born.

It is her German background that is influencing her vocational development. Her parents have been very strict; she must ask permission to do

Fig. 8-15 (left) — Case Study #15

PROFILE— STRONG VOCATIONAL INTEREST BLANK —FOR WOMEN (Form TW398)

BASIC INTEREST SCALES — PLOTTED SCORE

SCALE	
PUBLIC SPEAKING	48
LAW/POLITICS	45
MERCHANDISING	55
OFFICE PRACTICES	53
NUMBERS	40
PHYSICAL SCIENCE	52
MECHANICAL	52
OUTDOORS	55
BIOLOGICAL SCIENCE	49
MEDICAL SERVICE	49
TEACHING	52
SOCIAL SERVICE	45
SPORTS	45
HOMEMAKING	40
RELIGIOUS ACTIVITIES	53
MUSIC	51
ART	49
PERFORMING ARTS	49
WRITING	53

Non-Occupational Scales: AACH 45 · DIV 53 · FMII 46 · OIE 63

Administrative Indices: TR 398 · UNP 8 · FC 12 · LP 26 · IP 55 · DP 20

OCCUPATIONAL SCALES

OCCUPATION	STD SCORE		OCCUPATION	STD SCORE
I MUSIC TEACHER	-2		VII ARMY-ENLISTED	38
ENTERTAINER	36		NAVY-ENLISTED	37
MUSICIAN PERFORMER	31		ARMY-OFFICER	25
MODEL	43		NAVY-OFFICER	35
II ART TEACHER	16		VIII LAWYER	15
ARTIST	18		ACCOUNTANT	16
INTERIOR DECORATOR	10		BANKWOMAN	22
III NEWSWOMAN	24		LIFE INS. UNDERWRITER	10
ENGLISH TEACHER	20		BUYER	22
LANGUAGE TEACHER	25		BUSINESS ED TEACHER	20
IV YWCA STAFF MEMBER	28		IX HOME ECON. TEACHER	35
RECREATION LEADER	26		DIETITIAN	32
DIRECTOR CHRISTIAN ED	10		X PHYSICAL ED TEACHER	31
NUN-TEACHER	-8		OCCUPATIONAL THERAPIST	21
GUIDANCE COUNSELOR	17		PHYSICAL THERAPIST	
SOCIAL SCIENCE TEACHER	18		PUBLIC HEALTH NURSE	21
SOCIAL WORKER	20		REGISTERED NURSE	
V SPEECH PATHOLOGIST	22		LIC. PRACTICAL NURSE	16
PSYCHOLOGIST	15		RADIOLOGIC TECHNOLOGIST	36
LIBRARIAN	23		DENTAL ASSISTANT	29
TRANSLATOR	35		XI EXECUTIVE HOUSEKEEPER	21
VI PHYSICIAN	16		ELEMENTARY TEACHER	25
DENTIST	17		SECRETARY	41
MEDICAL TECHNOLOGIST	25		SALESWOMAN	21
CHEMIST	-3		TELEPHONE OPERATOR	34
MATHEMATICIAN	10		INSTRUMENT ASSEMBLER	38
COMPUTER PROGRAMMER	38		SEWING MACHINE OPERATOR	19
MATH SCIENCE TEACHER	27		BEAUTICIAN	38
ENGINEER	24		AIRLINE STEWARDESS	41

DOUBLE LINE = AVERAGE SCORE FOR 1000 EMPLOYED ADULT WOMEN

NON-OCCUPATIONAL SCALES: AACH · DIV · FMII · OIE

ADMINISTRATIVE INDICES: TR · UNP · FC · LP · IP · DP

FIG. 8-15. Profile for Case Study #15.

Fig. 8-16 (right) — Case Study #16

PROFILE— STRONG VOCATIONAL INTEREST BLANK —FOR WOMEN (Form TW398)

BASIC INTEREST SCALES — PLOTTED SCORE

SCALE	
PUBLIC SPEAKING	57
LAW/POLITICS	65
MERCHANDISING	50
OFFICE PRACTICES	56
NUMBERS	65
PHYSICAL SCIENCE	57
MECHANICAL	57
OUTDOORS	60
BIOLOGICAL SCIENCE	50
MEDICAL SERVICE	57
TEACHING	52
SOCIAL SERVICE	52
SPORTS	56
HOMEMAKING	40
RELIGIOUS ACTIVITIES	50
MUSIC	53
ART	49
PERFORMING ARTS	54
WRITING	49

Non-Occupational Scales: AACH 54 · DIV 67 · FMII 44 · OIE 39

Administrative Indices: TR 398 · UNP 3 · FC 2 · LP 0 · IP 98 · DP 0

OCCUPATIONAL SCALES

OCCUPATION	STD SCORE		OCCUPATION	STD SCORE
I MUSIC TEACHER	30		VII ARMY-ENLISTED	38
ENTERTAINER	24		NAVY-ENLISTED	36
MUSICIAN/PERFORMER	27		ARMY-OFFICER	38
MODEL	10		NAVY-OFFICER	37
II ART TEACHER	17		VIII LAWYER	33
ARTIST	15		ACCOUNTANT	35
INTERIOR DECORATOR	8		BANKWOMAN	34
III NEWSWOMAN	17		LIFE INS. UNDERWRITER	30
ENGLISH TEACHER	18		BUYER	29
LANGUAGE TEACHER	19		BUSINESS ED TEACHER	26
IV YWCA STAFF MEMBER	32		IX HOME ECON. TEACHER	12
RECREATION LEADER	41		DIETITIAN	36
DIRECTOR CHRISTIAN ED	18		X PHYSICAL ED TEACHER	29
NUN-TEACHER	29		OCCUPATIONAL THERAPIST	41
GUIDANCE COUNSELOR	28		PHYSICAL THERAPIST	46
SOCIAL SCIENCE TEACHER	32		PUBLIC HEALTH NURSE	11
SOCIAL WORKER	20		REGISTERED NURSE	35
V SPEECH PATHOLOGIST	18		LIC. PRACTICAL NURSE	47
PSYCHOLOGIST	12		RADIOLOGIC TECHNOLOGIST	42
LIBRARIAN	32		DENTAL ASSISTANT	36
TRANSLATOR	25		XI EXECUTIVE HOUSEKEEPER	36
VI PHYSICIAN	36		ELEMENTARY TEACHER	43
DENTIST	37		SECRETARY	30
MEDICAL TECHNOLOGIST	42		SALESWOMAN	33
CHEMIST	37		TELEPHONE OPERATOR	37
MATHEMATICIAN	20		INSTRUMENT ASSEMBLER	25
COMPUTER PROGRAMMER	21		SEWING MACHINE OPERATOR	28
MATH SCIENCE TEACHER	39		BEAUTICIAN	21
ENGINEER	31		AIRLINE STEWARDESS	21

DOUBLE LINE = AVERAGE SCORE FOR 1000 EMPLOYED ADULT WOMEN

FIG. 8-16. Profile for Case Study #16.

anything except to go to school, and the permission is often denied. She has average ability to do college work and has entered fourth-year courses in German. She could surely succeed in the plan her parents have outlined for her, teaching their language, but she is beginning to question their authority and to make some of her decisions independently. Still, she has not been able to look realistically at the many choices open to her as an American college girl up to this point and, unfortunately, she has been so sheltered that she has missed many experiences that would help her to define herself as a person.

In counseling, the counselor helped her to view vocational choice as an ongoing process, pointed out the flexibility of various college curricula, encouraged her to try as many new things as possible both academically and nonacademically (a plan she adopted enthusiastically), and suggested that she return every few months to talk about her progress. Though seemingly unique, this case is illustrative of the problems created for young women by the fast-moving trend toward feminine freedom. As this girl started from a more traditional setting than most, the tensions have been magnified for her, but they differ only in intensity from those felt by many young women.

These illustrations are from a limited counseling setting; yet they typify situations common to the experiences of counselors working in a variety of settings. Every counselor who uses vocational interest inventories to counsel women finds that the profiles sometimes confirm choices, sometimes suggest alternatives, sometimes highlight conflicts between interests and circumstances, and sometimes expose vocational immaturity.

The assumptions that counselors make about women will determine how they use the new SVIB. A recent Ph.D. thesis by Friedersdorf (1969) concluded that male high school counselors expect college-bound women to be interested in feminine occupations—they do not expect women to like traditionally male occupations. Such attitudes influence how women are counseled. Only one negative reaction, verbal or nonverbal, to a high score on the Chemist or Mathematician scale may dissuade a young woman from considering a career in science; yet anyone with a high score on those scales is not going to be comfortable as a secretary or housewife. If the counselor assumes that young women's interests are unimportant—even though the evidence suggests that many women will work after marriage and that their interests develop later than those of men—he may allow his client to waste the best or only years she will have for education and training. An excellent rule to follow in the vocational counseling of women is, "Consider every suggestion, every high score seriously. A woman can decide not to use her education or training, but she cannot decide to use education or training which she does not have."

The new SVIB for women is designed to give the counselor and his counselee a maximum of information for discussion and planning. The counselor can negate its breadth by refusing to discuss high scores in unusual occupations, or by not being straightforward about potential conflicts between marriage and career.

Case 16 (Figure 8-16)

One further woman's profile is presented for two reasons: first, it provides an opportunity to discuss the LP, IP, and DP Administrative Indices—on this profile, they were 2, 98, and 0 respectively—and second, this case demonstrates the passionate hostility created in some women by occupational discrimination, and emphasizes the need for finding better ways for providing meaningful employment for women.

The LP, IP, and DP Administrative Indices show the percent of "Like," "Indifferent," and "Dislike" responses respectively to the occupational titles section of the booklet.

This woman answered "Like" to only 2 percent of the first 128 items, and "Indifferent" to the remainder. What does this mean? As she was tested in a research study, by mail, there was no counselor to turn to for information. What explanation is available was pieced together from a variety of sources, mainly the other information supplied by her, including her penciled-in comments on the test booklet.

She was 32 years old, married, had a Master's degree, and was working as a nursing aide. She was tested as a member of a group working for feminine equality, and the comments that she wrote across the test booklet made it clear that she believes in that cause with some fervor—and this fervor helps explain her scores on the Administrative Indices. At the end of the first section of the booklet, in which she had responded "Like" to only three items—"Governor of a State," "Opera Singer," and "Veterinarian for small animals"—she wrote in:

"Since in most of these occupations, I would be carrying out phoney, destructive, male-supremacist aims, I view them all with the apathy born of powerless contempt—except for being governor of a state, where I could befoul and louse up their system quite a bit in a short time before I was impeached. Also, some male operatic arias are good, and I wouldn't mind singing them, if I could sing." Some of her other pithy comments give further flavor to her feelings: After responding "Like" to #200, *"Acting as a cheer-leader,"* she penciled in: "I especially like to lead heckling and jeering groups. I like to participate in enraged mobs but, in that case, I like to be safely in the middle." After marking "Dislike" to #244, "*Socialists*," she noted, "I like female socialists—the male ones are usually just another brand of jockstrap phoney." After marking "No" to #346, "*I can correct others without giving offense*," she wrote, "It's always good to give offense when you correct others—they learn faster."

Clearly, this profile can't be handled in the usual way; considerable caution is necessary in drawing any conclusions. This woman had things other than vocational interests on her mind when she answered. Still, despite her unique approach to the first section, she answered the remainder of the inventory in a more-or-less usual fashion, and the overall profile seems meaningful. Her high scores on the Numbers, Physical Science, and Mechanical scales are consistent and seem reasonable, as does her high score on Law/Politics. Her lowest score among the Basic Scales was on the Homemaking scale; that should surprise no one, including her.

Among the Occupational scales, her highest scores were in the paramedical service areas—Group X; the moderately high Recreation Leader and Medical Technologist scores support that pattern.

Her high score on the Elementary Teacher scale is curious, and is difficult to explain.

On the Nonoccupational scales, the results suggest that she is academically oriented (she does have a Master's degree), that her interests are considerably more diverse than the average woman's (surprising, considering how she responded to the first section, but most of the items on the Diversity of Interests scale are located further on in the booklet), that she is not greatly different from the average woman on the MFII scale (which emphasizes that this scale has more to do with art and cultural activities than with traditional feminine domesticity) and that she leans strongly toward extroversion (... cheering mobs ...).

Yet, although the profile can be made to appear reasonable, there are enough inconsistencies in all of this so that interpretations must be guarded, particularly because of the LP, IP, and DP percentages. Before any counseling took place based on these results, the counselor should directly raise the question of her style of answers. This is not to imply that she shouldn't be allowed any pattern of responses to the SVIB that she pleases, but it would be grossly inaccurate to suggest to her that her results can be interpreted in the traditional manner.

The intensity of this woman's feelings emphasizes the dire need for some changes in the occupational treatment of women. At the very least, they must be given opportunities that they think are interesting, dignified, and productive—both financially and emotionally. To do this will require a great deal of wisdom and imagination, for there certainly will continue to be conflicts in the career choices of young women. Even if the differences between the sexes are all culturally induced and even if the cultural forces creating these differences were all to evaporate overnight, each sex will retain some unique qualities. Women, for example, will continue to bear children, search for taller men as marriage partners, and worry about being sexually assaulted; men will continue to dominate occupations requiring physical strength—the construction trades, police and military work, pro football; they will be less troubled by emotional shifts brought on by physiological changes; and they will still commit most of the crimes of violence. Differences will persist.

But one can attend to differences between people without treating some of them as inferior. Each individual is unique, and the use of interest inventories helps to mirror the individual's uniqueness, and to suggest vocational alternatives particularly suited for that individual. With women, at this point in our society, such approaches seem particularly important.

CHAPTER 9

Stability of Measured Interests within Occupations over Long Time Spans

Do the characteristic interests of occupational groups change over time?

This is an important question for the counseling psychologist who needs to know something of the nature of these groups, and it is an absolutely crucial point for psychometricians involved in the development of vocational interest inventories. If occupational interest patterns do change, then interest inventories should be continually revised. As such revisions wipe out accumulated data on existing forms, disrupt on-going research programs, and require substantial amounts of time and money, some effort should be expended to determine if frequent revision is necessary; that is the purpose of this chapter.

To study change over time is not easy as data collected many years earlier are not always accessible and, even when available, they are usually not organized as one would wish. However, as the SVIB has been in existence almost 40 years, some completed inventories are available, already "aged," that permit some exploration of change over time.

Studies of Change over Time
Checks on Scale Validities

Relevant information can be grouped into four categories: the first includes those validity studies that are continually being published on the SVIB scales. If occupational groups are changing rapidly, then scales developed years ago should no longer be valid, but that is clearly not the case. Several recent studies of groups such as medical students (Thrush and King, 1965), life insurance salesmen (Ferguson, 1958, 1960), men and women psychologists (Campbell, 1965b, 1968a), and policemen (Matarazzo, Allen, Saslow, and Wiens, 1964) make it clear that the SVIB scales still discriminate between occupations. A brief review of just two such studies will provide the flavor of the results.

Portions of this chapter were published earlier in the *Personnel and Guidance Journal* and *Measurement and Evaluation in Guidance*

PROFILE — STRONG VOCATIONAL INTEREST BLANK FOR MEN

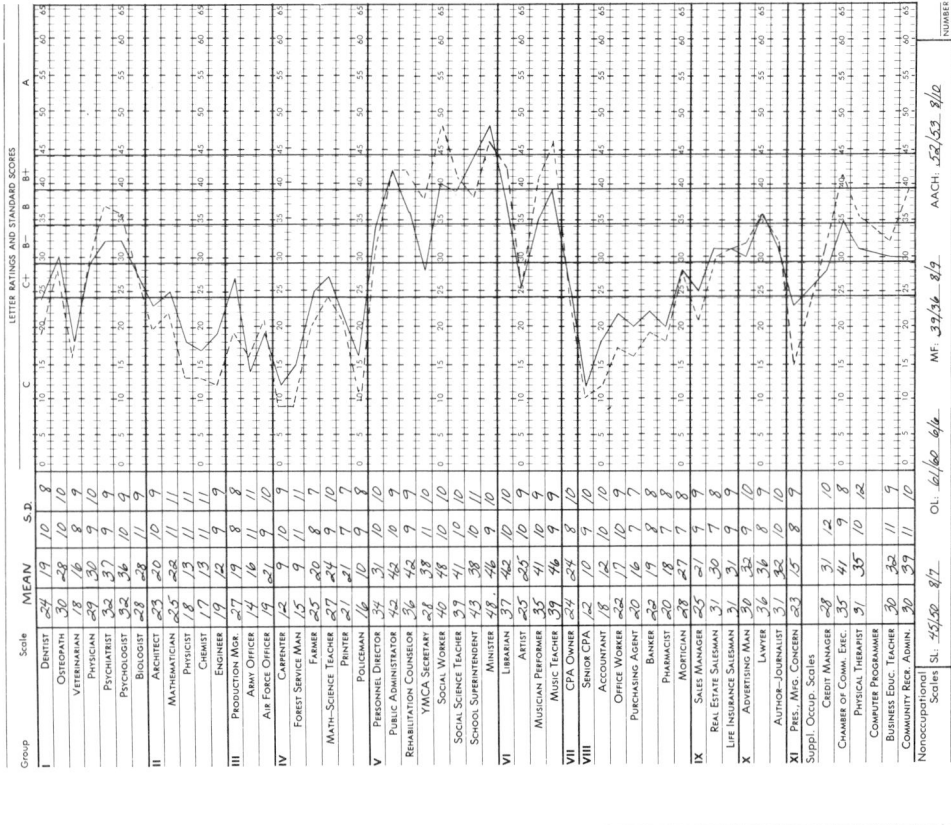

FIG. 9-2. *Mean profiles for 98 ministers tested in 1927 (solid line) and ministers who were serving in the same churches in 1965 (broken line).*

FIG. 9-1. *Mean profiles for 251 California lawyers tested in 1930 (broken line) and 79 Minnesota lawyers tested in 1948 (solid line).*

In an unpublished study in 1948, Berdie and Hagenah tested 70 lawyers in Minnesota who had been classified by the Minnesota Law School as good practitioners. The comparison between these Minnesota lawyers, tested in 1948, and Strong's sample, drawn from the California Bar Association and tested about 20 years earlier, is shown in Figure 9-1. Obviously, there was a great deal of similarity between the groups, even though they came from different geographical areas, were sampled by different techniques, and were tested 20 years apart. Note that both groups scored highest on the Lawyer scale.

Another group validity study, concerned with the Policeman scale, was reported by Matarazzo and his associates from the University of Oregon Medical School. They found considerable similarity between successful police applicants in Portland in 1959–62 and earlier applicants for the same positions. Their conclusion was: "The comparisons make clear that the 1959–62 police recruit is a remarkable facsimile ... of the police officer appointed to the same force in 1946–1947" (Matarazza *et al.*, 1964, p. 132).

While these validity generalization studies demonstrate that there is some stability in the characteristics of occupations, they are not sufficient to establish that fact conclusively. For one thing, the time spans were not very long—12 years in the case of the policemen, and 20 years for the lawyers—but the main reason for prudence is that it is naïve and contrary to common sense to believe that occupations are static and unchanging. Before that conclusion is acceptable, the evidence must be absolutely unassailable.

Restandardization of Specific Scales

There is a second kind of study that provides further relevant data. For various reasons, several occupations have been studied a second time to review the appropriateness of the original scale. The occupations are as follows: psychologists (Kriedt, 1949), accountants (Strong, 1949), physicians (Strong and Tucker, 1952), personnel directors (Kriedt, Stone, and Paterson, 1952), and women social workers (McCornack, 1956). In each case, a new scale was developed and compared with the original scale developed in the 1930's.

Two of these new scales, Accountant and Personnel Director, were so similar to the original scales that no changes were made. In the three studies dealing with psychologists, social workers, and physicians, there were some changes and revised scales were published. However, even in these instances, the changes were mild; for example, the revised Physician scale correlated .85 with the original scale.

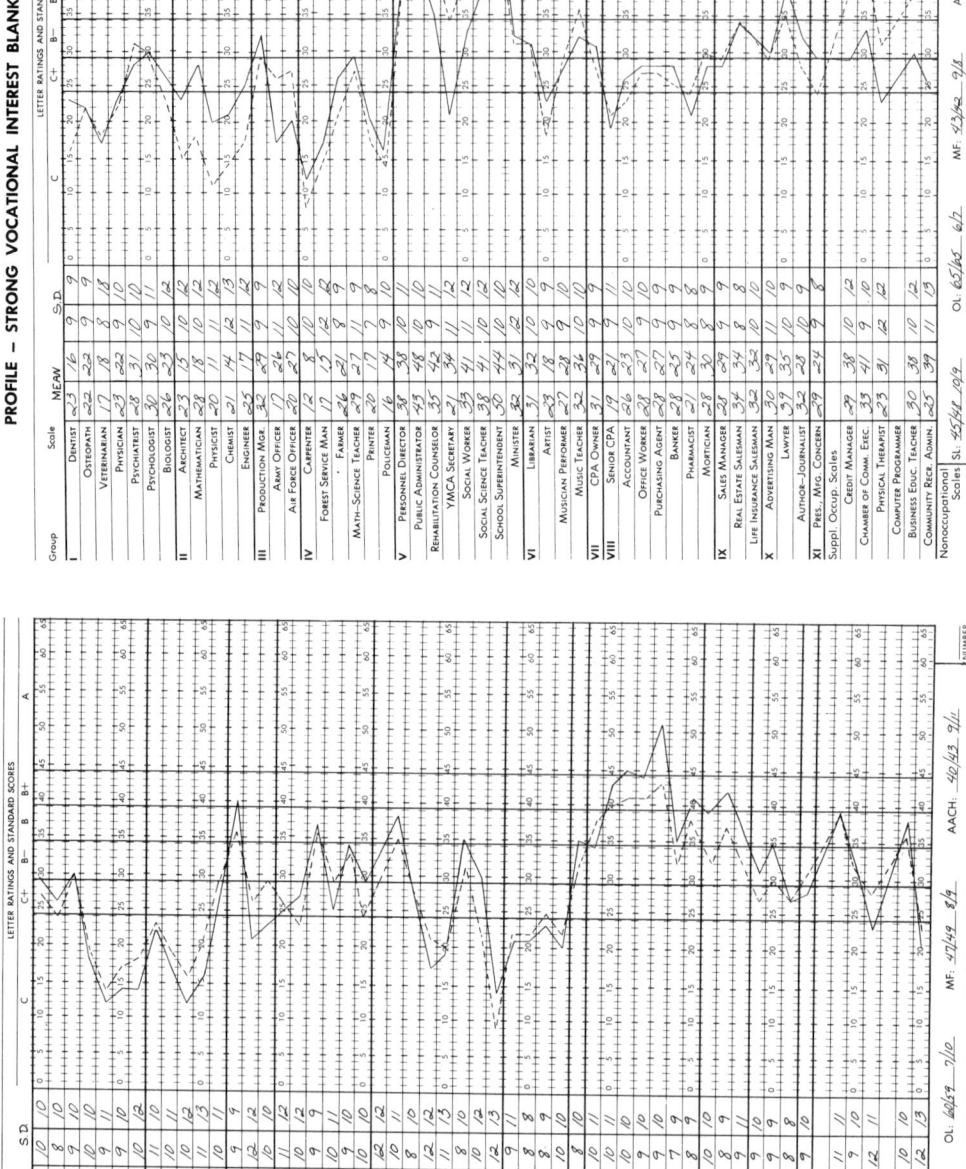

PROFILE – STRONG VOCATIONAL INTEREST BLANK FOR MEN

FIG. 9-3. Mean profiles for 93 bankers tested in 1934 (solid line) and bankers in the same jobs in the same banks in 1964 (broken line).

PROFILE – STRONG VOCATIONAL INTEREST BLANK FOR MEN

FIG. 9-4. Mean profiles for 149 school superintendents tested in 1930 (solid line) and the same individuals in the same jobs in 1964 (broken line).

Even these mild differences might be traced to sources other than changes in the occupation. Usually, the second study was methodologically better than the first, that is, the sampling was better or the sample was larger, and these sampling changes may have been sufficient to explain the changes. For example, the original 1930 Physician scale was based almost solely on the graduates of Stanford Medical School, while the 1950 Physician scale was based on a random sample of the American Medical Association. This difference in sampling method may have been sufficient to explain the difference between the original and revised scale. The same comments apply to both the psychologist and social worker studies.

1930's vs. 1960's: Matched Samples

To overcome these limitations, a third approach has been attempted, using a technique designed to hold the sampling constant within occupations over a long time span (Campbell, 1966a, 1966b). Essentially, what was done was to go back to some of the original criterion occupations, and test the men in the 1960's who were holding the exact jobs as those men tested by E. K. Strong in the 1930's. To do this, it was, of course, necessary to use occupations where individual positions could be precisely specified.

The occupations used, and the sampling control used for each of them, were:

1. Ministers. Strong's original 1927 ministers were matched with the ministers who were serving in the same churches in 1965 (Figure 9-2).

2. Bankers. Strong's original 1934 bankers were matched with the men who were holding the same jobs in the same banks in 1964 (Figure 9-3).

3. School Superintendents. Strong's original 1930 superintendents were matched with the men who were superintendents of the same school systems in 1965 (Figure 9-4).

4. Corporaton Presidents. Strong's original 1935 presidents were matched with the men who were presidents of the same companies in 1964 (Figure 9-5).

The number of matched pairs for each of the four occupations is shown in Figures 9-2 through 9-5, which present the mean profiles for all of these groups. With the exception of the corporation president sample, the N was a fairly substantial proportion of the original group. Sample shrinkage in each occupation was due to two sources: one, the original subject couldn't be matched for some reason (for example, the bank had failed, or the company had merged with a larger one); or, two, the current incumbent refused to fill in the SVIB. The corporation president sample was more vul-

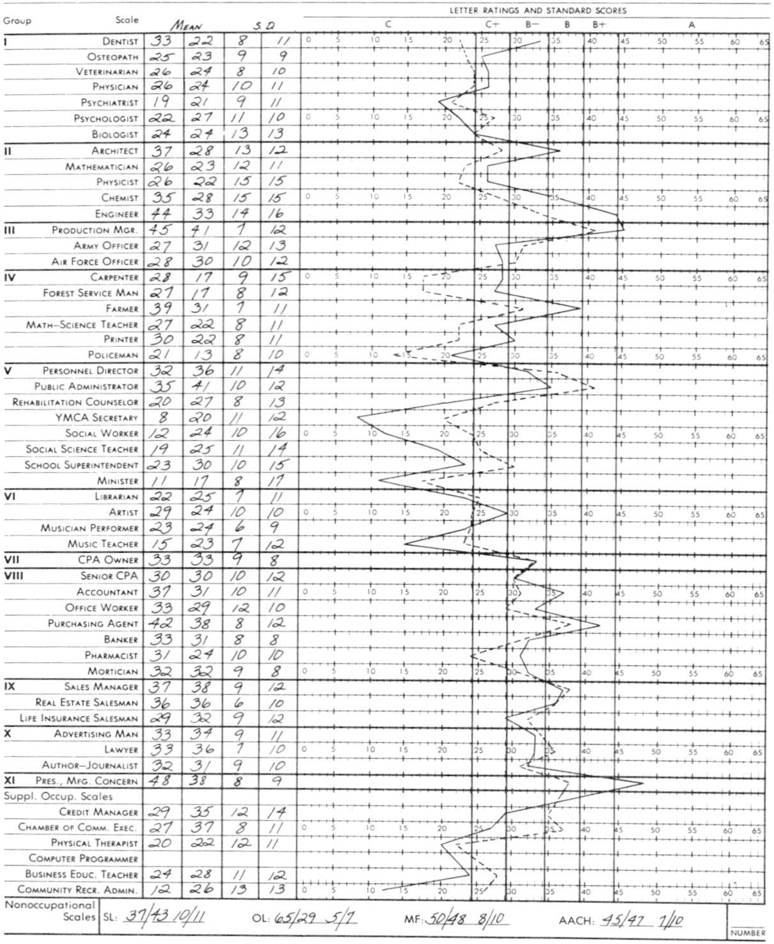

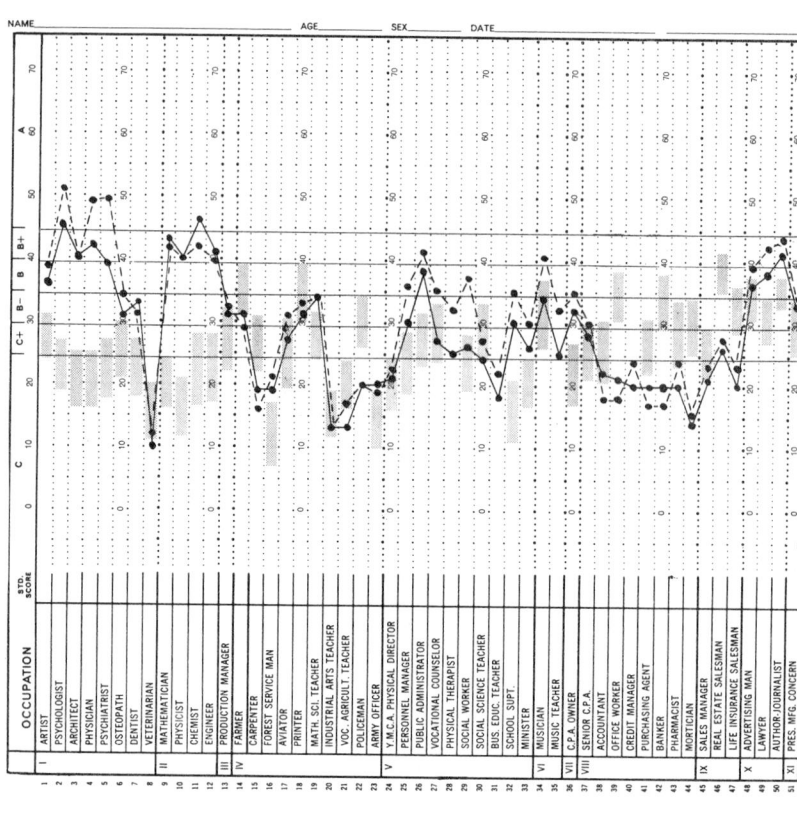

FIG. 9-6. *Mean SVIB profiles for 25 early (solid line) and 25 recent (broken line) presidents of the American Psychological Association.*

FIG. 9-5. *Mean profiles for 25 corporation presidents tested in 1935 (solid line) and presidents of the same corporations tested in 1964 (broken line).*

nerable to both of these than were the samples from banks, schools, or churches.

Inspection of the four pairs of profiles in Figures 9-2 through 9-5 shows hardly any shifts common to all of the groups. There was a faint tendency for all of the occupations, with the exception of bankers, to show a slight increase in social service interests and a slight decrease in scientific interests, but the changes were mild and inconsistent.

In general, the profiles were surprisingly similar, which suggests strongly that the scales are still relevant for today's occupations.

One distressing note is that the more recently tested sample in each occupation tended to score higher on the more recently developed scales. Although the trend was not completely consistent, where there were differences, they were usually on the newer scales, leading to the conclusion that there is some "modernity factor" in the more recently developed scales. Further discussion of this point is continued in the next chapter.

One further replication has been done, with a slightly different design, using psychologists as subjects. Instead of working with pairs of psychologists holding the same job, one position, that of president of the American Psychological Association, has been studied by examining the characteristic interests of the men holding that position over a long time span.

In Figure 9-6, the average profile of 25 men who were presidents of the American Psychological Association before 1939 is compared with the profile of 25 APA presidents since that time.

While the similarity was dramatic, there were some small but relevant differences. The more recent presidents tended to score higher on the biological science scales and slightly lower on the physical science scales. The more recent ones also scored higher on the social service scales. Profiles for all of these presidents have been published in an earlier article (Campbell, 1965b), and one of the more intriguing findings was that the latest available SVIB profile from an APA president (from the president in 1965) was a close duplication of the earliest available SVIB profile from an APA president (from the president in 1900).

Basic Interest Scale Means over 30 Years

The fourth source of data showing stability over time within occupations are the mean scores for many occupational samples on the Basic Interest Scales reported in Chapter 3 and 4. Those results show a great deal of similarity between samples from the same occupation tested many years apart. Scientists scored high on the Science scale, whether tested in the 1930's or the 1960's; ministers from both 1930 and 1964 scored high on the

Religious Activities scale; writers scored high on the Writing scale over these three decades—nothing surprising about these results, of course, except that one continually hears that occupations are undergoing major changes.

Some Conclusions

None of these four types of data reveal any great changes; indeed, they clearly indicate that there is considerable stability across time within occupations on interest measures, much more than one might expect intuitively. These studies collectively imply that individuals in the 1930 culture were similar in their interest patterns to those in the 1964 culture, and that the mechanisms of occupational choice—whatever they may be—are fairly constant over long time periods. For example, somehow men with banking interests gravitated into the banking business 30 years ago, and men with those same interest patterns are found in the same jobs today.

But cultures change, occupations come and go, and one wonders what happens to those individuals who today have the interest patterns of yesterday's occupations. For example, what happens to the men who today have interests similar to the blacksmiths of earlier generations?

The answer to that question appeared almost accidentally when about 60 blacksmiths were tested recently at the University of Minnesota, using the Minnesota Vocational Interest Inventory (MVII). Their results on the MVII Area Scales (scales with homogeneous item content, similar to the SVIB Basic Interest Scales) showed clearly that the blacksmiths of yesterday are the mechanics of today. The mechanical cluster of interests has emerged intact though there have been dramatic changes in the demands of society.

Homogeneous scales, such as the MVII Area Scales or the SVIB Basic Interest Scales, offer one means of studying the evolution of occupations as they are not dependent on the composition of any single occupational sample. As new occupations come into being, their relationship—in measured interests—to existing occupations can be more easily determined.

Some Speculations

The above conclusion of stability among existing occupations is cautious and based on substantial data; let me now do some far out speculating. If we but had the data, I think we could find similarities in interest patterns within occupations extending back to the edge of civilization, or at least back to the time when occupational groups began to appear. For example, the activities of some kinds of merchants have been similar from the bazaar shopkeepers of the Middle Ages to the door-to-door entrepreneurs of the current century. Or consider the military officers of history. Transporting men over long distances, worrying about logistical matters, sleeping in mud and cold, operating within an authoritarian chain-of-command are timeless activities.

One can think of many other examples. There have always been writers, scientists of one stripe or another, men who like to preach to others, men who like to administer the affairs of the larger group, others who are concerned with beauty and aesthetics. There have always been men in brutal occupations—those in charge of throwing Christians to the lions have been paralleled more recently by the Nazi stormtroopers. There have always been explorers, and one might muse over the similarity of interests between men such as Sir Francis Drake, Magellan, Columbus, and their current-day counterparts, the American and Soviet astronauts. Anyone who would step out of a spaceship with nothing but a rope between him and the stars must surely have something in common with a fellow who thinks at any moment he might sail over the edge of the world.

That men choose different ways to interact with their environment is already known; that there is some consistency across generations in these modes of interaction seems now to be a reasonable assumption.

This general stability in interest patterns over time is reassuring in the context of the revision of interest inventories. Although some mild change was detected—and that is discussed at greater length in the next chapter—the magnitude was not large, far smaller than the differences between unrelated occupations. Moreover, this source of change over time is not as crucial as other factors in planning revisions. The rate of obsolescence of individual items will probably force revision sooner than actual change in occupations, e.g., the recent SVIB revisions were motivated more by the need to do something about items such as "Literary Digest" (a magazine out of print for years) and "Aviator" than by any obvious change in occupations.

CHAPTER 10

Changing Interests over Time
within Society in General

The data presented in the preceding chapter demonstrate that occupational samples tested in the 1930's are quite similar in measured interests to comparable samples tested in the 1960's. Still, although the major finding was stability, there were several hints that some changes had occurred in the frequency of response to some of the SVIB items. The research reported in this chapter was an attempt to isolate and study those general shifts that appear in all, or most, of these occupational samples, shifts that apparently can be attributed to a change in the interests of the general population.

Matched Samples: 1930's and 1960's

The sampling technique, used in the last chapter, of matching men from the 1930's with their occupational counterpart of the 1960's has several advantages; it holds constant several variables such as general type of occupational activity, geographic differences, socio-economic level, and other unpredictable characteristics. One disadvantage is that new occupational trends, not represented in the former samples, can not appear. If, for example, a "new breed" of bankers is emerging, perhaps computer specialists, they could not appear in the "bankers '34 versus '64" comparison because only jobs in existence in the 1930's and their later parallels were included. As a partial solution to this problem, some other occupations were used in this phase, with no attempt to match exactly jobs from the 1930's with the 1960's. These groups included:

Veterinarians. A sample of Iowa veterinarians tested in 1949 (N = 310) were compared with a sample tested in 1966 (N = 478). Both groups were collected under the direction of T. E. Hannum, Iowa State University, using essentially the same sampling technique each time, i.e., surveying the membership of the Iowa Veterinarians Association. (See Hannum, 1950, and Alsip, 1966.)

Pilots. A sample collected in 1940 (N = 509) by Strong was compared with a sample collected in 1960 (N = 198) by Lt. Col. Frank Winter.

Strong's sample included a mixture of commercial pilots, military pilots, and FAA instructors; Winter's sample included only Air Force officers. (See Winter, 1963.)

Accountants. Strong's sample of CPAs from the American Institute of Accountants tested in 1944 ($N = 611$) were compared with a sample of Minnesota CPAs tested in 1966 ($N = 304$) by John Rhode (see Strong, 1949, and Rhode, 1966).

YMCA Staff Members. Strong's YMCA Physical Directors tested in 1929 and YMCA Secretaries tested in 1927 were combined into one sample ($N = 326$) and compared with a sample of YMCA Staff Members tested in 1961 ($N = 184$). The 1961 data were collected through the offices of the Psychological Corporation and the Personnel Services Office of the National Council of YMCAs.

Musicians. Strong's sample tested in 1952 ($N = 441$) was compared with the members of the Minneapolis Symphony Orchestra tested in 1966 ($N = 53$).

These five occupations, along with the four from the preceding chapter, were used to study changing responses between the 1930's and 1960's.

The technique used to detect shifts was to isolate those items showing large and consistent response percentage shifts between the samples tested in the 1930's and those tested in the 1960's. Figure 10-1 illustrates this method graphically by showing the changing response percentages for the item, "College Professor," one of those showing the greatest increase in popularity. The increase in percent responding "Like" was roughly constant—about 20 percent—over all occupations, no matter what percent of the original group responded "Like." For example, the increase among the bankers was from 9 percent to 29 percent, among ministers from 82 percent to 95 percent.

Figure 10-2 shows similar data for an item that has decreased in popularity, "Thrifty people." Again the change in percent responding "Like" was similar over the groups although the absolute level of response varied substantially and in a meaningful way. The bankers of the 1930's found "Thrifty people" more appealing than did other groups and the same was still true in the 1960's. The musicians fell at the bottom of the distribution both times.

"Changing" Items, and Construction of a Cultural Change Scale

Items were defined as "changed" if there was a shift of 10 per cent or more between the old and new groups on either the "Like" or "Dislike" response in a majority (5 of 9) of the occupations. These items were drawn together into a single measure called the "Cultural Change" scale; those

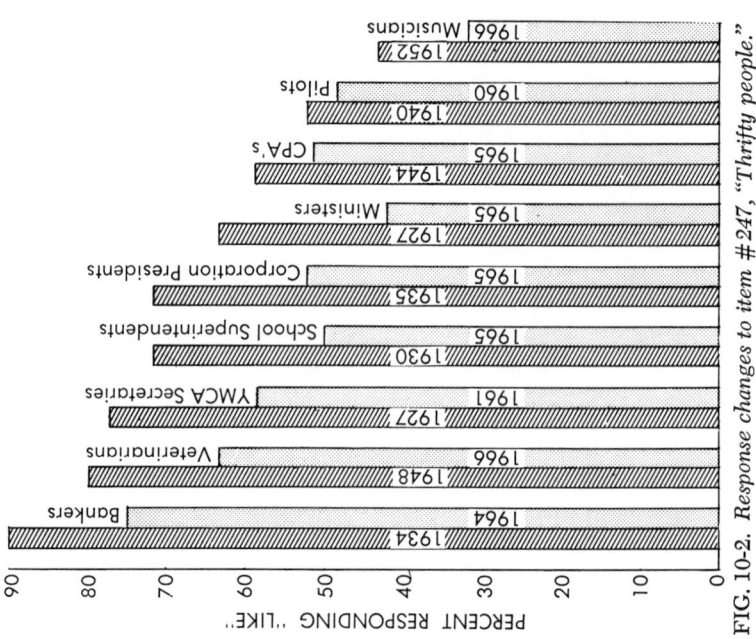

FIG. 10-2. *Response changes to item #247, "Thrifty people."*

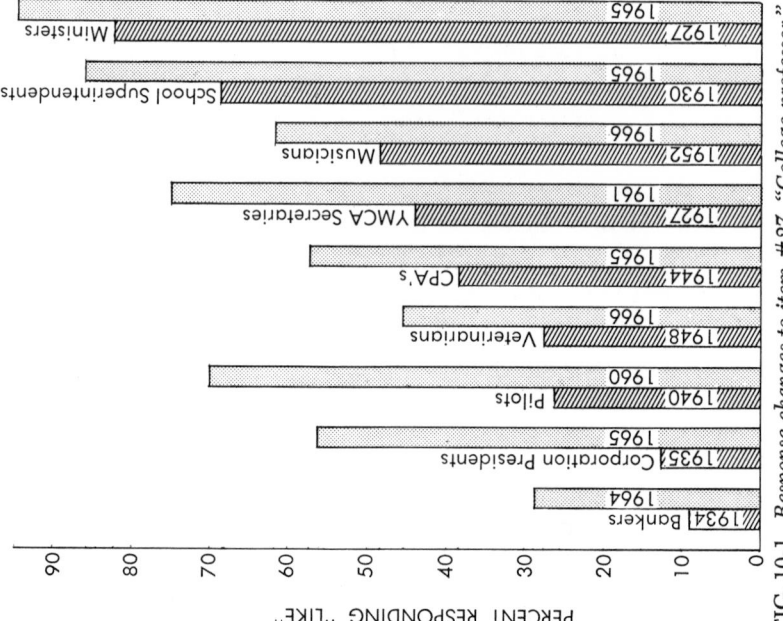

FIG. 10-1. *Response changes to item #27, "College professor."*

items that have increased in popularity were weighted:

Like +1   Indifferent 0   Dislike −1

Items that have decreased in popularity were weighted in the opposite direction:

Like −1   Indifferent 0   Dislike +1

This has the net effect of collecting all the changes together into one scoring scale which can then be applied to the individual's SVIB answers; his score will give an indication of how many of these changed items he has selected. Just what the score means for a single individual is not apparent but for a group it should provide some index of the psychological point in time that the group was tested.

The first validation check was to score the groups used in scale development. If the scale works as it should, there should be a substantial difference between the occupations tested in 1930 and their counterparts tested in 1960. These data are presented in Figure 10-3. For some of the occupations, a sample was available for cross-validation purposes. Those were the men from the 1930 sample who, for various reasons, could not be matched up with anyone today. As the figure shows, the scale discriminated well between the 1930 and 1960 samples within each occupation, with the exception of musicians, where the time difference was considerably smaller. Also, the cross-validation samples from the 1930's scored at the same level as the validation samples, a reassuring finding. The standard deviation of this scale is roughly 10 so the scale separated these samples by about one and one-half standard deviation, a very significant difference both practically and statistically.

The Meaning of the Cultural Change Scale

With these positive validation results available, it is now fruitful to study the flavor of this scale in an attempt to understand the nature of the interests that are changing.

Items Weighted

Table 10-1 shows the items selected for the Cultural Change (CC) scale; those gaining in popularity over time were weighted plus, those losing were weighted minus. (To call some of these items more popular is misleading; "less unpopular" would be more accurate. The item "Auctioneer" is a good example; the increase in popularity actually came about because 25 percent more men in the recent samples responded "Indifferent" rather than "Dislike.")

TABLE 10-1. ITEM WEIGHTS FOR THE MEN'S CULTURAL CHANGE SCALE

Item Number	Items weighted positively	Item Number	Items weighted negatively
	OCCUPATIONS		
1	Actor	56	Machinist
3	Architect	74	Private Secretary
6	Astronomer		
8	Auctioneer		
9	Author of novel		
12	Auto Racer		
14	Airplane Pilot		
17	Building Contractor		
26	Minister, Priest or Rabbi		
27	College Professor		
29	Dentist		
40	Foreign Correspondent		
41	Governor of a State		
44	Interpreter		
45	Inventor		
47	Judge		
51	Criminal Lawyer		
67	Pharmacist		
72	Politician		
79	Sports Page Reporter		
82	School Teacher		
89	Social Worker		
92	Stock Broker		
	SCHOOL SUBJECTS		
107	Calculus	121	Industrial Arts
135	Typewriting		
	AMUSEMENTS		
155	Sight-seeing trips	139	Hunting
171	Sports pages in newspapers	143	Boxing
		147	Bird watching
		163	Art galleries
		167	Symphony concerts
		172	Poetry
		180	Popular mechanics magazines
		182	Educational movies or TV
	ACTIVITIES		
196	Interviewing men for a job	190	Operating machinery
198	Interviewing clients	191	Handling horses
199	Making a speech	194	Decorating a room with flowers
203	Teaching adults	223	Methodical work
204	Calling friends by nicknames	224	Regular hours for work
205	Being called by a nickname		
225	Continually changing activities		
	TYPES OF PEOPLE		
243	People who assume leadership	247	Thrifty people
248	Spendthrifts	258	Very old people
255	Foreigners		
271	Fashionably dressed people		
	FORCED CHOICE ITEMS		
289*	Teach others the use of the machine	282*	Operate the new machine
		292*	Steadiness and permanence of work
290*	Interest the public in the machine through public address	342	Outside work vs Inside work
		348	Present a report in writing vs Present a report verbally
296*	Opportunity to ask questions and to consult about difficulties	349	Listening to a story vs Telling a story
311*	President of a Society or Club		
324	Head waiter vs Lighthouse keeper		
326	Selling things house to house vs Gardening		
328	Develop plans vs Execute plans		
334	Taking a chance vs Playing safe		

TABLE 10-1 (*continued*)

Item Number	Items weighted positively	Item Number	Items weighted negatively
343	Work in which you move from place to place vs Work where you stay in one place		
344	Great variety of work vs Similarity in work		

PERSONAL CHARACTERISTICS

Item Number	Items weighted positively	Item Number	Items weighted negatively
369	Have more than my share of novel ideas	395	Complaints annoy me...rarely... sometimes...quite a bit
379	Have good judgment in appraising values		
398	My advice is asked for...by many...by few...by almost nobody		

*Items not used in final version of scale.

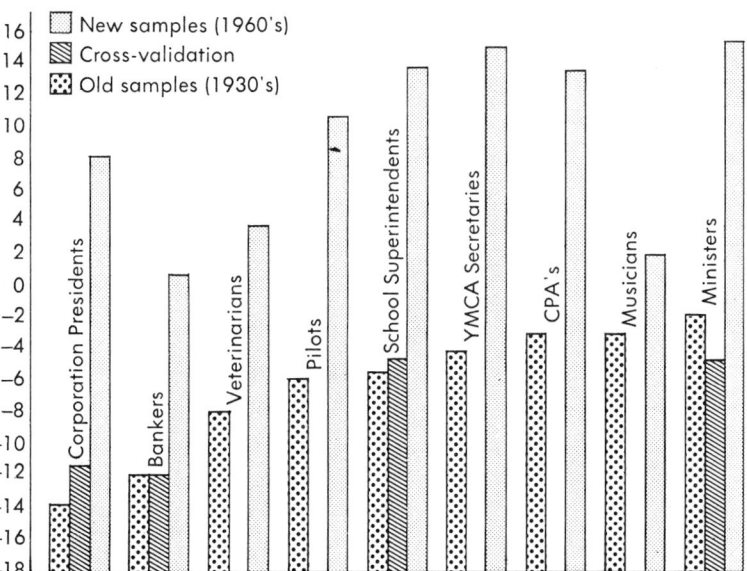

FIG. 10-3. *Mean scores for old and new occupational samples on the Men's Cultural Change scale.*

The section on "Activities" contains the items that are most useful in understanding the scale. The items gaining in popularity include "Interviewing clients," "Interviewing men for a job," "Teaching adults," and "Being called by a nickname." The items decreasing in popularity include "Operating machinery," "Handling horses," and "Methodical work." This contrast of working with people versus working outdoors or with your hands seems to be one of the major dimensions of this Cultural Change scale.

Correlations with Nonoccupational Scales

A second way to gain some understanding of this scale is to look at its correlations with the SVIB Nonoccupational scales. Those correlations are:

Occupational Introversion–Extroversion	−.62
Occupational Level	.31
Specialization Level	.29
Diversity of Interests	.28
Masculinity–Femininity	−.17
Academic Achievement	−.16

The highest correlation was with the Occupational Introversion–Extroversion scale. This scale, described in Chapter 5, has a strong flavor of dealing with others, especially in social service settings. Occupations which score high, toward the introverted end, include Physicist, Mathematician, and Artist. Occupations scoring low, toward the extroverted end, include Community Recreation Director, Chamber of Commerce Executive, and YMCA Staff Member. The negative correlation here indicates that the CC scale is oriented toward extroverted activities and suggests that these are the activities gaining in popularity over time in our society.

Correlations with Basic Interest Scales

A third way of trying to understand what the CC scale reflects is to look at its correlations with the Basic Interest Scales; those figures are rank-ordered in Table 10-2.

The pattern of these correlations again suggests the extroversion-introversion dimension as all the scales with high correlations are concerned with dealing with people. The scales with the lowest correlations are those most oriented toward the outdoors and blue-collar activities. Note that the Science scale has a negative correlation with the CC scale; this is surprising, as one intuitively thinks that scientific activities are growing in popularity within our culture.

Let me review what we have learned thus far.

TABLE 10-2. CORRELATIONS BETWEEN THE MEN'S CULTURAL CHANGE SCALE AND
THE MEN'S BASIC INTEREST SCALE

Law/Politics	.63	Military Activities	.11
Public Speaking	.61	Music	.07
Business Administration	.49	Religious Activities	.06
Merchandising	.44	Mathematics	.06
Sales	.40	Technical Supervision	.06
		Art	.00
Writing	.35	Medical Service	−.07
Recreational Leadership	.35	Mechanical Activities	−.11
Office Practices	.31	Science	−.14
Adventure	.27		
		Agriculture	−.20
Social Service	.16	Nature	−.32
Teaching	.15		

First, there are several items on the SVIB that show shifts in popularity over the last 30 years.

Second, it is possible to collect these items together into a single scale to discriminate between occupations tested in the 1930's and those tested in the 1960's.

Third, the content of this scale, though heterogeneous, is related positively to the so-called extroverted activities and negatively to blue-collar and outdoor activities.

Fourth, all of the above suggests a general shift in the interests of the general population toward more verbal activities; outdoor and skilled trades activities have become less popular while interests in other areas remain at about the same level.

Cultural Change Scale vs. Year Tested

One final set of data confirm the above conclusions. An extensive check of the relationship between this scale and year tested was made by scoring all available male occupational samples that have been tested with the SVIB. Table 10-3 shows the mean CC score for each of these samples, the year tested, the number in each sample, and the name of the investigator; the groups are arranged in rank order according to their mean score on the CC scale. The highest mean score was found in the sample of Control Data computer salesmen. As this scale, in a peculiar sort of way, reflects "modern" interests, it seems altogether fitting that whatever "modern" interests are, computer salesmen have more of them than anyone else.

The CC mean for these samples is plotted visually in Figure 10-4 against year tested, and the substantial relationship is obvious; the correlation was .85.

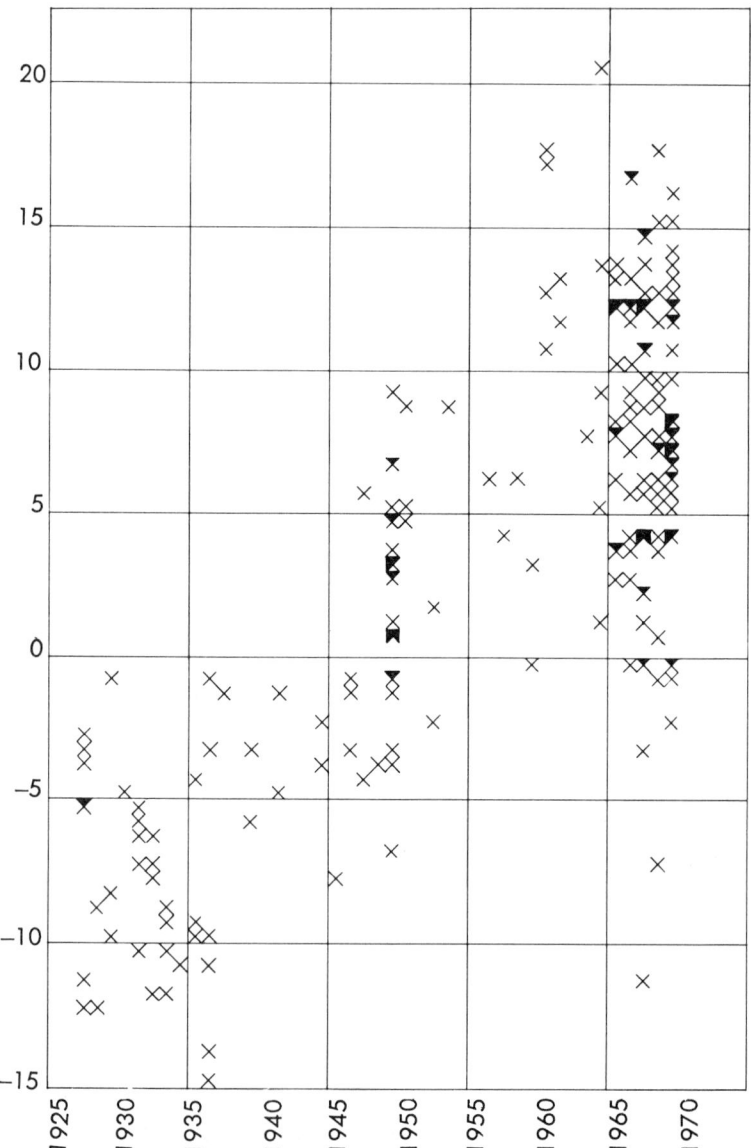

FIG. 10-4. *Mean cultural change score versus year tested for 202 male occupational sample. Each X is the mean "cultural change" score for an occupational sample. X indicates two X's.*

Table 10-3. Mean Scores on the Men's Cultural Scale Versus Year Tested for 202 Male Occupational Samples

Cultural Change Mean Score	Year Tested	N	Sample	Tested by
20.9	1964	190	Salesmen, Computer	C.I. Stein
17.6	1960	100	Salesmen, 3M	W.K. Kirchner
17.5	1968	199	Sales Managers (1968)	1*
17.4	1960	100	Salesmen, 3M applicants	W.K. Kirchner
16.5	1966	13	Football Coaches	1
16.3	1966	76	Salesmen, Life Insurance (1966)	1
16.0	1969	231	Personnel Directors (1969)	1
15.4	1969	257	Department Store Managers	M.D. Dunnette
15.1	1968	228	Advertising Men (1968)	1
14.8	1967	86	Minnesota State Legislators	R. Willow
14.5	1967	54	Social Workers (1967)	1
14.2	1969	189	Public Administrators (1969)	1
13.8	1964	350	Community Recreation Directors	K.B. Roys
13.7	1969	237	Investment Fund Managers	1
13.7	1965	97	Ministers (1965)	1
13.5	1967	252	Psychologists (1967)	1
13.3	1966	49	Salesmen, Encyclopedia	1
13.2	1965	115	Minnesota Elementary Teachers	C.A. Winkle
13.1	1969	250	Salesmen, Life Insurance (1969)	1
13.0	1961	184	Y.M.C.A. Staff Members	H.G. Seashore
12.9	1960	400	Chamber of Commerce Executives	2**
12.8	1969	239	Social Science Teachers (1969)	1
12.8	1967	203	High School Counselors	1
12.6	1968	868	Business School Professors	J.G. Rhode
12.4	1969	712	Army Officers(1969)	1
12.3	1967	283	Newsmen	1
12.3	1967	89	Psychiatrists(1967)	1
12.3	1969	177	Lawyers(1969)	1
12.3	1965	304	Certified Public Accountants (1965)	J.G. Rhode
12.2	1966	32	Actors (1966)	1
12.1	1967	177	Political Scientists	J.E. Rossmann & O.J. Lips
12.1	1965	645	Navy Officers	R.R. Stephenson & N.M. Abrahams
12.0	1965	153	School Superintendents (1965)	1
12.0	1966	61	Salesmen, Steel	R. F. Berdie
11.8	1961	192	Student Personnel Workers	A.B. Clark III
11.7	1969	207	School Superintendents (1969)	1
11.5	1968	44	Guidance Counselors (1968)	Janet Francis & G. Blanton
11.3	1966	93	Danforth Fellows	J.E. Rossmann & J.C. Bentley
11.3	1969	498	Ministers (1969)	D. Hultgren
10.9	1967-68	309	Judges & Lawyers	1
10.7	1968	223	English Teachers	1
10.6	1969	176	Buyers (1969)	1
10.6	1960	200	Air Force Officers	Col. F. Winter
10.4	1965	198	Sociologists	J.E. Rossmann & O.J. Lips
10.1	1966	16	Astronauts	1
9.7	1969	175	Salesmen, Real Estate (1969)	1
9.7	1968	44	Policemen (1968)	L.J. Klappauf
9.6	1967	99	Economists	J.E. Rossmann & O.J. Lips
9.4	1964	542	Computer Programmers	D.K. Perry & W.M. Cannon
9.2	1968	130	Food Scientists	C.O. Willis
9.2	1966	72	Physical Therapists (1966)	R. T. Flint
9.1	1949	16	Marketing Psychologists	P.H. Kriedt
8.9	1966	287	Priests (1966)	Rev. R. Lepak
8.8	1967	132	Judges	1
8.7	1968	463	High School Math Science Teachers (1968)	W.J. Lonner & S.E. Williamson
8.6	1950	113	Unitarian Ministers (1950)	2
8.5	1953	400	Social Workers (1953)	R.L. McCornack
8.4	1966	50	Interpreters	1
8.1	1965	385	Petroleum Engineers	J.B. Alford
8.0	1969	210	Dental Educators	1
8.0	1969	240	Physicians (1969)	1
8.0	1969	320	Funeral Directors (1969)	1
7.9	1968	1028	Engineers (1968)	J.C. Johnson
7.9	1967	451	Teaching Brothers	Rev. O'Toole
7.8	1963	405	Optometrists	N.E. Acree
7.8	1965	51	3 & 4 Star Generals & Admirals	1
7.7	1969	164	Purchasing Agents (1969)	1
7.6	1969	421	College Professors	1
7.6	1965	25	Corporation Presidents (1965)	1
7.4	1968	208	Architects (1968)	1
7.3	1969	196	Policemen (1969)	1
7.2	1969	378	Chiropractors	1
7.1	1968	205	Pharmacists (1968)	1
7.1	1966	460	Physiatrists	G. T. Athelstan
7.1	1969	171	Bankers (1969)	1
6.8	1969	232	Dentists (& Dental Educators, 1969)	1
6.8	1949	114	Guidance Psychologists	P.H. Kriedt
6.6	1949	272	Rehabilitation Counselors	N.E. Acree
6.5	1969	250	Chemists (1969)	1
6.4	1969	164	Dentists	1
6.3	1967	111	County Sheriffs	1
6.3	1968	65	Agricultural Extension Agents	J.W. Longest
6.2	1969	119	Army Sergeants	1
6.2	1956	323	Business Education Teachers	R.V. Bacon
6.1	1965	28	State Governors	1

(table continued next page)

Table 10-3 (*continued*)

Cultural Change Mean Score	Year Tested	N	Sample	Tested by
6.1	1958	452	Credit Managers	2
5.9	1967	258	Photographers	1
5.9	1969	223	Mathematicians (1969)	1
5.8	1947	149	Clinical Psychologists (1947)	E.L. Kelly
5.6	1968	288	Highway Patrolmen	1
5.5	1966	93	N.A.S.A. Scientists	M.D. Dunnette & J.C. Johnson
5.3	1967-69	473	Anthropologists	J.E. Rossmann, O.J. Lips, & Shirley Be
5.3	1964	510	University of Minnesota Freshmen	1
5.2	1949	108	Industrial Psychologists	P.H. Kriedt
5.2	1950	463	Army Officers (1950)	Army Personnel Research Office
5.0	1969	395	Vocational Agricultural Teachers	C.D. Norenberg
4.9	1950	275	Guidance Counselors (1950)	Brown
4.9	1949	219	Clinical Psychologists	P.H. Kriedt
4.6	1967	571	University of Minnesota I.T. Freshmen	R. Taylor
4.5	1949	69	Social Psychologists	P.H. Kriedt
4.4	1966	769	Men-In-General (1966)	1
4.3	1967	192	Interior Decorators	1
4.3	1957	350	Physical Therapists (1957)	2
4.3	1969	260	Foresters	1
4.2	1969	466	Cartographers	A. L. Benton
4.2	1968	230	Physicists (1968)	1
4.2	1966	357	University of Minnesota I.T. Freshmen	1
4.1	1967	82	Animal Husbandry Professors	1
4.1	1969	225	Musicians (1969)	1
4.1	1967	47	Astronomers	1
3.9	1968	252	Medical Technologists	1
3.9	1966	510	Veterinarians (1966)	T.E. Hannum & J.E. Alsip
3.7	1965	64	Generals and Lt. Generals, retired	1
3.7	1949	1045	Psychologists (1949)	P.H. Kriedt
3.5	1965	54	North Dakota Elementary Teachers	Beulah Hegdahl
3.4	1949	65	Statistical Psychologists	P.H. Kriedt
3.4	1959	425	Librarians	J.S. Winters
3.1	1949	404	Psychiatrists (1949)	E.K. Strong, Jr. & A.C. Tucker
3.0	1949	44	Child Psychologists	P.H. Kriedt
2.9	1966	53	Minneapolis Symphony	1
2.9	1965	84	Pulitzer Prize Winners	1
2.7	1949	96	Pediatricians	E.K. Strong, Jr. & A.C. Tucker
2.5	1949	154	Educational Psychologists	P.H. Kriedt
2.2	1967	256	German Psychologists	W.J. Lonner
2.1	1967	109	North Hennepin Jr. College Students	1
1.6	1952	493	Music Teachers (1952)	2
1.4	1949	79	Lawyers (1949)	R.I. Berdie & Theda Hagenah
1.2	1967	1490	Ferris State Students	R. Taylor
1.0	1964	102	Bankers (1964)	1
.8	1949	256	Experimental Psychologists	P.H. Kriedt
.7	1968	178	Artists (1968)	1
.6	1949	71	Orthopedic Surgeons	E.K. Strong, Jr. & A.C. Tucker
.6	1949	209	Internists	E.K. Strong, Jr. & A.C. Tucker
.5	1949	48	Neurological Surgeons	E.K. Strong, Jr. & A.C. Tucker
-.1	1967	35	V.A. Hospital Schizophrenic Patients	1
-.2	1969	122	Tool & Die Makers	1
-.4	1959	342	Biologists	C.A. Lindsay
-.6	1966	42	National Institute of Arts & Letters Members	1
-.7	1967	62	Colonels	1
-.9	1969	120	Electricians	1
-1.1	1936	217	Social Science Teachers (1936)	2
-1.2	1946	55	County Welfare Workers	Strate
-1.2	1968	143	German Medical Students	Gendel
-1.2	1949	111	Radiologists	E.K. Strong, Jr. & A.C. Tucker
-1.3	1969	339	Skilled Tradesmen	1
-1.3	1949	188	Surgeons	E.K. Strong, Jr. & A.C. Tucker
-1.4	1929	69	Unitarian Ministers (1929)	2
-1.8	1946	150	Music Teachers (1946)	Kleist
-1.8	1937	30	Actors (1937)	2
-1.9	1949	84	Urologists	E.K. Strong, Jr. & A.C. Tucker
- 1.9	1941	550	Public Administrators (1941)	2
- 2.5	1944	612	Certified Public Accountants (1944)	2
- 2.6	1952	450	Musicians (1952)	2
- 2.9	1969	97	Carpenters (1969)	1
- 3.0	1927	113	Y.M.C.A. Secretaries	2
- 3.7	1927	147	Personnel Directors (1927)	2
- 3.7	1936	289	High School Math Science Teachers (1936)	2
- 3.8	1949	534	Physicians (1949)	E.K. Strong, Jr. & A.C. Tucker
- 3.9	1967	126	German Accountants	W.J. Lonner
- 3.9	1946	158	Buyers (1946)	2
- 3.9	1939	179	Salesmen, Pacific Gas & Electric	2
- 4.0	1949	155	Pathologists	E.K. Strong, Jr. & A.C. Tucker
- 4.1	1927	250	Ministers (1927)	2
- 4.2	1948	118	Machinists	2
- 4.2	1944	354	Owners of Certified Public Accounting Firms	2
- 4.6	1947	309	Pharmacists (1947)	M. Schwebel
- 4.6	1935	41	Emporium Buyers	2

334

TABLE 10-3 (*continued*)

Cultural Change Mean Score	Year Tested	N	Sample	Tested by
- 5.0	1930	190	School Superintendents (1930)	2
- 5.2	1941	510	Pilots	2
- 5.5	1927	216	Y.M.C.A. Physical Directors	2
- 5.7	1927	251	Lawyers (1927)	2
- 5.7	1931	169	Advertising Men (1931)	2
- 6.3	1939	585	Osteopaths	2
- 6.4	1931	310	Salesmen, Life Insurance (1931)	2
- 6.6	1932	228	Sales Managers (1932)	2
- 6.9	1931	297	Chemists (1931)	2
- 7.0	1949	310	Veterinarians (1949)	T.E. Hannum
- 7.6	1932	243	Salesmen, Real Estate (1932)	2
- 7.6	1968	235	Farmers (1968)	D.W. Priebe
- 7.6	1931	248	Authors	2
- 8.0	1945	360	Funeral Directors (1945)	2
- 8.1	1932	345	Accountants	2
- 8.5	1929	135	Salesmen, Auto	2
- 9.0	1933	506	Men-In-General (1933)	2
- 9.0	1928	326	Office Workers	2
- 9.6	1935	216	Production Managers	2
- 9.9	1933	240	Architects (1933)	2
-10.3	1936	270	Printers	2
-10.3	1935	169	Corporation Presidents (1935)	2
-10.4	1929	181	Mathematicians (1929)	2
-10.7	1931	219	Purchasing Agents (1931)	2
-10.8	1933	254	Policemen (1933)	2
-11.0	1936	406	Forest Service Men	2
-11.2	1934	247	Bankers (1934)	2
-11.5	1927	172	Physicists (1927)	2
-11.7	1967	77	Farmers (1967)	K.R. Krause
-12.1	1932	239	Dentists (1932)	2
-12.3	1933	231	Artists (1933)	2
-12.5	1927	339	Physicians (1927)	2
-12.6	1928	513	Engineers (1928)	2
-14.4	1936	241	Farmers (1936)	2
-15.2	1936	181	Carpenters (1936)	2

1* Tested by this author
2**Tested by E.K. Strong, Jr.

Changing Interests Among Women

This entire project of studying change over time has been replicated among women's occupations by Diane Hill, using the samples of women tested by Strong in the 1930's versus the samples tested in the 1960's at Minnesota. The same technique as that described above for the Men's form, that of matching samples from the same occupation, was followed here. Because so many more occupations have been retested during 1966–68 for the Women's SVIB revision, many more pairs were available. The occupations used are listed in Table 10-5. The same technique of isolating items showing about 10 percent or more shift in percent response among a majority of the pairs was adopted here to identify the "changing" items and those items are listed in Table 10-4.

The validation samples were then scored on this scale, and their results are listed in Table 10-5; the scale clearly did an effective job of separating samples tested in the 1930's from those tested in the 1960's—the differences between the pairs in most samples amounted to about two standard deviations.

TABLE 10-4. ITEMS WEIGHTED ON THE WOMEN'S CULTURAL CHANGE SCALE

PLUS WEIGHTS (Liked more or disliked less)	MINUS WEIGHTS (Liked less or disliked more)

OCCUPATIONS

1* Actress	22 Chemist
9 Author, childrens' books	48 Housekeeper
15 Beauty specialist	55 Landscape Gardener
24 College Professor	58 Librarian
42 Foreign Correspondent	83 Private Secretary
51 Interpreter	102 Scientific Research Worker
57 Criminal Lawyer	120* Tea Room Proprietress
62* Fashion Model	
67 Missionary	
81 Politician	
86 Professional Dancer	
116 Grade School Teacher	

AMUSEMENTS

142 Amusement Parks	132* Camping out
156 Womens' Page	139* Bird watching
	150 Attending lectures
	152 Symphony concerts
	157 Poetry

ACTIVITIES

173* Expressing judgements publicly, regardless of what others say	177 Repairing electrical wiring
178 Doing your own laundry work	180 Arguments
200* Acting as cheerleader	209 Regular hours for work
210 Continually changing activities	212 Contributing to charities
	214 Looking at a collection of rare laces

TYPES OF PEOPLE

227 Religious people	226 Thrifty people
241 Fashionably dressed people	235* Physically sick people

SCHOOL SUBJECTS

365* Bible history	367 Botany
	374 Economics
	381 Ancient Languages

FORCED CHOICE ITEMS

275 Co-workers--congenial, competent and adequate in numbers	267 Steadiness and permanence of work
286 President of a Society	268 Opportunity for promotion
300 House-to-house canvassing	309 Preparing a meal
313 Follow own career after marriage	351 Plan my work in detail
321* Travel alone and make own preparations	
355 Discuss my ideals with others	

* -- These items were slightly reworded in the new booklet.

All available samples of employed women have been scored on the Women's Cultural Change scale, and their means are rank-ordered in Table 10-6. Again, as with the male samples, the ordering was closely related to year tested; the correlation between scale mean and year tested was .88, though this was somewhat inflated because most of the observations fell around two points. Still, the relationship was high; to emphasize that, a scatterplot of mean scores versus year tested is presented in Figure

TABLE 10-5. MEAN AND STANDARD DEVIATIONS FOR THE OLD (1930's) AND NEW (1960's) OCCUPATIONAL SAMPLES ON THE WOMEN'S CULTURAL CHANGE SCALE

Occupations	c. 1930 N	Mean	S.D.	c. 1960 N	Mean	S.D.	Mean Difference
Librarians	425	-14.1	6.0	410	-0.4	6.6	+13.7
Math-Science Teachers	467	-13.8	6.1	308	-1.5	7.6	+12.3
Nurses	396	-13.0	5.7	263	3.7	6.8	+16.7
Lab Technicians	356	-12.8	6.6	345	-3.0	6.8	+ 9.8
Dieticians	416	-12.6	6.2	327	-1.6	7.3	+11.0
Physicians	414	-12.2	6.0	329	-2.5	6.3	+ 9.7
Home Ec Teachers	420	-11.6	6.2	373	0.9	7.3	+12.5
English Teachers	293	-11.5	6.5	352	3.1	7.7	+14.6
YWCA Staff	202	-11.4	6.1	282	4.2	6.8	+15.6
Secretaries	452	-10.8	7.3	366	2.1	7.7	+12.9
Social Science Teachers	395	-10.0	6.4	183	3.2	7.4	+13.2
Occupational Therapists	162	-10.7	6.3	607	1.3	7.3	+12.0
Life Insurance Sales	205	- 9.8	6.6	187	2.3	7.3	+12.1
Artists	402	- 9.8	6.5	297	-1.7	6.2	+ 8.1
Women-in-General	500	- 9.4	8.1	1000	1.5	7.8	+10.9
Psychologists	380	- 9.0	6.3	275	1.4	6.7	+10.4
Authors-Journalists	402	- 8.3	6.4	189	5.1	7.4	+13.4
Lawyers	373	- 7.6	7.1	235	2.0	7.3	+ 9.6
H S Phys Ed Teachers	101	- 5.9	5.6	310	4.2	6.6	+10.1
Physical Therapists	450	- 5.8	6.8	267	0.0	7.2	+ 5.8

10-5, and that shows there was hardly any overlap on this scale between the 1930's and the 1960's samples.

The content of the Women's Cultural Change scale, like the men's is factorially complex, and can best be understood by looking at its correlations with the Basic Interest Scales, and the Nonoccupational Scales; that information is presented in Table 10-7.

The general relationships look similar to those found among the men's occupations; the emphasis is on extroverted, out-going, people-oriented activities. The positive correlations are not as high as those found among the men's groups, but the negative ones are higher, showing less interest among today's women in outdoors, mathematical, and scientific activities.

Once again, one can conclude that the American society is producing more extroverts.

Cultural Change Mean Score	Year Tested	N	Sample	Investigator[1,2]
6.86	1965	72	Fashion Models	1
6.11	1967	23	Director, Christian Education (Baptist)	1
5.14	1966	189	Newspaper Women	1
5.01	1968	199	Recreation Leaders	
4.69	1967	262	Beauticians	Jacqueline Boaz
4.21	1967	282	YWCA Staff	1
4.21	1967	310	Physical Education Teachers	1
3.89	1967	67	Director, Christian Education (Lutheran)	1
3.72	1967	263	Baccalaureate Nurses	1
3.44	1967	434	Director, Christian Education	1
3.43	1967	130	Director, Christian Education (Methodist)	1
3.16	1967	183	Social Science Teachers	1
3.12	1967	352	English Teacher	1
3.08	1967	347	Guidance Counselors	1
2.99	1967	214	Director, Christian Education (Presbyterian)	1
2.84	1968	61	Extension Agent	J. Longest
2.67	1966	30	Photographers	1
2.55	1967	366	Secretaries	1
2.55	1967	287	Language Teacher	1
2.34	1967	187	Life Insurance Underwriters	1
2.30	1967	82	Wives of Social Workers	1
2.08	1967	359	Art Teachers	1
2.05	1967	235	Lawyers	1
1.54	1967	1000	Women-In-General	1
1.42	1965	324	Speech Pathologists	1
1.37	1966	275	Psychologists	1
1.30	1966	607	Occupational Therapists	R. Flint and L. Miller
1.25	1967	307	WAC Officers	1
1.10	1967	191	WAVES - Officers	1
.91	1967	373	Home Economics Teachers	1
.83	1967	300	Business Education Teachers	1
.72	1967	307	Radiology Technicians	1
.57	1966	129	Telephone Operators	1
.19	1964	199	Computer Programmers	D. P. Perry
.16	1967	420	Non-Professional Women-In-General	1
.11	1966	172	Interior Decorators	1
.05	1966	267	Physical Therapists	R. Flint
-.01	1967	325	Elementary Teacher	1
-.05	1967	130	Interpreters-Translators	1
-.13	1967	335	Accountants	1
-.15	1968	271	Bank Women	
-.41	1967	418	Dental Assistant	1
-.44	1967	410	Librarians	1
-.51	1967	218	WAC Enlisted	1
-.84	1966	243	Salesladies	1
-.96	1966	268	Public Health Nurses	Constance Carmody
-.99	1967	106	Wives of Animal Husbandry Professors	1
-1.03	1966	89	Assemblers and Inspectors	1
-1.20	1967	213	WAVES Enlisted	1
-1.53	1967	308	Mathematics-Science Teachers	1
-1.59	1967	327	Dieticians	1
-1.71	1967	297	Artists	1
-2.00	1952	290	Music Performers	2
-2.44	1967	295	Munsingwear Sewing Machine Operators	1
-2.46	1967	329	Physicians	1
-2.82	1967	80	Wives of Physicists	1
-2.89	1966	79	Mathematicians--M.A.	1
-3.05	1967	345	Medical Technologists	1
-3.15	1961	494	Sister Teacher	Sister Mary David Olheiser
-3.20	1952	448	Music Teacher	2
-4.08	1967	77	Wives of Farmers	K. Krause
-4.08	1966	119	Mathematician--Ph.D.	1
-4.16	1967	281	Executive Housekeepers	1
-4.17	1959	324	Engineers	2
-4.38	1959	322	Visiting Nurses	Eileen Koehler
-4.68	1966	173	Chemists	1
-4.76	1967	222	Licensed Practical Nurses	1
-5.11	1953	464	Social Workers	R.L. McCornack
-5.80	1957	450	Physical Therapists	Sarah S. Rogers
-5.87	1939	100	College Physical Education Teachers	Patricia Collins
-6.90	1939	101	High School Physical Education Teachers	2
-7.58	1941	452	Stenographers	2
-7.62	1938	373	Lawyers	2
-8.26	1938	402	Authors	2
-8.69	1941	54	Ready-to-Wear Saleswomen	2
-8.73	1941	250	Business Education Teachers	H. F. Koepke
-8.95	1942	380	Psychologists	2
-8.97	1941	427	General Office Workers	2
-9.16	1942	204	Buyers	2
-9.36	1934	500	Women-In-General	2

TABLE 10-6 (*continued*)

Cultural Change Mean Score	Year Tested	N	Sample	Investigator
-9.76	1941	402	Artists	2
-9.79	1941	205	Life Insurance Salesmen	2
-10.72	1942	162	Occupational Therapists	2
-10.79	1941	395	Social Science Teacher	2
-10.87	1934	402	Housewives	2
-11.35	1934	202	YWCA Secretaries	2
-11.54	1934	293	English Teachers	2
-11.62	1941	420	Home Economics Teachers	2
-11.96	1942	195	Dentists	2
-12.22	1941	414	Physicians	2
-12.63	1941	416	Dieticians	2
-12.78	1941	356	Laboratory Technicians	2
-12.97	1934	396	Nurse	2
-13.75	1941	467	Mathematics-Science Teachers	2
-14.13	1934	425	Librarian	2

1 = Tested by Center for Interest Measurement Research, University of Minnesota
2 = Tested by E. K. Strong, Jr.

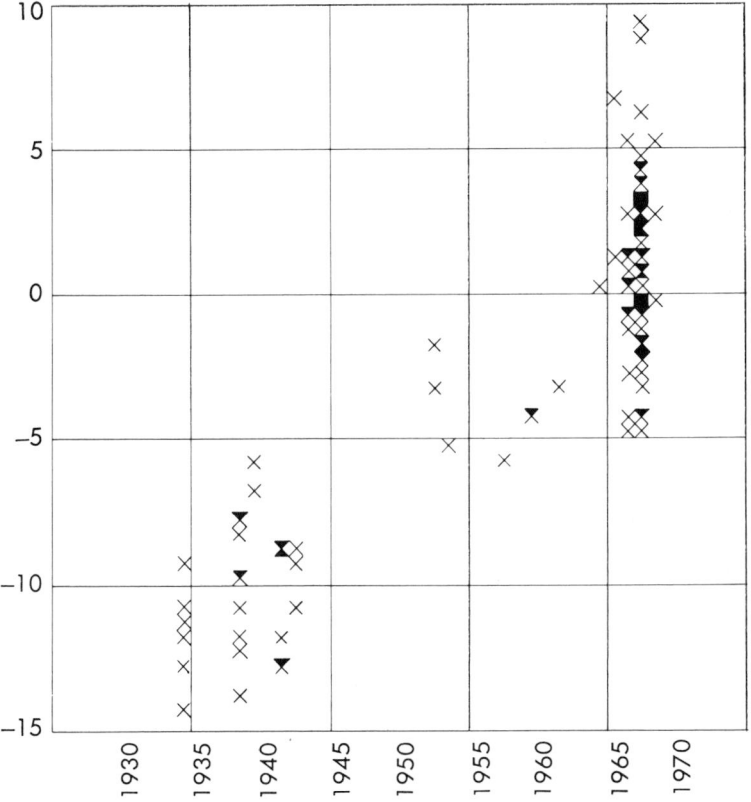

FIG. 10-5. *Mean cultural change score versus year tested for 95 female occupational samples. Each X is the mean "cultural change" score for an occupational sample. X indicates two X's.*

339

TABLE 10-7. CORRELATIONS BETWEEN THE WOMEN'S CULTURAL CHANGE SCALE
AND THE WOMEN'S BASIC INTEREST AND NONOCCUPATIONAL SCALES

Basic Interest Scales

Performing Arts	.30	Homemaking	.07
Social Service	.29	Sports	.04
Writing	.27	Office Practices	−.07
Public Speaking	.26	Biological Science	−.14
Law/Politics	.20	Medical Service	−.14
Teaching	.20	Outdoors	−.21
Religious Activities	.16	Numbers	−.33
Art	.14	Physical Science	−.44
Music	.12	Mechanical	−.52
Merchandising	.12		

Women's Nonoccupational Scales

Occupational Introversion–Extroversion	−.32	Diversity of Interest	.16
Academic Achievement	−.25	Femininity–Masculinity (II)	.08

Implications of the Cultural Change Research

Practical Implications for Interest Inventories

So much for the data; what are the implications of this research?

I have pondered at some length as to the meaning of this score for a single individual and must admit that I am baffled. Only wry applications come to mind: "Well, you might have taken this test last week but, according to this score, you're living in about 1943." I can see no serious, beneficial application of this score in the counseling situation.

Certainly the findings have some implications for the revision of interest inventories though, again, just what is implied is not clear. One's first reaction—that all inventories should be restandardized every few years—is too extreme for the changes were not that large. Roughly one-fourth of the SVIB items were classified as "changed," using a liberal definition, i.e., only a 10 percent shift or more in response. Clearly, the majority had not changed much in popularity over this time span; these stable items plus the 100 new items that were added in the 1966 revision will continue to provide a useful up-to-date item pool.

Still, some changes should be considered. Several alternatives are possible, none of them very appealing. One could calibrate each scale against year established, and add or subtract some constant from the individual's score. Or calibrate each person as he takes the SVIB by determining his score on the CC scale, from that determine the "psychological year he is living in" and adjust his remaining standard scores accordingly. A third possibility would be simply to report this score on the profile and let the counselor make the necessary modifications in his interpretation. None of these alternatives are very practical.

The technique that has been adopted was the modification of the "Men-in-General" group used to establish the SVIB scales. If the Men-in-General sample can be tested during the same period as the occupational samples, the effect of the time-dependent items should be canceled out and only those items truly characteristic of the occupational group will emerge from the item analysis. To accomplish this, the Men-in-General group used in the 1966 revision included men tested between 1927 and 1965, the same span used to test the criterion samples. This helped but did not completely solve the problem; most men tested today score higher on the more recently developed scales. Further work is still necessary.

As an immediate practical solution for the Women's booklet, a new Women-in-General sample was collected during 1966–67 as part of the data collection for the current revision. While this should solve the immediate problem, the quandary of how to deal with a slight but continual shift in interests over the years is unresolved.

Theoretical Implications for Understanding Society

Finally, what does this research tell us about our society? In trying to understand what has caused these shifts, psychologists have no advantage over any thoughtful man on the street for we know essentially nothing about the factors that cause changes in measured interests.

And we know nothing about how people develop these interests initially. Some men are interested in science, some in sales, and we know these interests are negatively correlated. Yet we are completely uninformed about how these two different types of people develop. Did they come from different backgrounds? Was one group successful in scientific activities in their early days, the other in interpersonal relationships, or do they simply have different genetic makeups? If interests are traceable to genetic factors, then there would be a plausible explanation for this shift toward extroversion. Extroverts probably tend to marry more often, and perhaps have more children. Thus the genetic pool within our society may be slowly shifting toward extroversion.

Other research has established a direct genetic link for extroversion-introversion. Gottesman (1963), using the MMPI with fraternal and identical twins, reported evidence for the inheritability of this trait. In a similar project being conducted with Dr. Robert Nichols of the National Merit Scholarship Corporation, using the SVIB with 19-year-old male fraternal

TABLE 10-8. MEAN SCORES ON THE OCCUPATIONAL INTROVERSION–EXTROVERSION
SCALE FOR MEN IN VARIOUS MARITAL CATEGORIES

		OIE Scores			
		Test (Age 16)		Retest (Age 52)	
	N	Mean	SD	Mean	SD
Never married	54	58	13	55	14
Married, no children	202	57	13	53	13
Married with children	958	56	13	50	13
Total	1,214				

and identical twins, preliminary data indicates that the correlations on the OIE scale between identical twins is higher than between fraternal twins (.53 to .27 respectively among males). Presumably, the difference here represents the genetic component.

Further data supporting this chain of thought are presented in Table 10-8. Means and SD's on the OIE scale are listed for various marital categories of the 52-year-old men in the Basic Interest Scale norm group. These data do, indeed, show that the rank-ordering on extroversion is from high to low:

1. Men who married and had children.
2. Men who married but had no children.
3. Men who did not marry.

(High scores on the OIE scale indicate introversion; low scores indicate extroversion.)

Although the mean differences were quite small, they were consistent in direction and suggest that introverts are not as likely to replace themselves as are extroverts—and, if there is a genetic link, the genetic pool would be slowly shifting toward extroversion.

One caution: the changes found earlier in this chapter cannot all be explained by genetic shift, as the time span is much too short. Other factors are clearly involved, but have not yet been identified. Such information may, of course, lead us to the conclusion that one effective way to change the vocational attitudes of the population might be through genetic mechanisms. That would be exciting scientifically but depressing sociologically. In any event, we must learn more about this.

CHAPTER 11

An Informal History of the SVIB

The SVIB has the longest history of any current widely used psychological inventory. First published in 1927, it has been the subject of extensive research for the past 40 years. Much has been learned about the meaning of a person's answers to this inventory, and more knowledge is continually coming into existence. Though our areas of ignorance are still great, they are at least becoming better identified, permitting a more efficient concentration of effort, and the coming years should see a substantial expansion of our understanding of what interests are, how they can be measured and how these measures can be used to make life more pleasant.

This is a brief history of the SVIB; it is not a technical report in the usual sense as the development of this inventory is reviewed from a historical rather than a psychometric viewpoint. Those who wish more detailed technical information should refer to the preceding sections of this Handbook.

The history of a psychological test is not a thrilling saga; there have been no gatherings in dusty squash courts to see if the gadget will really work, no agonizing waits to see if the graft or transplant survives, no tension ridden countdowns. Like most science, it has been a succession of drab and trivial activities with only an occasional significant statistic to brighten the day. Even when results look bright and promising, in the social sciences skepticism is so essential until several replications are completed that any thrill of a new breakthrough is dampened by the necessity of oozing under, over and around the barriers of ignorance until it is certain that the key— and not simply more error variance—has appeared. This means one is never sure just when it was that he learned what he now knows is true.

Lively times have not been entirely absent; any research with people creates its own sparks, whether angry letters from participants, friendly

---

This chapter was originally prepared as a chapter for *Advances in Psychological Assessment*, edited by Paul McReynolds, published by Science and Behavior Books, Palo Alto, California (1968).

testimonials from the audience, or professional disagreements over the philosophy, techniques, or—not the least—finances of the operations. The 1966 revision of the Men's SVIB involved two major investigators separated by fifty years in age and training, two others, more tangential but with bright, innovative and occasionally disruptive ideas, a family who justifiably feels possessive about the inventory, a university press publisher who values quality over profit, commercial distributors with somewhat different feelings, four scoring services with a variety of approaches, and a host of professionals who, from years of personal use, feel the Strong is in some sense "their" test. With these diverse outlooks and in the absence of corporation-chart-block-diagram lines of command and communication, the pot boiled occasionally.

However, for the most part, things have been staid and most of the issues have been no more controversial than "What color paper shall we use?", "Do we need 200 or 400 people to establish a new scale?", "In this form letter to women chemists, what salutation shall we use: Dear Madam . . . Dear Mesdames . . . Dear Dr. . . . , To Whom It May Concern . . . ?" (Eventual solution—Dear Chemist:).

Some Historical Trends

Those associated with the SVIB, especially its originator, Professor E. K. Strong, Jr., have continually insisted on an active research program; they have especially encouraged longitudinal studies so that the place of inventoried interests in long-range career development can be better understood. Even if there were no intrinsic academic reasons for studying the SVIB's history, this emphasis on long-term projects would make it essential; to comprehend fully the results of studies over time, one must know something about the background of the research.

An appropriate place to begin is with two charts showing trends over time. Figure 11-1 shows the number of booklets (for the Men's form only) printed each year since the SVIB was first published. The narrow line is the number actually printed, the broad line is a three-year floating average, a better technique for identifying trends. The line is generally upward with a sizable spurt in 1947, obviously reflecting the counseling of the returning veterans of World War II. Most of the postwar booklets have been reuseable forms so that more recent printing figures are a gross underestimate of the number of men who have filled in the SVIB each year. A rough guess is that each booklet is used approximately 2 to 4 times, so perhaps 300,000 to 500,000 men now complete the Strong annually. This corresponds roughly to the collective volume of the commercial scoring services.

The second trend, in Figure 11-2 shows the number of technical publications—directly related to the SVIB—appearing each year since 1926.

This figure was built from the list of SVIB references in the 6th *Mental Measurements Yearbook* (Buros, 1965). By 1967, the total number of publications was well over 800, a level of activity which would have amazed and gratified Dr. Strong.

As a further shorthand for reviewing the history of the SVIB, Table 11-1 has been prepared. Here are listed historical highlights in three columns: the first deals with the SVIB, the second with Professor Strong's career—for it is meaningless to study the SVIB without reference to his life—and a third column presenting some of the flavor of the times.

Early History

The genesis of psychological tests and inventories in America dates back to about 1900. The first attempt to deal specifically with interests was probably made by E. L. Thorndike, reported in the *Popular Science Monthly* (1912), "The permanence of interests and their relation to abilities." In this project, 100 college students were asked to rank-order their interests as they remembered them in elementary school, in high school, and currently. Then they were asked to rank-order their abilities for the same periods. Thorndike computed correlations between the various rank-orders and (perhaps going a bit beyond his data) concluded:

These facts unanimously witness to the importance of early interests. They are shown to be far from fickle and evanescent. . . . Interests are also shown to be symptomatic, to a very great extent, of present and future capacity or ability. Either because one likes what he can do well, or because one gives zeal and effort to what he likes, or because interests and ability are both symptoms of some fundamental feature of the individual's original nature, or because of the combined action of all three factors, interest and ability are bound very closely together. The bond is so close that either may be used as a symptom for the other almost as well as for itself.

We have since learned that the relationship between interests and abilities is much more complex.

A second early attempt was a questionnaire developed by T. L. Kelley (1914) asking questions such as: "If you had the opportunity, which one of the following would you attend, supposing each one of them to be first class of its kind?" (Then follow 14 amusements, such as "Circus" and "Grand Opera.")

Kelley's questionnaire apparently was not noticed by others, and the real beginning of the interest inventory as we know it was at the Carnegie Institute of Technology in Pittsburgh shortly after World War I. An active

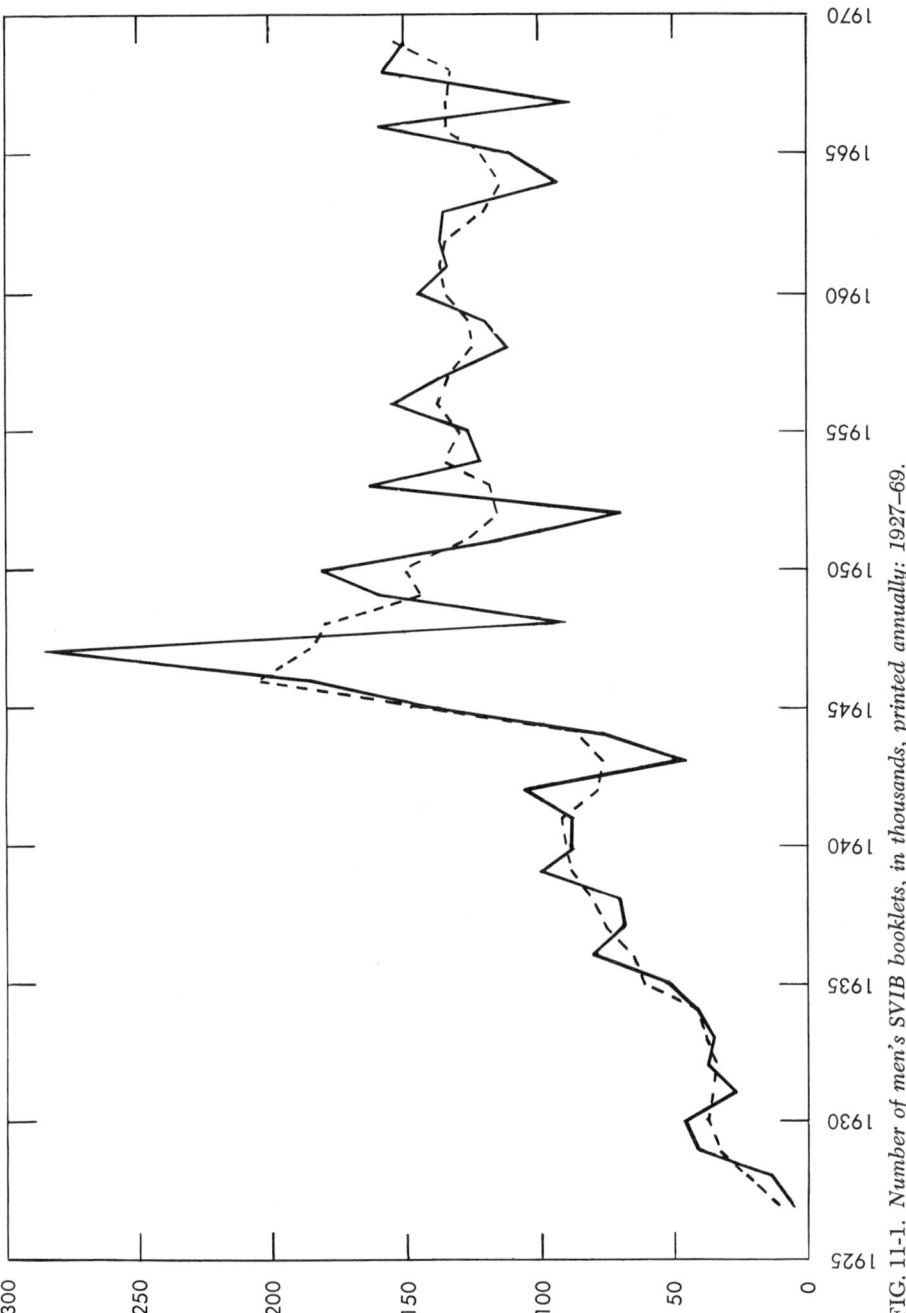

FIG. 11-1. *Number of men's SVIB booklets, in thousands, printed annually: 1927–69.*

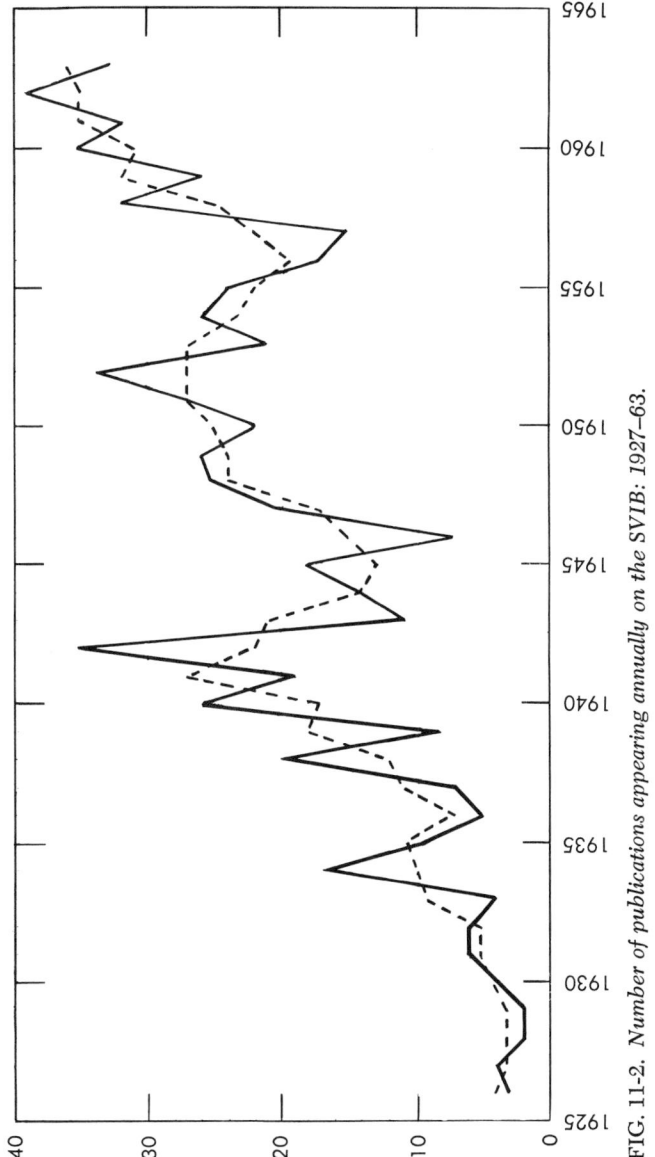

FIG. 11-2. Number of publications appearing annually on the SVIB: 1927–63.

TABLE 11-1. NOTEWORTHY EVENTS IN THE HISTORY OF THE SVIB

Strong Vocational Interest Blank	Edward K. Strong, Jr.	Historical Context
	1884 EKS born in Syracuse, New York	1884 Grover Cleveland elected U. S. President
	1902 EKS's father takes pastorate in San Francisco	
	1906 EKS earns B.A. in Biology from U. of California (Berkeley); takes job briefly with U.S. Forest Service.	1906 San Francisco earthquake; galleys of U.C. 1906 yearbook destroyed at print shop so EKS's class had none
	1909 EKS earns M.A. from Berkeley, leaves for Columbia to study with Cattell and Thorndike	1909 Peary acclaimed for reaching North Pole
	1911 EKS marries Margaret Hart, student at Barnard; receives Ph.D. from Columbia; publishes first technical paper, "The effect of various types of suggestion upon muscular activity," Psych. Review; spends next three years doing research on advertising methods	1911 "Alexander's Rag Time Band" published
	1912 Daughter, Margaret, born; she later marries Thomas Harrell, currently Professor of Psychology in Business School at Stanford	
	1914-1917 EKS joins psychology faculty at George Peabody College, Nashville, Tennessee	
	1914 Son Edward born; currently a physician in San Francisco	
		1915 Sinking of Lusitania; America edges toward war.
	1916 Daughter Frances born; she later marries Ralph Berdie, currently Professor of Psychology at Minnesota	
	1917-1919 EKS serves with Army Committee on Classification of Personnel	1917 U.S. enters World War I
1919 Yoakum's seminar at Carnegie Tech prepares 1,000 item pool of interest items.	1919 EKS publishes Introductory Psychology for Teachers, Warwick and York	1919 World War I ends, U. S. Senate votes not to enter League of Nations.
	1919-1923 EKS teaches at Carnegie Institute of Technology, Pittsburgh.	
		1920 Harding elected U. S. President; Prohibition comes in; America enters Roaring Twenties.
	1922 EKS publishes The Psychology of Selling Life Insurance, Harper and Brothers	1921-1923 Chinese Communist party founded.
1923 Karl Cowdery builds 263 item inventory for project under Strong	1923 EKS moves to Stanford as Professor of Psychology in School of Business; publishes (with R. S. Uhrbrock) Job Analysis and the Curriculum, Williams and Wilkins.	
	1925 EKS publishes The Psychology of Selling Advertising, McGraw Hill.	
	1926 EKS publishes (at age 42) first article on interest measurement, "An interest test for personnel managers," Journal of Personnel Research	
1927 EKS publishes 420 item SVIB, building from Carnegie Tech work and Cowdery's project--Stanford University Press is publisher.		1927 Lindbergh flies the Atlantic; Stalin takes over Russia.
1928 First SVIB Manual published.		
		1929 "Black Thursday" stock market crash.
	1931 EKS publishes Change of Interests with Age, Stanford University Press	

348

TABLE 11-1 (continued)

rong Vocational Interest Blank	Edward K. Strong, Jr.	Historical Context
		1932 Franklin D. Roosevelt pledges "New Deal" for American public, elected U. S. President
)33 Women's SVIB copyrighted; 410 items, 262 in common with Men's Form.	1933 EKS publishes Vocational Aptitudes of second generation Japanese in the United States, and Japanese in California, Stanford University Press.	
		1934 DPC born in Bridgewater, Iowa
)35 First Manual for Women's Form		
)38 Major revision of Men's Form--400 items; "Modern" profile adopted	1938 EKS publishes Psychological Aspects of Business, McGraw Hill.	1938 B. F. Skinner publishes Behavior of Organisms, D. Appleton Century Co.
		1939 Germany invades Poland; World War II starts
)41 John G. Darley at Minnesota publishes first monograph on SVIB, Clinical Aspects and Interpretation of the SVIB, Psychological Corporation		1941 Japanese bomb Pearl Harbor; U. S. enters war
	1943 EKS publishes Vocational Interests of Men and Women, Stanford University Press; awarded Butler Medal from Columbia University for this work	
		1945 World War.II ends
)46 Women's form revised to parallel Men's Form--400 items; Elmer Hankes in Minneapolis invents first automatic scoring machine for SVIB		
	1948 EKS begins follow-up study of Stanford students tested in 1920's, 30's.	1948 Truman upsets Dewey for U. S. Presidency.
	1949 EKS retires from Stanford	
		1952 Eisenhower elected, goes to Korea to review war
)55 U. of Minnesota has symposium on SVIB; results published in The Strong Vocational Interest Blank: Research and Uses, edited by W. L. Layton, University of Minnesota Press; John G. Darley and Theda Hagenah publish Vocational Interest Measurement, University of Minnesota Press	1955 EKS comes to Minnesota to talk about revision; publishes Vocational Interests Eighteen Years After College, University of Minnesota Press	1955 Rock 'n Roll music comes in: "See you later Alligator" published; Elvis Presley begins climb to fame ; Iron Curtain countries sign Warsaw Pact
		1957 Russia launches Sputnik
)58 All SVIB criterion group data transferred to Minnesota for computer analysis	1958 EKS gives Walter Bingham Lecture at Minnesota , "Satisfactions and interests," published in American Psychologist	
)59 First "modern" SVIB Manual published by Consulting Psychologists Press.		
		1960 Kennedy elected U.S. President; launches New Frontier
)62 National Computer Systems, Minneapolis, builds first SVIB scoring machine using digital computer	1962 EKS makes last visit to Minnesota to review revision decisions with Berdie, Campbell, and Clark	1962 John Glenn orbits the earth
)63 U. of Minnesota establishes Center for Interest Measurement Research; remainder of EKS files shipped to Minnesota; Measurement Research Center, Iowa City, enters SVIB scoring field	1963 [December 4] EKS passes away in Palo Alto, California	1963 John F. Kennedy assassinated
	1964 EKS's last publication appears: "Proposed scoring changes for the SVIB" (with Campbell, Berdie, and Clark) Journal of Applied Psychology	1964 Johnson swamps Goldwater for U. S. presidency.
)66 Major revision of Men's Form published-- 399 items		
)69 Major revision of Women's Form published -- 398 items		1969 Man reaches the moon

group of industrial psychologists, headed by Walter Bingham, attacked many applied psychological problems, including the problem of measuring interests. Douglas Fryer, in his 1931 book, *The Measurement of Interests,* summarized the early activities:

The earliest investigation in this [Carnegie Tech] group undertaking was one by Bruce Moore in which an attempt was made to measure the mechanical and social interests of engineers (Moore, 1921). Other early investigations from this source were studies made by Ream (1924), who endeavored to distinguish by their interests between successful and unsuccessful salesmen, and by Freyd (1924), who continued the research of Moore in a further attempt to distinguish by their interests between mechanical and social groups of people. Miner's work (1922) upon the inventorying method was a factor in this undertaking which has made the measurement of interests a feasible enterprise.

... further work has continued in the development of a standardized inventory along the line laid down by its beginnings. Research under the direction of Strong at Stanford University and Paterson at the University of Minnesota has been most fruitful in increasing the scope and standardization of the inventories and the development of scoring keys designating the interests of various social groups (Fryer, 1931, p. 61).

One focus of the work at Carnegie Tech, about 1919, was a seminar conducted by C. S. Yoakum; under his direction, a group of graduate students prepared an extensive pool of items for interest inventories. This pool, about 1,000 items, has had considerable historical influence, as the following inventories are direct descendants from Yoakum's seminar (and most other modern inventories have probably borrowed from them in one way or another):

The Carnegie Interest Inventory, 1921
The Carnegie Interest Analysis, 1923
Occupational Interests, published by Freyd in 1923
The Interest Report Blank, by Cowdery at Stanford in 1924
The General Interest Inventory, by Kornhauser in 1927
The Purdue Interest Report Blank, by Remmers in 1929
Strong's Vocational Interest Blank, 1927, developed mainly from Cowdery's inventory with the addition of several more items
The Minnesota Interest Inventory, Paterson in the early 1930's (not to be confused with Clark's Minnesota Vocational Interest Inventory, developed during the 1950's)
The Interest Analysis Blank, by Hubbard at Minnesota in the mid-1930's, using Paterson's blank as a beginning

Some of the early activity at Carnegie Tech was described in a 1927 letter from Professor J. B. Miner of Kentucky to Strong; a condensed version is printed below. Miner's letter mirrors the early thinking, and his sharp comment makes it clear that professional sensitivities over citations and credits have always been with us. (In the collection of old inventories at Minnesota are two from the 1920's. They are identical down to the last comma and period, except that one carries a copyright from Carnegie Tech, the other from the University of Kentucky.)

Lexington, Kentucky
August 22, 1927

MY DEAR STRONG:

You suggest that I describe the sequence of events starting with my Vocational Analysis Blank. As far as I have been able to trace it, it was like this: the idea of paired interest-contrasts occurred to me as a method of getting records of interests which might later be worked up for discriminating vocational interests. I included it in the first blank "An Analysis of Vocational Interests" which was tried out in the Pittsburgh high schools in 1918. The paper of 1921 summarized the results, but included only the suggestion of using the interest-contrasts for discovering unusual interests of students: Did a student have an interest like 1 in 15, etc.

Bruce Moore apparently paid no attention to my method of recording interests, did not even mention it in his thesis although he must have seen the blank as I think he worked out his plan there at Tech. He seems to have been the first to use the occupational names to discriminate groups. Ream, Freyd, you, and Cowdery have since tried and modified his method. . . . I think my first blank also contained the first attempt to make a functional classification of occupations so that students or adults would consider certain behavior resemblances and interest likenesses rather than the U.S. Census classification . . .

My method for evaluating the psychograph of interests has, I think, one essentially correct idea. Those in each occupational group should be compared with those in a random group of people of the sort that would make the choices contemplated . . . (J. B. Miner).

The last paragraph reports the genesis of "Men-in-General," a central concept in Strong's method of measuring interests.

Development of the SVIB at Stanford

In 1923 the industrial psychology program at Carnegie Tech was discontinued. At an informal gathering after the farewell banquet, someone asked Bingham what he thought the major contribution of the program had been. He replied, as Strong recollected later, that the measurement of interests would probably prove to be the most important.

This impressed Strong, and when he joined the Stanford faculty the next year, recruited in part by Lewis Terman, who was then working on his high IQ students, one of the first projects carried out under Strong's direction was a thesis by Karl Cowdery on the interests of physicians, engineers, and lawyers. Strong later summarized the study:

Cowdery finds that the five groups—(a) freshmen and sophomores planning to be engineers; (b) junior and seniors in engineering school; (c) engineers in graduate work; (d) engineers with less than 5 years practical experience; and (e) engineers with more than 5 years practical experience—all score approximately the same on the interest test. The same holds true with respect to physicians and lawyers. . . . If all this is correct, it means that what is measured by this test is present in men prior to technical training and practical experience and presumably leads to their vocational choice and is not a resultant of that vocational choice (Strong, 1927).

The middle 1920's were active years; the landmarks were Strong's first publication in interest measurement in 1926, the copyright of the booklet in 1927, and the distribution of the first Manual—a mimeographed document—in 1928. The state of the art then can perhaps be best understood by quoting extensively from that Manual:

There has been such an insistent demand from many to use this test for one purpose or another that the author feels constrained to issue these instructions although very much remains to be done before the test should be considered as properly standardized . . .

It is believed that scores on this test are indicative of whether or not a young man would like the work of a given occupation. His score is a measure of how nearly his interests agree with those of the average man successfully engaged in that occupation.

It will be some time before the validity of this test can be exactly determined. The results so far obtained seem to show that the test has genuine merit. Nevertheless, the test should be used only by those who approach the problem of vocational guidance with an experimental point of view and who will use the test results with proper safeguards. [Note: This caution about experimental point of view appeared in the 1928, 1929, 1930, and 1931 manuals, disappearing in 1933 after the first longitudinal data became available—DPC.]

If a man scores low, for example, in the interests of lawyers, it means that he would not like that occupational environment. If he scores high, the score may be interpreted in three ways depending upon how he scores in other interests. First, if he scores higher in law than any other occupation, presumably he should enter law. Second, if he scores higher in some other occupation than in law, he possibly should enter that other occupation. But third, he may better plan his career to utilize his interests in two or more occupations. Thus, if he scores high in both law and engineering, he might prepare for both and become a patent attorney, or a lawyer specializing in engineering problems. . . .

Practical use of the test for vocational guidance purposes must be based for some time to come on several assumptions, which our data suggest are true. Nevertheless, extensive research is necessary before these assumptions can be viewed as established.

The first assumption is that a man will be more effective in his vocational career and also be happier if he is engaged in work that he likes than if he is forced to do many things he dislikes.

Second, men who have continued to work at a given occupation for a considerable period of time, and are considered to be successfully earning a living must like that occupational environment fairly well (or at least like it better than any other they can enter).

Third, it is assumed that interests as measured by this test are fairly permanent from the time one enters college to later life, and that they are not particularly affected by technical training and practical experience. In other words, the interests of a young man of 20 are largely responsible for his choice of career. If such interests are very strong, the man becomes an artist, accountant, or lawyer, almost regardless of present-day environmental factors; if these interests are weak, the environmental factors play a very much larger role in determining what he does in life.

The 1928 Manual listed these scales:

Now Available

Advertising	Journalist
Architect	Lawyer
Certified Public Accountant	Minister
Chemist	Psychologist
Engineer	School Teacher and Administrator

Under Development

Author	Electrical Engineer
Artist (painter)	Mechanical Engineer
Farmer	Mining Engineer
Life Insurance Salesman	Purchasing Agent
District Manager (Specialty)	YMCA General Secretary
Civil Engineer	

Expected Soon

Banker	Personnel Manager
Credit Manager	Physician
Office Worker	Real Estate Salesman

In the 1929 Manual under the heading "To whom the test should be given" are the following paragraphs:

The scales and norms are based upon *adult men*. Our results indicate that in the case of *college men* (20 to 30 years of age) that the test can be used with success.

There are no data upon *high school boys*. Their scores probably average lower than what these boys will obtain ten years later. Allowance should be made for this constant error in the test.

There are no data on *women*. It is very questionable whether women should be scored upon this test. They should not be given their ratings unless an emphatic statement is made that no one knows the significance of their ratings.

Validity and reliability concerned Strong from the beginning. Though he felt concurrent validity—the ability of the test to separate adult occupations—had been established early, he was concerned with predictive validity to the end of his career. In his first publication on this specific topic,

"The diagnostic value of the vocational interest test" (Strong, 1929), he reported:

One hundred and fifty-six seniors of the Class of 1927 at Stanford filled out the Vocational Interest Blank two weeks before graduation. In January 1928 they reported their occupational choice. Comparison of these two sets of data show:
1. 46 percent have entered the occupation on which they scored highest on on the test.
2. 20 percent have entered the occupation on which they scored second highest.
3. 11 percent have entered the occupation on which they scored third highest. . . .

only 18 percent have entered an occupation for which, according to the test, they have no interest.

His early concern for reliability was stated clearly in "Permanence of interest of adult men" (Strong and McKenzie, 1930):

If interests are constantly changing, either back and forth or in some progressive manner, their determination may be of use in diagnosing an individual's present condition, but they will be of little significance in guidance for the future. It is extremely important, then, that the permanence of interests be ascertained.

The present study reports the permanence of interests of adult men over a period of a year and a half. Records were obtained from 100 ministers and 100 certified accountants upon the Cowdery Interest Blank in April and May, 1925. In December of 1926, these men were asked to fill out the Strong Interest Blank. Complete records were obtained from 61 ministers and 32 certified public accountants. . . . A marked degree of permanence (correlations between .74 and .90) was found for interests over a period of a year and a half.

During the early years, Strong was continually collecting information from other occupations and adding new scales to the profile. As the number of scales increased, he began to search for meaningful ways to group them. He asked L. L. Thurstone, who was then working on his factor analysis methods, for help and from that resulted a profile with five occupational groups. Thurstone's letter transmitting the findings, dated the week before the stock market crash, will interest many psychometricians:

Chicago, Illinois
October 23, 1929

DEAR STRONG:

The table of intercorrelations that you sent me shows five constellations of varying strength. I found it rather interesting to apply my new method of constellation analysis to your table, especially as I do not know what most of your symbols are. Now that I have the symbols arranged in several constellations, I think I can make a fairly good guess as to the meanings. . . .

The first two constellations are very strong. They are conspicuous clusters.

I venture the guess that since the symbols E and F are associated with Chemistry, they probably refer to engineering and farming but, of course, this might be entirely wrong. I have been wondering whether the notation Ad may refer to administration or advertising but, at any rate, it forms a very strong cluster with L and J which may possibly be law and journalism.

The third constellation is a fairly strong one but not so strong as the first two.

The fourth and fifth constellations are not so conspicuous as the others but they nevertheless form definite clusters.

I had the idea for this scheme for analyzing constellations when we were in Pittsburgh but, for some reason, I had never tried it out on any data until I did so on your table of correlations.

I believe we are on the track of a method of analyzing constellations of traits, which lends itself to a very refined mathematical development and which I believe may turn out to be much more powerful and flexible than the Spearman two factor analysis for which I have, however, very great respect. I am not yet sure that my method is novel but it seems that I would have heard about it if it had been used before. . . .

Cordially,
L. L. Thurstone

P.S. [in handwriting]: It would be a joke on us as psychologists if by any chance R should represent Real Estate and PS Psychology but here I am only guessing.

The Advent of Scoring Machines

By 1930, then, a useful though limited system for measuring interests had evolved. Materials had been prepared, printed, and made available for distribution, scoring techniques had been developed, and some basic psychometric information had been accumulated. The remaining hurdle was the data-processing problem. Interest inventories are nothing more than questionnaires that can be empirically keyed; to make them practically useful, techniques to score them in bulk have to be devised and the history of the SVIB has been greatly influenced by the availability of data processing systems.

The first information on scoring machines for the SVIB appeared in the 1930 Manual. Scanning these comments makes one appreciate how far we have come:

At the present time, [scoring] arrangements can be made with Dr. Ben Wood, Columbia University, Mr. P. H. Rulon, University of Minnesota, or the author. The author charges $2.00 for scoring a blank on all twenty-two scales . . . [Note: 1970 prices range from about 30¢ to $1.00 depending on volume scored, for about 75 scales—DPC.]

The procedure for scoring on the Hollerith machine, as developed by Mr. Rulon, is as follows: A Hollerith card is provided for liking, another for indifference, and another for disliking each of the 420 items, making 1,260 cards in all. Each of these cards has punched on it the appropriate scores for the twenty-two occupational scales. When a blank is scored, cards are taken from the file corresponding to the circlings [responses] on the blank; cards can be "pulled" for approximately five blanks an hour. The cards are then run through the tabulator and totals for ten scales recorded. They must be run through twice more to obtain the totals for the remaining scales. When this has been accomplished, the cards are run through the sorter and finally returned to the files to be used again.

At Stanford we have found twenty-five duplicates sufficient, thus employing 31,500 cards in all. The cards are kept in open files 15″ × 10¾″ with two partitions 15″ × 4″ that run longitudinally. Heavy cardboard dividers keep the cards separated. These are deeply notched so as to fit over the two partitions. The assistant pulls out with his right hand the like, indifferent, or dislike card, according as the blank is marked opposite item one, and places it on the table, while with his left hand he pulls the first divider forward, exposing the cards for item two. This is repeated for the 420 items.

Then, as now, data-processing systems depended on people, and people are wondrously ingenious in mastering these systems for their own ends; one such episode was reported in a reminiscing letter from Mrs. Thomas Harrell (Strong's daughter and office manager during the 1930's):

We had some problems that didn't seem funny at the time . . . Using the scoring device for the tabulator as demonstrated by IBM, one could score about 6 blanks an hour. One of the scorers, probably someone with a musical bent, discovered you could get the same results by maintaining a speed in rhythm with the machine—there would be no incessant clanking as one card at a time finished a cycle—and you could go twice as fast. But you had to maintain the beat or you would be selecting the response for item #48 on the card for #47, or some such confusion. . . .

It was a messy deal—the students felt, with some justification, that they were giving a fair day's work for their time so long as they were doing the quota. We couldn't just raise the quota to 12 since there were some people who couldn't manage to stay on the beat, and we needed every scorer we had because the machines were going 24 hours a day.

How we solved this problem I don't remember, but we did.

The 1930's: Continuing Research

With the system in operation, Strong turned his energies to expanding the framework of knowledge surrounding his inventory. In 1932, he contacted the Stanford seniors tested in 1927 and reported in the 1935 Manual:

On the basis of a 5-year follow-up of these Stanford seniors, it may be concluded that:

1. Men continuing in an occupation obtain a higher interest score in it than in any other occupation.
2. Men continuing in an occupation obtain a higher interest score in it than men entering some other occupation.
3. Men continuing in an occupation obtain higher scores in it than men who

change from that occupation to some other (based on relatively few data).
4. Men changing from some other occupation to occupation A score higher in A prior to the change than they did in other occupations.

In 1934 Strong published on the relationship between interests and sales ability. He had done some earlier work but was too cautious to publish: "The data in the first table show such surprising correlation between life insurance interests scores and production that, at the time (1927), the writer did not feel warranted in publishing them until they could be substantiated by further evidence" (Strong, 1934). That article includes the table reproduced here as Table 11-2.

TABLE 11-2. LIFE INSURANCE SALES PRODUCTION VERSUS RATINGS ON THE SVIB LIFE INSURANCE SALESMAN SCALE

GROUP	Number	Years of Experience	Average Annual Paid-for Production	Percent Having Various Life Insurance Interest Ratings				
				C	B-	B	B+	A
Criterion group of agents ----288		At least 3 years	$100,000 up	1	2	6	16	75
L. I. general agents --------204				3	1	8	15	73
Company W --------------------108		At least 3 years	225,648	2	2	4 .	15	77
Company W --------------------102		At least 4 years	207,980	2	2	4	15	77
Agency X, all given a contract ----------------- 20		Complete record	205,000	10	0	15	35	40
Agency X, all writing $100,000 a year for at least a year --------------15		Complete record	285,000	7	0	13	40	40
Agency Y --------------------37		At least 3 years	106,000	11	5	19	33	32
Group Z, rated as "failures," "unhappy," "not doing as well as they should" etc.---73		3.5 years	66,000	32	5	23	18	22
Group Z, rated as "failures" (included in above)---------46		2.6 years	41,000	35	7	30	17	11
1927 Stanford Seniors, 5 years after graduation ---------222				73	8	12	4	3

During the early 1930's, Strong worked on many more mundane technical issues, such as comparing various methods of deriving item weights, studying the effect of sample size, and exploring the influence of age and sex on the scoring scales.

While involved in these practical questions, Strong paused in his presidential address to the Western Psychological Association in 1933 (at a convention where a demonstration of television was one of the notable features) to ponder the schism between basic and applied science:

It has been my observation that when students read Hull's statement that 30 percent efficiency is about the upper limit to aptitude testing, they tend to throw up their hands and say, "What's the use?" Is this a fair and appropriate reaction?

Pure and applied scientists approach a question of this sort from two different points of view. The former seeks perfection; he longs for correlations of unity. Moreover, to a very large degree, he selects the problems he would solve and he very nimbly dodges those that do not look promising. The applied scientist, on the other hand, must attempt the solution of problems which are thrust upon him and, moreover, he must solve them some way or other and usually within a short period of time. Is it any wonder then that any contribution that bears upon the problem is highly prized by him? Is it any wonder that the pure scientist frequently views the solutions of the applied scientist with sarcasm and that the latter feels hurt that his contribution is not appreciated?

He expressed the same feelings years later after retirement and always felt mild chagrin that his work had not been more influential on the main stream of psychology, especially psychological theory. His perception was certainly accurate; when interest measurement is covered in introductory psychology textbooks, for example, it is usually presented only as a useful technique in vocational guidance; in the text currently used for the introductory course at, of all places, Minnesota, there is no mention of E. K. Strong, the SVIB, or vocational interests.

The 1938 Revision

During the decade 1927–37, Strong continually made changes to improve the system. The Manual—an 8-page "throwaway" booklet—was rewritten almost every year, the scoring weights were lowered from an initial range of ± 30 in 1927, to ± 15 in 1930, to ± 4 in 1938 (and to ± 1 in 1966), items in the booklet were changed, the arrangement of scores on the profile varied from year to year, and none of this was very disruptive as the operation was still small and under his day-to-day control. (The situation today is very different. We have evolved from a one-man hip-pocket operation into a bureaucracy, with all that that implies: on the one hand, organizational inertia, vested interests, and committee decisions; on the other, a capacity for amassing a wide range of talent, sufficient funds to free the researcher from clerical drudgery, and enough power to have some influence on what is happening "out there.")

Then, in 1938, a major revision of the Men's form was published, incorporating all of the changes that had been accumulating. The major ones were:

1. The Men-in-General reference group was changed from what was essentially a collection of all the blanks Strong had in his files to a group representing a sampling of occupations based on the U.S. Census with incomes over $2,500, usually professional and higher level business groups.

2. The occupational criterion groups were increased in size, where possible, to a minimum of 250.

3. The derivation of item weights was changed slightly.

4. Raw scores were converted to standard scores using means and stand-

ard deviations instead of percentiles, and the letter ratings (A, B+, B, . . .) were based on standard deviation units instead of quartiles.

5. Occupations were clustered on the profile into eleven groups—essentially the same profile that is used today.

The 1938 booklet and profile achieved widespread use in the next 28 years, and are the forms familiar today to most psychologists.

Five years later, in 1943, Strong published his massive book, *The Vocational Interests of Men and Women,* a work crammed with solid data that had been accumulating for twenty years. Though it is not a book for easy reading, it was well received and even now continues to sell. For this, Columbia University presented Strong with the Butler Medal, an award presented to their alumni for high achievement.

In 1946, a revision of the Women's Form, parallel to the 1938 men's revision, was published, but the Women's Form remained a slightly neglected little sister. There were fewer scales on the profile (25 vs. 38 for the Men's); the occupational groupings were not as well worked out, and there was nothing comparable to the Occupational Level or Interest Maturity scales. Still, the Women's Form had two advantages derived from Strong's experience with the Men's Form: first, the criterion samples were larger, usually over 400; second, the items in the booklet were probably better as Strong was learning more about what constitutes a good item; for example, the Women's booklet has 128 occupational titles, which are good items, the Men's booklet only 100.

Even though he added these improvements, working with the Women's Form was never one of Strong's favorite activities; in all of the longitudinal studies that he did, working especially with the Stanford students, not a single woman was included.

With these exceptions, the level of activity in the early 1940's was low. World War II siphoned off manpower and energy, as well as funds, and only projects promising immediate military payoff were started. Nothing came of them.

Scoring Becomes Automated

After the war, the tempo picked up again and in 1946 came a breakthrough with an immediate and lasting impact. Elmer Hankes, an engineer in Minneapolis, built the first automatic scoring and profiling machine for the SVIB. An article in the *Minneapolis Star-Journal,* July 8, 1946, described it:

The exterior appearance of the machine is deceptive. What looks like a crude wooden desk, with some mysterious dials on a 10-inch panel, actually contains three miles of fine wiring, 40,000 separate parts—including 37,000 resistors—and 80,000 hand-soldered connections.

When in operation, this collection of gadgets scores electronically the vocational interest test perfected by Dr. E. K. Strong of Stanford University.

The device is in use today in the very place that Hankes built it—the living room of his small apartment . . .

This machine, with its later modifications, was the only source of automatic scoring and profiling for the next several years. Although several offices, including Strong's, continued to score the SVIB using the IBM tabulator or IBM 805 scoring machine, these operations were inefficient and accounted for a progressively smaller portion of the scoring volume.

In 1962–63, several new SVIB scoring services were established, reflecting the Zeitgeist of the digital computer. National Computer Systems in Minneapolis built a flexible system around an optical scanner hooked into a Control Data Computer, Measurement Research Center in Iowa City offered scoring services on the electronic scanners developed by E. F. Lindquist for scoring his and other achievement tests, and Dela Data, working closely with Consulting Psychologists Press in Palo Alto, designed a service around IBM Mark Sense cards. TestScor, Elmer Hankes' company, also switched in 1962 from an analog to digital-type scoring machine. The new technology and fresh competition reduced scoring costs by a factor of three or four, and also encouraged vast improvements in tangential services, such as provisions for item response tabulations and descriptive statistics. Such trends will undoubtedly continue.

Strong's Retirement

In 1949 Strong retired from Stanford University but not from his research. The 1951 Manual reflects his activity; for the first time appeared the mean score on the relevant occupational scale for each occupation and for men-in-general. It seems inconceivable now that the SVIB could have existed for over twenty years before this basic information was published; the data had been available earlier, but it apparently had not seemed important to include them in the Manual. (The American Psychological Association's *Technical Recommendations for Psychological Tests and Diagnostic Techniques* did not appear until 1954.) The more extensive information of mean scores for all samples on all SVIB scales was not published until 1959, and even then the table had many gaps. One's first thought—that this information became available then because of the advent of large computers in the late 1950's—is inaccurate; to the end, Strong did these calculations by hand, usually using computational short-cuts derived in the 1930's or a small desk calculator.

The 1951 Manual also included Strong's first report on his longitudinal follow-up of Stanford students. Because these data provide the most important foundation for the use of the SVIB, I am quoting him at length:

Since the Vocational Interest Test is mainly used to aid in vocational counseling, it is not sufficient for the test to have high validity in differentiating adults; it must be demonstrated that interests do not change appreciably over a considerable period of time and that there is a reasonable degree of agreement between interest test scores and vocational choice . . .

A 20-year follow-up of 670 Stanford freshmen, seniors, and graduate students shows a high degree of agreement between interest scores in 1927–30 and occupations engaged in in 1949. For example, 137 of these students became physicians. The distribution of their physician interest scores, expressed in percentages, is given in Table [11-3], in comparison with the scores of the criterion group of physicians. The students scored nearly as high as the criterion group.

TABLE 11-3. DISTRIBUTION OF PHYSICIAN INTEREST SCORES OF CRITERION GROUP AND OF 137 STUDENTS WHO BECAME PHYSICIANS

Rating	Students	Criterion Group
A	70	64
B+	12	13
B	8	10
B−	5	8
C	5	5
Mean	50	47.8
Sigma	10	10.3

Among the 670 students, 132 had A ratings and 67 had B+ ratings in physician interest. How many of these 199 students became physicians? Of the 132 men with A ratings, 53 percent became physicians? Assuming that the students could have entered 100 different occupations, then on this basis the chance that anyone would go into medicine is 1 percent. If, however, they have an A rating on the physician scale, there is a 53 percent chance they will become physicians.

The remaining 47 percent did not go into every imaginable pursuit. Five percent became dentists or biologists, occupations which correlate .80 to .90 with physician interests. Eight percent became architects, psychologists, and chemists (correlation .70–.75) and 14 percent became engineers, writers, and geologists (correlation .52–.62). Altogether, 80 percent of those with A ratings became physicians or entered an occupation whose interests correlate .50 or higher with that of a physician.

Of the 67 students with B+ ratings in physician interest, 21 percent became physicians; 3 percent, biologists; 10 percent, architects, psychologists, or chemists; and 28 percent, engineers, writers or geologists—a total of 62 percent.

The 1950's and 1960's: Regrouping

In the 1950's Strong again became concerned with the revision of the men's booklet. Many of the items had become outdated, and a few other changes seemed necessary. From his correspondence files and notes, it is clear that he spent many hours pondering how to proceed. There were two types of questions, technical and administrative. The first included issues such as: Which items are obsolete? Which are useless? Should the test be shortened? Lengthened? Should the scoring system be changed? Should the profile be rearranged?

The second group, the administrative questions, filtered down to: Who should do the work?

The first questions had to be largely ignored until the second was answered, and not much progress was made for several years. Probably Strong felt unable, because of his advancing years and lack of knowledge about modern data-processing equipment, to undertake it himself; whatever the reason, he did seek advice from many people as to the best way to proceed. During his several visits to Minnesota in these years, several groups assembled, talked about the problem, and disassembled. Finally, through the mysterious way of group processes, three people emerged as the guiding force for the SVIB revision: Strong, Kenneth Clark, then Chairman of the Psychology Department at Minnesota, and Ralph Berdie, Strong's son-in-law, and then Director of the Student Counseling Bureau at Minnesota.

The technical work began. All of the criterion group inventories were shipped to Minnesota and the task of preparing them for computer analysis began. Strong tackled the question of which items to change, Clark and Berdie began the data analysis. I became involved as a graduate student who was supposed to know something of computers. During the next few years, due to Strong's illness, Clark's leaving Minnesota to become a Dean, and Berdie's extensive administrative responsibilities, I was swept to the center of the vacuum and there have remained.

During this unsettled time, Berdie, while on leave in India, wrote to Strong with some suggestions for future arrangements. Strong's reflective answer is relevant here:

> Palo Alto, California
> December 15, 1962
>
> Dr. Ralph Berdie
> Ford Foundation
> Calcutta, India
> DEAR RALPH:
>
> Your letter of October 16 raises the question as to the best way to keep the vocational interest measurement research both centralized and active. If there is a central person or agency, this will provide a focus for communication and will facilitate reporting of research underway and completed. This stimulates conducting research and makes it easier to obtain support, particularly financial support, for research.

The Vocational Interest Research has been supported almost entirely by profit from scoring blanks. In early days funds were received from the Carnegie Corporation and the Laura Spellman Fund. But no such funds have been received since some time before the last war.

The University [Stanford] has supplied space for my research and accounting of funds but has made no contribution or received any money from the Research Bureau. It did take over the obligation to supply pensions to my employees at the time I retired.

I shall not be able to continue direction of the Research Bureau very much longer. Mrs. Nicholson, my assistant for many years, retired this year but does give some time to it. The other two employees can handle the scoring but not research. Income from scoring just about maintains the present office activities.

What is the Vocational Interest Research? It is the name I gave to my research. It is associated by many people with Stanford University and recognized by the University. For many years it has been financed by profit from scoring blanks. It has been a place to which people have turned for advice in their research. It has helped many in their research by supplying blanks and varying amounts of statistical service. When I am gone, there will be nothing left except the name and some records. Profits from scoring have decreased in recent years and presumably will be too slight to keep the office going.

Has the University acquired "squatter's rights" in the name and the records? Will the University insist on keeping both or permit those assets to be transferred elsewhere?

As far as I know, there is no one at Stanford that is interested in my research or would be willing to take charge of the Bureau. My daughter and her husband, Thomas Harrell, are more interested than anyone but have their own commitments and say they would not want this added responsibility. There is no one at the University Press who is competent to direct research: there is no reason why there should be . . .

The two places that occur to me where a bureau of vocational research might be established are at the University of Colorado and of Minnesota because of the presence there of Ken Clark and yourself, respectively. There is no reason why such research should not be carried out in both places and, in fact, in other places as well. For various reasons I believe it would be best at the present time to centralize activities at one place. Later on, similar research might be established at other locations.

I don't believe it makes much difference how the unit is set up—as an institute, or what. The important thing is that there is a man really interested in such a project, and facilities by which he can carry on his research. Dave Campbell appeals to me as such a man, but I don't know whether he would want to devote his time to such an enterprise. It is not necessary for him to devote full time. I carried on a full teaching program in the Graduate School of Business until I retired in 1949 and directed research in my spare time.

I think your suggestion is excellent that the advisory committee formulate what should be done to transfer the research bureau from Stanford to Minnesota, or elsewhere. This constitutes an organization that is respected and can deal with the necessary negotiations.

I have not talked this matter over with anyone at Stanford and will not do so until I hear from you. There may be complications I have not thought of; many become exercised when they think they are going to lose something even though they have not concerned themselves previously.

Sincerely,

E. K. STRONG, JR.

In the fall of 1963, the University of Minnesota formally established the Center for Interest Measurement Research, and located it administratively within the Student Counseling Bureau, which is under the direction of the Office of the Dean of Students. Shortly after that, the remaining files from Stanford were shipped to Minnesota, and a general announcement over the signature of F. E. Terman, Stanford Vice-President and Provost (and son of the man who helped bring Strong to Stanford 40 years earlier), was released:

After serving customers for more than a quarter of a century, Dr. Edward K. Strong has announced the closing of the Strong Vocational Research Bureau, effective September 1, 1963. Dr. Strong has not been well for several months, and his illness has prevented him from participating as fully as he would prefer in the activities of the Bureau. I am certain you will understand the reluctance with which he has made the decision.

Professor Strong is one of our most distinguished emeritus professors, and soon he will complete his fortieth year at Stanford. During his tenure he has been a tireless and thorough researcher, continuing to improve his tests and the criteria for their evaluation. He designed his service particularly for the guidance of counselors and administrators in education and business, and more recently he extended the applicability of his techniques for us in the professions. In addition to his research, Professor Strong won admiration among colleagues and students as a skillful and understanding teacher . . .

Dr. Strong passed away the following December in Palo Alto.

The 1966 (Men's) and 1969 (Women's) Revisions

In 1966 another revision of the Men's form was published; the changes made are summarized in Appendix A of this Handbook. The similar revision of the Women's form was completed in 1969; those details are also covered in Appendix A.

The main technical change has been the introduction of the Basic Interest Scales to both the Men's and Women's profiles; these scales have considerable promise for increased understanding of the peculiar pattern of interests within each individual. Other additions have been the Administrative Indices, which take advantage of the computer's capabilities to detect possible problems in test administration and scoring, and more Nonoccupational scales, which permit more specific interpretations.

Along with these revisions, much of the research during the 1960's at Minnesota has capitalized on the presence of Strong's extensive files. Studies of change within occupations over time have been done by comparing current samples with those tested by Strong in the 1930's (see Chapters 9 and 10); profiles of outstanding people have been sifted out of Strong's groups for special treatment (see Chapter 7); 15- and 16-year-old boys originally tested by Strong in 1930 have been located, retested, and used to establish normative data for both teenagers and adults on the Basic Interest Scales (see Chapter 3). Further revision work is planned, as reported in Appendix E.

This chapter has been a brief history of one of the country's best-known psychological inventories. It has not been a critical review; some biases have crept—or more accurately—marched in boldly. I have been greatly impressed by E. K. Strong's methodicalness and persistence in pursuing this research, and believe he made a substantial contribution to our understanding of human nature. He immersed himself so completely in this work and studied each problem with such absorption that one is hesitant to criticize any of his techniques without overwhelming justification.

Of course, a critical perspective is still essential, especially in psychological testing; I have observed that psychological instruments exert almost charismatic control over their authors, and most of them treat their tests as objectively as they treat their children. Professor Strong managed better than anyone else I know to maintain, over forty years, a strictly empirical orientation toward his inventory—almost all decisions were based on data, not emotion—and that is surely one of the reasons that the SVIB has withstood so well the test of time. I hope his successors can do as well.

Appendices

The 1966 Revision of the Men's SVIB and the 1969 Revision of the Women's SVIB

This appendix presents a detailed discussion of the 1966 revision of the Men's SVIB—the changes that were made, the rationale for the changes, and the results of the changes.

As any revision disrupts the system to some extent, a definite attempt was made to maintain continuity between the old and new forms whenever possible. Thus, the familiar form of the booklet and profile were retained, and all plans for revisions were made within this framework.

Several exploratory studies were made to help guide the revision (see Strong, 1962, 1963; Strong, Campbell, Berdie, and Clark, 1964; Campbell, 1963; Campbell, 1966c); the following decisions and actions result from these studies.

Nature of the Revision

First, 109 of the 400 items in the booklet have been replaced with new items. The replaced items were either those that were clearly out of date, those that did not separate occupations well—usually because they were either very popular or very unpopular items—or those in poor taste: e.g., "Deaf mutes." Roughly 50 other items were slightly rephrased to bring them up to date or, in a few instances, to lower the required reading level. New items were selected as replacements to represent areas not well covered in the 1938 booklet, such as artistic and philosophic activities, and occupations concerned with recent technological advances in electronics and related areas. Table D-2 lists all of the 109 old and new items.

Second, for the immediate future, the scales will be based on the 291 unchanged items, and all of the original item analysis has been redone to make that possible.

Third, the scoring system has been simplified, both by reducing the number of items that appear on each scale, and by reducing the range of item weights from ±4 to ±1. Considerable research has shown that the new scoring system is comparable to the old one, and, of course, it has the considerable virtue of simplicity (Strong et al., 1964). But even with these changes, hand-scoring is still so laborious that most users will continue to use the scoring services.

Fourth, most of the scales are based on the criterion groups tested by Strong in the 1930's. Although this would seem at first glance to be extremely unwise—because of changes within occupational groups since the 1930's—considerable research has indicated substantial similarities in interest patterns between occupations then and now (for further information, see p. 315). But whenever new groups have been available for the SVIB, they have been used. Thus, the Air Force Officer scale—which replaced the Aviator scale—is based on a recently tested group; the YMCA Secretary scale is also derived from a new group (for details, see Appendix B).

Fifth, the composition of the Men-in-General (MIG) reference group has been changed. Strong's 1938 group included men from business and professional occupations, weighted according to the proportion of each occupation in the general population. This created some problems as the group tended to be dominated by businessmen, with only a relatively small number of men from scientific and cultural occupations. While correcting for this bias, we also discovered that it was necessary to have some recently tested individuals within the reference group, a point discussed at greater length below. Consequently, the MIG group used for the current revision includes a sampling of men from a wide variety of occuaptions spread throughout the interest domain, and includes men tested throughout the period 1925 to 1965. A detailed listing is given in Appendix C.

Sixth, a number of new scales have been added to the profile, and a few old ones have been dropped. Some of the new scales are helpful in better understanding the groupings of occupations on the profile; for example, the Army Officer and Air Force Officer scales have been added to Group III, a group which formerly included only the Production Manager scale. These new scales serve to define this cluster of interests as one flavored by "direct supervision of others in technical work." An analogous situation occurred when the addition of the Artist and Librarian scales to Group VI, formerly called the Musician group, helped identify that cluster as a general Aesthetic-Cultural grouping. A few of the old scales were dropped because the original criterion group data have been lost and no re-analysis could be done. One former nonoccupational scale—the Interest Maturity scale—was eliminated because it has consistently failed to hold up in validity studies.

Seventh, two new nonoccupational scales, Academic Achievement and Occupational Introversion-Extroversion, were added in 1966, and three others, Age-Related, Diversity of Interests, and Managerial Orientation, were added in 1969.

Eighth, in 1969, six Administrative Indices were added to the profile to help ensure greater accuracy in test administration and scoring.

Ninth, a number of minor changes have been made for practical purposes. The shaded area on the profile, the so-called "chance" area, has been adjusted to represent the middle third of the MIG distribution; in the past it has represented the scores of tests answered by throwing dice (see Campbell, 1963). The range of scores plotted on the profile has been changed: the range had been from −10 to 75; it is now from 20 to 60. (The actual range of scores has not been changed, only the plotted range. Scores that fall outside of 20 to 60 will be printed in the standard score column but plotted as either 20 to 60 as appropriate.) Finally, the length of the inventory has been decreased by one item, from 400 to 399; this has been done to make it easier to quickly identify the new booklets and answer sheets. For the same reason, the color of the booklet has been changed from yellow to blue.

Problems with the Revision

The above listing comprises the easily identifiable changes that were made; a disgression is necessary here to discuss some unexpected complexities that came to light during this work.

In November 1964, the initial stages of the revision were completed, as discussed above, but with two important differences: the MIG group used was the same one that Strong had been using for years; and many more new scales were included on the routine profile. All of the standardization data on this revision looked good, and the validity data for the new scales looked especially good, as these scales were doing a much better job of separating their occupational groups from the MIG group than almost any of the former scales. Because these new scales were in most cases based on larger samples, and because the sampling methods used had been more precise than those of the earlier studies, these findings seemed reasonable, indeed gratifying.

For unrelated reasons that are unimportant now, the publication of the revision was delayed for several months. In this interim period, arrangements were made to administer the revised SVIB to various groups. As the results began to sift back, a distressing trend began to appear; almost all of the new groups scored high (in the B+ and A ranges) on almost all of the new scales. Because the groups tested included occupations as diverse as computer programmers, petroleum engineers, sociologists, ministers, and school superintendents, and because the new scales included a variety such as Physical Therapist, Credit Manager, Chamber of Commerce Executive, and Business Education Teacher, it was disturbing to find all of these groups scoring high on all of these scales.

At that point, publication plans were suspended until the trouble could be located and corrected.

After extensive analysis, the following explanation seemed the most reasonable. Although interest patterns within occupations have been found to be stable over time, these patterns are based on *scale* scores, not on *item* responses. On the other hand, the building of new scales depends on item statistics, and in some cases these are apparently vulnerable to shifts over time. About twenty items have been located on the SVIB that appear to have much different endorsement frequencies today than they did 30 years ago. Consequently, any occupational group tested today will answer these twenty items differently than Strong's Men-in-General did and, thus, these items will be incorporated into the corresponding occupational scale. Since any person who is tested today is likely to answer the twenty items in the same way as the occupational group did, his score on that scale will be increased to that extent. A similar result will inflate his score on all new scales. This inflation will also make the men comprising the occupational group appear more different from MIG than they really are, and thus inflate the validity statistics.

The trend was particularly pronounced among the new scales developed for business occupations, a result traceable to the composition of the MIG group, with its heavy representation of businessmen. Because of this bias, there were fewer "honest" item differences between the business occupations and the MIG group, and the "time-shift" items were more likely to appear as discriminating items and therefore to be included in the occupational scale.

Once identified, the problem had to be corrected. The most obvious solution was to collect a new men-in-general group, but then the inverse problem would appear; i.e., the old occupational scales would likely be affected in just the opposite manner.

The eventual solution adopted was to use a MIG group with the composition described earlier, a group drawn equally from most of the occupational groups that have been tested with the SVIB, with particular attention paid to sampling from all areas of the interest domain, and from groups tested over the entire time span, 1925–65. Hopefully, this method will remove the businessman bias from the reference group and, by basing the item statistics on a group spread over a long time period, reduce the effects of change over time. For a complete description of the new MIG group, see Appendix B.

During the spring, summer, and fall of 1965, the final stages of this revision of the SVIB were completed, using the new MIG group to develop scales. Validity and reliability statistics, scale interrelationships, follow-up analyses, and normative data for various groups were all regenerated for the new scales, and are reported in the text of this Handbook. The change in reference groups did alleviate the problem described earlier but there are still puzzles in the data. (Many of them were always there; it is only recently that we have had the data-processing techniques necessary to identify them.) *Some* recently tested groups still score higher on *some* recently developed scales than seems reasonable, but the patterns are not consistent. Only time and further research will completely untangle the threads.

One specific finding isolated by this work is that the scales most recently developed for the old (1938) version of the SVIB have been affected to some extent by this time-shift bias. Thus, scales developed for the SVIB in the late 1950's and early 1960's, such as Librarian, Credit Manager, and Chamber of Commerce Executive, have included some of the items that have changed in endorsement frequency; this has had two results; first, the reported validities of these recent scales, measured by percent overlap with Strong's 1938 MIG group, have been inflated; and second, "modern subjects" tend to score too high on these scales.

To demonstrate these phenomena, four pairs of SVIB profiles are presented in Figures A1 to A4. Each pair of profiles consists of scores from the 1938 scales and scores from the 1966 scales. (In the following discussion, the term "1938 scales" refers to scales developed by using the original MIG group and ± 4 weights, i.e., the 1938 methods; the actual scales have often been developed more recently.) In each case, the actual people tested were the same; the scores used were assembled simply by scoring the same answer sheets two different ways—once for the 1938 item composition, once for the 1966 item composition. Four groups were chosen to represent four characteristic situations, as follows:

1. An old group—policemen, originally tested in 1933—used to establish the the Policeman scale in 1938 (Figure A-1).

2. A new group—librarians, originally tested in 1959—used to establish the Librarian scale in 1960 (Figure A-2).

3. An in-between group—psychologists, originally tested in 1948—used to establish the Psychologist scale in 1949 (Figure A-3).

4. An in-between group—lawyers(originally tested in 1949—not used to establish a scale but to cross-validate a scale developed in 1933 (Figure A-4).

The profiles for these groups should be inspected with the following points in mind: first, it is desirable, in general, that occupational groups score low on all scales other than their own; and second, if our rationale for explaining the change over time is correct, then the 1966 scales should work better with the recently tested occupational group, i.e., the librarians, and poorer with the earliest tested group, i.e., policemen, with psychologists and lawyers falling between.

Though there is no single index we may inspect to determine whether this pattern of results does in fact occur, inspection of all four pairs of profiles indicates that the data usually support the assertion that the new scales are better among the new occupations and work less well with old occupations. For example, on the 1938 scales, the librarians scored 41 or above on four other scales; on the 1966 scales, the highest score on a scale other than their own is 40. The four 1938 scales where the librarians had their highest scores are scales that all have been developed since 1940, i.e., psychologist (1949), Public Administrator (1941), Music Performer (1952), and Music Teacher (1952). They are also all nonbusiness occupations.

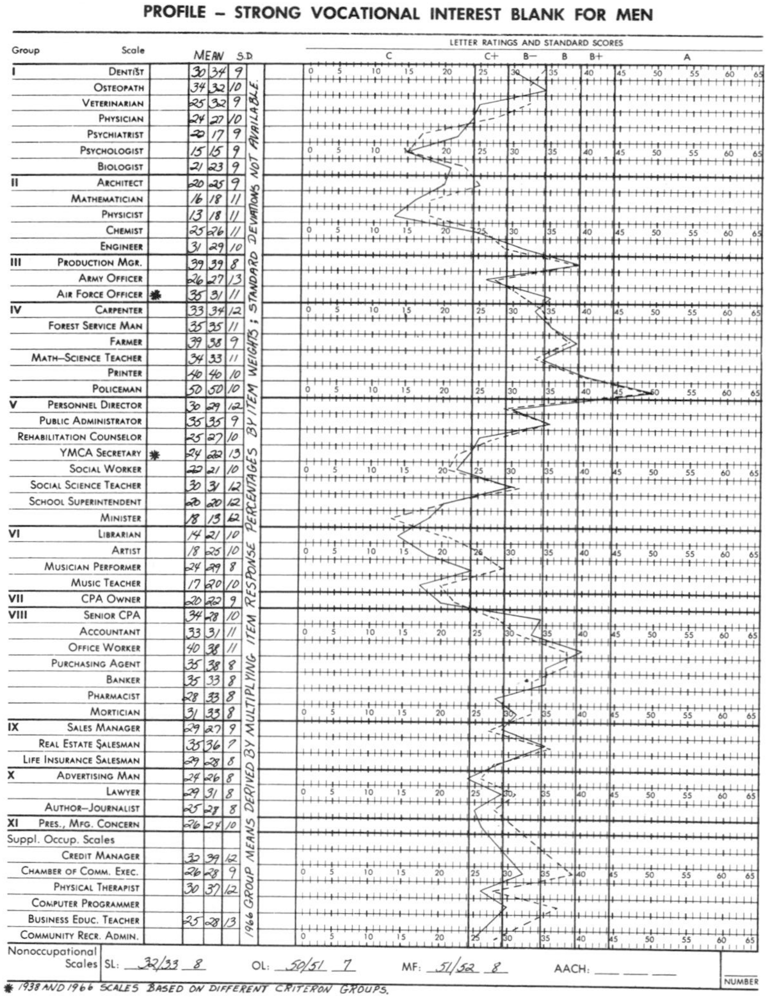

FIG. A-1. *Mean profiles of Policemen's scores on 1938 and 1966 scales.*

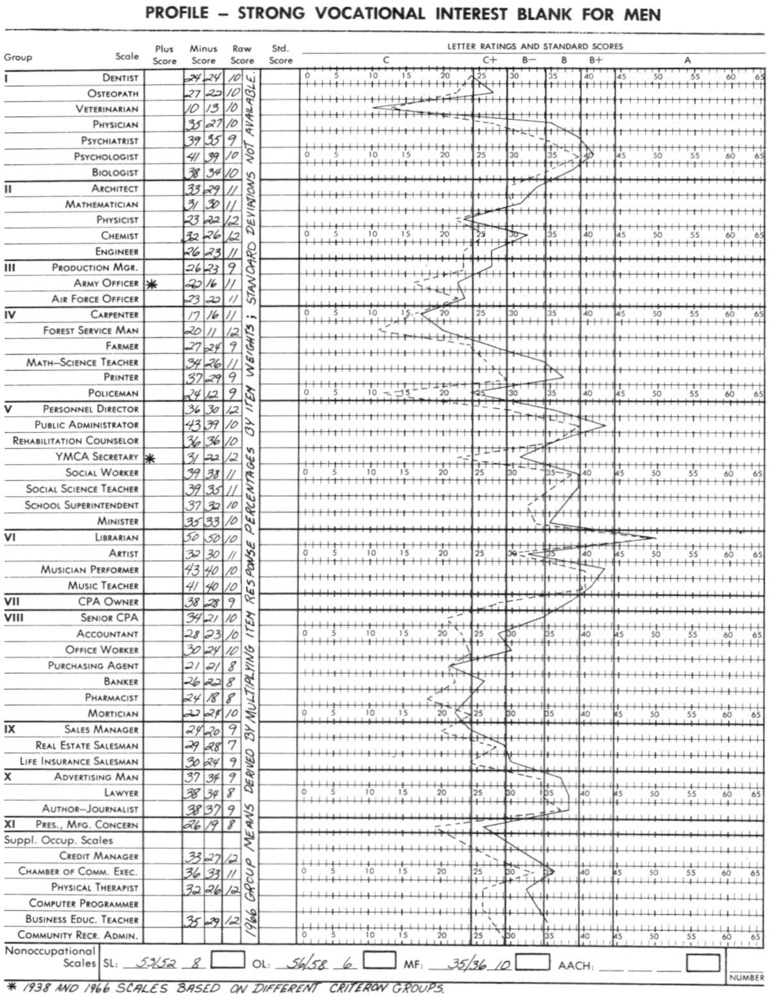

FIG. A-2. *Mean profiles of Librarians' scores on 1938 and 1966 scales.*

374

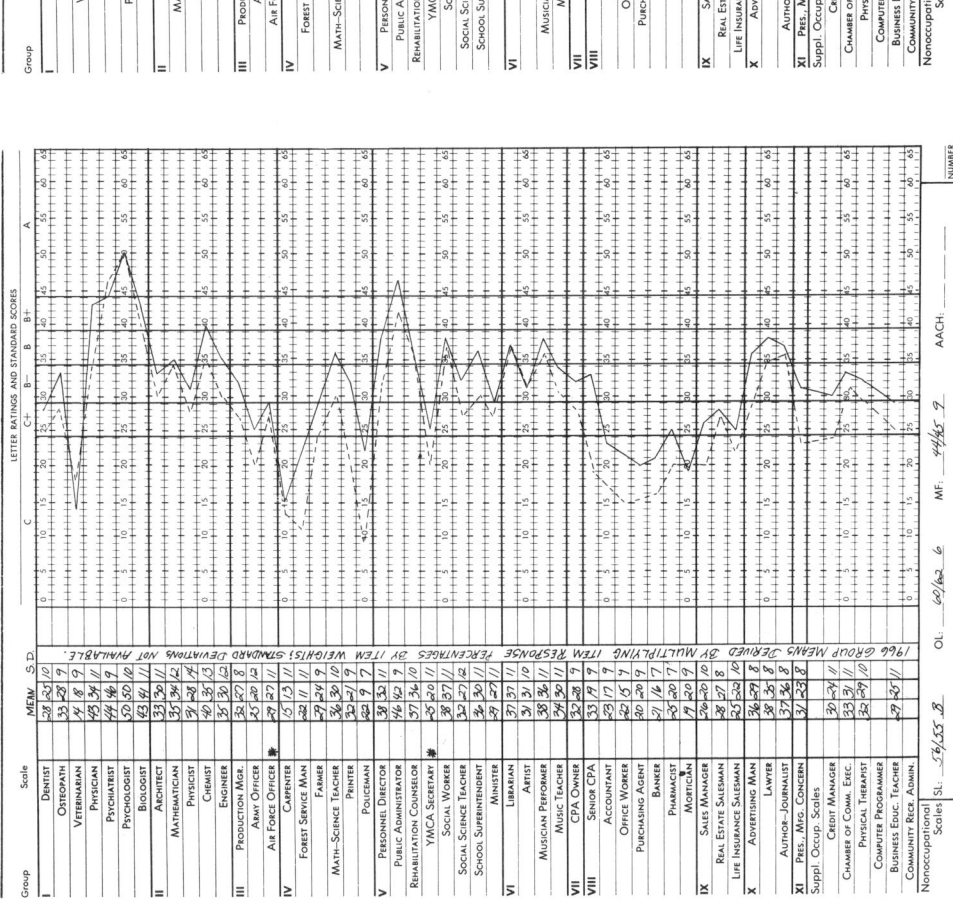

FIG. A-4. *Mean profiles of Lawyers' scores on 1938 and 1966 scales.*

FIG. A-3. *Mean profiles of Psychologists' scores on 1938 and 1966 scales.*

375

TABLE A-1. TEST-RETEST RELIABILITIES OF 1938 VERSUS 1966 SVIB SCALES

	Test–Retest Time Span			
	8-Year Reliabilities		30-Day Reliabilities	
	1938 Form	1966 Form	1938 Form	1966 Form
Q3	.65	.66	.92	.91
Median	.60	.60	.89	.90
Q1	.56	.54	.88	.87
Range	.43–.74	.45–.72	.82–.94	.79–.95

All of these research findings lead to the conclusion that recency of testing of the MIG group is not necessarily desirable, that testing spread over time might be more advantageous. Indeed, such a spread seems absolutely necessary for any inventory that is continually being used to develop new scales. Apparently it is necessary either to have a reference group that is spread throughout a considerable time period, or to do all of the testing and scale development at one time, and then never add any new scales.

Chapters 9 and 10 have longer discussions of the above points.

Psychometric Comparisons between the 1938 and 1966 Forms

Validity comparisons between the 1938 and 1966 forms, based on percent overlap with the MIG group, are difficult to make because of the problems discussed above. In general, the overlaps are higher (that is, poorer) by about 3 to 5 percentage points on the new form, but the original validity figures were slightly inflated, especially on the more recently developed scales, as discussed earlier.

Separation between occupational groups is slightly better with the new form, as can be seen in Figures A-1 to A-4.

Test-retest reliabilities are essentially the same for the two forms. For example, for two test-retest groups, comparison of scale reliabilities between the two forms on common scales produces the results shown in Table A-1.

Correlations between the 1938 and 1966 scales—e.g., between the 1938 Dentist and 1966 Dentist scales—are reported in the last column of Table A-1. The median correlation is .84.

The 1969 Revision of the Women's Form

Throughout the development of the SVIB, the Women's Form has been a favored but slightly neglected little sister of the Men's Form. Favored because whenever some improvement has been hammered out for the Men's Form, it has been incorporated into the Women's, usually with less disruption; slightly neglected because whenever research on a specific topic has been completed on the Men's Form, the researcher has usually gone on to other areas rather than completing an unexciting replication on the Women's booklet. Thus, for example, the Women's Form has never had an Occupational Level Scale, nor a Specialization Level Scale; much less longitudinal research has been done on women; fewer test-retest samples have been collected; fewer samples of successful women have been studied.

Even so, because the prior research on the Men's Form has been directly applied to the Women's Form, it has, in many ways, been superior to the Men's. In particular, the experience gained in the 1966 revision of the Men's booklet has helped greatly in carrying out the 1969 revision of the Women's; for example, most of the women's occupations, and a new Women-in-General sample, have been retested as a result of the discovery that some items change in popularity over time.

For many of the more recent development, the Men's and Women's booklets have been treated more or less concurrently. The Basic Scales are a good illustration; all of that work was done in tandem. The future will likely see more parallel efforts with the two booklets.

The following section reports the details of the 1969 Women's revision, much as did the preceding section for the 1966 Men's revision.

The Revision of the Items in the Women's Booklet

The changes made in the items in the Women's booklet paralleled those made in the 1966 revision of the Men's booklet. Out-dated items were either discarded or reworded in more modern terms; invalid items—those that have never discriminated well between occupations—were replaced; and some items in bad taste were eliminated in favor of other items. A few items were rephrased to lower the required vocabulary level. An example of each of these situations follows:

	Old Item	New Item
Outdated, discarded	Governess "Vanity Fair"	Supermarket Checkout Clerk Biographies
Outdated, reworded	Aviatrix Manikin	Airplane Pilot Fashion Model
Invalid (because usually marked disliked)	Factory Manager Proofreader	Electronics Technician Nurse's Aid
Poor taste	"Mannish" women Negroes	Ballet Dancers Public Opinion Interviewers
Simplified vocabulary	Activities possessing thrills and uncertainties	Thrilling, dangerous activities

The last two items, "Typewriting" and "Zoology" were dropped so that the revised women's booklet would have a unique number of items, 398.

A total of 111 items were discarded and replaced by new ones; two were discarded and not replaced.

The selection of the new items followed several guidelines: first, whenever they seemed suitable, items were taken from the new Men's Form; second, items with a strong occupational orientation were favored; third, an attempt was made to include more items from the lower end of the women's occupational hierarchy, for example, "Supermarket Checkout Clerk" and "Nurse's Aid"; fourth, attempts were made to make the items quite specific to avoid any ambiguity—such as "Manager of children's nursery at resort hotel," "Sales manager of large bookstore"; fifth, items such as "Computer Operator," "News Photographer," and "Weather Forecaster" were included to increase the diversity of the item pool. A listing of the discarded items and their replacements is in Table D-4.

One section of the booklet that has changed more than the others was Part IV—Types of People. Here the individual is asked to answer "Like," "Indifferent," and "Dislike" to various types of people. This is a troublesome section because a few respondents, perhaps one percent, become annoyed by this item content. They comment, "I react to people as individuals, not as members of some group." That is a reasonable complaint, one that is hard to find fault with.

Still, the main purpose of the SVIB is to detect differences in preferences which are related to occupational membership, and attraction to different types of people is certainly related to the choice of an occupation. Take, for example, the answers to one of the more controversial items, "Religious people." In Table A-2 are listed, in rank-order form, the percentages of several occupational groups answering "Like" to this item. Clearly, the response to this item is related to occupational membership: three times as many Music Teachers and YWCA staff members answered "Like" compared with women psychologists and physicians. Thus, the test constructor is faced with a dilemma: it is a useful item as it clearly elicits answers relevant to occupational choice, but it is a bad item because it inquires into a sensitive area—religion.

One solution to this quandary is to develop some way of collecting this information from people without forcing them to make decisions that they do not care to make; there should be no attempt to trick, mislead, or deceive—the task should simply be modified to make it more palatable. To this end, the instructions in this "Types of People" section of the booklet have been modified to emphasize the occupational nature of these choices, and some of the items have been changed to further emphasize this orientation.

The old instructions read: "Show your feeling about these different kinds of people. Do not think of various possibilities or of exceptional cases. 'Let yourself go' and record that feeling that comes to mind as you read each item."

TABLE A-2. PERCENTAGE OF VARIOUS WOMEN'S OCCUPATIONAL SAMPLES
RESPONDING "LIKE" TO RELIGIOUS PEOPLE
(All form WA's)

Percent Responding "Like"	Occupational Samples	Percent Responding "Like"	Occupational Samples
69	Music Teachers	39	Fashion Models; Life Insurance
65	YWCA Staff Members		Saleswomen
57	Physical Therapists; Musicians	38	Occupational Therapists
49	Buyers	37	Dietitians; Artists
46	Home Economics Teachers;	36	Nurses
	Business Education Teachers;	35	Steno-Secretaries; Physical Ed-
	Social Science Teachers		ucation Teachers; Lawyers
45	Office Workers	34	English Teachers; Authors
44	Math-Science Teachers	31	Lab Technicians; Dentists
42	Social Workers; Engineers	30	Librarians
41	Speech Pathologists; Women-	27	Physicians
	in-General (1946)	20	Psychologists

The new instructions read: "People tend to choose jobs where they can work with individuals they enjoy. Please indicate here your feelings about having day-to-day contact with the following types of people. Work fast—don't think of specific examples—give the first impression that comes to mind."

In addition the following items have been changed:

Item No.	Old Item	New Item
216	Conservative people	Highway construction workers
217	Energetic people	High school students
218	Democrats	College professors
219	Prohibitionists	Jet pilots
220	Republicans	Male hairdressers
221	Optimists	Corporation executives
222	Pessimists	Girls who enter beauty contests
224	People who assume leadership	Long-haul truck drivers
228	Irreligious people	Housewives
239	Beachcombers	Racing car drivers
245	Independents in politics	People who like to gamble

In general, more occupationally oriented items have been substituted for those that were more personality oriented.

These changes in Section IV were made after most of the standardization data had been collected for the new Women's booklet; thus there is some concern that the modified instructions will affect the responses to the unchanged items in this section. If that were true, then scoring weights based on data collected using the previous instructions could not be used with the changed booklet.

To test this possibility, the two forms of the revised booklet, identical except for the changed instructions and eleven changed items in Section IV, were given to random samples from two women's occupations; secretaries and accountants.

For this comparison, the following sample sizes were available:

	"Old" Revised Form	"New" Revised Form
Secretaries	36	29
Accountants	133	78

The major issue was whether the groups answering the new forms responded differently to the unchanged items in Section IV than did the groups answering the old forms. Relevant data on that point at the item response level are in Table A-3, where the groups are compared on their answers to the 29 items in Section IV (where the groups were working from different instructions) and the 360 items in the remainder of the booklet (where they were working from the same instructions). On the 11 items that were completely changed, no comparisons were made.

Table A-3 shows there was a tendency for about 6–7 percent of each sample to change their responses to the 29 Part IV items, from the "Like" end of the continuum toward the "Dislike" end. Among the secretaries, the shift was mainly from "Like" to "Indifferent." Among the accountants, the shift was mainly from "Indifferent" to "Dislike." Apparently women are more prone to respond negatively to types of people when asked to consider them as co-workers than they are when they are merely asked for a general reaction.

Still, the shift was a mild one, and was not a sufficiently large disadvantage to outweigh the advantage of changing the instructions.

Further support for this conclusion comes from inspecting the mean differences at the scale level for the two groups answering the differing forms

TABLE A-3. DIFFERENCES IN PERCENT RESPONSES FOR TWO GROUPS RESPONDING TO "OLD" REVISED VERSUS "NEW" REVISED WOMEN'S BOOKLET

	Accountants		Secretaries	
	360 Items, Identical Instructions	29 Part IV Items, Changed Instructions	360 Items, Identical Instructions	29 Part IV Items, Changed Instructions
Differences responding "Like":				
Mean difference (Old-new)	+1.1	+0.1	− 0.3	− 7.4
SD	6.7	9.4	10.7	10.6
Differences responding "Dislike":				
Mean difference (Old-new)	+0.2	6.1	− 2.3	+ 0.9
SD	6.3	7.5	9.4	8.6

of the booklet. Among the secretary sample, only one mean difference—out of 50 scales—between the two groups was statistically significant at the .05 level; among the accountants, none were.

Thus, the changes in instructions for Part IV have been incorporated in the published version of the SVIB booklet.

While this all may seem trivial, particularly when viewed against the more serious unsolved technical problems, Section IV has raised more antagonism among research participants than any other portion. Something had to be done—hopefully the modified instructions and items will help.

Collecting the New Women's Occupational Samples

Three general types of women's occupations have been tested in this restandardization: first, those groups already on the profile, tested for replacement purposes; second, occupations not on the profile but which counselors have frequently expressed interest in, such as interior decorator and scientist; third, some nonprofessional occupations—those requiring little or no post–high school training—to determine if the SVIB is useful at this level.

A few of the original profile occupations were not retested. Engineers, music teachers, and musician performers had been tested more recently, so those original criterion groups were used in the revision. Women dentists were not retested because so few women enter that occupation that it doesn't seem worth the expense. No new sample of housewives was collected mainly because it is very difficult now to decide who is or is not a housewife.

Some of the new occupational samples are small, for women in them were difficult to contact; fashion models, nightclub and TV entertainers, and language interpreters were three examples of that problem. Even so, scales have been developed for those groups as this information is particularly useful as little other data are available on these groups.

The 1968 Women-in-General Sample

The composition of the 1968 Women-in-General (WIG) sample is described in Appendix C, along with their percentage response to each SVIB item.

The purpose of the Women-in-General sample is to act as a reference group to provide a base rate of response for each SVIB item. Because the WIG sample is used for this basic purpose, its composition is quite important, yet no one knows just what this composition should be. Just what are "Women in General?"

Several guidelines were followed in defining the 1968 WIG sample; they were a result of a variety of researches on both the Men's and Women's booklet and were:

1. The sample should be large both to increase the stability of the item

statistics and to dilute the impact of any single individual, or subset of individuals. The final sample contained 1,000 women.

2. The sample should be diverse, again to dilute the impact of any subgroup, and to insure sampling from all variety of interest patterns. The final sample included women from 42 occupations and several miscellaneous groups; the latter, which included diverse individuals such as high school students, were used to round out the sample to 1,000, and to add more diversity.

3. The women in the WIG sample should be drawn from the same general population as those women in the criterion groups, and also from the same population that the SVIB will be used with in normal practice. These are usually conflicting goals; the women in the criterion groups were older, averaging about 40 years old, while the average age of those filling in the SVIB for counseling purposes is probably around 20, extending down to 16 and 17. The first goal of the two is probably more crucial from the item analysis standpoint, so it was given more weight, but at least some teenagers were included as a slight nod to the second goal.

4. Earlier research with the Men's Form, discussed on p. 370 and in more detail in Campbell (1968c), has suggested that there should be a fairly broad time span in testing the reference group, especially if scales continue to be developed. This was not done here as all of the WIG were tested between 1964 and 1968. Whether this will be a problem remains to be seen.

The 1968 Scales

Scale development followed the techniques described in Chapter 2, and psychometric qualities of the resulting scales are also reported there.

Some Interim Scales

During the revision, about 1965–68, some interim scoring scales were developed to permit immediate scoring of the new criterion group inventories so that the participating individuals could receive their results. As these women were filling in the revised inventory, they could not be scored on the then existing scales. To wait until all groups had been tested and new scales had been developed would have meant a delay of at least 24 months in returning results.

Consequently, a set of scoring scales directly analogous to those for the 1966 Men's revision were constructed. The percent responses of Strong's original criterion and Women-in-General samples to the items common to the old (Form M) and new (TW 398) were contrasted, and scales were built.

These scales could be used on either the old or new booklets, and were used to generate the profile for all of the women tested in the revision, and were used in two published studies (Harmon and Campbell, 1968; Campbell and Soliman, 1968a). Although all of the usual statistics were not calculated for these scales, there is no reason to doubt that they were less useful than their parallels in the Men's revision. Of course, the final scales published in 1969 differ from these interim scales in that they include all 398 items, are based on a new Women-in-General sample and, in most cases, on new criterion samples.

Other Changes

Several other changes were made in the 1969 revision. They have already been reported earlier in the text of this Handbook and listed here only for completeness. The other changes were (1) the addition of the Basic Interest Scales to the profile, (2) the introduction of the Administrative Indices, and (3) the addition of the Diversity of Interest and Occupational Introversion-Extroversion scales to the profiles.

The Occupational Criterion Groups

The Occupational Scales for the SVIB contrast the interests of men or women in specified occupations with those of a general reference group, Men, or Women-in-General. To better understand what is measured by these empirical scales, it is helpful to know the characteristics of each occupational sample; a brief description of each of them is given below. Most of the people in these groups have been in their occupations at least three years; virtually all of them were between 25 and 55 years old. For most groups, some expression of satisfaction with the occupation was required for inclusion. Wherever possible, some minimum standard of success, such as professional certification, or membership in a professional society, or supervisory ratings, was established and used to eliminate the "marginal" members of the occupation.

For some groups, responses were available for some individuals on the Cowdery Blank, a precursor of the SVIB with some identical items (see pp. 408–9). Where the N is given as one number plus another number, the second number represents the N from the Cowdery Blanks. In those instances, the norms are based on the first number only.

For each criterion group, mean age and education are listed, and also date tested. Appropriate references are also cited.

Appendix E has descriptions of the newer men's criterion samples; scales based on these samples will be published soon.

Occupation	N	Mean Age	Mean Education	Year Tested	References	Composition and Comments
ACCOUNTANT	345	37	12.3	1932	Strong, 1949	160 general accountants, 54 cost accountants, 65 auditors, and 66 comptrollers and treasurers. All junior accountants; see SENIOR CPA scale (below).
ADVERTISING MAN	169 +62	38	14.0	1927, 1935		104 advertising managers and 65 advertising agency men; also 62 agency advertisers responding on Cowdery Blank.
AIR FORCE OFFICER	200	36	16.0	1960	Winter, 1963	Drawn from 8,000 Air Force Officers requesting advanced formal training through Institute of Technology of the Air University, U.S. Air Force, Wright-Patterson Air Force Base, Ohio, during 1959–62. Sample restricted to Regular Air Force officers, Captains or higher, Line Officers. Average Promotion List service, 12 years. About 10 per cent received commissions through Service Academy, others through other routes. Most had science and/or engineering educational backgrounds. Pilots, about 60 per cent. Cross-validation sample of 200 closely resembled initial sample on all characteristics, including score on SVIB Air Force Officer scale. Data collected and made available by Lt. Col. Frank Winter, United States Air Force.
ARCHITECT	240	43	14.4	1927, 1936		Members of California State Board of Architecture.
ARMY OFFICER	463	39	16.+	1950	Feifel *et al.*, 1952	All West Point graduates. Sample drawn from upper half, on basis of army efficiency ratings, of 1810 officers. Predominantly field grade officers, minimum 8 years' experience since graduation from United States Military Academy. Average experience, 18 years. Data collected and made available by Dept. of Army, Personnel Research Office.
ARTIST	231 +46	43	11.9	1933		123 painters, 79 commercial artists, 20 sculptors, and 9 cartoonists.
AUTHOR–JOURNALIST	248	45	14.3	1928, 1935		148 journalists, 68 authors of fiction, 25 authors of nonfiction, and 7 playwrights and poets. Authors listed in *Who's Who in America;* newspaper editors designated in *Editor & Publisher Year Book.*
BANKER	247	46	12.2	1934	Campbell, 1966A	Includes 172 members of Minneapolis Federal Reserve System; of these, 95 were with banks that opened immediately after 1933 Bank Holiday, and 77 were bankers from national banks and designated "good bankers" by qualified expert. Remaining blanks obtained through Psychological Corporation, New York, and from miscellaneous sources.

(table continued next page)

Occupation	N	Mean Age	Mean Education	Year Tested	References	Composition and Comments
BIOLOGIST	342	44		1959	Herman *et al.*, 1962	Roughly 54 per cent teachers, 34 per cent research workers, 10 per cent administrators, and 2 per cent miscellaneous. All listed in *American Men of Science;* all hold advanced degree other than M.D.
BUSINESS EDUCATION TEACHER	323	40	16.8	1956	Bacon, 1958	Employed in public secondary schools. All completed 30 or more college credits in business courses, and reported satisfaction with occupation. Average experience, 9 years. Data collected and made available by Dr. R. V. Bacon.
CARPENTER	181	43	12.2	1936		All union members. 55 per cent from California, 24 per cent from Minnesota, remaining 21 per cent from rest of country.
CPA OWNER	354 +68	37	14.3	1944	Strong, 1949	Owners, partners, and managers of accounting firms. All certified CPA's in California or New York; members of American Institute of Accountants. See also SENIOR CPA scale (below) and ACCOUNTANT scale (above).
SENIOR CPA	612	-38	14.4	1944	Strong, 1949	Members of American Institute of Accountants, classified as partners, managers, seniors, semi-seniors, and juniors. This scale, seniors; ACCOUNTANT scale, juniors; CPA OWNER scale, partners primarily, managers secondarily.
CHAMBER OF COMMERCE EXECUTIVE	400	40	15.5	1960		Half of group Chamber of Commerce Executives; other half, managers of trade associations. Scale represents both groups equally well. Average experience, 10 years. Developed with assistance of Clifton Corporation, Washington, D.C., for U.S. Chamber of Commerce.
CHEMIST	297	35	16.8	1927, 1935		Industrial chemists; all members of American Chemical Society. College professors not included.
COMMUNITY RECR. ADMINISTRATOR	350	36	16.2	1964	Roys, 1967	Sample drawn from membership lists of 41 state associations. All between 25 and 55 years old, minimum 3 years' experience, minimum 2 years' college. All reported job satisfaction. Data collected and made available by Dr. Keith Roys, Department of Physical Education, University of Missouri.
COMPUTER PROGRAMMER	500	33	B.A.	1965	Perry & Cannon, 1967	All male, minimum 2 years' experience, jobs primarily nonsupervisory programming tasks. All reported job satisfaction. On cross-validation, satisfied programmers scored higher than dissatisfied ones. Data collected by Dr. Dallas Perry and William Cannon, System Development Corp.
CREDIT MANAGER	452	43	14.9	1958		Average experience, 16 years. Collected with cooperation of Credit Research Foundation, Inc., New York.

Occupation	N	Mean Age	Mean Education	Year Tested	References	Composition and Comments
Dentist	239	42	14.9	1932	Heist, 1960 Kirk *et al.*, 1963	Representative sampling of dentists in California. Obtained with cooperation of Dr. A. R. McDowell, then Dean of the College of Physicians and Surgeons, San Francisco.
Engineer	513	44	15.4	1928	Strong, 1952 Dunnette *et al.*, 1964	92 mining engineers, 126 mechanical engineers, 147 civil engineers, and 148 electrical engineers.
Farmer	241	38	14.6	1936		75 per cent graduates of California or Oregon agricultural college, minimum five years' experience. Remaining 25 per cent non - college - graduates, minimum three years' experience.
Forest Service Man	406	38	14.2	1936		186 District Rangers, 160 Forest Supervisors, and 60 Foresters. Obtained through P. P. Pitchlynn, Assistant Regional Forester, U.S. Forest Service, San Francisco.
Lawyer	251 +73	39	17.0	1927	Campbell, 1966B	174 lawyers in general civil practice, 53 corporation lawyers, and 24 criminal lawyers, judges, and district attorneys. All members of California Bar Association.
Librarian	425	40	17.3	1959	Winters, 1962	Sampling from professional librarian organizations. Average experience, 12 years. Data collected and made available by Dr. J. S. Winters.
Life Insurance Salesman	310	40	13.6	1927, 1935	Bills, 1952 Ferguson, 1958	About one-third managers, two-thirds agents. About one-fourth of agents Chartered Life Underwriters. About half of agents from Phoenix Mutual Life Insurance Company; remainder from about 50 different life-insurance companies.
Math–Science Teacher	289	34	16.4	1936		Minnesota high school teachers of mathematics, and of physical and biological sciences. Obtained through T. J. Berning of Minnesota State Department of Education.
Mathematician	181	46	18.8	1929		Designated in *American Men of Science;* college professors included.
Minister	250	43	18.2	1927		112 Presbyterians, 85 Methodists, 43 of other denominations. More than three-fifths from Pacific Coast; others represent rest of country.
Mortician	360	45	13.0	1945		Prepared with cooperation of F. A. Cutler, National Selected Morticians.
Music Teacher	493	41	17.0	1952		Average experience, 17 years. Selected by, and scale developed with assistance of *Music Journal.*
Musician Performer	450	36	13.6	1952		123 from 1938 criterion group, 327 selected by *Music Journal;* scale developed with assistance of that journal. Includes orchestra players, jazz musicians, and symphony conductors. Average experience, 18 years.

(table continued next page)

Occupation	N	Mean Age	Mean Education	Year Tested	References	Composition and Comments
OFFICE WORKER	326	33	11.5	1928		214 office clerks, bookkeepers, and stenographers; 92 office managers; and 20 credit managers.
OSTEOPATH	585	38	15.8	1939		Full-time practicing osteopaths.
PERSONNEL DIRECTOR	147	41	14.7	1927	Kriedt et al, 1953	Sample carefully selected by competent authorities.
PHARMACIST	309	41		1947	Schwebel, 1951	All registered in New York State. Same proportions of urban and rural pharmacists as found in United States. All reported job satisfaction. Data collected and made available by Dr. Milton Schwebel, New York University.
PHYSICAL THERAPIST	350	33	16.5	1957		Average experience, 6.5 years. Developed with assistance of American Physical Therapy Association, with help of Sarah Rogers.
PHYSICIAN	534	41	M.D.	1949	Strong & Tucker, 1952	Representative sample of physicians in United States. Collected with assistance of Association of American Medical Colleges and Dr. Helen Gee.
PHYSICIST	172	43	18.5	1929		Listed in *American Men of Science;* college professors included.
POLICEMAN	254	35	10.4	1933	Dubois & Watson, 1950 Matarazzo et al., 1964	From cities of Berkeley, Los Angeles, and Palo Alto, California; Cincinnati, Ohio; Duluth, Minnesota; and Wichita, Kansas.
PRESIDENT, MFG. CONCERN	169	48	13.1	1935		73 blanks obtained through Psychological Corporation, 89 blanks from presidents of manufacturing concerns listed in *Thomas' Register of American Manufacturers* and in *Moody's Industrials,* and 7 from miscellaneous sources.
PRINTER	270	36	10.8	1936		82 linotype operators, 86 compositors, 39 proprietors and foremen of printing shops, and 63 printers with varied duties. Primarily from Great Lakes and Pacific Coast states. More than one-third obtained through Oakland, California, Typographical Union.
PRODUCTION MANAGER	216	43	13.3	1935		114 blanks obtained through Psychological Corporation, 28 blanks returned from mailings to men listed in *Thomas' Register of American Manufacturers,* and 74 from miscellaneous sources.
PSYCHIATRIST	404	39	M.D.	1949	Strong & Tucker, 1952 Betz, 1967	Representative sample of those certified by the American Board of Psychiatry and Neurology.
PSYCHOLOGIST	1045	44	Ph.D.	1948	Kriedt, 1949 Klein et al., 1962	89 per cent of the 1201 members of American Psychological Association who received their Ph.D. degree before 1943, tested in 1948. Includes 108 industrial, 65 statistical, 44 child, 219 clinical, 154 educational, 256 experimental, 114 guidance, 16 marketing, and 69 social psychologists.

Occupation	N	Mean Age	Mean Education	Year Tested	References	Composition and Comments
PUBLIC ADMINISTRATOR	550			1941	Strong, 1947	59 in personnel work, 53 in departments of agriculture and commerce, and in T.V.A., 48 in public welfare work, 46 in Forest Service, 45 hospital superintendents, 41 city managers, 28 in statistical work, 26 in engineering work, 25 in public health, 24 in finance, 16 prison wardens, 15 in taxation, 14 chemists, 13 in recreation, 11 in Social Security, 9 reform school superintendents, 5 office managers, and remainder miscellaneous.
PURCHASING AGENT	219	40	11.8	1927, 1935		Members of Purchasing Agents' Associations of Northern California; Los Angeles, California; Washington, D.C.; and Cleveland, Ohio.
REAL ESTATE SALESMAN	243	40	12.1	1928, 1936		Men listed in *California Real Estate Directory.*
REHABILITATION COUNSELOR	272	50	17.5	1949	Acree, 1960	All vocational rehabilitation counselors employed by Veterans Administration. Average experience, 12 years.
SALES MANAGER	228	42	13.0	1928, 1935		Obtained through Psychological Corporation and from Sales Managers Association of San Francisco.
SCHOOL SUPERINTENDENT	190	46	16.9	1930		From cities of 10,000 population or over, in all parts of United States.
SOCIAL SCIENCE TEACHER	217	34	16.4	1936		Minnesota high school social science teachers, obtained through T. J. Berning of Minnesota State Department of Education.
SOCIAL WORKER	400	39	18.3	1953	McCornack, 1956 Klein *et al.*, 1962	From 44 states. About 83 per cent with two or more years' graduate education in social work. Average experience, 11 years.
VETERINARIAN	310	44	DVM	1949	Hannum, 1950 Hannum, 1955	All but 14 from Iowa, predominantly graduates of Iowa State University. Practically all in general practice. Data collected by Dr. T. E. Hannum, Iowa State University.
YMCA SECRETARY	184	30.+	17.0	1961		Selected in 1960 and tested in 1961 by identifying young, recently certified Senior Secretaries, or those within one year of certification. All had B.A.'s plus 30 hours' graduate work; most with minimum 3 years' experience, remainder at least 2 years. All 35 or younger. Represents about 40 per cent of men meeting these criteria on nationwide basis; selection not biased toward region, size of agency, source of education, or role in YMCA. Data collected and made available through offices of late Dr. Harold Seashore, Psychological Corporation, and Mr. Richard Lancaster, Senior Secretary, Personnel Services, National Council of YMCAs.

Description of Women's Criterion Groups

Occupation	N	Mean Age	Mean Education	Mean Experience	Percent Married	Year Tested	Composition and Comments
							As discussed in the text, all women in these samples, except where noted, had a minimum of three years' experience, and reported they enjoyed their work.
Accountant	335	45	14.6	17	44	1967	Selected from a national sample of the American Society of Women Accountants.
Army Enlisted	218	42	12.6	14	12	1967	Senior enlisted Wacs (E-7, 8, 9!s). Data gathered with the assistance of Lt. Col. Mary Kelly, Deputy Director, Women's Army Corps, (retired).
Army Officer	307	41	15.8	14	15	1967	WAC Captains (35%), Majors (49%), and Lt. Cols. (16%). Data gathered through the assistance of Lt. Col. Mary Kelly, Deputy Director, Women's Army Corps, (retired).
Artist	297	57	15.5	29	52	1967	Non-commercial artists listed in Who's Who in American Art, 1966. All those selected had exhibited their works.
Art Teacher	359	46	16.6	10	52	1967	Selected from names supplied by the National Art Education Association and certified teachers in the Iowa Educational Directory.
Bankwomen	271	49	13.0	23	55	1968	Members, National Association of Bankwomen. Sampled proportionately by job title from overall roster.
Beautician	263	30	11.8	7	82	1966	Selected from women licensed in Minnesota between 1954 and 1963. Sample includes women living in Wisconsin, Iowa, North Dakota, and South Dakota.
Business Education Teacher	300	42	16.4	14	64	1967	Most of the teachers' groups were drawn from three states, Minnesota, Iowa, and Colorado. Within each state, an attempt was made to balance samples between urban (i.e., Minneapolis-St. Paul, Des Moines, and Denver) and rural areas. Information was secured from the Departments of Education and their directories. Wherever the necessary information was available, only teachers trained in the field they were teaching in were used, e.g., Phys. Ed. Teachers who had majored in Phys. Ed.
Buyer	204	34	12.4	13	--	1942	Heads of merchandise departments, nearly all in department stores.
Chemist	173	47	19.9	19	36	1966	Selected from American Chemical Society Directory, all with Ph.D.'s.
Computer Programmer	262	32	14.1	5	--	1964,66	Female programmers employed by the government, private industry, research and development companies who deal primarily in programming for business, scientific pursuits and military systems. Data gathered by Dallis Perry and William Cannon (see Perry and Cannon, 1968).
Dental Assistant	418	39	12.6	12	59	1966	Selected from those members of the American Dental Assistant Association who belonged three years or more.
Dentist	195	40	16.0	16	--	1934,42	Appreciable percentage of all women dentists in the country when tested.
Dietitian	327	44	16.6	15	49	1967	Selected from names supplied by the American Dietetic Association.

Occupation	N	Mean Age	Mean Education	Mean Experience	Percent Married	Year Tested	Composition and Comments
irector, Christian Education	434	45	16.2	11	36	1967	Presbyterian, Methodist, Lutheran, and Baptist educators, whose names were supplied by the Council on Education, Board of Education of the Methodist Church, American Baptist Convention, Lutheran Church and United Presbyterian Church.
lementary School Teacher	325	44	15.9	17	63	1966	Urban sample selected from Directory of Minneapolis schools, 1965-1966. Suburban and rural sample provided by Minnesota State Department of Education.
nglish Teacher	352	41	16.4	12	67	1967	SEE GENERAL COMMENT UNDER BUSINESS EDUCATION TEACHER.
ngineer	325	37	15.9	10	--	1959	Data gathered from membership of the Society of Women Engineers.
ntertainer	104	34	13.5	13	71	1966-67	Selected from listings in Variety, show business magazines and broadway programs. The sample is small because it is difficult to reach these women.
xecutive Housekeeper	281	53	12.0	10	54	1967	Selected from membership of the National Executive Housekeepers Association, Inc.
uidance Counselor	347	48	17.5	9	51	1967	Members of the National Association of School Counselors. Data gathered with the assistance of Mrs. Gloria Blanton and Mrs. Janet Francis.
ome Economics Teacher	373	39	16.3	11	70	1967	SEE GENERAL COMMENT UNDER BUSINESS EDUCATION TEACHER. (No Colorado teachers were included in this sample.)
nstrument Assembler	89	45	11.4	14	78	1966	Assembly line workers of a large electronics firm. 561 SVIBs were mailed out, 183 (33%) returned. After eliminating those with less than 3 years' experience or those who did not enjoy the work, only 89 remained.
nterior Decorator	172	52	14.7	23	52	1966	All certified members of the American Association of Interior Decorators.
anguage Teacher	287	42	16.5	13	58	1967	SEE GENERAL COMMENT UNDER BUSINESS EDUCATION TEACHER. (Milwaukee, Wisconsin city schools language teachers also included here.)
awyer	235	49	18.0	18	60	1967	National sample selected from 1966 Martindale-Hubbell Law Directory.
brarian	410	45	17.5	13	47	1967	Selected from Who's Who in Library Science, 1966. All participants had at least a Master's Degree.
censed Practical Nurse	222	51	11.7	15	58	1967	National sample of members of the American Federation of Licensed Practical Nurses.
fe Insurance Underwriter	188	53	13.9	15	40	1967	Members of the Women Leader's Roundtable of the National Association of Life Underwriters--all have sold at least $250,000 worth of life insurance in one year's time.
thematician	119	49	20.0	20	43	1966	All Ph.D. mathematicians drawn from 1966 Directory of American Mathematical Society.
th-Science Teacher	308	44	16.5	15	61	1967	SEE GENERAL COMMENT UNDER BUSINESS EDUCATION TEACHER.
dical Technologist	345	39	15.8	14	43	1967	National sample selected from the American Society of Medical Technologists.

(table continued next page)

Occupation	N	Mean Age	Mean Education	Year Tested	References		Composition and Comments
Model	72					1965-67	Requests sent to modeling agencies in the US and Europe. (Data very difficult to collect. see Campbell, 1967).
Musician Performer	290	34	15.5	14	--	1952	Includes women who are mainly performers. Developed with the assistance of the Music Journal.
Music Teacher	450	44	16.5	20	--	1952	Includes women who are mainly teachers. Developed with the assistance of the Music Journal.
Navy Enlisted	213	32	12.3	10	13	1967	Enlisted WAVES in their second or further enlistment. In general, slightly lower ranks than the WAC enlisted sample. Data gathered with the assistance of Dr. Martin Wiskopf and Al Goin, Bureau of Naval Personnel, and C. D. Nace, Assistant Chief of Naval Personnel.
Navy Officer	191	36	16.5	12	12	1967	WAVE line officers: Lt. J.G. (19%), Lt. (37%), Lt. Cmdr (26%), Cmdr (14%), and Cpts (1%). Data gathered with the assistance of Dr. Martin Wiskopf and Al Goin, Bureau of Naval Personnel, and C. D. Nace, Assistant Chief of Naval Personnel.
Newswoman	189	43	15.5	14	46	1966	National sample of women engaged full time as staff members of a newspaper--selected from Editor and Publisher's Yearbook, 1966.
Nun-Teacher	494	39	16.2	18	00	1961	Roman Catholic sister-teachers from 41 states: 252 elementary teachers, 242 secondary teachers; all had 4 year college degrees. Data collected by Sister Mary David Olheiser, O.S.B., Ph.D., College of St. Benedict, St. Joseph, Minnesota (see Olheiser, 1962).
Occupational Therapist	607	32	--	--	72	1966	Data collected from two sources. Leland Miller, Director of Occupational Therapy, University of Kansas, provided national sample of 200 psychiatric OT's, and 188 non-psychiatric OT's. Robert Flint, American Rehabilitation Foundation, Minneapolis, Minnesota provided 219 OT's from a sample of Minnesota OT's who had completed training since 1960. 46% of these were not currently employed though 75% of these intend to return to occupational therapy when family responsibilities permit.
Physical Education Teacher (High School)	310	35	16.4	10	52	1967	SEE GENERAL COMMENT UNDER BUSINESS EDUCATION TEACHER.
Physical Therapist	267	34	--	--	68	1966	A sizable proportion of the PT's who had received their training in Minnesota since 1960. Both employed and non-employed women included here. Data was furnished by Robert Flint, American Rehabilitation Foundation, Minneapolis.
Physician	321	48	19.5	18	58	1967	National sample selected from American Medical Association Directory, 1965.
Psychologist	275	43	20.0	13	47	1966	National sample selected from American Psychological Association Directory, 1966, all with Ph.D.'s. (see Campbell and Soliman, 1968.)
Public Health Nurse	268	36	14.3	6	--	1964	Nurses working in public health nursing agencies (city or county health departments, visiting nurse agencies, school nursing services). Data collected by Miss Constance Carmody.

Occupation	N	Mean Age	Mean Education	Year Tested	References		Composition and Comments
Radiologic Technologist	307	34	12.8	10	48	1967	National sample selected from membership of the American Society of Radiologic Technologists.
Recreation Leaders	199	42	15.2	13	--	1968	National sample of women recreation leaders. Data collected by Miss Jacquelyn Boaz.
Registered Nurse	263	31	16.3	6	74	1967	Nurses with Baccalaureate degrees licensed in the state of Minnesota--names provided by Minnesota State Board of Nursing.
Saleswoman	243	52	11.7	15	73	1966	Members of Dayton, Inc. of Minneapolis sales staff.
Secretary	366	36	12.8	12	53	1967	Secretaries from the University of Minnesota, Pillsbury Company, Dow Chemical, 3M, and from the membership of the National Secretaries Association.
Sewing Machine Operator	295	45	10.5	11	79	1967	All Munsingwear, Inc. employees classified as piecework employees from plants in Arkansas, Texas, Illinois, Minnesota, Wisconsin, Alabama, and Oklahoma.
Social Science Teacher	183	42	16.4	14	63	1967	SEE GENERAL COMMENT UNDER BUSINESS EDUCATION TEACHER.
Social Worker	464	44	17.8	15	--	1953	Members of the American Association of Social Workers from 42 states. Predominantly in areas of direct service or supervision of those giving direct service. About 70 percent with two or more years graduate education in social work. Data collected by Dr. R. L. McCornack (see McCornack, 1956).
Speech Pathologist	353	44	18	16	--	1965	Selected from 1964 Directory of American Speech and Hearing Association. All held advanced clinical certification or MA or PhD. 52 percent spent most of their time in clinical practice, 43 percent in teaching, remainder in miscellaneous activities. 38 percent employed by a college or university, 25 percent in elementary or secondary schools, remainder in various agencies or private practice. Data collected with assistance of Dr. Hildred Schuell, Aphasia Section, VA Hospital, Minneapolis (see Campbell and Schuell, 1967).
Stewardess	443	24	13.3	3	00	1967	Northwest Orient Airlines stewardesses with more than 6 months' experience.
Telephone Operator	129	38	11.8	13	75	1966	Sample provided by Northwestern Bell Telephone Company from Minneapolis, and Bell Telephone in Colorado. Two-thirds of Minnesota operators were from metropolitan areas and one-third from rural areas.
Translator	130	42	16.2	13	59	1966-67	Members of the American Translators Association or the International Association of Conference Interpreters who listed English as a major language; women listed in Translators and Translators in Science and Technology, 1965; U.N. interpreters; others from miscellaneous sources.
YWCA Staff Member	282	40	16.4	10	48	1967	YWCA Staff Members with a minimum of BA degree. Data gathered with the assistance of Miss Mary-Alice Thomas, National Board of YWCA, New York.

The Men- and Women-in-General Samples

Several Men-in-General samples have been used to develop the scoring scales; their composition is reported in this Appendix, and their item response percentages are reported in the following tables.

Men-in-General Samples
The 1938 MIG (Form M). Table C-1

This sample was generated by Strong in the mid-1930's to provide item-analysis statistics for Form M. As composed in 1938, the sample was representative of business and professional men earning $2,500 per year and upward. Some occupations (e.g., draftsmen, postmasters) were excluded because they earned under $2,500 per year. Such earnings are, of course, equivalent to much higher figures today. The sample included 4,746 individuals, but responses were averaged within occupations, then weighted according to the number of each occupation per 1,000 population. For example, 114 blanks from architects were used, but weighted only 1. In the list that follows, the weight given to each occupational group is shown in parentheses; the larger figures are the numbers of individuals actually represented in each group: 114 architects (1), 226 artists (1), 122 editors and journalists (1), 60 advertising men (1), 148 chemists (1), 564 college professors (1), 238 dentists (2), 382 engineers (6), 195 lawyers (4), 99 YMCA staff members (2), 245 ministers (3), 337 physicians (4), 282 teachers (6), 193 city school superintendents (1), 329 Certified Public Accountants (1), 50 farm owners and managers (13), 25 retail-store owners (4), 5 lumbering officials (1), 50 presidents of manufacturing concerns (7), 25 sales managers (2), 25 production managers (2), 25 advertising managers (2), 7 officials of railroads (3), 4 officials of trucking or taxi concerns (3), 25 hotel managers and owners (2), 5 wholesale dealers (2), 7 government officials (4), 4 funeral directors (1), 50 bankers (2), 6 building contractors (4), 50 office managers (1), 332 accountants (5), 14 credit managers (1), 120 purchasing agents (1), 25 traveling salesmen (5), 220 life insurance salesmen (2), 126 real estate salesmen (2), 12 brokers (2).

In 1966, 500 blanks were drawn from this sample, using these same proportions, and used for calculating the percent overlap statistics.

TABLE C-1. ITEM RESPONSE PERCENTAGES FOR THE 1938 MEN-IN-GENERAL SAMPLE (FORM M)

Item Number	L	I	D	Item Number	L	I	D	Item Number	L	I	D	Item Number	L	I	D	Item Number	L	I	D	Item Number	L	I	D	Item Number	L	I	D	Item Number	L	I	D
1	21	32	47	51	24	27	49	101	57	24	19	151	18	32	50	201	32	39	29	251	6	48	46	301	36	38	26	351	19	29	52
2	33	38	29	52	43	27	30	102	38	45	17	152	36	37	27	202	42	39	19	252	83	16	1	302	14	26	60	352	74	22	4
3	37	40	23	53	13	43	44	103	74	16	10	153	21	43	36	203	43	37	20	253	3	44	53	303	56	37	7	353	57	32	11
4	22	29	49	54	8	25	67	104	35	44	21	154	48	35	17	204	40	37	23	254	48	37	15	304	50	37	13	354	10	13	77
5	24	40	36	55	25	36	39	105	29	36	35	155	39	36	25	205	39	38	23	255	10	62	28	305	6	39	55	355	59	18	23
6	26	44	30	56	32	37	31	106	38	42	20	156	32	41	27	206	58	30	12	256	21	52	27	306	37	45	18	356	17	38	45
7	26	41	33	57	52	37	11	107	29	41	30	157	8	41	51	207	82	14	4	257	50	43	7	307	19	53	28	357	8	72	20
8	8	27	65	58	18	52	30	108	52	34	14	158	28	41	31	208	8	41	51	258	32	47	21	308	17	45	38	358	28	69	3
9	32	38	30	59	18	47	35	109	53	34	13	159	21	40	39	209	58	27	15	259	60	21	19	309	29	50	21	359	20	68	12
10	31	41	28	60	34	38	28	110	29	43	28	160	17	39	44	210	25	29	46	260	4	21	75	310	6	47	47	360	17	55	28
11	13	35	52	61	18	45	37	111	61	32	7	161	5	28	67	211	15	33	52	261	3	53	44	311	51	31	18	361	54	24	22
12	12	25	63	62	37	30	33	112	45	39	16	162	56	33	11	212	49	31	20	262	4	56	40	312	21	31	48	362	71	12	17
13	19	27	54	63	30	28	42	113	77	20	3	163	59	33	8	213	5	27	68	263	3	61	36	313	27	38	35	363	59	27	14
14	30	36	34	64	5	28	67	114	54	39	7	164	68	27	5	214	30	35	35	264	23	64	13	314	42	44	14	364	67	20	13
15	10	33	57	65	33	39	28	115	58	27	15	165	59	31	10	215	27	41	32	265	16	64	20	315	19	58	23	365	31	41	28
16	12	29	59	66	39	33	28	116	76	18	6	166	75	20	5	216	41	36	23	266	10	58	32	316	26	53	21	366	56	30	14
17	35	40	25	67	9	37	54	117	19	38	43	167	56	31	13	217	25	36	39	267	5	38	57	317	26	40	34	367	75	16	9
18	35	37	28	68	14	30	56	118	39	41	20	168	16	45	39	218	44	38	18	268	2	19	79	318	17	49	34	368	36	20	44
19	28	38	34	69	39	30	31	119	57	34	9	169	8	29	63	219	27	44	29	269	11	55	34	319	22	50	28	369	26	36	38
20	24	46	30	70	15	41	44	120	69	20	11	170	3	24	73	220	20	47	33	270	41	23	36	320	28	36	36	370	85	11	4
21	20	38	42	71	16	28	56	121	48	37	15	171	50	36	14	221	36	39	25	271	38	54	8	321	45	33	22	371	88	10	2
22	19	33	48	72	18	28	54	122	41	36	23	172	36	46	18	222	41	41	18	272	5	40	55	322	28	36	36	372	84	11	5
23	35	36	29	73	7	41	52	123	29	35	36	173	51	34	15	223	48	32	20	273	10	66	24	323	71	15	14	373	58	17	25
24	41	37	22	74	8	43	49	124	49	35	16	174	70	26	4	224	85	11	4	274	6	46	48	324	31	21	48	374	30	28	42
25	8	39	53	75	43	30	27	125	52	32	16	175	49	43	8	225	30	30	40	275	2	23	75	325	9	16	75	375	59	33	8
26	14	29	57	76	20	35	45	126	57	30	13	176	24	63	13	226	89	9	2	276	5	43	52	326	7	14	79	376	65	30	5
27	33	30	37	77	14	32	54	127	54	34	12	177	40	50	10	227	5	19	76	277	5	61	34	327	34	30	36	377	12	20	68
28	34	40	26	78	17	42	41	128	58	24	18	178	83	15	2	228	2	19	79	278	2	66	32	328	48	24	28	378	66	23	11
29	7	24	69	79	15	40	45	129	64	30	6	179	53	38	9	229	7	29	64	279	1	66	33	329	35	38	27	379	58	35	7
30	23	36	41	80	13	41	46	130	50	33	17	180	49	41	10	230	75	20	5	280	73	26	1	330	77	22	1	380	58	22	20
31	36	36	28	81	37	34	29	131	41	34	25	181	43	43	14	231	15	28	57	281	36	32	32	331	38	25	37	381	53	36	11
32	32	41	27	82	21	31	48	132	38	31	31	182	71	25	4	232	6	37	57	282	44	40	16	332	54	28	18	382	50	38	12
33	30	40	30	83	44	31	25	133	34	45	21	183	80	17	3	233	28	40	32	283	38	47	15	333	59	26	15	383	55	40	5
34	50	31	19	84	41	41	18	134	53	41	6	184	29	47	24	234	85	11	4	284	44	29	27	334	52	25	23	384	56	33	11
35	9	38	53	85	13	40	47	135	21	51	28	185	24	39	37	235	56	35	9	285	30	47	23	335	44	22	34	385	79	20	1
36	6	29	65	86	20	38	42	136	38	56	6	186	29	35	36	236	89	9	2	286	7	51	42	336	39	19	42	386	63	29	8
37	37	28	35	87	20	38	42	137	56	34	10	187	33	35	32	237	5	32	63	287	33	32	35	337	48	17	35	387	90	8	2
38	2	18	80	88	17	45	38	138	65	24	11	188	43	29	28	238	2	19	79	288	22	40	38	338	51	11	38	388	67	15	18
39	19	35	46	89	34	34	32	139	54	21	25	189	31	48	21	239	7	29	64	289	54	25	21	339	48	38	14	389	20	59	21
40	26	39	35	90	13	36	51	140	55	33	12	190	54	26	20	240	75	20	5	290	24	21	55	340	77	14	9	390	4	33	63
41	30	41	29	91	19	40	41	141	77	19	4	191	47	31	22	241	3	27	70	291	28	35	37	341	36	28	36	391	15	32	53
42	20	37	43	92	19	39	42	142	61	31	8	192	40	42	18	242	88	10	2	292	37	45	18	342	52	29	19	392	19	36	45
43	18	38	44	93	39	25	36	143	29	41	30	193	49	31	20	243	47	25	28	293	41	39	20	343	17	27	56	393	15	52	33
44	13	40	47	94	16	32	52	144	25	49	26	194	29	49	22	244	5	40	55	294	10	51	39	344	69	20	11	394	39	58	3
45	47	13	40	95	32	42	26	145	37	41	22	195	39	31	30	245	52	42	6	295	60	31	9	345	16	44	40	395	37	52	11
46	36	12	52	96	4	26	70	146	51	23	26	196	35	35	30	246	16	41	43	296	46	46	8	346	79	16	5	396	3	28	69
47	19	41	40	97	3	11	86	147	47	41	12	197	51	37	12	247	74	22	4	297	5	44	51	347	34	42	24	397	33	53	14
48	19	29	52	98	5	35	60	148	39	34	27	198	47	41	12	248	14	35	51	298	52	44	4	348	34	23	43	398	44	53	3
49	24	36	40	99	23	43	34	149	18	51	31	199	18	51	31	249	32	14	54	299	60	25	15	349	50	35	15	399	7	52	41
50	36	35	29	100	11	33	56	150	12	43	45	200	12	43	45	250	32	44	24	300	24	44	32	350	34	24	42	400	XX	XX	XX

395

Table C-2. Item Response Percentages for the 1966 Men-in-General Sample to the Common Items of Form M and Form T399

Item No.	L	I	D	Item No.	L	I	D	Item No.	L	I	D	Item No.	L	I	D	Item No.	L	I	D	Item No.	L	I	D	Item No.	L	I	D	Item No.	L	I	D
1	28	33	39 a	51	30	28	43	101	60	22	18	151	22	31	48	201	36	42	21	251	8	53	39	301	XX	XX	XX	351	22	34	44
2	31	40	29	52	33	38	33	102	34	47	19	152	XX	XX	XX	202	48	34	18	252	XX	XX	XX	302	XX	XX	XX	352	49	36	XX
3	46	36	18	53	17	39	44	103	70	20	10	153	29	44	28	203	58	29	13	253	XX	XX	XX	303	XX	XX	XX	353	49	XX	15
4	29	28	43	54	9	23	68	104	37	41	22	154	57	32	11	204	49	35	16	254	XX	XX	XX	304	XX	XX	XX	354	51	24	25
5	32	36	32	55	28	38	34	105	26	38	35	155	52	32	16 a	205	46	38	16	255	29	61	10	305	XX	XX	XX	355	XX	XX	XX
6	33	41	26	56	25	36	38	106	43	41	16	156	XX	XX	XXb	206	64	29	8	256	XX	XX	XX	306	XX	XX	XX	356	XX	XX	XX
7	34	38	28	57	38	38	24	107	32	40	29	157	XX	XX	XXb	207	84	14	2	257	XX	XX	XX	307	XX	XX	XX	357	XX	XX	XX
8	8	26	66	58	43	40	17	108	54	30	15	158	36	41	24	208	60	29	XX	258	43	48	9	308	XX	XX	XX	358	XX	XX	XX
9	41	36	23	59	XX	XX	XX	109	56	35	9	159	24	40	36	209	60	29	12	259	XX	XX	XX	309	XX	XX	XX	359	XX	XX	XX
10	41	36	22	60	XX	XX	XX	110	34	40	26	160	XX	XX	XXb	210	25	31	45	260	XX	XX	XX	310	XX	XX	XX	360	XX	XX	XX
11	12	32	55	61	18	45	37	111	56	34	10	161	XX	XX	XXb	211	15	34	51	261	44	50	6	311	67	16	17	361	57	23	20
12	14	25	61	62	44	32	25	112	47	36	18	162	XX	XX	XXb	212	54	29	17	262	7	44	49	312	21	32	48	362	61	25	13
13	20	31	48	63	10	34	56	113	75	21	4	163	57	33	10	213	XX	28	XX	263	9	71	20	313	25	34	41	363	61	25	13
14	40	32	28	64	33	36	31	114	52	40	8	164	XX	XX	XXb	214	28	40	32	264	10	56	34	314	38	46	16	364	64	22	14
15	21	34	55	65	36	35	31	115	59	25	16	165	XX	XX	XXb	215	XX	40	XX	265	59	36	5	315	16	56	28	365	33	40	27
16	XX	XX	XX b	66	26	35	39	116	72	21	7	166	XX	XX	XXb	216	XX	39	XX	266	59	XX	XX	316	32	49	19	366	XX	XX	XX
17	36	39	25	67	15	41	44	117	22	38	41	167	59	29	12	217	24	39	37	267	XX	XX	XX	317	25	42	32	367	37	22	41
18	33	40	27	68	XX	XX	XXb	118	43	38	19	168	XX	XX	XXb	218	39	44	17	268	XX	XX	XX	318	16	51	33	368	37	22	41
19	36	37	27	69	26	34	40	119	59	32	9	169	XX	44	XXb	219	27	38	29	269	XX	XX	XX	319	36	43	21	369	31	37	33
20	29	45	26	70	25	40	35	120	64	29	13	170	XX	47	XXb	220	20	47	33	270	67	31	2	320	20	38	42	370	XX	XX	XX
21	18	36	46 b	71	19	36	46	121	53	33	14	171	56	32	12	221	36	39	24	271	42	29	29	321	XX	XX	XX	371	XX	XX	XX
22	XX	XX	XX	72	20	27	53	122	44	37	19	172	35	46	18	222	XX	XX	18	272	42	42	15	322	34	36	30	372	XX	XX	XX
23	38	36	25	73	12	44	44	123	XX	33	37	173	52	35	13	223	41	33	26	273	44	44	12	323	34	22	43	373	58	16	26
24	42	39	19	74	13	37	50	124	54	34	50	174	XX	XX	XXb	224	52	28	18	274	22	46	33	324	34	22	XX	374	28	29	43
25	18	43	39	75	37	XX	XXb	125	51	38	XXb	175	XX	XX	XXb	225	41	28	31	275	25	51	24	325	37	11	79	375	59	34	7
26	17	32	51	76	XX	32	24	126	58	34	8	176	XX	XX	XXb	226	37	39	24	276	26	36	5	326	10	11	XX	376	68	29	4
27	48	28	24	77	14	30	56	127	55	32	13	177	63	29	7	227	63	29	9	277	17	31	52	327	XX	XX	XX	377	XX	XX	XX
28	XX	XX	XX b	78	25	42	33	128	58	31	11	178	35	36	29	228	48	43	9	278	22	38	28	328	38	33	28	378	67	23	10
29	13	30	57	79	26	34	37	129	66	32	6	179	47	38	15	229	21	38	41	279	38	44	24	329	49	27	24	379	59	34	7
30	26	38	35	80	19	43	38	130	53	39	8	180	54	38	8	230	43	31	26	280	22	27	51	330	61	22	17	380	58	22	19
31	42	37	20	81	30	36	33	131	48	32	20	181	XX	XX	XXb	231	16	27	57	281	31	41	29	331	22	25	53	381	53	37	10
32	35	37	25	82	34	31	35	132	42	36	22	182	72	24	4	232	39	36	15	282	39	42	15	332	29	30	41	382	47	41	12
33	36	37	27	83	48	30	22	133	42	34	15	183	XX	XX	XX	233	29	36	35	283	44	44	12	333	42	29	44	383	51	41	8
34	XX	XX	XX b	84	22	38	41	134	50	34	15	184	40	42	18	234	82	14	4	284	22	46	33	334	27	29	44	384	XX	XX	XX
35	37	38	25	85	15	38	47	135	26	41	23	185	25	40	34	235	47	39	14	285	25	51	24	335	62	18	20	385	28	28	20
36	XX	XX	XX	86	31	31	35	136	45	41	14	186	34	35	30	236	XX	12	XX	286	26	15	26	336	60	25	15	386	63	28	8
37	32	31	37	87	XX	XX	XXb	137	57	32	11	187	35	36	29	237	XX	36	XX	287	17	31	52	337	24	20	56	387	XX	XX	XX
38	XX	XX	XX b	88	16	43	40	138	62	27	3	188	47	27	24	238	22	35	XX	288	22	38	39	338	24	20	56	388	71	13	16
39	XX	XX	XX	89	22	34	44	139	51	30	19	189	40	36	24	239	38	36	XX	289	38	44	17	339	26	45	29	389	XX	XX	XX
40	37	36	27	90	10	32	58	140	58	32	10	190	52	30	18	240	68	26	6	290	22	27	51	340	XX	XX	XX	390	XX	XX	XX
41	34	37	28	91	22	35	44	141	XX	XX	XXb	191	45	34	21	241	5	31	65	291	31	41	29	341	32	31	37	391	16	33	51
42	24	36	40	92	19	19	43	142	64	28	8	192	43	40	17	242	83	14	8	292	39	39	22	342	41	38	22	392	33	38	22
43	20	39	40	93	45	26	29	143	28	38	34	193	49	35	16	243	50	29	21	293	50	36	21	343	71	22	25-53a	393	14	57	29
44	18	42	40	94	19	40	42	144	27	43	30	194	23	XX	30	244	40	XX	XX	294	13	XX	XX	344	15	19	10	394	22	22-25-53a	
45	53	34	13 b	95	12	28	60	145	39	32	29	195	38	29	33	245	40	53	7	295	40	53	7	345	61	46	40	395	35-54-11 a		
46	XX	XX	XX	96	XX	XX	XXb	146	48	29	24	196	42	34	24	246	62-32-6 a			296	62	32	6 a	346	10	21	35	396	XX	XX	XX
47	40	36	24	97	5	14	81	147	41	42	17	197	26	34	40	247	7	38	55	297	32	47	36	347	44	21	35	397	XX	XX	XX
48	25	32	42	98	9	35	56	148	41	36	22	198	48	33	19	248	21	33	55	298	7	58	16	348	37	27	36	398	48	51	2
49	21	41	38	99	20	44	37	149	XX	XX	XXb	199	40	31	XXb	249	58	XX	36	299	58	26	17	349	43	40	17	399	7-55-38 a		
50	35	38	28	100	19	32	49	150	XX	XX	XXb	200	19	38	43	250	34	48	18	300	28	44	28	350	40	26	34	400	XX	XX	XX

a = Lined-out items have been dropped as the MIG percentages do not reflect current base rates.

b = X-ed items were changed from Form M to Form T399. See Appendix A text.

The 1966 MIG (Form M and Form T399). Table C-2

For item-analysis purposes in the 1966 revision, Men-in-General item-response percentages were generated by averaging the percent response to each item for the 56 occupational groups listed below. This is essentially similar to taking equal size samples from these groups, then tallying the percent responses of that entire sample. Guidelines for selecting occupations to be included were to use (1) as many groups as possible, to minimize effect of any single group; (2) as many nonbusiness groups as possible, to reduce businessman bias; (3) groups tested over a wide range of years, to minimize effects of sampling within a short span; (4) groups spread throughout the vocational interest domain. The numbers in each group and year tested are listed in Appendix B. For the few groups not found there, the data are listed in parentheses below. The occuaptions sampled included were: Accountant, Advertising Man, Air Force Officer, Architect, Army Officer, Artist, Author-Journalist, Aviator (510; 1940), Banker, Biologist, Business Education Teacher, Senior CPA, Carpenter, Chamber of Commerce Executive, Chemist, Community Recreation Administrator, Credit Manager, Dentist, Engineer, Farmer, Forest Service Man, Lawyer, Librarian, Life Insurance Salesman, Math-Science Teacher, Mathematician, Minister, Mortician, Music Teacher, Musician Performer, Office Worker, Osteopath, Personnel Director, Pharmacist, Physical Therapist, Physician, Policeman, President—Manufacturing Concern, Printer, Production Manager, Psychiatrist, Psychologist—Experimental (256; 1948), Psychologist—General, Public Administrator, Purchasing Agent, Real Estate Salesman, Rehabilitation Counselor, Sales Manager, School Superintendent, Social Science Teacher, Social Worker, Veterinarian, YMCA Physical Director (216; 1929), YMCA Secretary I (113; 1927), YMCA Secretary II.

The response percentages are given for only those items in common between Form M and Form T399.

The 1969 MIG (Form T399). Table C-3

Following is a listing of the 1969 Men-in-General sample. Chapter 2 contains a discussion of the general strategy in selecting men-in-general samples, and that strategy has been followed here. The general purpose was to select a diversified sample from all parts of the occupational spectrum. As a guide, the Basic Interest Scale areas were used to make up rough categories. Although there is considerable overlap between some of these areas, such as Science and Mathematics, they did provide considerable guidance in selecting subjects.

An initial glance at some of the categories makes it appear that some areas are more heavily weighted than others, but this is misleading because of the interrelations between the groups. In the Writing category

COMPOSITION OF THE 1969 MEN-IN-GENERAL SAMPLE

AREA	OCCUPATION	N
AGRICULTURE		50
	Farmers and Ranchers 40	
	Florists 10	
ADVENTURE.		45
	Astronauts 10	
	Highway Patrolmen. 20	
	Policemen. 15	
ART.		55
	Interior Decorators 10	
	Architects 20	
	Photographers. 10	
	Artists. 15	
BUSINESS MANAGEMENT		60
	Personnel Directors. 15	
	High Level Executives. 10	
	Dept. Store Managers 20	
	Investment Brokers 15	
LAW/POLITICS		40
	Federal Judges. 10	
	State Governors. 10	
	Political Scientists (Ph.D.s). 10	
	Lawyers. 10	
MATHEMATICS		30
	Mathematicians (Ph.D.s). . . . 10	
	Physicists (Ph.D.s). 10	
	Astronomers. 10	
MECHANICAL		30
	Skilled Craftsmen 15	
	Unskilled Laborers 15	
MEDICAL SERVICE		40
	Physicians 10	
	Psychiatrists. 10	
	Pharmacists. 10	
	Medical Technologists. 10	
MERCHANDIZING.		50
	Advertising Men 15	
	Business School Faculty 15	
	Economists (Ph.D.s) 10	
	Funeral Directors 5	
	Mortuary Science Students . . . 5	
MILITARY ACTIVITIES.		30
	Navy Admirals 10	
	Army Generals 10	
	Army Colonels (Retired) 10	
MUSIC.		25
	Symphony Members. 20	
	Composers 5	
NATURE		50
	Agricultural Extension Agents .10	
	Animal Husbandry Professors . .10	
	Forest Service Personnel. . . .20	
	Veterinarians 10	

AREA	OCCUPATION	N

OFFICE PRACTICES. 45
      Bankers 15
      Office Managers 15
      Small Businessmen 15

PUBLIC SPEAKING 35
      Newsmen 15
      Actors. 10
      State Legislators. 10

RECREATIONAL LEADERSHIP 15
      Football Coaches 5
      Physical Therapists. 10

RELIGIOUS ACTIVITIES. 40
      Catholic Priests 20
      Protestant Ministers 20

SALES 40
      Encyclopedia Salesmen. 10
      Life Insurance Salesmen. 20
      Realtors 10

SCIENCE 50
      Chemists (Ph.D.s). 10
      Psychologists (Ph.D.s) 10
      NASA Scientists-Engineers. . . . 5
      Anthropologists (Ph.D.s) 15
      Nobel Prize Winners. 10

SOCIAL SERVICE 50
      Guidance Counselors 15
      Social Workers. 15
      Social Science Teachers 20

TEACHING 50
      English Teachers. 15
      Math. Teachers. 15
      Superintendents 10
      Graduate Students 10

TECHNICAL SUPERVISION. 30
      Engineers 30

WRITING 15
      Newspaper Reporters. 10
      Poets 5

MISCELLANEOUS 125
      Schizophrenics (VA Clinic) . . . 5
      19 Year-Old Twins 20
      H. S. Seniors 20
      Junior College Students 10
      Liberal Arts College Freshmen . 20
      Engineering College Freshmen. . 20
      Miscellaneous 30
      (Selected from a variety of sources to emphasize
      diversity -- includes an inventor, a magician, a
      concert pianist, a puppeteer, etc.)

Total 1,000

TABLE C-3. ITEM RESPONSE PERCENTAGES FOR THE 1969 MEN-IN-GENERAL SAMPLE (FORM T399)

Item	L	I	D
1	43	28	29
2	28	37	35
3	55	31	14
4	31	29	40
5	41	34	25
6	39	40	21
7	39	32	29
8	33	33	34
9	51	30	19
10	37	37	26
11	15	26	59
12	29	25	46
13	26	34	40
14	58	27	15
15	8	34	58
16	28	42	30
17	38	40	22
18	27	36	37
19	40	35	25
20	35	42	23
21	11	33	56
22	22	42	36
23	30	37	33
24	34	42	24
25	15	46	38
26	21	35	44
27	58	28	14
28	51	33	16
29	12	36	52
30	24	40	36
31	44	36	20
32	32	41	27
33	29	41	30
34	42	38	20
35	26	42	32
36	11	28	61
37	33	33	34
38	9	29	62
39	22	35	43
40	48	31	21
41	43	29	28
42	22	38	40
43	21	41	38
44	23	41	36
45	61	29	10
46	49	38	13
47	48	33	19
48	24	34	42
49	15	39	46
50	35	36	29

Item	L	I	D
51	42	31	27
52	28	41	31
53	14	34	52
54	8	23	69
55	41	39	40
56	20	39	41
57	39	36	25
58	33	45	22
59	25	39	36
60	39	30	33
61	17	47	36
62	43	31	26
63	12	36	52
64	45	33	22
65	30	42	32
66	30	33	37
67	16	44	40
68	41	31	28
69	46	33	21
70	23	38	39
71	30	32	38
72	32	29	39
73	11	51	38
74	5	29	66
75	35	36	29
76	52	30	18
77	18	31	51
78	28	45	27
79	31	35	34
80	21	40	39
81	24	34	42
82	44	34	22
83	42	32	26
84	32	31	37
85	19	36	45
86	41	35	24
87	14	37	49
88	17	44	39
89	26	34	40
90	12	34	54
91	17	36	47
92	31	37	32
93	41	27	32
94	20	38	42
95	10	24	66
96	26	42	32
97	5	14	81
98	11	38	51
99	16	42	42
100	16	42	42

Item	L	I	D
101	60	22	18
102	41	36	23
103	64	25	11
104	47	32	21
105	26	39	35
106	44	39	17
107	41	31	28
108	45	33	22
109	53	33	14
110	38	33	29
111	47	40	13
112	43	34	23
113	49	25	6
114	48	40	12
115	58	24	18
116	69	24	7
117	23	37	40
118	41	38	21
119	57	29	14
120	63	23	14
121	41	42	26
122	32	31	36
123	11	42	47
124	34	38	28
125	53	34	13
126	57	31	12
127	51	32	17
128	51	30	19
129	62	28	10
130	40	44	16
131	53	31	16
132	43	33	24
133	42	42	16
134	43	40	17
135	43	40	18
136	46	40	14
137	53	33	14
138	63	25	12
139	50	25	25
140	52	37	11
141	21	46	33
142	67	26	7
143	20	33	47
144	35	41	24
145	48	32	20
146	38	34	28
147	24	40	36
148	39	34	27
149	28	39	33
150	64	23	13

Item	L	I	D
151	22	26	52
152	46	33	21
153	38	43	19
154	66	28	6
155	72	22	6
156	39	43	18
157	35	37	28
158	30	42	28
159	26	39	35
160	17	30	53
161	40	41	19
162	50	33	17
163	42	39	19
164	26	44	30
165	27	34	39
166	30	43	27
167	46	30	24
168	43	37	20
169	24	46	30
170	47	40	13
171	59	27	14
172	33	38	29
173	46	39	15
174	47	37	16
175	29	42	29
176	49	41	10
177	22	43	35
178	54	37	9
179	71	24	5
180	44	39	17
181	24	48	28
182	62	31	7
183	31	44	25
184	39	39	22
185	30	35	35
186	36	36	33
187	34	34	32
188	39	34	27
189	31	34	35
190	42	34	24
191	42	40	18
192	32	48	20
193	43	35	22
194	14	45	41
195	34	31	35
196	42	37	21
197	22	36	42
198	41	36	23
199	39	39	13
200	22	36	42

Item	L	I	D
201	40	44	16
202	52	35	13
203	61	29	10
204	54	38	8
205	48	40	12
206	58	34	8
207	78	19	3
208	25	41	34
209	46	36	18
210	29	22	49
211	22	36	42
212	50	33	17
213	10	29	61
214	48	35	17
215	21	42	37
216	66	26	8
217	34	41	25
218	46	41	14
219	26	41	33
220	20	43	37
221	55	33	12
222	66	27	29
223	27	41	32
224	38	37	25
225	56	28	16
226	26	43	32
227	65	29	6
228	18	47	13
229	44	43	38
230	36	30	34
231	36	26	40
232	58	32	10
233	28	38	34
234			a
235			a
236	86	12	2
237	35	42	23
238	40	30	30
239	22	42	36
240	61	31	8
241	18	33	61
242	78	18	4
243	64	27	9
244	18	52	30
245	45	48	7
246	39	40	41
247	39	49	12
248	11	47	42
249	33	60	7
250	31	54	15

Item	L	I	D
251	12	52	36
252	66	30	4
253	46	43	11
254	41	57	2
255	47	49	4
256	15	54	31
257	58	33	9
258	32	53	15
259	25	60	15
260	63	30	7
261	36	53	11
262	18	54	28
263	38	52	10
264	61	36	3
265	32	60	8
266	42	50	8
267	7	43	50
268	38	55	7
269	39	55	6
270	23	46	31
271	46	46	8
272	10	44	46
273	8	65	27
274	15	56	29
275	28	52	20
276	51	43	6
277	43	50	7
278	40	45	6
279	45	53	2
280	58	37	5
281	66	26	27 b
282	37	45	22 b
283	31	44	10 b
284	47	47	24 b
285	21	55	24
286	27	45	28 b
287	29	54	17
288	23	37	40 b
289	37	45	11 b
290	27	30	24 b
291	38	42	22 b
292	23	42	35 b
293	38	54	20 b
294	42	29	34 b
295	61	29	10
296	6	48	40 b
297	37	57	b
298	18	54	28 b
299	62	40	19 b
300	30	40	30

Item	L	I	D
301	29	38	33 b
302	10	22	68 b
303	49	43	8 b
304	29	52	18 b
305	26	42	32 b
306	32	43	25 b
307	26	43	31 b
308	41	46	13 b
309	39	42	19 b
310	19	40	41 b
311	69	13	18 b
312	12	31	57 b
313	24	36	40 b
314	36	48	16 b
315	12	54	34 b
316	35	48	17 b
317	32	52	27 b
318	16	52	32 b
319	41	40	19 b
320	20	41	39 b
321	83	8	9
322	44	23	51
323	26	37	21
324	34	26	40
325	32	32	31
326	12	14	74
327	40	43	17
328	48	25	27
329	45	53	25
330	54	37	13
331	66	23	56
332	37	27	36
333	37	28	35
334	40	28	31
335	59	17	24
336	68	18	14
337	31	27	42
338	21	23	56
339	25	49	26
340	78	17	5
341	43	27	29
342	44	32	24
343	40	24	36
344	79	13	8
345	19	46	35
346	40	22	38
347	45	26	29
348	29	24	47
349	33	37	30
350	48	26	26

Item	L	I	D
351	27	28	45
352	24	20	56
353	41	27	32
354	8	41	51
355	50	22	28
356	53	30	17
357	52	32	16
358	30	48	22
359	29	26	45
360	43	26	31
361	53	26	21
362	39	17	44
363	59	26	15
364	58	25	17
365	41	35	24
366	32	14	54
367	52	18	30
368	38	20	42
369	44	31	25
370	27	38	35
371	62	16	22
372	53	14	33
373	58	14	28
374	34	24	42
375	57	32	11
376	70	25	5
377	39	29	32
378	61	22	17
379	63	30	7
380	43	26	31
381	49	37	14
382	46	39	15
383	50	39	11
384	75	17	8
385	30	25	45
386	60	32	8
387	63	14	16
388	71	14	15
389	7	45	48
390	58	39	3
391	20	42	38
392	16	29	55
393	16	49	35
394	11	68	22
395	45	26	23
396	45	26	29
397	35	50	15
398	53	44	3
399	6	36	58

a=These items were changed at the last minute in Form T399N. They should not be used in the new scales.

b=These forced choice items will probably be dropped in the next revision. In anticipation of that, they should not be used in the new scales.

for example, there are only 15 individuals: 10 newspaper reporters and 5 poets. Yet the "Writing" section of the domain of interests is well-represented by groups categorized in other areas, such as the newsmen in Public Speaking, the psychologists in Science, and the political scientists in Law/ Politics.

Clearly some arbitrary decisions had to be made in constituting this sample and they generally followed the strategies outlined in Chapter 2. Specifically, careful attention was paid to achieving diversity within the sample, and to avoiding over-representation of any one area.

The item response percentages for this group are given in Table C-3. Note that no percentages are given for items 234 and 235; these items were changed on form T399N, which was used for some of this data collection, so they cannot be used in future scales. Also note the asterisks for items 281 to 320. These are the forced-choice items on the SVIB; because they are difficult to work with statistically and many respondents are confused by the item format, they will probably be dropped in the next revision cycle. To minimize confusion at that stage, researchers should not use these items in building future scales.

Women-in-General Samples
The 1946 WIG (Form W). Table C-4

This sample was built from the following: 402 authors, 425 librarians, 402 artists, 400 physicians, 195 dentists, 205 life insurance saleswomen, 432 social workers, 293 high school English teachers, 396 high school social science teachers, 467 high school math-science teachers, 250 high school physical education teachers, 373 lawyers, 202 YWCA secretaries, 396 nurses, 271 stenographer-secretaries, 416 dietitians, 356 laboratory technicians, 420 home economics teachers, 380 psychologists, 162 occupational therapists, 204 buyers, 54 ready-to-wear clothing saleswomen, 201 junior and senior high school students, 215 freshman and sophomore college students, 200 junior and senior college students, and a remaining 102 from miscellaneous sources. The total N was 7,819. To have each occupation equally represented, the data for each group were reduced to percentages, and percentages were totaled and divided by 26.

The 1968 WIG (Form TW398). Table C-5

A sample of 1,000 women were selected to be a group with diverse interests. Twenty women in each of the following occupations were included: Army—Enlisted, Army Officer, Art Teacher, Artist, Beautician, Business Education Teacher, Chemist, Dental Assistant, Dietitian, Director—Christian Education, Elementary Teacher, English Teacher, Entertainer, Executive Housekeeper, Fashion Coordinator, Home Economics Teacher, Instrument Assembler, Interior Decorator, Language Teacher, Librarian, Licensed Practical Nurse, Life Insurance Underwriter, Math-Science Teach-

TABLE C-4. ITEM RESPONSE PERCENTAGES FOR THE 1946 WOMEN-IN-GENERAL SAMPLE (FORM W)

Item	L	I	D	Item	L	I	D	Item	L	I	D	Item	L	I	D	Item	L	I	D	Item	L	I	D	Item	L	I	D	Item	L	I	D
1	20	40	40	51	35	41	24	101	18	45	37	151	77	18	5	201	24	34	42	251	11	49	40	301	70	18	12	351	62	17	21
2	35	32	33	52	35	42	23	102	40	30	30	152	80	16	4	202	61	27	12	252	52	33	15	302	35	42	23	352	41	46	13
3	17	27	56	53	25	36	39	103	40	34	26	153	96	4	0	203	53	27	20	253	44	48	8	303	61	24	12	353	78	21	1
4	32	37	31	54	28	33	39	104	40	31	29	154	77	20	3	204	30	36	34	254	42	45	13	304	66	24	10	354	54	32	14
5	44	38	18	55	53	31	16	105	36	27	37	155	20	44	36	205	59	18	4	255	38	58	4	305	10	32	58	355	52	14	34
6	52	30	18	56	18	33	49	106	45	30	25	156	48	39	13	206	78	18	4	256	72	24	4	306	14	53	33	356	60	34	6
7	11	29	60	57	17	25	58	107	21	32	47	157	66	27	7	207	28	46	12	257	28	60	12	307	43	32	25	357	21	57	22
8	25	33	42	58	42	37	21	108	17	32	54	158	54	38	8	208	64	24	12	258	17	74	9	308	25	31	41	358	24	29	40
9	41	40	19	59	7	17	76	109	16	29	54	159	43	33	24	209	74	18	8	259	17	51	32	309	55	30	14	359	2	24	74
10	52	34	14	60	53	29	18	110	7	28	65	160	17	41	42	210	44	18	25	260	70	27	3	310	30	27	40	360	27	51	22
11	27	36	37	61	41	32	27	111	41	23	36	161	47	40	13	211	62	26	12	261	41	51	8	311	49	31	20	361	7	31	62
12	34	31	35	62	14	25	61	112	31	34	35	162	68	30	2	212	63	33	4	262	5	22	73	312	86	9	5	362	60	9	27
13	36	30	34	63	15	40	45	113	18	32	55	163	65	30	5	213	24	37	39	263	6	38	56	313	33	22	45	363	57	15	28
14	11	32	57	64	13	33	54	114	22	31	47	164	74	21	3	214	40	40	21	264	20	49	31	314	36	34	30	364	60	25	15
15	14	25	61	65	21	36	43	115	25	32	43	165	52	41	7	215	49	36	15	265	8	19	73	315	50	23	27	365	40	41	19
16	40	30	30	66	9	29	62	116	31	31	38	166	79	19	2	216	52	12	36	266	40	24	36	316	18	44	38	366	25	33	42
17	18	26	56	67	13	24	63	117	38	26	36	167	36	58	6	217	84	14	2	267	40	43	17	317	65	28	6	367	70	16	14
18	51	26	23	68	22	36	42	118	28	29	43	168	89	9	2	218	12	37	51	268	29	42	29	318	11	16	47	368	19	36	45
19	30	43	27	69	41	36	23	119	29	33	38	169	3	22	80	219	16	13	71	269	16	51	33	319	68	16	16	369	18	18	26
20	17	31	52	70	64	24	12	120	30	30	40	170	39	48	13	220	17	24	59	270	57	25	18	320	54	33	13	370	54	32	14
21	21	30	49	71	14	20	66	121	9	26	65	171	21	54	25	221	70	23	7	271	15	50	35	321	35	35	30	371	55	29	16
22	32	32	36	72	16	38	46	122	11	20	69	172	26	45	29	222	24	13	63	272	7	46	47	322	42	26	32	372	54	29	17
23	29	45	26	73	37	35	28	123	15	29	56	173	27	37	36	223	45	32	23	273	23	51	26	323	52	31	13	373	86	11	3
24	44	31	25	74	17	26	57	124	52	28	20	174	58	28	14	224	45	38	17	274	58	23	19	324	27	19	54	374	53	33	14
25	17	30	53	75	16	33	51	125	6	19	55	175	63	19	8	225	61	31	8	275	34	40	26	325	6	34	52	375	65	19	16
26	13	38	49	76	29	26	45	126	10	35	55	176	27	34	39	226	52	34	14	276	52	35	13	326	78	14	8	376	70	21	9
27	13	37	50	77	50	27	23	127	75	20	5	177	24	29	47	227	38	29	33	277	24	43	33	327	47	28	16	377	43	42	15
28	54	28	18	78	56	27	17	128	25	35	40	178	25	25	45	228	11	44	45	278	53	35	12	328	50	41	6	378	49	19	32
29	42	31	27	79	34	42	24	129	80	14	6	179	86	12	2	229	33	48	19	279	25	38	37	329	44	38	9	379	69	18	13
30	9	24	67	80	28	38	34	130	76	17	7	180	34	24	42	230	80	19	1	280	33	55	12	330	28	20	52	380	48	38	14
31	33	33	34	81	30	35	35	131	55	33	12	181	24	38	38	231	52	35	8	281	17	40	43	331	27	32	41	381	44	28	28
32	16	39	45	82	29	38	33	132	69	19	12	182	44	30	26	232	57	37	6	282	31	53	16	332	31	16	72	382	64	23	13
33	44	33	23	83	26	26	41	133	44	44	14	183	51	34	15	233	33	55	12	283	21	41	38	333	21	31	17	383	86	11	3
34	34	29	37	84	11	33	65	134	67	16	10	184	30	25	42	234	55	28	17	284	21	30	49	334	49	18	33	384	24	41	35
35	44	37	19	85	20	42	38	135	78	16	6	185	63	22	15	235	35	48	17	285	18	45	37	335	18	68	10	385	69	22	9
36	42	36	22	86	32	36	32	136	46	25	29	186	43	26	31	236	35	51	14	286	45	22	33	336	45	25	29	386	63	28	9
37	45	30	25	87	36	27	35	137	29	40	35	187	30	37	33	237	22	48	30	287	21	42	37	337	21	17	47	387	35	34	31
38	14	36	50	88	19	27	34	138	29	33	33	188	44	36	20	238	27	43	30	288	18	37	45	338	42	24	33	388	66	26	8
39	2	20	78	89	20	42	38	139	52	33	15	189	63	20	17	239	8	34	17	289	43	46	11	339	18	47	33	389	51	28	21
40	28	27	45	90	33	38	31	140	31	34	35	190	57	25	18	240	39	34	18	290	16	60	24	340	16	60	20	390	38	32	30
41	54	35	11	91	30	35	35	141	63	26	11	191	49	30	21	241	57	40	3	291	32	50	18	341	90	7	3	391	61	26	13
42	50	31	19	92	29	38	33	142	27	34	39	192	58	28	14	242	8	35	57	292	34	40	26	342	85	13	2	392	40	41	19
43	19	31	50	93	26	26	41	143	17	17	66	193	48	30	22	243	16	21	63	293	15	50	35	343	84	10	6	393	78	16	6
44	14	41	45	94	11	24	65	144	32	36	32	194	69	25	6	244	49	45	6	294	49	31	20	344	63	14	23	394	40	28	32
45	14	25	61	95	20	42	38	145	44	36	24	195	63	27	10	245	41	46	13	295	21	32	47	345	34	25	41	395	21	39	40
46	47	31	22	96	32	36	32	146	32	32	36	196	80	15	5	246	27	63	10	296	27	17	56	346	65	9	26	396	58	31	11
47	27	35	38	97	36	38	35	147	60	30	10	197	78	17	5	247	6	43	51	297	16	21	63	347	12	30	58	397	60	23	17
48	33	31	36	98	19	38	41	148	79	18	4	198	63	24	13	248	50	40	10	298	45	25	30	348	24	17	5	398	24	34	42
49	43	38	19	99	20	36	44	149	73	23	4	199	56	29	15	249	61	20	19	299	61	20	19	349	59	24	34	399	43	36	21
50	65	26	9	100	33	36	31	150	58	30	12	200	6	16	78	250	8	18	74	300	2	24	74	350	35	30	35	400	49	32	19

402

TABLE C-5. ITEM RESPONSE PERCENTAGES FOR THE 1969 WOMEN-IN-GENERAL SAMPLE (FORM TW398)

Item Number	L	I	D	Item Number	L	I	D	Item Number	L	I	D	Item Number	L	I	D	Item Number	L	I	D	Item Number	L	I	D	Item Number	L	I	D	Item Number	L	I	D
1 a	41	27	33	51 a	49	32	19	101	17	37	47	151 a	17	33	50	201	25	34	41	251 a	9	59	32	301	44	30	25	351	49	21	30
2 a	20	28	52	52	44	35	21	102	32	30	38	152	62	24	14	202	64	26	10	252 a	43	48	9	302	37	36	6	352 a	37	49	14
3	15	21	64	53	28	35	37	103	42	28	30	153 a	44	41	15	203 a	40	19	41	253	35	51	14	303	66	24	9	353 a	35	16	49
4	33	34	33	54	26	34	43	104	21	34	45	154 a	74	22	4	204 a	18	21	53	254 a	12	66	23	304	68	24	9	354	45	39	16
5	50	31	20	55	45	29	26	105	36	26	38	155	22	36	42	205 a	66	21	12	255	39	58	4	305 a	29	33	38	355	70	14	16
6	62	22	16	56	17	33	49	106	45	30	25	156	64	27	8	206 a	52	27	21	256	75	21	4	306	13	27	59	356 a	63	36	1
7	14	27	59	57	26	27	46	107	19	31	49	157	30	37	26	207	57	37	26	257	39	48	14	307 a	26	35	36	357 a	11	65	24
8	27	29	44	58	33	35	32	108	16	29	55	158 a	42	32	26	208	61	28	11	258	26	68	6	308	19	35	46	358 a	20	42	37
9	52	29	19	59	6	17	78	109	17	24	59	159 a	30	30	40	209	60	25	14	259	14	46	40	309	50	34	16	359 a	43	22	35
10	54	29	17	60	47	30	22	110 a	39	25	36	160 a	10	23	67	210	56	30	14	260	69	27	3	310	28	35	37	360	34	55	11
11	21	35	44	61	40	30	30	111	34	22	44	161 a	72	22	5	211	69	25	6	261	42	47	11	311	48	32	20	361	4	23	73
12	35	25	40	62 a	35	26	40	112	38	29	33	162 a	54	33	13	212	53	41	6	262	6	24	70	312 a	41	30	29	362	50	19	31
13	31	29	40	63 a	25	30	45	113	17	33	50	163 a	17	33	50	213	31	41	28	263	6	42	51	313	37	35	28	363	54	25	21
14	19	27	52	64	31	29	58	114	29	28	43	164 a	30	36	34	214	29	36	28	264	18	58	24	314	32	39	29	364	65	25	10
15	31	27	42	65 a	37	35	28	115	26	32	42	165 a	37	31	31	215 a	17	28	76	265	5	19	76	315	48	28	24	365	54	33	14
16	38	30	32	66 a	18	27	55	116 a	32	30	38	166 a	32	34	34	216 a	XX	XX	XXb	266	33	36	31	316	56	41	3	366	30	29	41
17	20	26	53	67	27	32	41	117	44	25	31	167 a	15	32	53	217 a	XX	XX	XXb	267	21	44	35	317	30	24	46	367	46	34	20
18	50	26	24	68	50	33	17	118	35	27	38	168 a	35	27	38	218 a	XX	XX	XXb	268	21	44	35	318	70	20	10	368	23	20	49
19	40	36	24	69	40	33	27	119	29	30	41	169 a	29	30	41	219 a	XX	XX	XXb	269	20	60	20	319 a	17	51	32	369	40	28	32
20	19	29	52	70	60	24	16	120	21	28	51	170 a	21	28	51	220 a	XX	XX	XXb	270	63	23	15	320 a	45	31	24	370	48	36	16
21	26	30	44	71 a	47	33	20	121 a	14	30	56	171	21	56	23	221 a	18	49	33	271	18	49	33	321	.			371	55	27	18
22	26	30	44	72	31	25	44	122 a	47	29	24	172	48	29	24	222 a	46	46	47	272	7	46	47	322	39	26	35	372	55	27	18
23	54	45	28	73 a	19	25	56	123	28	28	55	173	34	40	26	223	84	15	1	273	17	53	30	323	42	43	14	373	46	31	22
24	22	29	19	74	14	25	60	124 a	49	31	20	174	32	32	16	224 a	15	35	30	274	55	21	24	324	16	16	42	374	36	40	24
25 a	49	29	30	75	25	29	46	125 a	8	20	72	175	61	26	13	225 a	26	37	24	275	45	35	20	325	17	37	46	375	57	27	16
26 a	41	29	30	76	29	29	42	126 a	17	40	43	176	26	34	40	226	51	39	11	276 a	36	35	29	326 a	41	24	35	376	67	24	9
27	55	26	19	77	22	36	42	127 a	22	32	45	177	14	22	43	227	48	40	11	277	50	41	9	327	31	44	25	377	43	40	17
28	9	33	23	78	42	27	31	128	31	24	45	178	41	34	25	228 a	16	47	XX	278	16	47	37	328 a	39	27	33	378	41	26	33
29 a	25	34	41	79	30	32	28	129 a	35	35	31	179	75	19	6	229 a	33	47	20	279	37	44	11	329	46	37	17	379	67	22	11
30	26	29	45	80	41	29	29	130	42	25	28	180	21	25	54	230 a	36	60	4	280 a	31	43	26	330	58	25	17	380	48	33	19
31	25	34	41	81	19	23	58	131 a	37	34	29	181	23	37	29	231	53	40	7	281	22	43	36	331	18	33	49	381	35	35	33
32	17	37	46	82 a	32	36	33	132	39	24	19	182	34	39	19	232	60	38	2	282 a	19	33	48	332 a	21	40	39	382	64	24	12
33	37	37	33	83	29	31	40	133	34	34	34	183	62	25	14	233 a	18	58	24	283	28	44	28	333	28	29	19	383	78	17	4
34	37	28	30	84	21	24	54	134	62	22	16	184	31	32	37	234 a	33	50	17	284 a	40	48	12	334 a	48	27	26	384	22	40	41
35	43	37	23	85 a	18	23	58	135	28	28	24	185	67	24	10	235	22	52	26	285 a	21	41	39	335	39	32	28	385 a	36	33	31
36	43	37	20	86	39	23	38	136 a	39	29	32	186	54	23	23	236 a	48	45	7	286	48	20	33	336	68	19	13	386	62	35	11
37	31	30	31	87	49	28	26	137	55	23	22	187	32	45	31	237 a	19	53	28	287	22	38	40	337	53	29	18	387	40	35	25
38 a	11	30	59	88	49	26	23	138	35	36	23	188	47	36	17	238 a	65	29	6	288	24	30	46	338 a	11	29	61	388	67	26	8
39 a	30	26	44	89 a	11	24	66	139	38	30	33	189	68	19	13	239 a	XX	XX	XXb	289	40	49	12	339	28	36	27	389	52	28	21
40	26	29	45	90 a	28	22	50	140	33	29	38	190	64	25	12	240 a	58	38	3	290	15	57	28	340	30	22	49	390	27	33	40
41	47	34	19	91	39	32	30	141	70	21	9	191 a	52	31	18	241	65	33	2	291	34	48	18	341 a	48	17	34	391	51	32	17
42 a	53	27	21	92	32	36	32	142 a	44	33	23	192 a	21	30	49	242 a	37	48	56	292	37	48	15	342 a	47	19	35	392	39	36	25
43 a	7	20	73	93	29	28	43	143	72	20	8	193	39	31	30	243 a	43	48	9	293	15	49	36	343 a	16	45	39	393	73	21	7
44 a	18	26	56	94	16	25	59	144	49	28	32	194	61	30	10	244 a	13	61	26b	294	40	40	20	344	67	10	23	394	40	28	32
45	43	28	53	95 a	43	31	26	145	28	23	26	195	58	30	12	245 a	XX	XX	XX	295	26	34	40	345	50	38	11	395	24	30	47
46	46	31	32	96	34	34	30	146 a	40	42	18	196 a	80	17	4	246 a	66	31	3	296	33	18	49	346	69	24	6	396	59	30	11
47	27	36	37	97	29	36	35	147	65	28	4	197 a	29	47	24	247 a	86	12	2	297	15	20	65	347	70	13	18	397	61	27	12
48	26	28	46	98	20	37	43	148	66	24	10	198	52	34	14	248 a	56	38	6	298	46	26	28	348 a	13	21	18	398	25	36	39
49	46	35	19	99 a	28	35	37	149 a	55	33	13	199	46	32	22	249 a	37	59	5	299	68	17	15	349	61	30	9				
50	69	21	9	100	25	38	37	150	43	38	19	200	22	25	53	250	19	41	40	300	3	37	60	350	43	37	60				

a = Items changed between Form W and Form TW398 booklets. These data are for the latter booklet.

b = Items revised after all criterion group data had been collected, so they were ignored in scale construction. See text, Appendix A.

403

er, Mathematician, Medical Technologist, Model (N=12), Navy—Enlisted, Navy Officer, Newswoman, Occupational Therapist, Photographer, Physical Education Teacher (HS), Physician, Psychologist, Radiologic Technologist, Saleswoman, Sewing Machine Operator, Social Science Teacher, Stewardess, Telephone Operator, Translator, YWCA Staff Member. The group also included 100 miscellaneous adults, and 68 miscellaneous high school students.

The Various Forms of the SVIB Booklets

This appendix contains information on all of the forms of the SVIB, including the following: (1) a reproduction of the booklets, (2) instructions for converting answers from one form of the booklet to another, where that is possible for scoring purposes, (3) lists of item changes between various forms of the booklet, and (4) a list of the items common to the current men's and women's booklet, Forms T399 and TW398.

This information has been included here for two purposes: first, to capture some of the historical flavor of the development of the booklets, and second, to aid the many investigators doing longitudinal research, using SVIB answer sheets filled in many years earlier.

Men's Forms

Cowdery's Booklet

As reported in greater detail in Chapter 11, the SVIB originally grew from some items gathered together in 1923 by Karl Cowdery, a student working under Strong's direction at Stanford. Cowdery's booklet is reproduced in Figure D-1. That booklet contained 293 items; some of the more notable ones were:

Lighthouse Tender	Missourians
People with hooked noses	Sunday Blue Laws

Forms A and B

Strong's first booklet, Form A, was published in 1927 and is reproduced in Figure D-2. He used 175 of the better Cowdery items and added 245 of his own, for a total of 420. Several different item formats were used in Form A, as Strong was interested in comparing different ways of presenting items. Form B was identical to Form A, except that the questionnaire on the front page was designed for students instead of employees.

Forms M and MM

In 1938, Strong published a revised booklet, Form M, reproduced in Figure D-3. The number of items was reduced from 420 to 400—because 400 items would fit onto an IBM answer sheet—by discarding the poorest

20 items. With a few minor exceptions, the remaining items were left in the same order and renumbered consecutively. Table D-1 has precise instructions for converting answers from Form A to Form M order. After answers are so converted, they can then be scored on the 1938 and 1966 scoring scales, and Set 1 of the Men's Basic Scales.

The identical items on Forms A and M did not necessarily have the same item number, and this plagued Strong's research for the rest of his life, for he always had to have two sets of scoring keys. Even now, when computers make such problems simpler, this is a nuisance, and we have worked to maintain consistent item numbers.

At the last moment before publishing Form M, Strong decided to eliminate the item "Negroes." To replace it, he added number 400, "Worry considerably about mistakes . . . Worry very little, Do not worry." This item had been in the earlier Form A but was discarded from the booklet when the new criterion groups were tested; thus, no Men-in-General response percentage had been derived for it. Consequently, this item in Form M served strictly for filler and was never used on any of the scoring scales.

Just why Strong eliminated the item "Negroes" is not recorded; probably it was for public relations purposes—yet eight years later, in 1946, when the revised women's booklet was published, the item was retained, and stayed in until taken out in the 1969 revision.

Form MM is identical to Form M, except it was designed to be used with a separate answer sheet so the response positions were not printed in the booklet.

Forms T399 and T399R

In 1966, a revised men's booklet was published, Form T399; that booklet is reproduced in Figure D-4. The general changes have already been described in Appendix A, and a list of all of the changed items is in Table D-2. The item content of Forms T399 and T399R is identical; the only difference is that the former is designed for use with a separate answer sheet, while the latter allows the person to respond directly in the booklet.

Using this booklet, Form T399R, the person's responses have to be transferred to IBM cards or an answer sheet to permit machine scoring. Another booklet is available, Form T399N, which is a combination booklet-and-answer-sheet. With this, the individual can mark directly onto the booklet, and then the booklet can be unfolded and run through an optical scanner like any other answer sheet.

Because T399N is the primary form used in collecting data from new criterion groups, two items were changed as a concession to public relations. Section V, Types of People, irritates some people, as they don't like to respond to categories of people. To make the task more palatable, the instructions were modified slightly to emphasize the relationship of these items to vocational membership, and the first two items were changed from "personality" items to vocational interest items. The changes were:

	Old Item	New Item
234	Progressive people	Highway construction workers
235	Conservative people	High school students

These changes have markedly decreased the number of complaints about this section.

Because 109 items have been changed between the Form M and Form T399 booklets, the latter cannot be scored on the 1938 scoring scales. However, because the 1966 scales are based on only the 291 common items, these scales can be used with the responses to either booklet.

Items common to the current men's and women's booklets, Forms T399 and TW398, are listed in Table D-5.

Women's Forms

Forms WA and WB

These booklets, identical except for the covering page, had 410 items, were published in 1933, and were quite similar in format to the analogous men's booklets. Form WA is reproduced in Figure D-5.

Forms W and WM

Form W, reproduced in Figure D-6, was published in 1946 and had 400 items; all of them appeared in the earlier Form WA booklet in exactly the same order but not numbered the same. The 10 discarded items, listed in Table D-3, came from all sections of the booklet, and after they were removed, the remaining items were renumbered consecutively. The transposition of responses from Form WA to Form W order can be accomplished relatively easily by simply lining out the 10 discarded items and renumbering. When this conversion has been done, the responses can be scored on the women's Set 1 Basic Scales, or the 1946 Occupational Scales—but not on Set 2 or the 1969 Occupational Scales.

Form WM is identical to Form W except that it was designed to be used with a separate answer sheet.

Forms TW398 and TW398R

These revised booklets, published in 1969, have 296 items in common with the earlier Form W booklet. The common items are in exactly the same order and have exactly the same item numbers. The list of items changed from Form W to Form TW398 is given in Table D-4. Form TW398 is reproduced in Figure D-7.

Items common to the current men's and women's booklets, Forms T399 and TW398, are listed in Table D-5.

PART II
Occupations

After each of the occupations listed below there are three letters.
Draw a circle around one of the letters for each occupation as follows:

Draw a circle around L if you like that kind of work
Draw a circle around I if you are indifferent to that work
Draw a circle around D if you dislike that kind of work

You are not to think of the occupation as if you were choosing it
for your profession. You are assuming that you have the ability to do the
work of any of the occupations, and that you are indicating whether or not
you like the kind of work involved in the various occupations, regardless
of the relative financial return or social standing incidental to each.
Indicate only your interest and satisfaction in doing the kind of work.

Draw a circle around one letter after every occupation:

Actor	L	I	D	Locomotive Engineer	L	I	D
Architect	L	I	D	Machinist	L	I	D
Army Officer	L	I	D	Magazine Writer	L	I	D
Artist	L	I	D	Marine Engineer	L	I	D
Astronomer	L	I	D	Mechanical Engineer	L	I	D
Athletic Director	L	I	D	Missionary	L	I	D
Auctioneer	L	I	D	Musician	L	I	D
Auto Salesman	L	I	D	Newspaper Reporter	L	I	D
Auto Racer	L	I	D	Naval Officer	L	I	D
Auto Repairman	L	I	D	Novelist	L	I	D
Aviator	L	I	D	Office Clerk	L	I	D
Bank Teller	L	I	D	Office Manager	L	I	D
Baseball Player	L	I	D	Orchestra Conductor	L	I	D
Bookkeeper	L	I	D	Pharmacist	L	I	D
Building Contractor	L	I	D	Photographer	L	I	D
Carpenter	L	I	D	Physician	L	I	D
Cashier	L	I	D	Poet	L	I	D
Certified Public	L	I	D	Politician	L	I	D
Accountant				Printer	L	I	D
Chauffeur	L	I	D	Private Secretary	L	I	D
Chef	L	I	D	Railway Conductor	L	I	D
Chemist	L	I	D	Rancher	L	I	D
Civil Service Employee	L	I	D	Real Estate Salesman	L	I	D
Clergyman	L	I	D	Scientific Research Worker	L	I	D
Consul	L	I	D	Secret Service Man	L	I	D
Dentist	L	I	D	Ship Officer	L	I	D
Draftsman	L	I	D	Shop Foreman	L	I	D
Editor	L	I	D	Social Worker	L	I	D
explorer	L	I	D	Specialty Salesman	L	I	D
Factory Manager	L	I	D	Statistician	L	I	D
Factory Worker	L	I	D	Stock Broker	L	I	D
Farmer	L	I	D	Steeplejack	L	I	D
Fisherman	L	I	D	Street Car Conductor	L	I	D
Floorwalker	L	I	D	Street Car Motorman	L	I	D
Foreign Correspondent	L	I	D	Surgeon	L	I	D
Forest Ranger	L	I	D	Teacher	L	I	D
Gardener	L	I	D	Toolmaker	L	I	D
Hotel Keeper or Manager	L	I	D	Traveling Salesman	L	I	D
Interpreter	L	I	D	Typist	L	I	D
Judge	L	I	D	Watchmaker	L	I	D
Labor Arbitrator	L	I	D				
Landscape Gardener	L	I	D				
Lawyer	L	I	D				
Librarian	L	I	D				
Lighthouse Tender	L	I	D				

INTEREST ANALYSIS

PROFESSIONAL GROUPS

The information requested on this blank is to be held absolutely
confidential. The purpose of gathering it is to study the interests
of two groups of persons, those who are already established in a definite profession, and those who are in the process of selecting or
preparing for the same professions.

Below are a number of facts and questions, many of which may
seem foolish, but from just such items are often selected definite
indicators that have been of assistance in vocational guidance and
advice to those who are choosing their life work.

If you will co-operate by filling in all the requested material
we may find something that is worth while for further use.

PART I.
General

Name . . . . Date . . . .

Address . . . .

Profession . . . . If specialized, what branch . . . . .

Age . . . . . Nationality . . . .

How far had you gone in school when you chose your present profession?

. . . .

Did you make your decision independently? Yes--No. . . . .

Which influenced you most:- other persons, your own desires, circumstances?
(underline)

At what other occupations have you worked? . . . .

. . . .

If at more than one, which did you enjoy most? . . . .

Did you plan definitely on some other occupation as permanent before

deciding on the present one? Yes--No. What was it? . . . . . .

Father's occupation or profession. . . . .

Occupations of relatives whose work has interested you:

Relative . . . . Occupation

. . . .

. . . .

Draw a circle around one of the three letters after each of the items listed below indicating your interest as in the previous list. If you are in doubt as to your attitude use your own judgement as to your most frequent attitude.

Draw a circle around L if you like the item
Draw a circle around I if you are indifferent to it
Draw a circle around D if you dislike the item.

Draw a circle around one of the letters after every item.

Fat Men — L I D
Fat Women — L I D
Thin Men — L I D
Thin Women — L I D
Tall men — L I D
Tall Women — L I D
Short Men — L I D
Short Women — L I D
Blondes — L I D
Brunettes — L I D
Very old people — L I D
Children — L I D
Cripples — L I D
Side show freaks — L I D
People with gold teeth — L I D
People with receding foreheads — L I D
People with protruding jaws — L I D
Chinless people — L I D
People with hooked noses — L I D
Cross-eyed people — L I D
Blind people — L I D
Deaf mutes — L I D
Feeble people — L I D
People with eyes close together — L I D
Men who wear beards — L I D
Bowlegged people — L I D
Self-Conscious people — L I D
People slow making decisions — L I D
Very Polite — L I D
Progressive people — L I D
Conservative people — L I D
Energetic people — L I D
Absent-minded people — L I D
People with opinions opposite to your own — L I D
People less intelligent than you — L I D
People more intelligent than you — L I D
People who borrow things — L I D
Quick tempered people — L I D
Optimists — L I D
Pessimists — L I D
People who forgive very quickly — L I D
Grudge-holders — L I D
People who assume leadership — L I D
People easily led — L I D

Jealous people — L I D
Conceited people — L I D
People who have made fortunes in business — L I D
Forgetful people — L I D
Emotional people — L I D
Thrifty people — L I D
Spendthrifts — L I D
Stingy people — L I D
Talkative people — L I D
Religious people — L I D
Irrelious people — L I D
People who have done you favors — L I D
People for whom you have done favors — L I D
People who get rattled easily — L I D
Witty people — L I D
Educated people — L I D
Immoral people — L I D
Cautious people — L I D
Sick people — L I D
People who have no sense of humor — L I D
Nervous people — L I D
People who always agree with you — L I D
People who talk very loud — L I D
People who talk very low — L I D
People who talk very fast — L I D
People who talk very slow — L I D
People who talk about themselves — L I D
Methodical people — L I D
Fashionably dressed people — L I D
Carelessly dressed people — L I D
Southerners — L I D
New Englanders — L I D
Westerners — L I D
Missourians — L I D
Golf — L I D
Fishing — L I D
Professional Baseball — L I D
Tennis — L I D
Swimming — L I D
Football — L I D
Driving an automobile — L I D

Taking long walks — L I D
Checkers — L I D
Chess — L I D
Poker — L I D
Solitaire — L I D
Billiards — L I D
Dancing — L I D
Summer resorts — L I D
Amusement Parks — L I D
Picnics — L I D
Excursions — L I D
Smokers — L I D
Conventions — L I D
Pet animals — L I D
Pet dogs — L I D
Pet cats — L I D
Pet monkeys — L I D
Pet parrots — L I D
Pet canaries — L I D
Sporting pages — L I D
Love stories — L I D
Detective stories — L I D
Harold Bell Wright — L I D
"Life" — L I D
"Literary Digest" — L I D
"New Republic" — L I D
"System" — L I D
"National Geographic Magazine" — L I D
"American Mechanics" — L I D
"Popular Mechanics" — L I D
"Atlantic Monthly" — L I D
"Arts and Crafts" — L I D
William S. Hart — L I D
Charlie Chaplin — L I D
Mary Pickford — L I D
Douglas Fairbanks — L I D
Cowboy movies — L I D
Educational movies — L I D
Travel movies — L I D
Social problem movies — L I D
Serial movies — L I D
Vaudeville — L I D
Musical Comedy — L I D
Listening to a story — L I D
Telling a story — L I D
Being the butt of a joke — L I D
Arguments — L I D
Interviews — L I D
Working alone — L I D
Making a speech before a crowd — L I D
Opening a conversation with a stranger — L I D

Being left to yourself — L I D
Teaching — L I D
Organizing a play — L I D
Working with tools — L I D
Repairing electrical wiring — L I D
Cabinet making — L I D
Minor repairs, miscellaneous — L I D
Digging in the garden — L I D
Meeting and directing people — L I D
Taking responsibility — L I D
Methodical work — L I D
Meeting new situations — L I D
Adjusting difficulties of others — L I D
Regular hours for work — L I D
Continually changing activity — L I D
Living in the city — L I D
Living in the country — L I D
Sunday Blue Laws — L I D

When you were in school:

Art — L I D
Botany — L I D
Chemistry — L I D
Civics — L I D
Commercial subjects — L I D
Economics — L I D
English Composition — L I D
Geology — L I D
History — L I D
Languages, ancient — L I D
Languages, modern — L I D
Literature — L I D
Mathematics — L I D
Manual Training — L I D
Mechanical drawing — L I D
Music — L I D
Penmanship — L I D
Physics — L I D
Psychology — L I D
Physiology — L I D
Public Speaking — L I D
Shop work — L I D
Sociology — L I D
Spelling — L I D
Zoology — L I D

FIG. D-1 (continued). *The Cowdery Booklet (c. 1923).*

FIG. D-1 (continued). *The Cowdery Booklet (c. 1923).*

FIG. D-1 (continued). *The Cowdery Booklet (c. 1923).*

FIG. D-1 (continued). *The Cowdery Booklet (c. 1923).*

VOCATIONAL INTEREST BLANK

By EDWARD K. STRONG, JR.
Professor of Psychology, Stanford University
Copyright 1927 by STANFORD UNIVERSITY PRESS, Publishers

Group............

Key number............

Date............

It is possible with a fair degree of accuracy to determine by this test whether one would like certain occupations or not. The test is not one of intelligence or school work. It measures the extent to which one's interests agree or disagree with those of successful men in a given profession.

Your responses will, of course, be held strictly confidential.

Name............ Age............ Sex............

Occupation (e.g. Carpenter)............ Years of Experience............

Just what do you do?............

Name of Firm and Address............

Address to which correspondence should be sent............

Last grade reached in school (e.g. Grammar 6th, High School 2nd, College 4th)............

Did you select your present occupation or was it more or less thrust upon you? Selected it............ Thrust upon me............

What occupations, other than your present one, have you at one time or another engaged in?............

What occupations have you frequently day-dreamed of entering?............

Remarks............

Before turning the page record the time (e.g., 10 minutes after 3 o'clock)............

FIG. D-2 (next 4 pages). *The SVIB, Form A (1927)*.

Parts Ia and Ib. Occupations. Indicate after each occupation listed below whether you would like that kind of work or not. Disregard considerations of salary, social standing, future advancement, etc. Consider only whether you would like to do what is involved in the occupation.

Draw a circle around L if you like that kind of work.
Draw a circle around I if you are indifferent to that kind of work.
Draw a circle around D if you dislike that kind of work.

Work rapidly. Your first impressions are desired here. Answer all the items. Many of the seemingly trivial and irrelevant items are very useful in diagnosing your real attitude.

Occupation	L	I	D
Actor (not movie)	L	I	D
Advertiser	L	I	D
Architect	L	I	D
Army Officer	L	I	D
Artist	L	I	D
Astronomer	L	I	D
Athletic Director	L	I	D
Auctioneer	L	I	D
Author of novel	L	I	D
Author of technical book	L	I	D
Auto Salesman	L	I	D
Auto Racer	L	I	D
Auto Repairman	L	I	D
Aviator	L	I	D
Bank Teller	L	I	D
Bookkeeper	L	I	D
Building Contractor	L	I	D
Buyer of merchandise	L	I	D
Carpenter	L	I	D
Cartoonist	L	I	D
Cashier in bank	L	I	D
Certified Public Accountant	L	I	D
Chemist	L	I	D
Civil Engineer	L	I	D
Civil Service Employee	L	I	D
Clergyman	L	I	D
College Professor	L	I	D
Consul	L	I	D
Dentist	L	I	D
Draftsman	L	I	D
Editor	L	I	D
Electrical Engineer	L	I	D
Employment Manager	L	I	D
Explorer	L	I	D
Factory Manager	L	I	D
Factory Worker	L	I	D
Farmer	L	I	D
Floorwalker	L	I	D
Florist	L	I	D
Foreign Correspondent	L	I	D
Governor of a State	L	I	D
Hotel Keeper or Manager	L	I	D
Interior Decorator	L	I	D
Interpreter	L	I	D
Inventor	L	I	D
Jeweler	L	I	D
Judge	L	I	D
Labor Arbitrator	L	I	D
Laboratory Technician	L	I	D
Landscape Gardener	L	I	D
Lawyer, Criminal	L	I	D
Lawyer, Corporation	L	I	D
Librarian	L	I	D
Life Insurance Salesman	L	I	D
Locomotive Engineer	L	I	D
Machinist	L	I	D
Magazine Writer	L	I	D
Manufacturer	L	I	D
Marine Engineer	L	I	D
Mechanical Engineer	L	I	D
Mining Superintendent	L	I	D
Musician	L	I	D
Music Teacher	L	I	D
Office Clerk	L	I	D
Office Manager	L	I	D
Orchestra Conductor	L	I	D
Pharmacist	L	I	D
Photo Engraver	L	I	D
Physician	L	I	D
Playground Director	L	I	D
Poet	L	I	D
Politician	L	I	D
Printer	L	I	D
Private Secretary	L	I	D
Railway Conductor	L	I	D
Rancher	L	I	D
Real Estate Salesman	L	I	D
Reporter, general	L	I	D
Reporter, sporting page	L	I	D
Retailer	L	I	D
Sales Manager	L	I	D
School Teacher	L	I	D
Scientific Research Worker	L	I	D
Sculptor	L	I	D
Secretary, Chamber of Commerce	L	I	D
Secret Service Man	L	I	D
Ship Officer	L	I	D
Shop Foreman	L	I	D
Social Worker	L	I	D
Specialty Salesman	L	I	D
Statistician	L	I	D
Stock Broker	L	I	D
Surgeon	L	I	D
Toolmaker	L	I	D
Traveling Salesman	L	I	D
Typist	L	I	D
Undertaker	L	I	D
Watchmaker	L	I	D
Wholesaler	L	I	D
Worker in Y.M.C.A., K. of C., etc.	L	I	D

FIG. D-2 (continued). *The SVIB, Form A (1927)*.

410

Part II. Amusements. Indicate in the same manner as in Part I whether you like the following or not. If in doubt, consider your most frequent attitude. *Work rapidly.* Do not think over various possibilities. Record your first impression.

Golf
Fishing
Hunting
Tennis
Driving an automobile
Taking long walks
Boxing
Checkers
Chess
Poker
Bridge
Solitaire
Billiards
Observing birds (nature study)
Solving mechanical puzzles
Playing a musical instrument
Performing sleight-of-hand tricks
Collecting postage stamps
Chopping wood
Drilling in a company
Amusement parks
Picnics
Excursions
Smokers
"Rough house" initiations
Conventions
Full-dress affairs
Auctions
Fortune tellers
Animal zoos
Art galleries
Museums
Vaudeville
Musical comedy
Symphony concerts
Pet canaries
Pet monkeys
Snakes
Sporting pages
Poetry
Detective stories
"Literary Digest"
"Life"
"New Republic"
"System"
"National Geographic Magazine"
"American Magazine"
"Popular Mechanics"
"Atlantic Monthly"
"Arts and Crafts"
Cowboy movies
Educational movies
Travel movies
Social problem movies

FIG. D-2 (continued). *The SVIB, Form A (1927).*

Part III. School Subjects. Indicate as in Part II your interest when in school.

Algebra
Agriculture
Arithmetic
Art
Bible Study
Bookkeeping
Botany
Calculus
Chemistry
Civics
Dramatics
Economics
English Composition
Geography
Geology
Geometry
History
Languages, ancient
Languages, modern
Literature
Mathematics
Manual Training
Mechanical Drawing
Military Drill
Music
Nature Study
Penmanship
Philosophy
Physical Training
Physics
Physiology
Psychology
Public Speaking
Shop work
Shorthand
Sociology
Spelling
Typewriting
Zoology

Part IV. Activities. Indicate your interests as in Part II.

Work rapidly.

Repairing a clock
Making a radio set
Adjusting a carburetor
Repairing electrical wiring
Cabinetmaking
Operating machinery
Handling horses
Giving "first-aid" assistance
Raising flowers and vegetables
Decorating a room with flowers
Arguments
Interviewing men for a job
Interviewing prospects in selling
Interviewing clients
Making a speech
Organizing a play
Opening a conversation with a stranger
Teaching children
Teaching adults
Calling friends by nicknames
Meeting and directing people
Taking responsibility
Meeting new situations
Adjusting difficulties of others
Drilling soldiers
Pursuing bandits in sheriff's posse
Doing research work
Acting as yell-leader
Writing personal letters
Writing reports
Entertaining others
Bargaining ("swapping")
Looking at shop windows
Buying merchandise for a store
Displaying merchandise in a store
Expressing judgments publicly regardless of criticism
Being pitted against another as in a political or athletic race
Being left to yourself
Methodical work
Regular hours for work
Continually changing activities
Continuing at same work until finished
Studying latest hobby, e.g., Einstein theory, Freud, etc.
Developing business systems
Saving money
Contributing to charities
Raising money for a charity
Living in the city
Climbing along edge of precipice
Looking at a collection of rare laces
Looking at a collection of antique furniture

FIG. D-2 (continued). *The SVIB, Form A (1927).*

Part V. Peculiarities of People. Record your first impression. Do not think of various possibilities or of exceptional cases. "Let yourself go" and record the feeling that comes to mind as you read the item.

Progressive people
Conservative people
Energetic people
Absent-minded people
People who borrow things
Quick-tempered people
Optimists
Pessimists
People who are natural leaders
People who assume leadership
People easily led
People who have made fortunes in business
Emotional people
Thrifty people
Spendthrifts
Talkative people
Religious people
Irreligious people
People who have done you favors
People who get rattled easily
Gruff men
Witty people
Foreigners
Negroes
Cautious people
Sick people
Nervous people
Very old people
Cripples
Side-show freaks
People with gold teeth
People with protruding jaws
People with hooked noses
Blind people
Deaf mutes
Self-conscious people
People who always agree with you
People who talk very loudly
People who talk very slowly
People who talk about themselves
Methodical people
Fashionably dressed people
Carelessly dressed people
People who do not believe in evolution
Socialists
Bolshevists
Independents in politics
Teetotalers
Men who chew tobacco
Women cleverer than you are
Men who use perfume
People who chew gum
Athletic men

411

Part VI. *Order of Preference of Activities.* Indicate which three of the following ten activities you would enjoy most by checking opposite them in column one; also indicate which three you would enjoy least by checking opposite them in column two. Be sure to mark 3 in each column.

First 3 choices / Last 3 choices

( ) ( ) Develop the theory of operation of a new machine, e. g., auto
( ) ( ) Operate (manipulate) the new machine
( ) ( ) Discover an improvement in the design of the machine
( ) ( ) Determine the cost of operation of the machine
( ) ( ) Supervise the manufacture of the machine
( ) ( ) Create a new artistic effect, i.e., improve the beauty of the auto
( ) ( ) Sell the machine
( ) ( ) Prepare the advertising for the machine
( ) ( ) Teach others the use of the machine
( ) ( ) Interest the public in the machine through public addresses

Indicate in the same way what you consider are the three most important factors affecting your work; also the three least important factors. Be sure to mark 3 in each column.

Most important 3 factors / Least important 3 factors

( ) ( ) Salary received for work
( ) ( ) Steadiness and permanence of work
( ) ( ) Opportunity for promotion
( ) ( ) Courteous treatment from superiors
( ) ( ) Opportunity to make use of all of one's knowledge and experience
( ) ( ) Opportunity to ask questions and to consult about difficulties
( ) ( ) Opportunity to understand just how one's superior expects work to be done
( ) ( ) Certainty one's work will be judged by fair standards
( ) ( ) Freedom in working out one's own methods of doing the work
( ) ( ) Co-workers—congenial, competent, and adequate in number

Indicate in the same way the three men you would most like to have been; also the three you would least like to have been.

First 3 choices / Last 3 choices

( ) ( ) Luther Burbank, "plant wizard"
( ) ( ) Enrico Caruso, singer
( ) ( ) Thomas A. Edison, inventor
( ) ( ) Henry Ford, manufacturer
( ) ( ) Charles Dana Gibson, artist
( ) ( ) J. P. Morgan, financier
( ) ( ) J. J. Pershing, soldier
( ) ( ) William H. Taft, jurist
( ) ( ) Booth Tarkington, author
( ) ( ) John Wanamaker, merchant

Indicate in the same way the three positions you would most prefer to hold in club or society; also the three you least prefer to hold.

First 3 choices / Last 3 choices

( ) ( ) President of a Society
( ) ( ) Secretary of a Society
( ) ( ) Treasurer of a Society
( ) ( ) Member of a Society
( ) ( ) Chairman, Arrangement Committee
( ) ( ) Chairman, Educational Committee
( ) ( ) Chairman, Entertainment Committee
( ) ( ) Chairman, Membership Committee
( ) ( ) Chairman, Program Committee
( ) ( ) Chairman, Publicity Committee

FIG. D-2 (continued). *The SVIB, Form A (1927).*

Part VII. *Comparison of Interest between Two Items.* Indicate your choice of the following pairs by checking in the first space if you prefer the item to the left, in the second space if you like both equally well, and in the third space if you prefer the item to the right. Assume other things are equal except the two items to be compared.

Work rapidly.

( ) ( ) ( ) Street-car motorman — Street-car conductor
( ) ( ) ( ) Policeman — Fireman (fights fire)
( ) ( ) ( ) Chauffeur — Chef
( ) ( ) ( ) Head waiter — Lighthouse tender
( ) ( ) ( ) House to house canvassing — Retail selling
( ) ( ) ( ) House to house canvassing — Gardening
( ) ( ) ( ) Repair auto — Drive auto
( ) ( ) ( ) Develop plans — Execute plans
( ) ( ) ( ) Do a job yourself — Delegate job to another
( ) ( ) ( ) Persuade others — Order others
( ) ( ) ( ) Deal with things — Deal with people
( ) ( ) ( ) Plan for immediate future. — Plan for five years ahead
( ) ( ) ( ) Activity which produces tangible returns. — Activity which is enjoyed for its own sake
( ) ( ) ( ) Taking a chance. — Playing safe
( ) ( ) ( ) Definite salary — Commission on what is done
( ) ( ) ( ) Work for yourself — Carry out general program of superior who is respected
( ) ( ) ( ) Work which interests you with modest income — Work which does not interest you with large income
( ) ( ) ( ) Work in a large corporation with little chance of becoming president until age of 55. — Work for self in small business
( ) ( ) ( ) Selling article, quoted 10% below competitor — Selling article, quoted 10% above competitor
( ) ( ) ( ) Small pay, large opportunities to learn during next 5 years — Good pay, little opportunity to learn during next 5 years
( ) ( ) ( ) Work involving few details. — Work involving many details
( ) ( ) ( ) Outside work — Inside work
( ) ( ) ( ) Change from place to place. — Work in one location
( ) ( ) ( ) Great variety of work. — Similarity in work
( ) ( ) ( ) Physical activity — Mental activity
( ) ( ) ( ) Emphasis upon quality of work. — Emphasis upon quantity of work
( ) ( ) ( ) Technical responsibility (head of a department of 25 people engaged in technical, research work) — Supervisory responsibility (head of a department of 300 people engaged in typical business operation)
( ) ( ) ( ) Present a report in writing. — Present a report verbally
( ) ( ) ( ) Listening to a story. — Telling a story
( ) ( ) ( ) Playing baseball — Watching baseball
( ) ( ) ( ) Amusement where there is a crowd. — Amusement alone or with one or two others
( ) ( ) ( ) Nights spent at home. — Nights away from home
( ) ( ) ( ) Reading a book. — Going to movies
( ) ( ) ( ) Belonging to many societies. — Belonging to few societies
( ) ( ) ( ) Few intimate friends. — Many acquaintances
( ) ( ) ( ) Many women friends — Few women friends
( ) ( ) ( ) Fat men — Thin men
( ) ( ) ( ) Tall men — Short men
( ) ( ) ( ) Jealous people — Conceited people
( ) ( ) ( ) Jealous people — Spendthrifts
( ) ( ) ( ) People who talk very low — People who talk very loudly
( ) ( ) ( ) People who talk very fast. — People who talk very slowly

FIG. D-2 (continued). *The SVIB, Form A (1927).*

now and what you have done. Check in the *first* column ("Yes") if the item really describes you, in the *third* column ("No") if the item does not describe you, and in the *second* column (?) if you are not sure. (Be frank in pointing out your weak points, for selection of a vocation must be made in terms of them as well as your strong points.)

YES   ?   NO

- Usually start activities of my group
- Usually drive myself steadily (do not work by fits and starts)
- Win friends easily
- Usually get other people to do what I want done
- Usually liven up the group on a dull day
- Am quite sure of myself
- Accept just criticism without getting sore
- Have mechanical ingenuity (inventiveness)
- Have more than my share of novel ideas
- Can carry out plans assigned by other people
- Can discriminate between more or less important matters
- Am inclined to keep silent (reticent) in confidential and semi-confidential affairs
- Am always on time with my work
- Remember faces, names, and incidents better than the average person
- Can correct others without giving offense
- Able to meet emergencies quickly and effectively
- Get "rattled" easily
- Can write a concise, well-organized report
- Have good judgment in appraising values
- Plan my work in detail
- Follow up subordinates effectively
- Put drive into the organization
- Stimulate the ambition of my associates
- Show firmness without being easy
- Win confidence and loyalty
- Smooth out tangles and disagreements between people
- Am approachable
- Discuss my ideals with others

Worry considerably about mistakes	( )	( )	Worry very little ... Do not worry
Feelings easily hurt	( )	( )	Feelings rarely hurt
Usually ignore feelings of others	( )	( )	Consider them sometimes ... Carefully consider them
Loan money to acquaintances	( )	( )	Loan only to certain people ... Rarely loan money
Rebel inwardly at orders from another, obey when necessary	( )	( )	Carry out instructions with little or no feeling ... Enter into situation and enthusiastically carry out program
When caught in a mistake, usually make excuses	( )	( )	Seldom make excuses ... Practically never make excuses
Best-liked friends are superior to me in ability	( )	( )	Equal in ability ... Inferior in ability
Handle complaints without getting irritated	( )	( )	Become annoyed at times ... Lose my temper at times
Borrow frequently (for personal use)	( )	( )	Borrow occasionally ... Practically never borrow
Tell jokes well	( )	( )	Seldom tell jokes ... Practically never tell jokes
My advice sought by many	( )	( )	Sought by few ... Practically never asked
Frequently make wagers	( )	( )	Occasionally make wagers ... Never make wagers

Record the time when you finished this page.

Number of minutes required to fill out the blank.

Be Sure You Have Not Omitted Any Part; Note Particularly the Second Columns on Pages 2 and 4.

FIG. D-2 (continued). *The SVIB, Form A (1927).*

Occupation	A	Ad	B	B	CI	CPA	O	D	E	L	M	P	Psy	S
Ia														
Ib														
II														
III														
IV														
V														
VI														
VII														
VIII														
Total														
Rating														

Occupation	T	T-A	X	LI						
Ia										
Ib										
II										
III										
IV										
V										
VI										
VII										
VIII										
Total										
Rating										

FIG. D-2 (continued). *The SVIB, Form A (1927).*

413

VOCATIONAL INTEREST BLANK FOR MEN (Revised)

By EDWARD K. STRONG, JR.

Professor of Psychology, Stanford University

Published by Stanford University Press, Stanford University, California

It is possible with a fair degree of accuracy to determine by this test whether one would like certain occupations or not. The test is not one of intelligence or school work. It measures the extent to which one's interests agree or disagree with those of successful men in a given occupation.

Your responses will, of course, be held strictly confidential.

Date............

1. Name............
2. Age............
3. Sex............
4. Address to which correspondence should be sent............

If you are still attending school or expect to return to school, answer items 5–12; if you have left school, answer items 13–20. Any additional remarks may be entered at 21.

5. Grade I am now in: Grammar School 1 2 3 4 5 6 7 8   High School 1 2 3 4   College 1 2 3 4 5 6 7 (DRAW A CIRCLE AROUND APPROPRIATE CLASS)

6. School grade I expect to complete............
7. School subjects I am now most interested in............
8. School subjects I expect to specialize in later on............
9. Occupation I am planning to enter............
10. Sure of this............ Not sure............
11. Jobs I have been employed at (e.g., clerical, retail selling, farming, giving number of months employed at each)............
12. Occupations I have formerly considered entering............

To be Answered by Those Who Have Left School

13. Last grade you finished in school (e.g., Grammar 6th, High School 2nd, College 4th)............
14. What technical or business courses have you taken? (Underline those you finished)............
15. Occupation (e.g., Carpenter)............
16. Years of experience in it............
17. Just what do you do?............
18. Why did you select the above occupation?............
19. What occupations, other than your present one, have you at one time or another engaged in?............
20. What occupations, if any, have you in mind entering? Why?............
21. Remarks............

414

Part L. Occupations.

Indicate after each occupation listed below whether you would like that kind of work or not. Disregard considerations of salary, social standing, future advancement, etc. Consider only whether or not you would like to do what is involved in the occupation. You are not asked if you would take up the occupation permanently, but merely whether or not you would enjoy that kind of work, regardless of any necessary skills, abilities, or training which you may or may not possess.

Draw a circle around L if you like that kind of work
Draw a circle around I if you are indifferent to that kind of work
Draw a circle around D if you dislike that kind of work

Work rapidly. Your first impressions are desired here. Answer all the items. Many of the seemingly trivial and irrelevant items are very useful in diagnosing your real attitude.

No.	Occupation	L	I	D
1	Actor (not movie)	L	I	D
2	Advertiser	L	I	D
3	Architect	L	I	D
4	Army Officer	L	I	D
5	Artist	L	I	D
6	Astronomer	L	I	D
7	Athletic Director	L	I	D
8	Auctioneer	L	I	D
9	Author of novel	L	I	D
10	Author of technical book	L	I	D
11	Auto Salesman	L	I	D
12	Auto Racer	L	I	D
13	Auto Repairman	L	I	D
14	Aviator	L	I	D
15	Bank Teller	L	I	D
16	Bookkeeper	L	I	D
17	Building Contractor	L	I	D
18	Buyer of merchandise	L	I	D
19	Carpenter	L	I	D
20	Cartoonist	L	I	D
21	Cashier in bank	L	I	D
22	Certified Public Accountant	L	I	D
23	Chemist	L	I	D
24	Civil Engineer	L	I	D
25	Civil Service Employee	L	I	D
26	Clergyman	L	I	D
27	College Professor	L	I	D
28	Consul	L	I	D
29	Dentist	L	I	D
30	Draftsman	L	I	D
31	Editor	L	I	D
32	Electrical Engineer	L	I	D
33	Employment Manager	L	I	D
34	Explorer	L	I	D
35	Factory Manager	L	I	D
36	Factory Worker	L	I	D
37	Farmer	L	I	D
38	Floorwalker	L	I	D
39	Florist	L	I	D
40	Foreign Correspondent	L	I	D
41	Governor of a State	L	I	D
42	Hotel Keeper or Manager	L	I	D
43	Interior Decorator	L	I	D
44	Interpreter	L	I	D
45	Inventor	L	I	D
46	Jeweler	L	I	D
47	Judge	L	I	D
48	Labor Arbitrator	L	I	D
49	Laboratory Technician	L	I	D
50	Landscape Gardener	L	I	D
51	Lawyer, Criminal	L	I	D
52	Lawyer, Corporation	L	I	D
53	Librarian	L	I	D
54	Life Insurance Salesman	L	I	D
55	Locomotive Engineer	L	I	D
56	Machinist	L	I	D
57	Magazine Writer	L	I	D
58	Manufacturer	L	I	D
59	Marine Engineer	L	I	D
60	Mechanical Engineer	L	I	D
61	Mining Superintendent	L	I	D
62	Musician	L	I	D
63	Music Teacher	L	I	D
64	Office Clerk	L	I	D
65	Office Manager	L	I	D
66	Orchestra Conductor	L	I	D
67	Pharmacist	L	I	D
68	Photo Engraver	L	I	D
69	Physician	L	I	D
70	Playground Director	L	I	D
71	Poet	L	I	D
72	Politician	L	I	D
73	Printer	L	I	D
74	Private Secretary	L	I	D
75	Railway Conductor	L	I	D
76	Rancher	L	I	D
77	Real Estate Salesman	L	I	D
78	Reporter, general	L	I	D
79	Reporter, sporting page	L	I	D
80	Retailer	L	I	D
81	Sales Manager	L	I	D
82	School Teacher	L	I	D
83	Scientific Research Worker	L	I	D
84	Sculptor	L	I	D
85	Secretary, Chamber of Commerce	L	I	D
86	Secret Service Man	L	I	D
87	Ship Officer	L	I	D
88	Shop Foreman	L	I	D
89	Social Worker	L	I	D
90	Specialty Salesman	L	I	D

—2—

FIG. D-3 (next 4 pages). The SVIB, Form M (1938).

... consider your most frequent attitude. *Work rapidly.* Do not think over various possibilities. Record your first impression.

	L I D
91 Statistician	L I D
92 Stock Broker	L I D
93 Surgeon	L I D
94 Toolmaker	L I D
95 Traveling Salesman	L I D
96 Typist	L I D
97 Undertaker	L I D
98 Watchmaker	L I D
99 Wholesaler	L I D
100 Worker in Y.M.C.A., K. of C., etc.	L I D

Part II. School Subjects. Indicate as in Part 1 your interest when in school.

	L I D
101 Algebra	L I D
102 Agriculture	L I D
103 Arithmetic	L I D
104 Art	L I D
105 Bookkeeping	L I D
106 Botany	L I D
107 Calculus	L I D
108 Chemistry	L I D
109 Civics	L I D
110 Dramatics	L I D
111 Economics	L I D
112 English Composition	L I D
113 Geography	L I D
114 Geology	L I D
115 Geometry	L I D
116 History	L I D
117 Languages, ancient	L I D
118 Languages, modern	L I D
119 Literature	L I D
120 Mathematics	L I D
121 Manual Training	L I D
122 Mechanical Drawing	L I D
123 Military Drill	L I D
124 Music	L I D
125 Nature Study	L I D
126 Philosophy	L I D
127 Physical Training	L I D
128 Physics	L I D
129 Psychology	L I D
130 Physiology	L I D
131 Public Speaking	L I D
132 Shop work	L I D
133 Sociology	L I D
134 Spelling	L I D
135 Typewriting	L I D
136 Zoology	L I D

3

FIG. D-3 (continued). *The SVIB, Form M* (1938).

	L I D
137 Golf	L I D
138 Fishing	L I D
139 Hunting	L I D
140 Tennis	L I D
141 Driving an automobile	L I D
142 Taking long walks	L I D
143 Boxing	L I D
144 Chess	L I D
145 Poker	L I D
146 Bridge	L I D
147 Observing birds (nature study)	L I D
148 Solving mechanical puzzles	L I D
149 Performing sleight-of-hand tricks	L I D
150 Collecting postage stamps	L I D
151 Drilling in a company	L I D
152 Chopping wood	L I D
153 Amusement parks	L I D
154 Picnics	L I D
155 Excursions	L I D
156 Smokers	L I D
157 "Rough house" initiations	L I D
158 Conventions	L I D
159 Full-dress affairs	L I D
160 Auctions	L I D
161 Fortune tellers	L I D
162 Animal zoos	L I D
163 Art galleries	L I D
164 Museums	L I D
165 Vaudeville	L I D
166 Musical comedy	L I D
167 Symphony concerts	L I D
168 Pet canaries	L I D
169 Pet monkeys	L I D
170 Snakes	L I D
171 Sporting pages	L I D
172 Poetry	L I D
173 Detective stories	L I D
174 "Time"	L I D
175 "Judge"	L I D
176 "New Republic"	L I D
177 "System"	L I D
178 "National Geographic Magazine"	L I D
179 "American Magazine"	L I D
180 "Popular Mechanics"	L I D
181 "Atlantic Monthly"	L I D
182 Educational movies	L I D
183 Travel movies	L I D
184 Social problem movies	L I D
185 Making a radio set	L D

	L I D
186 Repairing a clock	L I D
187 Adjusting a carburetor	L I D
188 Repairing electrical wiring	L I D
189 Cabinetmaking	L I D
190 Operating machinery	L I D
191 Handling horses	L I D
192 Giving "first aid" assistance	L I D
193 Raising flowers and vegetables	L I D
194 Decorating a room with flowers	L I D
195 Arguments	L I D
196 Interviewing men for a job	L I D
197 Interviewing prospects in selling	L I D
198 Interviewing clients	L I D
199 Making a speech	L I D
200 Organizing a play	L I D
201 Opening conversation with a stranger	L I D
202 Teaching children	L I D
203 Teaching adults	L I D
204 Calling friends by nicknames	L I D
205 Being called by a nickname	L I D
206 Meeting and directing people	L I D
207 Taking responsibility	L I D
208 Meeting new situations	L I D
209 Adjusting difficulties of others	L I D
210 Drilling soldiers	L I D
211 Pursuing bandits in sheriff's posse	L I D
212 Doing research work	L I D
213 Acting as yell-leader	L I D
214 Writing personal letters	L I D
215 Writing reports	L I D
216 Entertaining others	L I D
217 Bargaining ("swapping")	L I D
218 Looking at shop windows	L I D
219 Buying merchandise for a store	L I D
220 Displaying merchandise in a store	L I D
221 Expressing judgments publicly regardless of criticism	L I D
222 Being pitted against another as in a political or athletic race	L I D
223 Methodical work	L I D
224 Regular hours for work	L I D
225 Continually changing activities	L I D
226 Developing business systems	L I D
227 Saving money	L I D
228 Contributing to charities	L I D
229 Raising money for a charity	L I D
230 Living in the city	L I D
231 Climbing along edge of precipice	L I D
232 Looking at a collection of rare laces	L I D
233 Looking at a collection of antique furniture	L I D

FIG. D-3 (continued). *The SVIB, Form M* (1938).

... tional cases. Let yourself go and record the feeling that comes to mind as you read the item.

	L I D
234 Progressive people	L I D
235 Conservative people	L I D
236 Energetic people	L I D
237 Absent-minded people	L I D
238 People who borrow things	L I D
239 Quick-tempered people	L I D
240 Optimists	L I D
241 Pessimists	L I D
242 People who are natural leaders	L I D
243 People who assume leadership	L I D
244 People easily led	L I D
245 People who have made fortunes in business	L I D
246 Emotional people	L I D
247 Thrifty people	L I D
248 Spendthrifts	L I D
249 Talkative people	L I D
250 Religious people	L I D
251 Irreligious people	L I D
252 People who have done you favors	L I D
253 People who get rattled easily	L I D
254 Gruff men	L I D
255 Foreigners	L I D
256 Sick people	L I D
257 Nervous people	L I D
258 Very old people	L I D
259 Cripples	L I D
260 Side-show freaks	L I D
261 People with gold teeth	L I D
262 People with protruding jaws	L I D
263 People with hooked noses	L I D
264 Blind people	L I D
265 Deaf mutes	L I D
266 Self-conscious people	L I D
267 People who always agree with you	L I D
268 People who talk very loudly	L I D
269 People who talk very slowly	L I D
270 People who talk about themselves	L I D
271 Fashionably dressed people	L I D
272 Carelessly dressed people	L I D
273 People who don't believe in evolution	L I D
274 Socialists	L I D
275 Bolshevists	L I D
276 Independents in politics	L I D
277 Men who chew tobacco	L I D
278 Men who use perfume	L I D
279 People who chew gum	L I D
280 Athletic men	L I D

Part VI. Order of Preference of Activities. Indicate which three of the following ten activities you would enjoy most by checking (√) opposite them in column 1; also indicate which three you would enjoy least by checking opposite them in column 3. Check the remaining four activities in column 2.

	1	2	3	
281	( )	( )	( )	Develop the theory of operation of a new machine, e.g., auto
282	( )	( )	( )	Operate (manipulate) the new machine
283	( )	( )	( )	Discover an improvement in the design of the machine
284	( )	( )	( )	Determine the cost of operation of the machine
285	( )	( )	( )	Supervise the manufacture of the machine
286	( )	( )	( )	Create a new artistic effect, i.e., improve the beauty of the auto
287	( )	( )	( )	Sell the machine
288	( )	( )	( )	Prepare the advertising for the machine
289	( )	( )	( )	Teach others the use of the machine
290	( )	( )	( )	Interest the public in the machine through public addresses

Indicate in the same way what you consider are the three most important factors affecting your work; also the three least important factors. Check the remaining four items in column 2. **Be sure you have marked three items under 1, three items under 3, and four items under 2.**

	1	2	3	
291	( )	( )	( )	Salary received for work
292	( )	( )	( )	Steadiness and permanence of work
293	( )	( )	( )	Opportunity for promotion
294	( )	( )	( )	Courteous treatment from superiors
295	( )	( )	( )	Opportunity to make use of all one's knowledge and experience
296	( )	( )	( )	Opportunity to ask questions and to consult about difficulties
297	( )	( )	( )	Opportunity to understand just how one's superior expects work to be done
298	( )	( )	( )	Certainty one's work will be judged by fair standards
299	( )	( )	( )	Freedom in working out one's own methods of doing the work
300	( )	( )	( )	Co-workers—congenial, competent, and adequate in number

Indicate in the same way the three men you would most like to have been; also the three you would least like to have been. Check the remaining four men in column 2.

	1	2	3	
301	( )	( )	( )	Luther Burbank, "plant wizard"
302	( )	( )	( )	Enrico Caruso, singer
303	( )	( )	( )	Thomas A. Edison, inventor
304	( )	( )	( )	Henry Ford, manufacturer
305	( )	( )	( )	Charles Dana Gibson, artist
306	( )	( )	( )	J. P. Morgan, financier
307	( )	( )	( )	J. J. Pershing, soldier
308	( )	( )	( )	William H. Taft, jurist
309	( )	( )	( )	Booth Tarkington, author
310	( )	( )	( )	John Wanamaker, merchant

Indicate in the same way the three positions you would most prefer to hold in club or society; also the three you would least prefer to hold. Check the remaining four in column 2.

	1	2	3	
311	( )	( )	( )	President of a Society or Club
312	( )	( )	( )	Secretary of a Society or Club
313	( )	( )	( )	Treasurer of a Society or Club
314	( )	( )	( )	Member of a Society or Club
315	( )	( )	( )	Chairman, Arrangement Committee
316	( )	( )	( )	Chairman, Educational Committee
317	( )	( )	( )	Chairman, Entertainment Committee
318	( )	( )	( )	Chairman, Membership Committee
319	( )	( )	( )	Chairman, Program Committee
320	( )	( )	( )	Chairman, Publicity Committee

Part VII. Comparison of Interest between Two Items. Indicate your choice of the following pairs by checking (√) in the first space if you prefer the item to the left, in the second space if you like both equally well, and in the third space if you prefer the item to the right. Assume other things are equal except the two items to be compared.

Work rapidly.

321	Street-car motorman	( ) ( ) ( )	Street-car conductor
322	Policeman	( ) ( ) ( )	Fireman (fights fire)
323	Chauffeur	( ) ( ) ( )	Chef
324	Head waiter	( ) ( ) ( )	Lighthouse tender
325	House to house canvassing	( ) ( ) ( )	Retail selling
326	House to house canvassing	( ) ( ) ( )	Gardening
327	Repair auto	( ) ( ) ( )	Drive auto
328	Develop plans	( ) ( ) ( )	Execute plans
329	Do a job yourself	( ) ( ) ( )	Delegate job to another
330	Persuade others	( ) ( ) ( )	Order others
331	Deal with things	( ) ( ) ( )	Deal with people
332	Plan for immediate future	( ) ( ) ( )	Plan for five years ahead
333	Activity which produces tangible returns	( ) ( ) ( )	Activity which is enjoyed for its own sake
334	Taking a chance	( ) ( ) ( )	Playing safe
335	Definite salary	( ) ( ) ( )	Commission on what is done
336	Work for yourself	( ) ( ) ( )	Carry out program of superior who is respected
337	Work which interests you with modest income	( ) ( ) ( )	Work which does not interest you with large income
338	Work in a large corporation with little chance of becoming president until age of 55	( ) ( ) ( )	Work for self in small business
339	Selling article, quoted 10% below competitor	( ) ( ) ( )	Selling article, quoted 10% above competitor
340	Small pay, large opportunities to learn during next 5 years	( ) ( ) ( )	Good pay, little opportunity to learn during next 5 years
341	Work involving few details	( ) ( ) ( )	Work involving many details
342	Outside work	( ) ( ) ( )	Inside work
343	Change from place to place	( ) ( ) ( )	Working in one location
344	Great variety of work	( ) ( ) ( )	Similarity in work
345	Physical activity	( ) ( ) ( )	Mental activity
346	Emphasis upon quality of work	( ) ( ) ( )	Emphasis upon quantity of work
347	Technical responsibility (head of a department of 25 people engaged in technical, research work)	( ) ( ) ( )	Supervisory responsibility (head of a department of 300 people engaged in typical business operation)
348	Present a report in writing	( ) ( ) ( )	Present a report verbally
349	Listening to a story	( ) ( ) ( )	Telling a story
350	Playing baseball	( ) ( ) ( )	Watching baseball
351	Amusement where there is a crowd	( ) ( ) ( )	Amusement alone or with one or two others
352	Nights spent at home	( ) ( ) ( )	Nights away from home
353	Reading a book	( ) ( ) ( )	Going to movies
354	Belonging to many societies	( ) ( ) ( )	Belonging to few societies
355	Few intimate friends	( ) ( ) ( )	Many acquaintances
356	Many women friends	( ) ( ) ( )	Few women friends
357	Fat men	( ) ( ) ( )	Thin men
358	Tall men	( ) ( ) ( )	Short men
359	Jealous people	( ) ( ) ( )	Conceited people
360	Jealous people	( ) ( ) ( )	Spendthrifts

Occupational Scoring Tables (FIG. D-3, Form M)

Occupation	Artist	Psychologist	Architect	Physician	Dentist	Mathematician	Engineer	Chemist	Production Manager	Farmer
Raw Score										
Standard Score										
Rating										

Occupation	Carpenter	Printer	Mathematics Science Teacher	Policeman	Forest Service	Y.M.C.A. Physical Director	Personnel	Y.M.C.A. General Secretary	Social Science Teacher	City School Superintendent
Raw Score										
Standard Score										
Rating										

Occupation	Minister	Musician	Certified Public Accountant	Accountant	Office Worker	Purchasing Agent	Banker	Sales Manager	Real Estate Salesman	Life Insurance Salesman
Raw Score										
Standard Score										
Rating										

Occupation	Advertising Man	Lawyer	Author-Journalist	President, Mfg Concern	Occupational Level	Masculinity-Femininity	Internal Maturity	Aviator
Raw Score								
Standard Score								
Rating								

Occupation										
Raw Score										
Standard Score										
Rating										

-8-

FIG. D-3 (continued). *The SVIB, Form M* (1938).

Part VIII. Rating of Present Abilities and Characteristics. Indicate below what kind of a person you are right now and what you have done. Check in the *first* column ("Yes") if the item really describes you, in the *third* column ("No") if the item does not describe you, and in the *second* column (?) if you are not sure. (Be frank in pointing out your weak points, for selection of a vocation must be made in terms of them as well as your strong points.)

YES ? NO

361 Usually start activities of my group
362 Usually drive myself steadily (do not work by fits and starts)
363 Win friends easily
364 Usually get other people to do what I want done
365 Usually liven up the group on a dull day

366 Am quite sure of myself
367 Accept just criticism without getting sore
368 Have mechanical ingenuity (inventiveness)
369 Have more than my share of novel ideas
370 Can carry out plans assigned by other people

371 Can discriminate between more or less important matters
372 Am inclined to keep silent (reticent) in confidential and semi-confidential affairs
373 Am always on time with my work
374 Remember faces, names, and incidents better than the average person
375 Can correct others without giving offense

376 Able to meet emergencies quickly and effectively
377 Get "rattled" easily
378 Can write a concise, well-organized report
379 Have good judgment in appraising values
380 Plan my work in detail

381 Follow up subordinates effectively
382 Put drive into the organization
383 Stimulate the ambition of my associates
384 Show firmness without being easy
385 Win confidence and loyalty

386 Smooth out tangles and disagreements between people
387 Am approachable
388 Discuss my ideals with others

Check (√) in the first, second, or third column at the right according as the first, second, or third statement in each item below applies to you.

(1st) (2nd) (3rd)

389 (1) Feelings easily hurt — (2) Feelings hurt sometimes — (3) Feelings rarely hurt
390 (1) Usually ignore the feelings of others — (2) Consider them sometimes — (3) Carefully consider them
391 (1) Loan money to acquaintances — (2) Loan only to certain people — (3) Rarely loan money
392 (1) Rebel inwardly at orders from another, obey when necessary — (2) Carry out instructions with little or no feeling — (3) Enter into situation and enthusiastically carry out program
393 (1) When caught in a mistake usually make excuses — (2) Seldom make excuses — (3) Practically never make excuses
394 (1) Best-liked friends are superior to me in ability — (2) Equal in ability — (3) Inferior in ability
395 (1) Handle complaints without getting irritated — (2) Become annoyed at times — (3) Lose my temper at times
396 (1) Borrow frequently (for personal use) — (2) Borrow occasionally — (3) Practically never borrow
397 (1) Tell jokes well — (2) Seldom tell jokes — (3) Practically never tell jokes
398 (1) My advice sought by many — (2) Sought by few — (3) Practically never asked
399 (1) Frequently make wagers — (2) Occasionally make wagers — (3) Never make wagers
400 (1) Worry considerably about mistakes — (2) Worry very little — (3) Do not worry

Be Sure You Have Not Omitted Any Part: Note Particularly the Second Columns on Pages 2, 3, and 4.

-7-

FIG. D-3 (continued). *The SVIB, Form M* (1938).

Form T399

STRONG VOCATIONAL INTEREST BLANK FOR MEN

by Edward K. Strong, Jr.

Revised by

Edward K. Strong, Jr.	David P. Campbell	Ralph F. Berdie	Kenneth E. Clark
Stanford University	University of Minnesota	University of Minnesota	University of Rochester

> It is possible with a fair degree of accuracy to determine by this inventory whether or not you would like certain occupations. This is not a test of intelligence or special abilities. It does measure the extent to which your interests agree or disagree with those of successful men in a given occupation.

Some of your instructions for completing this inventory may be given orally; pay close attention. Then read the following directions carefully:

1. With this question booklet, you should have a **special answer sheet or cards** on which to record your responses. **Make no marks at all on this booklet;** it will be used again by other people.

2. There are 399 items, or questions, in this booklet. Be sure there are spaces for only 399 items on your answer sheet or cards. (Older answer sheets had 400 question spaces; they should not be used with this booklet.)

3. If you have been given a special pencil, use it. If not, mark with any soft, black, lead pencil. **Make a heavy, dark mark**—not a cross or check mark.

4. If you make a mistake or change your mind, **erase carefully and thoroughly.** Do not fold or crease your answer sheet in any way.

5. **You should make one mark for each of the 399 questions.** If you omit items, or make more than one mark, your test cannot be scored. If you are not familiar with a particular item, guess how you might feel about it and mark accordingly.

6. The instructions change somewhat from part to part; read the instructions for each part carefully.

7. Read the instructions on your answer sheet or card. And be sure to fill in your name and the other information requested on your answer sheet or card. In some cases, it is necessary to code your name by marking spots representing each letter.

8. Work quickly; first impressions usually give the best results with this inventory.

STANFORD UNIVERSITY PRESS
Stanford, California

Part I. Occupations. For each occupation listed below, indicate whether you would like that kind of work or not. Don't worry about whether you would be good at the job or about your lack of training for it. Forget about how much money you could make or whether you could get ahead in it. Think only about whether you would like the work done in that job.

Mark on the answer sheet in the space labeled **"L"** if you **like** that kind of work.
Mark in the space labeled **"I"** if you are **indifferent** (that is, don't care one way or another).
Mark in the space labeled **"D"** if you **dislike** that kind of work.

Work fast. Put down the first thing that comes to mind. Answer every one.

1 Actor
2 Advertising Man
3 Architect
4 Military Officer
5 Artist

6 Astronomer
7 Athletic Director
8 Auctioneer
9 Author of novel
10 Author of technical book

11 Auto Salesman
12 Auto Racer
13 Auto Mechanic
14 Airplane Pilot
15 Bank Teller

16 Designer, Electronic Equipment
17 Building Contractor
18 Buyer of merchandise
19 Carpenter
20 Cartoonist

21 Cashier in bank
22 Electronics Technician
23 Chemist
24 Civil Engineer
25 City or State Employee

26 Minister, Priest, or Rabbi
27 College Professor
28 Foreign Service Man
29 Dentist
30 Draftsman

31 Editor
32 Electrical Engineer
33 Employment Manager
34 Geologist
35 Factory Manager

36 Income Tax Accountant
37 Farmer
38 Labor Union Official
39 Art Museum Director
40 Foreign Correspondent

41 Governor of a State
42 Hotel Manager
43 Interior Decorator
44 Interpreter
45 Inventor

46 Photographer
47 Judge
48 Labor Arbitrator
49 Laboratory Technician
50 Landscape Gardener

51 Lawyer, Criminal
52 Lawyer, Corporation
53 Librarian
54 Life Insurance Salesman
55 Locomotive Engineer

56 Machinist
57 Magazine Writer
58 Manufacturer
59 High School Principal
60 Professional Baseball Player

61 Mining Superintendent
62 Musician
63 Music Teacher
64 Psychologist
65 Office Manager

66 Orchestra Conductor
67 Pharmacist
68 Public Relations Man
69 Physician
70 Playground Director

71 Poet
72 Politician
73 Printer
74 Private Secretary
75 Radio Announcer

76 Rancher
77 Real Estate Salesman
78 Reporter, General
79 Reporter, Sports page
80 Retailer

81 Sales Manager
82 School Teacher
83 Scientific Research Worker
84 Sculptor
85 Manager, Chamber of Commerce

86 Secret Service Man
87 Computer Operator
88 Shop Foreman
89 Social Worker
90 Specialty Salesman

91 Statistician
92 Stockbroker
93 Surgeon
94 Toolmaker
95 Traveling Salesman

96 Travel Bureau Manager
97 Funeral Director
98 Watchmaker
99 Wholesaler
100 Worker in Y.M.C.A.

2

FIG. D-4. (next 4 pages). *The SVIB, Form T399 (1966).*

FIG. D-4 (continued). *The SVIB, Form T399 (1966).*

418

Part II. School Subjects. Show as you did in Part I your interest in these school subjects, even though you may not have studied them.

101 Algebra
102 Agriculture
103 Arithmetic
104 Art
105 Bookkeeping

106 Botany
107 Calculus
108 Chemistry
109 Civics (government)
110 Dramatics

111 Economics
112 English Composition
113 Geography
114 Geology
115 Geometry

116 History
117 Languages, ancient
118 Languages, modern
119 Literature
120 Mathematics

121 Industrial Arts
122 Mechanical Drawing
123 Military Drill
124 Bible History
125 Nature Study

126 Philosophy
127 Physical Education
128 Physics
129 Psychology
130 Physiology

131 Public Speaking
132 Shop Work
133 Sociology
134 Spelling
135 Typewriting

136 Zoology

Part III. Amusements. Show in the same way as you did before whether or not you like these ways of having fun. Work rapidly. Do not think over various possibilities. Record your first feeling of liking, indifference, or disliking.

137 Golf
138 Fishing
139 Hunting
140 Tennis

141 Sketching pictures of wild animals
142 Hiking
143 Boxing
144 Chess
145 Poker

146 Bridge
147 Bird watching
148 Solving mechanical puzzles
149 Religious music
150 Camping out

151 Drilling in a military company
152 Playing the piano
153 Amusement parks
154 Picnics
155 Sight-seeing trips

156 Stag parties
157 Jazz concerts
158 Conventions
159 Formal dress affairs
160 Electioneering for office

161 Going to church
162 Horseback riding
163 Art galleries
164 Leading a Boy Scout troop
165 Writing a one-act play

166 Science fiction magazines
167 Symphony concerts
168 Night clubs
169 Church young people's group
170 Biographies

171 Sports pages in newspapers
172 Poetry
173 Detective stories
174 Skiing
175 Planning a large party

176 Telling jokes
177 Business methods magazines
178 Travel magazines
179 Weekly news magazines
180 Popular mechanics magazines

181 Reading the Bible
182 Educational movies or TV
183 Magazines about art and music
184 Social problem movies
185 Making a radio or hi-fi set

Part IV. Activities. Indicate your interests as before.

186 Repairing a clock
187 Adjusting a carburetor
188 Repairing electrical wiring
189 Cabinetmaking
190 Operating machinery

191 Handling horses
192 Giving "first-aid" assistance
193 Raising flowers and vegetables
194 Decorating a room with flowers
195 Arguments

196 Interviewing men for a job
197 Interviewing prospects in selling
198 Interviewing clients
199 Making a speech
200 Organizing a play

201 Starting a conversation with a stranger
202 Teaching children
203 Teaching adults
204 Calling friends by nicknames
205 Being called by a nickname

206 Meeting and directing people
207 Taking responsibility
208 Making statistical charts
209 Adjusting difficulties of others
210 Drilling soldiers

211 Pursuing bandits in a sheriff's posse
212 Doing research work
213 Acting as cheer-leader
214 Being a forest ranger
215 Writing reports

216 Looking at things in a hardware store
217 Bargaining ("swapping")
218 Looking at things in a clothing store
219 Buying merchandise for a store
220 Displaying merchandise in a store

221 Expressing opinions openly, regardless of what others say
222 Competitive activities
223 Methodical work
224 Regular hours for work
225 Continually changing activities

226 Developing business systems
227 Saving money
228 Contributing to charities
229 Raising money for a charity
230 Living in the city

231 Climbing along the edge of a precipice
232 Discussing the purpose of life
233 Looking at a collection of antique furniture

Part V. Types of People. Show your feeling about these different kinds of people. Do not think of various possibilities or of exceptional cases. "Let yourself go" and record the feeling that comes to mind as you read each item.

234 Progressive people
235 Conservative people

236 Energetic people
237 Military men
238 Aggressive people
239 Beachcombers
240 Optimists

241 Pessimists
242 People who are natural leaders
243 People who assume leadership
244 Ballet dancers
245 People who have made fortunes in business

246 Emotional people
247 Thrifty people
248 Spendthrifts
249 Famous chefs
250 Religious people

251 Irreligious people
252 Easygoing people
253 Artistic men
254 Public opinion interviewers
255 Foreigners

256 Physically sick people
257 Babies
258 Very old people
259 Women athletes
260 Outspoken people with new ideas

261 Musical geniuses
262 People who daydream a lot
263 Prominent artists
264 Outstanding scientists
265 Acrobats

266 Democrats
267 Prohibitionists
268 Republicans
269 Men who perform on TV
270 People who insist on having everything in its proper place

271 Fashionably dressed people
272 Carelessly dressed people
273 People who don't believe in evolution
274 Socialists
275 Nonconformists

276 Independents in politics
277 Men who live dangerously
278 Prominent businessmen
279 Prominent labor union men
280 Athletic men

3

4

FIG. D-4 (continued). *The SVIB, Form T399 (1966).*

FIG. D-4 (continued). *The SVIB, Form T399 (1966).*

Part VI. Order of Preference of Activities. Here are ten things you could do. **First read all ten.** Then select the **three things** you think you would like **most** to do, and mark them in the **first row** on the answer sheet, next to their numbers. Select the **three things** you would like **least** to do, and mark them in the **third row**. Then **mark the remaining four items in the middle row** where no marks have been made so far. (Some answer sheets use columns instead of rows.)

281 Develop the theory of operation of a new machine (for example, an auto)
282 Operate (manipulate) the new machine
283 Discover an improvement in the design of the machine
284 Determine the cost of operation of the machine
285 Supervise the manufacture of the machine
286 Create a new artistic effect (that is, improve the beauty of the machine)
287 Sell the machine
288 Prepare the advertising for the machine
289 Teach others the use of the machine
290 Interest the public in the machine through public addresses

Show in the same way the three things that mean the most to you in a job; then the three least important things. Mark the four items left over in the middle row.

291 Salary received for work
292 Steadiness and permanence of work
293 Opportunity for promotion
294 Courteous treatment from superiors
295 Opportunity to make use of all one's knowledge and experience
296 Opportunity to ask questions and to consult about difficulties
297 Opportunity to understand just how one's superior expects work to be done
298 Certainty that one's work will be judged by fair standards
299 Freedom in working out one's own methods of doing the work
300 Co-workers—congenial, competent, and adequate in number

Show in the same way the three occupations you would like most; then the three you would like least. Mark the remaining four in the middle row.

301 Plant scientist—develops new vegetables and flowers
302 Opera singer
303 Inventor
304 Manufacturer
305 Nationally known artist
306 Banker, financier
307 General of the Army
308 Member of the Supreme Court
309 Author of "best seller"
310 Manager of large department store

Show in the same way the three offices you would like most to hold in a club or society; then mark the three you would like least to hold. Mark the four offices left over in the middle row.

311 President of a Society or Club
312 Secretary of a Society or Club
313 Treasurer of a Society or Club
314 Member of a Society of Club
315 Chairman, Arrangements Committee
316 Chairman, Educational Committee
317 Chairman, Entertainment Committee
318 Chairman, Membership Committee
319 Chairman, Program Committee
320 Chairman, Publicity Committee

Please check to see that in each set of ten questions you have three marks in the first row, three in the third row, and four in the middle row.

420

FIG. D-4 (continued). *The SVIB, Form T399 (1966)*

Part VII. Preference between Two Items. Show here which of two different kinds of work or ways of doing things you like better. If you prefer the items on the left, mark in the **first row**; if you prefer the items on the right, mark in the **third** row. If you like **both the same** or if you **can't decide** which one you like better, mark in the **middle row.** Work rapidly. Make one mark for each pair.

321 Airline pilot .... Airline ticket agent
322 Policeman .... Fireman (fights fire)
323 Taxicab driver .... Policeman
324 Head waiter .... Lighthouse keeper
325 Take dancing lessons .... Take singing lessons

326 Selling things house to house .... Gardening
327 Repaint autos .... Grease autos
328 Develop plans .... Execute plans
329 Do a job yourself .... Tell somebody to do the job
330 Talk others into doing something .... Order others to do something

331 Deal with things .... Deal with people
332 Plan for immediate future .... Plan for five years ahead
333 Activity that produces tangible returns .... Activity that is enjoyed for its own sake
334 Taking a chance .... Playing safe
335 Definite salary .... Commission on what is done

336 Work for yourself .... Carry out program of superior who is respected
337 Thrilling, dangerous activities .... Quieter, safer activities
338 Work in a large corporation with little chance of becoming president until age 55 .... Work for self in small business
339 Selling something for less than others sell it .... Selling something for more than others sell it
340 Travel alone and make own preparations .... Travel with someone else who makes all the decisions

341 Work with few details .... Work with many details
342 Outside work .... Inside work
343 Work in which you move from place to place .... Work where you stay in one place
344 Great variety of work .... Similarity in work
345 Physical activity .... Mental activity

346 Work in an import-export business .... Work in a research laboratory
347 Technical responsibility (in charge of 25 people doing scientific or technical work) .... Supervisory responsibility (in charge of 300 people in typical business work)
348 Present a report in writing .... Present a report verbally
349 Listening to a story .... Telling a story
350 Playing baseball .... Watching baseball

351 Amusement where there is a crowd .... Amusement alone or with one or two others
352 Music and art events .... Athletic events
353 Reading a book .... Watching TV or going to a movie
354 Plumber .... Electrician
355 A few close friends .... Many acquaintances

356 Superintendent of hospital .... Warden of a prison
357 Vocational counselor .... Public health officer
358 Travel to outer space .... Explore bottom of ocean
359 Dog trainer .... Juvenile parole officer
360 Appraise real estate .... Repair, restore antiques

6

FIG. D-4 (continued). *The SVIB, Form T390 (1966)*

A NOTE TO PROFESSIONAL USERS OF THE SVIB

The following comments are directed to counselors, personnel workers, and research psychologists.

In 1966, this revised version of the SVIB was published to bring the questions in the inventory up to date. Many items were slightly reworded, and some were changed substantially. During the revision, several occupational scales **were** added to the profile, and the scoring system was changed.

The revised scales correlate highly with the older scales, and the reliabilities and validities of the revised scales are essentially the same as those of the older scales.

A complete discussion of this revision can be found in the 1966 Manual for the Strong Vocational Interest Blank.

The revised booklet is designated Form T399 and contains 399 items. (The older booklet contained 400 items.) Instructions in this booklet emphasize that a 399-item answer sheet should be used with Form T399 to prevent confusion. Actually, during 1966–67, either the revised (399-item) answer sheet or the old (400-item) answer sheet can be used, as they can both be scored with the revised scales. However, new scales will soon be developed for the revised booklet, and for this reason the changeover to the new answer sheet should be made as quickly as possible.

> If the old answer sheet is used with the revised booklet, the instructor should ask the person being tested to ignore instruction (2) on the front page of this booklet, and to begin the **test** by marking the answer sheet as requested in the special boxed instruction at the bottom of page 7.

Unless specifically requested otherwise, scoring services will use the revised scales for all answer sheets. Under certain conditions, inventories completed before 1966 can be scored on both the old and the revised scales. Inventories completed after 1966—with the revised booklet—can be scored on the revised scales only. More detailed information is available in the Manual for the SVIB. If questions arise, consult your scoring service or the publisher.

FIG. D-4 (continued). *The SVIB, Form T399 (1966).*

Part VIII. Your Abilities and Characteristics. Show here what kind of person you are and the kinds of things you do. If the item really describes you, mark in the first row (**Yes**); if the item does **not** describe you mark in the third row (**No**); and if you are not sure mark in the second row (**?**). (Be frank in pointing out your weak points, because these are as important as your strong points in choosing a career.)

361 Usually start activities of my group
362 Make decisions immediately, not after considerable thought
363 Win friends easily
364 Usually get other people to do what I want done
365 Usually liven up the group on a dull day

366 Keep detailed records of expenses
367 Prefer working alone to working on committees
368 Have mechanical ingenuity (inventiveness)
369 Have more than my share of novel ideas
370 Can prepare successful advertisements

371 Am concerned about philosophical problems, for example, religion, meaning of life, etc.
372 My grades in high school were a fairly accurate reflection of my abilities
373 Am always on time with my work
374 Remember faces, names, and incidents better than the average person
375 Can correct others without giving offense

376 Am able to meet emergencies quickly and effectively
377 Do my best work early in the morning
378 Can write a concise, well-organized report
379 Have good judgment in appraising values
380 Plan my work in detail

381 Follow up subordinates effectively
382 Put drive into the organization
383 Stimulate the ambition of my associates
384 Can be firm and show I mean it
385 Am slow-going and sure rather than quick-moving

386 Can smooth out tangles and disagreements between people
387 Have patience when teaching others
388 Discuss my ideals with others

For each question, choose from the three phrases the one that **best** describes you. Then mark your choice on the answer sheet: **first** row if your choice is (1), **middle** row for (2), or **third** row for (3).

389 Pay attention to details	(1) Very little	(2) Somewhat	(3) Very much
390 Worry about mistakes	(1) A good deal	(2) Very little	(3) Never
391 Lend money to	(1) Acquaintances	(2) Only certain people	(3) Hardly anyone
392 When it comes to taking orders from others and carrying them out	(1) I dislike to	(2) I don't care	(3) I do it cheerfully
393 When caught in a mistake, I make excuses	(1) Usually	(2) Seldom	(3) Practically never
394 Speak	(1) More slowly than others	(2) About average	(3) Faster than others
395 Complaints annoy me	(1) Rarely	(2) Sometimes	(3) Quite a bit
396 In my family, I am the	(1) Oldest (or only) child	(2) Youngest	(3) Neither oldest nor youngest
397 At a large conference, I prefer a seat	(1) In first 3 rows	(2) Halfway back	(3) In rear of room
398 My advice is asked for	(1) By many	(2) By few	(3) By almost nobody
399 Make bets	(1) Often	(2) Sometimes	(3) Rarely

> **NOTE: If your answer sheet has room for 400 items, fill in ALL THREE answers to item number 400; then write very plainly somewhere on the edge of the answer sheet, "I used Booklet Form T399."**

7

FIG. D-4 (continued). *The SVIB, Form T399 (1966).*

Group..............

Key number..............

VOCATIONAL INTEREST BLANK FOR WOMEN

By EDWARD K. STRONG, JR.
Professor of Psychology, Stanford University

Published by Stanford University Press, Stanford, California

It is possible with a fair degree of accuracy to determine by this test whether one would like certain occupations or not. The test is not one of intelligence or school work. It measures the extent to which one's interests agree or disagree with those of successful women in a given occupation.

Your responses will, of course, be held strictly confidential.

Name.............. Age.............. Sex..............

Last grade reached in school (e.g., Grammar 6th, High School 2d, College 4th).............. Married.............. Single..............

Occupation (e.g., Nurse).............. Years of Experience in Occupation..............

Just what do you do?..............

Name of Firm and Address..............

Address to which correspondence should be sent..............

Did you select your present occupation or was it more or less thrust upon you? Selected it.............. Thrust upon me..............

What occupations, other than your present one, have you at one time or another engaged in?..............

What occupations have you frequently day-dreamed of entering?..............

Remarks..............

Before turning the page record the time (e.g., 10 minutes after 3 o'clock)..............

FIG. D-5 (next 4 pages). *The SVIB, Form WA* (1933).

Parts Ia, Ib, and Ic. Occupations. Indicate after each occupation listed below whether you would like that kind of work or not. Disregard considerations of salary, social standing, future advancement, etc. Consider only whether or not you should like to do what is involved in the occupation. You are not asked if you would take up the occupation permanently, but merely whether or not you would enjoy that kind of work, regardless of any necessary skills, abilities or training which you may or may not possess.

Draw a circle around L if you like that kind of work
Draw a circle around I if you are indifferent to that kind of work
Draw a circle around D if you dislike that kind of work

Work rapidly. Your first impressions are desired here. Answer all the items. Many of the seemingly trivial and irrelevant items are very useful in diagnosing your real attitude.

#	Occupation	L	I	D
1	Actress (movie)	L	I	D
2	Actress (stage)	L	I	D
3	Accountant	L	I	D
4	Advertiser	L	I	D
5	Architect	L	I	D
6	Artist	L	I	D
7	Artist's Model	L	I	D
8	Athletic Director	L	I	D
9	Author of Children's Books	L	I	D
10	Author of Novel	L	I	D
11	Author of Technical Book	L	I	D
12	Aviatrix	L	I	D
13	Bacteriologist	L	I	D
14	Bank Teller	L	I	D
15	Beauty Specialist	L	I	D
16	Biologist	L	I	D
17	Bookkeeper	L	I	D
18	Buyer of Merchandise	L	I	D
19	Cartoonist	L	I	D
20	Cashier	L	I	D
21	Caterer	L	I	D
22	Chemist	L	I	D
23	Civil Service Employee	L	I	D
24	College Professor	L	I	D
25	Companion (to elderly person)	L	I	D
26	Confectioner	L	I	D
27	Cook	L	I	D
28	Costume Designer	L	I	D
29	Dean of Women	L	I	D
30	Dentist	L	I	D
31	Dietitian	L	I	D
32	Draftsman	L	I	D
33	Dramatist	L	I	D
34	Dressmaker	L	I	D
35	Editor	L	I	D
36	Educational Director	L	I	D
37	Employment Manager	L	I	D
38	Factory Manager	L	I	D
39	Factory Worker	L	I	D
40	Farmer	L	I	D
41	Florist	L	I	D
42	Foreign Correspondent	L	I	D
43	Governess	L	I	D
44	Government Clerk	L	I	D
45	Governor of a State	L	I	D
46	Hostess	L	I	D
47	Hotel Manager	L	I	D
48	Housekeeper	L	I	D
49	Illustrator	L	I	D
50	Interior Decorator	L	I	D
51	Interpreter	L	I	D
52	Inventor	L	I	D
53	Judge	L	I	D
54	Laboratory Technician	L	I	D
55	Landscape Gardener	L	I	D
56	Lawyer, Corporation	L	I	D
57	Lawyer, Criminal	L	I	D
58	Librarian	L	I	D
59	Life Insurance Salesman	L	I	D
60	Magazine Writer	L	I	D
61	Manager, Women's Style Shop	L	I	D
62	Manikin	L	I	D
63	Manufacturer	L	I	D
64	Mechanical Engineer	L	I	D
65	Milliner	L	I	D
66	Minister	L	I	D
67	Missionary	L	I	D
68	Museum Director	L	I	D
69	Music Composer	L	I	D
70	Musician	L	I	D
71	Naturalist	L	I	D
72	Nurse, Graduate General	L	I	D
73	Nurse, Public Health	L	I	D
74	Office Clerk	L	I	D
75	Office Manager	L	I	D
76	Opera Singer	L	I	D
77	Pharmacist	L	I	D
78	Physician	L	I	D
79	Playground Director	L	I	D
80	Poet	L	I	D

FIG. D-5 (continued). *The SVIB, Form WA* (1933).

Part Ic. Occupations, continued.

81 Politician
82 Postmistress
83 Private Secretary
84 Probation Officer
85 Proof Reader
86 Professional Dancer
87 Psychiatrist
88 Psychologist
89 Publisher
90 Purchasing Agent
91 Radio Lecturer
92 Radio Program Director
93 Radio Singer
94 Real Estate Saleswoman
95 Registrar
96 Reporter, General
97 Reporter, Women's Page
98 Retailer
99 Sales Manager
100 Scenario Writer
101 Scientific Illustrator
102 Scientific Research Worker
103 Sculptress
104 School Principal
105 Secret Service Woman
106 Social Worker
107 Specialty Saleswoman
108 Statistician
109 Stenographer
110 Stock Broker
111 Surgeon
112 Teacher, Art
113 Teacher, Commercial
114 Teacher, Dancing
115 Teacher, Domestic Science
116 Teacher, Grade School
117 Teacher, High School
118 Teacher, Kindergarten
119 Teacher, Music
120 Tea Room Proprietor
121 Telephone Operator
122 Traveling Saleswoman
123 Typist
124 Vocational Counsellor
125 Waitress
126 Wholesaler
127 Wife
128 Y.W.C.A. Secretary

Part II. Amusements.
Indicate in the same manner as in Part I whether you like the following or not. If in doubt, consider your most frequent attitude. Work rapidly. Do not think over various possibilities. Record your first impressions.

129 Dancing
130 Swimming
131 Taking long walks
132 Tennis
133 Camping
134 Golf
135 Riding horses
136 Driving an automobile
137 Bridge
138 Poker
139 Afternoon teas
140 Observing birds (nature study)
141 Travel cross country in an auto
142 Solving mechanical puzzles
143 Playing a musical instrument
144 Amusement parks
145 Picnics
146 Conventions
147 Formal affairs
148 Fortune tellers
149 Animal zoos
150 Art galleries
151 Museums
152 Attending lectures
153 Musical comedy
154 Symphony concerts
155 Plays
156 Movies
157 Financial pages
158 Women's pages
159 Poetry
160 Romantic stories
161 Detective stories
162 Movie magazines
163 "American Magazine"
164 "Atlantic Monthly"
165 "Good Housekeeping" magazine
166 "House and Garden" magazine
167 "Ladies Home Journal"
168 "National Geographic Magazine"
169 "New Republic"
170 "Reader's Digest"
171 "True Story" magazine
172 "Vanity Fair"

Part III. Activities.
Indicate your interest as in Part II.

173 Being the first to wear the very latest fashions
174 Being head of a civic improvement program
175 Expressing judgments publicly, regardless of criticism
176 Giving "first-aid" assistance
177 Raising flowers and vegetables
178 Operating machinery
179 Repairing electrical wiring
180 Doing your own laundry work
181 Decorating a room with flowers
182 Arguments
183 Interviewing men for a job
184 Interviewing clients
185 Attending church
186 Making a speech
187 Cooking
188 Sewing
189 Organizing a play
190 Opening a conversation with a stranger
191 Preparing dinner for guests
192 Teaching children
193 Teaching adults
194 Discussions of economic affairs
195 Discussions of politics
196 Reading editorial columns
197 Meeting and directing people
198 Taking responsibility
199 Meeting new situations
200 Adjusting difficulties of others
201 Doing research work
202 Acting as yell-leader
203 Writing reports
204 Entertaining others
205 Writing personal letters
206 Buying at an auction sale
207 Trying new cooking recipes
208 Looking at shop windows
209 Displaying merchandise in a store
210 Being left to yourself
211 Regular hours for work
212 Continually changing activities
213 Saving money
214 Contributing to charities
215 Raising money for a charity
216 Looking at a collection of rare laces
217 Studying the latest hobby, e.g., Einstein's theory, Freud, etc.

Part IV. Peculiarities of People.
Record your first impression. Do not think of various possibilities or of exceptional cases. "Let yourself go" and record the feeling that comes to your mind as you read the item.

218 Progressive people
219 Conservative people
220 Energetic people
221 Absent-minded people
222 People who borrow things
223 Very self-confident people
224 Optimists
225 Pessimists
226 People who are natural leaders
227 People who assume leadership
228 Very intellectual people
229 Emotional people
230 Thrifty people
231 Religious people
232 Irreligious people
233 People who are unconventional
234 People who have done you favors
235 People who take life seriously
236 Witty people
237 Foreigners
238 Negroes
239 Cautious people
240 Sick people
241 People with physical disabilities
242 Self-conscious people
243 People who always agree with you
244 People who tell you their troubles
245 People who talk very loudly
246 People who talk about themselves
247 Methodical people
248 Fashionably dressed people
249 Carelessly dressed people
250 "Mannish" women
251 Socialists
252 Independents in politics
253 Men who are indifferent to you.
254 Nervous people
255 Very old people
256 Women cleverer than you are
257 People who chew gum
258 Men who drink
259 Women who smoke
260 Athletic women
261 People who take chances on situations of doubtful outcome
262 People who have made fortunes in business

FIG. D-5 (continued). The SVIB, Form WA (1933).

FIG. D-5 (continued). The SVIB, Form WA (1933).

Part V. Order of Preference of Activities. Indicate which three of the following ten activities you would enjoy most by checking (√) opposite them in column one; also indicate which three you would enjoy least by checking opposite them in column two. Be sure to mark 3 in each column.

264 ( ) ( ) Design a new home
265 ( ) ( ) Have responsibility for care of new home
266 ( ) ( ) Discover an improvement in the design of the house
267 ( ) ( ) Determine the cost of building and furnishing the house

268 ( ) ( ) Supervise the furnishing of the house
269 ( ) ( ) Plan the landscaping
270 ( ) ( ) Sell "ideal" houses
271 ( ) ( ) Prepare the advertising for new houses to be offered for sale

272 ( ) ( ) Teach others how to furnish their homes
273 ( ) ( ) Interest the public in building their own homes through public addresses

Indicate in the same way what you consider are the three most important factors affecting your work; also the three least important factors. Be sure to mark 3 in each column.

274 ( ) ( ) Salary received for work
275 ( ) ( ) Steadiness and permanence of work
276 ( ) ( ) Opportunities for promotion
277 ( ) ( ) Courteous treatment from superiors

278 ( ) ( ) Opportunity to make use of all of one's knowledge and experience
279 ( ) ( ) Opportunity to ask questions and to consult about difficulties
280 ( ) ( ) Opportunity to understand just how one's superior expects work to be done
281 ( ) ( ) Certainty one's work will be judged by fair standards

282 ( ) ( ) Freedom in working out one's own methods of doing the work
283 ( ) ( ) Co-workers—congenial, competent, and adequate in number

Indicate in the same way the three women you would most like to have been; also the three you would least like to have been.

284 ( ) ( ) Jane Addams, social worker
285 ( ) ( ) Ethel Barrymore, actress
286 ( ) ( ) Madame Curie, scientist
287 ( ) ( ) Amelia Earhart, aviatrix

288 ( ) ( ) Edna Ferber, author
289 ( ) ( ) Mrs. F. D. Roosevelt, "first lady"
290 ( ) ( ) Madame Schumann Heink, singer
291 ( ) ( ) Helen Wills Moody, tennis champion

292 ( ) ( ) Frances Perkins, U.S. Secretary of Labor
293 ( ) ( ) Lillian M. Gilbreth, industrial engineer

Indicate in the same way the three positions you would most prefer to hold in club or society; also the three you least prefer to hold.

294 ( ) ( ) President of a Society
295 ( ) ( ) Secretary of a Society
296 ( ) ( ) Treasurer of a Society
297 ( ) ( ) Member of a Society

298 ( ) ( ) Chairman, Arrangement Committee
299 ( ) ( ) Chairman, Educational Committee
300 ( ) ( ) Chairman, Entertainment Committee
301 ( ) ( ) Chairman, Membership Committee

302 ( ) ( ) Chairman, Program Committee
303 ( ) ( ) Chairman, Publicity Committee

FIG. D-5 (continued). *The SVIB, Form WA* (1933).

Part VI. Comparison of Interest between Two Items. Indicate your choice of the following pairs by checking (√) in the first space if you prefer the item to the left, in the second space if you like both equally well, and in the third space if you prefer the item to the right. Assume other things are equal except the two items to be compared.

Work rapidly.

304 ( ) ( ) ( ) Physical education director. ... Magazine writer
305 ( ) ( ) ( ) Statistician ... Social worker
306 ( ) ( ) ( ) Aviatrix ... Stenographer
307 ( ) ( ) ( ) Teacher ... Saleswoman

308 ( ) ( ) ( ) House to house canvassing ... Retail selling
309 ( ) ( ) ( ) Permanence of residence ... Frequent change of residence
310 ( ) ( ) ( ) Develop plans ... Execute plans
311 ( ) ( ) ( ) Do a job yourself ... Delegate job to another

312 ( ) ( ) ( ) Persuade others ... Order others
313 ( ) ( ) ( ) Evenings in company of women friends ... Evenings in company of men friends
314 ( ) ( ) ( ) Deal with things ... Deal with people
315 ( ) ( ) ( ) Many men friends ... Few men friends

316 ( ) ( ) ( ) Activity which produces tangible returns ... Activity which is enjoyed for its own sake
317 ( ) ( ) ( ) Preparing a meal ... Making a dress
318 ( ) ( ) ( ) Taking a chance ... Playing safe
319 ( ) ( ) ( ) Work for yourself ... Carry out general program of superior who is respected

320 ( ) ( ) ( ) Work which interests you with modest income ... Work which does not interest you with large income
321 ( ) ( ) ( ) Follow own career after marriage ... Follow home and social activities after marriage
322 ( ) ( ) ( ) Work involving few details ... Work involving many details
323 ( ) ( ) ( ) Be married with small income ... Be single and earn your own living

324 ( ) ( ) ( ) Working for men ... Working for women
325 ( ) ( ) ( ) Change from place to place ... Work in one location
326 ( ) ( ) ( ) Great variety of work ... Similarity in work
327 ( ) ( ) ( ) Physical activity ... Mental activity

328 ( ) ( ) ( ) Be married ... Remain single
329 ( ) ( ) ( ) Travel alone and make preparations for the trip yourself ... Travel with someone who will make the necessary preparations for you
330 ( ) ( ) ( ) Present a report in writing ... Present a report verbally
331 ( ) ( ) ( ) Listening to a story ... Telling a story

332 ( ) ( ) ( ) Do your own housework ... Have someone else do your housework
333 ( ) ( ) ( ) Amusement where there is a crowd ... Amusement alone or with one or two others
334 ( ) ( ) ( ) People who are slow in making decisions ... People who are quick in making decisions
335 ( ) ( ) ( ) People who are always prompt and expect others to be on time also ... People who are seldom on time and who do not mind if others are late

336 ( ) ( ) ( ) Nights spent at home ... Nights spent away from home
337 ( ) ( ) ( ) Reading a book ... Going to movies
338 ( ) ( ) ( ) Going to a play ... Going to a dance
339 ( ) ( ) ( ) Activities possessing thrills and uncertainties ... Activities of a conservative nature

340 ( ) ( ) ( ) Belonging to many societies ... Belonging to few societies
341 ( ) ( ) ( ) Few intimate friends ... Many acquaintances

FIG. D-5 (continued). *The SVIB, Form WA* (1933).

Occupation	Score	Rating

Group...........................

Key Number.....................

Part VIII. School Subjects. Indicate whether you liked the following or not when in school. Work rapidly. Do not think over various possibilities. Record your first impressions.

372 Algebra .... L I D
373 Arithmetic .... L I D
374 Art .... L I D
375 Bible Study .... L I D

376 Bookkeeping .... L I D
377 Botany .... L I D
378 Calculus .... L I D
379 Chemistry .... L I D

380 Civics .... L I D
381 Domestic Science .... L I D
382 Dramatics .... L I D
383 Education (teacher training).... L I D

384 Economics .... L I D
385 English Composition............ L I D
386 Geography .... L I D
387 Geology .... L I D

388 Geometry .... L I D
389 History .... L I D
390 Journalism .... L I D
391 Languages, Ancient............. L I D

392 Languages, Modern.............. L I D
393 Literature .... L I D
394 Mechanical Drawing .... L I D
395 Music .... L I D

396 Nature Study .... L I D
397 Penmanship .... L I D
398 Philosophy .... L I D
399 Physical Training .... L I D

400 Physics .... L I D
401 Physiology .... L I D
402 Political Science .... L I D
403 Psychology .... L I D

404 Public Speaking .... L I D
405 Shorthand .... L I D
406 Sociology .... L I D
407 Spelling .... L I D

408 Statistics .... L I D
409 Typewriting .... L I D
410 Zoölogy .... L I D

Record the time when you finished this page..........

Number of minutes required to fill out the blank..........

BE SURE YOU HAVE NOT OMITTED ANY PART OF THE BLANK.

FIG. D-5 (continued). *The SVIB, Form WA (1933).*

Part VII. Rating of Present Abilities and Characteristics. Indicate below what kind of a person you are right now and what you have done. Check in the first column ("Yes") if the item really describes you, in the third column ("No") if the item does not describe you, and in the second column (?) if you are not sure. (Be frank in pointing out your weak points, for selection of a vocation must be made in terms of them as well as your strong points.)

YES ? NO

342 Usually start activities of my group..................... ( ) ( ) ( )
343 Usually drive myself steadily (do not work by fits and starts)..... ( ) ( ) ( )
344 Win friends easily..................... ( ) ( ) ( )
345 Usually get other people to do what I want done..... ( ) ( ) ( )

346 Am quite sure of myself.............................. ( ) ( ) ( )
347 Usually liven up the group on a dull day................ ( ) ( ) ( )
348 Accept just criticism without getting sore.............. ( ) ( ) ( )
349 Have mechanical ingenuity (inventiveness)............... ( ) ( ) ( )

350 Can carry out plans assigned by other people........... ( ) ( ) ( )
351 Can discriminate between more or less important matters..... ( ) ( ) ( )
352 Am inclined to keep silent (reticent) in confidential and semi-confidential affairs..... ( ) ( ) ( )
353 Am always on time with my work......................... ( ) ( ) ( )

354 Remember faces, names, and incidents better than the average person..... ( ) ( ) ( )
355 Can correct others without giving offense.............. ( ) ( ) ( )
356 Able to meet emergencies quickly and effectively....... ( ) ( ) ( )
357 Get "rattled" easily................................... ( ) ( ) ( )

358 Can write a concise, well-organized report............. ( ) ( ) ( )
359 Have good judgment in appraising values................ ( ) ( ) ( )
360 Plan my work in detail................................. ( ) ( ) ( )
361 Stimulate the ambition of my associates................ ( ) ( ) ( )

362 Win confidence and loyalty............................. ( ) ( ) ( )
363 Smooth out tangles and disagreements between people..... ( ) ( ) ( )
364 Discuss my ideals with others.......................... ( ) ( ) ( )

Check (√) in the (a), (b) or (c) column at the right according as the (a), (b), or (c) statement in each item below applies to you.

365 (a) Worry considerably about mistakes   (b) Worry very little   (c) Do not worry..... (a) ( ) (b) ( ) (c) ( )

366 (a) Feelings easily hurt   (b) Feelings hurt sometimes   (c) Feelings rarely hurt..... ( ) ( ) ( )
367 (a) Usually ignore the feelings of others   (b) Consider them sometimes   (c) Carefully consider them..... ( ) ( ) ( )

368 (a) Loan money to acquaintances   (b) Loan only to certain people   (c) Rarely loan money..... ( ) ( ) ( )

369 (a) Borrow frequently for personal use   (b) Borrow occasionally   (c) Practically never borrow..... ( ) ( ) ( )

370 (a) Tell jokes well   (b) Seldom tell jokes   (c) Practically never tell jokes..... ( ) ( ) ( )
371 (a) Frequently make wagers   (b) Occasionally make wagers   (c) Practically never make wagers..... ( ) ( ) ( )

PLEASE TURN TO LAST PAGE.

FIG. D-5 (continued). *The SVIB, Form WA (1933).*

425

Group............ Key number............ Form W

VOCATIONAL INTEREST BLANK FOR WOMEN (Revised)

By EDWARD K. STRONG, JR.
Professor of Psychology, Stanford University
Published by STANFORD UNIVERSITY PRESS, Stanford University, California

It is possible with a fair degree of accuracy to determine by this test whether one would like certain occupations or not. The test is not one of intelligence or school work. It measures the extent to which one's interests agree or disagree with those of successful women in a given occupation.
Your responses will, of course, be held strictly confidential.

Date..............

1. Name..............................
2. Age.............. 3. Sex..............
4. Address to which correspondence should be sent..............................

If you are still attending school or expect to return to school, answer items 5–12; if you have left school, answer items 13–20.
Any additional remarks may be entered at 21.

5. Grade I am now in: Grammar School 1 2 3 4 5 6 7 8   High School 1 2 3 4   College 1 2 3 4 5 6 7
6. School grade I expect to complete..............................
7. School subjects I am now most interested in..............................
8. School subjects I expect to specialize in later on..............................
9. Occupation I am planning to enter.............. 10. Sure of this.............. Not sure..............
11. Jobs I have been employed at (e.g., clerical, retail selling, giving number of months employed at each)..............................
12. Occupations I have formerly considered entering..............................

To be Answered by Those Who Have Left School

13. Last grade you finished in school (e.g., Grammar 6th, High School 2nd, College 4th)..............................
14. What technical or business courses have you taken? Underline those you finished)..............................
15. Occupation (e.g., Nurse).............. 16. Years of experience in it..............
17. Just what do you do?..............................
18. Why did you select the above occupation?..............................
19. What occupations, other than your present one, have you at one time or another engaged in?..............................
20. What occupations, if any, have you in mind entering? Why?..............................

21. Remarks..............................

FIG. D-6 (next 4 pages). *The SVIB, Form W (1946).*

Parts Ia, Ib, and Ic. Occupations. Indicate after each occupation listed below whether you would like that kind of work or not. Disregard considerations of salary, social standing, future advancement, etc. Consider only whether or not you should like to do what is involved in the occupation. You are not asked if you would take up the occupation permanently, but merely whether or not you would enjoy that kind of work, regardless of any necessary skills, abilities or training which you may or may not possess.

Draw a circle around L if you like that kind of work
Draw a circle around I if you are indifferent to that kind of work
Draw a circle around D if you dislike that kind of work

Work rapidly. Your first impressions are desired here. Answer all the items. Many of the seemingly trivial and irrelevant items are very useful in diagnosing your real attitude.

1 Actress (movie)	L I D	41 Florist	L I D
2 Actress (stage)	L I D	42 Foreign Correspondent	L I D
3 Accountant	L I D	43 Governess	L I D
4 Advertiser	L I D	44 Government Clerk	L I D
5 Architect	L I D	45 Governor of a State	L I D
6 Artist	L I D	46 Hostess	L I D
7 Artist's Model	L I D	47 Hotel Manager	L I D
8 Athletic Director	L I D	48 Housekeeper	L I D
9 Author of Children's Books	L I D	49 Illustrator	L I D
10 Author of Novel	L I D	50 Interior Decorator	L I D
11 Author of Technical Book	L I D	51 Interpreter	L I D
12 Aviatrix	L I D	52 Inventor	L I D
13 Bacteriologist	L I D	53 Judge	L I D
14 Bank Teller	L I D	54 Laboratory Technician	L I D
15 Beauty Specialist	L I D	55 Landscape Gardener	L I D
16 Biologist	L I D	56 Lawyer, Corporation	L I D
17 Bookkeeper	L I D	57 Lawyer, Criminal	L I D
18 Buyer of Merchandise	L I D	58 Librarian	L I D
19 Cartoonist	L I D	59 Life Insurance Salesman	L I D
20 Cashier	L I D	60 Magazine Writer	L I D
21 Caterer	L I D	61 Manager, Women's Style Shop	L I D
22 Chemist	L I D	62 Manikin	L I D
23 Civil Service Employee	L I D	63 Manufacturer	L I D
24 College Professor	L I D	64 Mechanical Engineer	L I D
25 Companion (to elderly person)	L I D	65 Milliner	L I D
26 Confectioner	L I D	66 Minister	L I D
27 Cook	L I D	67 Missionary	L I D
28 Costume Designer	L I D	68 Museum Director	L I D
29 Dean of Women	L I D	69 Music Composer	L I D
30 Dentist	L I D	70 Musician	L I D
31 Dietitian	L I D	71 Naturalist	L I D
32 Draftsman	L I D	72 Nurse, Graduate General	L I D
33 Dramatist	L I D	73 Nurse, Public Health	L I D
34 Dressmaker	L I D	74 Office Clerk	L I D
35 Editor	L I D	75 Office Manager	L I D
36 Educational Director	L I D	76 Opera Singer	L I D
37 Employment Manager	L I D	77 Pharmacist	L I D
38 Factory Manager	L I D	78 Physician	L I D
39 Factory Worker	L I D	79 Playground Director	L I D
40 Farmer	L I D	80 Poet	L I D

FIG. D-6 (continued). *The SVIB, Form W (1946).*

Part Ic. Occupations, continued.

81	Politician	L	I	D
82	Postmistress	L	I	D
83	Private Secretary	L	I	D
84	Probation Officer	L	I	D
85	Proof Reader	L	I	D
86	Professional Dancer	L	I	D
87	Psychiatrist	L	I	D
88	Psychologist	L	I	D
89	Publisher	L	I	D
90	Purchasing Agent	L	I	D
91	Radio Lecturer	L	I	D
92	Radio Program Director	L	I	D
93	Radio Singer	L	I	D
94	Real Estate Saleswoman	L	I	D
95	Registrar	L	I	D
96	Reporter, General	L	I	D
97	Reporter, Women's Page	L	I	D
98	Retailer	L	I	D
99	Sales Manager	L	I	D
100	Scenario Writer	L	I	D
101	Scientific Illustrator	L	I	D
102	Scientific Research Worker	L	I	D
103	Sculptress	L	I	D
104	School Principal	L	I	D
105	Secret Service Woman	L	I	D
106	Social Worker	L	I	D
107	Specialty Saleswoman	L	I	D
108	Statistician	L	I	D
109	Stenographer	L	I	D
110	Stock Broker	L	I	D
111	Surgeon	L	I	D
112	Teacher, Art	L	I	D
113	Teacher, Commercial	L	I	D
114	Teacher, Dancing	L	I	D
115	Teacher, Domestic Science	L	I	D
116	Teacher, Grade School	L	I	D
117	Teacher, High School	L	I	D
118	Teacher, Kindergarten	L	I	D
119	Teacher, Music	L	I	D
120	Tea Room Proprietor	L	I	D
121	Telephone Operator	L	I	D
122	Traveling Saleswoman	L	I	D
123	Typist	L	I	D
124	Vocational Counsellor	L	I	D
125	Waitress	L	I	D
126	Wholesaler	L	I	D
127	Wife	L	I	D
128	Y.W.C.A. Secretary	L	I	D

Part II. Amusements. Indicate in the same manner as in Part I whether you like the following or not. If in doubt, consider your most frequent attitude. Work rapidly. Do not think over various possibilities. Record your first impressions.

No.	Amusement			
129	Dancing	L	I	D
130	Swimming	L	I	D
131	Tennis	L	I	D
132	Camping	L	I	D
133	Golf	L	I	D
134	Riding horses	L	I	D
135	Driving an automobile	L	I	D
136	Bridge	L	I	D
137	Poker	L	I	D
138	Afternoon teas	L	I	D
139	Observing birds (nature study)	L	I	D
140	Solving mechanical puzzles	L	I	D
141	Playing a musical instrument	L	I	D
142	Amusement parks	L	I	D
143	Picnics	L	I	D
144	Conventions	L	I	D
145	Formal affairs	L	I	D
146	Fortune tellers	L	I	D
147	Animal zoos	L	I	D
148	Art galleries	L	I	D
149	Museums	L	I	D
150	Attending lectures	L	I	D
151	Musical comedy	L	I	D
152	Symphony concerts	L	I	D
153	Plays	L	I	D
154	Movies	L	I	D
155	Financial pages	L	I	D
156	Women's pages	L	I	D
157	Poetry	L	I	D
158	Romantic stories	L	I	D
159	Detective stories	L	I	D
160	Movie magazines	L	I	D
161	"American Magazine"	L	I	D
162	"Atlantic Monthly"	L	I	D
163	"Good Housekeeping" magazine	L	I	D
164	"House and Garden" magazine	L	I	D
165	"Ladies Home Journal"	L	I	D
166	"National Geographic Magazine"	L	I	D
167	"New Republic"	L	I	D
168	"Reader's Digest"	L	I	D
169	"True Story" magazine	L	I	D
170	"Vanity Fair"	L	I	D

Part III. Activities. Indicate your interest as in Part II.

171	Being the first to wear the very latest fashions	L	I	D
172	Being head of a civic improvement program	L	I	D
173	Expressing judgments publicly, regardless of criticism	L	I	D
174	Giving "first-aid" assistance	L	I	D
175	Raising flowers and vegetables	L	I	D
176	Operating machinery	L	I	D
177	Repairing electrical wiring	L	I	D
178	Doing your own laundry work	L	I	D
179	Decorating a room with flowers	L	I	D
180	Arguments	L	I	D
181	Interviewing men for a job	L	I	D
182	Interviewing clients	L	I	D
183	Attending church	L	I	D
184	Making a speech	L	I	D
185	Cooking	L	I	D
186	Sewing	L	I	D
187	Organizing a play	L	I	D
188	Opening conversation with a stranger	L	I	D
189	Preparing dinner for guests	L	I	D
190	Teaching children	L	I	D
191	Teaching adults	L	I	D
192	Discussions of economic affairs	L	I	D
193	Discussions of politics	L	I	D
194	Reading editorial columns	L	I	D
195	Meeting and directing people	L	I	D
196	Taking responsibility	L	I	D
197	Meeting new situations	L	I	D
198	Adjusting difficulties of others	L	I	D
199	Doing research work	L	I	D
200	Acting as yell-leader	L	I	D
201	Writing reports	L	I	D
202	Entertaining others	L	I	D
203	Writing personal letters	L	I	D
204	Buying at an auction sale	L	I	D
205	Trying new cooking recipes	L	I	D
206	Looking at shop windows	L	I	D
207	Displaying merchandise in a store	L	I	D
208	Being left to yourself	L	I	D
209	Regular hours for work	L	I	D
210	Continually changing activities	L	I	D
211	Saving money	L	I	D
212	Contributing to charities	L	I	D
213	Raising money for a charity	L	I	D
214	Looking at a collection of rare laces	L	I	D
215	Studying the latest hobby, e.g., Einstein's theory, Freud, etc.	L	I	D

Part IV. Peculiarities of People. Record your first impression. Do not think of various possibilities or of exceptional cases. "Let yourself go" and record the feeling that comes to your mind as you read the item.

216	Conservative people	L	I	D
217	Energetic people	L	I	D
218	Absent-minded people	L	I	D
219	People who borrow things	L	I	D
220	Very self-confident people	L	I	D
221	Optimists	L	I	D
222	Pessimists	L	I	D
223	People who are natural leaders	L	I	D
224	People who assume leadership	L	I	D
225	Emotional people	L	I	D
226	Thrifty people	L	I	D
227	Religious people	L	I	D
228	Irreligious people	L	I	D
229	People who are unconventional	L	I	D
230	People who have done you favors	L	I	D
231	People who take life seriously	L	I	D
232	Foreigners	L	I	D
233	Negroes	L	I	D
234	Cautious people	L	I	D
235	Sick people	L	I	D
236	People with physical disabilities	L	I	D
237	Self-conscious people	L	I	D
238	People who tell you their troubles	L	I	D
239	People who talk about themselves	L	I	D
240	Methodical people	L	I	D
241	Fashionably dressed people	L	I	D
242	Carelessly dressed people	L	I	D
243	"Mannish" women	L	I	D
244	Socialists	L	I	D
245	Independents in politics	L	I	D
246	Men who are indifferent to you	L	I	D
247	Nervous people	L	I	D
248	Very old people	L	I	D
249	Teetotalers	L	I	D
250	People who chew gum	L	I	D
251	Men who drink	L	I	D
252	Women who smoke	L	I	D
253	Athletic women	L	I	D
254	People who take chances on situations of doubtful outcome	L	I	D
255	People who have made fortunes in business	L	I	D

FIG. D-6 (continued). *The SVIB, Form W (1946).*

FIG. D-6 (continued). *The SVIB, Form W (1946).*

Part V. Order of Preference of Activities. Indicate which three of the following ten activities you would enjoy most by checking (√) opposite them in column 1; also indicate which three you would enjoy least by checking opposite them in column 3. Check the remaining four activities in column 2.

	1	2	3
256 Design a new home	( )	( )	( )
257 Have responsibility for care of new home	( )	( )	( )
258 Discover an improvement in the design of the house	( )	( )	( )
259 Determine the cost of building and furnishing the house	( )	( )	( )
260 Supervise the furnishing of the house	( )	( )	( )
261 Plan the landscaping	( )	( )	( )
262 Sell "ideal" houses	( )	( )	( )
263 Prepare the advertising for new houses to be offered for sale	( )	( )	( )
264 Teach others how to furnish their homes	( )	( )	( )
265 Interest the public in building their own homes through public addresses	( )	( )	( )

Indicate in the same way what you consider are the three most important factors affecting your work; also the three least important factors. Check the remaining four items in column 2. Be sure you have marked three items under 1, three items under 3, and four items under 2.

	1	2	3
266 Salary received for work	( )	( )	( )
267 Steadiness and permanence of work	( )	( )	( )
268 Opportunities for promotion	( )	( )	( )
269 Courteous treatment from superiors	( )	( )	( )
270 Opportunity to make use of all of one's knowledge and experience	( )	( )	( )
271 Opportunity to ask questions and to consult about difficulties	( )	( )	( )
272 Opportunity to understand just how one's superior expects work to be done	( )	( )	( )
273 Certainty one's work will be judged by fair standards	( )	( )	( )
274 Freedom in working out one's own methods of doing the work	( )	( )	( )
275 Co-workers—congenial, competent, and adequate in number	( )	( )	( )

Indicate in the same way the three women you would most like to have been; also the three you would least like to have been. Check the remaining four women in column 2.

	1	2	3
276 Jane Aidams, social worker	( )	( )	( )
277 Ethel Barrymore, actress	( )	( )	( )
278 Madame Curie, scientist	( )	( )	( )
279 Amelia Earhart, aviatrix	( )	( )	( )
280 Edna Ferber, author	( )	( )	( )
281 Mrs. F. D. Roosevelt, "first lady"	( )	( )	( )
282 Madame Schumann Heink, singer	( )	( )	( )
283 Helen Wills Moody, tennis champion	( )	( )	( )
284 Frances Perkins, U.S. Secretary of Labor	( )	( )	( )
285 Lillian M. Gilbreth, industrial engineer	( )	( )	( )

Indicate in the same way the three positions you would most prefer to hold in club or society; also the three you least prefer to hold. Check the remaining four in column 2.

	1	2	3
286 President of a Society	( )	( )	( )
287 Secretary of a Society	( )	( )	( )
288 Treasurer of a Society	( )	( )	( )
289 Member of a Society	( )	( )	( )
290 Chairman, Arrangement Committee	( )	( )	( )
291 Chairman, Educational Committee	( )	( )	( )
292 Chairman, Entertainment Committee	( )	( )	( )
293 Chairman, Membership Committee	( )	( )	( )
294 Chairman, Program Committee	( )	( )	( )
295 Chairman, Publicity Committee	( )	( )	( )

FIG. D-6 (continued). The SVIB, Form W (1946).

Part VI. Comparison of Interest between Two Items. Indicate your choice of the following pairs by checking (√) in the first space if you prefer the item to the left, in the second space if you like both equally well, and in the third space if you prefer the item to the right. Assume other things are equal except the two items to be compared.

Work rapidly.

296 Physical education director	( )	( )	( )	Magazine writer
297 Statistician	( )	( )	( )	Social worker
298 Aviatrix	( )	( )	( )	Stenographer
299 Teacher	( )	( )	( )	Saleswoman
300 House to house canvassing	( )	( )	( )	Retail selling
301 Permanence of residence	( )	( )	( )	Frequent change of residence
302 Develop plans	( )	( )	( )	Execute plans
303 Do a job yourself	( )	( )	( )	Delegate job to another
304 Persuade others	( )	( )	( )	Order others
305 Evenings in company of women friends	( )	( )	( )	Evenings in company of men friends
306 Deal with things	( )	( )	( )	Deal with people
307 Many men friends	( )	( )	( )	Few men friends
308 Activity which produces tangible returns	( )	( )	( )	Activity which is enjoyed for its own sake
309 Preparing a meal	( )	( )	( )	Making a dress
310 Taking a chance	( )	( )	( )	Playing safe
311 Work for yourself	( )	( )	( )	Carry out program of superior who is respected
312 Work which interests you with modest income	( )	( )	( )	Work which does not interest you with large income
313 Follow own career after marriage	( )	( )	( )	Follow home and social activities after marriage
314 Work involving few details	( )	( )	( )	Work involving many details
315 Be married with small income	( )	( )	( )	Be single and earn your own living
316 Working for men	( )	( )	( )	Working for women
317 Change from place to place	( )	( )	( )	Work in one location
318 Great variety of work	( )	( )	( )	Similarity in work
319 Physical activity	( )	( )	( )	Mental activity
320 Be married	( )	( )	( )	Remain single
321 Travel alone and make preparations for the trip yourself	( )	( )	( )	Travel with someone who will make the necessary preparations for you
322 Present a report in writing	( )	( )	( )	Present a report verbally
323 Listening to a story	( )	( )	( )	Telling a story
324 Do your own housework	( )	( )	( )	Have someone else do your housework
325 Amusement where there is a crowd	( )	( )	( )	Amusement alone or with one or two others
326 People who are slow in making decisions	( )	( )	( )	People who are quick in making decisions
327 People who are always prompt and expect others to be on time also	( )	( )	( )	People who are seldom on time and who do not mind if others are late
328 Nights spent at home	( )	( )	( )	Nights spent away from home
329 Reading a play	( )	( )	( )	Going to movies
330 Going to a play	( )	( )	( )	Going to a dance
331 Activities possessing thrills and uncertainties	( )	( )	( )	Activities of a conservative nature
332 Belonging to many societies	( )	( )	( )	Belonging to few societies
333 Few intimate friends	( )	( )	( )	Many acquaintances

FIG. D-6 (continued). The SVIB, Form W (1946).

Part VII. Rating of Present Abilities and Characteristics. Indicate below what kind of a person you are right now and what you have done. Check in the first column ("Yes") if the item really describes you, in the third column ("No") if the item does not describe you, and in the second column (?) if you are not sure. (Be frank in pointing out your weak points, for selection of a vocation must be made in terms of them as well as your strong points.)

	YES	?	NO
334 Usually start activities of my group............................	( )	( )	( )
335 Usually drive myself steadily (do not work by fits and starts)	( )	( )	( )
336 Win friends easily	( )	( )	( )
337 Usually get other people to do what I want done................	( )	( )	( )
338 Am quite sure of myself.................................	( )	( )	( )
339 Usually liven up the group on a dull day.......................	( )	( )	( )
340 Have mechanical ingenuity (inventiveness)....................	( )	( )	( )
341 Can carry out plans assigned by other people.................	( )	( )	( )
342 Can discriminate between more or less important matters.......	( )	( )	( )
343 Am inclined to keep silent (reticent) in confidential and semi-confidential affairs	( )	( )	( )
344 Am always on time with my work...........................	( )	( )	( )
345 Remember faces, names, and incidents better than the average person	( )	( )	( )
346 Can correct others without giving offense....................	( )	( )	( )
347 Able to meet emergencies quickly and effectively.............	( )	( )	( )
348 Get "rattled" easily.......................................	( )	( )	( )
349 Can write a concise, well-organized report..................	( )	( )	( )
350 Have good judgment in appraising values...................	( )	( )	( )
351 Plan my work in detail..................................	( )	( )	( )
352 Stimulate the ambition of my associates....................	( )	( )	( )
353 Win confidence and loyalty..............................	( )	( )	( )
354 Smooth out tangles and disagreements between people........	( )	( )	( )
355 Discuss my ideals with others............................	( )	( )	( )

Check (√) in the (a), (b), or (c) column at the right according as the (a), (b), or (c) statement in each item below applies to you.

			(a)	(b)	(c)
356 (a) Worry considerably about mistakes	(b) Worry very little	(c) Do not worry............	( )	( )	( )
357 (a) Feelings easily hurt	(b) Feelings hurt sometimes	(c) Feelings rarely hurt......	( )	( )	( )
358 (a) Loan money to acquaintances	(b) Loan only to certain people	(c) Practically never borrow..	( )	( )	( )
359 (a) Borrow frequently (for personal use)	(b) Borrow occasionally	(c) Practically never tell jokes	( )	( )	( )
360 (a) Tell jokes well	(b) Seldom tell jokes	(c) Practically never tell jokes	( )	( )	( )
361 (a) Frequently make wagers	(b) Occasionally make wagers	(c) Practically never make wagers	( )	( )	( )

PLEASE TURN TO LAST PAGE

Part VIII. School Subjects. Indicate whether you liked the following or not when in school. Work rapidly. Do not think over various possibilities. Record your first impressions.

362 Algebra	L	I	D
363 Arithmetic	L	I	D
364 Art	L	I	D
365 Bible Study	L	I	D
366 Bookkeeping	L	I	D
367 Botany	L	I	D
368 Calculus	L	I	D
369 Chemistry	L	I	D
370 Civics	L	I	D
371 Domestic Science	L	I	D
372 Dramatics	L	I	D
373 Education (teacher training)	L	I	D
374 Economics	L	I	D
375 English Composition	L	I	D
376 Geography	L	I	D
377 Geology	L	I	D
378 Geometry	L	I	D
379 History	L	I	D
380 Journalism	L	I	D
381 Languages, Ancient	L	I	D
382 Languages, Modern	L	I	D
383 Literature	L	I	D
384 Mechanical Drawing	L	I	D
385 Music	L	I	D
386 Nature Study	L	I	D
387 Penmanship	L	I	D
388 Philosophy	L	I	D
389 Physical Training	L	I	D
390 Physics	L	I	D
391 Physiology	L	I	D
392 Political Science	L	I	D
393 Psychology	L	I	D
394 Public Speaking	L	I	D
395 Shorthand	L	I	D
396 Sociology	L	I	D
397 Spelling	L	I	D
398 Statistics	L	I	D
399 Typewriting	L	I	D
400 Zoology	L	I	D

Record the time when you finished this page............

Number of minutes required to fill out the blank............

BE SURE YOU HAVE NOT OMITTED ANY PART OF THE BLANK, ESPECIALLY THE SECOND HALF OF PART I.

FIG. D-6 (continued). *The SVIB, Form W (1946).*

DO NOT WRITE IN THIS COLUMN

Occupation	Score	Rating
Author		
Librarian		
Artist		
Physician		
Dentist		
Life Insurance Saleswoman		
Social Worker		
Teacher of English		
Teacher of Social Sciences		
Lawyer		
Y.W.C.A. Secretary		
Teacher of Math. and Phys. Sciences		
Nurse		
Housewife		
Femininity-Masculinity		
Elementary School Teacher		
Physical Education Teacher		
Dietitian		
Laboratory Technician		
Home Economics Teacher		
Psychologist		
Occupational Therapist		
Buyer		

Group............
Key Number............

FIG. D-6 (continued). *The SVIB, Form W (1946).*

STRONG VOCATIONAL INTEREST BLANK FOR WOMEN

By EDWARD K. STRONG, JR.

Revised by

David P. Campbell
University of Minnesota

> It is possible with a fair degree of accuracy to determine by this inventory whether or not you would like certain occupations. This is not a test of intelligence or special abilities. It does measure the extent to which your interests agree or disagree with those of successful women in a given occupation.

Some of your instructions for completing this inventory may be given orally; pay close attention. Then read the following directions carefully:

1. With this question booklet, you should have a **special answer sheet or cards** on which to record your responses. **Make no marks at all on this booklet**; it will be used again by other people.

2. There are 398 items, or questions, in this booklet. Be sure there are spaces for only 398 items on your answer sheet or cards. (Older answer sheets had 400 question spaces; they should not be used with this booklet.)

3. If you have been given a special pencil, use it. If not, mark with any soft, black, lead pencil. **Make a heavy, dark mark**—not a cross or check mark.

4. If you make a mistake or change your mind, **erase carefully and thoroughly.** Do not fold or crease your answer sheet in any way.

5. **You should make one mark for each of the 398 questions.** If you omit items, or make more than one mark, your test cannot be scored. If you are not familiar with a particular item, guess how you might feel about it and mark accordingly.

6. The instructions change somewhat from part to part; read the instructions for each part carefully.

7. Read the instructions on your answer sheet or card. And be sure to fill in your name and the other information requested on your answer sheet or card. In some cases, it is necessary to code your name by marking spots representing each letter.

8. Work quickly; first impressions usually give the best results with this inventory.

STANFORD UNIVERSITY PRESS
Stanford, California

Copyright 1933 by the Board of Trustees of the Leland Stanford Junior University.
Copyright renewed 1961 by Edward K. Strong, Jr. Copyright © 1946, 1966, and 1968,
by the Board of Trustees of the Leland Stanford Junior University.
Printed in the United States of America.

Part I. Occupations. For each occupation listed below, indicate whether you would like that kind of work or not. Don't worry about whether you would be good at the job or about your lack of training for it. Forget about how much money you could make or whether you could get ahead in it. Think only about whether you would like the work done in that job.

Mark on the answer sheet in the space labeled "L" if you **like** that kind of work.
Mark in the space labeled "I" if you are **indifferent** (that is, don't care one way or another).
Mark in the space labeled "D" if you **dislike** that kind of work.

Work fast. Answer every one.

1 Actress
2 Dental Assistant
3 Income Tax Accountant
4 Advertiser
5 Architect

6 Artist
7 Artist's Model
8 Athletic Director
9 Author of children's books
10 Author of novel

11 Author of technical book
12 Airplane Pilot
13 Bacteriologist
14 Bank Teller
15 Beauty Specialist

16 Biologist
17 Bookkeeper
18 Buyer of merchandise
19 Cartoonist
20 Cashier in bank

21 Caterer
22 Chemist
23 City or State Employee
24 College Professor
25 Computer Operator

26 Children's Clothes Designer
27 Cook
28 Costume Designer
29 Dean of Women
30 Dentist

31 Dietitian
32 Draftsman
33 Dramatist
34 Dressmaker
35 Editor

36 Educational Director
37 Employment Manager
38 Electronics Technician
39 Manager of children's nursery at resort hotel
40 Farmer

41 Florist
42 Foreign Correspondent
43 Supermarket Checkout Clerk
44 Hospital Records Clerk
45 Governor of a State

46 Hostess
47 Hotel Manager
48 Housekeeper
49 Illustrator
50 Interior Decorator

51 Interpreter
52 Inventor
53 Judge
54 Laboratory Technician
55 Landscape Gardener

56 Lawyer, Corporation
57 Lawyer, Criminal
58 Librarian
59 Life Insurance Saleswoman
60 Magazine Writer

61 Manager, Women's Style Shop
62 Fashion Model
63 Professional Golfer
64 Mechanical Engineer
65 Church Worker

66 Courtroom Stenographer
67 Missionary
68 Art Museum Director
69 Music Composer
70 Musician

71 News Photographer
72 Nurse
73 Policewoman
74 Office Clerk
75 Office Manager

76 Opera Singer
77 Pharmacist
78 Physician
79 Playground Director
80 Poet

81 Politician
82 Portrait Photographer
83 Private Secretary
84 Probation Officer
85 Nurse's Aid

86 Professional Dancer
87 Psychiatrist
88 Psychologist
89 Railroad Reservations Clerk
90 Veterinarian for small animals

FIG. D-7 (next 4 pages). *The SVIB, Form TW398.*

FIG. D-7 (continued). *The SVIB, Form TW398.*

91 Radio Announcer
92 Radio Program Director
93 Radio-TV Singer
94 Real Estate Saleswoman
95 Receptionist

96 Reporter, General
97 Reporter, Women's Page
98 Retailer
99 Sales Manager of large bookstore
100 Scenario Writer

101 Scientific Illustrator
102 Scientific Research Worker
103 Sculptor
104 School Principal
105 Secret Service Woman

106 Social Worker
107 Specialty Saleswoman
108 Statistician
109 Stenographer
110 Stewardess

111 Surgeon
112 Art Teacher
113 Business Teacher
114 Dancing Teacher
115 Home Economics Teacher

116 Grade School Teacher
117 High School Teacher
118 Kindergarten Teacher
119 Music Teacher
120 Tea Room Proprietress

121 Supervisor in telephone office
122 Travel Bureau Manager
123 Typist
124 Vocational Counselor
125 Waitress

126 Weather Forecaster
127 X-Ray Technician
128 Y.W.C.A. Staff Member

FIG. D-7 (continued). The SVIB, Form TW398.

Part II. Amusements. Show in the same way as you did before whether or not you like these ways of having fun. Work rapidly. Do not dwell over various possibilities. Record your first feeling of liking, indifference, or disliking.

129 Chess
130 Jazz concerts

131 Sketching pictures of wild animals
132 Camping out
133 Golf
134 Horseback riding
135 Looking at things in hardware store

136 Bridge
137 Planning a large party
138 Afternoon teas
139 Bird watching
140 Solving mechanical puzzles

141 Playing the piano
142 Amusement parks
143 Hiking
144 Conventions
145 Formal dress affairs

146 Telling jokes
147 Travel magazines
148 Art galleries
149 Religious music
150 Attending lectures

151 Popular mechanics magazines
152 Symphony concerts
153 Reading the Bible
154 Movies
155 Financial pages in newspapers

156 Women's pages
157 Poetry
158 Collecting antique furniture
159 Performing scientific experiments
160 Electioneering for office

161 Educational movies or TV
162 Magazines about art and music
163 Making a radio or hi-fi set
164 Leading a Girl Scout troop
165 Writing a one-act play

166 Science fiction magazines
167 Business methods magazines
168 Night clubs
169 Church young people's group
170 Biographies

Part III. Activities. Indicate your interests as before.

171 Being the first to wear the very latest fashions
172 Being head of a civic improvement program
173 Expressing judgments publicly, regardless of what others say
174 Giving "first aid" assistance
175 Raising flowers and vegetables

176 Operating machinery
177 Repairing electrical wiring
178 Doing your own laundry work
179 Decorating a room with flowers
180 Arguments

181 Interviewing men for a job
182 Interviewing clients
183 Going to church
184 Making a speech
185 Cooking

186 Sewing
187 Organizing a play
188 Starting a conversation with a stranger
189 Preparing dinner for guests
190 Teaching children

191 Teaching adults
192 Operating office machines
193 Discussions of politics
194 Reading editorial columns
195 Meeting and directing people

196 Taking responsibility
197 Taping a bruised ankle
198 Adjusting difficulties of others
199 Doing research work
200 Acting as cheer-leader

201 Writing reports
202 Entertaining others
203 Watching an open-heart operation
204 Checking typewritten material for errors
205 Trying new cooking recipes

206 Organizing cupboards and closets
207 Displaying merchandise in a store
208 Being left to yourself
209 Regular hours for work
210 Continually changing activities

211 Saving money
212 Contributing to charities
213 Raising money for a charity
214 Looking at a collection of rare laces
215 Making statistical charts

Part IV. Types of People. People tend to choose jobs where they can work with individuals they enjoy. Please indicate here your feelings about having day-to-day contact with the following types of people. Work fast—don't think of specific examples—give the first impression that comes to mind.

216 Highway construction workers
217 High school students
218 College Professors
219 Jet Pilots
220 Male Hairdressers

221 Corporation Executives
222 Girls who enter beauty contests
223 People who are natural leaders
224 Long-haul truck drivers
225 Emotional people

226 Thrifty people
227 Religious people
228 Housewives
229 Nonconformists
230 Famous chefs

231 Artistic men
232 Foreigners
233 Public opinion interviewers
234 Men who live dangerously
235 Physically sick people

236 Musical geniuses
237 People who daydream a lot
238 Outspoken people with new ideas
239 Racing car drivers
240 Outstanding scientists

241 Fashionably dressed people
242 Carelessly dressed people
243 Ballet dancers
244 Socialists
245 People who like to gamble

246 Athletic men
247 Babies
248 Very old people
249 Men who perform on TV
250 People who insist on having everything in its proper place

251 Prominent labor union men
252 Military men
253 Women athletes
254 People who don't believe in evolution
255 People who have made fortunes in business

Be sure to read instructions for Part V on next page.

FIG. D-7 (continued). The SVIB, Form TW398.

Part V. Order of Preference of Activities. Here are ten things you could do. **First read all ten.** Then select the **three things** you think you would like **most** to do, and mark them in the **first row** on the answer sheet, next to their numbers. Select the **three things** you would like **least** to do, and mark them in the **third row.** Then **mark the remaining four items in the middle row.** (Some answer sheets use columns instead of rows.)

256 Design a new home
257 Have responsibility for care of new home
258 Discover an improvement in the design of the house
259 Determine the cost of building and furnishing the house
260 Supervise the furnishing of the house
261 Plan the landscaping
262 Sell "ideal" houses
263 Prepare the advertising for new houses to be offered for sale
264 Teach others how to furnish their homes
265 Interest the public in building their own homes through public addresses

Show in the same way the three things that mean the most to you in a job; then the three least important things. Mark the four items left over in the middle row.

266 Salary received for work
267 Steadiness and permanence of work
268 Opportunity for promotion
269 Courteous treatment from superiors
270 Opportunity to make use of all of one's knowledge and experience
271 Opportunity to ask questions and to consult about difficulties
272 Opportunity to understand just how one's superior expects work to be done
273 Certainty one's work will be judged by fair standards
274 Freedom in working out one's own methods of doing the work
275 Co-workers—congenial, competent, and adequate in number

Show in the same way the three occupations you would like most; then the three you would like least. Mark the remaining four in the middle row.

276 President, Women's College
277 Author of best-selling novel
278 Outstanding opera singer
279 Owner-manager of chain of women's shops
280 World-renowned scientist
281 Tennis champion
282 Wife of U.S. President
283 Famous actress
284 Prominent artist
285 Supreme Court Justice

Show in the same way the three offices you would like most to hold in a club or society; then mark the three you would like least to hold. Mark the four offices left over in the middle row.

286 President of a Society
287 Secretary of a Society
288 Treasurer of a Society
289 Member of a Society
290 Chairman, Arrangement Committee
291 Chairman, Educational Committee
292 Chairman, Entertainment Committee
293 Chairman, Membership Committee
294 Chairman, Program Committee
295 Chairman, Publicity Committee

Please check to see that in each set of ten questions you have three marks in the first row, three in the third row, and four in the middle row.

Part VI. Preference between Two Items. Show here which of two different kinds of work or ways of doing things you like better. If you prefer the items on the left, mark in the **first row**; if you prefer the items on the **right**, mark in the **third row.** If you like **both the same** or if you **can't decide** which one you like better, mark in the **middle row.** Work rapidly. Make one mark for each pair.

296 Physical education director .... Magazine writer
297 Statistician .... Social worker
298 Airplane pilot .... Stenographer
299 Teacher .... Saleswoman
300 House-to-house canvassing .... Retail selling

301 Take dancing lessons .... Take singing lessons
302 Develop plans .... Execute plans
303 Do a job yourself .... Tell somebody to do job
304 Talk others into doing something .... Order others to do something
305 Keep books on household finances .... Recover furniture

306 Deal with things .... Deal with people
307 Fashion magazines .... Household magazines
308 Activity which produces tangible returns .... Activity which is enjoyed for its own sake
309 Preparing a meal .... Making a dress
310 Taking a chance .... Playing safe

311 Work for yourself .... Carry out program of superior who is respected
312 Experiment with new beauty preparations .... Experiment with new office equipment
313 Follow own career after marriage .... Follow home and social activities after marriage
314 Work with few details .... Work with many details
315 Be married with small income .... Be single and earn your own living

316 Working for men .... Working for women
317 Work in which you move from place to place .... Work where you stay in one place
318 Great variety of work .... Similarity in work
319 Physical activity .... Mental activity
320 Be married to a research scientist .... Be married to a sales executive

321 Travel alone and make own preparations .... Travel with someone who makes all the decisions
322 Present a report in writing .... Present a report verbally
323 Listening to a story .... Telling a story
324 Do your own housework .... Have someone else do your housework
325 Amusement where there is a crowd .... Amusement alone or with one or two others

326 Work in an import-export business .... Work in a research laboratory
327 Spend a great deal of time on make-up before going out .... Go out without make-up
328 Be married to a rancher .... Be married to a corporation president
329 Reading a book .... Watching TV or going to a movie
330 Going to a play .... Going to a dance

331 Thrilling, dangerous activities .... Quieter, safer activities
332 Display merchandise in store window .... Arrange table settings for large banquet
333 A few close friends .... Many acquaintances

FIG. D-7 (continued). *The SVIB, Form TW398.*

FIG. D-7 (continued). *The SVIB, Form TW398.*

Part VII. Your Abilities and Characteristics. Show here what kind of person you are and the kinds of things you do. If the item really describes you, mark in the first row (**Yes**); if the item does **not** describe you mark in the third row (**No**); and if you are not sure mark in the second row (**?**). (Be frank in pointing out your weak points, because these are as important as your strong points in choosing a career.)

334 Usually start activities of my group
335 Have more than my share of novel ideas

336 Win friends easily
337 Usually get other people to do what I want done
338 Keep detailed records of expenses
339 Usually liven up the group on a dull day
340 Have mechanical ingenuity (inventiveness)

341 Prefer working alone to working on committees
342 Do my best work early in the morning
343 Can prepare successful advertisements
344 Am always on time with my work
345 Remember faces, names, and incidents better than the average person

346 Can correct others without giving offense
347 Able to meet emergencies quickly and effectively
348 My grades in high school were a fairly accurate reflection of my abilities
349 Can write a concise, well-organized report
350 Have good judgment in appraising values

351 Plan my work in detail
352 Stimulate the ambition of my associates
353 Enjoy tinkering with small hand tools
354 Can smooth out tangles and disagreements between people
355 Discuss my ideals with others

For each question, choose from the three phrases the one that **best** describes you. Then mark your choice on the answer sheet: **first** row if your choice is (1), **middle** row for (2), or **third** row for (3).

356 Worry about mistakes	(1) A good deal	(2) Very little	(3) Never
357 Complaints annoy me	(1) Rarely	(2) Sometimes	(3) Quite a bit
358 Lend money to	(1) Acquaintances	(2) Only certain people	(3) Hardly anyone
359 In my family, I am the	(1) Oldest (or only) child	(2) Youngest	(3) Neither youngest nor oldest
360 At a large conference, I prefer a seat	(1) In first 3 rows	(2) Half-way back	(3) In rear of room
361 Make bets	(1) Often	(2) Sometimes	(3) Rarely

PLEASE!

DON'T STOP

There's more on back page

Part VIII. School Subjects. Show as before your interest in these school subjects, even though you may not have studied them.

362 Algebra
363 Arithmetic
364 Art
365 Bible History

366 Bookkeeping
367 Botany
368 Calculus
369 Chemistry
370 Civics (government)

371 Home Economics
372 Dramatics
373 Education (teacher training)
374 Economics
375 English Composition

376 Geography
377 Geology
378 Geometry
379 History
380 Journalism

381 Ancient Languages
382 Modern Languages
383 Literature
384 Mechanical Drawing
385 Woodworking

386 Nature Study
387 Penmanship
388 Philosophy
389 Physical Education
390 Physics

391 Physiology
392 Political Science
393 Psychology
394 Public Speaking
395 Shorthand

396 Sociology
397 Spelling
398 Statistics

NOTE: If your answer sheet has room for 400 items, please fill in ALL THREE answers to item 399.

FIG. D-7 (continued). *The SVIB, Form TW398.*

FIG. D-7 (continued). *The SVIB, Form TW398.*

433

TABLE D-1. INSTRUCTIONS FOR CONVERTING ANSWERS TO MEN'S BOOKLET FORM A TO FORM M ORDER

Instructions for Converting Answers to Men's Booklet Form A to Form M Order

Form A of the SVIB had 420 items, Form M had 400, all of which were included in Form A, but in a different order. The transposition task is complicated because the items in Form A were not numbered. By following these instructions exactly, an individual's answers to the Form A booklet can be converted to the Form M order. These instructions assume the researcher is transferring by hand an individual's answers from a Form A booklet to a separate answer sheet. The same steps could, of course, be performed by a computer.

Section I

1. Record the first 100 answers in the exact order given

Section II

1. Skip to answer position 137 on the answer sheet and record the next seven responses, 137-143, in order. (These will be responses #101-107 on the Form A booklet.

2. Skip the response to the item "Checkers"

3. Record next three responses in positions 144, 145, and 146. (Here, and in all following steps, do not skip any numbers on the answer sheet when skipping items in the booklet.)

4. Skip response to "Solitaire" and "Billiards"

5. Record next responses in 147, 148.

6. Skip response to "Playing a musical instrument"

7. Record next responses in 149-181.

8. Skip responses to "Arts and Crafts" and "Cowboy Music"

9. Record next responses in 182-184.

10. In position 185 on the answer sheet, record individual's response to the second item in part IV, "Making a radio set."

Section III

1. Continue on in booklet, but go back to position 101 on the answer sheet.

2. Record next responses in 101-104.

3. Skip response to "Bible study"

4. Record next responses in 105-125.

5. Skip response to "Penmanship."

6. Record next responses in 126-132.

7. Skip response to "Shorthand"

8. Record next responses in 133-36.

Section IV

2. Record next response in position 186.

3. Skip response to "Making a radio set" (This response has already been entered in position 185)

4. Record next responses in 187-222.

5. Skip response to "Being left to yourself"

6. Record next responses in 223-225.

7. Skip responses to "Continuing at same work until finished" "studying latest hobby"

8. Record next responses in 226-233.

Section V

1. Record next responses in 234-254.

2. Skip response to "Witty people."

3. Record next response in 255.

4. Skip responses to "Negroes" and "Cautious people."

5. Record next responses in 256-270.

6. Skip response to "Methodical people."

7. Record next responses in 271-276.

8. Skip response to "Teetotalers."

9. Record next response in 277.

10. Skip response to "Women cleverer than you."

11. Record next responses in 278-280.

Section VI

1. Record next responses in 281-320. In this section, the responses to the left are to be treated as "Like" responses, those to the right as "Dislike" response. When an item has been left blank, the "Indifferent" response position on the answer sheet should be filled in.

Section VII

1. Record next responses in 321-360.

2. Skip response to "People who talk very low" "People who talk very fast"

Section VIII

1. Record next responses in 361-388.

2. Record response to next item, "Worry considerably about mistakes" in response position 400.

3. Record next responses in 389-399.

TABLE D-2. ITEM CHANGES BETWEEN MEN'S BOOKLETS FORM M AND FORM T399

Item Number	SVIB Form M	SVIB Form T399	Item Number	SVIB Form M	SVIB Form T399
16	Bookkeeper	Designer, Electronic Equipment	164	Museums	Leading a Boy Scout troop
22	Certified Public Accountant	Electronics Technician	165	Vaudeville	Writing a one-act play
28	Consul	Foreign Service Man	166	Musical-comedy	Science fiction magazines
34	Explorer	Geologist	168	Pet canaries	Night clubs
36	Factory Worker	Income Tax Accountant	169	Pet monkeys	Church young people's group
38	Floorwalker	Labor Union Official	170	Snakes	Biographies
39	Florist	Art Museum Director	174	"Time"	Skiing
46	Jeweler	Photographer	175	"Judge"	Planning a large party
59	Marine Engineer	High School Principal	176	"New Republic"	Telling jokes
60	Mechanical Engineer	Professional Baseball Player	177	"System"	Business methods magazines
64	Office Clerk	Psychologist	178	"National Geographic Magazine"	Travel magazines
68	Photo Engraver	Public Relations Man	179	"American Magazine"	Weekly news magazines
75	Railway Conductor	Radio Announcer	181	"Atlantic Monthly"	Reading the Bible
87	Ship Officer	Computer Operator	183	Travel movies	Magazines about art and music
96	Typist	Travel Bureau Manager	208	Meeting new situations	Making statistical charts
124	Music	Bible History.	214	Writing personal letters	Being a forest ranger
141	Driving an automobile	Sketch pictures of wild animals	216	Entertaining others	Looking at things in a hardware store
149	Performing sleight-of-hand tricks	Religious music	218	Looking at shop windows	Looking at things in a clothing store
150	Collecting postage stamps	Camping out	222	Being pitted against another as in a political or athletic race	Competitive activities
152	Chopping wood	Playing the piano	237	Absent-minded people	Military men
156	Smokers	Stag parties	239	Quick-tempered people	Beachcombers
157	"Rough house" initiations	Jazz concerts	244	People easily led	Ballet dancers
160	Auctions	Electioneering for office	249	Talkative people	Famous chefs
161	Fortune tellers	Going to church	252	People who have done you favors	Easygoing people
162	Animal zoos	Horseback riding	253	People who get rattled easily	Artistic men

(table continued next page)

435

Item Number	SVIB Form M	SVIB Form T399	Item Number	SVIB Form M	SVIB Form T399
254	Gruff Men	Public opinion interviewers	308	William H. Taft, jurist	Member of the Supreme Court
256	Sick people	Physically sick people	309	Booth Tarkington, author	Author of "best seller"
257	Nervous people	Babies	310	John Wanamaker, merchant	Manager of large department store
259	Cripples	Women athletes	321	Street-car motorman vs Street-car conductor	Airline pilot vs Airline ticket agent
260	Side-show freaks	Outspoken people with new ideas	323	Chauffeur vs Chef	Taxicab driver vs Policeman
261	People with gold teeth	Musical geniuses	325	House to house canvassing vs Retail selling	Take dancing lessons vs Take singing lessons
262	People with protruding jaws	People who daydream a lot	327	Repair auto vs Drive auto	Repaint autos vs Grease autos
263	People with hooked noses	Prominent artists	337	Work which interests you with modest income vs Work which does not interest you with large income	Thrilling, dangerous activities vs Quieter, safer activities
264	Blind people	Outstanding scientists	340	Small pay, large opportunities to learn during next 5 years vs Good pay, little opportunity to learn during next 5 years	Travel alone and make own preparations vs Travel with someone else who makes all the decisions
265	Deaf mutes	Acrobats	346	Emphasis upon quality of work vs Emphasis upon quantity of work	Work in an import-export business vs Work in a research laboratory
266	Self-conscious people	Democrats	352	Nights spent at home vs Nights away from home	Music and art events vs Athletic events
267	People who always agree with you	Prohibitionists	354	Belonging to many societies vs Belonging to few societies	Plumber vs Electrician
268	People who talk very loudly	Republicans	356	Many women friends vs few women friends	Superintendent of hospital vs Warden of prison
269	People who talk very slowly	Men who perform on TV	357	Fat men vs Thin men	Vocational counselor vs Public health officer
270	People who talk about themselves	People who insist on having everything in its proper place	358	Tall men vs Short men	Travel to outer space vs Explore bottom of ocean
275	Bolshevists	Non-conformists	359	Jealous people vs Conceited people	Dog trainer vs Juvenile parole officer
277	Men who chew tobacco	Men who live dangerously	360	Jealous people vs Spendthrifts	Appraise real estate vs Repair, restore antiques
278	Men who use perfume	Prominent business men	362	Usually drive myself steadily (do not work by fits and starts)	Make decisions immediately, not after considerable thought
279	People who chew gum	Prominent labor union men	366	Am quite sure of myself	Keep detailed records of expenses
301	Luther Burbank, "plant wizard"	"Plant wizard"--develops new vegetables and flowers	367	Accept just criticism without getting sore	Prefer working along to working on committees
302	Enrico Caruso, singer	Opera singer	370	Can carry out plans assigned by other people	Can prepare successful advertisements
303	Thomas A. Edison, inventor	Inventor	371	Can discriminate between more or less important matters	Am concerned about philosophical problems, e.g., religion, meaning of life
304	Henry Ford, manufacturer	Manufacturer	372	Am inclined to keep silent (reticent) in confidential and semi-confidential affairs	My grades in high school were a fairly accurate reflection of my abilities
305	Charles Dana Gibson, artist	Nationally known artist			
306	J. P. Morgan, financier	Banker, financier			
307	J. J. Pershing, soldier	General of the Army			

Table D-2 (*continued*)

Item Number	SVIB Form M	SVIB Form T399
377	Get "rattled" easily	Do my best work early in the morning
384	Show firmness without being easy	Can be firm and show I mean it
385	Win confidence and loyalty	Am slow-going and sure rather than quick-moving
387	Am approachable	Have patience when teaching others
389	Feelings easily hurt...hurt sometimes...rarely hurt	Pay attention to details very little... somewhat...very much
390	Usually ignore the feelings of others...consider them sometimes...carefully consider them	Worry about mistakes..a good deal... very little...never
392	Rebel inwardly at orders from another, obey when necessary... carry out instructions with little or no feeling...enter into situation and enthusiastically carry out program	When it comes to taking orders from others and carrying them out... I dislike to...I don't care.... I do it cheerfully
394	Best-liked friends are superior to me in ability..equal in ability..inferior in ability	Speak more slowly than others... about average...faster than others
396	Borrow frequently (for personal use)...borrow occasionally... practically never borrow	in my family, I am the oldest (or only) child..youngest..neither youngest nor oldest
397	Tell jokes well..seldom tell jokes.. practically never tell jokes	At a large conference, I prefer a seat..in first 3 rows..half-way back...in rear of room

Table D-3. Form WA Items Omitted from Form W Booklet

Form WA Item Number	Item
131	Taking long walks
141	Travel cross country in an auto
218	Progressive people
229	Very intellectual people
236	Witty people
243	People who always agree with you
245	People who talk very loudly
257	Women cleverer than you are
348	Accept just criticism without getting sore
367	Usually ignore the feelings of others

TABLE D-4. ITEM CHANGES BETWEEN WOMEN'S BOOKLETS FORM W AND FORM TW398

Item Number	SVIB Form W	SVIB Form TW398	Item Number	SVIB Form W	SVIB Form T398
2	Actress (stage)	Dental Assistant	130	Swimming	Jazz concerts
25	Companion (to elderly person)	Computer Operator	131	Tennis	Sketching pictures of wild animals
26	Confectioner	Children's Clothes Designer	135	Driving an automobile	Looking at things in hardware store
38	Factory Manager	Electronics Technician	137	Poker	Planning a large party
39	Factory Worker	Manager of children's nursery at resort hotel	143	Picnics	Hiking
43	Governess	Supermarket Checkout Clerk	146	Fortune tellers	Telling jokes
44	Government Clerk	Hospital Records Clerk	147	Animal zoos	Travel magazines
63	Manufacturer	Professional Golfer	149	Museums	Religious music
65	Milliner	Church Worker	151	Musical comedy	Popular mechanics magazines
66	Minister	Courtroom Stenographer	153	Plays	Reading the Bible
71	Naturalist	News Photographer	158	Romantic stories	Collecting antique furniture
73	Public Health Nurse	Policewoman	159	Detective stories	Performing scientific experiments
82	Postmistress	Portrait Photographer	160	Movie magazines	Electioneering for office
85	Proofreader	Nurse's Aid	161	"American Magazine"	Educational movies or TV
89	Publisher	Railroad Reservations Clerk	162	"Atlantic Monthly"	Magazines about art and music
90	Purchasing Agent	Veterinarian for small animals	163	"Good Housekeeping" magazine	Making a radio or hi-fi set
95	Registrar	Receptionist	164	"House and Garden" magazine	Leading a Girl Scout troop
99	Sales Manager	Sales Manager of large bookstore	165	"Ladies Home Journal"	Writing a one-act play
110	Stock Broker	Stewardess	166	"National Geographic" magazine	Science fiction magazines
121	Telephone Operator	Supervisor in telephone office	167	"New Republic"	Business methods magazines
122	Traveling Saleswoman	Travel Bureau Manager	168	"Reader's Digest"	Night clubs
126	Wholesaler	Weather Forecaster	169	"True Story" magazine	Church young people's group
127	Wife	X-Ray Technician	170	"Vanity Fair"	Biographies
129	Dancing	Chess	192	Discussions of economic affairs	Operating office machines
			197	Meeting new situations	Taping a bruised ankle
			203	Writing personal letters	Watching an open-heart operation

No.		
204	Buying at an auction sale	Checking typewritten material for error
206	Looking at shop windows	Organizing cupboards and closets
215	Studying the latest hobby, e.g., Einstein's theory, Freud, etc.	Making statistical charts
216	Conservative people	Highway construction workers
217	Energetic people	High School students
218	Absent-minded people	College Professors
219	People who borrow things	Jet pilots
220	Very self-confident people	Male Hairdressers
221	Optimists	Corporation Executives
222	Pessimists	Girls who enter beauty contests
224	People who assume leadership	Long-haul truck drivers
228	Housewives	Irreligious people
229	People who are unconventional	Nonconformists
230	People who have done favors for you	Famous chefs
231	People who take life seriously	Aritstic men
233	Negroes	Public opinion interviewers
234	Cautious people	Men who live dangerously
236	People with physical disabilities	Musical geniuses
237	Self-conscious people	People who daydream a lot
238	People who tell you their troubles	Outspoken people with new ideas
239	People who talk about themselves	Racing car drivers
240	Methodical people	Outstanding scientists
243	"Mannish" women	Ballet dancers
245	Independents in politics	People who like to gamble
246	Men who are indifferent to you	Athletic men

No.		
247	Nervous people	Babies
249	Teetotalers	Men who perform on TV
250	People who chew gum	People who insist on having everything in its proper place
251	Men who drink	Prominent labor union men
252	Women who smoke	Military men
254	People who take chances on situations of doubtful outcome	People who don't believe in evolution
276	Jane Addams, social worker	President, Women's College
277	Ethel Barrymore, actress	Author of best-selling novel
278	Madame Curie, scientist	Outstanding opera singer
279	Amelia Earhart, aviatrix	Owner-manager of chain of women's shops
280	Edna Ferber, author	World-renowned scientist
281	Mrs. F.D. Roosevelt, "first lady"	Tennis champion
282	Madame Schumann Heink, singer	Wife of U.S. President
283	Helen Wills Moody, tennis champion	Famous actress
284	Frances Perkins, U.S. Secretary of Labor	Prominent artist
285	Lillian M. Gilbreth, industrial engineer	Supreme Court Justice
301	Permanence of residence vs Frequent change of residence	Take dancing lessons vs Take singing lessons
305	Evenings in company of women friends vs Evenings in company of men friends	Keep books on household finances vs Recover furniture
307	Many men friends vs Few men friends	Fashion magazines vs Household magazines
312	Work which interests you with modest income vs Work which does not interest you with large income	Experiment with new beauty preparations vs Experiment with new office equipment
320	Be married vs Remain single	Be married to a research scientist vs Be married to a sales executive

(table continued next page)

439

Item Number	SVIB Form W	SVIB Form T398
326	People who are slow in making decision decisions vs People who are quick in making decisions	Work in an import-export business vs Work in a research laboratory
327	People who are always prompt and expect others to be on time also vs People who are seldom on time and who do not mind if others are late	Spend a great deal of time on make-up before going out vs Go out without makeup
328	Nights spent at home vs Nights spent away from home	Be married to a rancher vs Be married to a corporation president
332	Belonging to many societies vs Belonging to few societies	Display merchandise in store window vs Arrange table settings for large banquet
335	Usually drive myself steadily (do not work by fits and starts)	Have more than my share of novel ideas
338	Am quite sure of myself	Keep detailed records of expenses
341	Can carry out plans assigned by other people	Prefer working alone to working on committees
342	Can discriminate between more of less important matters	Do my best work early in the morning
343	Am inclined to keep silent (reticent) in confidential and semi-confidential affairs	Can prepare successful advertisements
348	Get "rattled" easily	My grades in high school were a fairly accurate reflection of my abilities
353	Win confidence and loyalty	Enjoy tinkering with small hand tools
357	Feelings...easily hurt...hurt sometimes...rarely hurt	Complaints annoy me...rarely...sometimes... quite a bit
359	Borrow frequently (for personal use)...occasionally... practically never borrow	In my family, I am the...Oldest (or only) child...Youngest...Neither youngest nor oldest
360	Tell jokes well...Seldom tell jokes ...Practically never tell jokes	At a large conference, I prefer a seat...In first 3 rows...Half-way back...In rear of room
385	Music	Woodworking
399	Typewriting	Left Out
400	Zoology	Left Out

TABLE D-5. ITEM NUMBERS OF THE 249 ITEMS COMMON TO THE MEN'S (FORM T399 AND T399R) AND WOMEN'S (TW398 AND TW398R) BOOKLETS

Women's Number	Men's Number	Women's Number	Men's Number	Women's Number	Men's Number	Women's Number	Men's Number	Women's Number	Men's Number
1	1	98	80	176	190	253	259	341	367
3	36	102	83	177	188	254	273	342	377
4	2	103	84	179	194	255	245	343	370
5	3	104	59	180	195	266	291	344	373
6	5	105	86	181	196	267	292	345	374
8	7	106	89	182	198	268	293	346	375
10	9	107	90	184	199	269	294	347	376
11	10	108	91	187	200	270	295	348	372
12	14	111	93	188	201	271	296	349	378
14	15	119	63	190	202	272	297	350	379
18	18	122	96	191	203	273	298	351	380
19	20	128	100	195	206	274	299	352	383
20	21	129	144	196	207	275	300	354	386
22	23	130	157	198	209	286	311	355	388
23	25	131	141	199	212	287	312	356	390
24	27	132	150	200	213	288	313	357	395
25	87	133	137	201	215	289	314	358	391
30	29	134	162	207	220	290	315	359	396
32	30	135	216	209	224	291	316	360	397
35	31	136	146	210	225	292	317	361	399
37	33	137	175	211	227	293	318	362	101
38	22	139	147	212	228	294	319	363	103
40	37	140	148	213	229	295	320	364	104
42	40	141	152	215	208	301	325	365	124
45	41	142	153	223	242	302	328	366	105
47	42	143	142	225	246	303	329	367	106
50	43	144	158	226	247	304	330	368	107
51	44	145	159	227	250	306	331	369	108
52	45	146	176	229	275	308	333	370	109
53	47	147	178	230	249	310	334	372	110
54	49	148	163	231	253	311	336	374	111
55	50	149	149	232	255	314	341	375	112
56	52	151	180	233	254	317	343	376	113
57	51	152	167	234	277	318	344	377	114
58	53	153	181	235	256	319	345	378	115
59	54	157	172	236	261	321	340	379	116
60	57	160	160	237	262	322	348	381	117
68	39	161	182	238	260	323	349	382	118
70	62	162	183	240	264	325	351	383	119
75	65	163	185	241	271	326	346	384	122
77	67	164	164	242	272	329	353	386	125
78	69	165	165	243	244	331	337	388	126
79	70	166	166	244	274	333	355	389	127
80	71	167	177	246	280	334	361	390	128
81	72	168	168	247	257	335	369	391	130
83	74	169	169	248	258	336	363	393	129
88	64	170	170	249	269	337	364	394	131
91	75	173	221	250	270	338	366	396	133
94	77	174	192	251	279	339	365	397	134
96	78	175	193	252	237	340	368		

The Forthcoming Revision of the Men's SVIB

This appendix reports the final steps of the Men's revision cycle that was started in the early 1960's. This work was completed just as this Handbook was finished, and the basic psychometric data for the new scales have been included here in skeleton form.

Throughout the past several years, many changes have been made to improve the SVIB. Foremost among these has been the attempt to modernize it with new items, new scoring techniques, and new criterion groups. This has been done in three main stages: (1) The first was the modifications made in the items; those changes first appeared in 1966 on the Men's Form, in 1969 on the Women's Form. (2) The second was the introduction of new scoring scales, most importantly, the Basic Interest Scales; they first appeared on both profiles in 1969. (3) The third has been the collection of new occupational criterion samples, and new Men- and Women-in-General samples. New scales for the Women appeared in 1969 and have been reported on in Chapter 2. The new scales for the Men's Form are just now being completed.

These new occupational scales are directly comparable in derivation to the earlier scales, and the assumption is made here that they will operate essentially as their predecessors did; that is, they will have about the same validities and reliabilities, high and low scores will mean about the same, and counselors can use these scales just as they have those on earlier profiles. The data reported in the several tables of this appendix all suggest that this is a reasonable assumption.

Sample Descriptions

Table E-1 contains brief descriptions of the samples used to develop the scales. As before, the samples were restricted to men who had at least 3 years of experience, who said they enjoyed their work, and, whenever the necessary information was available, who exceeded at least a minimum level of competence such as occupational certification or perhaps earning an advanced degree in the field.

The sample sizes were quite variable, ranging from an uncomfortably small number (119) of Army sergeants to an extravagantly large number (1,028) of engineers. The median sample size is 250. Just how large a criterion sample must be is a difficult question to answer; Strong began originally in the 1920's and 1930's with samples of 200–250. Later he decided they were too small and adopted a goal of 400. In my work, I have become convinced that that is unnecessarily large (see Harmon, 1968) and have opted for spending the time, energy, and funds in collecting two different samples of 200 instead of one of 400. With this approach it is necessary to strive for more homogeneous samples, and to make certain that men who are performing the occupation in some unusual manner are not included. In general, the samples included here have been more closely screened on these variables than were those used in the past.

Scale Derivation Data

Table E-2 contains the basic data for each scale: number of items scored, percent difference between the criterion and Men-in-General samples required for inclusion of the items in the scale, standard score mean and standard deviations for the Men-in-General sample, overlap between Men-in-General and the criterion sample, the correlation between the revised scale (1971) and the earlier (1966) scale, and the means and standard deviations of the sample used to calculate this correlation.

The median overlap for the new scales was 35 percent, indicating an average separation between the criterion samples and Men-in-General of 1.9 standard deviations. On this index, the Vocational Agriculture Teacher scale was best, showing a 2.6 standard deviation separation between the criterion sample and Men-in-General; the College Professor scale was poorest, showing only a 1.1 standard deviation separation. The College Professor sample was a diverse one, tending in the direction of a specialized Men-in-General sample; thus, it is not as different from the Men-in-General sample as are specific occupational samples.

Mean Scores of the Criterion Samples on the 1971 Scales

Table E-3 has the mean scores of the criterion samples on all 72 scales. These data are crucial in showing how well scales separate occupations from each other, as well as from Men-in-General. As with the older scales, these occupations show a meaningful rank order on any given scale, and these data are meaningful in understanding the structure of vocational interests. These relationships were used in determining the order of the scales on the profile.

There are no means for some of the samples; that is because they were tested with the earlier version of the booklet (Form M), and those booklets cannot be scored with the new scales. For those samples, their new scale is based on the common items between Form M and Form T399.

Mean Scores of Other Miscellaneous Groups

Several other groups have been tested and scored on the new scales; means for them appear in Table E-4. Some of them provide cross-validation information, as they were drawn from the same occupation as some of the criterion samples. In general, the scales held up well under cross-validation; most of the samples averaged at least 45 on the relevant scale and a few even had averages higher than 50, the criterion sample average.

Scale Intercorrelations

Table E-5 has the intercorrelations between the occupational scales; these data were also used in establishing scale order on the profile.

Table E-6 has the intercorrelations between the Occupational Scales and the Basic Interest Scales, and Table E-7 has the correlations between the Occupational Scales, and the Nonoccupational Scales, the Like, Indifferent, and Dislike percentages, and the Holland Scales—see the next section for an explanation of the latter scales.

The means and standard deviations for the sample used to calculate these correlations is given in Table E-8a, b.

The Holland Scales

John Holland (1966) has proposed an occupational classification system that conforms fairly well with the SVIB occupational groupings. To tie the two systems more closely together, six SVIB scoring scales have been developed to correspond to the six Holland occupational types. His six types are (1) Realistic, (2) Intellectual, or investigative, (3) Artistic, (4) Social, (5) Economic, and (6) Conventional.

In his book, *The Psychology of Vocational Choice* (1966), he presents a detailed discussion of these types.

The six scales were developed very simply—by studying Holland's descriptions of the six types and selecting 20 items for each category that represented the occupational descriptions. Each scale was discussed with Holland and, between us, we made some modifications based on our mutual knowledge of item validities, intercorrelations, and popularities.

The final 20 items selected for each scale are listed in Table E-9. To score older versions of the SVIB, a second set of 14 items each was developed—these included only items appearing on both Form M (1938) and Form T399 (1966). The six items eliminated from each scale are asterisked in Table E-9. The sample used to establish the scale intercorrelations was scored on both sets; their means and standard deviations are given in Table E-8b. Scores on the shorter set (Set 1) can be converted to the longer set (Set 2) by using the formula for each scale:

$$\text{Set 2 Score} = \left(\frac{\text{Set 1 Score} - \text{Mean}_{\text{Set 1}}}{\text{S.D.}_{\text{Set 1}}} \right) \text{S.D.}_{\text{Set 2}} + \text{Mean}_{\text{Set 2}}.$$

The conversion error depends on the magnitude of the correlation between the Set 1 and 2 scales. This correlation is .97 or .98 for 5 of 6 and .94 for the other, so the conversion is not greatly in error.

The main benefit of developing a set of Holland scales for the SVIB is to permit the insertion of the SVIB archival data into Holland's occupational structure. To that end, all of our occupational samples have been scored with these six scores and the means are reported in Tables E-10 to E-15. The means of the samples tested with the earlier forms have been converted as suggested above. (The Converted Score columns in Tables E-10 to E-15 are simply the raw scores +20, to eliminate negative scores. This is how they will eventually appear on the profile.)

Scale Intercorrelations

The scale intercorrelations for the Holland scales, both sets, are reported in Tables E-16 and E-17.

The Use of the Holland Scales

The Holland scales will be used to fill the need for a few, simple, general indices to summarize the entire profile. I had hoped the Basic Scales would fill that need, but there are too many of them (22) for simplicity, though they have proved very useful in other ways.

Now, there will be three main types of information on the profile: first, the six broad categories; second, the 22 Basic Scales, which are content-oriented, and third, the empirical occupational scales, which will tie the first two types into the occupational world.

TABLE E-1. DESCRIPTIONS OF THE 1971 MEN'S CRITERION SAMPLES

ample	N	Year Tested	Tested by	Mean Age	Mean Yrs Ed	Mean Yrs Exp	Composition and Comments
dvertising Men	228	1968	CIMR	41	15.1	14.5	Account Executives listed in the Standard Directory of Advertising Agencies June,(1968).
ir Force Officers	200	1960	Col. F. Winter	36	16.0	12	Drawn from 8,000 Air Force Officers requesting advanced formal training through Institute of Technology of the Air University, U.S. Air Force, Wright-Patterson Air Force Base,Ohio,during 1959-62. Sample restricted to Regular Air Force officers, Captains or higher,Line Officers. Most had science and/or engineering educational backgrounds. About 60 percent were pilots. Cross-validation sample of 200 closely resembled initial sample on all characteristics, including score on SVIB Air Force Officer scale.
nthropologists	473	1969 1967	S. Beran & J. Rossmann	42 40	Ph.D. Ph.D.	13.0 15	Anthropologists teaching at institutions offering graduate degrees in Anthropology. All had Ph.D.'s--all members of the American Assoc. of Anthropologists. Two samples collected by Jack Rossman and Shirley Beran.
rchitects	208	1968	CIMR	46	16.8	20.5	Selected from architects listed in the 1968 Directory of the American Institute of Architects(AIA)
rmy Officers	712	1969	CIMR	35	17.1	12.9	All West Point graduates from the classes of 1950-1962
rmy Sergeants	119	1969	CIMR	34	12.5	14.1	Random sample of sergeants, E7's or higher, drawn from the Washington,D.C. Department of Defense telephone directory.
rtists	178	1968	CIMR	49	15.8	25.9	Non-commercial artists listed in Who's Who in American Art, 1966 edition. All had exhibited their works.
ankers	171	1968	CIMR	49	14.7	24.3	National sample of bank presidents and vice-presidents listed in the Martindale-Hubbell Law Directory, 1968, Vols I-IV.
iologists	342	1959	C.A. Lindsay	44	n/a	n/a	Roughly 54 percent teachers, 34 percent research workers, 10 percent administrators, and 2 percent miscellaneous. All listed in American Men of Science; all hold advanced degree other than M.D.
usiness Administration Professors	868	1968	J.G. Rhode	43	19.7	13.6	National sample of business administration professors in management, marketing, accounting, finance and production.
usiness Education Teachers	323	1956	R.V. Bacon	40	16.8	9	Employed in public secondary schools. All completed 30 or more college credits in business courses, and reported satisfaction with occupation.
uyers	176	1969	CIMR	42	14.0	15.8	National sample of department store buyers listed in Sheldon's Retail Directory of the United States(1969).
artographers	466	1969	A.L. Benton	43	13.8	18.5	Civilian employees of the US Army Topographic Command.
ertified Public Accountants	304	1965	J.G. Rhode	n/a	n/a	n/a	Minnesota Certified Public Accountants.
hamber of Commerce Executives	400	1960	E.K. Strong, Jr.	40	15.5	10	Half of group Chamber of Commerce Executives; other half, managers of trade associations. Scale represents both groups equally well. Developed with assistance of Clifton Corporation, Washington,D.C., for U.S. Chamber of Commerce.
hemists	250	1969	CIMR	43	19.8	15.8	Random sample of Ph.D. chemists listed in American Men of Science, Physical and Biological Sciences, 11th edition.

(table continued next page)

445

Sample	N	Year Tested	Tested by	Mean Age	Mean Yrs Ed	Mean Yrs Exp	Composition and Comments
Chiropractors	378	1969	CIMR	44	16.4	16.0	National sample of chiropractors selected from membership lists of state associations of chiropractors. Collected with assistance from J.V. Durlacher, D.C., Assistant Director of Admissions, Palmer College of Chiropractic.
College Professors	421	1969	CIMR	n/a	n/a	n/a	National sampling of college professors from 37 disciplines compiled in 1969 from data collected by CIMR since 1966.
Community Recreation Administrators	350	1964	K.B. Roys	36	16.2	n/a	Sample drawn from membership lists of 41 state associations. All were between 25 and 55 years old and had a minimum of 2 years of college.
Computer Programmers	542	1964	D.K. Perry & W.M. Cannon	33	B.A.	n/a	Computer programmers , minimum 2 year experience, in primarily non-supervisory programming tasks. On cross-validation, satisfied programmers scored higher than dissatisfied ones
Credit Managers	452	1958	E.K. Strong, Jr.	43	14.9	16	Collected with cooperation of Credit Research Foundation,Inc.,New York.
Dentists	232	1969	CIMR	45	19.1	17.4	Dental practitioners and dental educators selected from the 1968 directory of the American Dental Association and tested with the assistance of Dr. Lawrence Meskin.
Department Store Managers	257	1969	M.D. Dunnette	n/a	n/a	n/a	Department store managers from Penny's, Inc.
Elementary Teachers	123	1965	C.A. Winkle	n/a	n/a	n/a	Graduates of the University of Minnesota College of Education with a major in elementary education.
Engineers	1028	1968	J.C. Johnson	n/a	n/a	n/a	National sample of engineers, drawn from all specialities.
English Teachers	223	1968	CIMR	35	17.0	10.2	From the directory of high school teachers provided by the Minnesota Department of Education.
Farmers	235	1968	D.W. Priebe	38	11.4	17.0	Minnesota farmers attending Agriculture Extension meetings conducted by the University of Minnesota extension agents.
Food Scientists	130	1968	C.O. Willis	n/a	n/a	n/a	Mostly Ph.D.'s, all in food production or processing research.
Foresters	260	1969	CIMR	40	16.6	14.3	National sample of foresters listed the 1968 directory of the Society of American Foresters. Included forest rangers and men in the forestry industry, but no professors of forestry.
Funeral Directors	-320	1969	CIMR	43	14.1	21.0	Members from 21 states of the National Funeral Directors Association. Collected with the assistance of Ronald C. Slator, Professor of Mortuary Science University of Minnesota.
Guidance Counselors	203	1967	H.B. Engen	37	18	5.0	Selected from the membership of the Iowa Personnel and Guidance Association.
Highway Patrolmen	288	1968	CIMR	40	12.6	12.3	Selected from roster provided by the Minnesota Highway Patrol.
Interior Decorators	192	1967	CIMR	46	15.2	19.7	National sample of members of the American Institute of Interior Design
Investment Fund Managers Managers	237	1969	CIMR	40	16.9	13.2	Portfolio managers participating in Institutional Investors Seminar, New York, January, 1969. All registered members of the New York Stock Exchange Data collected with the assistance of Miss Heidi Fiske.
Journalists	283	1967	CIMR	n/a	n/a	n/a	Newspaper reporters and television news broadcasters.

Sample	N	Year Tested	Tested by	Mean Age	Mean Yrs Ed	Mean Yrs Exp	Composition and Comments
Lawyers	309	1967-68	CIMR	n/a	n/a	n/a	Combined grouping of the national sample of 132 federal judges including District Taxation, Court of Appeals, and Supreme Court judges, and the national sample of 177 lawyers selected from the Martindale-Hubbell Law Directory, 1968, Vol.I-IV.
Librarians	425	1959	J.S. Winters	40	17.3	12	Sampling from professional librarian organizations.
Math-Science Teachers	463	1968	W.J. Lonner & S.E. Williamson	n/a	n/a	n/a	Drawn from National Science Foundation science institute courses.
Mathematicians	223	1969	CIMR	43	19.7	16.0	National sample of Ph.D. mathematicians listed in American Men of Science, Physical and Biological Sciences, 11th edition.
Medical Technologists	252	1968	CIMR	37	15.9	12.2	Members of the American Society of Medical Technologists. Data collected with the assistance of Mr. Stephen Friedheim, Executive Director of ASMT.
Ministers	498	1969	D. Hultgren	n/a	n/a	n/a	Includes protestant ministers from the following denominations: American Baptist, Southern Baptist, American Lutheran Church, Lutheran Church in America, Lutheran (Missouri Synod), United Methodist, Presbyterian Church in the U.S., United Presbyterian Church in U.S.A., Disciples(Christian Church), Protestant Episcopal, Reformed Church in American, United Church of Christ, Church of God(Anderson, Indiana).
Music Teachers	493	1952	E.K. Strong, Jr.	41	17.0	17	Selected by and scale developed with the assistance of Music Journal.
Musicians	225	1969	CIMR	43	13.7	19.5	A combined sample of Minneapolis Symphony members and members of the St. Paul Musicians' Association, 1968, and the Minneapolis Musicians' Association, 1967.
Navy Officers	645	1965	R.R. Stephenson & N.M. Abrahams	n/a	n/a	n/a	Career naval officers
Optometrists	405	1963	N.E. Acree	n/a	n/a	n/a	Members of the American Optometric Association.
Personnel Directors	231	1969	CIMR	43	16.4	14.2	Personnel directors and managers of companies with over 500 employees who were listed in the College Placement Annual, 1969.
Petroleum Engineers	385	1965	J.B. Alford	37	16.2	11.3	Texas petroleum engineers who were members of the Society of Petroleum Engineers of American Institute of Mining, Metallurgical and Petroleum Engineers (AIME). Collected with the assistance of Joe Alford, Executive Director of AIME.
Pharmacists	205	1968	CIMR	41	16.1	16.6	Pharmacists registered in the state of Minnesota and members of the Minnesota State Pharmaceutical Association, 1967
Photographers	258	1967	CIMR	42	14.4	18.0	Photo journalists and photographers who were members of the American Society of Magazine Photographers.
Physical Therapists	350	1957	E.K. Strong, Jr.	33	16.5	6.5	Developed with assistance of American Physical Therapy Association with help of Sarah Rogers.
Physicians	240	1969	CIMR	40	20.1	12.5	National sample selected from the American Medical Association.Directory, 1968.
Physicists	230	1968	CIMR	45	20.0	17.5	Selected from physicists listed in Faculties in Physics and Astronomy in the United States.
Policemen	196	1969	CIMR	39	12.7	12.1	City policemen from Minneapolis, Minnesota. Includes all members of department except clerical personnel.

(table continued next page)

Sample	N	Year Tested	Tested by	Mean Age	Mean Yrs Ed	Mean Yrs Exp	Composition and Comments
Political Scientists	177	1967	J.E. Rossmann O.J. Lips	n/a	n/a	n/a	Random sample of persons attending the Midwest Conference of Political Scientists, January, 1967. All had Ph.D.'s.
Priests	287	1966	Rev. R. Lepak	n/a	n/a	n/a	Includes Catholic priests of the Archdiocese of St. Paul and Minneapolis.
Psychiatrists	404	1949	E.K. Strong, Jr. & A.C. Tucker	39	M.D.	n/a	Representative sample of those certified by the American Board of Psychiatry and Neurology.
Psychologists	245	1967	CIMR	44	20.0	14.3	National sample from the American Psychological Association Directory (1966 edition)
Public Administrators	189	1969	CIMR	44	17.0	14.6	Chapter officers of the American Society for Public Administrators.
Purchasing Agents	164	1969	CIMR	44	14.1	15.0	Members of the Twin City Association of Purchasing Agents. Collected with assistance from the president, Will: Peter.
Rehabilitation Counselors	272	1949	N.E. Acree	50	17.5	12	Vocational rehabilitation counselors employed by Veteran's Administratio.
Sales Managers	199	1968	CIMR	44	14.7	15.4	Vice-presidents in charge of sales marketing and company owners who we members of the Sales and Marketing Executive Clubs of St. Paul and Minneapolis.
Salesmen, Computer	190	1964	C.I. Stein	n/a	n/a	n/a	Control Data Corporation computer salesmen.
Salesmen, Life Insurance	250	1969	CIMR	46	14.3	17.0	Salemen listed in directory of Minnesota State Association of Life Underwriters. Includes members of t Million Dollar Club in Minnesota.
Salesmen, Real Estate	175	1969	CIMR	48	12.8	14.7	Brokers and salesmen listed in State of Minnesota Roster of Licensed Rea Estate-Business Opportunity and Salesmen, 1967.
School Superintendents	207	1969	CIMR	50	18.2	21.4	National sample selected from the Directory of American Association of School Administrators, 1968
Skilled Tradesmen	339	1969	CIMR	42	11.6	18.0	National sample of carpenters, electricians, and tool & die makers from 14 major cities.
Social Science Teachers	239	1969	CIMR	38	17.0	12.2	High school social science teachers in Minnesota selected from roster provided by Minnesota State Department of Education.
Social Workers	400	1953	R. L. McCornack	39	18.3	11	From 44 states. About 83 percent wit two or more years' graduate educatio in social work.
Sociologists	198	1965	J.E. Rossmann & O.J. Lips	n/a	n/a	n/a	Members of the Midwestern Sociological Association, all having Ph.D.'s.
Veterinarians	510	1966	T.E. Hannum & J.E. Alsip	n/a	n/a	n/a	Iowa veterinarians.
Vocational Agriculture Teachers	395	1969	C.D. Norenberg	40	16.6	14.5	Vocational agriculture teachers from Minnesota, North Dakota, South Dakot and Wisconsin who were listed in the 1967 edition of the National Vocational Agriculture Teachers Director
YMCA Staff Members	184	1961	H.G. Seashore & R. Lancaster	30	17.0	n/a	Selected in 1960 and tested in 1961 identifying young, recently certifie Senior Secretaries, or those within one year of certification. All had B.A.'s plus 30 hours' graduate work; most with minimum 3 years' experienc remainder at least 2 years. All 35 or younger. Represents about 40 per cent of men meeting these criteria on nationwide basis.

SCALE	Minimum Scored Difference	No. of Scored Items	Men-In-General Standard Scores Mean	S.D.	Percent Overlap MIG vs Criterion Group	Correlation	Mean	SD(Old)	Mean	SD(New)
dvertising Man	17%	79	28.01	13.66	35%	.56	32.60	9.85	34.98	11.55
ir Force Officer	17%	76	28.86	12.63	35%	.94	29.35	11.99	28.41	12.55
nthropologist	22%(13) **	96	25.32	15.07	33%					
rchitect	15%	67	20.33	16.97	27%	.74	26.37	11.25	24.24	14.65
rmy Officer	17%	61	29.59	12.76	37%	.79	21.89	14.24	29.14	11.70
rmy Sergeant	16%	54	30.83	13.44	42%					
rtist	23%(13)	103	24.83	14.17	30%	.90	29.66	10.10	28.15	12.27
anker	15%	85	28.58	12.46	34%	.77	18.53	9.79	22.32	11.34
iologist	15%	81	27.28	14.08	35%	.91	31.20	13.69	30.84	12.79
usiness School Prof	14%	58	32.31	12.56	43%					
usiness Ed Teacher	15%	69	27.28	13.09	33%	.93	29.87	11.86	27.70	12.28
uyer	16%	60	24.03	16.21	32%					
artographer	16%	51	35.36	13.30	53%					
P Accountant	14%	70	22.37	15.42	28%	.70	23.13	13.06	21.01	13.88
ham Comm Executives	16%	74	32.47	12.60	44%	.93	36.97	10.34	35.67	11.16
hemist	16%	75	25.43	16.35	35%	.86	26.51	14.70	29.44	13.95
hiropractor	13%	59	33.43	12.55	46%					
ollege Professor	15%	61	37.47	12.16	57%					
omm Rec Administrator	18%	70	26.93	15.80	37%	.89	30.88	12.95	30.47	14.14
omputer Programmer	12%	55	33.79	13.59	49%	.84	35.81	12.89	37.25	12.62
redit Manager	16%	77	27.33	15.02	36%	.94	29.99	12.95	26.33	13.57
entist	13%	46	29.31	11.81	34%	.58	24.71	10.40	30.63	11.46
ept Store Manager	22%(13)	85	24.73	13.85	29%					
lementary Teacher	14%	58	32.62	13.64	46%					
ngineer	14%	61	34.03	13.42	50%	.61	21.43	11.33	33.64	12.55
nglish Teacher	15%	70	30.87	14.08	43%					
armer	25%(15)	82	22.65	13.47	24%	.87	22.52	9.63	13.28	9.91
ood Scientist	14%	75	31.92	12.25	42%					
orester	14%	76	29.50	13.87	39%	.80	11.17	13.15	20.62	12.25
uneral Director	17%	79	27.27	14.66	36%	.71	26.47	9.85	24.58	13.21
uidance Counselor	16%	80	28.18	13.04	34%					
ighway Patrolman	18%	81	24.44	16.97	34%					
nterior Decorator	21%(13)	81	26.38	10.28	24%					
nvestment Fund Mgrs	15%	83	29.22	11.80	34%					
ournalist	17%	93	28.60	13.90	37%	.78	35.02	9.60	36.00	11.75
awyer	14%	68	31.58	13.81	44%	.65	33.89	9.18	35.79	10.87
ibrarian	16%	73	23.22	15.64	30%	.86	40.92	11.89	34.07	13.27
ath Science Teacher	14%	62	31.21	14.34	44%	.80	27.76	10.24	34.27	13.61
athematician	20%(13)	86	27.58	13.64	35%	.93	24.08	12.44	30.18	12.01
edical Technologist	14%	64	24.78	15.36	32%					
inister	18%	75	22.83	14.02	25%	.86	29.36	14.96	31.87	12.53
usic Teacher	14%	80	26.10	12.39	29%	.80	36.27	12.70	32.67	12.72
usician	13%	48	32.18	12.99	44%	.68	41.13	11.49	40.82	12.51
avy Officer	14%	52	30.57	14.21	42%					
ptometrist	13%	63	28.92	13.30	37%					
ersonnel Director	17%	79	32.86	12.47	44%	.84	28.64	13.12	35.94	11.12
etroleum Engineer	15%	64	31.70	13.66	44%					
harmacist	14%	71	25.75	15.07	33%	.73	23.39	9.05	22.90	12.86
hotographer	19%	94	26.67	13.89	33%					
hysical Therapist	14%	72	31.60	12.40	41%	.91	35.56	12.14	33.95	12.04
hysician	14%	75	29.30	13.34	38%	.74	32.86	14.00	34.70	12.35
hysicist	21%(13)	91	17.46	18.18	25%	.88	19.86	12.93	21.35	15.48
olicemen	16%	74	29.39	14.83	41%	.74	16.20	10.44	25.55	14.78
olitical Scientist	20%(13)	92	24.55	14.77	30%					
riest	15%	78	28.67	13.84	37%					
sychiatrist	14%	74	21.76	14.46	25%	.86	37.47	12.75	32.03	12.47
sychologist	17%	81	28.95	14.44	39%	.82	36.45	11.87	40.63	12.42
ublic Administrator	14%	77	34.01	12.97	49%	.88	36.93	11.57	38.52	10.65
urchasing Agent	14%	85	32.37	14.77	48%	.64	21.87	11.72	26.69	13.59
ehab Counselor	15%	78	27.79	12.08	31%	.91	37.98	11.14	33.07	11.06
ales Managers	20%(13)	81	23.55	15.07	29%	.70	23.19	11.41	22.46	13.76
alesman,Computer	22%(14)	78	22.15	14.98	27%					
alesman,Life Insurance	19%	84	23.72	13.46	26%	.73	27.93	10.82	19.53	11.89
alesman,Real Estate	18%	59	27.20	14.56	35%	.66	31.03	8.85	20.74	12.64
chool Superintendent	14%	83	31.00	14.89	44%	.65	26.37	11.78	31.09	13.07
killed Tradesman	19%	77	25.63	15.34	34%	.83	12.43	11.79	15.69	12.64
ocial Science Teacher	16%	83	32.49	13.28	45%	.84	31.34	12.00	34.07	11.59
ocial Worker	14%	84	26.16	15.99	36%	.91	38.13	13.31	35.98	13.74
ociologist	17%	87	24.65	15.20	31%					
eterinarian	14%	84	26.47	14.37	33%	.71	19.17	8.32	18.56	11.41
ocational Ag Teacher	21%(13)	69	17.96	17.05	20%					
MCA Staff Member	16%	71	26.32	14.68	34%	.90	32.29	13.39	32.27	13.40

 * Based on diverse sample of 150 adults
 ** Minimum scored difference for Indifferent Response
   For all other scales, 10% was minimum

TABLE E-3. MEAN SCORES OF THE CRITERION SAMPLES ON THE 1971 SCALES

Column (Group) abbreviations: CP = College Professor, An = Anthropologist, PS = Political Scientist, BA = Bus. Adm. Professor, So = Sociologist, Py = Psychologist, Pt = Psychiatrist, Ph = Physician, De = Dentist, Bi = Biologist, Ch = Chemist, Px = Physicist, Ma = Mathematician, En = Engineer, PE = Petroleum Engineer, CPr = Computer Programmer, Ca = Cartographer, MT = Math-Sci. Teacher, FS = Food Scientist, MTe = Med. Technologist, PT = Physical Therapist, Op = Optometrist, AF = Air Force Officer, AO = Army Officer, NO = Navy Officer, AS = Army Sergeant, Ve = Veterinarian, VA = Voc. Ag. Teacher, Fa = Farmer, Fo = Forester, SC = Skilled Craftsman, HP = Highway Patrolman, Po = Policeman, PD = Personnel Dir., PA = Pub. Administrator, SST = Soc. Sci. Teacher

Scales	CP	An	PS	BA	So	Py	Pt	Ph	De	Bi	Ch	Px	Ma	En	PE	CPr	Ca	MT	FS	MTe	PT	Op	AF	AO	NO	AS	Ve	VA	Fa	Fo	SC	HP	Po	PD	PA	SST
College Professor	50	38	36	42	39	42	35	39	36	41	40	34	40	36	28	39	35	35	32	29	34	27	28	33	37	30	33	30	28	36	32	27	29	33	38	30
Anthropologist	55	50	42	42	44	47	37	40	37	46	43	42	47	33	21	35	34	33	29	24	25	21	22	18	19	16	14	3	18	24	22	16	16	18	24	17
Political Scientist	50	42	50	36	38	38	34	31	25	37	31	33	41	26	18	32	28	24	19	21	21	18	21	15	15	20	9	1	11	24	21	11	20	27	32	26
Bus. Adm. Professor	42	42	51	50	49	37	29	31	27	31	32	25	35	33	30	37	32	29	31	34	22	23	30	26	24	26	22	10	16	26	26	22	22	40	40	31
Sociologist	39	44	49	49	42	47	30	27	22	38	24	24	32	26	28	33	25	28	18	28	23	25	19	19	19	19	14	6	12	18	12	13	16	24	33	26
Psychologist	42	45	38	37	44	50	38	37	23	35	36	39	39	33	24	24	33	28	28	30	30	33	32	29	27	30	29	14	11	21	17	15	19	31	35	25
Psychiatrist	35	37	34	29	30	39	50	40	35	37	37	37	41	34	18	38	32	30	29	32	40	30	30	28	29	28	22	6	18	28	13	12	16	23	25	18
Physician	39	40	31	31	27	37	40	50	48	44	41	38	38	41	36	40	38	36	34	42	38	50	37	36	30	42	24	15	18	28	26	16	26	24	24	21
Dentist	36	37	25	27	22	28	35	48	50	38	38	38	38	41	40	40	38	38	36	36	38	48	41	41	31	44	32	20	22	33	35	18	27	24	24	20
Biologist	41	46	37	31	38	35	37	40	34	50	37	47	44	36	36	40	34	34	35	36	34	50	31	31	34	36	36	22	28	50	34	19	26	19	25	19
Chemist	40	43	31	32	24	38	37	37	31	37	50	55	49	37	34	31	31	34	32	50	37	55	35	34	31	35	29	21	28	38	32	18	27	17	25	13
Physicist	34	42	33	25	24	44	37	27	21	49	49	50	45	25	18	19	27	34	32	44	37	50	32	32	23	45	24	18	21	25	16	6	18	28	28	16
Mathematician	40	47	41	35	32	39	41	32	30	44	49	50	50	32	30	50	43	43	40	46	44	50	41	40	40	50	18	16	19	27	16	7	18	21	32	18
Engineer	36	33	26	32	26	28	34	41	38	36	37	46	50	50	47	44	43	39	40	44	41	39	39	38	36	34	20	21	16	36	40	18	21	32	32	27
Petroleum Engineer	28	21	18	30	28	24	18	36	35	36	34	33	40	41	50	40	41	39	40	40	40	36	34	35	34	39	35	35	25	41	45	38	40	37	29	26
Computer Programmer	39	35	32	37	30	38	38	40	37	40	39	38	48	41	50	44	44	42	40	46	44	40	42	35	37	41	34	25	26	42	44	37	38	32	29	32
Cartographer	35	34	28	32	25	33	32	38	38	34	31	27	43	43	44	50	50	40	50	40	50	36	40	30	39	32	31	25	26	38	42	43	43	35	35	30
Math-Sci. Teacher	35	33	24	29	28	40	30	35	38	34	34	34	43	39	40	50	40	50	44	50	50	37	44	36	35	34	36	44	42	43	48	43	43	31	35	32
Food Scientist	32	29	22	31	18	36	32	41	36	35	32	32	37	40	40	40	37	37	50	50	35	50	37	37	50	35	36	30	32	40	40	35	34	25	26	30
Med. Technologist	29	24	17	34	28	30	32	39	36	36	50	35	36	44	40	40	35	37	35	50	36	35	36	34	34	26	28	18	21	19	37	34	34	28	31	26
Physical Therapist	30	25	21	22	23	31	28	38	38	37	37	37	38	38	39	42	36	38	37	41	50	37	34	32	38	32	31	21	24	35	36	40	31	28	31	24
Optometrist	28	21	23	23	25	31	28	39	41	31	31	34	35	37	42	40	36	35	36	41	39	50	33	33	37	28	24	20	22	31	33	37	32	33	31	28
Air Force Officer	27	22	21	30	18	26	28	34	41	35	34	23	30	36	36	35	30	30	35	31	36	36	50	40	30	28	30	24	30	35	38	37	37	30	31	27
Army Officer	25	18	24	30	18	25	33	29	29	34	34	23	32	35	42	35	30	35	40	31	36	36	50	50	37	33	30	22	30	40	38	37	37	37	31	27
Navy Officer	26	19	23	32	19	27	23	37	29	40	35	28	35	40	40	38	39	35	40	34	37	37	49	40	50	37	33	23	37	40	40	40	40	39	37	32
Army Sergeant	21	16	22	26	16	23	23	35	34	44	41	17	32	30	42	39	35	40	31	36	40	32	42	42	50	50	33	30	35	41	41	43	42	35	32	37
Veterinarian	19	14	9	22	14	20	18	34	30	36	36	18	36	32	35	30	32	36	34	36	44	42	29	29	29	27	50	35	35	36	35	33	33	22	19	27
Voc. Ag. Teacher	9	3	1	10	6	6	7	15	20	22	15	7	7	18	30	25	28	28	24	24	42	32	22	24	24	24	46	50	42	50	44	30	30	15	19	14
Farmer	16	16	11	16	12	11	7	18	22	19	19	18	19	14	26	26	26	26	24	25	35	33	22	32	32	27	26	42	50	50	38	33	33	16	14	22
Forester	27	27	24	24	18	21	16	32	33	21	13	16	39	27	26	38	37	39	36	36	36	36	37	37	32	32	27	33	44	50	44	42	40	25	28	29

Occupation	1	2	3	4	5	6	7	8	9	10	11	12	13	14	15	16	17	18	19	20	21	22	23	24	25	26	27
Skilled Craftsman	19	19	10	17	14	24	29	28	26	24	35	35	32	30	32	28	32	32	37	48	34	50	39	35	19	17	21
Highway Patrolman	13	8	6	13	10	23	26	19	11	11	31	32	32	34	28	34	33	34	40	36	37	41	50	45	29	21	36
Policeman	20	15	16	21	19	28	29	23	16	15	34	36	32	34	32	40	37	34	40	37	41	25	49	50	33	31	36
Personnel Director	29	24	32	36	35	33	31	28	23	24	33	31	28	29	27	39	35	31	34	33	18	24	31	31	43	50	39
Pub. Administrator	35	32	42	42	41	33	32	33	31	31	34	33	29	36	32	41	37	31	38	18	34	24	31	37	37	48	40
Soc. Sci. Teacher	26	21	33	32	30	28	29	21	17	19	31	31	26	29	27	35	29	25	33	27	31	27	25	20	38	42	40
Rehab. Counselor	29	24	33	32	35	29	27	27	24	27	25	28	27	29	28	29	28	26	31	18	25	30	27	38	37	37	36
YMCA Staff Member	22	15	22	26	27	26	25	29	13	14	23	24	27	29	26	31	31	30	39	26	25	20	28	27	34	34	38
Elem. Teacher	34	30	35	34	39	35	33	32	30	29	32	34	37	37	31	34	31	28	36	19	33	31	35	30	39	39	44
Guidance Counselor	23	15	25	28	28	26	26	22	16	18	27	28	31	31	30	32	32	30	39	26	33	26	32	39	39	33	43
School Supt.	26	17	29	33	30	29	29	25	19	20	29	31	31	33	30	39	36	32	41	26	33	33	34	45	42	43	43
Community Rea. Adm.	20	12	21	25	25	25	26	19	12	12	25	26	28	31	31	32	31	28	35	21	28	22	32	33	40	35	40
Social Worker	31	29	40	38	38	27	23	25	25	24	20	23	21	23	24	26	19	19	23	5	21	11	20	25	38	40	36
Minister	26	22	29	29	29	25	22	26	25	22	19	20	23	23	23	20	19	20	23	11	18	13	18	18	29	29	30
Priest	32	30	37	31	35	31	36	26	27	27	24	25	27	25	28	24	25	24	28	16	22	20	24	24	34	34	36
English Teacher	35	36	40	39	39	31	29	28	29	29	26	26	29	28	27	26	27	24	28	16	26	26	24	29	36	36	40
Music Teacher	33	33	35	34	34	28	33	30	33	31	23	24	23	29	24	19	20	20	24	17	15	20	18	15	28	30	27
Librarian	35	40	42	36	36	25	22	25	36	35	22	18	19	18	12	18	20	12	13	5	17	12	24	24	24	32	22
Musician	39	42	57	40	40	35	33	37	42	40	22	26	30	30	33	22	26	26	30	26	30	23	25	30	30	30	25
Artist	34	42	34	33	29	29	27	30	37	36	22	26	30	31	30	15	16	20	14	20	15	20	15	16	16	21	17
Architect	29	35	22	20	27	28	30	30	36	33	26	24	19	23	22	16	13	17	10	16	21	25	20	17	24	25	5
Photographer	36	43	36	29	36	31	37	35	37	35	24	20	23	25	21	19	18	21	15	19	22	20	17	28	38	35	19
Interior Decorator	29	31	30	28	29	23	25	22	21	22	22	22	21	24	22	20	22	24	14	15	19	25	28	27	27	27	30
Advertising Man	29	30	33	31	34	26	27	22	22	22	20	21	19	27	20	26	24	22	19	14	22	15	19	25	38	35	30
Journalist	34	40	45	34	38	29	29	26	29	30	21	23	21	23	21	25	24	21	14	13	22	14	19	23	33	35	31
Lawyer	34	32	47	40	39	33	27	28	27	28	24	27	23	27	20	32	29	27	25	16	26	15	24	27	41	42	37
CPA	16	5	18	30	19	18	13	16	18	19	25	21	21	20	20	34	28	25	21	21	23	19	19	24	35	40	27
Investment Fund Mgr.	31	32	37	39	35	29	29	32	29	29	28	25	31	31	21	36	34	33	32	18	28	19	24	35	40	39	26
Banker	21	13	22	29	20	21	16	19	21	19	35	34	22	22	25	37	30	32	22	28	19	30	30	40	34	34	31
Chamb. Comm. Exec.	28	23	33	36	32	29	22	26	26	23	34	30	26	26	28	33	32	26	34	24	31	24	33	31	33	46	38
Dept. Store Mgr.	17	9	16	22	20	22	10	17	10	12	30	31	34	34	23	30	26	31	23	22	21	20	36	38	35	34	31
Buyer	13	5	16	24	17	20	12	26	4	6	31	23	14	26	17	31	31	25	21	21	24	27	33	40	42	32	30
Purchasing Agent	21	14	17	28	22	29	34	18	18	18	40	39	32	39	34	40	45	41	39	42	44	43	41	40	35	38	38
Credit Manager	19	10	22	29	22	22	24	13	13	13	35	35	24	31	28	35	29	33	25	28	21	31	32	35	35	40	36
Bus. Ed. Teacher	22	15	25	29	25	22	24	22	12	13	29	27	26	28	28	32	33	27	26	19	23	24	27	36	33	37	31
Pharmacist	16	7	10	20	15	29	32	29	12	13	31	33	30	33	38	28	41	38	34	33	29	33	36	39	41	23	31
Chiropractor	28	23	24	29	32	23	23	29	23	23	33	39	34	39	39	34	43	37	29	34	34	37	39	34	35	34	37
Funeral Director	15	8	14	22	17	15	7	9	7	9	22	23	31	29	17	30	37	36	27	29	23	34	34	36	36	29	33
Sales Manager	15	8	16	24	19	14	8	8	8	7	26	25	27	24	31	29	25	27	18	18	25	23	26	38	38	31	29
Life Ins. Salesman	15	8	17	22	16	21	7	14	7	10	26	29	26	30	21	26	29	26	25	23	21	17	26	15	32	30	31
Real Estate Salesman	14	7	14	23	16	20	24	8	8	11	31	34	33	35	38	28	32	35	35	35	28	33	35	35	28	**33**	24
Computer Salesman	17	9	15	24	21	23	21	19	15	14	31	24	24	25	14	22	18	20	22	24	22	18	24	34	29	34	24

(table continued next page)

Table E-3 (*continued*)

Scales \ Groups	Rehab. Counselor	YMCA	Elem. Teacher	Guidance Counselor	School Supt.	Community Rec. Adm.	Social Worker	Minister	Priest	Eng. Teacher	Music Teacher	Librarian	Musician	Artist	Architect	Photographer	Inter. Decorator	Advertising Man	Journalist	Lawyer	CPA	Investment Fund Mgr.	Banker	Chamb. Comm. Exec.	Dept. Store Mgr.	Buyer	Purchasing Agent	Credit Manager	Bus. Ed. Teacher	Pharmacist	Chiropractor	Funeral Director	Sales Manager	Life Ins. Salesman	Real Estate Salesman	Computer Salesman
College Professor				32	33			39	39	39			41	53	44	47	40	37	43	40		40	32		24	27	28			30	35	27	26	26	26	
Anthropologist				18	17			23	25	24			29	45	32	39	30	24	32	26		27	18		10	15	15			17	20	14	12	12	13	
Political Scientist				23	24			30	31	31			25	36	34	35	35	28	41	35		31	22		16	19	14			14	26	16	18	18	14	
Bus. Adm. Professor				32	34			35	34	35			31	34	34	35	35	39	40	42		43	34		32	34	30			29	29	28	35	32	28	
Sociologist				27	25			34	33	33			27	36	26	31	24	25	37	33		26	16		15	17	14			16	19	14	13	11	10	
Psychologist				28	26			34	32	33			33	44	35	42	35	36	38	34		35	22		23	24	20			23	28	20	24	21	10	
Psychiatrist				24	22			28	27	25			24	32	31	23	22	25	18	27		23	17		15	15	16			15	15	15	15	12	10	
Physician				24	26			31	31	27			32	38	35	37	28	25	31	29		30	22		20	19	25			23	36	25	18	19	19	
Dentist				25	27			28	27	24			32	38	34	36	33	28	25	29		29	27		24	23	29			34	39	33	20	21	24	
Biologist				22	24			27	28	27			30	41	34	33	29	22	29	28		25	21		13	15	20			38	26	17	10	10	13	
Chemist				17	19			24	24	20			29	36	33	32	20	18	24	24		26	18		11	13	18			24	23	12	10	8	11	
Physicist				8	10			15	17	13			21	35	26	27	14	10	20	18		18	9		-2	1	6			10	12	1	-2	-3	0	
Mathematician				22	22			25	26	25			30	41	34	35	26	23	30	28		30	23		13	17	19			21	22	15	14	14	16	
Engineer				32	33			30	24	27			33	29	37	32	25	28	24	28		32	31		34	29	39			38	35	30	30	28	31	
Petroleum Engineer				31	32			26	24	21			29	17	31	29	25	25	26	26		31	36		38	32	42			41	34	34	34	22	26	
Computer Programmer				32	33			31	29	27			35	28	37	30	25	26	26	29		33	32		32	29	37			37	33	28	22	22	26	
Cartographer				34	36			34	31	30			36	28	37	30	26	27	26	28		30	33		35	32	41			40	38	34	28	26	32	
Math-Sci. Teacher				32	33			30	26	29			31	28	37	26	17	20	18	22		24	23		30	23	32			38	34	25	35	20	24	
Food Scientist				32	33			30	25	25			31	24	33	30	28	21	23	27		32	32		39	32	32			40	35	33	33	24	
Med. Technologist				24	25			27	25	21			27	18	25	26	22	23	26	22		16	20		24	19	28			38	32	28	13	13	17	
Physical Therapist				39	36			38	34	34			30	24	29	26	27	27	26	28		24	28		36	28	35			40	40	36	33	30	29	
Optometrist				35	33			30	26	25			27	18	31	23	22	27	17	28		29	30		36	32	37			45	40	38	32	31	32	
Air Force Officer				29	32			26	23	24			27	16	30	23	21	27	26	28		27	29		34	36	36			34	31	33	30	27	30	
Army Officer				33	39			27	26	27			23	13	28	20	22	32	28	31		34	35		43	36	37			31	31	33	40	35	34	
Navy Officer				34	37			30	25	28			26	11	29	22	20	30	26	29		33	33		42	35	40			36	30	33	39	32	33	
Army Sergeant				37	37			28	27	28			26	13	23	16	23	26	24	27		27	38		43	39	39			37	32	41	35	35	38	
Veterinarian				30	28			23	21	18			20	12	19	23	18	24	27	31		22	31		31	27	34			41	34	40	29	24	28	
Voc. Ag. Teacher				31	27			18	14	16			11	-2	8	2	3	6	1	11		9	21		25	18	27			26	23	25	13	20	28	
Farmer				22	20			15	17	16			17	17	19	17	18	13	12	15		17	24		21	22	27			26	23	26	20	25	30	
Forester				32	32			25	21	25			25	21	31	21	19	22	19	23		26	32		30	26	38			34	32	30	29	28	32	

Skilled Craftsman
Highway Patrolman
Policeman
Personnel Director
Pub. Administrator
Soc. Sci. Teacher
Rehab. Counselor
YMCA Staff Member
Elem. Teacher
Guidance Counselor
School Supt.
Community Rea. Adm.
Social Worker
Minister
Priest
English Teacher
Music Teacher
Librarian
Musician
Artist
Architect
Photographer
Interior Decorator
Advertising Man
Journalist
Lawyer
CPA
Investment Fund Mgr.
Banker
Chamb. Comm. Exec.
Dept. Store Mgr.
Buyer
Purchasing Agent
Credit Manager
Bus. Ed. Teacher
Pharmacist
Chiropractor
Funeral Director
Sales Manager
Life Ins. Salesman
Real Estate Salesman
Computer Salesman

TABLE E-4. MEAN SCORES OF MISCELLANEOUS SAMPLES ON THE 1971 SCALES

	Animal Husbandry Professors	Astronauts	Astronomers	Carpenters 1969	Colonels - Retired	Danforth Fellows	Dental Educators	Economists	Electricians	Extension Agents (Ag.)	Generals - Retired	Generals & Admirals	German Accountants	German Medical Students	German Psychologists	Governors	Guidance Counselors 1968	I. T. Minnesota Freshmen 1966	I. T. Minnesota Freshmen 1967	Judges, Federal District	Legislators, Minnesota State	McKnight Fellows (Actors 1966)	N.A.S.A. Scientists	N.I.A.L. Members	North Hennepin County Jr. College	O'Toole Teaching Brothers	Physiatrists	Physical Therapists 1966	Psychiatrists 1967	Salesmen, Encyclopedia	Salesmen, Steel	Schizophrenic Patients at V.A. Hosp.	Sheriffs - County	Social Workers 1967	Tool & Die Makers
GROUP N	82	16	47	93	62	93	210	99	120	65	64	51	126	143	256	28	44	357	571	132	86	50	39	46	109	451	460	72	89	49	61	35	111	54	122
Professor	42	40	54	31	35	54	45	50	32	33	35	36	45	50	53	34	37	38	37	43	31	50	44	57	28	40	43	35	49	30	27	30	27	40	33
Anthropologist	28	27	44	22	21	41	33	38	22	19	22	22	37	43	46	19	22	26	25	29	14	42	32	48	19	27	28	21	36	15	14	18	16	26	21
Political Scientist	22	35	48	14	18	45	25	41	18	18	26	24	37	33	42	37	30	15	14	39	26	42	22	45	11	29	25	16	36	24	18	18	13	31	9
Bus. Ad. Prof.	34	32	45	17	23	44	25	44	50	34	26	24	40	34	40	25	38	24	24	43	36	39	34	42	18	33	35	26	44	36	32	23	21	37	19
Sociologist	24	21	40	11	20	48	29	44	18	20	19	21	30	34	44	37	34	19	19	36	26	36	40	42	16	32	36	20	48	28	23	16	16	38	13
Psychologist	28	26	42	14	21	48	36	43	17	24	22	23	37	43	50	24	35	25	23	36	26	47	32	47	16	31	37	14	43	14	20	23	11	31	18
Psychiatrist	28	22	37	9	22	38	35	34	12	22	21	33	35	38	42	25	30	17	16	32	19	30	26	37	5	25	26	12	42	18	15	25	24	28	16
Physician	38	22	44	22	22	32	35	29	32	30	21	29	33	40	38	21	26	31	31	32	23	35	40	39	19	31	45	22	37	20	23	22	28	25	30
Dentist	40	38	38	30	29	32	48	38	32	30	30	30	35	40	38	24	26	31	28	32	18	34	37	37	17	29	44	21	37	37	14	19	19	25	34
Biologist	40	31	47	24	31	40	40	38	26	27	30	30	35	40	42	22	26	29	28	32	18	34	37	46	29	29	37	29	37	14	14	19	19	25	27
Chemist	35	37	53	26	38	42	38	40	30	37	23	27	33	36	36	17	21	36	35	28	16	32	43	40	17	26	36	27	37	11	15	8	14	23	30
Physicist	25	27	48	18	42	39	35	35	28	11	16	16	31	34	37	8	13	26	25	22	6	29	34	42	8	19	25	15	30	1	2	20	3	16	17
Mathematician	33	32	49	24	26	42	35	42	26	21	24	18	35	31	31	21	25	31	28	32	18	31	31	37	17	29	31	24	37	17	14	19	16	26	26
Engineer	41	48	43	41	38	31	41	35	47	37	35	41	29	33	28	27	29	47	47	27	29	28	50	40	35	30	40	40	36	17	34	33	36	29	47
Petroleum Engineer	39	44	34	41	40	22	34	29	46	36	39	41	30	27	19	30	26	43	44	24	31	16	44	42	36	26	35	38	27	28	39	30	37	22	45
Computer Programmer	39	43	48	36	36	42	35	45	41	34	35	39	34	34	32	25	32	49	49	29	27	30	49	37	33	33	41	38	37	23	30	37	32	29	44
Cartographer	40	41	42	32	43	32	40	35	50	44	35	39	28	32	30	32	30	48	48	26	25	45	46	38	38	33	42	38	33	26	33	31	41	29	50
Math-Science Teacher	42	43	44	34	33	34	41	32	42	38	29	36	21	35	29	20	30	45	46	22	28	27	41	43	30	34	39	39	34	33	37	31	34	28	42
Food Scientist	41	41	34	35	33	26	40	30	38	38	32	36	32	35	29	30	29	36	36	25	30	25	41	21	23	29	40	40	30	13	20	28	34	28	39
Med. Technologist	39	32	36	29	28	25	39	25	31	31	22	25	19	30	24	19	29	36	36	18	18	16	38	19	30	28	41	43	30	34	37	37	28	21	37
Physical Therapist	36	33	28	31	30	24	38	27	37	32	24	26	26	40	27	27	37	32	33	28	33	24	34	37	34	34	45	45	35	29	33	29	40	36	38
Optometrist	36	35	30	30	30	24	38	27	35	32	24	26	29	29	27	27	34	36	36	36	31	18	35	41	18	41	41	40	35	30	30	30	41	30	35
Air Force Officer	33	40	31	35	38	23	31	28	40	32	36	39	22	22	19	27	27	39	39	24	29	18	38	15	31	25	33	34	28	26	33	28	36	24	40
Army Officer	29	43	22	40	42	29	27	27	30	31	46	46	24	17	17	36	30	26	30	30	36	18	32	12	28	28	32	32	26	35	38	29	40	29	30
Navy Officer	31	46	28	31	30	24	29	22	35	34	44	44	31	22	17	30	38	38	38	25	35	21	39	9	32	26	34	34	30	31	40	38	37	26	35
Army Sergeant	29	28	20	42	12	15	26	21	41	34	40	37	28	17	18	35	32	38	38	25	13	12	29	9	34	22	38	38	18	25	32	33	46	26	40
Veterinarian	43	30	18	36	31	10	29	14	35	38	31	30	27	24	29	30	29	30	30	18	27	6	29	9	34	22	38	38	18	30	30	26	35	19	35

Occupation	Scores (left to right)
Voc. Ag. Teacher	31 17 6 33 21 -2 17 3 33 38 18 21 19 19 21 2 19 6 9 21 27 8 19 31 30 15 33
Farmer	26 21 19 40 24 9 17 14 37 29 20 20 30 30 20 15 20 20 23 20 24 11 18 23 31 14 36
Forester	41 38 30 43 36 17 34 23 44 42 35 39 32 24 27 15 21 13 30 36 33 24 23 30 32 25 44
Skilled Tradesman	28 29 25 50 30 10 26 16 51 30 25 28 24 19 18 14 21 9 37 16 39 15 15 30 33 16 49
Highway Patrolman	27 31 12 42 30 5 23 9 42 34 29 31 21 16 40 19 24 13 42 20 48 13 15 36 36 21 41
Policeman	28 35 17 40 35 15 28 18 42 35 35 36 27 33 31 30 27 17 35 22 37 6 22 30 29 30 41
Personnel Adm.	27 30 22 24 32 29 30 31 26 36 36 37 33 23 34 26 42 33 35 47 31 35 43 30 35 39 26
Pub. Administrator	31 33 29 22 35 36 33 40 25 36 39 28 36 23 23 45 43 29 41 45 35 41 39 38 34 44 25
Soc. Sci. Teacher	27 25 18 27 31 36 35 32 26 27 39 31 36 18 22 22 44 30 28 31 33 28 31 28 27 42 28
Rehab. Counselor	27 20 22 17 30 31 25 30 19 32 35 30 31 31 36 18 22 24 27 35 29 36 31 28 34 38 21
Y.M.C.A.	23 22 12 18 22 25 24 20 19 35 25 28 27 19 16 16 30 22 28 30 27 20 35 35 34 38 21
Elementary Teacher	31 32 30 24 29 38 32 27 41 29 31 34 36 26 19 33 42 16 31 43 35 35 30 38 35 31 28
Guidance Counselor	30 22 15 25 28 22 27 23 26 36 37 30 37 21 19 26 45 20 28 35 35 35 39 37 35 44 27
Superintendent	31 28 18 25 34 27 23 20 25 41 36 30 36 19 19 33 44 27 31 33 47 31 30 29 36 19 25
Community Rec. Adm.	26 24 11 21 26 22 25 19 23 38 29 28 24 19 27 16 33 20 34 42 38 25 36 36 23
Social Worker	22 18 23 9 25 38 28 30 24 11 34 20 40 11 15 13 35 13 32 35 25 39 38 26 23 44 14
Minister	21 17 23 11 20 34 26 34 26 13 32 16 37 18 13 12 38 11 34 25 23 11 32 23 30 19 14
Priest	24 21 29 16 25 43 33 17 30 27 33 39 39 17 18 41 41 18 42 37 30 25 28 30 23 40 17
English Teacher	27 22 30 18 25 44 42 19 32 32 19 38 38 19 18 42 30 39 35 29 25 27 42 20
Music Teacher	25 18 33 17 28 37 26 31 28 22 34 32 26 15 26 37 32 23 20 14 32 11 34 32 15 32 19
Librarian	22 17 37 10 36 10 22 36 20 25 35 33 21 14 24 20 33 15 19 21 35 32 11 29 15
Musician	26 27 42 30 22 27 20 21 29 44 36 37 30 30 31 38 49 21 21 32 31
Artist	22 22 36 21 18 39 29 31 26 24 16 29 38 21 28 16 46 26 50 41 40 29 32 20 16 13 20
Architect	17 25 34 26 16 29 31 26 14 16 19 29 34 24 17 7 40 29 15 19 9 13 21 11 15 26
Photographer	21 26 36 20 18 42 30 33 20 20 42 30 21 22 30 21 50 27 19 28 26 22 24 17 28 20
Interior Decorator	20 20 25 21 22 30 27 28 18 23 21 37 39 17 23 23 27 49 19 20 32 35 20 23 28 20
Advertising Man	19 22 20 15 20 33 27 28 15 25 25 22 18 14 16 33 43 19 33 20 32 41 34 24 34 15
Journalist	22 26 29 14 24 43 28 35 14 21 29 26 32 15 16 40 46 23 30 18 37 33 26 23 36 14
Lawyer	27 26 27 15 31 41 28 40 15 28 37 24 37 16 15 25 35 39 16 34 25 41 42 21 40 16
CPA	22 24 12 20 29 10 15 23 22 22 32 28 33 23 25 33 21 19 19 32 18 25 22 22
Investment Fund Mgr.	24 29 27 21 26 21 21 21 32 47 36 28 21 25 34 21 24 20 32 38 28 22 29 18
Banker	28 26 14 29 36 14 29 23 27 29 40 31 42 24 31 36 14 29 27 21 39 40 31 32 25 27
Chamb. Comm. Exec.	26 29 20 23 32 20 23 24 34 36 43 40 24 38 29 27 30 33 48 43 26 35 25
Dept. Store Mgr.	20 24 9 22 24 30 30 28 35 35 44 22 31 31 30 18 27 27 38 26 35 24
Buyer	12 17 3 21 13 14 16 19 26 28 12 34 13 22 34 11 20 18 20 17 44 41 38 29 24 20
Purchasing Agent	31 33 17 41 36 29 24 42 41 34 37 34 33 26 31 8 38 30 25 40 46 32 43 31 43
Credit Manager	25 25 13 24 34 16 21 23 36 32 32 36 22 39 14 27 29 23 39 40 34 29 26
Bus. Ed. Teacher	26 20 17 25 30 19 24 25 25 34 31 39 21 21 35 11 27 28 30 36 34 32 30 27
Pharmacist	32 23 12 31 27 8 26 14 32 38 29 17 30 6 25 2 30 38 19 29 35 35 22 34
Chiropractor	34 30 24 38 26 38 25 34 40 27 34 40 28 31 40 25 30 20 33 41 43 40 37 38 34
Funeral Director	24 21 7 31 27 11 22 15 29 34 25 27 34 33 23 24 37 14 18 8 32 20 41 40 33 27 29
Sales Manager	17 21 6 18 21 13 18 16 27 25 26 28 13 24 13 17 17 13 8 20 22 21 46 39 21 27 17
Life Ins. Salesman	19 18 7 23 23 12 14 15 20 27 24 28 28 31 14 23 19 11 25 18 38 45 21 28 24 19
Real Estate Salesman	22 23 7 34 27 10 16 15 32 27 27 36 30 17 15 18 11 6 27 18 43 43 35 30
Computer Salesman	19 28 12 16 20 18 19 19 25 24 27 24 19 21 34 17 19 7 19 23 40 37 19 24 25 19

TABLE E-5. SCALE INTERCORRELATIONS FOR THE 1971 SCALES

Groups / Scales

Scale (row)	SocSciTch	PubAdmin	PersDir	Policeman	HwyPatrol	SkilledCraft	Forester	Farmer	VocAgTch	Veterin.	ArmySgt	NavyOff	ArmyOff	AirForceOff	Optom.	PhysTher	MedTech	FoodSci	MathSciTch	Cartog.	CompProg	PetroEng	Engineer	Mathem.	Physic.	Chemist	Biolog.	Dentist	Physic.	Psychiatr	Psychol.	Sociol.	BusAdmProf	PolSci	Anthro	CollProf
College Professor	-.60	-.32	-.48	-.68	-.72	-.37	-.30	-.48	-.70	-.55	-.85	-.51	-.63	-.38	-.20	-.21	.13	-.11	.18	-.13	.13	-.38	.01	.86	.88	.73	.84	.52	.63	.69	.82	.76	.40	.68	.86	1.00
Anthropologist	-.73	-.51	-.62	-.76	-.66	-.20	-.28	-.18	-.66	-.47	-.71	-.59	-.74	-.47	-.38	-.49	-.12	-.11	.18	-.24	-.05	-.39	-.11	.90	.87	.62	.79	.37	.38	.46	.63	.60	.35	.66	1.00	
Political Scientist	-.15	.04	-.09	-.82	-.88	-.79	-.73	-.59	-.84	-.72	-.67	-.62	-.56	-.70	-.40	-.51	-.40	-.51	-.42	-.64	-.39	-.72	-.56	.56	.49	.18	.42	.01	.09	.53	.74	.83	.73	1.00		
Bus. Adm. Professors	-.06	.36	.19	-.59	-.68	-.61	-.64	-.57	-.63	-.54	-.33	-.20	-.19	-.30	.00	-.43	-.24	-.23	-.25	-.43	-.11	-.34	-.31	.40	.33	.16	.17	-.08	.01	.44	.62	.66	1.00			
Sociologist	-.13	.12	-.12	-.62	-.77	-.71	-.57	-.71	-.75	-.74	-.69	-.48	-.46	-.45	-.20	-.19	-.07	-.31	-.07	-.32	-.08	-.58	-.29	.55	.57	.41	.52	.19	.34	.71	.88	1.00				
Psychologist	-.20	.12	-.01	-.62	-.74	-.71	-.49	-.71	-.66	-.72	-.78	-.40	-.40	-.40	-.20	-.10	-.35	-.06	.31	-.25	-.07	-.48	-.11	.55	.59	.47	.56	.35	.64	.80	1.00					
Psychiatrist	-.19	.17	-.15	-.35	-.77	-.48	-.29	-.73	-.51	-.46	-.62	-.20	-.20	-.07	.25	.22	.35	.17	.31	.00	.26	-.19	.12	.47	.55	.56	.63	.50	.64	1.00						
Physician	-.41	-.16	-.27	-.10	-.13	-.02	.23	-.38	-.17	.02	-.51	-.10	-.15	.14	.34	.44	.68	.50	.67	.41	.53	.20	.52	.45	.50	.75	.84	.84	1.00							
Dentist	-.45	-.29	-.34	-.06	-.15	.06	.16	-.23	-.16	.14	-.39	-.15	-.10	.14	.36	.37	.64	.42	.54	.32	.43	.14	.14	.45	.50	.63	.74	1.00								
Biologist	-.72	-.46	-.60	-.10	-.13	.03	.16	-.23	-.19	.02	-.51	-.06	-.15	.22	.36	.04	.09	.50	.67	.41	.43	.14	.10	.80	.83	.68	1.00									
Chemist	-.72	-.34	-.53	-.28	-.26	.16	.20	-.15	-.14	-.14	-.47	-.28	-.28	.21	.23	.08	.58	.32	.66	.44	.66	.25	.56	.80	.83	1.00										
Physicist	-.80	-.46	-.65	-.62	-.54	-.04	-.09	-.18	-.51	-.34	-.64	-.34	-.56	-.16	-.08	-.26	.25	-.04	.35	.09	.35	-.09	.22	.96	1.00											
Mathematician	-.82	-.50	-.65	-.61	-.61	-.08	-.19	-.13	-.56	-.38	-.62	-.41	-.62	-.26	-.17	-.42	.09	-.15	.19	-.05	.23	-.16	.10	1.00												
Engineer	-.28	-.34	-.53	-.28	-.26	.16	.20	-.15	-.14	.17	.17	.46	.46	.86	.51	.56	.65	.32	.85	.89	.74	.85	1.00													
Petroleum Engineer	-.11	.10	-.11	.65	.71	.75	.73	.41	.67	.60	.64	.83	.53	.83	.64	.44	.51	.75	.66	.79	.74	1.00														
Computer Programmer	-.34	.01	-.11	.33	.29	.50	.50	.04	.27	.20	.13	.56	.34	.77	.66	.48	.82	.71	.81	.84	1.00															
Cartographer	-.16	.01	-.08	.59	.58	.67	.73	.25	.55	.41	.36	.63	.45	.84	.61	.59	.77	.71	.77	1.00																
Math-Sci. Teacher	-.27	.01	-.15	.59	.58	.44	.58	.32	.35	.32	-.01	.49	.49	.68	.60	.61	.83	.72	1.00																	
Food Scientist	-.03	.27	-.05	.56	.48	.42	.58	-.01	.35	.40	-.01	.68	.32	.68	.69	.61	.72	1.00																		
Med. Technologist	-.21	-.01	-.12	.34	.28	.37	.47	-.06	.29	.37	.05	.42	.28	.64	.69	.65	1.00																			
Physical Therapist	.38	.34	.30	.42	.52	.18	.48	-.17	.48	.34	.17	.50	.55	.61	.58	1.00																				
Optometrist	.08	.34	.29	.42	.48	.24	.27	-.11	.34	.38	.30	.65	.65	.70	1.00																					
Air Force Officer	.04	.28	.23	.75	.71	.63	.69	.42	.65	.47	.65	.74	.74	1.00																						
Army Officer	.51	.64	.69	.78	.68	.25	.42	.02	.58	.39	.64	.87	1.00																							
Navy Officer	.25	.47	.46	.75	.70	.44	.53	.15	.60	.45	.59	1.00																								
Army Sergeant	.37	.26	.33	.62	.52	.53	.38	.55	.71	.57	1.00																									
Veterinarian	.03	-.04	.19	.52	.77	.71	.63	.62	.76	1.00																										
Voc. Ag. Teacher	.30	.08	.08	.26	.87	.71	.76	.62	1.00																											
Farmer	-.22	-.51	-.37	.26	.56	.80	.52	1.00																												
Forester	-.09	-.13	-.09	.49	.75	.77	1.00																													
Skilled Craftsman	.29	-.36	-.29	.66	.75	1.00																														
Highway Patrolman	.29	.11	.20	.91	1.00																															
Policeman	.46	.34	.40	1.00																																
Personnel Dir.	.72	.90	1.00																																	
Pub. Administrator	.77	1.00																																		
Soc. Sci. Teacher	1.00																																			

TABLE E-5 (continued)

Scales \ Groups	Computer Salesman	Real Estate Salesman	Life Ins. Salesman	Sales Manager	Funeral Director	Chiropractor	Pharmacist	Bus. Ed. Teacher	Credit Manager	Purchasing Agent	Buyer	Dept. Store Mgr.	Chamb. Comm. Exec.	Banker	Investment Mgr.	CPA	Lawyer	Journalist	Advertising Man	Interior Decorator	Photographer	Architect	Artist	Musician	Librarian	Music Teacher	English Teacher	Priest	Minister	Social Worker	Community Rec. Adm.	School Supt.	Guidance Counselor	Elem. Teacher	YMCA	Rehab. Counselor
College Professor	-.50	-.90	-.72	-.61	-.81	-.39	-.77	-.72	-.76	-.83	-.68	-.64	-.52	-.70	.13	-.61	.13	.51	.11	.33	.81	.71	.85	.61	.59	.45	.29	.22	.12	.05	.54	-.58	-.52	.03	-.48	-.18
Anthropologist	-.69	-.78	-.66	-.71	-.85	-.65	-.76	-.80	-.84	-.85	-.67	-.74	-.58	-.58	.27	-.62	-.02	.48	-.01	.38	.78	.63	.89	.48	.41	.24	.02	.12	-.22	-.21	-.21	-.58	-.66	.30	-.69	-.41
Political Scientist	-.35	-.55	-.20	-.25	-.47	-.36	-.69	-.37	-.43	-.77	-.20	-.36	-.05	-.32	.52	-.37	.64	.85	.44	.64	.69	.22	.69	.53	.68	.53	.42	.49	.26	.38	-.33	-.27	-.17	.07	-.19	-.18
Bus. Adm. Professor	-.04	-.19	.03	.04	-.52	-.22	-.36	-.37	-.04	-.42	.08	-.09	.21	.03	.68	.15	.63	.51	.32	.31	.33	-.02	.26	.29	.47	.32	.20	.29	.13	.33	-.16	-.01	-.04	-.07	-.07	-.32
Sociologist	-.27	-.44	.03	-.30	-.52	-.07	-.65	-.33	-.42	-.69	-.31	-.38	-.09	-.55	.25	-.41	.47	.67	.52	.44	.67	.58	.63	.59	.78	.61	.59	.55	.42	.49	-.20	-.22	-.16	.30	-.12	-.27
Psychologist	-.13	-.68	-.44	-.38	-.51	-.07	-.64	-.38	-.24	-.66	-.29	-.20	-.36	-.56	.08	-.29	.47	.38	.27	.44	.78	.38	.68	.64	.67	.57	.57	.48	.45	.46	-.06	-.08	-.28	.30	-.15	-.12
Psychiatrist	-.06	-.63	-.60	-.35	-.40	.07	-.35	-.20	-.37	-.44	-.30	-.20	-.07	-.47	.08	-.31	.47	.38	-.06	.22	.49	.53	.45	.50	.67	.57	.23	.55	.27	.60	-.02	-.08	-.27	.38	-.37	-.35
Physician	-.09	-.19	.03	-.18	-.42	.14	-.19	-.41	-.24	-.30	-.39	.00	-.36	.10	.50	-.29	-.10	-.02	-.06	-.11	-.25	.15	.39	.33	.30	.25	.23	.48	.17	.60	-.06	-.21	-.28	-.12	-.37	-.04
Dentist	.13	-.68	-.44	-.35	.42	.14	-.06	-.38	-.37	-.27	-.51	.11	-.40	.13	.08	-.33	-.23	-.02	-.06	-.01	-.15	.60	.36	.24	.30	.19	.06	.17	.08	-.08	-.15	-.29	-.27	.04	-.05	-.16
Biologist	-.55	-.86	-.79	-.70	-.75	-.38	-.51	-.66	-.41	-.74	-.74	-.26	-.40	-.64	.19	-.42	-.15	.19	-.06	.16	.58	.60	.70	.47	.49	.19	.09	.17	.08	-.15	-.56	-.60	-.54	.15	-.55	-.28
Chemist	-.32	-.71	-.78	-.63	-.72	-.33	-.38	-.56	-.53	-.45	-.72	-.26	-.60	-.55	.16	-.29	-.28	-.08	-.36	-.20	.38	.68	.46	.34	.31	.13	-.06	-.13	-.09	-.26	-.51	-.53	-.55	-.09	-.54	-.31
Physicist	-.57	-.82	-.79	-.76	-.86	-.57	-.65	-.74	-.75	-.74	-.78	-.17	-.70	-.59	.08	-.45	-.14	-.20	-.26	.08	.59	.68	.70	.44	.41	.21	-.06	-.13	-.17	-.26	-.73	-.70	-.66	-.24	-.70	-.40
Mathematician	-.62	-.86	-.79	-.72	-.88	-.56	-.68	-.75	-.75	-.79	-.74	-.42	-.72	-.50	.21	-.42	-.11	.27	-.25	.15	.59	.60	.73	.42	.39	.17	.12	-.09	-.26	-.32	-.81	-.75	-.67	-.36	-.75	-.44
Engineer	.30	-.71	-.78	-.63	-.08	.16	.53	.03	.50	.68	-.20	.36	-.16	.26	-.31	.55	-.52	-.74	-.37	-.74	-.22	-.04	-.61	-.40	-.38	-.38	-.30	-.33	-.08	-.14	-.51	.34	.13	.05	.18	-.13
Petroleum Engineer	.44	-.82	-.79	-.76	-.22	.19	.61	.25	.77	.81	.59	.77	.02	.33	.07	.69	-.80	-.45	.00	-.54	-.57	-.43	-.79	-.52	-.44	-.32	-.11	-.09	-.17	.02	.14	.73	.52	.27	.61	-.40
Computer Programmer	.20	.03	-.39	-.16	-.14	.07	.17	.03	.64	.23	-.24	.37	-.21	-.09	-.29	.27	-.71	-.61	-.24	-.56	-.35	-.41	-.20	-.48	-.01	-.12	-.22	-.25	-.07	-.16	-.05	.21	.28	-.15	.07	-.07
Cartographer	.25	.24	-.28	-.05	-.19	.24	.37	.14	.21	.46	-.12	-.05	-.15	-.03	.07	.26	-.56	-.52	-.43	-.63	-.15	-.27	-.36	-.10	-.20	-.25	-.25	-.34	-.09	-.18	-.24	.07	.11	.09	-.04	-.12
Math-Sci. Teacher	.18	-.24	-.18	-.19	-.43	.07	.40	-.09	.08	.11	-.39	.08	-.08	-.30	-.25	.35	-.29	-.44	-.13	-.48	-.25	.15	-.18	-.12	-.14	-.12	-.17	-.12	.12	-.08	-.28	.31	.33	.20	.24	-.09
Food Scientist	.56	.13	.04	.29	.23	.48	.33	.26	.37	.52	.11	.40	.18	.10	-.25	.09	-.53	-.52	-.38	-.45	-.25	.03	-.19	.03	-.23	-.14	-.02	.24	.12	-.06	.13	.06	.13	.20	.24	.17
Med. Technologist	.16	.04	-.01	-.15	-.02	.31	.44	.08	.12	.21	-.28	-.00	-.19	-.21	-.59	.09	-.40	-.53	-.01	-.44	-.32	-.19	-.41	-.18	-.07	.08	.28	.02	.17	.34	.02	.50	.46	.20	.03	.03
Physical Therapist	.46	.06	-.41	-.28	.34	.71	.40	.41	.41	.51	.07	.42	.24	.09	-.15	.12	-.18	-.48	-.04	-.59	-.41	.03	-.37	-.40	-.05	.08	.28	.08	.09	.34	.64	.06	.46	.60	.07	.38
Optometrist	.16	.22	-.01	-.28	.36	.57	.44	.40	.12	.20	.20	.42	.42	.24	-.15	.42	-.52	-.42	-.01	-.74	-.32	-.37	-.74	-.16	.05	.08	.25	.24	.07	.15	.34	.34	.38	.21	.35	.27
Air Force Officer	.55	.34	.06	.26	.29	.35	.50	.38	.50	.68	.16	.36	.16	.26	-.31	.55	-.39	-.74	-.37	-.74	-.55	-.04	-.61	-.40	-.38	-.38	-.30	-.33	-.08	-.14	-.31	.34	.05	.07	.18	.07
Army Officer	.83	.64	.55	.70	.64	.56	.61	.66	.77	.81	.59	.77	.62	.54	-.07	.69	-.03	-.45	.00	-.54	-.61	-.43	-.79	-.52	-.44	-.32	-.11	-.09	-.28	-.15	.66	.73	.52	.27	.61	.41
Navy Officer	.70	.52	.52	.48	.45	.39	.58	.49	.64	.64	.13	.55	.37	.44	-.13	.44	-.18	-.61	-.26	-.69	-.61	-.60	-.73	-.48	-.48	-.46	-.30	-.23	-.27	-.06	.41	.51	.28	.02	.33	.19
Army Sergeant	.44	.77	.52	.21	.65	.21	.74	.63	.69	.78	.54	.54	.16	.34	-.11	.68	-.26	-.63	-.45	-.51	-.83	-.60	-.61	-.63	-.63	-.45	-.30	-.38	-.46	-.20	.16	.69	.36	-.15	.08	-.08
Veterinarian	.15	.44	.32	.09	.42	.26	.66	.23	.30	.55	.08	.20	-.07	.34	-.41	.37	-.72	-.72	-.57	-.62	-.66	-.34	-.59	-.59	-.63	-.53	-.54	-.46	-.28	-.07	.16	.16	.15	.00	.04	-.21
Voc. Ag. Teacher	.35	.15	.33	.29	.11	.36	.33	.48	.49	.78	.25	.37	.13	.40	-.50	.44	-.51	-.62	-.46	-.47	-.73	-.41	-.73	-.46	-.60	-.48	-.59	-.78	-.53	-.25	.39	.41	.34	.56	.24	-.00
Farmer	.38	.38	.07	-.02	.09	-.27	.33	.01	.00	.32	-.06	-.14	-.36	.31	-.55	.16	-.69	-.62	-.67	-.35	-.47	-.22	-.32	-.40	-.60	-.55	-.72	-.71	-.66	-.18	-.28	-.25	-.21	-.56	-.37	-.57
Forester	-.08	.18	.08	-.08	.07	-.08	.38	.08	.09	.48	-.12	-.06	-.15	.22	-.47	.24	-.58	-.83	-.69	-.59	-.70	-.37	-.74	-.42	-.73	-.64	-.69	-.71	-.53	-.75	-.15	-.15	-.23	-.44	-.31	-.24
Skilled Craftsman	.04	.28	.31	-.02	.47	.37	.65	.39	.48	.80	.23	.42	.42	.35	-.15	.45	-.26	-.59	-.39	-.74	-.61	-.37	-.73	-.70	-.73	-.43	-.35	-.41	-.19	-.27	.59	.36	.26	-.02	.27	-.49
Highway Patrolman	.42	.60	.31	.31	.56	.57	.61	.74	.60	.84	.36	.58	.56	.29	.30	.45	.63	.10	.48	.30	-.27	.03	-.48	-.16	-.53	-.48	-.35	-.15	-.19	.02	.61	.54	.38	.43	.49	-.08
Policeman	.56	.56	.56	.49	.73	.57	.61	.74	.73	.84	.70	.75	.88	.43	.52	.54	.63	.05	.48	.30	-.27	-.42	-.48	-.19	-.53	-.48	-.06	-.08	-.48	-.02	.59	.54	.38	.26	.49	.16
Personnel Director	.61	.60	.79	.81	.73	.56	.28	.69	.73	.49	.85	.75	.93	.43	.30	.54	.05	.10	.48	-.30	-.30	-.42	-.48	-.16	-.53	-.18	.25	.40	-.08	.73	.79	.84	.66	.43	.82	.79
Pub. Administrator	.50	.44	.60	.81	.56	.56	.28	.69	.73	.49	.85	.75	.88	.52	.27	.54	.63	.10	.48	-.09	-.27	-.42	-.48	-.19	.08	.18	.35	.46	.54	.73	.73	.84	.66	.46	.75	.82

(table continued next page)

457

TABLE E-5 (continued)

Groups / Scales (correlation matrix). The group columns, read left to right, are: Computer Salesman, Real Estate Salesman, Life Ins. Salesman, Sales Manager, Funeral Director, Chiropractor, Pharmacist, Bus. Ed. Teacher, Credit Manager, Purchasing, Buyer, Dept. Store Mgr., Chamb. Comm. Exec., Banker, Investment Mgt., CPA, Lawyer, Journalist, Advertising Man, Interior Decorator, Photographer, Architect, Artist, Musician, Librarian, Music Teacher, English Teacher, Priest, Minister, Social Worker, Community Rec. Adm., School Supt., Guidance Counselor, Elem. Teacher, YMCA, Rehab. Counselor.

Each scale (row) is listed with its correlations, ending at the 1.00 diagonal.

Scale	Correlations (Computer Salesman → diagonal)
Soc. Sci. Teacher	.61 .57 .69 .75 .74 .64 .44 .75 .70 .56 .70 .76 .80 .39 −.06 .36 .51 .10 .44 −.02 −.39 −.61 −.56 −.28 −.07 .08 .43 .48 .54 .67 .85 .82 .82 .58 .77 .72
Rehab. Counselor	.59 .24 .48 .64 .53 .60 .22 .67 .62 .33 .60 .64 .78 .26 .13 .31 .68 .22 .54 −.18 −.12 −.31 −.28 .09 .35 .49 .55 .69 .73 .87 .72 .78 .75 .63 .77 1.00
YMCA Staff Member	.73 .45 .63 .79 .70 .65 .44 .72 .73 .55 .75 .83 .84 .23 −.08 .34 .03 .03 .50 .11 −.33 −.45 −.51 −.18 −.06 .21 .44 .54 .64 .71 .93 .87 .86 .67 1.00
Elem. Teacher	.37 −.10 .08 .35 .27 .62 .11 .37 .25 .14 .20 .39 .43 −.23 −.34 −.10 .44 .22 .48 .11 −.02 .02 −.08 .26 .41 .49 .76 .73 .83 .72 .67 .50 .51 1.00
Guidance Counselor	.58 .50 .65 .67 .69 .59 .52 .74 .72 .56 .62 .76 .73 .47 −.06 .44 .39 −.05 .26 −.06 −.49 −.60 −.58 −.32 −.09 .15 .28 .46 .53 .60 .84 .85 1.00
School Supt.	.81 .59 .73 .86 .77 .69 .53 .81 .83 .66 .75 .85 .86 .54 −.00 .57 .42 −.16 .41 −.14 −.51 −.58 −.67 −.33 −.15 .11 .28 .40 .61 .61 .90 1.00
Community Rec. Adm.	.41 −.03 .27 .49 .73 .69 −.06 .45 .36 .06 .40 .43 .67 −.04 −.20 −.02 .76 .32 .70 .34 −.40 −.44 −.58 −.25 −.12 .14 .41 .45 .61 .64 1.00
Social Worker	.38 .59 .60 .36 .73 .52 −.02 .45 .24 .66 .20 .33 .50 .32 .09 .40 .59 .32 .53 .34 −.16 −.11 −.01 .25 .53 .63 .79 .82 .82 1.00
Minister	.41 −.14 .16 .49 .31 .52 −.06 .45 .12 .06 .16 .33 .50 −.04 −.20 −.20 .59 .33 .53 −.14 −.40 −.44 −.58 .25 .51 .65 .80 .91 1.00
Priest	.21 −.22 .14 .26 .14 .33 −.17 .21 .12 −.17 .16 .22 .41 .21 .09 −.19 .71 .55 .57 .28 .16 −.03 .01 .42 .53 .65 .81 1.00
English Teacher	.08 −.10 .08 .35 −.04 −.14 −.23 .09 .09 .01 .01 .08 .31 −.42 −.15 −.36 .60 .69 .59 .35 .42 .29 .16 .45 .65 .82 1.00
Music Teacher	−.34 −.47 −.17 −.01 −.07 .14 −.35 −.08 −.08 −.35 .01 −.08 .15 −.28 .02 −.41 .43 .43 .49 .66 .46 .33 .44 .70 .82 1.00
Librarian	−.29 −.60 −.40 −.25 −.32 −.06 −.45 −.25 −.23 −.52 −.17 −.30 −.03 −.39 .09 −.42 .54 .54 .38 .57 .53 .43 .54 .74 1.00
Musician	−.33 −.61 −.42 −.29 −.34 −.12 −.48 −.37 −.37 −.56 −.20 −.32 −.18 −.46 .09 −.51 .16 .42 .38 .65 .69 .60 .68 1.00
Artist	−.40 −.71 −.74 −.51 −.75 −.19 −.52 −.65 −.56 −.49 −.56 −.51 −.52 −.66 .19 −.56 .10 .64 .27 .60 .93 .70 1.00
Architect	−.42 −.72 −.45 −.38 −.60 −.26 −.79 −.65 −.60 −.76 −.57 −.47 −.31 −.63 .26 −.68 −.25 .16 .09 .26 .67 1.00
Photographer	−.32 −.28 .32 −.02 −.62 −.07 −.37 −.11 −.71 −.48 −.42 −.12 −.52 −.65 −.08 −.68 .24 .71 .49 .60 1.00
Interior Decorator	−.23 −.41 −.06 −.06 −.05 −.05 .37 .15 .13 −.26 .13 −.15 −.11 −.15 .26 .38 .36 .63 .61 1.00
Advertising Man	.30 .02 .38 .41 .15 .22 −.22 −.20 .20 .16 .35 .27 .41 .09 .39 −.17 .69 .63 1.00
Journalist	.30 .41 .38 .55 .20 .15 −.22 −.34 .20 −.16 .58 .10 .59 −.33 .45 −.43 .57 1.00
Lawyer	.64 .70 .60 .55 .56 .26 .59 .60 .76 .67 .58 .61 .53 .75 .46 −.08 1.00
CPA	.13 .16 .34 .26 −.02 −.23 .59 .15 .76 −.26 .34 .13 .53 .34 .24 1.00
Investment Mgt.	.48 .80 .77 .62 .66 .15 .57 −.34 .72 −.21 .27 .27 .55 .75 1.00
Banker	.81 .61 .80 .92 .75 .61 .39 .62 .80 .66 .76 .65 .55 1.00
Chamb. Comm. Exec.	.84 .61 .79 .91 .82 .68 .61 .77 .84 .72 .85 .85 1.00
Dept. Store Mgr.	.70 .79 .79 .89 .85 .58 .61 .76 .83 .77 .85 1.00
Buyer	.70 .80 .61 .79 .79 .57 .79 .80 .89 .85 1.00
Purchasing	.70 .80 .71 .71 .84 .58 .71 .77 .83 1.00
Credit Manager	.76 .74 .66 .73 .85 .57 .79 .91 1.00
Bus. Ed. Teacher	.64 .68 .71 .81 .83 .58 .66 1.00
Pharmacist	.59 .55 .66 .67 .77 .55 1.00
Chiropractor	.26 .70 .44 .67 .70 1.00
Funeral Director	.56 .70 .80 .81 1.00
Sales Manager	.64 .73 .85 1.00
Life Ins. Salesman	.88 .84 1.00
Real Estate Salesman	.73 1.00
Computer Salesman	1.00

TABLE E-6. CORRELATIONS BETWEEN THE 1971 MEN'S OCCUPATIONAL SCALES AND THE BASIC INTEREST SCALES

	Pub. Speaking	Law/Politics	Bus. Mgt.	Sales	Merchandising	Office Practices	Mil. Activities	Tech. Supervision	Mathematics	Science	Mechanical	Nature	Agriculture	Adventure	Rec. Leadership	Med. Service	Soc. Service	Relig. Activities	Teaching	Music	Art	Writing
College Professor	-29	-32	-72	-77	-72	-58	-48	-70	14	30	-19	12	-22	-22	-38	03	-07	-12	18	41	42	40
Anthropologist	-47	-49	-78	-79	-76	-66	-51	-70	-02	12	-30	-06	-29	-29	-52	-19	-32	-38	-10	13	19	15
Political Scientist	-03	-07	-42	-46	-38	-39	-46	-59	-15	-26	-70	-22	-51	-45	-51	-20	10	-11	18	34	31	44
Bus. Adm. Professor	15	16	00	-11	-06	-19	-39	-27	11	-07	-50	-43	-66	-39	-40	-17	00	-18	14	16	03	28
Sociologist	03	00	-38	-46	-36	-32	-44	-51	01	06	-38	-03	-39	-31	-36	00	27	02	40	50	49	60
Psychologist	03	-01	-36	-42	-36	-44	-45	-50	04	20	-26	06	-32	-20	-30	12	19	-09	36	53	56	58
Psychiatrist	01	-01	-27	-35	-29	-28	-17	-34	27	44	-08	19	-21	-21	-21	34	23	10	45	57	50	49
Physician	-08	-11	-38	-44	-38	-29	02	-28	45	73	36	51	21	17	03	54	04	20	30	45	40	34
Dentist	-22	-24	-41	-41	-37	-29	03	-36	29	62	23	37	14	13	00	52	-02	05	11	25	31	18
Biologist	-39	-48	-71	-74	-67	-46	-26	-61	29	50	01	28	-07	-20	-36	17	-21	-03	11	31	32	25
Chemist	-31	-30	-52	-58	-61	-38	-28	-33	56	73	32	22	-04	-04	-20	16	-24	-03	09	25	17	13
Physicist	-44	-42	-73	-77	-78	-54	-45	-59	33	45	-03	02	-24	-22	-42	-04	-29	-21	01	21	15	12
Mathematician	-49	-45	-75	-78	-80	-57	-50	-64	27	31	-18	-11	-34	-29	-49	-16	-38	-28	-07	12	06	06
Engineer	-01	05	11	02	-03	07	27	36	60	79	87	30	34	41	30	30	-18	08	-01	04	-06	-11
Petroleum Engineer	07	15	37	28	23	24	38	56	56	59	78	10	30	40	33	22	-28	07	-13	-19	-39	-39
Computer Programmer	-08	01	04	-06	-08	14	15	19	69	80	73	19	12	22	15	29	-12	08	04	13	02	-06
Cartographer	00	05	18	08	10	29	28	38	51	72	87	36	38	37	29	35	-10	14	-04	03	01	-15
Math-Sci. Teacher	-05	03	-06	-09	-16	-04	17	15	63	89	72	40	34	36	30	49	00	21	24	10	00	-03
Food Scientist	21	24	33	27	23	19	34	43	53	67	72	34	34	39	29	50	00	16	07	12	03	-06
Med. Technologist	-02	-02	-01	-02	-06	17	23	09	58	82	63	38	25	17	24	59	10	37	21	26	15	00
Physical Therapist	35	34	30	27	26	28	49	38	26	51	66	54	52	36	57	64	47	53	39	26	24	19
Optometrist	17	28	42	35	36	36	28	36	56	62	50	06	00	18	18	56	10	14	12	09	-06	-10
Air Force Officer	23	30	45	37	32	34	49	62	54	61	84	19	33	44	39	29	-09	13	-02	-08	-20	-17
Army Officer	50	57	74	64	62	47	59	74	31	21	49	05	26	45	47	26	17	20	11	-07	-22	-12
Navy Officer	35	46	60	49	47	36	51	69	46	42	65	04	24	48	40	28	-04	10	-01	-10	-32	-26
Army Sergeant	18	25	64	56	57	61	49	64	02	-10	30	-19	13	16	27	-09	-07	-01	-23	-49	-52	-48
Veterinarian	-06	-02	22	28	25	34	41	30	17	19	36	21	47	27	32	36	-19	15	-20	-43	-49	-53
Voc. Ag. Teacher	16	17	46	46	41	48	46	63	11	15	63	31	56	32	43	14	00	21	-04	-40	-41	-41
Farmer	-36	-29	02	09	02	19	13	22	-08	-13	25	-06	27	05	05	-29	-44	-15	-48	-60	-58	-64
Forester	-03	-03	14	09	10	16	37	44	29	45	78	55	67	41	42	19	-23	.15	-10	-19	-20	-21
Skilled Tradesman	-29	-21	09	09	12	18	24	36	20	32	68	11	36	24	19	-06	-41	-13	-38	-42	-43	-57
Highway Patrolman	21	29	45	46	37	33	59	67	10	20	68	21	56	55	60	21	-04	14	-14	-39	-43	-37
Policeman	39	44	56	56	50	42	63	75	13	23	72	30	56	61	66	29	15	26	04	-12	-16	-08
Personnel Director	65	62	80	66	73	38	24	56	-05	18	03	-05	00	10	24	12	43	21	24	11	03	11
Public Administration	72	71	74	58	63	33	20	52	07	-02	07	-08	-09	06	21	13	48	24	36	20	07	24
Soc. Sci. Teacher	60	61	69	65	70	49	27	51	-31	-36	-03	06	17	11	42	16	63	37	36	04	06	20
Rehab. Counselor	54	49	60	44	55	38	12	33	-02	-10	-05	10	-05	-16	06	21	68	41	53	37	31	37
YMCA Staff Member	60	53	67	60	64	40	31	48	-09	-12	07	12	22	15	47	27	66	44	41	19	18	22
Elem. Teacher	40	30	26	21	33	27	16	15	03	13	13	43	22	13	28	45	70	50	67	56	59	61
Guidance Counselor	43	42	62	54	56	44	26	40	-08	-18	-02	02	12	-04	40	19	64	46	33	-01	-06	01
School Supt.	66	57	81	66	73	49	37	60	04	-10	16	07	17	11	39	17	52	44	37	10	-03	09
Community Rec. Adm.	59	49	71	64	70	46	35	54	-02	-06	22	23	32	21	56	31	64	47	40	16	14	22
Social Worker	56	47	35	25	35	19	05	10	-19	-15	-15	14	-07	-15	07	20	73	41	57	50	53	60
Minister	55	34	21	17	22	18	10	10	00	02	-01	31	08	-02	09	36	71	66	68	54	53	58
Priest	42	28	09	06	10	07	-04	-08	-10	-14	-28	12	-12	-19	-06	22	69	56	63	63	53	58
English Teacher	41	22	-03	00	05	-03	-02	-12	-23	-08	-14	29	02	-05	10	20	60	40	65	60	66	82
Music Teacher	07	-18	-09	-16	-03	04	-26	-29	-11	-26	13	-26	13	-32	-55	02	48	33	55	67	68	51
Librarian	-01	-13	-24	-29	-16	-01	-29	-38	-03	01	-28	08	-36	-48	-45	02	31	17	43	65	66	64
Musician	-21	-36	-31	-36	-21	-08	-48	-41	-02	00	-24	12	-28	-28	-51	00	11	01	23	72	73	43
Artist	-37	-48	-75	-74	-66	-59	-50	-73	-18	-05	-36	10	-19	-26	-45	-16	-15	-22	00	34	48	37
Architect	-34	-41	-56	-58	-50	-34	-27	-44	12	37	23	31	05	-03	-25	07	-19	-11	00	43	59	32
Photographer	-15	-27	-59	-60	-51	-56	-47	-60	-17	-04	-30	15	-15	-13	-09	-08	-02	-21	11	43	56	50
Interior Decorator	-15	-32	-20	-19	00	-06	-36	-48	-49	-54	-65	-09	-35	-48	-60	-20	15	-11	07	36	55	25
Advertising Man	44	27	20	18	30	-08	-07	-05	-40	-36	-34	05	-13	-02	-04	01	-51	04	26	41	56	59
Journalist	10	08	-34	-33	-27	-42	-30	-50	-39	-39	-67	-11	-33	-19	-23	21	-08	16	30	39	56	
Lawyer	55	51	21	12	18	-03	-09	-04	-31	-34	-49	-10	-29	-19	-10	-01	40	20	35	30	22	51
CPA	30	43	67	55	54	47	28	57	35	06	20	-34	-10	17	30	00	-05	01	-19	-29	-55	-30
Investments Mgr.	05	12	08	00	04	-22	-29	-19	-12	-32	-55	-54	-56	-22	-37	-36	-23	-51	-25	-10	-14	-07
Banker	20	23	66	56	60	47	22	51	-02	-33	-04	-40	-13	-08	09	-24	-10	-08	-27	-37	-51	-42
Chamb. Comm. Exec.	68	63	80	71	76	42	23	55		-11	-28	-05	-12	-04	04	26	45	23	22	12	06	18
Dept. Store Mgr.	51	54	80	71	78	47	34	61	-03	-14	15	-04	14	25	43	20	38	18	07	-01	-05	-04
Buyer	45	44	83	74	86	57	23	55	-20	-43	-07	-22	-11	01	07	-07	26	02	-04	-05	-06	-10
Purchasing Agent	37	42	81	73	74	61	51	82	06	34	55	08	34	35	36	16	14	20	-06	-22	-28	-30
Credit Manager	48	53	87	77	81	67	41	71	09	-09	22	-08	07	09	31	15	31	26	06	-06	-17	-14
Bus. Ed. Teacher	45	44	87	78	83	76	32	70	-03	-17	19	-06	04	-04	21	09	43	29	21	02	-04	-07
Pharmacist	18	23	65	65	68	60	41	55	10	11	29	03	19	19	33	39	12	22	-11	-25	-31	-42
Chiropractor	55	50	58	57	61	39	37	45	00	12	32	36	32	29	33	58	54	43	34	25	28	18
Funeral Director	45	44	81	78	84	69	37	59	-14	-29	10	-03	14	11	22	21	37	25	03	08	-11	-22
Sales Manager	63	58	81	77	80	40	31	60	-10	-23	07	-06	05	17	28	09	33	14	12	02	-02	03
Life Ins. Salesman	47	45	72	71	68	36	21	52	-20	-48	-16	-25	-01	04	18	-10	22	07	-06	-23	-34	-19
Real Estate Salesman	35	42	75	80	73	48	34	66	-12	-32	10	-27	06	18	27	-08	03	-01	-24	-43	-49	-42
Computer Salesman	69	69	77	72	66	36	36	65	25	14	33	00	13	34	38	26	30	21	17	07	-06	02

TABLE E-7. CORRELATIONS BETWEEN THE 1971 MEN'S OCCUPATIONAL SCALES, AND THE NONOCCUPATIONAL SCALES, LIKE, INDIFFERENT, DISLIKE PERCENTAGES, AND THE HOLLAND SCALES

	Academic Achievement	Age Related	Diversity of Interest	M-F II	Managerial Orientation	Occupational Intro.-Extro.	Occupational Level	Specialization Level	Liberalism-Conservatism	Cultural Change	A-B (1969)	Like Percentage	Indifferent Percentage	Dislike Percentage	Realistic II	Intellectual II	Artistic II	Social II	Persuasive II	Enterprising II	Conventional II	Realistic I	Intellectual I	Artistic I	Social I	Persuasive I	Enterprising I	Conventional I
College Professor	71	36	-20	-52	-20	29	19	51	54	-11	48	-18	-23	38	-32	33	44	-19	-10	-75	-47	-27	33	44	-12	-08	-77	-44
Anthropologist	44	17	-45	-35	-30	57	09	33	51	-30	31	-40	-31	63	-42	07	15	-49	-33	-84	-61	-39	11	14	-40	-27	-82	-58
Political Scientist	45	14	-28	-49	-17	09	40	40	83	03	64	-19	-42	57	-73	-14	29	-06	11	-51	-41	-69	-15	30	03	16	-47	-33
Bus. Adm. Professor	40	08	-21	-11	18	-09	57	54	55	26	42	-13	-20	31	-63	02	04	-09	27	-17	-11	-59	04	05	01	31	-15	-17
Sociologist	66	32	01	-14	-14	-08	28	61	73	10	66	-03	-19	21	-46	17	49	13	26	-44	-24	-41	15	49	23	28	-44	-21
Psychologist	67	36	04	-53	-13	-13	39	66	61	23	46	10	-21	22	-37	31	58	08	29	-39	-36	-33	52	58	19	29	-42	-36
Psychiatrist	77	56	22	-46	05	-16	41	62	39	14	23	19	-17	02	-16	54	52	19	28	-32	-08	-13	72	52	27	17	-33	-11
Physician	76	54	27	-33	06	02	13	37	00	06	15	27	-06	-16	29	61	48	07	06	-34	-08	32	61	44	-04	-16	-38	-09
Dentist	62	43	15	-26	-03	16	04	27	01	-04	74	15	-11	-01	17	54	33	07	-13	-34	-11	19	47	32	05	17	-37	-10
Biologist	72	47	-13	-43	-26	46	09	37	28	-31	06	-14	-18	29	-10	46	30	-02	-29	-73	-30	-07	48	27	-04	-28	-71	-28
Chemist	70	41	-07	-19	-15	36	08	46	04	-13	06	-05	01	03	11	68	21	-26	-20	-58	-13	14	72	18	-24	-19	-61	-18
Physicist	65	30	-33	-27	-24	61	14	43	38	-24	18	-31	-31	36	-22	41	05	-40	-31	-80	-37	-18	45	13	-34	-28	-81	-39
Mathematician	56	19	-45	-23	-27	61	14	37	38	-26	-36	-41	-16	49	-35	27	02	-51	-37	-83	-42	-31	32	04	-44	-32	-83	-43
Engineer	22	26	28	23	20	02	01	18	-68	08	-55	39	12	-44	74	70	-33	-07	00	08	19	73	52	-01	-12	02	-06	19
Petroleum Engineer	-07	04	21	54	26	01	00	-06	-84	12	-26	31	21	-46	71	48	07	-10	-05	32	46	68	45	-35	-18	-06	28	31
Computer Programmer	38	26	28	11	16	06	05	28	-49	04	-45	30	18	-43	54	74	03	-07	-03	00	43	54	52	05	-09	-03	31	29
Cartographer	12	23	38	20	02	-01	-19	06	-68	-02	-19	35	32	-60	76	61	08	-02	-01	17	52	75	63	-03	-07	-05	12	39
Math-Sci. Teacher	49	34	35	13	13	-02	19	21	-43	15	-17	35	23	-49	60	84	06	13	-01	-05	19	60	84	06	09	-07	-10	11
Food Scientist	22	28	46	17	34	-23	13	13	-66	23	-09	58	-04	-43	66	66	05	09	17	35	41	64	64	05	07	-05	29	31
Med. Technologist	51	40	44	-02	06	-06	-01	17	-41	01	-26	33	23	-50	51	78	18	21	-03	04	41	69	78	15	15	-06	00	35
Physical Therapist	22	40	67	-02	18	-51	-06	04	-45	25	-44	63	17	-68	70	56	32	61	33	36	41	69	56	30	54	13	30	40
Optometrist	27	20	44	24	28	-24	22	16	-46	30	-21	40	19	-52	37	64	-04	17	16	40	52	37	51	-06	15	-10	38	44
Air Force Officer	-01	14	40	42	33	-21	01	11	-78	21	-35	46	24	-61	77	54	-14	04	17	42	56	75	56	-17	-02	13	36	41
Army Officer	-18	-01	49	42	53	-54	-04	-04	-63	46	-58	60	05	-54	57	24	-16	32	40	70	55	53	23	-17	25	37	66	47
Navy Officer	-11	-02	39	51	44	-34	14	00	-72	40	-54	35	22	-58	64	40	-24	12	26	55	51	62	41	-26	06	24	50	37
Army Sergeant	-57	-27	12	56	19	14	-16	-35	-61	03	-64	12	26	-35	35	-21	-51	02	-27	31	61	43	-18	-57	-05	-04	58	53
Veterinarian	-26	-07	15	50	00	13	-23	-52	-62	-06	-70	03	27	-29	47	11	-51	-02	-05	31	35	11	11	-52	-13	-52	30	32
Voc. Ag. Teacher	-45	02	26	50	08	-10	-26	-41	-74	01	-54	24	33	-52	70	07	-41	17	-05	51	47	66	07	-43	08	-07	48	42
Farmer	-61	-34	-34	45	-30	56	-52	-62	-48	-42	-42	-31	22	04	27	-31	-65	-39	-56	04	12	25	-25	-66	-46	-55	07	09
Forester	-16	23	20	32	01	09	-28	-20	-75	-10	-54	25	25	-45	83	31	-15	-06	-12	18	27	80	32	-19	-14	-13	19	19

460

Skilled Craftsman	-38	-09	-08	47	-05	39	-39	-33	-76	-31	-73	-05	27	-22	61	11	-46	-34	-43	10	26	57	17	-49	-40	-43	08	17
Highway Patrolman	-46	-12	30	59	18	-17	-31	-39	-81	14	-54	29	33	-56	79	11	-38	12	06	49	37	74	11	-39	04	03	45	29
Policeman	-35	-04	51	28	39	-20	-31	-76	27	-37	52	30	-72	-26	83	19	-07	32	33	62	47	79	16	-09	24	28	57	40
Personnel Director	-20	06	39	12	57	-73	51	10	-18	56	17	58	-22	-26	11	-06	07	51	58	72	34	09	-12	08	51	58	71	30
Pub. Administrator	01	19	43	11	52	-82	53	35	-09	61	23	56	-10	-36	11	10	12	53	71	62	40	10	06	12	56	70	59	33
Soc. Sci. Teacher	-33	-01	44	07	20	-74	11	-15	-03	45	11	49	01	-42	14	-24	09	71	57	69	35	13	-32	10	69	55	69	40
Rehab. Counselor	14	39	48	-21	29	-73	49	26	12	41	31	60	-25	-25	-02	05	01	71	56	51	51	-01	-01	30	74	54	51	43
YMCA Staff Member	-10	10	54	00	39	-82	27	-04	-14	49	17	63	-15	-38	19	01	22	78	55	65	34	18	-06	23	75	51	63	37
Elem. Teacher	33	34	60	-48	04	-61	10	19	14	32	34	67	-32	-46	21	27	64	76	52	65	23	22	17	64	75	45	31	30
Guidance Counselor	-14	12	41	11	31	-65	14	-16	-11	36	07	45	-13	-24	08	-07	-05	73	33	53	37	06	-11	-02	70	29	56	43
School Supt.	-16	16	48	17	48	-80	34	02	-27	46	02	57	-04	-43	27	00	02	67	53	55	50	24	-04	03	63	50	72	48
Community Rec. Adm.	-13	14	60	05	39	-82	36	-04	-25	43	05	65	-03	-50	35	05	20	77	55	73	43	33	-01	20	73	50	69	43
Social Worker	23	39	45	-41	18	-75	19	39	35	38	51	50	-20	-21	-11	02	54	71	66	72	16	-10	-06	53	76	64	24	23
Minister	40	40	48	-51	08	-67	38	28	26	33	47	56	-16	-30	06	20	60	77	49	31	-07	07	11	59	77	51	30	26
Priest	37	35	31	-63	-05	-53	09	39	48	26	58	42	-12	-23	-22	05	40	57	49	03	-10	-05	-03	75	66	55	03	16
English Teacher	45	50	11	-76	-10	-22	25	40	50	41	16	16	-27	13	-34	-01	62	42	12	-12	03	-31	-03	62	48	10	-08	00
Music Teacher	57	42	05	-79	-30	-03	13	52	61	44	09	05	-17	09	-39	08	62	18	17	-27	02	-34	07	62	26	13	-23	10
Librarian	42	21	00	-79	-29	14	03	31	50	33	37	07	-26	20	-36	05	68	01	-04	-30	-13	-30	04	66	09	-06	-28	-05
Musician	40	19	-33	-61	-33	40	01	29	60	13	45	-26	-38	58	-43	-04	45	-30	-19	-74	-62	-39	04	45	-23	-16	-73	-54
Artist	46	31	-05	-53	-21	32	-11	40	13	04	19	-15	11	11	09	33	58	-19	-16	-51	-25	12	35	55	-23	-15	-53	-26
Architect	41	19	19	-62	-19	32	09	08	60	32	56	-05	-43	46	-36	01	57	-17	05	-57	-58	-31	-01	56	-08	08	-59	-53
Photographer	03	06	-18	-67	-19	08	13	63	-08	42	56	-12	-46	55	-66	-46	40	00	-10	-16	-28	-64	-48	41	07	-08	-10	-15
Interior Decorator	04	08	19	-45	25	-54	31	38	33	15	58	41	-45	11	-26	-22	60	32	56	22	-19	-26	-28	61	37	56	23	14
Advertising Man	26	02	-14	-48	-11	-11	29	77	17	41	02	-02	-46	47	-59	-26	42	07	30	-36	-52	-57	-31	44	14	33	-34	-41
Journalist	20	16	12	-23	17	-54	33	53	46	24	22	30	-29	10	-40	-15	28	37	62	11	-06	-38	-21	30	42	65	12	-01
Lawyer	-23	-20	17	59	41	-27	32	-06	38	50	31	07	-45	-28	21	06	-49	-31	53	58	58	19	09	-50	-27	22	53	44
CPA	-06	-18	-35	08	35	00	55	32	-48	31	16	25	07	-23	-59	-26	-17	-35	07	-05	-20	-58	-23	-14	-27	15	-03	-28
Investment Fund Mgr.	-52	-24	-10	46	35	-16	26	24	32	22	-33	-10	-41	13	01	-36	-53	-05	-02	55	44	-02	-32	-51	-09	00	58	39
Banker	-23	-01	39	09	48	-79	44	09	-40	51	-33	54	-19	-26	03	-16	09	51	64	75	36	02	-20	09	52	63	75	35
Chamb. Comm. Exec.	-32	-06	45	22	53	-68	33	-11	-39	48	01	63	-21	-31	26	-06	-01	46	43	79	44	23	-10	-01	43	41	76	41
Dept. Store Manager	-50	-17	25	16	40	-54	28	-12	-39	28	-04	39	-18	-15	00	-37	-10	26	34	80	43	00	-39	-10	27	33	82	41
Buyer	-50	-07	40	46	34	-43	-03	-26	-22	21	-46	47	17	-55	62	00	-26	34	21	81	61	57	00	-26	18	18	78	54
Purchasing Agent	-50	-07	40	46	34	-58	-03	-26	-76	21	-46	47	07	-46	28	-03	-17	41	37	81	68	25	-05	-18	38	34	81	62
Credit Manager	-33	-01	43	32	40	-58	24	-11	-46	33	07	47	08	-46	22	-13	-09	52	34	83	68	19	-15	-10	50	30	85	67
Bus. Ed. Teacher	-35	02	41	16	25	-54	12	-11	-35	23	-23	47	08	-46	35	08	-35	24	00	69	55	31	08	-35	16	-05	70	53
Pharmacist	-34	-12	35	42	19	-25	-08	-41	-57	15	41	30	22	-46	41	24	30	64	49	69	39	40	16	28	60	42	65	39
Chiropractor	-02	21	62	-04	26	-70	07	-03	-27	41	07	64	04	-57	21	-23	-16	44	27	85	56	27	-27	-16	39	24	86	57
Funeral Director	-48	-13	40	23	29	-54	07	-34	-38	24	-21	40	06	-38	16	-14	01	42	53	82	33	12	-18	02	41	52	81	29
Sales Manager	-35	-04	37	20	58	-76	40	00	-28	50	06	52	-13	-29	-03	-41	-33	28	30	69	23	-06	-43	-30	26	31	71	23
Life Ins. Salesman	-54	-24	09	35	38	-50	33	-30	-22	-05	26	-19	12	-02	20	-33	-50	11	16	78	37	15	-33	-48	06	16	79	31
Real Estate Salesman	-70	-38	10	57	34	-33	02	-39	49	27	-36	17	12	-02	20	-33	-50	11	16	78	37	15	-33	-48	06	16	79	31
Computer Salesman	-11	00	50	30	61	-76	14	63	-42	03	62	-03	-48		36	24	03	43	61	77	43	34	20	03	40	58	72	34

TABLE E-8a. MEANS AND STANDARD DEVIATIONS OF THE SCALE INTERCORRELATION
SAMPLE—OCCUPATIONAL SCALES

Scale	Mean	S.D.	Scale	Mean	S.D.	Scale	Mean	S.D.
College Professor	42.8	10.9	Navy Officer	32.0	13.2	Musician	40.8	12.5
Anthropologist	28.8	12.9	Army Sergeant	24.9	12.1	Artist	28.2	12.3
Political Scientist	31.7	12.4	Veterinarian	18.6	11.4	Architect	24.2	14.6
Bus. Ad. Professor	38.5	10.2	Voc. Ag. Teacher	7.4	13.6	Photographer	32.3	12.2
Sociologist	35.9	12.4	Farmer	13.3	9.9	Interior Decorator	30.8	11.2
Psychologist	40.6	12.4	Forester	20.6	12.2	Advertising Man	35.0	11.6
Psychiatrist	32.0	12.5	Skilled Tradesmen	15.7	12.6	Journalist	36.0	11.8
Physician	34.7	12.4	Highway Patrolman	16.0	15.1	Lawyer	35.8	10.9
Dentist	30.6	11.5	Policeman	25.6	14.8	Cert. Pub. Acc't.	21.0	13.9
Biologist	30.8	12.8	Personnel Director	35.9	11.1	Investment Fund Mgr.	31.5	10.2
Chemist	29.4	14.0	Public Administrator	38.5	10.6	Banker	22.3	11.3
Physicist	21.4	15.5	Soc. Sci. Teacher	34.1	11.6	Chamber Comm. Exec.	35.7	11.2
Mathematician	30.2	12.0	Rehab. Counselor	33.1	11.1	Dept. Store Mgr.	26.5	12.9
Engineer	33.6	12.6	YMCA Staff Member	32.3	13.4	Buyer	23.0	15.2
Petroleum Engineer	26.5	13.4	Elementary Teacher	43.8	12.2	Purchasing Agent	26.7	13.6
Computer Programmer	37.2	12.6	Guidance Counselor	30.6	11.3	Credit Manager	26.3	13.6
Cartographer	34.4	12.8	School Superintend.	31.1	13.1	Bus. Ed. Teacher	27.7	12.3
Math-Science Teacher	34.3	13.6	Community Rec. Adm.	30.5	14.1	Pharmacist	22.9	12.9
Food Scientist	32.7	11.5	Social Worker	36.0	13.7	Chiropractor	35.6	11.2
Med. Technologist	28.2	14.3	Minister	31.9	12.5	Funeral Director	24.6	13.2
Physical Therapist	34.0	12.0	Priest	38.9	12.6	Sales Manager	22.5	13.8
Optometrist	32.3	12.5	English Teacher	40.6	12.0	Life Ins. Salesman	19.5	11.9
Air Force Officer	28.4	12.6	Music Teacher	32.7	12.7	Real Estate Salesman	20.7	12.6
Army Officer	29.1	11.7	Librarian	34.1	13.3	Computer Salesman	24.0	13.3

TABLE E-8b. MEANS AND STANDARD DEVIATIONS OF THE SCALE INTERCORRELATION
SAMPLE—ALL OTHER SCALES

BASIC INTEREST SCALES (Set 2)			NON-OCCUPATIONAL SCALES			HOLLAND SCALES		
Scale	Mean	S.D.	Scale	Mean	S.D.	Scale	Mean	S.D.
Public Speaking	54.8	10.0	Academic Achievement	56.0	12.9	Realistic-II	-1.4	9.4
Law-Politics	56.3	10.0	Age Related	44.2	9.9	Intellectual-II	8.8	7.5
Bus. Management	49.5	10.8	Diversity of Interest	57.1	9.7	Artistic-II	8.1	9.1
Sales	48.2	9.0	Masc-Femininity II	44.5	12.7	Social-II	5.7	8.2
Merchandising	49.5	10.6	Manager. Orientation	39.6	9.8	Enterprising-II	-3.4	7.9
Office Practices	48.3	10.7	Occ. Int.-Extroversion	42.0	11.7	Conventional-II	-1.2	7.0
Military Activities	47.7	9.7	Occupational Level	47.8	10.1			
Technical Supervision	43.0	12.1	Specialization Level	62.1	8.2	Realistic-I	-1.3	6.8
Mathematics	50.2	11.3	Liberal-Conservative	56.1	11.9	Intellectual-I	6.0	5.9
Science	52.1	9.9	Cultural Change	11.9	9.8	Artistic-I	5.9	6.7
Mechanical	43.8	11.4	A-B 1969	57.1	11.6	Social-I	4.5	5.9
Nature	46.0	10.5				Enterprising-I	-2.8	6.2
Agriculture	43.3	11.0	ADMINISTRATIVE INDICES			Conventional-I	.25	5.2
Adventure	57.1	11.7	Scale	Mean	S.D.			
Rec. Leadership	48.0	11.1	Total Responses	8.8	.5			
Medical Service	55.4	10.2	Infrequent Responses	7.1	1.2			
Social Service	59.6	11.7	Form Check	11.9	2.9			
Religious Act.	54.0	12.0	First 100 Likes	36.5	13.4			
Teaching	57.6	9.9	First 100 Indifferent	29.8	16.1			
Music	59.0	10.1	First 100 Dislikes	33.6	16.4			
Art	59.0	10.2						
Writing	59.5	8.1						

TABLE E-9. ITEM COMPOSITION OF THE HOLLAND SCALES

REALISTIC		INTELLECTUAL		ARTISTIC	
Item Number	Item	Item Number	Item	Item Number	Item
4*	Military Officer	3	Architect	1	Actor
12	Auto Racer	6	Astronomer	5	Artist
13	Auto Mechanic	10	Author tech book	9	Author of Novel
14	Airplane Pilot	23	Chemist	20	Cartoonist
17	Building Contractor	34*	Geologist	30*	Art Museum Director
19*	Carpenter	45	Inventor	43	Interior Decorator
24	Civil Engineer	64*	Psychologist	46*	Photographer
37	Farmer	69	Physician'	62	Musician
55	Locomotive Engineer	83	Sci Research Worker	66	Orchestra Conductor
76	Rancher	93*	Surgeon	71	Poet
88	Shop Foreman	106	Botany	84	Sculptor
94	Tool Maker	107	Calculus	104	Art
102	Agriculture	108	Chemistry	110	Dramatics
121*	Industrial Arts	120	Mathematics	141*	Sketch pictures of animals
122	Mechanical Drawing	125*	Nature Study	163	Art galleries
139*	Hunting	128	Physics	172	Poetry
180*	Pop Mech Magazines	129	Psychology	183*	Magazines about art and music
189	Cabinetmaking	144*	Chess	233	Look at coll of antique furn
190	Operating Machine	212	Do research work	261*	Musical geniuses
214*	Be forest ranger	264*	Outstanding sci	263*	Prominent artists

SOCIAL		ENTERPRISING		CONVENTIONAL	
Item Number	Item	Item Number	Item	Item Number	Item
7*	Athletic Director	8*	Auctioneer	15	Bank Teller
26	Minister,Priest, Rabbi	11	Auto Salesman	21	Cashier in bank
33	Employment Manager	18	Buy merchandise	25	City of State Employee
59*	High School Principal	42	Hotel Manager	36*	Income Tax Accountant
70	Playground Director	54	Life Ins Salesman	65	Office Manager
82	School Teacher	77	Real Estate Salesman	74	Private Secretary
89	Social Worker	80	Retailer	91*	Statistician
100	Worker in YMCA	81	Sales Manager	103	Arithmetic
133	Sociology	85	Manager, Chamber Comm	105	Bookkeeping
161*	Go to church	90	Speciality Salesman	111	Economics
164*	Leading Boy Scouts	92*	Stockbroker	134	Spelling
169*	Church youth group	95*	Traveling Salesman	135	Typewriting
184	Soc problem movies	99	Wholesaler	177*	Bus Methods magazines
192	Give "first aid" asst	197	Interview prospects	208*	Make statistical charts
196	Interview men for job	201	Start conversation	223	Methodical work
202	Teaching children	217*	Bargaining (swapping)	224	Reg hours for work
203	Teaching adults	219	Buying merchandise	226*	Developing bus systems
209	Adjust difficulties	238*	Aggressive people	227	Saving money
228	Contribute to charity	243*	People assume ldrship	247	Thrifty people
257*	Babies	245	Made fortune in bus	270*	Insist on thing in proper place

* Eliminated from Set 1 Scales

TABLE E-10. MEAN SCORES FOR 202 SAMPLES ON THE HOLLAND REALISTIC SCALE

Converted Score	Raw Score	
30	10.0 to 10.49	Machinists/Tool & Die Makers/Voc Ag Teachers
	9.5 to 9.99	Skilled Tradesmen/Highway Patrolmen
29	9.0 to 9.49	Electricians/Farmers(1968)/Carpenters(1969)/Policemen(1968)
	8.5 to 8.99	Foresters/Farmers(1967)/Policemen(1969)
28	8.0 to 8.49	County Sheriffs/Orthopedic Surgeons
	7.5 to 7.99	
27	7.0 to 7.49	Air Force Officers/Carpenters(1936)/Pilots
	6.5 to 6.99	Ag Ext Agents/Engineers(1968)/Purchasing Agents(1969)/Army Officers(1950)
26	6.0 to 6.49	Astronauts/Cartographers
	5.5 to 5.99	Farmers(1936)/Generals & Admirals/Neurological Surgeons/Physical Therapists(1966)/Forest Service Me Petroleum Engineers
25	5.0 to 5.49	Math-Sci Teachers(1968)/Radiologists/Vets(1966)/NASA Scientists/Urologists/Army Officers(1969)/ Food Scientists
	4.5 to 4.99	Navy Officers/Physical Therapists(1957)
24	4.0 to 4.49	Elementary Teachers(NoDak)/No Hennepin Jr. Coll Stu/U of M Fresh(1967)/VA Schizophrenic Patients
	3.5 to 3.99	Army Sergeants/Generals and Lt Generals/High School Counselors/Surgeons/Pharmacists(1968)/U of M Fresh (1966)/Computer Programmers/Dentists/Medical Techs/Chiropractors/Vets(1949)/Animal Husb Profs
23	3.0 to 3.49	Architects(1968)/Dental Ed/Dentists and Dental Ed(1969)/Dept Store Mgrs/Salesmen,Real Estate(1969)/ Corp Pres(1965)/Engineers(1928)/Policemen(1933)/Physiatrists/Physicians(1969)/Colonels
	2.5 to 2.99	MIG(1966)/Optometrists/Pediatricians/School Supers(1969)/Comm Rec Direcs/Salesmen,Computer
22	2.0 to 2.49	Biologists/Public Admins(1941)/Credit Mgrs/Legislators/Production Mgrs/Salesmen,Steel/Soc Sci Teachers(1969)/Salesmen,PG&E/Math-Sci Teachers(1936)/Printers
	1.5 to 1.99	Bankers(1934)/Bankers(1964)/Ministers(1969)/Salesmen,3M/Elementary Teachers(Minn)/Chemists(1931)/ Funeral Direcs(1969)/Psychologists(Exp)/CPA(1944)/Chemists(1969)/County Welfare Workers/Osteopaths
21	1.0 to 1.49	Ferris State Stu/Pathologists/Personnel Direcs(1927)/Personnel Direcs(1969)/Salesmen,3M applicants/ YMCA PD/YMCA Staff/Business Ed Teachers/Sales Mgrs(1968)
	.5 to .99	Bankers(1969)/Physicians(1949)/Public Admins(1969)/Social Workers(1967)/Dentists(1932)/English Teachers/Physicists(1927)/Psychiatrists(1949)/Psychologists(Industrial)
20	0 to .49	Musicians(1969)/Physicists(1968)/Salesmen,Auto/Salesmen,Life Insurance(1969)/CPA(1965)
	-.5 to -.01	MIG(1933)/Ministers(1927)/U of M Fresh(1964)/Architects(1933)/Governors/Music Teachers(1946)/Priest (1966)/Psychologists(Market)/Purchasing Agents(1931)/Ministers(1965)/School Supers(1965)/Social Workers(1953)/Psychiatrists(1967)/Teaching Brothers/Guidance Counselors(1950)/Accountants/Cham Comm Execs/Funeral Direcs(1945)/Office Workers/Psychologists(1949)
19	-1.0 to -.51	Internists/Rehab Counselors/YMCA Secs/Astronomers/Buyers(1969)/Unitarian Ministers(1950)/College Profs/Lawyers(1969)/Photographers/Psychologists(Ed)
	-1.5 to -1.01	Salesmen,Encyclopedia/Advertising Men(1968)/Physicians(1927)/Soc Sci Teachers(1936)/Corp Pres(1935) Guidance Counselors(1968)/Psychologists(Child)/Psychologists(Statistical)/Musicians(1952)/Judges and Lawyers
18	-2.0 to -1.51	Buyers(1946)/Psychologists(1947)/Psychologists(Clinical)/Psychologists(Guidance)/Investment Mgrs/ Mpls Symphony/Sales Mgrs(1932)/Buyers for Emporium/Interpreters/Sociologists
	-2.5 to -2.01	Judges/Salesmen,Real Estate(1932)/Anthropologists/Mathematicians(1969)/German Med Students
17	-3.0 to -2.51	Football Coaches/Music Teachers(1952)/School Supers(1930)/Mathematicians(1929)/Pharmacists(1947)/ Student Personnel Workers/Artists(1968)/Business Adm Profs/Librarians/Psychologists(1967)/Economist
	-3.5 to -3.01	Actors(1966)/Lawyers(1949)/Salesmen,Life Insurance(1966)/Artists(1933)/Unitarian Ministers(1929)
16	-4.0 to -3.51	Actors(1937)/Newsmen/Psychologists(Social)/CPA Owners/Interior Decorators/Salesmen,Life Insurance (1931)
	-4.5 to -4.01	Danforth Fellows
15	-5.0 to -4.51	Lawyers(1927)
	-5.5 to -5.01	Advertising Men(1931)
14	-6.0 to -5.51	Political Scientists/Pulitzer Prize Winners
	-6.5 to -6.01	Authors
13	-7.0 to -6.51	NIAL Members
	-7.5 to -7.01	Psychologists(German)
12	-8.0 to -7.51	
	-8.5 to -8.01	Accountants(German)

464

Table E-11. Mean Scores for 202 Samples on the Holland Intellectual Scale

Converted Score	Raw Score	
34	14.0 to 14.49	Physicists(1927)
	13.5 to 13.99	Chemists(1969)/Psychologists(Exp)/Neurological Surgeons
33	13.0 to 13.49	Psychologists(Statistical)
	12.5 to 12.99	Astronomers/Biologists/Pathologists/Physicists(1968)/Chemists(1931)
32	12.0 to 12.49	Physicians(1969)/Psychiatrists(1949)/Urologists/NASA Scientists/Pediatricians/Internists/Orthopedic Surgeons
	11.5 to 11.99	Astronauts/Psychologists(Educ)/Physiatrists/Medical Techs/Psychologists(1949)
31	11.0 to 11.49	Psychologists(Industrial)/Psychologists(1947)/Psychologists(Social)/Mathematicians(1929)/Psychologists(Clinical)/Surgeons/Psychiatrists(1967)/Air Force Officers/Radiologists
	10.5 to 10.99	Math-Sci Teachers(1968)/Psychologists(Guidance)/Mathematicians(1969)/Dental Ed/Animal Husbandry Profs/Math-Sci Teachers(1936)/Psychologists(Child)
30	10.0 to 10.49	Engineers(1928)/Machinists/Physicians(1949)/Engineers(1968)/Food Scientists/Computer Programmers/Optometrists/Psychologists(Market)
	9.5 to 9.99	Danforth Fellows/College Profs/Physical Therapists(1957)/Physical Therapists(1966)/Psychologists(1967)
29	9.0 to 9.49	Anthropologists/Salesmen,Computer/U of M Fresh(1967)/Economists/Army Officers(1950)/Petroleum Engineers
	8.5 to 8.99	Cartographers/Dentists/Physicians(1927)/Dentists and Dental Ed(1969)/U of M Fresh(1966)/German Med Students/Pharmacists(1968)
28	8.0 to 8.49	CPA(1944)/Generals and Admirals/Navy Officers/Elementary Teachers(Minn)/Osteopaths/Pilots/Mpls Symphony/Policemen(1968)
	7.5 to 7.99	Army Officers(1969)/Chiropractors/Dentists(1932)/Student Personnel Workers/Foresters/Sociologists
27	7.0 to 7.49	Architects(1968)/Rehab Counselors/Business Admin Profs/Psychologists(German)/Pharmacists(1947)/Architects(1933)/Public Admin(1941)/Unitarian Ministers(1950)
	6.5 to 6.99	Generals & Lt Generals/Librarians/Ministers(1969)/Unitarian Ministers(1929)/Tool & Die Makers/CPA Owners/NIAL Members/Vets(1966)/YMCA PD/School Supers(1930)
26	6.0 to 6.49	CPA(1965)/Colonels/Corp Pres(1965)/Football Coaches/Credit Mgrs/Elementary Teachers(NoDak)/Guidance Counselors(1950)/Forest Service Men/Electricians/Interpreters/Ministers(1927)/Personnel Directors(1927)/Policemen(1969)/Ag Ext Agents/Production Mgrs/School Supers(1965)
	5.5 to 5.99	School Supers(1969)/Guidance Counselors(1968)/Musicians(1952)/Photographers/Accountants/County Welfare Workers/MIG(1966)/Public Admins(1969)/Social Workers(1953)/Voc Ag Teachers
25	5.0 to 5.49	Highway Patrolmen/Judges/Policemen(1933)/Skilled Tradesmen/Artists(1968)/Investment Mgrs/Political Scientists/Priests/Social Workers(1967)/Comm Rec Direcs/Musicians(1969)/Vets(1949)/Actors(1966)/Corp Pres(1935)/Purchasing Agents(1969)/Salesmen,3M/Salesmen,PG&E/Teaching Brothers
	4.5 to 4.99	Judges and Lawyers/Artists(1933)/YMCA Staff/Office Workers/Business Ed Teachers/Ministers(1965)/Music Teachers(1946)/Salesmen,Steel/YMCA Secs/Buyers for Emporium/Farmers(1936)/Lawyers(1949)/MIG(1933)/U of M Fresh(1964)
24	4.0 to 4.49	Dept Store Mgrs/Personnel Direcs(1969)/Cham Comm Execs/Lawyers(1969)/High School Counselors/Legislators/Printers/Music Teachers(1952)/Sales,3M applicants
	3.5 to 3.99	Actors(1937)/Carpenters(1936)/Pulitzer Prize Winners/Bankers(1964)/Lawyers(1927)/Sales Mgrs(1932)/Salesmen,Auto/County Sheriffs/English Teachers/Purchasing Agents(1931)
23	3.0 to 3.49	Advertising Men(1968)/Army Sergeants/Salesmen,Encyclopedia
	2.5 to 2.99	Sales Mgrs(1968)/VA Schizophrenic Patients/Advertising Men(1931)/Funeral Direcs(1969)/Governors/Accountants(German)/Soc Sci Teachers(1936)
22	2.0 to 2.49	Bankers(1969)/Newsmen/Soc Sci Teachers(1969)
	1.5 to 1.99	Buyers(1969)/Funeral Direcs(1945)/Salesmen,Life Insurance(1966)/Carpenters(1969)/Authors/Salesmen,Life Insurance(1931)/Salesmen,Real Estate(1969)/Buyers(1946)
21	1.0 to 1.49	No. Hennepin Jr Coll Stu/Salesmen,Life Insurance(1969)/Ferris State Stu/Bankers(1934)
	.5 to .99	Interior Decorators/Salesmen,Real Estate(1932)
20	0 to .49	
	-.5 to -.91	
19	-1.0 to -.51	Farmers(1967)
	-1.5 to -1.01	
18	-2.0 to -1.51	Farmers(1968)

465

TABLE E-12. MEAN SCORES FOR 202 SAMPLES ON THE HOLLAND ARTISTIC SCALE

Converted Score	Raw Score	
	15.5 to 15.99	Actors(1966)
35	15.0 to 15.49	
	14.5 to 14.99	
34	14.0 to 14.49	
	13.5 to 13.99	
33	13.0 to 13.49	
	12.5 to 12.99	Actors(1937)
32	12.0 to 12.49	Artists(1968)
	11.5 to 11.99	
31	11.0 to 11.49	
	10.5 to 10.99	Interior Decorators/NIAL Members
30	10.0 to 10.49	
	9.5 to 9.99	Mpls Symphony/Danforth Fellows/Photographers
29	9.0 to 9.49	Architects(1968)
	8.5 to 8.99	Pulitzer Prize Winners/Unitarian Ministers(1950)/Artists(1933)
28	8.0 to 8.49	Music Teachers(1952)
	7.5 to 7.99	Advertising Men(1968)
27	7.0 to 7.49	Architects(1933)/Ministers(1965)/English Teachers/Librarians/Musicians(1952)/Musicians(1969)
	6.5 to 6.99	Unitarian Ministers(1929)/Anthropologists
26	6.0 to 6.49	Newsmen/Psychiatrists(1967)/Ministers(1927)/Music Teachers(1946)/Psychologists(1967)
	5.5 to 5.99	College Profs/Neurological Surgeons/Physiatrists/Psychologists(1947)/Elementary Teachers(Minn.)
25	5.0 to 5.49	Psychologists(Clinical)/Political Scientists/Ministers(1969)/Sociologists
	4.5 to 4.99	Astronomers/Authors/Judges/Physicians(1969)/Social Workers(1953)/Economists/Physicists(1968)/Dental Educators/Interpreters
24	4.0 to 4.49	Psychiatrists(1949)/Psychologists(Social)/Advertising Men(1931)/Priests(1966)/Social Workers(1967)
	3.5 to 3.99	German Med Students/Psychologists(Exp)/Teaching Brothers/Pediatricians/Personnel Direcs(1927)
23	3.0 to 3.49	Student Personnel Workers/Judges & Lawyers/Psychologists(Ed)/Psychologists(Child)/Orthopedic Surgeons/Psychologists(1949)
	2.5 to 2.99	Biologists/Chemists(1969)/Elementary Teachers(No.Dak)/Psychologists(Guidance)/YMCA Secs/Mathematicians(1969)/Psychologists(German)/Public Admins(1969)/Salesmen,Encyclopedia
22	2.0 to 2.49	Lawyers(1969)/Dentists/Psychologists(Industrial)/Business Admin Profs/Chamber Comm Execs/Comm Rec Direcs/Salesmen,3M/Salesmen,3M applicants/Dentists and Dental Ed(1969)/Investment Mgrs/Guidance Counselors(1968)
	1.5 to 1.99	Personnel Direcs(1969)/Computer Programmers/Physical Therapists(1957)/Radiologists/YMCA Staff/Chiropractors/Football Coaches/Internists/Pathologists
21	1.0 to 1.49	Policemen(1968)/Psychologists(Market)/YMCA PD/NASA Scientists/Medical Techs/Salesmen,Life Insurance(1966)/Surgeons/Urologists
	.5 to .99	Astronauts/Dentists(1932)/Physicians(1949)/Soc Sci Teachers(1936)/Ag Ext Agents/Business Ed Teachers/Optometrists/Rehab Counselors/Physical Therapists(1966)/School Supers(1965)/Cartographers/Legislators
20	0 to .49	Guidance Counselors(1950)/Mathematicians(1929)/Public Admins(1941)/Math-Sci Teachers(1968)/Psychologists(Statistical)/School Supers(1930)/Food Scientists/Army Officers(1950)/Buyers(1969)/MIG(1966)/Printers/Salesmen,Computer/VA Schizophrenic Patients
	-.5 to -.01	Engineers(1968)/Generals & Admirals/Math-Sci Teachers(1936)/School Supers(1969)/Salesmen,PG&E/Buyers for Emporium/County Welfare Workers/Credit Mgrs/Physicists(1927)/Soc Sci Teachers(1969)
19	-1.0 to -.51	Lawyers(1927)/Lawyers(1949)/Dept Store Mgrs/Osteopaths/Physicians(1927)/Sales Mgrs(1968)/Salesmen, Steel/MIG(1933)/Navy Officers/Office Workers/Policemen(1969)/U of M Fresh(1964)
	-1.5 to -1.01	Foresters/Governors/Machinists/Salesmen,Life Insurance(1931)/Pharmacists(1968)/Purchasing Agents(196 CPA Owners/Accountants/Air Force Officers/Buyers(1946)
18	-2.0 to -1.51	Carpenters(1936)/Chemists(1931)/Funeral Direcs(1969)/CPA(1944)/Corp Pres(1965)/Colonels/Engineers(1928)/High School Counselors
	-2.5 to -2.01	Animal Husbandry Profs/Pilots/Policemen(1933)/Sales Mgrs(1932)/Army Officers(1969)/Tool & Die Makers/Corp Pres(1935)/U of M Fresh(1966)
17	-3.0 to -2.51	Army Sergeants/Bankers(1969)/Funeral Direcs(1945)/Forest Service Men/Petroleum Engineers/Salesmen,Auto/Salesmen,Life Insurance(1969)/CPA(1965)/Production Mgrs/U of M Fresh(1967)/Highway Patrolmen
	-3.5 to -3.01	County Sheriffs/Salesmen,Real Estate(1932)/Salesmen, Real Estate(1969)/Skilled Tradesmen/Generals & Lt Generals/Vets(1966)/Pharmacists(1947)
16	-4.0 to -3.51	Electricians/Carpenters(1969)/Farmers(1936)/Bankers(1964)/Purchasing Agents(1931)
15	-4.5 to -4.01	Bankers(1934)
	-5.0 to -4.51	Voc Ag Teachers/North Hennepin Jr. Coll Stu/Vets(1949)
14	-5.5 to -5.01	Accountants(German)/Ferris State Students
	-6.0 to -5.51	
13	-6.5 to -6.01	
	-7.0 to -6.51	Farmers(1967)
12	-7.5 to -7.01	
	-8.0 to -7.51	Farmers(1968)

466

TABLE E-13. MEAN SCORES FOR 202 SAMPLES ON THE HOLLAND SOCIAL SCALE

Converted Score	Raw Score	
	12.5 to 12.99	YMCA Staff
32	12.0 to 12.49	
	11.5 to 11.99	
31	11.0 to 11.49	YMCA Secretaries
	10.5 to 10.99	Ministers(1965)/Rehab Counselors/Social Workers(1953)/Guidance Counselors(1950)
30	10.0 to 10.49	High School Counselors/YMCA PD/Guidance Counselors(1968)
	9.5 to 9.99	Ministers(1969)
29	9.0 to 9.49	Unitarian Ministers(1950)/Soc Sci Teachers(1969)/Ministers(1927)/Student Personnel Workers/Social Workers(1967)/
	8.5 to 8.99	School Supers(1965)/School Supers(1969)/Comm Rec Direcs/Soc Sci Teachers(1936)
28	8.0 to 8.49	Elementary Teachers(NoDak)/Policemen(1968)/Priests(1966)
	7.5 to 7.99	Ag Ext Agents/Teaching Brothers/Bus Ed Teachers/Physical Therapists(1957)/Psychologists(Guidance)/Salesmen,3M applicants/Elementary Teachers(Minn)/Legislators/County Welfare Workers
27	7.0 to 7.49	Psychologists(1947)
	6.5 to 6.99	Dept Store Mgrs/Personnel Direcs(1969)/School Supers(1930)/Physical Therapists(1966)/Salesmen,3M/Salesmen,Encyclopedia/Music Teachers(1952)
26	6.0 to 6.49	English Teachers/Voc Ag Teachers
	5.5 to 5.99	Psychologists(Ed)
25	5.0 to 5.49	Math-Sci Teachers(1968)/Physiatrists/Danforth Fellows/Math-Sci Teachers(1936)/Psychologists(Clinical) Football Coaches/Sociologists
	4.5 to 4.99	County Sheriffs/Cham Comm Execs/Credit Mgrs/VA Schizophrenic Patients
24	4.0 to 4.49	Public Admins(1969)/Unitarian Ministers(1929)/Medical Techs/Salesmen,Life Insurance(1969)/Chiropractors/Highway Patrolmen/Psychiatrists(1949)/Psychiatrists(1967)/Psychologists(Child)/Music Teachers(1946)/Personnel Direcs(1927)/Salesmen,Life Insurance(1966)
	3.5 to 3.99	Pediatricians/Pharmacists(1968)/Salesmen,Steel/Policemen(1969)/Funeral Direcs(1969)/Psychologists(Market)/Sales Mgrs(1968)
23	3.0 to 3.49	Judges/Physicians(1969)/Purchasing Agents(1969)/Psychologists(1967)/Librarians/Psychologists(1949)/Governors
	2.5 to 2.99	Psychologists(Industrial)/Psychologists(Social)/Public Admins(1941)/Army Officers(1969)/Machinists/Psychologists(German)/Vets(1966)/Buyers(1969)/Optometrists
22	2.0 to 2.49	Generals & Lt Generals/Lawyers(1969)/Army Sergeants/Lawyers(1949)/Dental Educators/Interpreters/Salesmen,Computer/Judges & Lawyers
	1.5 to 1.99	Animal Husbandry Profs/Salesmen,Real Estate(1969)/Air Force Officers/Policemen(1933)/Cartographers/Salesmen,PG&E
21	1.0 to 1.49	Advertising Men(1968)/Colonels/Foresters/Orthopedic Surgeons/Osteopaths/Salesmen,Life Insurance(1931)/Bus Admin Profs/CPA(1965)/Dentists and Dental Ed(1969)/Food Scientists/Internists
	.5 to .99	Bankers(1964)/Buyers for Emporium/Mpls Symphony/Musicians(1952)/Musicians(1969)/Pharmacists(1947)/Psychologists(Statistical)/Urologists/College Profs/Buyers(1946)/Generals & Admirals/Navy Officers/Newsmen/Political Scientists/Tool & Die Makers/Dentists/Vets(1949)
20	0 to .49	Astronauts/Office Workers/Salesmen,Auto/Accountants/Electricians/Skilled Tradesmen/Biologists/Computer Programmers/German Med Students/Neurological Surgeons/Physicians(1949)/Surgeons/Engineers(1968)/Actors/(1966)/Chemists(1969)/Funeral Direcs(1945)/MIG(1966)
	-.5 to -.01	Radiologists/NASA Scientists/Forest Service Men/Army Officers(1950)/CPA(1944)/Economists/Corp Pres(1965)/Production Mgrs/Psychologists(Exp)
19	-1.0 to -.51	Bankers(1969)/Farmers(1968)/MIG(1933)/Pathologists/U of M Fresh(1964)/CPA Owners/Carpenters(1969)/Petroleum Engineers/No Hennepin Jr. Coll Stu
	-1.5 to -1.01	Printers/Sales Mgrs(1932)/Interior Decorators/Investment Mgrs
18	-2.0 to -1.51	Astronomers/Lawyers(1927)/Actors(1937)/Bankers(1934)/Carpenters(1936)/Corp Pres(1935)/Ferris State Stu/Mathematicians(1929)/Architects(1968)/Physicians(1927)
	-2.5 to -2.01	Farmers(1936)/Farmers(1967)/Physicists(1968)/Photographers/Salesmen,Real Estate(1932)/U of M Fresh(1967)/Pulitzer Prize Winners
17	-3.0 to -2.51	Dentists(1932)/U of M Fresh(1966)/Chemists(1931)/Mathematicians(1969)/Purchasing Agents(1931)/Advertising Men(1931)/Pilots
	-3.5 to -3.01	Accountants(German)/Physicists(1927)
16	-4.0 to -3.51	Engineers(1928)/Anthropologists/Artists(1968)
	-4.5 to -4.01	
15	-5.0 to -4.51	NIAL Members/Architects(1933)
	-5.5 to -5.01	Authors
14	-6.0 to -5.51	
	-6.5 to -6.01	Artists(1933)

467

Converted Score	Raw Score	
	9.5 to 9.99	Salesmen,3M applicants
29	9.0 to 9.49	Salesmen,3M
	8.5 to 8.99	Dept Store Mgrs/Sales Mgrs(1968)
28	8.0 to 8.49	Salesmen,Life Insurance(1969)
	7.5 to 7.99	Salesmen,Encyclopedia
27	7.0 to 7.49	Salesmen,PG&E
	6.5 to 6.99	Salesmen,Real Estate(1969)
26	6.0 to 6.49	Salesmen,Auto/Salesmen,Computer/Buyers(1946)/Buyers(1969)
	5.5 to 5.99	
25	5.0 to 5.49	Business Ed Teachers/Elementary Teachers(Minn)/Salesmen,Life Insurance(1966)
	4.5 to 4.99	Buyers for Emporium
24	4.0 to 4.49	Policemen(1968)
	3.5 to 3.99	Credit Mgrs/Funeral Directors(1969)/Purchasing Agents(1969)/Salesmen,Life Insurance(1931)
23	3.0 to 3.49	Pharmacists(1968)/YMCA Secs/Cham Comm Execs
	2.5 to 2.99	Sales Mgrs(1932)/Salesmen,Real Estate(1932)
22	2.0 to 2.49	Funeral Directors(1945)/Legislators/Pharmacists(1947)
	1.5 to 1.99	Personnel Directors(1969)/County Welfare Workers/Voc Ag Teachers
21	1.0 to 1.49	Guidance Counselors(1950)/Soc Sci Teachers(1969)/Comm Rec Directors/Office Workers
	.5 to .99	Ag Ext Agents/VA Schizophrenic Patients/Purchasing Agents(1931)/Rehab Counselors/YMCA Staff
20	0 to .49	Chiropractors/High School Counselors/School Supers(1965)/School Supers(1969)/Advertising Men(1968)/ Food Scientists/Policemen(1969)/Psychologists(Market)/Soc Sci Teachers(1936)
	-.5 to -.01	Bankers(1969)/Army Sergeants/Guidance Counselors(1968)/Elementary Teachers(NoDak)
19	-1.0 to -.51	County Sheriffs/Highway Patrolmen/Air Force Officers/Army Officers(1969)/Bankers(1964)/No Hennepin Jr Coll Stu/Ministers(1969)/Vets(1966)
	-1.5 to -1.01	Machinists/YMCA PD/Bankers(1934)/CPA(1965)/Football Coaches/Corp Pres(1935)/Interior Decorators/ Public Admins(1969)
18	-2.0 to -1.51	Governors/Physical Therapists(1966)/Accountants/Cartographers/Optometrists/Personnel Directors(1927) Petroleum Engineers/Farmers(1968)
	-2.5 to -2.01	Advertising Men(1931)/Ferris State Stu/Social Workers(1953)/Tool & Die Makers/Carpenters(1969)/ Investment Mgrs/MIG(1966)/Navy Officers/Skilled Tradesmen
17	-3.0 to -2.51	Music Teachers(1952)/Corp Pres(1965)/Electricians/Engineers(1968)/Physical Therapists(1957)/MIG(1931) Production Mgrs/U of M Fresh(1964)/Vets(1949)/Army Officers(1950)/English Teachers/Farmers(1967)/ Foresters/Math-Sci Teachers(1936)/
	-3.5 to -3.01	Lawyers(1969)/Music Teachers(1946)/CPA(1944)/Medical Techs/Ministers(1965)/Policemen(1933)
16	-4.0 to -3.51	Colonels/Farmers(1936)/Carpenters(1936)/Musicians(1969)/Public Admins(1941)/Generals & Admirals/ Business Admin Profs/Computer Programmers/Ministers(1927)/Physiatrists/Priests(1966)/School Supers (1930)/Social Workers(1967)
	-4.5 to 4.01	Animal Husbandry Profs/Dentists/Lawyers(1949)/Osteopaths/Dentists & Dental Ed(1969)/Math-Sci Teachers(1968)/Urologists/Printers/Psychologists(Guidance)/Student Personnel Workers/Unitarian Ministers(1950)
15	-5.0 to -4.51	Astronauts/Judges and Lawyers/Orthopedic Surgeons/U of M Fresh(1967)/Teaching Brothers/Internists/ Forest Service Men
	-5.5 to -5.01	Pilots/Radiologists/CPA Owners/Musicians(1952)/Physicians(1969)
14	-6.0 to -5.51	Dentists(1932)/Librarians/Psychologists(1947)/Generals and Lt Generals/Psychologists(Ed)/U of M Fresh(1966)/Psychiatrists(1967)
	-6.5 to -6.01	Salesmen,Steel/Dental Educators/Psychiatrists(1949)/Architects(1968)/Neurological Surgeons/ Pediatricians
13	-7.0 to -6.51	Judges/Physicians(1949)/Psychologists(1967)/Surgeons/NASA Scientists
	-7.5 to -7.01	Sociologists/Chemists(1931)/Lawyers(1927)/Newsmen/Psychologists(1949)/Engineers(1928)/Psychologists (Statistical)
12	-8.0 to -7.51	Chemists(1969)/Economists/Psychologists(Clinical)/Internists/Photographers
	-8.5 to -8.01	College Profs/Mpls Symphony/Architects(1933)/Unitarian Ministers(1929)
11	-9.0 to -8.51	Biologists/Psychologists(Child)/Physicians(1927)
	-9.5 to -9.01	Actors(1966)/Political Scientists/Pathologists/Psychologists(Exp)
10	-10.0 to -9.51	Danforth Fellows/Psychologists(Social)
	-10.5 to -10.01	Astronomers/Mathematicians(1929)/Mathematicians(1969)/Actors(1937)
9	-11.0 to -10.51	Artists(1968)/Authors/Pulitzer Prize Winners/Accountants(German)
	-11.5 to -11.01	Physicists(1968)/Physicists(1927)/Artists(1933)
8	-12.0 to -11.51	Anthropologists/German Medical Students
	-12.5 to -12.01	
7	-13.0 to -12.51	Psychologists(German)
	-13.5 to -13.01	NIAL Members

468

Converted Score	Raw Score	
27	7.0 to 7.49	Bankers(1934)/Business Ed Teachers
	6.5 to 6.99	Bankers(1964)
26	6.0 to 6.49	Office Workers/Accountants
	5.5 to 5.99	Policemen(1968)
25	5.0 to 5.49	County Welfare Workers
	4.5 to 4.99	Credit Mgrs/Soc Sci Teachers(1936)
24	4.0 to 4.49	CPA(1944)/Bankers(1969)
	3.5 to 3.99	Colonels/Dept Store Mgrs/Elementary Teachers(NoDak)/Army Sergeants
23	3.0 to 3.49	Guidance Counselors(1950)/School Supers(1930)/Voc Ag Teachers/Math-Sci Teachers(1936)/Rehab Counselors/Policemen(1933)
	2.5 to 2.99	Purchasing Agents(1931)/High School Counselors/Purchasing Agents(1969)/School Supers(1969)/CPA (1965)/YMCA Secs/CPA Owners/Guidance Counselors(1968)/School Supers(1965)
22	2.0 to 2.49	Printers/Cartographers/Public Admins(1941)/Public Admins(1969)/Ag Ext Agents/Carpenters(1936)/ Pharmacists(1968)/Accountants(German)/Funeral Direcs(1969)/Governors
	1.5 to 1.99	Legislators/Librarians/Medical Techs/Army Officers(1969)/Buyers(1969)/Comm Rec Direcs/Ministers (1927)/YMCA PD
21	1.0 to 1.49	Buyers for Emporium/Funeral Direcs(1945)/Generals & Admirals/Mathematicians(1929)/VA Schizophrenic Patients/Vets(1966)/Generals and Lt Generals/Forest Service Men/Salesmen,PG&E/Farmers(1936)
	.5 to .99	Business Admin Profs/Music Teachers(1952)/Salesmen,3M/MIG(1933)/Personnel Direcs(1927)/Pharmacists (1947)/Soc Sci Teachers(1969)/U of M Fresh(1964)/Highway Patrolmen(1967)/Production Mgrs/ Salesmen,R al Estate(1969)/Air Force Officers/Army Officers(1950)/Personnel Direcs(1969)/Salesmen, Auto
20	0 to .49	Foresters/Physical Therapists(1957)/Sales Mgrs(1932)/Salesmen,3M applicants/Salesmen,Life Insurance (1931)/Salesmen,Life Insurance(1969)/Cham Comm Execs/Tool & Die Makers/Vets(1949)/YMCA Staff/ Elementary Teachers(Minn)/Farmers(1968)/Ferris State Students/Physiatrists/Animal Husbandry Profs/ County Sheriffs/Ministers(1969)/Buyers(1946)/Chiropractors/Computer Programmers/Corp Pres(1935)/ Lawyers(1949)/Machinists/Optometrists/Social Workers(1953)/Ministers(1965)
	-.5 to -.01	Navy Officers/Petroleum Engineers/Policemen(1969)/Psychologists(Guidance)/Dentists(1932)/Economists/ MIG(1966)/Math-Sci Teachers(1968)/Music Teachers(1946)/Physical Therapists(1966)/Salesmen,Real Estate(1932)/Electricians/Osteopaths/Radiologists/Skilled Tradesmen/Salesmen,Steel
19	-1.0 to -.51	Lawyers(1969)/Psychologists(Educ)/Sociologists/U of M Fresh(1966)/Urologists/Chemists(1931)/ Engineers(1928)/Lawyers(1927)/Pediatricians/Football Coaches/Psychologists(Statistical)/Student Personnel Workers/Teaching Brothers/Food Scientists/Judges and Lawyers/Salesmen,Encyclopedia/Corp Pres(1965)/Engineers(1968)/Psychologists(1947)
	-1.5 to -1.01	U of M Fresh(1967)/Carpenters(1969)/No Hennepin Jr Coll Stu/Physicists(1927)/Judges/Priests/English Teachers/Musicians(1969)/Dentists and Dental Ed(1969)/Investment Mgrs
18	-2.0 to -1.51	Biologists/Pilots/Dental Ed/Neurological Surgeons/Orthopedic Surgeons/Psychiatrists(1949)/Patholo- gists/Physicians(1969)/Psychologists(1949)/Psychologists(Child)/Psychologists(Social)/Sales Mgrs (1968)/Unitarian Ministers(1929)
	-2.5 to -2.01	Social Workers(1967)/NASA Scientists/Unitarian Ministers(1950)/Chemists(1969)/Musicians(1952)/ Physicians(1949)/Psychologists(Market)/College Profs/Political Scientists/Salesmen,Life Insurance (1966)
17	-3.0 to -2.51	Physicians(1927)/Salesmen,Computer/Internists/Psychologists(Exp)/Psychologists(1967)/Astronomers/ Psychologists(Clinical)
	-3.5 to -3.01	Architects(1968)/Interpreters/Psychiatrists(1967)/Psychologists(Industrial)/Surgeons/Mathematicians (1969)/Physicists(1968)/Mpls Symphony/Advertising Men(1931)
16	-4.0 to -3.51	Architects(1933)/Advertising Men(1968)/Astronauts/Interior Decorators
	-4.5 to -4.01	
15	-5.0 to -4.51	Newsmen/Pulitzer Prize Winners
	-5.5 to -5.01	Authors/Danforth Fellows
14	-6.0 to -5.51	NIAL Members/Psychologists(German)/Actors(1937)/Anthropologists
	-6.5 to -6.01	
13	-7.0 to -6.51	Photographers/German Medical Students
	-7.5 to -7.01	
12	-8.0 to -7.51	Artists(1933)
	-8.5 to -8.01	Actors(1966)
11	-9.0 to -8.51	Artists(1968)

TABLE E-16. SCALE INTERCORRELATIONS FOR THE HOLLAND SCALES AND NONOCCUPATIONAL SCALES

	AACH	AR	DIV	MFII	MO	OIE	OL	SL	LC	CC	A-B	LP	IP	DP	R-II	I-II	A-II	S-II	E-II	C-II	R-I	I-I	A-I	S-I	E-I	C-I
Academic Achievement	1.00	.50	.18	-.42	-02	-03	35	54	35	16	42	14	-09	-03	-10	67	44	16	-43	-04	-05	67	44	18	-45	-04
Age Related		1.00	.20	-.33	03	-21	32	41	05	00	11	28	-06	-16	21	41	34	33	-10	09	24	38	29	36	-11	09
Diversity of Interests			1.00	-.12	19	-59	01	09	-21	28	11	55	11	-56	43	39	40	53	46	45	42	34	36	51	40	47
Masculinity-Femininity II				1.00	31	00	02	-27	-51	26	-46	-21	31	-13	23	02	-75	-20	21	08	19	05	-76	-24	-05	-10
Managerial Orientation					1.00	-48	50	29	-26	43	12	23	-08	-11	11	18	-07	13	34	04	07	18	-03	13	18	-24
Occ. Intra-Extroversion						1.00	-33	-24	06	-57	-31	-53	-05	49	-21	-13	00	-70	-59	-26	-20	-06	-34	-70	-54	-10
Occupational Level							1.00	36	15	41	38	20	-43	26	-25	17	00	14	02	-01	-26	17	01	17	04	-04
Specialization Level								1.00	23	22	33	19	-07	-08	-05	36	41	04	-14	-04	-03	37	41	12	-17	-12
Liberalism-Conservatism									1.00	00	57	-27	-21	43	-76	-21	30	08	-43	-41	-71	-22	33	16	-38	-30
Cultural Change										1.00	29	44	-01	-35	14	30	06	35	35	00	16	24	08	35	27	-06
A-B (1969)											1.00	15	-40	28	-39	06	48	25	-21	-35	-39	00	49	30	-22	-29
Like Percentage												1.00	-41	-43	50	34	45	51	48	41	51	28	44	47	44	42
Indifferent Percentage													1.00	-66	27	13	-15	01	17	19	26	14	-17	00	14	10
Dislike Percentage														1.00	-67	-41	-22	-43	-52	-56	-68	-37	-19	-39	-50	-44
Realistic II															1.00	39	09	18	33	36	98	37	05	10	25	29
Intellectual II																1.00	23	13	-08	14	40	98	21	11	-14	05
Artistic II																	1.00	34	-03	-04	12	17	98	37	04	03
Social II																		1.00	38	25	17	06	34	97	37	32
Enterprising II																			1.00	52	30	-12	-04	36	97	48
Conventional II																				1.00	37	15	-07	21	51	94
Realistic I																					1.00	38	07	11	22	29
Intellectual I																						1.00	16	04	-18	06
Artistic I																							1.00	36	-06	01
Social I																								1.00	35	28
Enterprising I																									1.00	49
Conventional I																										1.00

Calculated on Psychology 126 Sample
N = 150

TABLE E-17. INTERCORRELATIONS BETWEEN THE MALE BASIC SCALES, AND THE NONOCCUPATIONAL AND HOLLAND SCALES

	AACH	AR	DIV	MFII	MO	OIE	OL	SL	LC	CC	A-B	LP	IP	DP	R-II	I-II	A-II	S-II	E-II	C-II	R-I	I-I	A-I	S-I	E-I	C-I
Public Speaking	00	06	34	10	36	-73	21	24	-06	59	23	50	01	-42	21	10	18	46	49	25	19	04	19	43	45	21
Law/Politics	-09	-03	39	31	33	-66	23	14	-12	67	18	43	10	-45	20	15	03	36	50	27	19	09	02	35	44	22
Business Management	-40	-07	35	29	41	-56	16	-07	-42	34	-25	49	05	-45	27	-09	-14	38	84	59	25	-12	-14	37	85	51
Sales	-45	-19	33	30	31	-55	04	-16	-37	32	-20	37	14	-45	21	-11	-15	34	89	44	17	-14	-14	32	91	41
Merchandising	-42	-08	38	14	31	-52	08	-13	-33	25	-20	46	06	-44	21	-20	-02	34	90	53	19	-22	-03	33	91	49
Office Practices	-28	-09	35	01	-07	-21	-12	-23	-31	-02	-33	37	15	-45	24	-14	-04	27	61	84	23	-15	-06	23	63	87
Military Activities	-17	-03	36	21	24	-28	-11	-13	-49	10	-18	30	15	-39	51	10	-06	14	36	31	44	06	-06	06	36	31
Technical Supervision	-43	-06	28	38	28	-41	-05	-12	-63	24	-40	47	17	-56	57	01	-16	25	71	50	55	00	-18	22	69	44
Mathematics	56	19	22	13	17	02	24	22	-25	12	-11	17	09	-23	25	68	-02	-03	-06	32	27	74	-02	-06	-09	23
Science	58	38	28	09	11	02	07	34	-33	17	-09	26	19	-40	46	92	12	00	-12	14	46	93	09	-02	-18	03
Mechanical	-02	24	36	21	11	-13	-22	08	-74	04	-45	43	29	-64	90	50	08	09	26	38	88	50	04	05	19	28
Nature	23	53	42	-31	-15	-15	-19	-04	-15	-05	-07	37	08	-38	53	35	46	28	03	07	53	30	42	24	-02	10
Agriculture	-09	23	33	07	-06	-16	-27	-30	-42	04	-22	33	14	-41	70	16	13	26	15	13	71	13	10	18	09	14
Adventure	-10	-25	38	27	22	-21	-20	-08	-43	37	-03	33	12	-39	58	26	07	02	21	04	58	22	06	-03	12	-02
Rec. Leadership	-12	-07	35	36	24	-40	-10	-16	-40	39	-13	37	16	-46	55	19	00	37	27	14	53	16	01	27	22	11
Medical Service	39	28	54	-03	05	-27	03	-02	-17	32	10	39	13	-45	33	59	24	35	19	18	34	52	22	32	16	19
Social Service	16	33	46	-29	03	-60	14	07	23	24	36	42	-09	-26	01	06	36	86	28	18	02	01	35	89	29	28
Religious Activities	22	30	34	-19	-10	-40	02	-06	-05	12	13	35	08	-36	25	21	28	71	17	26	23	15	28	57	16	34
Teaching	43	47	36	-36	06	-44	17	34	22	23	24	37	03	-33	08	24	40	40	11	13	11	18	40	71	09	17
Music	51	38	35	-68	-07	-27	13	40	23	04	38	39	-16	-17	02	26	77	36	-02	08	05	22	74	38	-05	14
Art	36	38	37	-79	-13	-25	-06	35	33	-10	41	36	-15	-14	-02	14	93	29	-03	00	01	08	89	34	-03	08
Writing	47	35	26	-58	-06	-37	09	50	42	17	48	39	-15	-18	-01	13	74	34	-08	-08	03	09	74	36	-08	-03

Calculated on Psychology 126 sample
N = 150

Item Composition of the Occupational Scales

In Table F-1 is a listing of the items in the Men's booklet with an indication of how each item is scored on each of the occupational scales. While there are several patterns of response weights for each item on a scale, the patterns can be grouped into either positive or negative clusters. An example of positive weighting would be weights of +1, 0, −1 for the Like, Indifferent, and Dislike responses respectively; an example of negative weighting would be −1, −1, +1. In Table F-1, items weighted in the positive direction are indicated by a plus sign (+), those weighted in the negative direction are indicated by a minus sign (−). The actual weights, of course, were determined by contrasting the criterion group and Men-in-General item response percentages.

Similar information for the Women's scales is presented in Table F-2.

These listings will make it possible for users of the SVIB to study the makeup of each scale, and should be useful in further understanding the meaning of the scores on each scale.

TABLE F-1. ITEMS WEIGHTED ON THE MEN'S OCCUPATIONAL SCALES

Occupational Scales (columns, across scale 1–70):

College Professors · Anthropologists · Political Scientists · Bus. Admin. Professors · Sociologists · Psychologists · Psychiatrists · Physicians · Dentists · Biologists · Chemists · Physicists · Mathematicians · Engineers · Petroleum Engineers · Computer Programmers · Cartographers · Math-Science Teachers · Food Scientists · Med. Technologists · Physical Therapists · Optometrists · Air Force Officers · Army Officers · Navy Officers · Army Sergeants · Veterinarians · Voc. Agri. Teachers · Farmers · Foresters · Skilled Tradesmen · Highway Patrolmen · Policemen · Personnel Directors · Public Administrators · Soc. Sci. Teachers · Rehab. Counselors · YMCA Staff Members · Elementary Teachers · Guidance Counselors · School Supts. · Commun. Rec. Admins. · Social Workers · Ministers · Priests · English Teachers · Music Teachers · Librarians · Musicians · Artists · Architects · Photographers · Interior Decorators · Advertising Men · Journalists · Lawyers · CPA's · Investment Fund Mgrs. · Bankers · Chamb. Com. Execs. · Dept. Store Managers · Buyers · Purchasing Agents · Credit Managers · Bus. Ed. Teachers · Pharmacists · Chiropractors · Funeral Directors · Sales Managers · Life Ins. Salesmen · Real Estate Salesmen · Computer Salesmen

Item legend:

1 ACTOR
2 ADVERTISING MAN
3 ARCHITECT
4 MILITARY OFFICER
5 ARTIST

6 ASTRONOMER
7 ATHLETIC DIRECTOR
8 AUCTIONEER
9 AUTHOR OF NOVEL
10 AUTHOR OF TECHNICAL BOOK

11 AUTO SALESMAN
12 AUTO RACER
13 AUTO MECHANIC
14 AIRPLANE PILOT
15 BANK TELLER

16 DESIGNER, ELECTRONIC EQUIPMENT
17 BUILDING CONTRACTOR
18 BUYER OF MERCHANDISE
19 CARPENTER
20 CARTOONIST

21 CASHIER IN BANK
22 ELECTRONICS TECHNICIAN
23 CIVIL ENGINEER
24 CITY OR STATE EMPLOYEE
25 CITY OR STATE EMPLOYEE

26 MINISTER, PRIEST, OR RABBI
27 COLLEGE PROFESSOR
28 FOREIGN SERVICE MAN
29 DENTIST
30 DRAFTSMAN

474

(table continued next page)

31 EDITOR
32 ELECTRICAL ENGINEER
33 EMPLOYMENT MANAGER
34 GEOLOGIST
35 FACTORY MANAGER

36 INCOME TAX ACCOUNTANT
37 FARMER
38 LABOR UNION OFFICIAL
39 ART MUSEUM DIRECTOR
40 FOREIGN CORRESPONDENT

41 GOVERNOR OF A STATE
42 HOTEL MANAGER
43 INTERIOR DECORATOR
44 INTERPRETER
45 INVENTOR

46 PHOTOGRAPHER
47 JUDGE
48 LABOR ARBITRATOR
49 LABORATORY TECHNICIAN
50 LANDSCAPE GARDENER

51 LAWYER, CRIMINAL
52 LAWYER, CORPORATION
53 LIBRARIAN
54 LIFE INSURANCE SALESMAN
55 LOCOMOTIVE ENGINEER

56 MACHINIST
57 MAGAZINE WRITER
58 MANUFACTURER
59 HIGH SCHOOL PRINCIPAL
60 PROFESSIONAL BASEBALL PLAYER

61 MINING SUPERINTENDENT
62 MUSICIAN
63 MUSIC TEACHER
64 PSYCHOLOGIST
65 OFFICE MANAGER

66 ORCHESTRA CONDUCTOR
67 PHARMACIST
68 PUBLIC RELATIONS MAN
69 PHYSICIAN
70 PLAYGROUND DIRECTOR

71 POET
72 POLITICIAN
73 PRINTER
74 PRIVATE SECRETARY
75 RADIO ANNOUNCER

76 RANCHER
77 REAL ESTATE SALESMAN
78 REPORTER, GENERAL
79 REPORTER, SPORTS PAGE
80 RETAILER

TABLE F-1 (*continued*)

Column headings (occupations):

Computer Salesmen · Real Estate Salesmen · Life Ins. Salesmen · Sales Managers · Funeral Directors · Chiropractors · Pharmacists · Bus. Ed. Teachers · Credit Managers · Purchasing Agents · Buyers · Dept. Store Managers · Chamb. Com. Execs. · Bankers · Investment Fund Mgrs. · CPA's · Lawyers · Journalists · Advertising Men · Interior Decorators · Photographers · Architects · Artists · Musicians · Music Teachers · Librarians · English Teachers · Priests · Ministers · Social Workers · Commun. Rec. Admins. · School Supts. · Guidance Counselors · Elementary Teachers · YMCA Staff Members · Rehab. Counselors · Soc. Sci. Teachers · Public Administrators · Personnel Directors · Policemen · Highway Patrolmen · Skilled Tradesmen · Foresters · Farmers · Voc. Agri. Teachers · Veterinarians · Army Sergeants · Navy Officers · Army Officers · Air Force Officers · Optometrists · Physical Therapists · Med. Technologists · Food Scientists · Math-Science Teachers · Cartographers · Computer Programmers · Petroleum Engineers · Engineers · Mathematicians · Physicists · Chemists · Biologists · Dentists · Physicians · Psychiatrists · Psychologists · Sociologists · Bus. Admin. Professors · Political Scientists · Anthropologists · College Professors

Legend:

A1 SALES MANAGER
A2 SCHOOL TEACHER
A3 SCIENTIFIC RESEARCH WORKER
A4 SCULPTOR
A5 MANAGER, CHAMBER OF COMMERCE

A6 SECRET SERVICE MAN
A7 COMPUTER OPERATOR
A8 SHOP FOREMAN
A9 SOCIAL WORKER
90 SPECIALTY SALESMAN

91 STATISTICIAN
92 STOCKBROKER
93 SURGEON
94 TOOLMAKER
95 TRAVELING SALESMAN

96 TRAVEL BUREAU MANAGER
97 FUNERAL DIRECTOR
98 WATCHMAKER
99 WHOLESALER
100 WORKER IN Y.M.C.A.

101 ALGEBRA
102 AGRICULTURE
103 ARITHMETIC
104 ART
105 BOOKKEEPING

106 BOTANY
107 CALCULUS
108 CHEMISTRY
109 CIVICS (GOVERNMENT)
110 DRAMATICS

111 ECONOMICS
112 ENGLISH COMPOSITION
113 GEOGRAPHY
114 GEOLOGY
115 GEOMETRY

116 HISTORY
117 LANGUAGES, ANCIENT
118 LANGUAGES, MODERN
119 LITERATURE
120 MATHEMATICS

121 INDUSTRIAL ARTS
122 MECHANICAL DRAWING
123 MILITARY DRILL
124 BIBLE HISTORY
125 NATURE STUDY

126 PHILOSOPHY
127 PHYSICAL EDUCATION
128 PHYSICS
129 PSYCHOLOGY
130 PHYSIOLOGY

131 PUBLIC SPEAKING
132 SHOP WORK
133 SOCIOLOGY
134 SPELLING
135 TYPEWRITING

136 ZOOLOGY
137 GOLF
138 FISHING
139 HUNTING
140 TENNIS

141 SKETCHING PICTURES OF WILD ANIMALS
142 HIKING
143 BOXING
144 CHESS
145 POKER

146 BRIDGE
147 BIRD WATCHING
148 SOLVING MECHANICAL PUZZLES
149 RELIGIOUS MUSIC
150 CAMPING OUT

151 DRILLING IN A MILITARY COMPANY
152 PLAYING THE PIANO
153 AMUSEMENT PARKS
154 PICNICS
155 SIGHT-SEEING TRIPS

156 STAG PARTIES
157 JAZZ CONCERTS
158 CONVENTIONS
159 FORMAL DRESS AFFAIRS
160 ELECTIONEERING FOR OFFICE

(table continued next page)

TABLE F-1 (*continued*)

	College Professors	Anthropologists	Political Scientists	Bus.Admin. Professors	Sociologists	Psychologists	Psychiatrists	Physicians	Dentists	Biologists	Chemists	Physicists	Mathematicians	Engineers	Petroleum Engineers	Computer Programmers	Cartographers	Math-Science Teachers	Food Scientists	Med. Technologists	Physical Therapists	Optometrists	Air Force Officers	Army Officers
161 GOING TO CHURCH	-	-				-						-	-		+					+				
162 HORSEBACK RIDING																								
163 ART GALLERIES	+					+	+	+		+		+												
164 LEADING A BOY SCOUT TROOP		-	-										-											
165 WRITING A ONE-ACT PLAY						+																		
166 SCIENCE FICTION MAGAZINES																+								
167 SYMPHONY CONCERTS	+	+	+		+	+	+	+		+	+	+	+											
168 NIGHT CLUBS											-		-											
169 CHURCH YOUNG PEOPLES GROUP		-	-			-							-							+				
170 BIOGRAPHIES	+		+															-						
171 SPORTS PAGES IN NEWSPAPERS		-										-									+			
172 POETRY	+				+		+			+					-									
173 DETECTIVE STORIES																		-						
174 SKIING					-			+											+					+
175 PLANNING A LARGE PARTY													-											
176 TELLING JOKES																								
177 BUSINESS METHODS MAGAZINES	-	-	-	+	-	-						-	-		+			-	+					
178 TRAVEL MAGAZINES																								
179 WEEKLY NEWS MAGAZINES																								+
180 POPULAR MECHANICS MAGAZINES			-	-										+			+			+	+	+	+	
181 READING THE BIBLE		-				-																		
182 EDUCATIONAL MOVIES OR TV																					+	+		
183 MAGAZINES ABOUT ART AND MUSIC																		-						
184 SOCIAL PROBLEM MOVIES					+	+	+								-						+			-
185 MAKING A RADIO OR HI-FI SET			-					+			+	+		+	+	+	+	+	+	+			+	
186 REPAIRING A CLOCK								+			+			+	+	+	+	+	+	+	+		+	
187 ADJUSTING A CARBURETOR			-											+	+	+	+	+	+		+		+	
188 REPAIRING ELECTRICAL WIRING			-				+	+			+			+	+	+	+		+	+	+	+	+	
189 CABINETMAKING														+			+		+		+			
190 OPERATING MACHINERY			-											+	+				+		+		+	

	Navy Officers	Army Sergeants	Veterinarians	Voc. Agri. Teachers	Farmers	Foresters	Skilled Tradesmen	Highway Patrolmen	Policemen	Personnel Directors	Public Administrators	Soc. Sci. Teachers	Rehab. Counselors	YMCA Staff Members	Elementary Teachers	Guidance Counselors	School Supts.	Commun. Rec. Admins.	Social Workers	Ministers	Priests	English Teachers	Music Teachers	Librarians	Musicians
161 GOING TO CHURCH			+	+	+							+				+	+	+			+				
162 HORSEBACK RIDING			+																						
163 ART GALLERIES		-	-	-	-	-	-	-											+	-			+	+	
164 LEADING A BOY SCOUT TROOP								+										+		-					
165 WRITING A ONE-ACT PLAY			-	-	-	-	-	-	-							-						+			
166 SCIENCE FICTION MAGAZINES												-													
167 SYMPHONY CONCERTS		-	-	-	-		-	-				-				-			+	+	+		+	+	+
168 NIGHT CLUBS	+	+										+								-					
169 CHURCH YOUNG PEOPLES GROUP			+		+											+	+	+		+	+				
170 BIOGRAPHIES					-		-								+					+	+	+			
171 SPORTS PAGES IN NEWSPAPERS												+		+		+	+	+						-	-
172 POETRY			-	-			-	-							+				+	+	+	+	+	+	
173 DETECTIVE STORIES															-										
174 SKIING	+																								
175 PLANNING A LARGE PARTY										+															
176 TELLING JOKES																									
177 BUSINESS METHODS MAGAZINES			+							+	+						+					-			
178 TRAVEL MAGAZINES																									
179 WEEKLY NEWS MAGAZINES	+										+	+													
180 POPULAR MECHANICS MAGAZINES				+			+	+	+												-				
181 READING THE BIBLE																	+			+	+				
182 EDUCATIONAL MOVIES OR TV													+						+				+		
183 MAGAZINES ABOUT ART AND MUSIC			-	-		-	-	-								-					+				+
184 SOCIAL PROBLEM MOVIES						-	-					+	+	+		+			+	+	+	+	+	+	
185 MAKING A RADIO OR HI-FI SET	+						+																		+
186 REPAIRING A CLOCK	+						+																		
187 ADJUSTING A CARBURETOR	+			+	+	+	+	+	+																
188 REPAIRING ELECTRICAL WIRING	+			+			+	+	+												-				
189 CABINETMAKING						+	+	+																	
190 OPERATING MACHINERY			+	+	+	+	+	+	+																

	Artists	Architects	Photographers	Interior Decorators	Advertising Men	Journalists	Lawyers	CPA's	Investment Fund Mgrs.	Bankers	Chamb. Com. Execs.	Dept. Store Managers	Buyers	Purchasing Agents	Credit Managers	Bus. Ed. Teachers	Pharmacists	Chiropractors	Funeral Directors	Sales Managers	Life Ins. Salesmen	Real Estate Salesmen	Computer Salesmen
161 GOING TO CHURCH	-		-					+						+			+		+		+	+	
162 HORSEBACK RIDING																							
163 ART GALLERIES	+	+	+	+				-						-			-		-		-	-	
164 LEADING A BOY SCOUT TROOP	-											+											
165 WRITING A ONE-ACT PLAY	+		+		+	+				-				-			-		-				
166 SCIENCE FICTION MAGAZINES										-													
167 SYMPHONY CONCERTS	+		+	+																		-	
168 NIGHT CLUBS												+		+			+		+	+			
169 CHURCH YOUNG PEOPLES GROUP	-		-						-					+			+		+				
170 BIOGRAPHIES						+	+																
171 SPORTS PAGES IN NEWSPAPERS			-	-				+		+					+		+						
172 POETRY	+							-						-			-		-		-		
173 DETECTIVE STORIES																							
174 SKIING									+			+											+
175 PLANNING A LARGE PARTY				+	+							+							+	+			
176 TELLING JOKES																							+
177 BUSINESS METHODS MAGAZINES	-				+	-		+	+	+		+	+	+			+	+	+	+	+	+	+
178 TRAVEL MAGAZINES																							
179 WEEKLY NEWS MAGAZINES																							
180 POPULAR MECHANICS MAGAZINES						-	-		-					+		+		+					
181 READING THE BIBLE									-														
182 EDUCATIONAL MOVIES OR TV										-											-		
183 MAGAZINES ABOUT ART AND MUSIC	+	+	+	+				-		-				-			-						
184 SOCIAL PROBLEM MOVIES										-						+							
185 MAKING A RADIO OR HI-FI SET				-							-										-		+
186 REPAIRING A CLOCK																					-		
187 ADJUSTING A CARBURETOR				-		-	-		-					+									
188 REPAIRING ELECTRICAL WIRING									-					+				+					
189 CABINETMAKING		+												+									
190 OPERATING MACHINERY				-	-	-	-		-					+									

191 HANDLING HORSES
192 GIVING FIRST-AID ASSISTANCE
193 RAISING FLOWERS AND VEGETABLES
194 DECORATING A ROOM WITH FLOWERS
195 ARGUMENTS

196 INTERVIEWING MEN FOR A JOB
197 INTERVIEWING PROSPECTS IN SELLING
198 INTERVIEWING CLIENTS
199 MAKING A SPEECH
200 ORGANIZING A PLAY

201 STARTING A CONVERSATION WITH A STRANGER
202 TEACHING CHILDREN
203 TEACHING ADULTS
204 CALLING FRIENDS BY NICKNAMES
205 BEING CALLED BY A NICKNAME

206 MEETING AND DIRECTING PEOPLE
207 TAKING RESPONSIBILITY
208 MAKING STATISTICAL CHARTS
209 ADJUSTING DIFFICULTIES OF OTHERS
210 DRILLING SOLDIERS

211 PURSUING BANDITS IN A SHERIFFS POSSE
212 DOING RESEARCH WORK
213 ACTING AS CHEER-LEADER
214 BEING A FOREST RANGER
215 WRITING REPORTS

216 LOOKING AT THINGS IN A HARDWARE STORE
217 BARGAINING (SWAPPING)
218 LOOKING AT THINGS IN A CLOTHING STORE
219 BUYING MERCHANDISE FOR A STORE
220 DISPLAYING MERCHANDISE IN A STORE

221 EXPRESSING OPINIONS OPENLY, REGARDLESS O
222 COMPETITIVE ACTIVITIES
223 METHODICAL WORK
224 REGULAR HOURS FOR WORK
225 CONTINUALLY CHANGING ACTIVITIES

226 DEVELOPING BUSINESS SYSTEMS
227 SAVING MONEY
228 CONTRIBUTING TO CHARITIES
229 RAISING MONEY FOR A CHARITY
230 LIVING IN THE CITY

231 CLIMBING ALONG THE EDGE OF A PRECIPICE
232 DISCUSSING THE PURPOSE OF LIFE
233 LOOKING AT A COLLECTION OF ANTIQUE FURNI
234 HIGHWAY CONSTRUCTION WORKERS
235 HIGH SCHOOL STUDENTS

236 ENERGETIC PEOPLE
237 MILITARY MEN
238 AGGRESSIVE PEOPLE
239 BEACHCOMBERS
240 OPTIMISTS

(table continued next page)

TABLE F-1 (*continued*)

Column headings (occupations, left to right across the table):

Computer Salesmen · Real Estate Salesmen · Life Ins. Salesmen · Sales Managers · Funeral Directors · Chiropractors · Pharmacists · Bus. Ed. Teachers · Credit Managers · Purchasing Agents · Buyers · Dept. Store Managers · Chamb. Com. Execs. · Bankers · Investment Fund Mgrs. · CPA's · Lawyers · Journalists · Advertising Men · Interior Decorators · Photographers · Architects · Artists · Musicians · Librarians · Music Teachers · English Teachers · Priests · Ministers · Social Workers · Commun. Rec. Admins. · School Supts. · Guidance Counselors · Elementary Teachers · YMCA Staff Members · Rehab. Counselors · Soc. Sci. Teachers · Public Administrators · Personnel Directors · Policemen · Highway Patrolmen · Skilled Tradesmen · Foresters · Farmers · Voc. Agri. Teachers · Veterinarians · Army Sergeants · Navy Officers · Army Officers · Air Force Officers · Optometrists · Physical Therapists · Med. Technologists · Food Scientists · Math-Science Teachers · Cartographers · Computer Programmers · Petroleum Engineers · Engineers · Mathematicians · Physicists · Chemists · Biologists · Dentists · Physicians · Psychiatrists · Psychologists · Sociologists · Bus. Admin. Professors · Political Scientists · Anthropologists · College Professors

Row labels:

241 PESSIMISTS
242 PEOPLE WHO ARE NATURAL LEADERS
243 PEOPLE WHO ASSUME LEADERSHIP
244 BALLET DANCERS
245 PEOPLE WHO HAVE MADE FORTUNES IN BUSINESS

246 EMOTIONAL PEOPLE
247 THRIFTY PEOPLE
248 SPENDTHRIFTS
249 FAMOUS CHEFS
250 RELIGIOUS PEOPLE

251 IRRELIGIOUS PEOPLE
252 EASYGOING PEOPLE
253 ARTISTIC MEN
254 PUBLIC OPINION INTERVIEWERS
255 FOREIGNERS

256 PHYSICALLY SICK PEOPLE
257 BABIES
258 VERY OLD PEOPLE
259 WOMEN ATHLETES
260 OUTSPOKEN PEOPLE WITH NEW IDEAS

261 MUSICAL GENIUSES
262 PEOPLE WHO DAYDREAM A LOT
263 PROMINENT ARTISTS
264 OUTSTANDING SCIENTISTS
265 ACROBATS

266 DEMOCRATS
267 PROHIBITIONISTS
268 REPUBLICANS
269 MEN WHO PERFORM ON TV
270 PEOPLE WHO INSIST ON HAVING EVERYTHING I

271 FASHIONABLY DRESSED PEOPLE
272 CARELESSLY DRESSED PEOPLE
273 PEOPLE WHO DONT BELIEVE IN EVOLUTION
274 SOCIALISTS
275 NONCONFORMISTS

276 INDEPENDENTS IN POLITICS
277 MEN WHO LIVE DANGEROUSLY
278 PROMINENT BUSINESSMEN
279 PROMINENT LABOR UNION MEN
280 ATHLETIC MEN

281 DEVELOP THE THEORY OF OPERATION OF A NEW
282 OPERATE (MANIPULATE) THE NEW MACHINE
283 DISCOVER AN IMPROVEMENT IN THE DESIGN OF
284 DETERMINE THE COST OF OPERATION OF THE M
285 SUPERVISE THE MANUFACTURE OF THE MACHINE

286 CREATE A NEW ARTISTIC EFFECT (THAT IS, I
287 SELL THE MACHINE
288 PREPARE THE ADVERTISING OF THE MACHINE
289 TEACH OTHERS THE USE OF THE MACHINE
290 INTEREST THE PUBLIC IN THE MACHINE THROU

291 SALARY RECEIVED FOR WORK
292 STEADINESS AND PERMANENCE OF WORK
293 OPPORTUNITY FOR PROMOTION
294 COURTEOUS TREATMENT FROM SUPERIORS
295 OPPORTUNITY TO MAKE USE OF ALL ONES KNOW

296 OPPORTUNITY TO ASK QUESTIONS AND TO CONS
297 OPPORTUNITY TO UNDERSTAND JUST HOW ONES
298 CERTAINTY THAT ONES WORK WILL BE JUDGED
299 FREEDOM IN WORKING OUT ONES OWN METHODS
300 CO-WORKERS---CONGENIAL, COMPETENT, AND A

301 PLANT SCIENTIST---DEVELOPS NEW VEGETABLE
302 OPERA SINGER
303 INVENTOR
304 MANUFACTURER
305 NATIONALLY KNOWN ARTIST

306 BANKER, FINANCIER
307 GENERAL OF THE ARMY
308 MEMBER OF THE SUPREME COURT
309 AUTHOR OF BEST SELLER
310 MANAGER OF LARGE DEPARTMENT STORE

311 PRESIDENT OF A SOCIETY OR CLUB
312 SECRETARY OF A SOCIETY OR CLUB
313 TREASURER OF A SOCIETY OR CLUB
314 MEMBER OF A SOCIETY OR CLUB
315 CHAIRMAN, ARRANGEMENTS COMMITTEE

316 CHAIRMAN, EDUCATIONAL COMMITTEE
317 CHAIRMAN, ENTERTAINMENT COMMITTEE
318 CHAIRMAN, MEMBERSHIP COMMITTEE
319 CHAIRMAN, PROGRAM COMMITTEE
320 CHAIRMAN, PUBLICITY COMMITTEE

(table continued next page)

TABLE F-1 (*continued*)

Item	College Professors	Anthropologists	Political Scientists	Bus.Admin. Professors	Sociologists	Psychologists	Psychiatrists	Physicians	Dentists	Biologists	Chemists	Physicists	Mathematicians	Engineers	Petroleum Engineers	Computer Programmers	Cartographers	Math-Science Teachers	Food Scientists	Med. Technologists	Physical Therapists	Optometrists	Air Force Officers	Army Officers
321 AIRLINE PILOT...AIRLINE TICKET AGENT																								
322 POLICEMAN...FIREMAN (FIGHTS FIRE)												-												+
323 TAXICAB DRIVER...POLICEMAN		+						-																-
324 HEAD WAITER...LIGHTHOUSE KEEPER							+												+			+		
325 TAKE DANCING LESSONS...TAKE SINGING LESS																								
326 SELLING THINGS HOUSE TO HOUSE...GARDENIN										-														
327 REPAINT AUTOS...GREASE AUTOS																								
328 DEVELOP PLANS...EXECUTE PLANS				+	+	+				+		+	+			+								
329 DO A JOB YOURSELF...TELL SOMEBODY TO DO								+																-
330 TALK OTHERS INTO DOING SOMETHING...ORDER								-																
331 DEAL WITH THINGS...DEAL WITH PEOPLE							-			+	+	+	+	+		+				+	-		+	
332 PLAN FOR IMMEDIATE FUTURE...PLAN FOR FIV																							-	
333 ACTIVITY WHICH PRODUCES TANGIBLE RETURNS															+				+					+
334 TAKING A CHANCE...PLAYING SAFE							-													-	-	-		
335 DEFINITE SALARY...COMMISSION ON WHAT IS			+		+			-	-	+						+	+					-		
336 WORK FOR YOURSELF...CARRY OUT PROGRAM OF								+	+							-	-			-		+		-
337 THRILLING, DANGEROUS ACTIVITIES...QUIETE																								+
338 WORK IN A LARGE CORP WITH LITTLE CHANCE.			+		+			-	-		+	+	+	+		+						-		
339 SELLING SOMETHING FOR LESS THAN OTHERS..									-										-			-	+	
340 TRAVEL ALONE AND MAKE OWN PREPARATIONS..																								
341 WORK WITH FEW DETAILS...WORK WITH MANY D									-	-						-			-	-	-	-	-	
342 OUTSIDE WORK...INSIDE WORK			+	-	-	-	-				-	-	-			-				-		-		
343 WORK IN WHICH YOU MOVE FROM PLACE TO PLA							-		-	-	-	-	-			-			+	-	-	-	+	+
344 GREAT VARIETY OF WORK...SIMILARITY IN WO							-															-		
345 PHYSICAL ACTIVITY...MENTAL ACTIVITY	-		-	-	-	-	-			-		-	-			-					+	-		+
346 WORK IN AN IMPORT-EXPORT BUSINESS...WORK	-	-				-		-	-		-	-	-	-			-	-	-	-				
347 TECHNICAL RESPONSIBILITY...SUPERVISORY P	+	+			+	+	+	+	+	+	+	+	+	+		+	+	+	+	+	+	+		-
348 PRESENT A REPORT IN WRITING...PRESENT A																								
349 LISTENING TO A STORY...TELLING A STORY																								
350 PLAYING BASEBALL...WATCHING BASEBALL																		+			+			+

Item	Navy Officers	Army Sergeants	Veterinarians	Voc. Agri. Teachers	Farmers	Foresters	Skilled Tradesmen	Highway Patrolmen	Policemen	Personnel Directors	Public Administrators	Soc. Sci. Teachers	Rehab. Counselors	YMCA Staff Members	Elementary Teachers	Guidance Counselors	School Supts.	Commun. Rec. Admins.	Social Workers	Ministers	Priests	English Teachers	Music Teachers	Librarians
321 AIRLINE PILOT...AIRLINE TICKET AGENT																								
322 POLICEMAN...FIREMAN (FIGHTS FIRE)						+		+	+															
323 TAXICAB DRIVER...POLICEMAN	-	-				-		-	-															
324 HEAD WAITER...LIGHTHOUSE KEEPER						-	-			+				+		+	+		+		+		+	
325 TAKE DANCING LESSONS...TAKE SINGING LESS																				-	-	-		
326 SELLING THINGS HOUSE TO HOUSE...GARDENIN						-								+										
327 REPAINT AUTOS...GREASE AUTOS																								
328 DEVELOP PLANS...EXECUTE PLANS									-			-					-							
329 DO A JOB YOURSELF...TELL SOMEBODY TO DO	-		+							-	-		-	-			-		-					
330 TALK OTHERS INTO DOING SOMETHING...ORDER										+									+					
331 DEAL WITH THINGS...DEAL WITH PEOPLE					+		+			-	-	-	-	-		-	-	-	-	-	-			
332 PLAN FOR IMMEDIATE FUTURE...PLAN FOR FIV															+		-				+			
333 ACTIVITY WHICH PRODUCES TANGIBLE RETURNS																						-		
334 TAKING A CHANCE...PLAYING SAFE													-			-							-	-
335 DEFINITE SALARY...COMMISSION ON WHAT IS		+	-										+		+	+			+	+		+	+	+
336 WORK FOR YOURSELF...CARRY OUT PROGRAM OF	-		+			-			-		-				-				-			-		-
337 THRILLING, DANGEROUS ACTIVITIES...QUIETE								+	+							-								
338 WORK IN A LARGE CORP WITH LITTLE CHANCE.			-		-					+	+													+
339 SELLING SOMETHING FOR LESS THAN OTHERS..			-										+						+	+				+
340 TRAVEL ALONE AND MAKE OWN PREPARATIONS..																								
341 WORK WITH FEW DETAILS...WORK WITH MANY D																					+		-	-
342 OUTSIDE WORK...INSIDE WORK			+	+	+	+		+	+		-		-			-		+	-				-	-
343 WORK IN WHICH YOU MOVE FROM PLACE TO PLA	+								+				-						-				-	-
344 GREAT VARIETY OF WORK...SIMILARITY IN WO																								
345 PHYSICAL ACTIVITY...MENTAL ACTIVITY			+	+	+	+	+	+	+		-		-	+				+	-					-
346 WORK IN AN IMPORT-EXPORT BUSINESS...WORK										+		+					+							
347 TECHNICAL RESPONSIBILITY...SUPERVISORY P		-	+							-	-	-		-			-	-						
348 PRESENT A REPORT IN WRITING...PRESENT A																	-							+
349 LISTENING TO A STORY...TELLING A STORY																								
350 PLAYING BASEBALL...WATCHING BASEBALL												+	-	+			+						-	-

Item	Musicians	Artists	Architects	Photographers	Interior Decorators	Advertising Men	Journalists	Lawyers	CPA's	Investment Fund Mgrs.	Bankers	Chamb. Com. Execs.	Dept. Store Managers	Buyers	Purchasing Agents	Credit Managers	Bus. Ed. Teachers	Pharmacists	Chiropractors	Funeral Directors	Sales Managers	Life Ins. Salesmen	Real Estate Salesmen	Computer Salesmen
321 AIRLINE PILOT...AIRLINE TICKET AGENT																								
322 POLICEMAN...FIREMAN (FIGHTS FIRE)																								
323 TAXICAB DRIVER...POLICEMAN		+											-											
324 HEAD WAITER...LIGHTHOUSE KEEPER												+				+	+				+	+		+
325 TAKE DANCING LESSONS...TAKE SINGING LESS	-																							
326 SELLING THINGS HOUSE TO HOUSE...GARDENIN												+									+	+	+	+
327 REPAINT AUTOS...GREASE AUTOS					+																			
328 DEVELOP PLANS...EXECUTE PLANS			+								-				-	-				-		-		
329 DO A JOB YOURSELF...TELL SOMEBODY TO DO									-			-	-	-		-			+		-			-
330 TALK OTHERS INTO DOING SOMETHING...ORDER												+												
331 DEAL WITH THINGS...DEAL WITH PEOPLE		+	+					-			-	-	-			-				-	-	-	-	-
332 PLAN FOR IMMEDIATE FUTURE...PLAN FOR FIV							+																	
333 ACTIVITY WHICH PRODUCES TANGIBLE RETURNS									+	+	+		+	+	+	+					+			+
334 TAKING A CHANCE...PLAYING SAFE				+			+			+							-				+			+
335 DEFINITE SALARY...COMMISSION ON WHAT IS			-	-	-	-		-	-	-				-			+		-	-	-	-	-	-
336 WORK FOR YOURSELF...CARRY OUT PROGRAM OF		+		+			-	+								-	-		+	+		+		
337 THRILLING, DANGEROUS ACTIVITIES...QUIETE				+							-													
338 WORK IN A LARGE CORP WITH LITTLE CHANCE.		-	-	-	-		+	-	-		+		+			+		-	-	-		-	-	
339 SELLING SOMETHING FOR LESS THAN OTHERS..			-	-	-	-			-	-			+		-		+				-			-
340 TRAVEL ALONE AND MAKE OWN PREPARATIONS..																								
341 WORK WITH FEW DETAILS...WORK WITH MANY D			-																			+		
342 OUTSIDE WORK...INSIDE WORK	-		-	+				-	-					-		-	-	-				+		
343 WORK IN WHICH YOU MOVE FROM PLACE TO PLA				+				-	+		-				-	-	-	-	-			+		+
344 GREAT VARIETY OF WORK...SIMILARITY IN WO									+															
345 PHYSICAL ACTIVITY...MENTAL ACTIVITY								-	-	-									+					
346 WORK IN AN IMPORT-EXPORT BUSINESS...WORK					+	+		+		+	+		+	+	+					+	+	+	+	
347 TECHNICAL RESPONSIBILITY...SUPERVISORY P		+	+	+		-		-	-	-	-	-	-	-	-	-	-			-	-	-	-	
348 PRESENT A REPORT IN WRITING...PRESENT A							+		+							+					-	-		-
349 LISTENING TO A STORY...TELLING A STORY																								-
350 PLAYING BASEBALL...WATCHING BASEBALL					-								+											+

351 AMUSEMENT WHERE THERE IS A CROWD...AMUSE
352 MUSIC AND ART EVENTS...ATHLETIC EVENTS
353 READING A BOOK...WATCHING TV OR GOING TO
354 PLUMBER...ELECTRICIAN
355 A FEW CLOSE FRIENDS...MANY ACQUAINTANCES

356 SUPERINTENDENT OF HOSPITAL...WARDEN OF A
357 VOCATIONAL COUNSELOR...PUBLIC HEALTH OFF
358 TRAVEL TO OUTER SPACE...EXPLORE BOTTOM O
359 DOG TRAINER...JUVENILE PAROLE OFFICER
360 APPRAISE REAL ESTATE...REPAIR RESTORE AN

361 USUALLY START ACTIVITIES OF MY GROUP
362 MAKE DECISIONS IMMEDIATELY, NOT AFTER CO
363 WIN FRIENDS EASILY
364 USUALLY GET OTHER PEOPLE TO DO WHAT I WA
365 USUALLY LIVEN UP THE GROUP ON A DULL DAY

366 KEEP DETAILED RECORDS OF EXPENSES
367 PREFER WORKING ALONE TO WORKING ON COMMI
368 HAVE MECHANICAL INGENUITY (INVENTIVENESS
369 HAVE MORE THAN MY SHARE OF NOVEL IDEAS
370 CAN PREPARE SUCCESSFUL ADVERTISEMENTS

371 AM CONCERNED ABOUT PHILOSOPHICAL PROBLEM
372 MY GRADES IN HIGH SCHOOL WERE A FAIRLY A
373 AM ALWAYS ON TIME WITH MY WORK
374 REMEMBER FACES, NAMES, AND INCIDENTS BET
375 CAN CORRECT OTHERS WITHOUT GIVING OFFENS

376 AM ABLE TO MEET EMERGENCIES QUICKLY AND
377 DO MY BEST WORK EARLY IN THE MORNING
378 CAN WRITE A CONCISE, WELL-ORGANIZED REPO
379 HAVE GOOD JUDGMENT IN APPRAISING VALUES
380 PLAN MY WORK IN DETAIL

381 FOLLOW UP SUBORDINATES EFFECTIVELY
382 PUT DRIVE INTO THE ORGANIZATION
383 STIMULATE THE AMBITION OF MY ASSOCIATES
384 CAN BE FIRM AND SURE RATHER THAN QUICK
385 AM SLOW-GOING AND SURE RATHER THAN QUICK

386 CAN SMOOTH OUT TANGLES AND DISAGREEMENTS
387 HAVE PATIENCE WHEN TEACHING OTHERS
388 DISCUSS MY IDEALS WITH OTHERS...VERY LITTLE.
389 PAY ATTENTION TO DETAILS...A GOOD DEAL...VER
390 WORRY ABOUT MISTAKES...A GOOD DEAL...VER

391 LEND MONEY TO...ACQUAINTANCES...ONLY CER
392 WHEN IT COMES TO TAKING ORDERS...I DISLI
393 WHEN CAUGHT IN A MISTAKE, I MAKE EXCUSES
394 WEAK...MORE SLOWLY THAN OTHERS...ABOUT
395 COMPLAINTS ANNOY ME...RARELY...SOMETIMES

396 IN MY FAMILY, I AM THE...OLDEST...YOUNGE
397 AT A LARGE CONFERENCE I PREFER SEAT...
398 MY ADVICE IS ASKED FOR...BY MANY...BY FE
399 MAKE BETS...OFTEN...SOMETIMES...RARELY
400 BLANK

TABLE F-2. ITEMS WEIGHTED ON THE WOMEN'S OCCUPATIONAL SCALES

Column headers (occupational scales), left to right:

Music Teachers, Entertainers, Musician Performers, Models, Art Teachers, Artists, Interior Decorators, Newswomen, English Teachers, Language Teachers, YWCA Staff Members, Recreation Leaders, Dirs. of Christian Ed., Nun-Teachers, Guidance Counselors, Soc. Sci. Teachers, Social Workers, Speech Pathologists, Psychologists, Librarians, Translators, Physicians, Dentists, Med. Technologists, Chemists, Mathematicians, Computer Programmers, Math-Sci. Teachers, Engineers, Army--Enlisted, Navy--Enlisted, Army Officers, Navy Officers, Lawyers, Accountants, Bankwomen, Life Ins.Underwriters, Buyers, Bus. Ed. Teachers, Home Ec. Teachers, Dieticians, Phys. Ed. Teachers, Occ. Therapists, Physical Therapists, Pub. Health Nurses, Registered Nurses, Lic. Practical Nurses, Radiol. Technologists, Dental Assistants, Exec. Housekeepers, Elementary Teachers, Secretaries, Saleswomen, Telephone Operators, Instrument Assemblers, Sewing Machine Ops., Beauticians, Airline Stewardesses

Row items:

1 ACTRESS
2 DENTAL ASSISTANT
3 INCOME TAX ACCOUNTANT
4 ADVERTISER
5 ARCHITECT
6 ARTIST
7 ARTISTS MODEL
8 ATHLETIC DIRECTOR
9 AUTHOR OF CHILDRENS BOOKS
10 AUTHOR OF NOVEL
11 AUTHOR OF TECHNICAL BOOK
12 AIRPLANE PILOT
13 BACTERIOLOGIST
14 BANK TELLER
15 BEAUTY SPECIALIST
16 BIOLOGIST
17 BOOKKEEPER
18 BUYER OF MERCHANDISE
19 CARTOONIST
20 CASHIER IN BANK
21 CATERER
22 CHEMIST
23 CITY OF STATE EMPLOYEE
24 COLLEGE PROFESSOR
25 COMPUTER OPERATOR
26 CHILDRENS CLOTHES DESIGNER
27 COOK
28 COSTUME DESIGNER
29 DEAN OF WOMEN
30 DENTIST

31 DIETITIAN
32 DRAFTSMAN
33 DRAMATIST
34 DRESSMAKER
35 EDITOR

36 EDUCATIONAL DIRECTOR
37 EMPLOYMENT MANAGER
38 ELECTRONICS TECHNICIAN
39 MANAGER OF CHILDRENS NURSERY AT RESORT H
40 FARMER

41 FLORIST
42 FOREIGN CORRESPONDENT
43 SUPERMARKET CHECKOUT CLERK
44 HOSPITAL RECORDS CLERK
45 GOVERNOR OF A STATE

46 HOSTESS
47 HOTEL MANAGER
48 HOUSEKEEPER
49 ILLUSTRATOR
50 INTERIOR DECORATOR

51 INTERPRETER
52 INVENTOR
53 JUDGE
54 LABORATORY TECHNICIAN
55 LANDSCAPE GARDENER

56 LAWYER, CORPORATION
57 LAWYER, CRIMINAL
58 LIBRARIAN
59 LIFE INSURANCE SALESWOMAN
60 MAGAZINE WRITER

61 MANAGER, WOMENS STYLE SHOP
62 FASHION MODEL
63 PROFESSIONAL GOLFER
64 MECHANICAL ENGINEER
65 CHURCH WORKER

66 COURTROOM STENOGRAPHER
67 MISSIONARY
68 ART MUSEUM DIRECTOR
69 MUSIC COMPOSER
70 MUSICIAN

71 NEWS PHOTOGRAPHER
72 NURSE
73 POLICEWOMAN
74 OFFICE CLERK
75 OFFICE MANAGER

76 OPERA SINGER
77 PHARMACIST
78 PHYSICIAN
79 PLAYGROUND DIRECTOR
80 POET

(table continued next page)

485

Table F-2 (*continued*)

Column headings (left to right):

Music Teachers · Entertainers · Musician Performers · Models · Art Teachers · Artists · Interior Decorators · Newswomen · English Teachers · Language Teachers · YWCA Staff Members · Recreation Leaders · Dirs. of Christian Ed. · Nun-Teachers · Guidance Counselors · Soc. Sci. Teachers · Social Workers · Speech Pathologists · Psychologists · Librarians · Translators · Physicians · Dentists · Med. Technologists · Chemists · Mathematicians · Computer Programmers · Math-Sci. Teachers · Engineers · Army--Enlisted · Navy--Enlisted · Navy Officers · Army Officers · Lawyers · Accountants · Bankwomen · Life Ins. Underwriters · Buyers · Bus. Ed. Teachers · Home Ec. Teachers · Dieticians · Phys. Ed. Teachers · Occ. Therapists · Physical Therapists · Pub. Health Nurses · Registered Nurses · Lic. Practical Nurses · Radiol. Technologists · Dental Assistants · Exec. Housekeepers · Elementary Teachers · Secretaries · Saleswomen · Telephone Operators · Instrument Assemblers · Sewing Machine Ops. · Beauticians · Airline Stewardesses

Row key:

81 POLITICIAN
A2 PORTRAIT PHOTOGRAPHER
A3 PRIVATE SECRETARY
A4 PROBATION OFFICER
A5 NURSES AID

86 PROFESSIONAL DANCER
A7 PSYCHIATRIST
A8 PSYCHOLOGIST
A9 RAILROAD RESERVATIONS CLERK
90 VETERINARIAN FOR SMALL ANIMALS

91 RADIO ANNOUNCER
92 RADIO PROGRAM DIRECTOR
93 RADIO-TV SINGER
94 REAL ESTATE SALESWOMAN
95 RECEPTIONIST

96 REPORTER, GENERAL
97 REPORTER, WOMENS PAGE
98 RETAILER
99 SALES MANAGER OF LARGE BOOKSTORE
100 SCENARIO WRITER

101 SCIENTIFIC ILLUSTRATOR
102 SCIENTIFIC RESEARCH WORKER
103 SCULPTRESS
104 SCHOOL PRINCIPAL
105 SECRET SERVICE WOMAN

106 SOCIAL WORKER
107 SPECIALTY SALESWOMAN
108 STATISTICIAN
109 STENOGRAPHER
110 STEWARDESS

486

(table continued next page)

111 SURGEON
112 TEACHER, ART
113 TEACHER, COMMERCIAL
114 TEACHER, DANCING
115 TEACHER, DOMESTIC SCIENCE

116 TEACHER, GRADE SCHOOL
117 TEACHER, HIGH SCHOOL
118 TEACHER, KINDERGARTEN
119 TEACHER, MUSIC
120 TEA ROOM PROPRIETRESS

121 SUPERVISOR IN TELEPHONE OFFICE
122 TRAVEL BUREAU MANAGER
123 TYPIST
124 VOCATIONAL COUNSELOR
125 WAITRESS

126 WEATHER FORECASTER
127 X-RAY TECHNICIAN
128 YWCA SECRETARY
129 CHESS
130 JAZZ CONCERTS

131 SKETCHING PICTURES OF WILD ANIMALS
132 CAMPING OUT
133 GOLF
134 HORSEBACK RIDING
135 LOOKING AT THINGS IN HARDWARE STORE

136 BRIDGE
137 PLANNING A LARGE PARTY
138 AFTERNOON TEAS
139 BIRD WATCHING
140 SOLVING MECHANICAL PUZZLES

141 PLAYING THE PIANO
142 AMUSEMENT PARKS
143 HIKING
144 CONVENTIONS
145 FORMAL DRESS AFFAIRS

146 TELLING JOKES
147 TRAVEL MAGAZINES
148 ART GALLERIES
149 RELIGIOUS MUSIC
150 ATTENDING LECTURES

151 POPULAR MECHANICS MAGAZINES
152 SYMPHONY CONCERTS
153 READING THE BIBLE
154 MOVIES
155 FINANCIAL PAGES IN NEWSPAPERS

487

Column headings (occupations):

Airline Stewardesses
Beauticians
Sewing Machine Ops.
Instrument Assemblers
Telephone Operators
Saleswomen
Secretaries
Elementary Teachers
Exec. Housekeepers
Dental Assistants
Radiol. Technologists
Lic. Practical Nurses
Registered Nurses
Pub. Health Nurses
Physical Therapists
Occ. Therapists
Phys. Ed. Teachers
Dieticians
Home Ec. Teachers
Bus. Ed. Teachers
Buyers
Life Ins. Underwriters
Bankwomen
Accountants
Lawyers
Navy Officers
Army Officers
Navy--Enlisted
Army--Enlisted
Engineers
Math-Sci. Teachers
Computer Programmers
Mathematicians
Chemists
Med. Technologists
Dentists
Physicians
Translators
Librarians
Psychologists
Speech Pathologists
Social Workers
Soc. Sci. Teachers
Guidance Counselors
Nun-Teachers
Dirs. of Christian Ed.
Recreation Leaders
YWCA Staff Members
Language Teachers
English Teachers
Newswomen
Interior Decorators
Artists
Art Teachers
Models
Musician Performers
Entertainers
Music Teachers

Row items:

156 WOMENS PAGES
157 POETRY
158 COLLECTING ANTIQUE FURNITURE
159 PERFORMING SCIENTIFIC EXPERIMENTS
160 ELECTIONEERING FOR OFFICE
161 EDUCATIONAL MOVIES OR TV
162 MAGAZINES ABOUT ART AND MUSIC
163 MAKING A RADIO OR HI-FI SET
164 LEADING A GIRL SCOUT TROOP
165 WRITING A ONE-ACT PLAY
166 SCIENCE FICTION MAGAZINES
167 BUSINESS METHODS MAGAZINES
168 NIGHT CLUBS
169 CHURCH YOUNG PEOPLES GROUP
170 BIOGRAPHIES
171 BEING THE FIRST TO WEAR THE VERY LATEST
172 BEING HEAD OF A CIVIC IMPROVEMENT PROGRA
173 EXPRESSING JUDGMENTS PUBLICLY, REGARDLES
174 GIVING FIRST AID ASSISTANCE
175 RAISING FLOWERS AND VEGETABLES
176 OPERATING MACHINERY
177 REPAIRING ELECTRICAL WIRING
178 DOING YOUR OWN LAUNDRY WORK
179 DECORATING A ROOM WITH FLOWERS
180 ARGUMENTS
181 INTERVIEWING MEN FOR A JOB
182 INTERVIEWING CLIENTS
183 GOING TO CHURCH
184 MAKING A SPEECH
185 COOKING

186 SEWING
187 ORGANIZING A PLAY
188 STARTING A CONVERSATION WITH A STRANGER
189 PREPARING DINNER FOR GUESTS
190 TEACHING CHILDREN

191 TEACHING ADULTS
192 OPERATING OFFICE MACHINES
193 DISCUSSIONS OF POLITICS
194 READING EDITORIAL COLUMNS
195 MEETING AND DIRECTING PEOPLE

196 TAKING RESPONSIBILITY
197 TAPING A BRUISED ANKLE
198 ADJUSTING DIFFICULTIES OF OTHERS
199 DOING RESEARCH WORK
200 ACTING AS CHEER-LEADER

201 WRITING REPORTS
202 ENTERTAINING OTHERS
203 WATCHING AN OPEN-HEART OPERATION
204 CHECKING TYPEWRITTEN MATERIAL FOR ERRORS
205 TRYING NEW COOKING RECIPES

206 ORGANIZING CUPBOARDS AND CLOSETS
207 DISPLAYING MERCHANDISE IN A STORE
208 BEING LEFT TO YOURSELF
209 REGULAR HOURS FOR WORK
210 CONTINUALLY-CHANGING ACTIVITIES

211 SAVING MONEY
212 CONTRIBUTING TO CHARITIES
213 RAISING MONEY FOR A CHARITY
214 LOOKING AT A COLLECTION OF RARE LACES
215 MAKING STATISTICAL CHARTS

216 HIGHWAY CONSTRUCTION WORKERS
217 HIGH SCHOOL STUDENTS
218 COLLEGE PROFESSORS
219 JET PILOTS
220 MALE HAIRDRESSERS

221 CORPORATION EXECUTIVES
222 GIRLS WHO ENTER BEAUTY CONTESTS
223 PEOPLE WHO ARE NATURAL LEADERS
224 LONG-HAUL TRUCK DRIVERS
225 EMOTIONAL PEOPLE

226 THRIFTY PEOPLE
227 RELIGIOUS PEOPLE
228 HOUSEWIVES
229 NONCONFORMISTS
230 FAMOUS CHEFS

(table continued next page)

Column headings (left to right):

Music Teachers · Entertainers · Musician Performers · Models · Art Teachers · Artists · Interior Decorators · Newswomen · English Teachers · Language Teachers · YWCA Staff Members · Recreation Leaders · Dirs. of Christian Ed. · Nun--Teachers · Guidance Counselors · Soc. Sci. Teachers · Social Workers · Speech Pathologists · Psychologists · Librarians · Translators · Physicians · Dentists · Med. Technologists · Chemists · Mathematicians · Computer Programmers · Math-Sci. Teachers · Engineers · Army--Enlisted · Navy--Enlisted · Army Officers · Navy Officers · Lawyers · Accountants · Bankwomen · Life Ins. Underwriters · Buyers · Bus. Ed. Teachers · Home Ec. Teachers · Dieticians · Phys. Ed. Teachers · Occ. Therapists · Physical Therapists · Pub. Health Nurses · Registered Nurses · Lic. Practical Nurses · Radiol. Technologists · Dental Assistants · Exec. Housekeepers · Elementary Teachers · Secretaries · Saleswomen · Telephone Operators · Instrument Assemblers · Sewing Machine Ops. · Beauticians · Airline Stewardesses

Row items:

231 ARTISTIC MEN
232 FOREIGNERS
233 PUBLIC OPINION INTERVIEWERS
234 MEN WHO LIVE DANGEROUSLY
235 PHYSICALLY SICK PEOPLE
236 MUSICAL GENIUSES
237 PEOPLE WHO DAYDREAM A LOT
238 OUTSPOKEN PEOPLE WITH NEW IDEAS
239 RACING CAR DRIVERS
240 OUTSTANDING SCIENTISTS
241 FASHIONABLY DRESSED PEOPLE
242 CARELESSLY DRESSED PEOPLE
243 BALLET DANCERS
244 SOCIALISTS
245 PEOPLE WHO LIKE TO GAMBLE
246 ATHLETIC MEN
247 BABIES
248 VERY OLD PEOPLE
249 MEN WHO PERFORM ON TV
250 PEOPLE WHO INSIST ON HAVING EVERYTHING I
251 PROMINENT LABOR UNION MEN
252 MILITARY MEN
253 WOMEN ATHLETES
254 PEOPLE WHO DONT BELIEVE IN EVOLUTION
255 PEOPLE WHO HAVE MADE FORTUNES IN BUSINES
256 DESIGN A NEW HOME
257 HAVE RESPONSIBILITY FOR CARE OF NEW HOME
258 DISCOVER AN IMPROVEMENT IN THE DESIGN OF
259 DETERMINE THE COST OF BUILDING AND FURNI
260 SUPERVISE THE FURNISHING OF THE HOUSE

490

(table continued next page)

261 PLAN THE LANDSCAPING
262 SELL IDEAL HOUSES
263 PREPARE THE ADVERTISING FOR NEW HOUSES T
264 TEACH OTHERS HOW TO FURNISH THEIR HOMES
265 INTEREST THE PUBLIC IN BUILDING THEIR OW

266 SALARY RECEIVED FOR WORK
267 STEADINESS AND PERMANENCE OF WORK
268 OPPORTUNITY FOR PROMOTION
269 COURTEOUS TREATMENT FROM SUPERIORS
270 OPPORTUNITY TO MAKE USE OF ALL OF ONES K

271 OPPORTUNITY TO ASK QUESTIONS AND TO CONS
272 OPPORTUNITY TO UNDERSTAND JUST HOW ONES
273 CERTAINTY ONES WORK WILL BE JUDGED BY FA
274 FREEDOM IN WORKING OUT ONES OWN METHODS
275 CO-WORKERS--CONGENIAL, COMPETENT, AND AD

276 PRESIDENT, WOMENS COLLEGE
277 AUTHOR OF BEST-SELLING NOVEL
278 OUTSTANDING OPERA SINGER
279 OWNER-MANAGER OF CHAIN OF WOMENS SHOPS
280 WORLD-RENOWNED SCIENTIST

281 TENNIS CHAMPION
282 WIFE OF U. S. PRESIDENT
283 FAMOUS ACTRESS
284 PROMINENT ARTIST
285 SUPREME COURT JUSTICE

286 PRESIDENT OF A SOCIETY
287 SECRETARY OF A SOCIETY
288 TREASURER OF A SOCIETY
289 MEMBER OF A SOCIETY
290 CHAIRMAN, ARRANGEMENT COMMITTEE

291 CHAIRMAN, EDUCATIONAL COMMITTEE
292 CHAIRMAN, ENTERTAINMENT COMMITTEE
293 CHAIRMAN, MEMBERSHIP COMMITTEE
294 CHAIRMAN, PROGRAM COMMITTEE
295 CHAIRMAN, PUBLICITY COMMITTEE

296 PHYSICAL EDUCATION DIRECTOR...MAGAZINE W
297 STATISTICIAN...SOCIAL WORKER
298 AIRPLANE PILOT...STENOGRAPHER
299 TEACHER...SALESWOMAN
300 HOUSE-TO-HOUSE CANVASSING...RETAIL SELLI

301 TAKE DANCING LESSONS...TAKE SINGING LESS
302 DEVELOP PLANS...EXECUTE PLANS
303 DO A JOB YOURSELF...TELL SOMEBODY TO DO
304 TALK OTHERS INTO DOING SOMETHING...ORDER
305 KEEP BOOKS ON HOUSEHOLD FINANCES...RECOV

TABLE F-2 (*continued*)

	Music Teachers	Entertainers	Musician Performers	Models	Art Teachers	Artists	Interior Decorators	Newswomen	English Teachers	Language Teachers	YWCA Staff Members	Recreation Leaders	Dirs.of Christian Ed.	Nun-Teachers	Guidance Counselors	Soc. Sci. Teachers	Social Workers	Speech Pathologists	Psychologists	Librarians	Translators	Physicians	Dentists	Med. Technologists	Chemists	Mathematicians	Computer Programmers	Math-Sci. Teachers	Engineers	Army--Enlisted	Navy--Enlisted	Army Officers	Navy Officers	Lawyers	Accountants	Bankwomen	Life Ins.Underwriters	Buyers	Bus. Ed. Teachers	Home Ec. Teachers	Dieticians	Phys. Ed. Teachers	Occ. Therapists	Physical Therapists	Pub. Health Nurses	Registered Nurses	Lic. Practical Nurses	Radiol. Technologists	Dental Assistants	Exec. Housekeepers	Elementary Teachers	Secretaries	Saleswomen	Telephone Operators	Instrument Assemblers	Sewing Machine Ops.	Beauticians	Airline Stewardesses
306 DEAL WITH THINGS...DEAL WITH PEOPLE					+				-	-	-	-	-		-	-	-	-					+	+	+		+		+								-								-						+				+			
307 FASHION MAGAZINES...HOUSEHOLD MAGAZINES		+																																									-				-			-	-	-						+
308 ACTIVITY WHICH PRODUCES TANGIBLE RETURNS																																		+				+		+																		
309 PREPARING A MEAL...MAKING A DRESS					-												+	+															+							-			-															
310 TAKING A CHANCE...PLAYING SAFE		+									+	+																				+								-												-			-	-		
311 WORK FOR YOURSELF...CARRY OUT PROGRAM OF						+	+							-			-					+	+	-			-						-	+		-	+	-						-			-	-	-	-			-	-		-		
312 EXPERIMENT WITH NEW BEAUTY PREPARATIONS.		+																		-		-			-	-		-		-	-	-		-	-	-			-											-							+	+
313 FOLLOW OWN CAREER AFTER MARRIAGE..FOLLOW		+	+			+	+						-	-	+			+	+		+	+	+		+	+								+	+											-							-	-				-
314 WORK WITH FEW DETAILS...WORK WITH MANY D																	+										-								-	-	+	-																				
315 BE MARRIED WITH SMALL INCOME...BE SINGLE		-	+														+													-	-	-	-		-										+	+								+				
316 WORKING FOR MEN...WORKING FOR WOMEN											-			-			-																+					+						-			-		+				+			-		+
317 WORK IN WHICH YOU MOVE FROM PLACE TO PLA		+		+						-													-							+	+	+	+			-		-	-	-												-						+
318 GREAT VARIETY OF WORK...SIMILARITY IN WO											+	+	+	-									-				+						+		+												-					-	+	-	-			+
319 PHYSICAL ACTIVITY...MENTAL ACTIVITY								-	-	-		+			-	-	-	-	-	-	-				-	-								-	-	-		-				+		+				+	+						+		+	+
320 BE MARRIED TO A RESEARCH SCIENTIST...BE							-												+		+	+		+	+	+										-	-		-														-	-			-	-
321 TRAVEL ALONE AND MAKE OWN PREPARATIONS..			-	-										-			-	-												+															-													
322 PRESENT A REPORT IN WRITING...PRESENT A		-									-							-									+										-															+	+					
323 LISTENING TO A STORY...TELLING A STORY				-					-				-					-					+															+													+							
324 DO YOUR OWN HOUSEWORK...HAVE SOMEONE ESL		-		-		-	-	-						+	-		-	-	-	-	-	-	-						-			-	-	-	-		-			+				+			+	+			+	+		+	+	+	+	+
325 AMUSEMENT WHERE THERE IS A CROWD...ALONE																			-		-	-				-																											+				+	
326 WORK IN AN IMPORT-EXPORT BUSINESS...WORK					+		+		+	+	+	+				+			-			-		-	-	-		-				+		+			+		+	+				-			-	-					+	+				+
327 SPEND A GREAT DEAL OF TIME ON MAKE-UP BE		+																		-		-			-	-		-														-		-													+	+
328 BE MARRIED TO A RANCHER...BE MARRIED TO							-																							+	+			-		-	-					+																
329 READING A BOOK...WATCHING TV OR GOING TO																			+	+	+	+			+									+								-									-					-	-	
330 GOING TO A PLAY...GOING TO A DANCE									+				+							+					+																	-						-			-					-	-	-
331 THRILLING, DANGEROUS ACTIVITIES...QUIETE				+																									+		+					-						+					-			-		-		-	-	-		+
332 DISPLAY MERCHANDISE IN STORE WINDOW...AR					+																									+	+									-	-					-	-			-								
333 A FEW CLOSE FRIENDS...MANY ACQUAINTANCES	-																		+		+					+	+															-															-	
334 USUALLY START ACTIVITIES OF MY GROUP	+										+	+	+	+									-									+					+	+										-							-	-		
335 HAVE MORE THAN MY SHARE OF NOVEL IDEAS		+			+	+	+	+											+																																							

336 WIN FRIENDS EASILY
337 USUALLY GET OTHER PEOPLE TO DO WHAT I WA
338 KEEP DETAILED RECORDS OF EXPENSES
339 USUALLY LIVEN UP THE GROUP ON A DULL DAY
340 HAVE MECHANICAL INGENUITY, INVENTIVENESS

341 PREFER WORKING ALONE TO WORKING ON COMMI
342 DO MY BEST WORK EARLY IN THE MORNING
343 CAN PREPARE SUCCESSFUL ADVERTISEMENTS
344 AM ALWAYS ON TIME WITH MY WORK
345 REMEMBER FACES, NAMES, AND INCIDENTS BET

346 CAN CORRECT OTHERS WITHOUT GIVING OFFENS
347 ABLE TO MEET EMERGENCIES QUICKLY AND EFF
348 MY GRADES IN HIGH SCHOOL WERE A FAIRLY A
349 CAN WRITE A CONCISE, WELL-ORGANIZED REPO
350 HAVE GOOD JUDGMENT IN APPRAISING VALUES

351 PLAN MY WORK IN DETAIL
352 STIMULATE THE AMBITION OF MY ASSOCIATES
353 ENJOY TINKERING WITH SMALL HAND TOOLS
354 CAN SMOOTH OUT TANGLES AND DISAGREEMENTS
355 DISCUSS MY IDEALS WITH OTHERS

356 WORRY ABOUT MISTAKES...A GOOD DEAL...VER
357 COMPLAINTS ANNOY ME...RARELY...SOMETIMES
358 LEND MONEY TO...ACQUAINTANCES...ONLY CER
359 IN MY FAMILY, I AM THE...OLDEST OR ONLY
360 AT A LARGE CONFERENCE PREFER A SEAT...IN

361 MAKE BETS...OFTEN...SOMETIMES...RARELY
362 ALGEBRA
363 ARITHMETIC
364 ART
365 BIBLE HISTORY

366 BOOKKEEPING
367 BOTANY
368 CALCULUS
369 CHEMISTRY
370 CIVICS, GOVERNMENT

371 HOME ECONOMICS
372 DRAMATICS
373 EDUCATION, TEACHER TRAINING
374 ECONOMICS
375 ENGLISH COMPOSITION

376 GEOGRAPHY
377 GEOLOGY
378 GEOMETRY
379 HISTORY
380 JOURNALISM

(table continued next page)

493

TABLE F-2 (*continued*)

Subject areas:

- 381 LANGUAGES, ANCIENT
- 382 LANGUAGES, MODERN
- 383 LITERATURE
- 384 MECHANICAL DRAWING
- 385 WOODWORKING
- 386 NATURE STUDY
- 387 PENMANSHIP
- 388 PHILOSOPHY
- 389 PHYSICAL EDUCATION
- 390 PHYSICS
- 391 PHYSIOLOGY
- 392 POLITICAL SCIENCE
- 393 PSYCHOLOGY
- 394 PUBLIC SPEAKING
- 395 SHORTHAND
- 396 SOCIOLOGY
- 397 SPELLING
- 398 STATISTICS
- 399 TYPEWRITING
- 400 ZOOLOGY

Occupations (columns):

Music Teachers; Entertainers; Musician Performers; Models; Art Teachers; Artists; Interior Decorators; Newswomen; English Teachers; Language Teachers; YWCA Staff Members; Recreation Leaders; Dirs. of Christian Ed.; Nun-Teachers; Guidance Counselors; Soc. Sci. Teachers; Social Workers; Speech Pathologists; Psychologists; Librarians; Translators; Physicians; Dentists; Med. Technologists; Chemists; Mathematicians; Computer Programmers; Math-Sci. Teachers; Engineers; Army--Enlisted; Navy--Enlisted; Army Officers; Navy Officers; Lawyers; Accountants; Bankwomen; Life Ins. Underwriters; Buyers; Bus. Ed. Teachers; Home Ec. Teachers; Dieticians; Phys. Ed. Teachers; Occ. Therapists; Physical Therapists; Pub. Health Nurses; Registered Nurses; Lic. Practical Nurses; Radiol. Technologists; Dental Assistants; Exec. Housekeepers; Elementary Teachers; Secretaries; Saleswomen; Telephone Operators; Instrument Assemblers; Sewing Machine Ops.; Beauticians; Airline Stewardesses

494

References

References

Abrahams, N. M., Idell Neumann, and W. H. Githens (1968a). The Strong Vocational Interest Blank in predicting NROTC officer retention. Part I, Validity and reliability, U.S. Naval Personnel Research Activity, Technical Bulletin STB 68–7, January.

——— (1968b). The Strong Vocational Interest Blank in predicting NROTC officer retention. Part II, Fakability. U.S. Naval Personnel Research Activity, Technical Bulletin STB 68–9, February.

Acree, N. E. (1960). Vocational interests of rehabilitation counselors. Graduate thesis, George Peabody College for Teachers.

Alsip, J. E. (1966). Differential responses of veterinarians to the revised Strong Vocational Interest Blank for men. Master of Science thesis, Iowa State University.

Athelstan, G. T. (1966). An exploratory investigation of response patterns associated with low profiles on the Strong Vocational Interest Blank for men. Unpublished doctoral dissertation, University of Minnesota.

Bacon, R. V. (1958). A study of the interest patterns of men business teachers in public secondary schools. Unpublished doctoral dissertation, University of California at Los Angeles.

Benjamin, D. R. (1967). A thirty-one year longitudinal study of engineering students' interest profiles and career patterns. Unpublished doctoral dissertation, Purdue University.

Bentley, J. C., and J. E. Rossmann (1969). Vocational exploration of future college teachers. *Personnel and Guidance Journal, 47*, 435–439.

Benton, A. L., and S. I. Kornhauser (1948). A study of "score faking" on a medical interest test. *Journal of the Association of American Medical Colleges, 23*, 57–60.

Berdie, R. F. (1960). Strong Vocational Interest Blank scores of high school seniors and their later occupational entry. *Journal of Applied Psychology, 44*, 161–165.

——— (1965). Strong Vocational Interest Blank scores of high school seniors and their later occupational entry, II. *Journal of Applied Psychology, 49*, 188–193.

Berdie, R. F., and D. P. Campbell (1968). The measurement of interests.

In *Handbook of psychological measurement*, D. K. Whitla (ed.). New York: Addison-Wesley.

Betz, Barbara J. (1962). Experiences in research in psychotherapy with schizophrenic patients. In H. H. Stripp and L. Luborsky (eds.), *Research in psychotherapy*. American Psychological Association, 2, 41–60.

—— (1963). Bases of therapeutic leadership in psychotherapy with the schizophrenic patient. *American Journal of Psychotherapy, 17*, 196–212.

—— (1967). Studies of the therapist's role in the treatment of the schizophrenic patient. *American Journal of Psychiatry, 123*, 963–971.

Bills, Marian A. (1952). A tool of selection that has stood the test of time. In *Applications of psychology: Essays to honor Walter V. Bingham, L. L. Thurstone (ed.)*. New York: Harper.

Brandt, J. E. (1967). The effect of personality adjustment on the predictive validity of the Strong Vocational Interest Blank. Dissertation, University of Iowa.

Brandt, J. E., and A. B. Hood (1968). Effect of personality adjustment on the predictive validity of the Strong Vocational Interest Blank. *Journal of Counseling Psychology, 15*, 547–551.

Buros, O. K. (ed.) (1965). The sixth mental measurements yearbook. Highland Park, New Jersey: Gryphon Press.

Campbell, D. P. (1963). Chance on SVIB: dice or men? *Journal of Applied Psychology, 47*, 127–129.

—— (1965a). *The results of counseling: twenty-five years later*. Philadelphia: Saunders.

—— (1965b). The vocational interests of APA presidents. *American Psychologist, 20*, 636–644.

—— (1966a). Stability of interests within an occupation over thirty years. *Journal of Applied Psychology, 50*, 51–56.

—— (1966b). The stability of vocational interests within occupations over long time spans. *Personnel and Guidance Journal, 44*, 1012–1019.

—— (1966c). The 1966 revision of the Strong Vocational Interest Blank. *Personnel and Guidance Journal, 44*, 744–749.

—— (1966d.) Occupations ten years later of high school seniors with high scores on the SVIB life insurance salesman scale. *Journal of Applied Psychology, 50*, 369–372.

—— (1966e). *Manual for the Strong Vocational Interest Blank*. Stanford, Calif.: Stanford University Press.

—— (1967a). The vocational interests of beautiful women. *Personnel and Guidance Journal, 45*, 968–972.

—— (1968c). Changing patterns of interests within the American society. *Measurement and Evaluation in Guidance, 1*, 1, 36–49.

Campbell, D. P., and Hildred Schuell (1967b). The vocational interests of women in speech pathology and audiology. *Asha, 9*, 67–72.

Campbell, D. P., and A. M. Soliman (1968*a*). The vocational interests of women in psychology. *American Psychologist, 23,* 158–163.

Campbell, D. P., J. H. Stevens, E. H. Uhlenhuth, and C. B. Johansson (1968*b*). An extension of the Whitehorn-Betz A-B scale. *Journal of Nervous and Mental Diseases, 146,* 417–421.

Carkhuff, R. R., and J. Drasgow (1963). The confusing literature on the OL scale of the SVIB. *Journal of Counseling Psychology, 10,* 283–288.

Clark, K. E. (1961). *Vocational interests of non-professional men.* Minneapolis: University of Minnesota Press.

Darley, J. G. (1941). *Clinical aspects and interpretation of the Strong Vocational Interest Blank.* New York: Psychological Corporation.

Darley, J. G., and Theda Hagenah (1955). *Vocational interest measurement.* Minneapolis: University of Minnesota Press.

DuBois, P. H., and R. I. Watson (1950). Selection of patrolmen. *Journal of Applied Psychology, 34,* 90–95.

Dunnette, M. D., P. Wernimont, and N. Abrahams (1964). Further research and vocational interest differences among several types of engineers. *Personnel and Guidance Journal, 42,* 484–493.

Feifel, H., N. V. Steenberg, H. Brogden, and W. Klieger (1952). Measurement of the interests of army officers. Department of the Army, Personnel Research Section, Report #973.

Ferguson, L. W. (1958). Life insurance interest, ability, and termination of employment. *Personnel Journal, 11,* 189–193.

———— (1960). Ability, interest, and aptitude. *Journal of Applied Psychology, 44,* 126–131.

Freyd, M. (1924). The personalities of the socially and the mechanically inclined. *Psychological Monographs, 33,* 151.

Fricke, B. G. (1968). What about paper-and-pencil personality and interest testing? Paper presented at the meetings of the American Personnel and Guidance Association, Detroit.

Friedersdorf, Nancy (1969). A comparative study of counselor attitudes towards the further educational and vocational plans of high school girls. Unpublished dissertation, University of Michigan.

Fryer, D. (1931). *The measurement of interests.* New York: Henry Holt.

Galinsky, M. D., and Irene Fast (1969). The use of the SVIB with identity problems. *Journal of College Student Personnel, 10,* 177–181.

Garry, R. (1953). Individual differences in ability to fake vocational interests. *Journal of Applied Psychology, 37,* 33–37.

Gehman, W. S. (1957). A study of ability to fake scores on the Strong Vocational Interest Blank for Men. *Educational and Psychological Measurement, 17,* 65–70.

Gottesman, I. I. (1963). Heritability of personality: a demonstration. *Psychology Monographs, 77,* No. 9.

References

Gray, C. W. (1959). Detection of faking in vocational interest measurement. Unpublished doctoral dissertation, University of Minnesota.

Hannum, T. E. (1950). Response of veterinarians to the SVIB for men. *Iowa Academy of Science Proceedings, 57*, 381–384.

——— (1960). Correlates of achievement in a veterinary medicine curriculum. *Iowa Academy of Science Proceedings, 67*, 459–462.

Hannum, T. E., and J. B. Thrall (1955). Use of the SVIB for prediction in veterinary medicine. *Journal of Applied Psychology, 39*, 249–252.

Harmon, P. A. (1960). Personality characteristics of dental students. *Educational Record, 41*, 240–252.

Harmon, Lenore W. (1969). The predictive power over 10 years of measured social service and scientific interests among college women. *Journal of Applied Psychology, 53*, 193–198.

Harmon, Lenore W., and D. P. Campbell (1968). Use of interest inventories with nonprofessional women: stewardesses versus dental assistants. *Journal of Counseling Psychology, 15*, 17–22.

Heist, P. A. (1960). Personality characteristics of dental students. *Educational Record, 41*, 240–252.

Herman, L. M., C. Lindsay, and M. L. Zeigler (1962). Vocational scale for biologists. *Journal of Applied Psychology, 46*, 170–174.

Hill, Diane S., and D. P. Campbell (1969). The changing interests of women. Paper presented at the meetings of the Midwestern Psychological Association, Chicago.

Holland, J. L. (1966). *The psychology of vocational choice*. Waltham, Mass.: Blaisdell.

Holmen, M. G. (1954). Specialization level scale for the Strong Vocational Interest Blank. *Journal of Applied Psychology, 38*, 159–163.

Hoppock, R. H., H. A. Robinson, and P. J. Zlatchin (1948). Job satisfaction researches of 1946–47. *Occupations, 27*, 167–176.

Hoyt, D. P., J. L. Smith, Jr., and S. Levy (1957). A further study in the prediction of interest stability. *Journal of Counseling Psychology, 4*, 228–233.

Hutchins, E. B. (1964). The AAMC longitudinal study: implications for medical education. *Journal of Medical Education, 39*, 265–277.

Hutchinson, J. C., Jr. (1952). Vocational interest and job satisfaction of women elementary teachers. Unpublished doctoral dissertation, New York University.

Johansson, C. B. (1970). Strong Vocational Interest Blank test-retest correlations for different age groups and over varying intervals.

Johnson, J. C., and M. D. Dunnette (1968). Validity and test-retest stability of the Nash Managerial Effectiveness scale on the revised form of the Strong Vocational Interest Blank. *Personnel Psychology, 21*, 283–293.

Joselyn, E. G. (1968). The relationship of selected variables to the stability of measured vocational interest of high school students. Unpublished doctoral dissertation, University of Minnesota.

Kates, S. L. (1950). Rorschach responses related to vocational interests and job satisfaction. *Psychological Monographs, 64,* 1–34.

Kelley, T. L. (1914). Educational guidance. An experimental study in the analysis and prediction of ability of high school pupils. T. C. Columbia University *Contributions to Education,* No. 71.

Kelly, E. L., and D. W. Fiske (1951). *The prediction of performance in clinical psychology.* Ann Arbor: University of Michigan Press.

Kelso, D. F., and E. S. Bordin (1948). The ability to manipulate occupational stereotype inherent in the Strong Vocational Interest Test. *American Psychologist, 3,* 352–353 (abstract).

King, L. A. (1957). Stability measures of Strong Vocational Interest Blank profiles. *Journal of Applied Psychology, 41,* 143–147.

Kirchner, W. K. (1961). "Real-life" faking on the Strong Vocational Interest Blank by sales applicants. *Journal of Applied Psychology, 45,* 273–276.

Kirk, Barbara A., R. W. Cummings, and H. R. Hackett (1963). Personal and vocational characteristics of dental students. *Personnel and Guidance Journal, 41,* 522–527.

Klein, F. L., D. M. McNair, and M. Lorr (1962). SVIB scores of clinical psychologists, psychiatrists, and social workers. *Journal of Counseling Psychology, 9,* 176–179.

Kriedt, P. H. (1949). Vocational interests of psychologists. *Journal of Applied Psychology, 33,* 482–488.

Kriedt, P. H., C. H. Stone, and D. G. Paterson (1952). Vocational interests of industrial relations personnel. *Journal of Applied Psychology, 36,* 174–179.

Kroger, R. O. (1967). Effects of role demands and test-cue properties upon personality test performance. *Journal of Consulting Psychology, 31,* 304–312.

Kuder, G. F. (1966). *Occupational Interest Survey General Manual.* Chicago: Science Research Associates, Inc.

Kunce, J. T. (1967). Vocational interests and accident proneness. *Journal of Applied Psychology, 51,* 223–225.

Kunce, J. T., and B. Brewer (1966a). Neuropsychiatric patients, accident proneness, and interest patterns. *Journal of Psychology, 63,* 287–290.

Kunce, J. T., and B. Worley (1966b). Interest patterns, accidents and disability. *Journal of Clinical Psychology, 22,* 105–107.

Layton, W. L. (1958). *Counseling use of the Strong Vocational Interest Blank.* Minneapolis: University of Minnesota Press.

Longstaff, H. P. (1948). Fakability of the Strong Interest Blank and the Kuder Preference Record. *Journal of Applied Psychology, 23,* 360–369.

McArthur, C. (1954). Long term validity of the Strong Interest Test in two subcultures. *Journal of Applied Psychology, 38,* 346–354.

McArthur, C., and Lucia B. Stevens (1955). The validation of expressed interests as compared with inventoried interests: a 14 year follow-up. *Journal of Applied Psychology, 39,* 184–189.

McCornack, R. L. (1956). Vocational interests of male and female social workers. *Journal of Applied Psychology, 40,* 11–13.

McNair, D. M., D. M. Callahan, and M. Lorr (1962). Therapist "type" and patient response to psychotherapy. *Journal of Consulting Psychology, 26,* 425–429.

Mahoney, T. A., T. H. Jerdee, and A. N. Nash (1960). Predicting managerial effectiveness. *Personnel Psychologist, 13,* 147–163.

Martin, Ann (1964). Development and successive refinement of an academic interest scale for the SVIB. *Educational and Psychological Measurement, 24,* 841–852.

Matarazzo, J. D., Bernadene V. Allen, G. Saslow, and A. Wiens (1964). Characteristics of successful policemen and firemen applicants. *Journal of Applied Psychology, 48,* 123–133.

Miner, J. B. (1922). An aid to the analysis of vocational interests. *Journal of Educ. Res., 5,* 311–323.

Moore, B. V. (1921). Personnel selection of graduate engineers. *Psychological Monographs, 30,* 138.

Mosier, C. I. (1937). Factors influencing the validity of a scholastic interest scale. *Journal of Educational Psychology, 28,* 188–196.

Nash, A. N. (1965). Vocational interests of effective managers: a review of the literature. *Personnel Psychology, 18,* 21–37.

——— (1966). Development of an SVIB key for selecting managers. *Journal of Applied Psychology, 50,* 250–254.

Nolting, E., Jr. (1967). A study of female vocational interests: pre-college to post-graduation. Unpublished doctoral dissertation, University of Minnesota.

Olheiser, Mary D. (1962). Development of a sister teacher interest scale for the Strong Vocational Interest Blank for women. Unpublished doctoral dissertation, Boston College.

Paterson, D. G. (1946). Vocational interest inventories in selection. *Occupations, 25,* 152–153.

Perry, D. K., and W. M. Cannon (1967). Vocational interests of computer programmers. *Journal of Applied Psychology, 51,* 28–34.

——— (1968). Vocational interests of female computer programmers. *Journal of Applied Psychology, 52,* 31–35.

Priebe, D. W. (1968). An interest inventory of Minnesota farmers. Unpublished doctoral dissertation, University of Minnesota.

Ream, M. J. (1924). *Ability to sell; its relation to certain aspects of personality and experience.* Baltimore: Williams and Wilkins.

Rhode, J. G. (1966). The measurement of vocational interests for certified public accountants over a thirty year period. Unpublished master's thesis, University of Minnesota.

——— (1969). Vocational interests of Business Administration professors. Unpublished doctoral dissertation, University of Minnesota.

Robinson, H. A. (1953). Job satisfaction researches in 1952. *Personnel and Guidance Journal, 32*, 22–25.

Rothney, J. W. M. (1967). A review of E. K. Strong, D. P. Campbell, R. F. Berdie, and K. E. Clark, Strong Vocational Interest Blank (revised). Stanford, California: Stanford University Press, 1966. *Journal of Counseling Psychology, 14*, 187–191.

Roys, K. B. (1967). Vocational interests of community recreation administrators using the SVIB. *Journal of Applied Psychology, 51*, 539–543.

Scheller, T. G. (1967). A study of the academic aptitude, occupations, and occupational satisfaction of a sample of men with low intensity interests. Unpublished doctoral dissertation, University of Minnesota.

Schletzer, Vera M. (1963). A study of the predictive effectiveness of the Strong Vocational Interest Blank for job satisfaction. Unpublished doctoral dissertation, University of Minnesota.

——— (1966). SVIB as a predictor of job satisfaction. *Journal of Applied Psychology, 50*, 5–8.

Schwebel, M. (1951). *The interests of pharmacists.* New York: Columbia University Press.

Steinmetz, H. C. (1932). Measuring ability to fake occupational interest. *Journal of Applied Psychology, 16*, 123–130.

Stephenson, R. R. (1961). Predicting SVIB profiles of high ability male arts college freshmen. *Personnel and Guidance Journal, 39*, 650–653.

——— (1965). A comparison of responses to a vocational interest test taken under standard conditions at recruiting stations and responses to the same test taken as a self-administered test at home. Paper presented at the meetings of the American Personnel and Guidance Association, Minneapolis.

Steward, V. (1947). The problem of detecting fudging on vocational interest tests. *Personnel Reports for Sales Executives.* Los Angeles, January.

Stewart, L. H. (1964). Selected correlates of the specialization level of the Strong Vocational Interest Blank. *Personnel and Guidance Journal, 42*, 867–873.

Stone, V. W. (1960). Measured vocational interests in relation to intraoccupational proficiency. *Journal of Applied Psychology, 44*, 78–82.

Stordahl, K. E. (1954). Permanence of interests and interest maturity. *Journal of Applied Psychology, 38*, 339–340.

Strong, E. K., Jr. (1927). Differentiation of certified public accountants from other occupational groups. *Journal of Educational Psychology, 18*, 227–238.

——— (1929). Diagnostic value of the vocational interest test. *Educational Record, 10*, 59–68.

References

———— (1931). *Change of interests with age*. Stanford: Stanford University Press.

———— (1934). Interests and sales ability. *Personnel Journal, 13*, 204–216.

———— (1943). *Vocational interests of men and women*. Stanford: Stanford University Press.

———— (1947). Differences in interests among public administrators. *Journal of Applied Psychology, 31*, 18–38.

———— (1949). Vocational interests of accountants. *Journal of Applied Psychology, 33*, 474–481.

———— (1952). Nineteen year follow-up of engineer interests. *Journal of Applied Psychology, 36*, 65–74.

———— (1955). *Vocational interests 18 years after college*. Minneapolis: University of Minnesota Press.

———— (1959). *Strong Vocational Interest Blank Manual*. Palo Alto, Calif.: Consulting Psychologists Press.

———— (1962). Good and poor interest items. *Journal of Applied Psychology, 46*, 269–275.

———— (1963). Reworded versus new interest items. *Journal of Applied Psychology, 47*, 111–116.

Strong, E. K., Jr., D. P. Campbell, R. F. Berdie, and K. E. Clark (1964). Proposed scoring changes for the Strong Vocational Interest Blank. *Journal of Applied Psychology, 48*, 75–80.

Strong, E. K., Jr., and H. McKenzie (1930). Permanence of interest of adult men. *Journal of Social Psychology, 1*, 152–159.

Strong, E. K., Jr., and A. C. Tucker (1952). Use of vocational interest scales in planning a medical career. *Psychological Monographs, 66*, 341.

Thomas, R. R. (1955). Permanence of measured interests of women over 15 years (abstract). *American Psychologist, 10*.

Thorndike, E. L. (1912). The permanence of interests and their relation to abilities. *Popular Science Monthly, 18*, 449–456.

Thrush, R. S., and P. T. King (1965). Differential interests among medical students. *Vocational Guidance Quarterly*, Winter, pp. 120–123.

Tilton, J. W. (1937). The measurement of overlapping. *Journal of Educational Psychology, 28*, 656–662.

Trimble, J. T. (1965). Ten year longitudinal follow-up study of inventoried interests of selected high school students. Unpublished doctoral dissertation, University of Missouri.

Verburg, W. A. (1952). Vocational interests of retired YMCA secretaries. *Journal of Applied Psychology, 36*, 254–256.

Wallace, W. L. (1950). The relationship of certain variables to discrepancy between expressed and inventoried vocational interest. *American Psychologist, 5*, 354 (abstract).

Whitehorn, J. C., and Barbara J. Betz. (1960). Further studies of the doctor as a crucial variable in outcome of treatment with schizophrenic patients. *American Journal of Psychiatry, 117,* 215–223.

Williamson, E. G. (1937). An analysis of the Young-Estabrooks studiousness scale. *Journal of Applied Psychology, 21,* 260–264.

Williamson, E. G., and E. S. Bordin (1950). Evaluating counseling by means of a control-group experiment. In *Readings in modern methods of counseling,* A. H. Brayfield (ed.). New York: Appleton-Century-Crofts, Inc., pp. 511–520.

Winter, F. (1963). Development of a USAF officer's interest scale. Unpublished master's thesis, University of California at Los Angeles.

Winters, J. S. (1962). Inventoried interests of male librarians. Unpublished doctoral dissertation, New York University.

Young, C. W., and G. H. Estabrooks (1936). *Scale for measuring studiousness by means of the SVIB for men.* Stanford: Stanford University Press.

Index

AACH, *see* Academic achievement scale
Ability and interests, 62–66 *passim. See also* Success and interests
Abrahams, N. M., 20–21, 135, 387, 447
Academic achievement scale, 50f, 52–53, 71, 194, 330, 370; men, 195–203; women, 203–5; use of, 205–8; in case study, 295, 297, 302, 309
Academically gifted women, 177
Academic success and interests, 65. *See also* Academic achievement scale
Accident proneness index, 194–95
Accountants, 51, 57, 121, 132, 317, 325, 385f, 445; accounting students, 15, 55, 151; women, 52, 177, 390
Accuracy of SVIB, 49, 54–55. *See also* Validity
Acree, N. E., 135f, 389, 447f
Actors, 132, 230, 261
Administration of the SVIB, 10–11; problems in, 248–49
Administrative Indices, 248–59, 370
Advances in Psychological Assessment, 343n
Adventure scale, 93, 105, 109, 115, 119, 121, 129, 139, 151, 261, 323; in case study, 290, 298f
Advertising men, 51, 57, 132, 385, 445
Age level for using SVIB, 11
Age-related interests scale, 208–21, 292, 370
Agricultural extension agents, 132
Agriculture scale, 93, 139, 150; in case study, 290f
Air force officers, 50, 132, 325, 370, 385, 445
Airline stewardesses, *see* Stewardesses
Alford, J. B., 135, 447
Allen, Bernadene V., 315, 388
Alsip, J. E., 123, 137, 324, 448
American Institute of Accountants, 325
American Medical Association, 29, 319
American Psychological Association, 13,

65, 82, 208, 260–61; presidents of, 65, 261, 270, 321. *See also* Psychologists
American Psychologist, 261
Animal husbandry professors, 132. *See also* College professors
Answer sheets, 3, 10; problems with, 249
Anthropologists, 132, 445
Applicants faking the SVIB, 17–24. *See also* Faking
Aptitude tests and interests, 64, 196. *See also* MSAT
Architects, 50, 132, 385, 445; students, 55
Army: officers, 50, 132, 205, 230, 270f, 385, 445; sergeants, 132, 445; women, 52–53, 177, 390
Army officer scale, 26–28
AR scale, 208–21, 292, 370
Artistic scale, Holland's 443, 463, 466. *See also* Art scale
Artists, 28–29, 51, 63, 226, 261, 271, 330, 385, 445; on basic interest scales, 132; students, 176, 191; women, 52, 177, 390
Art scale: men, 93, 119, 129f, 140, 271, 284; women, 159, 175, 181, 191; in case study, 289, 299
Art teachers, 52, 177, 390
Association of American Medical Colleges, 18, 71, 120–21
Astronauts, 132, 208, 231, 261, 272, 323
Astronomers, 132
Athelstan, G. T., 135, 280–81
Authors, 28–29, 51, 57, 132, 208, 230, 261, 323, 385; women, 177. *See also* Journalists, Newsmen
Automobile salesmen, 136, 448
Autonomy, scale for, 103
Aviator scale, 370

Bacon, R. V., 132, 386, 445
Bankers, 48, 51, 81, 123, 132, 319, 321, 325, 385, 445; women, 52, 177, 390
Basic interest scales: plotted on profile, 6–7; and faking, 18–19; purpose, 88;

construction, 88–92; norm sample, 153; and occupational scales, 155; interpretation, 156–57. *See also individual scales by name*
Beauticians, 52, 177, 390
Benjamin, D. R., 66–67, 82, 119
Bentley, J. C., 133, 270
Benton, A. L., 15, 133, 445
Beran, Shirley, 132, 445
Berdie, R. F., 33, 55–57, 59, 81, 134, 137, 151–52, 210–11, 315, 362, 369
Berning, T. J., 387
Betz, Barbara J., 64, 388
Bias in sample, 115
Bills, Marion A., 387
Bingham, W. V., 350f
Biological science scale, 159, 181, 191. *See also* Science scale
Biologists, 50, 132, 385, 445
Blacksmiths, 322
Blanton, Gloria, 134, 178, 391
Boaz, Jacquelyn, 393
Bordin, E. S., 15, 119
Boring, E. G., 82–83
Brandt, J. E., 62–63, 68
Breadth of interests, *see* Diversity of interests
Buros, O. K., 345
Business education teachers, 51, 132, 386, 445; women, 52, 177, 390
Business management scale, 94, 119, 140, 150, 271; in case study, 290, 295
Business school professors, 132, 150–51. *See also* College professors
Business students, 14
Buyer, 132, 445; women, 52, 177, 390. *See also* Purchasing agent

California Bar Association, 315
Campbell, D. P., 33, 57–59, 64, 82f, 123, 173, 261, 315, 363, 369, 382
Cannon, W. M., 68, 133, 386, 390, 446
Carmody, Constance, 179, 392
Carnegie Institute of Technology, 345, 350
Carnegie Interest Analysis, 350
Carnegie Interest Inventory, 350
Carpenter, 50, 133, 386
Cartographers, 133, 445
Cartoonists, 230, 270
Case studies, 286–312
Center for Interest Measurement Research, 21, 138, 364
Certified Public Accountants, 121. *See also* Accountants
Chamber of Commerce executives, 51, 133, 330, 386, 445
Change of interest: among society, 34–42; with age, 57, 129, 151, 173–76; on

AACH scale, 198–200; on all SVIB scales, 211; on AR scale, 217; mathematical curve, 219; case studies, 287. *See also* Reliability *and* Stability of interests
Change of Interests with Age, 286
Cheating on SVIB, *see* Faking
Chemists, 48, 50, 133, 246, 271, 386, 445; women, 52, 177, 390
Chiropractors, 133, 446
Clark, A. B., III, 137
Clark, K. E., 33, 350, 362f, 369
Clerical workers, 67
Cluster analysis, 88–92. *See also* Basic interest scales
College professors, 132f, 150–51, 325, 442, 446
College students, 66–67, 71, 83, 112–19, 171–72, 286; emotionally distressed, 62–63
Collins, Patricia, 179
Colonels, 133. *See also* Army officers
Columbia University, 355, 358
Common items, men's and women's booklets, 6
Community recreation directors, 133, 330, 386, 446
Composers, 208, 230, 270f
Compulsivity, scale for, 103
Computer programmers, 68, 133, 371, 386, 446; women, 52, 390
Computer salesmen, 137, 331 448
Concurrent validity, *see* Validity
Connecticut College for Women, 173
Construct validity, *see* Validity
Consulting Psychologists Press, 360
Content validity, *see* Validity
Conventional scale, Holland's, 443, 463, 469
Corporation presidents, 51, 133, 205, 231, 270, 319, 388
Counselors, *see* Guidance counselors; High school counselors; Rehabilitation counselors
County sheriffs, 133
Cowdery, Karl, 350f, 384, 405, 408–9
CPA: owner, 51, 386; senior, 51, 386. *See also* Accountants
Creativity and interests, 225
Credit managers, 28, 51, 133, 386, 446
Criterion samples, 25, 29–30, 177–80; description of, 358, 380, 384–93, 441–42
Cross-validation, 33, 65; evidence for, 47–48, 271, 443; on specific scales, 68, 195, 227, 327
Cultural Change scale: men, 325–35; women, 335–40; use of, 340–41
Cummings, R. W., 387

Cutler, F. A., 387

Danforth fellows, 133, 230, 270
Darley, J. G., 275, 277–78, 281
Data processing, 355–56
Dela Data, 360. *See also* Scoring agencies
Dental assistants, 52, 177, 390
Dentists, 50, 153, 387, 446; women, 52, 177, 390; students, 55, 151; educators, 133
Department store managers, 133, 446
Dictionary of Occupational Titles, 87
Dieticians, 52, 177, 390
Directors, Christian education, 52, 177, 391
Discrepancies: between basic and occupational scales, 283; between stated and measured interests, 285–86
Dishonest answers, *see* Faking
Dislike percentage, 255–59, 280
Dislike responses, 280
Diversity of Interests scale, 52–53, 221–26, 330, 370; in case study, 297
DIV scale, 221–26, 330, 370; in case study, 297
Doctors, *see* Medical students; Physicians
DP index, 255–59, 280
DuBois, P. H., 388
Dunnette, M. D., 16, 34, 133, 135, 226, 232, 387, 446

Economists, 133
Educational level: and interests, 123; prediction of, 197–99, 202. *See also* Academic achievement scale; High school students
Electricians, 133
Elementary teachers, 67, 133, 176, 191, 446; women, 52, 177, 391
Emotionally distressed students, 62–63
Empirical weights, 34. *See also* Scale construction
Empiricism, 194
Encyclopedia salesmen, 230, 270–71
Engen, H. B., 134, 446
Engineers, 42, 48, 50, 133, 275, 350f, 371, 387; students, 14f, 55, 66, 82, 119, 129f, 151; women, 52, 178, 391; new sample, 446
English teachers, 133, 446; women, 52, 177f, 391
Enterprising scale, Holland's, 443, 463, 468
Entertainers, 52, 178, 391
Error detection, 248. *See also* Faking, Administrative Indices
Estabrooks, G. H., 196
Ethics, code of, APA, 261

Executive housekeepers, 52, 178, 391
Explanation of profile scores, 87, 138–50, 273–74, 282. *See also individual scales by name*
Explorers, 323
Expressed versus measured interests, 286–312 *passim*
Extraversion, 331, 337. *See also* Occupational introversion-extraversion

Factor analysis, 276, 354–55. *See also* Cluster analysis
Faking the SVIB, 14–24; literature review, 14–16; real-life faking, 16; among applicants, 17–19; simulated faking, 21; conclusions about, 22–23; detection of, 23–24; and scoring errors, 248
Farmers, 50, 66, 133, 387, 446
Fashion models, *see* Models
Fast, Irene, 273
Faunce, Patricia, 177
FC index, 249–50
Femininity–masculinity scale, 52–53, 232–36. *See also* Masculinity–femininity scale
Ferguson, L. W., 315, 387
Finnie, Bruce, 71, 113
Fiske, D. W., 65
Flat profiles, 280–82
Flint, R. T., 135, 179, 392
FMII, *see* Femininity–masculinity scale
Food scientists, 134, 446
Football coaches, 133, 205, 231, 270
Forest service men, 50, 134, 387, 446
Form check index, 249–50
Forms, *see* Answer sheets; Profile forms; Test booklets
Francis, Janet, 134, 178, 391
Freyd, M., 350f
Fricke, B. G., 14
Friedersdorf, Nancy, 311–12
Fryer, Douglas, 350
Funeral directors, 51, 133, 276, 387, 446

Galinsky, M. D., 273
Garry, R., 15
Gee, Helen, 71, 388
Gehman, W. S., 16
General Interest Inventory, 350
Generals, 134. *See also* Army officers
Genetics and interests, 341–42
Githens, W. H., 20–21
Giving the SVIB, 10–11. *See also* SVIB, administration of
Goin, A., 392
Good impression scales, *see* Faking
Gottesman, I. I., 341
Governors, 133, 208, 230, 270

Grade point, prediction of, 196–97
Graduate students, 270
Gray, C. W., 14–17
Guidance counselors, 134, 446; women, 52, 178, 391. *See also* High school counselors; Student personnel worker

Hackett, H. R., 387
Hagenah, Theda, 134, 275, 277–78, 281, 315
Hand-scoring, 369
Hankes, Elmer, 359f
Hannum, T. E., 123, 137, 324, 389, 448
Harmon, Lenore W., 59–60, 302–3, 382, 442
Harrell, Thomas, 363
Harrell, Thomas, Mrs., 356
Harvard University, 60, 68, 71, 82, 113, 199
Hegdahl, Beulah, 133
Heifner, Betty, 113
Heist, P. A., 387
Herman, L. M., 386
High school counselors, 134
High school students, 55, 58f, 61, 81f, 221; tested in 1930, 107–8, 198–99, 217
High scores: BIS scales, 139–50, 176; occupational scales, 278–79, 280–82
Highway patrolmen, 134, 446
Hill, Diane S., 335
Holland, J. L., 443
Holland scales, 443–44. *See also* Artistic scales; Conventional scales; Enterprising scales; Intellectual scales; Realistic scales; Social scales
Hollerith machine, 355
Holmen, M. G., 244
Home economists, 52, 176, 178, 191, 391
Homemaking scale, 103, 159, 181, 191; in case study, 309, 313
Hood, A. B., 62–63
Hoppock, R. H., 67
Housewives, 178
Hoyt, D. P., 209
Hull, Clark, 357
Hultgren, D., 134, 447
Hutchins, E. B., 18, 71
Hutchinson, J. C., Jr., 67

IBM, 805; scoring machine, 360
IBM mark sense cards, 360
Identity problems and SVIB, 273–74
Inconsistent scores, 283
Indifferent percentage, 255–59
Instrument assemblers, 52, 178, 391
Intellectual scale, Holland's, 443, 463, 465

Intercorrelations, *see* Item intercorrelations; *list of table headings for correlations between scales*
Interest Analysis Blank, 350
"Interest Archives," 205, 260
Interest maturity scale, 194, 209, 217, 220–21
Interest Report Blank, 350
Interests and abilities, early research, 345. *See also* Aptitude tests; Success
Interests and age, 208–21. *See also* Change of interest
Interior decorators, 134, 446; women, 52, 178, 391
Internists, 135
Interpretation of profile, 87, 138–50, 273–74; problems, 282. *See also* individual scales by name
Interpreters, 52, 134
Introversion, 331, 337. *See also* Occupational introversion–extraversion scale
Investment fund managers, 134, 446
Iowa State University, 303, 324
IP index, 255–59
Item analysis: occupational scales, 26–28, 29f, 33f; basic interest scales, 88–92; AACH scale, 195–96; AR scale, 213; DIV scale, 223; MO scale, 227; MF scale, 232–33; OL scale, 243; SL scale, 243–44; FC index, 249–50; UNP index, 251–53; CC scales, 325–26, 335; new scales, 401. *See also* Scale construction
Item changes, 5, 369, 378; initial pool, 350; women's booklet, 377–80. *See also Appendix D*
Item characteristics, 6, 102, 156, 378
Item content, 6, 102, 156, 323, 378; interpretation of, 201; AACH scale, men and women, 201, 204; AR scale, 215; DIV scale, 222; MO scale, 228; MF and FM scales, 234; OIE scale, men and women, 240, 242; OL scale, 244; SL scale, 246; FC index, 252; UNP index, men and women, 254, 255
Item intercorrelations, 89–91
Item obsolescence, 323
Item response percentages, 30, 33, 378; shifts over time, 325–26, 340, 371–72. *See also* Men-in-general
Item stability, 68–69
Item weights, 102; changes in, 358, 369; new scales, 473. *See also* Item analysis; Scale construction

Jenson, Paul, 16
Job applicants, faking the SVIB, 17–24

Job descriptions, 153–54
Job satisfaction: in criterion samples, 29; and interests, 60–61, 62f, 67f; in Basic scales norm sample, 108
Johansson, C. B., 64, 82, 232
Johnson, J. C., 34, 133, 135, 226, 232, 446
Joselyn, E. G., 221
Journalists, 57, 134, 208, 230, 270f, 446; students, 55, 151. *See also* Authors; Newsmen; Newswomen
Judges, federal, 134, 230, 270f
Junior college students, 81, 112, 172

Kates, S. L., 67
Kelley, T. L., 345
Kelly, E. L., 16, 65, 136
Kelly, Mary, 390
Kelso, D. P., 15
King, P. T., 315
King, Stanley, 71, 113
Kingsley, G. G., 81
Kirchner, W. K., 16ff, 137; Kirchner's hunch, 18
Kirk, Barbara A., 387
Klappauf, L. J., 136
Klein, F. L., 388f
Koehler, Eileen, 180
Koepke, H. F., Jr., 177
Kornhauser, S. I., 15, 350
Krause, K. B., 133
Kriedt, P. H., 81, 136, 317, 388
Kroger, R. O., 21–22
Kuder, G. F., 32
Kuder Preference Record, 14
Kunce, J. T., 194

Laboratory technicians, 59, 178. *See also* Medical technologists
Lancaster, R., 448
Language interpreters, 52, 134
Language teachers, 52, 178, 391
Law/Politics scale: men, 94, 141, 150, 271; women, 160, 182; in case study, 289, 295, 298, 313
Lawyers, 51, 57, 134, 315, 351, 373, 387; law students, 55, 129, 151; women, 52, 178, 391; new sample, 446
Layton, W. L., 275, 279f
LeBold, William, 66
Legislators, 134
Lepak, R., 136, 448
Letter ratings, 54f, 59, 274–75, 278
Levy, S., 209, 500
Librarians, 51, 134, 176, 191, 373, 387, 447; women, 52, 178, 391
Licensed practical nurses, 52, 178, 391
Lie scale, *see* Faking

Life insurance salesmen, 14–15, 51, 66, 205, 230, 270–71, 315, 357, 387; women, 52, 178, 391; new sample, 448
Like Percentage, 255–59; in case study, 291, 293, 298, 312f
Lindquist, E. F., 360
Lindsay, C., 132, 386, 445
Lips, O. J., 132f, 136f, 448
Longest, J. W., 132
Longstaff, H. P., 15
Lonner, W. J., 134, 447
Lorr, M., 388f
Low scores, 139–50, 277–78
LP index, 255–59; in case study, 291, 293, 298, 312f

McArthur, C., 60–61, 68
McCornack, R. L., 137, 180, 317, 389, 393, 448
McDowell, A. R., 386
Machinists, 134
McKenzie, H., 354
McKnight fellows, 230, 261, 270
McNair, D. M., 388f
McReynolds, Paul, 343n
Mail: sending results, 13; in collecting data, 19–20
Maladjustment and the SVIB, 280
Managerial effectiveness, 226–32 *passim*
Managerial orientation scale, 194, 226–32, 271, 370; in case study, 297
Manual, SVIB, first published, 352–53
Martin, Ann, 196
Masculinity–femininity scale, 16, 50f, 194, 232–36; problems with, 234–35; use of, 236; in case study, 293, 313
Mathematical curve showing age change, 219
Mathematicians, 50, 134, 259, 330, 387, 447; women, 52, 178, 391
Mathematics scale, 94, 119, 141, 150f, 283; in case study, 289f, 295. *See also* Numbers scale
Math-Science Teachers, 50, 134, 387, 447; women, 52, 179, 391
Mattarazzo, J. D., 315, 388
Mawardi, Betty H., 179
Measurement of Interests, The, 350
Measurement Research Center, 360. *See also* Scoring agencies
Mechanical scale: men, 95, 142, 150, 271; women, 160, 183; in case study, 291, 305, 313
Medal of Science, 230, 271f
Medical service scale: men, 96, 121, 142, 153; women, 161, 182, 191; in case study, 291

Medical specialists, 243–44. *See also individual specialists by name*
Medical students, 15ff, 18–19, 55, 71, 119–21, 129, 151, 199, 217, 315. *See also* Physicians
Medical technologists, 134, 447; women, 52, 179, 391
Mencken, H. L., 260
Men-in-general, 7, 25ff, 29–32, 92, 251–52, 275, 358, 372–76; 1938 sample, 31f, 275, 370, 394f; 1966 sample, 31f, 341, 370, 396f; 1969 sample, 31f, 397–99, 400, 442. *See also* Women-in-general
Mental Measurement Yearbook, 345
Merchandising scale: men, 96, 143, 150, 153; women, 161, 183; in case study, 290, 295
MFII, *see* Masculinity–femininity scale
Military activities scale, 96, 109, 119, 129, 143, 284; in case study, 290f, 301
Military officers, 323. *See also* Air Force officers; Army officers; Navy offiicers
Millay, Edna St. Vincent, 260
Miller Analogies Test, 65
Miller, L. D., 179, 392
Miner, J. B., 350
Minister, 28–29, 50, 134, 319, 371, 387, 447; Unitarian ministers, 137
Minneapolis Star-Journal, 359–60
Minneapolis Symphony Orchestra, 134, 325
Minnesota Interest Inventory, 350
Minnesota Mining and Manufacturing (3M), 17
Minnesota Multiphasic Personality Inventory, 62f, 237, 239, 280, 341
Minnesota Scholastic Aptitude Test, 196–97, 202, 206
Minnesota Symphony Orchestra, 134, 325
Minnesota Vocational Interest Inventory, 322, 350
Missing items, 249
MMPI, *see* Minnesota multiphasic personality inventory
Models, 52, 178, 392
Modernity factor, 321, 331, 372
Money managers, 134, 446
Moore, B. V., 350f
Morticians, *see* Funeral directors
MO scale, *see* Managerial orientation scale
Mosier, C. I., 196
MSAT, *see* Minnesota scholastic aptitude test
Musicians, 51, 134f, 230, 270, 325, 387, 447; women, 52, 179, 392
Music scale: men, 97, 109, 119, 129f, 144; women, 162, 175, 184, 191; in case studies, 289f, 299
Music teacher, 51, 135, 387, 447; women, 52, 179, 392
MVII, *see* Minnesota vocational interest inventory

Nace, C. D., 392
NASA scientists, 134
Nash, A. N., 226, 232
National Computer Systems, 4, 360. *See also* Scoring agencies
National Council of YMCAs, 325
National Institute of Arts and Letters, 208, 230, 261; members of, 134
National Merit Scholarship Corporation, 341
Nature scale, 97, 115, 119, 129f, 144, 191; in case study, 290, 295. *See also* Outdoors scale
Navy: officers, 20, 134, 205, 231, 270f, 447; ROTC applicants, 19–21; women, 52, 179, 392
Neurological surgeons, 135
Neurotics, 64
Neumann, Idell, 20–21
New scales, *see* Scale construction
Newsmen, 134. *See also* Journalists
Newswomen, 52, 179, 392
Nichols, Robert, 341
Nobel prize winners, 230, 270, 272
Nolting, E., Jr., 173, 176, 250
Nonoccupational scales, use of, 195. *See also scales by name*
Norenberg, C. D., 137, 448
Norms: men's BIS scales, 107–8; women's BIS scales, 158; for inventories by age, 220. *See also* Standard scores *and individual scales by name*
Numbers scale, 162, 184; in case study, 303, 307, 313. *See also* Mathematics scale
Nun-Teacher, 52, 179, 392
Nurses, 52, 179f, 392f

Occupational groups, 275–77. *See also* Criterion samples
Occupational Interests, 350
Occupational introversion–extraversion scale, 52–53, 236–43, 330f, 337, 370; in case study, 290f, 295, 299; for twins, 342; for parents, 342
Occupational level scale, 50–51, 194, 243
Occupational samples, *see* Criterion samples
Occupational scales: plotted on profile, 7; disadvantages of, 87f; versus Basic

scales, 155–56; most recent revision, 441–73. *See also* Scale construction
Occupational similarities, 48
Occupational success, *see* Success
Occupational therapists, women, 52, 176, 179, 191, 392
Occupations, change in, 315–42 *passim*; outdated, 322–23
Office practices scale: men, 98, 115, 145, 150, 153; women, 162, 185; in case study, 290, 309
Office worker, 51f, 134, 179, 388
Olheiser, Mary David, 179, 392
OL scale, 50–51, 194, 243
Omitted items, 249
Optometrists, 134, 447
Orthopedic surgeons, 135
Osteopaths, 50, 134, 388
O'Toole, Rev., 137
Outdoors scale, 163, 175, 185, 191. *See also* Nature scale
Outstanding men, 260–72 *passim*. *See also* Success

Packard, R. E., 133
Paterson, D. G., 14, 317, 350, 388
Pathologists, 135
Pattern of scores, 275–77
Pediatricians, 135
Percent overlap, 42f, 68; table of, 43; for new scales, 442
Performance and interests, 65–66. *See also* Success
Performing arts scale, 163, 175, 186
Perry, D. K., 68, 133, 386, 390, 446
Personality scales, 103. *See also* OIE, MF, DIV scales
Personality tests and interests, 62–63. *See also* MMPI
Personnel directors, 50, 135, 317, 388, 447
Petroleum engineers, 135, 447
Pharmacists, 51, 67, 135, 388, 447
Photographers, 135, 447; women, 179
Phys. ed. teachers, 52, 179, 392
Physiatrists, 135
Physical science scale, 164, 186, 191; in case study, 313. *See also* Science scale
Physicians, 50, 54f, 57, 62, 153, 243–44, 275, 317, 351, 388; women, 52, 176, 179, 191, 392; on basic interest scales, 135; new sample, 447. *See also* Medical students *and medical specialists by name*
Physical therapists, 50, 135, 388, 447; women, 52, 179, 392
Physicists, 48, 50, 136, 271, 285, 330, 388, 447

Pilots, 136, 324
Pitchlynn, P. P., 387
Poets, 230, 261
Policemen, 50, 136, 271, 315, 373, 388, 447
Political scientists, 136, 448
Predictive validity, *see* Validity
Presidents, APA, *see* American Psychological Association; Psychologists
Presidents, corporation, 51, 133, 205, 231, 270, 319, 388
Priebe, D. W., 66, 133, 446
Priests, 136f, 448
Primary patterns, 276, 281
Printer, 50, 136, 388
Privacy, and SVIB scores, 260. *See also* Secrecy
Production managers, 50, 136, 388
Professors, *see* College professors
Profile changes, prediction of, 220–21
Profile forms, 3, 6–10
Profile shape, 282; pattern, 275–77
Prominent people, 205, 260
Psychiatrists, 50, 135, 448
Psychological Corporation, 325
Psychologists, 50, 81ff, 123, 136, 173, 176, 208, 230, 315, 317, 373; women, 52, 180, 392; APA presidents, 65, 261, 270ff, 321; students, 65; criterion samples, 388, 448
Psychology of Vocational Choice, The, 443
Psychotherapists, 64
Public administrator, 50, 136, 389, 447
Publications on SVIB, 345
Public speaking scale: men, 98, 119, 145, 150; women, 164, 187; in case study, 290f, 298
Pulitzer prize winners, 136, 208, 230, 270
Purchasing agent, 51, 136, 389, 448. *See also* Buyer
Purdue Interest Report Blank, 350
Purdue University, 66, 82, 119, 129

Qualifications for using SVIB, 11–12
Questions, *see* Items

Radiologic technologists, 52, 179, 393
Radiologists, 136
Random responding, 280
Range of interests, *see* Diversity of interests
Raw scores, conversion to standard scores, 35. *See also* Standard scores
Reaction to SVIB, 312–13
Real estate salesmen, 51, 137, 389, 448
Realistic scale, Holland's, 443, 463f

Ream, M. J., 350f
Recreational leadership scale, 98, 109, 129, 146, 271. *See also* Sports scale
Recreation leaders, 52, 393. *See also* Community recreation leaders
Rehabilitation counselor, 50, 136, 389, 448
Reject patterns, 277–78
Reliability: odd-even, 69; men's occupational scales, 70–83 *passim*; women's, 83–86 *passim*; men's BIS, 105–6, 112–30, 151, women's BIS, 171–76; AACH scale, 199–200; MO scale, 228; 1938 vs. 1966 form, 376
Religious activities scale: men, 99, 109, 119, 121, 146, 173, 285, 322; women, 165, 175, 187; in case study, 290
Remmers, R. E., 350
Research booklets, 4
Research problems, 319–20
Response set, 92, 254; in case study, 299–300
Response stability, 68–69
Results, reporting to clients, 13, 261, 282
Revealing test results, 13, 261, 282
Revision of interest inventories, 315, 340, 344, 441–73
Revision, SVIB: reasons for, 361–62; changes, 364; most recent, 441–72
Rhode, J. G., 121, 132f, 150–51, 325, 445
Robinson, H. A., 67
Rogers, Sarah, 179, 388
Rossmann, J. E., 132f, 136f, 270, 445, 448
ROTC applicants, 19–21
Rothney, J. W. M., 14
Roys, K., 133, 386, 446
Rulon, P. H., 355

Sales interests, and eventual occupation, 58–59
Sales managers, 51, 137, 389, 448
Salesmen, 17, 136–37, 53–55, 271f, 279, 285, 350, 448
Sales scale, 99, 129, 147, 153, 155, 271; in case study, 290f, 295, 301
Saleswomen, 52, 180, 393
Sample size of criterion samples, 358, 442
Saslow, G., 315, 388
Scale construction, 26–28, 29f, 33f, 43, 45, 102, 401, 442; Basic interest scales, 88–92. *See also* Item analysis *and individual scales by name*
Scheller, T. G., 281–82
Schizophrenics, 64
Schletzer, Vera M., 55–57, 59, 67, 81, 151–52, 210–11
School superintendents, 51, 137, 319, 371, 389, 448
Schuell, Hildred, 180, 393

Schwebel, M., 67, 135, 388
Science interests, and eventual occupation, 58–59
Science scale, 100, 119, 121, 147, 153, 155, 271f, 321; in case study, 289f, 295. *See also* Biological science; Physical science
Science teacher, *see* Math-science teacher
Scientists, 153–55, 271, 323. *See also* NASA scientists
Scoring agencies, 11, 248
Scoring machines, 355–56, 359–60
Seashore, H. G., 137, 448
Secondary patterns, 276, 281f
Secrecy and test scores, 13, 83, 282
Secretaries, 52, 180, 393
Selection: use of SVIB, 12; use of AACH scale, 208
Set 1 and Set 2 scales, 88–89, 173. *See also* Basic interest scales
Sewing machine operators, 52, 180, 393
Sex differences, 314. *See also* Masculinity–femininity scale
Shaded area, 7, 35, 370–71
Sheriffs, 133
Skilled tradesmen, 137, 448
SL scale, 50–51, 194
Smith, J. L., Jr., 209, 500
Social scale, Holland's, 443, 463, 467
Social science teachers, 51, 137, 389, 448; women, 52, 180, 393
Social service interests, 57
Social service scale: men, 100, 121, 130, 148, 150, 283f; women, 165, 188; in case study, 299
Social workers, 51, 59, 137, 176, 191, 317, 389, 448; women, 52, 180, 393
Socio-economic level and interests, 60–61, 243
Sociologists, 137, 371, 448
Soliman, A. M., 83, 173, 382
Specialization level scale, 50–51, 194
Speech pathologist, 52, 180, 393
Sports scale, 165, 188. *See also* Recreational leadership scale
Stability of interests, 119, 130; general conclusions, 86. *See also* Change of interest; Reliability
Standard scores, 28, 35, 108, 158, 359
Standards for Educational and Psychological Tests and Manuals, 13
Stanford University, 67, 81, 110, 115–19, 196, 220, 350, 354, 361; Medical School, 319; seniors, 356
State legislators, 134
Stein, C. I., 136, 448
Stein, M., 177
Steinmetz, H. C., 14

Stephenson, R. R., 19, 135, 275, 447
Stevens, J. H., 60–61, 64
Steward, V., 14–15
Stewardesses, 52, 180, 259, 393
Stewart, L. H., 247
Stone, C. H., 317, 388
Stordahl, K. E., 209
Store managers, 133, 446
Strong, E. J., Jr.: on SVIB scores, 2; scale construction, 29; men-in-general, 30–33; study of Stanford students, 49–54, 67–68, 115–19; on interest changes, 86, 209; files, 260, 286–87, 319; on research, 344f, 357–58; early history, 348–49; WPA presidential address, 357–58; recognition by psychologists, 358; awarded medal, 359; retirement, 360; letter to Berdie, 362–64; death, 364; contributions, 365; mentioned, 5, 14, 81ff, 107–8, 138, 173, 198–99, 317, 324–25, 335, 344, 350–65 *passim*
Student personnel workers, 137
Success and interests, 2, 62–66 *passim*, 208, 260–72 *passim*; in criterion samples, 29; in computer programmers, 68
Surgeons, 136
SVIB, 1, 3; time to complete, 11; scoring agencies, 11; age level for use, 11; use in selection, 12; use by untrained persons, 13; number printed, 344; publications on, 345; assumptions behind, 352–53; first manual, 352; revision, 361–62, 364

T-Scores, *see* Standard scores
T399, *see* Test booklets
Taxidermist, 24
Teaching scale: men, 101, 115, 119, 129f, 148, 150; women, 166, 175, 189, 191; in case study, 290f, 299, 301
Teenagers, *see* High school students
Technical Recommendations for Psychological Tests and Diagnostic Techniques, 360
Technical supervision scale, 101, 119, 149; in case study, 290
Telephone operators, 52, 180, 393
Terman, Lewis, 351, 364
Test administration, 10–11; by mail, 20; environment, 21–22; instructions, 378–81
Test booklets, 3–6, 405–7, 407–21; Form T399, 4, 249f, 396, 406, 418–21, 435; Form T399R, 4, 406; Form T399N, 4, 249; Form M, 4, 249f, 382, 396, 405, 414–17, 434f; Form TW398, 4–5, 171, 249f, 382, 407, 430–33, 438; Form TW398N, 5, 249; Form TW398R, 5,

407; Form W, 249f, 407, 426–29, 438; Form A, 405, 410–13, 434; Form B, 405; Form MM, 406; Form WA, 407, 422–25, 437; Form WB, 407; Form WM, 407; number printed, 344. *See also* Women's booklet
Tests, misuse of, 1–2
TestScor, 360. *See also* Scoring agencies
"Things versus people" dichotomy, 239
Thomas, Mary-Alice, 393
Thomas, R. R., 83, 173
Thorndike, E. L., 345
Thorndike Intelligence Test, 64
Thrifty people, 325
Thrush, R. S., 315
Thurstone, L. L., 354–55
Tilton, J. W., 42
Tilton percent overlap, 42–43. *See also* Percent overlap
Time shift, 321, 371–76
Time to complete the SVIB, 11
Tool and die makers, 137
Total responses index, 249
Translators, 52, 180, 393. *See also* Interpreters
Trimble, J. T., 61–62, 68, 81, 115, 221
TR index, 249
Tucker, A. C., 135f, 317, 388, 448
Twins and interests, 341–42
Tyrone Guthrie Theater, 230, 270

U.S. Army Reserve, 71, 113
Uhlenhuth, E. H., 64
Unanswered items, 249. *See also* Total response index
Unitarian ministers, 137
University of California at Berkeley, 21
University of Iowa, 62
University of Kentucky, 350
University of Michigan, 16
University of Minnesota: medical school, 18; general college, 81, 113, 173; college of liberal arts, 86, 113, 173, 195, 275; law school, 315; mentioned, 17, 67, 71, 81, 83, 113, 115, 119, 151, 171, 173, 176, 199, 209, 226, 232, 239, 260, 270, 280, 322, 350, 358
University of Missouri, 113–15
University of Wisconsin, Milwaukee, 302
UNP index, 251–54
Unpopular index, 251–54
Urologists, 136
User's qualifications, 11–12

Validity: concurrent, 42–46, 131–38, 176, 281, 287; problems in determining, 49, 54–55, 62; predictive, 59–63, 151, 176, 281, 287, 354; for BIS scales, 130–57,

passim, 176; content, 131; construct, 200–203; 1938 vs. 1966 forms, 376
Validity scales, *see* Administrative indices; Faking
Verburg W. A., 81
Veterinarians, 50, 123, 137, 276, 324, 389, 448
Vocational agriculture teachers, 137, 448
Vocational Interests of Men and Women, 29, 359

Wallace, W. L., 15
Warman, Roy, 179
Watson, R. I., 388
Welfare workers, 133, 177
Wernimont, P., 387
Western Psychological Association, 357
Whitehorn, J. C., 64
Widespread interests, 278. *See also* Diversity of interests
Wiens, A., 315, 388
Williamson, E. G., 119, 196
Williamson, S. E., 134, 447
Willis, C. O., 134, 446
Willow, R., 134
Wilson, Rosena M., 179
Winkle, C. A., 133, 446
Winter, F., 132, 324–25, 385, 445

Winters, J. S., 134, 387, 447
Wiskopf, M., 392
Women: occupational planning, 193; problems in counseling, 302–12. *See also* Masculinity–femininity scale
Women-in-general, 7, 158, 252, 341, 382f; 1946 sample, 158, 401f; 1968 sample, 158, 341, 401–4. *See also* Men-in-general
Women's booklet, 4, 6; advantages of, 359, 376–77. *See also* Test booklets
Women's interim scales, 382–83
Wood, B., 355
Writing scale: men, 101, 119, 129f, 149f, 322; women, 166, 189; in case study, 299

X-ray technicians, 52, 179, 393

YMCA staff, 50, 81, 123, 130, 137, 325, 330, 389, 448; women, 52, 180, 393
Yoakum, C. S., 350
Young, C. W., 196

Zeigler, M. L., 386
Zlatchin, P. J., 67
Zytowski, D., 303